PUBLIC PAPERS OF THE PRESIDENTS

OF THE UNITED STATES

PUBLIC PAPERS OF THE PRESIDENTS

OF THE UNITED STATES

Dwight D. Eisenhower

1960–61

Containing the Public Messages, Speeches, and

Statements of the President

JANUARY 1, 1960, TO JANUARY 20, 1961

PUBLISHED BY THE
OFFICE OF THE FEDERAL REGISTER
NATIONAL ARCHIVES AND RECORDS SERVICE
GENERAL SERVICES ADMINISTRATION

U.S. GOVERNMENT PRINTING OFFICE: 1961

FOREWORD

THERE HAS BEEN a long-felt need for an orderly series of the Public Papers of the Presidents. A reference work of this type can be most helpful to scholars and officials of government, to reporters of current affairs and the events of history.

The general availability of the official text of Presidential documents and messages will serve a broader purpose. As part of the expression of democracy, this series can be a vital factor in the maintenance of our individual freedoms and our institutions of self-government.

I wish success to the editors of this project, and I am sure their work through the years will add strength to the ever-growing traditions of the Republic.

Dwight D. Eisenhower

v

PREFACE

IN THIS VOLUME are gathered most of the public messages
and statements of the President of the United States that were
released by the White House during the period January 1, 1960—
January 20, 1961. Similar volumes covering the years 1953
through 1959 are also available. Volumes covering the remainder of 1961 and the period April 12, 1945—January 20,
1953, are under preparation.

This series was begun in response to a recommendation of the
National Historical Publications Commission (44 U.S.C. 393).
The Commission's recommendation was incorporated in regulations of the Administrative Committee of the Federal Register
issued under section 6 of the Federal Register Act (44 U.S.C.
306). The Committee's regulations, establishing the series, are
reprinted at page 1093 as "Appendix D."

The first extensive compilation of the messages and papers of
the Presidents was assembled by James D. Richardson and published under Congressional authority between 1896 and 1899. It
included Presidential materials from 1789 to 1897. Since then,
there have been various private compilations, but no uniform,
systematic publication comparable to the *Congressional Record*
or the *United States Supreme Court Reports*.

For many years Presidential Proclamations have been published
in the *United States Statutes at Large*. The Federal Register Act
in 1935 required that Proclamations, Executive Orders, and some
other official Executive documents be published in the daily
Federal Register; but the greater part of Presidential writings

and utterances still lacked an official medium for either current publication or periodic compilation. Some of them were interspersed through the issues of the *Congressional Record* while others were reported only in the press or were generally available only in mimeographed White House releases. Under these circumstances it was difficult to remember, after a lapse of time, where and in what form even a major pronouncement had been made.

CONTENT AND ARRANGEMENT

The text of this book is based on Presidential materials issued during the period January 1, 1960—January 20, 1961. A list of White House releases from which final selections were made is published at page 1067 as "Appendix A."

Proclamations, Executive Orders, and similar documents required by law to be published in the *Federal Register* and *Code of Federal Regulations* are not repeated. Instead, they are listed by number and subject under the heading "Appendix B" at page 1086.

The President is required by statute to transmit numerous reports to Congress. Those transmitted during the period covered by this volume are listed at page 1091 as "Appendix C."

The items published in this volume are presented in chronological order, rather than being grouped in classes. Most needs for a classified arrangement are met by the subject index. For example, a reader interested in veto messages will find them listed in the index under the heading "veto messages."

The dates shown at the end of item headings are White House release dates. In instances where the date of the document differs from the release date that fact is shown in brackets immediately following the heading. Other editorial devices, such as text notes, footnotes, and cross references, have been held to a minimum.

Remarks or addresses were delivered in Washington, D.C., unless otherwise indicated. Similarly, statements, messages, and letters were issued from the White House in Washington unless otherwise indicated.

Original source materials, where available, have been used to protect against substantive errors in transcription. In maintaining the integrity of the text (and in solving many other problems in the Eisenhower volumes), valuable assistance was furnished by L. Arthur Minnich, Jr., and William J. Hopkins of the White House staff, and by Robert R. Bolton of the National Archives and Records Service.

The planning and publication of this series is under the direction of David C. Eberhart of the Office of the Federal Register. The editor of the present volume was Warren R. Reid, assisted by Mildred B. Berry and Dorothy M. Jacobson. Frank H. Mortimer of the Government Printing Office developed the typography and design.

WAYNE C. GROVER
Archivist of the United States

JOHN L. MOORE
Administrator of General Services

May 15, 1961

CONTENTS

CONTENTS

PUBLIC PAPERS OF DWIGHT D. EISENHOWER

LIST OF ITEMS

List of Items

List of Items

List of Items

List of Items

Page

174 Address "Beyond the Campus" Delivered at the Commencement Exercises of the University of Notre Dame. June 5, 1960

461

175 Exchange of Messages Between the President and President Alessandri Concerning the Disaster in Chile. June 8, 1960

467

176 Letter to Governor Underwood of West Virginia on Further Federal Activities in Aid of Chronic Labor Surplus Areas. June 12, 1960

469

177 Statement by the President Recorded Before Leaving for the Far East. June 12, 1960

470

178 Remarks Upon Arrival at Elmendorf Air Force Base, Anchorage, Alaska. June 12, 1960

472

179 Veto of Bill for the Relief of Our Lady of the Lake Church, Mandeville, Louisiana. June 13, 1960

474

180 Veto of Bill Concerning the Defense of Suits Against Federal Employees Operating Government Motor Vehicles. June 13, 1960

475

181 Veto of Bill for the Relief of Grand Lodge of North Dakota, Ancient Free and Accepted Masons. June 13, 1960

476

182 Remarks Upon Arrival at the International Airport in Manila. June 14, 1960

477

183 Address Before a Joint Session of the Philippine Senate and House of Representatives. June 15, 1960

478

184 Remarks to the Staff of the U.S. Embassy and the American Community in Manila. June 15, 1960

485

185 Toast by the President at a Dinner Given in His Honor by President Garcia. June 15, 1960

486

186 Remarks at the University of the Philippines Upon Receiving an Honorary Degree. June 16, 1960

489

187 Remarks at a Luncheon Given by the Chamber of Commerce in Manila. June 16, 1960

492

List of Items

List of Items

List of Items

List of Items

List of Items

List of Items

List of Items

List of Items

List of Items

Dwight D. Eisenhower

1960-61

1 ¶ Letter to the Attorney General on Receiving His Report on Deceptive Practices in Broadcasting Media. *January* 1, 1960

[Released January 1, 1960. Dated December 31, 1959]

Dear Mr. Attorney General:

Thank you for the informative report relating to deceptive practices in broadcasting media which you prepared at my request and submitted to me on December 30, 1959.

The report indicates that there may be further developments and that the governmental bodies concerned have not completed all of the action which they may be considering. I would therefore appreciate it if you continued to follow the matter for me. Please advise me of developments and report your recommendations from time to time as you consider it appropriate.

Sincerely,

DWIGHT D. EISENHOWER

NOTE: "The Report to the President by the Attorney General on Deceptive Prac- tices in Broadcasting Media" was pub- lished by the Government Printing Office (54 pp., 1959).

2 ¶ Exchange of New Year Greetings Between the United States and the Soviet Union. *January* 4, 1960

Nikita S. Khrushchev
Chairman, Council of Ministers, U.S.S.R.

Kliment Efremovich Voroshilov
Chairman, Presidium of the Supreme Soviet, U.S.S.R.

On behalf of the American people, I thank you for your kind New Year's message. I share the hope which you have expressed for a further improvement in the relations between our two countries. The

United States seeks the achievement of a just and lasting peace in a world where all questions are settled by peaceful means alone. I can assure you that my Government will continue its best efforts to reach that goal. Please accept my good wishes for you and your families and the people of the Soviet Union for the coming year.

DWIGHT D. EISENHOWER

NOTE: The message from Mr. Khrushchev and Mr. Voroshilov follows:

On the eve of the New Year we send to you, Mr. President, and to the people of the United States of America sincere greetings and best wishes from the peoples of the Soviet Union and from ourselves personally. It is possible to note with deep satisfaction that in the past year there were undertaken joint efforts in the search of ways for closer relations of our States, for ensurance of such a situation in which the unresolved international questions would be decided by peaceful means only. Entering the New Year, we would like to hope sincerely that these joint efforts will guarantee a new triumph of reason, and that a start will be made to solve the most important problem of our times—the general and complete disarmament and the liberation of mankind from the burden of armament.

Let this New Year be the year of a further improvement in the relations between our countries. The realization of this hope which is so dear to the hearts of both the Soviet and American peoples would undoubtedly bring nearer the time when, thanks to the efforts of both countries, the relations between them could be built on the foundation of enduring friendship and mutually advantageous cooperation for the good of our nations, for the good of peace in the entire world. It is exactly in this way that we evaluate the meaning of exchange visits by the leading statesmen of both countries. These meetings make it possible to ensure that historical turning point in the relations between our countries, as well as in the international situation as a whole, which leads to the deliverance of all people from the dread of a new war.

With best wishes for happiness and health to you personally and to your entire family.

N. KHRUSHCHEV
K. VOROSHILOV

The messages were released at Augusta, Ga.

3   ¶ Statement by the President on the Death of Representative Simpson of Pennsylvania. *January 7, 1960*

IT IS with profound regret that I have learned this morning of the passing of Representative Richard M. Simpson, a veteran and distinguished legislator who for many years has courageously and conscientiously served his District, the Nation and the Republican Party.

Mrs. Eisenhower and I join Americans all across the country in extending deepest sympathy to his family. His passing is a grievous loss to our nation, and a personal loss to me.

NOTE: Representative Simpson had served as chairman of the House Republican Congressional Committee since 1953.

4 ¶ Annual Message to the Congress on the State of the Union. *January 7, 1960*

[Delivered in person before a joint session]

Mr. President, Mr. Speaker, Members of the 86th Congress:

Seven years ago I entered my present office with one long-held resolve overriding all others. I was then, and remain now, determined that the United States shall become an ever more potent resource for the cause of peace—realizing that peace cannot be for ourselves alone, but for peoples everywhere. This determination is shared by the entire Congress—indeed, by all Americans.

My purpose today is to discuss some features of America's position, both at home and in her relations to others.

First, I point out that for us, annual self-examination is made a definite necessity by the fact that we now live in a divided world of uneasy equilibrium, with our side committed to its own protection and against aggression by the other.

With both sides of this divided world in possession of unbelievably destructive weapons, mankind approaches a state where mutual annihilation becomes a possibility. No other fact of today's world equals this in importance—it colors everything we say, plan, and do.

There is demanded of us, vigilance, determination, and the dedication of whatever portion of our resources that will provide adequate security, especially a real deterrent to aggression. These things we are doing.

All these facts emphasize the importance of striving incessantly for a just peace.

Only through the strengthening of the spiritual, intellectual, economic and defensive resources of the Free World can we, in confidence, make progress toward this goal.

Second, we note that recent Soviet deportment and pronouncements suggest the possible opening of a somewhat less strained period in the relationships between the Soviet Union and the Free World. If these pronouncements be genuine, there is brighter hope of diminishing the

3

intensity of past rivalry and eventually of substituting persuasion for coercion. Whether this is to become an era of lasting promise remains to be tested by actions.

Third, we now stand in the vestibule of a vast new technological age—one that, despite its capacity for human destruction, has an equal capacity to make poverty and human misery obsolete. If our efforts are wisely directed—and if our unremitting efforts for dependable peace begin to attain some success—we can surely become participants in creating an age characterized by justice and rising levels of human well-being.

Over the past year the Soviet Union has expressed an interest in measures to reduce the common peril of war.

While neither we nor any other Free World nation can permit ourselves to be misled by pleasant promises until they are tested by performance, yet we approach this apparently new opportunity with the utmost seriousness. We must strive to break the calamitous cycle of frustrations and crises which, if unchecked, could spiral into nuclear disaster; the ultimate insanity.

Though the need for dependable agreements to assure against resort to force in settling disputes is apparent to both sides yet as in other issues dividing men and nations, we cannot expect sudden and revolutionary results. But we must find some place to begin.

One obvious road on which to make a useful start is in the widening of communication between our two peoples. In this field there are, both sides willing, countless opportunities—most of them well known to us all—for developing mutual understanding, the true foundation of peace.

Another avenue may be through the reopening, on January twelfth, of negotiations looking to a controlled ban on the testing of nuclear weapons. Unfortunately, the closing statement from the Soviet scientists who met with our scientists at Geneva in an unsuccessful effort to develop an agreed basis for a test ban, gives the clear impression that their conclusions have been politically guided. Those of the British and American scientific representatives are their own freely-formed, individual and collective opinion. I am hopeful that as new negotiations begin, truth—not political opportunism—will be the guiding light of the deliberations.

Still another avenue may be found in the field of disarmament, in which the Soviets have professed a readiness to negotiate seriously. They have not, however, made clear the plans they may have, if any, for mutual inspection and verification—the essential condition for any extensive measure of disarmament.

There is one instance where our initiative for peace has recently been successful. A multi-lateral treaty signed last month provides for the exclusively peaceful use of Antarctica, assured by a system of inspection. It provides for free and cooperative scientific research in that continent, and prohibits nuclear explosions there pending general international agreement on the subject. The Treaty is a significant contribution toward peace, international cooperation, and the advancement of science. I shall transmit its text to the Senate for consideration and approval in the near future.

The United States is always ready to participate with the Soviet Union in serious discussion of these or any other subjects that may lead to peace with justice.

Certainly it is not necessary to repeat that the United States has no intention of interfering in the internal affairs of any nation; likewise we reject any attempt to impose its system on us or on other peoples by force or subversion.

This concern for the freedom of other peoples is the intellectual and spiritual cement which has allied us with more than forty other nations in a common defense effort. Not for a moment do we forget that our own fate is firmly fastened to that of these countries; we will not act in any way which would jeopardize our solemn commitments to them.

We and our friends are, of course, concerned with self-defense. Growing out of this concern is the realization that all people of the Free World have a great stake in the progress, in freedom, of the uncommitted and newly emerging nations. These peoples, desperately hoping to lift themselves to decent levels of living must not, by our neglect, be forced to seek help from, and finally become virtual satellites of, those who proclaim their hostility to freedom.

Their natural desire for a better life must not be frustrated by withholding from them necessary technical and investment assistance. This is a problem to be solved not by America alone, but also by every nation cherishing the same ideals and in position to provide help.

In recent years America's partners and friends in Western Europe and Japan have made great economic progress. Their newly found economic strength is eloquent testimony to the striking success of the policies of economic cooperation which we and they have pursued.

The international economy of 1960 is markedly different from that of the early postwar years. No longer is the United States the only major industrial country capable of providing substantial amounts of the resources so urgently needed in the newly-developing countries.

To remain secure and prosperous themselves, wealthy nations must extend the kind of cooperation to the less fortunate members that will inspire hope, confidence and progress. A rich nation can for a time, without noticeable damage to itself, pursue a course of self-indulgence, making its single goal the material ease and comfort of its own citizens—thus repudiating its own spiritual and material stake in a peaceful and prosperous society of nations. But the enmities it will incur, the isolation into which it will descend, and the internal moral and physical softness that will be engendered, will, in the long term, bring it to disaster.

America did not become great through softness and self-indulgence. Her miraculous progress and achievements flow from other qualities far more worthy and substantial—

—adherence to principles and methods consonant with our religious philosophy

—a satisfaction in hard work

—the readiness to sacrifice for worthwhile causes

—the courage to meet every challenge to her progress

—the intellectual honesty and capacity to recognize the true path of her own best interests.

To us and to every nation of the Free World, rich or poor, these qualities are necessary today as never before if we are to march together to greater security, prosperity and peace.

I believe the industrial countries are ready to participate actively in supplementing the efforts of the developing countries to achieve progress.

The immediate need for this kind of cooperation is underscored by the strain in our international balance of payments. Our surplus from foreign business transactions has in recent years fallen substantially short of the expenditures we make abroad to maintain our military establishments overseas, to finance private investment, and to provide assistance to the less developed nations. In 1959 our deficit in balance of payments approached $4 billion.

Continuing deficits of anything like this magnitude would, over time, impair our own economic growth and check the forward progress of the Free World.

We must meet this situation by promoting a rising volume of exports and world trade. Further, we must induce all industrialized nations of the Free World to work together in a new cooperative endeavor to help lift the scourge of poverty from less fortunate nations. This will provide for better sharing of this burden and for still further profitable trade.

New nations, and others struggling with the problems of development, will progress only if they demonstrate faith in their own destiny and possess the will and use their own resources to fulfill it. Moreover, progress in a national transformation can be only gradually earned; there is no easy and quick way to follow from the oxcart to the jet plane. But, just as we drew on Europe for assistance in our earlier years, so now do those new and emerging nations that have this faith and determination deserve help.

Over the last fifteen years, twenty nations have gained political independence. Others are doing so each year. Most of them are woefully lacking in technical capacity and in investment capital; without Free World support in these matters they cannot effectively progress in freedom.

Respecting their need, one of the major focal points of our concern is the South Asian region. Here, in two nations alone, are almost five hundred million people, all working, and working hard, to raise their standards, and in doing so, to make of themselves a strong bulwark against the spread of an ideology that would destroy liberty.

I cannot express to you the depth of my conviction that, in our own and Free World interests, we must cooperate with others to help these people achieve their legitimate ambitions, as expressed in their different multi-year plans. Through the World Bank and other instrumentalities, as well as through individual action by every nation in position to help, we must squarely face this titanic challenge.

All of us must realize, of course, that development in freedom by the newly emerging nations, is no mere matter of obtaining outside financial assistance. An indispensable element in this process is a strong and continuing determination on the part of these nations to exercise the national discipline necessary for any sustained development period. These qualities of determination are particularly essential because of the fact that the process of improvement will necessarily be gradual and laborious rather than revolutionary. Moreover, everyone should be aware that the development process is no short term phenomenon. Many years are required for even the most favorably situated countries.

I shall continue to urge the American people, in the interests of their own security, prosperity and peace, to make sure that their own part of this great project be amply and cheerfully supported. Free World decisions in this matter may spell the difference between world disaster and world progress in freedom.

Other countries, some of which I visited last month, have similar needs.

A common meeting ground is desirable for those nations which are prepared to assist in the development effort. During the past year I have discussed this matter with the leaders of several Western Nations.

Because of its wealth of experience, the Organization for European Economic Cooperation could help with initial studies. The goal is to enlist all available economic resources in the industrialized Free World— especially private investment capital. But I repeat that this help, no matter how great, can be lastingly effective only if it is used as a supplement to the strength of spirit and will of the people of the newly-developing nations.

By extending this help we hope to make possible the enthusiastic enrollment of these nations under freedom's banner. No more startling contrast to a system of sullen satellites could be imagined.

If we grasp this opportunity to build an age of productive partnership between the less fortunate nations and those that have already achieved a high state of economic advancement, we will make brighter the outlook for a world order based upon security, freedom and peace. Otherwise, the outlook could be dark indeed. We face what may be a turning point in history, and we must act decisively.

———————

As a nation we can successfully pursue these objectives only from a position of broadly based strength.

No matter how earnest is our quest for guaranteed peace, we must maintain a high degree of military effectiveness at the same time we are engaged in negotiating the issue of arms reduction. Until tangible and mutually enforceable arms reduction measures are worked out, we will not weaken the means of defending our institutions.

America possesses an enormous defense power. It is my studied conviction that no nation will ever risk general war against us unless we should be so foolish as to neglect the defense forces we now so powerfully support.   It is world-wide knowledge that any nation which might be tempted today to attack the United States, even though our country might sustain great losses, would itself promptly suffer a terrible destruction. But I once again assure all peoples and all nations that the United States, except in defense, will never turn loose this destructive power.

During the past year, our long-range striking power, unmatched today in manned bombers, has taken on new strength as the Atlas intercontinental ballistic missile has entered the operational inventory.   In fourteen recent test launchings, at ranges of over 5,000 miles, Atlas has been striking on an average within two miles of the target.   This is less than the length of a jet runway—well within the circle of total destruction.   Such performance is a great tribute to American scientists and engineers, who in the past five years have had to telescope time and technology to develop these long-range ballistic missiles, where America had none before.

This year, moreover, growing numbers of nuclear-powered submarines will enter our active forces, some to be armed with Polaris missiles.   These remarkable ships and weapons, ranging the oceans, will be capable of accurate fire on targets virtually anywhere on earth.   Impossible to destroy by surprise attack, they will become one of our most effective sentinels for peace.

To meet situations of less than general nuclear war, we continue to maintain our carrier forces, our many service units abroad, our always ready Army strategic forces and Marine Corps divisions, and the civilian components.   The continuing modernization of these forces is a costly but necessary process, and is scheduled to go forward at a rate which will steadily add to our strength.

The deployment of a portion of these forces beyond our shores, on land and sea, is persuasive demonstration of our determination to stand shoulder-to-shoulder with our allies for collective security.   Moreover, I have directed that steps be taken to program our military assistance to these allies on a longer range basis.   This is necessary for a sounder collective defense system.

Next I refer to our effort in space exploration, which is often mistakenly supposed to be an integral part of defense research and development.

First, America has made great contributions in the past two years to the world's fund of knowledge of astrophysics and space science.   These discoveries are of present interest chiefly to the scientific community; but they are important foundation-stones for more extensive exploration of outer space for the ultimate benefit of all mankind.

Second, our military missile program, going forward so successfully, does *not* suffer from our present lack of very large rocket engines, which are so necessary in distant space exploration. I am assured by experts that the thrust of our present missiles is fully adequate for defense requirements.

Third, the United States is pressing forward in the development of large rocket engines to place much heavier vehicles into space for exploration purposes.

Fourth, in the meantime, it is necessary to remember that we have only begun to probe the environment immediately surrounding the earth. Using launch systems presently available, we are developing satellites to scout the world's weather; satellite relay stations to facilitate and extend communications over the globe; for navigation aids to give accurate bearings to ships and aircraft; and for perfecting instruments to collect and transmit the data we seek. This is the area holding the most promise for early and useful applications of space technology.

Fifth, we have just completed a year's experience with our new space law. I believe it deficient in certain particulars and suggested improvements will be submitted shortly.

The accomplishment of the many tasks I have alluded to requires the continuous strengthening of the spiritual, intellectual, and economic sinews of American life. The steady purpose of our society is to assure justice, before God, for every individual. We must be ever alert that freedom does not wither through the careless amassing of restrictive controls or the lack of courage to deal boldly with the giant issues of the day.

A year ago, when I met with you, the nation was emerging from an economic downturn, even though the signs of resurgent prosperity were not then sufficiently convincing to the doubtful. Today our surging strength is apparent to everyone. 1960 promises to be the most prosperous year in our history.

Yet we continue to be afflicted by nagging disorders.

Among current problems that require solution are:

—the need to protect the public interest in situations of prolonged labor-management stalemate;

—the persistent refusal to come to grips with a critical problem in one sector of American agriculture;

—the continuing threat of inflation, together with the persisting tendency toward fiscal irresponsibility;

—in certain instances the denial to some of our citizens of equal protection of the law.

Every American was disturbed by the prolonged dispute in the steel industry and the protracted delay in reaching a settlement.

We are all relieved that a settlement has at last been achieved in that industry. Percentagewise, by this settlement the increase to the steel companies in employment costs is lower than in any prior wage settlement since World War II. It is also gratifying to note that despite the increase in wages and benefits several of the major steel producers have announced that there will be no increase in steel prices at this time. The national interest demands that in the period of industrial peace which has been assured by the new contract both management and labor make every possible effort to increase efficiency and productivity in the manufacture of steel so that price increases can be avoided.

One of the lessons of this story is that the potential danger to the entire Nation of longer and greater strikes must be met. To insure against such possibilities we must of course depend primarily upon the good common-sense of the responsible individuals. It is my intention to encourage regular discussions between management and labor outside the bargaining table, to consider the interest of the public as well as their mutual interest in the maintenance of industrial peace, price stability and economic growth.

To me, it seems almost absurd for the United States to recognize the need, and so earnestly to seek, for cooperation among the nations unless we can achieve voluntary, dependable, abiding cooperation among the important segments of our own free society.

Failure to face up to basic issues in areas other than those of labor-management can cause serious strains on the firm freedom supports of our society.

I refer to agriculture as one of these areas.

Our basic farm laws were written 27 years ago, in an emergency effort to redress hardship caused by a world-wide depression. They were continued—and their economic distortions intensified—during World War II in order to provide incentives for production of food needed to sustain a war-torn free world.

Today our farm problem is totally different. It is that of effectively adjusting to the changes caused by a scientific revolution. When the original farm laws were written, an hour's farm labor produced only one-fourth as much wheat as at present. Farm legislation is woefully out-of-date, ineffective, and expensive.

For years we have gone on with an outmoded system which not only has failed to protect farm income, but also has produced soaring, threatening surpluses. Our farms have been left producing for war while America has long been at peace.

Once again I urge Congress to enact legislation that will gear production more closely to markets, make costly surpluses more manageable, provide greater freedom in farm operations, and steadily achieve increased net farm incomes.

Another issue that we must meet squarely is that of living within our means. This requires restraint in expenditure, constant reassessment of priorities, and the maintenance of stable prices.

We must prevent inflation. Here is an opponent of so many guises that it is sometimes difficult to recognize. But our clear need is to stop continuous and general price rises—a need that all of us can see and feel.

To prevent steadily rising costs and prices calls for stern self-discipline by every citizen. No person, city, state, or organized group can afford to evade the obligation to resist inflation, for every American pays its crippling tax.

Inflation's ravages do not end *at the water's edge*. Increases in prices of the goods we sell abroad threaten to drive us out of markets that once were securely ours. Whether domestic prices, so high as to be noncompetitive, result from demands for too-high profit margins or from increased labor costs that outrun growth in productivity, the final result is seriously damaging to the nation.

We must fight inflation as we would a fire that imperils our home. Only by so doing can we prevent it from destroying our salaries, savings, pensions and insurance, and from gnawing away the very roots of a free, healthy economy and the nation's security.

One major method by which the Federal government can counter inflation and rising prices is to insure that its expenditures are below its revenues. The debt with which we are now confronted is about 290 billion dollars. With interest charges alone now costing taxpayers about 9½ billions, it is clear that this debt growth must stop. You will be glad to know that despite the unsettling influences of the recent steel strike, we estimate that our accounts will show, on June 30, *this* year, a favorable balance of approximately $200 million.

I shall present to the Congress for 1961 a *balanced* budget. In the area of defense, expenditures continue at the record peace-time levels of the last several years. With a single exception, expenditures in every major category of Health, Education and Welfare will be equal or greater than last year. In Space expenditures the amounts are practically doubled. But the over-all guiding goal of this budget is national *need*— not response to specific group, local or political insistence.

Expenditure increases, other than those I have indicated, are largely accounted for by the increased cost of legislation previously enacted.[1]

[I repeat, this budget will be a balanced one. Expenditures will be 79 billion 8 hundred million. The amount of income over outgo, described in the budget as a Surplus, to be applied against our national debt, is 4 billion 2 hundred million. Personally, I do not feel that any amount can be properly called a "Surplus" as long as the nation is in debt. I prefer to think of such an item as "reduction on our children's inherited mortgage." Once we have established such payments as normal practice, we can profitably make improvements in our tax structure and thereby truly reduce the heavy burdens of taxation.

[In any event, this one reduction will save taxpayers, each year, approximately 2 hundred million dollars in interest costs.]

This budget will help ease pressures in our credit and capital markets. It will enhance the confidence of people all over the world in the strength of our economy and our currency and in our individual and collective ability to be fiscally responsible.

In the management of the huge public debt the Treasury is unfortunately not free of artificial barriers. Its ability to deal with the difficult problems in this field has been weakened greatly by the unwillingness of the Congress to remove archaic restrictions. The need for a freer hand in debt management is even more urgent today because the costs of the undesirable financing practices which the Treasury has been forced into are mounting. Removal of this roadblock has high priority in my legislative recommendations.

---

[1] At this point the President interpolated the two paragraphs shown in brackets.

Still another issue relates to civil rights.

In all our hopes and plans for a better world we all recognize that provincial and racial prejudices must be combatted. In the long perspective of history, the right to vote has been one of the strongest pillars of a free society. Our first duty is to protect this right against all encroachment. In spite of constitutional guarantees, and notwithstanding much progress of recent years, bias still deprives some persons in this country of equal protection of the laws.

Early in your last session I recommended legislation which would help eliminate several practices discriminating against the basic rights of Americans. The Civil Rights Commission has developed additional constructive recommendations. I hope that these will be among the matters to be seriously considered in the current session. I trust that Congress will thus signal to the world that our Government is striving for equality under law for all our people.

Each year and in many ways our nation continues to undergo profound change and growth.

In the past 18 months we have hailed the entry of two more States of the Union—Alaska and Hawaii. We salute these two western stars proudly.

Our vigorous expansion, which we all welcome as a sign of health and vitality, is many-sided. We are, for example, witnessing explosive growth in metropolitan areas.

By 1975 the metropolitan areas of the United States will occupy twice the territory they do today. The roster of urban problems with which they must cope is staggering. They involve water supply, cleaning the air, adjusting local tax systems, providing for essential educational, cultural, and social services, and destroying those conditions which breed delinquency and crime.

In meeting these, we must, if we value our historic freedoms, keep within the traditional framework of our Federal system with powers divided between the national and state governments. The uniqueness of this system may confound the casual observer, but it has worked effectively for nearly 200 years.

I do not doubt that our urban and other perplexing problems can be solved in the traditional American method. In doing so we must realize that nothing is really solved and ruinous tendencies are set in motion by yielding to the deceptive bait of the "easy" Federal tax dollar.

Our educational system provides a ready example. All recognize the vital necessity of having modern school plants, well-qualified and adequately compensated teachers, and of using the best possible teaching techniques and curricula.

We cannot be complacent about educating our youth.

But the route to better trained minds is not through the swift administration of a Federal hypodermic or sustained financial transfusion. The educational process, essentially a local and personal responsibility, cannot be made to leap ahead by crash, centralized governmental action.

The Administration has proposed a carefully reasoned program for helping eliminate current deficiencies. It is designed to stimulate classroom construction, not by substitution of Federal dollars for state and local funds, but by incentives to extend and encourage state and local efforts. This approach rejects the notion of Federal domination or control. It is workable, and should appeal to every American interested in advancement of our educational system in the traditional American way. I urge the Congress to take action upon it.

There is one other subject concerning which I renew a recommendation I made in my State of the Union Message last January. I then advised the Congress of my purpose to intensify our efforts to replace force with a rule of law among nations. From many discussions abroad, I am convinced that purpose is widely and deeply shared by other peoples and nations of the world.

In the same Message I stated that our efforts would include a reexamination of our own relation to the International Court of Justice. The Court was established by the United Nations to decide international legal disputes between nations. In 1946 we accepted the Court's jurisdiction, but subject to a reservation of the right to determine unilaterally whether a matter lies essentially within domestic jurisdiction. There is pending before the Senate, a Resolution which would repeal our present self-judging reservation. I support that Resolution and urge its prompt passage. If this is done, I intend to urge similar acceptance of the Court's jurisdiction by every member of the United Nations.

Here perhaps it is not amiss for me to say to the Members of the Congress, in this my final year of office, a word about the institutions we respectively represent and the meaning which the relationships between our two branches has for the days ahead.

I am not unique as a President in having worked with a Congress controlled by the opposition party—except that no other President ever did it for quite so long! Yet in both personal and official relationships we have weathered the storms of the past five years. For this I am grateful.

My deep concern in the next twelve months, before my successor takes office, is with our joint Congressional-Executive duty to our own and to other nations. Acting upon the beliefs I have expressed here today, I shall devote my full energies to the tasks at hand, whether these involve travel for promoting greater world understanding, negotiations to reduce international discord, or constant discussions and communications with the Congress and the American people on issues both domestic and foreign.

In pursuit of these objectives, I look forward to, and shall dedicate myself to, a close and constructive association with the Congress.

Every minute spent in irrelevant interbranch wrangling is precious time taken from the intelligent initiation and adoption of coherent policies for our national survival and progress.

We seek a common goal—brighter opportunity for our own citizens and a world peace with justice for all.

Before us and our friends is the challenge of an ideology which, for more than four decades, has trumpeted abroad its purpose of gaining ultimate victory over all forms of government at variance with its own.

We realize that however much we repudiate the tenets of imperialistic Communism, it represents a gigantic enterprise grimly pursued by leaders who compel its subjects to subordinate their freedom of action and spirit and personal desires for some hoped-for advantage in the future.

The Communists can present an array of material accomplishments over the past fifteen years that lends a false persuasiveness to many of their glittering promises to the uncommitted peoples.

The competition they provide is formidable.

But in *our* scale of values we place freedom first—our whole national existence and development have been geared to that basic concept and are responsible for the position of free world leadership to which we have succeeded. It is the highest prize that any nation can possess; it is one that Communism can never offer. And America's record of material accomplishment in freedom is written not only in the unparalleled prosperity of our own nation, but in the many billions we have devoted to the reconstruction of Free World economies wrecked by World War II and in the effective help of many more billions we have given in saving the independence of many others threatened by outside domination. Assuredly we have the capacity for handling the problems in the new era of the world's history we are now entering.

But we must use that capacity intelligently and tirelessly, regardless of personal sacrifice.

The fissure that divides our political planet is deep and wide.

We live, moreover, in a sea of semantic disorder in which old labels no longer faithfully describe.

Police states are called "people's democracies."

Armed conquest of free people is called "liberation."

Such slippery slogans make more difficult the problem of communicating true faith, facts and beliefs.

We must make clear our peaceful intentions, our aspirations for a better world. So doing, we must use language to enlighten the mind, not as the instrument of the studied innuendo and distorter of truth.

And we must live by what we say.

On my recent visit to distant lands I found one statesman after another eager to tell me of the elements of their government that had been borrowed from our American Constitution, and from the indestructible ideals set forth in our Declaration of Independence.

As a nation we take pride that our own constitutional system, and the ideals which sustain it, have been long viewed as a fountainhead of freedom.

By our every action we must strive to make ourselves worthy of this trust, ever mindful that an accumulation of seemingly minor encroachments upon freedom gradually could break down the entire fabric of a free society.

So persuaded, we shall get on with the task before us.

So dedicated, and with faith in the Almighty, humanity shall one day achieve the unity in freedom to which all men have aspired from the dawn of time.

DWIGHT D. EISENHOWER

NOTE: This is the text of the document which the President signed and transmitted to the Senate and the House of Representatives (H. Doc. 241, 86th Cong., 2d sess.).

The Address as reported from the floor appears in the Congressional Record of January 7, 1960 (vol. 106, p. 135).

5 ¶ Letter to Senator Cooper on Federal Programs and Activities in Aid of Chronic Labor Surplus Areas.   *January 8*, 1960

Dear John:

In response to your letter of December 31, 1959, I assure you that I share your deep concern in respect to areas with substantial and persistent unemployment.

I trust that it will hearten you and others to know that fourteen agencies of the Executive Branch have been contributing either direct or indirect assistance in such areas. The scope of these undertakings has been steadily enlarged. Last year I directed an intensification of these Federal efforts, which, I hope, will provide further help for existing local business and in creating job opportunities and attracting new businesses to these areas.

The substance of existing Federal programs and activities in chronic labor surplus areas range from specialized technical assistance in fields such as area development, small business enterprise, employment counseling and surveys, financial assistance programs of loans and grants for urban renewal, public facilities, state and local industrial development corporations, the procurement of goods and services and construction of government facilities.

In magnitude of impact, the defense and civilian procurement programs are impressive in their contribution to the economies of virtually all of the labor surplus areas.

Among specific examples that have been reported to me, reflecting both the extent and diversity of Federal assistance, are the following:

1. In the last fiscal year when unemployment was a widespread problem, 42.5% of the total procurement awards of the Department of Defense were made in labor surplus areas—temporary and chronic.

2. Of these total awards by the Department of Defense, set asides specifically reserved for labor surplus areas amounted to $96 million.

3. Two large operational offices of the Bureau of Census, Department of Commerce, have been placed in labor surplus areas (Jeffersonville, Indiana, and Parsons, Kansas) to prepare for the censuses of population and agriculture.

4. A total of 21 urban renewal projects have been approved by the

Housing and Home Finance Agency in chronic labor surplus areas. These involve $58 million in Federal grant funds; 17 projects are under contract for execution and four are in the planning stage.

5. During the 15 month period ending October 1, 1959, the General Services Administration placed procurement contracts totaling over $408 million with suppliers in all labor surplus areas. This represents 62.3% of the total dollar value of contracts awarded during this period.

These examples indicate that the benefits resulting from the Federal contribution in surplus labor areas have been widespread and substantial. Other programs and activities to improve community economic conditions are underway or planned. Two activities in particular deserve mention:

1. A new lending authority of the Small Business Administration provided for by the Small Business Investment Act of 1958 allows the making of mortgage loans (up to $250,000) to state and local development companies for local projects which assist small business. The Act also provides for the licensing of Small Business Investment Companies to provide equity capital and long-term debt funds to small business concerns. Already 24 loans to state and local development corporations amounting to $2.7 million have been approved, and 57 small business investment companies have been licensed.

2. Action has been taken to establish closer working relations between Federal programs and state and local efforts. The Office of Area Development in the Department of Commerce has been channelling Federal technical assistance to state and local groups, including industrial development corporations. This office acts as a clearinghouse on the methods and experiences of communities which have successfully coped with their economic problems.

Increased strength was added to Federal programs last year through creation of an Interdepartmental Committee to Coordinate Federal Area Assistance Programs. This committee has been coordinating the numerous diversified undertakings of the Departments and agencies in urban-industrial regions and now is intensifying these joint efforts.

Members of the Committee include the Under Secretary of Commerce, Chairman; the Deputy Postmaster General; the Under Secretary of Interior; the Under Secretary of Agriculture; the Under Secretary of Labor; the Under Secretary of Health, Education, and Welfare; the Assistant Secretary of Defense (Supply & Logistics); the Administrator of the General Services Administration; the Administrator of the Federal Aviation Agency; the Administrator of the Small Business Administration; the Administrator of the Housing and Home Finance Agency; the Director of the Office of Civil and Defense Mobilization; the Special Assistant to the President for Public Works; and a member of the Council of Economic Advisers.

This Committee complements the long-established Committee for Rural Development Program with which it is working in close cooperation.

Our policy is twofold: Efficient coordination among Federal agencies and full cooperation by these Federal agencies with state and local governments and private individuals and organizations that seek to help areas with substantial and persistent unemployment.

The national economy is at a very high level. We all want people in areas with chronic unemployment to share more in this overall prosperity. Through joint Federal, local and private efforts, which help these areas to help themselves, considerable improvement in regional economic conditions has been realized. Through more intensified efforts of the Federal coordinating committee above described, which I believe meets the purpose suggested by your bill, I anticipate that additional industrial activity can be stimulated and more job opportunities made available.

In addition, as you well know, I have repeatedly urged that the Congress pass legislation which I have specifically proposed to assist areas of urgent need. This legislation would give the government additional authority and finances to help these areas once again to become fully productive elements in the national economy. I am hopeful that the Congress will soon approve my recommendations in this regard.

With warm regard,

Sincerely,

Dwight D. Eisenhower

NOTE: Senator Cooper of Kentucky was the ranking minority member of the Senate's Special Committee on Unemployment Problems, and the sponsor of a resolution providing for an interagency task force to formulate plans for the development of the economic potential of underdeveloped regions. His letter of December 31, 1959, emphasized the need for informing communities in areas of chronic unemployment concerning the programs of Federal agencies. The letter was released with the President's reply.

On April 20, 1960, the White House released a preliminary report by the Interdepartmental Committee to Coordinate Federal Urban Area Assistance Programs. The report, entitled "Federal Programs of Assistance to Labor Surplus Areas" (55 pages), is in the form of a manual, with index, for use by local officials or private organizations seeking the cooperation of the Federal Government in resolving labor surplus area problems. See also Item 176.

6 ¶ Special Message to the Congress on Removal of the Interest Rate Ceiling on Government Bonds. *January* 12, 1960

To the Congress of the United States:

As I said in my State of the Union Message, the Treasury is being prevented from taking debt management actions that are fully consistent with the public interest because of the artificial interest rate ceiling on new Treasury medium-term and long-term issues.

In a special message to the Congress on June 8, 1959, I urged the removal of this archaic restriction on flexible debt management. Congressional inaction on that request has resulted in a much more rapid increase in short-term debt than would otherwise have occurred. As a result, short-term Treasury borrowing costs have risen to the highest levels in several decades and the ability of debt management to operate in a manner consistent with sound principles of sustained economic growth has been seriously undermined.

I deem it imperative, therefore, that this restrictive ceiling be removed. I am asking the Secretary of the Treasury to transmit to the Congress proposed legislation designed to attain this objective.

DWIGHT D. EISENHOWER

7 ¶ The President's News Conference of *January* 13, 1960

THE PRESIDENT. I have no announcements.

Q. Marvin L. Arrowsmith, Associated Press: Mr. President, there have been demands that this country protest and try to block Russia's announced plans to use the central Pacific to test a powerful new missile. How do you feel about this?

THE PRESIDENT. Well, I didn't know it was moon missile. Somebody said larger propulsive engines; isn't it?

Q. Mr. Arrowsmith: I think that's it.

THE PRESIDENT. The United States has always claimed the right in the high seas to use areas there for valid scientific experiment, and has, in doing so, notified everybody concerned, and then taken the proper measures to warn away from the areas involved anyone that might be damaged.

We did this in the central Pacific. We have assumed that this was within the meaning and spirit of international law; and if there is any contrary view, why, it would have to be, I think, studied in that context as to the requirements of international law.

Therefore, it would seem very unusual for us to make a protest when we have done the same thing ourselves and intend to do it again.

Q. Merriman Smith, United Press International: Mr. President, what do you think of the revived suggestion, this time from former President Truman, that you take some ranking Democrats with you to the May summit meeting? Are you considering such a thing?

THE PRESIDENT. As a matter of fact, I am not commenting on anybody else's suggestion. It is a thing that always comes up whenever there is any international conference. Indeed, so far as I know, it has always been the practice, where there was any prospect of any treaties to be signed, to bring somebody of the opposite party into these conferences, particularly from the Senate, so that when the matter of confirmation came up there could be someone to explain the details of the agreements.

Now, I have never looked at the composition. As a matter of fact, during the Casablanca and Teheran and Yalta and Potsdam conferences, I have no idea whether there were any Republicans there. I wasn't interested in those days whether a man was a Republican or a Democrat.

But there are, of course, certain circumstances where you could say such-and-such a thing is valuable. It is one of those things that is never forgotten and is kept in mind. Certainly if there came up an occasion when you would believe that there was something that might come to a head, whether it be a treaty signed, I would certainly think it would be a good idea to have others along.

Q. Ray L. Scherer, National Broadcasting Company: Mr. President, two questions about your December trip. You were acclaimed by millions of people, perhaps more people than anyone else in history. Have you had a chance to ponder the meaning of this and, two, can you tell us anything about the substance of your talk with Mr. Nehru?

THE PRESIDENT. Well, the first part, I think, is very simple. I believe that there have been a lot of people through the nations that I visited, that were a little bit of the belief that they have been accused of being unfriendly of the American; they have an opposite feeling and they wanted to express it. I believe it is just that simple. Certainly so many young people never knew of an old soldier of World War II—they were too young for that; they didn't come out for any personal thing particularly, although, of course, some of the older ones and some of them who may have been friends and associates of mine in the war did.

Largely this was an attempt to express for the United States some affection and respect for American efforts to promote a peaceful world.

Now, I could say only this about my conversations with Mr. Nehru: I talked to many people, and I wouldn't be at liberty to talk about the specific subjects. The talks with him were not only interesting; particularly those when we were alone were very instructive to me and I think showed a very splendid grasp of the situation, particularly in the areas in which he is so deeply involved.

Q. Robert C. Pierpoint, CBS News: Mr. President, could you tell us your reaction to the withdrawal of Governor Rockefeller and the resulting semiautomatic candidacy of Vice President Nixon?

THE PRESIDENT. Well, I was just as much astonished as you were. By the way, he tried to call me up and to give me some advance information. I believe he was very much annoyed because he had given the thing for release at 6:30, and it was released at 2; and so he called me after it was already on my desk in the form of the ticker tape.

I would just say that I was just as astonished as anybody else, but I just take his statement at face value and that's that.

I do agree that it does give a certain atmosphere of no competition, you might say, on the nomination. [*Laughter*]

Q. William Knighton, Jr., Baltimore Sun: Mr. President, under those circumstances, however, do you feel you want to give a formal declaration of support to the Vice President before the convention?

THE PRESIDENT. You know, the only thing I know about the Presidency the next time is this: I can't run. [*Laughter*] But someone has raised the question that were I invited, could I constitutionally run for Vice President, and you might find out about that one. I don't know. [*Laughter*]

Q. Mrs. May Craig, Portland (Maine) Press Herald: Mr. President, in a speech last summer you advocated help to the Middle East in development.

The first stage of the Aswan Dam in Egypt has now begun with Soviet help. Are you considering offering help from us to Egypt in further stages of the Aswan Dam?

THE PRESIDENT. We are trying to do that now, Mrs. Craig, through the World Bank.

The World Bank today, in my opinion, is the most knowledgeable instrument that belongs to the West to bring about, first, the probable value of these various public works, and on top of that the best way to go into it, to support the thing.

For example, you will remember when we were into the Aswan business, the dam business—[*laughter*]—well, I don't want to be accused of profanity around here—[*laughter*]—we at that time had the World Bank as the central affair.

We were to put in a certain amount of money, Britain was to put in a certain amount of money; and so we have gone pretty well on that theory, that they have got a very fine engineering exploratory service. Then, of course, this special Fund of the United Nations is doing a very fine job in what you might call the pre-exploratory efforts. All in all, I would say we would look at the Aswan Dam in the same way we would anything else—from that basis.

Q. Robert J. Donovan, New York Herald Tribune: Speaking of Vice President Nixon, sir, could you comment on his role in the steel settlement, and tell us how you feel about the settlement itself?

THE PRESIDENT. Well, it's a very simple affair, really. We'd had this long deadlock, and then there was no evidence of progress even after the invocation of the injunctional proceedings under Taft-Hartley. So, it seemed that possibly new personalities to act as some kind of mediators between the contending parties might be helpful; and I asked Mr. Mitchell, with Mr. Nixon, to act in that capacity.

Now, they were deadlocked; they would not come together, would not reach an agreement. So, finally, these people, acting as mediators, by going to each side separately and working—apparently a very intensive area of working and a period of working—proposed a solution that was somewhere between the two positions.

There are certain facts that ought to be noted. Mr. Blough very properly said this was not an agreement forced by anybody; it was forced by circumstances. Two of the important circumstances were these: the can and the aluminum contracts had already been solved and written; the other one was that all of the information to both sides was that the workers were absolutely going to reject what had been advertised as the last offer of the companies.

You are in that kind of a position when they brought this forward—this proposal. Any idea that there was threat or pressure brought to bear upon the companies is silly.

First of all, I don't know what pressure you could bring of a practical nature. Both sides did, on the contrary, voluntarily accept this solution. They did so, first of all, saying that there would be no immediate price rises—the first time it has happened, by the way, in any steel contract that I know of since World War II; secondly, if the can or the aluminum contracts had been applied—their terms, been applied—to steel, this would have been a higher settlement than the compromise settlement that was reached. So the final word on the thing was, at least the hope was expressed, that if the kind of cooperation that they now believe could be expected between labor and the companies was pursued vigorously we might indeed avoid any price rises as a result of this contract.

Of course there are other influences always at work; for example, higher taxes in OASI, as they come in, and all the rest of it. But that was the thing that happened, and it is the whole story as far as I know it.

Q. Frank van der Linden, Nashville Banner: Sir, Gen. Maxwell Taylor, in his new book, is proposing a single Chief of Staff for all the services, and a much larger defense budget of something like $50 to $55 billion a year. Could you give us your views with regard to both those points?

THE PRESIDENT. Well, I should think he has the right to his own opinion.

Q. Sarah McClendon, Manchester (N.H.) Union Leader: Sir, there seems to be sort of an attitude of kissing off defense adequacy, the subject even in your State of the Union Message; and your Republican leaders, as they came out of the White House yesterday, they seemed to think any question of adequacy here is partisanship.

Now, isn't this more of a serious situation? This Polaris submarine you referred to in your State of the Union Message, you said we would have some entering with missiles into the active forces this year. Do you mean "some" means one or more?

THE PRESIDENT. Wait just a minute. Are you asking a question or making a speech?

Q. Mrs. McClendon: I am asking two questions, sir.

THE PRESIDENT. O.K.

Q. Mrs. McClendon: Two questions, sir; with an introduction.

One is, is it not more serious, this question of adequacy of defense more serious, than just to kiss it off as a partisan matter; and, two, will the submarines, the nuclear submarines, with the missile that we get this year, be more than one?

THE PRESIDENT. I am not exactly certain as to the time each one of these comes off the ways. I know, and I think the budget shows, how many have been authorized each year. They know that the testing of the Polaris missile is going ahead, and the last one, the very last one that they have just had, has been successful.

I don't take it very kindly—the implied accusation that I am dealing with the whole matter of defense on a partisan basis.

First of all, I don't have to be partisan; and, second, I want to tell you this: I've spent my life in this, and I know more about it than almost anybody, I think, that is in the country, because I have given my life to it, and on a basis of doing what is good for the Government and for the country.

I believe that the matter of defense has been handled well and efficiently in the proposals that will be before the Congress within a matter of a day or so; and I think those people that are trying to make defense a partisan matter are doing a disservice to the United States.

Q. David Kraslow, Knight Newspapers: Mr. President, the Cuban Government apparently has rejected another protest concerning the illegal seizure and confiscation of American property. Does the administration plan to take any steps beyond the sending of notes to secure equity for American property owners?

THE PRESIDENT. In this particular stage of this particular problem, I don't think it would be best to comment at the moment as to the things that may be available to us.

Q. Don Oberdorfer, Knight Newspapers: Mr. President, you asked the Congress to study the recommendations of the Commission on Civil Rights in your State of the Union Message. Do you agree with the majority of the Commissioners that a law is needed to provide Federal registrars when Negroes are denied the right to register or vote?

THE PRESIDENT. As a matter of fact, I don't even know whether it is constitutional.

What the Commissioners said: this was one plan that they thought might have some measure of validity and, therefore, they wanted to study it.

Now, the way I feel about this civil rights, we have one bill that was put in last year in which extensive hearings have been had; and I should like to see the Congress act decisively on this particular proposal, and such other proposals that now become almost controversial from the moment that they are presented would not enter into the process of examining and passing the bill that was already put before the Congress.

What I am trying to get at is, I have no objection to the study of the others. As a matter of fact, I want to study them because I would like to see what everybody thinks about it. My big problem is, though, let's get this bill already proposed on which they have had hearings, let's get that acted on.

Q. Roscoe Drummond, New York Herald Tribune: Mr. President, you have said on more than one occasion that you thought that there were a number of Republican leaders who would be qualified to be the presidential nominee. I would like to ask whether you think it is accurate to say that the Republican leaders in the main do not welcome a contest for the presidential nomination, as has been said, and what do you think of that statement?

THE PRESIDENT. I suppose you refer to the statement of Mr. Rockefeller—I mean in his announcement—in which he said, I think, those controlling the party—something of that kind. Now, if we are talking about political leaders, some of them have no position in the hierarchy of Republican machinery; that is, they are not members of the National Committee, they are not State or county chairmen, or anything of that kind. All I have said is this: there are a number of them that I think are very, very highly qualified people. I have said this ever since 1954, I guess. But I do not know whether they welcome any contest or not.

I am sure of this: some of the leaders think that any contest is good because of whipping up interest, even if they know, or think they know, who is going to win. But I suppose there are other ways; for example, in '56 it seemed to be perfectly well known, once I accepted, that I was going to be the nominee, and I don't see that it hurt that election particularly. [*Laughter*]

Q. Felix Belair, New York Times: Mr. President, in recent days the papers have been carrying a statement from a former British Prime Minister, Mr. Eden, highly critical of the United States foreign policy, particularly in Indochina and that general area, critical of Mr. Dulles.

Well, the way we operate, as you well know, is not to disclose papers that would confirm or throw light on our position at that time.

THE PRESIDENT. Yes.

Q. Mr. Belair: I wonder if in the present instance you might make it possible for us to receive some guidance so that the public could get the true picture of what really happened?

THE PRESIDENT. Well, of course, I do not comment on memoirs, and I must say at times there has been a bit of provocation. [*Laughter*]

I think here that, as an official matter, I wouldn't do it. But remember this: Secretary Dulles was a very forceful man. He could very well talk about possibilities and ask people about possibilities that might by them be considered as proposals, when they were not meant that at all. It was to put out an idea and study it.

I do know this, that there was never any plan developed to be put into execution in the particular instance that has been talked about.

Now, on the other hand, I must say this: I have known Mr. Eden for many years, from the very beginning of World War II. I have known him in positions of responsibility, and he is not an irresponsible person. So I think whatever he is doing, he is writing the story as he believes it to be.

Q. Mr. Belair: What I was wondering, Mr. President, was whether you would look sympathetically on—I mean I understand *you* could not possibly comment on this business—but would you look sympathetically on some authorized person in, say, the State Department, advising the press and supporting the contrary view, if there is a contrary view?

THE PRESIDENT. Well, Mr. Belair, I would have to talk to them. I hadn't thought of that, but I will talk to them about it.

Q. Edward T. Folliard, Washington Post: Mr. President, to go back to the question of defense, some critics of the administration's defense program are saying that in talks with Chairman Khrushchev, you would be at a disadvantage because of the prospect that the United States will be second best in the missile field. Do you think that argument has any merit, Mr. President?

THE PRESIDENT. Well, let's put it this way: such an argument as that presupposes that I come to any conversation in the feeling of inferiority— that I am a little bit frightened. I assure you I am not.

I believe in the United States power, and I believe it is there not to be used but to make certain that the other fellow doesn't use his. I am not in the slightest degree disturbed by such a possibility as you speak of.

Q. L. Edgar Prina, Washington Star: From what your Air Chief General White said at the Press Club Monday, he believes that the virtual cancellation of the B–70 program was a budgetary decision, certainly not an Air Force decision, and he indicated that he might make his views known on Capitol Hill. Do you have any comment on it?

THE PRESIDENT. I will say this: it is certainly not a budgetary decision because there is money in the budget and, as I pointed out, there was a surplus that I hoped we could pay off some of our debts.

It was my conviction as to the necessity for particular weapons at a particular time. The B–70, as an operational weapon, is going to take a long time to produce, and we certainly ought to be in a pretty strong position in many other ways before those years elapse.

Q. Ronald W. May, Madison (Wis.) Capital Times: Mr. President, Representative Kastenmeier of Wisconsin has suggested that there might be a change in our traditional policy of not using chemical, germ, or poison gas warfare first. He said that Army people have indicated that they believed that maybe we should change our policy and use these first, either in a large war or even in a small war. Is this true?

THE PRESIDENT. I will say this: no such official suggestion has been made to me, and so far as my own instinct is concerned, is to not start such a thing as that first.

Q. Raymond P. Brandt, St. Louis Post Dispatch: Can you tell us how you reached the $4.2 billion surplus for fiscal 1961?

THE PRESIDENT. Easily; $84 billion of revenue, and 79.8 of expenditures.

Now, we did it on this basis, Mr. Brandt: we took a $510 billion GNP. Already, we are accused that it is too conservative. I saw one in a financial page the other day, a guess of 524; I saw where several bankers said 514.

We made ours 510; and on the basis of such a GNP and our tax rates, why, it was very simple to get a pretty accurate estimate of our expected revenues. Of course, we are hopeful that the Congress will see the wisdom of the recommendations we have made in the expenditure side, and by that means we hope to have that much to put on the debt.

Q. Mr. Brandt: I can see how you get your 84, but how do you get the 79.8?

THE PRESIDENT. I put that—yes, I said that in the State of the Union Message. It is the total amount of the budget.

Q. Mr. Brandt: Is that variable?

THE PRESIDENT. Well, look: now, let's don't pretend that anyone has got a sacrosanct judgment on something that reaches 18 months ahead. Of course, there are going to be some needs that are increased, and some that probably are decreased—hopefully. But that is our best guess at this time.

A budget, after all, is not a paper that you go to jail on if you happen to be a little bit wrong. A budget is an estimate, a plan for expenditures and revenues, and you get your balances on that basis.

But I do point out that it is absolutely necessary that we have savings to put on this debt that we are passing on to someone else; and possibly we seem to think it will be all right for us and them to increase it. I think the kind of alleged economist that says that the United States can afford to keep piling this debt on and on and on is not one to be very highly respected as an economist.

Q. Lillian Levy, National Jewish Post: Mr. President, it is reported that our authorities in Berlin have put a lid on press information and requests about officials in the Bonn Government accused of former Nazi affiliations. The excuse offered is that this information might be embarrassing to the Bonn Government. Would you comment on such a reason for a news ban?

THE PRESIDENT. You will have to go to the State Department. I haven't heard any such thing as this. I thought it was all in the papers; at least I have read in the papers about the things that have been going on; so I think you will have to go to the State Department.

Q. Miss Levy: Well, the report was in the *Post* this morning that press requests for such information are being turned down by our military authorities who have records of Nazi, of officials in the Bonn Government who are accused of former Nazi affiliation.

THE PRESIDENT. That is a very "iffy" question. But I assure you of this, that a local military commander is not going to get into political affairs and give out information that has to do about the politics of individuals or anybody else. This is not his business, and while there may be reports of this kind that come to the Defense Department and are passed on to State, the last thing I would think of any local military commander would be to get into any such thing as that.

Marvin L. Arrowsmith, Associated Press: Thank you, Mr. President.

NOTE: President Eisenhower's one hundred and seventy-seventh news conference was held in the Executive Office Building from 10:33 to 11:02 o'clock on Wednesday morning, January 13, 1960. In attendance: 253.

8 ¶ Letter to Gordon Gray Designating Him Chairman of the Operations Coordinating Board. *January* 13, 1960

Dear Mr. Gray:

I hereby designate you Chairman of the Operations Coordinating Board, vice Mr. Robert D. Murphy, to perform duties in accordance with Executive Order 10700 dated February 25, 1957, as amended, in addition to your other duties. I know that you are thoroughly familiar with the work of the OCB through your service as a member of the Board since July 1958. In view of your continuing responsibility as the principal supervisory officer of the work of the National Security Council in formulating national security policies including those assigned by me to the OCB for coordination, you are in a position to provide impartial and objective guidance and leadership to the Board.

This new assignment is one step which I feel should be taken toward enabling the President to look to one office for staff assistance in the whole range of national security affairs.

I reiterate the importance I attach to the Board's responsibilities.

Sincerely,

DWIGHT D. EISENHOWER

NOTE: Mr. Gray was serving as Special Assistant to the President for National Security Affairs.

9 ¶ Letter to Karl G. Harr, Jr., Concerning His Duties With the Operations Coordinating Board. *January* 13, 1960

Dear Mr. Harr:

I have today designated Mr. Gordon Gray, Chairman of the Operations Coordinating Board, vice Mr. Robert D. Murphy. Under this new arrangement I will look to Mr. Gray to give impartial and objective leadership and guidance for the work of the OCB as well as the work of the National Security Council and its Planning Board.

Within the framework of your duties as my Special Assistant, you are requested henceforth to make a special contribution to two major areas of the Operations Coordinating Board's work in addition to continuing to discharge your responsibilities with respect to the normal work of the OCB. The first of these is in taking the lead in initiating new proposals to the Board for actions within the framework of national security policies in response to opportunity and changes in the situation. The second is in placing particular emphasis on seeing that Board actions implementing national security policies contribute fully to the climate of foreign opinion the United States is seeking to achieve in the world.

You will, of course, continue as Vice Chairman of the OCB and I will expect you to continue to present OCB reports to the National Security Council as you have been doing since your appointment as my representative on the Board in March 1958.

Sincerely,

DWIGHT D. EISENHOWER

NOTE: Mr. Harr was serving as Special Assistant to the President for Security Operations Coordination.

10 ¶ Special Message to the Congress on Transfers From the Department of Defense to the National Aeronautics and Space Administration. *January 14, 1960*

To the Congress of the United States:

In pursuance of the provisions of section 302 of the National Aeronautics and Space Act of 1958 I transmit herewith a transfer plan headed "Making certain transfers from the Department of Defense to the National Aeronautics and Space Administration." This message, together with the transfer plan, constitutes the report to the Congress, relative to the transfers, as required by the provisions of section 302.

Under the National Aeronautics and Space Act of 1958, the National Aeronautics and Space Administration (NASA) has primary responsibility for the Nation's program of space exploration. The Department of Defense has responsibility for the Nation's defense program, including the development and operation of space vehicles for defense purposes.

I have recently reviewed the needs and requirements of the two agencies in their respective fields. It is clear that NASA, in order to carry on a vigorous and effective program for the exploration of space, both manned and unmanned, requires boosters for space vehicles greatly exceeding the thrust of any boosters now available. Furthermore, there is at present no clear Department of Defense requirement for such very large boosters. For this reason I assigned sole responsibility for development of space vehicle boosters of very high thrust to NASA last November. In carrying out this responsibility NASA will be fully responsive to specific requirements of the Department of Defense for the development of very large boosters for future military missions. At the same time the Department of Defense and NASA will continue with a coordinated program for the development of boosters based on the current intercontinental ballistic missile (ICBM) and the intermediate range ballistic missile (IRBM) and growth versions of those missiles.

On the basis of this assignment of responsibility the National Aeronautics and Space Administration has assumed technical direction of the Saturn booster project which was previously under the direction of the Department of Defense. This booster which promises to increase greatly the Nation's ability to explore space is being developed by the Army Ballistic Missile Agency and will soon constitute the major workload of the Development Operations Division of that Agency.

The foregoing reflects the pertinent arrangements as they now exist. I have concluded that it is in the best interest of the Nation to take another step at this time—to provide NASA with an organization capable of and equipped for developing and operating large space vehicle boosters and conducting related research. This can be done by transferring to NASA the Development Operations Division of the Army Ballistic Missile Agency and certain supporting personnel. At the same time it is recognized that the Army must continue to be able to discharge its responsibilities for development of missile systems. The transfer plan forwarded herewith is designed to accomplish these purposes.

In carrying out the transfer plan every effort will be made to prevent the dislocation or disruption of ongoing missile or space vehicle projects. The development of military weapons systems and related programs, currently being worked on by the Development Operations Division, will be continued by the Army, utilizing the skills of the transferred personnel as requested by the Army, on a reimbursable basis.

The transfer of personnel, property, and funds, under the plan, will be accomplished in such manner as to serve the objectives I have outlined.

I urge the Congress to allow the transfer plan transmitted herewith to take effect.

DWIGHT D. EISENHOWER

NOTE: The plan entitled "Making Certain Transfers from the Department of Defense to the National Aeronautics and Space Administration" became effective on March 15, 1960. It is published in the Federal Register of March 16 (25 F.R. 2151) and in the 1960 Supplement to title 3 of the Code of Federal Regulations.

11 ¶ Special Message to the Congress Recommending Amendments to the National Aeronautics and Space Act.   *January* 14, 1960

To the Congress of the United States:

I recommend that the Congress enact certain amendments to the National Aeronautics and Space Act of 1958 to clarify management responsibilities and to streamline organizational arrangements concerning the national program of space exploration.

Prior to establishment of the National Aeronautics and Space Administration, the Department of Defense had been responsible for all of the nation's space activities, including those of a nonmilitary nature such as the Vanguard satellite project designed for United States participation in the scientific activities of the International Geophysical Year. When the new agency came into existence, with the duty of carrying out a program of space exploration, it became necessary to transfer the nonmilitary projects, with their supporting facilities and personnel, to the new agency from the Department of Defense. The Act empowered the President to make such transfers. I exercised this authority on October 1, 1958, when I transferred to NASA responsibility for Project Vanguard and certain other space-related projects previously under the direction of the Department of Defense. I exercised it for the second time on December 3, 1958, when I directed the transfer to NASA of the Jet Propulsion Laboratory at Pasadena, California. And today I am transmitting a report advising the Congress of my intention to transfer to NASA the Development Operations Division of the Army Ballistic Missile Agency. The authority granted to the President has thus been used to center in NASA direction of all of the nation's nonmilitary space activities, and to provide NASA with the facilities and personnel needed to carry out this task.

The Act, however, contains a number of provisions which tend to obscure the responsibility of NASA for planning and directing a national program of space exploration and peaceful space activity. For example, there is inherent in it the concept—which I believe to be incorrect—of a single "comprehensive program" of space activities embracing both civilian and military activities, and it implies that a multiplicity of unnamed agencies might have responsibility for portions of such a program.

In an effort to deal with these problems, the Act established a scheme of organization of considerable complexity. First, Section 201(e) of the Act imposes upon the President an unusual degree of personal responsibility for developing this "comprehensive" space program and of surveying its operations in detail. Second, the Act established the National Aeronautics and Space Council and gave it the sole function of advising the President with respect to the performance of his statutory duties. Third, it made provision for a Civilian-Military Liaison Committee, which was given no other duty than providing a channel of advice and consultation between NASA and the Department of Defense.

I have become convinced by the experience of the fifteen months since NASA was established that the Act needs to be amended so as to place responsibility directly and unequivocally in one agency, NASA, for planning and managing a national program of nonmilitary space activities. This requires, first of all, elimination of those provisions which reflect the concept of a single program embracing military as well as nonmilitary space activities. In actual practice, a single civil-military program does not exist and is in fact unattainable; and the statutory concept of such a program has caused confusion. The military utilization of space, and the research and development effort directed toward that end, are integral parts of the total defense program of the United States. Space projects in the Department of Defense are undertaken only to meet military requirements. The Department of Defense has ample authority outside the National Aeronautics and Space Act of 1958 to conduct research and development work on space-related weapons systems and to utilize space for defense purposes; and nothing in the Act should derogate from that authority.

I am also convinced that it is no longer desirable to retain in the Act those provisions which impose duties of planning and detailed surveying upon the President. We have come to the end of a transitional period during which responsibilities for a broad range of activities were being shifted to NASA from the Department of Defense and NASA's capabilities for discharging those responsibilities were being developed. From now on it should be made clear that NASA, like the Department of Defense in the military field, is responsible in the first instance for the formulation and execution of its own program, subject, of course, to the authority and direction of the President.

With the repeal of the statutory enumeration of Presidential duties, the National Aeronautics and Space Council should be abolished, since its only function is to advise the President in the performance of those duties. The repeal would not, however, affect another provision of the Act which provides that the Administrator of NASA and the Secretary of Defense may refer to the President for decision those matters concerning their respective areas of responsibility on which they are unable to reach agreement. This provision should be retained in the law.

The Civilian-Military Liaison Committee should also be eliminated. The statute should go no further than requiring that NASA and the Department of Defense advise, consult, and keep each other fully informed with respect to space activities within their respective jurisdictions; it should not prescribe the specific means of doing so.

Finally, the Act should contain safeguards against undesirable duplication by NASA and the Department of Defense in developing the major tools of space exploration. Although a civilian space exploration program is clearly distinguishable from the military utilization of space for defense purposes, both NASA and the Department of Defense may have similar or identical requirements for launch vehicles used to propel and guide spacecraft into orbit about the earth or toward other celestial bodies. I propose that the Act be amended to provide that the President shall assign responsibility for the development of each new launch vehicle, regardless of its intended use, to either NASA or the Department of Defense. Responsibility for development of the new vehicle should in no way determine responsibility for its use in space activities.

Amended as I have recommended, the National Aeronautics and Space Act of 1958 would become the organic act of an independent civilian agency having a well defined statutory responsibility for which it is answerable to both the President and to Congress.

I have requested the Administrator of the National Aeronautics and Space Administration to transmit to the Congress draft legislation incorporating the foregoing recommendations, and I urge that they be enacted by the Congress at the earliest possible date.

DWIGHT D. EISENHOWER

12 ¶ Letter to T. Keith Glennan, Administrator, National Aeronautics and Space Administration, on High Thrust Space Vehicles. *January* 14, 1960

Dear Dr. Glennan:

As we have agreed, it is essential to press forward vigorously to increase our capability in high thrust space vehicles.

You are hereby directed to make a study, to be completed at the earliest date practicable, of the possible need for additional funds for the balance of FY 1960 and for FY 1961 to accelerate the super booster program for which your agency recently was given technical and management responsibility.

Consistent with my decision to assign a high priority to the Saturn development, you are directed, as an immediate measure, to use such additional overtime as you may deem necessary on this project.

Sincerely,

DWIGHT D. EISENHOWER

NOTE: The White House announced on February 1, at Denver, Colo., that as a result of Dr. Glennan's study the President had approved an amendment in the fiscal year 1961 appropriation request for NASA adding $113 million to accelerate progress on Saturn and other elements of the Nation's super booster program.

13 ¶ Annual Budget Message to the Congress: Fiscal Year 1961. *January* 18, 1960

To the Congress of the United States:

With this message, transmitting the Budget of the United States for the fiscal year 1961, I invite the Congress to join with me in a determined effort to achieve a substantial surplus. This will make possible a reduction in the national debt. The proposals in this budget demonstrate that this objective can be attained while at the same time maintaining required military strength and enhancing the national welfare.

This budget attests to the strength of America's economy. At the same time, the budget is a test of our resolve, as a nation, to allocate our resources prudently, to maintain the Nation's security, and to extend economic growth into the future without inflation.

In highlight, this budget proposes:

1. Revenues of $84 billion and expenditures of $79.8 billion, leaving a surplus of $4.2 billion. This surplus should be applied to debt reduction, which I believe to be a prime element in sound fiscal policy for the Nation at this time.

2. New appropriations for the military functions of the Department of Defense amounting to $40.6 billion, and expenditures of $41 billion. These expenditures, which will be slightly higher than the 1960 level, will provide the strong and versatile defense which we require under prevailing world conditions.

3. Increased appropriations (including substantial restoration of congressional reductions in the 1960 budget), and a virtual doubling of expenditures, for nonmilitary space projects under the National Aeronautics and Space Administration. This furthers our plans to keep moving ahead vigorously and systematically with our intensive program of scientific exploration and with the development of the large boosters essential to the conquest of outer space.

4. Nearly $4.2 billion in new appropriations for mutual security programs, an increase of about $950 million above appropriations for the current year, with an increase of $100 million in expenditures. This increase in program is needed to accelerate economic and technical assistance, chiefly through the Development Loan Fund, and to strengthen free world forces, in particular the forces of the North Atlantic Treaty Organization, with advanced weapons and equipment.

5. A record total of expenditures, $1.2 billion, for water resources projects under the Corps of Engineers and the Bureau of Reclamation. In addition to funds for going work, this amount provides for the initiation of 42 new high-priority projects, which will require $38 million in new appropriations for 1961, and will cost a total of $496 million over a period of years.

6. Substantially higher expenditures in a number of categories which under present laws are relatively uncontrollable, particularly $9.6 billion for interest; $3.9 billion to help support farm prices and income; $3.8 billion for veterans compensation and pensions; and $2.4 billion in aid to State and local governments for public assistance and employment security activities.   The aggregate increase in these relatively uncontrollable expenditures is more than $1 billion over 1960.

7. Research and development expenditures of $8.4 billion—well over one-half of the entire Nation's expenditures, public and private, for these purposes—in order to assure a continuing strong and modern defense and to stimulate basic research and technological progress.

8. Recommendations for prompt legislative action to increase taxes on highway and aviation fuels, and to raise postal rates.   These measures are needed to place on the users a proper share of the rising costs of the Federal airways and postal service, and to support the highway program at an increased level.

9. Recommendations to extend for another year present corporation income and excise tax rates.

10. A constructive legislative program to achieve improvements in existing laws relating to governmental activities and to initiate needed actions to improve and safeguard the interests of our people.

In short, this budget and the proposals it makes for legislative action provide for significant advances in many aspects of national security and welfare.   The budget presents a balanced program which recognizes the priorities appropriate within an aggregate of Federal expenditures that we can soundly support.

I believe that the American people have made their wishes clear: The Federal Government should conduct its financial affairs with a high sense of responsibility, vigorously meeting the Nation's needs and opportunities within its proper sphere while at the same time exercising a prudent discipline in matters of borrowing and spending, and in incurring liabilities for the future.

Budget Totals

During the present fiscal year we have made encouraging progress in achieving sound fiscal policy objectives.   The deficit of $12.4 billion in fiscal 1959, which was largely caused by the recession, is expected to be followed by a surplus of $217 million in the current year.   To safeguard this small surplus, I am directing all Government departments and agencies to exercise strict controls over the expenditure of Federal funds. Even so, the slender margin of surplus can be attained only if economic growth is not interrupted.

For the fiscal year 1961, I am proposing a budget surplus of $4.2 billion to be applied to debt retirement. In my judgment this is the only sound course. Unless some amounts are applied to the reduction of debt in prosperous periods, we can expect an ever larger public debt if future emergencies or recessions again produce deficits.

In times of prosperity, such as we anticipate in the coming year, sound fiscal and economic policy requires a budget surplus to help counteract inflationary pressures, to ease conditions in capital and credit markets, and to increase the supply of savings available for the productive investment so essential to continued economic growth.

The budget recommendations for 1961 lay the groundwork for a sound and flexible fiscal policy in the years ahead. A continuance of economic prosperity in 1962 and later years can be expected to bring with it further increases in Federal revenues. If expenditures are held to the levels I am proposing for 1961 and reasonable restraint is exercised in the future, higher revenues in later years will give the next administration and the next Congress the choice they should rightly have in deciding between reductions in the public debt and lightening of the tax burden, or both. Soundly conceived tax revision can then be approached on a comprehensive and orderly basis, rather than by haphazard piecemeal changes, and can be accomplished within a setting of economic and fiscal stability.

Budget expenditures in 1961 are estimated at $79.8 billion, which is $1.4 billion more than the 1960 level. The total increase is attributable to (1) an increase of more than $1 billion in relatively uncontrollable expenditures for farm price supports fixed by law, interest on the public debt, veterans compensation and pensions, and public assistance grants, and (2) an increase of about $500 million in expenditures because of commitments made in prior years for Federal housing programs, for civil public works projects and other construction, for loans under the mutual security program, and for other programs.

New activities and expansion of certain other programs have been included on a selective basis of need. These increases are offset by reductions in other existing programs, including the proposed elimination of the postal deficit.

New obligational authority recommended for the fiscal year 1961 totals

$79.4 billion. This is $306 million less than the amounts already enacted and recommended for 1960, and $401 million less than estimated expenditures in 1961.

Budget receipts under existing and proposed legislation are expected to rise substantially to $84 billion in 1961. This compares with the revised estimate of $78.6 billion for 1960 and actual receipts of $68.3 billion in 1959.

MANAGEMENT OF THE PUBLIC DEBT

Achievement of the proposed budget surplus will provide an opportunity to offset part of the deficits incurred in the fiscal years 1958 and 1959 largely because of the recession. The corresponding reduction of the public debt will reduce Government competition with private industry, individuals, and State and local governments for investment funds and will help ease the pressure on interest rates. Along with the recommended removal of the interest rate ceiling on long-term Federal debt, this will help hold down budget expenditures for interest, which now amount to almost one-eighth of the whole budget.

Statutory debt limit.—It is estimated that the public debt, which stood at $284.7 billion on June 30, 1959, will be $284.5 billion on June 30, 1960, and will decline to $280 billion at the end of fiscal 1961. Thus, the budget surplus estimated for fiscal 1961 will permit the Government to end the year with desirable operating leeway within the permanent debt limit of $285 billion. However, the fluctuating seasonal pattern in receipts will again require a temporary increase in the debt limit during the fiscal year 1961, since the present temporary limit of $295 billion expires on June 30, 1960. It is expected that the request for a new temporary limit will be for less than the present $295 billion if the Congress accepts my budgetary proposals.

Interest ceiling.—Effective management of a debt of this size requires a reasonable distribution among securities maturing at different times. Three-fourths of all marketable Treasury securities outstanding today come due in less than five years, of which $80 billion will mature in less than a year. As long as the rate that would have to be paid on newly issued bonds exceeds the present statutory ceiling of 4¼%, it is impossible to issue and sell any marketable securities of over five years' maturity.

Exclusive reliance on borrowing in a limited sector of the market is an expensive and inefficient way to manage the debt. Inflationary pressures increase as the volume of short-term and hence highly liquid securities mounts, especially if these securities are acquired by commercial banks. Further, effective monetary policy becomes more difficult when the Treasury has to refinance often. To make possible prudent and flexible management of the public debt, to permit sale of a modest amount of intermediate and longer term bonds when market conditions warrant such action, and to keep the average maturity of the debt from constantly shortening, it is imperative that the Congress immediately act to remove the 42-year-old 4¼% limitation on interest rates on Government securities maturing after five years.

BUDGET RECEIPTS

Estimated budget receipts of $84 billion in the fiscal year 1961 assume a high and rising level of economic activity in calendar year 1960. Specifically, this revenue estimate is consistent with an increase in the gross national product from about $480 billion for calendar 1959 to about $510 billion for calendar 1960. Personal incomes and corporate profits are expected to rise considerably beyond last year's levels, which were depressed somewhat by the long duration of the steel strike. The accompanying table shows the sources of Government receipts for the fiscal years 1959, 1960, and 1961.

BUDGET RECEIPTS

[Fiscal years. In billions]

Source	1959 actual	1960 estimate	1961 estimate
Individual income taxes.........................	$36. 7	$40. 3	$43. 7
Corporation income taxes.......................	17. 3	22. 2	23. 5
Excise taxes....................................	8. 5	9. 1	9. 5
All other receipts..............................	5. 8	7. 0	7. 3
Total.....................................	68. 3	78. 6	84. 0

The estimates for 1961 assume (1) extension of present tax rates and (2) the adoption of modifications recommended last year for certain tax laws. These are summarized in the following paragraphs.

Extension of present tax rates.—In order to maintain Federal revenues, it is necessary that the present tax rates on corporation profits and certain excises be extended for another year beyond their scheduled expiration date of June 30, 1960. The scheduled reductions in the excise tax rates on transportation of persons and the scheduled repeal of the tax on local telephone service, which were enacted in the last session of the Congress, should be similarly postponed.

Improvement of the tax system.—The recent tax revision hearings of the Ways and Means Committee have provided valuable information bearing on changes in the tax laws. The Treasury will continue to work in cooperation with the committees of the Congress in developing sound and attainable proposals for long-range improvement of the tax laws.

As the development of a comprehensive tax revision program will take time, the Congress should consider this year certain changes in the tax laws to correct inequities. These include amendments of the laws on taxation of cooperatives, now before the Congress, and a number of technical changes on which the Treasury Department has been working with committees of Congress. There is also before the Congress an amendment to prevent unintended and excessive depletion deductions resulting from the computation of percentage depletion allowances on the selling price of finished clay, cement products, and mineral products generally; unless the problem is satisfactorily resolved in a case now pending before the Supreme Court, the need for corrective legislation in this area will continue.

Under existing law, administration of the depreciation provisions is being hampered by the attempts of some taxpayers to claim excessive depreciation before disposing of their property. If gain from the sale of depreciable personal property were treated as ordinary income, the advantage gained in claiming excessive depreciation deductions would be materially reduced and the taxpayer's judgment as to the useful life of his property could more readily be accepted. Accordingly, I recommend that consideration be given to a change in the law which would treat such gain as ordinary income to the extent of the depreciation deduction previously taken on the property.

Aviation fuel taxes.—To help defray the cost of the Federal airways system, the effective excise tax rate on aviation gasoline should be promptly increased from 2 to 4½ cents per gallon and an equivalent excise tax should be imposed on jet fuels, which now are untaxed. The conversion from piston engines to jets is resulting in serious revenue losses to the Government. These losses will increase unless the tax on jet fuels is promptly enacted. The revenues from all taxes on aviation fuels should be credited to general budget receipts, as a partial offset to the budgetary costs of the airways system, and clearly should not be deposited in the highway trust fund.

Changes in fees and charges.—The cost of other Federal programs which provide measurable special benefits to identifiable groups or individuals should be recovered through charges paid by beneficiaries rather than by taxes on the general public. Whenever feasible, fees or charges should be established so that the beneficiaries will pay the full cost of the special services they receive. To help accomplish this purpose, I have directed that further work be done by the departments and agencies on a carefully defined inventory of Federal services which convey such special benefits. In the meantime, the Congress is requested to act favorably on the postal rate proposals described in this message and on a number of other specific proposals now pending before it or planned to be submitted this year for increased fees or charges for special services.

ESTIMATED SAVINGS TO THE GENERAL TAXPAYERS FROM MORE ADEQUATE FEES AND CHARGES

[In millions]

Proposal	Fiscal year 1961	Full annual effect
Increase postal rates	$554. 0	$554. 0
Support highway expenditures by highway-user taxes:		
Replace future diversion of general excise taxes to trust fund with increased motor fuel tax or other user charges	....	850. 0
Transfer financing of forest and public land highways to trust fund	39. 0	36. 0
Charge users for share of cost of Federal airways:		
Increase taxes on aviation fuels	72. 0	88. 0
Transfer aviation fuel taxes from highway trust fund to general fund	17. 0	20. 0
Revise fees for noncompetitive oil and gas leases	....	14. 0
Recover administrative costs of Federal crop insurance	....	6. 4
Increase patent fees	3. 7	3. 7
Increase miscellaneous fees now below costs	8. 0	8. 9
Total savings	693. 7	1, 581. 0

RECEIPTS FROM AND PAYMENTS TO THE PUBLIC

The program of responsible fiscal policy represented by a balanced budget with a substantial surplus is reinforced by an even greater surplus of total cash receipts from the public over cash payments to the public.

In this more comprehensive measure of Federal financial activity, obtained by consolidating budget, trust fund, and certain other Federal transactions, receipts from the public are estimated at $102.2 billion in 1961 and payments to the public at $96.3 billion, resulting in an excess of $5.9 billion of receipts.

This excess of receipts will be used to repay cash the Government has previously borrowed from the public. Repayment of such debt owed to the public will be greater than the amount of public debt retired, because the Government trust funds are expected to add to their holdings of public debt securities to the extent that trust fund receipts exceed trust fund expenditures. This will reduce the debt held by the public in like amount by shifting ownership to the trust funds.

For the fiscal year 1960, on the other hand, an excess of payments to the public of $542 million is estimated, despite the anticipated budget surplus of $217 million. This situation reflects the fact that total disbursements of trust funds will exceed their receipts in 1960, notably in the old-age and survivors insurance, unemployment, and highway trust funds.

FEDERAL GOVERNMENT RECEIPTS FROM AND PAYMENTS TO THE PUBLIC

[Fiscal years. In billions]

	1959 actual	1960 estimate	1961 estimate
Receipts from the public......................	$81.7	$94.8	$102.2
Payments to the public........................	94.8	95.3	96.3
Excess of payments over receipts...........	−13.1	−.5	....
Excess of receipts over payments...........	....	....	+5.9

REVIEW OF MAJOR FUNCTIONS

The following sections of this message discuss the legislative and budget recommendations for 1961 in terms of the major purposes which they fulfill. The following table compares the estimated expenditures for each of the nine major functional categories with the actual figures for 1959 and the latest estimate for 1960.

The expenditure totals for 1960 and 1961 include expenditures under both existing and proposed legislation. The allowance for contingencies is intended to provide for unforeseen increases in existing programs, and for proposed new programs not separately itemized.

BUDGET EXPENDITURES

[Fiscal years. In millions]

Function	1959 actual	1960 estimate	1961 Estimate	1961 Percent of total
Major national security................	$46, 426	$45, 650	$45, 568	57. 1
International affairs and finance........	3, 780	2, 066	2, 242	2. 8
Commerce and housing................	3, 421	3, 002	2, 709	3. 4
Agriculture and agricultural resources...	6, 529	5, 113	5, 623	7. 0
Natural resources....................	1, 669	1, 785	1, 938	2. 4
Labor and welfare....................	4, 421	4, 441	4, 569	5. 7
Veterans services and benefits..........	5, 174	5, 157	5, 471	6. 9
Interest............................	7, 671	9, 385	9, 585	12. 0
General government..................	1, 606	1, 711	1, 911	2. 4
Allowance for contingencies...........	....	75	200	. 3
Total........................	80, 697	78, 383	79, 816	100. 0

The figures for 1961 allocate to the separate programs for the first time the dollar equivalent of expenditures for U.S. Government programs of foreign currencies received from the sale abroad of surplus U.S. agricultural commodities under Public Law 480.

MAJOR NATIONAL SECURITY

Our national objective remains as before—peace with justice for all peoples. Our hope is that the heavy burden of armaments on the world may be lightened.

But we should not delude ourselves. In this era of nuclear weapons and intercontinental missiles, disarmament must be safeguarded and verifiable. The problems involved in achieving reductions of armaments with safety and justice to all nations are tremendous. Yet we must face up to these problems, for the only alternative is a world living on the edge of disaster.

While seeking the true road to peace and disarmament we must remain strong. Our aim at this time is a level of military strength which, together with that of our allies, is sufficient to deter wars, large or small, while we strive to find a way to reduce the threat of war. This budget, in my judgment, does that.

Expenditures of the Department of Defense in 1961 will continue to emphasize the modernization of our Armed Forces. Military assistance for our allies under the mutual security program will also reflect the growing importance of modern weapons and missiles in the continued strengthening of the free world defense forces.   The Atomic Energy Commission is continuing its weapons programs on a high level and will move forward with research and development on the peaceful applications of atomic energy.   Expenditures for stockpiling and for expansion of defense production will decline further, since most of the stockpile objectives have been met.

DEPARTMENT OF DEFENSE—MILITARY.—New appropriations of $40,-577 million are recommended for the military functions of the Department of Defense for 1961.   Expenditures in 1961 are estimated at $40,995 million.   These amounts exclude funds for the development of the Saturn space project which I have proposed be transferred to the National Aeronautics and Space Administration.

MAJOR NATIONAL SECURITY

[Fiscal years. In millions]

Program or agency	Budget expenditures			Recommended new obligational authority for 1961
	1959 actual	1960 estimate	1961 estimate	
Department of Defense—Military:				
Military functions:				
Military personnel:				
Present programs..............	$11, 801	$11, 959	$12, 124	¹ $11, 813
Proposed legislation, retirement pay.........................			22	24
Operation and maintenance.......	10, 384	10, 137	10, 321	10, 527
Procurement....................	14, 410	13, 943	13, 602	13, 085
Research, development, test, and evaluation....................	2, 859	3, 680	3, 917	3, 910
Construction...................	1, 948	1, 670	1, 359	1, 188
Revolving funds.................	−169	−444	−350	30
Subtotal.....................	41, 233	40, 945	40, 995	40, 577
Military assistance................	2, 340	1, 800	1, 750	2, 000
Atomic energy......................	2, 541	2, 675	2, 689	2, 666
Stockpiling and expansion of defense production......................	312	230	134	39
Total.......................	46, 426	45, 650	45, 568	² 45, 282

¹ Additional obligational authority available by transfer: $350 million.

² Compares with new obligational authority of $45,517 million enacted for 1959 and $44,749 million (including $25 million in anticipated supplemental appropriations) estimated for 1960.

Strategy and tactics of the U.S. military forces are now undergoing one of the greatest transitions in history. The change of emphasis from conventional-type to missile-type warfare must be made with care, mindful that the one type of warfare cannot be safely neglected in favor of the other. Our military forces must be capable of contending successfully with any contingency which may be forced upon us, from limited emergencies to all-out nuclear general war.

Forces and military personnel strength.—This budget will provide in the fiscal year 1961 for the continued support of our forces at approximately the present level—a year-end strength of 2,489,000 men and women in the active forces. The forces to be supported include an Army of 14 divisions and 870,000 men; a Navy of 817 active ships and 619,000 men; a Marine Corps of 3 divisions and 3 air wings with 175,000 men; and an Air Force of 91 combat wings and 825,000 men.

If the reserve components are to serve effectively in time of war, their basic organization and objectives must conform to the changing character and missions of the active forces. Quality and combat readiness must take precedence over mere numbers. Under modern conditions, this is especially true of the ready reserve. I have requested the Secretary of Defense to reexamine the roles and missions of the reserve components in relation to those of the active forces and in the light of the changing requirements of modern warfare.

Last year the Congress discontinued its previously imposed minimum personnel strength limitations on the Army Reserve. Similar restrictions on the strength of the Army National Guard contained in the 1960 Department of Defense Appropriation Act should likewise be dropped. I strongly recommend to the Congress the avoidance of mandatory floors on the size of the reserve components so that we may have the flexibility to make adjustments in keeping with military necessity.

I again proposed a reduction in the Army National Guard and Army Reserve—from their present strengths of 400,000 and 300,000, respectively, to 360,000 and 270,000 by the end of the fiscal year 1961. These strengths are considered adequate to meet the essential roles and missions of the reserves in support of our national security objectives.

Military personnel costs.—About 30% of the expenditures for the Department of Defense in 1961 are for military personnel costs, including pay for active, reserve, and retired military personnel. These expenditures are estimated to be $12.1 billion, an increase of $187 million over

1960, reflecting additional longevity pay of career personnel, more dependents, an increased number of men drawing proficiency pay, and social security tax increases (effective for the full year in 1961 compared with only 6 months in 1960). Retired pay costs are increased by $94 million in 1961 over 1960, partly because of a substantial increase in the number of retired personnel. These increased costs are partially offset by a decrease of $56 million in expenditures for the reserve forces, largely because of the planned reduction in strength of the Army Reserve components during 1961.

Traditionally, rates of pay for retired military personnel have been proportionate to current rates of pay for active personnel. The 1958 military pay act departed from this established formula by providing for a 6% increase rather than a proportionate increase for everyone retired prior to its effective date of June 1, 1958. I endorse pending legislation that will restore the traditional relationship between retired and active duty pay rates.

Operation and maintenance.—Expenditures for operating and maintaining the stations and equipment of the Armed Forces are estimated to be $10.3 billion in 1961, which is $184 million more than in 1960. The increase stems largely from the growing complexity of and higher degree of maintenance required for newer weapons and equipment.

A substantial increase is estimated in the cost of operating additional communications systems in the air defense program, as well as in all programs where speed and security of communications are essential. Also, the program for fleet modernization will be stepped up in 1961 causing an increase in expenditures. Further increases arise from the civilian employee health program enacted by the Congress last year.

Other factors increasing operating costs include the higher unit cost of each flying hour, up 11% in two years, and of each steaming hour, up 15%. In total, these increases in operating costs outweigh the savings that result from declining programs and from economy measures, such as reduced numbers of units and installations, smaller inventories of major equipment, and improvements in the supply and distribution systems of the Armed Forces.

In the budget message for 1959, and again for 1960, I recommended immediate repeal of section 601 of the Act of September 28, 1951 (65 Stat. 365). This section prevents the military departments and the Office of Civil and Defense Mobilization from carrying out certain transactions involving real property unless they come into agreement with the Committees on Armed Services of the Senate and the House of Representatives. As I have stated previously, the Attorney General has advised me that this section violates fundamental constitutional principles. Accordingly, if it is not repealed by the Congress at its present session, I shall have no alternative thereafter but to direct the Secretary of Defense to disregard the section unless a court of competent jurisdiction determines otherwise.

Basic long-line communications in Alaska are now provided through Federal facilities operated by the Army, Air Force, and Federal Aviation Agency. The growing communications needs of this new State can best be met, as they have in other States, through the operation and development of such facilities by private enterprise. Legislation has already been proposed to authorize the sale of these Government-owned systems in Alaska, and its early enactment is desirable.

Procurement, research, and construction.—Approximately 45% of the expenditures for the Department of Defense are for procurement, research, development, and construction programs. In 1961, these expenditures are estimated at $18.9 billion, compared to $19.3 billion in 1960. The decreases, which are largely in construction and in aircraft procurement, are offset in part by increases for research and development and for procurement of other military equipment such as tanks, vehicles, guns, and electronic devices. Expenditures for shipbuilding are estimated at about the same level as in 1960.

New obligational authority for 1961 recommended in this budget for aircraft procurement (excluding amounts for related research and construction) totals $4,753 million, which is $1,390 million below that enacted for 1960. On the other hand, the new authority of $3,825 million proposed for missile procurement (excluding research and construction) in 1961 is $581 million higher than for 1960. These contrasting trends in procurement reflect the anticipated changes in the composition and missions of our Armed Forces in the years ahead.

The Department of Defense appropriation acts for the past several years have contained a rider which limits competitive bidding by firms in other countries on certain military supply items. As I have repeatedly stated, this provision is much more restrictive than the general law, popularly known as the Buy American Act. I urge once again that the Congress not reenact this rider.

The task of providing a reasonable level of military strength, without endangering other vital aspects of our security, is greatly complicated by the swift pace of scientific progress. The last few years have witnessed what have been perhaps the most rapid advances in military technology in history. Some weapons systems have become obsolescent while still in production, and some while still under development.

Furthermore, unexpectedly rapid progress or a technological breakthrough on any one weapon system, in itself, often diminishes the relative importance of other competitive systems. This has necessitated a continuous review and reevaluation of the defense program in order to redirect resources to the newer and more important weapons systems and to eliminate or reduce effort on weapons systems which have been overtaken by events. Thus, in the last few years, a number of programs which looked very promising at the time their development was commenced have since been completely eliminated. For example, the importance of the Regulus II, a very promising aerodynamic ship-to-surface missile designed to be launched by surfaced submarines, was greatly diminished by the successful acceleration of the much more advanced Polaris ballistic missile launched by submerged submarines.

Another example is the recent cancellation of the F–108, a long-range interceptor with a speed three times as great as the speed of sound, which was designed for use against manned bombers in the period of the mid-1960's. The substantial progress being made in ballistic missile technology is rapidly shifting the main threat from manned bombers to missiles. Considering the high cost of the F–108 system—over $4 billion for the force that had been planned—and the time period in which it would become operational, it was decided to stop further work on the project. Meanwhile, other air defense forces are being made effective, as described later in this message.

The size and scope of other important programs have been reduced from earlier plans. Notable in this category are the Jupiter and Thor intermediate range ballistic missiles, which have been successfully developed, produced, and deployed, but the relative importance of which has diminished with the increasing availability of the Atlas intercontinental ballistic missile.

The impact of technological factors is also illustrated by the history of the high-energy fuel program. This project was started at a time when there was a critical need for a high-energy fuel to provide an extra margin of range for high performance aircraft, particularly our heavy bombers.

Continuing technical problems involved in the use of this fuel, coupled with significant improvements in aircraft range through other means, have now raised serious questions about the value of the high-energy fuel program. As a result, the scope of this project has been sharply curtailed.

These examples underscore the importance of even more searching evaluations of new major development programs and even more penetrating and far-ranging analyses of the potentialities of future technology. The cost of developing a major weapon system is now so enormous that the greatest care must be exercised in selecting new systems for development, in determining the most satisfactory rate of development, and in deciding the proper time at which either to place a system into production or to abandon it.

Strategic forces.—The deterrent power of our Armed Forces comes from both their nuclear retaliatory capability and their capability to conduct other essential operations in any form of war. The first capability is represented by a combination of manned bombers, carrier-based aircraft, and intercontinental and intermediate range missiles. The second capability is represented by our deployed ground, naval, and air forces in essential forward areas, together with ready reserves capable of effecting early emergency reinforcement.

The Strategic Air Command is the principal element of our long-range nuclear capability. One of the important and difficult decisions which had to be made in this budget concerned the role of the B-70, a long-range supersonic bomber. This aircraft, which was planned for initial operational use about 1965, would be complementary to but likewise competitive with the four strategic ballistic missile systems, all of which are scheduled to become available earlier. The first Atlas ICBM's are now operational, the first two Polaris submarines are expected to be operational this calendar year, and the first Titan ICBM's next year. The Minuteman solid-fueled ICBM is planned to be operational about mid-1963. By 1965, several or all of these systems will have been fully tested and their reliability established.

Thus, the need for the B-70 as a strategic weapon system is doubtful. However, I am recommending that development work on the B-70 airframe and engines be continued. It is expected that in 1963 two prototype aircraft will be available for flight testing. By that time we should be in a much better position to determine the value of that aircraft as a weapon system.

I am recommending additional acquisitions of the improved version of the B–52 (the B–52H with the new turbofan engine) and procurement of the B–58 supersonic medium bomber, together with the supporting refueling tankers in each case. These additional modern bombers will replace some of the older B–47 medium bombers; one B–52 can do the work of several B–47's which it will replace. Funds are also included in this budget to continue the equipping of the B–52 wings with the Hound Dog air-to-surface missile.

In the coming fiscal year additional quantities of Atlas, Titan, and Polaris missiles also will be procured. I am recommending funds for 3 additional Polaris submarines to be started in the coming fiscal year and for the advance procurement of long leadtime components on 3 more—making a total of 15 Polaris submarines and the appropriate number of missiles. Funds to continue the development and to initiate production of the first operational quantities of the Minuteman are also included in this budget.

Thus, four strategic ballistic missile systems will be in development and production during the coming fiscal year. These, together with the manned bomber force, the carrier-based aircraft, the intermediate range ballistic missiles, and the tactical aircraft deployed abroad, ensure our continued capability to retaliate effectively in the event of an attack upon ourselves or our allies.

In order to ensure, insofar as practicable, the safety and readiness of these forces, we have substantially completed the dispersal of Strategic Air Command aircraft and the construction of alert facilities. These measures will permit a large portion of all our manned bombers and supporting tankers to get off the ground within 15 minutes after receiving warning of an attack.

I have also authorized the Department of Defense to begin to acquire a standby airborne alert capability for the heavy bombers. This will entail the procurement of extra engines and spare parts, and the training of the heavy bomber wings with the ability to conduct an airborne alert. It is neither necessary nor practical to fly a continuous airborne alert at this time. Such a procedure would, over a relatively short period of time, seriously degrade our overall capability to respond to attack. What I am recommending is a capability to fly such an alert if the need should arise and to maintain that alert for a reasonable period of time until the situation which necessitated it becomes clarified.

Attention is also being given to the safety and readiness of our land-based strategic missile forces. Except for the first several squadrons, strategic missiles will be dispersed in hardened underground sites. Measures are also being taken to shorten the reaction time of liquid-fueled missiles. The Minuteman, because it will be solid fueled, will have a quick reaction time and will lend itself to mobile use. The solid-fueled Polaris to be carried in submarines at sea is by its very nature highly invulnerable.

Air defense forces.—Much progress has been made in increasing the effectiveness of the North American Air Defense Command organized in 1957 as an integrated command of the United States and Canadian forces. The U.S. military elements—consisting of parts of all of our armed services—are integrated with Canada's Air Defence Command for maintaining an air defense capability for the entire North American Continent.

While we pay increasing attention to the growing threat of a potential enemy's ballistic missiles we should not lose sight of the fact that for the time being the manned bomber is the major threat. Although some $17 billion has already been invested in defense systems against manned bombers, excluding the cost of personnel and operation and maintenance, certain segments have yet to be completed. These were described in the Department of Defense air defense plan presented to the Congress last year. The funds recommended in this budget will substantially complete the programs outlined in that plan. Specifically, the last major elements of the Nike-Hercules surface-to-air missile program will be financed in 1961 and the Bomarc interceptor missile program will approach completion. The related radar warning, electronic control, and communication systems will also be further equipped and modernized.

In response to the increasing missile threat, we are pressing to completion a new system for the detection of ballistic missile attack—the ballistic missile early warning system. Construction has been under way for the last two years and the first segment is expected to be in operation in about a year.

To provide for an active defense against ballistic missile attack, I am recommending the continued development of the Nike-Zeus system, but it will not be placed in production during the coming fiscal year during which further testing will be carried out.

The Nike-Zeus system is one of the most difficult undertakings ever attempted by this country. The technical problems involved in detecting, tracking, and computing the course of the incoming ballistic missile and in guiding the intercepting Zeus missile to its target—all within a few minutes—are indeed enormous.

Much thought and study have been given to all of these factors and it is the consensus of my technical and military advisers that the system should be carefully tested before production is begun and facilities are constructed for its deployment. Accordingly, I am recommending sufficient funds in this budget to provide for the essential phases of such testing. Pending the results of such testing, the $137 million appropriated last year by the Congress for initial production steps for the Nike-Zeus system will not be used.

Sea control forces.—Control of sea and ocean areas and sea lanes of communication is an integral element in the maintenance of our national security. The naval forces which carry the primary responsibility for this mission will consist of 817 combatant and support ships, 16 attack carrier air groups, 11 antisubmarine air groups, and 41 patrol and warning air squadrons.

From new construction and conversion programs started in prior years, the Navy will receive during fiscal year 1961 an unusually large number of modern ships. These will include the fifth and sixth *Forrestal*-class attack carriers, the first nuclear-powered cruiser, nine guided missile destroyers, seven guided missile frigates, and six nuclear-powered submarines. Three more Polaris ballistic missile submarines and a converted guided missile cruiser will also be commissioned.

For the coming fiscal year I am recommending the construction of 20 new ships and conversions or modernizations of 15 others. Included among the new ships is an attack carrier. It is planned to construct this carrier with a conventional rather than a nuclear powerplant.

While it is generally agreed that a nuclear-powered attack carrier has certain military advantages, such as extended range and endurance at high sustained speeds, these advantages are not overriding as in the case of a submarine. In a submarine, nuclear power provides the critical advantage of almost unlimited operation, submerged at high speeds. This enables nuclear-powered submarines to carry out missions which no conventionally powered submarine, no matter how modern, could accomplish.

The advantages of nuclear power with respect to the carrier, however, are not comparable. The primary requirement in a carrier is up-to-date facilities to operate, safely and effectively, the most modern naval aircraft.

Use of a conventional powerplant will in no way prevent a carrier from functioning as a completely modern and mobile base for fleet aircraft for its foreseeable life. The additional $130 million which a nuclear-powered carrier would cost can be used to much greater advantage for other purposes. I therefore strongly urge the Congress to support this request for a conventionally powered aircraft carrier.

Tactical forces.—Elements of the ground, naval, and air forces comprise the tactical forces which are available to deal with cold war emergencies and limited war situations, in addition to performing essential tasks in the event of general war. Recommendations made in this budget provide funds for modernization and improvement in the effectiveness of our tactical forces.

Increased emphasis has been given in this budget to improving the mobility and firepower of the 14 Army divisions and other active combat elements of the Army and the 3 Marine Corps divisions. Additional quantities of new rifles and machineguns employing the standard NATO ammunition will be procured, as will combat and tactical vehicles of all kinds, including the new M60 tank, the M113 armored personnel carrier, self-propelled howitzers, trucks and jeeps. In recognition of the value of artillery in both nuclear and nonnuclear warfare, an entire new family of self-propelled artillery is introduced with this budget. This new artillery is lighter, more mobile, and, utilizing new ammunition, will have greater range than that of types currently available.

The Army and Marine Corps will also buy a wide variety of guided missiles and rockets such as: Sergeant, Honest John, Little John, and Lacrosse for medium and close range ground fire support; Davy Crockett for an integral infantry-unit close-range atomic support weapon; and Hawk and Redeye for defense of field forces against air attack. Army aircraft procurement proposed for 1961 is more than 35% higher than for the current year, and includes funds for surveillance aircraft and for utility and medium cargo helicopters.

The tactical forces of the Army are supported by the tactical air wings of the Air Force which will also be provided with an increased capability under these budget recommendations. Funds are provided for increased procurement of F–105 supersonic all-weather fighter bombers. These aircraft, with their low-altitude handling characteristics and large carrying capacities for both nuclear and nonnuclear weapons, will strengthen significantly the air support available to the Army ground units.

The three Marine divisions are tactically supported by three Marine aircraft wings, which will also receive quantities of new aircraft.

Military assistance.—The ability of the free world to deter aggression depends on the combined strength and determination of many countries. The total forces of the countries receiving aid under the military assistance program include about 5 million Army troops, 2,200 combatant ships, and over 25,000 aircraft, about half of which are jet. These forces make a vital contribution to the security of the free world, including the United States.

A committee of distinguished private citizens, the President's Committee to Study the United States Military Assistance Program, conducted an extensive and comprehensive analysis of the mutual security program during the last year. I have previously transmitted the reports of the Committee to the Congress. Many of the significant findings and recommendations of this group have been put into effect by the executive agencies; others are in the process of implementation. The military assistance program has been budgeted in 1961 with other activities and programs of the Department of Defense, and major changes are being made in the management, organization, and programing of military assistance.

Last spring I mentioned the possibility of requesting a supplemental appropriation as suggested by the Committee largely to expedite modernization of NATO forces. However, in view of the time factor involved in securing a separate authorization and appropriation for 1960, a supplemental request this year is not practical.

The new obligational authority of $2 billion recommended for fiscal year 1961 for the military assistance program will provide the training and quantities of materiel required to support the forces in the countries receiving aid. Because of the long leadtime required for many items, procurement must be started in 1961 in order to provide the necessary deliveries in future years. During recent years, deliveries have been maintained only by drawing down the backlog of undelivered items by an amount ranging from $500 to $800 million per year. The backlog has now been reduced to the point where adequate deliveries in the future must depend on new appropriations.

The defense of Western Europe in this era of modern weapons is costly and must be accomplished through the combined efforts of all NATO countries. Many of these countries have now assumed the financial responsibility for producing or purchasing conventional arms and equipment which the United States previously supplied. At the same time, the 1961 military assistance program squarely faces the pressing need for new and costly weapons for which the free world still looks for help from the United States. In addition, it provides for an intensified training effort to assure effective use and maintenance of the new equipment by allied forces.

This budget also provides for military assistance to countries which are building defenses against aggression and subversion in other parts of the world. These countries border on aggressive regimes, or are confronted with strong internal subversive elements. Many of them have joined in mutual defense organizations such as the Southeast Asia Treaty Organization (SEATO) and the Central Treaty Organization (CENTO), or with the United States in bilateral defense agreements. Assistance to these countries, most of which are in the Near East and the Far East, emphasizes primarily the strengthening of conventional forces in keeping with the nature of the threat in each area.

ATOMIC ENERGY ACTIVITIES.—In 1961 the expenditures for the Atomic Energy Commission are expected to remain at the 1960 level of about $2.7 billion. Substantial increases for research and development activities will be offset by reductions in procurement of uranium ore concentrates from United States and Canadian producers. These reductions will bring ore supplies into better balance with production requirements.

Development and production of nuclear weapons in 1961 will remain at the high levels of previous years. The vigorous development of military reactors for a variety of propulsion and power uses will continue. When the land-based prototype reactor for a destroyer is placed into operation in 1961 along with four other naval prototype reactors now operating, nuclear powerplants will be available for major types of naval combatant ships. Emphasis in naval reactor development in 1961 will be placed primarily on development of improved and longer lived reactor fuel. The development of nuclear ramjet engines for missiles, of nuclear aircraft engines, and of nuclear electric powerplants for use at remote military bases will be carried forward.

Peaceful uses of atomic energy.—Expenditures in 1961 for development of civilian electric power from atomic energy are estimated at $250 million. Of this amount, $185 million is for research and development and $65 million is for construction of civilian power reactors and related development facilities. The estimated expenditures include amounts from proposed new appropriations of $40 million for assistance to private and public power groups in developing and building demonstration nuclear powerplants, and alternatively for such direct Government construction as may be considered necessary. The number, type, and size of reactors built and the nature of the assistance provided will be determined by the Commission after considering the state of technology and the cooperation proposed by industry.

Expenditures by the Commission for research in the physical and life sciences in 1961 will again increase substantially to over $210 million. This level of research will help the United States to continue its leadership in the study of the behavior of the basic matter of the universe and the effects of radiation on man and his environment. The largest part of the increase will be used to place in operation in the next 18 months three new particle accelerators in the multibillion electron-volt energy range, including the alternating gradient synchrotron at Brookhaven National Laboratory.

In support of the civilian space program, the Atomic Energy Commission will continue development of nuclear-powered rockets and small, long-lived nuclear power sources for space vehicles. Development work on thermonuclear power and on applications of nuclear explosives to a variety of civilian uses will continue in 1961.

STOCKPILING AND DEFENSE PRODUCTION EXPANSION.—Most of the objectives for the stockpile of strategic and critical materials have been met. Receipts of materials under contracts to promote expansion of defense production are continuing at a reduced rate, as the number of such contracts still in effect declines. Hence, expenditures for stockpiling and expansion of defense production are estimated to decline from $230 million in 1960 to $134 million in 1961.

Amendments to outstanding contracts are now being negotiated where practicable, so as to minimize the delivery of materials no longer required for stockpiling. Arrangements are also under way to dispose of materials excess to stockpile objectives whenever disposal will not seriously disrupt markets or adversely affect our international relations.

INTERNATIONAL AFFAIRS AND FINANCE

The United States is continuing to support programs to maintain world peace and to improve economic conditions throughout the free world. In helping to improve economic conditions, we are being joined in larger measure by our friends in the free world who have now reached a high level of prosperity after recovering from the ravages of war. Accordingly, multilateral programs are being expanded. At the same time, the pressing need for economic development requires the continuation of substantial economic assistance under the mutual security program.

Expenditures for international affairs and finance are estimated to be $2.2 billion in the fiscal year 1961. This amount is $177 million higher than estimated expenditures for 1960, mainly because of larger disbursements by the Development Loan Fund under prior commitments.

MUTUAL SECURITY PROGRAM.—Through the mutual security program as a whole the United States helps promote stability and economic growth in less-developed countries and helps strengthen the defenses of the free world. For these purposes new obligational authority of $4,175 million is recommended in fiscal year 1961, an increase of $949 million over the amount enacted for 1960 (of which $700 million is for military assistance). Expenditures are estimated to be $3,450 million, an increase of $100 million over 1960.

The military assistance portion of this program is carried in the Department of Defense chapter and has been discussed in the major national security section of this message. Economic assistance is discussed in the following paragraphs in this section.

Development Loan Fund.—The Development Loan Fund was established in 1957 in order to provide capital to less-developed countries, when capital is not available from other sources. The capital is provided on favorable terms, often including the option to repay in the borrower's own currency. By the end of the fiscal year 1960, the Fund will have made commitments for an estimated 148 loans totaling some $1,400 million. More than three-fourths of the projects it is financing are for roads, railroads, electric power generation, and industry, including industrial development banks. Because many of these projects require several years for construction, expenditures have thus far been relatively small. However, in the fiscal year 1961 they are estimated to be $300 million, an increase of $125 million over 1960. New obligational authority of $700 million is requested for 1961, an increase of $150 million over the amount enacted for 1960. This will provide the loan funds essential to our foreign policy objective of assisting in the economic growth of the less-developed countries of the free world.

Technical cooperation.—Technical and administrative skills are no less important for the newly developing countries than capital. Through the technical cooperation program, American experts are sent abroad to transmit the skills required in a modern economy and foreign technicians are brought to the United States for training.

INTERNATIONAL AFFAIRS AND FINANCE

[Fiscal years. In millions]

Program or agency	Budget expenditures			Recommended new obligational authority for 1961
	1959 actual	1960 estimate	1961 estimate	
Economic and technical development:				
Mutual security—economic:				
Development Loan Fund................	$66	$175	$300	$700
Technical cooperation..................	169	170	175	206
Defense support......................	881	740	730	724
Special assistance.....................	257	250	255	268
Other...............................	120	105	110	101
Contingencies........................	30	110	130	175
Subtotal, mutual security—economic.....	1,524	1,550	1,700	2,175
International Monetary Fund subscription...	1,375	......	......	....
Inter-American Development Bank.........	......	80	......	....
Export-Import Bank.....................	390	−56	−7	....
Emergency relief abroad and other........	113	140	131	116
Conduct of foreign affairs:				
Administration of foreign affairs...........	211	205	197	205
Philippine claims:				
Present program.......................	24	......	......	....
Proposed legislation....................	......	......	49	49
Other................................	2	5	3	2
Foreign information and exchange activities:				
United States Information Agency..........	109	110	124	124
Department of State, exchange of persons....	22	24	36	36
President's special international program.....	8	7	8	9
Total..............................	3,780	2,066	2,242	[1] 2,715

[1] Compares with new obligational authority of $6,982 million enacted for 1959 and $2,697 million (including $49 million of anticipated supplemental appropriations) estimated for 1960. The 1959 authorization included $3,175 million for the International Bank for Reconstruction and Development and $1,375 million for the International Monetary Fund.

MUTUAL SECURITY PROGRAM

[Fiscal years. In millions]

Program	Budget expenditures			Recommended new obligational authority for 1961
	1959 actual	1960 estimate	1961 estimate	
Military assistance..........................	$2, 340	$1, 800	$1, 750	$2, 000
Economic (including technical) assistance......	1, 524	1, 550	1, 700	2, 175
Total, mutual security................	3, 864	3, 350	3, 450	[1] 4, 175

[1] Compares with new obligational authority of $3,448 million enacted for 1959 ($1,515 million military, $1,933 million economic) and $3,226 million enacted for 1960 ($1,300 million military, $1,926 million economic).

For the fiscal year 1961, new obligational authority of $206 million is requested, which is $25 million over the amount enacted for 1960, in order to permit an increase in the bilateral programs. It will also permit a higher contribution to the United Nations technical assistance program and the related special fund; as other governments increase their contributions for the United Nations programs, the United States contribution, which is two-fifths of the total, also increases.

Defense support.—Many of the less-developed countries participating in the common defense maintain large military forces whose cost imposes a severe strain upon their limited economic resources. In order to help maintain political and economic stability and to prevent the cost of necessary defensive forces from unduly hindering economic development, the United States provides economic aid principally by supplying commodities for consumption and raw materials and machinery for industrial production. For the fiscal year 1961, new obligational authority of $724 million is requested, an increase of $29 million over the amount enacted for 1960.

Special assistance.—New obligational authority of $268 million is requested for economic assistance to promote economic and political stability in various countries of the free world where the United States is not supporting military forces, and for certain other special programs. In several instances, this assistance indirectly relates to military bases maintained by the United States.

The appropriation recommended for special assistance in 1961 is $23 million above the amount enacted for 1960. Additional programs are proposed to help improve conditions in Africa, largely for education, public health, and administration.

Increased funds will also be devoted to certain worldwide health programs in conjunction with the World Health Organization of the United Nations. The largest of these is the malaria eradication program, now in its fourth year. In addition numerous public health projects are supported through technical cooperation.

Other mutual security programs.—Other programs include assistance to refugees and escapees; grants of atomic research equipment, including reactors, to the less-developed countries for training and research in nuclear physics; support of the NATO science program; and the United States contribution to the United Nations Children's Fund. For the fiscal year 1961, new obligational authority of $101 million is requested, an increase of $1 million above the amounts enacted for 1960.

Contingencies.—Experience has shown that economic and military assistance is also required in some international situations which cannot be foreseen or for which it is not possible to estimate in advance the specific amount needed. To cover situations of this type, new obligational authority of $175 million is requested.

OTHER ECONOMIC AND TECHNICAL DEVELOPMENT.—More resources from countries of the free world are being channeled into economic development by increasing the capital funds of international organizations. In the past year the capital of the International Bank for Reconstruction and Development was doubled and that of the International Monetary Fund increased by half.

The Inter-American Development Bank, with planned total resources of $1 billion, including $450 million from the United States, is expected to begin operations before the close of this fiscal year. Expenditures of $80 million are estimated in the fiscal year 1960 as the first installment of the U.S. cash investment in the Bank. In addition, guarantee authority of $200 million will be made available, on the basis of which the Bank can sell its bonds to private investors.

Last October the Governors of the International Bank for Reconstruction and Development unanimously approved in principle a U.S. proposal for an International Development Association, which will be closely affiliated with the Bank. Under this proposal, the Association will make loans on more flexible terms than the Bank is able to offer under its charter, such as loans repayable in the currency of the borrowing country. In addition, it is expected that the charter of the Association will contain provisions under which a member could provide to the Association, for use in lending operations, other member country currencies which it holds. The draft charter of the Association is being prepared and will probably be submitted to the member governments early this year. Legislation authorizing U.S. participation and making financial provision for membership will be transmitted to the Congress at the appropriate time.

Private investment.—The United States is trying to encourage more reliance on private enterprise in foreign economic development. During the past year, the Department of State and the Business Advisory Council of the Department of Commerce have both completed special studies on ways to increase the role of private investment and management abroad. Tax treaties, with investment incentive clauses, are now being negotiated with many countries. More trade missions are being sent abroad. Several of the less-developed countries are opening business information offices in this country. As a result of these various activities, more private investment in the less-developed areas should be forthcoming. To provide an additional incentive, U.S. taxation of income earned in the less-developed areas only should be deferred until repatriated.

Export-Import Bank.—The oldest Federal agency specializing in foreign lending and the largest in terms of foreign loan volume is the Export-Import Bank. In the fiscal year 1961 the Bank plans to devote an increasing share of its program to transactions which support economic development abroad. At the same time the Bank plans to finance its operations without requiring net budgetary expenditures by encouraging more participation by private lenders in its loan program and by using funds obtained from repayments on its large outstanding portfolio.

Eligibility for assistance.—Amendments to the Battle Act to revise the eligibility requirements for assistance to certain countries are pending before the Congress. It is highly desirable that they be enacted.

CONDUCT OF FOREIGN AFFAIRS.—The Department of State is making plans to strengthen further the administration of foreign affairs in the fiscal year 1961. The disarmament staff is being expanded in preparation for discussions on disarmament soon to begin in Geneva and for the continuation of the negotiations on the suspension of nuclear tests. Language training programs will also be expanded. New diplomatic and consular posts will be opened in Africa, Latin America, South Asia, and

Eastern Europe. For these and other activities, new obligational authority of $205 million is requested for the fiscal year 1961.

Legislation is recommended to remove certain reservations on acceptance by the United States of jurisdiction of the International Court of Justice (the World Court).

Legislation will be requested for payment in the fiscal year 1961 of certain war damage claims of the Philippine Government against the United States in the amount of $73 million. These claims will be partially offset by an amount, now estimated at approximately $24 million, owed to the United States by the Philippine Government. Pending legislation should be enacted in fiscal year 1960 to authorize compensation of $6 million to displaced residents of the Bonin Islands.

FOREIGN INFORMATION AND EXCHANGE ACTIVITIES.—New obligational authority totaling $168 million is requested for foreign information and exchange activities in the fiscal year 1961. The United States Information Agency plans to expand its programs in Africa and Latin America, including construction of a new Voice of America transmitter in Africa. The Agency will make greater use of the growing number of television facilities overseas. The expansion of domestic radio transmitting facilities, begun last year in order to improve oversea reception, will continue. Exchanges of key persons with about 80 other countries will be increased, with special emphasis on leaders and teachers.

COMMERCE AND HOUSING

The improvements made in recent years in Federal programs for outer space exploration, aviation, highways, the postal service, housing, urban renewal, and small business will be further extended by this budget.

Expenditures for all commerce and housing programs in the fiscal year 1961 are estimated at $2.7 billion, which is $293 million less than the estimated expenditures for 1960. Proposed legislation to provide adequate postal rates will reduce sharply the net budget expenditures of the Post Office Department. Expenditures for other programs, however, especially space exploration and the promotion of aviation, will increase substantially.

SPACE EXPLORATION AND FLIGHT TECHNOLOGY.—The National Aeronautics and Space Administration is carrying forward the nonmilitary space projects started by the Department of Defense and has initiated additional programs that will lay the foundations for future exploration and use of outer space. Estimated expenditures of $600 million during the fiscal year 1961, nearly double the expenditures in 1960, will carry forward the programs now under way and those becoming the agency's responsibility in 1961. Appropriations of $802 million for 1961, together with anticipated supplemental appropriations for 1960 of $23 million to restore substantially the Congressional reduction in the space program last year, are recommended to finance these programs. Legislation is being submitted to authorize the appropriations required for 1961 and to provide permanent authorization for later years.

I am assigning to this new agency sole responsibility for the development of space booster vehicles of very high thrust, including Project Saturn. This assignment includes the transfer of certain facilities and personnel of the Army Ballistic Missiles Agency. With the imminent completion of the Jupiter missile project this outstanding group can concentrate on developing the large space vehicle systems essential to the exploration of space. Certain amendments to the National Aeronautics and Space Act of 1958 will be proposed to clarify the organization and streamline the management of the space programs.

At the present time Soviet scientists have the advantage in the weight of the payloads that they can hurl into space. This weight advantage stems from the earlier start of the Soviet development of very large rocket boosters that they considered necessary for their intercontinental ballistic missile program. Because of the relatively advanced state of our nuclear warheads, however, we were able, after a much later start, to develop an effective ICBM using a smaller rocket booster.

Our space programs are based on a systematic and technically sound approach to the complicated scientific and engineering problems involved. This approach will assure continued demonstrable achievements. Project Mercury has a high priority and we should be ready to attempt actual manned space flights within the next two years. Progress on the development of very high thrust engines and the vehicles to use them will make it possible, in the not too distant future, to launch much larger space vehicles and thus extend the conquest of space.

For the near future satellites and space probes will continue to depend primarily on Thor and Atlas missiles as boosters, with the Delta and Agena upper stages providing improved performance and reliability. These vehicles will make possible a wide variety of highly useful scientific experiments which will provide essential information for future explora-

COMMERCE AND HOUSING

[Fiscal years. In millions]

Program or agency	Budget expenditures			Recommended new obligational authority for 1961
	1959 actual	1960 estimate	1961 estimate	
Space exploration and flight technology.......	$145	$325	$600	$802
Promotion of aviation:				
Federal Aviation Agency..................	441	567	681	717
Civil Aeronautics Board..................	53	60	69	72
Promotion of water transportation:				
Department of Commerce.................	200	257	263	299
Coast Guard.............................	229	276	281	285
Panama Canal Company.................	7	4	14	....
Provision of highways.....................	30	45	¹ 3	(¹)
Postal service:				
Public service costs........................	......	37	49	49
Postal deficit............................	774	567	554	554
Proposed rate revisions.....................	......	......	−554	−554
Community development and facilities:				
Urban Renewal Administration............	77	197	172	305
Other....................................	31	39	31	27
Public housing programs....................	97	130	148	159
Other aids to housing:				
Federal Savings and Loan Insurance Corporation:				
Under present legislation.................	−41	−50	−57	....
Proposed premium increase..............	......	......	−28	....
Federal Housing Administration...........	−51	−76	−120	....
Federal National Mortgage Association......	842	56	111	150
College housing loans.....................	180	186	148	....
Veterans housing loans....................	113	230	−12	....
Farm housing loans and other.............	43	−122	36	11
Other aids to business:				
Small Business Administration..............	107	102	120	66
Proposed area assistance legislation..........	......	......	10	57
Other....................................	32	48	48	64
Regulation of commerce and finance..........	58	58	64	66
Civil and defense mobilization................	46	56	68	76
Disaster loans and relief.....................	8	8	8	....
Total..............................	3, 421	3, 002	2, 709	² 3, 204

¹ Reflects proposed financing of Federal-aid highways in national forests and public lands from highway trust fund.

² Compares with new obligational authority of $2,929 million enacted for 1959 and $3,789 million (including $71 million of anticipated supplemental appropriations) estimated for 1960.

tion of outer space by manned and unmanned vehicles. Somewhat later the Centaur project will provide an Atlas-boosted space vehicle with further improved capabilities and establish the technology of very high energy propulsion for space vehicles. In all of these projects, the success of the space vehicle launchings depends on a strong continuing program of supporting research and ground testing.

TRANSPORTATION AND COMMUNICATION.—The detailed review of transportation problems and policies which I requested last year is now nearing completion in the Department of Commerce. This study should provide a sound basis for administrative actions and for legislation that may be needed to assure adequate and balanced growth of all branches of the Nation's transportation system.

Aviation.—Primarily because of the airways modernization program now under way, expenditures of the Federal Aviation Agency will increase by $114 million to an estimated $681 million in fiscal year 1961. New obligational authority of $717 million is requested mainly for procurement and operation of radar equipment, airport landing aids, communications, and other facilities needed to handle the rapidly growing volume of air traffic safely and efficiently and for establishment and enforcement of air safety standards. Research and development activities are being accelerated to insure the further improvements in equipment and techniques required to meet future aviation needs.

The Federal Aviation Agency is already making increasing use of military facilities, and steps are under way to achieve a closer integration of air defense and civil air traffic control networks. Over the next few years the Agency will also assume traffic control functions now performed by military personnel at airbases throughout the world, with significant savings in cost.

Expenditures for subsidy payments to the airlines by the Civil Aeronautics Board are estimated at $69 million in 1961, an increase of $31 million, or 80%, over the $38 million actually spent in 1958. Almost all of the subsidy will go to local service airlines, including helicopter operations in three major metropolitan areas and intra-Alaska service. This rise and the prospect of even higher subsidies in the future make necessary the consideration of proposals to reduce the dependence of these airlines on the Government.

Airway user charges.—Consistent with the principle that special beneficiaries of Government programs should pay the cost of those benefits, the users of the Federal airways should ultimately be expected to pay their full share of rising capital and operating costs. Accordingly, the effective tax on aviation gasoline should be raised from 2 to 4½ cents per gallon and the same tax should also be levied on jet fuels, which are now tax-free. Receipts from all aviation fuel taxes should be retained in the general fund rather than transferred to the highway trust fund as at present. These actions will increase revenues to the general fund by an estimated $89 million in fiscal year 1961.

Promotion of water transportation.—Expenditures of the Department of Commerce to aid water transportation will be sharply higher in both 1960 and 1961 than in 1959, primarily because of higher levels of payments required under past commitments for ship operating and construction subsidies. A supplemental appropriation of $32 million will be requested for the current year to meet increased operating subsidy obligations caused by lower earnings of the shipping industry and to permit prompt payment of subsidies accrued.

Efforts to maintain a U.S. merchant fleet adequate, along with the ships of our allies, to meet national defense requirements are seriously hampered by high operating costs. To preserve the capability of our merchant fleet without placing an undue burden on the taxpayer will require willingness by ship operators, maritime labor, and the Government to explore and adopt new solutions.

This budget provides for expanded work on advanced ship designs that could bring sharply reduced operating costs. By extending the operation of war-built vessels, which comprise more than 70% of the subsidized fleet, over a somewhat longer period, the results of this research can be more fully exploited in replacement plans. The Secretary of Commerce is also undertaking a special study of sailing requirements and competitive conditions of maritime trade routes and services, in the hope of discovering opportunities to increase the benefits flowing from the public investment in this area.

I repeat the request made last year that the 3½% interest rate ceiling on ship mortgage loans made by the Maritime Administration be replaced by authority to charge the Government's full cost for such loans.

Work will continue on widening sections of the Panama Canal from 300 to 500 feet to facilitate the movement of increased ship traffic. Largely as a result of this program and the increased disbursements for the $20 million Balboa Bridge, which is being built to fulfill a treaty commitment with the Republic of Panama, expenditures of the Panama Canal Company in 1961 will be $10 million higher than in 1960.

Highways.—Federal payments of $2,728 million from the highway trust fund in 1961 will enable the States to proceed with construction of the Interstate System at a level consistent with the pay-as-you-build principle established by the Highway Revenue Act of 1956 and reaffirmed by the Congress in 1959. Last year I recommended that highway fuel taxes be increased by 1½ cents per gallon for a period of five years to meet estimated expenditure requirements. The Congress after months of delay enacted an increase of only 1 cent for less than two years.

As a result of both the delay and the failure to provide the full amount of revenue requested, the roadbuilding program has been slowed below a desirable rate of progress. The apportionments to the States for future construction had to be reduced and a plan had to be established to time reimbursements to the States so that the trust fund could be kept in balance. By timely action and planning, however, potential failures to reimburse States promptly for want of funds in the trust fund have been avoided, and equitable and proportionate programs in every State have been established.

I urge the Congress again to increase the highway fuel tax by another one-half cent per gallon and to continue the tax at 4½ cents until June 30, 1964. This will permit the construction program for the Interstate System to proceed at a higher and more desirable level. I request repeal of the diversion of excise taxes enacted last year for the period July 1, 1961, to June 30, 1964. New reports giving estimates of the cost of completing the Interstate System and recommendations on the allocation of costs among future highway beneficiaries will become available in 1961. At the appropriate time, further recommendations will be made to the Congress for the ensuing conduct and financing of the program.

A temporary advance of $359 million from the Treasury to the trust fund was necessary in fiscal 1960 to balance out the monthly flow of revenues and expenditures within the fiscal year, but this will be repaid by June 30, 1960. A similar temporary advance of $200 million will be required in the fiscal year 1961, repayable before the end of that year.

During this session of the Congress, funds should be authorized for 1962 and 1963 for regular Federal-aid highway programs and for forest and public lands highways. In view of the limited resources available to the trust fund and the priority requirements of the Interstate System, it is recommended that authorizations for the regular programs for each of these years be reduced to $900 million from $925 million provided for 1961. Annual authorizations of $33 million for forest highways and $3 million for public lands highways are also recommended.

Finally, I again request that the financing of forest and public lands highways be transferred from the general fund to the highway trust fund. Most of these highways are integral parts of the Federal-aid systems, and they should be financed in the same way.

Postal service.—The Post Office Department is intensifying its efforts to improve service and to hold down the persistent postal deficit while handling a growing volume of mail. Initial steps have been taken to mechanize mail processing and to reduce serious congestion at major distribution centers. Ultimately, modern mail processing plants will be established in all principal urban areas to assure prompt and efficient deliveries.

The Postal Policy Act of 1958 established the policy that postal rates should be adjusted whenever necessary to recover postal expenses, excluding the costs of certain public services as fixed by appropriation acts. Over the past 13 fiscal years, 1947–59, the Federal budget has had to finance postal deficits totaling $6.8 billion, which is almost half of the increase in the national debt during that time. At the average rate of interest on the outstanding debt the taxpayers are paying well over $200 million annually in interest for the unwillingness of the Congress to take timely action to increase postal rates.

For fiscal 1961, a postal service deficit of $554 million is estimated with postage rates now in effect or scheduled, after designating $49 million as attributable to public services. Rate increases enacted in 1958 were substantially less than needed to meet the deficit at that time and made no allowance for the pay increase for postal employees then enacted. Since then, increased railroad rates (up $55 million), costs of modernization (up $80 million), and the new employee health insurance program ($39 million) have widened the gap between revenues and expenditures.

Accordingly, legislation is again proposed to increase first-class and airmail rates by 1 cent and to raise other rates and fees by enough to cover the postal deficit. I urge the Congress to act promptly on these proposals, which will be submitted in the near future.

HOUSING AND COMMUNITY DEVELOPMENT.—I have presented to each of the past two sessions of the Congress a comprehensive program of legislation for the Government's housing and community development programs. Some of these recommendations were enacted in the Housing Act of 1959. This year, legislation will be requested only for the authority necessary to continue important existing programs and provide necessary flexibility in interest rates. The authorization of additional funds for these programs should be subject to appropriation action.

Urban renewal.—In the decade since Federal grants were first authorized, urban redevelopment has become recognized as essential to the future vitality of our cities, and planning has been initiated on 647 projects in 385 communities. However, only 26 projects have been completed. An additional 355 projects for which Federal funds have been obligated are now under way, but progress on many of these has been slow.

The budget, accordingly, places major emphasis on accelerating program progress. Sixty-five projects are scheduled for completion in 1960 and 1961. At the same time, the number of projects under way is expected to increase from 355 at the end of 1959 to 510 at the end of 1961. The acquisition of land for these projects in 1961 is estimated at more than double, and the sale of land to redevelopers at nearly triple, the 1959 amounts. As a result of the increased rate of activity, a supplemental appropriation of $50 million will be necessary in the current year to pay capital grants for projects nearing completion under prior contracts. Since the Housing Act of 1959 provided new contract authority for capital grants of $350 million for 1960 and $300 million for 1961, no additional obligational authority will be necessary for this program for 1961.

Public facility loans.—The authority of the Housing and Home Finance Agency to borrow $100 million from the Treasury for loans to small communities for needed public facilities will be exhausted early in 1961. An additional $20 million will be required to meet loan applications through the end of the fiscal year 1961. Legislation is recommended to authorize the provision in annual appropriation acts of this amount and such future increases as may be necessary.

Public housing programs.—By the end of fiscal year 1961, about 500,000 federally-aided public housing units will be occupied and an additional 125,000 units will be under contract for Federal contributions. In the allocation of new contracts authorized in the Housing Act of 1959 emphasis is being given to projects which will be constructed in the near future. The 1959 act authorized 37,000 added units of public housing, to be available until allocated. Accordingly, no additional authorization is requested. Increases of $18 million in 1961 expenditures result primarily from rising Federal contributions to local authorities under past contracts.

Federal Savings and Loan Insurance Corporation.—The share accounts of savings and loan associations insured by the Federal Savings and Loan Insurance Corporation have increased fivefold over the past 10 years. With a continuation of this rate of growth, the insurance reserve of the Corporation cannot reach levels commensurate with the mounting insurance liability without an increase in the present premium rate. I am, accordingly, recommending legislation to restore the higher premium rate in effect prior to 1949, to remain in force until the reserve exceeds 1% of the share accounts and borrowings of insured institutions. At the same time, the statutory goal of a reserve equal to 5% of such accounts and borrowings exceeds potential needs and should be reduced to 2%. In addition, the Corporation should be given authority to borrow from private sources, both to increase the available sources of funds to levels adequate to meet any temporary borrowing needs and to reduce its potential dependence upon the Federal Government.

Insurance of private mortgages.—The mortgage insurance programs of the Federal Housing Administration will continue in 1961 to underwrite a substantial share of the mortgages on residential housing. While it is difficult to forecast mortgage insurance requirements, the general mortgage insurance authorization of the Federal Housing Administration now appears to be adequate to meet demands for mortgage insurance until the next Congress is in session.

Sharp fluctuations in the demand for mortgage insurance during recent years have caused the funds available for personnel under appropriation act limitations to be inadequate in periods of heavy demand to provide the staff required by the Federal Housing Administration for prompt service on applications. Supplemental funds are usually not made available in time to meet this problem. To correct this situation, appropriation language is being requested to permit use of additional income for such expenses when actual demand exceeds the budget estimate.

Legislation should also be enacted to extend the authority for insurance of loans on home improvements. This program, which makes a major contribution to modernization of existing homes, would otherwise expire on October 1, 1960.

Last year legislation was recommended to provide some flexibility in maximum interest rates on mortgages originated under the housing loan and guarantee programs of the Veterans Administration and under certain mortgage insurance programs of the Federal Housing Administration. The action taken by the Congress was inadequate, and some of these programs are now seriously hampered by their inability at present maximum interest rates to attract adequate private capital. The Veterans Administration should be given the same flexibility to adjust its interest rates to market conditions which is now possessed by the Federal Housing Administration in its basic mortgage insurance programs. In addition, the maximum interest rate of 4½% on insured mortgages on armed services family housing should be removed.

Veterans housing loans.—The direct housing loan program of the Veterans Administration, which has been extended several times, terminates July 25, 1960, and I am asking for no further authorization. At that time, over $1 billion of loans will be outstanding, and the program will have provided over 150,000 loans to veterans. There is no longer justification for continuing this readjustment program.

Mortgage purchases.—The authority of the Federal National Mortgage Association to borrow from the Treasury to purchase mortgages under its special assistance program will be exhausted during 1961. I am recommending legislation which would permit future increases in authorizations to be subject to appropriation review. An additional $150 million is requested for 1961 for this program. The additional funds will be used chiefly to buy mortgages on housing in urban renewal areas, on housing for the relocation of displaced families, and on housing for the elderly.

Special assistance for these mortgages is intended to be transitional, and an increasing proportion of total financing should in the future be obtained from private sources. With annual financing requirements in excess of $1 billion already in sight for these programs, the need can be met only with the full and active support of local communities and private financial institutions.

At the same time, mortgage purchases by the Association's secondary market operations trust fund will continue at high levels. Expenditures for such purchases are estimated at $1,047 million in 1960 and $975 million in 1961. These purchases will be almost wholly financed through the sale of debentures to the public and the purchase of common stock by mortgage sellers. Budget expenditures of $50 million, however, will be necessary for the additional Treasury purchases of the preferred stock of the Association required to support the mortgage purchase program.

College housing.—No additional authorizations are proposed for the existing college housing direct loan program. The housing needs of our colleges and universities represent only a part of the need for new university facilities of all types. These needs should be considered as a whole and within the framework of the general problems of education. I have, accordingly, recommended the termination of the college housing program and the enactment of legislation authorizing a new program of grants and loan guarantees for college facilities, to be administered by the Department of Health, Education, and Welfare (discussed under labor and welfare programs).

SMALL BUSINESS.—The increase in financial assistance to small businesses under the Small Business Investment Act of 1958 will continue in 1961. I recommend the enactment of legislation previously proposed to the Congress to encourage the formation of additional investment companies by liberalizing the authority of these companies, thus expanding the supply of private capital available to small businesses. Other loans by the Small Business Administration will continue at a high level, but less new obligational authority is recommended because repayments on outstanding loans will increase. Efforts to assist small businesses in obtaining a fair share of Federal Government procurement and surplus property will also continue. In order to facilitate small business financing, the Securities Act of 1933 should be amended to extend the privilege of simplified filings to a wider range of security issues.

AREA ASSISTANCE.—Despite the rapid economic recovery in the Nation as a whole, unemployment remains high in a relatively small number of local areas. The chronic problems in these communities reflect primarily basic changes in consumer buying habits, production methods, and industry location patterns. Some localities and States have properly taken the initiative in measures designed to meet these problems. In addition, the Department of Commerce, with the cooperation of 13 other Federal agencies, is intensifying existing Federal programs to encourage and support this local initiative. More help is required. Therefore, for the past four years, I have requested expanded legislative authority, primarily for loans and grants, to supplement existing Federal,

State, and local programs. Prompt enactment of this legislation is important. The budget includes an estimated $57 million in appropriations as the initial amount necessary to provide the proposed additional Federal aid.

REGULATION OF COMMERCE AND FINANCE.—The general growth of the economy, newly legislated responsibilities, and the increased complexity of the problems which confront the regulatory agencies require increases in funds for most of them. The largest single increase in this category will permit the Federal Communications Commission to make a thorough study of ultrahigh frequency television to determine whether channels in this range can be used to meet the needs of the expanding television industry.

I again recommend legislation to strengthen the antitrust laws, including extending Federal regulation to bank mergers accomplished through the acquisition of assets, requiring businesses of significant size to notify the antitrust agencies of proposed mergers, empowering the Attorney General to issue civil investigative demands in antitrust cases when civil procedures are contemplated, and authorizing the Federal Trade Commission to seek preliminary injunctions in merger cases where a violation of law is likely.

CIVIL AND DEFENSE MOBILIZATION.—Preparations for nonmilitary defense have been seriously hindered by the unwillingness of Congress to provide appropriations to carry out programs authorized by the 1958 amendments to the Federal Civil Defense Act. Funds are again being requested for 1961, as well as in a supplemental appropriation for 1960, to help States and localities strengthen their full-time civil defense organizations. Increased funds are also required to finance greater purchases of radiological instruments for donation to the States; for expansion of the emergency preparedness activities of other Federal agencies; and to carry on the national fallout shelter policy.

In accordance with the national fallout shelter policy, the Federal departments and agencies have been directed to include fallout shelters when appropriate in the design of new buildings for civilian use, and funds for such shelters are included in the budget requests of the various agencies. In addition, the budget of the General Services Administration includes $6 million for a new fallout shelter program at certain Federal relocation sites and in some existing Federal buildings.

AGRICULTURE AND AGRICULTURAL RESOURCES

In the fiscal year 1961, Federal programs for agriculture will again have a heavy impact on the budget, primarily because of continued high agricultural production and the past unwillingness of the Congress to make appropriate modifications in the long-established price support laws. The longer unrealistic price supports are retained, the more difficult it will be to make the adjustments in production needed to permit relaxation of Government controls over farm operations.

Last year I proposed to the Congress urgently needed legislation relating to price supports. Very little of that program was enacted. I recommend that the Congress give this important matter early consideration.

Particularly urgent now is legislation to put wheat price supports on a more realistic basis. Stocks of wheat are continuing to rise in spite of our efforts to move wheat abroad through the International Wheat Agreement, sales for foreign currencies, and grants to disaster victims and needy people. The carryover of wheat stocks is expected to rise to almost 1.4 billion bushels by July 1, 1960, an amount that would provide for more than two years of domestic consumption without any additional production.

The wheat surplus problem has been a long time in the making and cannot be solved overnight. In fact, wheat legislation enacted in this session cannot be made applicable before the 1961 crop. The fact that any significant effect on the budget would be delayed until the fiscal year 1962 underlines the need for prompt action at this session of the Congress.

Authority to bring additional land into the conservation reserve expires after the 1960 crop year. Legislation is proposed to extend this authority through the 1963 crop year and to expand the program by increasing the basic limitation on the amount of payments that may be made in any calendar year from $450 million to $600 million. Specific authority will be requested for the Secretary of Agriculture to give special consideration, in allocating conservation reserve funds, to those States and regions where curtailment of production of wheat or other surplus commodities is consistent with long-range conservation and production-adjustment goals. The rental rates needed to induce farmers to withdraw cropland from production under the conservation reserve depend on the income prospects from farming, which in turn are a reflection of the levels of price supports. Therefore, the future authorization for the conservation reserve program should not be increased above the 1960 level unless needed price support legislation is enacted for wheat.

AGRICULTURE AND AGRICULTURAL RESOURCES

[Fiscal years. In millions]

Program or agency	Budget expenditures			Recommended new obligational authority for 1961
	1959 actual	1960 estimate	1961 estimate	
Stabilization of farm prices and farm income:				
Commodity Credit Corporation—price support, supply, and purchase programs	$2, 775	$1, 828	$2, 279	$1, 250
Commodity Credit Corporation—special activities (other than acreage reserve of the soil bank):				
Public Law 480	1, 022	1, 055	1, 172	881
International Wheat Agreement	48	49	68	49
National Wool Act	20	94	70	51
Other	347	243	124	423
Soil bank—acreage reserve:				
Program total	673	6	......	....
Under CCC special activities	(64)	(5)	......	....
Removal of surplus agricultural commodities	141	110	110	271
Sugar Act	67	74	78	74
Other	34	41	48	47
Subtotal	5, 126	3, 499	3, 950	3, 046
Financing rural electrification and rural telephones	315	334	355	200
Financing farm ownership and operation:				
Farm Credit Administration	5	6	8	2
Farmers Home Administration	246	236	221	216
Conservation of agricultural land and water resources:				
Conservation reserve:				
Existing program total	175	365	362	362
Under CCC special activities	(4)	(30)	......	....
Proposed legislation	......	......	32	32
Agricultural Conservation Program Service:				
Program total	246	244	233	243
Under CCC special activities	(7)	(1)	(−12)	....
Soil Conservation Service (including watershed protection and Great Plains program)	125	130	137	136
Research and other agricultural services	291	298	325	333
Total, agriculture and agricultural resources	6, 529	5, 113	5, 623	[1] 4, 570

[1] Compares with new obligational authority of $5,421 million enacted for 1959 and $5,099 million (including $704 million in anticipated supplemental appropriations) estimated for 1960.

Estimated expenditures for agricultural programs in fiscal 1961 are $5.6 billion, which is $510 million more than the estimate for the current year but $907 million less than was spent in 1959. Total new authority to incur obligations requested for agriculture and agricultural resources in 1961 is $4.6 billion. This amount includes $1.3 billion to restore, to the extent necessary, the capital impairment of the Commodity Credit Corporation resulting from previous price support losses and $1.4 billion to reimburse the Corporation for estimated costs and losses through the fiscal year 1960 of other programs financed through that agency.

Stabilization of farm prices and farm income.—Most of the recent year-to-year variations in expenditures for agriculture and agricultural resources reflect changes in expenditures for price supports and other programs to stabilize farm prices and farm income. During the five fiscal years, 1955–59, Federal spending for these programs has accounted for 70% to 80% of the total for all agricultural programs. In the fiscal year 1961, these programs are estimated to cost $3.9 billion, an increase of $450 million over 1960, but a decrease of $1.2 billion from 1959.

Under present laws, price support expenditures for agricultural commodities cannot be controlled through regular budgetary processes. They are the result, mainly, of the loans and commodity purchases that the Commodity Credit Corporation is required to make, and the other price- and income-supporting programs that the Corporation is required to finance, under existing laws. These expenditures reflect the volume of production, consumption, and exports of price-supported commodities, which, in turn, are influenced by such uncertain factors as the weather and domestic and foreign economic conditions.

The budget estimate for 1961 reflects the residual effect of the large 1958 and 1959 crops and assumes that yields on price-supported crops for the 1960 crop year will be in line with recent averages; also exports of farm commodities in the fiscal year 1961 may be down somewhat from the high level expected in 1960.

The Sugar Act expires on December 31, 1960. To give sugar producers maximum time for production planning, action should be taken early in the present session of the Congress to continue this program.

We are continuing to use our surplus agricultural production in many ways for constructive purposes overseas through the "food for peace" program. Under the Agricultural Trade Development and Assistance Act of 1954 (Public Law 480), surplus wheat, cotton, corn, rice, and other commodities are being sold abroad for foreign currencies. These currencies are used principally as loans or grants for the economic development and common defense in foreign countries, and to a lesser extent to finance various U.S. programs abroad. Surplus commodities are also being given to foreign governments for emergency relief needs and to private relief organizations in support of their programs abroad; over 60 million needy people benefited this past year from these donation programs. Last year the executive branch proposed certain amendments which, if enacted, would have made this surplus disposal program more effective. It is recommended that the Congress again consider these amendments.

Rural electrification and telephones.—About 96% of our farms now have central station electric service, as compared with 11% in 1935. The expanding use of power in the areas served by electric cooperatives financed by the Rural Electrification Administration continues to require substantial amounts of new capital every year to provide additional generating capacity and heavier transmission and distribution facilities. More than one-half of the total power sales by the REA system are made to rural industrial, recreational, and other nonfarm customers. These nonfarm users now comprise over 80% of the new customers being added.

The Rural Electrification Administration currently finances the capital needs of the cooperatives by borrowing from the Treasury at the statutory interest rate of 2% and relending at the same rate. Legislation is proposed under which REA would (*a*) borrow from the Treasury at not to exceed the average rate of interest payable by the Treasury on recently issued long-term marketable obligations, and (*b*) make future electric and telephone loans at the same rate plus one-fifth of 1% to cover administrative expenses and estimated losses. Legislation now before the Congress to place the operations of this agency on a revolving fund basis should also be enacted.

It is vital, looking ahead, that legislation be developed to enable telephone as well as electric borrowers to obtain funds from a mutually owned financing institution to meet the needs for the future growth of these borrowers. Under this longer range plan, loans would also be available from the Rural Electrification Administration to meet special circumstances. The Secretary of Agriculture will work with REA cooperatives and other interested parties in developing such a proposal.

Farm ownership and operation.—In 1961, new direct loans and administrative expenses of the Farmers Home Administration are proposed in an amount equal to estimated collections on outstanding loans. Loans are made to borrowers who are unable to obtain credit from other sources at interest rates currently prevailing in their communities in order to finance farm ownership and enlargement, farm operations, and soil and water conservation. Direct loans for farm ownership and soil and water conservation are supplemented with private loans insured by the Federal Government.

The present authority of the Secretary of Agriculture to make loans to farmers and ranchers is the cumulative result of the enactment of many separate laws over a long period of years. The legislation now before the Congress to simplify, consolidate, and improve the authority of the Secretary of Agriculture to make these types of loans should be enacted. Also, the pending legislation to require the States to share a greater part of the costs of farm disaster relief assistance should be enacted.

Conservation of agricultural resources.—Expenditures under the conservation reserve program are expected to be $394 million in the fiscal year 1961. Of this amount $362 million will be needed to fulfill commitments incurred in the crop years 1956 through 1960 under existing authority, and $32 million will be used for conservation practice payments and additional operating expenses under proposed legislation to extend this program for three years. Under the proposed legislation it is planned to add about 9 million additional acres to the program during the 1961 crop year, bringing the total at the end of that crop year to about 37 million acres. Increases in expenditures required for the 1961 crop year program will occur mainly in 1962 and later fiscal years.

In both the 1959 and 1960 appropriation acts, the Congress maintained the agricultural conservation program at levels which far exceeded my recommendations. As a result, expenditures of the Agricultural Conservation Program Service are estimated to be $244 million in 1960 and $233 million in 1961. The advance authorization for the 1961 agricultural conservation program, which will affect primarily fiscal year 1962 expenditures, should be limited to $100 million. The lower program recommended, together with other public aids for soil and water conservation, will meet the Nation's high-priority conservation needs.

Federal policy on cost-sharing assistance in the future should be concentrated on conservation measures which will foster needed shifts to less intensive uses of cropland, and assistance should be eliminated for practices which increase capacity to produce agricultural commodities already in surplus supply. Continuation of cost sharing for output-increasing practices would directly conflict with the recommended expansion of the conservation reserve program under which cropland is removed from production.

New obligational authority of $43 million is recommended for the upstream watershed programs, including $28 million for projects under the Watershed Protection and Flood Prevention Act. Of this amount, $5 million is provided to initiate construction on projects involving an estimated total Federal cost of $29 million.

New obligational authority of $10 million is requested for the Great Plains conservation program, the same as for 1960. Under this program conducted in designated counties of the 10 Great Plains States, the Federal Government provides cost-sharing and technical assistance to farmers who enter into long-term contracts to make needed adjustments of land use on their farms.

Research and other agricultural services.—Expenditures for research, education, and other agricultural services, exclusive of programs financed with foreign currencies, will be about $8 million higher in the fiscal year 1961 than in 1960. This amount will provide increased support for the research programs on pesticide residues and on industrial uses of farm commodities. It will also provide increased support for the rural development program which is making an important contribution to the solution of the economic problems of rural areas arising out of technological changes in agriculture and inadequate employment opportunities.

In addition, it is estimated that $19 million will be spent in 1961 for the purchase of foreign currencies, obtained from the sale of surplus farm commodities, to be used for research and market development work abroad. This compares with approximately $12 million in foreign currencies to be used for this purpose in 1960.

NATURAL RESOURCES

The recommendations in this budget for Federal natural resource programs take into account their great importance to the Nation's economic growth and security.

The estimated total of $1.9 billion to be spent in the fiscal year 1961 for natural resources is more than has been spent for this purpose in any previous year. The increase of $152 million over 1960 is predominantly for water resources programs.

Water resources.—The Corps of Engineers and the Bureau of Reclamation will spend an estimated $1.2 billion in the fiscal year 1961 to construct, maintain, and operate flood control, navigation, irrigation, power, and related projects. This record total includes, in addition to operating costs, $965 million to continue construction on projects started in 1960 or prior years, $12 million for advance planning, and $18 million for the first-year expenditures on 42 proposed new starts. These new projects, as well as three new construction starts by the Tennessee Valley Authority and one by the International Boundary and Water Commission, are recommended in this budget in the interest of balanced development of water resources.

For the Corps of Engineers, appropriations (as distinct from the expenditures previously discussed) of $21 million are required for starting 31 new projects and for an additional number of smaller projects costing less than $400,000 each. The estimated commitments for these new projects total $301 million. Appropriations of $6 million for 1961 are recommended for the Bureau of Reclamation to begin construction on six projects with total estimated commitments of $184 million, and $11 million for loans which will be used by local groups to start work on five small reclamation projects.

I again recommend that the Congress authorize the Fryingpan-Arkansas project in Colorado.

To carry forward the joint development of the waters of the Rio Grande, construction should be started on the Amistad (Diablo) Dam, in accordance with the treaty of February 3, 1944, between the United States and Mexico. I urge the Congress to enact promptly the legislation now needed to authorize negotiation of an agreement for this construction. Funds will be requested for the U.S. share of the first-year cost of this project following enactment of the legislation. Provision is made in this budget to begin modification of the lower Rio Grande levee system.

Under legislation enacted during the past session, the Tennessee Valley Authority plans to issue an estimated $115 million of revenue bonds in 1961. These funds will be used to help finance construction of a second unit in the Paradise steam powerplant and of other units under way, including new generating capacity in the eastern part of the TVA area. The Authority will start construction of the Melton Hill project for navigation and power. In accordance with this administration's policy, and as authorized under the Tennessee Valley Authority Act as amended by the recently enacted revenue bond legislation, the power facilities portion of this project will be financed from net power proceeds and revenue bonds, and the remaining portion will be financed from appropriations. With the completion of the Wilson lock, the present lock at Wheeler Dam will be a bottleneck for shipping on the Tennessee River. Appropriations are therefore recommended for 1961 to begin construction of a new lock at Wheeler Dam.

NATURAL RESOURCES

[Fiscal years. In millions]

Program or agency	Budget expenditures			Recommended new obligational authority for 1961
	1959 actual	1960 estimate	1961 estimate	
Land and water resources:				
Corps of Engineers.........................	$779	$860	$910	$936
Department of the Interior:				
Bureau of Reclamation.................	246	234	300	314
Power marketing agencies..............	33	40	40	40
Indian lands resources.................	57	62	57	41
Public domain and other..............	33	36	40	38
Saint Lawrence Seaway Development Corporation...............................	15	7	4	....
Tennessee Valley Authority...............	7	35	73	21
Federal Power Commission...............	7	7	8	8
Department of State and other............	5	6	9	9
Mineral resources..........................	71	66	64	63
Forest resources...........................	201	223	222	191
Recreational resources.....................	86	87	87	54
Fish and wildlife resources..................	68	70	71	68
General resource surveys and other..........	60	53	53	53
Total.............................	1, 669	1, 785	1, 938	[1] 1, 836

[1] Compares with new obligational authority of $1,742 million enacted for 1959 and $2,538 million (including $32 million of anticipated supplemental appropriations) estimated for 1960.

Research for converting sea water and brackish water into fresh water, carried on cooperatively by the Department of the Interior and non-Federal groups, has progressed to the point where some processes are in the development stage. Construction will begin in 1960 at Freeport, Tex., on a demonstration plant for conversion of sea water, and $1.5 million is recommended in the 1961 budget for the Federal cost of building the first brackish water plant as well as a second sea water plant. Advance planning will be completed in 1961 on two additional demonstration plants.

Cost-sharing on flood protection projects.—It is essential that legislation be promptly enacted to establish a consistent basis for cost-sharing on projects which provide flood protection benefits. At the present time, the various Federal agencies responsible for flood protection operate under different and confusing cost-sharing standards. The non-Federal contributions vary from zero to over 60%. This intolerable situation should be corrected. Legislation now before the Congress would require generally that identifiable non-Federal interests receiving flood protection benefits bear at least 30% of the costs of flood protection. The value of lands, easements, and rights-of-way contributed locally would be included as part of this non-Federal share. The cost of operation and maintenance would also be a State or local responsibility.

Mineral resources.—Amendments to the Helium Act were recommended last year to carry out a long-range plan for conserving helium. This lightweight nonflammable gas is important to the Nation's atomic energy and missile programs, and known deposits of it are extremely limited. Under the legislation proposed, private industry would be encouraged to finance, build, and operate plants which would make helium available for conservation by the Department of the Interior. Prompt enactment is needed to check the waste of this essential gas.

The Bureau of Mines will continue its research on improved methods of production and utilization of coal and other minerals. Legislation is again recommended to grant authority to the Secretary of the Interior to contract for coal research, thus allowing the Secretary to use outside scientific resources to assist the coal industry.

Other resource programs.—In the fiscal year 1961, programs for conserving and developing the resources of the public domain and Indian lands will be carried on at about the 1960 levels. Although total expenditures for forest resources are estimated at about the same level in 1961 as in 1960, some increases are provided in 1961 to carry forward the long-range program of the Forest Service for conservation and development, including added facilities and services to accommodate campers and picnickers. It is expected that these increased expenditures will be offset by a decrease in the unusually large 1960 outlays for fighting forest fires.

Receipts from the timber, grazing, and mineral resources on these public lands are estimated to increase to a total of over $400 million in 1961, including revenues from mineral leases on the Outer Continental Shelf. To obtain a more adequate return for use of federally-owned resources, legislation is again recommended to revise the fee schedule for noncompetitive oil and gas leases on public domain lands.

In the interest of improving efficiency and providing convenience for the non-Federal parties concerned, certain functions with respect to land and timber exchanges should be transferred from the Secretary of the Interior to the Secretary of Agriculture by legislation embodying the basic provisions of Reorganization Plan No. 1 of 1959, which was disapproved by the Congress. In these exchanges, the Government obtains non-Federal lands in exchange for national forest lands administered by the Secretary of Agriculture or for timber on such lands. This legislation is needed to simplify the work relating to these land exchanges.

Each year more of our citizens use and enjoy the national parks. Expenditures of $86 million estimated for the National Park Service in 1961 for recreational resources will provide for additional urgently needed facilities and services for visitors, for maintenance and operation of the present facilities, and for selective acquisition of lands to add to existing park areas.

Before it is too late we should take steps to preserve, for public benefit, part of the remaining undeveloped shore areas. I hope, therefore, that the Congress will enact during this session the legislation proposed in the last session to permit the Secretary of the Interior to select and acquire for the national park system three areas which would be of national significance because of their outstanding natural and scenic features, recreational advantages, and other public values.

Contract authority is available to finance planned construction of parkways, roads, and trails in the national parks and forests and on Indian lands during 1961. Beginning in 1962, this construction should be financed by direct appropriations, and the budget so contemplates.

Recent legislation increased the fee charged to hunters of migratory birds and earmarked these revenues for acquisition of lands for refuges and nesting areas. In 1961 land acquisitions from these revenues will be four times those of the current year. Other proposed increases in expenditures for fish and wildlife resources are mainly for fishery research.

LABOR AND WELFARE

Budget expenditures for labor and welfare programs in the fiscal year 1961 are estimated to reach an all-time high of $4.6 billion, of which three-fourths will take the form of grants to States and localities. The total expenditures are estimated to be $128 million more than for the current year. The largest increase is for promotion of public health, mainly for research and hospital construction, as a result of much larger appropriations by the Congress in previous years. Significant increases are also estimated for the support of basic research provided by the National Science Foundation and for the defense education and public assistance programs of the Department of Health, Education, and Welfare.

Budget expenditures for labor and welfare programs will be more than double the amount a decade ago. During the same period, trust fund expenditures for these programs, including social security and unemployment compensation, will have quintupled to an estimated $16.2 billion in 1961.

New obligational authority recommended for 1961 totals $4.5 billion, about the same as for 1960 but $356 million more than for 1959. Reductions from 1960 are recommended in the grant-in-aid programs for assistance to schools in federally-affected areas, for hospital construction, and for waste treatment works construction. Larger appropriations are proposed for other presently authorized activities in the fields of science, vocational rehabilitation, education, welfare, and health. In addition, a number of new programs are recommended to meet important national needs, particularly in the education and labor fields.

In the last several years great strides forward have been made in the social security, welfare, and health fields. The Secretary of Health, Education, and Welfare is continually reviewing the various programs in these fields for the purpose of determining where improvements should be made. As needs for improvement are found, appropriate recommendations will be made.

EDUCATION AND RESEARCH.—Our Nation seeks to foster a climate of freedom and creativity in which education, the arts, and fundamental science can flourish. The Federal Government helps in the attainment of these objectives through programs for support of basic research, aid to educational institutions, and training assistance to individuals in various fields important to the national interest. In this budget I recommend

LABOR AND WELFARE

[Fiscal years. In millions]

Program or agency	Budget expenditures			Recommended new obligational authority for 1961
	1959 actual	1960 estimate	1961 estimate	
Promotion of education:				
National Science Foundation, science education.................................	$51	$54	$59	$70
Department of Health, Education, and Welfare:				
Defense education program..............	78	134	170	171
Assistance to schools in federally-affected areas...............................	216	234	207	171
Vocational education and other...........	63	67	67	69
Other, primarily Bureau of Indian Affairs....	60	60	62	65
Promotion of science, research, libraries and museums:				
National Science Foundation, basic research..	55	71	101	122
Department of Commerce:				
Bureau of the Census...................	23	91	36	29
National Bureau of Standards and other....	12	22	33	50
Other.................................	27	37	50	45
Labor and manpower:				
Temporary extended unemployment compensation.................................	447	−7	......	....
Grants for administration of employment service and unemployment compensation.....	306	323	311	326
Other.................................	91	99	124	126
Promotion of public health:				
National Institutes of Health, research grants and activities.........................	265	364	390	400
Grants for construction of health research facilities....................................	23	26	29	25
Hospital construction grants..............	136	144	161	126
Grants for construction of waste treatment facilities...............................	36	45	45	20
Other.................................	243	271	279	276
Public assistance.........................	1, 969	2, 056	2, 087	2, 087
Correctional and penal institutions...........	39	46	48	57
Other welfare services:				
School lunch and special milk programs......	218	234	234	225
Other.................................	61	71	76	79
Total..............................	4, 421	4, 441	4, 569	[1] 4, 538

[1] Compares with new obligational authority of $4,182 million enacted for 1959 and $4,543 million (including $22 million in anticipated supplemental appropriations) estimated for 1960.

increased appropriations for high-priority education and research programs and enactment of new legislation to authorize additional aids to education.

I am recommending repeal of the provision of the National Defense Education Act that prohibits payments or loans from being made to any individual unless he executes an affidavit that he does not believe in or belong to any organization that teaches the illegal overthrow of the Government. This affidavit requirement is unwarranted and justifiably resented by a large part of our educational community which feels that it is being singled out for this requirement.

Education.—Expenditures for the education-aid programs authorized by the National Defense Education Act of 1958 will increase sharply in 1961. During the current school year more than 100,000 students from 1,368 colleges, about four times the number of students last year, are expected to borrow from college loan funds to which the Government makes repayable advances. A supplemental appropriation of nearly $10 million is proposed to enlarge this loan program for 1960. A small increase in appropriations is recommended for 1961 pending further experience on the rate at which loans will be made to students. Increases are also proposed for fellowships for prospective college teachers; for grants to States for science, mathematics, and foreign language teaching equipment; for research in the educational use of television and other media; for contracts with universities for training of counselors and for foreign language training; and for grants to States for vocational training in occupations requiring scientific skills.

Appropriations of $70 million are requested for aids to science education programs administered by the National Science Foundation, an increase of $3 million over the amount provided in 1960.

The budget includes the same aggregate amount for vocational education programs as was appropriated this year, but with shift in emphasis. The need for Federal assistance in the vocational education programs begun in 1917 for the purpose of stimulating training in agriculture, home economics, industrial trades, and distributive occupations is not as great as for promotion of training in new science-age skills. Thus as increased funds for training needs in new skills are provided under the National Defense Education Act, Federal assistance for the older programs is being reduced by a corresponding amount.

Appropriations recommended for 1961 to assist school districts whose enrollment comes partially from children whose parents work or reside on Federal property are $54 million below those enacted for 1960 and are in line with requirements under legislation proposed by the administration last year. The appropriation recommended for these programs is the maximum which I believe should be provided. The substantial increase in Federal employment during World War II, which led to the enactment of this legislation in 1950, has been superseded by a relatively stable Federal establishment. In many cases, the presence of Federal installations in the communities adds to rather than detracts from the revenue base for the support of schools. This is particularly true where parents employed by the Government live on private property which is subject to State and local taxation even though they earn their income on nontaxable Federal property. The proposed legislation would discharge more equitably the Federal responsibility in these districts, and its prompt enactment by the Congress is recommended.

The pressing need now is not for aid to federally-affected districts on the basis initiated in 1950 but for general aid to help localities with limited resources to build public schools. Despite encouraging progress in the rate of school construction, many school districts are still finding it difficult to avoid overcrowding and double sessions as enrollments continue to mount. Moreover, increasing secondary school enrollments require facilities which are much more costly than elementary school classrooms. Last year the administration recommended legislation authorizing annual Federal advances to local school districts to pay up to half the debt service (principal and interest) on $3 billion of bonds to be issued in the next five years for school construction. This legislation is designed to stimulate, not supplant, additional State and local effort. Affirmative action should be taken this year on that proposal.

Congressional approval of the administration's proposals for aid to higher educational institutions is also essential. The enrollment growth facing colleges and universities from 1960 to 1975 brings a need for additional academic, housing, and related educational facilities. To help colleges finance the construction required, the administration's proposal would authorize Federal guarantees of $1 billion in bonds with interest subject to Federal taxation, and would provide Federal grants, payable over 20 years, equal to 25% of the principal of $2 billion of bonds. This program would provide aid on a much broader basis, and result in the construction of much larger total amounts of college facilities per dollar of Federal expenditures, than the present more limited college housing loan program which should be allowed to expire.

Basic research.—To provide a strong foundation of fundamental scientific knowledge for the Nation's future advancement, this budget provides, in various functional categories including major national security, expenditures totaling more than $600 million for support of basic research in 1961.

Appropriations of $122 million are recommended for support of basic research by the National Science Foundation, an increase of $34 million over 1960. The total includes $79 million for basic research projects and $15 million for grants to universities for modernization of graduate level laboratories under a program initiated in 1960. Increased support is also provided for scientific work of the Bureau of Standards, including funds for two new laboratories, as a first step in the construction of completely new facilities for the agency.

Oceanography.—Federal support of oceanography and related marine sciences is being substantially augmented by several agencies under a long-range program developed by the Federal Council on Science and Technology to strengthen the Nation's effort in this field. This program stems from a study undertaken by the National Academy of Sciences at the request of several agencies. The expansion of oceanographic research will be undertaken by the Navy, the Departments of Commerce and the Interior, and the National Science Foundation. Funds are provided for the construction of new vessels and the replacement of obsolete vessels, and for increased support for research by private institutions.

Government statistical services.—Adequate and timely national statistical information is essential for recording and appraising the performance of the Nation's economy, and for formulating public and private policies. Activities planned in various agencies for the fiscal year 1961 will help close significant gaps in our statistical information and make improvements in current data. Obligations for these purposes in the various functional categories of the budget are estimated at $62 million, including $20 million for the decennial census and other periodic statistical programs.

This budget includes funds for tabulating and processing basic economic and demographic data collected through the Eighteenth Decennial Census, and for the final publication of the results of the 1958 censuses of business, manufactures, and mineral industries. Other recommendations include the initiation of a new series on the service trades and the improvement of data on retail trade, on consumer prices, on health, on crop and livestock production, and on State and local government finances.

LABOR AND MANPOWER.—Last year the administration recommended and the Congress enacted much-needed legislation designed to protect workers and the public from racketeering, corruption, and abuse of democratic processes which had been disclosed in the affairs of a few labor unions. To assure effective and efficient administration of this new law, the budget recommends supplemental appropriations in 1960 for the National Labor Relations Board and the newly established Bureau of Labor-Management Reports in the Department of Labor. Increased appropriations are proposed for both agencies for 1961. Additional funds needed by the Department of Justice will be requested later when requirements can be better determined.

Appropriations of $326 million are requested in the fiscal year 1961 for grants to the States to administer the Federal-State employment security system with its network of 1,800 offices throughout the country. These grants are now financed from an earmarked Federal tax and the transactions involved increase both budget receipts and expenditures, even though these funds cannot be used for general Government purposes. Legislation proposed by the administration last year for financing this program through the unemployment trust fund should be enacted. Amounts equal to the proceeds from this tax could then be placed directly in the trust fund from which the necessary grants could be appropriated and an adequate balance could be maintained as a reserve for employment security purposes. The administration of the program would then be financed in essentially the same way as other major social insurance programs.

The job placement services and unemployment compensation payments provided through the State employment security offices are important for a smoothly operating free labor market in a growing economy. These services and payments provide also for security against economic hardship for the work force covered by the system. I again urge the enactment of legislation to extend unemployment compensation to some 3 million workers, primarily those employed in small enterprises. Some States have recently made encouraging progress in increasing the duration and level of benefits, but more needs to be done and additional States should take these steps.

Action is needed to strengthen the financial position of the unemployment compensation system. Although the reserves of most States proved adequate in the past recession, a few were and still are in a precarious condition. Moreover, reserve funds in most States have fallen behind the growth in payrolls during the last decade, and in certain States could be inadequate in the event of future economic distress. I have asked the Secretary of Labor to make a study of this problem and to report to me his conclusions.

Previously proposed amendments to strengthen the basic authority in the Welfare and Pension Plan Disclosure Act should be enacted, and the protection of the Fair Labor Standards Act should be extended to several million additional workers in accordance with previous recommendations. Legislation is likewise again proposed to assure equal pay for equal work, and to strengthen and improve laws governing hours of work and overtime pay on direct Federal and certain federally-aided construction projects.

PUBLIC HEALTH.—Advances in medical technology and the spread of private health insurance have played important roles in raising the level of health services for our rapidly growing population. At the same time, the growing demand for better health care has contributed to shortages of facilities, medical and scientific manpower, and supporting health workers, as well as to the rising cost of medical and hospital services.

In order to deal effectively with these developments, the Federal Government has expanded its public health programs and is actively seeking solutions to the Nation's health problems. Expenditures in the fiscal year 1961 are estimated to total $904 million, which is $53 million more than in 1960 and nearly three times the level five years earlier. The largest part of the increase is for medical research and training of research workers through programs of the National Institutes of Health, for which the estimated expenditures of $390 million in 1961 will be four times as great as five years ago. Expenditures for hospital construction grants are estimated at $161 million in 1961, a threefold increase during the same period.

The Department of Health, Education, and Welfare will insist on maintaining high standards in determining the acceptability of medical research projects for Federal support. As I indicated last August in approving the 1960 appropriations for the Department, it is essential that Federal grants for these projects be so administered that medical manpower is not unduly diverted from other pressing needs and that Federal funds are not substituted for funds from private sources. The 1960 appropriation of $400 million for the National Institutes of Health will not be entirely committed this year even with advanced funding of certain training programs. I am recommending that 1961 appropriations to the National Institutes of Health continue at the high level of 1960.

The recommended appropriation for the Hill-Burton hospital construction program for 1961 is consistent with the levels achieved by this program before the 1958 recession. It will assure that sufficient new general hospitals can be financed to keep pace with population growth, cover current obsolescence rates, and provide for 6,000 new beds to reduce the backlog of needs. The remainder of this program, covering diagnostic and other special facilities, would approximate the 1959 and 1960 levels.

The 1961 appropriation proposed for construction of waste treatment facilities is the same as that requested for 1960. It represents the maximum amount which I believe is warranted for a construction program which is and should remain primarily a State and local responsibility.

Larger appropriations are proposed for other health programs where present or impending needs create urgent priorities. Emerging health problems of increasing seriousness to our population arise from the complexities of the environment in which we live. To cope with the far-reaching problems of environmental health on a more systematic and intensive basis, this budget provides substantial increases to the Public Health Service for air pollution, water pollution, and radiological health control activities. These increases for radiological health, together with the stepped-up activity by the Atomic Energy Commission and other agencies, will permit a greatly intensified effort by the Federal Government in this field. In order to provide for more effective Federal air and water pollution control activities, the Secretary of Health, Education, and Welfare will make legislative recommendations to strengthen the enforcement provisions of the Water Pollution Control Act and to authorize greater Federal leadership in combating air pollution.

Rapid technological developments in the production, processing, and marketing of foods, drugs, and other products likewise underline the necessity for more research and action for the protection of the consumer. To meet this need, the budget continues to emphasize an orderly expansion of the Food and Drug Administration, expenditures for which will be more than double those five years ago.

SOCIAL INSURANCE AND OTHER WELFARE.—The social security insurance system now provides basic protection against loss of income from death, disability, and retirement to about 85% of our labor force. Another 8% are covered under the railroad retirement system and other public retirement systems.

Social security and public assistance.—At the present time 10 million of the 16 million people aged 65 and over are receiving monthly old-age or survivors insurance benefits. This vast insurance system, which will pay $11.7 billion in old-age, survivors, and disability benefits to 14.6 million people of all ages in 1961, is administered at a cost of about 2% of the social security taxes.

Our social insurance and public retirement systems provide basic protection to the worker and his family. For those who have no such protection and whose incomes are insufficient to meet basic needs, the Federal Government shares, through grants to the States, in providing four categories of public assistance payments. These are (1) old-age assistance, (2) aid to the blind, (3) aid to dependent children, and (4) aid to the permanently and totally disabled. In 1961, the Federal share for payments, made to an estimated monthly average of 5.9 million beneficiaries, will total an estimated $2.1 billion, or about 58% of the total Federal-State-local public assistance expenditures. This contrasts with Federal expenditures of $1.1 billion, representing a Federal share of 52%, for payments to 4.9 million individuals in 1950.

Public assistance has long been recognized as primarily a responsibility of the State and local governments, because need for these payments in individual cases can best be determined at the local level. I am particularly concerned about the growing Federal share, especially because it tends to weaken this sense of State and local responsibility.

While we are spending hundreds of millions for aid to the needy, there are large gaps in our knowledge of the causes of dependency and of the best ways to alleviate or prevent it. I believe that appropriations to initiate a program of research and demonstration projects designed to identify and alleviate these causes are highly necessary and I have so recommended in this budget.

Military service credits.—It has long been recognized that military service should be counted towards the rights of employees under the various public retirement programs. Likewise, where employees are not required to make payroll contributions during military service, the trust funds from which benefits based on such service are paid should be re-imbursed by the Government. However, the Federal Government should not, as required under the Railroad Retirement Act, pay more than the true cost of such benefits or pay to both the railroad retirement account and to the old-age, survivors, and disability insurance trust funds for the same military service benefits.

Accordingly, I repeat my earlier recommendation that the Federal Government should reimburse the railroad retirement account only for the actual added cost of benefits resulting from military service. Pending action on legislation dealing with substantial overpayments found by the Comptroller General, no provision is made in this budget for further Federal military service payments to either the railroad retirement account or the old-age, survivors, and disability insurance trust funds.

Other welfare services.—This budget includes recommended appropriations for vocational rehabilitation totaling $72 million for the fiscal year 1961, primarily for grants to help the State agencies rehabilitate an estimated 93,000 individuals, about 6% more than in 1960.

Grants to all school systems in the States through the school lunch and special milk programs of the Department of Agriculture are estimated at $234 million in 1961, approximately the same as in 1960. These programs will provide improved diets for 11.8 million children, on the average, in 1961. The 1961 amount is in addition to the commodities which are distributed to the schools through the disposal programs classified in this budget under agriculture and agricultural resources.

The health, employment, income, and other needs of the increasing number of elderly people in our population can be met only through the combined efforts and cooperation of private, local, State, and Federal organizations and agencies. The White House Conference on Aging, to be held in January 1961, and the State conferences which precede it should help point the way toward more productive and satisfying living for our aged citizens.

The realization of our aspirations for a better society in the years to come will in large measure depend upon the way in which our children and youth are prepared to realize their maximum potential. This will be the vital concern of the White House Conference on Children and Youth, which will be held in March 1960 and through which private and public organizations will endeavor to bring their wisest and most expert counsel together on this vitally important matter.

VETERANS SERVICES AND BENEFITS

Expenditures for veterans programs are estimated to rise by $314 million to $5.5 billion in 1961, chiefly because of additional pension cases and higher pension rates, both authorized by the Veterans' Pension Act of 1959. The increase for pensions, amounting to $438 million, will be partly offset by a decrease of $128 million in readjustment benefit expenditures.

Programs of the Veterans Administration, providing compensation and pension, medical, and readjustment benefits for the Nation's veterans, rank fourth in size among all Government functions in this budget. Total expenditures for these programs, as presently authorized, will continue to increase in future years as our veterans advance in age. The 23 million living veterans, together with the dependents and survivors of veterans, comprise a total of 81 million people, a considerable proportion of whom are potential recipients of one or more types of benefits.

This country has provided a wide range of benefits and services for war veterans and their families to meet needs resulting from military service. Disability and death compensation benefits have been provided for veterans who were injured in the service or for their survivors. The Servicemen's and Veterans' Survivor Benefits Act of 1956 improved the death benefit structure both for wartime and peacetime servicemen. In 1957, general disability compensation rates were increased by 10%, and a still larger increase was enacted in the basic rate for the totally disabled.

A first-rate hospital and medical care program is also being provided. During the past year a long-range policy for stabilizing the Veterans Administration's hospital program at 125,000 beds has been established, and beginning with the 1961 budget a 12-year hospital modernization program is being initiated that will ultimately cost $900 million.

The 21 million veterans who served during World War II or the Korean conflict were eligible for benefits from the highly successful readjustment programs. For the 16 million World War II veterans the GI bill provided unemployment and self-employment compensation payments to 9.7 million veterans; education and training benefits to 8.4 million veterans; and loan assistance to 5 million veterans for the acquisition or improvement of homes, farms, and businesses. Except for the loan guarantee and direct loan programs, which will terminate on July 25, 1960, the World War II readjustment benefits have essentially expired. Similar readjustment programs, which will continue into 1965 for veterans of the Korean conflict, have already provided 2.3 million veterans with education and training benefits and 700,000 with loans. The special unemployment compensation program for Korean conflict veterans which ends in 1961 has aided 1.3 million veterans. No further extension or liberalization of these benefits is needed.

The long-standing veterans pension program also provides special assistance to war veterans for needs not arising from military service. The Veterans' Pension Act of 1959 was an important step in the modernization of the program. It eliminated the disparity in eligibility for pensions between the widows of World War I veterans and those of later wars, and provided higher benefits for all persons who could demonstrate need under a new sliding scale income test. No further liberalization of the laws concerning pensions for non-service-connected disability is proposed.

In addition to the special veterans programs, a great majority of veterans participate in the general social security, health, and welfare programs which are financed wholly or in part by the Federal Government. In the future these general programs will provide with increasing adequacy for the economic security needs of our elderly population, of which veterans and their widows will constitute a large and increasing proportion for several decades.

VETERANS SERVICES AND BENEFITS

[Fiscal years. In millions]

	Budget expenditures			Recommended new obligational authority for 1961
Program or agency	1959 actual	1960 estimate	1961 estimate	
Readjustment benefits:				
Education and training....................	$574	$445	$316	$286
Loan guarantee and other benefits..........	133	115	124	124
Unemployment compensation..............	44	8	......	....
Compensation and pensions:				
Service-connected compensation............	2,070	2,071	2,066	2,066
Non-service-connected pensions.............	1,153	1,278	1,716	1,716
Burial and other allowances................	52	58	58	58
Hospitals and medical care.................	875	906	928	933
Hospital construction......................	45	60	63	75
Insurance and servicemen's indemnities........	35	36	31	49
Other services and administration............	193	180	169	168
Total..............................	5,174	5,157	5,471	[1] 5,476

[1] Compares with new obligational authority of $5,125 million enacted for 1959 and $5,176 million (including $114 million in anticipated supplemental appropriations) estimated for 1960.

Readjustment benefits.—Readjustment assistance is expected to decline significantly from 1960 to 1961, primarily because of the reduction in the number of veterans of the Korean conflict participating in educational or vocational training programs. An average of 225,000 veterans will receive training in 1961, compared to 325,000 in 1960 and 425,000 in 1959. Educational benefits for war orphans, which were enacted in 1956, are expected to total over $17 million in 1961.

Peacetime ex-servicemen are recognized as being in a different category from wartime veterans because of the different conditions under which they serve. Those who serve in peacetime undergo fewer rigors and hazards than their combat comrades. The disruption of their educational plans and careers is minimized under peacetime selective service procedures. While on active service they now receive substantial pay and benefits, and they return to civilian life under more favorable conditions after receiving valuable training while in service.

To discharge its responsibility to peacetime ex-servicemen, the Federal Government has provided unemployment compensation, employment service and reemployment rights, and service-connected disability or death compensation. One additional benefit should be added to these in accord with my earlier recommendations: a program of vocational rehabilitation for those with substantial service-connected disabilities. On the other hand, I oppose the establishment of special educational and loan guarantee programs for peacetime ex-servicemen. Such benefits are not justified because they are not supported by the conditions of military service. Moreover, they would be directly contrary to the incentives which have been provided to encourage capable individuals to make military service a career.

Compensation and pensions.—Expenditures for compensation for service-connected disabilities and deaths will show only a minor change in 1961. A reduction in the number of World War I and II veterans on the rolls will be offset somewhat by the addition of veterans of the Korean conflict and peacetime ex-servicemen. Compensation will be paid for an estimated 2.4 million cases during 1961.

The net impact of the 1959 law governing non-service-connected pensions is to add several hundred thousand new cases to the rolls at an estimated additional cost of $284 million in 1961 and an estimated cumulative cost of $9 billion during the next 40 years. Expenditures are also increasing because of the growing number of World War I veterans reaching age 65. Approximately 40% of all World War I veterans over 65 are now receiving pensions. An average of 1.9 million veterans and families of deceased veterans are expected to receive pensions in 1961; this is 26% more than in 1960 and 38% more than in 1959.

Hospital and medical services.—The budget includes $928 million of expenditures in 1961 for hospital and medical care for veterans. The increase of $22 million from 1960 is to continue improvements in the staffing and quality of service in the hospitals and to meet the higher costs of hospital and medical care generally. Hospital and domiciliary care will be provided during the year for an average of 141,250 beneficiaries per day, and a total of 2,300,000 veterans will receive medical or dental care for service-connected disabilities in outpatient clinics.

Hospital construction.—As a first step toward an orderly 12-year program for modernization of existing veterans' hospital facilities, an appropriation of $75 million is proposed for 1961. Of this total, $53 million is for construction of replacement hospitals at Cleveland, Ohio (800 beds); Washington, D.C. (700 beds); and Martinez, Calif. (500 beds). The remainder is for a large number of modernization projects.

Administration.—The general operating expenses of the Veterans Administration are expected to decline approximately 7% in 1961, reflecting decreased workloads in loan and educational programs, improved administrative procedures particularly in insurance operations, and the application of modern electronic equipment to recording and paying veterans benefits.

INTEREST

Interest payments are estimated to rise $200 million to $9.6 billion in the fiscal year 1961. These payments, almost entirely for interest on the public debt, represent 12% of budget expenditures.

For a year and a half now, market rates of interest have been increasing, reflecting inflationary pressures, the high level of investment demands in our economy and heavy Federal borrowing required by the 1958 and 1959 budget deficits. The rise in market rates requires the Treasury to pay higher interest on securities issued to refinance the heavy volume of maturing obligations, which were issued when interest rates were lower.

It is imperative that the Congress lift the present legal ceiling of 4¼% on interest rates on all Government obligations having maturities of more than five years. Otherwise, interest payments could rise even more

INTEREST

[Fiscal years. In millions]

Item	Budget expenditures			Recommended new obligational authority for 1961
	1959 actual	1960 estimate	1961 estimate	
Interest on public debt.....................	$7,593	$9,300	$9,500	$9,500
Interest on refunds of receipts...............	70	75	75	75
Interest on uninvested funds................	9	9	10	10
Total..............................	7,671	9,385	9,585	9,585

sharply. The current interest rate on shorter term securities is now higher than on long-term bonds, and the continued need to limit financing to the short-term market tends to raise interest rates more than if the financing could be spread over both the short- and long-term markets.

GENERAL GOVERNMENT

Expenditures for general government activities are estimated to rise by $200 million to $1.9 billion in the fiscal year 1961, primarily because of increased construction of Government buildings and a new appropriation to the civil service retirement fund required by law.

Federal financial management.—There is growing evidence that a considerable amount of revenue is lost annually to the Government because of the failure of some individuals and businesses to report fully the income which they have received. The existence of such a condition seriously weakens the integrity of our tax system, and places an unfair share of the total tax burden upon the vast majority of citizens who conscientiously report all of their taxable income. This budget includes an increase of $29 million for the Internal Revenue Service, primarily to strengthen its enforcement programs, including initiation of an electronic computer system. I urge its approval as the first step in a long-range plan to prevent this revenue loss. The additional costs should be recovered many times through increased tax collections in later years.

General property and records management.—The efficient and economical operation of many Federal agencies is hindered by inadequate office space, much of which is rented. Accordingly, new obligational authority of $185 million is recommended for fiscal year 1961 for the planning and construction of additional general office space. Although no funds for such construction were appropriated for 1960, expenditures will rise in 1961 as outlays for new construction are added to those for construction initiated in prior years. In addition, the estimate for the legislative functions includes increased expenditures for a new office building for the House of Representatives.

GENERAL GOVERNMENT

[Fiscal years. In millions]

Program or agency	Budget expenditures			Recommended new obligational authority for 1961
	1959 actual	1960 estimate	1961 estimate	
Legislative functions............................	$102	$121	$146	$95
Judicial functions..............................	47	50	53	53
Executive direction and management...........	12	13	14	14
Federal financial management..................	566	560	591	595
General property and records management.....	291	384	432	469
Central personnel management and employment costs...................................	205	198	251	251
Civilian weather services......................	46	52	58	63
Protective services and alien control...........	216	218	229	230
Territories and possessions, and the District of Columbia.................................	89	96	126	124
Other general government.....................	30	20	12	15
Total.................................	1, 606	1, 711	1, 911	¹ 1, 910

¹ Compares with new obligational authority of $1,795 million enacted for 1959 and $1,645 million (including $7 million in anticipated supplemental appropriations) estimated for 1960.

The General Services Administration, in collaboration with other agencies, has developed a new program for improved use of excess personal property by Federal agencies, and faster, more efficient disposal of surplus property. This involves more effective screening of such property and simplifying the procedures under which agencies are advised of its availability for other uses.

Central personnel management.—The Civil Service Commission and the Bureau of the Budget have recently recommended a long-range policy on financing the civil service retirement system. I hope the Congress will speedily enact these recommendations, which would assure continued availability in the fund of the full amount of the net accumulations from employee contributions and establish a definite basis for meeting the Government's share of the costs consistent with the principle that its full faith and credit support the authorized benefits.

A new appropriation of $46 million for payments to the civil service retirement fund is requested for 1961 to finance the costs of new or increased benefits enacted in 1958 for certain widows or widowers of former Federal employees and for certain retired employees. The law provides that these particular benefits cannot be continued after July 1, 1960, unless such an appropriation is made. Recipients of these benefits should enjoy the same assurance of uninterrupted payment as do other annuitants of the civil service retirement system, and the Federal liability in their case is not different from that for other benefits under this program. Accordingly, I recommend that the Congress consider, in connection with the legislation referred to in the preceding paragraph, authorizing the civil service retirement and disability fund to bear the future cost of these particular benefits without a specific appropriation.

The budget provides approximately $120 million to pay the Government's share of the Federal Employees Health Benefits Act of 1959, which becomes effective in the fiscal year 1961, and which will provide opportunity for approximately 2 million employees and 2.4 million dependents to have reasonable protection against the cost of both basic and major health care. This program will add substantially to employee fringe benefits, which in the aggregate now compare very favorably with those provided to employees in private industry.

In 1958 immediately following enactment of a 10% general salary increase for Federal civilian employees, I proposed to the Congress a review of all compensation systems in the three branches of the Federal Government, directed toward adoption of an equitable employee compensation policy. This recommendation was renewed in my budget message for the 1960 fiscal year.

It has been more than 30 years since a thorough-going review has been made of the manner in which the Federal Government compensates its employees. There are now dozens of pay plans in the executive branch alone. Review and coordination of the excessive number of pay plans now in existence are the most effective means of removing inequities which adversely affect the Government's ability to recruit and retain qualified personnel in some fields. Continued patching of individual Federal salary systems in not satisfactory as a substitute for a comprehensive Federal pay policy, which should be developed either by authorizing a Joint Commission such as I proposed or by some other equally effective means. Pending development and adoption of such a comprehensive policy, a general pay raise would be unwarranted, unfair to the taxpayers of the United States, and inequitable as among employees compensated under different and unrelated pay systems.

The budget estimates for the Post Office Department assume legislative action to continue that part of the 1958 salary increase for postal field service employees which expires on January 20, 1961.

Civilian weather services.—Appropriations totaling $63 million are recommended for the fiscal year 1961 for the Weather Bureau. The $12 million increase over the amounts enacted for 1960 will permit expanded research, weather observation, and forecasting services. These improvements are necessary primarily to keep pace with advances in air traffic controls. Research projects include intensive investigation of hurricanes and tornadoes, and the development of a semiautomatic system for the collection and analysis of weather data.

Hawaii.—Our Union was greatly strengthened in 1959 by the admission of the States of Alaska and Hawaii. As in the case of Alaska, comprehensive legislation will be necessary to enable Hawaii to take its place as the equal of the other 49 States. Recommendations will be transmitted to the Congress concerning those changes needed in Federal laws in order to bring Hawaii under the same general laws, rules, and policies as are applicable to the other States.

Territories, Possessions, and District of Columbia.—Completion of action on statehood for Alaska and Hawaii makes it all the more urgent that legislation to provide home rule for the District of Columbia be enacted without delay. Both equity and efficiency require that the people of the Nation's Capital be given a voice in their own local government and that the role of the Federal Government be limited to matters of Federal concern.

Legislation will shortly be proposed to the Congress to establish a Government corporation to develop an improved mass transportation system in the National Capital metropolitan area, pending creation of an interstate agency to assume this responsibility.

To foster further development of democratic institutions and in keeping with the growth of local self-government, action should be taken to authorize the Virgin Islands and Guam to be represented in the Congress through nonvoting resident commissioners.

Intergovernmental relations.—There are many problems requiring attention of the recently established Advisory Commission on Intergovernmental Relations. Foremost among these are the problems of allocation of tax sources among various levels of government and rapid growth of metropolitan areas.

An aspect of intergovernmental relations requiring attention in both the legislative and executive branches involves a series of court decisions permitting local taxation of federally-owned property in the hands of contractors and leaseholders. This matter should be resolved in the context of the broader subject of Federal payments in lieu of taxes.

Other recommendations.—Legislation enacted in the last session of Congress to amend the immigration and nationality laws failed to cover several significant proposals, including modification of the quota system. Prompt action is needed on these remaining items.

To strengthen the Government's hand in restraining inflationary forces, I urge that the Employment Act of 1946 be amended to make reasonable price stability an explicit goal of Federal economic policy, coordinate with the goals of maximum production, employment, and purchasing power now specified in that Act.

I urge the Congress to enact the remaining six points of the civil rights program that I recommended last year. The Civil Rights Commission, extended for an additional two years by the last session of Congress, continues its important work and has developed additional constructive recommendations, particularly for protecting the right of every citizen to vote. I hope these recommendations will also be earnestly considered by the Congress.

I also recommend that the Congress create additional Federal judgeships, as proposed by the Judicial Conference, and strengthen Federal laws against organized crime.

Legislation will be submitted to increase the authorization for appropriations for the Commission on International Rules of Judicial Procedure in order that it may complete its work successfully.

It is important that legislation now before the Congress be enacted to provide reimbursement to Americans for certain property damage in Europe and the Far East during World War II for which compensation has not previously been authorized.

I again recommend that a system be devised for suitable recognition in the United States for distinguished achievement in various fields of endeavor.

IMPROVEMENTS IN BUDGETING, ORGANIZATION, AND MANAGEMENT

The decisions made by Government are vital to so many aspects of our national life that improvement of the procedures through which these decisions are made should be a continuing major goal. A substantial number of important specific steps can and should be taken to improve these practices.

Revisions in authorization and appropriation procedure.—Contract authority and authorizations to spend from debt receipts in basic legislation outside the appropriation process are generally inconsistent with sound standards of budget practice. The recommendations being placed before the Congress in this budget are based upon the principle that authority to make budget obligations and expenditures, whether financed from receipts or borrowing, should be granted by the Congress only in appropriation acts.

The Congress has shown a growing tendency to require the annual enactment of authorizing legislation before appropriations may be made. Space programs, some mutual security programs, military and atomic energy construction in this budget, and much of defense procurement beginning in fiscal 1962, will require separate authorizations before appropriations can be considered. Under this procedure these programs receive a duplicating review each year. At the same time the value of legislative consideration and expression of long-range program objectives and amounts is largely lost, and agency personnel devote an inordinate amount of time to the congressional process at the expense of effective administration of the continuing program. I hope the Congress will find it possible generally to make authorizing legislation cover program requirements for longer periods of time.

In the interest of good government, methods to expedite the authorization and appropriation processes should be found. In order to facilitate early consideration, and also to show the Government program more fully, this budget includes specific proposed appropriations for a number of programs for which authorizing legislation must also be renewed. In most of these cases, proposals for such legislation will be submitted in a very short time. This procedure should be an improvement over the past practice of delaying submission of detailed estimates until the renewing legislation has been enacted.

Before the executive budget is presented to Congress annually, the most careful consideration is given to the relationships of spending to receipts and borrowing, and to relative priorities of various programs. When the budget reaches the Congress, however, its consideration is usually fragmented because of the distribution of responsibilities among the various committees and subcommittees. I believe that the Congress should find means by which it can more effectively examine the budget as a whole and base its actions on the overall fiscal situation.

Provision for item veto.—In passing the Alaska and Hawaii statehood acts, the Congress again recognized the value of an item veto by a chief executive by approving provision for its use in their State constitutions. Forty-one State Governors now have item veto authority. Many Presidents have recommended it, but the Congress has not yet granted the President of the United States that power. I again recommend it.

Control of foreign currencies.—The Government receives from its operations considerable quantities of foreign currencies each year. Much of this currency is earmarked for grants to and loans in the country concerned, and some is available for programs of the U.S. Government. In many countries the currencies available to us are needed for conducting normal U.S. operations, yet such use is prevented in some cases by statutes or by the international agreements under which the currencies are received.

As a result of a detailed study, this budget includes provisions to bring under budget and appropriation controls all foreign currencies available for U.S. agency operations which are received from the sale of surplus agricultural commodities. This change will not alter total appropriations or expenditures, but will increase those of the agencies using the currencies and decrease those of the Commodity Credit Corporation. Accordingly, I intend that no more allocations be made for uncontrolled use after the current fiscal year except for country grants and loans committed in international agreements, and I recommend that at an appropriate time the Congress remove from the laws the provisions which permit uncontrolled use for other purposes. I am also instructing that in future negotiations of international agreements we endeavor to avoid restrictions which would limit our ability to apply normal budget and appropriation controls to the use of those currencies which are earmarked for U.S. agency operations.

Improved funding for public enterprises.—Major business-type activities of the Government should, with few exceptions, operate on a self-sustaining basis. Their budgets and accounts should permit ready comparison of their expenses and revenues. They should have simplicity in their financing structure and the flexibility in expenditures necessary to meet unforeseen business conditions, but should be expected to keep their obligations and expenditures within the resources provided by Congress for that purpose, and should be subject to annual review and control by the Congress. Accordingly, I recommend that the Rural Electrification Administration, the Farmers Home Administration, the Bureau of Reclamation, the power-marketing agencies of the Department of the Interior, and the loan guarantee programs of the Veterans Administration be financed through revolving funds. Similar recommendations may be made in due time for other business-type activities.

Legislation is again being recommended to bring under budget review the activities of those few Government corporations which are now exempt from such review, but possess authority to draw money from the Treasury or to commit the Treasury for future expenditures. This can best be done by including them under the budget provisions of the Government Corporation Control Act.

Revision of budget presentation.—In this budget more than half of the 626 appropriation accounts of the executive branch have been presented on a cost basis. The remaining appropriations, including those for the Department of Defense, will be converted to this basis as soon as possible. This budget also provides for accrued expenditure limitations for 12 appropriations, in accordance with legislation enacted in 1958. Such limitations are recommended to permit closer congressional control over annual expenditures.

The customary totals of budget receipts and budget expenditures are distorted by the inclusion in both of interest and other payments by public enterprise funds to the general fund of the Treasury. Such interfund payments amounted to $355 million in the fiscal year 1959, and are estimated at $737 million for 1960 and $779 million for 1961. While this duplication does not affect the amount of the budget surplus or deficit, it does overstate the size of the budget receipts and expenditures. To correct this it is planned that such amounts, while still shown within the figures for the affected agencies, will be eliminated from budget totals in financial statements on Government operations beginning with the fiscal year 1961. I also plan to present the 1962 budget so as to remove this duplication. However, in order to preserve full comparability with previous budgets, no such adjustments are shown in the amounts in this document. If adjustments had been made, the net totals would appear as follows:

ADJUSTED BUDGET TOTALS, EXCLUDING INTERFUND PAYMENTS

[Fiscal years. In billions]

	1959 actual	1960 estimate	1961 estimate
Budget receipts..............................	$67. 9	$77. 9	$83. 2
Budget expenditures..........................	80. 3	77. 7	79. 0
Budget deficit............................	12. 4	....	....
Budget surplus.............................	....	. 2	4. 2

Strengthening of organization and management.—From the beginning of this administration I have placed emphasis on obtaining the best possible executive ability in the administration of the widespread and diverse activities of the Federal Government and on providing the best organizational structure in which officials can carry out their responsibilities. This continued emphasis is essential not only to operate the complex machinery of government effectively, but also to meet the constant flow of new problems of organization and management.

In recent years several major organizational improvements have been made, including the establishment of the Department of Health, Education, and Welfare, the Federal Aviation Agency, and the National Aeronautics and Space Administration, as well as new organizational structures for defense programs and for civilian and defense mobilization activities. The many actions taken on recommendations of the two Hoover Commissions have also resulted in more efficient administration.

The Reorganization Act of 1949, as amended, under which numerous executive agencies and functions have been reorganized, contains a limitation of June 1, 1959, for the transmittal of reorganization plans by the President to the Congress. Accordingly, this authority is not now available. I urgently recommend that this cutoff date be removed in order to permit continued use of that act by me and by my successor in improving the management and organization of the executive branch.

The search for better management and operations is a never-ending process. Like all large organizations, the Federal Government continues to have management problems. For example, property management offers an enormous challenge, and in the past year greater attention has been focused on it. Application of new data-processing techniques to

Government operations is under constant study. The Post Office Department is improving its operations by installing modern methods of mail handling and transportation. The Treasury Department is using up-to-date data-processing equipment to achieve more effective administration of disbursements and revenue collection. These are but a few of many examples, and this budget provides for further improvements.

At my request, the heads of all Government agencies will give renewed emphasis to the review of management procedures and operating activities to make sure that the most modern methods, techniques, and equipment are in use. All agency heads have been encouraged to continue to search for the best practices in other Government agencies, in business, or in industry, to apply them in their own agencies to the extent possible during the term of this administration, and to leave to their successors a legacy of plans for further improvement.

The plans presented in this budget meet the Nation's immediate needs and will support continuing sound economic growth in the future. The achievement of these plans, however, will in the last analysis depend on the people themselves.

I believe our people have the determination to hold expenditures in check, to pay their own way without borrowing from their children, to choose wisely among priorities, and to match sound public policy with private initiative. It is that determination which is the key to continued progress and sound growth with security. It is that determination which reinforces the recommendations I have made.

DWIGHT D. EISENHOWER

NOTE: As printed above, the following have been deleted: (1) illustrative diagrams and highlight summaries; (2) references to special analyses appearing in the budget document.

14 ¶ Toasts of the President and Prime Minister Kishi of Japan. *January* 19, 1960

Mr. Prime Minister, Mr. Foreign Minister, and distinguished guests:

It is a very great personal honor to welcome here in Washington the Prime Minister of Japan and his associates in government. They are here to sign, with us, a treaty of mutual cooperation and security.

This year is the centennial of an occasion very similar to this one. A predecessor of mine, 100 years ago, welcomed to this city the first Japanese diplomatic mission to the United States—indeed, the first diplomatic mission that in modern times the Japanese had sent abroad.

During those hundred years, tremendous changes have taken place. In our technology, in science, the changes have been such as to be revolutionary. And in the thinking of our two peoples, there has been likewise a great change. We have come to the realization that we were not, each of us, truly independent of ourselves and of others, but that there is among the nations—certainly the nations of the free world—a great and growing interdependence.

In 1860 Japan was just emerging from an isolation centuries old and almost complete in its character. The United States was living in an isolation of a different kind. We were so protected by two vast ocean areas that we had no real interest in the rest of the world, and certainly felt ourselves to be immune from the quarrels and struggles and problems and even the privations that others experienced.

We have come a long way from that time. In 1960, our two countries represented here today are leaders in an effort to bring the free nations of the world into a closer cooperation through which they may achieve a better security for themselves and for realizing for all people the peace in freedom that they seek.

The signing of this treaty this afternoon will, all of us hope, mark one significant step in progress toward that goal.

I am hopeful that all of you present, after we have had our coffee in the Blue Room, will be guests at that signing, which will take place in the East Room immediately after we leave the Blue Room.

It has been a particular delight for me to have Mr. Kishi, an old friend of mine, here representing his country this morning. We had a chance, because of this visit, to remark upon the tremendous changes, the tremendous progress that has been made in the last 2 years between the relations of our two countries. We agreed that there is ground for great confidence that these relations will be sound and will grow ever stronger.

Now of course, for both of us, it would have been a little bit more enjoyable and possibly even more profitable to have had these conversations on the golf course. But in spite of the uncooperative character of the season, we did have these talks and both of us agreed that they have been not only interesting but fruitful.

And it is in that belief and conviction that I propose a Toast to the Monarch whose able Prime Minister is our honored guest today.

Gentlemen, and Madam, will you please join me in raising our glasses to His Majesty, the Emperor of Japan.

NOTE: The President proposed this toast at a luncheon in the state dining room at the White House at 2:06 p.m. In his opening words he referred to Aiichiro Fujiyama, Japanese Minister of Foreign Affairs. In the closing paragraph the words "and Madam" referred to Madam Harue Yamashita, Member of the Japanese House of Representatives.

An unofficial translation of Prime Minister Kishi's response follows:

Mr. President, Mr. Speaker, and other honorable guests:

Today I and my associates have the privilege of discussing political affairs with the President, for which I offer thanks from the bottom of my heart. Further, the President's generous Toast has touched me deeply, for which I am also thankful.

In the two and a half years which have passed since I first met with the President to discuss matters of mutual concern and mutual cooperation, we have seen great progress toward achieving a position of equality and mutual trust. That we have done so is a blessing for the peoples of both our countries. Moreover, it also contributes in a great degree toward the achievement of that peace in the world which all peoples wish for.

We all know that the President works constantly, with all of his energies, toward achieving peace in the world, with justice and freedom. Not only we in Japan, but the peoples of the entire world are well aware of this, and we all praise you for your activities, Mr. President. We pray for your success in your purposes.

As the President has already explained, my purpose in coming to the United States at this time is to sign the new treaty of mutual cooperation and security between Japan and the United States. But this year, as the President has also indicated, marks the end of the first century since the first amicable diplomatic contact between our two countries.

Throughout that hundred years, never with the exception of a brief few do I believe that we have had relations of anything less than a mutually profitable nature. I hope that in the coming hundred years that we will achieve even more progress toward a new relationship based on trust and cooperation.

I think that what we are doing today is significant for both the peace of the world and for the prosperity of the peoples of the world. I hope that our friendship continues in this way through the next century, without even a few years such as those which blotted our relations in the past.

I hope that the work we do here today will gain for us more than the hundred years of peaceful and cooperative relations that my predecessors gained. I know that we will continue to work hard to achieve this.

In reply to the remarks of the President, I would like to thank him from the bottom of my heart. I would like to toast the health of the President, and pray that he may continue to work so energetically for the peace of the world and for the prosperity of all of the American people. Thank you.

15 ¶ Remarks at the Signing of the Treaty of Mutual Cooperation and Security Between Japan and the United States. *January* 19, 1960

THE SIGNING TODAY of the Treaty of Mutual Cooperation and Security between Japan and the United States is truly a historical occasion at which I am honored to be present. This treaty represents the fulfillment of the goal set by Prime Minister Kishi and myself in June of 1957 to establish an indestructible partnership between our two countries in which our relations would be based on complete equality and mutual understanding. The treaty likewise reflects the closeness and breadth of our relations in the political and economic as well as security fields.

It is equally fitting that the Treaty of Mutual Cooperation and Security should be signed in the hundredth year after the first treaty between our two countries came into effect. On May 22, 1860, the first Japanese delegation to the United States exchanged ratifications of the Treaty of Amity and Commerce between our two countries. The subsequent hundred years have brought unbelievable progress and increasing prosperity to both our countries. It is my fervent hope that the new treaty signed today will usher in a second hundred years of prosperity and peace in freedom which the peoples of our countries and of all countries so earnestly desire.

NOTE: The ceremony was held in the East Room at the White House following the luncheon in honor of Prime Minister Kishi. The text of the treaty and related documents are published in the Department of State Bulletin (vol. 42, p. 184).

At the conclusion of the ceremony President Eisenhower presented Prime Minister Kishi with a reproduction of the original medal struck at the U.S. Mint in Philadelphia in 1860 commemorating the arrival of the first Japanese diplomatic mission.

On the following day the White House announced that Prime Minister Kishi had invited the President to visit Japan on the occasion of the Japanese-American Centennial, and that the President had accepted the invitation and would visit Japan about June 20.

16 ¶ Joint Statement Following Discussions With Prime Minister Kishi of Japan. *January* 19, 1960

THE PRESIDENT of the United States and the Prime Minister of Japan conferred at the White House today prior to the formal signing of the Treaty of Mutual Cooperation and Security between Japan and the

United States. Their discussions were devoted chiefly to a broad and comprehensive review of current international developments, and to an examination of Japanese-American relations. Japanese Minister of Foreign Affairs Fujiyama and American Secretary of State Herter also took part in the White House talks. Later the Prime Minister and his party conferred with the Secretary of State on matters of mutual concern to the two countries.

I.

The President and the Prime Minister first discussed the international situation. The President told the Prime Minister of the profound impression made upon him during his recent trip to South Asia, the Near East, Africa and Europe by the overwhelming desire throughout these areas for early realization of the goals of the United Nations, international peace, respect for human rights, and a better life. In discussing the international situation, the President stated his determination to exert every effort at the impending Summit meeting to achieve meaningful progress toward these goals. The Prime Minister expressed full agreement and support for the President's determination.

In this connection, the President and the Prime Minister agreed that disarmament, with the essential guarantees of inspection and verification, is a problem of urgent and central importance to all nations, whose resolution would contribute greatly to reducing the burden of armaments and the risk of war. They expressed the further hope that early agreement can be reached on an adequately safeguarded program for the discontinuance of nuclear weapons tests. They concluded that the world is entering a period affording important opportunities which they have every intention of exploring most seriously, but only on the basis of tested performance not merely promises. Both leaders recognized that all of man's intellect, wisdom and imagination must be brought into full play to achieve a world at peace under justice and freedom. They expressed the conviction that, during this period and particularly until all nations abide faithfully by the purposes and principles of the UN and forego the resort to force, it is essential for free nations to maintain by every means their resolution, their unity and their strength.

II.

The President and the Prime Minister considered the security relationship between the United States and Japan in the light of their evaluation of the current international situation and declared that this close relationship is essential to the achievement of peace in justice and freedom. They are convinced that the partnership and cooperation between their two nations is strengthened by the new treaty which has been drawn up on the basis of the principles of equal sovereignty and mutual cooperation that characterize the present relationship between the two countries. Both leaders look forward to the ratification of the treaty and to the celebration this year of the centennial of Japan's first diplomatic mission to the United States as further demonstrations of the strength and continuity of Japanese-American friendship.

In reviewing relations between Japan and the United States since their last meeting in June of 1957, the President and the Prime Minister expressed particular gratification at the success of efforts since that time to develop the new era in relations between the two countries, based on common interest, mutual trust, and the principles of cooperation.

Both the President and the Prime Minister looked ahead to continued close cooperation between the two countries within the framework of the new Treaty of Mutual Cooperation and Security. They are convinced that the treaty will materially strengthen peace and security in the Far East and advance the cause of peace and freedom throughout the world. They are convinced also that the treaty will foster an atmosphere of mutual confidence. In this connection, the Prime Minister discussed with the President the question of prior consultation under the new treaty. The President assured him that the United States Government has no intention of acting in a manner contrary to the wishes of the Japanese Government with respect to the matters involving prior consultation under the treaty.

The President and the Prime Minister also discussed the situation in Asia. They reaffirmed their belief that they should maintain close contact and consultation with relation to future developments in this area. They agreed that Japan's increasing participation in international discussion of the problems of Asia will be in the interest of the free world.

III.

The President and the Prime Minister agreed that the expansion of trade among free nations, the economic progress and elevation of living standards in less developed countries are of paramount importance, and will contribute to stability and progress so essential to the achievement of peace in the world.

The President and the Prime Minister exchanged views on the European economic and trade communities and on the role that can be played by the industrialized free world countries in the economic development of the less developed areas. Both leaders called particular attention to the urgent desire of peoples in the less developed areas of the world for the economic advancement without which they cannot preserve their freedom. They stressed the role which increasingly must be played by the industrialized nations of the free world in assisting the progress of the less developed areas. The President particularly referred to the increasing role the Japanese people are playing in the economic development of free Asia.

In considering economic relations between the United States and Japan, the President and the Prime Minister recognized that trade between their two nations is of great benefit to both countries, noting that the United States is the largest purchaser of Japanese exports, and Japan is the second largest buyer of American goods. They expressed gratification at the growth of mutually profitable trade between the two countries. They reaffirmed their conviction that the continued and orderly expansion of world trade, through the avoidance of arbitrary and new unnecessary trade restrictions, and through active measures to remove existing obstacles, is essential to the well-being and progress of both countries.

The Prime Minister stressed the importance of the United States and Japan consulting on a continuing basis with regard to economic matters of mutual interest. The President expressed full agreement to this view.

IV.

The President expressed his particular gratification that the Prime Minister could come to Washington on this occasion so important in United States-Japanese relations. The Prime Minister expressed his appreciation for the opportunity to meet again with the President.

The President and the Prime Minister agreed that their talks will contribute to the continued strengthening of the United States-Japanese partnership.

17 ¶ Annual Message Presenting the Economic Report to the Congress. *January* 20, 1960

To the Congress of the United States:

I present herewith my Economic Report, as required by Section 3(a) of the Employment Act of 1946.

The Report was prepared with the advice and assistance of the Council of Economic Advisers and of the heads of the executive departments and independent agencies directly concerned with the matters it discusses. It summarizes the economic developments of the year and the steps taken in major areas of economic policy to promote the sound expansion of employment, production, and income. It also puts forward a program for the year 1960 which, in the context of present and prospective economic conditions, would effectively implement the purposes of the Employment Act.

The major conclusions and recommendations of the Report are set forth below, in part in the words of the Report itself.

By the first quarter of 1959, the recovery that started early in 1958 had already carried production and income to levels higher than ever before attained in the American economy. A considerable further advance was scored during the remainder of 1959, despite the deep effect of the 116-day strike in the steel industry.

The Nation's output of goods and services in the fourth quarter of 1959 was at an annual rate of $482 billion. When adjusted for price changes, this rate of output was 3½ percent higher than the rate attained in the corresponding period in 1958. By December 1959, total employment had reached a record level, 66.2 million, on a seasonally adjusted basis. And personal income payments in December were at an annual rate of $391 billion, $24 billion greater than a year earlier. After adjustment for increases in prices, the rise in total personal income in 1959 represented a gain of nearly 5 percent in the real buying power of our Nation.

As we look ahead, there are good grounds for confidence that this economic advance can be extended through 1960. Furthermore, with appropriate private actions and public policies, it can carry well beyond the present year.

However, as always in periods of rapid economic expansion, we must avoid speculative excesses and actions that would compress gains into so short a period that the rate of growth could not be sustained. We must seek, through both private actions and public policies, to minimize and contain inflationary pressures that could undermine the basis for a high, continuing rate of growth.

Three elements stand out in the Government's program for realizing the objectives of high production, employment, and income set forth in the Employment Act: first, favorable action by the Congress on the recommendations for appropriations and for measures affecting Federal revenues presented in the Budget for the fiscal year 1961; second, use of the resulting surplus, now estimated at $4.2 billion, to retire Federal debt; third, action by the Congress to remove the interest rate limitation that currently inhibits the noninflationary management of the Federal debt. Numerous additional proposals, many of which are described in Chapter 4 of the Economic Report, will be made to supplement the Federal Government's existing economic and financial programs.

Following the budget balance now in prospect for the fiscal year 1960, these three elements of the 1960 program will strengthen and be strengthened by the essential contributions to sustainable economic growth made through the policies of the independent Federal Reserve System. Fiscal and monetary policies, which are powerful instruments for preventing the development of inflationary pressures, can effectively reinforce one another.

But these Government policies must be supplemented by appropriate private actions, especially with respect to profits and wages. In our system of free competitive enterprise and shared responsibility, we do not rely on Government alone for the achievement requires a blending of suit-growth. On the contrary, that achievement requires a blending of suitable private actions and public policies. Our success in realizing the opportunities that lie ahead will therefore depend in large part upon the ways in which business management, labor leaders, and consumers perform their own economic functions.

A well-informed and vigilant public opinion is essential in our free society for helping achieve the conditions necessary for price stability and vigorous economic growth. Such public opinion can be an effective safeguard against attempts arbitrarily to establish prices or wages at levels that are inconsistent with the general welfare. Informed public opinion is also necessary to support the laws and regulations that provide the framework for the conduct of our economic affairs.

Further progress is needed in establishing a broad public understanding of the relationships of productivity and rewards to costs and prices. It would be a grave mistake to believe that we can successfully substitute legislation or controls for such understanding. Indeed, the complex relationships involved cannot be fixed by law, and attempts to determine them by restrictive governmental action would jeopardize our freedoms and other conditions essential to sound economic growth.

Our system of free institutions and shared responsibility has served us well in achieving economic growth and improvement. From our past experience, we are confident that our changing and increasing needs in the future can be met within this flexible system, which gains strength from the incentive it provides for individuals, from the scope it affords for individual initiative and action, and from the assurance it gives that government remains responsive to the will of the people.

Dwight D. Eisenhower

NOTE: The message and the complete report (243 pages) are published in "Economic Report of the President, 1960" (Government Printing Office, 1960).

18 ❡ Remarks to Participants in the Young Republican National Leadership Training School. *January* 20, 1960

Mr. Chairman, ladies and gentlemen:

It is indeed a most unexpected and a very welcome reception that you have given me. I expected to find a bunch of desks and people having their pads and pencils out and working here in a sort of office. I don't know why I didn't expect it was a luncheon.

In a very few months we are going to come to a great decision in America. That decision has to be made by the electorate—the adult citizens of the United States.

My life has been largely spent in affairs that required organization. But organization itself, necessary as it is, is never sufficient to win a battle.

The first thing I would like to speak to you about is the cause, the purpose, for which you struggle. You have to believe something with your whole souls or you will never be effective in a political or any other campaign. You have to believe that government has a certain relationship to its citizen, certain responsibilities toward that citizen, including the responsibility to let the citizen alone when there should be no interference. You have got to understand how this kind of concept can translate into your daily and local problems; and then you must believe that this is the most important thing at this moment to get done.

I don't think that I need to say anything about the enthusiasm with which you do this. Your very presence here attests to the enthusiasm you have for the venture in which you are already launched. But we need, then, in the kind of organizations that I have known, to know why we are fighting, what we are fighting for—and to have leaders to organize and crystallize these thoughts, these ideals, these purposes, make them plain to the entire group, and then organize it so that it is invincible.

This is what I know you are doing. You are here as leaders. Organization should be carried down to the last detail. If we as Republicans don't make certain that every citizen, be he Democrat, Independent, or Republican, has had the opportunity to hear our explanation, then to that extent we have failed. If we are incapable of bringing to him at least the sense of the earnestness of our own convictions, we have likewise failed. If he is so rooted in tradition or preconception, or just plain stubbornness that he doesn't recognize your wisdom, why that's too bad. There are some like that, of course.

But you must make sure that you give your story to this man in the best way you possibly can.

The last thing is these leaders. I would hope that every one of you would put your whole selves, your whole souls, into the matter of seeing that the people you put in the positions of leadership—not merely the man you nominate for President, or for Governor, or county chairman or State chairman—but the person you select as a precinct worker, right down the line—have an organization, a purpose for which to work, and the leaders, including yourselves, to make this whole thing effective.

Finally, let's not forget this one thing: just hard work—hard work in recruiting.

Many years ago there was a Kansas farmer boy. His name was Bristow. He had one great act to his credit at least: he appointed me to West Point. [*Laughter*] But he was not a great speaker—there was nothing brilliant about him.

One day a colleague, comparing him with another, said this man was a racy, speedy horse; he was showy, fast, and handy. He said Bristow was more a Clydesdale—he was made for draft work—he did the heavy work. But he said he noticed that whatever Bristow went after he achieved. Just the plain ability to stay in, day after day, carrying the burden, never quitting, is one of the things that Bristow was famous for. And he said one little thing that is going to be the last word I say to you. He said, "Just remember this: in public life moral and political courage cannot be attained after you enter that service. You must have it before, if you are going to do your part in sustaining the moral and political courage of the nation itself."

I have talked far longer than I meant. I just can't tell you how grateful I am to each of you for what you are doing to keep up and preserve moderate government, and to get the kind of candidates you can support—not only you support, because you are Young Republicans, but that you can get a lot of other people to support. I don't mean that they have to be matinee idols. You have an example right in front of you where that wasn't important—but I do say they must be leaders, people who believe with their whole hearts in what you are working for— and then we will win.

Good luck to you. I will see a lot of you, I hope, here and there in the months to come until we can have another victory celebration in early November.

Goodbye and good luck.

NOTE: The President spoke at the Willard Hotel in Washington. At the conclusion of his remarks, Ned Cushing, Chairman of the Young Republican National Federation, presented a citation to the President on behalf of the faculty of the Young Republican National Leadership Training School.

19 ¶ Remarks at the Annual Midwinter Meeting of the National Association of Real Estate Boards. *January 25, 1960*

President Udall, and ladies and gentlemen:

I have been talking to your President about this group, about the hour that you had to get up this morning in order to be at breakfast on time, and about the work you are doing. I noticed that he kept stressing that this is bipartisan. He apparently was afraid I was going to make a political speech. And you know, I am, because I am going to try to convince those people who are of another persuasion—so far as political parties are concerned—that what President Udall has been talking about and that what I have been talking about is to their interest. I should like to see them all banded together, and therefore, as they go out the door this morning, I would like to see them take another little oath of allegiance to the proper party and get behind these things.

One of the reasons that I was anxious to come is because I know of your work in the great effort to prevent the debasement of our currency. But I am not going to talk about that kind of program and the ones that are related to it particularly. What I want to talk about is something a little broader and a little deeper.

I know you people know all the risks there are to inflation because of excessive Federal spending. If we indulge in fiscal irresponsibility and irresponsible debt management, you know what it means. Therefore, I am not going to waste your time. What I am going to try to talk about is this: our mission—as people who do understand—is to inform others who are going along in a sort of cloud, believing that one party or another has all the virtues and the other none, or who are completely uninterested, particularly if registering and taking part in political action interferes with their golf or their shooting or any other recreation.

I believe the greatest problem in America today is not simply keeping our currency from being debased and eroded. It is the need of understanding, the understanding of the United States about the issues that we face.

People who oppose budgets that are balanced say, "Well, you think more of a balanced budget than you do about the education of some poor lad out in Kansas."

If you say anything about America's responsibility for giving real leadership in the world in order that we may have an opportunity to see people follow the course of freedom—living in freedom—and maintain themselves against any kind of incursion from an atheistic philosophy, we see it attacked by saying "giveaway programs."

To my mind there is nothing that can be more futile, and nothing that can be more indicative of an abysmal ignorance—if there is no demagoguery in it at all, but just ignorance—than to say that the programs the United States carries out in the world are "giveaway programs."

Do we want peace?   Do we want the free world strong, or do we not?

I was reading a history of the United States by a man named Muzzey, and he talks about the amount of investment capital that flowed into our country in the fifties to seventies which was largely responsible for the tremendous expansion in our continent during those years.   In 1873 there was a sudden money panic in Austria, and it spread in Europe, and suddenly there was no capital coming into the United States.   This country was in a panic.   From 1873, really, to 1879 it never came out of it.

We in our turn have the chance to help people invest properly, in their own freedom, in their own dignity, in their own security.   If we don't do something like this, those people are going to be abandoned, and we are going to pay the bill in a very, very much higher currency than the mere dollars that we lend to them—or indeed at times grant to them—in order to keep this kind of peaceful program working and operating in the world.

We need, of course, other countries—other industrial countries. What I am getting at is this: do you learn the facts?   And, as you talk the facts, supporting the Government in economy, in efficiency, and preserving our dollar, are you taking these other great issues and getting your friends—all of the other realtors in the world that you can get hold of—and letting them see what the issues are?

That is the biggest problem today, because if the United States is informed—even if you have to do it by injection—our people will make the right decisions.   There is no question about that.

We have had some of the difficult questions in the last few years brought to the people through the help of bodies such as this—for example, economy last year, and before that, the reorganization of the Defense Department.   As quickly as people became aroused, there was no question about what Congress would do.

So, first, I think my message is: congratulations for what you are doing—and the expression of the hope that you will go even a little deeper into the relationship of the United States Government with you, with your community, with your State, and with other nations.   It isn't good enough to say, "Oh, well, so and so is Secretary of State, or so and so is Director of the Budget, or Secretary of the Treasury, so we can just forget it."

We have to know.

You have to give your honest convictions, not because a man is a Democrat or a Republican or even a Populist or anything else. You have to do it because you believe something. And if you believe it on the basis of facts—and you can make enough other people believe those same facts—you will have in your hands the mightiest force there is in the United States: an informed public opinion.

I come here because I know your record up to this point, and I hear your program being discussed as to what you are going to be doing next year. So I just come here to ask you: work harder, deeper, wider, for one cause only—the United States of America.

I am very proud that I have been asked to come to see you this morning. I am really, truly complimented that I find so many ladies have found it possible to get up this time of the morning to come to such a meeting.

Thank you all very much indeed.

NOTE: The President spoke at the May-flower Hotel in Washington. In his open-ing words he referred to James M. Udall, President of the Association.

20   ¶ Statement by the President on the Occasion of the 80th Birthday of General of the Army Douglas MacArthur. *January* 26, 1960

AS GENERAL OF THE ARMY Douglas MacArthur reaches four score years of a life that in service and in distinction has had few equals in all our history, I speak for every citizen in expressing to him warm felicitations and the wish that he may have many more years of fruitful and rewarding activity.

For more than a half century of active military service, in both World Wars and the Korean conflict as well, General MacArthur's name has been a symbol of courage, of patriotism, and of inspired generalship. To-gether these earn him a foremost place in the hearts of our people, and in the annals of our military endeavors. I value most highly my own years of service with this great leader and soldier. With Americans every-where, I salute General MacArthur on his eightieth birthday.

21   ❡ The President's News Conference of
January 26, 1960

THE PRESIDENT. Good morning. I am ready for questions.

Q. Merriman Smith, United Press International: Mr. President, the Cuban Premier, Fidel Castro, recently has stepped up the character and intensity of his attacks on the United States, and the American Government is apparently very concerned about this, as reflected in your meeting yesterday with Secretary Herter and Ambassador Bonsal.

What, if anything, can you do about this situation, Mr. President? Do you feel that specific action is required by the American Government to preserve its position against these Castro attacks?

THE PRESIDENT. Well, you are perfectly correct. We are concerned and, more than that, we are perplexed. We don't know really the foundation of these accusations that are made not only by the Prime Minister but appear in the publications in Cuba.

Now, we have had these conferences with Secretary Herter and Ambassador Bonsal, trying to understand more about the motives and what they are really hoping to do. Over the last 2 days, now, with Mr. Herter and Mr. Bonsal, we have prepared a written restatement of our policy, as of now, concerning Cuba. It's in written form and you will get it. [*Addresses Mr. Hagerty*] Where is it?

Mr. Hagerty: Outside.

THE PRESIDENT. Outside?

Mr. Hagerty: Yes, sir.

THE PRESIDENT. Right outside the door. You can get a copy.

So it explains our position and exactly what our policy is in the circumstances.[1]

Q. J. Anthony Lewis, New York Times: Mr. President, in your State of the Union Message you made reference to the Civil Rights Commission proposals and said they deserved a thorough study. Since then, the Attorney General has been studying them and reportedly thinking of some alternative ideas. Do you have anything now that you can say about the proposals?

THE PRESIDENT. Yes. The Attorney General has another plan that he thinks, within the framework of existing law, will improve very much

---
[1] See Item 22.

the procedures that have been followed. It is somewhat technical—exactly what the jurisdiction and the action possible for judges to take. So I would suggest, to get the thing exactly so it is not subject to misinterpretation, you should go to him; because it is a legalistic amendment that it would be difficult for me to describe in detail.

Q. Chalmers M. Roberts, Washington Post: Mr. President, the last few days there has been some dispute over Secretary Gates with reference to estimates of Soviet military capabilities, and he has expressed the idea that we have changed our estimate from one based on capability to one based on intention. Could you tell us whether you, yourself, have had a part in this? Could you give us your thinking as a soldier on the reliability of an estimate that takes intentions into consideration?

THE PRESIDENT. I don't think it's exactly correct—what you are now giving as a premise of your question. There was a premise to the effect that you just now suggest contained in a question put to Mr. Gates; he rather ignored that, and therefore his statements were subject to misinterpretation. Certainly his meaning was subject to misinterpretation.

Frankly, what is really happening is that we have better estimates than we had in the past in this field.

Let me call your attention to a little bit of history. Only 3 or 4 years ago there was a great outcry about the alleged bomber gap in favor of the Russians, and there was a great deal of talk about it and, actually, I think we got more—a billion dollars or something like that, $900 million more—for bombers that year than I asked for. Subsequent intelligence investigation showed that that estimate was wrong and that, far from stepping up their production of bombers, the Soviets were diminishing it or even eliminating that production.

Now, I think that we should never talk about an argument between intention and capability. Both of these things are, of course, necessary when you are making any intelligence estimate.

Let me point this out: we've got all of the power that would be necessary to destroy a good many countries. We have no intention of using it. And the whole world knows that.

We also know a number of things about the Soviets. Naturally we think that our intentions, stated intentions, are more trustworthy than those of people hostile to us.

I do say that this whole business of intelligence, of producing intelligence and an intelligence estimate, is a very intricate and a very complex thing. You cannot take any one basis, any one channel of thought, to make a proper estimate on which a government or a commander can act.

I would just say this: I think that Mr. Gates will find ways of clarifying exactly what he meant; because, in my opinion, he is a very splendid civil servant.

Q. William McGaffin, Chicago Daily News: Mr. President, in view of the international prestige at stake, why are we not moving with a greater sense of urgency to catch up with Russia in the field of space exploration?

THE PRESIDENT. Just start at that again. How did you start it, how did you start that question?

Q. Mr. McGaffin: I said, in view of the international prestige at stake.

THE PRESIDENT. Is it?

Q. Mr. McGaffin: Well, sir, do you not feel that it is?

THE PRESIDENT. Not particularly, no. We have got a record in 5 years in space exploration that is not only admirable, but I think is one to be proud of.

The Soviets have made some very spectacular achievements, but I don't think that we should begin to bow our heads in shame, because in a few years we have gotten up and gone past them in many fields of this work, when they have been working on it ever since 1945.

So I would think that once in a while we ought just to remember that our country is not asleep, and it is not incapable of doing these things; indeed, we are doing them.

Now, I don't deny that this spectacular achievement more excites the public imagination than does the good, hard, steady work of the scientists that are keeping satellites in the air and getting from them information all the time. It is more spectacular, and it has more effect on the casual reader. But in the actual examination of these two programs, I think we've got a pretty good record.

Q. Felix Belair, New York Times: Mr. President, since we last met, the former British Prime Minister, Mr. Eden, has had another recollection, this one about Suez. And he says that the decision to go into Suez by Britain and France was made in June, or many months before the October going in, and that you, sir, were privy to that decision.

THE PRESIDENT. Well, I don't like to comment on memoirs. As I have said, I think, here several times, Mr. Eden is a very good friend of mine, been one for years, and I had great confidence in him.

Now I do recall this about the decision—or not decision, the action at Suez. As a matter of fact, I'll tell you one or two footnotes of history that might be interesting. I made it clear that the United States was going to stand by its interpretation of United Nations policy and the Charter. This meant that we would apply this to anybody, those that we thought our closest friends as well as those that we thought were in another category.

At about this time—I have forgotten just exactly at what time the invasion started——

Q. Mr. Belair: October, wasn't it?

THE PRESIDENT. Well, sometime in early October, Mr. Eban was going back to Israel for a short time. He came in to see me. And I told him I'd hoped that he would not allow any misinterpretation of sentiment in this country to sway him. Particularly because of possible Jewish sympathy for what seemed to be an intention building up around the mobilization of Israel at that time, I hoped he would not allow this to sway his judgment as to what this administration would do in doing its very best to prevent any outbreak of hostilities and the, you might say, settlement of international issues by force.

I told him that if he thought that this would have any iota of influence on the election or that that would have any influence on me, he should disabuse his mind about it.

In addition to that, both Foster Dulles and I went to great pains to show to Britain and to France what we would do under that set of circumstances. As far as the decision itself was concerned, for the 2 weeks just prior to the action, Foster Dulles told me, there wasn't a single item that came in from the British Foreign Office; as a matter of fact, he referred to it as "a blackout of news."

Now, that is all I recall from this time.

I am not trying to impugn anybody else's memory or anybody's interpretation of the facts as they were then. We had telephone calls—transAtlantic—in order to try to keep this thing on the rails. But that was our own attitude; that I know.

Q. James B. Reston, New York Times: Mr. President, two other points on Mr. Belair's question.

First, were there recordings of the telephone calls back and forth between Washington and London at that time; and, secondly, are you putting in train any kind of historical, orderly way of gathering the historical material of the last 8 years together?

THE PRESIDENT. Well, you know, Mr. Reston, for a good many years I've tried personally to keep a diary. And every evening I find that I have been a little-bit too tired, and I was going to do it tomorrow morning.

Some of these calls were occasionally from my own room. It just struck me that I'd better get hold of Mr. Eden or someone else and talk to him, Mr. Churchill, or someone. I cannot recall for sure whether I always came back and gave the gist—I'm sure I always told it verbally to Secretary Dulles.

Now, as far as it can be done through my official acts, and even in conversations, there is an orderly record made. For example, one of the types of correspondence that is going to the Presidential Library that will be built to take my papers will be Foster Dulles' personal notations of the conversations between ourselves, because that was a personal thing between him and me. All the others of his papers, as you know, are going to the Dulles Wing of the Princeton Library, as they properly should. He himself made that decision, and it is in his will. And his executors have the direction to keep those.

There are a thousand other things we keep over here in the White House. The Secretary, and my own personal secretary, people like that, keep a record. The trouble is it gets so voluminous until you get experts to winnow it down, it's going to be a very difficult thing to do.

Q. Mr. Reston: How far did you get with that diary, sir?

THE PRESIDENT. Me?

Q. Mr. Reston: Yes.

THE PRESIDENT. I started, as I recall, in Panama in 1921, and I found that, from time to time, as I looked back, oh, I'd find three or four notes over the period of 5 years; and I decided that it wasn't very much. [*Laughter*]

Q. Harold R. Levy, Newsday: Sir, aside from any thought of economic reprisal against Cuba, it has been suggested that our present sugar quota system should be dropped, or at least modified, to permit free competition among producing nations. Do you think such a step would be feasible or desirable?

THE PRESIDENT. As I say, I refer you to my statement as to what our policy is.

But I do want to say this: the American people still have the greatest affection and the greatest interest in the Cuban people. We are not going to be party to reprisals or anything of that kind. At this moment it is not our time to do it, and certainly we are not going to intervene in their internal affairs. But when you read the whole statement, if you have further questions, why, come back to the next press conference and I'll be glad to try to answer them.

Q. Sarah McClendon, El Paso Times: Sir, Mr. Gates has said that he did not make the intelligence decisions and he was not a member of the United States Intelligence Board which uses this intent, or approach. And then when we went to get the names of the U.S. Intelligence Board, we were told that two members had recently been added, about the time, I believe, they started making this new type of approach. But we couldn't get the names. Don't you think that the American people have the right to know who is making these decisions that may affect their security?

THE PRESIDENT. I hadn't thought of this question at all. I'll ask——

Q. Mrs. McClendon: Well, could you ask them to get those names?

THE PRESIDENT. No, no; I won't say that. I'll just ask them what the procedure is.

Q. Raymond P. Brandt, St. Louis Post-Dispatch: The joint congressional committee on your Economic Report has made a voluminous study and report which differs somewhat from your Economic Report. This brings up the question of your National Goals Commission, because they apparently established some goals. What is the status of your Goals Commission, and will they make a similar study?

THE PRESIDENT. The study I am talking about is, first of all, to be bipartisan, and that I could not say for the kind of economic report to which you have just referred. This is to be bipartisan, done by scholars and experienced people. I hope that, at long last, we've gotten the thing on the rails and it will get to business. I am disappointed that its report necessarily will not be available in the time that I would hope it could have been, but it has been a long-term job getting it done.

Now, I just point out about this report [1] which I hear is coming out this noon: always before, it has been the practice that, after the Joint Economic Committee gets the President's report and recommendation, they hold hearings; and then they make a report. Well, they're doing it this time without hearings, apparently.

---

[1] Senate Report 1152, 86th Congress (Government Printing Office, 1960).

Q. Rutherford M. Poats, United Press International: Sir, while we appreciate that you have not announced, and therefore presumably not made your plans as to additional travel in the Far East, I wonder whether you can tell us now what your thinking is about the desirability and your own personal hopes as to whether you can extend your travels to visit some of the other countries which have invited you in that area.

THE PRESIDENT. This is a big point: time. How can you, during the time that the Congress is in session, how can you so stretch this time as not to get into difficulty in your own country?

Now, we have jet planes and all that sort of thing, but let us take this one point. A bill comes in; frequently, although I am kept informed while I am here what is going on, I have to sign it or refuse to sign it in a matter of 2 hours before the final minute for the action. If I'm gone too long, I run into the difficulty of not having the benefit of that kind of consultation and, therefore, my own constitutional duties are to that extent neglected.

While I can make certain provisions, and always have been able to do so, to hold some of these bills before they leave the Capitol and come to the White House, this is not a process that ought to be usual. And so the thing becomes a question of time.

Naturally, as long as I am going to be in the Far East, I should like to go to a number of places. Some of the people are old friends of mine. But the visit that I talked about was made possible only by the authority of the Soviet Government to permit my leaving it by the eastern exit. That makes it possible for me to go at least to Tokyo.[1]

Beyond that, I haven't studied the thing in detail.

Q. Spencer Davis, Associated Press: Mr. President, further along that line, is there a possibility of a second trip out to the Far East when time permits?

THE PRESIDENT. You know one thing—come next July there is no one going to be interested in what my visits are, either you people or anybody else. [*Laughter*]

Q. Donald H. Shannon, Los Angeles Times: Going back to Mr.

---

[1] On January 17 the White House announced that as a result of personal exchanges between the President and Chairman Khrushchev it had been agreed that the President would visit the Soviet Union June 10–19, 1960. On January 20 the White House announced that the President would visit Japan about June 20. On April 12 a further release stated that the President's visit to Japan would take place June 19–23, and that he would make a brief visit to Korea on June 22.

McGaffin's question about space exploration, Mr. President, you distinguished between space exploration and defense in your State of the Union Message, but a great many people feel that the subjects are not really distinguishable. I wonder if you could say something along your—your views, how you divide them up?

THE PRESIDENT. I doubt that I can say anything more than I said in my State of the Union Message, because I assure you that I worked 3 months on that, and it represents my very definite, fixed conclusion. These things are different. They are for different purposes.

Now, no one has ever denied that if the Defense Department can find some space activity that can contribute to its defense, well, quite naturally, we'd exploit it. But the difference between space activity as such and defense is really quite marked, and not nearly as confused as it is, for example, between, say, Air Force and Navy and the Navy and the Army, and all of the three of them put together.

Q. Robert G. Spivack, New York Post: Mr. President, I'd like to get back to your earlier answer to the question about civil rights. Without getting into the technicalities of what the Attorney General is working on, is the alternative that he is proposing an alternative to the Federal registrars proposal or to the civil rights bill that now is bottled up in the House Rules Committee?

THE PRESIDENT. Oh no, he's not making—we stand by the recommendations we've already made. But he thinks he's got a scheme that will make the insurance of the voting right more firm, and that is the thing you should talk to him about so then you know exactly what he's got in mind.

Q. Mrs. May Craig, Portland (Maine) Press Herald: Mr. President, our railroads complain that they suffer from competition with Government-subsidized shipping, aviation, highway transport. Now, if we are planning to put the Minuteman and other solid fuel missiles on railroad cars as mobile launching pads, how are we going to save the railroads from being ruined by this competition and not here when we need them?

THE PRESIDENT. Well, I thought your question was a pretty good one until you got the Minuteman in it. [*Laughter*] No one knows exactly how those things will happen now.

No one could be more concerned than I am about the railroads. I think that they are governed by antiquated laws and regulations; and, frankly, I think some of the trouble is their own.

In the great golden days of the seventies and early eighties, when everybody could get rich by either building a railroad or pretending he was going to and selling stock—if you will read in some of the parts of those late sixties and early seventies, you will find it mostly scandal—well, everybody wanted an independent railroad. I think our railroad systems are proliferated into so many different independent things—of course, everybody likes to be president, don't forget that—so you've got these things that are not always economic and efficient. But even allowing for that, I believe we ought to have a real overhaul of all the regulations and the controls, and give them a chance to be prosperous.

I guess 4 years ago now, I had a Cabinet meeting that proposed, in a transportation report, just something of that order. As a matter of fact, my transportation committee remains alive.

I am all for some reform in this whole thing in the railroads, I assure you.

Q. Thomas N. Schroth, Congressional Quarterly: Speaking of next July, sir, last Saturday the Democrats had a great many attacks to make on your administration, and particularly on Vice President Nixon. One of them called him a "juvenile delinquent." Do you care to comment on the remarks of the Democrats last Saturday?

THE PRESIDENT. Well, I couldn't comment except to laugh.

Q. William H. Y. Knighton, Jr., Baltimore Sun: Mr. President, at the last press conference, you yourself raised a very interesting point when you suggested that we get an opinion whether a second term President should run for Vice President.

THE PRESIDENT. Not "should"—I said "could."

Q. Mr. Knighton: Could—yes, sir; could. We can't get an official opinion in our status, but you can. Have you, and if you can run, will you? [*Laughter*]

THE PRESIDENT. I'll tell you this much—I'll be more like these non-running candidates; I'll be cagey—the afternoon of that press conference, there was a note on my desk saying a report from the Justice Department—I don't know whether the Attorney General himself signed this, but the report was, it was absolutely legal for me to do so. That stopped it right there, as far as I'm concerned.

Q. William J. Eaton, United Press International: Mr. President, there was a great deal of criticism of the Taft-Hartley law during the steel dispute. Do you plan to ask Congress to revise the emergency procedures of that law to deal more adequately with major strikes?

THE PRESIDENT. I have asked the Attorney General, the Secretary of Commerce, Secretary of Labor, and the Chairman of the Economic Advisers to study this matter thoroughly, so that in some timely fashion, if there is anything I should or could do, I'd like to know.

Q. Lillian Levy, National Jewish Post and Opinion: Mr. President, a clause was written in the last appropriation legislation empowering you to withhold aid to foreign countries which discriminate against American citizens on the basis of race or creed. Are you contemplating taking such action against countries that have continually so discriminated, or do you have another remedy that you think would be more effective?

THE PRESIDENT. I have seen no specific case of this kind brought before me on my desk for a long time, and I'll just have to take a look before I can state what my policy will be, for this reason: these exceptions are written in the law so as to put the specific cases before the President and make him decide whether or not such-and-such a thing is to the best interests of the United States.

Now quite frequently such a decision has to conflict with, you might say, the normal or general policy. You have to do it because of specific cases. That is all I can say, because I don't know the cases you are talking about this morning.

Q. Miss Levy: I was referring specifically to Saudi Arabia, which for several years has discriminated against our citizens.

THE PRESIDENT. I think the recommendation of the State Department would be—I'd stop there and then if they have anything to tell me, why, I'll be glad to take it up again.

Marvin L. Arrowsmith, Associated Press: Thank you, Mr. President.

NOTE: President Eisenhower's one hundred and seventy-eighth news conference was held in the Executive Office Building from 10:31 to 11:01 o'clock on Tuesday morning, January 26, 1960. In attendance: 235.

22 ¶ Statement by the President Restating United States Policy Toward Cuba.
January 26, 1960

SECRETARY HERTER and I have been giving careful consideration to the problem of relations between the Governments of the United States and Cuba. Ambassador Bonsal, who is currently in Washington, shared in our discussions. We have been, for many months, deeply concerned and perplexed at the steady deterioration of those relations reflected especially by recent public statements by Prime Minister Castro of Cuba, as well as by statements in official publicity organs of the Cuban Government. These statements contain unwarranted attacks on our Government and on our leading officials. These attacks involve serious charges none of which, however, has been the subject of formal representations by the Government of Cuba to our Government. We believe these charges to be totally unfounded.

We have prepared a re-statement of our policy toward Cuba, a country with whose people the people of the United States have enjoyed and expect to continue to enjoy a firm and mutually beneficial friendship.

The United States Government adheres strictly to the policy of non-intervention in the domestic affairs of other countries, including Cuba. This policy is incorporated in our treaty commitments as a member of the Organization of American States.

Second, the United States Government has consistently endeavored to prevent illegal acts in territory under its jurisdiction directed against other governments. United States law enforcement agencies have been increasingly successful in the prevention of such acts. The United States record in this respect compares very favorably with that of Cuba from whose territory a number of invasions directed against other countries have departed during the past year, in several cases attended with serious loss of life and property damage in the territory of those other countries. The United States authorities will continue to enforce United States laws, including those which reflect commitments under Inter-American treaties, and hope that other governments will act similarly. Our Government has repeatedly indicated that it will welcome any information from the Cuban Government or from other governments regarding incidents occurring within their jurisdiction or notice, which would be of assistance to our law enforcement agencies in this respect.

Third, the United States Government views with increasing concern the tendency of spokesmen of the Cuban Government, including Prime Minister Castro, to create the illusion of aggressive acts and conspiratorial activities aimed at the Cuban Government and attributed to United States officials or agencies. The promotion of unfounded illusions of this kind can hardly facilitate the development, in the real interest of the two peoples, of relations of understanding and confidence between their governments. The United States Government regrets that its earnest efforts over the past year to establish a basis for such understanding and confidence have not been reciprocated.

Fourth, the United States Government, of course, recognizes the right of the Cuban Government and people in the exercise of their national sovereignty to undertake those social, economic and political reforms which, with due regard for their obligations under international law, they may think desirable. This position has frequently been stated and it reflects a real understanding of and sympathy with the ideals and aspirations of the Cuban people. Similarly, the United States Government and people will continue to assert and to defend, in the exercise of their own sovereignty, their legitimate interests.

Fifth, the United States Government believes that its citizens have made constructive contributions to the economies of other countries by means of their investments and their work in those countries and that such contributions, taking into account changing conditions, can continue on a mutually satisfactory basis. The United States Government will continue to bring to the attention of the Cuban Government any instances in which the rights of its citizens under Cuban law and under international law have been disregarded and in which redress under Cuban law is apparently unavailable or denied. In this connection it is the hope of the United States Government that differences of opinion between the two governments in matters recognized under international law as subject to diplomatic negotiations will be resolved through such negotiations. In the event that disagreements between the two governments concerning this matter should persist, it would be the intention of the United States Government to seek solutions through other appropriate international procedures.

The above points seem to me to furnish reasonable bases for a workable and satisfactory relationship between our two sovereign countries. I should like only to add that the United States Government has confidence in the ability of the Cuban people to recognize and defeat the intrigues of international communism which are aimed at destroying democratic institutions in Cuba and the traditional and mutually beneficial friendship between the Cuban and American peoples.

23 ¶ Address in Los Angeles to the Nationwide Republican "Dinner With Ike" Rallies. *January 27,* 1960

Mr. Vice President, Chairman Morton, fellow Republicans, and all other supporters of good government:

First, may I thank the Los Angeles audience here for the warmth of your personal welcome. I am deeply grateful. And I must say a word to all those workers, all those good Republicans that made this dinner such a success and started this year off as a good Republican one. And on top of that, I am overwhelmed by the verbal tributes that have come from my friends and associates and that we have heard over the television. It is indeed a proud moment for me.

Before leaving early in December for a tour of foreign nations, I received a letter from a young lady, who lives in Arvada, Colorado. It reads:

"My dear Mr. President,

"I have just turned 21 years of age. I am now old enough to vote and mature enough to take part in political elections.

"My problem is, which party am I best suited to serve. I thought you would be able to help me by telling me what the Republican Party stands for. What are its goals and in what way may I help it to achieve them?"

Since that time, her letter has been much on my mind. Thinking about this evening's program, I asked friends to invite her and her husband to the Denver dinner, in the hope that I may convince her that she wants to be a Republican. So—Shirley Jean, to you, and I trust, to all other young or undecided voters I can reach, here is my answer.

First of all—I am sure what you mean to ask is not what party you can best serve, but rather through what party you can best serve your country.

I start by observing that no party, at any one time, embraces all of the policies and beliefs any of us might deem ideal. Yet a major party, through its platforms, programs, record, and leaders, takes on a character and appearance of its own before the public.

Tonight, we are concerned with Republican beliefs—with what Republicans have accomplished, particularly over the past 7 years—and with how we are trying to perform the tasks ahead.

Republican conviction, since the days of Lincoln, has always held that people are supreme. Our party first came into power to bring equal protection of the law to our people.

Republicans insist that the personal, political, and economic freedoms of the individual are his most precious possessions and are inseparable. If any one of these is lost, eventually all others must disappear. Never should a citizen transfer any of his own rights and responsibilities to government, except in those cases where necessity clearly demands. Indeed, the first and more sacred responsibility of government is to help people protect their inalienable individual freedoms. Now these convictions form the foundation of the entire Republican structure of political doctrine and practice.

It is true that government has to do many things which, individually, we cannot do for ourselves. So, for example, local governments provide police protection and street maintenance. But the principle still holds true; governments must refrain from unnecessary meddling in the daily, normal problems of living and working.

Now today one of the sharpest controversies in public life is centered on economic freedom. Many feel that economic life has become so complicated that individuals and private business cannot function fairly and profitably. They hold that economic progress now depends largely upon Federal intervention and Federal appropriations.

Republicans flatly reject the argument that the Nation can pump its way to permanent prosperity by an outpouring of Federal dollars. We are opposed to those extremists who argue that the Federal Government should become the master mechanic of our economy—with sweeping authority to tinker with the free processes of the competitive enterprise system. That system provides the best possible protection to our own personal and political freedoms and to individual opportunity. Moreover, it is the most productive system ever devised.

Only when an activity is operated most efficiently as a practical national monopoly should it be a Federal responsibility, as for example, interstate highways and the handling of the mails. But the production of the automobiles on the highways, or the stationery we use in the mails, should always be privately done.

Now we go to a second basic Republican doctrine. A healthy, free society requires a wide diffusion of power and responsibility. Power belongs to all the people, and citizens should never permit its excessive concentration in any hands—industrial combines, labor groupments, or even government.

Concentration of power is dangerous and susceptible to abuse.　It courts disaster for the individual.

Already too much power and responsibility—and tax money—have drifted to Washington.

Therefore, in all those things that must be done by government we strive to have the responsibility borne by local and State governments, which are closest to the people.

But even adherence to this Republican conviction finds the Federal Government carrying immense responsibilities.　The list is a long one. For example—the Government must develop a national defense in which our citizens can have confidence.　It must so manage its fiscal and financial affairs as to prevent the debasement of our currency, thus helping to protect the citizens' savings, pensions, and insurance from erosive inflation.

It must assist in developing water power; conserving and reclaiming land resources; cooperating with States and institutions in education; relieving hardships in areas where individuals are not able to find employment; in supporting medical, agricultural, and other research so that American science and technology will be able to meet every challenge of the future; helping eliminate the vast and difficult problems in agriculture as well as the human and material blight that is imposed upon many of our cities by crowded slums; developing a cooperative program among Federal, State, and city authorities to reduce the hazards of travel on America's skyways.　There are dozens of other Federal responsibilities.

And for this reason the National Government owes it to every citizen to see that all of these approved programs—some of them costing billions of dollars—are performed efficiently and economically.　Integrity in Government is mandatory.

The Republican record in all these things is one to merit the confidence of every American citizen.

Let us look at specific cases:

Providing an effective defense is a vital service that the Federal Government must perform in a world divided by opposing ideologies.　This is a nonpartisan subject—but of such vast importance that it is necessary for us to take note of its administration these past 7 years.

The real test is to provide security in a way that effectively deters aggression but does not itself weaken the values and institutions we seek to defend. This demands the most careful calculation and balance, as well as steadiness of purpose, not to be disturbed by noisy trumpeting about dazzling military schemes or untrustworthy programs. Neither effort nor expense has been spared to provide a sure defense. Moreover, we have not wasted our strength or resources.

Because of our insistence upon adequacy and efficiency, our country is, over-all, the strongest power on earth, both militarily and economically.

Nevertheless, America's unchanging goal for decades has been the pursuit of peace—through negotiation from a position of strength, in concert with other nations that share our ideals.

We and our loyal friends are striving to make it possible for the new or less industrialized nations to strengthen themselves economically and where necessary, militarily—so that all of us together can live and prosper in peace. These programs we call Mutual Security. They comprise part of our whole effort to keep the free world strong, safe, and free. There is no more vital program that is to be executed within the Federal Government.

Reviewing the foreign field over these 7 years:

The independence of South Korea has been sustained. Iran was saved for the free world.

The explosive situation in Trieste was resolved. Austria is now a free nation. Stability has returned to Jordan and Lebanon.

Today, there is no war. The international atmosphere recently shows signs of improvement.

Now we seek ironclad self-enforcing agreements on the grave issues of nuclear test suspension, arms control, the status of Germany and Berlin. Progress is slow and frustrations many, but we shall continue to approach the task with patience, firmness, and candor.

Though national security and programs for strengthening the free world are costly, we can provide for them adequately and can do so while keeping ourselves economically solvent and fiscally sound. But to do this we must, first, make the national need our sole guide for expenditures. Extravagance and security are mutually hostile—and in prosperous times like the present, only Federal extravagance can plunge us needlessly and deeper into debt.

Republicans believe that America is tired of a constantly growing debt—with annual bills for interest alone well over nine billion dollars.

We want to stop the cowardly habit of passing our own obligations as a mortgage to our children. This is a first Republican determination.

So, when we consider a new Federal project, we ask ourselves whether it is truly necessary, or does it merely serve the selfish desire of some particular group? Is it of such importance to the Nation as to justify either an increase in taxes or an addition to our debt—which spurs a constant rise in prices, and a cheapening of the currency.

Do we want or need to saddle the taxpayer with ever greater taxes?

And Republicans say No! And they have acted and are acting accordingly.

This good Republican record extends into many fields. Consider education.

Today, the Federal Government is aiding America's schools and colleges in many vital ways. Among these is a program for constructing great numbers of additional classrooms, to supply great deficiencies. But, again, the Republican policy is to help the States help themselves—not to allow a Federal take-over of America's institutions of learning.

In agriculture our purpose is to assist the farmer in meeting adverse conditions over which he has no control; flood, drought, and unreasonable fluctuations in the price of farm products. Antiquated legislation in this field has built up huge and costly surpluses that depress prices and rapidly grow unmanageable. Republicans have devised and supported legislation to help correct these conditions, but the majority opposition in Congress has prevented its passage. We want our farms to be run by farmers, not Washington bureaucrats. And above all we want our farmers to receive their fair share of the Nation's income.

The Department of Health, Education, and Welfare has, in 6 years, spent over one billion dollars in Federal aid for medical research seeking to find cures for killing and crippling diseases. The discoveries made are immediately available to any individual or group who can use them. At the same time we are determined that the Federal Government is not going to displace the family doctor.

This is just another example of Republican efforts—and there are many others—to satisfy human needs, with government help where necessary, but not through government domination.

To pay for costly and highly publicized "phony" panaceas for all our problems, many politicians seem to believe that money by the bale can be printed without shrinking—a kind of Sanforized dollar! Well, we know better!

And it is the unshakable aim of the Republican Party to make certain that your dollar will buy today and tomorrow as much as it did yesterday.

In the 7 years just preceding 1953 our general price structure went up an unconscionable 48%. In the 7 Republican years since 1953 the price rise has been held to 10%. This record is one for every thinking citizen to applaud, but it is not good enough—we Republicans propose to make it better.

If we are to hold down prices, one thing we must do is avoid excessive governmental spending so you may have more money for the things you want for yourself.

The Republican program this year avoids any increase in the debt. Next year that debt will be reduced by a substantial amount.

And remember—more Americans are working than ever before. Real per capita income has never been higher. This is true prosperity. In every way, America enters this new decade stronger than ever before.

One other point—Republicans have faith in America, her strength, her destiny. Yet in late years, the tendency to disparage the unmatched power and prestige of our country has become an obsession with noisy extremists. Time and again we hear spurious assertions that America's defenses are weak; that her economic expansive force can be sustained only by Federal spending; that her educational and health efforts are deficient. In this kind of preachment, political morticians are exhibiting a breast beating pessimism in the American system.

Of this I am certain; America's economic strength is not in Washington, D.C., nor in public spending. It is in the creativeness and industry and spirit of our people.

Fellow Republicans, our duty is to make certain that our party is always better qualified than any other to guide our national destiny.

This involves a deep sense of individual responsibility.

In the great and divinely-ordained sweep of time, it is our children who live at the forward edge of history. The future belongs to them and to those who are to follow. We must not by our actions or inaction today, tarnish the bright prospects for that future.

And so I close, Shirley Jean, with a postscript directed at a most vital part of your question—what you can do to help achieve these Republican goals.

First, study carefully the great issues facing our Nation.

Second, see your precinct leader and volunteer for doing some of the tasks he will have for you.

Next, make certain to register; don't let your husband and your friends forget to register.

Fourth, bring all your enthusiasm to the business of getting able, personable, Republican candidates to run for public office.

Fifth, vote. Get everybody else to vote.

Sixth, every day of your life support your Nation in its search for a peace with justice, and take an active part in preserving and strengthening those values that in America we place above all else—freedom, equality of opportunity, and human dignity.

So doing, you will be a good Republican and a great citizen.

Thank you and good night.

[Following his formal address the President said:]

I have been asked to make an announcement. As one who has spent a great deal of his life traveling back and forth to Europe and this country and all over the world, I know only too well how wonderful it sounds in a meeting of this kind to hear one of our traditional patriotic songs. As a salute to our beloved country, I am going to ask Mr. Gordon MacRae and his closed circuit cross-country chorus, the collegiate singers and the Howard University Choir, and all of you seated in this great dinner across the Nation, to stand and sing "God Bless America."

Mr. MacRae, would you please lead off.

[The President's response upon receiving a gold medal award follows:]

Thank you, Mr. Chairman, and everybody here, both for my wife and for myself.

This is indeed a great honor. The title of the medal itself is enough to overwhelm one with emotion, and I know that my wife will share my pride and my very great appreciation of this most generous—over-generous act.

On the part of you, Mr. Chairman, and your organization, to all of you—thank you.

NOTE: The President spoke at 7:40 p.m. in the Pan Pacific Auditorium in Los Angeles. The address was broadcast by closed-circuit television to similar dinner-rallies in 83 cities.

The President was introduced by the Vice President, speaking in Chicago. U.S. Senator Thruston Morton of Kentucky, Chairman of the Republican National Committee, served as toastmaster, speaking in New York. The young lady from Arvada, Colo., to whom the President referred, was Mrs. Shirley Jean Havens.

The presentation of the gold medal bearing the inscription "Peace and Prosperity" was made by Harold Ramser, Chairman of the Republican State Central Committee and of the Los Angeles dinner.

24 ¶ The President's News Conference of *February 3, 1960*

THE PRESIDENT. Good morning.

I have one correction I want to make for a statement I made in my last press conference. I said that Ambassador Eban was actually in my office when I made a particular statement about my attitude toward the impending Suez crisis at that time. I have had the staff look up the records. Actually, Foster Dulles came to my office at 6 o'clock in the evening, stating that he was to see Mr. Eban in a few minutes, and I made the same statement that I gave you last night [time] but I made it to him. I had confused that incident from what I said then with other visits, or at least another visit of Mr. Eban.

So, again, it shows that my memory, at least, is not perfect.

Q. Marvin L. Arrowsmith, Associated Press: Some California Republicans seem to be rather surprised that you did not mention Vice President Nixon in your Los Angeles speech. Now that Mr. Nixon seems to have no opposition for your party's presidential nomination, do you intend to stick to your announced policy of endorsing no one before the convention?

THE PRESIDENT. I admit that such a concern now seems to be a bit academic. But it has been my policy, and I think it is a correct one— we're all human, and we don't know what is around the next corner. I maintain that there are a number of Republicans, eminent men, big men, that could fulfill the requirements of the position; and until the nominations are in as a matter of history, why, I think I should not talk too much about an individual.

I have so often, because of his close association with me, had opportunity and the occasion to express my admiration and respect for the Vice President, I am quite sure at least he is not unaware of my sentiments in this regard.

Q. Merriman Smith, United Press International: Mr. President, the burden of some recent statements on Capitol Hill, primarily by generals, has been that we are well behind the Russians in missile development, with little or no prospect of catching up with them in the near future. I'd like to ask you, sir, as far as man's effort to enter space, as well as the development of military missiles, do you feel any sense of urgency in catching up with the Russians?

THE PRESIDENT. I am always a little bit amazed about this business of catching up. What you want is enough, a thing that is adequate. A deterrent has no added power, once it has become completely adequate, for compelling the respect of any potential opponent for your deterrent and, therefore, to make him act prudently.

I saw Monday morning in the *Congressional Record*—just after I got back from California—that day's *Congressional Record* had a statement of America's history in missile development. It's a very comprehensive one. I commend it to your attention to show what has been done—with a very slow start and with a complete neglect for a period—in the period, particularly in ICBM and IRBM development. And the record, I insist, is one to be at least quite gratified about.

As I recall, for 1960 there is, for missiles of all kinds, appropriated $6,690 million. This, it seems to me, is getting close to the point where money itself will [not] bring you any speed, any quicker development.

Q. Rowland Evans, Jr., New York Herald Tribune: Mr. President, you mentioned the word "deterrent" in your answer to that last question. Yesterday, General Power said that our deterrent of heavy bombers cannot be properly safeguarded unless it is put on a full air alert. You discussed this with us before, but in view of General Power's testimony yesterday, would you give your view on that question?

THE PRESIDENT. No; too many of these generals have all sorts of ideas. But I do point this out: I have got the Secretary of Defense, whom I trust, and who I know is honest in his study, analysis, and conclusions. That is Secretary Gates. And beneath him, assisting him, is the Chairman of the Chiefs of Staff, whom I similarly trust; and the Joint Chiefs of Staff, with those two, are my military advisers. I have been long enough in the military service that I assure you that I cannot be particularly disturbed because everybody with a parochial viewpoint all over the place comes along and says that the bosses know nothing about it.

Now, I don't think anyone's trying to impugn the patriotism and the earnestness and the integrity of the group I have just mentioned. I think, myself, they are the ablest people we could get. That's the reason they were selected.

Q. Alan S. Emory, Watertown Times: As the No. 1 Republican in the country, sir, are you seriously concerned about the future and the vigor of the Republican Party, and do you think the party needs more crusaders?

THE PRESIDENT. Well, I know it ought to have a lot more recruits. [*Laughter*]

Now, you say vigorously, or whether I am concerned. I don't know whether that's the right word. I am genuinely interested to see the Republicans telling their story more eloquently and better than they have in the past, more often and on a more widespread basis, and to get these recruits that we need.

Q. Robert C. Pierpoint, CBS News: Mr. President, quite aside from the military implications of the space race, I believe your head of the USIA, George Allen, said recently before Congress that he feels we are in a race to space with the Russians, whether we want to be or not, and that also the United States prestige seems to be low because of our lag behind the Russians.

Now, I think that last week you told us that you don't believe that the international prestige of the United States is at stake in this race. I wonder if you could straighten out that confusion.

THE PRESIDENT. I made a long trip; and certainly if there wasn't an evidence that the prestige of America was rather high, then I was very badly mistaken in my own conclusions. And I think that most of the people of this group that went along with me, that they would have been mistaken.

It is idle to say that just exactly as we like to see this country ahead in every single activity that seems to us worthwhile, we want to see them ahead in space. This is a spectacular area in which we are now working. But let us remember this one thing: the reason for going into space, except for those activities that are carried on by the Defense Department as having some value to the security of the country, is purely scientific. Therefore, you are not talking about racing them in finding the particular items or in naming the particular course that you are going to run in this race; you work out a proper and an appropriate plan of scientific exploration, and you follow it positively, rather than trying to follow along behind somebody else.

Now, I have said time and again that because the Soviets are far ahead in this very large booster and engine, that, so far as distant space exploration is concerned, they are going to be ahead in that regard for some time, because it takes time to get that engine built.

Just taking over, this Saturn project from the Army: I have, after long study by the space agency, determined that the amount of money that we took over with that particular thing was not sufficient; and there's another hundred million being devoted, or at least recommended for devotion, to it. I believe it will be appropriated; and I believe that implies not only the determination of the United States to go ahead rapidly with this thing, I believe that we can look forward at the proper time to success.

Q. Ray L. Scherer, National Broadcasting Company: In the general context of the so-called spirit of Camp David, do you think the fact that the lend-lease talks came to nothing indicates anything about the general Soviet desire to negotiate on outstanding issues?

THE PRESIDENT. Again, I must repeat myself. I wasn't aware of any spirit of Camp David. I have heard it quoted a number of times, and I think that it was originated by people other than ourselves. No one denied that the talks there went on in an atmosphere that was personally friendly. That's the only way the spirit of Camp David could be defined.

But I think that these difficulties, when in this instance the Soviets tried to put two or three other problems together with the lend-lease talks, was a typical maneuver and there was nothing done. But it doesn't mean that sooner or later there won't be something done.

Q. William H. Knighton, Jr., Baltimore Sun: Mr. President, don't you think the country ought to have the benefit of your advice as to who you think the other Republicans are who could be President?

THE PRESIDENT. Well, I'll tell you what: there's a number of them, and I am not going into the business of nominating people. That's not my job. I want to make this very clear: I am not dissatisfied with the individual that looks like he will get it, not by any manner of means. I just simply say there's a number that could perform the duties of the office with distinction.

Q. Mrs. May Craig, Portland (Maine) Press Herald: Mr. President, there is concern in the Capital for fear you may feel it necessary to give atomic information, or even actual custody of atomic weapons, to those countries where we're going to have bases for nuclear weapons. Do you want to do that and, if so, inasmuch as we took our bases out of France on that quarrel with De Gaulle, would that mean we might put nuclear bases back into France?

THE PRESIDENT. Well, you've got about a three-barreled question there.

But, Mrs. Craig, the law itself says what information the Executive can give to particular nations, and it defines rather accurately the nations to whom you can give this information. As far as giving away the bombs, this cannot be done under existing law.

I do believe this: that where we are allied with other nations and we are trying to arm ourselves in such a way as to make certain of our defense, we should try to arm them in such methods and ways as will make that defense more strong and more secure.

I would not ever, even if the law permitted, give away information that was still, in our opinion, withheld from the Soviets themselves. But when the Soviets have the information and know-how to do things, it's pretty hard for me to understand why we don't do something with our allies, as long as they themselves stand with us firmly in defending against the probable aggressive intent of communism.

Q. Charles H. Mohr, Time Magazine: You made clear in an earlier answer, Mr. President, how strongly you felt that SAC was not vulnerable to being wiped out in an enemy attack. Since this is at the heart of the current argument, I wonder if you could tell us whether you believe that we would get strategic warning of any enemy missile attack or, if you don't believe that, could you give us some of the reasons why you feel that SAC is not vulnerable, in a period of 2 or 3 years, to a very crippling blow.

THE PRESIDENT. If you will take the things that the Soviets could probably do 3 or 4 years from now and then we sit right where we are now and do nothing, well, that's a different story.

I just say this: I don't believe that anyone today can destroy all of our capabilities for retaliation, and they cannot destroy today enough of them that we couldn't retaliate very effectively to the point of destructiveness to them.

Now, as we go ahead, they will go ahead. But I would say that 3 years from now, if we are working as hard as we do now, we are going to be in the same relative position.

Q. Chalmers M. Roberts, Washington Post: In view of your answer to Mrs. Craig's question and the fact that the nuclear test negotiations at Geneva seem to be stalled, Mr. President, do you feel that it's becoming really impossible to stop the spread of nuclear weapons to the so-called "fourth" countries, or do you still look upon the test ban negotiations as a way to do this? Are you prepared to keep on with the moratorium?

THE PRESIDENT. Of course, if you had real test bans that applied to all nations, then the only way other nations could get weapons would be through sale, transfer, or gift.

Of course, it concerns any thoughtful individual as to the problem of the spread of these weapons to smaller and other nations, as the process of their manufacture may become more simple and as just through, you might say, the method of absorption the necessary know-how becomes more widespread.

I am of the belief that, if you could have now a ban on all testing that everybody could have confidence in, it would be a very, very fine thing to stop this—for this very reason, if no other: it is a very expensive business, to begin with. The very first bomb we produced, I think, cost America $2 billion or more before we ever had the very first one. Since that time, although you'd have to look this up, I think our appropriations have never been below $2 billion a year. So it is an expensive business.

Q. Mr. Roberts: Could I ask, sir, are you prepared, in face of the difficulties at Geneva, to keep our negotiator there more or less indefinitely? You put the moratorium on sort of a day-to-day basis months ago.

THE PRESIDENT. I want to keep him there as long as there is the slightest chance of success. We should get this kind of agreement as soon as we can.

Q. Laurence H. Burd, Chicago Tribune: Mr. President, where do you expect to be and what do you expect to be doing one year from now?

THE PRESIDENT. I hope, out in the desert or down shooting quail in Georgia—or maybe just sitting in a rocking chair.

Q. Felix Belair, New York Times: Have you decided yet, Mr. President, in connection with the Panama Canal, what form of visible evidence of titular sovereignty should be displayed over the canal?

THE PRESIDENT. I'll tell you, Mr. Belair, here is a question that, if it had been asked me 3 years, I'd have known exactly what I would have said. One of the earliest tours I had in my military service was in Panama. I learned to know the people pretty well. I stayed there something over 3 years, I think, from '21 onward—6 years after I got out of West Point.

I think that not all of the difficulties that have come about have been entirely because of their demands. It is perfectly true there was a treaty made many, many years ago, more than 50, now. And the conditions of that treaty were changed from time to time as the whole condition of affairs in the world so demanded, just exactly like our Constitution has been amended 22 times.

I think that at times, because we did buy the territory—and everyone knows that the primary source of revenues for the Panamanian nation is the wealth that is brought there through the canal operations—that we suddenly decide that we must be a little bit too stern in our treatment of them. They are people that are sensitive. I don't know exactly now what you can do, because we have people that have suddenly gotten themselves into a state that believes that even if you ever had, for example, a flag flown as a courtesy to the nation in which titular sovereignty still resides, that this would be a very, very great abdication of American rights and responsibility. I think that this is getting a little bit beyond the rule of reason, because the treaty says that the United States may act, and in all respects can act, as if it were completely sovereign. Such language means that there is a titular sovereignty in the other nation, in my opinion.

So I haven't decided any particular thing.[1]

Q. David Kraslow, Knight Newspapers: Mr. President, there seems to be considerable pressure in Congress for amending the Social Security Act this year. Can you tell us, sir, if the administration is planning to recommend any changes in the Social Security Act and what those changes might be, generally?

THE PRESIDENT. There is under consideration a possible change to run up the taxes by a quarter of a percent to make greater provision for the care of the aged.

There has been no conclusion reached in the administration; I have not yet made any recommendation on it.

---

[1] On April 19 the White House announced at Augusta, Ga., that the President had that day approved a nine-point program for improvement of relations between the United States and Panama with reference to operations in the Canal Zone (Department of State Bulletin, vol. 42, p. 798).

Later, on September 17, the Associate Press Secretary to the President announced that the President had "as a voluntary and unilateral decision on the part of the Government of the United States, approved and directed the flying of the flag of the Republic of Panama together with the United States flag on a daily basis in Shaler's Triangle in the Canal Zone."

Q. John Scali, Associated Press: Mr. President, of late, Premier Khrushchev has started to talk, both publicly and privately, about Berlin and the Soviet demand that the West sign a separate peace treaty with East Germany. In his January 14 speech to the Supreme Soviet, he said that, unless the West agreed to a separate peace treaty with East Germany, the Soviets would go ahead and sign one with all the consequences that would flow from that. Now, do you regard such talk as violating the understanding that you reached with him at Camp David on the removal of threats from the Berlin situation?

THE PRESIDENT. I'll say this: at Camp David nor anywhere else did he ever retreat from the statement that he had a right, if he so wanted, to make a separate treaty with East Germany; bringing to everybody's attention, of course, the fact that the West had made a special treaty with West Germany. But when he adds that this would immediately—when he talks about the consequences—make all of East Germany, including West Berlin, a sovereign, cutting it off from connections from the West, well, that, of course, would be a very grave situation that would be brought about.

Q. Carleton Kent, Chicago Sun-Times: Mr. President, the Senate yesterday passed a proposed constitutional amendment which abolishes the poll tax, gives the District of Columbia citizens the right to vote and Governors the right to appoint temporary members of the House under certain wartime conditions. How do you feel about this?

THE PRESIDENT. I think they make pretty good sense. Certainly I would think the poll tax, where you abolish it only for Federal elections, and to give the residents of the District the right to vote for the national ticket, I think are reasonable and should be done.

The other one is one that I think is brought about by the realization of the catastrophes that could occur if there should ever be the tragedy of war.

Now, I might add I have a couple more that I think ought to be added. I think Congressmen ought to be elected for 4 years, at the same time with the President, that is, the lower House, so called, the House of Representatives. I think also that the item veto should be an authority of the President and so stated in the national Constitution; because I know one thing: that would defeat pork barrels.

Q. Garnett D. Horner, Washington Star: Awhile ago, sir, while you were talking about the atomic weapons and information to allies, I got the impression that you might lean toward favoring changing the law so that you could provide allies with custody of weapons that Russia has or knows how to make. Was that correct or wrong impression?

THE PRESIDENT. From the very beginning, from what I knew about allied cooperation, and so on, I have always been of the belief that we should not deny to our allies what your potential enemy already has. We do want allies to be treated as partners and allies, and not as junior members of a firm who are to be seen but not heard.

So I would think that it would be better, for the interests of the United States, to make our law more liberal, as long as we classify our countries as those that we are confident, by our treaties and everything else, they'd stand by us, and stand by us in time of trouble.

Q. Edward P. Morgan, American Broadcasting Company: I would like to pursue this discussion about our relative progress with the Soviet Union from a different angle.

Have you considered the possibility that the American public may be confused by a psychological aspect of our struggle with the Russians? They may have more missiles than we. They did beat us to the moon. Their rate of economic growth now is faster than ours, and they are, net, turning out, for example, more trained engineers than we do. Now, individually, none of these factors is decisive. But cumulatively, is it not possible that a state of mind, a dangerous state of mind, is being created under which we would be in a position or be forced into a position to accept a posture of second-best in everything or anything.

THE PRESIDENT. Well, I think here and there you can find that in a country as big as Russia you are going to be certainly second-best; didn't they win the Olympic games last time?

Q. Mr. Morgan: I believe they did, sir, in many events.

THE PRESIDENT. Well, what did we do with that?

Let's remember this: if they find an athlete, they take him, and it's a national responsibility to train him and build him up until he's the best there is in the world, if they can make him such.

Now we have a free enterprise; we place above all other values our own individual freedoms and rights; and we believe, moreover, that the operation of such a system in the long run produces more, not only more happiness, more satisfaction, and pride in our people, but also more goods, more wealth.

Let's remember that dictatorships have been very efficient. Time and time again, look how we were overawed, almost, by Hitler's early years—overrunning Poland, and then overrunning the West, and going into Africa. Of course, we talked about this great efficiency. This is dictatorship.

If you take our country and make it an armed camp and regiment it, why, for a while you might do it with great morale, too, if you could get people steamed up like you did in wars; you might do this thing in very greater tempo than we now are doing it.

Democracy, we hope, is an enduring form of government. We are, therefore, trying to do these things at the same time we keep these values.

I would like to see our people—and I admit that they get disturbed and probably at times alarmed about something, particularly when the headlines give it an interpretation far beyond its true meaning, like hitting the moon. I've heard people say, "Well, soon there'll be colonies on the moon and they'll be shooting at the earth from the moon." I saw that in one story.

Well, this is long after you and I will be gone; that, I'll assure you.

Now, what we should think about and talk about more in the world are the values which we do treasure. They don't have them. And since we believe that in the long run men do learn to have this same belief about the same values, I believe that there is just as much of the seeds of self-destruction in the Communist system as they claim is in ours—they claim the inherent conflicts within our system are going to destroy it.

I think our people ought to have greater faith in their own system. Let's remember, you people are the bosses of the American Government—you the people, by your votes and your representatives, and so what do you want? All right, you can make the decisions. All you have to do is to inform yourselves and you will make good decisions. And that is exactly what we are doing, to say we want these things or we don't want them. So let's just be sure that we don't kid ourselves that somebody else, different from ourselves—because people in government are just you people. All right, then it's your responsibility to make sure that you are secure, that you are not alarmed and certainly not hysterical.

Q. Mr. Morgan: Then, sir, you don't feel that there is a basic danger of defeatism under the present circumstances?

THE PRESIDENT. Put it this way: none in my soul; I'll tell you that.

Marvin L. Arrowsmith, Associated Press: Thank you, Mr. President.

NOTE: President Eisenhower's one hundred and seventy-ninth news conference was held in the Executive Office Building from 10:29 to 11:02 o'clock on Wednesday morning, February 3, 1960. In attendance: 225.

25 ¶ Citation Accompanying Awards for Oceanographic Research. *February 4, 1960*

THE PRESIDENT of the United States takes pleasure in presenting awards to:

    MR. JACQUES PICCARD

    LIEUTENANT DON WALSH, U.S. NAVY

    DR. ANDREAS B. RECHNITZER

    LIEUTENANT LAWRENCE A. SHUMAKER, U.S. NAVY

CITATION:

For outstanding contributions to the United States and science in the field of oceanographic research.

These officers and distinguished scientists are richly deserving of the appreciation and acclaim of the Government and the people of the United States. Their marked professional skill and resourcefulness, their scientific studies and courageous efforts while conducting operations at great personal risk, culminated on 23 January 1960 in a dive by the bathyscaph Trieste to the unprecedented depth of 37,800 feet, the deepest spot on the ocean floor known to man. This dive and others before it were made in the interest of science and to collect data for the United States Navy in this previously unexplored area of the earth. This, the first penetration of the deepest parts of the ocean, impressively demonstrates that the United States is in the forefront of oceanographic research.

As President of the United States, I extend the nation's recognition and gratitude for your resourcefulness, courage and devotion to duty and your contributions to our country and to all free men. I offer my personal congratulations.

NOTE: The President presented the awards in his office at the White House, as follows: to Mr. Piccard, the Distinguished Public Service Award; to Lieutenant Walsh, the Legion of Merit; to Dr. Rechnitzer, the Distinguished Civilian Service Award; to Lieutenant Shumaker, the Navy Commendation Ribbon with Metal Pendant.

26 ¶ Memorandum Concerning a Career Executive Development Program in All Departments and Agencies. *February* 5, 1960

To the Heads of Executive Departments and Agencies:

Our government faces the possible loss of two-thirds of its top career managers over the next ten years. A survey of 751 career officials in grades GS–16, 17 and 18, indicates that two out of every three will be eligible for retirement during the next decade. Further, two out of every five will be eligible for retirement by 1963. In addition, of course, there will be certain losses because of death, disability and resignation. This situation emphatically and clearly points to the importance of instituting a positive program which will assure the filling of the anticipated vacancies with persons of outstanding leadership ability, creative imagination and sound judgment.

Upon each of us rests the responsibility for seeing to it that the critically important functions of the top career management positions continue to be carried out by persons of the highest competence. Nothing less will satisfy our obligation to the American people for effective and efficient administration of their government's programs.

To properly discharge this responsibility, careful planning will be needed in each agency and on a government-wide scale. Employees with executive potential in positions below the top career levels must be identified, trained and developed over a period of time to increase their capacity to perform the complex functions of career managers.

The success or failure of our efforts to identify, select and develop competent career managers will determine the future effectiveness of government operations, both here and abroad. I have asked my Special Assistant for Personnel Management to provide leadership to the departments and agencies in taking such steps as may be necessary to see to it that we continue to have the best available executive talent for these top civil service posts. He will work with you and the Civil Service Commission toward this goal.

In the last analysis, however, the results of the quest for topnotch administrators in the career service will depend on the steps each agency takes to find persons of executive potential and to train and develop them for the responsibilities that lie ahead.   I know each of you shares my concern that the ablest persons are selected for top career civil service positions. I expect you to give personal leadership towards the achievement of this objective within your organization.

Dwight D. Eisenhower

NOTE: See also Items 27 and 28.

27   ¶ Memorandum Directing the Special Assistant for Personnel Management To Provide Leadership in the Career Executive Development Program. *February* 5, 1960

Memorandum for the Special Assistant to the President for Personnel Management:

As you know, the government faces a continuing loss each year of some of the executives filling the top career management positions.

To meet this problem, we must be assured a continuing supply of well-trained career employees to replace those leaving the service. The military services, of course, have well-developed programs for the replacement of top officers going out of the service. I understand the civilian services generally have none.

While I fully realize that the same requirements and conditions do not apply with equal force to the military and civilian services of government, both must have an adequate and continuing supply of well-trained and competent leaders and managers if they are to meet the demands of today's world.

Career men and women are the backbone of any organization. Without able career managers, government, in particular, cannot function effectively and efficiently.

I am most anxious that we, in this Administration, do our utmost to see to it that the government has a sound program for the selection, development and training of its career civil servants.

Therefore, as my Special Assistant for Personnel Management, you will take the leadership in the development of a government-wide program to meet this objective. With respect to positions in the competitive Civil

Service, you will, of course, cooperate with and depend upon the Civil Service Commission. In regard to other personnel systems, you will cooperate with the heads of the agencies concerned.

All department and agency heads are being advised of my concern in this matter.

DWIGHT D. EISENHOWER

NOTE: Eugene J. Lyons was serving as Special Assistant to the President for Personnel Management. See also Items 26 and 28.

28 ¶ Memorandum to the Chairman, Civil Service Commission, on the Career Executive Development Program. *February* 5, 1960

Memorandum for the Chairman of the Civil Service Commission:

No area of personnel management is of greater importance to sound administration than the selection and development of highly competent career administrators. As an indication of my personal concern in the matter I have sent the attached letter to the heads of all executive departments and agencies.

You will note that I have asked my Special Assistant for Personnel Management to assume responsibility for providing leadership in instituting service-wide action programs and to cooperate with the Civil Service Commission and the departments and agencies in stimulating better executive selection and development programs within agencies.

Therefore, it is my wish that you work with The Special Assistant for Personnel Management in devising methods for strengthening and coordinating existing programs and in developing new ones. As the operating arm for the largest segment of the Federal personnel management field, the Commission will continue to provide assistance to the departments and agencies in strengthening their executive development programs.

In this connection please review existing Civil Service programs concerned with recruitment and examining, position classification, career and employee development and take whatever steps may be necessary to strengthen them and to achieve maximum coordination.

In addition, the Commission will assemble periodically and report to me, information summarizing significant developments and progress being made by the departments and agencies in this area.

Because of your own long-time interest in this phase of Federal personnel management, I am confident that I can depend on you to help to make this program successful.

DWIGHT D. EISENHOWER

NOTE: Roger W. Jones was serving as Chairman of the Civil Service Commis-   sion.
See also Items 26 and 27.

29 ¶ Letter to Dr. Henry Wriston on His Acceptance of the Chairmanship of the Commission on National Goals. *February 7, 1960*

[Released February 7, 1960. Dated February 5, 1960]

Dear Henry:

I am glad to learn that you have agreed to accept the Chairmanship of the Commission on National Goals, and that this study will be carried forward through the American Assembly. As I have indicated in our conversations, I am hopeful that the panel will develop a broad outline of coordinated national policies and programs for the next decade and longer, and that it will, in the process, set up a series of goals in various areas of national activity.

While I would hope that your report could be completed before my term of office is ended, I am far more concerned about the breadth and depth of the study than in the exact timing of its completion. I am appending hereto a brief memorandum outlining in general terms some of my reasons for requesting you to participate in this inquiry.

I should like to emphasize my desire that the inquiry be conducted free of any direct connection with me or other portions of the Federal government. However, all Federal agencies will cooperate with you in any way you may desire, as will my staff.

With many thanks for your willingness to undertake this important assignment.

Sincerely,

DWIGHT D. EISENHOWER

NOTE: Dr. Wriston is president of the American Assembly, an affiliate of Columbia University. President Eisenhower had been closely associated with the Assembly during his term as the university's president. (See Item 86.)

For the President's memorandum concerning the Commission on National Goals, together with a list of members, see Item 30.

30　¶ Memorandum Concerning the Commission on National Goals.　*February* 7, 1960

[Released February 7, 1960. Dated February 5, 1960]

THE PRESIDENT'S hopes for the Commission were stated in his State of the Union message in January, 1959, as follows:

"We can successfully sustain security and remain true to our heritage of freedom if we clearly visualize the tasks ahead and set out to perform them with resolution and vigor. We must first define these tasks and then understand what we must do to accomplish them.

"If progress is to be steady we must have long-term guides extending far ahead, certainly five, possibly even ten years . . . They must be goals that stand high, and so inspire every citizen to climb always toward mounting levels of moral, intellectual and material strength . . ."

The genesis of the study is rooted in our tradition and our history. Ours is a land carved out of a hostile wilderness, populated by people filled with a spirit of freedom and adventure, made strong by sheer perseverance, and dominated always by strong moral and religious beliefs. It was logical that for several generations we devoted all our energies to growing—developing our vast lands and resources, building a way of life. But the industrial revolution which we helped nurture has now reached a stage that makes it impossible for us to live in isolation.

We are now the strongest nation on the earth. This fact brings with it the realization that with power comes responsibility. We have found ourselves in a position in which the entire Free World looks to us for leadership and help, in the first instance against an aggressive Communist conspiracy, supported by rapidly growing economic and military strength, but more broadly in the worldwide struggle for realization of decent conditions of life.

But behind these problems of our external relationships, lie the more basic issues of realizing our own ideals for the development of American society. Unless we can press forward toward these goals, in an era of vast technological change and development, we shall not be able to fulfill our world role or, most basically of all, be true to ourselves and to the ideals on which this nation is based.

The Commission on National Goals is being asked to identify the great issues of our generation and describe our objectives in these various areas. To do so will be to give us the basis for coordinated policies in both the domestic and international areas.

One American aspiration is to develop a world in which all peoples will be living at peace under cooperative policies with maximum standards of living and opportunity for all. But more specifically, the Commission undoubtedly will want to consider how within a framework of free decision-making our economy can best be developed to meet the Communist challenge and simultaneously progress toward established goals. The Commission will also want to consider how our educational and other social institutions can best be shaped to develop mind and spirit; how individual well-being, health, and initiative can be nurtured without undesirable centralization of authority and responsibility; and how the various levels of our government can best contribute to the nation's welfare.

Since a universal understanding of basic issues and goals is, in a free government, necessary to its own perpetuation, one of the greatest accomplishments of the Commission could well be the outline of effective methods for producing this understanding.

The Commission has the opportunity to sound a call for greatness to a resolute people, in the best tradition of our Founding Fathers. It is no wonder that a nation so recently thrust into a position of world leadership is sometimes bewildered by its new role. That we have emerged so rapidly and accepted so readily our position of leadership is but another proof of our resilience. Now we must cast our eyes ahead toward the future. Some obstacles along this path will be frightening. Many decisions we must make are not easy. But through the haze of indecision one sees the strong and vibrant image of a future America—where modern-day pioneers, with deep religious conviction, develop the richness of a free society, where the dignity of each and every individual is recognized and his ability to enjoy life is enhanced.

NOTE: A copy of the President's memorandum was transmitted to each member of the Commission. In addition to Dr. Henry Wriston, President of the American Assembly, Graduate School of Business, Columbia University, who was designated chairman, and Frank Pace, Chairman of the Board, General Dynamics Co., Inc., who was designated vice chairman, the members as announced by the White House were: James Killian, President of the Corporation, Massachusetts Institute of Technology; Alfred Gruenther, President, American National Red Cross; Clark Kerr, President, University of California; Learned Hand, Retired United States Circuit Judge for the 2d Circuit, New York; Erwin Canham, Editor-in-Chief, Christian Science Monitor, and President, United States Chamber of Commerce; Colgate Darden, former President of the University of Virginia and former Governor of Virginia; James Conant, former President of Harvard and former Ambassador to the Federal Republic of Germany; George Meany, President, AFL–CIO; and Crawford Greenewalt, President, E. I. DuPont de Nemours and Co., Inc.

31 ¶ Remarks at Dedication of the Veterans of Foreign Wars Memorial Building. *February* 8, 1960

Mr. Chairman, Commander Feldmann, distinguished guests, comrades-in-arms of past years, and friends:

It is an honor to participate in this moving tribute to American veterans, living and dead. The emblem of the Veterans of Foreign Wars, here established, will be, I am told, perpetually lighted, symbolizing the Nation's eternal gratitude for the service and sacrifice of those who served its colors in the cause of freedom.

The struggle for freedom does not stop when the guns of war cease firing. Nor will it stop so long as freedom is suppressed or threatened anywhere in the world.

Freedom makes its rightful claim upon the daily life of everyone who enjoys its benefits. No deed is too small to count. Every one of us contributes in his own way to the strength of America, and the strength of this country is dedicated to the preservation of freedom.

So our efforts add up to more than simply our own health, our own well-being and economic development. They answer the disbelieving and the doubtful that in freedom man can achieve his rightful destiny; and that men of all nations and races can live in dignity together as they seek the common goal of peace with justice.

Our daily preoccupations too often divert us from our duty in the service of this noble cause. We accept freedom much as the air we breathe. We lose sight of the connection between our own acts and the vigor of our governmental representatives in preserving the values we deem priceless. We tend to forget the high price that was paid for the privilege of living in freedom, and the price that would be exacted from all mankind if freedom should ever be allowed to shrivel and weaken in the earth.

This is why it is well for us to pause, to acknowledge our debt to those who paid so large a share of freedom's price. As we stand here in grateful remembrance of the veterans' contributions we renew our conviction of individual responsibility to live in ways that support the eternal truths upon which our Nation is founded, and from which flows all its strength and all its greatness.

Thank you very much.

NOTE: The President spoke at noon at the site of the new national memorial on Maryland Avenue near the Capitol. In his opening words he referred to U.S. Representative James E. Van Zandt of Pennsylvania, chairman of the dedication committee, and Louis G. Feldmann, Commander in Chief of the Veterans of Foreign Wars.

32 ¶ Special Message to the Congress on Agriculture.   *February* 9, 1960

To the Congress of the United States:

I urgently call attention, once again, to a most vexing domestic problem—the low net income of many of our farmers and excessive production of certain farm products, largely due to economic distortions induced by years of Federal interference.

We are most fortunate that our problem in agriculture is over-abundance rather than a shortage of food. But it defies common sense to continue to encourage, at the cost of many millions of tax dollars, the building of ever larger excess supplies of products that, as they accumulate, depress farm prices and endanger the future of our farmers.

The wheat situation is particularly acute. Federal funds tied up in wheat approximate $3½ billion. Although this means that well over thirty percent of the total funds invested in inventories and loans of the Commodity Credit Corporation goes for wheat, this crop provides only six percent of the cash receipts from sales of farm products. The government sustains a net cost of more than $1,000 a minute—$1,500,000 every day—the year around, to stabilize wheat prices and income.

Day by day this program further distorts wheat markets and supplies. Its only future is ever higher cost. Inexorably it generates ever larger surpluses which must be expensively stored. Ultimately, if our government does not act quickly and constructively, the danger is very real that this entire program will collapse under the pressure of public indignation, and thousands of our farming people will be hurt.

I think the American people have every right to expect the Congress to move promptly to solve situations of this kind. Sound legislation is imperatively needed. We must quickly and sensibly revise the present program to avoid visiting havoc upon the very people this program is intended to help. Every additional day of delay makes a sound solution more difficult.

I have repeatedly expressed my preference for programs that will ultimately free the farmer rather than subject him to increasing governmental restraints. I am convinced that most farmers hold the same view. But whatever the legislative approach, whether toward greater freedom or more regimentation, it must be sensible and economically sound and not a political poultice. And it must be enacted promptly. I will approve any constructive solution that the Congress wishes to develop, by "constructive" meaning this:

First, that price support levels be realistically related to whatever policy the Congress chooses in respect to production control, it being recognized that the higher the support the more regimented must be the farmer.

Second, that price support levels not be so high so as to stimulate still more excessive production, reduce domestic markets, and increase the subsidies required to hold world outlets.

Third, for reasons long expressed by the Administration, that we avoid direct subsidy payment programs for crops in surplus; likewise, we must avoid programs which would invite harmful counter measures by our friends abroad, or which, while seeking to assist one group of farmers, would badly hurt other farmers.

Within these three guidelines, I am constantly ready to approve any one or a combination of constructive proposals. I will approve legislation which will eliminate production controls, or make them really effective, or allow the farmers themselves to choose between realistic alternatives. I am willing to gear supports to market prices of previous years, or to establish supports in accordance with general rather than specific provisions of law, or to relate price supports to parity.

I recognize that these observations are general in nature. They are intentionally so in order to leave the Congress room for alternative constructive approaches to this problem. If the Congress should so act, I urge an orderly expansion of the Conservation Reserve Program up to 60,000,000 acres, with authority granted the Secretary of Agriculture to direct the major expansion of this Program to areas of greatest need.

In connection with the expansion of the Conservation Reserve, the Department of Agriculture stands ready to assist, if desired, with the development of sound legislative criteria governing the administration of this program in the light of its experience gained through its operations of the past four years.

As part of the Conservation Reserve Program, I would be willing to accept an authorization, with proper safeguards, to the Secretary of Agriculture to make payments in kind in whole or in part for the reduction of acreage devoted to crops in surplus and retirement of this acreage from cultivation, provided measures are included to keep production below total consumption while the payment-in-kind procedure is being used. Lacking such safeguards, a payment-in-kind procedure would overload the free market and thereby depress prices.

My views as regards the price support program for wheat are clear. I prefer the following approach:

Acreage allotments and marketing quotas for wheat should be eliminated beginning with the 1961 crop—thus freeing the wheat farmers—and thereupon price-support levels should be set as a percentage of the average price of wheat during the three preceding calendar years. The Secretary of Agriculture will furnish the Congress the details of this approach.

Here I wish to comment somewhat more specifically on corn, a crop tremendously important to many thousands of our farmers.

Just over a year ago, by a referendum margin of almost 3 to 1, our corn farmers decided upon a new program that liberalizes corn acreage and adjusts corn price supports. This program is still new, and I believe it would be wise to give it a chance to demonstrate what it can do. In order to help the producers adjust to this new program, it is intended to use the expanded Conservation Reserve Program to provide a voluntary means of removing substantial acreage of corn and other feed grains from production.

On the administrative side, I want briefly to mention three programs highly important to agriculture.

The Food for Peace Program, initiated pursuant to my recommendations of last year, has been vigorously advanced. On my recent trip abroad, I saw many constructive results from these efforts and the need and opportunity for even greater use of this humanitarian program. Clearly we should continue to do our utmost to use our abundance constructively in the world-wide battle against hunger. The law we enacted in 1954, known as Public Law 480 of the Eighty-Third Congress, has been especially helpful to us in waging this battle.

Next, an aggressive Utilization Research Program is under way to develop new markets and new uses for farm products. The 1961 Budget now before Congress recommends additional appropriations for utilization research, and additional local currencies being acquired under Public Law 480 transactions will be devoted to this purpose.

A Coordinator for Utilization Research will shortly be named by the Secretary of Agriculture with the sole mission of concentrating on finding and promoting productive new uses for farm products.

The Rural Development Program, to assist rural people in low income areas to achieve a better living, is also being accelerated.

This program, initiated in my 1954 Message, is now well beyond the demonstration stage and is going steadily forward in 30 States and Puerto Rico. Other States are now starting this important work. I have also recommended more funds for this program in the pending Budget.

Finally, I repeat my conviction that the public, and farmers particularly, are entitled to sound legislative action on the problems I have mentioned. The Congress can act within a broad latitude of proposals and still comply with the recommendations I have made.

If the Congress wishes to propose a plan as an alternative to the course here recommended, so long as that plan is constructive, as I have indicated herein, I will approve it. The Department of Agriculture will cooperate fully with Congressional Committees and with individual Members of Congress in helping to prepare such alternative programs as they may wish to have considered.

The important thing for farmers, and for all other Americans, is for us to act sensibly and to act swiftly.

I urge the Congress so to act in order that the farmers and public generally may plan accordingly.

DWIGHT D. EISENHOWER

33　¶ Remarks After Inspecting the Missile Test Center, Cape Canaveral, Florida.
February 10, 1960

WELL, it was an interesting day, and I have been wanting to come here for a long time, so it's a trip that's another realization of an ambition.

Obviously, it is the most highly instrumented place you can imagine, and certainly the personnel show every evidence of a high degree of competence.

So from my viewpoint it was a very worthwhile trip, and I hope it has been for you fellows.

Good luck to you.

NOTE: The President spoke at the airstrip before boarding a plane to return to Washington. His remarks were addressed primarily to the reporters who accompanied him.

34　¶ The President's News Conference of
February 11, 1960

THE PRESIDENT. I have a statement, but you won't have to take notes, because I believe there will be copies outside. This affects the negotiations for nuclear weapons tests at Geneva.

[*Reading*] The United States is today presenting in Geneva a proposal, involving the ending of nuclear weapons tests, to end the apparent deadlock in the negotiations. This Government has stood, throughout, for complete abolition of weapons testing subject only to the attainment of agreed and adequate methods of inspection and control. The present proposal is designed to end nuclear weapons tests in all the environments that can now be effectively controlled.

It would end forthwith, under assured controls:

(1) all nuclear weapons tests in the atmosphere;

(2) all nuclear weapons tests in the oceans;

(3) all nuclear weapons tests in those regions in space where effective controls can now be agreed to; and

(4) all nuclear weapons tests beneath the surface of the earth which can be monitored.

This proposal will permit, through a coordinated program of research and development, a systematic extension of the ban to the remaining areas, especially those involving underground tests, for which adequate control measures appear not to be possible now.

These are initial but far-reaching and yet readily attainable steps toward a complete ban on nuclear weapons tests. If adopted, they will prevent increases in the level of radioactivity in the atmosphere and so allay worldwide concern. They are steps which offer an opportunity to consolidate the important progress made in the negotiations thus far. It is our hope that the Soviet Union will join with us in this constructive beginning.[1] [*Ends reading*]

Questions.

Q. Merriman Smith, United Press International: Mr. President, every day the public is being subjected to a new chapter in the controversy over the missile gap between this country and Russia. Now, this argument, as you are well aware, is being waged in public by men who are supposed to be expert in the defense requirements of the country. Is there anything you can say to us today to explain this controversy to the public; and, in this connection, sir, are you thinking of a nationwide speech on this subject?

THE PRESIDENT. First of all, let me understand the first part of your question, Mr. Smith. You say, "waged by people who are supposed to be expert." Are you speaking now about the people of the Defense Department?

Q. Mr. Smith: Of the Defense Department and on Capitol Hill, too, sir.

THE PRESIDENT. I should think this: it would be fair to use the description "expert" with respect to the people in the Defense Department. That is what they're for. [*Laughter*]

They do have different ideas, and the trouble of it is that because one Chief or one Secretary or one individual or one technician, far down the line, has a particular idea and exploits this idea and publicizes it highly,

---

[1] On the same day the White House released a further statement, covering the same ground but in somewhat greater detail. The statement noted that the new proposal included provision for a program of joint research and experimentation by the United Kingdom, the USSR, and the United States to improve the detection of small tests underground and thus permit the extension of the ban to such tests. It also noted that extensive research and experimentation was already under way in the United States to improve detection instruments and techniques. The White House statement is printed in the Department of State Bulletin (vol. 42, p. 327).

that this, according to him, becomes the great judgment to be made in the defense of this country.

Defense of this country is a very wide and comprehensive problem. It is not decided by such a matter as can you make three or two particular weapons in a particular week, or such numbers as that. It is a matter that involves the study and investigations of many staffs, reaching many months into the future.

So these struggles that you talk about among the people in the Defense Department are those things that are brought about when they are required, apparently, and then leaks occur, as to their personal attitude toward the particular weapon or the particular weapons system, and then that becomes a matter of argument.

This I deplore, particularly the methods of publicizing it and making it look like any one of these particular points is the real problem to solve in America's defense.

I want to point out again—possibly I don't need to—that I have been in the military service a long time. I am obviously running for nothing. I want only my country to be strong, to be safe, and to have a feeling of confidence among its people so they can go about their business. And I just want to point out that in the decisions that I have to make—and there are many of them—in the approval of such a system, that I have heard all of the arguments, pro and con, in this individual type of an opinion of which I have been speaking. I have done the best I can, and I am doing it with one idea in mind only—America.

Q. Pat Munroe, Chicago American: Could you fill us in, sir, on the Vice President's role in reshaping the farm message?

THE PRESIDENT. Well, this is the first that I have heard about him reshaping it. I required that he read it, because there seems to be a great probability that in the next few months he is going to be defending what I believe, and the administration believes, is the best way to approach this problem. Naturally, he is completely aware of everything that is in the message, but this is the first I have heard of any reshaping.

Q. William McGaffin, Chicago Daily News: Mr. President, you're nearing the end of your term, and you've had a good 7 years of experience with it. Could you tell us, sir, what you think will be the major problems of the man who succeeds you and whether you think they will be any more difficult than the problems that you've had to deal with?

THE PRESIDENT. I think what you are suggesting now is we have sort of an informal conversation, rather than any exposition of specific problems.

The fact is that I think there are two things we must remember. America has become a leader in the world. In many of these aspects it is almost a decisive leader. This means that the problems that come to the presidential desk—whether it's a small farm in Dickinson County, Kansas, or a village problem somewhere, or urban renewal, or difficulty in the Mideast or with the Russians, whatever—these things have to be viewed in a broad world context, and then they have to be studied very earnestly, both on their short-term and their long-term effects.

I don't believe that anyone can predict what the next President's problems are really going to be. I have tried to describe, time and again, the ones that I see as important as of this moment and the methods in which I approach them. In so doing, I hope that I am helping to establish a pattern for solving these problems in the manner of reasonable men, never giving way to the so-called ultraliberal that has no other purpose than to give your money away for some pet theory of his own, and on the other hand, to repudiate reaction like you would the devil and all his works.

You've just got to approach these things with the best advice, the best knowledge, the best judgment that the individual or the occupant of the chair can bring to bear, and then solve them. I will point out there is one problem that is always with us, will never be properly or at least perfectly solved, but which all of us must work at.

It is this. You people right here have a very big function to perform. The biggest problem there is for the United States today is to make sure that her own people—her own people—understand the basic issues that face us, and form their own judgment. If we can inform these people properly, then we can be sure that the health and vigor of the democracy will solve them properly. Our great danger is that we are sometimes led down blind alleys by demagogues, or we're too lazy to inform ourselves, or we just say that some popular figure will solve them for us. We've got to inform ourselves. This is the greatest problem. And if we ever solve that one, we can do all the others without any difficulty.

Q. Chalmers M. Roberts, Washington Post: Mr. President, in relation to your statement about the test ban problem, I think there is one question that you left unanswered, and that is this. Assuming that the Soviet Union would accept this proposal, during the period of the development of new techniques to extend the ban on certain of the underground test problems, would the United States during that period resume underground testing?

THE PRESIDENT. It's a question that, of course, itself has not yet been resolved. I have already told you that laboratory testing—not of weapons testing, but of just the nuclear science—go on all the time. But when it comes down to weapons testing, that is something that we would have to decide with our own allies.

Q. Mr. Roberts: Would that be subject to negotiation as part of this proposed agreement with the Russians?

THE PRESIDENT. Well, no. We are not going to make an agreement, Mr. Roberts, when we can't know, when we cannot have any information as to whether or not it will be carried out by the other fellow as well as ourselves. That's what the problem is about. You see, we have been asked, time and again, to stop all testing and, indeed, to eliminate all bombs just by everybody unilaterally and voluntarily doing so. This is the kind of a system we will not accept. We say there must be adequate examination, verification, and enforcement.

Q. Charles W. Roberts, Newsweek: In connection with the first question asked you today, sir, when the congressional leaders came out of your office on Tuesday, they said that they thought the hearings on Capitol Hill concerning our defense—that some people, apparently running for office, had performed a disservice to the country and, furthermore, by undermining morale, that they had also breached security. Do you accept both of these charges?

THE PRESIDENT. Well, I didn't read them. I have heard them for the first time right now.

I am trying to keep my own statements outside the partisan field. I am trying to dedicate, as I have in the past, my efforts toward securing the United States in the fields of foreign relations and in defense. I think we should be big enough not to seek headlines. I think we should be big enough to put our heads together and see if we can get a real solution.

While I admit I have not specifically answered your question, I am giving you my belief about the whole matter.

Q. Felix Belair, New York Times: Mr. President, is there any ready answer to published suggestions that it is somehow defeatist to spend not quite so much money for defense or bigger defense and more and more for fancy tail fins and other things like that? That has been written about lately.

THE PRESIDENT. I don't quite understand your question.

Q. Mr. Belair: Well, you see, the argument seems to suggest, sir— and it came up yesterday at Canaveral—that much more could be spent, for instance, on missile development, to put us nearer to where the Russians now are. The argument seems to ignore what you have already said about our defense planning being based more on the adequacy of a deterrent. But the argument attributes to you, sir, the view that in all of these expenditures we must always have an eye on the budget, to maintain our fiscal responsibility, and that in emphasizing the need for a balanced budget, we thereby hold down expenditures for these purposes to a point that is not really necessary in our economy.

THE PRESIDENT. In this present case it would seem to me their argument is not too good, because I have put in the budget $4,200 million for surplus.

Now, if anyone, by any kind of hysterical argument, is going to make me say that fiscal responsibility in this country is not important; indeed, if they can prove that you can continue to go deeper and deeper and deeper into debt, without finally paying a very great cost in the Nation's security, I'd like to see how they prove their case.

Now, that does not mean that any budget I've ever put up has been put together on the basis of just achieving a balanced budget. I have tried to calculate and form the judgments about the needs of the United States, and I must say that I try to put need above pressure-group inducement, before local argument, before every kind of any pressure except that that America needs. I don't believe in putting luxury and extravagance ahead of need. But having satisfied the need, I believe we should go ahead with such policies and programs that the United States believes will be helpful and are in keeping with our Constitution and our institutions, and at the same time get this fiscal business into such control that we can have prosperity in the future as well as thinking we have it merely when we begin to debase our currency.

Q. Lambert Brose, Lutheran Layman: Mr. President, last fall, in connection with the TV quiz scandals, District Attorney Hogan stated that more than 100 people had committed perjury before a New York State grand jury—I think it was New York State. I am sure the American people bear no personal malice toward these individuals, and maybe this is a State matter.   But do you have any information, sir: one, whether indictments will be brought—I think only one or two have—and, two, if indictments are not brought, do you think this might undermine confidence somewhat in our system of equal justice under law?

THE PRESIDENT. As you say, it obviously is a State matter.

Now, I don't think it's necessary here for me to stress the importance I put on, you might say, public morality.   I believe that public morality finally became involved in this matter, and I think that every echelon of government that may have a responsibility ought to be working on the matter and see that it doesn't happen again.

Q. John Scali, Associated Press: Mr. President, Premier Khrushchev had some very blunt things to say to Italy's President, Mr. Gronchi, this week about world affairs generally.   He talked about West Berlin, Germany, and Russia's power, generally.   And among the things Mr. Khrushchev is quoted as saying is this: "Our flag is flying on the moon.   This means something.   Is this not enough to prove the superiority of communism over capitalism?"   What do you think of such remarks?

THE PRESIDENT. I think it's crazy.

I tried to point out to you the other day that in an industrial complex of the strength of Russia's, with its vast territory and resources, its people, and its great imaginative and competent scientists, that if it wants to put all of its strength in a particular field of activity—and, remember, secretly undertaken—of course it can come out with spectacular achievements.   And let's not try to blind ourselves about it.   But my contention is we should not be hysterical when dictatorships do these things.

As a matter of fact, Hitler was rather successful in keeping secret from many people the strength of the forces he actually had when he went in 1939 into Poland, and how much he had with which to smash the Western allies in Western Europe.

All of these things are possible, but they are not things that we should, in what we believe is a broader and better type of civilization, let dismay us.

Q. Sarah McClendon, El Paso Times: Sir, in view of your own expressed philosophy that defense should not be a partisan issue, do you not think it was wrong for six top officials of the Defense Department to accept invitations to speak at fundraising "Dinners with Ike," planned by the Republican Party?

THE PRESIDENT. No, I don't think so.   As a matter of fact, are you going to change all the traditions and the habits of America since we formed two parties way back at the time of Jefferson and Hamilton?

Q. Mrs. McClendon: Well, sir——

THE PRESIDENT. Now, just a minute, and I'll finish your question.

These people are politically appointed. They are not, and should not, indulge in talking about the failures of others of which I personally, and on both sides of the House, believe there have been many in years going past. Certainly they did in the Indian wars, if we want to get back to a place that is certainly nonpartisan. [*Laughter*]

For these people to report what they're doing and why they're doing it and to show the reasoning in which they have reached their decisions is far from harmful; it is helpful, in my opinion.

Q. John R. Gibson, Wall Street Journal: Mr. President, on the disarmament question, is it your feeling that the U.S., Britain, and Russia pretty well have to reach an agreement on the nuclear test situation before there is much chance for making any further headway on the broader disarmament question, either at the 10-nations meeting or at the summit conference meeting?

THE PRESIDENT. I am not now trying to express the opinions of any study group or any opinions other than my own. I believe that we are probably tackling the most difficult of all problems in this disarmament thing when we put all our attention on nuclear testing and nuclear use. Here is something, our scientists have testified over the years, that even if today you stop manufacturing plutonium and U–235, you could still conceal such an amount of destructive power that, to start at this end of the thing to establish the kind of inspection systems that are necessary, we are probably taking the most thorny thing and allowing that to keep us from other places.

Now, in testing I think the program that we put forward today is a good one and ought to lead finally to even a better one. But I think that we should look at disarmament on such a broad scale that we can find the areas where we can make progress, but not letting this one bar us from some progress along the line. Only as we make progress of this kind is there going to be a real lessening of tension.

Q. Marvin L. Arrowsmith, Associated Press: Mr. President, do you have any new appraisal of our missile program on the basis of your visit to Canaveral yesterday?

THE PRESIDENT. On that one I think, possibly except for some secret specification or something else, I think you people learned just exactly as much as I did.

I would say this, as I said that day: I was impressed by the business-like atmosphere in this whole facility. There seemed to be a minimum of extravagance and luxury and a maximum of efficiency and competence and real dedication to the problem at hand. I felt this: I came back with a very much better feeling than I had before I went down there.

Q. Spencer Davis, Associated Press: The Chinese Communists, sir, have said that they would not take part in any disarmament agreement in which they had no hand in formulating. At what point, sir, do you think they should come into a worldwide disarmament agreement?

THE PRESIDENT. Well, it's perfectly clear that such a big territory and such a great population could not be ignored when you are talking about general disarmament. Once we can make any kind of progress between the West and the Soviets and its satellites, I think that there will have to be some kind of mechanism in which we can bring these people into some kind of agreement, if it is going to be successful.

Q. M. Stewart Hensley, United Press International: Mr. President, with respect to the nuclear test ban, you say that you are proposing to ban the underground tests which can be verified. Is Ambassador Wadsworth going to, at the Geneva talks, put any specific level on that thing? In other words, there's been disagreement between the Russians and our scientists on this, whether it's below 20 kilotons, 30 kilotons, and so forth. Are you going to propose any specific threshold there, or is that a subject for negotiation?

THE PRESIDENT. I think it is a subject for negotiation, but it will, of course, have to go back finally to our technical people—what their conclusions are.

Q. Jack Raymond, New York Times: Mr. President, there have been various figures published on Soviet-United States missile strength. Do you believe that these have damaged the security of the country?

THE PRESIDENT. That what?

Q. Mr. Raymond: Do you believe these figures that have been published have damaged the security of the country, and do you expect to do anything about that?

THE PRESIDENT. I don't think the figures mean a lot.

Q. Edward V. Koterba, United Features Syndicate: Mr. President, somewhat in line with your reply to Mr. McGaffin, there have been some published suggestions that you become an honorary Senator after your term as President. What are your thoughts about accepting an official job as advice-giver after 1960?

THE PRESIDENT. Well, I would think that that's one of those questions that the answer would have to await the offer.

Q. Earl H. Voss, Washington Star: Mr. President, if the Russians accept your new proposal on nuclear tests, could you give us your evaluation of the effect this would have on nuclear weapons development? I have in mind particularly our theories which I understand have been proved that, according to the "big hole" theory, large nuclear explosions can be concealed.

THE PRESIDENT. Well, the very large ones, I don't think could be concealed, not practically, and certainly not periodically.

I would think this: the proposal, with all its ramifications, is going to be studied and discussed. I think we should better wait to see what are the objections and the supporting arguments that are brought forward at Geneva before we try to make conclusions of exactly what the effect will be. There could be all kinds of proposals, but all of them, as I see it, would bring some kind of inspection that so far has not been agreed to by the Soviets.

Q. Jerry O'Leary, Washington Star: Mr. President, the Senators passed a $1,800 million education bill with teachers' salaries as well as buildings. Would you like to see the House scale that down some?

THE PRESIDENT. To go further than that, I would say this: I do not believe the Federal Government ought to be in the business of paying a local official. If we're going into that, we'll have to find out every councilman and every teacher and every other person that's a public official of any kind, or public servant, and try to figure out what his right salary is. I can't imagine anything worse for the Federal Government to be into.

Q. Edward P. Morgan, American Broadcasting Company: Mr. President, speaking of public morality and basic issues as we have been today, at the congressional "payola" hearings yesterday a disc jockey likened the giving of gifts and money by record companies to these record spinners, as they're called, to the exercise of competing for a teacher's favors with an apple. And he went on to say—I'm quoting his testimony from the *New York Times:* "This seems to be the American way of life, which is a wonderful way of life. It's primarily built on romance—I'll do for you, what will you do for me?"

On the eve of Lincoln's birthday, do you have any comments on those things?   [*Laughter*]

THE PRESIDENT. I don't think that the shades of Lincoln would have possibly any great approval for what I might think and say.   But I'll tell you this, that when we get to the place where the right of people to use the airwaves, under license of Government, and then they can use this just for personal gain over and above the purposes for which they're hired, then I think there is public morality involved.   And I think this fellow, whoever he was, talking that way just hadn't thought through the implications of the, let's say, the alibi that he was setting forth.

Marvin L. Arrowsmith, Associated Press: Thank you, Mr. President.

NOTE: President Eisenhower's one hundred and eightieth news conference was held in the Executive Office Building from 10:30 to 11:01 o'clock on Thursday morning, February 11, 1960.   In attendance: 235.

35   ¶ Remarks Recorded in Observance of the 50th Anniversary of the Boy Scouts of America. *February* 12, 1960

My fellow citizens:

I have long been interested and active in the Boy Scouts of America, both as a member of its National Executive Board, and more recently as its Honorary President.   In that capacity, I have the special privilege of calling upon our Nation to join in honoring the 50th anniversary of this great youth movement.

For half a century the men who have led this virile movement have been making a great and wise investment in time and energy voluntarily given.   The dividend they have reaped has been a rich one.   Today the Scouting movement counts a membership of 5 million boys and men— and women, too.   Over 30 million boys have been members since its founding here in Washington just 50 years ago.

In thousands of churches, schools, meeting halls of all kinds, Scouts and their leaders are rededicating themselves to the Scout Oath.   These 32 words might well serve as an appropriate guide for good citizenship at any age level——

"On my honor I will do my best to do my duty to God and my country and to obey the Scout law; to help other people at all times; to keep myself physically strong, mentally awake and morally straight."

The active and abiding interest of the adult citizens of this Nation is important to the furtherance of this great movement. I ask that you join with the Boy Scouts as they celebrate this anniversary by giving them that active support—by your helping your son—or another's—to become a Scout; by volunteering as an adult leader; by making available the resources needed.

Thank you very much.

36 ¶ Special Message to the Congress on the Mutual Security Program. *February* 16, 1960

To the Congress of the United States:

A year ago in my message to the Congress on the Mutual Security Program, I described it as both essential to our security and important to our prosperity. Pointing out that our expenditures for Mutual Security are fully as important to our National Defense as expenditures for our own forces, I stated that the Mutual Security Program is not only grounded in our deepest self-interest but springs from the idealism of the American people which is the true foundation of our greatness. It rests upon five fundamental propositions:

(1) That peace is a matter of vital concern to all mankind;

(2) That to keep the peace, the free world must remain defensively strong;

(3) That the achievement of a peace which is just depends upon promoting a rate of world economic progress, particularly among the peoples of the less developed nations, which will inspire hope for fulfillment of their aspirations;

(4) That the maintenance of the defensive strength of the free world, and help to the less developed, but determined and hard working, nations to achieve a reasonable rate of economic growth are a common responsibility of the free world community;

(5) That the United States cannot shirk its responsibility to cooperate with all other free nations in this regard.

It is my firm conviction that there are only a few in the United States who would deny the validity of these propositions. The overwhelming support of the vast majority of our citizens leads us inexorably to mutual security as a fixed national policy.

The Mutual Security Program is a program essential to peace. The accomplishments of the Mutual Security Program in helping to meet the many challenges in the mid-20th Century place it among the foremost of the great programs of American history. Without them the map of the world would be vastly different today. The Mutual Security Program and its predecessors have been an indispensable contributor to the present fact that Greece, Turkey, Iran, Laos, Vietnam, Korea and Taiwan, and many nations of Western Europe, to mention only part, remain the home of free men.

While over the past year the Soviet Union has expressed an interest in measures to reduce the common peril of war, and while its recent deportment and pronouncement suggest the possible opening of a somewhat less strained period in our relationships, the menace of Communist imperialism nevertheless still remains. The military power of the Soviet Union continues to grow. Increasingly important to free world interests is the rate of growth of both military and economic power in Communist China. Evidence that this enormous power bloc remains dedicated to the extension of Communist control over all peoples everywhere is found in Tibet, the Taiwan Straits, in Laos and along the Indian border.

In the face of this ever-present Communist threat, we must, in our own interest as well as that of the other members of the free world community, continue our program of military assistance through the various mutual security arrangements we have established. Under these arrangements each nation has responsibilities, commensurate with its capabilities, to participate in the development and maintenance of defensive strength. There is also increasing ability of other free world nations to share the burden of this common defense.

Obviously, no one nation alone could bear the cost of defending all the free world. Likewise, it would be impossible for many free nations long to survive if forced to act separately and alone. The crumbling of the weaker ones would obviously and increasingly multiply the threats to those remaining free, even the very strongest.

Collective security is not only sensible—it is essential.

That just peace which has always been and which remains our primary and common goal can never be obtained through weakness. The best assurance against attack is still the possession and maintenance of free world strength to deter attack.

The nations of Europe are increasingly assuming their share of the common defense task. None of our NATO partners other than Greece, Turkey, and Iceland now requires nor receives any economic assistance. Indeed, in rising volume, these nations are now providing economic assistance to others. Our NATO allies are also meeting their military needs to an increasing degree; several major countries now require no help. Our military programs in NATO countries today are largely designed and executed as joint cost sharing arrangements whereby vital additional defense needs are met through mutual effort.

It is clear that while every possibility to achieve trustworthy agreements which would reduce the peril of war must be explored, it would be most foolish to abandon or to weaken our posture of common deterrent strength which is so essential a prerequisite to the exploration of such possibilities. The need is for steadfast, undramatic, and patient persistence in our efforts to maintain our mutual defenses while working to find solutions for the problems which divide the World and threaten the peace.

The Mutual Security Program is a program essential to world progress in freedom. In addition to its mutual defense aspects, it also is the American part of a cooperative effort on the part of free men to raise the standards of living of millions of human beings from bases which are intolerably low, bases incompatible with human dignity and freedom.

Hundreds of millions of people throughout the world have learned that it is not ordained that they must live in perpetual poverty and illness, on the ragged edge of starvation. Their political leaders press the point home. In a variety of ways this drive is moving forward by fits and starts, often uncertain of its direction. It is sometimes involved in free world struggle against Communism, sometimes not. It is clearly in the interests of the United States that we assist this movement so that these countries may take their places as free, independent, progressing and stable members of the community of nations. It is equally clear that it would be against our interests if this forward movement were stifled or hindered. The result would be to breed frustration and explosive threats to political and economic stability in areas around the world.

Equally with military security, economic development is a common necessity and a common responsibility. An investment in the develop-

ment of one part of the free world is an investment in the development
of it all. Our welfare, and the welfare of all free men, cannot be divided—we are dependent one on the other. It is for each of us, the strong
and the weak, the developed and the less developed, to join in the great
effort to bring forth for all men the opportunity for a rewarding existence in freedom and in peace. World economic expansion and increase
in trade will bring about increased prosperity for each free world nation.

New challenges, with corresponding opportunities, are now visible before us: the acceleration of the achievement of independence of peoples
in Africa; the growing restlessness in the less developed areas; and the
increasing potential for partnership and assistance to these areas as a result
of the continued growth of the now healthy economies of the industrialized Western European nations and of Japan, Canada and Australia.

Free World cooperation is becoming the watchword of this effort. In
the past year the capital of the International Bank for Reconstruction
and Development was doubled and that of the International Monetary
Fund was increased by half. In addition, a United States proposal for
an International Development Association to be affiliated with the International Bank for Reconstruction and Development has been accepted
in principle and a draft charter recently has been submitted to member
governments. I expect to transmit to the Congress recommendations
on this matter in the near future. The industrialized nations of Europe,
together with Japan and Canada, are notably stepping up their participation in cooperative efforts among themselves and with the less developed countries to promote growth. Similar approaches will be discussed
at a meeting of representatives of a number of nations, to be held in Washington in March.

In our own Western Hemisphere society of nations, we are now joined
in a great new venture, the Inter-American Development Bank. This
new institution, formed in partnership with our neighboring nations,
should prove of immense value in promoting the more rapid development
of the member nations. Our participation in this joint effort is significant of the special interest which we have in the progressive development
of our neighbors. Together with the very considerable dimensions of
private and government investment taking place in the hemisphere, and
the mutually beneficial technical cooperation we have so long enjoyed
with our neighbors, it should serve to accelerate progress.

Thus the military and economic resources which we provide through the Mutual Security Program to help create and maintain positions of strength are properly to be regarded as what they are—investments in the common defense and welfare and thus in our own security and welfare. This is a *Mutual* Security Program.

Our concepts are sound, our policies of proven value, and our will to meet our responsibilities undiminished and constant.

THE PROPOSALS FOR FISCAL YEAR 1961

The form and general structure of the Mutual Security Program for fiscal year 1961 remains essentially that which has stood the test of experience.   In the administration of the various mutual security programs, changes have been instituted in organization, programming, and management controls.   It was in part for the purpose of analyzing and making recommendations for improving the administration of the program that I appointed last year a distinguished group of citizens headed by General Draper.   Many of the recommendations that they made have already been put into effect.   We are constantly seeking additional management improvements to meet the program needs and difficult problems of operating these diverse programs on a world-wide basis.   The categories of activity are the same as those with which the Congress is familiar.   Adjustments in the nature and dimension of activity are proposed which reflect and are responsible to the changes in the world scene, in the degrees of need and of capability for self-help.   These adjustments also are consistent with an analysis of future needs and of future changes and capability for self-help.   This forward analysis was, in part, conducted in conformance with the requirement of law that plans of future grant economic assistance be developed and presented to the Congress.   The detailed plans and conclusions on future assistance will be submitted to the Congress in the near future.

MILITARY ASSISTANCE

For Military Assistance I am requesting in the pending Department of Defense budget an appropriation of $2 billion.   This is more than was requested, or than was provided for fiscal year 1960.   The request for a larger appropriation is not made in order to increase the proportionate share of United States participation in the common defense.   Nor does it reflect an intent to embark on a vast expansion of the military assistance program.

The amount requested for military assistance within the Defense budget is in my considered judgment, and in that of the Joint Chiefs of Staff, a need for our defense equally compelling and of equal importance with the needs of our own services provided for elsewhere in the Defense budget.

The amount requested is the result of careful and detailed review of the needs of our allies to enable them to maintain the level of combat effectiveness made possible by previous military assistance and to provide, mostly on a cost sharing basis, for certain essential force improvement projects. Without adequate provision for maintenance, the monies previously spent would be largely wasted. And without force improvement, without the provision of more advanced weapons, the free world forces would inevitably fall behind in their ability to counter modernized aggressor forces.

The fact, if it is a fact, of reductions in Soviet military manpower, does not alter the need for the maintenance of our collective defense. Soviet military power, as Mr. Khrushchev's own statements make clear, remains great. Our plans have never attempted to match Soviet armed manpower; they have been and are designed to deter aggression. Of special importance is the maintenance of a strong and effective deterrent posture in the NATO alliance. As indicated earlier, the improving economic position of Western Europe as a whole makes it possible for Europe to share increasingly in the cost of the common defense, and for certain major European countries to maintain their defense efforts without United States assistance. At the same time, the requirements for modernization and improvement are of such dimension that our participation in joint cost sharing projects with certain European countries over the immediate future is still essential. Provision for such contributions is included in the proposed program.

The amount requested for fiscal 1961 is consistent with the recommendations of the bipartisan committee of distinguished citizens headed by General Draper, which I appointed last year to review our policies and programs. This committee strongly urged the maintenance of a delivery program of approximately $2 billion annually. In recent years, annual deliveries have averaged about $2.2 billion. Deliveries in FY 1960, however, reflecting the reduced appropriations of recent years, will fall back to $1.8 billion or less. Unexpended balances carried over from previous years have now been reduced to a minimum and deliveries in future years will closely approximate the annual appropriation level.

In my considered judgment, an appropriation of $2 billion for FY 1961 is the minimum amount consistent with the maintenance of a firm and adequate collective defense posture. Anything less in effect precludes essential modernization and improvement of forces and limits us to a bare maintenance program.

ECONOMIC ASSISTANCE

DEFENSE SUPPORT

For twelve of the nations with whom we are joined in collective or mutual security arrangements, we have for some years been contributing not only military resources required in the common defense but economic resources in the measure needed to permit the maintenance of such defenses without incurring political or economic instability. This category of resource contribution we term *Defense Support*—economic resources to assure a defense posture. These 12 countries maintain forces of over 3,000,000 men, more than the total number in the United States Armed Forces, and each of these underdeveloped countries, except for Spain, is part of the exposed land and off-shore island belt that forms the immediate southern and eastern boundary of the Sino-Soviet empire. Requirements in this Defense Support category have decreased somewhat; for fiscal year 1961 I am requesting for these programs $724 million or $111 million less than I asked for last year. This reduced requirement reflects in some measure a gradual but perceptible improvement in the economic situations in these countries. More than half, 56 per cent, is for the three Far Eastern countries of Korea, Taiwan and Vietnam which have the common characteristics that they are divided countries facing superior Communist forces on their borders, forces which the Communists previously have demonstrated their willingness to use, thereby compelling these frontier nations to support armed forces far in excess of their unaided capacities to maintain. The amounts requested for these purposes represent the least we can contribute and retain confidence that adequate defenses will be maintained.

SPECIAL ASSISTANCE

Another category of international cooperation in the Mutual Security Program is the provision of economic resources to other nations where such resources are essential to the maintenance of their freedom and stability. This category of cooperation we term Special Assistance. I am requesting $268 million for these purposes in fiscal year 1961. Such provisions will enable us, for example, to continue aid to the young nations of Morocco, Libya and Tunisia, to strengthen the stability of Jordan and the Middle East, to combat the encroachment of Communist influence in Afghanistan, and to undergird the economies in Bolivia and Haiti. Special Assistance will also enable our continued participation in such vital programs as the world-wide anti-malaria campaign.

AID TO DEVELOPMENT

The achievement of economic progress, of growth, depends on many things. Through collective security arrangements, through defensive measures, by giving military aid and defense support, we and other nations can achieve a measure of security and stability within which the process of development is possible and can be fostered. The primary and essential prerequisite internally is the determination to progress and take the actions needed and to make the sacrifices required. No matter how great the determination, however, there will remain tremendous needs for both technical improvement and capacity and for development capital. If a pace of development is to be achieved which will meet the essential demands of these peoples, outside help is a necessity.

TECHNICAL COOPERATION

Through our long established program of Technical Cooperation and by our contributions to the United Nations activities in the technical assistance field, we make a major contribution toward the satisfaction of this thirst and need for growth in knowledge and technical capacity. The Mutual Security Program proposed for Fiscal Year 1961 continues these vital activities and provides for the enlargement and extension of our technical assistance programs in the newly emerging nations of Africa. For bilateral technical assistance I request $172.5 million; for our participation in United Nations technical assistance programs I ask $33.5 million; and to supplement our much larger bilateral program with our neighbors to the south, I ask $1.5 million for the program of technical assistance which we conduct in cooperation with them through the Organization of American States.

AFRICA

Of inescapable interest to the United States in the world today is the increasing assumption of self-government by the peoples of the great Continent of Africa, especially in the area South of the Sahara. This vast area deserves and commands the full attention and assistance of the free world if it is to develop its institutions and its economy under freedom. While the needs of Africa South of the Sahara for development capital are real and can be expected to grow, there is an imperative and immediate requirement for increased education and training. The request for appropriations for Special Assistance includes an amount of $20 million for a special program to be instituted for the improvement of education and training in Africa South of the Sahara, with particular emphasis to be given to the meeting of needs which are common to all the countries of the area. It is my belief that this initial effort must grow significantly in the immediate years ahead and complement similar efforts on the part of other Free World nations so that the capacity of the new and other developing nations in Africa to manage and direct their development can be strengthened and increased rapidly and effectively. Without such strengthening and development of education and training, the pre-conditions of vigorous economic growth cannot be established.

DEVELOPMENT LOAN FUND

In the field of development assistance, the Development Loan Fund is proving to be an increasingly effective instrument for response to those needs which cannot be satisfied from private investment, the World Bank or other like sources. It has assisted in the installation of basic facilities, such as power and transportation, necessary for growth in the less developed areas. Particularly important are the expanded activities of the Development Loan Fund in the field of private enterprise. The Development Loan Fund is opening new opportunities to build an effective partnership with American private enterprise wherein the private resources of the country can make an increased contribution to development in the less developed nations. The history of the Development Loan Fund activity over the past two years indicates that the flow of such loan capital has tended to respond to the degree of need and of capability. In other words, those areas where the determination and the will to progress are greatest and the capacity to use such resource effectively is the greatest, have been the leading recipients of loan assistance from the Development Loan Fund. I request $700 million for the Development Loan Fund for use beginning in fiscal year 1961.

SOUTH ASIA

Over the past two years a major share of Development Loan Fund loans have been made to the two great nations of South Asia, India and Pakistan, where half a billion people are deeply committed and irrevocably determined to develop and maintain institutions of their own free choice, and to raise their standards of living to levels of decency. The force and drive of this great effort is unmistakable; it warrants the full and warm support of the free world. We have joined with other nations in helping these countries; we envisage the total public and private effort to assist South Asia not only continuing but expanding. An increased amount is expected to be devoted to this great cause from the resources requested for the Development Loan Fund for Fiscal Year 1961 as these countries increase even further their own self-help efforts.

THE INDUS BASIN DEVELOPMENT

A development of major significance in South Asia is the substantial progress being made under the auspices of the World Bank to effect a solution to the complex and difficult problem of the use of the waters of the Indus River Basin as between India and Pakistan. Vital interests of both countries are involved; the solution must involve a plan whereby the waters, on which the agriculture, the food supplies, and the economies of the region depend, can be equitably developed and shared. It is anticipated that an agreement on such a development plan may be reached in the near future. Essential to its fruition is the willingness of nations outside South Asia to assist in the development plan, the cost of which cannot be borne by these nations unaided. Under World Bank auspices, plans are being developed whereunder the Bank, British Commonwealth nations, West Germany, and the United States will each contribute to the costs of the development plan and the supervision and management of the enterprise will be undertaken by the Bank. We propose to provide a measure of assistance to this activity through the Mutual Security Program in fiscal year 1961 and in subsequent years as needs arise. To assure that we can effectively participate in this multilateral undertaking, I am asking for authorization to exercise flexibility in the application of regulations normally applied to bilateral undertakings, if and when such exceptional action is required for this great project. The solution of this troublesome international issue should be of great assistance in promoting a peaceful and cooperative resolution of other divisive issues and encourage a maximum concentration on the major goals of peace and prosperity.

REPUBLIC OF CHINA

The Mutual Security Program can be expected also to be responsive to the needs of other areas and countries as their determination and capacity to employ development capital grows. We have received proposals from the Government of the Republic of China for an expanded and accelerated program of economic reform and development to which we are giving close and careful attention. The vigorous and skilled population on Taiwan, the record of growth in investment and output, the very real potential for acceleration, offer a prospect for a convincing demonstration that under free institutions a pace and degree of achievement can eventually be obtained in excess of that resulting under totalitarianism. For this purpose, we envisage the full employment of both grant and loan assistance to hasten the day of ultimate viability and self-sustaining growth.

CONTINGENCY FUND AND OTHER PROGRAMS

In addition to the major categories of cooperation which I have mentioned, Military Assistance and Defense Support, Special Assistance, Technical Cooperation and the Development Loan Fund, I am asking also for a Contingency Fund of $175 million and for $101 million to continue a variety of small but important programs.

The Contingency Fund is an essential safeguard against the unforeseen or not wholly predictable need. The record of the past several years clearly demonstrates its value as enabling prompt and effective response to the altering course of international events.

The $101 million requested for other programs will permit our continued participation in UNICEF, in refugee programs and in the foreign programs for peaceful uses of atomic energy. It also will provide for administrative costs to administer the economic and technical programs.

For the total Mutual Security Program I ask $4.175 billion. The need for these amounts has been examined and re-examined with great care in the Executive Branch. I am entirely satisfied that the needs for which funds are sought are needs which must be met and that the funds sought are the most reasonable estimates of requirements we can produce. There is no question but that the nation can afford the expenditures involved; I am certain we cannot afford to ignore the needs for which they are required.

CONCLUSION

The United States is a privileged nation. Its citizens enjoy a measure of prosperity and well-being and an extent of liberty under free institutions unequalled in the history of the world. Our ideals and our ideology place upon us a responsibility for leadership and for cooperation with other nations and other peoples which we accept willingly and with pride.

My recent travels impressed upon me even more strongly the fact that free men everywhere look to us, not with envy or malice but with hope and confidence that we will in the future as in the past be in the vanguard of those who believe in and will defend the right of the individual to enjoy the fruits of his labor in peace and in freedom. Together with our fellow men, we shall not fail to meet our responsibilities.

DWIGHT D. EISENHOWER

37   ¶ Memorandum on the 1960 Red Cross Campaign.   *February* 17, 1960

[Released February 17, 1960. Dated February 16, 1960]

Memorandum for the Heads of Executive Departments and Agencies:

During the month of March, the American National Red Cross conducts its annual campaign for members and funds. This is one of the three campaigns authorized within the Executive Departments and Agencies. However, those local Red Cross chapters that obtained financial requirements through partnership in Federated Fund Campaigns will not make their appeals at this time.

By Congressional Charter, the Red Cross is required to provide welfare services to members of the Armed Forces and their families at home and overseas. It maintains a program of Disaster Preparedness and Relief. It offers other vital services in the fields of First Aid and Water Safety, Home Nursing, and various youth training programs.

The American people have long provided the volunteers and the funds that make this great work possible. I urge employees of the Federal Government and members of the military establishments to continue their fine record in support of the Red Cross.

DWIGHT D. EISENHOWER

38 ¶ The President's News Conference of *February* 17, 1960

THE PRESIDENT. Good morning. I am ready for questions.

Q. Marvin L. Arrowsmith, Associated Press: Mr. President, just before your trip in December, you went on nationwide television and radio to discuss that tour. Do you plan to do the same thing in connection with your South American tour and, if so, is there any possibility of your talk dealing as well with national defense?

THE PRESIDENT. I'm expecting to make a television talk of 15 minutes at 6:15 on Sunday evening. I'm leaving early Monday. The talk will be in the general tone of the one that I made before I went to Asia, and I would suppose that such items as security and strength and so on would, of course, be included.

Q. Robert G. Spivack, New York Post: Mr. President, in recent weeks, spokesmen for the Navy seem to have admitted that it discriminates against American ships in trade with Israel.

In the view of—judgment of—critics it does this by discouraging the owners of such ships from bidding on transportation that involves the use of Arab ports, because the Arabs refuse to accommodate the vessel. The effect, these critics say, is to comply with the Arab boycott of Israel. Would you say that this was in line with our foreign policy?

THE PRESIDENT. Certainly not within our policy. Right after the Suez incident, you recall that the United States joined in saying that if the operation of the canal was not so conducted as to be fair to the traffic of all nations, that this should be a cause of action by the united group. I believe this matter has been up in the United Nations; I know it has— well, I believe it has, put it that way. Certainly the United States has always stood for that principle.

I didn't know about the incidents to which you refer, and I would suggest you ask the Navy Department itself about that.

Q. Warren W. Unna, Washington Post: In this morning's paper, sir, there is an account of an Air Force Reserve Training Manual which is casting reflection on the integrity of the church and possible Communist infiltration of it, as well as the people's right to know what is going on in their Government. I wondered if you'd seen this, and if you have any comment on it, sir?

THE PRESIDENT. It was brought to my attention this morning. I understand the Secretary of Air found out about it very recently, that he has recalled the thing and repudiates it as a statement of Air Force policy.

Q. Charles W. Roberts, Newsweek: Sir, in view of the increasing importance of the Vice Presidency and the ever-present possibility that he might succeed to the Presidency, do you feel that the vice presidential nominee of your party should be handpicked by the presidential nominee as he has been traditionally in the past, or that there should be an open convention, or that perhaps the vice presidential contenders compete in State primaries?

THE PRESIDENT. Well, I wouldn't know any reason for them abstaining from competition in primaries.

One thing we must remember: if we are going to have this closer relationship between President and Vice President, which during these last 7 years has been rather violative of tradition, then these two have to be people that are friends. They have to be people that have a certain mutual respect. That comes about because of the fact that the presidential nominee has some say in who the vice presidential nominee is.

In my own case I don't mind telling you, in 1952 I put down a list of men who would be completely acceptable to me. It was not a long one, but it was certainly comprehensive, and I gave—turned over—to the Convention, or the people in charge of it—I said you can take anybody here and the Convention can have its nominations and so make and give their decision.

There are a lot of factors of that kind in the thing, but I do believe that only in few instances, probably, has there been any case where the nominee, the presidential nominee, has complete authority in this matter.

Q. Felix Belair, New York Times: Can you say, sir, whether in your opinion the United States should pay more for Cuban sugar than the price made available by that government to Russia?

THE PRESIDENT. Well, you're getting into a question we've been studying a long time around this Government. The treaty with Cuba is one of long standing, concerning their preferred position in our sugar market. We must not forget that we want to be dealing in such a way that the Cuban people, who are our friends, are treated justly and there is no action taken that in the long run would be detrimental to them.

As I understand it from this latest report coming out of Mikoyan's visit, the Cubans are proposing to sell sugar at the world price and, as far as I can see, on more of a barter basis. We pay more than the world price, and we pay in completely convertible currency, so that they have complete freedom.

Now, there have been a number of traditional economic relationships that have been either repudiated or disturbed or changed by the Cubans in the last few months. I would hope that this whole thing can be worked out so that the Cuban people will not suffer, and that the relationships between those people and our people will remain firm.

Q. Laurence H. Burd, Chicago Tribune: Mr. President, in your farm message last week, you suggested to Congress that you would now be willing to accept some things such as stricter controls that you seemed to oppose before. Was that change prompted by, as some people suggested, by the hope that it might help the Republicans win more votes in the Farm Belt this year?

THE PRESIDENT. Well, it wasn't done in that particular thing, but I would hope that it would appeal to a lot of people and, therefore, get more votes; of course I do.

The point is, last year I suggested two different methods; before that, I have sent down time and again a rather detailed bill, list of recommendations, that I thought would help the situation. It has gone so long and in such a bad way that no cure can be brought about rapidly, nor in a revolutionary fashion. Everybody knows that.

So I put down what I preferred, but I said within certain guidelines I would accept anything that didn't violate just good sense and trying to get the matter better on the rails.

About controls, I said they must be realistically related to support prices. And that has a very deep meaning in that phrase.

Q. Charles H. Mohr, Time Magazine: Mr. President, Chancellor Adenauer has expressed anxiety that any new interim agreement on West Berlin might erode the Western position there, and be worse than the situation that now prevails. He also seems obviously worried about allied intentions. What are those——

THE PRESIDENT. Allied what?

Q. Mr. Mohr: Intentions.

THE PRESIDENT. All right.

Q. Mr. Mohr: And May 16 is some time off, but can you talk any about what these intentions are? And especially in view of the fact you once called that situation abnormal.

THE PRESIDENT. Of course the situation is abnormal. But this is what would be my answer to your question: the three Western Powers of Britain, France, and the United States, in a variety of ways keep in very close touch and collaboration with the Government of the Federal Republic. We certainly expect, to go to the summit, that any views to be expressed there will represent the common convictions of the four of us. Now, that is all I can say in detail in that matter.

Q. Lambert Brose, Lutheran Layman: Mr. President, you referred before to Mr. Mikoyan's visit to Cuba. And a month or two ago, J. Edgar Hoover, talking about another famous Russian's visit to our country, said that Mr. Khrushchev's visit had some effect in making Americans more receptive to communism. Since it's the FBI's job to detect subversive activities in this country, is Mr. Hoover perhaps understandably but unduly sensitive and apprehensive in this matter, or do you think his contention might have some merit?

THE PRESIDENT. I haven't talked to Mr. Hoover about the effect of Mr. Khrushchev's visit. I have stayed in very close touch with him over the years. He is a man for whom I have the greatest respect, not only for his views but for him as a character, as a public servant.

Now, this is what I do know about his views: once I proposed that we study a matter of just inviting a very great number of Russians, particularly students, into our country. He looked it over and said it would not increase the difficulties in his department whatsoever.

What he thinks about this one, I don't know; I've never talked to him about it.

Q. Robert C. Pierpoint, CBS News: Mr. President, in view of Vice President Nixon's troubles in his visit to Latin America, I wonder if the Secret Service or any of our other organizations of that nature are particularly concerned about your personal safety during your trip to Latin America and, if so, could you tell us what special measures they may have taken?

THE PRESIDENT. On the contrary; they have said no word to me about it. And, remember, the Secret Service limit their efforts to giving information and help to the local people. Our Secret Service have no authority in these sovereign countries, and certainly they couldn't widen or, by their own volition, establish a more firm security establishment.

This is what I feel about it: in any place in the world you have some elements that want to cause a little trouble and to show a little bit of discourtesy. They might here. But when you've got a purpose that is directed toward the vast bulk of the people that you meet, you just can't worry about these things; and I don't think the Secret Service worries too much about those. Certainly they haven't told me they do.

Q. Ray L. Scherer, National Broadcasting Company: Mr. President, we note that the father of your daughter-in-law is about to embark on a career in Florida politics. I'm wondering, as another old Army man who got into politics, if you had any friendly advice for Colonel Thompson. [*Laughter*]

THE PRESIDENT. Well, I'll tell you, Mr. Scherer, I learned about this this morning, because my wife seems to read the paper in which there is this kind of news, so she called me in to read it to me. Now, that's all I know about it. And I think if he wanted any advice from me, he'd ask for it.

Q. John Scali, Associated Press: Mr. President, a few days ago France exploded its first atomic bomb. Since then, there have been reports that the French may explode a second one, and possibly a hydrogen device later. Are you concerned by this French action, or do you regard it as strengthening the overall defensive capacity of the West?

THE PRESIDENT. If you go back to 1947, one of the arguments that Mr. Baruch presented in the United Nations, in the committee of which he was the chairman, and to the Russians, that one of the great risks we wanted to avoid was that of having many nations developing this kind of a device, this kind of a weapon.

I think it's only natural that first Britain and then France have done this, in the circumstances of life as we now understand them and know them. I would hope that we could get the kind of agreements among the larger nations, that have already done this thing to make sure that other nations don't want to go into the expense of going into this kind of an armament race, that would stop this whole thing in its tracks.

This is not easy. We must realize that this spirit of nationalism of which we hear so much is not felt just by the underdeveloped nations, the ones that the people want to be suddenly independent; it is felt by all of us. The matters of pride and national prestige impel people to do things, I think at times, that would not be necessary.

But I would say this, that our great hope is for agreement where we can stop the thing where it is.

Q. M. Stewart Hensley, United Press International: Mr. President, in this connection the Russians yesterday at Geneva turned down the plan you proposed last week to ban all tests except the smaller underground ones. They countered with a proposal under which they would permit Western inspection teams to make a limited number of checks of any suspicious explosion in the Soviet Union. Do you think this means we're getting closer together on this? What do you think about their counter?

THE PRESIDENT. First of all, as a practical measure, I thought the proposal we put forward was a very good one, and it would certainly establish a very good position while we went along with the technical and political conversations that might lead toward the total ban that both sides profess to want.

Now, the Soviet proposal does seem to change the criteria that they are ready to observe, which would establish the need for inspection. But when they say a limited number, obviously you've got a very long argument coming in, because now you get into the old numbers racket that everybody seems to love so much; just exactly what is adequate would be a very difficult thing.

I say this: it does seem to be a move away from a position that formerly looked completely rigid, and it certainly is going to be studied.

Q. John Herling, Editors Syndicate: Mr. President, President George Meany yesterday said that business groups and the Eisenhower administration have joined hands in raising quote, "the phantom of runaway inflation" as a means of depressing wages. Do you care to comment on this observation by Mr. Meany, and do you regard the whole problem of wages, prices, and inflation as a fit subject for the forthcoming summit conference on labor-management relations?

THE PRESIDENT. Well, I'm not going to comment on Mr. Meany's remarks, one reason being that he makes his remarks in an entire speech; I haven't read it, and therefore I don't know its context.

To accuse somebody else of bad faith, in my opinion, is just not a way to win arguments. I try to take anybody's convictions and expressed opinions and weigh them against facts and logic as I understand them. I'm not trying to say that someone is guilty of pushing a particular doctrinaire position or doing anything else merely because, in this case, the administration believes that we should have sound fiscal arrangements, avoid deficits that we pass on to our children and therefore spur inflation. Inflation, in the long run, in my mind, is a tremendous and always-present difficulty and risk that we must face every day of our life, as long as we live, in a free country.

Q. Lillian Levy, National Jewish Post and Opinion: Mr. President, in a speech recently, Senator Javits said that it would be in the best interests of this country to join with Israel in a mutual defense pact. He pointed to the fact that Soviet arms and military personnel are flowing into the middle east Arab countries, and expressed the view that a defense pact with Israel would serve as a deterrent to any Soviet-inspired or -encouraged Arab military action there. In view of present tensions in the area, would you comment on Senator Javits' recommendation?

THE PRESIDENT. As a matter of fact, I didn't read this particular recommendation. I have heard similar ones from many people.

The United States, as a matter of policy, has never been a major supplier of arms for Israel and doesn't intend to be, nor to any other country in the area.

As a matter of fact, I went to the United Nations and, making a talk about the whole Mideast situation, said if these countries could get together in any kind of a program or plan for the economic development of the whole region, the United States would be greatly interested in dealing with the whole group.

Now, with regard to the allegations of the arms the Soviet are sending in there; of course they have. We know they've been in that area, but Israel has also been getting arms from Britain and France for a long time. Frankly, I think we're sending arms to enough nations, really. I think somebody else ought to carry a little responsibility.

Q. Richard L. Wilson, Cowles Publications: Mr. President, there is common speculation in the political community that there may be a difference in approach toward public problems between you and Vice President Nixon in the sense that Nixon would be more a man of action, you more a man to wait until events developed to see whether action was required.

He has stated recently, for example, that there should be a month-by-month examination of our military posture and military—whether our security in the military field is greater now.

Would you, based on your experience with Mr. Nixon, would you be able to discuss or characterize any variations in approach that you might have, as distinguished from his approach?

THE PRESIDENT. All of us are human, and consequently, I don't believe there are any two men in the world, or two individuals, who would find exactly the same methods or use exactly the same procedures in trying to solve a difficult problem.

Mr. Nixon has been close to me now for something over 7 years. In all that time, I know of no occasion when he's been excluded from any important group that is conferring for the making of policy or deciding upon action, and never once that I know of has Mr. Nixon been at any major variance with me.

I think I've made clear many, many times the great respect I have for his capacities and for his character, and I would expect him to have some kind of different methods. He doesn't work with people the way I do; he has his own methods. I've had mine, developed probably over a good many years, and possibly I think they're pretty good.

But I certainly have no thought of trying to guide him as to what he will or should do.

One other comment to your question: far from waiting each month to weigh defense requirements and defense production, we have the National Security Council, in which nobody is barred from bringing up any fear or any matter, any preoccupation on his mind, any anxiety or conviction. Of course, we have to work by agenda, but everybody there is just as free to express his opinion as a man can be. So the matter of reviewing constantly our defensive requirements and measures we take to meet them is a thing that is a day-by-day process.

Q. Raymond P. Brandt, St. Louis Post-Dispatch: Mr. President, in your mutual security message yesterday, you said that in March there would be a meeting of representatives of many nations to study the pooling of foreign aid. Could you tell us who will be at that meeting, what will be their objective?

THE PRESIDENT. Well, I can't tell you exactly at this moment; because if the final charter for the meeting has been drawn up, why, I have not yet read it.

I have visited a number of governments and individuals, talking about this matter. I've found a very great concern about it, and everybody feeling that there is a common responsibility.

There's one thought which I very definitely put into my message that I believe we should talk about a little bit. It is this: we are not just a mere group of industrialized and, say, relatively wealthy nations seeking to give something or put something into another nation according to our ideas of what will help them. I personally believe the whole free world should be in a cooperative effort to raise the world economy. I believe that, in doing the kind of thing that we are now talking about, we will be raising our own prosperity, our own well-being, and our own security. So, I believe that the smallest country can contribute something. As long as it's got the will and the heart to do the major portion of the work itself which must be done, it can increase its output of raw materials, all of the things that it needs to get the foreign exchange which will enable it to purchase from others. In the same way, we get a better market, but we give them better markets all the time.

I really think this whole matter is not just of a group of, let's say, "have" nations meeting to see how they will distribute the load that falls on them. I think in the long run we must have a congress of all the free nations where we can work this out.

Q. Mr. Brandt: Does that mean you are going to use the U.N. more than you have done in the past?

THE PRESIDENT. To my mind, of course, the United Nations is something that should be strengthened. I think it's done good work in so many areas; but there are, of course, difficulties because of its particular composition. In any event, I want to get over the cooperation between the primary user and the giver so that we will have an expanding world economy, rather than just saying we are helping some particular group.

I really believe, again I must tell you, there is no program that the United States is pursuing now that is so much to our own interests as this one of mutual security. I realize it's the whipping boy for everybody that wants to have another dam built or something else done in his area. It's got the political appeal of just an ordinary clod out in the field— none; so therefore it makes a good whipping boy.

But if the United States as a whole can be waked up to our best interests, this program will be supported generously.

Q. Sarah McClendon, Manchester (N.H.) Union Leader: Sir, our Air Force sent a safety crew to Newfoundland to board the plane of Mikoyan to see that he got safely to Cuba. Now, I realize, as the Air Force says, that this is done for reciprocity; but why would we have to send one of our Air Force crews into another country to board the plane of a Russian official to see that he gets into a third country, so that he can go down there and malign us? [*Laughter*]

THE PRESIDENT. Ma'am, I thought I kept rather closely in touch with all the affairs of this Government. There are certainly many, and I think I do in most of the important things. This is the first time I heard it. I commend you to Secretary Sharp; ask him what he thinks, why this is done. I don't know.

Q. David Kraslow, Knight Newspapers: Mr. President, will the administration's recommendations on the Sugar Act contain a provision designed specifically to deal with unfavorable developments in Cuba?

THE PRESIDENT. No. I say what we are doing now is studying the program with everybody that is interested, both outside and inside Government, and that program is not yet ready to go to the Congress.

Q. Charles E. Shutt, Telenews: Mr. President, two of the many charges that your defense critics have made against you and your administration are that the administration has been complacent in advising the people of the danger we face in world affairs. The other is that economy may stand in the way of developing some weapon or a series of weapons we may need.

Sir, do you believe that the administration has misled the American people in any way, or that any money has been withheld from any weapon we might need?

THE PRESIDENT. If anybody—anybody—believes that I have deliberately misled the American people, I'd like to tell him to his face what I think about him. This is a charge that I think is despicable; I have never made it against anyone in the world, and I wouldn't unless he were in a bar of justice somewhere to be tried for something that was intolerable.

I would like to see somebody—people like yourselves—take the whole history of our defense organization from 1945 until this minute, and see what has been done. Frankly, this Nation unilaterally disarmed, and it wasn't until the danger or the great surprise attack in Korea came about that we started in the other direction. In almost every field of development we were behind. We had to change our policy at that time, back in 1950, and from that time on, we sought one thing—adequacy; adequacy in our power to deter and defend ourselves, and particularly to help these areas which are so exposed to the menace of Communist imperialism so that they may give a reasonable defense of themselves and their lives and their rights, while their allies could come to their assistance. This is what I believe we've been trying to do with all our might.

I get tired of saying that defense is to be made an excuse for wasting dollars. I don't believe we should pay one cent for defense more than we have to.

But I do say this: our defense is not only strong, it is awesome, and it is respected elsewhere.

Marvin L. Arrowsmith, Associated Press: Thank you, Mr. President.

NOTE: President Eisenhower's one hundred and eighty-first news conference was held in the Executive Office Building from 10:29 to 11:02 o'clock on Wednesday morning, February 17, 1960. In attendance: 205.

39 ¶ Special Message to the Congress Recommending U.S. Participation in the International Development Association. *February* 18, 1960

To the Congress of the United States:

I herewith submit to the Congress the Articles of Agreement for the establishment of the International Development Association. I recommend legislation authorizing United States membership in the Association and providing for payment of the subscription obligations prescribed in the Articles of Agreement.

The Association is designed to assist the less-developed countries of the free world by increasing the flow of development capital on flexible terms. The advisability of such an institution was proposed by Senate Resolution 264 of 1958. Following this Resolution, the National Advisory Council on International Monetary and Financial Problems undertook a study of the question. The Council's conclusions and the favorable response of representatives of other governments who were consulted during the course of the study have resulted in the Articles of Agreement which satisfy the objectives of that Resolution and which I am submitting herewith. The accompanying Special Report of the Council describes the Articles in detail.

We all know that every country needs capital for growth but that the needs are greatest where income and savings are low. The less-developed countries need to secure from abroad large amounts of capital equipment to help in their development. Some part of this they can purchase with their current savings, some part they can borrow on conventional terms, and some part is provided by private foreign investors. But in many less-developed countries, the need for capital imports exceeds the amounts they can reasonably hope to secure through normal channels. The Association is a multilateral institution designed to provide a margin of finance that will allow them to go forward with sound projects that do not fully qualify for conventional loans.

In many messages to the Congress, I have emphasized the clear interest of the United States in the economic growth of the less-developed countries. Because of this fundamental truth the people of our country are attempting in a number of ways to promote such growth. Technical and economic aid is supplied under the Mutual Security Program. In addition, many projects are assisted by loans from the Export-Import Bank, and we also participate with other free world countries in the International Bank for Reconstruction and Development which is doing so much to channel funds, mainly from private sources, to the less-developed areas. While we have joined with the other American Republics in the Inter-American Development Bank, there is no wide international institution which, like our Development Loan Fund, can help finance sound projects requiring a broad flexibility in repayment terms, including repayment in the borrower's currency.

Conceived to meet this need, the International Development Association represents a joint determination by the economically advanced countries to help accelerate progress in the less-developed countries. It is highly gratifying that so many other free world countries are now ready to join with us in this objective.

The Association is a cooperative venture, to be financed by the member governments of the International Bank. It is to have initial subscriptions totaling one billion dollars, of which the subscription of the United States would be $320.29 million and the subscriptions of the other economically-strong countries would be $442.78 million. The funds made available by these countries would be freely convertible. The developing countries would subscribe $236.93 million, of which ten per cent would be freely convertible. Members would pay their subscriptions over a five year period and would periodically re-examine the adequacy of the Association's resources.

The International Development Association thus establishes a mechanism whereby other nations can join in the task of providing capital to the less-developed areas on a flexible basis. Contribution by the less-developed countries themselves, moreover, is a desirable element of this new institution. In addition, the Association may accept supplementary resources provided by one member in the currency of another member. Thus, some part of the foreign currencies acquired by the United States primarily from its sales of surplus agricultural commodities may be made available to the Association when desirable and agreed to by the member whose currency is involved.

The Articles of Agreement give the Association considerable scope in its lending operations so that it can respond to the varied needs of its members. And because it is to be an affiliate of the International Bank, it will benefit from the long and successful lending experience of the Bank. By combining the Bank's high standards with flexible repayment terms, it can help finance sound projects that cannot be undertaken by existing sources. With a framework that safeguards existing institutions and traditional forms of finance, the Association can both supplement and facilitate private investment. It will provide an extra margin of capital that can give further momentum to growth in the developing countries on terms that will not overburden their economies and their repayment capacities.

The peoples of the world will grow in freedom, toleration and respect for human dignity as they achieve reasonable economic and social progress under a free system. The further advance of the less-developed areas is of major importance to the nations of the free world, and the Association provides an international institution through which we may all effectively cooperate toward this end. It will perform a valuable service in promoting the economic growth and cohesion of the free world. I am convinced that participation by the United States is necessary, and I urge the Congress to act promptly to authorize the United States to join with the other free nations in the establishment of the Association.

Dwight D. Eisenhower

NOTE: The Articles of Agreement of the International Development Association and the Special Report of the National Advisory Council on International Monetary and Financial Problems are printed in House Document 345 (86th Cong., 2d sess.).

40 ¶ Statement by the President on the Birth of a Son to Queen Elizabeth II and Prince Philip. *February* 19, 1960

I KNOW that all Americans join with Mrs. Eisenhower and myself in congratulating Her Majesty, Queen Elizabeth II, and Prince Philip on the birth of their new son and are delighted by the news that the Queen and her son are doing well. May the Prince have a long, happy and useful life.

41 ¶ Message to the King of Denmark on the Death of Prime Minister Hansen. *February* 20, 1960

Your Majesty:

The people of the United States join me in expressing deepest sympathy to Your Majesty and to the people of Denmark at the passing of Prime Minister Hansen.

I came to know him personally during the course of meetings both in Europe and the United States. He was a statesman whose absence will be felt keenly in the future by all of us who appreciated his humanitarian views and valued his many contributions to international understanding.

DWIGHT D. EISENHOWER

42 ¶ Radio and Television Address to the American People on the Eve of South American Trip. *February* 21, 1960

[Delivered from the President's Office at 6:15 p.m.]

My friends:

Early tomorrow I start a journey to several of our Latin American neighbors, with three major purposes in mind. These are: to learn more about our friends to the south; to assure them again that the United States seeks to cooperate with them in achieving a fuller life for everyone in this hemisphere; and to make clear our desire to work closely with them in the building of a universal peace with justice.

Our interest in our sister Republics is of long standing, and of deep affection. This, in itself, is reason sufficient for the journey. But in these days of world tension, of awakening ambitions, and of problems caused by the growing interdependence of nations, it is vital for national partners to develop better understandings and to improve common programs.

The bonds among our American Republics are not merely geographic; rather they are shared principles and convictions. Together we believe in God, in the dignity and rights of man, in peace with justice, and in the right of every people to determine its own destiny. In such beliefs our friendship is rooted.

Yet even among close comrades, friendships too often seem to be taken for granted. We must not give our neighbors of Latin America cause to believe this about us.

So I shall reaffirm to our sister Republics that we are steadfast in our purpose to work with them hand in hand in promoting the security and well-being of all peoples of this hemisphere. To do so calls for a sustained effort that is, unfortunately, sometimes impeded by misunderstandings.

One such misunderstanding, at times voiced in Latin America, is that we have been so preoccupied with the menace of Communist imperialism and resulting problems of defense, that we have tended to forget our southern neighbors. Some have implied that our attention has been so much directed to security for ourselves and to problems across the oceans to the west and east, that we neglect cooperation and progress within this hemisphere.

It is true that we have given first priority to worldwide measures for security against the possibility of military aggression. We have made many sacrifices to assure that this security is and will be maintained.

But I hope to make clear, on my journey, that our military programs at home and abroad have been designed for one purpose only—the maintenance of peace, as important to Latin America as to us.

That there is need for these programs, postwar history clearly proves. For the first 5 years following World War II, we in the United States, hopeful of a global and durable peace, pursued a policy of virtual disarmament. But, the blockade of Berlin, the military weakness of our European friends living face to face with the Communist menace, and finally the Korean war—together with arrogant threats against other peaceful nations—belatedly made it clear to us that only under an umbrella of military strength could free nations hope to make progress toward an enduring and just peace. World uneasiness rose to the point of alarm.

Since then our Nation has developed great arsenals of powerful weapons to sustain the peace. We have created a great deterrent strength—so powerful as to command and to justify the respect of knowledgeable and unbiased observers here at home and abroad.

Our many hundreds of Air Force bombers deployed the world over— each capable of unleashing a frightful destruction—constitute a force far superior to any other, in numbers, in quality, and in strategic location of bases. We have, in addition, a powerful nuclear force in our aircraft carriers and in our host of widely deployed tactical aircraft. Adding constantly to these forces are advanced types of missiles steadily augmenting the armaments of all ground and other military units.

As for longer range ballistic missiles, from a standing start only 5 years ago, we have literally leaped forward in accomplishments no less than remarkable. Our Atlas missile, already amazingly accurate, became operational last year. Missiles of intermediate range are in forward bases. The first Polaris missile submarine—an almost invulnerable weapon—will soon be at sea. New generations of long-range missiles are under urgent development.

Collectively, this is a force not unduly dependent upon any one weapon or any one service, not subject to elimination by sudden attack, buttressed by an industrial system unmatched on this earth, and unhesitatingly supported by a vigorous people determined to remain free. Strategically, that force is far better situated than any other that could be brought to bear against us.

As we have strengthened these defenses, we have helped to bolster our own and free world security by assisting in arming 42 other nations—our associates in the defense of the free world. Our part in this indispensable effort is our Mutual Security Program. It makes possible a forward strategy of defense for the greater security of all, including our neighbors to the south.

I am certain that our Latin American neighbors, as well as you here at home, understand the significance of all these facts.

We have forged a trustworthy shield of peace—an indestructible force of incalculable power, ample for today and constantly developing to meet the needs of tomorrow.   Today, in the presence of continuous threat, all of us can stand resolute and unafraid—confident in America's might as an anchor of free world security.

But we all recognize that peace and freedom cannot be forever sustained by weapons alone.   There must be a free world spirit and morale based upon the conviction that, for free men, life comprehends more than mere survival and bare security.   Peoples everywhere must have opportunity to better themselves spiritually, intellectually, economically.

We earnestly seek to help our neighbors in this hemisphere achieve the progress they rightly desire.

We have sought to strengthen the Organization of American States and other cooperative groups which promote hemispheric progress and solidarity.

We have invested heavily in Latin American enterprise.

New credits, both public and private, are being made available in greater volume than ever before.   Last year, these approximated one billion dollars.   Our outstanding loans and investments in Latin America now exceed eleven billion dollars.

With our sister Republics, we have just established the Inter-American Development Bank.   With them we hope that this new billion dollar institution will do much to accelerate economic growth.

Additionally, we have expanded technical cooperation programs throughout the Americas.

To improve our own knowledge of our neighbors' needs, we recently established a distinguished panel of private citizens under the chairmanship of the Secretary of State.[1]   This National Advisory Committee will, by continuous study of inter-American affairs, help us at home better to cooperate with our Latin American friends.   Members of this committee will accompany me on my journey tomorrow.

This will be a busy trip, for our neighbors' problems are many and vexing; the lack of development capital—wide fluctuations in the prices of their export commodities—the need for common regional markets to

---

[1] The National Advisory Committee for Inter-American Affairs. See 1959 volume, this series, Item 287 and note.

foster efficiency and to attract new credits—the need to improve health, education, housing, and transportation.

All these are certain to be subjects of discussion in each of the countries I visit.

And wherever I go, I shall state again and again the basic principles and attitudes that govern our country's relationships in this hemisphere.

For example:

Our good partner policy is a permanent guide, encompassing non-intervention, mutual respect, and juridical equality of States.

We wish, for every American nation, a rapid economic progress, with its blessings reaching all the people.

We are always eager to cooperate in fostering sound development within the limits of practical capabilities; further, we shall continue to urge every nation to join in help to the less fortunate.

We stand firmly by our pledge to help maintain the security of the Americas under the Rio Treaty of 1947.

We declare our faith in the rule of law, our determination to abide by treaty commitments, and our insistence that other nations do likewise.

We will do all we can to foster the triumph of human liberty throughout the hemisphere.

We condemn all efforts to undermine the democratic institutions of the Americas through coercion or subversion, and we abhor the use of the lie and distortion in relations among nations.

Very recently, in a faraway country that has never known freedom—one which today holds millions of humans in subjugation—impassioned language has been used to assert that the United States has held Latin America in a colonial relationship to ourselves.

That is a blatant falsehood.

In all history no nation has had a more honorable record in its dealings with other countries than has the United States.

The Philippines are independent today—by their own choice.

Alaska and Hawaii are now proud partners in our federated, democratic enterprise—by their own choice.

Puerto Rico is a Commonwealth within the United States system—by its own choice.

After the two World Wars and the Korean war, the United States did not annex a single additional acre, and it has sought no advantage of any kind at the expense of another.

And in all of Latin America, I repeat, we adhere honorably and persistently to the policy of nonintervention.

It is nonsense to charge that we hold—or that we desire to hold—any nation in colonial status.

These are but a few of the matters that friends in this hemisphere need to talk about. I look forward with the keenest pleasure to exchanging views with the Presidents of Brazil, Argentina, Chile, and Uruguay, and with their colleagues.

It is my profound hope that, upon my return, I shall be able to report to you that the historic friendship and trust among the nations of this hemisphere have been strengthened, and that our common cause—justice and peace in freedom—has been reaffirmed and given new life.

Good evening, and to my Latin American friends, *buenos tardes.*

NOTE: The President departed from Andrews Air Force Base on February 22 at 8:30 a.m. His itinerary included stopovers at Ramey Air Force Base, Puerto Rico; Brasilia, Rio de Janeiro, and São Paulo in Brazil; Buenos Aires, Mar del Plata, and San Carlos de Bariloche in Argentina; Santiago, Chile; and Montevideo, Uruguay. On his return trip he stopped again at Ramey Air Force Base, Puerto Rico. He returned on March 7, arriving at Andrews Air Force Base at 3:01 p.m.

43 ¶ Remarks Upon Arrival at International Airport, San Juan, Puerto Rico. *February* 22, 1960

Governor Muñoz Marin:

Thank you very much indeed for your words of welcome.

Naturally, I am delighted that my first stop on this 15,000-mile journey is in Puerto Rico. To all of you, I bring greetings from your fellow citizens of the 50 States of the Republic. I bring their best wishes for your continued success in making this island a unique demonstration of how free men and women work together for their mutual good. For Puerto Rico is truly unique. We are happy that Puerto Rico is a proud, free, self-governing Commonwealth, joined to the United States of America by her own choice.

This island, in the Caribbean waters between two great continental land masses, has been stirred by two mighty currents of history, enriched by two great treasuries of culture.

Out of them, Puerto Rico has fashioned its own way of life, blending the best of the old and the new.

Your program of development—rooted in self-confidence, self-help, and self-achievement—has aroused tremendous interest in every area of the free world. To other peoples now struggling to realize their aspirations and ambitions, the Commonwealth of Puerto Rico has demonstrated that courage, persistence, faith in one's fellow men and a God-given destiny can open up ways through barriers and obstacles that might appear to be insurmountable.

By what you have accomplished for yourselves, by the help you have given others toward a like accomplishment for themselves, you have made for the Commonwealth a record of achievement in which many other people around the globe have found hope and inspiration.

Although the hours I spend here must be few, I know that I shall leave tomorrow morning sharing some of the hope and some of the inspiration that are inescapable on this island.

Thank you very much.

NOTE: The President spoke at 12:07 p.m. He was met by Governor Luis Muñoz Marin and other members of the Puerto Rican Government.

44 ¶ Veto of Bill To Amend the Federal Water Pollution Control Act. *February 23, 1960*

[Released February 23, 1960. Dated February 22, 1960]

To the House of Representatives:

I am returning herewith, without my approval, H.R. 3610, an enrolled bill "To amend the Federal Water Pollution Control Act to increase grants for construction of sewage treatment works, and for other purposes."

The bill would authorize an increase in Federal grants to municipalities for assistance in the construction of sewage treatment works from $50 million to $90 million annually, and from $500 million to $900 million in the aggregate.

Because water pollution is a uniquely local blight, primary responsibility for solving the problem lies not with the Federal Government but rather must be assumed and exercised, as it has been, by State and local governments. This being so, the defects of H.R. 3610 are apparent.

By holding forth the promise of a large-scale program of long-term Federal support, it would tempt municipalities to delay essential water pollution abatement efforts while they waited for Federal funds.

The rivers and streams of our country are a priceless national asset. I, accordingly, favor wholeheartedly appropriate Federal cooperation with States and localities in cleaning up the Nation's waters and in keeping them clean. This Administration from the beginning has strongly supported a sound Federal water pollution control program. It has always insisted, however, that the principal responsibility for protecting the quality of our waters must be exercised where it naturally reposes—at the local level.

Polluted water is a threat to the health and well-being of all our citizens. Yet, pollution and its correction are so closely involved with local industrial processes and with public water supply and sewage treatment, that the problem can be successfully met only if State and local governments and industry assume the major responsibility for cleaning up the nation's rivers and streams.

The Federal Government can help, but it should stimulate State and local action rather than provide excuses for inaction—which an expanded program under H.R. 3610 would do.

The following are steps which I believe the Federal Government should take so that our rivers and streams may more rapidly be relieved of the pollution blight.

First, I am requesting the Secretary of Health, Education and Welfare to arrange for a national conference on water pollution to be held next December. This conference will help local taxpayers and business concerns to realize the obligation they have to help prevent pollution. It is unconscionable for one town or city deliberately to dump untreated or inadequately treated sewage into a stream or river without regard to the impact of such action on the lives of down-stream neighbors. Local taxpayers should be willing to assume the burdens necessary to bring such practices to a halt. Businessmen and industrialists must face up to the expenditures they must make if industrial pollutants are to be removed from the nation's waters. In short, the proposed conference will provide a forum in which all concerned can confront and better appreciate their mutual responsibility for solving this pressing problem.

Second, where the issue is of an interstate nature and the problem is beyond the powers of a single State, or where it is otherwise appropriate to assist State enforcement actions, the Federal Government should have authority to move more quickly and effectively in directing the application of control measures that will swiftly correct such intolerable pollution. In accordance with the 1961 Budget Message, recommendations will be submitted to the Congress for strengthening the enforcement provisions of the Federal Water Pollution Control Act.

Third, the Federal Government should continue to provide modest financial assistance for the administration of control programs by States and interstate water pollution control agencies. Because such programs rest upon a solid foundation of local cooperative action, they properly merit Federal encouragement and assistance. An extended life for this program is recommended in the 1961 Budget.

Fourth, the Federal Government, through research and technical assistance, can be of material help in contributing to our knowledge of water pollution—its causes, its extent, its impact and methods for its control. Increased Federal effort in this respect is also provided for in the 1961 Budget.

These measures will provide Federal authority that accords with the proper Federal, State, and local roles in water pollution abatement. I urge their early consideration by the Congress.

Dwight D. Eisenhower

NOTE: The veto message was released in Washington.

45 ¶ Remarks at the Civic Reception for President Eisenhower in Brasilia. *February 23, 1960*

Mr. President, Dr. Pinheiro, citizens of Brasilia:

I am most grateful for the cordial welcome you have extended to me. I am glad that my return to this hospitable land has taken place in this magnificent new city, a living testimony to your own tireless efforts, Mr. President, and a symbol of Brazilian progress. It is an inspiration to get this new glimpse of the vision and energy which characterize modern Brazil and its leadership.

Brasilia has captured the imagination of my fellow countrymen who have visited here and, who, on their return home, have been lavish in their praise of the wonders they have seen.

For several reasons, Brasilia fascinates citizens of the United States. In the first place, your decision to carve a beautiful city out of the wilderness reminds us of our own decision many years ago to move the capital of our fledgling nation from Philadelphia to the District of Columbia.

In the second place, this pioneering venture recalls to our minds the rolling advance of our own frontier—the winning of the American West— a process which was barely accomplished when I was a youngster. Indeed, having now witnessed the speed with which Brasilia is being completed, I understand why Brazil itself is sometimes described as a "country in a hurry." Brasilia is an epic worthy of this nation's vast possibilities and aspirations.

And thirdly, one senses here a "boom" spirit not unlike that which pervaded frontier western communities in the United States such as my boyhood town of Abilene, Kansas.

It has been said, somewhat facetiously, that Brazil and the United States—both influenced by the stern demands of the frontier—ought to get along well together because each has so many of the other's faults. At least we are both willing to confess that we do have faults. And of course we get along well because we have many of the same virtues— we are, indeed, much alike. Our vast expanses of land have many similarities in physiography and resources. Our constitutional systems and forms of government are similar. The people of both our countries have various national origins, gaining strength from diversity. Both countries are forever committed to democracy, human dignity, and freedom with justice.

Our common heritage will be emphasized for us when you inaugurate your new capital next April 21—Tiradentes Day. It was in 1787, when Thomas Jefferson, then our Minister in France, gave sympathetic counsel to José Joaquim da Maia, emissary of Tiradentes and his little band of Inconfidentes. Those Brazilian patriots—to recall the observation of Joaquim Nabuco—had their eyes fixed on the new democracy to the north at a time when, here, even to think of independence was a crime. Your freedom and ours were won by men of dauntless courage and passionate vision, and it is these qualities in our peoples today that will carry us forward to the brighter future so eloquently dramatized by this new city of the frontier.

To you, Dr. Pinheiro, and your thousands of associates, has been entrusted the enormous task of transplanting the inspired dream of planners into reality. I congratulate you for the marvels you are fashioning.

And now to the workers assembled here and through them to all Brazilian labor, I bring special greetings. May your toil be fruitful in advancing Brazil's development and well-being. May your hands be firmly clasped with those of the workers of the United States and the entire free world in the building of a richer life, in freedom, for yourselves, your children, and all generations to follow.

I thank all of you here for the honor you today have done me and my country. This has been a moving and memorable experience.

I thank you for the privilege of being here.

NOTE: The President spoke at the Central Platform. Earlier, upon his arrival about 1:45 p.m. at the Brasilia Airport, the President was met by President Juscelino Kubitschek de Oliveira, members of the Brazilian Cabinet, and U.S. Ambassador John M. Cabot.

Dr. Israel Pinheiro, to whom the President referred, was in charge of the construction of Brasilia.

46   ¶ Joint Statement of the President and President Kubitschek of Brazil.
February 23, 1960

THE PRESIDENTS of the United States of Brazil and of the United States of America, Juscelino Kubitschek de Oliveira and Dwight D. Eisenhower, meeting together in the new city of Brasilia, soon to be the capital of Brazil, reaffirm the joint determination of the two nations to defend the following principles:

1. The democratic freedoms and the fundamental rights of man, wherein are included the fight against racial discrimination and the repudiation of any attempt against religious freedom and of any limitation on the expression of thought. These are inalienable conquests of civilization which all free men have the duty to protect, bearing in mind the sacrifices of the soldiers of both countries in the last war, and the need to prevent repetition of the causes which led to the loss of so many young and precious lives.

2. The belief that the aspiration of the peoples of the Americas to an ever-improving way of life, moral and material, presents one of the great challenges and opportunities of our time. This challenge should be met by joining together, ever more closely and harmoniously, the

efforts of all countries within the inter-American community in order that, through coordinated action, there may be an intensification of measures capable of combating underdevelopment in the vast area of the American continents.

3. The full implementation of the principles of political and economic solidarity contained in the Charter of the Organization of American States and in the Mutual Assistance Treaty of Rio de Janeiro.

4. The recognition that economic advancement cannot be disassociated from preservation of peace and democratic rights, and that the effort of each nation must be complemented by hemisphere action helping all Americans to achieve the improved living standards which will fortify belief in democracy, freedom and self-determination of peoples. To this end, the Presidents reaffirm their solidarity with the principles approved by all the nations of America within the scope of Operation Pan America and assure their wholehearted support to the Organization of American States and to those other entities which already are formulating measures to help achieve these ends. This will pave the way to the realization of the inter-American ideals, economic as well as political.

Acknowledging that joint efforts of the American nations have already achieved much, but firm in the conviction that action still more fruitful should be taken, the two Presidents are confident that the hemispheric crusade for economic development will lead toward greater prosperity and harmony for all.

NOTE: This statement, released at Brasilia, was read by Secretary of State Christian A. Herter and Foreign Minister Horacio Lafer at the site of the monument commemorating President Eisenhower's visit to Brasilia.

47 ¶ Message to the Congress Transmitting Second Annual Report on U.S. Aeronautics and Space Activities. *February 24, 1960*

[Released February 24, 1960. Dated February 22, 1960]

To the Congress of the United States:

In accordance with Section 206(b) of the National Aeronautics and Space Act of 1958, I am transmitting herewith the second annual report on the Nation's activities in the fields of aeronautics and space.

During 1959, the Nation's space effort moved forward with purpose and its accomplishments were many, as this report recounts.   In the short period of a single year, a program of great complexity and scope was aligned so that the scientists of many organizations in and out of Government could pool and coordinate their knowledge and skills.   Much information of far-reaching significance was acquired on the frontiers of science and technology; substantial gains were made, ranging from advances in aircraft and space vehicle design to greatly improved understanding of the environment in which our planet exists and by which its natural forces and life are conditioned.

The year was also one of transition.   The national space program grew in breadth and depth—benefiting greatly from the tremendous efforts of the American scientists, engineers, and technicians who, in the short space of the past five years, have performed miraculously in developing United States rocket technology.

This Report details the steps taken during 1959 to establish a firm foundation for a dynamic program of space exploration, and it summarizes the contributions of Federal agencies toward the paramount goal: the conquest of space for the benefit of all mankind.

DWIGHT D. EISENHOWER

NOTE: The message and report, which were released in Washington, are printed   in House Document 349 (86th Cong., 2d sess.).

48   ¶ Remarks Upon Arrival at the Naval Ministry in Rio de Janeiro.   *February 24, 1960*

President Kubitschek, Your Excellencies, and citizens of Rio de Janeiro:

It is a privilege and a particular pleasure to meet again your distinguished President and a privilege to return to this great country with which over the years we have enjoyed fruitful relations in a tradition of friendship.

When I visited Brazil in 1946, I came as a former commander of allied military forces to pay personal tribute to the gallant Brazilian people for their invaluable contributions to our common victory in World War II.

Now, in response to your President's gracious invitation and to my long-held desire to reciprocate the courtesy which he did us in visiting the United States as President-elect, I come here as the representative of 180 million citizens of the United States. They share with you this fervent wish: that war and all forms of coercion be forever banished from the earth; that leaders of all nations hearken to the prayers of their peoples for peace—for a peace founded on mutual respect, understanding, and collaboration—a peace in which the race of armaments will give way to a constructive, cooperative attack against disease, ignorance, and poverty—a peace which makes neighborliness such as that enjoyed by our two countries a reality throughout the world.

It is impossible to enter Rio de Janeiro without feeling the inspiring impact of this city's scenic grandeur. But Rio has more than natural beauty.

For decades this city has become a symbol of Brazil's cultural contributions to the world.

In the halls of Rio, great principles have been proclaimed, righteous determinations formed.

Here, in 1942, the Foreign Ministers of the American Republics voiced this hemisphere's determination to defend itself against a Fascist aggression. Here representatives of the Americas met in 1947 to proclaim in solemn treaty that an attack on one American Republic would be an attack on all. That treaty has enabled the nations of this hemisphere to live in peace, free of the fear that any one of them, however weak or small, would have its independence challenged by any other, however strong or large.

Brazil and the United States have always lived together in peace and friendship. Constant cooperation has been mutually beneficial. I hope that my brief visit here will emphasize the desire of my Government and all the people of my country to strengthen bonds of friendship with you. We seek only greater understanding of one another, a mutual conviction that all problems existing between us can be resolved to the benefit of both nations, and a lasting partnership in efforts to build a stronger, freer hemisphere—a stronger, freer world.

Mr. President, I am grateful for the generosity of your welcome and remarks, and to all of you, thank you very much.

NOTE: The President spoke at 11:22 a.m.

49 ¶ Address Before a Joint Session of the Congress of Brazil. *February 24, 1960*

Mr. President, Members of the Congress, fellow citizens of the New World, ladies and gentlemen:

Mr. President, I think you must understand how deeply touched I am by the scene which here before me spreads. I see here represented in the members of this body the spirit, the intellect, and the character of the great Brazilian nation, a nation which is surging forward to heights as yet unimagined, even by ourselves.

Beyond this, I am grateful for the generous statements directed to my country and to me by those who have preceded me today. I am proud that I have been invited the second time by the representative body of Brazil to meet with them for a brief period, and I am more proud of the fact that your spokesmen have greeted me and my country as a country and as an individual that with them work to support and forward the priceless values that make men free and fight those influences which tend or would want to regiment or enslave them.

It is, then, with a sense of singular honor that I come before you, the elected representatives of the people of the United States of Brazil.

But the warm glow of personal pleasure is tempered by the realization that we share awesome responsibilities which this profoundly moving occasion prompts me to discuss with you.

If the burdens of my office permitted, I would travel to the largest cities and the remotest villages of all the Americas, to speak of these responsibilities and of how, together, we may possibly bear them successfully. Since I cannot do this, I trust that what I say here will be accepted by the governments and peoples of all the Western Hemisphere nations as an expression of hope from the millions of my country to the millions who constitute Latin America.

It is fitting, I think, that I should do this here, at the beginning of my present journey, for you of Brazil and we of the United States of America have always worked together for the spiritual unity and material advancement of the hemisphere. If it were physically possible for us to do so, I am sure we would speak with a single voice to all our neighbors of this vast continent.

Not long ago, you and we shared anxieties, suffering, and tragedy in an agony of worldwide war. Many of your families, as of ours, paid a heavy price in order that the rule of law and moral suasion might replace the rule of naked force. To pay homage to the gallant Brazilian soldiers, airmen, and sailors who fought side by side with others of the free world I came here 14 years ago. I know that your brave men, who knew the horrors of war, pray with me now, that their children and their children's children will find a better way—so that in the future the deep, abiding desires of humanity will prevail over the arrogance and ambitions of misguided or willful leaders; that consultations will replace coercion; that mutual understanding will eliminate threat and crude accusation; that the earth, casting aside the sterile use of resources for arms, will yield its rich bounty to all who are willing to work in freedom.

I am confident that I shall not be thought presumptuous in suggesting that we—our two nations—could speak with a single voice. For our basic ideas have a common inspiration: man, in his sonship under God, is endowed with dignity, entitled to equality in all human and political relations, and destined, through the employment of consecrated intelligence, to shape a world harmonious with basic moral law. Adhering to these beliefs, we have established similar governmental systems; we have constantly maintained friendly relations unmarred by a single explosive incident; and we have worked together to establish and strengthen the Organization of American States, the United Nations, and other cooperative international organizations.

We of the United States admire Brazil for its enviable record of constructive leadership in hemisphere and world affairs, and we salute your statesmen who have played decisive parts in critical international situations, even some involving the United States and one or more of our sister Republics.

Speaking with one voice, then—your country and mine—we would say, I know, that the first responsibility of leadership in any nation is to work for the welfare of its own people, its own land. We would emphasize that heavy reliance must be placed upon the creative talents of the people themselves, with government a helpful partner. While we recognize that success or failure in the whole domestic enterprise is largely a nation's own responsibility, we would look for any needed outside temporary assistance to speed our development. Certainly my country did this from its establishment as a free nation until late in the nineteenth century. And in receiving and using these honors, our sovereignty was not violated—nor was our self-reliance diminished.

You now are experiencing, primarily due to your own persistent labors, a remarkable industrial and economic growth. Yesterday, on what was once a remote plateau, I saw your growth revealed in the stone and steel of an emerging and magnificent new capital—a symbol of the vision and sturdy confidence which characterize modern Brazil. This surging growth is evident everywhere in this seaport city of Rio, and tomorrow I shall see what I am told is the most rapidly growing city in the world— São Paulo.

We of the United States are proud that our public and private agencies have responded to the best of their ability to your requests for temporary assistance. United States public and private investments and loans in Brazil now total about two and a half billion dollars. To this could be added the loans of international financial agencies which obtain the major part of their funds from the United States.

These are mighty, but only supplemental aids. The time will come when Brazil, through its own efforts, will experience both the benefits and the complexities of being a creditor nation, and others will be seeking your help—a seeking which I know will not be unrewarded.

Our second responsibility is to all our good neighbors of this hemisphere.

We, Brazil and the United States, hold the common, burning conviction that relations among these sister nations must be characterized by mutual respect, juridical equality, independence, respect for each human being, regardless of his race, creed, or color, and a willingness to help one another promote the well-being of all our peoples.

Neither of us covets one acre of land from another. We do not wish to prosper at another's expense. We do not wish to impose our particular form of democracy upon another. Rather, fervently and persistently, while avoiding all forms of intervention, we proclaim our hope that the nations of the hemisphere will each, according to its own genius and aspirations, develop and sustain free government. We pray that all of us will reject cruel tyranny, for tyranny is, in simple essence, the outright denial of the teachings of Christ. May each of us in every appropriate way, and especially by example, work for the strengthening of democratic institutions.

You of Brazil have constantly shown your desire for the Americas to be a community of free democratic nations, united by the common ideal of hemispheric cooperation and solidarity. You, like we, insist upon freedom of choice for every country. And you, like we, aspire to the day when poverty, hunger, illiteracy, and discrimination in all forms will become relics of the past.

In proposing Operation Pan America, Brazil has taken an important initiative for the democratic development of the entire hemisphere. The high purpose of this imaginative proposal of your distinguished President—to attack the problem of underdevelopment by cooperative effort— is one which my government endorses. It is for this reason that we have joined with Brazil in requesting an early meeting of the Committee of Nine; this Committee should accelerate the formulation of the specific projects needed to translate this plan into a working reality.

Permit me here to renew a pledge, which I have made repeatedly: the United States itself stands ready, and will continue to urge other free nations to be ready to join in a gigantic effort: to devote substantial portions of the savings made possible by disarmament to vast constructive programs of peaceful development. We embrace this idea despite the fact that we are now carrying such heavy burdens throughout the world that our own internal and external financial situation requires great caution in management—and incidentally, this aid includes significant volumes of public and private capital and technical assistance to Latin America.

Pending that achievement, I assure you that my government, while honoring its commitments outside this hemisphere is in no mood to allow its special responsibilities among the American States to go by default. Indeed, these commitments and responsibilities are part and parcel of the same problem—preserving the strength and unity of the free world.

This brings me to the third responsibility which we may speak of in common voice—that which involves the larger world.

This is truly a time of fateful decision. Nations now possess power so terrible that mutual annihilation would be the only result of general physical conflict. War is now utterly preposterous. In nearly every generation the fields of earth have been stained with blood. Now, war would not yield blood—only a great emptiness for the combatants, and the threat of death from the skies for all who inhabit the earth. To strive ceaselessly, honestly, and effectively for peace is today the imperative responsibility of every statesman—of yours, of ours, of all countries.

At the same moment of this great crisis, we face anew decisions involving tyranny or freedom, totalitarianism or democracy. Our shared view on this issue is so eloquent and so clear that any words of mine would not be enlightening.

And, perhaps inseparable from the decision of freedom or slavery, we face the philosophic issue which today brings fear, misgiving, and mistrust to mankind. In contrast to our adherence to a philosophy of common sonship, of human dignity, and of moral law, millions now live in an environment permeated with a philosophy which denies the existence of God. That doctrine insists that any means justifies the end sought by the rulers of the state, calls Christianity the "sigh of the oppressed," and, in short, seeks to return mankind to the age-old fatalistic concept of the omnipotent state and omnipotent fate.

You of Brazil and we of my country do not say that this philosophy shall not be held; that peoples may not return to that unenlightened system of tyranny, if they so wish. We would feel a great sorrow for them, but we would respect their right to choose such a system. Here is the key to our policy—the right to choose. Human beings everywhere, simply as an inalienable right of birth, should have freedom to choose their guiding philosophy, their form of government, their methods of progress.

But we—you of Brazil and we of the United States—would consider it intervention in the internal affairs of an American State if any power, whether by invasion, coercion, or subversion, succeeded in denying freedom of choice to the people of any of our sister Republics.

To work throughout the world for a guaranteed peace, free of all outside interference, and for rising levels of human well-being, in justice and in freedom—this is the greatest of the responsibilities which you of Brazil and we of the United States now share.

It is to confer with your distinguished President and his colleagues about these bilateral but hemispheric and global problems that I am making my brief trip to Brazil and your neighbors in this great Southland.

May God cast his grace upon us and guide us in this noble purpose.

Thank you very much.

NOTE: The President spoke at 4:38 p.m. at the Tiradentes Palace in Rio de Janeiro. His opening words "Mr. President" referred to Vice President João Goulart.

Operation Pan America was proposed by Brazil in a memorandum dated August 9, 1958, following the exchange of messages between Presidents Eisenhower and Kubitschek in May and June of that year (see 1958 volume, this series, Item 133). The memorandum of August 9, 1958, is published in Operación Panamericana, Compilación de Documentos II (Presidencia de la República, Servicio de Documentación, Rio de Janeiro, 1958).

The Committee of Nine, to which the President referred, is a subcommittee of the Special Committee of the Council of the Organization of American States to Study the Formulation of New Measures for Economic Cooperation (Committee of 21).

50 ¶ Remarks to the Members of the Supreme Court of Brazil. *February* 24, 1960

Mr. Chief Justice, Justices of the Supreme Court of the United States of Brazil, and my Brazilian friends:

I have been privileged to call upon the President of the Brazilian Republic. I have just completed a meeting with the legislative body of this great country. Now it is my great privilege and honor to pay a call upon the third branch—equal branch of equal status in the Brazilian Government.

To have been invited once before this august body was in itself a great privilege and an honor. To have been invited back again, Mr. Chief Justice, is an honor that I consider almost unique.

It is my simple concept that the Supreme Court in a Federal Republic exists to make certain that the rule of law will flourish and will not be weakened by any processes that are not approved by the constitution and as interpreted by that Supreme Court.

In my country, the Supreme Court has attained a position in the minds of the average citizen of grandeur, almost of veneration.

I have been examining the history of your Supreme Court. I see the parallels, between its formation and its history, with our own. I know from the picture you have in the window that you give the same respect to the memory of John Marshall that we do. I have also heard of a great jurist of yours named Luís Barbosa who in your country and in his term took the same occasion as did John Marshall to assert the right, the absolute unchallenged right of the Supreme Court to place interpretation upon any law, and to determine whether or not it was in consonance with the Constitution.

Clothed with this kind of responsibility and with this kind of authority, the Supreme Court stands as a true guardian of justice for the individual. And I submit that the reason for republican or democratic government is to protect the individual in his rights which we—you and ourselves—

believe are his, because of the fact of his creation, because he has been created in the image of his God. I can see, therefore, that the decisions of such a body as this, its opinions, are more than mere decisions for application in a particular case and to make certain that the rights of a particular citizen have been protected, or that the law has not been allowed to go astray in its application in some other branch of the government. It is more important—the court is more important than merely to do this. As I see it, the court is also a teacher. Because the real strength of democracy is in the hearts and minds and the understandings of people, not merely the august members of this great body.

In my country, and I think it is possibly true in yours, a man who has been honored by being given a chair in this body is thereby removed from partisan politics. Partisan politicians do much to inform our public. Sometimes they merely try to influence. As I see it, the man now in this kind of position, with this authority, with this opportunity to study without bias, cannot merely influence, he can inform. And I say that in all forms of free government the only final force, the only final authority, is public opinion. And if it be informed public opinion, then in truth democracy is truly working. If the rule of law is to be substituted for the rule of the sword, if persuasion is to take the place of fighting on the battlefield, then the kind of public opinion that I speak of must be strong in all free nations.

And so I salute this body for the opportunity that belongs to each of you, because as a group we know that, just like in my own country, this institution is venerated. Your words carry weight. And your words will be heeded. Consequently, when you say we must substitute the rule of law for force, all will heed, all will help—which is all important.

So, Mr. Chief Justice, and Justices of the Supreme Court of Brazil, I come here to pay my respects, but those words are merely formalities by themselves. My visit has a far deeper meaning to me than mere formality. I do want to pay my respects to this court and to its functions, and what I think it can and will do in helping Brazil toward the destiny that is certain to belong to that nation as long as it lives in the institutions of freedom and pushes forward on the course that it is now pursuing.

Thank you very much indeed.

NOTE: The President spoke in the Federal Room of the Supreme Court building at Rio de Janeiro. His opening words "Mr. Chief Justice" referred to Chief Justice Luiz Galloti.

51   ¶ Toast by the President at a Dinner Given in His Honor by President Kubitschek in Rio de Janeiro. *February 24, 1960*

Mr. President, Madame Kubitschek, distinguished guests, and friends:

First, Mr. President, may I thank you sincerely for the generosity of your remarks about my country and about me, and for your generous hospitality toward me and to my party. I deeply regret that my wife could not be here to participate in this most gracious ceremony in which you and your lovely wife are the host and hostess. I think the reasons that she could not come are known, but I assure you her regret is very deep.

Mr. President, this afternoon, in meeting with the assembled Congress of the United States of Brazil, I tried to outline the convictions that I hold as to the common role that your country and mine have in the attempt to better the standards of living for all peoples, in order that democracy and the freedom, of which you so eloquently speak, can be thereby strengthened.

On this trip with me, as you know, are Secretary Herter, Assistant Secretary Rubottom, and the citizen members of the new United States Advisory Committee on Inter-American Affairs. The fact that these gentlemen are accompanying me symbolizes the high importance we of my country attach to good relations with all the nations of Latin America. I know that what we are all learning here, and shall observe throughout this trip, will be helpful to us as we seek constantly to work for hemispheric solidarity.

I should say, Mr. President, that the strong feelings I felt about the need for cooperation, which were the feelings that led me to make this trip, have been emphasized and greatly strengthened by the meetings I have held with you and with your associates during the past hours that I have been able to spend in your great nation.

The friendly relations of our two countries—now stronger and more meaningful than ever before—have an inspiring history. The beautiful home of the Brazilian Foreign Ministry reminds one of thrilling diplomatic traditions.

Here I should like to say if I mispronounce names, it's because of my ignorance and not because of any intent. Itamaraty is symbolic of the principles enunciated by Baron do Rio Branco, a great hero to us, as to you.   Here worked such dedicated statesmen as Joaquim Nabuco and Afranio de Malo France, who stood resolutely for the abiding friendship of our two countries.   And here labored Oswaldo Aranha, a firm friend, whose recent passing is deeply mourned in the United States.

I raise my glass in tribute to all who have in these halls worked so patiently and gloriously for the principles of freedom, independence, and abiding cooperation—and to you, President Kubitschek, both for your deeds of friendship and for your staunch support of inter-American solidarity.

Ladies and gentlemen: the President!

NOTE: The President proposed the toast at a dinner at the Itamaraty, the Foreign Ministry in Rio de Janeiro.

52   ¶ Remarks Upon Arrival at Congonhas Airport, São Paulo, Brazil.   *February* 25, 1960

Mr. President, Governor Carvalho Pinto, Mayor de Barros, citizens of São Paulo:

Yesterday I referred to a rumor I have often heard—that São Paulo is the fastest growing city in the world—center of Brazilian commerce and industry.   Certainly it is a sincere personal pleasure to have this opportunity today to witness firsthand the mighty achievements of this fabulous community.

In addition to seeing evidence of Brazil's remarkable economic and industrial growth, I have another very special and, to me, deeply moving, mission to perform in your city.   Later today, I shall have the honor of paying homage to those brave soldiers of Brazil who were my comrades-in-arms during World War II.

My nation—and all free nations—have reason to remember with gratitude Brazil's partnership in two World Wars.

You made your bases available for our common cause—bases which were truly springboards to victory.   On land, sea, and air, Brazilian cooperation was of inestimable value in defeating our enemies and preserving a way of life we cherish.   Gallant Brazilian blood, shed with ours, must ever remind us of our solemn, common covenant to preserve the peace, with justice and freedom for all.

I thank all of you for the warmth and cordiality of your welcome, Governor and Mr. Mayor.   It is a real privilege to be here.

NOTE: The President spoke at 9:45 a.m. He was met by Governor Carlos Alberto Carvalho Pinto, Mayor Adhemar de Barros, Dr. Potado Rus de Mello Juqueira, President of the Legislative Assembly, Dsembargador Joao Marcelino Gonzaga, President of the Court of Justice, and other officials.

53   ¶ Address by the President at a Luncheon Given in His Honor in São Paulo.
February 25, 1960

Mr. President, Governor Carvalho Pinto, and other Governors here present, ladies and gentlemen:

I am deeply grateful for the generous welcome my associates and I have received in São Paulo.   And I must personally express to you my deep gratitude for the warmth of the welcome with which you have greeted me in this hall.

This is my first visit to your great city, the industrial heart of Brazil. Here in your factories and workshops, much of the economic future of Brazil is being forged.   It is indeed a privilege to meet personally so many leaders of São Paulo's progressive government, industry, and agriculture.

I do not wonder, as I look around me and see what Paulista energy and intiative have achieved, that you take pride in your city and state, and especially in the fact that in this area great opportunities exist for men of energy, talent, and initiative to carve for themselves important places in the life of the nation.   This country, like my own, provides opportunities to all, however humble their origins and whatever the circumstances of their birth.

Opportunity, without discrimination—this is one vital aspect of democracy both in Brazil and the United States.   The humblest may become the highest—through his own efforts.

Our societies are designed to permit everyone to pursue family welfare and happiness in liberty, and also to promote the well-being of all, not just a few, of the people.

We believe fervently that no one should be denied the chance for or the fruits of self-betterment because of his race, his religion, sex, class, or political beliefs. In short, in both our countries we make the concept of the dignity of the individual a living reality, knowing that, given a chance, each person is capable of running his affairs with wisdom, dedication, and due respect for the rights of others.

At this point in history, our countries may differ in economic development, but this difference can and will disappear, for Brazil is on the march. It is today a universal Brazilian aspiration to develop the country's resources, to extend the blessings of education to all, to realize the nation's immense potentialities. Let me say to you most earnestly that we pray for your success. And we rejoice in your progress not only because you and we are friends but also because we know that the progress of Brazil and of all the nations which aspire to develop rapidly will make a happier and more peaceful world for everyone.

Three hundred years ago there was little but forbidding wilderness in the United States of America. Great natural resources existed, as they exist in Brazil. But there were no houses, transportation facilities, utilities, factories, institutions of learning and culture. A hundred years ago half our people were engaged in agriculture; industry was beginning to expand. Even 60 years ago there was not a single industrial research laboratory in the United States. Today we have a mature, highly diversified economy. This has been obtained by the hard work and frugal management of the American people. And of course we are proud of what we have accomplished. But we take even greater satisfaction in the means we have employed. All our progress has been protective of personal freedom, political freedom, economic freedom—in my judgment, inseparable elements of true liberty. Other nations have amassed wealth. However, in no nation, ancient or modern, totalitarian or free, have the rights of the individual been more zealously safeguarded.

Sheer material wealth can of course be accumulated, and scientific miracles can be achieved, by authoritarian methods. But let us not be misled by the boasts that fill the air. The production of goods—either capital or consumer goods—is not an end in itself, nor is it a sound criterion for judging economic and governmental systems. Production is only one element in the human enterprise on this earth. You and I believe that each of us is an inviolable spiritual entity, capable of reaching the heights of creative thought. Each is endowed with the right to build social and cultural institutions compatible with our finest instincts, and more deeply devoted to the protection of human dignity and to love of

God than to the mere acquisition of material things. We see then that production, to be praiseworthy, must serve these nobler ends. Faced with no other choice, you and we in the United States would choose poverty in freedom, rather than prosperity in slavery.

But of course we need make no such choice, for freedom in the long run yields also the most productive economic system ever devised by man. The reason for this is simple. Every human being is capable of greatness. Given opportunity and responsibility, he will reach the heights. Controlled man may become an efficient automaton, but with the limitations and the joylessness of men in lock-step parade.

The proponents of Marxism-Leninism seek to belittle the American system. They speak of the "exploited masses." Certainly anyone who has studied history knows that capitalism, in its early stages, was often exploitative. But it is ridiculous to pretend that conditions of the 18th and early 19th centuries exist today in the economic life of the United States.

Our socially-conscious private-enterprise system benefits all the people, owners and workers alike. It has resulted in high productivity, high consumption, high wages, and reasonable returns on investment. Balanced progress is our watchword.

São Paulo is, I think it can fairly be said, the outstanding example of Brazilian private initiative and of Brazilian balance in development. Here is a concentration of factories which produce much of what all Brazil consumes. You are now helping to provide the means by which the remainder of Brazil will similarly progress. And the rewards of your production are indeed exciting.

In freedom the Brazilian worker is happily demonstrating the joys of life under a democratic system. He knows that you do not consider the accumulation of wealth to be the privilege of a few—rather that the true aim of production is to contribute to the greater well-being of the many.

I wish that all the world could see what I have seen today in this city—a demonstration that a dynamic economy, based on private enterprise and free labor, redounds to the benefit of the worker, the consumer, the public at large and the state which embodies their sovereign will.

I am sure that your workers, as ours in the United States, have attained positions of influence, honor, and prestige. Surely the old concept of "the exploited masses" deserves to be discarded, along with the idea of state omnipotence and the divine right of kings.

I take real pleasure in noting the modest but significant contributions which United States capital has made to the prosperity of São Paulo and Brazil. It cannot be coincidence that this area, in which foreign capital is most heavily concentrated, is also the most prosperous in Brazil.

We too benefited much from foreign capital in the period of our development. Late in the 19th century, foreign investments in the United States were as large as those in Brazil today. In fact, I think if we should take the price of today's dollars, the investments that then were made in our country were many times the amount that I am just speaking of. But at that time the revenue of our national government was only one-third as great as yours is now.

The contributions of United States private enterprise to Brazilian development are matched in other fields. We have sought to express our friendship and our interest in your development through loans of the Export-Import Bank and other public lending institutions, through our Point IV work, the re-loaned funds derived from the sale of agricultural surpluses, our support of the international coffee pact, grants by our private foundations, and through the backing we have given President Kubitschek's imaginative Operation Pan America proposal.

Within our financial and economic capacity, we shall continue to support Brazilian development. In view of the modest part we have had in your growth, it is, then, the more heartening to see the mighty contributions which São Paulo is making to the majestic future of our traditional friend and ally, the United States of Brazil.

And in closing, I should like to repeat the sense of the quotation that the Governor took from Thomas Jefferson, the United States wants to march forward as a true partner and brother to Brazil, as we seek earnestly toward that brightest goal of all mankind: peace with justice.

I thank you. Thank you again.

NOTE: The President spoke at 2:30 p.m. at the Fasano Restaurant. He was joined by President Kubitschek at the luncheon, which was given by the Industrial Association, the Commercial Association, and the Federation of Rural Associations of São Paulo. Antonio de Visale, President of the São Paulo Federation of Industries, introduced President Eisenhower.

54   ¶ Remarks at the Airport in São Paulo Upon Leaving for Rio de Janeiro.   *February* 25, 1960

Mr. President, Governor, and citizens of São Paulo:

As I say a friendly farewell to the leaders and people of São Paulo, I want to express my warm thanks for the cordial welcome and the many courtesies which have been extended to my associates and me during our short stay here.

I was greatly impressed by what I was able to see of your magnificent city during the day.   São Paulo, leader in Brazilian commerce and industry, is surely characterized by energy, growth, and the spirit of progress.

You receive here each year vast quantities of goods, especially capital goods, from the United States, and of course you ship a tremendous volume of products, especially coffee, to the United States.   The two-way trade of the United States and Brazil has long been of high importance to both countries.   We are your major consumer; you a major customer of ours.   I am glad to have learned in my conversations here today that there is a minimum of friction in these trade matters.   And this is good news.

I might point out that we of the United States are the most insatiable coffee drinkers in the world—indeed, we buy nearly 60 percent of your coffee exports.   And I doubt that you would have a surplus here if you drank as much coffee as we do.

On leaving São Paulo, I want to say how happy I am to have met Governor Carvalho Pinto, the state and municipal authorities, and to have been privileged to make a personal visit to this tremendous city.

Thank you again, sincerely, for your cordiality, your kindness, and your hospitality.

NOTE: The President's opening words "Mr. President" referred to President Kubitschek who accompanied him on the return flight to Rio de Janeiro.

55   ¶ Statement by the President Upon Leaving Brazil.   *February* 26, 1960

I MUST NOW say farewell to the leaders and people of this vast and beautiful country.   I do so with a full heart weighed down by the tragic accident which cost the lives of Brazilians and Americans yesterday.

I wish, nevertheless, on leaving Brazil to express my deep gratitude for the magnitude of the reception accorded me and my associates since our arrival among you only a few days ago. I am beginning to understand that sentiment which you Brazilians describe so poignantly with the word *saudade*.

I interpret the cordiality of your greeting as evidence of Brazilian friendship for my countrymen. I assure you that this friendship is earnestly reciprocated.

I saw your sparkling new capital at Brasilia—a symbol of Brazilian progress.

In São Paulo I saw firsthand the phenomenal development which forecasts Brazil's emergence as one of the world's new industrial giants.

And here in your present capital of Rio de Janeiro old memories of unsurpassed scenic beauty and traditional Carioca hospitality have been rekindled.

During the past few days my associates and I have had an opportunity to talk with your distinguished President and other leaders of your country. All of us hope and believe that these conversations will enable us to understand better not only Brazilian aspirations but also how our collaboration can become more effective to our mutual benefit.

As I proceed on this trip, I feel that a significant beginning in fulfilling its purpose has been made here. My desire, in the countries I am visiting, is to emphasize the importance we of the United States attach to hemispheric solidarity; to seek ways in which cooperation among the Americas may be even more fruitful, and to proclaim here as I have repeatedly done in other areas the supreme desire of the United States to do all it can to help bring about peace with justice, in freedom, to all humankind.

For your friendship and your many kindnesses, I thank you, and now, goodbye.

NOTE: The President left from Galeao Airport, Rio de Janeiro, at 8 p.m.

In the opening paragraph the President referred to the collision of a U.S. Navy transport plane with a Brazilian airliner over Guanabara Bay. The Navy transport plane was carrying U.S. Navy bandsmen and members of an anti-submarine team.

The statement was released in Rio de Janeiro.

56 ¶ Remarks Upon Arrival at Ezeiza Airport, Buenos Aires. *February* 26, 1960

Mr. President, Your Excellencies, ladies and gentlemen:

With genuine pleasure and satisfaction, I greet you in friendship as I begin my visit in the Republic of Argentina.

My pleasure is in realizing a long-cherished wish to view this beautiful land, and in returning officially the visit which your President and Mrs. Frondizi graciously made to my country.

My satisfaction derives from the knowledge that our commitment to common aspirations provides one stone in the structure of world peace.

I am especially happy that my visit occurs during the 150th anniversary of your nation's valiant fight for freedom. With pride in our own long adherence to the democratic vision, we of my country salute you, and welcome this opportunity to join our voices joyously with yours in your meaningful celebration.

I bring all of you the heartfelt good wishes of the Government and the people of the United States of America. In the few days we shall be here among you, we hope to meet many of you personally, to enjoy the grandeur of your world-famed capital, to visit several other of your beautiful cities, and, at least from the air, to obtain a panoramic perspective of your vast and noble country.

Al gran pueblo Argentino, Salud!

NOTE: The President spoke at 11 a.m. He was met by President Arturo Frondizi, Foreign Minister Diogenes Toboada, and U.S. Ambassador Willard L. Beaulac.

57 ¶ Remarks at the U.S. Embassy Residence in Buenos Aires Upon Receiving the Key to the City. *February* 26, 1960

I AM DEEPLY HONORED not only for the presentation of this key, symbolic of the friendly spirit of your country for the United States, but for the generosity of the terms in which your Mayor has described the ideals and democratic aspirations that bind his country with mine.

If I may be personal, I should like to tell you a bit of a story. Forty-five years ago now, I was just preparing to graduate from West Point—

our military school in the United States. I had been badly injured and the medical corps decided that I should not become a lieutenant in the Army. I was called before the board and I think they thought that I would be a heartbroken young man. I said, "Well, it's all right with me, if you just give me my diploma, I am going down to the Argentine." They were a bit surprised, and I said, "Well, it strikes me to be a fine place to go."

Now by the favorable action of the board, my intent of that time was spoiled, but it was never given up. For 45 years I have held the hope to go and meet the people of this beautiful city, and to visit this great country. I know I shall have a wonderful trip—[*helicopter noise*]—to renew that urge of mine to come back here than any other thing I could possibly have said when he said, "Argentina is going to be one of the great leading democracies not only of the Western World but all the world." And with that kind of ambition, I am for him one hundred percent, and I feel that it is a great privilege for me to come back to return his friendly call.

Mr. Mayor, again I thank you for the honor.

NOTE: The key to the city was presented by Mayor Hernan M. Giralt.

The missing text was later reconstructed by Ambassador Beaulac. In a memorandum dated July 26, 1960, the State Department informed the White House that the Ambassador believed the portion in question should read as follows, the missing words being italicized: "I know I shall have a wonderful trip. *I told President Frondizi in Washington about my early plan to come to Argentina and my talk with him served more* to renew that urge of mine to come back here than any other thing I could possibly have said when he said 'Argentina is going to be one of the great leading democracies not only of the Western World but all the world.' "

58 ¶ Address Before a Joint Session of the National Congress of Argentina. *February 26, 1960*

Mr. President, Honorable Members of Congress, ladies and gentlemen:

First, an expression of my warm gratitude for the cordiality with which you have received me in this hall. I cannot fail to mention what I have just seen in the streets of your beautiful city. I have seen crowds on those streets, I have seen the smiles on their faces, the flowers in their hands, and I have heard their shouts and cries of welcome. To me, this can mean one thing only: that the people of the Argentine, like the people of the United States, are proud that they are free men and they want to stand together as partners in our never-ceasing search for a just peace in which all men can prosper and better themselves, their families, their communities and their nations.

I am honored by this opportunity to address the Congress of the Argentine Republic. To you, and through you and to all your people, I bring friendly greetings from my government and my fellow citizens. I convey to you our unbounded admiration for the courageous efforts you are making under the inspiring leadership of President Frondizi to strengthen respect for human dignity and human rights, and to build institutions which will eternally guarantee the free exercise of those rights.

Though the people of the United States do not know your history, philosophy, and aspirations as well as they should—and this is a shortcoming which, despite distance and dissimilar language, simply must be overcome—nonetheless they are mindful of the extraordinary efforts you are making to restore your national economy. We hope and expect that the solid economic foundations you have been building will soon result in improved living standards.

I am happy that Argentina has created conditions which have made it possible for some of our credit agencies to extend to it a significant program of dollar credits. During the past few years, public and private lending agencies of the United States, and international financial institutions to which we contribute substantially, have joined in lending to Argentina approximately a billion dollars. This is the most intensive program of financial cooperation to have been yet carried out in the history of this hemisphere.

In a nation that is truly determined to develop, capital is one essential instrument of production. If there is a shortage of capital, production and living standards suffer simultaneously. But new capital, if accompanied by other instruments of production, including technical proficiency—in this case provided by Argentina itself—quickly translates into more production, more and better-paid jobs, and higher living standards. Everybody gains in the process.

We of the United States are highly gratified that we have been able to be of some assistance in your march toward a better life.

In words so candid and clear that no one in all the Americas can possibly misunderstand me, I wish to emphasize again our deep desire:

First, to see every one of the American Nations make steady economic progress, with the blessings of this advance reaching all of its people;

Second, to cooperate in every sound way we can, within the limits of our ability, in helping the American Nations attain their just aspirations— we also wish to persuade them and others to join in a world-wide effort to help the less developed nations to progress in freedom;

Third, while adhering strictly to a policy of non-intervention and mutual respect, to applaud the triumph of free government everywhere in the world. We do not urge emulation of the United States, but we do know that human beings, sacred in the sight of God, and more majestic than any institutions they may create, will in the long sweep of history never be content with any form of slavery or coercion;

Fourth, to bring ever closer the realization of a world in which peace with freedom is guaranteed, and in which the mighty productive power of man can work constructively for the betterment of all humankind.

As perhaps you know, I have recently traveled in Europe, the Middle East, and India. I am now at the half-way point in this all-too-brief trip through South America. In June I shall go to the Soviet Union and Japan. When those journeys have been completed, I shall have visited many countries, large and small; industrial and agricultural communities; highly developed nations and some newly emerging. In all these travels I have had one paramount interest: to assure everybody of my Nation's peaceful intent and to do what I can to promote the cooperation of all in the cause of peace and freedom.

I have emphasized that we seek peace, but only in freedom. If peoples were willing to give up their liberty and their personal dignity, they could readily have peace—a peace in which a single great power controlled all other nations.

Genghis Khan, Tamerlane, Alexander the Great, Napoleon, Hitler, and others sought to establish that kind of peace. But always peoples and nations have rebelled against their false, self-serving doctrines. We do not want an imposed peace. We want a cooperative peace in which the peoples of every nation have the right of free choice—the right to establish their own institutions, to live by their own cardinal concepts, and to be free of external pressure or threat.

These are deep-seated desires held passionately in common by the peoples of the United States and Argentina. We hope to see machines capable of destruction turned exclusively to constructive purposes.

These shared aspirations spring from a common heritage:

Both our countries won their independence from European powers. The drafters of our Declaration of Independence proclaimed that "all men are created equal, endowed by their Creator with certain inalienable rights, among them life, liberty, and the pursuit of happiness." In Argentina, Esteban Echeverria said: "Equality and liberty are . . . the two poles of . . . Democracy . . ." In the United States, Abraham Lincoln described democratic government as "of the people, by the people, and for the people." In Argentina, Juan Alberdi declared: "Public freedom is no more than the sum . . . of the freedoms of all." The Constitution of the United States carefully separated the legislative, executive, and judicial branches of our government. In Argentina, the great liberator, José de San Martin, stated: "Displaying the most excellent principles matters not at all, when he who makes the law, he who carries it out, is also he who judges it."

Your founding fathers and ours acted upon the same great hopes and expressed—almost identically—the same wisdom. This is of course not surprising: the vision of true freedom cannot be dimmed by a barrier of language or distance.

It was once possible to think of democratic freedom as a matter of purely national concern. But now, in a world of exacting interdependence, freedom must be fostered, developed, and maintained cooperatively among many nations. Hence, across national boundaries, among peoples and governments, a constant increase in mutual understanding must prevail. Based on that understanding, political, cultural, and economic cooperation will succeed, with benefits for all.

Unhappily, until the last threat of force has been suppressed, there must also be military cooperation, for no single nation, no matter how mighty, can alone protect the freedom of all. Together, however, the nations which cherish independence can command a power so great that no potential aggressor could violate the peace without inviting his own destruction.

Can the ugly external threat which faces us impose such physical strains upon us as to impair or destroy our heritage? With confidence our two nations emphatically and jointly say "No." I have heard some say that the more a country develops its technology and science, the more "materialistic" it becomes and the less it possesses or cherishes the cultural aspects of life. But of course science, technology, and richness of culture must, and do, march forward hand in hand.

Surely scientific advances that make possible the conquering of human disease; that remove drudgery from the household; that yield shorter working hours with leisure for the arts and recreation—surely these are not inimical to the fulfillment of man's spiritual aspirations.

No single technological development in all history did more to advance the cultures of the world than the invention of the printing press. Modern technological miracles have speeded communications to the point that an event in a remote part of Africa is known minutes later in Buenos Aires. They have enabled us to move from one part of the world to any other in a matter of hours.

With these so-called "materialistic" advances, we have the means of obtaining accurate information, and more knowledge, faster. These accomplishments are helpful in developing that genuine human understanding on which all other cooperative actions among peace-longing nations can be based.

I have watched, with much satisfaction, the increasing amount of news published in each of our countries about the other—and the increasing number of books translated from each of our languages into the other's. I have observed, too, the growing numbers of our teachers, students, businessmen, labor leaders, and others who are exchanging visits between us.

My country was recently honored by the visit of a number of distinguished members of this Congress, who traveled extensively in the United States and conferred with their fellow legislators and other American citizens. Also, legislators from the United States have visited Argentina on numerous occasions. I can think of nothing more useful to our relations than such exchanges.

But it is not possible for everyone to travel great distances. So our schools and universities, the press, books, philosophic societies, study groups, and government—all these must work ceaselessly to promote better understanding between us, as well as among all the Americas. And there must be interchanges to the maximum degree possible—of ideas, of persons, of techniques. I hold the unshakeable conviction that the greatest single impediment to abiding, mutually-helpful cooperation among nations desiring peace with freedom is not opposing policies, or different aspirations, or insoluble conflicts—serious as these sometimes are. No, the most persistent, single impediment to healthy, effective cooperation is the lack of deep and abiding understanding, and the trust that flows from understanding. Here, then, in this effort to increase mutual understanding among all nations, is the basic problem. It is one that every citizen, in your country and mine, can help to solve. Overcoming it will build the surest foundation for the kind of cooperative progress and the just peace we all seek.

Again, I convey to you the admiration of the people of the United States for the courage and determination with which Argentina is facing its problems. We wish you every success. I am also happy to assure you of the continued readiness of my government to cooperate with you to the extent that such cooperation is feasible, is welcomed, and may contribute to the well-being of your great country.

I thank you for the privilege of addressing you, the elected representatives of the Argentine people.

NOTE: The President spoke at approximately 5 p.m. His opening words "Mr. President" referred to Senator José Maria Guido, Provisional President of the Argentine Senate.

59 ¶ Toast by the President at a Dinner Given in His Honor by President Frondizi in Buenos Aires. February 26, 1960

Mr. President, ladies and gentlemen:

I have in my hand a few brief notes which I had expected to use as a basis for the remarks I should make to you this evening.

Inspired by some of the words of your President, I am sure that I will wander somewhat from the notes, so on behalf of my interpreter I apologize for such errors as may be made in their interpretation.

With deep sincerity, I thank you, Mr. President, for your gracious hospitality, for your heartwarming expression of friendship, and for your eloquent statement of Argentina's aspirations and future.

Although I have been here in your beautiful land for only a few hours, I have already learned much and have been deeply impressed by all that I have seen and heard. Especially impressive are your courage to face up to difficult problems, your demonstrated capacity to solve them, and your determination to construct now a dependable economic base on which to build soundly in the future.

Indeed, Mr. President, in making this statement, I do not express only my own personal opinions—your foresight, your integrity, your dedication to the truth are recognized throughout this hemisphere. To this I can testify.

Among the leaders of Argentina, as among your people, there is obviously a sense of purpose and destiny. Your land is vast and endowed with rich resources. Your people have great vigor. Though you are justly proud of your traditions, your eyes are focused on a future in which you envision orderly progress in freedom, not only for yourselves, but for all who have the courage to be self-reliant and to live in harmony with the cardinal concepts of their cherished philosophies.

We of the United States applaud you.

My visit to Argentina, and to several other countries of this great Southland, has two central purposes: I want to reaffirm the high importance we of the United States attach to friendly inter-American relations and to hemispheric solidarity; and, as I have done recently in other areas of the world, I wish to emphasize over and over again our passionate desire for a permanent, guaranteed peace, in freedom—a peace which will permit the creative talents of mankind to concentrate on finding constructive solutions to economic, social, and cultural problems.

Mr. President, this afternoon I spoke of one of the most difficult tasks lying before the men and women of the free world: the cultivation of mutual understanding.

Basic to this, though, is the most difficult problem of all; that is, making use of the intelligence and minds of people that make up a free country—to inform people, so that public opinion rather than being guided by demagogues or by falsehood, or by laziness or ignorance, is based upon the facts of the world, logically interpreted to each.

To my mind, this is not only a problem for the President and his closest associates; every single informed individual in any free democracy has this problem. And unless he performs it, there will be disaster.

We speak of the problem of obtaining outside capital. Indeed, I conceive this to be the easiest of the problems with which democracy is faced.

Capital is a funny thing. Give it the right conditions and the right promises, and you can't keep it away. There's money to invest all over this world.

You have just stated, sir, that here you give it juridical protection, you do not regard it as evil merely because it may come from abroad, you provide the conditions in which it can prosper.   And those conditions are, first of all, a people of heart and strength and courage who want to go ahead, who have the natural resources on which to build.   And then the capital will come.   Of this I am certain.

I know that you and your countrymen are working for dependable, abiding cooperation among the Americas, and for a world freed of threat and fear.   We are proud of our partnership with you.   And we pray that God will give you and your associates strength, sir, to carry out your great work to its complete success.

So it is with an unusual sense of privilege, and indeed admiration and respect that I lift my glass in friendship to President Frondizi, expressing the confident hope that the partnership of Argentina and the United States will ever grow stronger and more rewarding.

NOTE: The President proposed the toast at a dinner at the Plaza Hotel in Buenos Aires.

60 ¶ Remarks to the Members of the Supreme Court of Argentina.   *February* 27, 1960

Your Excellencies, Ministers of the Supreme Court, distinguished guests and friends:

I have paid my respects upon your President, and to your legislative branch.   The Western democracies have learned that true democracy exists only when those who interpret the law are completely free of the authority of the people who make the law and execute the law.   I think the words of José de San Martin on this matter were not only eloquent but were completely accurate.

So I felt that as I made this hurried trip to this great country and spent these few hours in your capital, that I would be remiss should I fail to pay my respects on the Supreme Court where the interpretation of law, the determination of its constitutionality, and the final word in determination that the rights of the individual are always protected—where all this work is done.

So, sir, I feel that it has been a great privilege for me, and a great honor, to have met this number of your judiciary in this country.

Thank you very much.

NOTE: The President spoke at the Palacio de Tribunales following remarks of welcome by Dr. Benjamin Villegas Basavilbaso, Acting President of the Supreme Court.   He left immediately for the airport in Buenos Aires for his flight at 9:25 a.m. to Mar del Plata.

61 ¶ Remarks Upon Arrival at the Provincial Hotel in Mar del Plata, Argentina. *February 27, 1960*

Honorable Mayor, Mr. President, citizens of the Argentine and of this lovely city, ladies and gentlemen:

Thank you for your generous welcome, and for the honor you do me in presenting me with a key to the city. I assure you I shall not misuse it. I am not privileged to be here long enough to do so.

Indeed, in recent months, I seem to travel so often, so fast, and so furiously, that I am given little opportunity to see any real estate—but I do see people. And to me, people are more important than anything else in the world.

And I must say to you that in the last few hours the people of Argentine and the people of this city have seized a warm and large spot in my heart, one that I shall cherish forever. And I assure you that whatever I can do to bring my people closer to yours, to make certain that you of your nation and we of our nation are stronger and better friends, that I shall do. However, from what I have already seen of the beautiful city of Mar del Plata, I wish I could remain longer than the few hours available to me. Even so, I shall carry with me vivid and pleasant memories of this short visit.

In Buenos Aires I was impressed by the majesty of its beauty, and by the bustling activity, and commerce, and industry. Since, however, I grew up far from my own national capital, and have lived in many parts of my country, I realize full well that the real strength of a nation lies in all its parts, not just its capital and its industrial cities.

As we flew to Mar del Plata, I was able to glimpse from the air some of your country's farmland, a few of the cattle-growing estancias, and some of the sheep-raising area. There is a native richness and even greater promise in this land. Its future is certain to be a bright one—the Argentines will make it so.

So I bring you the friendly wishes of the people of the United States, and again thank you earnestly for the warmth of your welcome, both along the streets and in this hall—and for the great honor you have done me in presenting to me this symbolic key.

NOTE: The President spoke at 11:55 a.m. following Mayor Todoro Bronzini's presentation of the key to the city. Earlier, upon his arrival at Camet Airport, the President was met by President Frondizi who accompanied him to the Provincial Hotel.

62 ¶ Remarks Upon Arrival at the Airport, San Carlos de Bariloche, Argentina. *February 27, 1960*

President Frondizi, Mayor Sacido, ladies and gentlemen:

I have heard much of the scenic and climatic wonders of Bariloche. With no more than the view from the plane and my first breaths of air in this gorgeous setting, it is already evident that my informants were not exaggerating.

I arrive among you with new and indelible impressions of another part of your country. On the way to Bariloche, we flew over Patagonia. Even at high altitude, we could note the remarkable progress being made in the development of that Province. It appears to me that Patagonia is to Argentina what the western frontier was to the United States of America a century ago. Few are the countries in the shrinking world of today which possess a physical frontier. They are indeed fortunate, for the world will soon need the products of such land, and conquering it is a great challenge to the vitality, spirit, and courage of a people. I know you are abundantly blessed with these qualities.

Here among you, I am to have an opportunity to discuss informally many hemispheric and world problems, as well as to have a few hours of rest and relaxation. For this, and for the warmth of your welcome, I am most grateful.

Salud!

NOTE: The President spoke at 4:35 p.m. after which the two Presidents left the air-port by helicopter for the Llao Llao Hotel.

63   ¶ Toast to President Frondizi at a Dinner
Given in His Honor by the President in San Carlos
de Bariloche.   *February 27, 1960*

Mr. President, and gentlemen:

Mr. President, it is a high honor to have you as my guest for these few
hours this evening.   And incidentally, as we sat down, I find that both
you and I were honored with the presentation from the National Park
Service of fishing licenses.   So if I am found fishing tomorrow, I don't
want to be arrested for breaking a law.

Had I the words to express my deepest thoughts, you would know the
full extent of my respect, admiration, and friendship for you, first felt
when you visited my country 13 months ago.   At that time you said in
an address before a joint session of the United States Congress, "Without
national development, no welfare or progress can exist.   When there is
misery and backwardness in a country, not only freedom and democracy
are doomed, but even national sovereignty is in jeopardy."

This is a basic truth.   And I would add one thought: when freedom,
democracy, and national sovereignty are in jeopardy in any country, they
are to some degree in jeopardy in all free countries of the world.

This is one strong reason why the United States is vitally interested in
the development, and general well-being of all free nations.   It is why
the United States—despite unmatched levels of taxation, heavy economic
and military burdens, and pressing internal problems—continues to make
sacrifices in helping other free nations with their problems of national
development.

Next to the attainment of a just and lasting peace, with freedom, no
hope consumes my mind and heart so much as this: that the nations of
the world arrive at a system of guaranteed disarmament, with a significant portion of the savings, thus achieved, employed in a continuous
program of assistance to those who need it, who would welcome it, and
who would work hard in using it.

Each hour of the 2 days I have been in your country has added to my
deep respect for your efforts to stabilize your economy, your determination to develop your nation soundly in ways that benefit all the people,
and the evident progress you are making.   What I have seen reflects the

virtues of a freely elected government, a dedicated and energetic leader, and the courage of an independent people.

Gentlemen: I invite you to join me in a Toast to President Frondizi, and to the abiding friendship of the peoples of Argentina and the United States.

NOTE: The President proposed the toast at 10:20 p.m. at the dinner given at the Llao Llao Hotel in San Carlos de Bariloche.

64 ¶ Message to President Kubitschek of Brazil on the Air Tragedy Over Rio de Janeiro. *February 28, 1960*

Dear Mr. President:

The Senate of the United States of America, shocked at the air tragedy last Thursday over Rio de Janeiro, has expressed its feeling in the following Resolution:

"Resolved, that the Senate of the United States of America hereby expresses its deep and profound anguish that, in the line of duty, members of the Armed Forces of the United States of America and citizens of the United States of Brazil have today met their creator in a tragic air accident in the city of Rio de Janeiro.

"In full knowledge that the peoples of the United States of Brazil and the United States of America have stood together, in war as in peace, and believing as it does that our friendship will ever grow stronger, it is the sense of the Senate that the sacrifices of these lives will long be remembered; and be it further

"Resolved, that the Senate hereby expresses its profound sympathy to the bereaved families and friends of those who have died.

"The President of the United States is hereby requested to communicate the sense of this resolution to the Government and people of Brazil."

In forwarding this resolution to you, not only do I assure you that it represents the sentiments of the entire nation, but I take this opportunity again to extend through you my own heartfelt sympathy to the Brazilian families who lost loved ones in this tragedy.

Sincerely,

DWIGHT D. EISENHOWER

NOTE: The message was released at San Carlos de Bariloche.

65 ¶ Statement of the President Recorded for the Opening of the 1960 Red Cross Campaign. *February 28, 1960*

My fellow Americans:

March is Red Cross Month.

Throughout our nation, the Red Cross will be seeking to raise the funds needed to keep it on the job. All of us need to come promptly and effectively to its support.

The Red Cross is truly an integral part of our national life—always ready to lend a helping hand to Americans in times of stress.

Each year the Red Cross participates in aiding our people in some 300 disasters. It provides food, shelter and medical care to the victims— and then helps those in need to rebuild or repair and refit their homes and to resume normal living. Even if Red Cross had no other humanitarian task, we would need to keep it strong for this purpose alone.

But disaster relief is only one of its many responsibilities. More than 3900 hospitals are provided blood collected by the Red Cross. With 100 million people participating in water sports every year, Red Cross classes in swimming, life saving and small craft safety are effective in keeping the drowning rate down. Equally important are the courses in first aid and home nursing.

In addition to doing all these things, more than half the time of Red Cross staff and volunteers and one-third of its budget are expended in assisting members of our armed forces and veterans who need help.

The Red Cross does many other good things. Above all, it typifies the spirit of man helping man. Now it is our turn to show that spirit by supporting this great work. I am sure all Americans will respond generously.

And to you two million volunteers who make this wonderful work possible, I extend my gratitude and my thanks to all workers and supporters of the American Red Cross.

NOTE: This statement, recorded prior to the President's departure on his South American trip, was released in Washington.

66 ¶ The Declaration of San Carlos de Bariloche: Joint Declaration by the President and President Frondizi of Argentina. *February 28, 1960*

THE PRESIDENTS of the Argentine Nation and of the United States of America, having conferred on matters relating to peace, freedom and cultural and material opportunities for the peoples of the Americas, have decided to issue a joint declaration.

They reaffirm the determination of their respective governments to foster improved living standards for the peoples of the Americas.

They agree that:

Improved living standards result from economic progress which in turn depends upon adequate economic policies, upon friendly international cooperation, and upon efficient utilization both of natural resources and of the talents and capacities of the individual citizen acting alone or in voluntary association with others.

Economic progress and improved living standards facilitate the development of strong and stable political institutions and enable countries to make a more effective contribution to international understanding.

Likewise whatever serves to reinforce democratic institutions contributes not only to political, economic and social progress but also to the improvement of relations among nations.

The inter-American system, an expression of the common experience of the peoples of the Americas, has proved itself an effective instrument for peace and for cooperative relations among countries.

Experience within the inter-American system has taught that non-intervention is the keystone of international harmony and friendship and that its corollary is mutual respect among nations, however large or small.

The efforts of the Government of the Argentine Republic and of the United States of America will continue to be directed to the attainment of these inter-American ideals.

DWIGHT D. EISENHOWER
ARTURO FRONDIZI

NOTE: The joint declaration, released at San Carlos de Bariloche, was signed in the main hall of the Llao Llao Hotel.

67 ¶ Remarks at the Airport in San Carlos de Bariloche Upon Leaving for Chile. *February 29, 1960*

President Frondizi, Mayor Sacido, and all citizens of Argentina:

I think there is some significance in the circumstance that gives me the privilege of saying my farewell to Argentina, here in the shadow of the majestic Andes. Possibly these eternal mountains might symbolize for all of us the strength, spiritual power, and unity of all the Americas.

How simple our world would be if in the management of human affairs all of us could be as sturdy and inspiring as are these evidences of God's creation.

We too must be sturdy, must be firm and unshakable, in our adherence to basic principles to which we have commonly subscribed. We of the Americas are pledged to nonintervention in the internal affairs of our sister Republics, and we adhere to a policy of mutual respect and juridical equality of States. We recognize our economic, social, and cultural interdependence, and strive to be helpful to one another.

So, in leaving you, I repeat that we of the United States recognize the mutual dependence of the nations of this hemisphere. We attach the highest possible importance to maintaining a friendly, unswerving partnership with you and the other Republics.

Above all, we support the right of self-determination and human dignity. We will oppose with all our strength any outside attempt to enslave or regiment the peoples of any of us.

From my visit here, I know you share these thoughts.

I carry with me deep impressions of the vastness and natural wealth of your land. How fortunate you are, in a world of growing population and terrible under-consumption, to have in your possession resources which could if necessary support ten times as many persons as now live here—how lucky the world is that there is an Argentina with such a potential.

I salute with profound respect the gallant efforts you are making to create the firm foundation on which generations of steady progress may be built.

And I shall never forget your warm hospitality. In a few days with you I have met a great many people, and my heart has been warmed both by your understanding and by the many evidences of sincere friendship.

I trust that my visit has contributed a little to your understanding of my country, as I have learned much about yours, for again I say: without genuine understanding there simply cannot be cooperative progress.

Thank you, President Frondizi, thank you all—and *hasta luego!*

NOTE: The President spoke at approximately 10:15 a.m.

68 ¶ Statement by the President Concerning the Recipients of the President's Award for Distinguished Federal Civilian Service. *February* 29, 1960

THE DISTINGUISHED service of these men in the fields of administration, accountancy, science, and medicine contribute much to the general welfare of our country and to the progress of our world in justice and freedom. Their achievements provide an inspiring example for all Government employees, each of whom must perform at peak levels of productive effort if we are to solve successfully the complex problems of our times.

I welcome this opportunity of giving wider attention to their work.

Among America's most cherished traditions are those which guarantee full opportunity for the development of the individual citizen and which reward the exercise of high ability, resourcefulness, and unfailing energy. The careers of these five individuals witness to the living vitality of these traditions.

NOTE: The President's words were released in Washington as part of an announcement concerning the awards "for exceptionally meritorious civilian service." The recipients selected by the President were: Andrew Barr, Chief Accountant, Securities and Exchange Commission, for "exceptional contributions to the development of accounting principles and meaningful accounting presentations of corporate financial affairs to investors [which] have materially aided the process of capital formation in the United States and advanced the cause of investor protection"; Hugh L. Dryden, Deputy Administrator, National Aeronautics and Space Administration, for "scientific and administrative leadership in planning and organizing American space exploration"; William J. Hopkins, Executive Clerk, White House Office, for "effective and impartial administration of the White House Office and his handling of the President's communications with the Congress" and "unselfish loyalty and high dedication to the service of the Presidency for three decades"; Dr. Winfred Overholser, Superintendent, St. Elizabeths Hospital, for "profound and far-reaching contributions in the field of mental health"; and Robert M. Page, Director of Research, Naval Research Laboratory, for "remarkable achievements in the field of electronics research, most particularly in the original development of radar."

Gold medals were presented by the President in a White House ceremony on March 7 at 11:30 a.m.

69 ¶ Remarks in Santiago in Response to Greetings by President Alessandri of Chile. *February* 29, 1960

Mr. President and gentlemen:

Mr. President, permit me to say that in a fairly long life, I have listened to a great many public statements. I have heard no more statesmanlike statement of this kind than the one I have just heard from you. I am grateful for what you have said.

I thank you for the cordiality of your welcome to me and my party. We have experienced also a heartwarming greeting from many people who gathered along the way from the airport, or assembled at this historic palace. To all who have so graciously bid us welcome, I express most earnest appreciation.

And, Mr. President, there seems to be no words in the English language, at least not in my vocabulary, that permit me to express properly the true appreciation I feel. I can say only that the affection that I believe that I saw in these crowds along the street, the affection for my people, is reciprocated from the bottom of my heart.

We have come to Chile to reaffirm the friendship of my people for yours, and to discuss with you and your associates many matters of hemispheric and world importance.

We hope to taste the flavor of this land, which is noted for its beauty, for the hospitality of its people, and the vigor of their traditions from the days of San Martin and O'Higgins. But beyond this, I keenly anticipate the serious discussions we shall have.

I am especially pleased that this visit could occur in the year in which your nation is celebrating its 150th anniversary of independence. On behalf of the people of the United States, who know full well the blessings of independence and freedom, I extend warm congratulations to you and all citizens of Chile.

Our two nations are justly proud of the peaceful, harmonious, and mutually helpful relations which have existed between us over these many years. To strengthen these relations still more is my devout wish, as I am sure it is yours.

Indeed, as the bonds between our two countries become ever stronger we help produce a greater solidarity among all our American States. Cooperation among us all is thus improved—as is also our common determination to oppose any aggression from outside, no matter what form it may take.

As you have most aptly put it, we of all the Americas must accept with enthusiasm our common destiny. And a principal purpose of my visit here is to demonstrate our eagerness to remove from our mutual relations any possible suspicion, fear, or restraint—to demonstrate our hope to work with you in perfect trust. In this effort the primary factor is the observance by all of the principle of nonintervention.

And among the members of my party are six distinguished private citizens who, with Secretary Herter and Assistant Secretary Rubottom, comprise our Government's newly established National Advisory Committee on Inter-American Affairs. These gentlemen are leaders in governmental, educational, industrial, labor, and cultural affairs, and are noted for their dedication to promoting hemispheric solidarity. They are charged with the task of constantly studying inter-American relations and formulating appropriate recommendations to our Government and private institutions. Thus they will help promote understanding of Latin America in the United States of America.

I personally have looked forward to this opportunity to confer with you, Mr. President, and with your colleagues, in the manner of good friends seeking to strengthen their understanding of one another's problems.

I have been told that Chileans have a vigorous tradition of free and candid speech, and that they welcome this quality in others. We, too, welcome open and honest expression of views, and thus I am sure our conversations will be fruitful.

In the words you have just spoken, Mr. President, you have given us all a comprehensive panorama of the ideas, the problems, the objectives with which we must be concerned. You have given our discussions a most constructive start. The citizens of the United States, when they read what you have just said, will applaud your words.

They and I agree wholeheartedly that our problems can be solved through more intensive cooperative effort.

It is the earnest hope of my countrymen that our two peoples will continue to work in harmony and good will toward the goal cherished by all democratic peoples—a world of peace and friendship in freedom.

Thank you for your kind invitation for us to visit you.

I repeat—we are delighted to be here, and are deeply moved by the reception given us.

NOTE: The President spoke at 4:07 p.m. at La Moneda Palace, official residence of President Jorge Alessandri Rodriguez. Earlier the President had been met at Los Cerrillos Airport by President Alessandri, other Chilean officials, and U.S. Ambassador Walter Howe.

70   ¶ Remarks at the American Embassy Residence in Santiago Upon Receiving a Scroll From the Chilean-American Cultural Institute. *February* 29, 1960

FOR A good many years I have been preaching that the only real need in the world is for peace, and you are going to get no peace except by understanding among nations. You see, all of us realize that no people wants war, and we are amazed that governments succeed, sometimes, in getting us into war.

The feeling for peace is universal, and if we could get together so well in our understanding that we would forbid governments to get us into war, there would be a great burden lifted from the backs of men.

We are spending so much of our substance, so much of our talent, so much of our man hours of work just for the destructive and sterile instruments of war, that it seems to me the greatest tragedy that almost has come to this world, particularly now, when we realize what one single bomb taken to each city can do.

It is time that this kind of thinking that you are doing in your way becomes universal, not only among all of the free nations; we have got to get better acquaintanceship with the people behind the Iron Curtain, because in their hearts there is this fundamental longing for peace. Hatred of war is just as firm in their hearts as it is in ours.

So, if we can do that, take one little step in the forwarding of such a great objective as this, then I think our efforts—indeed, our lives—are worth while. Because it is only by millions and millions of small efforts that this is going to come about.

So I accept this, not only with great pride in joining your organization, but because of my respect for the work which you are undertaking.

Thank you very much indeed.

NOTE: The President spoke at 6:05 p.m. after receiving an honorary membership in the Chilean-American Cultural Institute.

71 ¶ Toast by the President at a Dinner Given in His Honor by President Alessandri.
February 29, 1960

Mr. President:

In view of the shortness of my visit here in Chile, and in view of the importance of the matters we have been discussing, I would like to answer your toast at a little greater length than is my custom.

From my heart, Mr. President, I thank you for the sentiments you have so graciously expressed, and for the warm hospitality you have permitted my colleagues and me to experience here tonight.

My visit to Chile is in partial fulfillment of the keen desire I had when I became President of my country to visit all the nations of Latin America. Unfortunately, the tremendous pressures upon me during the past 7 years have permitted me to go only to Panama and Mexico, and now to four great Republics in this vast Southland, including this delightful and helpful visit with you, Mr. President, and your colleagues.

As you know, shortly after this trip is concluded, I shall go to Paris for a meeting with the leaders of Great Britain, France, and the Soviet Union. While I am too realistic to expect miracles, I do hope that in Paris we may reach some agreements which will lessen the tensions that divide and vex the world.

One of my purposes in coming to South America, even while our Congress is in session, is to consult with chiefs of state here about the many problems which today so perplex mankind. I know that you are as concerned as we are to have guaranteed disarmament replace the mad race for destructive power, to have honest negotiation replace arrogant threat, and to have truth replace blatant propaganda. Since you treasure freedom, independence, and human dignity as much as we, you have a vital stake in all that goes on in global affairs, and therefore most earnestly I have come to seek your views on these matters of transcendent importance. I am sure it is needless for me to assure you that the discussions with you, and with other chiefs of state I am seeing on this trip, are of incalculable importance to me and to all the free world. In short, I wish to go to Paris with a clear understanding of the views of our friends in this region.

Of course my colleagues and I are also seeking ways to strengthen the friendship and the fruitful cooperation of our two countries, and of all the nations of the hemisphere. We especially wish to learn all we can about Chile's economic development and the effectiveness of the substantial assistance extended by our official and private financial institutions.

We have so much to talk about, Mr. President—so many views to exchange—that I wish our stay here could be much longer.

Ladies and gentlemen, I propose a Toast to His Excellency, President Alessandri: may his term in office be notable for the democratic advance of his people, and may he enjoy God's gracious blessing; and to all the people of Chile: may they, in the joyous company of free men, go forward in liberty to a richer, fuller life.

NOTE: The President proposed the toast at a dinner at La Moneda Palace in Santiago.

72   ¶ Remarks to the Embassy Staff and to Members of Chilean-American Groups in Santiago. *March 1, 1960*

Mr. Ambassador, my fellow citizens, and friends of the United States in Chile:

I am delighted to see all of you this morning. It is heartening to meet individuals who are actually practicing a people-to-people program. Many of you, as members of our Embassy staff, devote much of your time to promoting Chilean-American understanding. But all of you are ambassadors of good will. I assure you this is encouraging to me.

To paraphrase the opening clause of the UNESCO constitution: since difficulties among nations begin in the minds of men, it is in the minds of men that good international relations must be constructed.

Unfortunately, as all of you must know, despite all the advances in modern communication, there exist in the American Republics serious misunderstandings which impede the resolution of many problems that beset us.

The people of the United States do not have as deep a knowledge of our sister American Republics as they should. But the American people do prize good relations with Latin America, not only because of an undoubted material interest, but also because we have a genuine fondness for all our neighbors. If the United States sometimes proposes or even takes actions which seem not in harmony with this feeling, it is, I assure you, not a mistake of the heart, but a lack of sufficient knowledge.

Unfortunately, too, serious misunderstandings of the United States exist in all our sister Republics. It is astounding, for example, to hear it said time and again that the United States is doing more for other areas of the world than it is for Latin America. Nothing could be more erroneous.

Certainly, the United States has given generously of its resources in helping rebuild vast areas that were destroyed in the common fight against Nazi tyranny, and in helping construct a defense perimeter for the protection of freedom. But these expenditures have benefited all free nations, including Latin America. And, at the same time, our public and private institutions have extended vast loans, technical assistance, and some grant-aid to help our sister Republics speed their development.

Investments and loans outstanding in Latin America now total more than $11 billion, and new private and public credits which become available each year amount to nearly $1 billion, with beneficial side effects of much more than this magnitude.

This movement of capital continues, even though today we find that because—and I mean North America—we find that because of the heavy burdens we carry and changes in international trade, we are experiencing an unfavorable financial balance in international transactions of several billion dollars a year.

Despite this, we are not decreasing our help to Latin America. Indeed, two new credit instrumentalities are coming into being, with a substantial share of their funds being provided by the United States. One of them, the Inter-American Development Bank, has just elected a distinguished Chilean as its first President.

I have actually heard it said in several countries that the United States "crushes the economies of Latin America in order to enrich itself." When

I first heard this, I did not take it seriously at all. And then I realized, although its falsity soon becomes apparent to any thoughtful person, those who said it spoke in dead earnest.

We of the United States want every American Republic to become strong economically—as well as politically and socially. If for no other reason, we would want this because our trade with each country will increase as that country improves its economy. But we also want it just as one wants to see members of his family succeed. And we want it, for we know that only strong nations in our divided world can be sure of retaining their precious freedom.

We want it in order that the undernourished and unhappy people of the world, wherever they may be, may have an opportunity to enjoy the blessings of bread, peace, and liberty.

Then I have heard it said that the United States supports dictators. This is ridiculous. Surely no nation loves liberty more, or more sincerely prays that its benefits and deep human satisfactions may come to all peoples than does the United States.

We do adhere, however, to a policy of self-determination of peoples. We subscribe to and have observed with constancy a cardinal principle of inter-American life—the policy of nonintervention. It is no contradiction of these policies to say that we do all we can to foster freedom and representative democracy throughout the hemisphere. We repudiate dictatorship in any form, right or left. Our role in the United Nations, in the Organization of American States, in two World Wars, and in Korea stands as a beacon to all who love freedom.

I could go on. There are many serious misunderstandings throughout the hemisphere, and one of the most effective contributions an individual can make to hemispheric solidarity is by helping directly to overcome these intellectual shortcomings.

Because of my schedule, my friends, I have only a very few minutes at this meeting. I regret it, because I would like to talk this morning at greater length.

This morning, I received a letter signed by some individuals who are officials in student bodies. They say they represent 25,000, I believe, university students.

This was a letter speaking to me, or of me, in the most respectful and even affectionate terms, but telling about the tremendous errors that the United States of America is making with respect to South America. It says that every bit of the work in the Organization of American States and similar organizations is all in favor of the rich nation, all in favor of the rich individual, is against the weak, whether it be a nation or an individual.

Now I am not going to detail all of the things where they believe the United States is in error. I want to point this out: before individuals who do not carry great responsibilities in the world make decisions and spread information, or what they call information, we should be sure of our facts, we should read history carefully. Let's don't read merely the sensational stories of the newspapers.

Only within the week I read an account of testimony given in Congress by a great friend of mine—been a friend of mine for 30 years. I was astonished when I saw this story reported. This morning I got the full text, and everything he said in it was exactly opposite to what I had been told was the fact in a short newspaper account which really apparently was seeking to be a bit sensational.

We must have the facts. We must go to the statistics that are accumulated by honest governments. We must go to history which has been written by historians. We must not talk about these matters with the voice of authority when we have no real information to do it.

Now these students happen to be the people that I am interested in more than any others in the world. The young people of today, with all of their opportunities for learning, the certainty that they are going to take over the responsibilities of government, of business, of the social order, and of education—these are the people in whom we must be interested.

If the United States is to help, we must have some understanding between us. The United States has never, at the end of two World Wars and Korea, added an acre to its territory. We have sought no advantage anywhere, either as a result of war or peaceful help that would give us an advantage at the expense of others.

We are not saints—we know we make mistakes, but our heart is in the right place, and we believe that aid given by the United States to the people who want to work, who welcome some help, who are energetically working for themselves to raise their standards of living, not merely for themselves as individuals but for every single individual in the nation, those are the people from which we get great satisfaction in helping.

I would hope that the students of this great nation could have little bit better sources of information, as seems evident they did not have in the very hasty, even rapid reading of most of the parts of this letter that I saw.

Now I would like to send to them my very warmest greetings. I believe in them, but I do hope, as I say, that they will come to their conclusions on the basis of fact.

I congratulate all of you for what you are doing here in Chile. Your efforts will strengthen still further the friendly working relations of Chile and the United States, and the good neighborliness of all the American Republics.

And I repeat to you one great truth: the peace that we all seek, in justice and in freedom, can be based only on one thing, mutual understanding. Unless we have that among peoples, and eventually governments, which are always seemingly behind the people rather than ahead of them—unless we have that kind of understanding—mutual understanding—we are not going to have true peace.

Each of you that helps in the tiniest way to bring about this understanding is thereby promoting the peace for himself, his children, and those who are to come after him.

It is a pleasure to see you—and good luck to all of you.

NOTE: The President spoke at 11 a.m. in the Windsor Theater in Santiago to members of the U.S. Embassy staff, the American community, the American Society of Chile, the Association of American Women in Chile, and the Chilean-American Chamber of Commerce. In his open- ing words he referred to U.S. Ambassador Walter Howe. Later he referred to Felipe Herrera, President of the Inter-American Development Bank.

The letter to the President from the Students Federation of Chile is published in the Department of State Bulletin (vol. 42, p. 648).

73 ¶ Address Before a Joint Session of the National Congress of Chile. *March 1, 1960*

Mr. President of the Senate, Mr. President of the Chamber, Members of the Congress of Chile:

It is a high honor indeed and a personal privilege for me to address the elected representatives of the free people of the Republic of Chile.

In this year—the 150th anniversary of the first movement toward independence by Chilean patriots—I bring to you and your people the warm greetings and congratulations of my countrymen.

We Americans glow with pride when we recall the early links between our two countries—when you were seeking your independence and our own was scarcely a generation old. It was not just coincidence, I suspect, that your first Congress was inaugurated on the fourth of July. That was in 1811, the 35th anniversary of our own Declaration of Independence. Later, in 1812, the first draft of your provisional Constitution was written in the home of Joel Poinsett, United States Consular representative to Chile. In the battle which helped bring final victory, one of my countrymen was the Chief of Staff of Lord Cochrane.

These early associations helped forge lasting bonds of friendship. Their firm base is a shared philosophy—faith in God, respect for the spiritual dignity of man, and the conviction that government must be the servant of the people.

During the past twenty-four hours I have had friendly and helpful discussions with your distinguished President. I have gained new insight into your problems and the efforts you are making to achieve economic stability and growth which will mean a better life for all your people.

We all know that in today's inter-dependent world no nation can live unto itself, or be immune to developments in other lands.

We in the Western Hemisphere are still young nations, still growing, still experimenting.

How much easier would be the tasks of our own internal development and of helping nations sustain liberty, if the awesome threat of conflict and coercion could be eliminated from the minds and affairs of men.

The quest for peace is the imperative of our time. War has become preposterous. And maintaining armaments is consuming resources which, if constructively used, could bring forth a new era of benefit for all mankind.

As you know, I recently visited a number of the nations of Europe, the Middle East, South Asia and Africa. There I had an opportunity to convey to millions the wish dearest to the hearts of my own countrymen; a world of free men living in peace and friendship.

Soon, with my colleagues in Great Britain and France, I will meet with the Chairman of the Council of Ministers of the Soviet Union. It is in part to prepare for this meeting that I have sought the opportunity to confer with the leaders of some of the Latin American nations. All of us hope fervently that out of this and subsequent international meetings may come understandings which will permit at least a partial relaxation of tensions and a modest advance along the road of lasting peace.

We seek to promote universal acceptance of the rule of law. We are determined to do all in our power to help the United Nations become an ever more effective instrument for peace. We support the International Court of Justice.

Though the road to guaranteed peace is a long one, we in the Western Hemisphere may take satisfaction that we among ourselves have made encouraging progress along that road. By providing guarantees of national independence and integrity to our own nations, we have set a useful example for the world. The Organization of American States has provided our American family of nations a valuable mechanism for consultation and has made possible the evolution of political and juridical doctrines in international relations which are accepted by all our republics. The vitality of our Organization was recently demonstrated in the meeting of Foreign Ministers which took place here in Santiago. Under the able chairmanship of your distinguished Foreign Minister, the meeting agreed to the strengthening of the Inter-American Peace Committee, and it gave new emphasis to two basic concepts of the Inter-American system: nonintervention and representative democracy.

With a long history of successful consultation, fortified by solemn agreements and machinery for the peaceful settlement of disputes, it is logical that leaders throughout the hemisphere should now have a new concern regarding the burden of armaments on the economies of the American Republics. Hence the initiative of His Excellency President Alessandri in suggesting that the time is ripe to find effective means of reducing the burden of armaments in Latin America has been hailed as an act of statesmanship.

Working out the procedures for achieving limitation and assuring compliance will not be easy. The level of armaments which a nation feels it must maintain to assure the safety of its people involves a decision which the sovereign authority of that country must make for itself. In reaching its decision, each government will have to balance the minimum requirements for security against the drain on its resources.

While the technical steps will be difficult, multilateral agreement can be achieved if each nation of the hemisphere has confidence that it need not fear unprovoked aggression.

It is precisely such confidence that our Inter-American system should provide. The Rio Treaty of 1947 provides, and I quote from that document, "that an armed attack by any State against an American State shall be considered as an attack against all the American States and, consequently, each one of the said Contracting Parties undertakes to assist in meeting the attack."

My Government supports this solemn agreement. Should any American Republic be the victim of aggression, the United States is ready to fulfill its treaty obligations with strength, promptness, and firmness.

Bearing in mind the guarantees provided by the Rio Treaty, I assure you that my Government is prepared to cooperate in any practical steps that may be initiated by the Government of Chile or any of her neighbors to reduce expenditures on armaments.

As arms expenditures decline, funds will be released for more productive purposes. This will be at best a gradual process. In the meantime, Chile, like other growing countries, will need capital for economic development. Here and elsewhere, that capital must come primarily from within; from the encouragement of savings, which depends on confidence in economic and political stability, and their intelligent investment; from a just and equitable tax system, strictly enforced; and from incentives to more efficient production and distribution, including the incentive of competition.

Yet domestic capital, while of first importance, will not always be sufficient to meet demands in a period of rapid growth. Hence Chile, like other countries, looks abroad for capital. I am glad that lending institutions in the United States have been able to grant substantial credits to the Government of Chile.

In addition, considerable other credits and equity capital have flowed into various sectors of your economy. Thus, United States copper companies have in the past three years invested more than $125 million in new capacity—which means more earnings, more tax revenue, and more jobs. Investments are either being made or planned in fabricating plants to use the output of your great steel mill. I have been happy to learn that your national power company has received approval for a loan from the International Bank which will permit needed expansion of your power supply; and that this will be supplemented by the investment of substantial private United States capital to increase power capacity in the Santiago-Valparaiso area. All this is good, since it will make important contributions to the growth of your country.

And yet the demand for more capital, in South America as in other parts of the world, continues. It is for this reason that during the past year the Congress of the United States—despite our own difficult situation with respect to international balances—has increased the resources of the Export-Import Bank, has approved the doubling of our subscription to the capital of the World Bank and has joined with you and your neighbors in the formation of the Inter-American Development Bank.

As this Bank starts its career, under the presidency of a distinguished Chilean, it, together with the other institutions I have mentioned, should do much to meet the need for long term credits.

I must emphasize, however, that the competition for both public and private credit is severe. Some charge that private capital in the more developed countries is seeking every opportunity to pour into the less developed countries in order to engulf their economies.

Nothing could be more erroneous. Investment capital is limited. Competition for it is keen in the United States and in many other countries. It will flow only to those areas where it is actively sought, welcomed, and treated fairly. More and more it seeks the partnership of local capital and local experience.

I congratulate your President and all of you on your efforts to strengthen the economy and fiscal situation of your country. You will thus create confidence for investment, both domestic and foreign.

As I have said, the principal impetus for any nation's economic development must be its own will—its own dedicated effort. Then, financial and technical assistance from abroad can be extremely helpful. So, too, can increased cooperation between neighbors. Working together, nations can increase trade and reduce costs of production, to their mutual benefit. These developments will attract additional credit. Hence the United States is sympathetic to the progress being made by Chile and her neighbors to establish some form of common market.

The United States, as the largest common market in the world, could not but look with favor on the efforts of other free nations—in Europe, Latin America, or elsewhere—to enhance their prosperity through the reduction of barriers to trade and the maximum use of their resources. We feel that a common market must be designed not only to increase trade within the region but to raise the level of world trade generally.

Members of the Chilean Congress: in mentioning briefly this afternoon our quest for peace and friendship in freedom, our common concern for reducing the burden of armaments, the need for development capital, and the benefits that may be derived from common planning, I have merely touched on several elements involved in our hopes for a better world for the future. What we do, or fail to do, will have its maximum impact on the lives of our children and grandchildren. The future is the domain of youth. More than ever before, our young people, living in a world of inter-dependence and rapid communication, must possess technical competence. They must develop inter-cultural understanding, possess high spiritual values and integrity, be imbued with a passion for cooperation, and be devoted to building societies in freedom, that yield benefits to all. Only then will they be able to use effectively all of their material resources, including capital. Hence, we now have the obligation to expand educational opportunities in each of our countries and provide for the maximum exchanges of students, teachers, and others. We must provide an environment which convinces our youth that only in a democratic society can there be the intellectual freedom they cherish, that there is no short-cut to a richer life, and that the path they must follow will demand courage and a deep and abiding faith in humanity.

These are values which for generations have been held dear in Chile, as they have been in my country. I trust that our sons and daughters will in the future give them even deeper meaning. From my visit to Chile and her neighbors I shall take back renewed faith in the lofty aspirations of free people and renewed courage to face the tasks during the time which remains to me as President of my country.

From my heart I thank you for the honor you have done me in inviting me to be with you today and for the cordial welcome you have given me.

I thank you.

NOTE: In his opening words the President referred to Senator Hernan Videla, President of the Senate, and Deputy Raul Juliet, President of the Chamber of Deputies. Later he referred to Foreign Minister German Vergara, who served as chairman of the meeting of the Foreign Ministers in Santiago, August 12–18, 1959.

74 ¶ Remarks Upon Receiving a Medal Presented by Members of the National Congress of Chile. *March 1, 1960*

Mr. President and Members of this Congress:

I cannot remember when I have been more deeply touched by any gift or any award than the one which you just accorded to me. But I do assure you that I need no symbol or any memento to keep buried deep in my heart and mind the pleasures and the interests—and indeed the instruction—I have received here in Chile.

This visit will always be one of my cherished memories. To have this medal as a visible token of your affection is indeed something for which I thank you from the very bottom of my heart—not only on my own behalf, and of my associates, but indeed on behalf of all my countrymen.

Thank you.

NOTE: The medal was presented by Senator Videla immediately following the President's address to the Chilean Congress (Item 73). The inscription reads "Congreso Nacional de Chile—Dwight D. Eisenhower, 1 March 1960."

75 ¶ Toast to President Alessandri at a Dinner Given in His Honor by the President.
March 1, 1960

Your Excellency President Alessandri:

Your presence here this evening does honor to my country, and to me. It is good, for a few hours, to have you in this American home, and to extend our hospitality to you and your associates.

May I say, Mr. President, that in the short time I have been here I have seen all the ingredients of progress.

I was greatly encouraged to meet with large groups which are fostering Chilean-American understanding, for I deeply believe that genuine understanding is the foundation of all fruitful cooperation.

From you personally I have learned more about your efforts to establish economic stability, and to set in motion giant forces for the improvement of production and the living standards of your people.

Your cooperation in promoting a common regional market is highly encouraging, for it promises greater intraregional trade and, once realized will create conditions attractive to foreign development capital.

Your views on disarmament must command the attention and respect of every thoughtful citizen in the hemisphere. Certainly every enlightened leader should aspire to transferring production from sterile to constructive purposes.

And of special significance I think, I have sensed in all the people I have met a will to work—a faith in their ability to solve their problems in their own way—and in freedom.

Finally, I have been impressed by Chile's deep sense of responsibility toward other nations—not only the republics of this hemisphere, but the larger world.

Mr. President, in appreciation of your leadership of a free and proud nation, and with earnest thanks for the hospitality which you and your people have extended to us, I salute you, and ask all to join me in a Toast to you.

NOTE: The President proposed the toast at a dinner given at the residence of U.S. Ambassador Walter Howe in Santiago.

76 ❡ Joint Statement Following Discussions With President Alessandri of Chile.
March 1, 1960

THE PRESIDENTS of the United States of America and of Chile, Messrs. Dwight D. Eisenhower and Jorge Alessandri, on the occasion of the visit to Santiago of President Eisenhower, from February 29 to March 2, 1960, exchanged views on various matters of common interest:

The Presidents discussed the collaboration of Chile and the United States of America in international organizations with a view to the realization of the common principles which guide the foreign policies of both countries.

In particular they exchanged ideas regarding the principal affairs of the world situation and, moreover, concerning measures which would make possible the strengthening of the inter-American system in accordance with the Declaration of Santiago, which was unanimously approved at the Fifth Meeting of Consultation of Ministers of Foreign Affairs, held in August, 1959.

They reaffirmed the urgency of seeking solutions for the problems of economic development and of improving living standards in America. They likewise reiterated that the inter-American system should be based on respect for human rights, the effective exercise of democracy, and non-intervention in the internal affairs of other States.

Economic matters of common interest, particularly those of hemispheric scope comprehended in Operation Pan America, were also discussed. Similarly, special attention was given to the armaments problem in the continent and to Chile's initiative in proposing that the nations of the Americas give their urgent consideration to this matter, with the objective of reaching an appropriate equilibrium within a general policy of limitation on arms purchases.

The financing of economic development, both public and private, was also discussed, as was the formation of various regional trade zones, both in Europe and the Americas, and their possible effects on the economies of this hemisphere.

Finally, programs of cultural collaboration were reviewed, with emphasis on the importance of disseminating scientific and technical knowledge.

NOTE: This statement was released at Santiago, Chile.

The Declaration of Santiago is pub-lished in the Department of State Bulletin (vol. 41, p. 342).

77 ¶ Remarks at Los Cerrillos Airport in Santiago Upon Leaving for Uruguay.   *March 2, 1960*

Dr. Del Rio, ladies and gentlemen:

All too swiftly, the time has come for our departure from this magnificent land.   On behalf of the members of my party and myself, I thank all of you sincerely for the hospitality and kindness you have shown us.

We have been heartened by the friendly and informative discussions we have held with His Excellency President Alessandri and other leaders of your government.   I trust that they have found these conversations to be as helpful as we have.

As we prepare to embark, my mind goes back many years—to a time when both our countries were very young.   In those days many pioneers in my country journeyed to the Western United States by sea, around South America.   Thousands of them put into Chilean ports to rest from their arduous journey and to prepare for the northward part of their voyage.

Now, we could reach the capital of my country in a matter of hours— a journey which would have taken those pioneers many months.

Technology has indeed shrunk the world. Today all men are close neighbors.

Technology has given us the means of achieving a full life. But whether the possibility is realized is in the hands and minds of men.

Will men everywhere strive for the ideals of peace, freedom, and progress which our sturdy forefathers sought?

So far as Chile and the United States—and the nations of this hemisphere—are concerned, the answer is obviously a resounding "Yes!"

I leave with profound admiration for Chile's efforts for internal stability and progress, and for your noble work in the world community.

Goodbye—and thanks to all once again for your hospitality and friendship.

NOTE: The President's opening words referred to Dr. Sotero del Rio, Minister of the Interior and senior member of the Chilean Cabinet.

78 ¶ Remarks Upon Arrival at Carrasco Airport, Montevideo. *March* 2, 1960

Mr. President of the National Council of Government, ladies and gentlemen:

The friendly reception you have accorded my associates and me is especially gratifying, for to me it is indicative of the strong spiritual kinship between the governments and peoples of Uruguay and of the United States.

The fame of your democratic institutions has earned the applause of every American—school children and adults alike. We salute you, not only for your adherence to democratic principles in your own country, but also for your continuing contributions to hemispheric solidarity, to the Organization of American States, and to the United Nations. By deeds you have eloquently demonstrated your devotion to the concept of building a world characterized by peace, justice, and freedom.

I bring you this heartfelt message from all the people of my country: we treasure our partnership with you, and all our sister Republics in this hemisphere. We want this partnership to be a model of mutually helpful cooperation among sovereign states—some large, some small, but each equally contributing to the unity of purpose and effectiveness of the whole. How to make our partnership better shine as a beacon light to mankind will be the substance of my conversations with you, Mr. President, and with your associates in government.

I am delighted to be here, and look forward eagerly to meeting many of you during my short stay.

Thank you very much.

NOTE: The President spoke at 2:10 p.m. He was greeted by President Benito Nardone and the other members of the National Council of Government, Foreign Minister Homero Martinez, and U.S. Ambassador Robert F. Woodward.

79 ¶ Remarks Upon Receiving a Medal From the President of the Departmental Council of Montevideo.   *March 2, 1960*

Mr. President, Mr. Mayor, and members of the City Council of Montevideo:

It is indeed a very great honor that you do me to give me this medal as a symbol of the medal of honor of Montevideo.   It is indeed a unique occasion.

To stand here in the shadow of this obelisk, a memorial to constitutional government, in a country that worships—venerates the doctrines of Artigas, one of the great champions of liberty and freedom of all time, this is an occasion that warms the very depths of my heart.

I could only say that this medal, if ever earned at all, has been earned by the people of the United States, who with the people of Uruguay have been champions of freedom, have worked for freedom, have been ready to sacrifice for freedom.   And no stronger bonds could hold together two people more firmly.

So, sir, as I thank you, the citizens of Montevideo—as a matter of fact, all Uruguay—I do so as one who believes in exactly the same sentiments that you have just expressed concerning liberty, independence, and human dignity.

Thank you.

NOTE: The President spoke at the obelisk at approximately 3 p.m.   His opening words "Mr. President, Mr. Mayor" referred to President Nardone and Daniel Fernandez Crespo, President of the Departmental Council of Montevideo.

The medal, which was presented by Mr. Crespo, bears the inscription "Homenaje de Montevideo, El Concejo Departamental al Presidente Dwight Eisenhower."

80   ¶ Address Before a Joint Session of the National Congress of Uruguay.   *March 2, 1960*

Mr. President, distinguished members of the Congress, ladies and gentlemen, citizens of Uruguay:

Before I give to you my communications, the thoughts that I have wanted to say to you, I want to express something of my feelings concerning the welcome that has been given me by Montevideo—all the way along the beaches, through the streets with their majestic buildings, and by a people that seemed to be expressing the utmost in friendship.

My only regret is that every member in every dwelling in the farms and cities of my country could not have seen this day, because they would have realized that this people was trying to say "We are with you, in believing in freedom, in our dedication to liberty, and because we are so joined with you we send across these oceans to you from North America, our very best wishes."

I deem it a high honor to address you, the democratically elected representatives of the people of Uruguay.

I bring you from my people and my government earnest expressions of friendship and good will.

The United States shares with Uruguay an abiding desire to live in freedom, human dignity, and peace with justice.

The great wonder of history is that leaders—knowing that peoples everywhere, regardless of economic station, race, or creed, possess a burning desire to achieve these values—still have been unable to prevent the world from becoming tragically divided by mistrust, threat, and even overt hostility.

In our time, the destructive power available for misuse is awesome. We have now reached the point in human progress where the choice before us is mutual annihilation or abiding cooperation in the construction of the peace that lives as a cherished dream in the hearts of people everywhere.

At this fateful time, the people of the United States find themselves carrying unbelievably heavy burdens.   They do this not just in their own interest, but for the benefit of all who cherish freedom—all who believe that human affairs should be managed in harmony with basic moral law. They do this for all who are deeply convinced that peoples have the inalienable right to live in peace, with their creative energies devoted exclusively to building the social, cultural, and economic institutions consonant with their own desires.

My country makes these sacrifices with no avaricious end in view. The United States does not covet a single acre of land that belongs to another. We do not wish to control or dictate to another government. We do not desire to impose our concepts of political, cultural, or economic life upon either the largest or the smallest, the strongest or the weakest, of the nations of the earth. We believe that the people of every nation are endowed with the right of free choice, and that the most sacred obligation of the world community is to guarantee such choice to all.

Need I document these assertions? The Philippines today are independent—by their own choice. Alaska and Hawaii are now, proudly, equal partners in our federated, democratic enterprise—by their own choice. Puerto Rico is a Commonwealth within the United States system—by its own choice. After World War I, World War II, and the Korean War, the United States did not in any way enrich itself at another's expense—even from former enemies.

Indeed, it did the opposite. We offered substantive help to others, first for reconstruction, and then, because of thundering threats, for the creation of a cooperative defense system to protect the free world from deliberate attack or the miscalculation of arrogance.

I am aware of the feeling of many people in Latin America that the United States, while giving bounteously for postwar reconstruction and mutual security, has been less generous with our good neighbors of this hemisphere.

I am the first to acknowledge the fallibility of nations and leaders, even those with the best intentions. But I ask you and all our good friends of the Americas to consider this:

The aid we gave to Europe after the Great War helped restore that area as a producer and buyer, to the benefit of Latin America as well as to ourselves. During the war, the trade of Latin America with the United States increased six-fold, and has been sustained at a higher level since then.

The resources we have exported for the construction of a defense perimeter have been for the benefit of all who desire freedom, independence and the right to be unmolested as they work for the improved well-being of their own people.

These efforts have required our people to impose upon themselves the most burdensome levels of taxation in our national history.   They have caused us to forego doing as much as we otherwise would in some internal projects.   They have brought difficulties in our international financial affairs.   But—let me emphasize this—the assistance flowing to Latin America from the United States, in the form of private and public loans and technical aid, has been higher in recent years than ever before. Indeed I wonder if many realize the extent, both in mass and beneficial effect, of the capital going into Latin American enterprises from United States sources?   In the last fiscal year, for example, the private and public funds made available in Latin America from the United States and its companies approximated one billion dollars—and it is difficult to set a figure representing the subsidiary benefits brought about by the creation of new jobs, new markets, and new enterprises.

Yes, while we have known holocausts of anxiety, suffering, and great human tragedy three times in this century, we have not turned inward to indulge in self-pity.   We have willingly extended the hand of friendship and cooperation, and in this process we have attached no greater importance to solid, abiding partnerships with any area than we have with those of the American republics.

Of course we face vexatious problems requiring constant attention. We have them.   You do.

As for our bilateral problems, the record clearly reveals that they have been susceptible of solution when the healing balm of understanding has been applied.

I am keenly aware that all of Latin America—and Uruguay is no exception—is plagued by the fluctuation of raw commodity prices.   Latin America has need for industrialization, diversification, education, health facilities, and capital to speed development.

Progress in any nation is and must be largely the task of its own people, institutions, and leaders.   But the United States stands ready to help in any way it soundly can, within the framework of our world responsibilities and the limits of our resources.   Further, we work for the time—not distant I hope—when all the nations of the world in attaining greater prosperity will progressively share in programs of assistance to less developed countries.   Indeed, I would go further: I believe it is the duty of every nation, no matter how large or small, how weak or strong, to contribute to the well-being of the world community of free men.   For a time, perhaps some can supply only certain skills, or personnel, or spiritual support. The important consideration is that we should all accept a common sense of responsibility for our common destiny.

I am sure you hold the concept, as we do, that every human being, given an opportunity to do so, will make his contribution to the general welfare. You must feel, as we surely do, that hunger and privation must be eliminated from the earth by the cooperative effort of peoples and of governments of good will. We are certain, as you must be, that the cooperative effort of free working men and women, dedicated to and living under democratic principles, can out-produce the regimented working force of any nation suffering under dictatorial control.

Nations must constantly explore new opportunities to be helpful to one another. Who would have thought, a few years ago, that six nations of Europe would now be joined in a common effort to enlarge trade opportunities, to lower production costs, and thus to improve living standards? Or that seven other nations would develop a loose confederation for cooperation with those six? Yet these developments are under way. They can contribute to the growth of the free world, provided of course that both blocs operate with due regard for the interests of other countries.

Here in Montevideo last month, you were host to a meeting of the representatives of eight nations, at which was taken an important formal step toward the creation of a common market in which Uruguay would be a participant. You are dealing here with the possibility of widening each nation's markets in such a way that you increase the efficiency of many industries and thus greatly enhance the opportunity to obtain credits to hasten development. I congratulate you.

The beginning point of all cooperation—or between individuals, or between groups within a single society, or between nations—is genuine human understanding.

The conclusion, within the next few days, of a Fulbright Agreement between Uruguay and the United States for the exchange of students and professors is an important step in this direction.

Surely we of Uruguay and the United States should not fail in developing the knowledge about one another, and the abiding understanding, on which dependable cooperation can be based. I know you respect our democratic processes, our system of economic freedom, our adherence to those cardinal concepts of human dignity and consecrated intelligence which we draw from our religious philosophy.

Certainly we admire you. The people of Uruguay, like the people of the United States, came from many different places, but all were guided by passionate desires for freedom, justice, and opportunity. Under a great leader, José Artigas, you struggled for independence, even as we did under George Washington. And then you set to work.

We have watched the development of democratic institutions in Uruguay with unbounded admiration. We have been impressed with your individualism—with the development of the flaming spirit of liberty, justice, and self-discipline in the citizens of Uruguay. And we have applauded your successes as you have battled against human want, without sacrifice of human liberty.

It is no wonder that, in a world in which millions have been subjected to the philosophy and fetters of vicious tyranny, we feel a deep spiritual relationship to you.

We have worked well together in helping build the most influential regional organization on earth, the Organization of American States—in helping make the United Nations an instrument of true promise for international cooperation—and in seeking the solution to the problem of transcendent importance: peace, with justice, in freedom.

Controlled, universal disarmament is now imperative. The billions now living demand it. That we can make it our children's inheritance is our fondest hope.

The United States is deeply committed to a ceaseless search for genuine disarmament, with guarantees that remove suspicions and fears. Nearly seven years ago I said what I now re-pledge: the United States "is ready to ask its people to join with all nations in devoting a substantial percentage of its savings achieved by disarmament to a fund for world aid and reconstruction."

Members of the Congress: I profoundly thank you for the honor of meeting with you, for your generous hospitality and for the friendly greetings of the Uruguayan people whom you represent. May God favor you in your efforts to promote the interests of your people in freedom, and inspire you to still greater effort in our common struggle to achieve a world which lives in harmony under moral law.

NOTE: The President spoke at 6:05 p.m. at the Legislative Palace. His opening words "Mr. President" referred to Senator Juan Carlos Raffo Fravega, President of the General Assembly and of the Senate.

Toward the close of his address the President quoted from an address before the American Society of Newspaper Editors on April 16, 1953 (see 1953 volume, this series, p. 179).

81 ¶ Remarks Upon Receiving a Medal Presented by the President of the General Assembly. *March 2, 1960*

Mr. President:

I am most grateful for this medal. I have only one regret, that the message that I delivered to your Congress was not so eloquent as I could have wished in expressing the true affection that the United States has for Uruguay, and the feeling of brotherly comradeship with them that we always cherish.

Could I have put those thoughts in the proper words, they would have been more valuable. But I do thank you very much.

NOTE: The medal was presented to the President by Senator Raffo at a reception immediately following the President's address to the National Congress (Item 80). The inscription reads "El Poder Legistivo al Presidente Dwight Eisenhower, 2 March 1960—Republica Oriental del Uruguay."

82 ¶ Toast of the President at a Dinner Given in His Honor by President Nardone of Uruguay. *March 2, 1960*

Mr. President of the National Council of Government:

I deeply appreciate your gracious remarks. I interpret your words as an expression of the abiding friendship which happily exists between the peoples and governments of Uruguay and the United States.

My associates and I are grateful for this opportunity to be with you and Senora de Nardone, and this distinguished company of Uruguayans. We sincerely thank you for your hospitality, which has enabled us to know you better and to appreciate at firsthand the admirable, warm qualities of Uruguay's people and their leaders.

This has been a deeply moving experience—one that has stirred us profoundly, not only because of its warm human quality, but because we know that this expression of friendship is a recognition of our common love of liberty and justice, our common devotion to representative government, our common conviction that all men, in their sonship, are endowed with dignity and inalienable rights.

It was here in Montevideo, more than a quarter of a century ago, that the policy of nonintervention in the affairs of other nations was formalized and thus became a living reality. Our governments have, even in adversity, honorably, persistently, and consistently adhered to this policy. Our dedicated hope is that our example will be noted and emulated by all the nations of this earth.

Bearing in mind our shared ideals and purposes, Mr. President, I lift my glass to you and to the Uruguayan people while expressing the hope that we may find even more effective methods for cooperative progress toward peace, freedom, and ever-rising levels of human well-being.

NOTE: The President proposed the toast at the dinner given at the presidential residence in Montevideo.

83 ¶ Remarks to the Staff of the U.S. Embassy in Montevideo. *March* 3, 1960

MY FIRST COMMENT, my friends, is that this seems to be a very efficient embassy, because there are so few people compared to what I have run into in a good many places in the Far East and Mideast. The number seems to be kept down here, something that pleases my heart because I am quite sure that a lot of us make work for others.

I have just one little thought that may be worth while expressing: the very deep conviction that everybody in a foreign country from America is an ambassador. We have the head of a mission, and we call him Mr. Ambassador. But the more I have seen and known of foreign relations—and I've been in it for a good many years, because they started me off in the Philippines in 1935 after some training in Panama—I have come to the conclusion that America is judged by what each of us does, says, and how we act.

Now this is, in the mass, so terribly important that each individual is often very apt to forget it. And he says, "To hell with it, this is my life and I am going to live it as I please"—and so on. But when we undertake service, particularly in the United States Government, to a certain extent you have adopted a code, a code of conduct that demands the best you have—in spirit and intelligence and perseverance.

I think, therefore, that each person here and in every other embassy can feel they have a very great responsibility.

But they can feel more than that. They have a great opportunity, because there is nothing that's going to be so important to these youngsters right here in the front—and their youngsters—than going about the work of producing a peace. Nothing can be more difficult, nothing more important.

But if each of us can feel he has done a little bit, whether it's a President trying to meet a crowd and make them believe that the United States truly wants peace, or whether it's a secretary who's showing always the courtesy and the politeness that some visitor expects, or if it's merely a good "Good morning" from an American as they pass someone on the street—I think this is one of the great jobs we can do outside, you might say extracurricular, because I know you are all busy.

But the fact is, if we can't make progress along this line, I am rather pessimistic about this poor old world. But I don't think we have to be pessimistic. We can do our part and possibly we will get representatives of other countries to do theirs.

And there is another place, where I have started meeting with some of my friends that are influential in corporations, to get them to try to tell these same things to their representatives abroad. Because if all of our commercial friends coming out looking for business, if they do it in a way that shows their concern in the country they are visiting, as well as their own pocketbooks, I think we will make tremendous progress.

I didn't mean to come out here to say anything more than "Hello," but when I see what I believe to be the great opportunity that lies in the hands of this collective group, I can't fail to say we serve America best when we are doing our job for the world best.

So, good luck to you, and while I probably won't be this way again, until after I am free at least—and if I am, maybe I will come down here and be one of these tourists of whom I speak.

Thank you—and good luck.

NOTE: The President spoke at 8:15 a.m. from the rear portico of the U.S. Embassy residence.

84 ¶ The Declaration of Montevideo: Joint Declaration by the President and the National Council of Government of Uruguay.
March 3, 1960

THE NATIONAL COUNCIL of Government of the Oriental Republic of Uruguay and the President of the United States of America have agreed to make the following declaration defining the basic principles which, in each of their countries, govern the international relations of their respective peoples and inspire the ideal of freedom which binds them:

1. The sacred respect for human rights and dignity, the strengthening of their democratic institutions and the repudiation of all manner of anti-democratic actions or penetration;

2. The wide and growing acceptance of these same principles throughout the Americas in accordance with juridical standards freely accepted by the participating states, and, therefore, in strict compliance with the principles of nonintervention;

3. The most sincere and wholehearted support of institutions and organizations for international cooperation which promote both universally and regionally, in accordance with the rules of international law, the consolidation of peace, the strengthening of international security and the parallel economic, social and cultural development of the American nations, as well as the rest of the world.

4. Both countries will endeavor to increase their economic, social and cultural cooperation directly and through international organizations.

5. This declaration shall be known as the Declaration of Montevideo.

DWIGHT D. EISENHOWER
BENITO NARDONE

NOTE: The declaration was released at Montevideo.

85 ¶ Remarks at Carrasco Airport, Montevideo, Upon Leaving for Puerto Rico.　*March 3*, 1960

Mr. President, and people of Uruguay:

The warm hospitality which you, Mr. President, and your fellow citizens have shown to me and to my party has impressed itself indelibly on my mind. My deep personal faith in the goodness of people, in the sanctity of the human spirit, and in the burning desire of people for freedom to progress in their chosen way, has received here renewed strength. I am grateful to you for a memorable demonstration which will encourage and inspire me in the months to come.

My departure from your lovely country marks the end of my all-too-brief visit to this great southern area. Since duties at home would not permit me to visit all the nations of the hemisphere, I have hoped that this trip would be recognized throughout the continent as an expression of the deep respect and affection held by the people of the United States for all the people of Latin America. To all of them, if I may, I wish to say this:

The good neighbor and good partner policy is a firm, unswerving guide to all the actions of my Government which affect Latin America.

We adhere firmly to the policy of nonintervention.

We wish to see all the Americas progress together rapidly, in freedom.

We are ever ready to cooperate with you in fostering sound development.

We always stand ready to consult with our good neighbors on economic, political, social, and security problems, both on a bilateral and multilateral basis.

We reaffirm our pledge to help maintain the security of the Americas under the Rio Treaty, and to cooperate in achieving a realistic program of disarmament.

We declare our faith in a realm of law, our determination to abide by treaty and related international commitments, and our insistence that other nations do likewise.

We repudiate and condemn all efforts to undermine the democratic institutions of the hemisphere through coercion, subversion, or blatant lie.

We will do all in our power to spread the blessings of freedom in the hemisphere, and to work for a solidarity among free peoples.

And now, Mr. President, goodbye to you, to Senora de Nardone, to all your friendly citizens, and to the people of this majestic Southland.

86 ❡ Remarks at Dorado, Puerto Rico, at a Meeting of the American Assembly.
March 4, 1960

Governor Muñoz Marin, President Wriston, members of the Assembly, and fellow citizens of this hemisphere:

I should apologize, I think, before beginning this little talk, because I face a distinguished people who know a very great deal about the subject that I expect to talk about; and the other is that I have just learned, while sitting at the head table, that your report has been completed. And after I gave my conclusions, they said, "Well, it's identical," and I think they should have added, "Well, then, you don't have to give the speech"! But in the hope that there may be one or two points of some interest, I will indulge myself to take advantage of you for a few minutes.

When I first visited the proposed site for the American Assembly at Arden House 10 years ago, I could hardly have foreseen that in the year 1960 I should be addressing a regional meeting of the Assembly in Puerto Rico; or that I would come before you having just completed 2 journeys, totaling almost 40,000 miles, with visits to 15 countries on 4 continents.

But I assure you I am delighted to be with you here in a renewal of my personal association with the American Assembly. And I must confess to some pride that this meeting is a major expansion of what was for me little more than a dream 10 years ago.

You will permit me, I hope, a few minutes of reminiscence about my early thinking on the Assembly and my participation in its establishment.

Even before I went to Columbia as its President, out of some experience in war and in Washington I had come to feel very strongly that there was a need for a forum or council in which could be utilized the best minds of the Nation.

To do this, my associates and I believed we should attempt to set up specific problems of national interest, where in a proper setting the best academic and practical minds could be assembled for the necessary analyses. Their examination of each of these could take place in an atmosphere free from the pressures of partisan politics and special interests. Then, solutions might be suggested, founded in sound principle and wide knowledge, undistorted by pleas for the expedient and immediately popular.

We felt that many of the problems confronting the American people often were apparently impossible of solution, and hopelessly confused, because even the most critical question could easily become a political football or an excuse for sensationalism and even hysteria.

Matters affecting the future of the Republic, its world leadership and responsibilities deserved, we thought, the serious, deliberate, calm study their importance merited.

Shortly after my arrival at Columbia, I was invited by the present President of the American Assembly, my friend, Henry Wriston, to participate in the monthly deliberations of the Council on Foreign Relations. There in our discussions of various international concerns we tried, with the help of expert and specialized counsel, to suggest courses of action in the field of foreign relations that were designed directly for the correction, improvement, or clarification of the situation under study. Our proposals were formulated within the context of the enlightened self-interest of the United States of America. They were not reached under the influence of the politically palatable, the quick and easy, the supposedly popular.

The same quality of work on a much larger scale—the study of all problems affecting our people and the future of the Republic—could be ideally undertaken, I thought, at Columbia University. There we had available immense resources in the faculty and libraries and trained research people—a unique pool of human knowledge and written knowledge. By testing faculty proposals before groups of businessmen and leaders in all professions, we felt we would provide for such proposals a validity not otherwise likely to be had.

In 1949, with the trustees and my associates on the campus, we began work on this idea. By early 1950 we had a home for the American Assembly, at Arden House, given to the University by Governor Averell Harriman. I thought this venture so important that I wrote hundreds of letters and flew the length and breadth of this country time and again to raise the necessary money. It came in—often in generous amounts— and before I left for SHAPE in January of 1951 a healthy start for the American Assembly was assured.

As you know, the studies of the Assembly have been many and varied, ranging from our relations with Western Europe to wages, prices, profits and productivity. They have had a substantial impact on American thinking throughout Government and in the communities of our own country.

But even in the planning days, a decade ago, I felt that the Assembly's deliberations eventually should be concerned with the subject on which I expect to speak briefly today—the common destiny, the common interests, the common aspirations of the American Republics and Commonwealth members, Netherlands and French communities.

Our hemisphere, from the polar cap to the Antarctic ice, is a geographical unity. For the advantages of all its nations the hemispheres should be characterized by mutually-helpful economic cooperation. With proper respect to the sovereignty of its states and the cultural heritages of its peoples, there should be a mutual security unity and, in its philosophy of representative free government, complete political harmony. These purposes, it seems to me, indicate a need to exploit for the good of almost half a billion people of the Americas—and their numbers daily increase—the new mastery of space and natural resources, of science and machines.

If I have to apologize for my voice, I could do so by saying I left most of it in South America.

Ignorance of each other, misunderstanding of each other, lack of mutual and cooperative planning in our common purposes: these, I think, are the principal obstacles in our path. To do something toward their reduction was a principal purpose of the journey I have just finished.

Wherever I went, I stated again and again the basic principles and attitudes that govern our country's relationships in this hemisphere.

For example: our good neighbor—good partner policy is a permanent guide, encompassing nonintervention, mutual respect, and juridical equality of states.

We wish, for every American nation, a rapid economic progress with its blessings reaching all the people.

We are always eager to cooperate in fostering sound development within the limits of practical capabilities; further, we shall continue to urge every nation to join in help to the less fortunate.

We declare our faith in the rule of law, our determination to abide by treaty commitments, and our insistence that other nations do likewise.

Everywhere I found in the nations I visited a general agreement that these principles have been actually practiced by the United States. I found, too, inescapable evidence that many in every country knew little of our record and more who misunderstand our purposes. But identically the same can be said of North Americans in their ignorance and misunderstanding of Latin America.

Here the American Assembly can play a tremendous and useful role. Its participants are recognized everywhere for their experience in human affairs, their broad knowledge, their professional competence—and above all their good will and their dedication to truth. Particularly to the young people, those who will manage the affairs of this hemisphere in a few years, the members of the Assembly can be honest teachers and wise counsellors.

And the problems that confront us are immense. Many countries of Latin America desperately need long-term financing of their development projects; technical assistance in their planning and execution; escape from dependence on one crop or one mineral; help in balancing budgets and substituting productive work for bureaucratic make-work; an end to inflation and a start on solidly, widely based economics. And their needs must be answered soon and effectively.

Panacea proposals, facile solutions, will lead only to disillusionment.

Above all, any thought of the United States alone developing a so-called master plan for the raising of living standards throughout the hemisphere has been rejected by us and by the leaders of the states I have just visited, including Surinam, and is foredoomed to failure.

Each nation of Latin America is highly individual. Each must analyze its own human and material resources, and develop a program of action, with priorities assigned. Then, national and international credit agencies should stand ready to be of assistance in making the program a reality. Obviously the major responsibility for a nation's development devolves upon its own people, its own leaders; its own pride, its own self-respect, its own self-interest demand that this be so. And, parenthetically, may I say I saw many evidences of this on the trip I have just completed. I visited what was nothing but a rural slum outside of Santiago—thousands of people living in hovels, whose poverty beggared description. But the government gave them a start. The government owned the ground of the area and then it laid out plots, and it built concrete floors.

On each of these floors were two families, in the center where the normal washroom and toilet facilities were. Then, they've got a new system of construction, one I had never seen, and yet may be a very practical thing in many countries. It is the making of bricks out of wood, and these bricks instead of being put together by cement, they have very heavy glue, and then they are nailed down to the block below—each block is about a foot long and about four inches square in cross-section.

Now the point is that all the rest of the work is done by self-help. Before work in the morning, after work in the evening, these families do this. The particular project I visited, I believe there were 4,102 cottages, of which about 600 have been developed in the weeks so far past, and they are going to have it finished before snow flies—before winter comes.

Now here is the point: never have I seen such a happy people, because they were doing this themselves, in crowds—and crowded around—workman after workman coming running to me, would I autograph one of the blocks that was going in his house? He wanted to show this as a show piece to his—even to his grandchildren, I suppose. And all he needed is a plumb bob, because once you get the walls straight, it seems like they are very, very strong. The inventor is convinced that he has hold of a very good idea, and these people are showing what self-respect and pride can be developed out of your ability to do something yourself, with a little bit of help—a helping hand from someone outside.

I assure you I think that the government is reaping great benefits, not only for the individuals thus helped, but for what it means in understanding on the part of all these people of its own government.

But nations which desire to advance rapidly surely do need public and private funds from abroad. And funds are available. First there is private capital always seeking good investment opportunity. The International Bank and the Export-Import Bank have had their funds greatly increased, and the new Inter-American Bank will soon be functioning. And behind all these is the instant readiness of the United States, on a government-to-government basis, to investigate cooperatively any special problem or need, and to make such arrangements as seem to fill the requirements.

As I said a few days ago to the Uruguayan Congress:

"We work for the time—not distant, I hope—when all the nations of the world in attaining greater prosperity will progressively share in programs of assistance to less developed countries. Indeed I would go further: I believe it is the duty of every nation, no matter how large or small, how weak or strong, how rich or poor, to contribute to the well-being of the world's community of free men. For a time, perhaps some can supply only certain skills, or knowledge, or personnel, or spiritual support. But all these are important too. And the most important consideration is that we should all accept a common sense of responsibility for our common destiny."

Only hard thinking and hard work will do the job. And they must be accompanied by a most determined drive to eliminate ignorance and to correct misunderstanding.

Here the American Assembly can help greatly. The need for your help is, I think, the greatest challenge to confront you since the founding of the Assembly 10 years ago.

So I congratulate the American Assembly for its venture into this whole area of study which is so profoundly important to the millions who inhabit this hemisphere—indeed, to all the free world.

Thank you very much.

NOTE: The President spoke at a luncheon meeting at the Dorado Beach Hotel. In his opening words he referred to Governor Luis Muñoz Marin and Dr. Henry Wriston, President of the American Assembly.

The report of the 16th American Assembly, to which the President referred in the opening paragraph, is published in "The United States and Latin America" (Columbia University Press, 1959).

87 ¶ Radio and Television Report to the American People on the South American Trip. *March 8,* 1960

[Delivered from the President's Office at 7 p.m.]

Good evening, friends:

My first words upon my return from the four American republics I have just visited must be a heartfelt expression of gratitude for the friendly receptions my associates and I experienced, wherever we went.

Millions endured for long hours along the streets the hot summer sun—and occasionally rain—to let us know of the enthusiastic good will they have for the government and people of the United States. In the nations of Latin America—indeed as I have found in all of the eighteen countries I have visited in my trips of recent months—there is a vast reservoir of respect, admiration and affection for the United States of

America. The expressions of this attitude by Latin American peoples and their leaders were so enthusiastic and so often repeated as to admit no possibility of mistake. Two or three insignificant exceptions to this may have made a headline, but they were only minor incidents, lost in the massed welcome.

This was a good will trip—but it was also much more. Members of my party and I held serious conversations and exchanged information on bilateral, hemispheric, and global problems with the four Heads of State, with Cabinet members, with leaders of labor, education, finance, and business.

Two impressions are highlighted in my mind.

First—Brazil, Argentina, Chile and Uruguay treasure as much as we do freedom, human dignity, equality, and peace with justice. In freedom, they are determined to progress—to improve and diversify their economies—to provide better housing and education—to work ceaselessly for rising levels of human well being.

Second, while certain problems are continental in scope, nonetheless each of the countries I visited—indeed, each of the twenty republics of Latin America—is highly individual. Each has its own unique problems and ideas regarding future development.

Hence, our cooperation with each republic must be tailored to its particular situation.

I was gratified to learn that, as the indispensable basis for their self-improvement, comprehensive surveys of resources, capacities, objectives, and costs have progressed rapidly in recent years. But each nation feels it must do more in this regard, and seeks help for this purpose. The United Nations has funds for such pre-development studies. The new Inter-American Bank also should be able to lend technical help. The studies of each country called for under "Operation Pan America" will likewise contribute to this end.

Once sound planning has made significant progress, a nation can formulate specific projects for action, with priorities established, and with confidence that each development will open still further opportunity to speed the spiral of growth.

The execution of any development program will of course depend primarily upon the dedicated efforts of the peoples themselves.

I was impressed, for example, by what I saw in Chile. I visited a low-cost housing project. The government had provided land and utilities. The home owners were helping one another build the new houses. They will pay for them monthly, over a period of years. Personal accomplishments brought pride to their eyes; self-reliance to their bearing! Their new homes are modest in size and character—but I cannot possibly describe the intense satisfaction they take in the knowledge that they themselves have brought about this great forward step in their living conditions.

In Argentina and Uruguay I witnessed encouraging sights—men building schools, homes, and roads—and, in Brazil, erecting a wholly new capital city.

The people of Latin America know that poverty, ignorance, and ill-health are not inevitable. They are determined to have their resources and labors yield a better life for themselves and for their children.

I assured them that most earnestly we of the United States want them to succeed. We realize that to speed improvement they need foreign capital. They want sound loans, public and private. Their repayment record on loans previously made is noteworthy.

International and United States lending agencies have recently had their funds greatly increased. The new Inter-American Development Bank will soon be functioning. I believe that each nation which has produced a well-conceived development program will find that these lending institutions will respond to their needs. Should this not be so in a particular situation, we of the United States would want to know the circumstances and do what we could to help to rectify the difficulty.

In our discussions I stressed that all nations—large or small, powerful or weak—should assume some responsibility for the advancement of humankind, in freedom. Though we of the United States will, within the framework of our world situation and economic capacity, assist all we can, we look for the time when all the free nations will feel a common responsibility for our common destiny. Cooperation among free nations is the key to common progress. Aid from one to another, if on a one way street basis only, and indefinitely continued, is not of itself truly productive.

The peoples of Latin America appreciate that our assistance in recent years has reached new heights, and that this has required sacrifice on our part.

I must repeat, however, what I said several times during my trip: serious misunderstandings of the United States do exist in Latin America.

And, indeed, we are not as well informed of them as we should be.

Many persons do not realize the United States is just as committed as are the other republics to the principles of the Rio Treaty of 1947. This Treaty declares that an attack on one American republic will in effect be an attack on all. We stand firmly by this commitment. This mutual security system, proved by time, should now enable some of the American republics to reduce expenditures for armaments, and thus make funds available for constructive purposes.

One editorial alleged that the United States did not accept the principle of nonintervention until 1959. In fact, our country has consistently abided by this hemispheric concept for more than a quarter of a century.

Another persistent misunderstanding which I sought to correct wherever I travelled is that we sometimes support dictators. Of course we abhor all tyrannical forms of government, whether of the left or of the right. This I made clear.

In Brazil, I explained another important item of our policy: we believe in the rights of people to choose their own form of government, to build their own institutions, to abide by their own philosophy. But if a tyrannical form of government were imposed upon any of the Americas from outside or with outside support—by force, threat, or subversion—we would certainly deem this to be a violation of the principle of nonintervention and would expect the Organization of American States, acting under pertinent solemn commitments, to take appropriate collective action.

On occasion I heard it said that economic advance in some American republics only makes the rich richer, and the poor poorer, and that the United States should take the initiative in correcting this evil. This is a view fomented by communists, but often repeated by well-meaning people.

If there should be any truth in this charge whatsoever, it is not the fault of the United States. So far as our purpose is involved, projects financed by our institutions are expected to yield widespread benefits to all, and, at the same time to conform to our policy of nonintervention. I know that the Latin American leaders I met also seek this same result.

Moreover, when internal social reform is required, it is purely an internal matter.

One of the most far-reaching problems of continental scope is this: in their exports, the Latin American republics are largely single commodity countries. The world market prices of what they sell fluctuate widely, whereas the prices of things they buy keep going up.

We have tried to be helpful in the cooperative study of this vexing situation. Many facts about supply, demand, production are widely comprehended for the first time. Thus, for example, with the facts about coffee understood, producing nations are cooperating in orderly marketing for this commodity with beneficial results.

The real solution is in agricultural and industrial diversification. Here, we are encouraged by the progress being made toward the creation of common markets. Large areas, relatively free of trade restrictions, will make for greater efficiency in production and distribution, and will attract new capital to speed development.

Despite such problems as these, our relationships with our sister republics have, with notable—but very few—exceptions, reached an all-time high. Leaders and populations alike attested to this truth. But an even firmer partnership must be our goal.

The republics of this hemisphere have a special relationship to one another. The United States is important to all of Latin America, as its largest buyer, as the main source of foreign investment capital, and as a bastion of freedom. Our southern neighbors are important to us, economically, politically, culturally, militarily. Indeed, no other area of the world is of more vital significance to our own future.

This interdependence must be comprehended by us, and by them. Each should know the policies, attitudes, aspirations, and capacities of the other. For, as I have said time and again, all fruitful, abiding cooperation must be based upon genuine mutual understanding of vital facts.

Exchanges of students, teachers, labor leaders, and others are helpful. Newspapers, magazines, all means of communication should accept the responsibility not merely of transmitting spectacular news, but of helping build the knowledge on which cooperative action may flourish.

In one respect our neighbors put us to shame. English is rapidly spreading as the second language in Latin America. Business executives, labor leaders, taxi drivers—most speak English well, learned in school or in bi-national institutes. The study of Spanish is increasing in our schools, but I wish that literally millions of Americans would learn to speak Spanish or Portuguese fluently, and to read the literature, histories, and periodicals of our sister republics.

H. G. Wells once said that civilization is a race between education and catastrophe. His thought is applicable to hemispheric relations. With common dedication to the highest ideals of mankind, including shared aspirations for a world at peace, freedom and progress, there is no insurmountable impediment to fruitful cooperation, save only insufficiency in mutual understanding. This is something that you and I—every single citizen, simply by informing himself—can do something about.

I hope each of us will do so.

Again, I express my gratitude to President Kubitschek, President Frondizi, President Alessandri, and President Nardone and all their peoples for providing me with a most instructive and rewarding experience.

And I convey to you their best wishes and warm greetings.

Thank you, and good night.

88 ¶ Remarks at a Dinner Given by the Indiana State Society in Honor of Minority Leader Charles A. Halleck. *March 10, 1960*

Mr. Halleck, Mr. Sam, distinguished guests, ladies and gentlemen:

I am just sort of a wanderer that dropped in on this party.

First of all, I am not from Indiana. Actually I was born in the district of my friend here, Mr. Sam. And all of these years he has allowed me to call myself his vicarious constituent to this moment.

I understand that about two-thirds of Indiana is here—the other third is probably snowbound.

As I understand it, they call today "Charlie Halleck Day," because he is Indiana's Man of the Year. I would like to say that for me, during a session at least, every day is "Charlie Halleck Day."

He once pleased me mightily. He said: "Mr. President, this is going to cost me a lot of votes, but I'll do it." That kind of loyalty to a leader of the party and to an administration is priceless. I know it. Everybody in the executive department knows it.

Indeed, I think that some of my very distinguished members of the opposition, of whom the chief one is here, knows it too. For that reason he not only has a great affection for Charlie but he respects him mightily.

A political party should stand for something. If the issues of our country are to be debated intelligently and properly, it is only proper that Americans just as good as we are should have political views that do not coincide with our own. That's why we have two major parties.

Among them both Charlie and I claim many, many friends—personal friends—no matter how much we may battle them in those factors and those subjects which are properly partisan or political.

I think it is only proper that I should say on Charlie's behalf—and my own—when it comes to matters that extend beyond the water's edge, we have had the cooperation and we have sought the cooperation of the opposition, which I think has been most effective for our country.

So as I come here not to praise Charlie, because he doesn't need it, but merely to recognize what he has done, and to be one of you in sharing a great privilege of saying, "Thank you, Mr. Halleck," I think it's a very good thing for us to realize that the politics in Washington should be—and I think most frequently is—a means by which we promote the welfare of America, not merely to satisfy the ambitions of any particular individual or any particular party, much as all of us are partisans.

I leave you with this thought: Charlie is doing a job not just for Republicans but above all and first of all for the United States of America. I am quite sure that my first Congressman would join with me in that tribute to this very topflight, fighting, tough little Hoosier.

God bless you, Charlie—and goodbye.

NOTE: The President spoke at the Shera-ton-Park Hotel in Washington. In his opening words "Mr. Sam" referred to the Honorable Sam Rayburn, Speaker of the House of Representatives.

89 ¶ Special Message to the Congress on Increasing the Postal Rates. *March* 11, 1960

To the Congress of the United States:

In the Budget Message I urged the enactment of legislation to increase postal rates in order to eliminate the postal deficit. Several facts indicate the urgency of such action by the Congress.

The Postal Policy Act of 1958 definitely states that postal rates and fees shall be adjusted from time to time as may be required to produce the amount of revenue approximately equal to the total cost of operating the postal establishment, less the amount attributable to the performance of public services. That Act directed the Postmaster General to submit to the Senate and House of Representatives no later than April 15th of this year the results of his survey of the need for the adjustment of postal rates and fees in accordance with this policy.

Because of the existing inadequate postal rates, the Post Office Department is losing $2 million every working day. In the thirteen years from July, 1946 to June, 1959 the postal deficits have been approximately as much as the entire cost of running the Federal government in 1938. The cumulative $6.8 billion postal deficit for these 13 years represents nearly one-half of the total increase in the Federal debt during this same thirteen year period. Interest charges alone on the debt represented by this cumulative deficit are costing our taxpayers some $200 million each year.

These huge postal deficits are phenomena of the years since World War II. In the years from 1900 to 1940 the losses of the Post Office Department averaged only $33 million a year. Since that time—excluding the war years—these losses have increased astronomically. The tremendous losses incurred since World War II have been due to the increases in cost of everything the Department uses or buys, and to the failure of the Congress to enact postal rate increases to pay for the added costs. For example, since the increase in the first-class letter rate in 1932 from 2 cents to 3 cents, costs have more than doubled, but the first-class letter rate has been increased only one-third. The annual losses on 2nd and 3rd class mail, now in the hundreds of millions of dollars, are likewise growing.

It is imperative that Congress implement the policy it wisely established in 1958 of providing that the Post Office Department shall operate on a self-supporting basis. The Postmaster General is transmitting to the Congress the Administration proposals for increases in postage rates on first, second, and third class mail to yield an estimated $550 million of new postal revenues in the 1961 fiscal year. Responsibility in the handling of our public affairs demands prompt action, in this session, to restore the Post Office Department to its traditional posture of budgetary good sense.

DWIGHT D. EISENHOWER

90   ¶ Letter to Frederick M. Eaton, U.S. Representative to the Ten-Nation Disarmament Conference in Geneva.   *March* 12, 1960

[Released March 12, 1960. Dated March 11, 1960]

Dear Ambassador Eaton:

The ten nations which will begin disarmament discussions at Geneva on March 15, 1960, have both the opportunity and a great responsibility to serve mankind. The interest of the United States in disarmament and my own strong personal feelings on this subject are well known. I want to take this opportunity to emphasize that the United States is prepared to explore every possible avenue to find a way toward general disarmament.

We must not be pessimistic because of the lack of success in past disarmament negotiations. Nor should we necessarily expect immediate, dramatic and far-reaching strides, although we would certainly welcome such progress. Rather, it should be our objective in these negotiations to contribute by carefully balanced, phased and safeguarded arms control agreements to the ultimate objective of a secure, free and peaceful world in which international disputes will be settled in accordance with the principles of the United Nations Charter.

As the United States Representative to the Ten-Nation Disarmament Conference, I know that you will exert every possible effort to reach agreement on measures which will lessen the danger of another armed conflict, ease the burden of armaments and thereby contribute to the attainment of the ultimate goal of general disarmament and a peaceful world. I should like you to convey to the other delegates at the Ten-Nation Disarmament Conference my earnest hope that the Conference will discharge its solemn obligation to mankind and thus contribute to this goal.

You may be assured that you carry with you my complete support and that of the people of the United States.

Sincerely,

DWIGHT D. EISENHOWER

91 ¶ Toasts of the President and Chancellor Adenauer of Germany. *March* 15, 1960

Mr. Chancellor and gentlemen:

Mr. Chancellor, in your time you have heard many brilliant toasts, you have been paid many well-deserved and very enthusiastic compliments.   In the tradition of American directness and simplicity, I want to say to you merely, "Welcome"—that this country, this capital city, this company at this table, extends to you a truly warm welcome.

We have respected the work that you have done in the rehabilitation of Germany and in leading it along the path of democracy.   We believe that under your leadership your nation and ours have grown in understanding and in friendship far beyond anything that has been their privilege to experience before you came to your high office.

Being an advocate of better understanding among people, I have had to apologize more than once about my inability to speak another language. The Germans found this out very well.   I was once told by Germans: "Apparently you know only one single German word and that is your own name."

Unfortunately, Mr. Chancellor, there are too many citizens in this country, bearing names just as Germanic as mine, who have the same difficulty.   But that doesn't mean that we are complacent, lazy, or lacking in energy in our seeking to establish with your country greater, better understanding, and better cooperation in the many programs that lie before us in common.

In order to pay a symbolic compliment to your people, and to your great leadership of those people, I am going to ask this company to join me in a Toast to your country, to President Luebke of the Federal Republic of Germany—the President!

NOTE: The President proposed the toast at a luncheon at the White House at 1 p.m.   Chancellor Adenauer responded (through an interpreter) as follows:

Mr. President and gentlemen:

You, Mr. President, have extended to us Germans here such cordial words, and given us such a great and warm reception—you have spoken to us with such warmth and frankness that I can only say

that this is symbolic of the relations existing between our two nations.

I remember my first visit to the United States of America back in 1953.   I was particularly impressed by the fine ceremony at Arlington Cemetery.   That was a deep and unforgettable impression.   I thought of my first visit to the Arlington Cemetery this morning when I paid a visit to the grave of the late Secretary Dulles.   In 1953 I had my first talk with you in the capacity as President of the United States of America, and I remember the conversation of ours of that time as if it had taken place only yesterday.

I was also impressed soon after I met you again, both here and in Bonn. I remember our first meeting was at Weisbaden, I think, when you were still Supreme Commander of SHAPE, in the residence of our friend, Mr. McCloy.

In the first speech and conversation I had with you as President of the United States of America, you spoke with refreshing and convincing frankness. At that time you also spoke about the problem of controlling disarmament—general disarmament.

Please, Mr. President and gentlemen, be convinced that after the defeat we had suffered, we were all the more grateful for the helpful hand that was extended

to us—to the German nation—by the Americans.

And I would also like to say, Mr. President, this morning when I left your office, I happened to meet in one of the offices here in the White House, the widow of General Marshall. I was deeply moved to meet Mrs. Marshall because we owe General Marshall a great debt of gratitude as the father of the Marshall Plan.

Relations have developed—personal relations—between our two countries which are not only guided by reason, but considerations of logic. But what is more important also is the great element which represents the mind and the heart. That in my opinion seems to be very significant.

[Then the Chancellor raised his glass and proposed a toast to a prosperous future of the United States of America, and to the health of the President.]

92 ¶ Joint Statement Following Discussions With Chancellor Adenauer. *March 15, 1960*

THE PRESIDENT and the Chancellor have had a pleasant and fruitful exchange of views on a number of subjects of mutual interest. Secretary of State Herter and German Foreign Minister von Brentano also participated in the conversation.

The talks were completely informal in nature and did not involve negotiations of any type. The participants believe that the exchange of views which occurred has resulted in a further coordination of the positions of the two Governments on a number of common problems.

Among the subjects touched upon in the course of the conversation were the current disarmament discussions in Geneva, East-West relations in general, the problem of Germany including Berlin, and European economic integration.

The President and the Chancellor reaffirmed their determination to continue their efforts to achieve the reunification of Germany in peace and freedom. They further agreed that the preservation of the freedom of the people of West Berlin, and their right of self-determination, must underlie any future agreement affecting the city.

The Chancellor and the President discussed the general situation with regard to European economic integration. The President reiterated the support of the United States Government for the goals of the European Communities, and for a strengthening of Atlantic economic cooperation. They welcomed the prospect that the United States and Canada would soon join more closely with the European countries in a reconstituted Organization for European Economic Cooperation. In this connection, they discussed the recent trade proposals of the European Economic Commission. They noted that, should proposals along these lines be adopted, the result would be a major contribution to a general lowering of world trade barriers.

93 ¶ The President's News Conference of *March* 16, 1960

THE PRESIDENT. I'm ready for questions.

Q. Merriman Smith, United Press International: Mr. President, for the benefit of some of us who were not present at a dinner you attended Saturday night—[*laughter*]—we understand that you made some remarks that were regarded as quite politically significant concerning the Vice President, and we wonder, sir, if you can reconstruct those remarks for us today?

THE PRESIDENT. First of all, I believe at this meeting, it says, no reporters are ever present. I'm certain that no guest would be guilty of talking about something in the public domain that should have been in the social domain.

But as long as it's out by some mysterious way, I don't mind clarifying what I had to say, or at least what I thought; what I had to say could not possibly be reconstructed because I was talking about the geographical areas in which certain people were sitting at a party.

But if anyone is wondering whether I have any personal preference or even bias with respect to this upcoming presidential race, the answer is yes, very definitely. [*Laughter*]

Q. Edward T. Folliard, Washington Post: Mr. President, you have indicated in one way or another that you hope to do something in the campaign insofar as your duties will permit. It's been suggested that you might make a keynote speech at the Republican Convention. Is that likely?

THE PRESIDENT. Well, I don't know. I haven't been invited. But I say this: I would want to give such support as I could. I think there are certain limits, for the simple reason that no candidate wants it to appear that he has someone that is the authority that has helped to nominate him and to put him in his position of prominence that he would now occupy. So I think there has to be very good judgment exercised. But if I am asked to give some help, why, I'd certainly want to try to do it.

Q. Mr. Folliard: Did you say, sir, that you have been invited to make the keynote speech?

THE PRESIDENT. No, I said I have not been invited—not invited.

Q. Edward P. Morgan, American Broadcasting Company: On the record, Mr. President, you have frequently spoken out, emphasized the importance of what you sometimes describe as human value, including moral courage. I wonder if you consider the current Gandhi-like passive resistance demonstrations of Negroes in the South as worthy of identification as manifestations of moral courage, or whether you disapprove of them?

THE PRESIDENT. It's difficult, Mr. Morgan, to give a sweeping judgment. Some are unquestionably a proper expression of a conviction of the group which is making them; others probably can be otherwise classified.

Now, let me make one thing clear. I am deeply sympathetic with the efforts of any group to enjoy the rights, the rights of equality that they are guaranteed by the Constitution. I do not believe that violence in any form furthers that aspiration, and I deplore any violence that is exercised to prevent them—in having and enjoying those rights. So, while I don't want to make any judgment because I am not in position to—I know about these as they come just briefly to my attention, I do not know what all of them are—I do know, though, that if a person is expressing such an aspiration as this in a perfectly legal way, then I don't see any reason why he should not do it.

Q. Charles H. Mohr, Time Magazine: Mr. President, in an earlier answer you suggested it might be a disadvantage to a candidate to have it thought that he had a patron. Do you think that it might also be a disadvantage to a candidate to have another powerful figure speaking out on the same issue but perhaps not in perfect coordination, and in such a case would you plan to broadly coordinate your position on policies and programs with the Republican nominee?

THE PRESIDENT. Well, if I happen to have any difference with him I would certainly not publicize it.

Now, so far as I know, there has never been between Mr. Nixon and myself, and that's who you are talking about—*[laughter]*—so far as I know, there has never been a specific difference in our points of view on any important problem in 7 years.

There has been free discussion in every meeting that I have ever held, and he has certainly been, always, not only free but even requested to give his honest opinions on these things. In certain details or points there naturally are differences that I have with everybody, because I seem to have a genius for that.

But I do say this: there has been never an important division of opinion or conviction. Therefore, if I were wanted in this field, in a perfectly proper and restricted activity, I would not feel the need to go down through every word of what I had to say with anybody, including Mr. Nixon himself.

Q. Felix Belair, New York Times: You have been represented, sir, as supporting the candidacy for Governor of Puerto Rico of Mr. Luis Ferré, whom you gave a ride to Washington, I think, from Ramey. If that is so, does it include his sponsorship of statehood for the Island?

THE PRESIDENT. No. I have talked to Mr. Ferré one time; that was when I got the opportunity. When he said he was coming to Washington, I said, "Come with me; I want to hear what you are talking about." He is a Republican candidate, I understand. I believe that he is not in any primary struggle or anything of that kind.

Now, he told me about his views. I said these are things that have not been the subject of party policy in the United States, so far as I understand; until they are brought up before that party and studied, well, I have not yet come to any conviction that I would want to express.

Q. Mr. Belair: Do you support his candidacy, is what I wondered. I mean aside from statehood?

THE PRESIDENT. I assume that like all other good Republicans, if I could vote there, I would vote Republican.

Q. William H. Y. Knighton, Jr., Baltimore Sun: Mr. President, in answer to Mr. Smith's question, you used the word "bias." Were you also speaking there of Mr. Nixon?

THE PRESIDENT. Was there any doubt in your mind?

Q. Mr. Knighton: No, sir. *[Laughter]*

Q. John Scali, Associated Press: A West German newspaper reported today that Premier Khrushchev in his latest letter to you has promised not to stir up any trouble between now and the next election. Could you tell us whether this is true, and could you discuss with us in general terms the letter that you got from the Soviet Premier?

THE PRESIDENT. First of all, I have made it clear I will not reveal the tenor and details of messages that pass back and forth between me and any other head of state or head of government unless there is some kind of agreement that this should be done, or because someone else has either deliberately or inadvertently exposed the correspondence; then, I would have to.

I can merely say this: the detail of which you speak had nothing whatsoever to do with the latest correspondence between Mr. Khrushchev and me.

Q. Sarah McClendon, El Paso Times: Sir, back to these racial problems in the South, you said they come to your desk briefly. Do we not feel that this situation is of so grave injustice on both sides that it requires your great attention? Could you not call a conference at the White House of Southern leaders to sit down and go over this thing and come to some constructive program about what could be done?

THE PRESIDENT. Do you know what I think? I think there ought to be biracial conferences in every city and every community of the South, which would be much better than trying to get up here and direct every single thing from Washington. I am one of those people that believes there is too much interference in our private affairs and, you might say, personal lives already. And I would like to diminish rather than increase it.

Now, when it comes to the matter of enforcing the Constitution, which is a different thing from having some kind of orderly or even disorderly activity that is involved in the matter of racial equality—that is a different thing than the United States trying to enforce the Constitution, because one is a local matter for local authorities; the other is something with which the United States must be concerned. That is why we are trying to get a civil rights bill through the Congress.

So, you must not in your thinking take a local incident, whether it be a protest meeting or a march through the streets or anything else; that is not in the same category as getting the voting rights of a Negro in the South protected and insured. That's entirely two different subjects.

Q. Lowell K. Bridwell, Scripps-Howard Newspapers: Mr. President, late last summer when you signed the legislation increasing the motor fuel tax one cent a gallon, I believe you requested General Bragdon to make a comprehensive survey of the highway program, particularly as it related to the interstate system. Can you tell us what were the principal findings of that survey and whether you have made any administrative changes as a result?

THE PRESIDENT. No, I couldn't say too much to you about it this morning because, first of all, it was a personal advisory thing to me. In other words, should I recommend to the Congress any differences or should there be any administrative changes within the present law, as to what we should do.

What I was really trying to find out from General Bragdon is, what are we doing and does it seem to accord with the law and the legislative history.

I have not had any thought of putting this out, because it's a matter between General Bragdon and myself.

Q. Spencer Davis, Associated Press: Mr. President, the United States has fought to preserve democracy in Korea, a country in which we express great concern. Do you have any comment on the election which they have just completed there, and is there a possibility that you may visit the country in June?

THE PRESIDENT. Well, no plans with respect to a visit; no plans are yet formalized for any other visits except those that I have already published.

Now, all the reports that I have are that there was some violence, which I deplore. I have no other information from which I could say that there had been any violation of democratic processes in the election itself.

Q. John M. Hightower, Associated Press: Mr. President, yesterday you had an opportunity to talk with Chancellor Adenauer. There have been many reports that the Chancellor was worried or concerned in some manner about your policy line on West Berlin in connection with a summit conference.

Could you tell us something of your discussion with him?

THE PRESIDENT. Well, I refer you to the joint statement which was issued last—I guess it was issued last evening—[*confers with Mr. Hagerty*]—issued last evening. That states, I think, the case exactly.

We agreed that there was no change in policy on either side.

Q. John R. Gibson, Wall Street Journal: On Cuba, sir, you have announced a policy of nonreprisals toward the Castro Government. In line with that, could you explain the reason for your changes in the sugar act that some Cubans are taking as a reprisal?

THE PRESIDENT. I think they have no justification for taking it for a reprisal whatsoever.

The United States consumes a very great amount of sugar every year, and there have been many activities taking place in Cuba that could easily endanger our source of supply. We have been getting on the order of 3,500,000 tons of sugar from Cuba yearly.

I have got the responsibility of trying to make sure that the United States gets the sugar it needs—one of the reasons that, if any of these supplying areas should fall down in supplying its quota, then I should have the right, in my opinion, to go to somebody else to get it. That's all it said, in effect.

I have flatly stated again and again that we are not trying to punish Cuba, particularly the Cuban people or even the Cuban Government. We are trying to get to a basis of agreement with them that is based upon justice, on international usage and law, and so that the interests of both sides are protected.

Q. Ruth S. Montgomery, Hearst Headline Service: Mr. President, can you tell us anything about your plans for retirement and whether you plan to write another book?

THE PRESIDENT. I must tell you, Miss Montgomery, that I have no plans whatsoever.

I am sure you would understand a number of publishers have suggested some possibilities of this kind. My reply has always been, I have no plans yet, I'll have to wait a few months.

Q. Earl H. Voss, Washington Star: Mr. President, the Soviet Union this morning has elaborated somewhat on Khrushchev's 4-year plan for full disarmament at Geneva. They have suggested in the first stage a cut in the armed forces of the United States, Russia, and Communist China, to 1.7 million men in a period of a year to 18 months.

Now, there is another provision that their 4-year package be accepted as a package, this would be a part of it.

Do you envision any kind of negotiation with Communist China over armed forces cuts in a disarmament plan?

THE PRESIDENT. If disarmament, and disarmament programs, come into the realm of practical negotiation and enforcement, as you go progressively along that road, you will unquestionably have to take into account the armaments of Red China. We are not yet into that stage.

The United States has proposed a plan for progressive disarmament and under stages. We think it is a practical and workable plan. We are trying to get the things that now seem within reach, trying to get them accomplished in the first stage, and to go on from there.

So, I should say that in our thinking there has to be a very great deal of progress before we are into the stage of worrying too much about Red China.

Q. Chalmers M. Roberts, Washington Post: Mr. President, Secretary Herter told us that you had ruled against any change in the 10,000-foot flight ceiling into Berlin. The Russians have backed down on the Berlin pass issue, and some people have seemed to conclude that there is some sort of a working agreement between yourself and Mr. Khrushchev, sort of a—let's not rock the boat before the summit.

Is there in fact any such agreement, or how do you explain this; such incidents as this seem to balance each other to some degree.

THE PRESIDENT. I don't explain anything, and there is no such agreement. I just tell the facts.

Now, you've been told the facts about the passes, and I believe that it was stated publicly—maybe it was speculation, I'm not sure whether it was—it was in a report that Mr. Khrushchev had been said to comment that he did not want to stir up any trouble just now, and because it was before the summit. He never said such a thing to me, and I am not sure that it is true.

Now, for myself, the Chiefs of Staff originally thought there might be an operational need for flying more than 10,000 feet, and therefore study and coordination with our allies was directed. When I came back from South America, the reports that came in were to the contrary, there was no operational need whatsoever. I said, therefore, we will drop it, we will not do it. That's all there was to it.

Q. Peter Lisagor, Chicago Daily News: Mr. President, as a result of your understanding with Mr. Khrushchev at Camp David last September, do you feel obliged to attempt to reach a settlement on Berlin in the forthcoming summit meeting?

THE PRESIDENT. What I have said, and said to him: within the limits that we would not abandon our position respecting our rights in Berlin, and our belief and our conviction that the Berlin question will never finally be settled except with the background of a settlement of a divided Germany, and remembering one more, that what has been called our juridical position will not be touched and will not be damaged—within that context I am perfectly ready to talk about Berlin and Germany at any time.

To deny that you will talk or try to negotiate as long as your position of right and principle has been established would, to my mind, be a great mistake.

Q. Frank van der Linden, Nashville Banner: Sir, Senator Humphrey of Minnesota and the Southern Democrats seem finally to have agreed on one subject, that is that Paul Butler should go out as Democratic National Chairman. I wondered, sir, if you would like to make that unanimous?

THE PRESIDENT. If the Democrats have any troubles, I am not going to try to help them out. [*Laughter*]

Q. David Kraslow, Knight Newspapers: Mr. President, did you find in South America as much concern over the behavior of the Castro Government as there is in the United States? And could you discuss this briefly with us, sir?

THE PRESIDENT. Well, they are concerned because no one understands exactly what is happening, but the talks I had with these several Presidents were confidential, and I wouldn't want to violate their confidences.

This matter, this subject, was brought up numbers of times with different ministers. So far as I can recall, there was no one that criticized the attitude of the United States as has been expressed by myself and by Mr. Herter—that is, of trying to find solutions for these difficulties, avoiding anything that sounds like bullyragging or dominating a weaker people.

We are friendly with the Cuban people and we want to get the kind of understanding with their government that will make mutual progress feasible.

Now, as I say, that policy which our friends down south know was, so far as I heard, approved by them.

Q. Thomas N. Schroth, Congressional Quarterly: Mr. President, two key points in the administration's civil rights bills, those covering Government contracts conditions and the aid to areas that are desegregating schools, have been cut out of the House version. Are you going to urge your Senate leaders to restore them when the bill gets to the Senate?

THE PRESIDENT. I shall continue to say that this bill was brought up after all kinds of conferences I could get. As you know, I am trying to find a moderate, reasonable path that points to progress. So, I believe in this bill, and I'm going to ask for it. Of course, I want the best bill the Congress will give me in this very troublesome and sensitive area.

Q. Lloyd M. Schwartz, Fairchild Publications: Businessmen seem to be somewhat apprehensive about the economic outlook which appears to have lost some of its luster since January. What is your own assessment for the economic outlook for the rest of the year?

THE PRESIDENT. I think it is very healthy and very fine.

Now, of course, people are always looking at curves of past performance, and they always want to have a recovery curve mounting more steeply. There were some rather bold predictions made as late as December and early January and even early February. I think that my own advisers have always counseled to take a moderate target, but they have always said this: the outlook for American business is indeed good.

Q. Clark R. Mollenhoff, Des Moines Register and Tribune: Mr. President, Vice President Nixon very recently established an independent advisory committee on agriculture to develop some kind of a farm program, independent of the administration. And I wondered if he had ever discussed with you this agricultural situation and expressed any dissatisfaction or anything like that.

THE PRESIDENT. As a matter of fact I know he was party with the agricultural program that I sent down to the Congress. I don't know about this development you speak of; I suspect it's something to bring into sharper focus some of the local problems that will be encountered in any campaign. I haven't talked further than that with the Vice President about it.

Q. L. Edgar Prina, Washington Star: Mr. President, in reply to an earlier question on lunch counter demonstrations, you said that you believed that all persons were guaranteed equal rights. Now, do you believe that Negroes have guaranteed rights to eat with whites at lunch counters, and if so, do you not then believe that the Federal Government has some role to play in the present situation?

THE PRESIDENT. So far as I know, this matter of types of segregation in the South has been brought time and again before the Supreme Court.

Now, I certainly am not lawyer enough or wise enough in this area to know when a matter is such as actually to violate the constitutional rights of the Negroes.

My own understanding is that when an establishment belongs to the public, opened under public charter and so on, equal rights are involved; but I am not sure that this is the case whatsoever.

I was talking about demonstrations, of marching in the streets, or any other kind of peaceful assembly that is trying to show what the aspirations and the desires of a people are. Those, to my mind, as long as they are in orderly fashion, are not only constitutional, they have been recognized in our country as proper since we have been founded.

Now, the different types, different ways in which resentment or defiance could be expressed, I couldn't possibly go into all those details; I don't know.

Q. Rutherford M. Poats, United Press International: Sir, a moment ago you described the Western disarmament plan as a practical step-by-step approach. Would you characterize for us, sir, the Soviet plan for a 4-year package approach to this problem?

THE PRESIDENT. Well, no, I don't want to characterize anything at the moment. I just believe that our plan is a better one on which to start for a disarmament in some scale than is theirs; but I don't want to characterize it with any adjective or in any other particular type.

Q. Donald H. Shannon, Los Angeles Times: Mr. Butler had some "leak" problems himself just recently and he was reported as having said that Senator Kennedy appears to have the leading role, as far as getting the Democratic nomination. I know it's no concern of yours, but if you will be involved very seriously in the campaign, as you said today, does it appear to you that Kennedy is out in front for the other party's nomination?

THE PRESIDENT. I didn't say I would be involved very seriously; I said if I were asked, and a candidate from my party thinks I can be useful, then I will do what I can. I am not going to make any predictions for the other side, but this is a political year, and I'll just keep still about it and be wiser. [*Laughter*]

Marvin L. Arrowsmith, Associated Press: Thank you, Mr. President.

NOTE: President Eisenhower's one hundred and eighty-second news conference was held in the Executive Office Building from 10:30 to 11 o'clock on Wednesday morning, March 16, 1960. In attendance: 248.

94 ¶ Remarks at the 16th Annual Washington Conference of the Advertising Council.
March 16, 1960

Mr. Gray and members of the Advertising Council:

I was reminded this morning that this is the eighth straight year I have had the honor of meeting this body. For me at least, this is a record with respect to any publicly constituted body. I feel privileged that again I can welcome you to the Capital City for your deliberations.

For 18 years you have been stimulating the Nation's conscience in areas where the voluntary work of great numbers of people has been necessary in order to promote worthwhile causes. I know you have been in such fields as conservation, organized charities, safety, prevention of accidents, and more recently in giving your efforts to the job of pointing out to our people the need for self-discipline, if we are to avoid debasement of our currency and prevent inflation.

Now I understand that you are taking under study what we should be trying to do in developing our most precious national asset: the intellectual capacity and skills of our people.

This is indeed a problem that needs study, analysis, and action. It is one, again, where I believe our efforts should be far more upon the voluntary side than on the governmental and directed side—certainly in any centralized government.

Quality rather than quantity is necessary. Yet we don't want to think of the production of any elite, intellectual corps. Just as we have to have in the military, for example, the brilliant brain to devise a new weapon, we also have to have better intelligence and better training to use it.

We need a betterment of all education in all levels. If we are going to meet the requirements of a constantly increasing complexity in our lives—governmental, political, industrial, and individual lives—we must take this matter very seriously indeed.

Our Government, private institutions and foundations, universities and schools have got to find the stimuli that will bring out for us the best. The worldwide contest in which we are engaged admits of no room for error or neglect or complacency.

Not long ago, I had a letter—as a matter of fact, two or three days ago—from a teacher who wrote to me about her experiences. She has

12 students—mentally retarded children about 12 to 13 years old and with an average IQ of below 50. She told me she had been trying every way she could to get these youngsters interested in anything—particularly interested in anything going on in the world at the moment. She found that she could interest the children by taking the news of the day of one of my recent trips. She was able to talk to the children about the need for peace, and the effort of trips such as this to promote peace, to put America better in the minds of children like themselves in different countries. Her children began daily to show a better comprehension of what was going on around them. And indeed, each one of them wrote to me a letter—three or four lines, it's true—but this thought came through: they didn't want war, they wanted peace; and complimenting me, they said they were thinking I was doing something about it, and that was why they wanted to thank me.

Now at the other end of the scale, I saw a piece in the paper about a little girl prodigy in a fight for her possession. From this end of the scale to the one clear down to the mentally retarded, we have a job to do, and I repeat: the more we can do it by voluntary action, the better it will be done.

I can't leave here before I refer again to the problem that I think for 8 straight years I have told this body is still the most important in our country. That is to get before the American public in widespread fashion the essentials of the issues that face us. It is not enough, I think, in this modern time, for a successful democracy just to place its trust in an individual or in a group of individuals. They must have enough information and comprehension of the great issues between ourselves and our opponents in the international world—the issues that determine internally whether we are going to be a sound, going economy, whether we are going ourselves to protect all the priceless values for which this Nation was established to protect, whether we are going to further them and try to live by them and vitalize them, so that our people can understand. This is truly the great problem that always is before our country.

It is not enough, then, to give our faith to slogans, even to individuals. We must think of our own comprehension. And I think no other body has done more in this regard in trying to inform America across the board of these things than has the Advertising Council.

So, as I try to express feebly many thanks for your work of the past 18 years, I must say to you that no one could be more convinced of the need for this kind of work that you are now doing than I am.

I think if we look always to the future and if we are going to experience that kind of progress in our country that we know is best for all of us— the workman, the employer, the professional man, the teacher, the student, the children, the old—the kind of work that is done to bring the facts of these great issues before our people is not only praiseworthy, but absolutely vital.

There's an old military statement which says, "You can do nothing positive except from a firm base." This means, if you were going to do anything positively in the field, you must have some place on which you can depend which is firmly established. You must have a base to depend on for your replacements, for your repairs, for your hospitalization, and so on. In the same way, if America is to do anything positive in the world, and lead the nations more surely and straightly down the road toward peace, we ourselves must be that firm base.

Since public opinion is the only force that has any validity in democracy it must be an informed public opinion. So not only do we think, therefore, of our country as an individualistic entity by itself, we think of it with a great mission in the world. We think of it from the standpoint of enlightened self-interest, but because also we are part of the great brotherhood of man. We must be informed. We must get a public opinion that supports those programs that intelligent, informed people believe are good for our Nation, good for promoting our ability to lead the world to that great objective that has been the goal of mankind certainly since the days of the Delphic League in Greece: a durable peace, with justice and in freedom.

So I find now, as some 8 years ago I was doing things for the first time, I am doing them now for the final time. As President, I will not again have the privilege of greeting you. I again assure you it has been a very great privilege to have these contacts with a body in which I find so many of my intimate friends, and alongside them others at least that I respect and admire, even if I do not have the privilege of their personal acquaintanceship and friendship.

So thank you again, and good luck—and keep going, that's all I can say.

NOTE: The President spoke at the District Red Cross Building. His opening words "Mr. Gray" referred to Gordon Gray, Special Assistant to the President for National Security Affairs, who served as chairman of the conference.

95   ¶ Special Message to the Congress Concerning the Administration's Program To Promote the Growth of Export Trade.   *March 17, 1960*

To the Congress of the United States:

Because increased exports are important to the United States at this time, the Administration has developed a program to promote the growth of our export trade.   While most of the public steps to be taken with this end in view can be accomplished under existing legislative authority, the cooperation and support of the Congress are vital to the success of this program.

Expanded exports can add substantially to the millions of jobs already generated for our people by export trade.   At the same time, our export surplus contributes significantly to our capacity to sustain our expenditures abroad for investment, private travel, maintenance of United States military forces, and programs of foreign economic cooperation.   To support these essential activities, which are reflected in our international balance of payments, we must, as I pointed out in my State of the Union Message, promote a rising volume of exports and world trade.

Unlike the sellers' markets of early post-war years when productive capacity abroad was limited, world markets have recently become highly competitive.   To expand exports in these circumstances demands a more vigorous effort by both Government and business to improve our capacity for international competition.

Through the trade agreements program we shall continue to work with other countries toward the removal of unnecessary obstacles to international trade and payments.   The discriminatory restrictions that other countries imposed at a time when they had serious balance of payments difficulties have been especially burdensome to our exports.   Economic improvement in many countries has removed the justification for such barriers, and with the assistance of the General Agreement on Tariffs and Trade and the International Monetary Fund, much has been accomplished in eliminating those restrictions.   We shall continue to seek the elimination of the discriminatory restrictions that still remain; we shall also continue to seek the general reduction of quantitative controls.

To assist our exporters to meet current international competition in

export financing arrangements, the Export-Import Bank will inaugurate
a new program of guarantees of non-commercial risks for short-term export credits. The Bank will also expand and improve its existing credit facilities for medium-term export transactions. These steps, which can
be taken under existing statutory authority, should improve the ability
of our exporters to compete in world markets. These arrangements will
be designed and administered to encourage full participation of commercial banks and other private sources of credit and guarantees.

To help our exporters in the development of their foreign sales, we
should improve the numerous Government services now available to
business firms and especially useful to our smaller producers. These services have been available all along, but we must infuse them with a new
purpose and strengthen them with additional resources. Accordingly,
I have directed comprehensive steps

—to strengthen the trade promotion services of the Department of Commerce, including its field offices located throughout the United States,

—to expand and give higher priority to the commercial activities of
the Foreign Service,

—to expand the agricultural trade promotion activities of the Department of Agriculture,

—to place greater emphasis on the prompt reporting of information
useful to American exporters,

—to establish new overseas trade centers,

—to make fuller use of international trade fairs, trade missions, and
other promotional means to stimulate the interest of foreign buyers in
United States products while continuing to emphasize the basic objectives
of the Special Program for International Understanding, and

—to emphasize the promotion of tourist travel to the United States.

The details of this program will be presented during the Congressional
hearings soon to be held on the expansion of United States trade and in
connection with a forthcoming request for the supplemental appropriations necessary for rapid progress in the export promotion program. Government promotion, however, can be effective only to the extent that it
stimulates and encourages private business efforts to expand sales abroad.
Government can help enlarge export opportunities, but it is American
business that must supply and sell the goods that world markets demand.

To this end I have asked the Secretary of Commerce in cooperation
with other department heads to enlist the efforts of the business com-

munity.   Consultations have already been held in connection with the preparation of this program.   In addition, a group of business leaders will be asked to organize an export drive by business, to enlist the active support of existing national and local business groups, to discover the sectors in which better results can be obtained, to assist and encourage businessmen newly entering the export field, to strengthen contacts with business groups abroad, and to develop an organization structure adequate to these purposes.

The individual steps in this export program are modest ones.   Their cumulative effect, however, will be substantial if American enterprise will make the necessary effort.   With the support of the Congress, this Government can both facilitate and give continued impetus to the expansion of our exports as free world economic progress continues to enlarge the potential for international trade.   The rising tide of productivity and prosperity in many nations creates a timely opportunity for mutual benefits from expanding world trade.   By pursuing this opportunity, we can promote vigorous economic growth both at home and abroad.

DWIGHT D. EISENHOWER

96   ¶ Special Message to the Congress on Immigration.   *March* 17, 1960

To the Congress of the United States:

I again urge the liberalization of some of our existing restrictions upon immigration.

The strength of this nation may be measured in many ways—military might, industrial productivity, scientific contributions, its system of justice, its freedom from autocracy, the fertility of its land and the prowess of its people.   Yet no analytical study can so dramatically demonstrate its position in the world as the simple truth that here, more than any other place, hundreds of thousands of people each year seek to enter and establish their homes and raise their children.

To the extent possible, without dislocating the lives of those already living here, this flow of immigration to this country must be encouraged. These persons who seek entry to this country seek more than a share in our material prosperity.   The contributions of successive waves of immigrants show that they do not bring their families to a strange land and learn a new language and a new way of life simply to indulge themselves with comforts. Their real concern is with their children, and as a result those who have struggled for the right of American citizenship have, in countless ways, shown a deep appreciation of its responsibilities. The names of those who make important contributions in the fields of science, law, and almost every other field of endeavor indicate that there has been no period in which the immigrants to this country have not richly rewarded it for its liberality in receiving them.

In the world of today our immigration law badly needs revision.

Ideally, I believe that this could perhaps be accomplished best by leaving immigration policy subject to flexible standards. While I realize that such a departure from the past is unlikely now, a number of bills have already been introduced which contain the elements of such an idea. The time is ripe for their serious consideration so that the framework of a new pattern may begin to evolve.

For immediate action in this session I urge two major acts.

First, we should double the 154,000 quota immigrants that we are presently taking into our country.

Second, we should make special provision for the absorption of many thousands of persons who are refugees without a country as a result of political upheavals and their flight from persecution.

The first proposal would liberalize the quotas for every country and, to an important extent, moderate the features of existing law which operate unfairly in certain areas of the world. In this regard, I recommend the following steps:

1. The removal of the ceiling of 2,000 on quotas within the Asiatic-Pacific triangle;

2. The basing of the over-all limitation on immigration on the 1960 census as soon as it is available in place of that of 1920 which is the present base;

3. The annual acceptance of $\frac{1}{6}$ of 1% of our total population;

4. Abandonment of the concept of race and ethnic classifications within our population, at least for the purposes of the increases in quotas I have recommended, by substituting as the base for computation the number of immigrants actually accepted from each area between 1924 and 1959. In other words the increase in the quota for Italy, for example, would not be based upon a percentage of a so-called Italian ethnic group

within our country, but upon a percentage of actual immigration from Italy between 1924 and 1959; and

5. The unused quotas of under-subscribed countries should be distributed among over-subscribed countries. This distribution should be in proportion to the quotas of the over-subscribed countries.

My second major proposal is for authorization for the parole into this country of refugees from oppression. They are persons who have been forced to flee from their homes because of persecution or fear of persecution based upon race, religion or political opinions, or they are victims of world political upheaval or national calamity which makes it impossible for them to return to their former homes.

This year has been designated World Refugee Year. The United States and sixty-eight other nations have joined together in an attempt to seek permanent solutions for the problems of these peoples. Nations who in the past have granted entry to the victims of political or religious persecutions have never had cause to regret extending such asylum. These persons with their intellectual idealism and toughness will become worthwhile citizens and will keep this nation strong and respected as a contributor of thought and ideals.

I have asked the Attorney General to submit a draft of legislation to implement the recommendations I have made. The Administration stands ready to supply whatever information is necessary to permit appropriate action by the Congress during its present session. If, notwithstanding my specific recommendations, the Congress should enact other or different liberalizations of our immigration law that are constructive, I will be glad to approve them.

DWIGHT D. EISENHOWER

97 ¶ Exchange of Messages Between the President and Chairman Khrushchev on the Rescue of Four Soviet Soldiers by the U.S.S. Kearsarge. *March 22, 1960*

Dear Mr. Chairman:

Thank you for your thoughtful message regarding the rescue of four Soviet soldiers by the men of the USS Kearsarge.

I am grateful for the happy outcome for these courageous men and am glad that our Navy was in a position to rescue them from the risks and hardships they had undergone.

Sincerely,

DWIGHT D. EISENHOWER

NOTE: The four Russians had been adrift 49 days before they were rescued west of Midway Island. They had been participating in exercises conducted by the Soviet Union off the Kurile Islands.

Chairman Khrushchev's message of March 16 follows:

Dear Mr. President:

Permit me to express to you, to the Government of the USA, and to the American Naval Command the feeling of deep gratitude for the rescue of four courageous Soviet soldiers who in the course of many days manfully struggled against the elements and hardships in the expanses of the Pacific Ocean.

The Soviet people see in the noble conduct of American sailors and the solicitous attitude toward Soviet young men on the part of American authorities the expression of an attitude of friendship which is developing between our two countries. It is to be hoped that this may serve the cause of further developing the relations between our two countries to which you and I have devoted no little time during the course of our recent conversations in the USA and for which, I hope, we will both spare no effort during our forthcoming meetings.

Respectfully,

N. KHRUSHCHEV

98 ¶ Remarks to a Group of Eisenhower Exchange Fellows. *March* 22, 1960

IN MY TRIPS around the world, I have run into some of your Fellows. Without exception they make a point to come to see me. I ran into two or three of them while I was in South America and one or two in Asia. From their reports, they are getting a lot of use out of this program. They believe that not only have they learned a lot themselves but they think they have been able by coming here to impart to our people a better appreciation of their cultures and their civilizations. And of course that means the kind of thing that brings benefits in both directions.

I always have one thing to stress when I meet an international group in my country. It is very simple. The development of a just peace is the imperative of our time. We are approaching more and more a critical period in this regard. Without peace we are burdened with defense mechanisms. Our minds are diverted from constructive purposes to those of worrying about our own safety, of our children, of our friends abroad. And finally we are upset all the time by the possibility that a really catastrophic occurrence could do much to destroy civilization.

I have come to put it almost as a truism in my own thinking that only through the exchange of information among peoples, resulting in better understanding of the basic issues in the world, are we going to have peace. I believe that governmental negotiation is principally, as of this moment, designed to get a better atmosphere in which peoples can work. I think, therefore, that on this side of the Iron Curtain, as we understand each other better, as we show a unity of purpose in great world problems, we will be stronger morally, spiritually, and economically, as we strive to better the people in our own countries. Moreover, by this kind of understanding, we will get renewed hope and renewed inspiration to help those on the other side to understand us better.

In the long run, this is the only thing that is going to lift these terrible burdens of sterile and unproductive armaments and give us an opportunity to develop ourselves as individuals, as human beings of dignity. Thus we will be able to achieve—each of us—what he believes will accord with his own aspirations.

So when you come over here, I welcome you not just as individuals that I want to see. I welcome you also as people that have been inspired to join a great crusade in the world—to help develop understanding among the nations of the world.

It's a peculiar thing that in spite of the growth of communications— the radio, the television, and magazines and newspapers—we still have to meet face to face to achieve mutual understanding.

And so, in the measure that you people can help, I thank each one of you, and my country thanks you for taking the trouble to come here to be a part of this great movement.

When I say I am glad to see you, I really mean that the whole Nation is glad to see you here.

NOTE: The Eisenhower Exchange Fellowships, established in 1953 in honor of the President, are awarded each year to 15 to 20 potential leaders from free nations overseas. In addition, 3 to 5 Americans are selected to go abroad as Eisenhower Fellows. The fellowships are nonpolitical and are independent of established educational institutions.

99 ¶ Exchange of Messages Between the President and the King of Morocco on the Earthquake at Agadir. *March* 23, 1960

[Released March 23, 1960. Dated March 2, 1960]

Your Majesty:

I have been deeply saddened by the news of the terrible earthquake which has caused so much loss of life and suffering at Agadir. Please accept the sincere condolences of the American people and myself in this great tragedy.

DWIGHT D. EISENHOWER

NOTE: This message was sent from Santiago, Chile. The message from King Mohamed V, dated March 12, follows:

His Excellency Dwight D. Eisenhower
President of the United States

We were particularly touched by the message of sympathy Your Excellency transmitted to us in your own name and that of the American people in connection with the disaster in Agadir.

We wish to express to Your Excellency and to your country, our friend, sincere appreciation for your deep concern over this tragic occurrence.

MOHAMED V

100 ¶ Address at the Opening Session of the White House Conference on Children and Youth, College Park, Maryland. *March* 27, 1960

Mrs. Brown, delegates to the White House Conference on Children and Youth, fellow citizens, and our guests from foreign lands:

It is truly an honor to greet you here tonight in the Free State of Maryland, one of the oldest of our family of States in America. It seems fitting, also, that we are gathered on the campus of one of the Nation's many great universities. An educational institution symbolizes the never-ending effort of society to help our young find the knowledge and the understanding through which they can move forward in the ongoing life of tomorrow.

I am not here, of course, as one pretending to any expertness on questions of youth and children—except in the sense that, within their own families, all grandfathers are experts on these matters. So it is not my purpose to advise you on what you should do at this conference, but it may be appropriate to suggest a few reasons why, to me, your mission here is so important.

First, then, you are working with the most precious resource of our Nation—indeed of the world: a whole generation who will someday make their country's policies and dispose its great power. The very life of America depends upon the wisdom and resourcefulness which they will bring to the basic problems with which they will then be confronted. And the responsibility for their early preparation belongs to the older citizen, not to the younger one.

Now second, this process of preparation for tomorrow's leadership grows increasingly difficult as rapid and momentous changes alter the look of tomorrow's world.

Half a century ago, when the first of these conferences met at the request of President Theodore Roosevelt, the automobile was just beginning to be a fairly common sight on the landscape of America. Radio was a laboratory toy, and television was yet even a dream. Bleriot had still to make his famous flight across the English Channel. Wars, though destructive, were so confined to particular areas that the remainder of the earth was only indirectly affected by their outbreak. Events, and news of events, moved slowly, and there was a feeling of permanence and stability in the world that people born in this century have never known. Parenthetically, may I say, this last change is the particular one that I feel to be the most significant of all those I have witnessed during my lifetime.

Now, in contrast, the world fairly shakes with the heavy tread of humanity on the march. Tonight, as I speak to you, an American space vehicle 2,310,000 miles away in its orbit around the Sun is telling what it sees and feels on its cosmic journey. Who can predict what miracles may be witnessed by those who sit at the Youth Conference ten years from now?

A billion people have been added to the earth since the first Youth Conference, a half billion more will arrive before the next one convenes. In America we race to prepare for the surge of children—fifty million of them—who will enter our homes during the next decade. Jet aircraft have shrunk our world by half during the past five years, and we no longer see anything unusual in lunching in New York and dining, the same day, in Lima, Peru. As this shrinking and crowding proceeds, the world—certainly the free world—must learn better how to live cooperatively together to the mutual benefit of all peoples. Clearly the rising generation must become more internationally minded and more diplomatically skillful than the one to which I belong.

A final reason I cite why your mission is important is because within the great context of change and accommodation there are certain great values which must neither be changed nor abandoned.

Young people today are, of course, the heirs to the greatest fund of knowledge and the most opulent store of material advantages any generation ever received. The high school student has vastly more information at his command than any of the early settlers of this land, no matter how brilliant. The student lives longer and more comfortably than did medieval royalty, and moves about in an environment increasingly devoted to his convenience and enjoyment.

Yet we know that these things are not the essence of civilization. For civilization is a matter of spirit; of conviction and belief; of self-reliance and acceptance of responsibility; of happiness in constructive work and service; of devotion to valued tradition. It is a religious faith; it is a shared attitude toward people and living which is felt and practiced by a whole people, into which each generation is born—and nurtured through childhood to maturity.

Now no sudden, perfunctory transfer, from parent to child, of these enduring doctrines and traditions is possible, for their usefulness depends upon the degree to which they are understood and appreciated. Their inheritance is a matter of patient and loving instruction on the part of the parent, and of the slow but consistent spiritual and intellectual growth on the part of youth.

Growing in these concepts, drawing strength from these beliefs our children understand, as we did not in our own youthful days, the need— now approaching the absolute—for peace with justice.

The universality of the hope for peace and the imperative character of its need cannot fail, around the globe, to develop in our youth the qualities of the heart and mind that will surely, one day, be inscribed on the permanent pillars of peace in freedom.

In this hope, among the things we teach to the young are such truths as the transcendent value of the individual and the dignity of all people, the futility and stupidity of war, its destructiveness of life and its degradation of human values. This kind of understanding will help make of them not only useful members of societies, but will increase their effectiveness in pursuing the goal of world peace. Through patient education in our homes, churches, and schools, free and peaceful societies will be perfected and perpetuated. Problems and circumstances change, priceless human qualities and values must never be lost. To assure this is also another part of the mission of this Conference.

Now there is a specific problem that could never be ignored in such a study as you are making.

Juvenile delinquency has increased each year for the past ten years, and has become not merely a local, but a world-wide, concern. The causes for this condition are multiple, and multiple measures must be used to weed them out.

Yet we must beware of a tendency to generalize pessimistically about our youth—to attribute to the many the failures of the few. Such terms as "lost," "misguided," or "off-beat," have had their counterparts in earlier generations.

I have an unshakable faith in the overwhelming majority of fine, earnest, high-spirited youngsters who comprise this rising generation. They possess a more intense intellectual curiosity than we of my age exercised when we were their age. They are wise for their years and they are fast learning the relationship between physical and mental fitness on the one hand, and satisfaction in accomplishment on the other. We strive to make certain that the number of failures is held to a minimum. And in this effort we have developed appropriate programs—physical, recreational, educational, moral, psychological, occupational. Underlying all these as both preventive and cure is a happy family; one that finds its greatest enjoyment as a group in such things as the family picnic, family games, the "cookout," or the home movies.

From the play pen to the campus our task is not to provide the conditions of an affluent existence for the young, but rather to teach them that such things have real value only as they are earned. We must see to it that our children grow up in a climate that encourages response to intellectual challenge, in self-reliance, initiative, and a healthy regard for hard work and the dignity of man. To do otherwise is to do a disservice to the young.

So as you enter into your deliberations beginning tomorrow, you will take note of the many changes and resulting problems that affect our well-being. You will discuss solutions for these problems. Guiding you constantly will be your overriding purpose—to expand the creative potential of our children and youth in freedom and dignity.

As the person responsible for calling you together, I felicitate our Nation on your readiness to undertake and persist in this noble task. I assure you of my deep appreciation of your effort. May every success attend you.

Thank you very much indeed.

NOTE: The President spoke at 9:15 in the Student Activities Building on the campus of the University of Maryland. His opening words "Mrs. Brown" referred to Mrs. Rollin Brown, former president of the National Congress of Parents and Teachers, who served as chairman of the President's National Committee for the 1960 White House Conference.

101   ¶ Joint Statement by the President and Prime Minister Macmillan at the Beginning of Their Conversations at Camp David.   *March 28, 1960*

THE PRIME MINISTER and I have agreed upon the following statement as we begin our conversations at Camp David:

The main object of this meeting, of course, is to consider the present state of the negotiations in Geneva for the suspension of nuclear tests. We will be studying the various aspects of the most recent Soviet proposal and what this proposal means to the free world.

This Geneva Conference has rightly attracted the attention of the entire world. It is dealing with a subject of interest to all people and not just the three countries engaged in the negotiation.

Certainly both of us are aware of the importance of arriving at a properly safeguarded agreement with the Soviet Union on the suspension of nuclear tests, both because of the intrinsic importance of this objective and because of the impetus which it might give to progress in the broader field of the reduction and control of armaments.

We are confident that out of our talks here will come agreement on how we proceed as partners in this all-important task of helping to bring a true and just peace to the world. With this explanation of the purpose of the meeting we are sure you will not expect to get too much in the way of spot news during the course of our discussions.

NOTE: This statement was released at Camp David, Md.

102   ¶ Joint Declaration by the President and
Prime Minister Macmillan on Nuclear Weapons
Tests.   *March 29, 1960*

PRESIDENT EISENHOWER and Prime Minister Macmillan have
discussed the present position of the nuclear tests conference at Geneva
between the United States, United Kingdom and the Soviet Union.

It has been, and remains, the earnest desire of both the United States
Government and Her Majesty's Government in the United Kingdom to
achieve, by international agreement, the total prohibition of all nuclear
weapons tests, under effective international control.

When the Geneva Conference began seventeen months ago, there was
reason to hope from the preliminary scientific discussions which had
preceded it that there would be no insuperable technical or scientific
difficulties in establishing an effective control system capable of detecting
nuclear tests of all kinds.   Subsequently, however, it appeared from further scientific research that in our present state of knowledge there are
great technical problems involved in setting up a control system which
would be effective in detecting underground nuclear tests below a certain
size.   It is, however, the sincere hope of the President and the Prime
Minister that an agreed program of coordinated scientific research, undertaken by the three countries, will lead in time to a solution of this problem.

Meanwhile, the President and the Prime Minister believe that progress
can be made towards their ultimate objective of a comprehensive agreement.   They have agreed that much has been accomplished in these
Geneva negotiations toward this objective.   They point out that in the
effort to achieve the early conclusion of a treaty there are a number of
important specific problems to be resolved.   These include the questions
of an adequate quota of on-site inspections, the composition of the Control Commission, control post staffing, and voting matters, as well as
arrangements for peaceful purposes detonations.   They believe that negotiation on these points should be speeded up and completed at the earliest
possible time.   The Prime Minister and the President have agreed that
as soon as this treaty has been signed and arrangements made for a
coordinated research program for the purpose of progressively improving
control methods for events below a seismic magnitude of 4.75, they will
be ready to institute a voluntary moratorium of agreed duration on nu-

clear weapons tests below that threshold, to be accomplished by unilateral declaration of each of the three powers. In order to expedite progress, the President and the Prime Minister have agreed to invite the Soviet Government to join at once with their two Governments in making arrangements for such a coordinated research program and putting it into operation.

It is to be understood that once the treaty is signed, ratification will have to follow the constitutional processes of each country.

The President and the Prime Minister have agreed to give instructions to their delegates at Geneva in accordance with the spirit of this declaration.

NOTE: This declaration was released at Camp David, Md.

103 ¶ The President's News Conference of *March* 30, 1960

THE PRESIDENT. Good morning. I have no announcements.

Q. Marvin L. Arrowsmith, Associated Press: Mr. President, in connection with the agreement you reached with Prime Minister Macmillan, do you have in mind a moratorium on small underground nuclear tests that would run beyond your term of office; and, if so, do you feel it would be binding on your successor?

THE PRESIDENT. You will recall that the agreement said that there would be unilateral pronouncement, unilateral action, and therefore it would be Presidential action. I think—my own idea is—that any successor would have the right to exercise his own judgment in the matter.

Q. Merriman Smith, United Press International: Mr. President, yesterday when this moratorium and the duration of it was under discussion at Camp David, did Vice President Nixon have a voice in determination of the American position on that moratorium?

THE PRESIDENT. Well, I couldn't possibly answer in particular detail. What happens is this: as you people have known for 7 years, every time there are important conferences, I do my best to have the Vice President present—for the simple reason, if I have an accident or anything happens to me, he has to take over. So, therefore, he is never denied opportunity for discussion in any meeting. But I could never tell you in detail what his particular ideas were, unless we happened to get in an argument of some kind about it.

Q. Ray L. Scherer, National Broadcasting Company: Mr. President, another question about Mr. Nixon. He has now twice declared in public speeches that he will not seek election on the record of the administration alone, but on the basis of an expanded program of his own. As far as you are concerned, is he now free to enunciate his own positions, even if they differ or go beyond yours; or is this a prerogative that Mr. Nixon has had all along?

THE PRESIDENT. Well, let us say this: Mr. Nixon has been part of this administration and certainly will be until January 20th next, so his voice has always been heard in any discussion as to policy.

Now, I should think he would be absolutely stupid if he said that you were going as far as the record of this administration would carry you and then stop. This world moves. I'll tell you, if I were not so fortunate as to be stopped here and don't have to go any further with this thing, certainly I would be looking for new ways and directions in which to carry on what I conceive to be the responsibilities of the Federal Government.

If he doesn't say that he is going to build on what has been so far accomplished, I think he would be very foolish. So, I completely applaud what he has to say about the thing.

Q. Carleton Kent, Chicago Sun-Times: Mr. President, Governor Collins, of Florida, recently declared that he felt it was morally wrong for operators of variety stores to take Negroes' money in other parts of the store and yet refuse to give them service at luncheon counters. Can you discuss your opinion of that problem?

THE PRESIDENT. I think I have made my position rather clear. I think that eventually the conscience of America is going to give to all of us equal economic and political rights, regardless of such inconsequential differences as race and so on.

As I tried to make it clear, every one of these incidents seems to have some specific slight difference, when compared with any other incident, and they bring up all sorts of possibilities of local interpretation and local action. I cannot possibly be familiar with all of them. I just stand by the fact that I think eventually the conscience of America will bring this about.

Q. John M. Hightower, Associated Press: Mr. President, could you help us understand a little better the negotiating situation which might arise in Geneva in the light of what you just said about the position of your successor on a nuclear test ban?

As I gather, if a treaty were drafted, it probably would not be completed under the most favorable circumstances for 6 weeks or 2 months or 3 months, something like that. That means that at most, the new— the unilateral declaration would be good for about 6 months. What would be the position thereafter? Would you be in position now, for example, to say to the Soviets that you believed the circumstances were such that your successor would surely continue the moratorium?

THE PRESIDENT. This is, I think, the main point in answering the question: every government understands the powers and limitations of each of the individuals who is responsible for negotiating. Therefore, while you would remind the other governments, it would practically be unnecessary for me to say that in our country we do have a separation of powers. Under a situation where you have a simultaneous and voluntary renunciation of testing for a stated period, if that period went beyond your own term of office, I personally think it would have to be reaffirmed by a successor, if it were to be effective.

I haven't asked the Attorney General for a specific ruling on this point, but I shall do that as soon as I can. That is my own feeling, that would be the answer.

Q. Rowland Evans, Jr., New York Herald Tribune: In view of your well-known concern over bipartisanship in foreign policy, sir, I wonder whether you would discuss the question of Democratic participation at the summit, and whether you think it might be advisable to have a Democrat at that Paris meeting, even if a treaty isn't ready for actual signing on May 16.

THE PRESIDENT. The man that I would think would be the principal one in the Senate who would want to have something to say about this is the chairman of the Foreign Relations Committee. I believe he has an understanding with Mr. Herter. I believe, as to the general effect, that when you are having what you hope to be intimate discussions with heads of governments, trying to uncover and discover areas where some kind of progress will be made, that there is no thought of making treaties or the kinds of agreements in which the Senate would be interested.

I think that Senator Fulbright has, before this, intimated or stated that he thought this was not the place for this kind of membership of the group that would go.

Now, I think I have never gone abroad without making some attempt to get a hold of the leaders of both parties, try to tell them what seems to be in the wind, what we are hoping to do, and sort of warning them that you didn't at the moment expect any treaties to be projected. Whenever there is any treaty projected, and we believe should be considered carefully, then I would certainly say you have to have Democratic participation.

Q. E. W. Kenworthy, New York Times: It's been a week and a half since Ambassador Bonsal returned to Havana, and in that time the attacks upon the United States have grown increasingly more violent. Are you satisfied that the Castro Government sincerely wishes to compose the differences with us through negotiation?

THE PRESIDENT. Really, I can't guess on the thing very much. I will say this: any progress in that direction has been disappointing to me. We have sent back Mr. Bonsal because we thought it was a better thing to do, in view of certain statements that had been made; but the whole thing, our attitude stands as it has been before. We stand ready to discuss all of the complaints that the Government of Cuba has against ours, and we certainly think it would be reasonable and decent in discussing them. That is as far as I can go.

Q. John R. Gibson, Wall Street Journal: There is a certain amount of concern, both here and in Western Europe, about the growing trade rivalries between our allies in Western Europe. Could you comment on our policy in this respect, and to what extent if any this has come up between you and the Prime Minister?

THE PRESIDENT. With respect to the Prime Minister, while he mentioned this subject casually to me, he did not in private conversations with me bring it up at all, beyond that. He knows there is a problem.

Now, for our point, our policy has been this: we stand for the policy of cooperating with others to eliminate or to reduce barriers to trade.

Unfortunately, some of these methods that are proposed, in certain instances would bring down, in other instances bring up, barriers. So, it is not an easy and simple problem, and it is the reason they are going to have this Paris trade council to discuss the thing. It is a delicate thing and it affects every country in Europe; not merely the Six or the Seven, but every other one.

Q. William McGaffin, Chicago Daily News: Mr. President, when the issue of ending nuclear tests was first raised in the 1956 campaign, you did not seem to think very much of the suggestion. As a footnote to history, it would be interesting if you could tell us what has caused you to come around to your present position.

THE PRESIDENT. I don't believe that there is any place you could find where I said I was against cessation of tests. I said I was against cessation of tests except by an arrangement which gave mutual right for inspection. At least this was my whole attitude toward disarmament, still is, and this inspection is only one of the fringe subjects—I mean the nuclear tests—the fringe subjects on the whole field of disarmament. So, I think there has been no basic difference, except to this extent: that if we could go so far in setting up these reciprocal intelligence—not intelligence, inspectional—systems, that underneath the so-called threshold we could certainly have a continuation of a moratorium that would permit opportunity for a joint or coordinated study and program for permanent elimination of those tests. But, remember, the heart of it is mutual inspection and verification.

Q. Richard L. Wilson, Cowles Publications: A couple of weeks ago, Mr. President, you were frank in stating your preference for Vice President Nixon as the Republican presidential nominee. I wondered if you could be equally frank with regard to the vice presidential nomination? How about Governor Rockefeller, for example?

THE PRESIDENT. Well, Mr. Wilson, I said this: we were talking, not between Mr. Nixon and any other Republican that had been mentioned—were there two candidates in the field, I would have to observe my self-imposed limitation that I had always before observed, whether in State or Federal officeseeking—we were talking about a candidate on my side and the numerous ones on the other. I had my preference, and I said even to the point of bias.

I would say this about the Vice President: certainly if Mr. Rockefeller were nominated, he would be one that would be acceptable to me; and I think I have said here several times, I think I can name a score of Republicans of real stature that would be acceptable in this office.

Q. Edward V. Koterba, United Features Syndicate: Sir, at some sessions of the White House Conference on Children and Youth, there has been some talk that the youth of today is soft, less rugged mentally and physically than the children of a few generations ago; and that also, in fact, that goes for the modern parent.

Do you agree, sir, that too many people in the United States these days are more interested in seeking pleasure and comfort and wealth than they are in building up our moral and physical values?

THE PRESIDENT. I'm not going to comment on the moral strength of the thing, because this is obviously something that really gets an expert.

I do believe that if we lose moral strength, we have lost our greatest asset.

Let's take this matter of physical fitness. It is not a matter that we deliberately set about doing; but here is what happens: we are a people that, when we see a new convenience or a new comfort in our lives, we go about it and try to earn enough to buy that kind of thing. So, in Europe today you see children, as you know, by the thousands, bicycling along the Holland roads and the Paris roads and so on. In our country, you don't see it. The children go to school by buses, and if they have to walk more than 4 or 5 blocks, I think their parents get a little bit frightened, there is so much traffic on the roads; and so they want to get them up there. So the child doesn't walk, he rides somewhere.

Here is what happens: the first of these youth fitness conferences that I called back about 1954, Mr. Kelly, from Philadelphia, who has been very interested in this, came down and gave me some statistics. He gave a whole series of physical tests that the children of the United States, I think about 15,000 here, and about four or five thousand in each of the European countries took. The alarming results were—well, they were very depressing.

Now, I think this: all of these people are trying to find ways of correcting this thing. But I don't think that it is anything that we deliberately did and said we wanted to be affluent and soft. It's just our mode of life has brought about something we have to overcome, that's all; and we have to do it very earnestly.

Q. J. F. Ter Horst, Detroit News: I'd like to jump, sir, from the youth to the aged, if I may.

There has been a lot of controversy on Capitol Hill and we understand also within administration circles regarding what kind of medical care should be provided for senior citizens. And, some of the administration critics have even gone so far as to say the President does not understand this problem because he has never had to defray his own medical bills. I wonder, sir, if you could help us understand what your position and what your philosophy is toward what the Government should really do for senior citizens and what they should do on their own.

THE PRESIDENT. Well, of course, I'll start off with this: you start off asking what the Government should do. There are lots of governments, and the thing I object to is putting everything on the Federal Government. I point out to you people all the time, if a city or a county or a State has to raise funds, if they have to do it even by borrowing, they have to go into the market with their bonds. The Federal Government tries to do that also, as long as it is fiscally responsible, but the Federal Government can print money. Nobody else can. So, it is always a little caution that you ought to tuck in the back of your minds when you think just of bringing in new responsibilities and new expenses in the Federal Government.

Now, to talk about this specific thing: I have, from the time this subject was discussed with me very thoroughly and exhaustively away back in 1951 and '52, I have been against compulsory insurance as a very definite step in socialized medicine. I don't believe in it, and I want none of it myself. I don't want any of it.

At the same time, there has been a great deal of progress made in this whole field. The number of people that have come under the voluntary health insurance programs has been very great, increasing rapidly. We still leave with ourselves, however, the problem of those people who are not indigent—taken care of under that State assistance act, I forget the name of it—but the people who are just too low incomed to take care of these catastrophic illnesses.

I think we have got to develop a voluntary program. As a matter of fact, in all our discussions inside the Cabinet, that is exactly what I've instructed the HEW Secretary to do: to get all the people that are interested—the insurance companies, the doctors, the older people, everybody that seems to have a real worthwhile opinion and conviction on this thing—get them in and work out what should be the responsibility of the individual and the city and the State and, finally, the Federal Government.

I want to point out at this time there is not a single State that has a program in this field. It seems to me that the problem does have enough of the local in its character that they should be just as interested as anybody else. Now, we are trying to develop a program that will show exactly where the Federal responsibility in this field should begin and where it should end.

Q. Frank Bourgholtzer, National Broadcasting Company: Mr. President, on this subject of committing your successor in office, are you considering a second and third summit conference; the second one, for example, immediately after the election, to which you would take your successor, and perhaps a third one next spring?

THE PRESIDENT. Why, I hadn't even thought of that. With all of my associates and friends in Europe, the subject is talked about in terms of we should have these things, oh, not at 4- or 5-year intervals, but fairly frequently. That is all that can be said now.

I would think this: after the election, no matter who is elected, I would think there would be a resurgence of all of the questions now placed about my ability to make, let's say, a 1-year moratorium; because I haven't got a year, you see. So the closer you get to next January, why, the more those questions would come up, and I would doubt whether it would be too useful. But if there were some emergency that came up that made it useful, why, of course I'd go.

Q. James B. Reston, New York Times: Mr. President, as I understand it, it would take a year or two to build these inspection sites in the Soviet Union. Now, does that mean that the treaty would be signed and that there would be no inspection for a couple of years before the system would be operating?

THE PRESIDENT. Well, I think the statement, as we stated yesterday, made that perfectly clear—that when the treaty was established and confirmed, then there would be no test under the threshold and you certainly wouldn't have any above, would you?

Q. Mr. Reston: No, but then you would have, then, for a period of 2 years, that you would have an uninspected system over the entire range, would you not?

THE PRESIDENT. Well, you would have people over there, and I think that it would begin gradually to develop in efficiency. You have to do something if you are going to get a system established that is going to be mutually acceptable as to its accuracy and reliability; well, then, you have to make some concessions as to stopping this whole business until you're sure of that, that is what I feel. I mean this: you have to put into it every safeguard so that there cannot be dilatory tactics used just to push you off for 10 years. As we said in this suggestion, a 4- or 5-year moratorium is just excessive.

Q. John Scali, Associated Press: Mr. President, the success of the offer that you and Prime Minister Macmillan put forward yesterday would seem to depend to a great extent on how serious and sincerely the Soviets would negotiate on this issue. Now, after months of deadlock on this problem, do you have any reason for believing that at this stage the Soviets are any more sincere in wanting such an agreement?

THE PRESIDENT. Again, I can't presume to describe in any accuracy what are the motives of somebody else.

Now, all the signs are that the Soviets do want a degree of disarmament, and they want to stop testing. That looks to me to be more or less proved.

But, the condition on which they want it, the conditions they want to establish for such an accomplishment, are things, of course, that are of their devising—which are, simply, common pronouncement; that's it, just a pronouncement by both parties. That is what they have always said.

They have come a long way since they said, "Now we are ready to establish these mutual systems." So the very fact that they have made this concession means that they want to negotiate further; no question in my mind.

Q. Charles E. Shutt, Telenews: Could you give us your views, sir, on current serious race problems now confronting South Africa?

THE PRESIDENT. Well, I think that I wouldn't want to say anything more about that than the Secretary of State has already said.

Naturally, when we see things of this kind where people are killed and there is so much violence, we deplore it. But it is a very touchy thing where I think that there are probably a lot of people within that country of understanding, human understanding, and want to get a better condition brought about. I'd like to see them do it.

Q. Robert C. Pierpoint, CBS News: Mr. President, reports have been published that Vice President Nixon is planning a trip to Communist China. I'd like to ask you, first of all, have you heard anything about these plans; and secondly, what is your reaction to the basic idea?

THE PRESIDENT. Well, that must be the most speculative "think piece" I ever heard of in a long time. [*Laughter*] He has never said such a word to me in his whole life; and I'll tell you, there are just no such plans of any kind.

Q. Edward P. Morgan, American Broadcasting Company: Two points on the problem of your successor, Mr. President: was it considered completely impracticable to have a Democrat along with Vice President Nixon at the Camp David briefings; and, second, what is your view on the suggestions that after the nominees are actually picked, they be given high level intelligence briefings?

THE PRESIDENT. The second part, to take that first—always we do that. They did it for me in 1952, and I did it in '56. As quick as the nominees are named, they begin to get it, and for this very practical reason: one of the two of them is the successor. He is the obvious successor, and so you have to keep him informed.

Mr. Nixon—after all, you people must remember, he is Vice President. He is not coming up just to negotiate or to talk, although as I said his opinion is always welcome. He is there because he might be the President of the United States tomorrow, or acting as such, anyway. Now, if that is so, you have got to keep him informed. How can he be ready to operate and act if he had to come out of a vacuum and go into all of the difficult details of such an office? So, it is entirely a different thing.

When the two nominees are set up, they will both be briefed steadily.

Q. Peter Lisagor, Chicago Daily News: Mr. President, the chief Soviet delegate at the Geneva test talks has said that the number of onsite inspections which has been an obstacle in the negotiations, is a matter to be decided politically. Would you then expect that this figure would be subject to agreement at a summit conference?

THE PRESIDENT. That could well be, if you had had now satisfactory progress in a program, and I think that that would be something that might be discussed and maybe even decided there.

I would just like to say one more thing about these summit meetings. If the summit meetings are all plenary meetings, sessions, with the whole room full—as a matter of fact you have a room full of people about like this, you have a big square table and you have around it as many people as you can crowd, and behind that you have two or three rows of so-called advisers—[*laughter*]—everybody is talking at everybody else, instead of talking with them. And they are also, because so many of these statements are published, they are talking to their own constituents. In other words, they are doing as good a propaganda job as they can. We would do the same if we could think of anything we haven't said already. [*Laughter*]

The summit meeting, if it has got any value, is this: four men sitting around the table with their interpreters and, without anybody having any checks of any kind, by exploring each other's minds, "What do you really want to do? What could we do?"—that's the kind of thing that you would do at a summit meeting.

Now, if you get an idea, what do you do? You have to put it now, to all these experts, because they are knowledgeable and they know their stuff. You give it to them and say, "Now, come up with a little scheme or a plan. Can we put out something now that could possibly be a basis of a treaty or at least a basis for a temporary action of some kind?" That's the kind of thing that takes place.

So, when you begin to visualize this tremendous group in a summit meeting, that's only the part of it that ought to be for show; the rest of it, in my opinion, the working part of it, ought to be in small groups like I have just described.

Q. Chalmers M. Roberts, Washington Post: If we could get away from the details of this test ban negotiation for a minute, I would like to ask you this, sir: why is it that you are trying to get a treaty? Is it because you think this would freeze nuclear weapons and make the world safer, or keep other countries from going into the business? What is the driving force behind your determination?

THE PRESIDENT. For me—now I am speaking personally at this moment—the driving force behind me is the belief that we should try to stop the spreading of this, what you might say, the size of the club. There are already four nations into it, and it's an expensive business. And it could be finally more dangerous than ever, merely because of the spreading of this knowledge and this know-how, particularly with newer ways coming up of manufacturing all of this U–235 and so on.

So that is really the big thing. Because as of now, I assure you, the power that exists in the arsenals, certainly of our own and we know of Russia's, is such a tremendous thing that I don't think that testing will necessarily make destruction more likely, I mean, of your enemy or of yourself—I don't mean enemy; I mean of anyone, any nation, or this one.

But the perfection of the peaceful uses of this thing, the perfection of the weapons themselves, in using one pound of something where two pounds was necessary before, that's the kind of thing that goes on all the time.

If we continue to do that, others are going to test in the fields that we have already covered, you see. Finally there will be any number of nations that have it, and I think it ought to be stopped.

Marvin L. Arrowsmith, Associated Press: Thank you, Mr. President.

NOTE: President Eisenhower's one hundred and eighty-third news conference was held in the Executive Office Building from 11 to 11:33 o'clock on Wednesday morning, March 30, 1960. Attendance: 243.

104 ¶ Statement by the President on the Launching of Satellite Tiros I. *April* 1, 1960

I CONGRATULATE Dr. T. Keith Glennan and the members of his Agency, the scientists and engineers, the supporting contractors and military services that contributed so magnificently to this achievement.

Once again, many elements of our scientific, technological and industrial communities have cooperated in the further development of our national program in space exploration under NASA's leadership.

NOTE: Satellite Tiros I was designed to aid in meteorological research through such means as the transmission to earth of pictures of cloud formation.

105 ¶ Statement by the President on the Fifth Anniversary of the Announcement of the Effectiveness of Polio Vaccine. *April* 4, 1960

APRIL 12, 1960, marks the fifth anniversary of an auspicious day for American parents—the announcement of the effectiveness of a vaccine against poliomyelitis.

In the intervening years, polio has been dealt a heavy blow but it has not been destroyed. The reason is clear; not enough Americans have had the full course of injections that are needed for the maximum protection afforded by the vaccine against polio.

Many people are needlessly risking death or lifetime handicap simply because they have failed to take advantage of one of medicine's great achievements.

To those who are still unvaccinated or only partially vaccinated, I urge renewed effort on this anniversary occasion. Make April 12 a new kind of V–Day—vaccination day—by calling your physician or health department to arrange for the polio shots you or your family need. Children under five years of age particularly need this protection.

106 ¶ Exchange of Telegrams Between the President and President Garcia on the Philippine Sugar Quota. *April 4, 1960*

[Released April 4, 1960. Dated March 30, 1960]

Dear Mr. President:

I have received your telegram of March 17 asking that I increase the Philippine sugar quota. As you know, the sugar quotas are determined by Congress and any modification would require Congressional action. Since the Sugar Act of 1948, as amended in 1956, expires this year, Congress is expected to consider its extension during the present session.

The Administration has been giving considerable thought to what recommendations it should make to Congress for its consideration. After weeks of most careful study of this problem, I have concluded that the time is not propitious to recommend any change in the present structure of quotas assigned to foreign countries.

Accordingly, I have recommended to the Congress only certain minimum changes in the present Sugar Act. The most important of these would give me the authority to reduce the quota for a calendar year for any foreign country, except, of course, the Philippines, and to make required replacements from any source when I determine it to be in the national interest or necessary to insure adequate supplies of sugar. I have requested this authority primarily to enable me to protect our sugar consumers should our supplies of sugar from foreign sources be endangered for any reason. The final decision as to whether I am to be given this authority, however, rests with Congress. I regret therefore that it has not been possible for me to comply with the wishes of the Philippine sugar producers. I wish to assure you, however, that the position of the Philippines has been given full consideration by the Administration in arriving at the position which I have recommended to Congress.

With assurances of my continued esteem,

Sincerely,

DWIGHT D. EISENHOWER

NOTE: President Garcia's telegram follows:

President Dwight Eisenhower
The White House

On behalf of the Filipino people, particularly those in the sugar industry, may I ask Your Excellency to increase the Philippine sugar quota by any amount you deem just and fair. May I state in this connection that present production capacity can absorb two hundred thousand tons more of additional quota. Your generous action on this request will give a tremendous boost to our economy which needs further stabilization.

Assuring you of the lasting gratitude of the Filipinos and of my own, I remain

Very sincerely yours,

CARLOS P. GARCIA

107 ¶ Remarks at a Rally Sponsored by the Republican Women's National Conference. *April 4, 1960*

Madam Chairman, Mr. Vice President, delegates to the 8th Republican Women's National Conference, and friends:

For me it is invariably a joyous occasion when I meet with my friends of the Republican Women's National Conference. Your enthusiasm is infectious and it's good to feel it again.

As a matter of fact, I got so enthused this evening that sitting here I am thinking of running for the national —. Well, nevertheless, I am thinking of running for the legislature of my adopted State. At least, again I have the opportunity of thanking all of you—which I do most earnestly—for the support you have given me, both in political campaigns and in the day-to-day business of administering the Government of the United States.

Many of you here probably know of a fact concerning women in politics that I discovered only recently. The first woman to address any presidential nominating convention was a Republican, who, back in 1892, said, "We are here to help, and we have come to stay." I cannot tell you how deeply appreciative I am of the continuing validity of that 60-year-old pledge. For in politics, I early learned that the ladies not only produce "helping power" but also seem to have the most "staying power."

For example, I see plenty of evidence that you are standing firmly by a decision that many of you here helped to make in 1952. That year our Republican Convention turned to a highly talented man for the vice presidential nomination. None of us has ever regretted that choice.

Now in this little talk I wrote some things about Dick Nixon, and I was astonished when he talked a little bit about me, because I am not running. But Dick Nixon has been a credit to the administration, to our party, and to our country. Since 1952 he has gained nearly 8 years of added governmental experience at the highest level—a tour of seasoning unmatched in the Nation's history. All of us know him as a man of integrity and deep faith—one who is intelligent, mature, and uniquely knowledgeable in the problems and personalities in the world scene. And along with this, he has that priceless gift, a sense of humor—indispensable in politics.

And finally and most important, he has Pat.

Now, this year we want to and expect to elect a Republican President and are striving to regain control of the House of Representatives and make real gains in the Senate. The need for this effort is one on which I can speak with some feeling. Not since 1954 have I served with a Congress controlled by our party. More than 5 consecutive years with an opposition Congress is, I'm told, a record for any President—although it is hardly one I wanted to make. In any event, we are setting our sights on obtaining a Republican House to work with my Republican successor.

It's not my purpose tonight to take off into oratorical orbit—already we have a number of senatorial hopefuls doing that, each hoping in the scramble to get into the chair I shall soon vacate. Instead, might I make just a few comments about the coming campaign, about our party, our record, and how we shall serve our country in the coming years.

As we approach this presidential election, each party should be prepared to examine the corridors of its conscience, the record of its performance and its program for future action.

For this our party stands well prepared.

First of all, it believes that political programs should be based on moral law. Moreover, the Republican Party has never rested its case upon promises and platforms alone; it has been a party of accomplishment.

From 1860 to 1960 it has achieved a record of responsible and brilliant performance that is boldly written across the pages of history.

Let's take a look at just the past 7 years.

What have we done to redeem the platform pledges made to the American people in 1952 and 1956?

The record is filled with such advances as improvements in the health and welfare of our people, the greater soundness, freedom, and growth of our economy, increased modernization and strengthening of our defenses, greater prestige abroad, and the initiation of a roadbuilding program that dwarfs anything of its kind in all history of all nations.

To cite in more detail just two examples of the way in which we have kept faith with the American voter:

Foremost, we stopped, on honorable terms, the fighting in Korea and, since, have kept the peace.

That peace cannot, because of the threat hanging like a cloud over the world, achieve the perfection we desire. But we do remember that during the past 7 years no American boy has lost his life in battle, nor has our Nation been depressed by daily casualty lists.

Since 1953 we have lived in an atmosphere where, with our allies, we are able constantly to strengthen the bonds of peace, regardless of the undeniable uneasiness and tension in the world.

We are well aware of and well understand the powerful threats, both implicitly and explicitly expressed by Communist imperialism, and the sacrifices we must make to uphold peace in freedom. And wherever freedom is threatened we have never temporized nor compromised—nor ever shall.

In this spirit we have made certain of our Nation's defenses—well knowing that from a position of strength we provide not only for military security but establish the only platform from which we can effectively pursue the objective of mutual disarmament and world peace.

In programming America's defense, we have insisted not only on sufficiency, but on balance—a balance that makes maximum use of our material resources, human energies, and national spirit, and is designed to counter every foreseeable risk.

To do otherwise would be to court disaster.

Now some, I know, have felt and expressed themselves individually as highly qualified to criticize adversely the comprehensive and painstaking calculations that responsible military, scientific, and governmental personnel have made in satisfying our defense requirements. For myself, I assure you that I have the highest personal confidence in those calculations, made by a great cooperating group of able and dedicated people.

I am convinced that our whole defensive structure has been accurately tailored in the light both of national needs and operational efficiency.

Our Nation is the most powerful in the world, and only the ignorant or the blind insist it to be otherwise.

But we—we Republicans—owe it to our people to make this clear to every citizen in the land.

And I earnestly hope you will drive home something else.

Here I refer to a second major area of Republican promise and performance.

Some opponents apparently feel there is no problem that cannot be solved by a subsidy—that all social and economic difficulties can be speedily resolved by tapping the treasury.

What a myth that is!

Extravagance and statesmanship can never be happily wedded.

We stand squarely with Lincoln in the conviction that government should undertake only that which the citizen cannot do properly for himself—that government should always be ready to give a helping hand but never a heavy handout.

Now when we express our belief in such things as "fiscal responsibility," "balanced budgets," "refusal to debase our currency," and the importance of local authority, we no doubt sound unspectacular to those people who want to dive deeply into the Federal Treasury.

But these subjects are not unspectacular to the family that has, in the past, encountered the rising costs and prices resulting from governmental irresponsibility; or to the housewife who must make the family budget stretch to cover the necessaries of life, with its emergencies; or to the worker whose savings and pensions are endangered whenever government permits the debasing of our money.

All these matters are basic to sound government. Moreover, good government does not seek to be spectacular; it seeks rather the progress and the happiness of the people it serves.

So we shall not deviate from principle; but our job is to make sure that the public better understands the Republican accomplishments of the past and the sound and enduring good to be found in its programs for the future.

If we do this, I have no doubt about which party the American people will turn to next November.

If we do our work well, all our people will appreciate the great advances in American influence in the world, and the growing effectiveness of foreign programs. They will realize that we have had marked success in preserving stability and promoting a great expansion in our economy.

Moreover, in two small cyclic recessions we have remained true to principle, refusing to heed the councilors of fear. We have pursued sane and helpful programs tailored to the true needs of our people. The result has been in each case a rebounding economy and a record rise in prosperity.

Under the policies our party has supported, our people are assured of becoming ever more prosperous according to the best judgment of the finest economic experts we can muster. Indeed, this year's Gross National Product—the broadest measure of the Nation's output of goods and services—will be more than $500 billion.

And if we spread the good news properly, the public will pay no attention to those who have developed an amazing, and what is to them seemingly an enjoyable, habit of making forecasts that drip with gloom, lack of faith, and self-doubt.

Although the political pessimist may voice despair about our future, I know that this audience will never believe that our Nation has lost the hardy traits of mind and spirit, the self-confidence and self-dependence, that have characterized the American people for over 300 years. Rather all of us here tonight assert that the history of our Nation—including that of its past 7 years—justifies fully our confidence in America for the journey ahead.

Our party is about to enter the second century since it first came to power. Over the years the core of Republican purpose has been to exalt individual opportunity and human dignity and to enthrone freedom. This purpose we all share, but we must remember that the driving force in a successful political party is the strength of spirit of its members. Only as we renew this spiritual power and enthusiasm will we bring our party up the slow climb to the summit where the election of a Republican President and a Republican Congress will again become the normal pattern.

And so, as I thank you again for your courtesy and express my admiration for the effort you are making, may I say this: in the confident spirit of the final resolution introduced at the convention that nominated

Lincoln, we read, "we adjourn to meet at the White House on March 4th next"—I bid you good night and I hope to see you at the Capitol when my Republican successor takes over on January 20th.

NOTE: The President spoke at 9:25 p.m. at the Uline Arena in Washington. His opening words "Mrs. Chairman" referred to Mrs. Clare B. Williams, Assistant Chairman of the Republican National Committee, who served as chairman of the rally.

108 ❡ Remarks of Welcome to President Lleras Camargo of Colombia at the Washington National Airport. *April* 5, 1960

Mr. President:

It is a particular honor for me and for the American people to welcome you here to this country that you know so well.

First of all, your country and ours has a long history of friendly associations, and we well remember the sacrifices that your country made in the late Korean conflict when you sent to the aid of the United Nations both military and naval forces.

But beyond this we have watched with the greatest interest your own leadership in the developing of your country, both in the spreading of the advantages of education, health facilities, democratic order, and in the leadership that has brought about the standing of Colombia ever higher among those nations that are true practices of democracy. We have seen how your efforts have resulted, and we are indeed admiring and most respectful of those accomplishments.

So when we have the opportunity today of welcoming you to this land, we do it as one that reveres those great values of freedom, of human dignity, and know that you stand with us in all of the measures that are necessary in the promotion of these values throughout the world and defeating any kind of threat that may be opposed against us.

So again I say to you, sir, welcome, and I sincerely hope that you and your party find in this country not only an instructive trip but a most enjoyable one for all of you.

And finally, that when you go back, you will convey to your own people the very best wishes and warm greetings from this, the people of this country.

Thank you very much.

109 ¶ Toasts of the President and President Lleras at the White House.   *April* 5, 1960

Mr. President, Señora Lleras, ladies and gentlemen:

It is indeed a great honor to welcome to this country, to this Capital, and to this table the President of Colombia. I am not so sure that I should couch this statement just in words of welcome, because the President is practically a Washingtonian. It occurred to me that by the time I have lived in Washington as long as he has, there will be a lot of people demanding that I say whether I was a Democrat or Republican. Now I don't think that you have to answer that question, and certainly I shall not ask it.

But indeed, to welcome back someone in the sense of a prodigal son returning home, this is quite an honor and indeed a great and enjoyable experience.

Our country is very proud of its relationship with Colombia. The history of our friendship—mutual friendship—is a bright one, and we had a great inspiration in the late Korean trouble when Colombia sent its troops to assist ours in repelling the Communist aggression in that area. This is something for which we have been eternally grateful, Mr. President, and we think it is symbolic of the strength of the friendship that our two peoples feel each for the other.

Because of this long experience of the President in his position here in the Organization of American States, and formerly as an Ambassador, we were quite prepared to understand and to appreciate the work he has done in these recent years as President of his own country. He is leading it into an advance that is making of it a democracy that is truly strong and dedicated to all those values that we hold so dear.

And it is because of such reasons as these that I count it a special privilege to symbolize our affection for the people of Colombia, and our admiration for its President, by asking you to join me in a Toast to the President of Colombia and Señora Lleras.

NOTE: The President proposed the toast at a state dinner at the White House. President Lleras responded as follows:

Mr. President:

I sincerely thank you for all your kind words and in particular for your refer- ences to my country. My companions and I have received with deep emotion and lasting gratitude the welcome which you, your Government, and your coun- trymen have extended to us. For my part, I interpret this as a testimonial of fraternity for a nation which I happen to have the privilege of representing, not— thank Heaven—against its will, but by its decision. I know quite well that the people of Colombia honestly and unreservedly share the sentiments of admiration and friendship I feel for the United States, and regard with enthusiasm your invitation and my visit, which are an eloquent way of indicating that the cooperation between our two nations is proceeding regularly and harmoniously.

We have, in moments of special difficulty, received the support of the American Government, and when support from us—physically scant, perhaps, but politically and morally important—has been necessary to maintain an international policy to which we have conjointly pledged ourselves, we have given it without the slightest hesitation. It is long since there has been between Colombia and the United States any difference which has not been settled with the greatest ease and in the shortest time possible. In the international organizations to which we belong, our agents collaborate to achieve the purposes clearly set forth in the Charters. Your Ambassadors in Colombia, Mr. President, have been welcome with an affection which they have invariably deserved. Ours here have been cordially treated, and there has never been anything to impair the effectiveness of their labors. Besides, it gives me pleasure to say that—though this is

the way the moral relationship between friendly peoples usually functions—the difference between your material circumstances and ours has in no way been emphasized, except insofar as this great power feels obliged to aid less developed countries, to give them technical, scientific, and financial assistance with the purpose of bettering our people's condition.

You, Mr. President, have recently had the opportunity of knowing directly the popular sentiments of Latin America towards the nation you so loftily represented in our countries. And I am sure that from your visit—which, unfortunately, could not be more extended and complete—you brought back with you the conviction that in that vast region of the world, which has been the oldest partner of the United States in her international policy, there are unsuspected possibilities of collaborating harmoniously to make this Hemisphere a worthy haven for man, for the highest human qualities and for liberty.

On reiterating to you and Mrs. Eisenhower my thanks, as well as those of Mrs. Lleras and my traveling companions, for all the acts of courtesy and friendship you have showered upon us, I should like to express, Mr. President, my best wishes for the continued greatness of the United States and the personal happiness of its President and Mrs. Eisenhower.

---

110 ¶ Toasts of the President and President Lleras at the Colombian Embassy. *April* 7, 1960

Mr. President, Señora, ladies and gentlemen:

Ordinarily when we have a visitor, a head of state from abroad, we always express the hope that the friendship between the two peoples we represent will be strengthened by such a visit.

In this case, I think it is a rather futile hope—I do not know how the friendship between our two countries could be stronger, and so I will content myself, Mr. President, by saying that the American people are proud of the friendship of your people for ours. We are grateful for it, and we reciprocate it.

And as a symbol of our affection for the people of Colombia, I ask this company to drink with me a Toast to the President of Colombia and Señora Lleras.

NOTE: The toast was proposed in response to a toast by President Lleras at a dinner which he gave in honor of President Eisenhower. The toast proposed by President Lleras follows:

Mr. President:

We have certainly no words to express our appreciation for the way in which you have treated us, Mr. President—you, and Mrs. Eisenhower, your government and your people. So, if we have no words, the best thing to do is to be silent.

But I invite all of you to drink a Toast to the President of the United States and Mrs. Eisenhower.

111 ¶ Statements by the President and President Lleras Following Their Discussions. *April 8, 1960*

THE PRESIDENT of the United States has had a valuable and friendly exchange of views with the President of Colombia on a number of subjects of mutual interest, including matters of special significance and concern in inter-American relations. The discussions between the two Presidents began at the White House on Wednesday, April 6, and continued at Camp David on Thursday, April 7. They were entirely informal in nature and without any agenda; no negotiations of any type were involved. They took place in an atmosphere of complete cordiality, frankness and mutual understanding.

During his four-day visit President Lleras addressed a Joint Meeting of Congress and he and the members of his party conferred with the Vice President, the Secretary of State, members of the Senate Foreign Relations Committee and other United States Government officials. After leaving Washington President Lleras will visit three other cities of this country and will meet and confer with governmental, cultural and business leaders.

The President is happy to confirm that there are no serious problems pending between the United States and Colombia and that relations between the two countries are characterized by a spirit of friendliness and mutual respect. He discussed at length with President Lleras the economic needs of Colombia and noted with satisfaction the return of Colombia to economic and financial stability under the present regime, a development largely made possible by the great efforts of the Colombian

Government and people and cooperation between the Colombian Government and official and private banks in the United States, together with support from international banking institutions. At the same time these discussions disclosed the need for increasing and diversifying Colombian agricultural and industrial production to keep pace with the rapid growth of population in that country, in which task all possible efforts will be made to cooperate with the Colombian Government.

The conversations dwelt also upon the basic problem of social and economic development which, as President Lleras has eloquently stated, "has no other objective than that of producing within the shortest period of time, with the full application of all public and private resources, a gradual rise in the standard of living of the entire population and a better distribution of income." The two Presidents found it a matter for rejoicing that in America war has been outlawed as an instrument of national policy, that Americans, north and south, live at peace with one another and wholeheartedly sympathize with and maintain their solidarity with the free nations of the world. They reaffirmed their support of the Organization of American States and their devotion to the defense of its ideals as voiced in its Charter and other significant inter-American agreements.

Finally, President Eisenhower expressed his conviction that a continuing personal relationship between the Chiefs of State of the two countries was an important element in maintaining the long tradition of friendship and cooperation between Colombia and the United States, and that the present visit signifies the determination of the two Chiefs of State and their two Governments to continue their collaboration on matters of mutual concern both directly and through international organizations, as befits two nations sharing a common faith in freedom, democracy and social justice.

NOTE: The statement by President Lleras follows:

The President of Colombia has had a most gratifying experience in his visit to the United States in response to the invitation from President Eisenhower. In his conversations with President Eisenhower, Secretary of State Herter and other high officials of the American Government he has had the opportunity to discuss problems that affect the hemisphere and their relation to world problems and, in particular, to those of Colombia. The President of Colombia found the same spirit of cooperation, understanding and good neighborliness that constantly has characterized relations between the two countries, as well as an intense and deep concern for the progress of the Latin American nations, their political and social stability and their economic development. Colombia has wished to make fully evident, on the occasion of this visit, its appreciation for the high degree of cooperation it has received from the Government of the United States in connection with the crisis suddenly made acute by the drop in coffee prices, that, had it continued, would have brought disaster to the producing countries. In this crisis, the United States assumed the position, unprecedented for a consumer country, of cooperating in the formulation of world-wide agreements designed to seek stability for this product. Likewise, the President of Colombia has wanted to attest his gratitude and that of his people for the financial aid given the economic policies of his Government, thanks to which it has been possible to reestablish the foreign credit of his country, to stabilize its currency and to open new prospects for economic development.

President Eisenhower and high officials of the American Government, as well as members of the United States Congress, have shown on this occasion special interest in intensifying the cooperation of their country with the efforts being made by the American Governments to raise the standards of living of their peoples. Also, the President of Colombia has found a clear expression of the respect, confidence and esteem in which the Government of the United States holds the Organization of American States as an instrument for studying, clarifying and resolving all problems that may arise concerning relations between our countries, when these cannot be resolved directly. It has been gratifying and stimulating to the Chief of the Colombian Government to confirm that he is in complete accord with President Eisenhower's concept that the juridical structure developed by the American states during the 71 years of their collaboration is one of the greatest contributions of our times to the predominance of a system of law in international relations, and with the need and desirability of strengthening the American regional organization by giving it the governments' strongest support.

It is also gratifying to the President of Colombia to state that, although it was not the aim of his visit to discuss any special aspect of cooperation between the two countries, he found in President Eisenhower, in the members of Congress and the Government and generally in all official circles, special desire to help resolve the serious problems of Colombia's growth and to enlist the American nation in the development of an economic and social policy that would serve the interests of the Colombian people, raise their standard of living and contribute to developing a state of prosperity and justice. In the course of our interviews through the normal channels, conversations will be carried forward on specific ways to cooperate in these efforts, that are intended to consolidate democracy and the order, peace and social justice of the hemisphere.

The President of Colombia wishes to express his highest appreciation for the way President Eisenhower, the American Government and people have received the Chief of a sister nation, turning this visit not only into an act of close friendship between nations but also into a very useful opportunity to examine new ways of intensifying long term and reciprocal political and economic cooperation.

112 ¶ Message to President Garcia of the Philippines on the Occasion of Bataan Day. *April 8, 1960*

Dear Mr. President:

Eighteen years ago today Filipinos and Americans, in common struggle against tyranny, gave new vigor to man's quest for peace in freedom.

It is fitting that we should pause each year to observe Bataan Day and to remind ourselves that liberty and justice are, indeed, worth whatever price we may be called upon to pay.

Eight years ago Filipinos and Americans were again fighting side-by-side to preserve the integrity of the Free World. I am confident that we will continue to work together to this end, and it is my profound hope that we will be able to safeguard our integrity without having thrust upon us again the necessity of taking up arms. The goals of our two peoples—the spiritual and material welfare of the individual, a free society dedicated to peace and justice—are deeply ingrained. The fact that they correspond to the aspirations of hundreds of millions of our fellow men should strengthen our determination to defend this heritage against any who would deny it to us.

On behalf of the American people, I wish to extend through you, Mr. President, my deep respect and affection for the Filipino people and their dedication to the democratic way of life. May we continue to draw common inspiration from the symbol of Bataan.

With high esteem,

Sincerely,

DWIGHT D. EISENHOWER

113 ¶ Veto of Bill for Relief of William J. Kaiser. *April* 11, 1960

To the House of Representatives:

I return herewith, without my approval, H.R. 6023, a bill "For the relief of William J. Kaiser."

The bill would relieve Mr. Kaiser of all liability to refund to the United States amounts improperly paid to him as sickness and unemployment benefits under the Railroad Unemployment Insurance Act while he was also receiving a pension as a retired member of the New York City Fire Department. The bill would further direct the Railroad Retirement Board to repay to Mr. Kaiser from the railroad unemployment insurance account of the unemployment trust fund the amounts already recovered from him.

The Railroad Unemployment Insurance Act itself provides that the

Railroad Retirement Board may extend equitable or compassionate relief in appropriate cases of overpayment when the Board finds recovery would be against equity or good conscience. This the Board did not do and there is no evidence available to me that indicates the Board's decision to have been erroneous.

The payments which the bill would require are not authorized by general law. More importantly, the money for the payments would have to come from a trust fund. The beneficiary has no valid claim to this money and its payment would constitute a discriminatory gift from funds which the Government holds in trust for railroad employees.

For these reasons, and because the bill would create an undesirable precedent, I am constrained to withhold my approval.

DWIGHT D. EISENHOWER

114 ¶ Veto of Bill for Relief of Mrs. Virginia Bond. *April* 11, 1960

To the House of Representatives:

I am returning herewith, without my approval, H.R. 7933, "For the relief of Mrs. Virginia Bond."

The $1,582.89 of death pension benefits authorized by this bill are for the period between Mrs. Bond's husband's death on June 29, 1957 and May 13, 1959, the effective date of the pension Mrs. Bond currently receives. The benefits provided by H.R. 7933 are retroactive and may not be paid under existing legislation. Such an exception to general law should be made only to correct a serious inequity or in other unusually meritorious circumstances. I find no such basis for approving this bill.

Mrs. Bond on July 11, 1957 filed a claim for death pension benefits with the Veterans' Administration. Had this claim been allowed Mrs. Bond's pension, because applied for within a year of her husband's death, would have been retroactive to the date of her husband's death. Her claim was denied, however, because it was determined that her husband's death was not due to his service—nor was the evidence in support of the claim sufficient to entitle Mrs. Bond to a non-service-connected death pension. This denial was affirmed on appeal.

On May 13, 1959, Mrs. Bond filed a second claim with new evidence and on the basis thereof she was awarded the death pension she is now receiving. The law, however, specifically requires that such a second claim be treated as a new claim. The effective date of the award, therefore, was the date of the second claim because it had been filed more than one year after the death of Mr. Bond.

This history affords no valid justification for the special relief the bill would accord. The language of the law requiring that second claims be treated as new claims is clear and unmistakable. Furthermore, the insufficiency of the evidence in support of the first claim is attributable to Mrs. Bond, not to the Government.

Because the bill would discriminate against others similarly situated and would create an undesirable precedent, I am constrained to withhold my approval.

DWIGHT D. EISENHOWER

115 ¶ Letter to the Co-Chairmen of the Joint Federal-State Action Committee on Receiving the Committee's Final Report. *April* 12, 1960

[Released April 12, 1960. Dated April 9, 1960]

Dear —————:

This acknowledges the receipt of the report of the Joint Federal-State Action Committee, submitted on April 7, 1960. I believe that continuation of the Committee alongside the Advisory Commission on Intergovernmental Relations would be duplication of effort. The Committee has worked well and earnestly toward the strengthening of our governmental system. It is my hope and expectation that the Advisory Commission will further the Committee's work and broaden its scope for the same purpose—to make our federal system an even more effective instrument to serve the American people.

In dissolving the Joint Federal-State Action Committee, I extend my thanks to the members, both the Governors and Federal officials, and to the joint staffs, for their work and interest in this project.

Sincerely,

DWIGHT D. EISENHOWER

NOTE: This is the text of identical letters addressed to Governor Robert Smylie of Idaho and Secretary of the Treasury Robert B. Anderson.

The Joint Federal-State Action Committee was established in response to the President's suggestion to the Conference of Governors at Williamsburg, Va., June 24, 1957 (1957 volume, this series, p. 494). The Committee's final report was published by the Government Printing Office (197 pp., 1960). A brief addendum was printed in November 1960.

The Advisory Commission on Intergovernmental Relations was established by Public Law 86–380 (73 Stat. 703).

116   ¶ Letter to the Governors Concerning Assumption by the States of Regulatory Functions Relating to Atomic Energy.   *April* 12, 1960

[Released April 12, 1960. Dated April 11, 1960]

Dear Governor —————:

I have often stressed the need to increase the functions and responsibilities of the States as a safeguard against excessive centralization of governmental power in this country. Public Law 86–373 was enacted in response to a recommendation by the Joint Federal-State Action Committee.

The law authorizes the Atomic Energy Commission to enter into agreements with the Governors of the States under which the States will assume responsibility for specified regulatory functions now performed by the Commission for the promotion and regulation of the peaceful uses of atomic energy. Following consultations with representative State groups, the Commission has prepared proposed criteria to guide both parties in reaching agreement on the transfer of these functions.

I have asked the Chairman of the Atomic Energy Commission to send copies of the proposed criteria to you. Your views, and those of the other Governors, will be important in determining the actual criteria to be applied. I request that you give this matter your personal attention and ask that you send your views as soon as possible to Mr. John A. McCone, Chairman of the Atomic Energy Commission. Mr. McCone and his staff will welcome an opportunity to meet with you or your representatives to discuss the proposed criteria and other aspects of the program authorized under Public Law 86–373.

This legislation is a constructive step toward a better distribution of functions between the Federal Government and the States. I know that you share with me the hope that more such steps to expand State responsibility will be taken in the future.

　　With best wishes,

Sincerely,

Dwight D. Eisenhower

NOTE: This is the text of identical letters sent to the Governors of all the States. It was released at Augusta, Ga.

　　The amendment of the Atomic Energy Act of 1954 with respect to cooperation with the States (Public Law 86–373; 73 Stat. 688) was approved September 23, 1959.

　　Copies of the criteria referred to by the President were released by the Office of Health and Safety, Atomic Energy Commission, Germantown, Md.

117 ¶ Statement by the President Upon Making Public the Second Interim Report of the Cabinet Committee on Price Stability for Economic Growth. *April* 17, 1960

THE CABINET COMMITTEE on Price Stability for Economic Growth under the chairmanship of Vice President Nixon has submitted to me a Second Interim Report entitled "Prospects for Price Stability." I am making this Report public because it deals with matters of continuing importance to all Americans.

　　The Report is encouraging because it reveals the substantial progress we have made in checking inflation and in creating favorable prospects for price stability and healthy economic growth. But the Report gives no cause for complacency. Both government and the public must be constantly alert to these problems. We must continue to manage our monetary and fiscal affairs in a responsible manner; we must be firm, yet flexible, in adjusting public policies to promote economic expansion and to meet changing economic conditions; and we must preserve and strengthen the institutions of our free, competitive economy.

　　In the last analysis, sound public policies derive their strength from public understanding and public support. This Report, I believe, will help to enlarge that public understanding and broaden that support upon which the success of future efforts so largely rests.

NOTE: The report (20 pp., mimeographed) was released with the President's letter, together with the following summary by the Committee of its conclusions:

　　1. Inflation has been, and the threat of

inflation will continue to be, a serious national problem.

2. We have the tools to curb inflation. On the whole, these tools have been used effectively during the past 8 years.

3. Most of the inflation that really hurts our old people and others on fixed incomes took place between the beginning of the Second World War and the end of the Korean War. Only 10 percent of the general price increase since 1939 has occurred since the Korean War.

4. It is not true that inflation stimulates economic growth. On the contrary, it creates waste, inefficiency, and hardship. It hurts our foreign markets, and it lessens the ability of American business to compete at home with imported goods.

5. While sound monetary and fiscal policies are the first line of defense against harmful increases in the price level, we cannot be complacent about cost increases springing from inefficiency and unsound practices of management, labor, or government.

6. Stability of the price level, though a necessary condition for the great expansion we expect in the 1960's, will not by itself assure economic growth. Growth requires research, imagination, initiative, thrift, constant efforts to increase efficiency, an improved investment climate, and vigilance in rooting out rigidities, whether governmental or private, that impede change in our economic system.

For the President's statement upon making public the first interim report, see the 1959 volume, this series, p. 484.

118   ¶ Letter to the Administrator of General Services Offering the President's Papers and Other Documentary Materials as a Gift to the United States.   *April* 19, 1960

[Released April 19, 1960. Dated April 13, 1960]

Dear Mr. Floete:

The papers of a President, which from the time of George Washington have been regarded as the personal property of the President, have, inescapably, a direct and important association with the history of our country. Believing that they should be permanently and generally available for study, I desire that my papers should be made so available and believe that this can best be done through a Presidential archival depository, as provided by the Federal Property and Administrative Services Act of 1949, as amended.

The Eisenhower Presidential Library Commission, an agency of the State of Kansas, now has under construction in the City of Abilene a library building, financed by public subscription, where it is proposed to house my Presidential and other papers. This building is appropriately situated on land adjacent to my boyhood home and to a museum, both of which are maintained by the Eisenhower Foundation, a non-profit corporation organized under the laws of Kansas.

When the Library building has been completed, the Commission intends to present it, together with equipment and grounds, as a gift to the United States, on condition that the United States will maintain and operate this Library as a Presidential archival depository under the provisions of the above cited Act.

Therefore, in furtherance of this plan and in accordance with the provisions of that Act, I now offer as a gift to the United States such of my papers and other documentary materials as are hereinafter described, on condition that these papers and materials will be accepted, preserved, and made available by the United States under the following terms:

1. Upon the close of my term in office, I shall cause to be transferred to the United States for deposit in the Library at Abilene the bulk of my papers in the White House office, estimated to include several million documents.

2. Other documents still in my possession, including the remainder of my Presidential papers, the papers accumulated by me before my inauguration as President, and other documentary materials, including books, still pictures, motion pictures, and sound recordings, shall be transferred to the United States for deposit in said Library from time to time as shall be agreed upon by the Administrator of General Services or his representative and me or my representative, except those papers and other documentary materials which shall, before or after my leaving the Office of President, be determined by me or my representative to be excluded from this offer by reason of private or personal interest in such papers or materials on my part or on the part of a member of my family.

3. The offer of the papers and other materials described in paragraphs 1 and 2 hereof is conditioned upon acceptance by the United States of the offer of the land and buildings comprising the Eisenhower Library at Abilene, Kansas, and upon its agreement to maintain and operate the Library at all times thereafter as a Presidential archival depository for the storage of such papers and other materials, in accordance with the provisions of the Federal Property and Administrative Services Act of 1949, as amended, such acceptance and agreement to be effected within 90 days after the end of the period described in the second proviso to section 507 (f)(1) of said Act.

4. All papers and other documentary materials which shall be transferred to the United States pursuant to the foregoing shall be kept in the

Library permanently, subject to the right of the Administrator of General Services in his discretion (a) to make temporary loans thereof to such persons, organizations, or institutions as he shall determine, (b) to dispose by sale, exchange, or otherwise of any such papers or documentary materials which the Archivist of the United States may determine to have no permanent or historical interest or to be surplus to the needs of said Library, and (c) to remove from said Library any or all such papers or documentary materials if he deems it necessary to preserve them from threatened destruction.

5. All papers and other documentary materials transferred to the United States pursuant to the foregoing shall be accessible at all reasonable times to me, my son, my representative, or to other persons authorized in writing by me or my son to have access to such papers.

6. It is my purpose to make the papers and other documentary materials donated to the United States by the terms of this instrument available for purposes of serious research as soon as possible and to the fullest extent possible. However, since the President of the United States is the recipient of many confidences from others, and since the inviolability of such confidences is essential to the functioning of the office of the Presidency, it will be necessary to withhold from public scrutiny certain papers and classes of papers for varying periods of time. In pursuance of this objective and in accordance with the provisions of Section 507(f)(3) of the Federal Property and Administrative Services Act of 1949, as amended, conditions are imposed on the use of my papers as provided in paragraphs 7 through 10 immediately following.

7. Subsequent to the execution of this instrument, the Administrator of General Services shall have the papers that are transferred to the United States reviewed and shall place under seal the following classes of materials:

a. Papers that are security-classified pursuant to law or Executive Order, until such classification shall be removed.

b. Papers the use of which may be prejudicial to the maintenance of good relations with foreign nations.

c. Papers containing statements made by or to me in confidence.

d. Papers relating to my family or private business affairs, and papers relating to the families or private business affairs of persons who have had correspondence with me.

e. Papers containing statements about individuals which might be used to injure or harass them or members of their families.

f. Such other individual files as I, or my representative, or the Administrator of General Services may specify.

8. Papers placed under seal shall not be made available to anyone or their contents divulged to anyone (including public officials) except (a) persons authorized under the terms of paragraph 5 above, and (b) officials and employees of the National Archives and Records Service when performing essential archival work processes on such papers under the supervision of the Administrator of General Services.

9. All papers placed under seal in accordance with the foregoing provisions shall be reexamined from time to time by officials and employees of the National Archives and Records Service under the direction of the Administrator of General Services and, subject to approval by me or my representative, shall be opened to research use as soon as the passage of time or other circumstances have removed the conditions that required that they be put under seal.

10. All competent private persons interested in using my papers for serious scholarly research shall be granted equal access to those that are not withheld from use according to the foregoing, subject to the regulations issued by the Administrator of General Services governing the use of papers and other documentary materials in the Library.

11. Title to my papers and other documentary materials and the literary property rights in my papers, shall pass to the United States as such papers and materials are transferred to the United States under the terms and conditions herein expressed, except that I reserve to myself and to my heirs (a) a right to make any use of any of these papers in writing for publication, and (b) literary property rights in any works that I have written or may hereafter write for publication. These reservations include the right to license any publisher of any such work.

12. My representative for purposes of paragraphs 2, 5, 7, 8 and 9 shall be such person or persons as I may designate in a letter filed with the Administrator of General Services. In the event that at any time after my death there should be no representative so designated, my representative shall be my son John Eisenhower, or such person or persons as he may designate in the same manner.

The detailed conditions described in this letter have been drawn up in accordance with known precedents and with the cooperation of officials of your office and of the National Archives. Permit me to express

my deep appreciation of the help that all these individuals have given me.
With personal regard,

Sincerely,

DWIGHT D. EISENHOWER

NOTE: Mr. Floete's reply, dated April 15, follows:

Dear Mr. President:

It gives me great pleasure to accept, in accordance with the provisions of the Federal Property and Administrative Services Act of 1949, as amended, your offer of certain papers and other documentary materials subject to the conditions prescribed in your letter of April 13, 1960.

Mr. John P. Harris, Chairman of the Eisenhower Presidential Library Commission, has written me on behalf of the Commission, offering to convey as a gift to the United States the land, building and equipment necessary to the establishment of the Eisenhower Library. The Commission's offer is subject to further action of the Kansas Legislature, which must give the Commission authority to convey title, but the Commission is confident this action will be taken at the 1961 session. The Commission has also offered the Library property for use in the meantime as a Presidential archival depository. Copies of Mr. Harris' letter and my reply are enclosed.

While final transfer of title will be delayed until the Kansas Legislature has acted, I understand that all necessary

steps under the laws of the United States and the State of Kansas can be completed so that the building will be constructed and available to house your papers by the time you leave Office. For this, every American is indebted not only to the Commission headed by Mr. Harris but also to the Governor's National Committee for the Eisenhower Presidential Library, of which Governor Docking and Senator Darby are co-chairmen.

Also, we are all deeply indebted to you, Mr. President, for making your papers available for preservation and use in a public institution. There they will be safeguarded, reviewed, and catalogued by professional archivists so that as time passes they may become increasingly available for use by all serious researchers who seek to know and understand the history of our times.

Because of the Library's national significance, it is a great privilege for us in GSA to participate in the preparations necessary for this important addition to our national archives system.

Respectfully,

FRANKLIN FLOETE

The President's letter and Mr. Floete's reply were released at Augusta, Ga., together with the exchange of letters between Mr. Harris and Mr. Floete.

---

119   ¶ Message to President Kubitschek of Brazil on the Occasion of the Inauguration of the New Capital, Brasilia.   *April* 21, 1960

[Released April 21, 1960. Dated April 19, 1960]

Dear Mr. President:

You will recall how greatly I was impressed during our meeting at Brasilia last February with the extraordinary accomplishment of the

Government and the people of Brazil in building this inspiring new capital. On this joyful occasion of the inauguration of your great city of the future, I wish to renew my congratulations to Your Excellency on your vision and achievement and on the splendid pioneering spirit of Brazil.

With warm regard,

Sincerely,

DWIGHT D. EISENHOWER

NOTE: This message was released at Augusta, Ga.

120   ❡ Remarks of Welcome to President de Gaulle of France at the Washington National Airport.   *April* 22, 1960

President de Gaulle:

It is a very great pleasure for me and for the American people to welcome you here, sir, with Madame de Gaulle, and members of your party.

There has been a long and very special relationship existing between the United States and France. We have shared 200 years of common experiences. We have been devoted to common ideals, and the men of our two countries have shed their blood in common cause.

Through all of these experiences and these adventures, the affection and the admiration of one people for another have never weakened—indeed they have strengthened. And it is a happy circumstance that your visit here today is symbolic of that continuing affection and admiration that these people have one for the other.

It is indeed a happy circumstance that I can welcome you for the first time on this soil not only as President of France but President of the French Community. Our people are just as anxious for the development of those countries under the sponsorship of France as is France itself, and indeed we hope that our ties of friendship with the entire Community will be as strong and as close as have those ties with the people of your country.

And now, finally, may I welcome you more especially personally. I met you first 18 years ago, in the dark days of a world war. From that time on our association has grown ever closer. And I must assure you—as I have assured my own people time and again—that the debt that the cause of freedom owes to General de Gaulle has not only been strong but it is one that is widely understood, appreciated, in this country—as indeed I think it is in all other portions of the free world.

I repeat my welcome on behalf of the American people, and for myself, to a man who in war and peace has proved such a great friend to all of those who love human dignity and are dedicated to the welfare of humans everywhere. We thank you for being here.

NOTE: President de Gaulle responded (through an interpreter) as follows:

From the bottom of my heart, thank you, Mr. President. Seeing you and listening to you, I feel once more in agreement. Here I am once again in the United States of America. I had not been here for 15 years. This time again on your invitation, that is, the invitation of a dear and illustrious friend. This is another proof that one does not resist President Eisenhower. It is also impossible to resist the powerful stream of events.

A grave international debate is going to take place in 3 weeks. Before joining this debate for France, it was indeed necessary that I converse with the President of the United States. In any case, I feel a deep satisfaction to visit and salute the great American people, dear to my heart and upon whom rests to a very great extent the fate of the entire free world.

121 ¶ Toasts of the President and President de Gaulle. *April 22, 1960*

Mr. President, Madame de Gaulle, and friends:

It is indeed a happy privilege for me to welcome President de Gaulle to this table on behalf of this company. My lasting respect and admiration for General de Gaulle began 18 years ago when I met him first in London. He and I were associates in a war, a desperate war, of which the hope was to gain a peace in which people could have faith and confidence.

At the end of that war we learned certain things about peace. One is that there is no peace merely because the cannons are still. Another is that many people talk about peace who are not talking honestly except as they conceive of a peace as a condition in which their opponents must surrender their privileges and rights and live in a state of serfdom.

Finally, we learn that peace is a rather delicate condition and characteristic, and it needs to be guarded with vigilance and with strength—with moral, intellectual, economic, and military strength.

Now General de Gaulle is a partner, with his country, of this country and this Government, in waging the peace. In waging the peace, we have other battles to fight. The campaigns and the battles against hunger, disease, privation, resentment, ignorance—all these are part of waging peace.

No single country can win this campaign by itself. We are proud indeed, in this country, that France with its great leader General de Gaulle is associated with us in this great effort—this worldwide effort; and more especially as a partner of ours in the great alliance of NATO, founded well over a decade ago to bring about a situation in which peace can be waged without fear and without bending to threat.

I can conceive of no more worthy partner that I should like to have at my side, in what efforts I can make towards waging the peace, than General de Gaulle. And for this reason I have a feeling of special honor in asking this company to join with me in a Toast to General de Gaulle, President of the French Republic and the French Community.

NOTE: The President proposed the toast at a state dinner at the White House. President de Gaulle responded (through an interpreter) as follows:

Mr. President:

Our two countries have given us—you and me—a sacred trust, that of Franco-American friendship. It seems to me that in our actions and in the performance of our duties, we have had the good fortune to preserve it and even to help it grow. Indeed, I do not believe that in the two countries since this flame was kindled, the United States and France have ever been closer to each other in mind and in spirit.

Once again, only a short while ago, Mr. President, Paris gave you magnificent testimony of this when you were there on an official visit. And this morning, Washington in return has just given an unforgettable truth: when the world is troubled, when danger hovers over the peoples, when those in authority face the task at one and the same time of opening the path of peace and finding the means to safeguard the right of man to liberty, this moral and political force constituted by the natural agreement of our two countries has a worth and an impact that are unparalleled.

The forthcoming international debate will no doubt afford a new opportunity for demonstrating this. But I must point out that in any case no one has contributed to it more eminently, more effectively in the light of history, than President Eisenhower, in time of war and in time of peace.

In saying this, Mr. President, I am expressing the sentiments that we feel, my wife and I, when we are with you and Mrs. Eisenhower. I am also expressing the cordial and trusting frankness that inspire me in the talks that we have begun.

I raise my glass to President Eisenhower, the Government of the United States, to the American people—the friend and ally of France.

122 ¶ Message to President Betancourt on the Occasion of the Sesquicentennial of Venezuela's Independence. *April* 23, 1960

[Released April 23, 1960. Dated April 18, 1960]

Dear Mr. President:

It gives me great pleasure to convey to Your Excellency and to the people of Venezuela warm greetings and hearty congratulations from the people of the United States and from myself on the occasion of the commemoration of the sesqui-centennial of the independence of the Republic of Venezuela. I am confident that the social, political, and economic progress of Venezuela and its people will continue in the years ahead.

Sincerely,

DWIGHT D. EISENHOWER

123 ¶ Remarks to Members of the National 4-H Conference. *April* 25, 1960

FIRST OF ALL, my thanks to both of you for acting as representatives of this group in giving me this little emblem. I don't know whether I can wear it all the time these next 9 months, but starting next January I see no reason why I shouldn't keep it about me all the time. As a matter of fact, I am very proud to be so designated because while my years will not allow me membership except on an honorary basis, still I would like to be one of your members.

I don't know how many times in the last 7 or 8 years I have had the opportunity of welcoming representatives of the 4-H groups. I remember that I helped to dedicate your headquarters out on Connecticut Avenue. At other times we have also met together. This shall be my final meeting, and I want to leave with you a little message. Possibly I have repeated it time and again, but I think it will not be tiring if I give to you something of what is in my heart and mind when I talk about the opportunities of 4-H people to do something for the world.

Humanity has common problems that cry out for solution. These are problems of starvation, misery, suffering, and disease throughout the world. Unless the battles against these evils are waged intensively and with increasing success, the kind of world that we want, for ourselves and for those who come after, is not going to be achieved.

Back of the solution of these problems we must have real understanding. This word is bandied about a great deal by people when they don't want to be specific. But I mean the understanding of the problem as a human—not because you are an American or because you are a Frenchman or a Brazilian or any other nationality. We all must take heed of a human problem and a human need and see why we cannot solve it by a cooperative effort, because we all should understand it on the same basis.

It is not necessarily true, I think, that we can always think as an individual from another nation. Each nation has its own traditions, its background, its history, its own heroes. That makes some difference of approach to most problems. But these problems I am talking about so clearly belong to all peoples, to all humans, that we can forget various kinds of nationality and achieve a very great deal of understanding among ourselves.

As we do that—as we reach greater understanding—there will be every day greater and newer fields open to us in which these same attributes of cooperative attitude can be exercised and brought to bear. We will all be happier and better people. By that I mean not just ourselves, because of the satisfaction of doing the decent thing, but actually in the development of greater spiritual, intellectual, cultural, and material strength in the world.

This is what we want to do.

This puts a great deal of responsibility on people who like yourselves already understand a great deal of these problems. It also opens a greater field of opportunity. Part of the responsibility is to make yourselves physically and mentally, intellectually and spiritually fit for the job. This is one of the great functions of the 4–H movement. It is one reason that I am so proud of it.

Because you all are classed now as young leaders, the opportunity you have is that you can influence others all over the world to show the same self-interest in their problems. Young people can all have the same dictates of conscience, of gratification of doing something decent for other humans.

Only as the whole world becomes better unified through the kind of understanding that you people are already doing so much to promote—

only as the world peoples understand each other's weaknesses and strengths and have greater sympathy for common problems—is there going to be greater assurance of a durable peace with justice.

This is what we all want.

Now my young friends, as I leave you and say goodbye, at least in my present capacity to 4–H, I tell you: no one could have more confidence in what young America can do, and will do, than I have. Since the earliest days of dealing with the youth of America in the military forces, I have developed the most tremendous respect for the capacity, the imagination, the dedication, and devotion of our youngsters. I don't want at this moment to be buttering you up. I don't mean that.

I mean you have got a tremendous responsibility, a great opportunity, and a great capacity to discharge your responsibilities and to take advantage of the opportunities to the benefit of America, yourselves, your families, and the whole world.

And so in my new capacity, you will probably see me again. But, as President, goodbye.

NOTE: The President spoke in the Rose Garden at the White House. In his opening sentence he referred to Brenda Ann Tjaden of Kansas and Jimmy McCor-mick of Tennessee, delegates to the Conference, who presented the President with a tie clasp bearing the 4–H emblem and inscribed with the words "Partner in 4–H."

124   ¶ Toast by the President at a Dinner Given in His Honor by President de Gaulle. *April 25, 1960*

Mr. President, Madame de Gaulle, and friends:

General de Gaulle, over two decades you and I have met in unusual circumstances, both in war and in peace. We have met in Casablanca and in Algiers, and in London and Paris. In all those meetings, many of which were important for the progress of events that were then afoot, I am sure I have never felt any greater sense of satisfaction at the outcome than I have of your visit here to Washington.

You have been able to meet the Members of our Congress, and to speak to them. You have spoken to them as a symbol of modern France. You have spoken indirectly to all the people who have seen you, both on the streets and on the family television. You have met the members of the Executive Department—and everywhere people say: General de Gaulle is a direct, forceful, and great man.

I have met this evening several of my friends from Congress. They have said words that mean just what I have now indicated, because of the speech that you made before them this noon.

Other millions will see you on their televisions, and the streets of New York, and other cities. To all of them you will be the symbol of a France that is regenerated, that has come back from the depths of World War II—again a great influence, marching on the side of all the other free nations, in favor of freedom, independence, and with human feeling for those nations less fortunate. You will be the spokesman for an ally that we have been fortunate to have ever since the Battle of Saratoga. As I recall—and my military history should be accurate—I think it was completed on October 17, 1777, and its principal result was that it brought France as the ally of America. Since that time France and America have been great friends—and your visit has made us greater friends. Of that I can assure you, on behalf of myself, the Government, and all of the people that you will meet.

And so for me it is an especial privilege to raise my glass to General de Gaulle, the President of the French Republic and the French Community. President de Gaulle!

NOTE: The President proposed the toast at the dinner given in his honor at the French Embassy Residence.

125 ¶ Joint Statement Following Discussions With President de Gaulle. *April* 25, 1960

THE PRESIDENT of the United States and the President of the French Republic have had a series of talks from April 22 to 25 on the occasion of the visit of General de Gaulle. The Secretary of State of the United States, the Minister of Foreign Affairs of France and the Ambassadors of the two countries have taken part in these talks.

The exchanges of views which they have had have permitted them to define more precisely the positions which will be taken at the Summit Conference on the questions which will be raised there.

The main purpose of this Conference in the view of the two Presidents is to achieve an easing of tensions in the international situation.

126 ¶ Exchange of Messages Between the President and the Shah of Iran on the Lar Earthquake Disaster. *April* 27, 1960

[Released April 27, 1960. Dated April 25, 1960]

Your Imperial Majesty:

I was deeply shocked to hear of the terrible tragedy that has befallen the people of Lar and the surrounding villages. I extend on behalf of the American people our profound sympathy to the victims of this unfortunate catastrophe.

Sincerely,

DWIGHT D. EISENHOWER

NOTE: The Shah of Iran's reply, dated April 26, follows:

The President
The White House

Deeply touched by your kind message of sympathy for the victims of the Lar earthquake. I hasten to express sincere thanks for the generous help which your Government is extending to us in this disaster.

MOHAMMAD REZA PAHLAVI

127 ¶ The President's News Conference of *April* 27, 1960

THE PRESIDENT. I have no announcements.

Q. Merriman Smith, United Press International: Mr. President, the new Acting President of Korea says he still expects you to visit there June 22d. Could you comment on that for us, sir; and in this connection, describe for us the role of the United States in the current Korean crisis—specifically, did this Government ever indicate to Korea that we thought President Rhee should leave office?

THE PRESIDENT. Well, you've got a number of barrels on your gun there, but I'll try to remember all your points.

First of all, I have no change of plans whatsoever. I expect to go to Korea.

Secondly, to charge America with interference in the internal affairs of Korea is not correct.

Now, we start off with this: Syngman Rhee is not only, has been not only a great man in his area, but he has been a tremendous patriot. I think he is one of those men that can be called "The father of his country." He fought for its independence from the moment it lost it, I think in 1910; he has never ceased; and as he has grown older, there would be no doubt that here and there there have been mistakes. Now, in this last election there were certain irregularities. And the most that I ever did, and this was as a friendly gesture for a man I know and respect and admire, I said that trouble could come out of such irregularities and hoped that they could be stopped. I said this through the State Department; I believe it was published. No interference of any kind was ever undertaken by the United States; and we had no part in inciting, or know anything about the inciting of, this difficulty.

Just exactly what is going to happen I don't know; but I do know this: both the Communist press of Peking and, I believe, of Moscow have expressed some disappointment that Mr. Rhee has again shown a statesmanlike attitude in saying, "All right, I'm still serving my people and I'll do what seems to be correct."

I might add this: there is no evidence whatsoever that there was any Communist inspiration for this unrest that was brought about.

Q. Edward P. Morgan, American Broadcasting Company: Mr. President, this question is based on a White House announcement yesterday, that Mr. Nixon might be called on to substitute for you at the summit. Perhaps you have emphasized no theme more emphatically than the need to go wherever it was necessary to go and do whatever it was necessary to do to obtain and secure peace. Could you suggest to us what overriding domestic developments outside of an outright emergency there might be that would call you away from summit deliberations?

THE PRESIDENT. Well, I think it's simple. Congress is in session and there are a number of bills that are important that are before the Congress. If they should come at an awkward time for me and I felt that they should be vetoed, now I have quite a tough time schedule. Any important bill that requires a veto not only requires the deepest study in the departments concerned, but it demands daily consultation with me; because I am the one that has got to be convinced that this is a bad bill or a good bill. Therefore you cannot do this, as I say, if these bills are important, from a distance.

Now, the only reason that I happen to have said this in this particular case, we don't know how long this summit meeting is going to be. In 1955 we had a pretty good understanding of the number of days. Everybody agreed that this time it should go as long as it was felt necessary. So, since I am leaving on the 14th and had to fix a date for my visit to Portugal on Sunday, I took the 23d, the 23d to the 24th. This is getting along at a rather long period. So, I said if domestic requirements did bring me back, I would have to ask Mr. Nixon to serve for me as the head of the delegation. This doesn't mean that I expect him to be there, but I simply put the warning.

Q. Mrs. May Craig, Portland (Maine) Press Herald: For more years than you have been in the White House, the pitiful children of the West Virginia unemployed coal miners have been starving for proper food. We do give them whatever surpluses we have. While you and Congress talk about helping the needy in foreign countries, isn't there something that you could do for needy Americans in this rich America of our own?

THE PRESIDENT. Well, Mrs. Craig, you say they haven't been helped. I thought they had. Now I'm not going to try to generalize here or make any alibis. I will find out exactly what has happened, because in talking to the Secretary of Agriculture over the years, I assumed that for those people that were really destitute, there were methods for helping them so that they got enough to eat.[1]

Q. Laurence H. Burd, Chicago Tribune: Mr. President, you and President de Gaulle agreed that disarmament should be a priority subject at the summit. If we should have substantial disarmament somewhere along the line, do you think it would send this economy into a tailspin?

THE PRESIDENT. Well, I can't believe that it would, for this simple reason: we are now scratching around to get money for such things as

---

[1] On April 28 the White House issued a press release in response to Mrs. Craig's question. The release referred to the lack of information and understanding about the amount of Federal assistance that had been made available to destitute children and families not only in West Virginia but throughout the Nation. It added "the facts are that very material assistance has been given to these groups. It should be made perfectly clear that by law and as a matter of policy all surplus foods are made available to needy persons in this country before they are made available for donation to needy persons abroad." The release then outlined in detail the nature and extent of Federal assistance in West Virginia through the school lunch program, through the making available to needy families of surplus commodities, and through social security.

The release concluded as follows: "The Federal Government shares with State and local governments in providing monthly public assistance payments to four needy groups of people—the aged, blind, disabled, and children. In fiscal year 1959 payments to these four groups totalled $34,383,000, of which $26,139,000 or 76 percent came from the Federal Government. Needy children and their families received the major share of this assistance—$21,531,000, of which $16,396,000 came from the Federal Government."

school construction, a bill that I recommended a year ago. We are trying to build our roads before they become obsolete, and have to get a new program to bring them around. There are all sorts of things to be done in this country in the way of reclamation and so on that have to take over the years. I see no reason why the sums which now are going into these sterile, negative mechanisms that we call war munitions shouldn't go into something positive. Moreover, a greater portion of it could go into investment in the foreign field which in the long run will make us more prosperous than will just putting them in tanks and airplanes.

Q. Mr. Burd: May I ask one more thing on that? What role do you see for the Government in this conversion period if there were disarmament, in the sense of helping industry or not helping them?

THE PRESIDENT. I think, Mr. Burd, you are making one assumption that probably is not correct; that is, that if you got some agreement, that instantly there would be a very—cutoff. I think the thing would be an almost imperceptible decline; and that could be picked up, I think, without any great trouble.

Q. Robert J. Donovan, New York Herald Tribune: Mr. President, in New York yesterday General de Gaulle renewed his pledge of self-determination for the Algerians. I wonder if you could comment on that and tell us anything else that you and General de Gaulle may have discussed on that point?

THE PRESIDENT. Yes. I asked him specifically whether he stood by his pledge, and his speech of September 16, 1959, in which he promised a self-determination for the Algerian people with the suggested three— under three methods. He said that he not only stood by that but that it was the continued policy, the official policy as well as his personal conviction about the situation.

Now, the reason I asked the question was because of one or two speeches that he had made, one of them I believe at Constantine, the language as interpreted to us here seemed to mean that he had hardened, that he had changed his attitude. I put the specific question, and I said on that basis, just as I did in September 1959, "I endorse what you are doing and wish you well in its progress."

Q. Peter Lisagor, Chicago Daily News: Mr. President, if it should develop that Vice President Nixon were to go to the summit meeting after you leave it, would you expect the other heads of government to stay on, or would you expect them to appoint representatives of comparable rank to continue the talks?

THE PRESIDENT. Well now, it wouldn't be more than for a couple of days, so they would stay. As a matter of fact I have notified my friends, including Mr. Khrushchev, that this is always a possibility, because when we were trying to discuss the matter of the probable length of the conference, I had to insert this one possible caveat. The others are not under the same kind of compulsion, under certain situations; so if I had to come back, if the thing ran more than 2 or at the outside 3 days that he'd do, I'd be right back there. But in the meantime I would have taken care of whatever I thought was necessary.

Q. David P. Sentner, Hearst Newspapers: Mr. President, inasmuch as our democratic attitude has brought about free elections in distant South Korea, could you tell us what is our current attitude towards the absence of free elections under the Castro regime in Cuba?

THE PRESIDENT. Well, you say we brought them about. I think that the Korean people brought them about. I believe the Koreans are dedicated to the self-expression of peoples. I believe that they are against communism and they have brought this about by their protests.

Now, I must say this: I deplore violence in these things. I have several times brought out that protests by peaceful assembly to bring to the attention of responsible officials the feelings of people, that's fine. I bitterly resent violence in connection with these things. So I think that we didn't do it. I did say to Mr. Rhee this could lead to trouble, if our reports are correct; but that's all.

Q. Robert C. Pierpoint, CBS News: Mr. President, I wonder if you could tell us some of your hopes for the summit conference in the light of two things: first of all, your visit with President de Gaulle; and, secondly, the recent belligerent statement by Khrushchev on Berlin.

THE PRESIDENT. Well, you mean the speech at Baku?

Q. Mr. Pierpoint: Yes.

THE PRESIDENT. Of course, when you come down to it, it is just a reiteration of the same old theme and the same old story.

I don't think that we should take that too seriously; but certainly if he means it as an ultimatum, which I don't believe he does, but if he does then I would have to reply just as I have to him before, and said to him, I shall never go to any meeting under a threat of force, the use of force or an ultimatum of any kind. I'm going there as a free representative of a free country if I go, and I'm sure he understands that. Therefore, I don't believe that his statement means a real change in policy. It's just a mere—more of the same.

Now, you say that you'd like to know about my hopes for the summit. I think the most we can hope for, at this time, is ease of tension, some evidence that we are coming closer together—sufficiently so that people have a right to feel a little bit more confident in the world in which they are living and in its stability.

How this might come about, I don't know. There are, of course, the subjects of ceasing of tests and with a controlled system for that, for developing some step in disarmament, and for greater contacts, particularly cultural contacts. I think that there are a number of ways in which this might begin, and that's about all you can say.

Q. Ray L. Scherer, National Broadcasting Company: A number of men in American public life recently have spoken up on how they feel about the injection of the religious issue into the political campaign. Could you tell us how you feel on that?

THE PRESIDENT. First of all, let me read two items from the American Constitution, article VI:

"The Senators and Representatives before mentioned, and the Members of the several State Legislatures, and all executive and judicial Officers, both of the United States and of the several States, shall be bound by Oath or Affirmation, to support this Constitution; but no religious Test shall ever be required as a Qualification to any Office or public Trust under the United States."

The second is the Bill of Rights and it is the first one of those rights:

"Congress shall make no law respecting an establishment of religion, or prohibiting the free exercise thereof; . . ."

Now, my answer, as far as I can give it, has been better given by the Constitution than in any words I can think of.

Q. John M. Hightower, Associated Press: Mr. President, if Mr. Khrushchev at the summit conference raises a very heavy pressure for his demands on Berlin, and in effect creates a crisis, would you regard such a development as blocking your hopes for an easing of tensions and for some agreement in the field of disarmament?

THE PRESIDENT. I reported to you people that Mr. Khrushchev said that he was going to raise this question, he was going to try to argue it, but that he was not putting any time limit upon an accomplishment.

I think that certainly at that moment he meant it. He knows that there are certain events coming around in the world. There are elections here and abroad and every place else; possibly he wants to see what's going to happen, I don't know. For example, there is a German election in which he is unquestionably interested. And he is probably hoping for some closer relations between West Germany and some of the border states, particularly like Poland. So there are other developments that he could expect or would hope to come about that would help to solve his problems from his viewpoint. But I think that is the reason that he sees there is no reason for putting down an ultimatum at this moment, because otherwise you just run into an immovable object and an irresistible force and there you are. Of course that would have a very great effect on the hopes that we have.

Q. Rutherford M. Poats, United Press International: Sir, I believe in listing your hopes and prospects for the summit you did not mention any settlement on Berlin or Germany. May we conclude from that and your answer just given that you do not have much, see much chance of any agreement there on that subject?

THE PRESIDENT. I think our position has been so clearly stated in speeches over the years, just recently one by the Vice President, one by Secretary Dillon, one by the Secretary of State. The point is that we are not going to give up the juridical position that we have.

It doesn't seem feasible or possible to me that any agreement could now be reached that would settle this whole thing; that we have to remember. But that does not mean that some kind of progress cannot be made, the side issue or side effect of which could be making a better approach toward Berlin in the months to come.

Q. Carleton Kent, Chicago Sun-Times: Mr. President, can you tell us anything of your administration's plans to send Congress a health insurance bill at this session?

THE PRESIDENT. I am preparing now a message for Congress giving my great concern about several bills. The only reason that is holding it up is that we have not yet been able to coordinate, to bring together the various aspects, you might say, of this great problem and try to make a sensible unit out of the literally dozens of different proposals and alternatives suggested.

Everybody agrees that in this field is a problem. Some of it, of course, is exemplified in very pitiful cases. There are all sorts of areas in which this is attacked—local, State, Federal, voluntary methods and every other kind of thing. The only thing to which I am utterly opposed is compulsory insurance in this field; and to put the matter in the OASI by adding on a half percent of taxes, half for the workman and half for the company, does not seem to me to be suitable because I regard that as a compulsory affair.

Q. Spencer Davis, Associated Press: Could you give us a better idea now of your travel plans for the Soviet Union, Japan, and Korea; and the possibility that you will not disappoint some of your Far Eastern friends by going to the Philippines and Taipei?

THE PRESIDENT. With this last part, every time you undertake a trip someone expresses a hope that you would go to another place. Now, if you continue this far enough, well, I couldn't get back here in time to vote next year. [*Laughter*]

Therefore, there has to be a compromise. I do my best in advance to explain my situation to those of our friends that might have an interest in it. So far, I have not felt able to enlarge the plans which include visits to Russia, Japan, and a very brief call in Korea.

The one in Russia, I don't believe the details are yet fixed sufficiently so that I could give you the actual schedule. I think in a few days I probably could—Mr. Hagerty says in a few days it could be.

Q. John Herling, National Newspaper Syndicate: At long last, sir, preparations are being made for that labor-management summit conference and in your January State of the Union Message you talked about the public interest which required such a getting together. May I ask, sir, why the public is not directly represented in such a proposed conference?

THE PRESIDENT. I think that they will be. First of all, we are starting out to get three representatives of labor and three of business to determine who they believe should be included in the membership of a committee that will do this. So I would rather see three businessmen and three recognized labor leaders determining on the composition of the final commission than I would to just name it myself. Frankly, the only thing I'm doing here is suggesting this thing and getting it started by putting the six individuals together, having seen George Meany and then Mr. Bannow. In this way I hope it will take just as much concern about the public interest as all of the rest of us are.[1]

Q. Sarah McClendon, El Paso Times: Sir, last December the 2d I asked you a question and you said you'd look into it, and that was about the ex parte conversations of Thomas Corcoran, a lawyer, with members of the Federal Power Commission, and actions that resulted in an increase in rates not once but at least twice. I wonder what you think about this?

THE PRESIDENT. Well, I don't recall, but I assure you this, that I told them to do it.

Do you have anything [*addresses Mr. Hagerty*]?

Mr. Hagerty: Yes, but it's too long an answer now. [*Laughter*]

THE PRESIDENT. Come over to Mr. Hagerty's office and see if he can give you the exact answer.

Q. Mrs. McClendon: Sir, I've been over there several times and asked that question——

THE PRESIDENT. Well, do you think you or I should do the correction for Mr. Hagerty? One of us will have to do it. [*Laughter*]

Q. E. W. Kenworthy, New York Times: Mr. President, several leading scientists last week testified before the Joint Committee on Atomic Energy that the art of concealing underground tests was outstripping the art of detecting them. Would the views of those scientists be taken into account in our negotiations at Geneva or at Paris and would we request an increase in the number of detection stations for a treaty on a nuclear test ban?

THE PRESIDENT. Well, you know the plan that we suggested was to agree on the methods for eliminating those above the atmosphere, those in the atmosphere, and those under the sea; and then, underground, down to I believe what they call a seismic index of 4.75 which is supposed to show a size, I believe, somewhere in the order of 20 kt. Up until that point, that would require an inspection system about like that that was laid out in 1958 at Geneva; but to go below that is going to take a very much more elaborate system.

---

[1] On April 26 the White House announced that the President had met with George Meany, President of the AFL-CIO, and that he would soon meet with Rudolph Bannow, President of the NAM, concerning the proposed conference. The release stated that the representatives of labor and of management would form a committee of six "to develop among themselves, without Government participation, understandings on the subject matters of the conference, select such additional conferees as they may decide upon, determine time and place of first meeting, and decide on other matters necessary to inaugurate a series of conferences."

What we have asked is for a group of the three countries that are working on this to get their scientists and see whether they can come up and develop the kind of plan that would be needed for these below the critical point. That is as far as it has gone.

I don't know, I have heard it said the number would have to be multiplied three times, or something of that kind, as to the number that was agreed first; but I am not sure.

Q. Charles W. Bailey, Minneapolis Tribune: Mr. President, earlier this year the Secretary of Agriculture indicated that a wheat bill raising price supports in any way would not fall within the guide lines you set down in your message. More recently Republican leaders have come away from meetings at the White House, including one meeting at which you were present, with the impression that it might be possible to have some small increase in wheat price supports in order to get a new piece of legislation this year. I wonder if you could help us out with your view on that.

THE PRESIDENT. Well, I am against higher price supports because the only effect I can see of them is that we put more and more wheat in storage; we have surpluses that overhang the market, depress prices, and make the problem much greater—greater and more severe.

Now, if there were any kind of reasonable plan, connected with other features of the thing that could bring something about that seemed to be reasonable and fair to the farmers, well, I would be glad to look at it. As I say, if it looks reasonable to me, I will approve it; because I am just to this point: I know that we are in a bad fix, the farmers are, and I have had correspondence recently with some of my farmer friends, individuals, to get statistics. I must say that it is one, though, that when you take all of the intricacies of actual problems affecting so many humans in such a great industry and then mix that up with politics you have got something that is very difficult indeed to solve.

Q. Richard E. Mooney, New York Times: Mr. President, Senator Bush has said that he has been advised by the White House that Mr. Connole will not be reappointed to the Federal Power Commission. You have received several representations on behalf of Mr. Connole's reappointment, most recently from a group of Mayors. Could you tell us first, are you not going to reappoint Mr. Connole; and second, why?

THE PRESIDENT. First—why—this: because it is my responsibility to appoint people and to get the best people I can. Mr. Connole came to see one of my staff in December to ask about his reappointment, and they said they'd look into it. I think I can get a better man, that's all.

Q. James B. Reston, New York Times: Mr. President, in his speech yesterday in Baku, Mr. Khrushchev repeated the threats which the Camp David communique was intended to remove. Now my question is whether you intend to let it stand where it is or will you communicate with him about the Baku speech?

THE PRESIDENT. I have made no particular decision on the point.

Q. Lillian Levy, National Jewish Post and Opinion: President Nasser recently stated that the Suez would remain closed to Israel's ships and shipping and that he has reached no understanding on this matter with you and Secretary General Hammarskjold. Under your leadership, sir, the 1956 Suez crisis was resolved; at that time the United States again reaffirmed the broad principle of free access through the Suez for all nations and expressed its faith that Nasser would uphold this principle.

Since Nasser has rejected it, are you considering now personal intervention, and do you have any reason to believe that your intervention would be less successful today than it was in '56?

THE PRESIDENT. I did say exactly what you said in 1956. Mr. Nasser has given as his reason for doing nothing since that time that they are in a state of war, that this doesn't apply.

Now, I don't know what you can do unless you want to resort to force in such affairs, and I'm certain that we're not trying to settle international problems with force. We have done everything we could to make it clear that we stand by our commitments and we think that other nations should do the same, particularly when it comes to the free use of the Suez Canal. But, I don't know that there is any idea whatsover of making a new step in this direction or new argument, because I think it's all been said.

Marvin L. Arrowsmith, Associated Press: Thank you, Mr. President.

NOTE: President Eisenhower's one hundred and eighty-fourth news conference was held in the Executive Office Build- ing from 10:28 to 11 o'clock on Wednesday morning, April 27, 1960. In attendance: 215.

128 ❡ Remarks of Welcome to the King and Queen of Nepal at the Washington National Airport. *April 27, 1960*

Your Majesties:

It is indeed a great honor to welcome you here to the United States. The American people are delighted that you have found it possible to lay down your own responsibilities long enough to come and make this visit to our country.

It is truly an historic occasion. This is the first time that a reigning monarch of Nepal has set foot on this continent, and we are indeed proud that you have found it possible to do so.

The friendly relations between your country and ours are a matter of common knowledge. They have long existed. They have been strong and cordial, and we are confident that your visit here will do much to strengthen them and sustain them.

So, sir, and to you, Your Majesty, we—the people, the Government, and I—join in saying welcome, and we hope that you find our country interesting, and that every minute of your stay here will be enjoyable.

NOTE: King Mahendra responded (through an interpreter) as follows:

Your Excellency, and ladies and gentlemen:

We are all very happy to be here on your very kind invitation. We heartily welcome this opportunity for the exchange of views with such a great leader as you, who have distinguished yourself in the service of your nation in both war and peace and have always stood for the cause of peace and freedom in the world.

We hope and trust that our visit will further strengthen the existing bonds of friendship and cordiality between our two countries.

We bring to you, Mr. President, the greetings and salutations of the people of Nepal and also through you, sir, convey their best wishes to the people of the United States.

During our visit in the United States in the next few days, we will be looking forward to meeting the people in the different parts of the country and acquiring a firsthand knowledge of the great achievements the American people have made in different spheres of national endeavor.

Your Excellency, we thank you from the bottom of our hearts for the kind and generous words of welcome you have just addressed to us, and take this opportunity to express our good wishes for the happiness and prosperity of this great land.

Thank you, Mr. President.

129 ¶ Toasts of the President and King Mahendra of Nepal.   *April 27, 1960*

Your Majesties and my friends:

It is indeed an honor for us to gather this evening to welcome to this Capital and to this house the King and Queen of Nepal. We are especially honored because it is the first time that a ruling monarch of Nepal has set foot on this land.

The times are gone when we feel that geography means much to the relations between countries. We have become neighbors through the miracle of modern inventions, communications, and transportation, and we have come to know more of each other. Up until now we have known about such countries as Nepal only by reports from a few adventurous travelers—a few of whom, Your Majesty, are here present this evening—but they have told us about a people that is sturdy, proud of its independence and its liberty, and determined to sustain it. Those are the qualities that Americans admire and respect, and try themselves to show.

It is certain, therefore, that as you go about this country, you will be greeted with the utmost friendliness, respect, and admiration, and indeed our great hope of knowing—through the members of your party and yourself and your gracious Queen—your people. I think that your visit here cannot fail to stimulate greater travel between our two peoples. This is all to the good, because this means a greater understanding among the peoples—and international understanding is the only foundation upon which true peace can be built.

And so, sir, as you come here as the representative and the ruler of your people, as through you we try to send to them greetings and our best wishes for their success and their continued progress, I know that this company will want to join me in raising our glasses to your health and happiness. Ladies and gentlemen, the King!

NOTE: The President proposed the toast at a state dinner at the White House. King Mahendra responded (through an interpreter) as follows:

Your Excellency, ladies and gentlemen:

With your permission, I would like to offer on behalf of the Queen, ourselves, and all those who have accompanied us, heartfelt thanks to the President for his most generous expression of goodwill to us and our people.

During this brief period of history of diplomatic and friendly association between our two countries, it is for the first time that a personal meeting between the two heads of state has taken place. In the long history of our nation, it is also the first time that an occupant of the Throne of Nepal has set foot on American soil. We welcome this opportunity of having a free and frank exchange of views on subjects of mutual interest, and especially on the means and possibility of further strengthening the friendly relations between our two countries, both of which share a common belief in the democratic way of life.

Mr. President, my government and people have always welcomed and appreciated the initiative and efforts on your part for the furtherance of the cause of

peace in the world. We would like to take this opportunity to offer our best wishes for the success of the summit conference due to be held next month, and venture to express the hope that the whole world will benefit by its outcome.

We are happy to receive this opportunity to meet the American people and their leaders in various spheres of their national life and activity.

Ladies and gentlemen, may we now request you all to join us in toasting the health and happiness of the President and Mrs. Eisenhower.

130   ¶ Joint Statement Following Discussions With King Mahendra.   *April* 28, 1960

THE PRESIDENT of the United States and His Majesty Mahendra Bir Bikram Shah Deva, King of Nepal, today held a friendly and fruitful discussion on various matters of mutual interest.

King Mahendra, who is visiting the United States upon the invitation of the President, has also addressed a joint session of the United States Congress. At the conclusion of his Washington stay on April 30, King Mahendra will begin a twelve-day coast-to-coast tour of the United States, during which he will meet with various civic, cultural, and business leaders.

The President expressed great admiration for the steps which have been taken under the leadership of King Mahendra to foster the growth of democracy in Nepal, as exemplified by the promulgation of a constitution by the King and by the holding of general elections in 1959 under the provisions of that constitution.

In their review of the world situation, the President and King Mahendra expressed their mutual concern with the vital problem of achieving lasting peace and establishing a world order based on international justice. They reaffirmed their determination to work toward those goals, the achievement of which will contribute immensely to the general progress, prosperity, and welfare of mankind.

The President and King Mahendra agreed that the American people and the Nepalese people have in common the virtues of tolerance, charity, and benevolence, which virtues should serve as the basis of relations between all nations. The President and King Mahendra agreed further that Nepal and the United States share a profound belief in the sovereignty and independence of nations and in genuine noninterference in the affairs of others. The President and King Mahendra agreed that any attempt by any nation to impose its own economic system or political beliefs on any other country should be condemned.

The President and King Mahendra expressed a common belief that social and economic progress should be achieved by all peoples in the manner of their own choosing and in government based on consent of the governed and the dignity of the human individual. In this spirit, the President assured King Mahendra of the continuing readiness of the United States to be of assistance to the Government of Nepal in its high objective of developing the resources of the country for the welfare of its people.

The President and King Mahendra expressed their mutual desire to maintain and further strengthen the cordiality and genuine friendship which has always characterized Nepalese-American relations and which has been so evident during the King's visit.

131 ¶ Remarks at the Annual Meeting of the U.S. Chamber of Commerce. *May 2, 1960*

Dr. Canham, Secretary Mueller, and members of the Chamber, and friends:

It is, of course, a distinct privilege to have the opportunity to meet with the members of the Chamber of Commerce during this convention. You have established in this country a very enviable reputation for making recommendations to the Government or for stating propositions before our people that are based upon principle and not expedience. This fact enhances your capacity and your opportunities in one broad function that I conceive to be very important: that of teachers.

It is not enough that a body of people understands a matter, places it before the Government or any other responsible body, and then to sit back in the belief that the duty of that body is completed.

The United States is a government in which public opinion is the motivating force behind everything that happens. It must be an informed public opinion if the things that happen are going to be good for the United States and good for humanity.

Consequently, those that understand must make their voices heard. Their responsibility to inform others is equal, indeed, to that of the responsibility of informing themselves.

I am going to speak for a short time on three subjects that each of you understands. Of this I am certain, because the official actions and recommendations and reports of the Chamber of Commerce have always supported them.

They are:

1. Reciprocal trade, or the importance of expanding foreign and international trade.

2. The programs of mutual security, by which we help other nations further to advance their economic standards and their living standards.

3. And, thirdly, here at home, the need for prudence in our fiscal affairs. We should cast from our minds the thought that money alone can solve all our problems. Only as we produce the people—the thinkers, the teachers, the technicians, the professional people that go along with great programs of welfare, education, and development—then, and then only, can money be used expeditiously, properly, and in a coordinated fashion to bring about the results we seek.

In the field of international trade, it would be unbecoming for me to appear before you as an expert. You people study these matters all the time. But I can express to you my own convictions in support of pronouncements you have made. Indeed, I can pause long enough to tell you that one of the reasons I think you are such a great organization is because you agree with me!

In speaking about foreign trade, we know that without liberalized trade there would be some four or five million of our people who would soon be out of jobs. You know this, but do all others?

It is important that people understand that a great deal of our employment is to produce the things that we send abroad. It is important for our people to understand that we are not a completely self-dependent nation, that there is a whole array of important minerals and products that we must obtain from the other parts of the world.

These areas are important to us both from our security and economic viewpoint. We must liberalize our trade policies or keep them liberal so that this trade can be advanced and increased all the time. As we grow, we need more trade. All along the line through trade we make other countries stronger in their industrial and economic output and standards. We give them hope—and hope is the thing that sustains them.

So both abroad and here we find that we do prosper, we do advance the causes of freedom and of peace through the business of trading and producing for the other fellow at such costs as he can buy and at such prices as we can pay.

———————

The mutual security program I shall mention only briefly, because tonight I expect, before another audience, to talk about this subject with the greatest emphasis of support that I personally can command. I believe it is one of the great programs through which the United States can lead toward world peace. Certainly people who believe in trade and commerce must be looking for world peace as strongly or even stronger than others.

I want to say one or two things about the mutual security program that occurred to me as simple examples of what I am talking about. No one here needs to be told of the vast importance it is to the world for the United States to cooperate closely with Canada and with Mexico. With these two countries we have long borders, and along them is found no soldier, no fort, no defensive or offensive arrangements of any kind. They are defended by friendship. That friendship must be based upon cooperative work—mutual understanding of problems and a constant, insistent effort to solve these problems to the mutual satisfaction of the parties concerned.

Now we understand this need and we are very proud of the results that have been achieved over the years. But modern transportation and modern communications have made every nation of the world our neighbor, except in the geographic sense. The cooperative efforts that have been so successful with Canada and with Mexico must be extended through every possible economic and trade factor that we can bring to bear so as to increase these friendships. The way is paved for us because we commonly worship and revere certain ideals: the dignity of the human, his rights, his equality before the law. These are the kind of concepts that create the atmosphere in which this kind of understanding of which I speak can be developed.

I can conceive of no greater accomplishment for the Chamber of Commerce, or indeed all of the friends and supporters of the Chamber of Commerce, than to bring these subjects and these matters affecting freer trade and mutual security to the understanding of our people, so that no longer do we hear such terms as "give-away," and the pretense that we neglect our own people in some of their needs and desires because we perform and pursue programs on the outside that are of the utmost importance to our own security and of world peace.

———

Finally, I mention a message that I shall this week send to the Congress, in which I want again to emphasize to them the importance of constructive legislation in certain areas. Along with this, I want to bring before their attention again the need for responsibility in handling the fiscal affairs of this Nation, not to believe that merely because you pass a bill that appropriates billions for some affair, some activity, that this instantly solves the problem that it is intended to solve.

The soundness of the dollar is as important to the world and to us as any other factor I can think of. By this, I mean we must avoid debasement of our currency. Too much of world stability and world peace hangs on it. All of us must bear these truths in mind, and they must be part of what we teach.

By no means must we ever be niggardly in doing for our own people those things that need to be done. We do not forget, and I know the Chamber does not forget, those words of Lincoln when he insisted that it was the responsibility of government to do for the individual that which he cannot do at all or so well do by himself alone. But Lincoln added this admonition when he continued to say that in all those incidents where the individual can do these things for himself, the government ought not to interfere.

So, my friends, in these days when we are spending necessarily and properly billions and billions—unprecedented peace-time billions—for the mere purpose of insuring our own safety, of carrying on programs that have been established in our books in all kinds of welfare and health programs—necessary ones—but in which our appropriations have gone up—even some of them in these past 7 years—about 4 times, we must look at the whole fiscal arrangements of this Nation with that same prudence that you, as the head of a family or as a housewife, does when he or she looks at the family budget and says, "Each month we are going deeper in debt.   From here where do we go?"

The resources of this Nation are incalculable, but they are not inexhaustible.

As long as we keep these homely truths in our minds and live them as principles, rather than expedients that might be thought profitable in an election year, I really believe that we can, with great confidence, move forward toward our own ideals of prosperity, greater opportunity for the pursuit of happiness at home, equality among ourselves in all things before the law, and achievement of a sounder position for attaining a permanent and durable peace abroad.

Thank you very much.

NOTE: The President spoke at Constitution Hall.   In his opening words he referred to Dr. Erwin D. Canham, President of the U.S. Chamber of Commerce, and Secretary of Commerce Frederick H. Mueller.

132   ¶ Address at a Dinner Sponsored by the Committee for International Economic Growth and the Committee To Strengthen the Frontiers of Freedom.   *May 2, 1960*

Mr. Vice President, Mr. Johnston, Dr. Bush, Your Excellencies and ladies and gentlemen of this distinguished audience:

Before I convey to you the thoughts that I have put down on paper for this purpose this evening, I want to give a word of explanation about my understanding about this meeting.

The invitation that I received requested that I add my voice to those who support the mutual security program of the United States and cooperation among the free nations of the world.   There was not a word said about any function honoring me, and I heard no such talk from either the Co-Chairmen or any of my staff.   So I want to take this moment to thank my friends from so many countries who have paid to me overgenerous and possibly undeserved compliments.

I want to say to them something that they already know—and I am sure you do—that the greetings that I received from so many places in Europe and Asia were simply one thing: the effort of great peoples to tell the people of the United States of their respect for them, their admiration and their affection. I was the messenger, and if I were a successful messenger in that office, in bringing that feeling from these countries to my own, then I am indeed happy and proud.

In any event, I thank you all for your compliments.

This gathering heartens every true believer in preparedness, freedom, and peace. That leaders from all across the land would assemble here—energetically to reaffirm support of mutual security—is good news indeed. This rededication could not come at a better time.

For trends are developing, particularly in Washington, that are profoundly disturbing.

Unless an alert citizenry takes effective action to support those in the Congress who champion the cause of mutual security, it could well result:

In jeopardizing an important part of the nation's defense;

In endangering our worldwide alliance structure;

And in weakening efforts to resist Communist expansion and to forge a just peace.

Two months ago I requested the Congress to continue adequate support of our long proven mutual security program. I asked an appropriation of $4 billion, 175 million—a sum one-twentieth of our Federal budget and one-tenth of our Defense budget. This amount is imperatively required.

The Secretary of State, the Secretary of Defense, the Joint Chiefs of Staff all share this conviction.

One bright development is that, in the past few days, the Committees of Congress legislatively concerned with our relations with other nations, have reasserted the overriding importance of our mutual security program to America's security and free world progress.

Only this evening I have been informed by Senators Fulbright and Dirksen that the Senate this evening acted constructively on this program in the authorizing legislation. The same has of course happened in the House.

But, at the same time, other groups strategically situated in Congress have proclaimed it as their fixed purpose to slash the appropriation for this mainstay of the free world by more than a billion dollars.

They cite isolated instances of malfunctioning in operational staffs as an excuse to attack a great program, which for 14 years has been indispensable in protecting America's stake in security, in free world cooperation, and in global peace. On such grounds and on the erroneous contention that our mutual security program is ineffectual, they would reduce it by twenty-five percent or more.

Every American citizen needs to understand what this would mean.

It would be, for America and all the free world, a crushing defeat in today's struggle between communistic imperialism and a freedom founded in faith and justice.

It would mean, within a matter of months, new international tensions and new international problems of the utmost gravity for every one of our citizens.

It would mean the virtual abandonment of an effort which has yielded our Nation greater benefits in security, better neighbors, and opportunities for expansion of profitable trade than has been achieved by any comparable expenditures for any other Federal purpose.

An America aroused can prevent these calamitous results, for in this Republic government must respond to the will of the people.

Mutual security has never been, nor is it now, Republican or Democratic. Like our own defense program, of which it is an essential part, it is bipartisan to the core.

This program was started 14 years ago by my Democratic predecessor. It was first enacted into law by the Republican 80th Congress. Both political parties, patriotically joined in the national interest, are its parents. And still today both parties are pledged to its support.

Here, specifically, are solemn promises made to the American people in the public document:

First, ". . . . we strongly favor collective defense arrangements . . . "

Second, "we believe that . . . America must support the efforts of underdeveloped countries . . ."

Third, ". . . we will intensify our cooperation with our neighboring republics . . ."

Here is another set of pledges:

First, "we shall continue to support the collective security system . . ."

Second, "where needed, we shall help friendly countries maintain such local forces and economic strength as provide a first bulwark against Communist aggression or subversion."

Third, "we will continue efforts with friends and allies to assist the underdeveloped areas of the free world . . ."

Now in their meaning, these two sets of pledges are identical. The first three are in the Democratic Platform of 1956. The last three are in the Republican Platform of the same year. These commitments still stand. America has the right to expect both parties to keep their word.

Indeed, even beyond the call of integrity, both parties have excellent reason to do so.

For mutual security has effectively supported freedom everywhere on earth. It has made possible a greater and mutually advantageous trade. No other investment has yielded greater dividends in terms of stability, security and free world morale.

This is the program that helped to save Greece from Communist guerrillas. It helped to rescue Turkey from economic collapse, restoring this critical area as a bastion of freedom. It helped to maintain Western Europe as a center of free—rather than communist—power and production. The importance of these victories is incalculable; every one of our citizens is today the stronger, the more prosperous, the more secure, thanks to mutual security.

In Asia, under SEATO and other security treaties, a million soldiers stand as a bulwark of liberty—sustained, again, by mutual security.

As I speak tonight our economic and military help gives support to the military might of 42 other nations, which stand poised in freedom's cause. For this they—and we—give heartfelt thanks to mutual security.

On five continents our economic and technical programs help struggling millions better their production and living standards. Only recently I looked into the faces of these many people. I have seen the desperate need of these people; I have felt their spirit. Most of all, I have witnessed their abiding faith in the greatness and goodness of America, and their love and respect for this land of the free. By helping to make their lives more meaningful and more rewarding, we have helped to keep bright their love of liberty and their determination to reject the soulless forces of communist materialism.

Moreover, America's efforts to help others have evoked a heartening response from other advanced industrial nations. In recent years they have doubled their direct aid to the less developed countries. In addition, in the new International Development Association other countries will put up three dollars for every two dollars put up by the United States.

The very moment when other countries are recognizing their responsibilities is no time for us to walk away from our own.

That such a program—its record shining with accomplishment, and its continuance solemnly pledged by both of our political parties—should now face a crippling cutback seems incredibly irresponsible. To me it is almost inconceivable.

Let America speak, and this will not be done.

Thus far I have mentioned past achievements.

But a great deal more cries out for attention.

Half a world away from us, for example, a great democracy, dedicated to peace, struggles with almost insuperable problems to demonstrate that Asians do not have to sacrifice freedom as payment for economic advance.

To the South our sister Republics need help to unlock the storehouses of their great wealth.

In Africa a seething continent is trying to telescope a thousand years of development into a few decades.

Around the world almost two billion people are living in a ferment of privation, misery, resentment and frustrated hope. They are imbued with an unshakable, even fanatical, determination to break through the spiritual and cultural stagnation imposed upon them by grinding poverty.

Mutual security has done much to help. The hope, confidence and energetic effort so inspired are slowly making progress in creating conditions in which prosperity, security and peace in freedom can flourish. But for lack of understanding the program has been steadily weakened while the need has grown more obvious and critical. Only the conscience and the down-to-earth common sense of all Americans, informed and aroused, can meet the need.

Facing us is a test of our resolve to make our government do the task it has to do to protect the safety of the American people.

The amount I have asked the Congress to provide for mutual security is the minimum required to meet the basic necessities of sheer defense and to keep alight a glimmer of hope in hundreds of millions of people arrayed with us on the side of freedom.

From all these facts we see that the free world needs America!

Just as importantly, America needs the world.

This means far more to us than soldiers and tanks and ships and missiles essential though these are.

Important it is that our allies contribute 5 million soldiers, 30,000 airplanes and 2,200 combatant ships to the common defense of freedom. But our involvement with our neighbors is far more basic than this.

Foreign trade is an example. It is, for America, a $30 billion a year business. To this trade four and a half million of our people owe their jobs with other nations.

For all of us there is great meaning in this: we export, on the average, a third of our cotton crop, just under a third of our wheat, and a fourth of our tractor production.

But this is only a part of our dependence on foreign trade.

The health of our economy depends upon materials owned by others. Manganese, chrome, tin, natural rubber, nickel are examples. As our economy grows, we depend increasingly upon others for such materials. Eight years ago we imported only about a twentieth of our iron ore. Today we have to import over a third of it.

Yes, America needs the world!

And this we must never forget: these needs are more than military and economic. They are technical, cultural and spiritual as well.

Great ideas originating with other peoples have vastly enriched our land.

Fellow Americans—even if we wanted to, we could not shut out the free world. We cannot escape its troubles. We cannot turn our backs on its hopes. We are an inseparable part of the free world neighborhood.

We must hold to these truths:

If nations friendly to us are weakened and imperiled, so are we.

If other friendly nations are strong and free, our own strength and freedom are more secure.

If other free nations prosper, so do we.

In these truths we see the fallacy of adding measurably to our own massive and adequate armaments at the expense of allied strength which is in many instances better located strategically than ours can ever be. No less dangerous is the annual argument that America should stint on strengthening the free world because this would give us more luxury in a comfortable isolation here at home.

This is sheer deadliness—a counsel of defeat and complacency. Logically carried out, it could end only in a militarized America. To the extent that this concept is indulged, it gravely menaces the people of the United States.

We can, here at home, arm to the teeth, and yet go down in total defeat if we let the rest of the world be swallowed up by an atheistic imperialism. By abandonment of struggling millions to lives of hopeless desperation, rich America might, for a time, live more extravagantly. But not for long! For a just peace, dependable security and real progress were never bought by destructive weapons and hard-hearted selfishness, but rather by education, by training, by constructive works—by cooperation.

Only by thinking of ourselves, and truly conducting ourselves, as brothers under God with those who, with us, want to live and grow in freedom, can we hope to solve problems in which failure will mean disaster for much of humanity. Victory in this effort will mean a shoulder-to-shoulder march to greater security, greater prosperity, and greater happiness for all. There, in those few words, is the very heart of mutual security.

So tonight, I restate to you this pledge of the Executive Branch of your government.

I pledge a continuing and energetic support of the principle and programs of mutual security.

And I call upon the leadership, and the rank and file, of both political parties, as well as upon all other sons and daughters of America, to see that those parties hold true to their pledges to give this program their support.

Of this I am certain. The path for America must be one of cooperation—cooperation among ourselves, and with our friends abroad who are dedicated to human dignity and from whom we draw strength as we impart of our own strength to them.

Together we shall confidently carry the burdens and sacrifices of sustaining security against any imperialistic design—as together we continue the search for peace, a search in which we shall persevere without tiring or ceasing until victory, at last, shall belong to all the earth.

Thank you, and good night.

NOTE: The President spoke at 10:30 p.m. at the Statler Hilton Hotel in Washington. In his opening words he referred to Vice President Nixon, Eric Johnston, Chairman of the Committee for International Economic Growth, and Dr. Vannevar Bush, Chairman of the Committee to Strengthen the Frontiers of Freedom.

133   ¶ Special Message to the Congress on the Legislative Program.   *May 3, 1960*

To the Congress of the United States:

Of this, presumably the last Congressional session during my term of office, four months have gone by.   Thus far the one major accomplishment is enactment of civil rights legislation.   Although Congress rejected certain of my recommendations in this area—those relating to equality of job opportunity and assistance to states attempting to desegregate their schools—the new civil rights measure is another important step toward the attainment of the ideal of equal rights before the law for every citizen.

With only two months apparently left in the session, we still have a great deal to get done for America.   I stress this now because, first, the time grows short in which to legislate prudently and wisely, without undue haste; and, second, too great a preoccupation with the events of an election year could seriously impede constructive effort.   With the Congress controlled by one party and the Executive Branch by the other, these difficulties could become severe.

We should jointly resolve that the shortness of time and political rivalries will not be allowed to prevent us from serving the American people effectively.   Matters are still pending that are vital to the health of our economy and to the nation's security and world peace; none of us can afford to electioneer at the expense of these.   Nor can we yield to the temptation to neglect projects that we know are essential to good government but possess little popular appeal, and at the same time overemphasize others in the hope of benefit to one party or the other, or individuals therein.

Relating these considerations to a few of the programs still pending, I refer, first, to our vital mutual security effort.

During most of our Nation's history, our growth was strongly influenced by two unique conditions.   First, for more than a century and a half two great oceans protected us from the violent struggles of the Old World.   Although in recent years we became engaged in two global wars, our relative isolation gave us months in which to assemble, train and equip our forces deliberately and unmolested.   Second, from the very beginning, our Nation's rapid expansion was encouraged by commercial and financial assistance from the nations of Europe. These countries provided us with valuable skills and the capital needed to accelerate the development of our resources, industries and commerce.

These conditions have radically changed. America emerged from World War II as the mightiest nation in a free world that, in the main, was exhausted and crippled. Soon thereafter we came to realize that new weapons of great power, speed and range had markedly reduced the value of our ocean shield. Our homeland, in any future major war, would be a prime target, and our warning time against surprise attack would be minutes, not months. Our security cannot now be achieved by methods and a level of effort believed adequate only a few years ago.

In a world, moreover, in which an aggressive ideology drives ceaselessly to destroy human freedom, it is now the United States to which aspiring free peoples, particularly in under-developed areas, must look, as America once did to others, for the technical knowledge and financial assistance needed to help them strengthen their economies and protect their independence.

Such changes as these gave rise to our mutual security program, one of the most necessary and successful enterprises America has undertaken throughout her history. Started more than a decade ago, the program helped to save Greece, forestalled economic collapse in Turkey and Western Europe, supported the countries of the SEATO Alliance, sustained the strength and independence of South Korea and the Republic of China, and made real progress, in under-developed nations on five continents, in combatting disease, poverty and suffering, and thus has strengthened the resistance of those areas to Communist penetration, propaganda and subversion. Clear it is that the mutual security program provides the surest path by which America can lead to and sustain a durable peace with justice.

Such a program serves the nation at large rather than any particular locality, section or group. Only with difficulty, therefore, can its great rewards be measured by individual communities and citizens. It inevitably follows that in the annual contests over the public use of tax revenues, there is a tendency to bypass the needs of this vital security program in favor of domestic projects that, urged by special groups, achieve a measure of support far greater than their over-all value to the nation warrants. Understandable this tendency is, but I deem it a great disservice to America to indulge it. The security of our country obviously demands that our mutual security program be carried forward at an adequate level.

I have asked new appropriations of $4.175 billions for this program for the 1961 fiscal year. Nearly half of this—a sum one-twentieth of our own defense budget—is to assist the military forces of the free world, comprising 5,000,000 soldiers, 2,200 combatant ships, and 30,000 aircraft. I need not remind the Congress of the low cost at which this force for freedom is sustained as compared to the cost of an aircraft carrier, a squadron of jet bombers, or an Army or Marine Corps division in our own defense structure.

Of the other parts of the program, one-third is for economic assistance required to help sustain these large forces abroad. The remainder consists of loans, technical assistance and grants to help under-developed nations. These are the funds that spell the difference between hopeless stagnation and progress for hundreds of millions of people who, with us, believe in freedom.

Congressional approval of these funds for mutual security will profoundly benefit our people. To our allies and to others with whom we discuss the great issues of our times, it will signify that a united America has not wearied in the discharge of its responsibilities, and that we are unshakable in our determination to attain a world order in which men are free to pursue their goals in peace. And I emphasize once again that, as we strive to build the kind of world in which America believes, our adversaries are not all included in the single word "Communism." They are distress and privation as well, and also the desperation of peoples when they realize that, lacking outside help, they struggle in vain to better their lives. Widespread chaos and misery cannot provide a world climate in which our free Republic can prosper and remain secure. There is for America no higher purpose or greater need than to measure up to her world leadership responsibilities.

I am keenly aware of the contention that, because of an adverse balance of payments, and because of certain failures in administration, America should curtail these mutual security efforts. We must, and do, strive for greater efficiency. Likewise, we do have a problem with balance of payments, but the way to meet this is by positive actions which expand exports. Neither difficulty can be met by withdrawing from our responsibilities for world leadership and from partnership in the protection of freedom. We need—in our own interests—greater human progress and economic growth throughout the world. We cannot achieve these by an assault either on mutual security or on liberal trade policies.

I congratulate the Congress for its actions thus far on the funds for mutual security in the authorizing legislation, and I reaffirm the imperative necessity of providing the appropriations that the authorization would allow.

———————

Next is agriculture, a subject on which I have commented repeatedly to the Congress.

In no domestic area do we have a more obvious need for corrective action. We cannot wonder that the patience of our farmers wears thin. By force of law the Government's surplus holdings, especially of wheat, continually increase. These overhang the market, depress prices, and impose an ever more onerous burden upon all citizens, our farmers particularly. I have offered many recommendations for attacking the problem through bipartisan action. Action there has been on occasion but, in respect to wheat especially, far less than needed or of a kind that would make our farmers' present troubles grow worse.

In an effort to break the legislative stalemate I recently advised the Congress that, within broad guidelines which I suggested, I would approve any constructive farm bill that the Congress might enact. There is as yet no agreement on the part of the two Houses of Congress on a constructive approach.

Meanwhile farmers grow more concerned about their future, and our people generally become increasingly unhappy as their government expends a thousand of their tax dollars every minute on the self-defeating wheat program. Lately I have noted, with deep concern, a growing disposition in certain Congressional quarters to favor proposals long ago rejected as unworkable, and which would obviously go beyond even the very broad limits I outlined almost three months ago.

I regret also the continuing tendency to rely, in agriculture, upon Federal controls, which inevitably create interference with the lives of our farm people. I still believe that America's farmers prefer, as certainly I do, the development of legislation which will promote progress for them toward economic equality and permit them the maximum freedom.

Surely it is time, in the interest of all Americans, for the Congress to face up to the admittedly difficult problems of agriculture. It is constructive results that farmers want and need. Indeed, I believe that all America is looking for this kind of action before this session adjourns.

Also badly needed is extension of the Sugar Act, soon to expire. At stake are an assured and stable supply of sugar for our people at reasonable prices and removal of the uncertainties now facing this industry. A four-year extension of the present program, modified to give the President authority to adjust quotas in order to assure America of an adequate sugar supply, is needed to give farmers and processors the time to plan. Appropriate recommendations are before the Congress. The interests of America require that legislation be enacted before the Congress adjourns.

I have repeatedly stated the need for legislation in other important areas. Some of these measures are of a kind that, at the expense of responsible government, tend to be shunted aside in an election year.

First is the urgent need of Federal Courts for enough judges to hear the greatly increased number of cases being filed each year. Regardless of expediency, justice calls for prompt action.

The Judicial Conference of the United States has recommended the creation of approximately 40 new judgeships. This recommendation is supported by the Administration and by virtually every important professional organization concerned with the administration of the courts.

We who advocate equal justice under law have a duty to make it effective. In certain districts injured people must wait over four years for justice or compromise their rights; innocent people who are defrauded are made a laughing stock because the delay in the courts deprives them of an effective remedy; justice is denied the weak because they cannot finance the delay necessary to be heard. Further neglect of this need is heartless. For all our people, I most earnestly urge swift action on the pending measure to increase the number of judgeships.

Next I refer to my request of last June to remove the statutory prohibition against the Treasury's paying more than 4¼ percent interest on Treasury bonds which are due more than five years after issuance.

The American people have a great deal at stake in this legislation, for failure to remove this interest rate restriction can have many serious consequences, including the forcing of a new upturn in living costs. The Treasury, under this restriction, continually faces the prospect of having to manage the government's $290 billion debt in ways that would unavoidably increase the upward pressures on prices and on the interest rate for the consumer credit so important to millions of our citizens.

Again, I stress the need for prompt removal of this harmful restriction.

We also owe it to America to provide adequate new revenues for the Highway Trust Fund (as my proposal for a gasoline tax increase would do), so that we may keep our very important highway program on schedule; and fiscal responsibility dictates that we not fail to raise postal rates and thus end the heavy drain on general revenues for postal services which Congress has said by law should be self-sustaining. Our other revenue proposals—notably, extension of certain excise taxes and an added tax on aviation fuel—also need to be approved.

Additionally, as I recently emphasized by special message to the Congress, we have compelling reasons to liberalize our immigration law during the course of this session. I remind the Congress, also, that this is World Refugee Year. Our country was one of those sponsoring this move in the United Nations. In harmony with the spirit of this resolution, and in keeping with America's tradition of leadership in humanitarian causes, we should press forward, in this session, with the refugee legislation I have recommended to the Congress.

I add two proposals of special importance to future Presidents of the United States. First is provision of Presidential office space. The Congress has met its own space requirements and those of the Supreme Court. Requirements for modern office facilities for the President, his staff and the news media assigned to the White House are no less necessary and urgent. Second, the need to carry forward Presidential powers to reorganize the Executive Branch is acute, in the interest of efficiency and economy in this huge government. Both of these authorizations are clearly essential. I again urge their approval before this session adjourns.

I refer now to a number of programs of intense interest to millions of our people—programs intended to initiate or enlarge benefits for various groups or sections of the nation. Such projects require objective analysis and a nicety of decision so that on the one hand there will be no neglect of essential Federal responsibility and on the other hand no surrender to the election-year temptation to overspend and over-reach. Responsibility respecting these will do credit to both parties but, more important, will benefit our people.

A comparison of 1952 and 1961 Federal expenditures shows the pace of the Federal advance in matters of this kind. Likewise it discloses the pressing need for prudence both as regards the level of these expenditures and the extent of Federal involvement in the problems of individual citizens. For labor, welfare and veterans programs, including payments from trust funds, cash payments to individuals were $11.7 billion in 1952. The comparable figure in the 1961 budget is $26.4 billion. Thus there has been a 125% increase in these programs during a period in which the population increased by 16%. This growth in payments far exceeds any increases required to match the 12% rise in living costs during this period.

Among such matters still pending I would mention, first, school construction legislation. Long ago the Administration asked Congress to approve a sound program to help colleges and universities and elementary and secondary schools meet their pressing construction needs. I have stressed that any such Federal assistance should be provided only to meet genuine need, and that it must preserve for the States, local communities and educational institutions their traditional responsibilities for education. The Administration's debt service plan for elementary and secondary schools, and its comparable plan for institutions of higher learning, both before the Congress for over a year, conform to these standards.

By these programs we would help to construct 75,000 additional elementary and secondary classrooms at a Federal cost, over the next 20 to 30 years, of $2.2 billion, and at a Federal cost of $500 million we would help build higher education facilities costing in the aggregate some $2 billion. The financing for the initiation of these programs is included in my 1961 budget.

It will be deeply disappointing if the Congress should fail to authorize such programs, and no less disappointing if, instead, programs that basically conflict with these standards should be passed.

Area redevelopment legislation also needs priority attention. I have long urged legislation authorizing loans and technical assistance to help areas afflicted with long-term, substantial unemployment resulting from technological changes. The purpose is to diversify these economies and thereby create new sources of private employment. With important local efforts to provide new jobs already underway, Federal help must be of a kind that strengthens and supplements rather than displaces or discourages those efforts.

I think it is basic that we reject the various schemes that would perpetuate insecurity by making distressed areas dependent upon the uncertainties of continued Federal subsidies, or that would pour Federal dollars into areas where distress has been temporary and which are competent to meet their problems themselves. Moreover, it will injure, not help the chronically affected areas if funds and loan advantages are indiscriminately broadcast to other areas that do not urgently require such assistance.

The only way this difficult problem can be sensibly solved is through healthy government-community cooperation that creates self-sustaining local economies. It cannot be solved by a dispiriting and misplaced benevolence on the part of the distant central government. The people who need this help are hopefully looking for truly constructive action this session. For this purpose I have recommended a Federal program amounting to $53 million, to be expended for loans and technical assistance.

The Secretary of Health, Education, and Welfare will present this week a new program which will enable older people truly in need of help to meet the calamity of catastrophic illness. This program will take full advantage of, and support, the progress that has been made by private effort; it will recognize the traditional Federal-State relations in various fields of assistance; and, additionally, it will not do violence to the private relationships that must continue to characterize the rendering of health care services.

Behind this program is a meticulous and thoughtful weighing of many alternatives. I believe the Congress will find this proposal of great value to our people most in need of medical protection in their later years. I urge this program in place of compulsory schemes which over a period of years would blight America's unexcelled medical standards and leave unaided large numbers of citizens we are striving to help.

The Fair Labor Standards Act likewise needs attention before these next 60 days elapse.

For several years I have urged expansion of coverage under this Act to include approximately three million additional wage earners. This is the most urgently needed change in this law, and I hope that the Congress will not fail to provide it.

The Secretary of Labor recently presented the Congress with information indicating that the minimum wage could be increased moderately without disruptive effects upon the economy. On the other hand we should, as responsible officials, stand firmly against an excessive increase which could cause unemployment and severe repercussions in many industries and areas of our country. It is of great importance to the well-being of the American people that we govern our actions in this area by economic facts rather than by political or social prejudice.

Nor, I believe, should we close this session without enacting various long-pending measures, mostly in the field of conservation—each of them important to all our people, but particularly to our citizens out West.

Among these measures I refer as examples to preservation of our priceless seashore areas, establishment of the Arctic Wildlife Range, permission to western communities to expand into public land areas, research assistance to the coal industry, and the Fryingpan-Arkansas and San Luis projects. Approval of these and similar pending bills will help to round out the program of natural resources development—now at a record level—which I presented last January in my Budget Message. We also need a solution of the Indian heirship problem and to give the people of Guam and the Virgin Islands a voice in the Congress.

As a general but most important consideration, I point again to the need of restraint in new authorizations for Federal spending. Our Federal accounts should balance with enough left over for a reasonable payment on the public debt, on which we are already paying for interest alone more than nine billion dollars per year. Proposals now before Congressional Committee would, if approved, raise our annual spending by tens of billions of dollars in 1961 and would disrupt Federal budgets over the next five years by many scores of billions.

For America's sake, we must resist the temptation, this year or any year, to overspend the taxpayer's hard-earned dollars and overcentralize responsibilities in the Federal Government. If we fail in this, we will weaken our hope of ever controlling Federal extravagance and will indefinitely postpone debt retirement and tax relief. At the same time we will debase our currency, invite the resurgence of inflationary forces, undermine local and state responsibility, and thus erode away America's strength at home and in the world.   We should avoid preemption of state and local functions and take genuine national need rather than glittering desirability as our guide in Federal expenditures.

Most taxpayers, I believe, are becoming more and more aware of the results of laws that, though sometimes carrying a surface appeal, far too often add unjustifiably to the tax burdens of the individual.

———

Finally, I repeat my hope that in the brief span remaining before adjournment the Executive Branch and the 86th Congress can work constructively together in the interest of America and avoid schism and stalemate.   The measures I have mentioned, and many others also calling for action this session, must go forward if we are to keep faith with our countrymen.   Let us remember, as Congressional deliberations proceed, that both the nation and the world are looking on.

With sound progress as our object, we can accomplish much despite the shortness of time left in this session.   Working together responsibly, we shall surely make America a stronger and better nation; and, so working, we shall brighten the cause of freedom and peace everywhere on earth.

DWIGHT D. EISENHOWER

134   ¶ Statement by the President on the Occasion of the Centennial of the First Japanese Diplomatic Mission to the United States.
May 3, 1960

ONE HUNDRED YEARS ago Japan sent its first Embassy to Washington to exchange ratifications of the Treaty of Amity and Commerce between Japan and the United States.   In extending a warm welcome to this Embassy, the President expressed, on behalf of the American people, his deep gratification at this beginning of closer relations with Japan.

This historic occasion laid the foundation for our friendship, and a remarkable cultural, economic, and political interchange between our two countries.   I am happy to say that the bonds of friendship between our two peoples are stronger today than ever before.

Japan and the United States are joined in a partnership based on mutual trust, mutual respect, and full cooperation. We are both dedicated to the task of helping build a better world, where there will be peace and justice for all.

DWIGHT D. EISENHOWER

135 ¶ Remarks at Fort Benning, Georgia, After Watching a Demonstration of New Army Equipment. *May* 3, 1960

Secretary Gates, Secretary Brucker, General Lemnitzer, General Harris, officers and men, and distinguished visitors:

At a time such as this, an old soldier is tempted to reminisce, but I think most of you are sufficiently old in the Service to know that is a dangerous habit to get into. I should like to go back to the days of 1911 when General Bradley and I entered the Academy and talk about the amazing differences that have come about when we think or see the infantry. There are soldiers here, comrades of mine, that date even further back than do General Bradley and I. But I think it is rather profitless; I think we must take the day as it is, life as it is, the developments that we have and that we know are going to come about.

I agree with what Secretary Brucker has to say about the importance of the man that is handling these things. But we must go back first to the scientist who is doing the research, who has the great skill and the patient hours that it takes to bring them finally into being in the pilot model form; and finally the great study and the work that must go into obtaining procurement with the greatest possible economy; and the fine instructors that tell us how to use them. This is a very laborious process.

America now has a defense problem that goes back to every village in our country. As the problem reaches the Armed Forces, everybody must not only learn a technique, he must get into his head that this is a nation defending itself, not a professional soldier defending somebody else. We are all working as a team.

From the very first demonstration that I saw this morning, I felt this oneness, this unity, of America producing these tremendous and wonderful weapons, with a great organization taking them from the producers

395

and the scientists and learning to use them so expertly. Every minute that I have been here I have wanted to give some salute to the entire team that does these things.

And finally, I want to talk just one word about the spirit that is behind all this. It is the finest type of patriotism. A day like this makes a man quite ready to call all those people mistaken, if not worse, who say that America has become soft and is not capable of defending itself.

In other words, gentlemen, I am so proud of you that I really have no words in which to express it. Far from thanking me for being here today, I thank you for letting me have such a wonderful time, to come back to old comrades—indeed to a spot which I have seen before in my service—and to have the satisfaction of talking with old friends. Or if they are not old friends individually, in spirit they are all American soldiers, as I was in the days when I was a junior, working then as you are today.

So, to each of you: congratulations, and thank you very much.

NOTE: The President spoke at 3:03 p.m. In his opening words he referred to Secretary of Defense Thomas S. Gates, Jr., Secretary of the Army Wilber M. Brucker, Gen. Lyman L. Lemnitzer, Chief of Staff of the U.S. Army, and Maj. Gen. Hugh P. Harris, Commanding General at Fort Benning and Commandant of the Infantry School. Later the President referred to General of the Army Omar N. Bradley (ret.), who was also present at the demonstration.

136 ¶ Statement by the President Upon Signing "Food for Peace" Agreement Between the United States and India.   *May 4, 1960*

THIS IS A CEREMONY, Mr. Ambassador and Minister Patil, in which I am both honored and delighted to participate.

The agreement that we have just signed is a practical application of the term "Food for Peace."

In a world marked too often by fears and distrust, it warms my heart to take part in an event which is the product of mutual respect and ever-growing friendship.

When I was in your country last December, I caught the spirit of progress that abounds in the new India. What we can do to lend encouragement, to lend a helping hand, we are most happy to do.

My thoughts go back to the day—it was December eleventh—when I was in New Delhi at the opening of the great World Agriculture Fair.

I recall the words of your Prime Minister, Mr. Nehru, when he said that "in this world today, the call is for ever greater cooperation between individuals, between groups, between nations."

When Mr. Nehru spoke of cooperation, he was speaking of true cooperation, joint effort in behalf of the common good. What we are observing here today is the signing of a cooperative agreement, freely entered into by each nation, pledged by each of us as equal partners in the world community.

This is the fifth and by far the largest of such agreements entered into by our two nations. By terms of these agreements, 587 million bushels of wheat and 22 million bags of rice, to be paid in rupees, will be moved to India over a four-year period. We are fortunate in having this means of sharing our abundance.

India is going forward with a zeal and determination that commands our unreserved admiration and respect. Its people are successfully embarked on the road to improved economic well-being in freedom.

The food that we make available under our special programs today will be reflected in India's accelerated progress tomorrow.

This is what we mean by "Food for Peace."

NOTE: The agreement was signed at the White House by the President and the Indian Minister of Food and Agriculture, S. K. Patil. In his opening words the President referred to Ambassador M. C. Chagla of India who was among those present at the signing.

In a White House release of the same date it was noted that the agreement, the fifth to be signed with India under the Agricultural Trade Development and Assistance Act, was unique in the following respects: (1) it was almost four times as large as any agreement previously signed with any country since the beginning of the program in 1954; (2) it was the first agreement to span a period of 4 years; (3) and it was the first agreement specifically designed to help a country in establishing substantial food reserves; one-fourth of the wheat and all of the rice being available for that purpose. The agreement was published in pamphlet form in the Treaties and Other International Acts Series (TIAS 4499; Government Printing Office, 1960).

On April 13, 1960, the White House announced the appointment of Special Assistant to the President Don Paarlberg as Food for Peace Coordinator. The release noted that the Food for Peace program, although based on the 1954 act, represented a new effort to explore with other surplus-producing nations all practical means of utilizing surpluses in the interest of reinforcing peace and the well-being of friendly peoples throughout the world—as was first announced by the President in his message on agriculture of January 29, 1959.

137   ¶ Statement by the President Upon Signing the Civil Rights Act of 1960.   *May* 6, 1960

I HAVE TODAY signed into law the Civil Rights Act of 1960. It is only the second civil rights measure to pass the Congress in 85 years. As was the case with the Act of 1957, recommendations of this Administration underlie the features of the Civil Rights Act of 1960.

The new Act is concerned with a range of civil rights problems. One title makes it a crime to obstruct rights or duties under Federal court orders by force or threat of force. That provision will be an important deterrent to such obstruction which interferes with the execution of Federal court orders, including those involving school desegregation. Provision is also made to assure free public education to all children of Armed Forces personnel in the United States where local public school facilities are unavailable. By authorizing the FBI to investigate certain bombings or attempted bombings of schools, churches and other structures, the Act will deter such heinous acts of lawlessness.

The new Act also deals significantly with that key constitutional right of every American, the right to vote without discrimination on account of race or color. One provision, which requires the retention of voting records, will be of invaluable aid in the successful enforcement of existing voting rights statutes. Another provision authorizes the use by federal courts of voting referees. It holds great promise of making the Fifteenth Amendment of the Constitution fully meaningful.

While I regret that Congress saw fit to eliminate two of my recommendations, I believe the Act is an historic step forward in the field of civil rights. With continuing help from all responsible persons, the new law will play an important role in the days ahead in attaining our goal of equality under law in all areas of our country for all Americans.

NOTE: The Civil Rights Act of 1960 is Public Law 86–449 (74 Stat. 86).

138 ¶ Exchange of Messages Between the President and Queen Juliana Upon Completion of the Monument Presented by the People of the Netherlands. *May* 6, 1960

[Released May 6, 1960. Dated May 5, 1960]

Your Majesty:

I am most grateful for your thoughtful message. It is indeed appropriate that today, the fifteenth anniversary of the liberation of your great country, should be the occasion of the presentation of the monument from you and the people of The Netherlands to the people of the United States. Personally and on behalf of all our citizens I assure you of our deep appreciation. The monument will remain a symbol of the enduring friendship between our peoples.

Sincerely,

DWIGHT D. EISENHOWER

NOTE: Queen Juliana's message, dated May 5, 1960, follows:

The President
The White House

At the commemoration of our liberation 15 years ago and at the completion of the monument of our gratitude I should like once again to emphasize the moral and material support your country gave us in so ample measure during and after the war. Gladly I take this opportunity, Mr. President, to send you and the people of the United States of America, also on behalf of the people of The Netherlands, my very best wishes for a peaceful and prosperous future.

JULIANA

The monument is a 49-bell carillon and tower which is located at Ridge Road and Marshall Drive near the Iwo Jima Monument in Arlington, Va.

139 ¶ Remarks at the Opening of the 1960 AFL–CIO Union-Industries Show. *May* 6, 1960

Mr. Meany, Mr. Lewis, and ladies and gentlemen:

It is with a distinct sense of honor—personal honor—that I have accepted this invitation to be with you on the opening of this great union-industrial exhibition. And I have been highly privileged by the opportunity to go with Mr. Meany and others in wandering for some three quarters of an hour around this armory so that I could see something of the exhibits that you all will see.

399

The reaction that I had is that of realizing anew what can be achieved by true cooperation. We have the scientist who conceives of some new idea applicable to industry, who proves its validity. We find the financier or a group of investors who are ready to put up the money to make the venture go. We find the management who organizes the whole into a productive enterprise, and we have those people who with their hands and their minds finally produce the wealth of the United States. And by this method, voluntarily arrived at by each of these groups, we will see some of the results in this exhibition.

Some of them are marvels of ingenuity and modern practice. Mr. Meany, who has often told me he was very expert in the plumber's trade, acknowledged himself today being bewildered and amazed by the things he has found in the plumbing facilities that he finds in here.

Now all of these things, these material advantages that each of us has in better living conditions, better clothes, better food better processed—all of these things that come to us, sometimes we probably don't look quite as far across the horizon as we should. And so I was particularly impressed by the fact in the AFL–CIO booth there is a little exhortation to each of us, to look to the less developed nations, to help them, so that we ourselves may do better.

We exhibit that kind of concern for our brother, under God, that we are exhorted to in the Bible or in any other religious doctrine, but at the same time, as we help our brother—as we help those people—we make this a more peaceful, a more prosperous, all in all a better world in which to live, with easier minds and with the certainty that spiritually, intellectually, and materially we all profit by this cooperation that I spoke of between the scientist and the financier and management and labor. But more than that, by cooperation among nations.

And because union labor, by the statement in its own booth, has brought our attention to this matter, I hope that each of you going through this wonderful exhibit will pause long enough to read that little sign.

And as I express this hope, as I told you before, it is an honor to have been invited to cut the ribbon which will open this show—which I will now do. Thank you.

NOTE: The President spoke at the National Guard Armory in Washington. In his opening words he referred to George Meany, President of the AFL–CIO, and Joseph Lewis, Director of the AFL–CIO Union-Industries Show.

140 ¶ Statement by the President Announcing the Forthcoming Visit of the Crown Prince and Princess of Japan. *May 7, 1960*

AT THE TIME of Prime Minister Kishi's visit last January, I expressed the hope that the Crown Prince and Princess would be able to visit the United States during the Centennial year of Japanese-American relations. I am now happy to announce that their Imperial Highnesses have accepted my invitation, and will be in Washington from September 27 to September 29.

They will be welcomed in the spirit of cordial friendship and mutual respect which characterizes relations between our two great nations.

141 ¶ Letter to Syngman Rhee Upon His Withdrawal From Political Life in Korea. *May 9, 1960*

[Released May 9, 1960. Dated May 5, 1960]

Dear Dr. Rhee:

The vastness of the events which have taken place in Korea has claimed the attention of the entire world. I can assure you that no one has followed them with more anxious sympathy than I.

With your voluntary withdrawal from political life, I am reminded ever more strongly of how much your country will remain in your debt. The rebirth of Korea in 1945 was the fruition of your long years of patient and arduous labor. Your tenacity and indomitable courage at a time when the Republic was the prey of Communist armies won the admiration of the entire Free World as well as the gratitude of all Koreans. Since then, under your guidance, Korea has recovered from the deepest wounds of that conflict and is today a monument to your life-long work.

I cannot but feel that your decision, momentous as it is, is yet another example of wisdom as well as selfless service. I assure you that the United States will continue to feel itself bound by strong ties of sympathy to Korea under your successors.

My best wishes for many years of health and happiness in the honored retirement which you have done so much to earn.

Sincerely,

DWIGHT D. EISENHOWER

142 ¶ Citation Accompanying Award of Legion of Merit to Captain Edward L. Beach, USN. *May* 10, 1960

THE PRESIDENT of the United States takes pleasure in presenting the Legion of Merit to

CAPTAIN EDWARD L. BEACH, UNITED STATES NAVY

for services as Commanding Officer of the U.S.S. TRITON during the first submerged voyage around the world.

CITATION:

For exceptionally meritorious conduct in the performance of outstanding service while serving on board the U.S.S. Triton from the 16th of February 1960 to the 10th of May 1960. As Commanding Officer, Captain Edward L. Beach, U.S. Navy, led his crew with courage, foresight and determination in an unprecedented circumnavigation of the globe, proving man's ability under trying conditions to accomplish prolonged submerged missions as well as testing new and complex equipment in the world's largest submarine. This historic voyage took his ship into strange waters under difficult and frequently unknown conditions, as a result, the Triton collected much valuable oceanographic information. Captain Beach's sound judgment, masterful leadership, professional skill and devotion to duty were in keeping with the highest traditions of the naval service.

DWIGHT D. EISENHOWER

NOTE: The presentation ceremony was held in the Conference Room at the White House. The text was read by Capt. E. P. Aurand, Naval Aide to the President. Captain Beach served as Naval Aide to the President from January 20, 1953, to February 15, 1957.

143 ¶ The President's News Conference of *May* 11, 1960

THE PRESIDENT [*reading*]. I have made some notes from which I want to talk to you about this U–2 incident.

A full statement about this matter has been made by the State Department, and there have been several statesmanlike remarks by leaders of both parties.

For my part, I supplement what the Secretary of State has had to say, with the following four main points. After that I shall have nothing further to say—for the simple reason I can think of nothing to add that might be useful at this time.

The first point is this: the need for intelligence-gathering activities.

No one wants another Pearl Harbor. This means that we must have knowledge of military forces and preparations around the world, especially those capable of massive surprise attacks.

Secrecy in the Soviet Union makes this essential. In most of the world no large-scale attack could be prepared in secret, but in the Soviet Union there is a fetish of secrecy and concealment. This is a major cause of international tension and uneasiness today. Our deterrent must never be placed in jeopardy. The safety of the whole free world demands this.

As the Secretary of State pointed out in his recent statement, ever since the beginning of my administration I have issued directives to gather, in every feasible way, the information required to protect the United States and the free world against surprise attack and to enable them to make effective preparations for defense.

My second point: the nature of intelligence-gathering activities.

These have a special and secret character. They are, so to speak, "below the surface" activities.

They are secret because they must circumvent measures designed by other countries to protect secrecy of military preparations.

They are divorced from the regular visible agencies of government which stay clear of operational involvement in specific detailed activities.

These elements operate under broad directives to seek and gather intelligence short of the use of force—with operations supervised by responsible officials within this area of secret activities.

We do not use our Army, Navy, or Air Force for this purpose, first, to avoid any possibility of the use of force in connection with these activities, and second, because our military forces, for obvious reasons, cannot be given latitude under broad directives but must be kept under strict control in every detail.

These activities have their own rules and methods of concealment which seek to mislead and obscure—just as in the Soviet allegations there are many discrepancies. For example, there is some reason to believe that the plane in question was not shot down at high altitude. The normal agencies of our Government are unaware of these specific activities or of the special efforts to conceal them.

Third point: how should we view all of this activity?

It is a distasteful but vital necessity.

We prefer and work for a different kind of world—and a different way of obtaining the information essential to confidence and effective deterrents. Open societies, in the day of present weapons, are the only answer.

This was the reason for my "open skies" proposal in 1955, which I was ready instantly to put into effect—to permit aerial observation over the United States and the Soviet Union which would assure that no surprise attack was being prepared against anyone. I shall bring up the "open skies" proposal again at Paris—since it is a means of ending concealment and suspicion.

My final point is that we must not be distracted from the real issues of the day by what is an incident or a symptom of the world situation today.

This incident has been given great propaganda exploitation. The emphasis given to a flight of an unarmed nonmilitary plane can only reflect a fetish of secrecy.

The real issues are the ones we will be working on at the summit—disarmament, search for solutions affecting Germany and Berlin, and the whole range of East-West relations, including the reduction of secrecy and suspicion.

Frankly, I am hopeful that we may make progress on these great issues. This is what we mean when we speak of "working for peace."

And as I remind you, I will have nothing further to say about this matter. [*Ends reading*]

Q. Robert J. Donovan, New York Herald Tribune: Mr. President, since our last visit, or conference, Prime Minister Khrushchev has made some pretty vigorous statements about your plans for bringing Mr. Nixon to the summit in case you had to come home. Do his comments in any way change your intentions?

THE PRESIDENT. No, indeed. And, I should clarify something. There seems to be some misunderstanding, because a friend from Congress, a friend indeed of the other party, told me the other day that he had never heard of the latter part of my press conference on this point where I said that if my absence from the conference had to be more than 2 or 3 days, I would be right back there. And I believe I remarked, although I am not sure, that the jet plane made this kind of a trip possible.

Now, as far as Mr. Khrushchev's statement, I can just say this: he has never asked me my opinion of some of his people. [*Laughter*]

Q. Charles H. Mohr, Time Magazine: In case, Mr. President, that the Soviet Union should reject your proposal for a surprise attack conference, or an "open skies" arrangement, do you think that the development of satellites like Samos and Midas will possibly in the next few years erase our worries on the score of surveillance; and also are you doing anything now to speed up those scientific projects?

THE PRESIDENT. I keep in touch with my Scientific Advisory Committee and operators, and I know of nothing we could do to speed these up. They are research items and as such no one can predict exactly what would be their degree of efficiency. So I couldn't make a real prediction of how useful they are going to be.

Q. Mr. Mohr: Sir, do you think that their development will ease our worries on the question of secrecy?

THE PRESIDENT. Well, I say, I just can't predict what the final results will be. Now, we do know this, right now. I believe it's Tiros that is sending back constantly pictures on the cloud cover all around the earth. That is admittedly a rather rough example of what might be done in photography, but that is being done constantly; and I don't know how many thousands of photographs have been taken. And they send them back on command.

Q. Laurence H. Burd, Chicago Tribune: Mr. President, last week you used the word "if" in connection with your trip to Russia. Have you changed any plans about that, or think you might?

THE PRESIDENT. No, not at all. I have no idea, but you can never tell from one day to the other what is happening in this world, it seems, so I just said "if." I put it in the positive sense, I think. I expect to go; put it that way.

Q. Felix Belair, New York Times: I know, Mr. President, you don't ordinarily tip your hand on disposition of pending legislation before you, but since the legislative leaders more than a week ago said you were very much opposed to the emergency housing bill, may I ask if you have had any change of view about it?

THE PRESIDENT. Well, what it says right now, I don't know; but I have said this: I am very definitely opposed of taking another billion dollars of Federal money and making use of it, making it available for direct loans when we don't need it.   And I think it's a very bad way to stimulate housing.

As a matter of fact, while I think there has been some little slowup in the housing field, there is indication it's coming up—back to the level of 1.2, something of that kind.   I see no reason for constantly getting excited about this one.

By the way, I've got another paper.   [*Laughter*]

Q. (Questioner unidentified): How many more?

THE PRESIDENT. This is something that is good news in this whole economic field, and that is what you are talking about.

I understand the employment rose 1.9 million between mid-March and mid-April, and has reached a total of 66.2 million.   This is the biggest April increase by far in the postwar period.   There was also a sharp drop in the number of unemployed persons, a decline of more than one-half million.

It has been reported by the Commerce Department that retail sales in April were more than 3 percent above March, and 5 percent above last April.

Finally, figures from the Department of Commerce today show that in the first quarter of this year, gross national product reached 500.2 billion.   This means that, in effect, the United States is producing goods and services at a rate of a half-trillion dollars for the first time in our history.

The achievement of these high levels of employment and production, at the same time that prices have been reasonably stable—the consumer price index has varied only one-quarter of one percent in the last 6 months—is proof of the great strength of our free enterprise system and its promise for the future.   And if we continue to act responsibly, I think it will keep going.

Q. Edward T. Folliard, Washington Post: Mr. President, do you think the outlook for the summit conference has changed, or has been changed, in the last week or so?

THE PRESIDENT. Not decisively at all, no.

Q. Mrs. May Craig, Portland (Maine) Press Herald: Mr. President, when you came into office you obtained a truce in Korea. Do you think a treaty now, an effort to get a treaty now would be useful, and will you discuss that with Mr. Rhee and the acting officials of Korea when you visit there?

THE PRESIDENT. Well, Mrs. Craig, I have no reason to believe that it would now be easy to achieve a treaty.

Now, as far as my trip to Korea is concerned, it is to be an official one. Assuming the permission of the people now in charge of Korea, and a proper opportunity, I should be glad to see Mr. Rhee who, as I have told you people, I have admired and respected over the years.

Q. Andrew F. Tully, Jr., Scripps-Howard Newspapers: Sir, I know this borders on your rule not to discuss personalities, but Mr. Truman has written an article in a magazine in which he says certain things about you, and I wonder if you would like to speak out in your own behalf for the record.

THE PRESIDENT. I just haven't time.

Q. Sarah McClendon, El Paso Times: Sir, now that you have been to Fort Benning and you have seen the wonderful display of modern Army weapons, I wonder if you don't realize that we need a stepping up of production of some of these weapons.

THE PRESIDENT. Well, I'd say this: of course, your question implies that you know very much more about the military than I do and it's probably true. [*Laughter*]

I can just say this: I do just as good as what the commonsense the Good Lord gave me and my own judgment and experience allow me to do.

Q. Pat Munroe, Chicago American: Mr. President, when an unfriendly cartoon or column appears in the press, that is unfriendly to you, we often hear people say, "I'll bet they won't let the President see that one." Now, what are your regular habits, sir, for keeping up with what we are saying about you?

THE PRESIDENT. Well, I don't know whether you can call it a habit, for the simple reason that it takes a lot of time if I was going to keep track of what all you people say. I take what I call the important sections of the Sunday papers that review world events, go over the things, and those are the things I study carefully. The kind of things that you talk of, cartoons and unfriendly quips, I just can't be bothered.

Q. Ruth S. Montgomery, Hearst Headline Service: Mr. President, to go back a minute, I am very puzzled about this statement by your predecessor. As I recall, you not only participated in the inaugural parade, but you also attended the inaugural ball that night, did you not, in '49?

THE PRESIDENT. I don't think I went to the ball. I had an invitation from Mr. Royall, then Secretary of the Army. He was very anxious, and he said the administration approved of his request, that I, as a five-star general, ride with him because I believe the Secretary of the Navy was going to have, oh, Admiral Nimitz or somebody, and he felt that he had to have one of these five-star generals which I still was then. So, I went along. Now, I think I went right back to Columbia that day.

Q. Miss Montgomery: I attended a party where you were that evening at George Allen's, and you and Mrs. Eisenhower went in and changed into evening attire and left for the ball.

THE PRESIDENT. Well, then, your memory is better than mine. [*Laughter*] Can I just say one thing: I have never advanced the theory that my memory is perfect, like a good many others.

Q. Merriman Smith, United Press International: Quite aside from your comment about the U–2 plane episode, sir, I wonder if you could give us your reaction to a rather denunciatory speech made this morning, right ahead of the summit meeting, by the Russian Foreign Minister. Mr. Gromyko attributes to this country deeds and efforts which he said amount to dangerous ways of balancing on the brink of war. He says that the United States has deliberately engaged in provocative acts in conjunction with some of our allies. Now, with statements like this, do you still maintain a hopeful attitude toward the summit?

THE PRESIDENT. I'd say yes. I have some hope, because these things have been said for many years, ever since World War II, and there is no real change in this matter.

I wonder how many of you people have read the full text of the record of the trial of Mr. Abel. Well, I think he was sentenced to 30 years. Now, this business of saying that you're doing things that are provocative, why, they had better look at their own record.

And I'll tell you this: the United States—and none of its allies that I know of—has engaged in nothing that would be considered honestly as provocative. We are looking to our own security and our defense and we have no idea of promoting any kind of conflict or war. This is just— it's absolutely ridiculous and they know it is.

Q. Henry N. Taylor, Scripps-Howard Newspapers: Sir, would it be trespassing on your request about the U–2 to ask if you could tell us something about any possible Soviet reconnaissance flights over the western part of the world, and our response to them, if any?

THE PRESIDENT. I could just say this: as far as I know, there has never been any over the United States.

Q. Holmes Alexander, McNaught Syndicate: Sir, this is a question about Quemoy and Matsu; two of the Democratic candidates have said that if elected they would try to get rid of that responsibility. I know you don't deal in personalities, but I wonder if you could tell us as a military man to what extent these islands help us control the air and sea over the Formosa Strait.

THE PRESIDENT. Well, I am not talking personalities because I don't know who said this. I will say this: if you go back to the Formosa doctrine, you will find that the responsibility is placed upon the President to determine, in the event of any attack upon Quemoy and Matsu, whether this is in fact a preliminary to or part of an attack against the Pescadores and Taiwan. If that is true, then he must participate because then it will be the defense of Formosa, one of our allies.

Now, as to the actual value of Matsu and Quemoy, of course we must remember how much this seems to mean to the morale of all the Chinese forces on Formosa. From their viewpoint, any desertion of those islands means a complete surrender—abject surrender. So, it is a factor that anyone who is going to have to make possible decisions in the future has to take into consideration when he talks about the abandonment of these sets of islands. And frankly, no President of the United States can do it by himself.

Now, he can withhold support to Taiwan, but are you going to destroy Taiwan? So, none of these problems is ever a simple, black and white thing. You have got a very great number of conflicting considerations and they take study and heart searching, and you hope and pray that you are right most of the time.

Q. Chalmers M. Roberts, Washington Post: Last week, sir, you announced that the U.S. would resume underground nuclear testing for purposes of protecting the detection and control system.[1]   There seems, however, to be some dispute as to whether this would be joint or coordinated, that is, this testing in conjunction with the Soviet Union.   Could you tell us what the argument there is, and what your own view is?

THE PRESIDENT. Well, I'll tell you, Mr. Roberts, having heard of this misunderstanding, I had a discussion with Dr. Kistiakowsky only this morning.   These things are not nuclear weapons testing.   They are for one simple—and as a matter of fact in many cases I don't think will involve any nuclear explosions except under the coordinated directions of a body made up of the U.K., U.S.S.R., and ourselves.   That's the way I understood the agreement, and I believe that you will find that they are not expected to have anything to do either with weapons development or the Plowshare Project, anything else except just finding out how good this testing of the weapons below 4.75 is.

Q. Mr. Roberts: Well, sir, is it your understanding that we would show everything involved, mechanism and so on, to the Soviets under this program?

THE PRESIDENT. Well, now, Mr. Roberts, there are some details I just can't get down to.   You know that.   But, I would think that everything that they found it necessary to see in order to determine whether this thing is effective, they would see and should see.

Now, I think that to get a little further on the thing you might get that statement of Dr. Kistiakowsky's and show it to him—[*confers with Mr. Hagerty*]

Mr. Hagerty just reminds me of what Dr. Kistiakowsky told me, another

---

[1] On May 7 a White House release stated that the President had that day announced approval of a major expansion of research and development directed toward an improved capability to detect and identify underground nuclear explosions.   The release added that the program, to be known as Project VELA, had grown out of the recommendations of the Panel on Seismic Improvement ("Berkner Panel"), and that it provided that "such nuclear explosions as are essential to a full understanding of both the capabilities of the presently proposed detection system and the potential for improvements in this system would be carried out under fully contained conditions and would produce no radioactive fallout."   The release further stated that Soviet negotiators at Geneva had concurred with the proposal that underground nuclear explosions should be conducted to improve the capability of the proposed control network; that they had also indicated a willingness to discuss research and development in the seismic detection area with the U.S. and the U.K.; and that agreement had been reached to convene a group of U.S.S.R., U.K., and U.S. scientists at Geneva on May 11 to exchange information on the seismic research activities of the three nations as a basis for future determination of the areas in which coordinated or joint research would be most fruitful.

point.   Our people are leaving tomorrow, they will meet there together—the U.S.S.R. and the U.K. and the U.S.—in determining exactly how we will do this.

Q. Charles W. Roberts, Newsweek: Sir, in connection with the Abel trial which you mentioned, the Soviet Government in that case made no effort to defend Colonel Abel.   I wonder if an American citizen were arrested by a foreign government and brought to trial as a spy, what the policy of this Government would be so far as his defense was concerned.

THE PRESIDENT. We would certainly offer the good offices of our Embassy, and see whether there was anything we could do. Of course it would be an internal matter there, and we would have to do it with the permission of the other country.   I think that if there is anything wrong diplomatically with my answer, you had better ask the State Department, but I think that would be the result.

Q. Robert C. Pierpoint, CBS News: Mr. President, many people seem to feel that the result of yesterday's elections in West Virginia once and for all buries the religious issue in politics in America. Do you agree with that premise, sir, and how do you feel about it?

THE PRESIDENT. Well, I don't know whether I agree completely with the conclusion or not.   Certainly I have made as strong a statement as I can, deploring the insertion of the religious issue in elections.   As a matter of fact, I think it is very, very bad for this country.   But as to what this election means, the only thing it means to me is—as a response to one question I said that I normally read only the Sunday papers, but I have read what the newspapers said were going to happen.   Now, this morning, I am a bit astonished.   [*Laughter*]

Q. Marvin L. Arrowsmith, Associated Press: Mr. President, you have said many times that you wouldn't go to the summit under any threats or ultimatums.

Yesterday, as you know, the Soviets in their note threatened retaliation against us if we continued to fly these planes over their territory.   Do you regard that kind of threat as within the category you were speaking of?

THE PRESIDENT. No.   I think that you have to set that aside in a special category.   I don't believe it's the kind of thing that you call an ultimatum at all.

Q. Edward P. Morgan, American Broadcasting Company: A point of clarification, Mr. President.   Do we infer correctly that your prepared statement this morning is the final, complete, and ultimate answer to your critics, friendly and hostile, on the subject?

THE PRESIDENT. I said that at this time I could see nothing more useful that I could say, so that's where I stand at this moment.

Q. Thomas N. Schroth, Congressional Quarterly: You said last summer, sir, that you planned to put before Congress at its final session a plan to reorganize the highest echelons of Government in order to relieve the burdens on some of the high officials. Can you give us any of the details of your plans and whether you expect to send them to Congress?

THE PRESIDENT. I've had to change my plan a little bit, because I became convinced that anything you did this year of extraordinary nature would probably be made political in some form or another. So I decided that regardless of who was elected to my present office, when I go up in January, as I must go under the Constitution—I must go make a statement—I'm going to put in then the plans that I have adverted to in these conferences before.

In general, it is to get closer, tighter day-by-day coordination in everything that touches upon the foreign field through one proper part of the plan; and the other, get all our business affairs, our types of procurement and making of contracts and all that, get that more tightly coordinated day in and day out.

The first one, I think, is tremendously important, because almost every department now has really heavy responsibilities in the foreign field. I think more and more we have to have not merely day-by-day meetings with the department heads concerned; it has to be closer, more tightly done than that.

Q. John Scali, Associated Press: Mr. President, you said in your initial statement that the Soviet account of the downing of this plane contained many discrepancies, and that there was reason to doubt that the plane was downed at a high altitude, as Mr. Khrushchev claims.

Can you tell us, sir, whether the administration at some future time intends to expose these discrepancies, and can you at this time without violating what you have said, give us any more details about how we believe this plane actually came down in the Soviet Union?

THE PRESIDENT. You raise a question that is really an auxiliary to the main issue, and so I don't mind saying this: take the pictures themselves, we know that they were not, or we believe we know that they are not pictures of the plane that was downed, and there are other things in their statements.

Now, I don't know what's going to happen in the future, but these things you can be sure will be carefully looked into. Again I say I do not foreclose any kind of statement that in the future may be necessary; I am saying that now I can see nothing more useful to say.

Q. John Herling, National Newspaper Syndicate: Mr. President, in reference to the drop in unemployment to which you referred, the hard core unemployment continues in many depressed areas, including West Virginia. Now, in view of that, sir, is Senator Dirksen correct in predicting that you plan to veto the depressed areas bill?

THE PRESIDENT. Well, if I don't approve of the particular depressed area bill, what do you expect me to do? As a matter of fact, as I have so far been reading this bill, the amounts there to be put under this greatly inflated bill of $251 million, or something like that, the amounts that are going into the areas like West Virginia, Southern Illinois, Pennsylvania, and Eastern Kentucky are less than they would be under ours. It's a shotgun—it's getting to be a pork barrel bill, as I see it. So I say I am not predicting anything; I am just saying this: I'll do what my judgment tells me to.

Q. Frank van der Linden, Nashville Banner: Sir, recently you proposed that the several southern cities having the problems of sit-in demonstrations should have biracial committees to meet and try to solve them.

Yesterday six of the stores in downtown Nashville admitted Negroes to the lunch counters. I wondered, sir, if you felt that was a solution to the problem, do you think that would be a pattern for the other cities to follow?

THE PRESIDENT. Let me say this: let us assume that I had the wisdom of a Solomon. I am still a good many hundred miles away from any of these cities, and any solutions to these problems must take into account local considerations and feelings and beliefs.

We here can talk and believe in the ideals that have been set up for us by the Constitution, and certainly we have a responsibility in helping to enforce or seeing that the constitutional rights guaranteed are not violated.

Now, when it comes to sit-ins, I am just not enough of a lawyer to say just exactly what they do mean—what they mean in the constitutional or legal terms. We, you and I, can talk about it in social terms and you might say on a moral standard, but this is something else.

I would say for that question, you ought to go to the Attorney General. I am just not that much of a lawyer.

Q. Raymond P. Brandt, St. Louis Post-Dispatch: In view of your emphasis on you might go back to the summit, if you had to come back here, have you any idea how long the Paris meeting will go on—how long do you think it will take you to get to some agreement?

THE PRESIDENT. Well, I don't know. But I just want to point this out: I hear that some—I don't know whether this is all of the others or not—do not like the simultaneous translations. Now, let us assume you have called an hour's conference, and one of you, for example, wants to make a, let's say, a 10-minute exposition. When you take seriatum translations, here is already a half hour of an hour's conference gone, and you have had only 10 minutes.

Now, these are very slow and laborious things, and consequently the possibility of prophesying how long this thing is going to be is really remote. Now, for my part, I am perfectly ready to work as many hours as an individual human can to get this thing along the line. I am prepared to go to this thing as long as there is any usefulness whatsoever promised, and even if I am called back—I know I have one date for 24 hours—I am still ready and prepared to go back. That is what I have been trying to insist, that I am not making my own convenience and my own duties here the decisive thing as to how long this conference will last.

Q. Lillian Levy, National Jewish Post and Opinion: Mr. President, are any changes in the present borders of West Germany part of the German question to be discussed at the summit? I ask this, sir, because this issue has been raised by a responsible West German leader and member of Adenauer's Cabinet who recently suggested that Germans be allowed to return to Sudetenland.

THE PRESIDENT. I didn't get the very first clause of your question.

Q. Mrs. Levy: Well, what I asked—were boundaries going to be part of the German question to be raised?

THE PRESIDENT. Well, at this time we wouldn't raise it. As a matter of fact, they've been living with these boundaries for a long time, and I would see at this moment no possibility of changing them except in methods that would be unacceptable. So, it might be raised by someone but I have no plan to do it.

Marvin L. Arrowsmith, Associated Press: Thank you, Mr. President.

NOTE: President Eisenhower's one hundred and eighty-fifth news conference was held in the Executive Office Build-ing from 10:27 to 11:01 o'clock on Wednesday morning, May 11, 1960. In attendance: 275.

144 ¶ Statement by the President on the Death of John D. Rockefeller, Jr.   *May* 12, 1960

THE PASSING of John D. Rockefeller, Jr., is a great loss to our nation. Life in America and, indeed throughout the world, has been enriched by his leadership in the planning and accomplishment of many programs for the public welfare.   These, in their enduring contribution to the growth and progress of our country and to the health and welfare of millions elsewhere, constitute a noble monument to his name and work. His place in our history will be both prominent and permanent.

Through the years I came to know Mr. Rockefeller as a churchman, philanthropist and a dedicated citizen.   In every aspect of his life, he won my deep admiration.   I share with millions a feeling of profound regret in the death of such a distinguished American.

145 ¶ Remarks to the Members of the American Helicopter Society.   *May* 12, 1960

President Alex, and my friends:

You will have noted that there have been a number of awards given this evening by the helicopter association, and until I stood up, all of them had been given in recognition of contributions made by these several individuals to the advancement of the helicopter as a vehicle for human travel.   In my case, it was not what I did for helicopters, it's what helicopters did for me.   And I think it's only appropriate, therefore, that I should try briefly to describe some of the things that they have done for me.

First of all, while it might have been possible for me to make three or four trips in the recent months that I have already completed without the use of the helicopter and the jet transport, it would indeed have been difficult and none of those trips could have been so extensive as it was. The saving of time in the great capitals of the world, in these large cities where often there are throngs gathered along the route are of course carefully scheduled as you come into the city, but in order to save valuable time as you go along to the next country, the helicopter is almost always used to go back to the airport, and occasionally indeed, to come in, as I believe was the case in Montevideo.

Without that kind of service, and the jet airplane, these trips would have been well nigh impossible. The convenience, the lack of wear and tear on the disposition, which at times wears thin anyway, I think, are among the advantages that all habitual users of helicopters are bound to experience. They are particularly, of course, useful in all the areas of crowded streets. When you have a traffic jam and you can hop over it and look down at it, two things happen. First, the Secret Service is not halting all of that traffic and therefore inspiring a good many hundreds, or thousands possibly, of people to despise your insides, but you yourself get such an exhilarated feeling. Boy, you look down and you say, "I don't have to work my way through *that!*"

In every kind of short trip from the city, where we find them appropriate, they are used invariably. To the units that have just been decorated this evening by your chairman, I owe a very great debt of gratitude. More than that, I owe my grateful thanks to the helicopter industry, to its presidents, its engineers, the people that support and believe in it—and indeed, also, to those other people who just use it.

Because I believe that as the advantages of this machine come more and more home to the consciousness of the American people, we will find a lot of travel that is much safer, at least in my opinion, than that on the road and possibly in the speedier airplane—fixed plane, that has to go, in any event, to fields of long runways. I land ordinarily at the back door of my farm, for example, after having taken off from the back door of the White House. And that is a great convenience, I assure you.

So as I express my thanks for this award, which really should have been given to all who have had a part in making the helicopter so useful, I say: good luck to all of you, and may your machines grow in numbers, and size, and one other item—silence.

NOTE: The President spoke at 10 p.m. at the Sheraton-Park Hotel in Washington. His opening words "President Alex" referred to Ralph Alex, President of the American Helicopter Society, who presented the President with a citation "for regular and extensive use of the helicopter."

146 ¶ Veto of the Area Redevelopment Bill. *May* 13, 1960

To the Senate of the United States:

I return herewith, without my approval, S. 722, the Area Redevelopment Bill.

For five consecutive years I have urged the Congress to enact sound area assistance legislation. On repeated occasions I have clearly outlined standards for the kind of program that is needed and that I would gladly approve.

In 1958 I vetoed a bill because it departed greatly from those standards. In 1959, despite my renewed urging, no area assistance bill was passed by the Congress.

Now in 1960, another election year, a new bill is before me that contains certain features which I find even more objectionable than those I found unacceptable in the 1958 bill.

The people of the relatively few communities of chronic unemployment—who want to share in the general prosperity—are, after five years, properly becoming increasingly impatient and are rightfully desirous of constructive action. The need is for truly sound and helpful legislation on which the Congress and the Executive can agree. There is still time and I willingly pledge once again my wholehearted cooperation in obtaining such a law.

———

S. 722 is seriously defective in six major respects which are summarized immediately below and discussed in detail thereafter.

1. S. 722 would squander the federal taxpayers' money where there is only temporary economic difficulty, curable without the special federal assistance provided in the bill. In consequence, communities in genuine need would receive less federal help for industrial development projects than under the Administration's proposal.

2. Essential local, State and private initiative would be materially inhibited by the excessive federal participation that S. 722 would authorize.

3. Federal financing of plant machinery and equipment is unwise and unnecessary and therefore wasteful of money that otherwise could be of real help.

4. The federal loan assistance which S. 722 would provide for the

construction of sewers, water mains, access roads and other public facilities is unnecessary because such assistance is already available under an existing Government program. Outright grants for such a purpose, a provision of S. 722, are wholly inappropriate.

5. The provisions for federal loans for the construction of industrial buildings in rural areas are incongruous and unnecessary.

6. The creation of a new federal agency is not needed and would actually delay initiation of the new program for many months.

I.

The most striking defect of S. 722 is that it would make eligible for federal assistance areas that don't need it—thus providing less help for communities in genuine need than would the Administration's proposal. S. 722, as opposed to the Administration bill, would more than double the number of eligible communities competing for federal participation in loans for the construction or refurbishing of plants for industrial use— the main objective of both bills. Communities experiencing only temporary economic difficulty would accordingly be made eligible under S. 722 and the dissipation of federal help among them would deprive communities afflicted with truly chronic unemployment of the full measure of assistance they so desperately desire and which the Administration bill would give them.

II.

Lasting solutions to the problems of chronic unemployment can only be forthcoming if local citizens—the people most immediately concerned— take the lead in planning and financing them. The principal objective is to develop new industry. The Federal Government can and should help, but the major role in the undertaking must be the local community's. Neither money alone, nor the Federal Government alone, can do the job. The States also must help, and many are, but in many instances and in many ways they could do much more.

Under S. 722, however, financing of industrial development projects by the Federal Government—limited to 35% under the Administration's proposal—could go as high as 65%, local community participation could be as low as 10% and private financing as little as 5%. Furthermore, although S. 722 conditions this assistance on approval by a local economic development organization, if no such organization exists one can be appointed from Washington.

III.

S. 722 would authorize federal loans for the acquisition of machinery and equipment to manufacturers locating in eligible areas. Loans for machinery and equipment are unnecessary, unwise and costly. Much more money would be required and unnecessarily spent, much less money would find its way into truly helpful projects, and manufacturers would be subsidized unnecessarily vis-a-vis their competitors.

IV.

S. 722 would authorize further unnecessary spending by providing both loans and grants—up to 100% of the cost—for the construction of access roads, sewers, water mains and other local public facilities.

Grants for local public facilities far exceed any appropriate federal responsibility. Even though relatively modest at the start, they would set predictably expensive and discriminatory precedents.

With regard to loans for such purposes, exemption from federal income taxes makes it possible today for local communities in almost every case to borrow on reasonable terms from private sources. Whenever such financing is difficult to obtain, the need can be filled by the existing Public Facility Loan Program of the Housing and Home Finance Agency—a program which S. 722 would needlessly duplicate and for which an additional $100 million authorization has already been requested.

V.

S. 722 would make a minimum of 600 rural counties eligible for federal loans for the construction of industrial buildings in such areas. The Rural Development Program and the Small Business Administration are already contributing greatly to the economic improvement of low income rural areas. Increasing the impact of these two activities, particularly the Rural Development Program, is a preferable course.

VI.

Finally, S. 722 would also create a new federal agency and would, in consequence, mean many unnecessary additions to the federal payroll and a considerable delay in the program before the new agency could be staffed and functioning effectively. None of this is necessary, for all that needs to be done can be done—much better and immediately—by the existing Department of Commerce.

Again, I strongly urge the Congress to enact new legislation at this session—but without those features of S. 722 that I find objectionable. I would, however, accept the eligibility criteria set forth in the bill that first passed the Senate even though these criteria are broader than those contained in the Administration bill.

Moreover, during the process of developing a new bill, I would hope that in other areas of past differences solutions could be found satisfactory to both the Congress and the Executive.

My profound hope is that sound, new legislation will be promptly enacted. If it is, our communities of chronic unemployment will be only the immediate beneficiaries. A tone will have been set that would hold forth, for the remainder of the session, the hope of sound and rewarding legislation in other vital areas—mutual security, wheat, sugar, minimum wage, interest rates, revenue measures, medical care for the aged and aid to education to mention but a few.

Only this result can truly serve the finest and best interests of all our people.

DWIGHT D. EISENHOWER

147 ¶ Remarks Upon Arrival at Orly Airport in Paris. *May* 15, 1960

ONCE AGAIN I am privileged to come to France, this beautiful France, to salute a great people and their leader. I have come here to join with the leaders of France, Great Britain and the Soviet Union in discussions of historic importance.

The American Government's participation is undertaken not to seek any advantage at another's expense; rather it hopes to prove equally with any other its sincere dedication to peace with justice.

Mankind knows that the effects of nuclear war would be not only horrible but universal. Mankind expects the participants in this summit meeting to work honestly and intelligently for measures toward genuine peace.

The hopes of humanity call on the four of us to purge our minds of prejudice, and our hearts of rancor. Far too much is at stake to indulge in profitless bickering. The issues that divide the free world from the Soviet bloc are grave and not subject to easy solution. But if goodwill exists on both sides, at least a beginning can be made. The West, I am sure, will meet Mr. Khrushchev halfway in every honest effort in this direction. America will go every foot that safety and honor permit.

It will be a pleasure to meet again with my old friends President de Gaulle and Prime Minister Macmillan. I hope to meet another friend, Chancellor Adenauer, this afternoon. I have talked with all three of these leaders in recent weeks, and we have had opportunity to discuss the issues before us. Unity on great principles and purposes strengthens the Western powers as the eyes of the world turn towards Paris. I pray that the grace of God will be with us to direct our efforts so that progress toward a just peace may be achieved.

148 ¶ Statement by the President Upon Signing the Mutual Security Act of 1960. *May* 16, 1960

I HAVE SIGNED into law the Mutual Security Act of 1960.

I am highly gratified by the action of the Congress on this measure. The Act embodies essentially all of the requests I have put forward as necessary for the successful continuation of the Mutual Security Program, and, with one regrettable exception, the Congress has resisted the addition of amendments which would adversely affect our foreign relations or impair the administration of the Program.

I believe it is impressive that, after extensive and searching hearings on the bill conducted by the authorizing committees of both Houses, the Congress concluded that substantially all of the funds requested are necessary for carrying forward important economic aspects of the Program. The same high degree of responsibility and regard for our national interests will, I trust, result in not only the full sums now authorized for certain economic programs but also in the full appropriations which I have requested as necessary to provide for the Development Loan Fund and the Military Assistance Program.

NOTE: The Mutual Security Act of 1960 is Public Law 86–472, signed by the President on May 14 (74 Stat. 134). The statement was released in Washington.

149 ¶ Message to the Congress Transmitting the Civil Service Commission's First Report Under the Government Employees Training Act.
May 16, 1960

[Released May 16, 1960. Dated May 14, 1960]

To the Congress of the United States:

The Government Employees Training Act (P.L. 85–507) directs the Civil Service Commission to submit annually to the President for his approval and transmittal to the Congress a report with respect to the training of employees of the Government under the authority of the Act. I am transmitting to you with this letter the Commission's report entitled, "Employee Training for Better Public Service."

It is my firm conviction that training has long been essential for the successful operation of Federal agencies. Today's demands, however, bring a new urgency to training, especially for our career managers. I have, therefore, recently asked all agency heads to strengthen their programs for the selection, development, and training of these key officials. This directive is in addition to that issued in 1955 which supported all types of training.

The action of the Congress in broadening authority to train Federal employees was a healthy and progressive move. The Commission's report shows that Federal officials have made intelligent use of their authority under the Act and that it has helped to meet an urgent need. I was particularly interested in the Commission's comments on "The Future," which point out two important areas needing improvement—Planning, and Budgeting and Scheduling for Training Activities.

The Commission's report is encouraging and its suggestions to the agencies sound. A good beginning has been made under the authority granted by the Congress.

DWIGHT D. EISENHOWER

NOTE: The 38-page report, dated May 1960, was published as a Senate Committee Print by the Senate Committee on the Post Office and Civil Service (Government Printing Office, 1960).
The message was released in Washington.

150 ¶ Veto of Bill for Relief of Universal Trades, Inc. *May 16, 1960*

[Released May 16, 1960. Dated May 14, 1960]

To the House of Representatives:

I return herewith, without my approval, H.R. 1456, a bill for the relief of Universal Trades, Incorporated.

The Renegotiation Board, in 1955, ordered Universal Trades, Incorporated, to refund to the Government $50,000 in excessive profits, subject to applicable Federal tax credits. The law provides a 90-day period, after the conclusion of the Renegotiation Board proceeding, in which to apply for a review of the case by The Tax Court of the United States. Universal Trades did not file such a petition.

Under H.R. 1456 jurisdiction would now be conferred on The Tax Court—some five years after the expiration of the 90-day period.

Universal Trades claims that income of $92,481.54 was improperly included in its 1952 renegotiation proceeding. A change in the company's accounting method did move this income from 1952 to 1953 for income tax purposes, but for renegotiation purposes no such transfer was made. This treatment was equitable, appropriate for renegotiation purposes, and in accordance with the Renegotiation Act.

Finally, no valid justification appears for the corporation's failure to file a petition with the Tax Court within the prescribed 90-day period. At all times before and after issuance of the Board's order, Universal Trades was in full possession of the facts pertaining to the accounting method used by the Board.

Under the circumstances, therefore, I am constrained to withhold my approval from the bill.

Dwight D. Eisenhower

NOTE: The veto message was released in Washington.

151 ¶ Veto of a Bill Relating to the Income Tax Treatment of Nonrefundable Capital Contributions to Federal National Mortgage Association. *May 16, 1960*

[Released May 16, 1960. Dated May 14, 1960]

To the House of Representatives:

I return herewith, without my approval, H.R. 7947 entitled "An Act Relating to the income tax treatment of nonrefundable capital contributions to Federal National Mortgage Association."

When a financial institution sells a mortgage to the Federal National Mortgage Association, the institution is required to purchase shares of Association common stock at par value in an amount equal to 2 percent of the unpaid principal of the mortgage. The market price for this common stock has been appreciably lower than its par value. H.R. 7947 would permit the financial institution to deduct as a business expense the difference between par value and market value when it sells the common stock it was required to purchase.

I am sympathetic with the objectives of the bill. But it provides for the retroactive application of the proposed amendment in a highly discriminatory manner. This is a defect which is sufficiently serious to require my disapproval. Generally, changes in the tax laws should only apply prospectively, for retroactive amendments result in substantial administrative problems. Wholly apart from this, however, the particular provision for retroactivity in H.R. 7947 would benefit only those taxpayers who previously claimed the deduction contrary to the announced position of the Internal Revenue Service; the bill would not permit refund or credit to those taxpayers who accepted the position of the Internal Revenue Service and paid their taxes. I cannot approve such discrimination.

In view of this defect, I withhold my approval from H.R. 7947.

DWIGHT D. EISENHOWER

NOTE: The veto message was released in Washington.

152   ¶ Special Message to the Congress Concerning the Proposed Freedom Monument. *May* 16, 1960

[Released May 16, 1960. Dated May 14, 1960]

To the Congress of the United States:

I am enclosing for the consideration of the Congress a report of the National Monument Commission submitted as directed by the Act of August 31, 1954. I have requested the Secretary of the Interior to submit to the Congress a proposed bill embodying the Commission's recommendations.

The Commission's report recommends an approved design for the Freedom Monument, asks that the Commission be authorized to erect the Monument, suggests that the number of private citizens serving on the Commission be increased from four to eight, asks the Congress to authorize the appropriation of $12 million as the Federal share of the cost of construction, and requests that the Commission be authorized to solicit private contributions for the remaining cost of the Monument.

The Act of August 31, 1954, created the National Monument Commission for the purpose of securing designs and plans for a useful monument to the Nation symbolizing to the United States and the world the ideals of our democracy as embodied in the five freedoms—speech, religion, press, assembly, and petition—sanctified by the Bill of Rights adopted by Congress in 1789 and later ratified by the States.

I believe it important that the story of the noble ideas which shaped our country's beginning, its course, its great moments, and the men who made it possible, be ever present in the minds of Americans. This purpose can be furthered in a variety of ways, but the simplest and most effective of all methods in my judgment is to present it impressively in visual form. The erection of the Freedom Monument would accomplish that objective. The National Capital area is adorned by a galaxy of memorials to individuals but nowhere in the Nation's Capital or this Nation can one find a memorial to the principles and ideals upon which our Government is based.

The Commission, since its creation, has placed the ideas I have mentioned on the drawing board. It is intimately acquainted with the problems involved in the erection of the Monument; it has advanced the memorial; and I recommend that the Commission be authorized to complete the task.

DWIGHT D. EISENHOWER

NOTE: The message was released in Washington. The report of the National Monument Commission was not printed.

153   ¶ Memorandum to Federal Agencies on the United Givers Fund Campaign in the National Capital Area.   *May* 16, 1960

[Released May 16, 1960. Dated May 14, 1960]

To the Heads of Executive Departments and Agencies:

This fall, the United Givers Fund will conduct its fifth annual Campaign in the National Capital Area.   Nearly 150 local and national agencies in Washington and nearby Maryland and Virginia—providing vitally needed health and welfare services to our community—will seek our voluntary support during this Campaign.

Among the agencies that benefit from our gifts are the six area chapters of the American National Red Cross, the Salvation Army, the Family Service Associations, the Boy and Girl Scouts, the Mental Health Associations and other health agencies, and the USO.   Scores of others provide Child Care, Care for the Aged, Hospital and Medical care and many other services to meet human needs.

I am happy to announce that the Honorable Robert B. Anderson, Secretary of the Treasury, has accepted the chairmanship of the Government Unit for the 1960 United Givers Fund Campaign.   I know that all Government personnel in the Washington area will want to join with him in making this fund-raising effort an outstanding success.

DWIGHT D. EISENHOWER

NOTE: The memorandum was released in Washington.

154 ¶ Statement by the President Concerning the Position Taken by Chairman Khrushchev at the Opening of the Summit Conference. *May* 16, 1960

HAVING BEEN INFORMED yesterday by General de Gaulle and Prime Minister Macmillan of the position which Mr. Khrushchev has taken in regard to this conference during his calls yesterday morning on them, I gave most careful thought as to how this matter should best be handled. Having in mind the great importance of this conference and the hopes that the peoples of all the world have reposed in this meeting, I concluded that in the circumstances it was best to see if at today's private meeting any possibility existed through the exercise of reason and restraint to dispose of this matter of the overflights, which would have permitted the conference to go forward.

I was under no illusion as to the probability of success of any such approach but I felt that in view of the great responsibility resting on me as President of the United States this effort should be made.

In this I received the strongest support of my colleagues President de Gaulle and Prime Minister Macmillan. Accordingly, at this morning's private session, despite the violence and inaccuracy of Mr. Khrushchev's statements, I replied to him on the following terms:

"I had previously been informed of the sense of the statement just read by Premier Khrushchev.

"In my statement of May 11th and in the statement of Secretary Herter of May 9th, the position of the United States was made clear with respect to the distasteful necessity of espionage activities in a world where nations distrust each other's intentions. We pointed out that these activities had no aggressive intent but rather were to assure the safety of the United States and the free world against surprise attack by a power which boasts of its ability to devastate the United States and other countries by missiles armed with atomic warheads. As is well known, not only the United States but most other countries are constantly the targets of elaborate and persistent espionage of the Soviet Union.

"There is in the Soviet statement an evident misapprehension on one

key point. It alleges that the United States has, through official statements, threatened continued overflights.   The importance of this alleged
threat was emphasized and repeated by Mr. Khrushchev.   The United
States has made no such threat.   Neither I nor my government has
intended any.   The actual statements go no further than to say that
the United States will not shirk its responsibility to safeguard against
surprise attack.

"In point of fact, these flights were suspended after the recent incident
and are not to be resumed.   Accordingly, this cannot be the issue.

"I have come to Paris to seek agreements with the Soviet Union which
would eliminate the necessity for all forms of espionage, including overflights.   I see no reason to use this incident to disrupt the conference.

"Should it prove impossible, because of the Soviet attitude, to come
to grips here in Paris with this problem and the other vital issues threatening world peace, I am planning in the near future to submit to the
United Nations a proposal for the creation of a United Nations aerial
surveillance to detect preparations for attack.   This plan I had intended
to place before this conference.   This surveillance system would operate
in the territories of all nations prepared to accept such inspection.   For
its part, the United States is prepared not only to accept United Nations
aerial surveillance, but to do everything in its power to contribute to the
rapid organization and successful operation of such international
surveillance.

"We of the United States are here to consider in good faith the important problems before this conference.   We are prepared either to
carry this point no further, or to undertake bilateral conversations between
the United States and the U.S.S.R. while the main conference proceeds."

My words were seconded and supported by my Western colleagues who
also urged Mr. Khrushchev to pursue the path of reason and common
sense, and to forget propaganda.   Such an attitude would have permitted
the conference to proceed.   Mr. Khrushchev was left in no doubt by me
that his ultimatum would never be acceptable to the United States.

Mr. Khrushchev brushed aside all arguments of reason, and not only
insisted upon this ultimatum, but also insisted that he was going to publish
his statement in full at the time of his own choosing.

It was thus made apparent that he was determined to wreck the Paris
conference.

In fact, the only conclusion that can be drawn from his behavior this morning was that he came all the way from Moscow to Paris with the sole intention of sabotaging this meeting on which so much of the hopes of the world have rested.

In spite of this serious and adverse development, I have no intention whatsoever to diminish my continuing efforts to promote progress toward a peace with justice. This applies to the remainder of my stay in Paris as well as thereafter.

NOTE: The President's statement of May 11 was read at his news conference of that date (Item 143). Secretary Herter's statement of May 9 is published in the Department of State Bulletin (vol. 42, p. 816).

This statement was released in Paris.

155 ¶ Joint Statement With President de Gaulle and Prime Minister Macmillan Concerning the Summit Conference. *May* 17, 1960

THE PRESIDENT of the United States, the President of the French Republic and the Prime Minister of the United Kingdom take note of the fact that because of the attitude adopted by the Chairman of the Council of Ministers of the Soviet Union it has not been possible to begin, at the Summit Conference, the examination of the problems which it had been agreed would be discussed between the four Chiefs of State or Government.

They regret that these discussions, so important for world peace, could not take place. For their part, they remain unshaken in their conviction that all outstanding international questions should be settled not by the use or threat of force but by peaceful means through negotiation. They themselves remain ready to take part in such negotiations at any suitable time in the future.

NOTE: Shortly before the release of the joint statement, the Press Secretary issued the following paper:

"The President understands from the invitation of President de Gaulle, the host and chairman, that the meeting which he has called for this afternoon will be a formal session of the Conference at the Summit. In this light, the Conference will address itself to the subjects which had originally been accepted for discussion.

"In accepting this invitation, the President of the United States assumes that acceptance by the Soviet representative of the same invitation to attend this meeting would constitute a withdrawal on his part of the 'conditions' which had already been refused by the President."

On May 18 it was announced that the President, the President of France, and the Prime Minister of Great Britain met for one hour at the Elysée Palace with their Foreign Ministers to hear the ministers report on their discussions that morning concerning the international situation then prevailing.   After the meet-ing the President remained for a farewell visit with President de Gaulle.

The joint statement was released in Paris.

156 ¶ Remarks at Orly Airport, Paris, Before Leaving for Lisbon.   *May* 19, 1960

AGAIN I HAVE the opportunity to say adieu to France.   I share the disappointment of my colleagues that because of our inability to convene the Summit Conference, we could make no progress toward easing the tensions that so plague mankind.   But I equally share their confidence that because of this setback we of the Western Allies, particularly France, Britain, and the United States, both through their governments and through their people, are joined even closer than before in their determined pursuit of peace with justice in the world.

And so now I say, or express my deep gratitude to the people of France who have made our stay here so enjoyable personally and who have been so generous in their extension of courteous hospitality.   It is a lovely country that I hope in the coming months and years to visit often.

Thank you all very much.

157 ¶ Remarks Upon Arrival at Portela Airport, Lisbon.   *May* 19, 1960

MR. PRESIDENT, I thank you most sincerely for your warm words of welcome.

It is 9 years since I last visited this lovely land.   It was a January day of beautiful sunshine, and I recall very vividly the opportunity I had to see from the vantage point of the Edward VII Park the lovely city of Lisbon.

Now I am particularly fortunate that I come back when you are celebrating your Fifth Centenary of Prince Henry the Great Navigator.   His studies and leadership were the very inspiration for the great age of exploration.   And the American people join your people in the salute to this great gentleman, a man whose genius did so much to enrich both our country and yours.

Finally, I come back to tell you that there are no great problems between the United States and Portugal.   Our entire history since the birth of my Nation has been that of friendship, and in friendship we are members of the United Nations; we are both members of the North Atlantic Treaty Organization, an alliance that seeks only security and peace. And our two nations, despite obstacles set in our paths by others, will continue the march towards peace and freedom.

Thank you very much.

NOTE: The President spoke at 9:58 a.m. He was met by President Américo Deus Rodriques Thomaz, Dr. C. Arreiro de Sreitas, Portuguese Chief of Protocol, and U.S. Ambassador C. Burke Elbrick.

158   ¶ Remarks to the Staff of the U.S. Embassy and the American Community in Lisbon.
May 19, 1960

THANK YOU very much.   Did you see that cartoon not long ago where it says, "The next speaker needs all the introduction he can get"?   Well, I rather feel that way, after coming from this last meeting in Paris.

While none of the world—certainly none of the free world—thought that there was going to be any great revolutionary gains, still we had a right to hope, I think, that there would be some further amelioration of those conditions that seem to cause so much disorder and tension in the world.   I think that you deserve to know that the Western representatives—the representatives of Great Britain and of France, and the company that went with me to Paris—did their very best to bring about this kind of condition.   And certainly every one of us answered abuse with decency and logic, and accusation with a simple statement of facts.

Now I think there is no reason to be particularly dismayed or disheartened.   This kind of struggle has been going on for a long time, but I think it does mean this: each of us, and particularly those who are living here all the time in an Embassy and in other activities that come under the general purview of the governmental activities of America, have to work a little bit harder.

We do know that we have a tremendous friend in Portugal.   We have to strengthen that friendship, because every time we have a setback in the effort to bring about better conditions between the two opposite camps of the world, this means that our own camp must be brought closer together by voluntary effort, by deeper convictions, by more dedication to the great cause of peace with justice in freedom.

So when I meet members of this kind of a colony—and I have done so now, I suppose, in the last few months in 15 or 16 countries—I never fail to get some inspiration, because I know that they are working so hard.

Perhaps leaders here and there may make mistakes, but at least they certainly never make the mistake of deprecating or of minimizing the value of the work you people are doing. So I say, rather than being dismayed, we have to tighten our belts, put our chins up a little higher, and if we can, be more eloquent in telling the story that we have.

To meet such a group as this, always far away—far from home, we feel somewhat like we are at home again. This is not only an inspiration, it is a great joy, a lot of fun—normally along with you come all the little youngsters, who sit in front and I really think I have more fun with them than I do some of you grownups, because I think possibly I am one of those simple creatures who thinks in those terms, and we get along famously.

But to each of you—first of all, I thank you for coming out, doing me the honor to come here to meet with me just briefly. I also repeat my appreciation for what you are doing, and in a more official sense, my gratitude and my thanks for what the people and those like you all around the world are doing to present the picture. And I will tell you flatly: I have gone many, many places, in different kinds of countries, and there's one book that was written that I felt did more disservice to the honest public servant of America, doing exactly what you people are doing, than any other.

There were obviously some elements of truth in what he said, but the exaggeration and the distortion to my mind were sickening.

So to you I want to say thanks, as earnestly as I can. And if I can say one more word: keep it up, and a little bit stronger, a little better, a little bigger.

I am very proud of every one of you.

Thank you very much.

NOTE: The President spoke at 12:55 p.m. in a reception room at Queluz Palace, his official residence while in Lisbon.

159   ¶ Toast by the President at a Luncheon Given in His Honor by President Thomaz at Ajuda Palace.   *May* 19, 1960

Mr. President, Mrs. Thomaz, ladies and gentlemen:

I am grateful for your words to me, my country, and the people of the United States.

In the past, hardy Portuguese explorers spent many months penetrating the uncharted distances between our two continents.   Today the space between us has been reduced to a few hours on a jet plane.   May this shrinking distance symbolize the ever more binding ties between our two nations.

Founding partners in the NATO alliance, we are of a like abiding confidence in its strength and in the ideals which it seeks to preserve and defend.

Ladies and gentlemen, to Portuguese-American friendship: may it be in the future as it has been in the past—warm, steadfast, and enduring.

Ladies and gentlemen, will you join me in a Toast to the President of Portugal.

160   ¶ Toast by the President at a Dinner Given in Honor of President Thomaz at Queluz Palace.   *May* 19, 1960

TODAY was a marvelous day.   After the deceptions that brought about the failure of our efforts to achieve a top level conference, the welcome which I received during my visit to Portugal was an antidote.   I am absolutely certain that other countries, too, will not feel discouraged at the result and the failure of our efforts.   On the contrary it will constitute an incentive to continue our attempts to achieve peace with justice.

In the past, all generations have had to face problems which appeared to them to be insoluble.   Our generation is no exception.   It also has problems to face all over the world.   There is the problem of the threat of communism, which by means of economic, financial, political, and subversive penetrations imperil what we are trying to defend.   But communism isn't the only problem that we have to face.   There are others equally difficult, such as sickness, misery, illiteracy, human suffering, and so many others. And we all know that if we leave them unsolved, we shall not be able to achieve our objectives of peace and justice. These problems know no geographical frontiers. And in order to solve all the difficulties which we shall have to face in all parts of the world, it will be essential for us to join our forces.

But if at times we feel disheartened and discouraged by the magnitude of the obstacles with which we are faced, all we need to do is to look back upon the Age of the Great Discoveries of Portugal, to encounter there the inspiration which is indispensable to us today.

The great Infante Don Henrique didn't lose heart in the face of the problems which he proposed to solve. He didn't lose courage in the course of his efforts and didn't turn back from the unknown, that unknown which terrified the peoples of the past, the unknown in which to adventure was the same as being lost. And there is also another great figure: Vasco da Gama. Both had the courage to put their shoulders to great undertakings. Neither of them hesitated in the face of mystery. Perhaps those two figures of your history may have contributed more to enrich the life of humanity than has the scientific knowledge of the two last decades.

But leaders of this stature exist also in the world of today. We have them with us. Observe your country and note the progress and the improvements brought about here during the nine years since my last visit under the leadership of your Prime Minister, Dr. Salazar.

That vision, courage, and tenacity of the Portuguese navigators we still find today to resolve great questions not so much for ourselves but for the benefit of others. What I see here did not occur by chance: it was necessary to make plans and the plans had to be carried out.

For this reason I am absolutely certain that the apparently insoluble problems of today can be solved by means of a close union between our peoples and our Governments. I am profoundly convinced that if we join our capacities, our energies—and intelligence, and the will of Portugal and of the United States, we shall be able to show the way to other countries—and then, together we shall achieve victory at the end of each daily road.

I toast this Nation—the happiness of the Portuguese people—symbolized by President Américo Thomaz who also represents courage, willpower, vision, the past and the future of the great Portuguese people.

161   ¶ Remarks at Portela Airport, Lisbon, Before Leaving for Washington.   *May* 20, 1960

Mr. President, and all citizens of this lovely and friendly country:

First of all, Mr. President, will you permit me a word of congratulations to the Armed Services for the beauty and character of the arrival and departure ceremonies.   Never have I seen any more impressive than this.

Twenty-four hours is far too short a time to spend in your lovely country.   As in my visit here in 1951, I have been impressed by the beauty of Portugal and by the friendliness and hospitality of the Portuguese people.   Equally impressive are the signs of real progress.   Today I saw whole communities which in my visit in 1951 did not exist.

Brief as this visit was, I believe it has been productive of many useful results.   My talks with President Thomaz and with the President of the Council, Dr. Salazar, have been conducted in a spirit of complete mutual understanding.   All of us realize that we are united in a common cause and that each of us, in his own way, shares a part of the responsibility of striving for a peaceful and better world.   Moreover, our talks together have once again affirmed the spirit of friendship and good will that has always characterized the relations between Portugal and the United States.

The time has come to say goodbye.   It is with the greatest reluctance that I take my leave after this pleasant stay with you.

But in the name of the American people, I salute the Portuguese nation, its distinguished leaders, and its wonderful, warm-hearted citizens.   My deepest gratitude and thanks go to all who have made this visit so pleasant and memorable.

NOTE: The President spoke at 9:40 a.m.

162   ¶ Remarks Upon Arrival at Andrews Air Force Base.   *May* 20, 1960

My good friends and fellow citizens:

After a trip of this kind you can well understand what it means to me to have this kind of a welcome.   I am deeply appreciative of the trouble that each of you took to come out to this spot. It truly means a lot to me.

As we planned for the Summit, the hopes of the world were not too high. The experience of the past years had denied us any right to believe that great advances toward the purposes we seek—peace with justice—could be achieved in any great measure. Yet, it seems that the identity of interest between ourselves and the Soviets in certain features was so obvious that logically we should have made some progress.

Certainly the subjects on which we wanted to talk were those that seemed so important to them—for example, disarmament; the widening of contacts so that we would have open societies, or slightly more open societies, dealing with each other; then the matter of Berlin and a divided Germany; and finally, as between Russia, and the U.K., and ourselves some agreement on a plan for control of nuclear testing.

Therefore, it was a mystery and remains a mystery as to why, at this particular moment, the Soviets chose so to distort and overplay the U–2 incident that they obviously wanted no talks of any kind, and in fact, made it impossible to begin them. I am not going to speculate today as to the future, but it is quite clear that since they wanted no talks whatsoever at this time that we can be watchful for more irritations, possibly other incidents that can be more than annoying, sometimes creating real problems.

For example, just today a half hour before I landed, it was reported to me that there is a C–47 missing in Western Germany. This is an unarmed, slow plane—no possibility of being used for military purposes—and in fact, I believe it had nine passengers aboard. There was some bad weather and its route took it near the Eastern German border. We do not know at this moment that any deliberate act delayed it, but at least it is overdue. And so, in the atmosphere in which we now have to think and live we cannot be sure that the worst has not happened.

Now, I may want to talk soon to the Nation about these matters, and for that part of it, I now stop. But I do want to tell all of you people about three or four encouraging features that I encountered. First of all was the assurance of the support of the home folks—from friends, and from the Joint Chiefs of Staff, from the political leaders of both parties, from newspaper comments and editorial comment of every kind. I was assured of the essential solidarity of the United States and of the sincerity of our peaceful purposes.

Secondly, was the conduct of my two principal colleagues of the West.

Mr. Macmillan and General de Gaulle were superb. They spoke with one voice with our delegation in support of those things that we thought right and decent and logical.

Thirdly, was an action on the part of the NATO Council yesterday when Secretary Herter reported to them while I was in Portugal. The NATO Resolution unanimously supported the three Western powers in what we were trying to do.

And finally, the Portuguese reception: in a way I think they wanted to provide the United States and the West—and even me personally—with something of an antidote for some of the disappointments we have felt. Government and citizens alike tried to outdo themselves in the warmth and cordiality of their receptions, and on top of that, in their assurances from every side—newspapers, the officials, common people coming in who were serving us in the Palace—everywhere they said, "The West, in effect, is right, and we want you to know it." And they used every possible way to do it. And for that day in Portugal yesterday I am grateful.

Finally, since most of you will understand that by our time here it was one o'clock when I arose this morning I am sure you expected nothing of eloquence. But I did want sincerely to give you some of my reactions, convictions, as of this moment, and to say again to each of you—thank you very much indeed.

NOTE: The President spoke at 3 p.m.

163 ¶ Radio and Television Report to the American People on the Events in Paris.
May 25, 1960

[Delivered from the President's Office at 8 p.m.]

My fellow Americans:

Tonight I want to talk with you about the remarkable events last week in Paris, and their meaning to our future.

First, I am deeply grateful to the many thousands of you, and to representatives in Congress, who sent me messages of encouragement and support while I was in Paris, and later upon my return to Washington. Your messages clearly revealed your abiding loyalty to America's great purpose—that of pursuing, from a position of spiritual, moral and material strength—a lasting peace with justice.

You recall, of course, why I went to Paris ten days ago.

Last summer and fall I had many conversations with world leaders; some of these were with Chairman Khrushchev, here in America. Over those months a small improvement in relations between the Soviet Union and the West seemed discernible. A possibility developed that the Soviet leaders might at last be ready for serious talks about our most persistent problems—those of disarmament, mutual inspection, atomic control, and Germany, including Berlin.

To explore that possibility, our own and the British and French leaders met together, and later we agreed, with the Soviet leaders, to gather in Paris on May 16.

Of course we had no indication or thought that basic Soviet policies had turned about. But when there is even the slightest chance of strengthening peace, there can be no higher obligation than to pursue it.

Nor had our own policies changed. We did hope to make some progress in a Summit meeting, unpromising though previous experiences had been. But as we made preparations for this meeting, we did not drop our guard nor relax our vigilance.

Our safety, and that of the free world, demand, of course, effective systems for gathering information about the military capabilities of other powerful nations, especially those that make a fetish of secrecy. This involves many techniques and methods. In these times of vast military machines and nuclear-tipped missiles, the ferreting out of this information is indispensable to free world security.

This has long been one of my most serious preoccupations. It is part of my grave responsibility, within the over-all problem of protecting the American people, to guard ourselves and our allies against surprise attack.

During the period leading up to World War II we learned from bitter experience the imperative necessity of a continuous gathering of intelligence information, the maintenance of military communications and contact, and alertness of command.

An additional word seems appropriate about this matter of communications and command. While the Secretary of Defense and I were in Paris, we were, of course, away from our normal command posts. He recommended that under the circumstances we test the continuing readiness of our military communications. I personally approved. Such tests are valuable and will be frequently repeated in the future.

Moreover, as President, charged by the Constitution with the conduct of America's foreign relations, and as Commander-in-Chief, charged with the direction of the operations and activities of our Armed Forces and their supporting services, I take full responsibility for approving all the various programs undertaken by our government to secure and evaluate military intelligence.

It was in the prosecution of one of these intelligence programs that the widely publicized U–2 incident occurred.

Aerial photography has been one of many methods we have used to keep ourselves and the free world abreast of major Soviet military developments. The usefulness of this work has been well established through four years of effort. The Soviets were well aware of it. Chairman Khrushchev has stated that he became aware of these flights several years ago. Only last week, in his Paris press conference, Chairman Khrushchev confirmed that he knew of these flights when he visited the United States last September.

Incidentally, this raises the natural question—why all the furor concerning one particular flight? He did not, when in America last September charge that these flights were any threat to Soviet safety. He did not then see any reason to refuse to confer with American representatives.

This he did only about the flight that unfortuately failed, on May 1, far inside Russia.

Now, two questions have been raised about this particular flight; first, as to its timing, considering the imminence of the Summit meeting; second, our initial statements when we learned the flight had failed.

As to the timing, the question was really whether to halt the program and thus forego the gathering of important information that was essential and that was likely to be unavailable at a later date. The decision was that the program should not be halted.

The plain truth is this: when a nation needs intelligence activity, there is no time when vigilance can be relaxed. Incidentally, from Pearl Harbor we learned that even negotiation itself can be used to conceal preparations for a surprise attack.

Next, as to our government's initial statement about the flight, this was issued to protect the pilot, his mission, and our intelligence processes, at a time when the true facts were still undetermined.

Our first information about the failure of this mission did not disclose whether the pilot was still alive, was trying to escape, was avoiding interrogation, or whether both plane and pilot had been destroyed. Protection of our intelligence system and the pilot, and concealment of the plane's mission, seemed imperative. It must be remembered that over a long period, these flights had given us information of the greatest importance to the nation's security. In fact, their success has been nothing short of remarkable.

For these reasons, what is known in intelligence circles as a "covering statement" was issued. It was issued on assumptions that were later proved incorrect. Consequently, when later the status of the pilot was definitely established, and there was no further possibility of avoiding exposure of the project, the factual details were set forth.

I then made two facts clear to the public: first, our program of aerial reconnaissance had been undertaken with my approval; second, this government is compelled to keep abreast, by one means or another, of military activities of the Soviets, just as their government has for years engaged in espionage activities in our country and throughout the world. Our necessity to proceed with such activities was also asserted by our Secretary of State who, however, had been careful—as was I—not to say that these particular flights would be continued.

In fact, before leaving Washington, I had directed that these U–2 flights be stopped. Clearly their usefulness was impaired. Moreover, continuing this particular activity in these new circumstances could not but complicate the relations of certain of our allies with the Soviets. And of course, new techniques, other than aircraft, are constantly being developed.

Now I wanted no public announcement of this decision until I could personally disclose it at the Summit meeting in conjunction with certain proposals I had prepared for the conference.

At my first Paris meeting with Mr. Khrushchev, and before his tirade was made public, I informed him of this discontinuance and the character of the constructive proposals I planned to make. These contemplated the establishment of a system of aerial surveillance operated by the United Nations.

The day before the first scheduled meeting, Mr. Khrushchev had advised President de Gaulle and Prime Minister Macmillan that he would make certain demands upon the United States as a precondition for beginning a Summit conference.

Although the United States was the only power against which he expressed his displeasure, he did not communicate this information to me. I was, of course, informed by our allies.

At the four power meeting on Monday morning, he demanded of the United States four things: first, condemnation of U–2 flights as a method of espionage; second, assurance that they would not be continued; third, a public apology on behalf of the United States; and, fourth, punishment of all those who had any responsibility respecting this particular mission.

I replied by advising the Soviet leader that I had, during the previous week, stopped these flights and that they would not be resumed.   I offered also to discuss the matter with him in personal meetings, while the regular business of the Summit might proceed.   Obviously, I would not respond to his extreme demands.   He knew, of course, by holding to those demands the Soviet Union was scuttling the Summit Conference.

In torpedoing the conference, Mr. Khrushchev claimed that he acted as the result of his own high moral indignation over alleged American acts of aggression.   As I said earlier, he had known of these flights for a long time.   It is apparent that the Soviets had decided even before the Soviet delegation left Moscow that my trip to the Soviet Union should be cancelled and that nothing constructive from their viewpoint would come out of the Summit Conference.

In evaluating the results, however, I think we must not write the record all in red ink.   There are several things to be written in the black. Perhaps the Soviet action has turned the clock back in some measure, but it should be noted that Mr. Khrushchev did not go beyond invective— a time-worn Soviet device to achieve an immediate objective.   In this case, the wrecking of the Conference.

On our side, at Paris, we demonstrated once again America's willingness, and that of her allies, always to go the extra mile in behalf of peace. Once again, Soviet intransigence reminded us all of the unpredictability of despotic rule, and the need for those who work for freedom to stand together in determination and in strength.

The conduct of our allies was magnificent.   My colleagues and friends—President de Gaulle and Prime Minister Macmillan—stood sturdily with the American delegation in spite of persistent Soviet attempts to split the Western group.   The NATO meeting after the Paris Conference showed unprecedented unity and support for the alliance and for the position taken at the Summit meeting. I salute our allies for us all.

And now, most importantly, what about the future?

All of us know that, whether started deliberately or accidentally, global war would leave civilization in a shambles. This is as true of the Soviet system as of all others. In a nuclear war there can be no victors—only losers. Even despots understand this. Mr. Khrushchev stated last week that he well realizes that general nuclear war would bring catastrophe for both sides. Recognition of this mutual destructive capability is the basic reality of our present relations. Most assuredly, however, this does not mean that we shall ever give up trying to build a more sane and hopeful reality—a better foundation for our common relations.

To do this, here are the policies we must follow, and to these I am confident the great majority of our people, regardless of party, give their support:

First. We must keep up our strength, and hold it steady for the long pull—a strength not neglected in complacency nor overbuilt in hysteria. So doing, we can make it clear to everyone that there can be no gain in the use of pressure tactics or aggression against us and our Allies.

Second. We must continue businesslike dealings with the Soviet leaders on outstanding issues, and improve the contacts between our own and the Soviet peoples, making clear that the path of reason and common sense is still open if the Soviets will but use it.

Third. To improve world conditions in which human freedom can flourish, we must continue to move ahead with positive programs at home and abroad, in collaboration with free nations everywhere. In doing so, we shall continue to give our strong support to the United Nations and the great principles for which it stands.

Now as to the first of these purposes—our defenses are sound. They are tailored to the situation confronting us.

Their adequacy has been my primary concern for these past seven years—indeed throughout my adult life.

In no respect have the composition and size of our forces been based on or affected by any Soviet blandishment. Nor will they be. We will continue to carry forward the great improvements already planned in these forces. They will be kept ready—and under constant review.

Any changes made necessary by technological advances or world events will be recommended at once.

This strength—by far the most potent on earth—is, I emphasize, for deterrent, defensive and retaliatory purposes only, without threat or aggressive intent toward anyone.

———————

Concerning the second part of our policy—relations with the Soviets— we and all the world realize, despite our recent disappointment, that progress toward the goal of mutual understanding, easing the causes of tensions, and reduction of armaments is as necessary as ever.

We shall continue these peaceful efforts, including participation in the existing negotiations with the Soviet Union. In these negotiations we have made some progress. We are prepared to preserve and build on it. The Allied Paris communique and my own statement on returning to the United States should have made this abundantly clear to the Soviet government.

We conduct these negotiations not on the basis of surface harmony nor are we deterred by any bad deportment we meet. Rather we approach them as a careful search for common interests between the Western allies and the Soviet Union on specific problems.

I have in mind, particularly, the nuclear test and disarmament negotiations. We shall not back away, on account of recent events, from the efforts or commitments that we have undertaken.

Nor shall we relax our search for new means of reducing the risk of war by miscalculation, and of achieving verifiable arms control.

———————

A major American goal is a world of open societies.

Here in our country anyone can buy maps and aerial photographs showing our cities, our dams, our plants, our highways—indeed, our whole industrial and economic complex. We know that Soviet attaches regularly collect this information. Last fall Chairman Khrushchev's train passed no more than a few hundred feet from an operational ICBM, in plain view from his window. Our thousands of books and scientific journals, our magazines, newspapers and official publications, our radio and television, all openly describe to all the world every aspect of our society.

This is as it should be. We are proud of our freedom.

Soviet distrust, however, does still remain. To allay these misgivings I offered five years ago to open our skies to Soviet reconnaissance aircraft on a reciprocal basis. The Soviets refused. That offer is still open. At an appropriate time America will submit such a program to the United Nations, together with the recommendation that the United Nations itself conduct this reconnaissance. Should the United Nations accept this proposal, I am prepared to propose that America supply part of the aircraft and equipment required.

This is a photograph of the North Island Naval Station in San Diego, California. It was taken from an altitude of more than 70 thousand feet. You may not perhaps be able to see them on your television screens, but the white lines in the parking strips around the field are clearly discernible from 13 miles up. Those lines are just six inches wide.

Obviously most of the details necessary for a military evaluation of the airfield and its aircraft are clearly distinguishable.

I show you this photograph as an example of what could be accomplished through United Nations aerial surveillance.

Indeed, if the United Nations should undertake this policy, this program, and the great nations of the world should accept it, I am convinced that not only can all humanity be assured that they are safe from any surprise attack from any quarter, but indeed the greatest tensions of all, the fear of war, would be removed from the world. I sincerely hope that the United Nations may adopt such a program.

As far as we in America are concerned, our programs for increased contacts between all peoples will continue. Despite the suddenly expressed hostility of the men in the Kremlin, I remain convinced that the basic longings of the Soviet people are much like our own. I believe that Soviet citizens have a sincere friendship for the people of America. I deeply believe that above all else they want a lasting peace and a chance for a more abundant life in place of more and more instruments of war.

———————

Finally, turning to the third part of America's policy—the strengthening of freedom—we must do far more than concern ourselves with military defense against, and our relations with, the Communist Bloc. Beyond this, we must advance constructive programs throughout the world for the betterment of peoples in the newly developing nations.

The zigs and zags of the Kremlin cannot be allowed to disturb our worldwide programs and purposes. In the period ahead, these programs could well be the decisive factor in our persistent search for peace in freedom.

To the peoples in the newly developing nations urgently needed help will surely come. If it does not come from us and our friends, these peoples will be driven to seek it from the enemies of freedom. Moreover, those joined with us in defense partnerships look to us for proof of our steadfastness. We must not relax our common security efforts.

As to this, there is something specific all of us can do, and right now. It is imperative that crippling cuts not be made in the appropriations recommended for Mutual Security, whether economic or military. We must support this program with all of our wisdom and all of our strength. We are proud to call this a nation of the people. With the people knowing the importance of this program, and making their voices heard in its behalf throughout the land, there can be no doubt of its continued success.

Fellow Americans, long ago I pledged to you that I would journey anywhere in the world to promote the cause of peace. I remain pledged to pursue a peace of dignity, of friendship, of honor, of justice.

Operating from the firm base of our spiritual and physical strength, and seeking wisdom from the Almighty, we and our allies together will continue to work for the survival of mankind in freedom—and for the goal of mutual respect, mutual understanding, and openness among all nations.

Thank you, and good night.

NOTE: On August 28, the White House made public an exchange of letters between James C. Hagerty, Press Secretary to the President, and the Joint Editorial Board of Moscow News and Nouvelles de Moscou. In a letter dated June 25, the Board returned copies of the President's address, received that day from the U.S. Embassy, stating that it was "directed essentially against the friendship between our peoples." The Press Secretary's letter, dated August 15, stated that the Board's letter confirmed the fact that the Soviet press is not free to publish or broadcast any viewpoint running counter to the policies of the Soviet Government.

164 ¶ Remarks of Welcome to the Delegates of SEATO at a Luncheon Given in Their Honor at the White House. *May 31, 1960*

Excellencies and distinguished guests:

It is a deep personal honor to welcome as our honored guests today the Council members, their senior civil and military advisers, the Secretary-General and the Chief of the Military Planning Office of the Southeast Asia Treaty Organization.

I have long held an unwavering conviction that our collective security arrangements are indispensable safeguards of freedom with justice in today's world. In an address called "The Chance for Peace" which I made soon after taking office in 1953 I advocated "united action" for Southeast Asia. This policy was realized in September 1954 when our eight countries concluded a solemn commitment at Manila. It was an extraordinary event when countries with such diversity and geographical separation united to preserve freedom and security and to promote the economic well-being and development of the peoples of the Treaty Area. I am particularly pleased that we have with us today two of those who were present on that historic occasion: Secretary-General Sarasin, who was then a member of the Thai delegation, and Senator Mansfield, a member of the American delegation.

We can take much satisfaction in the fact that our first objective of preventing further Communist domination through aggression or subversion in the Treaty Area has been realized. However, we cannot afford to relax our vigilance or slacken our cooperative efforts to further the high principles of the Pacific Charter.

No defensive alliance of which we are a member faces a greater challenge or protects a more vital segment of the free world than SEATO. Together we can continue to measure up to the task and, in the process, deepen our mutual understanding through intimate consultations such as those you are initiating today. Under these circumstances the responsibilities which devolve upon you who are directly charged with promoting SEATO's high objectives are indeed great.

NOTE: In the opening paragraph the President referred to His Excellency Pote Sarasin of Thailand, Secretary-General of SEATO, and Brigadier L. W. Thornton, C.B.E., of New Zealand, Chief of the Military Planning Office of SEATO. Later in his remarks he referred also to Mike Mansfield, U.S. Senator from Montana.

165 ⁋ Remarks to the Delegates to the Second Conference of Young Political Leaders From North Atlantic Treaty Countries. *June 1, 1960*

THIS IS INDEED a pleasure—to see so many young leaders in the political field from so many countries.

I think that today more than ever we have to take thought among ourselves as to just what we believe is the value of freedom—we all have rights within our own countries, of expressing ourselves whether it is agreement with government or bitter criticism of government from top to bottom. But always we have the right to guide our own lives as we please, as long as we don't trespass on the similar rights of others.

We have got, in these critical days to see that we are talking about the differences in the values that tyranny establishes for its people and those that we as free peoples establish for ourselves.

There was a very wise Frenchman who gave a good definition of free government, or democracy. He said it this way: "Freedom is merely the opportunity for self-discipline."

The point he was making was that if we as a free people in each of our countries do not have the self-discipline to perform those functions that will keep us free, then finally we will be regimented, or we will be disciplined by central power—no matter how it is exercised.

Let us remember that part of free government is the rules and regulations and methods by which we run our economy—how we obtain from our economy the products that we need, the productivity that will raise our standards of living and give us the opportunity to protect ourselves and to help others in need. That economy is part of free government. So even in the business and labor worlds we have this necessity for self-discipline.

To keep these things working properly, there has to be statesmanship, not merely as a few heads of government meet together—or try to meet together. It has got to be in every walk of life—the labor leader has got to talk with his employer, working men have to talk together, we ourselves have to make sure that we comprehend what we are talking about when we say "democracy" or "freedom" because it's just as much responsibility as it is opportunity.

447

This is a great thing I think we must all live with, think about, and practice.

Now I have got one other obsession: there is in our Constitution a little phrase "the pursuit of happiness." No one can ever guarantee he is going always to be a happy individual, but he can pursue happiness in his own way.

My own belief is this: this is a very noble, a very fine, objective.

You may find your happiness in some kind of religious devotion, some service to others as in the political field or in any other kind, charitable or business. If you are helping society of which you are a part, to my mind that is one of the great satisfactions we have. But in any event, no matter how you pursue happiness, try to get a little of it every day. I just don't believe long faces solve tough problems.

I hope there will never be another war, but to go back to war just a minute: staffs have the job of coming in and telling you how tough everything is—"The enemy's over there, and he's on this side, and he's behind you, too." They make everything tough. Well, finally, it used to be a habit of mine, after the gloom got a little bit thick in a group, let's say, a third of this size, I would say, "Well, you know one thing, it's a hard problem, but that's the reason your government sent such able people here."

Just try to look at it that way once in a while. Of course these are tough problems, but you have got the self-confidence that you can do something about it. If you can do something about it, you have gotten the satisfaction that is part of that happiness that all of us should seek and all of us should gain.

So, those words "pursuit of happiness," "responsibility," as well as "right and opportunity," these are the things that all of us, I believe, have to get imbedded in our brains, in our hearts, and in our souls, so that we have sort of an atmosphere ourselves—where we atmosphere ourselves into that kind of a situation that we can solve these problems decently.

What all of this is leading up to—I just talk along, I am not very orderly, let's say, in my discussions—but by doing this, we are showing such a common dedication to the great values that we deem priceless that we can all get close together.

I believe that today, and probably for some years—decades—to come, there will be a need for strong organizations, associations, and cooperation among ourselves. By this I mean among different nations, whether for example the Canadians and ourselves in North America—you people of Western Europe—we have got to be very, very close together.

We come close when we work on the solution of a problem, whether it's a tariff about zinc, a new air route across such and such a place, or any other kind of tough one that makes everybody mad. If we all see that we are working for the promotion of the basic values we are talking about, then all the other problems begin to get straightened out. And one diplomat says to another, "Well, we are all working for this same thing, now let's see how the devil"—excuse me—"how the dickens" (they'll never put that on the tape, I shouldn't have said it; I'm sorry)— in any event, how we can solve this specific problem when all of us are going after the same things.

So since I strongly believe that mutual understanding is really the key to peace, as we among ourselves achieve that understanding, we spread it a little bit, and somebody else comes into it. Finally, we don't have to be an exclusive club, we don't have to have just NATO type organizations—everybody can get in finally—even the Iron Curtains. When that has happened, then there will be real peace. Then we will really have achieved a lot of happiness. But there will be still problems, after you people have done all this, there will be problems for those that come after you, but they won't be the kind that keep all humanity in strain and tension.

I meant, when I came out here, merely to say welcome to Washington. I am delighted to see you at such a conference with such a fine objective. I understand you are going through the White House. There will be a few interesting things I think you will see there, but in any event, I want to thank each of you for coming out and giving me a chance to greet you, to say "Hello." I think that in every single one of your countries I have some friend—maybe a number. If you are so fortunate as to meet those people I call friends, give them my greetings, my very best wishes, and the hope that out of your meeting here comes closer understanding, some little step in progress toward peace, and certainly progress toward our strength in spirit and in brain and in heart to meet and solve the problems of our day.

Thank you a lot. It has been a lot of fun to see you.

NOTE: The President spoke on the South Lawn at the White House.

166 ¶ Remarks at a Dinner Commemorating the 50th Anniversary of the Boy Scouts of America. *June 1, 1960*

Mr. Chairman and distinguished guests:

I am here this evening to join all those, who by coming to this dinner, wanted to pay their tribute to the Boy Scouts of America and to their leaders, both their local leaders and national leaders, their instructors, and all those supporters that have made it possible to carry this movement forward through these 50 years so successfully.

Twenty-five years ago, I learned through a personal experience something about Boy Scout training that I have never forgotten. My family and I had gone into Mexico to visit on a large ranch. My son was then shortly past 12 years, and at that time there was a solo march required of the boys to make the next grade—probably First-Class Scout, Dr. Schuck—14 miles he had to march.

Now it happened that the gate of the ranch was exactly seven miles away from the house, so John decided that this would be his march, he would get this credit point while he was down in Mexico. So he announced his intention.

Well, there was nothing said, except that his mother and his doting grandmother both decided that there would have to be a car go along, and there would have to be orange juice, Coca Colas, and water, and everything that you would take along to make sure that he got through, to follow him through this wild country of cacti and greasewood and all the rest of it.

Well now, we had a "storm." This boy had decided that he was going to do something and he was going to have nobody going along in a boat escorting him as we did his swimming trick. He was going alone. And this got to be rather a hot argument.

And so, exercising what every man always thinks is his prerogative, I made the decision and said, "Go right ahead, John, that will be all right—go ahead."

Well, he started out because he had his dad's authority. But I was still in the house. And the very tough looks, to say nothing of the talk about a hard-hearted parent and an old soldier that didn't know better than to do this to his son.   I heard all the exaggerations about the occasional coyote that was found out on the ranch, and some of these old horn cows that were as gentle as a Hereford always is, but looks very large and big to the ladies—and about the rattlesnakes and all the other dangers.   And finally I had to surrender.

But I wasn't going to get in John's way.   So I took the station wagon and I wound around through the desert, staying away from that trail, but always making sure that I could come back and report that nothing was wrong.

Well, he made the trip back—there and back.   Came in in fine shape. And I found this: the tremendous pride that boy had in making sure— getting the self-confidence that he could do a thing by himself, that some of his doting parents did not think he could do.

And moreover, it occurred to me that possibly we are doing a little bit too much of the paternalistic care about our young, and we don't give them an opportunity to develop self-dependence.   And when I saw the pride that boy exhibited—not saying a word, but you could see his chest come up a little bit—and he combed his hair that evening.   He was a different boy, and he has been a different boy ever since, in my opinion.

And I think even the ladies of the household learned that they do have to allow the young birdling to spread its wings once in a while and try them out.   Boy Scouts have done this for the boy.   Scout leaders and the Boy Scout executives and even the Explorers helping the younger ones— they have done this for years.   In doing so they have made America a different country than it probably could have been.

Because of this lesson that I learned in this little homely incident, I have followed what is happening to these Boy Scouts.   Whenever it is possible for me to stop along the road and to see a group of Cubs or Brownies and Girl Scouts or Boy Scouts, I try to get a word—two or three words—two minutes—to see what they are thinking about, what their morale is.   And it is always at the top.

They get this morale, why?   Because they are trained or they are taught that they can render a service.   I might say that after I finally lose the loving care of the Secret Service, that should I be standing one day on the corner of a busy street and a Boy Scout sees this rather elderly-looking fellow looking a little doubtful, if he offers to take me across the street, he can do it.   Because the way these boys and their counterparts among the girls are growing up is to believe there is an honor and a satisfaction in doing a service for others. To my mind, that is the great thing about Scouting. It doesn't make any difference whether they wrap up their bed-rolls just right, or pitch their tent exactly right, or whether they do their cookout and burn the eggs and the bacon not fit to eat. As long as they have that feeling and that development— if they get the same feeling that we did when we read in our Bibles the Parable of the Good Samaritan and then as time comes along, if they individually and collectively begin to think of their nation in part as a "good Samaritan," doing the decent thing in this world, then I will tell you: Scouting is indeed doing something for all of us that is not only necessary but I would say vital to our vigor as a nation based upon a religious concept, but is ready to take on its own shoulders its duty with respect to itself, with respect to those that are less fortunate. Only in this way, in my opinion, is America going to be able to lead the way to that goal that mankind has sought so long, and so far so futilely, a peace with honor and with justice.

Thank you very much.

NOTE: The President spoke at the Sheraton-Park Hotel in Washington. His opening words "Mr. Chairman" referred to Charles W. Froessel, Chief Judge of the New York State Court of Appeals in Albany. Later in his remarks he addressed Dr. Arthur A. Schuck, Chief Scout Executive, Boy Scouts of America.

167 ¶ Letter to Senator Bennett on the Need for Legislation Authorizing the President To Make Adjustments in Sugar Quotas. *June 2, 1960*

[Released June 2, 1960. Dated June 1, 1960]

Dear Wallace:

Thank you for your May twenty-fifth letter with your observations on the allocation of possible 1960 domestic area sugar quota deficits. I also noted in the May twenty-seventh Congressional Record your comments made on the Senate Floor on the same subject.

Whether or not it would be determined to reallocate such deficits in a manner different from that now provided by law, I nevertheless attach particular importance to the recommendation that the President be given appropriate authority to adjust certain foreign quotas when he finds such action is called for—either in the national interest or to insure adequate domestic supplies of sugar. I hope most earnestly that Congress will act promptly on the sugar legislation recommended last March by this Administration, and I very much appreciate your own efforts, as well as the efforts of your colleagues joined with you, to see that the necessary legislative action on this subject is taken quickly.

　　With warm regard,

Sincerely,

DWIGHT D. EISENHOWER

NOTE: In his letter of May 25, 1960, released with the President's reply, Senator Bennett noted that whenever any domestic sugar-producing area was unable to fill its quota, the Secretary of Agriculture, under existing law, was required to determine the size of such deficit and to allocate a substantial part of it to Cuba. He further noted that estimated deficits in Puerto Rico and Hawaii would amount to 500,000 tons, and that Cuba's share of these deficits would be 160,000 tons unless the law was changed in time to permit adjustments. Senator Bennett further stated "there is every indication that the same situation will occur again next year, so a law extending the Act without change will not only confirm this year's windfall, but guarantee a similar one in 1961."

168 ❡ Statement by the President Upon Signing Bill Relating to the San Luis Unit of the Central Valley Project, California. *June 3, 1960*

IT IS WITH pleasure that I have today signed S. 44, authorizing the Secretary of the Interior to construct in California the San Luis Unit of the Central Valley Project and to enter into an agreement with the State of California with respect to its financing, construction and operation in order that there may be a joint Federal-State use of the San Luis Reservoir site. This legislation culminates cooperative Federal and State efforts which began five years ago. It constitutes a unique achievement in the field of water development and conservation and is consistent with the Administration's philosophy of partnership and teamwork in this field.

　　Negotiation of the agreement between the State and Federal agencies should be undertaken immediately and concluded with dispatch. It is my earnest hope that these negotiations will insure a clear-cut understanding of responsibilities and the early undertaking of this mutually advantageous Federal-State partnership in water development.

NOTE: As enacted, S. 44 is Public Law 86–488 (74 Stat. 156).

169 ¶ Veto of Bill Concerning Unlimited Income Tax Deductions for Certain Contributions to Charity.   *June 3*, 1960

To the House of Representatives:

I return herewith, without my approval, H.R. 6779 entitled "An Act To amend section 170 of the Internal Revenue Code of 1954 (relating to the unlimited deduction for charitable contributions for certain individuals)."

Existing law allows a taxpayer an unlimited deduction for charitable contributions if the sum of his contributions and federal income tax payments in the taxable year and in each of eight of the ten preceding taxable years exceeds 90 percent of his taxable income.

H.R. 6779 would provide that under certain circumstances the 90 percent test shall be considered satisfied in each of two consecutive years if the sum of the contributions and income tax payments for the two consecutive years exceeds 90 percent of the combined taxable income for such two years.   The bill is a temporary measure without effect after the 1968 taxable year.   It would also apply retroactively to taxable years beginning after December 31, 1956.

Nothing appears in the record on this bill that would justify a departure from the general rule that changes in the tax laws should apply only prospectively.   In actual fact, the retroactive feature of this bill is highly discriminatory.   Some taxpayers could avoid an otherwise assessable deficiency for 1957, 1958 or 1959 by using the bill's benefits to amend incorrect returns for those years, but other taxpayers who filed correct returns could not avail themselves of the bill's benefits to claim a refund for those years.

Although unable to approve this bill, I would be willing to sign new legislation provided it applied only prospectively and were truly designed to encourage substantial gifts to educational institutions and other recognized public charities.

DWIGHT D. EISENHOWER

170　¶ Veto of Bill Relating to Unemployment
Tax Credits of Successor Employers.
June 3, 1960

To the House of Representatives:

I return herewith, without my approval, H.R. 6482, entitled "An Act Relating to the credits against the unemployment tax in the case of certain successor employers."

To help finance the Federal-State unemployment compensation system, the Federal Government imposes on covered employers an annual tax of 3 percent on the first $3,000 of each employee's wages.

A special provision of law permits the wages paid each employee by a predecessor employer to be taken into account for purposes of the $3,000 annual limitation on taxable wages by an employer who succeeds to the business. This provision is intended to insure that taxes paid with respect to the wages of any one employee are not increased for any year as a result of the business changing hands during the year. This desirable purpose is thwarted under present law, however, whenever a predecessor does not qualify as an "employer" within the meaning of that word as it is defined in the Federal law.

H.R. 6482 would correct this situation, but it would do so, not just prospectively, but also retroactively to the beginning of 1951.

Strict avoidance of retroactive tax legislation, except in extraordinary and compelling circumstances not here in evidence, is essential to orderly tax administration, the Government's revenues and the fair treatment of taxpayers.

Although constrained, therefore, to disapprove the bill, I urge the Congress at its earliest opportunity to enact new legislation without retroactive effect.

DWIGHT D. EISENHOWER

171   ¶ Toasts of the President and Prime Minister
Diefenbaker of Canada.   *June 3, 1960*

Mr. Prime Minister, Mrs. Diefenbaker and friends of Canada and the United States:

Every member of this company feels a very definite sense of honor and distinction in the privilege of having with us tonight the Prime Minister of the great republic of Canada.

It would be a fitting occasion, since this is at least semiformal, to address you, sir, in sonorous phrases, telling about the history of our relations between our countries and expressing the admiration and respect we feel for you as the leader of that country.

Actually, we feel that here we are in the family. You are another of our best friends. You are the head not merely of a great republic that borders us on the north, you are the leader of a people that with us shares common ideals, common international purposes, and common culture and language.

So the sense of honor and distinction we have is more than that of an official character. It is extremely personal and cordial.

This afternoon the Prime Minister and I had a long talk, as we have in the past. I suppose it is two and a half years now and more that we have been discussing our common problems. And whether they would be of wheat or oil or any other difficult matter, they are dealt with as friends should deal with such problems: as a family deals with its own problems; and there emerges from these discussions the kind of compromise, the kind of composition of difficulties with which we can both live, and which can serve as guides for the future.

And the one thing that I want to take the privilege of repeating to you, that the Prime Minister said to me this afternoon, and in which it gives me the greatest pride and satisfaction, is this: "In the last two and a half years, Mr. President," he said, "the relations of Canada and the United States have reached the height of friendliness, cordiality, and true cooperation that has never before been attained so far as I know." "And," he said further, "to my mind those relations are a model for the world, if the world is truly seeking, through cooperation, to attain a just and permanent peace."

So you can understand how happy all of us are here, to say through me, that we are proud to have with us this great representative of Canada— and to ask all of you to join with me in a Toast to Her Majesty Queen Elizabeth the Second.

NOTE: The President proposed the toast at 9:57 p.m. at a state dinner at the White House. Prime Minister Diefenbaker responded as follows:

Mr. President:

May I say how deeply grateful I am to you for the opportunity that you have given my wife and me today, to enjoy a day that will always be memorable to us.

You summarized a moment ago the views that I expressed this afternoon, and those views I reiterate now: during the last several years that I have held the position of Prime Minister, our relations and the relations between our two countries, outstanding as they have been in the past, have not been excelled in any other period in our history.

And we owe quite a bit to you in the United States. As a matter of fact, if it hadn't been for Benjamin Franklin—and that is going back a little before our time—if it hadn't been for Benjamin Franklin, we wouldn't have had a Canada, because in 1761 the government of Great Britain gave serious consideration to trading us for the Island of Guadalupe.

And then again, as you Toasted Her Majesty the Queen, we have had differences in the past between the British people and the people of the United States, but as to the Senators here present, you recall on another occasion the only reason that the British have a Commonwealth at all is because there were thirteen Colonies in North America who took a strong and a firm stand in 1775.

And it was in that year—I like to remind people of the old country of this— it was in that year following Bunker Hill and Concord and Lexington that Benjamin Franklin went over to England and took with him a petition signed by several, some sixteen in number, who subsequently signed the Declaration of Independence. This was the Olive Branch Petition which set forth in regard to the experiences of recent months—

which had brought about bloodshed as between us and the mother country—that we will become your loyal and devoted servants for this and future generations, provided that you give to us the right of self-government within our own confines.

So in point of fact, if the Olive Branch Petition in 1775, prepared on July fifth of that year, the first signature of which was John Hancock's, had been accepted by the British government of that day, then the Toast that you drank tonight would have been the Toast that we in Canada would drink to you.

Sir, we recall too that we had quite interesting relationships with you during the 1860s and many of our people from Canada enlisted in the Northern army, and some loaned their money to the South; and when it was all over, they once more joined together and gave that reverence to the Union that has been characteristic of the people of this land and out of which the name of Lincoln earned eternal reverence everywhere where liberty is respected and regarded.

And we have had our relations over the years. We were together in two World Wars. We were together, particularly in the Second World War.

That unity which today was epitomized in the manner of the reception that began when you, Mr. Secretary [Herter], received my wife and me at the Airport, there is something about this relationship that I can't describe.

I come into your country. You come into mine. We don't always agree. We sometimes have our differences. But I will always look back on this day as one that represents, to me, the embodiment of those great and eternal principles of liberty. We get together. We discuss. We are not at all afraid. I did not look to see whether the coat of arms of the United States had any sound recording instruments in it. We speak freely. We understand each other.

I see the Chief Justice of the United

States here this evening. I think of how your shrines of freedom are our shrines— our shrines are your shrines. And that is the spirit in which we have met again today, a spirit of deep attachment to our respective countries, and only with that recognition in unity can we be assured among the free countries of the world of the maintenance of those things in which we believe.

And I assure everyone here that I come here not to discuss the great election that is about to take place, because after all one of the greatest elements in statesmanship is to view what takes place in another country with detachment, although even with interest. But I say to you, sir, that now that you approach the end of your service to the United States, you have earned from all of us in the free world not only affection, not only the realization that a few short years ago you led the legions of freedom, but in the last 8 years—and I was present when you received your nomination in the City of Chicago—in the intervening 7½ years you have become the embodiment of those principles to which each of us owes our common dedication to the United States of America; great in the opportunities that Providence has given it, magnificent in the manner in which it has discharged its responsibilities that today cover all the seven seas and all the continents.

To you, sir, as the leader of this Nation—this may be my last opportunity to do so, and not only on behalf of my own country but on behalf of the nations of the Commonwealth, which recognize the Queen either as the head of the Commonwealth or in the capacity of Queen of Canada—all of us owe to you, in these days of peace, the same debt of gratitude that we pay you for what you did in the days of war. I am not going to say any more than that.

Thank you, Mr. President, for what represents to me one of those occasions when idle sentiment and words do not convey the meaning I want to express.

To the people of the United States, may I say this: we live side by side, and the fact that we do, and have, in peace, for 150 years, is the greatest answer that can be given to the forces of communism everywhere in the world when they say that this Nation is a warlike and aggressive nation.

We give the people of the world the answer to that statement which has received at the hands of the Communists widespread circulation.

Sir, it has been a privilege to be here. My wife and I very much appreciate everything that has been done. Tomorrow, when I return to my own country, I shall tell the people of that country what they already know: that you and I recognize, and our countries recognize, that only in the maintenance of a unity of purpose and objective, and a common dedication, will the things for which we stand be finally successful.

I ask you, ladies and gentlemen, to rise and drink a Toast to the President of the United States.

172 ¶ Joint Statement Following Discussions With the Prime Minister of Canada. *June 4, 1960*

THE PRIME MINISTER of Canada, the Right Honorable John G. Diefenbaker, and the President of the United States have consulted on a wide range of subjects of both an international and bilateral nature. The Canadian Ambassador at Washington and the Secretary to the Canadian Cabinet assisted in the discussions, together with the United States Secretary of State and the United States Ambassador at Ottawa.

The Prime Minister and the President were in agreement on measures which should be taken to maintain the security of the free world. They reaffirmed their determination to continue to work for peace with justice. Particular attention was paid to the importance of achieving, with effective international control, an end to nuclear testing and progress toward general disarmament.

The Prime Minister and the President reviewed the course of relations between their countries during recent years and noted with pleasure the extent to which the problems arising in such relations have yielded to the process of friendly and continuing consultation. They considered that satisfactory means of carrying on such consultation have been established in personal exchanges as well as by regular diplomatic arrangements and the various joint committees that have been created. They expressed their belief that there has been established between the two countries a model for the relationship between neighbors.

173 ¶ Remarks at a Testimonial Dinner in Honor of Representative St. George, Bear Mountain State Park, New York. *June* 4, 1960

Mrs. St. George, Senator Keating, and my friends:

It is indeed difficult, in the circumstances in which I find myself, to discover words that seem applicable to this situation. I am here as a member of the Class from West Point of 1915, my 45th anniversary. The members of my class and their wives and their widows, their children and their grandchildren, have been here in this inn, trying with me to recapture something of the atmosphere of 1915, the year we graduated.

You know at that moment, while the first European war had started, we were still cadets, and the world seemed reasonably quiet—indeed, almost leisurely in its approach to every question public or private. We had no sense of urgency or tension: the United States was a long way from this war. And we have been talking about those times, when our great preoccupation really was to find out whether the tactical officers could discover any of the offenses that we were guilty of committing. Fortunately for me, they didn't discover all of them.

Now tonight we meet at a time of bewilderment. I don't like this term, or the using of the term that we are living always in crisis. We are not. There is no nation in this world that dares at this moment to attack the United States, and they know it.

But we wonder what is the outcome of every decent, proper gesture we make to those that live in the other camp. They live in a closed society, secrecy of intent—which we try to penetrate, and in my opinion properly—but we are certain of this: our problem is not only keeping ourselves strong—and by strong I don't mean merely militarily; I mean spiritually, intellectually, scientifically, economically, *and* militarily. And then we must make certain that all of those people who live with us, in the hope that those concepts of human dignity and freedom and liberty are going to prevail in the world, will stand always by our side in the determination that freedom and liberty will eventually triumph over tyranny.

We have staunch allies. And as a matter of fact, many of the excesses, particularly the ill-tempered expressions of Mr. Khrushchev, has really brought the West closer together than I have known it, ever since I have been occupying my present office.

Now I am talking about matters, for this moment, that are not partisan. They are bipartisan. But I want to say this: it is a tremendous satisfaction to me to know that the Republican Party believes in the kind of things that I have tried so haltingly to express to you.

My colleagues here in Government, Senator Keating and your guest of honor, Mrs. St. George, have in every single vote that has anything to do with these important world questions, stood exactly in the ranks, exactly like any soldier would when asked by his commander to do so.

So I want to say to you a very simple word—and I promised my classmates I would only be 5 minutes, and I think I have used 10 minutes already, but I just want to ask you to do this: look at the records of your Republican representatives in the Congress. Do they represent what you understand to be firm, sound, middle-of-the-road government that refuses to make government a centralized government capable of governing your lives in every single item, refuses to accede to the doctrine of collectivity or centralization, or is it the kind of philosophy that says "We want to live in liberty, in freedom"?

This is the kind of thing they have been supporting and, therefore, you support it not because of a word Republican, or because of some particular or special vote. You support it because you believe in what they believe: that the Government of the United States intends to do its full duty by every one of its citizens, but it shall never—in the words of Abraham Lincoln—do those things for the individual that he can do better for himself.

Now I just have a simple request of you. If you believe in the basic principles these representatives of yours, congressional and senatorial, if you believe in those basic principles, then not merely do I ask you that you register and you vote—I know good Republicans will do that—I ask you to go out and work as you have never worked before.

Because I tell you, this kind of policy, internally and externally, is the thing that will keep America strong, safe, and sure—for you and every single person that comes behind you.

This is what I hope to do myself, so far as it is proper and the people who will meet within a few short weeks to take over the direction of campaigns—I am ready to do my part.

And I tell you this, it will be an honor to be associated with such people as you are, as you do your part.

Thank you and good night.

NOTE: The President spoke at Bear Mountain Inn. The dinner was sponsored by the Republican County Committees of the 28th Congressional District of New York.

174 ¶ Address "Beyond the Campus" Delivered at the Commencement Exercises of the University of Notre Dame. *June 5, 1960*

Father Hesburgh, Your Eminence, Your Excellencies, members of the Clergy, members of the Graduating Class and the Trustees, faculty and students, and friends of Notre Dame:

I acknowledge with the deepest gratitude the receipt of the Honorary Doctorate of Notre Dame. And I am overwhelmed by the terminology of the Citation read to me. But I want to say to all of you that as I listened to what was said about Dr. Dooley, that I could not fail to believe that there are few if any men that I know who have equaled his exhibition of courage, self-sacrifice, faith in his God, and his readiness to serve his fellow men.

At Commencement time in our country a generation ago, a well-known Englishman felt an urge to tell us something about ourselves. The theme he selected was, "Why don't young Americans care about politics?"

He felt that the attitude of our young people toward civil government, at all levels, was like that of "the audience at a play."

My simple purpose today is to talk to you these next few minutes about the compelling need for all Americans to interest themselves seriously in politics.

There may be a plausible, if not necessarily a valid, explanation for the American's traditional indifference to politics.

Historically, the 19th Century in America was one of amazing growth. A wilderness needed conquering; vast resources had to be utilized; illiteracy had to be eliminated; a great economic machine, reaching to every corner of the world, had to be built. This unprecedented development commanded extraordinary talents in our private enterprise system. To people busy in productive life, government seemed not only remote but relatively unimportant. The demand for real skills in political pursuits was minimal.

Moreover, in that long period, a view developed that political life was somewhat degrading—that politics was primarily a contest, with the spoils to the victor and the public paying the bill. This belief had some justification at one period in our history, and may still persist in local situations.

In these circumstances, some of our highly talented people have refrained from offering themselves for public service—indeed, often to refuse to enter it.

But times have changed, and the change includes the character of government. The first major platform drafted in 1840 by a political party required only 500 words; in the last national election each major party used over 15,000 words to deal with the highlights of the principal issues. This thirtyfold growth in political platforms is illustrative of the increase of governmental influence over all our lives.

The need for the best talent in positions of political responsibility is not only great, but mounts with each stroke of history's clock.

A few years ago, government represented only a small fraction of the total national activity. Today, to support our national, state and local governments, and to finance our international undertakings, almost one-

fourth of the total national income is collected in taxes.   In every phase
of life, government increasingly affects us—our environment, our opportunities, our health, our education, our general welfare.

Government is, of course, necessary, but it is not the mainspring of
progress.   In the private sector of American life, commanding as it does
the productive efforts of our citizens, is found the true source of our
nation's vitality.   Government is not of itself a part of our productive
machinery.   Consequently its size, its growth, its operations can be justified only by demonstrated need.   If too dominant, if too large, its effect is
both burdensome and stifling.

Only an informed and alert citizenry can make the necessary judgments
as to the character and degree of that need.

We do not want a government with a philosophy of incessant meddling,
which imposes a smothering mist on the sparks of initiative.

We do not want a government that permits every noisy group to force
upon society an endless string of higher subsidies that solve nothing and
undermine the collective good of the nation.

We do not want governmental programs which, advanced, often
falsely, in the guise of promoting the general welfare destroy in the individual those priceless qualities of self-dependence, self-confidence, and a
readiness to risk his judgment against the trends of the crowd.

We do want a government that assures the security and general welfare
of the nation and its people in concord with the philosophy of Abraham
Lincoln, who insisted that government should do, and do only, the things
which people cannot well do for themselves.

This concept is particularly relevant to most activities encompassed by
the phrase "the general welfare."

But even with devotion to the principle that governmental functions
can be justified only by public need, government has become so pervasive
that its decisions inescapably help shape the future of every individual,
every group, every region, every institution.

Though we recognize this vast change—and though most persons in
public office are selfless, devoted people—we are still plagued by yesterday's
concept of politics and politicians.

Too many of our ablest citizens draw back, evidently fearful of being
sullied in the broiling activity of partisan affairs.

This must change.   We need intelligent, creative, steady political
leadership as at no time before in our history.   There must be more talent

in government—the best our nation affords. We need it in county, city, state—and in Washington.

Human progress in freedom is not merely something inscribed upon a tablet—not a matter to be shrugged off as a worry for others. Progress in freedom demands from each citizen a daily exercise of the will and the spirit—a fierce faith; it must not be stagnated by a philosophy of collectivity that seeks personal security as a prime objective.

Clearly, you—you graduates who enjoy the blessings of higher education have a special responsibility to exercise leadership in helping others understand these problems.

And, by no means, does your responsibility stop there. To serve the nation well you must, for example, help seek out able candidates for office and persuade them to offer themselves to the electorate. To be most effective you should become active in a political party, and in civic and professional organizations. You should undertake, according to your own intelligently formed convictions, a personal crusade to help the political life of the nation soar as high as human wisdom can make it.

Now some of you will become doctors, lawyers, teachers, clergymen, businessmen. Each of you will contribute to the national welfare, as well as to personal and family welfare, by doing well and honorably whatever you undertake. But a specialist, regardless of professional skill and standing, cannot fulfill the exacting requirements of modern citizenship unless he dedicates himself also to raising the political standards of the body politic.

Now I hope that some of you will enter the public service, either in elective, career, or appointive office. Most of the top posts in government involve manifold questions of policy. In these positions we have a special need for intelligent, educated, selfless persons from all walks of life.

I believe that each of you should, if called, be willing to devote one block of your life to government service.

This does not mean that you need become permanently implanted in government. Quite the contrary. In policy-forming positions we constantly need expert knowledge and fresh points of view. Some frequency of withdrawal and return to private life would help eliminate the dangerous concept that permanence in office is more important than the rightness of decision. Contrariwise, such a tour should not be so brief as to minimize the value of the contribution and diminish the quality of public service. Normally, a four-year period in these policy posts would seem to be a minimum. Most leaders from private life who enter the public service do so at a substantial sacrifice in the earning power of their productive years.

Although these personal sacrifices are, by most individuals, accepted as a condition of service, yet when these sacrifices become so great as to be unendurable from the family standpoint, we find another cause for the loss of talent in government.

We ought not to make it inordinately difficult for a man to undertake a public post and then to return to his own vocation. In government one must obviously have no selfish end to serve, but citizens should not, invariably, be required to divest themselves of investments accumulated over a lifetime in order to qualify for public office. The basic question to be determined in each case is this—is such divestment necessary to remove any likelihood that the probity and objectivity of his governmental decisions will be affected? And this question is proper and ethical whether the individual holds either elective or appointive office. We need to review carefully the conflict-of-interest restrictions which have often prohibited the entry into government of men and women who had much to offer their country.

But let me return to the more broadly-based consideration: that thinking Americans in all walks of life must constantly add to their own knowledge and help build a more enlightened electorate and public opinion. For herein lies the success of all government policy and action in a free society.

Leaders in America—and this comprehends all who have a capacity to influence others—must develop a keen understanding of current issues, foreign and domestic—and of political party organization, platform, and operations.

They must have critical judgments regarding actions being proposed or taken by legislatures and executives at all levels of government. They need to be knowledgeable so as not to be misled by catchwords or doctrinaire slogans.

Thus they can analyze objectively how such actions may affect them, their communities, and their country—and help others to a similar understanding.

Political understanding, widely fostered, will compel government to develop national and international programs truly for the general good, and to refrain from doing those things that unduly favor special groups or impinge upon the citizen's own responsibility, self-dependence, and opportunities.

Graduates of the Class of 1960: a half century ago, when I was about to enter West Point—and, incidentally, to meet shortly thereafter and to know that gridiron genius, Knute Rockne—our country was in what now seems to have been a different era. The annual Federal budget was below seven hundred million dollars. Today it has increased more than one hundredfold, and organized groups demand more and more services, both expensive and expansive. At the turn of the century there was a certain grace, calmness, and courtliness about human deportment and the movement of events.

Now we operate on a relentless timetable which we must race to keep events from overwhelming us.

Complicating the lives of all of us today we know that in the dimly-lit regions behind the Iron Curtain, eight hundred million people are denied the uncountable blessings of progress in freedom, and compelled by their masters to develop vast means of destructive power. Elsewhere, among the underdeveloped countries of the world, a billion people look to America as a beacon that confidently lights the path to human progress in freedom.

This is no time to whimper, complain, or fret about helping other peoples, if we really intend that freedom shall emerge triumphant over tyranny.

The enemies of human dignity lurk in a thousand places—in governments that have become spiritual wastelands, and in leaders that brandish angry epithets, slogans, and satellites. But equally certain it is that freedom is imperiled where peoples, worshipping material success, have become emptied of idealism. Peace with justice cannot be attained by peoples where opulence has dulled the spirit—where indifference ignores moral and political responsibility.

Too often there is, in politics as in religion, a familiar pattern of the few willing workers and the large number of passive observers.

Our society can no longer tolerate such delinquency.

We must insist that our educated young men and women—our future leaders—willingly, joyously play a pivotal part in the endless adventure of free government. The vital issues of freedom or regimentation, public or private control of productive resources, a religiously-inspired or an atheistic society, a healthy economy or depression, peace or war—these are the substance of political decisions and actions that you young people must be ready to participate in. Neglect by citizens of civic responsibilities will be a greater danger to a free America than any foreign threat can ever pose; but an enlightened, dedicated people, studiously and energetically performing their political duties will insure us a future of ever-rising standards of spiritual, cultural and material strength. These duties and these opportunities must demand the dedicated attention of all the people, and especially all who have so profoundly benefited from our vast educational system.

My heartiest congratulations on this splendid preparation that the members of this Graduating Class have received for exercising the leadership which this great Republic must have as it faces the problems, the trials and the bright opportunities of the future.

Thank you—and may God bless you.

NOTE: The President spoke at 2:05 p.m. on a platform erected in front of O'Shaughnessy Hall. His opening words "Father Hesburgh, Your Eminence" referred to the Reverend Theodore M. Hesburgh, President of the University of Notre Dame, and Giovanni Battista Cardinal Montini, Archbishop of Milan. He later referred to Dr. Thomas A. Dooley, cofounder of the Medico organization in northern Laos.

The citation accompanying the honorary degree called the President "the most eminent and most popular statesman of his time."

175 ¶ Exchange of Messages Between the President and President Alessandri Concerning the Disaster in Chile. *June* 8, 1960

Dear Mr. President:

I am deeply distressed at the indications of hardship and suffering being undergone now by the people of your nation and have just issued the following public statement:

"The people of the United States are appalled at the disaster that has struck the friendly, hard-working people of Chile. Earthquakes, tidal waves, avalanches and volcanic eruptions have brought extremely serious personal casualties and heavy material damage that will take years to overcome.

"Many people in Chile are homeless, injured and poorly clothed. It is now winter in Chile. The disaster area is one of heavy rainfall. Hence the extent of personal suffering being experienced by Chileans is almost beyond comprehension.

"The United States Government is doing all it can to assist the Government of Chile and the Chilean people in this catastrophe.

"In addition, I urge all our people promptly to demonstrate once again the great generosity so characteristic of them. The Chileans need help of many kinds—medicine, tents, clothing, food and other things. Cash contributions can be made to the American Red Cross. Contributions of material goods can be made through many voluntary organizations which, I am informed, are issuing local appeals. I have asked General Alfred M. Gruenther, President of the American Red Cross, to arrange for the coordination of this voluntary material assistance."

DWIGHT D. EISENHOWER

NOTE: President Alessandri's message follows:

Dear Mr. President:

I sincerely thank Your Excellency for the message you were so good as to transmit to me, informing me of the public appeal made by you to the people of the United States to give their generous assistance in the tragic, difficult emergency our country must meet as a result of the earthquakes, tidal waves, and volcanic eruptions that have caused great suffering and exceptionally serious material damage. Your Excellency's appeal,

the exemplary significance of which I wish to emphasize, reveals once more your warm friendship toward the people of Chile and admirably bespeaks the noble sentiments and Christian solidarity of the people of the United States, in whom we see the basis of your nation's greatness.

Accept, Excellency, the sincere thanks of the Government and people of Chile for your noble action, together with my deep personal gratitude.

JORGE ALESSANDRI RODRÍGUEZ

The statement quoted in the President's letter was released by the White House on May 27.

176 ¶ Letter to Governor Underwood of West Virginia on Further Federal Activities in Aid of Chronic Labor Surplus Areas. *June* 12, 1960

[Released June 12, 1960. Dated June 9, 1960]

Dear Governor Underwood:

Following my meeting with you and Senators Scott and Cooper on May fourth, I called together the appropriate officials in those Federal agencies having programs affecting chronic labor surplus areas, to again review pertinent activities within their province. As a result of this meeting a number of additional executive actions have been taken to further assist these areas. Knowing of your deep interest in this matter, I thought you would like to have a copy of a report to me which outlines these new actions.

May I take this occasion to also call to your attention the fact that bills have been introduced, both in the House and the Senate, designed to implement the suggestions which I made when I vetoed S. 722. In my opinion, the revised legislation which has been submitted on behalf of the Administration represents a sound and forthright program for assisting the states and localities in dealing with the problems of chronic unemployment. I am disturbed that hearings on this legislation have not been scheduled. It had been—and is—my hope that suitable legislation would be enacted at this session of the Congress.

In any event, we will continue to take every possible administrative action we can to assist chronic labor surplus areas in West Virginia and elsewhere.

With warm regard,

Sincerely,

DWIGHT D. EISENHOWER

NOTE: The report to which the President referred was in the form of a letter dated May 31, 1960, from Under Secretary of Commerce Philip A. Ray, Chairman of the Interdepartmental Committee To Coordinate Federal Urban Area Assistance Programs (see Item 5). The report, released with the President's letter, described additional Government action with special reference to Pennsylvania, Kentucky, and West Virginia.

For veto of the area redevelopment bill (S. 722), see Item 146.

177   ¶ Statement by the President Recorded Before Leaving for the Far East.   *June* 12, 1960

My friends:

Through recent weeks my mail has been heavy with personal messages from thousands of Americans and friends of America overseas—messages of calm faith that our decent peaceful purposes will not be obscured in the world's eyes by propaganda and invective.

These messages, written in fullness of heart, have been inspiring proof that, far from Washington and the world centers of power, men and women are deeply concerned with the world role of the Republic—for peace with justice in freedom.   To all those who have written and cabled me heartening words, I am most thankful.

As you know, there have been public warnings, based on a variety of considerations, that I should not visit the Far East at this time.   With these, I did not agree.   However, they moved me to re-think and to re-examine my individual responsibility within the American mission of free world leadership.

In that process, I decided neither to postpone nor to cancel my trip to the Far East.

This is the reason for my decision: so that I can continue to learn more about the immediate problems and purposes of our friends, and to continue to promote a better understanding of America abroad—which, particularly in the circumstances of the moment—is a compelling responsibility on me as the President of the United States.

If the trip now ahead of me were concerned principally with the support of a regime or a treaty or a disputed policy; if it were intended merely to bolster a particular program, or to achieve a limited objective, such a journey would have no real justification.   But this trip is not so concerned, not so intended.   Rather, it represents an important phase of a program whose paramount objective was, and is, to improve the climate of international understanding.

Toward that goal we have worked in many ways: for instance, by the exchange of students and by our economic assistance program.   Not the least among these means has been a long series of visits, through 7½ years, by chiefs of state and senior officials of other governments to the United States, and like trips abroad by myself, the Vice President, and our associates at all levels of American Government.

Never, I believe, in the history of international affairs has there been so massive a program of communications between government officials and between peoples. We should not permit unpleasant incidents and sporadic turmoil, inspired by misled or hostile agents, to dim for us the concrete and gratifying results. They have been to the great profit and to the great good of the entire world.

For one thing, America's sincere dedication to the pursuit of a permanent peace, with justice for all, is becoming more clearly understood than ever before, throughout the free world.

For another, the free world economy—including our own—has been steadily strengthened.

For a third, among most of the world's peoples there now is a genuine concensus of conviction that we can, by negotiation, solve even the most difficult of international problems.

We in truth have made immense progress. In the devout hope that I can help further, even a little, this forward movement, I go to the Philippines, Republic of China, Japan, and Korea.

In these countries we have many millions of warm and devoted friends, in every case the vast majority of the population. But because these are countries of freedom, where men and women are free to assemble, to speak out and to criticize, we must not expect a regimented unanimity on any subject—any more than we expect it here at home.

I am going to these countries:

Because with the Republic of the Philippines we have the closest ties of association beginning 6 decades ago, and because it was in the Philippines many years ago that we launched our first major program to help a developing people achieve a prosperous independence.

Because with the Republic of China we have helped demonstrate to the world that a free people can hold high its precious national heritage against all efforts to destroy it and can in adversity build soundly for the future without a fatal sacrifice of human values.

Because with Japan we have just completed our first century of relations and we can now so plan and order our partnership that through the new century ahead we may work together for the prosperity and peace of the entire world.

Because with Korea we have been joined since the establishment of its Republic in maintaining there a bulwark on the frontier of the free world, essential to the security of this Nation and the honor of the United Nations.

Our associations with these four nations are vital to our own security and to the security of the free world. In my personal mission through the next 2 weeks I shall strive to my utmost that our friendships may grow warmer, our partnerships more productive of good for us all.

I am stopping briefly in Okinawa where we have important responsibilities for the welfare of the Ryukyuan people.

I am also happy to visit our newest States, Alaska and Hawaii. They are important bridges of communication to the free nations of Asia.

I know that all Americans will want me to express their warm friendship to the peoples I shall visit. I know also that I shall bring back to you the friendly greetings of our Asian brothers.

And now—goodbye to all of you for a short while.

NOTE: The statement was recorded for broadcast over radio and television following the President's departure at 8:40 a.m. from Andrews Air Force Base.

178 ¶ Remarks Upon Arrival at Elmendorf Air Force Base, Anchorage, Alaska. *June* 12, 1960

Governor Egan, Mayor Byer, officers and men of the Alaskan Command, and my fellow citizens:

My first visit to Alaska since it became the 49th State in the Union means much to me as an individual American and as President.

On the personal side, thinking back to my boyhood, Alaska for all of us—at least in Kansas—was synonymous with gold and glamor of the Yukon and Klondike; the home of sourdoughs and Eskimos; best known through Jack London and Robert Service. We thought of it as a cruel Arctic region, a new and raw possession.

Incidentally, I had an uncle who came on that adventure, but he did not find the gold and he never talked to me about the glamor.

But Alaska was new. My father, for example, was a growing boy when the Russian flag still flew here. I question that many in that day ever dreamed it would achieve statehood within their life span.

Certainly I can assure you that never for a moment did it enter my head that one day as President of the United States I would urgently recommend statehood for Alaska and later welcome it as a State into our great Union.

As so many voices express worry and fear about the future, let us remember it usually turns out as good as the effort we put into it. And Alaska is an example.

Today, flying here through five time zones, across almost thirty-five hundred miles, at little less than the speed of sound, over fertile fields and prosperous cities, this trip is an index to North American growth in my own lifetime.

Beyond the physical, I reach this largest city of the 49th State knowing that I will find in its people, as indeed I have before, the great traits of all America: a tremendous energy for achievement, a courageous persistence in mastering natural resources for human good—boundless faith in country and in God.

The changes in less than a century hearten us as we view the future. For you, that future is bound to be a bright and useful one. You are no longer an Arctic frontier, you constitute a bridge to the continent of Asia and all its peoples.

To all of them—in your energy and persistence and faith—you exemplify the stimulus of freedom, its rewards and its spirit.

Through the years you will be for them a new and close demonstration of what free men and free women can accomplish, given challenge and opportunity and the will to work together.

It is good to be here to learn at first hand something of what you are doing, what you are hoping and planning for the future. My party and I truly value these few hours that we can spend with you.

Governor Egan, from the bottom of my heart, I thank you for your cordial welcome and for the mementoes that you have just mentioned as gifts to me here. I cannot tell you with what gratitude I express my feelings about your generous statements.

Thank you.

NOTE: The President spoke at 10:10 a.m. His opening words "Governor Egan, Mayor Byer" referred to William A. Egan, Governor of Alaska, and George H. Byer, Mayor of Anchorage.

Governor Egan presented the President with a gold medal commemorating the statehood of Alaska, and, on behalf of his daughter, Mrs. Jacqueline Grainger, a blue leather stamp album.

179 ¶ Veto of Bill for the Relief of Our Lady of the Lake Church, Mandeville, Louisiana. *June* 13, 1960

[Released June 13, 1960. Dated June 11, 1960]

To the House of Representatives:

I return herewith, without my approval, H.R. 5150, "For the relief of Our Lady of the Lake Church."

The bill would direct a refund to Our Lady of the Lake Church, Mandeville, Louisiana, of $1,284.17 in customs duties assessed on organ boarding imported from Germany. In support of the refund, it is asserted that the organ boarding was denied free entry despite its hand-carved panels which constitute original sculptures of the type granted duty-free status under applicable law.

The entry free of duty of certain sculptures is permitted, but an express provision of the applicable law excludes "any articles of utility." The Bureau of Customs has determined that the organ boarding in question is an article of utility within the meaning of the statute, and therefore does not meet the requirements for free entry.

The record contains no reason for granting special legislative relief in this case other than the belief that the law has been misinterpreted. Special legislation is not needed, however, in cases where the law may have been misinterpreted. General law provides procedures by which importers may challenge, administratively and in the courts, the Bureau of Customs' interpretations of the laws relating to importation. The Church did not avail itself of these procedures.

The bill would, therefore, discriminate in favor of a single importer who did not take advantage of the available remedies. Such a result would be unfair to other importers and would create an unwise and unsound precedent.

In view of the foregoing, I am constrained to withhold my approval of H.R. 5150.

DWIGHT D. EISENHOWER

NOTE: The veto message was released in Washington.

180 ¶ Veto of Bill Concerning the Defense of Suits Against Federal Employees Operating Government Motor Vehicles. *June* 13, 1960

[Released June 13, 1960. Dated June 11, 1960]

To the House of Representatives:

I return herewith, without my approval, H.R. 7577, "To amend title 28, entitled 'Judiciary and Judicial Procedure', of the United States Code to provide for the defense of suits against Federal employees arising out of their operation of motor vehicles in the scope of their employment, and for other purposes."

As originally introduced, this legislation provided that when a Government driver is sued in a state court on a claim resulting from his operation of a motor vehicle while acting within the scope of his employment, such action should be removed to the appropriate United States district court. There it would become an action against the United States under the Federal Tort Claims Act and be the plaintiff's exclusive judicial remedy. Government drivers would thus cease to be defendants and would be relieved of personal liability in such cases. These are desirable objectives.

The bill was amended, however, to require the consent of the plaintiff before any such action could be removed to a Federal court. This amendment is unfortunate, for any plaintiff, by refusing to give his consent, could prevent the conversion of the action to one under the Federal Tort Claims Act and thus thwart the sound purposes of the original bill. The amendment also makes the bill inconsistent internally and could give rise to needless litigation.

Although unwilling, therefore, to approve this bill, I would gladly sign new legislation corresponding to H.R. 7577 as first passed by the House of Representatives.

DWIGHT D. EISENHOWER

NOTE: The veto message was released in Washington.

181 ¶ Veto of Bill for the Relief of Grand Lodge
of North Dakota, Ancient Free and Accepted
Masons. *June* 13, 1960

[Released June 13, 1960. Dated June 11, 1960]

To the House of Representatives:

I return herewith, without my approval, H.R. 8417, "For the relief of
Grand Lodge of North Dakota, Ancient Free and Accepted Masons."

The bill would direct a refund to the Grand Lodge of North Dakota,
Ancient Free and Accepted Masons, of $1,155.26 in customs duties as-
sessed on masonic jewels, consisting of insignia and emblems composed of
metal and other material, imported from Canada. In support of the
refund, it is asserted that such jewels should have been granted duty-free
status under applicable law.

The entry free of duty of regalia and gems is permitted for the use of a
society incorporated or established solely for religious, philosophical, educational, scientific, or literary purposes, or for the encouragement of the
fine arts. The Bureau of Customs has determined, however, that fra-
ternal organizations, such as the Grand Lodge of North Dakota, do not
meet the requirements for free entry.

No reason has been advanced for granting special legislative relief in
this case other than the belief that the law has been misinterpreted. If
the law has been misinterpreted, however, there is no need for a special
bill. General law provides procedures by which importers may challenge,
administratively and in the courts, the Bureau of Customs' interpretations
of the law relating to importation. The Grand Lodge has not yet availed
itself of these procedures, but it still has the opportunity to do so.

The bill would, therefore, discriminate in favor of a single importer
who has not taken advantage of the available remedies. Such a result
would be unfair to other importers and would create an unwise and
unsound precedent.

Although the enrolled bill would provide for a refund of $1,155.26,
the Treasury Department has previously advised the Congress that the
amount of duties due upon final liquidation of this entry will be only
$375.34, and that the difference between this figure and the amount
deposited at the time of entry by the Grand Lodge will be refunded
administratively in any event.

In view of the foregoing, I am constrained to withhold my approval from the bill.

DWIGHT D. EISENHOWER

NOTE: The veto message was released in Washington.

182 ¶ Remarks Upon Arrival at the International Airport in Manila. *June* 14, 1960

Mr. President and my friends of the Philippine Islands:

This is indeed for me a homecoming. As I circled over your city, I saw the old familiar sights of the Laguna de Bay, the Baguio Mountains and the Pasig River, and finally this lovely coastline along which your city lies. Indeed these sights aroused in me sentiments and emotions that no eloquence of mine could ever adequately express.

I worked among you for more than 4 years. I came here as an assistant of General Douglas MacArthur, and only yesterday morning, or possibly—my days are getting mixed up—2 days ago, I called General MacArthur and had a conversation with him about these Islands, and this section of the world that he knew so well, and he asked me to convey to you his sincere conviction—strengthened with the years—that always there will be unity between the Philippines and the United States of America. And he asked me to convey to you, Mr. President, and to your people, his warmest greetings and his best wishes for your continued welfare.

The last time that I was enabled to come to see your country, was just after the conclusion of World War II. I then saw a city wrecked and living in destruction—everything torn to pieces. As I flew down over the city today, I saw what Philippine courage, Philippine energy, Philippine endurance and stamina could accomplish.

Manila is as beautiful as ever it was before—and more so. All over your country the ravages of war have been repaired, by your refusal to surrender to despair or to lose faith in your own destiny.

As I looked at these familiar sights, there was one thing, of course, that was missing: so many of my old friends of the years just preceding World War II—they are gone. So many of them paid the price that free men have been called upon to pay again and again for the defense of freedom, for the right of living as human people of dignity, to stand

477

straight under their God, and bow the knee to no one else.

I pay tribute to those great heroes, and to all who fought with them and beside them—both American and Filipino. I hope in a symbolic way to pay my respects when I go to some of the cemeteries where they are buried.

But to you the living, and among you are many of my old friends, I affirm again the determination of the United States to live with you as a true partner in defense of those ideals of liberty and human dignity in which we alike believe.

Between us, just as always it has been the case between members of a family, are some problems to be discussed and to be talked about and to negotiate. But that negotiation and those conferences take place in a spirit of common dedication to ideals that make us true partners. Therefore, no petty differences of any kind can ever tear apart these two great countries, which are certain together to march down the lane of the future—free, proud, prospering, and always friends.

Thank you very much.

NOTE: The President spoke at 5 p.m. He was met by President Carlos P. Garcia, officials of the Philippine Government, members of the diplomatic corps, and U.S. Ambassador John D. Hickerson.

183   ¶ Address Before a Joint Session of the Philippine Senate and House of Representatives. *June 15, 1960*

Mr. President of the Senate, Mr. Speaker of the House, Members of the Congress, distinguished guests, and my friends:

I am keenly sensible of the high honor this assembled body has paid to me and to my country by inviting me to be present here and to address this body, a body representing the political leadership of a great Republic in the Asian sector. I am indeed overwhelmed by your kindness and I can say only *mabuhay*.

You will understand the flood of memories that swept over me on coming back to this land, where I feel that I am revisiting an old home and old friends and renewing ties of long standing.

Here my wife and I spent four happy years, making friendships that we shall ever cherish. Here our son went to school and grew into young manhood.   Here I saw the first beginnings of this Republic and worked with men whose vision of greatness for the people of the Philippines has been matched by its realization.

Through many days I could talk of life as I knew it here a quarter of a century ago.   For hours on end I could make comparisons of what was in those days and what is now.   But I have only minutes in which I can address myself to this subject.

Even in the short space I have been here, however, I have been struck by the vigor and progress that is evident everywhere.   I see around me a city reconstructed out of the havoc and destruction of a world war.   I know of the Binga Dam; the Maria Cristina Power and Industrial Complex; the Mindinao highway system; rural electrification; the disappearance of epidemic diseases; the amazing growth of Manila industry.

Everywhere is inescapable physical evidence of energy and dedication and a surging faith in the future.   But of deeper significance is the creation here of a functioning democracy—a sovereign people directing their own destinies; a sovereign people concerned with their responsibilities in the community of nations.   Those responsibilites you have discharged magnificently even as you toiled to rebuild and to glorify your own land.

Certainly, we Americans salute Filipino participation in the Korean war; the example set the whole free world by the Filipino nurses and doctors who went to Laos and to Viet Nam on Operation Brotherhood; your contribution to SEATO and the defense of your neighbors against aggression; your charter membership and dynamic leadership in the United Nations; your active efforts to achieve closer cultural and economic relations with other Southeast Asian countries.

The stature of the Republic of the Philippines on the world scene is the creation of its own people—of their skill; their imagination; their courage; and, above all, their commitment to freedom.   But their aspirations would have gone unrealized were they not animated by a spirit of nationalism, of a patriotic love of their own land and its independence, which united and directed them in their efforts.

This spirit was described by your late great leader and my personal friend, Manuel Quezon, when he with great eloquence said: "Rightly conceived, felt and practiced, nationalism is a tremendous force for good. It strengthens and solidifies a nation.   It preserves the best traditions of the past and adds zest to the ambition of enlarging the inheritance of the people.   It is, therefore, a dynamic urge for continuous self-improvement. In fine, it enriches the sum total of mankind's cultural, moral, and material possessions through the individual and characteristic contribution of each people."

Significantly, President Quezon had this caution to offer, "So long as the nationalistic sentiment is not fostered to the point where a people forgets that it forms a part of the human family; that the good of mankind should be the ultimate aim of each and every nation; and that conflicting national interests are only temporary; and that there is always a just formula for adjusting them—nationalism then," he said, "is a noble, elevating and most beneficial sentiment."

In these words of clarity and timeless wisdom, President Quezon spoke a message forever applicable to human affairs, particularly fitted to the circumstances of this era.

Nationalism is a mighty and a relentless force. No conspiracy of power, no compulsion of arms can stifle it forever. The constructive nationalism defined by President Quezon is a noble, persistent, fiery inspiration; essential to the development of a young nation. Within its ideal my own country since its earliest days has striven to achieve the American dream and destiny. We respect this quality in our sister nation.

Communist leaders fear constructive nationalism as a mortal foe. This fear is evident in the continuing efforts of the Communist conspiracy to penetrate nationalist movements, to pervert them, and to pirate them for their own evil objectives.

To dominate—if they can—the eternal impulse of national patriotism, they use force and threats of force, subversion and bribery, propaganda and spurious promises. They deny the dignity of men and have subjected many millions to the execution of master plans dictated in faraway places.

Communism demands subservience to a single ideology, to a straitjacket of ideas and approaches and methods. Freedom of individuals or nations, to them is intolerable. But free men, free nations, make their own rules to fit their own needs within a universally accepted frame of justice and law.

Under freedom, thriving sovereign nations of diverse political, economic and social systems are the basic healthy cells that make up a thriving world community. Freedom and independence for each is in the interest of all.

For that very reason—in our own enlightened self-interest, in the interest of all our friends—the purpose of American assistance programs is to protect the right of nations to develop the political and social institutions of their choice. None, we believe should have to accept extremist solutions under the whip of hunger, or the threat of armed attack and domination.

We—free, self-governing peoples—readily accept that there is a great variety of political, social and economic systems in the world; and we accept the further fact that there is no single, best way of life that answers the needs of everyone, everywhere.

The American way satisfies the United States. We think it is best for us.

But the United States need not believe that all should imitate us. But what all of us do have in common with the free nations in Asia, Africa, Europe and Latin America are basic and weighty convictions, more important than differences of speech and color and culture.

Some of these convictions are: that man is a being capable of making his own decisions; that all people should be given a fair opportunity to use their God-given talents, to be worthy heirs of their fathers, to fulfill their destiny as children of God; that voluntary cooperation among groups and nations is vastly preferable to cooperation by force—indeed, voluntary cooperation is the only fruitful kind of effort in the long run.

True enough, in a too lengthy period of history, some European nations seemed convinced that they were assigned the mission of controlling the continents. But always powerful voices within those countries attacked the policy of their own governments. And we of the American Republics—twenty-one independent nations, once European colonies—denied in arms and in battle the validity of the assumed mission. Colonialism died there because true nationalism was a more potent force.

Since 1945, thirty-three lands that were once subject to Western control have peaceably achieved self-determination. These countries have a population of almost a billion people. During the same period, twelve countries in the Sino-Soviet sphere have been forcibly deprived of their independence. The question might be asked: Who are today the colonialists?

The basic antagonism of the Communist system to anything which it cannot control is the single, most important cause of the tension between the free nations in all their variety on the one hand, and, on the other, the rigidly controlled Communist bloc.

One purpose of the Communist system's propaganda is to obscure these true facts. Right now, the principal target is the United States of America. The United States is painted by the Communists as an imperialistic seeker of limitless power over all the peoples of the world, using them as pawns on the chessboard of war, exploiting them and their resources to enrich our own economy, degrading them to a role of beggarly dependence.

The existence, the prosperity, the prestige of the Republic of the Philippines proves the falsity of those charges. You, as a people, know that our American Republic is no empire of tyranny. Your leaders repeatedly have so testified to the world. But for a few minutes I should like to speak to you on what America stands for: what it stood for before I became President and what it will continue to stand for after I have left office.

More important than any one year, any one incident, or any one man is the role we have played through our whole history—the role we shall continue to play so long as our Republic endures.

Two hundred years, lacking sixteen, have passed since our forefathers proclaimed to the world the truths they held self-evident: that all men are created equal; that they are endowed with inalienable rights to life, liberty and the pursuit of happiness; that governments are instituted among men to secure those rights, deriving their just powers only from the consent of the governed.

On the day of that proclamation, you and we and scores of other now-free nations were colonies. Mankind everywhere was engaged in a bitter struggle for bare survival. Only a few by the accident of birth enjoyed ease without back-breaking toil. Naked power, more often than not, was the decisive element in human affairs. Most men died young after an all too short life of poverty.

Since then, free men—using their rights, embracing their opportunities, daring to venture and to risk, recognizing that justice and good will fortify strength—have transformed the world.

The wilderness and jungle of nature have been conquered. The mysteries of the universe are being unlocked. The powers of the elements have been harnessed for human benefit. The ancient tyrannies of hunger and disease and ignorance have been relentlessly attacked and ceaselessly reduced in their domains.

The evil of our forebears' times were manifold and entrenched and often accepted without murmur. But to free men who saw in their fellow men the image of God, who recognized in themselves a capacity to transform their circumstances and environment—to such free men, those evils were unbearable.

Not all of these evils were vanquished at the first assault. Indeed, many still survive. Not always was success persistently prosecuted to ultimate triumph. Free men, however mighty their inspiration, are humanly frail.

At times they may be fearful when they should be girding and bracing themselves for more vigorous effort; trading words when they should be working; bickering over trifles when they should be uniting on essentials; rioting when they should be calmly planning. Often they may dissipate their energies in futile and wasteful exercise. Often they are mistaken or for a while misled. Being human, these things are true about all of us. Nevertheless, the resources of free men living in free communities, cooperating with their neighbors at home and overseas, constitute the mightiest creative temporal force on earth.

In your sister Republic of the United States, the greatest achievement of our history is that our rebels against colonialism, against subjection, against tyranny, were the first in this era to raise the banner of freedom and decent nationalism, to carry it beyond our shores, and to honor it everywhere.

What we stood for in 1776, when we were fighting for our freedom, we still stand for in 1960.

To maintain our stand for peace and friendship and freedom among the nations, the United States must remain strong and always faithful to its friends, making clear that propaganda pressures, rocket rattling and even open aggression are bound to fail.

Beyond the guarantees of American strength, we seek to expand a collective security. SEATO demonstrates what can be accomplished. Since its inception not one inch of free Southeast Asia territory has been lost to an aggressor.

Collective security must be based on all fields of human endeavor, requiring cooperation and mutual exchange in the areas of politics, economics, culture and science. We believe in the expansion of relations between nations as a step toward more formal regional cooperation. In accord with this belief, we support the initiative taken by the Government of the Philippines during the past several years in establishing closer ties with its neighbors.

Patience, forebearance, integrity, an enduring trust, must between our two countries characterize our mutual relations. Never, I pray, will the United States because of its favored position in size and numbers and wealth, attempt to dictate or to exercise any unfair pressure of any kind, or to forget or to ignore the Republic of the Philippines—its equal in sovereign dignity. And never, I pray, will the Philippines deem it advantageous either at home or abroad to make a whipping boy of the United States. Each of us proudly recognizes the other as its sovereign equal.

And my friends, at this point I just want to interpolate one simple thought on the cooperative efforts for our own security, for advancing the standards of living of peoples, for everything that we do together, there are of course differences in the ability of each nation to make contributions.

Each of us as an individual is different from every other individual. Physically, mentally, and in the possession of the world's goods, we are somewhat different. But I submit, Members of the Congress, that there is one field where no man, no woman, no nation, need take a secondary place, and that is in moral leadership.

The spirit of a people is not to be measured by its size or its riches or even its age. It is something that comes from the heart, and from the very smallest nation can come some of the great ideas—particularly those great inspirational ideas that inspire men to strive always upward and onward.

Therefore, when I say that our two nations are sovereign equals, I mean it just in that spirit, in the sense that you have just as much to contribute to the world and to yourselves and to freedom as the greatest and the most powerful nation in the world.

Now finally, in this great cause of peace and friendship and freedom, we who are joined together will succeed. The eternal aspirations, purposes, ideals of humanity inspire and hearten and urge us to success.

But we face repeated challenges; endless temptations to relax, continuous campaigns of propaganda and threat. Let us stand more firmly together against them all.

And so doing, and with God's help, we shall march ever forward toward our destiny as free nations and great and good friends.

Thank you very much.

NOTE: The President spoke at 4 p.m. In his opening words he referred to Eulogio Rodriguez, President of the Senate, and Daniel Z. Romualdez, Speaker of the House of Representatives.

184 ¶ Remarks to the Staff of the U.S. Embassy and the American Community in Manila. *June* 15, 1960

Ladies and gentlemen:

In numerous places in the world I have been privileged to meet with the members of the United States diplomatic missions and the auxiliary forces and services that work with them.   Always I try to point out that each of you is in fact an ambassador.   You are representing America, and you are not doing it in the style that is described in very exaggerated fashion in "The Ugly American."   You are trying to show those qualities of integrity and of friendliness and readiness to cooperate with others for good, that recognition that men and women are, after all, children of God, and we try to treat each other in that way.

Now when I come to this spot, here is a country with whom we have had a long association, and before it took its completely independent place in the family of nations we had toward it a position of tutor and helper, in order that it could fittingly take over the heavy responsibilities of sovereignty.

It seems to me, therefore, that in this particular Embassy, and in each particular individual that is connected with it, from the youngest child that can think to the oldest employee, that we have a very special effort to place America before the consciousness of not only every Filipino but every visitor to this city that does not know our country as we know it.

I believe, in doing so, you are not only discharging one of the gravest responsibilities that belongs to a public servant in the United States, but I believe it is an effort that if we want to pursue it with our hearts and our minds, it is one of the most joyous and one of the most satisfying efforts that can come to anyone—that can be performed by anyone.   It is a great opportunity.

Now I served in this land something over 4 years myself, about a quarter century ago.   It is an entirely different land from what I knew then. The progress in everything, as I see it in the people, in their education, in the buildings and the streets—industries—it is amazing.   I see no limit to its future.

Therefore, we are not only fortunate to have this country as our great partner in the work that we do to pursue peace with justice and freedom, but we are very—indeed happy to have it.   And I think and I am quite sure each of you feels this way.

I do not mean by any manner of means to be lecturing you or implying that you have not been doing exactly what I am now talking about. What I do mean is that this is an effort that concerns me so deeply that I have been traveling for many thousands of miles just for this one purpose, on the part of the individual who for the moment is the spokesman for the United States, to say these things over and over again.   Because if there is one thing we want—I mean the United States wants—it is good, loyal friends, inspired by the same ideals of human dignity and decency that we ourselves cherish.   So I envy you your assignment.   I congratulate you for the way you have been doing it.   And I just say: double it in spades. Thank you very much indeed.   Goodbye.

NOTE: The President spoke at 4:45 p.m. at the American Embassy.

185   ¶ Toast by the President at a Dinner Given in His Honor by President Garcia.   *June* 15, 1960

Mr. President, Mrs. Garcia, and distinguished guests:

There are some of you at this dinner that attended a somewhat similar occasion in this very spot just a bit over 20 years ago.   There was a *despedida* given to my wife and me by President Quezon.   It was both a joyous and a sad occasion.   Two things had happened.   Europe was at war, and most of us believed that the United States could not prevent itself from getting embroiled.   So by agreement with President Quezon, I went back to the United States, and I was very happy that I was to be given the opportunity to help prepare, Mr. President, our country and its forces for the coming struggle.

The occasion was also sad, because we were leaving so many other friends that we had formed through 4 years of intimate association with them, working with them and playing with them.

Now I want to call your attention to those 20 years, not to review merely the record that history has written about them in science, in literature, in construction, and all the marvels of men's genius that we now enjoy.   I want to point out the pace at which we are now moving.

We had already achieved trans-Pacific air transport in 1938 or something of that kind, but those boats were flying boats and they could move only in daytime, they tied up at night and they were nothing at all like the later transports—the Constellations and the DC-7's and so on. They were followed in turn by the jets. And now the companies advertise that their jet is faster and faster—and possibly soon we will be going from breakfast to one spot in order to have dinner the night before in another, because in such fashion we will outrace the earth's movement.

Electronics was something only discussed in the laboratories by scientists. Our whole system of communications, of transport, and aids to aviation have all been developed in these 20 years.

And now let's think for a second of the time from Cleopatra to Napoleon. In all those centuries the pace of transportation never once moved forward. The ancient Egyptians had chariots, and while sailing ships had achieved some improvement, we were still dependent upon the wind to get across the oceans, and the horse or the camel was our best transport on land.

I think we should stop and recognize how this pace—let's say the curve of civilization—has leaped forward in leaps and bounds in these very few years. Even if we go back to the beginning of the Industrial Revolution, we still have a pace that, compared to the prior years, was like taking a race horse and comparing it to a snail.

This means, I think, that the years in front of us are going to be just as dramatic and are going to witness the same kind of changes we have in the past 20. I think that any individual here would have to have a bold imagination to sit down this evening and try to write out for himself what are going to be the achievements in the several sciences and arts in the coming 20 years.

President Garcia spoke of the need for preparation, and of the people he pointed out that won't fight and who are never prepared. We must fight. But above all we must be prepared. And I do not mean to fight wars as we have understood that.

Weapons have now come upon the scene that make war as we have understood it in the past a complete absurdity and really impossible and preposterous. They mean, in short—if used in the profusion that prophets sometimes predict—really the destruction of civilization as we know it. This cannot be.

And yet, with all of these changes certain to come upon us, we must keep a steady mind and a steady heart. We must keep a steady purpose.

We must look forward to those next 20 years, and we must be ready with every reasonable idea and conviction and faith that we can bring to bear, as we confer with our friends and even those that are hostile to us, to make certain that this world does not become so badly out of balance that only catastrophe can result.

When I talk about these dire possibilities, I do not mean to be pessimistic. I am quite sure that there was never in war a battle won by a pessimist. We must be optimists. But optimism by no means should beget complacency.

I believe that the time for working harder, more thoughtfully, in more dedicated fashion, is now with us. We must strengthen our spiritual powers in a deeper faith in the Almighty. We must dedicate ourselves more to the ideal of peace, not a peace of surrender, not a peace of appeasement—a decent, reasonable peace, permanent and with justice for all.

We must train ourselves—we must look to our educational processes, and in this way, though we may not in those 20 years—since that is the space I have chosen to speak about this evening—we must not for one moment give up this effort to induce those hostile to us to see things in a better light and to follow with us the path of reason.

But at the very least, we must make certain that associations among us—and by among us I mean all friends of freedom, the people that believe in the dignity of man and his rights under and given to him by the Almighty—these are the ideals in which we must bind ourselves closer together than ever before. And if the mighty forces that are available in all the free world will so bind themselves, will so dedicate themselves, will so work unremittingly, then no matter whatever may betide, we cannot be in danger. It is merely, as I see it, up to us.

Now the point of my remarks is this: over these 60 years we have gradually achieved better and better relations between our two countries—between the Philippines and the United States of America. Today I think they are stronger and better than they ever have been before. But I think they are not yet good enough. Because we must work as brothers, not as two people sitting across the table and arguing to the point that we can say there can be no agreement. We must have agreements, and they must be achieved in such a way as to satisfy the sense of reason and logic of both sides. Then we will go further and further forward, and we will be one element in that mighty team in the free world of making certain that peace with justice and in freedom will be a reality.

I cannot tell you how deep my faith is that this will come about, and one of the greatest factors in the development of this belief and this conviction and this faith is our association, our work with and our friendship between the United States and the Philippines.

So it is with a sense of, really, obligation to a great nation and its head that I ask this company to rise with me to drink a Toast to my friend, the President of the Philippines.

NOTE: The President proposed the toast at 9:48 p.m. at a dinner at the Malacañang Palace.

186   ¶ Remarks at the University of the Philippines Upon Receiving an Honorary Degree. *June* 16, 1960

Mr. President, faculty members and staff, students and friends of the Philippine University:

I express to you my deep and lasting gratitude for the honor you bestow on me today.   The kindness of the University of the Philippines in granting me the honorary degree of Doctor of Laws has a particular personal significance.

Mr. President, if the records of the Philippine University were so fortunate as to survive the destruction of the late war, you will find in your records an incident in which another American was awarded an honorary degree of Doctor of Laws.   This was General MacArthur. As a major, I was a staff officer with him and accompanied him to the exercises.

At that time it could scarcely ever have crossed my mind that one day, sir, I should be awarded the honorary degree of this great university, and indeed later as President of my own country to be privileged to carry back to you General MacArthur's personal greetings, transmitted to me only 3 or 4 days ago in Washington.

He said, "One of the high moments of my life in the Philippines was when I received the Honorary Doctorate of this great university."

This university stands as a visible monument to a tradition which your country and mine share. That tradition is: the right of the citizen to education on the basis of merit.

When I lived in Manila, the university was located in Ermita. At that time, the healthy growth of the school already required larger facilities, and the move to Diliman had begun. As one who has experienced the problems of an administrator in higher education, Mr. President, I congratulate you on the wonderful university which you have here, and on the strength and vitality of the educational tradition which you represent.

Now, sir, in order to get in perspective my own short experience as a president of a great university, I trust you will not be offended if I tell a story that was told years ago, at my expense.

The story was this, that in the university, when they found that a man was no longer a good professor, they made him a dean. But when he was no longer a good dean, they made him president.

I hasten, my friends, to add, the story applied only to me.

You and all who are associated with you—faculty, staff and students, friends and public officials—are joined in a noble human endeavor—the search for truth; the teaching of it; the preservation of truth for ages ahead.

In the long future before us, command of technical skills, knowledge, understanding of the past and a vision of what free men can accomplish, integrity in every public trust and in every personal responsibility, faith in ourselves and in our fellows and in the guiding hand of our Creator— all these qualities of mind and of spirit are essential, if our accomplishments are to match our hopes and our dreams.

Their possession far outweighs all physical defects and wants. Given them and a genuine fellowship, a sound partnership with other peoples of like mind and purpose, every physical lack can be filled; every physical resource developed in the fullest measure for our mutual good and the profit of mankind.

In these days when an aggressive and strong ideology proclaims a purpose of world domination, the free world cannot afford to neglect its own security—its moral, economic, intellectual, and material strength. But all too often we measure the place and the power and the prestige of a nation by its numbers and its riches in nature and in gold.

Population in men and women, of course, is an index to potential stature, if those men and women are eager in freedom to expand themselves and all their talents; growing in mastery of nature; ever more conscious of their dependence on their fellows; always devoted to supporting the prosperity, the dignity, the priceless freedom of their own nation and of all mankind.

We are so minded—we of the Philippines and the United States and of all the free world.

In numbers, we are mightier than all those who are allied against us and those still in bondage under them. Let us never for a moment forget this world fact: the bulk of the earth's people are joined with us in the eternal pursuit of freedom and dignity and justice for every single individual.

But our chief and most potent asset, in the battle for men's minds and their loyalty, is our commitment to the mutual interchange of knowledge and wisdom and culture; and our commitment to the mutual interchange of new skills; of our power in machines; of our mastery over nature.

Not all peoples and their nations are so minded. For them, no matter how immense their numbers may be, if the minds and souls within them are chained in the dictates of tyrannic master plans; conceived only for the purposes of those who rule; enforced by distant and pitiless bosses, the ultimate products will be: sterility in works, hopeless futility in spirit, increasing resentment that finally ignites revolt.

Tens of millions cannot forever be denied their freedom to venture on their own. They will not eternally remain chained to the mastery of other men.

In so speaking I merely echo a deep seated conviction expressed by José Rizal—scholar and writer and scientist, doctor of medicine, leader of men, patriot.

Were he here today in the land that he so fervently loved, in the halls of the learning that he pursued all his days, not one of us could equal him in praise of this university's purpose. None of us, I am certain, could hope to reach his heights of inspiration, or his exhortations that we use our every muscle of body, every talent of mind and soul toward the golden goal of peace and friendship with freedom among men and their nations. Nevertheless, in all humility and in recognition of his greatness in voice and thought, I venture to suggest that the core of his message might be this:

Filipinos, Americans, forever strengthen your brotherhood; forever grow together in knowledge; in wisdom; in your faith as children of

God so endowed by God that you can achieve, under His guiding providence, mastery of the universe for all people's good and His glory.

Again, my friends, I thank you very much.

NOTE: The President spoke at 10:11 a.m. His opening words "Mr. President" referred to Dr. Enrique Virata, Acting President of the University of the Philippines.

187 ¶ Remarks at a Luncheon Given by the Chamber of Commerce in Manila.   *June 16, 1960*

Mr. Orosa, Mr. Balatbat, Mr. Robie, members of the Philippine and American Chambers of Commerce, and my friends:

Some years ago I became President of Columbia University. I learned within 24 hours that a president of a university had to be ready to speak at the drop of a hat, but I learned something more: the trustees were expected to be ready to speak at the passing of the hat. Now the president of a university, according to my experience, is no more ready to speak than any member of any chamber of commerce that I know, whenever he gets a chance or opportunity to talk about his own home community. As a matter of fact, he doesn't even have to have any ready-made opportunity.

There was a Texan went to a neighboring State and was there at the time of a hanging. Well, it turned out that in that particular State there was a law that the condemned man, before the final act, had 5 minutes to say anything he wanted to in the world.

Well, this condemned man knew he was guilty and didn't know what he should talk about so he said he didn't want his 5 minutes. And the Texan immediately was on his feet and he said, "Mr. Sheriff, I submit, if the condemned can't use this 5 minutes, I can, to tell them about Texas." And he did, 5 minutes' worth!

Now as a sort of vicarious representative of the chamber of commerce of the Manila Hotel, I could do a little talking here about this place where I spent 4 very happy years with my wife. And I could be, I think, something of a speaker for the Chamber of Commerce of Manila and of the Philippines, because my duties here took me to every sector of these Islands. I think in those days we had constructed 94 separate stations, and I am sure that I visited, at one time or another, each of them.

But within the few hours that I have to spend in Manila, I want to tell you a little bit about the impression I have of progress, progress in which you people—both the Philippine and the American Chambers of Commerce—have had a part. Your industrial skyline has changed immeasurably. Within the city itself, the changes are so great that I have been unable—and would have been unable to find myself in any place in the city except with the aid of a friend riding with me. Even the Luneta seems to have changed. It has a big bandstand I never saw before and other buildings to the left.

Now these instances of progress are not confined to the city. Secretary Serrano and I went out to Fort McKinley this morning. I was amazed at the factories that have gone up and are going up. The industrial housing that is springing up everywhere, the kind of thing that shows a thriving city, and more than that, a vibrant, dynamic, energetic people. This progress is so great that it could possibly induce complacency.

But I want to talk to you for a moment about the problems that are unsolved, that still are to be done. In all the world there is greater need for education, for better understanding, for a freer flow of information, for more success in our fight against disease, for better housing, better comfort. In short, better living standards for all peoples. And this means, particularly for the newly developing countries, a better average income, which they must have.

In these problems and all their related auxiliaries, there is a challenge to every man and woman of goodwill in this whole world; because the things of which I speak are the substance out of which universal peace will finally emerge.

If all people are ready to share their efforts, their hearts, their dreams with others, and then share their material possessions to make better the lot of the less fortunate, this will finally be peace.

Because, let us remember, it is greed, it is selfishness, it is lack of consideration for the other, it is a narrow pursuit of material goods and wealth that makes for struggle everywhere in the world. And it breaks up the cooperation that we need so desperately, if we are truly to reach our goal.

Now by no means do I mean that anyone should slack off his efforts to gain more for himself, for his family, and for his community. This is the motive, this is the incentive that makes us work harder. But the point of it is, what then do we do, because whatever we gain we do as a part of

493

society of which we are a part, and we owe that society our help, our leadership, our assistance in every single area in which any of the problems to which I have adverted has not been solved.

And how much more so, if the free world is to bind itself together tightly to make certain that the concepts of human dignity, freedom, liberty, equality before the law for all people—I say if these concepts are to triumph, they will do it only as free man and free nations find themselves ready to help each other. The strongest helping the weaker, and the weaker always able to put something in the "pot" to make this operation go better and faster.

There is no such thing as a nation too poor to help. As I pointed out in a talk yesterday, any man or any nation may be poor in material goods. It may be weak physically, or weak militarily, but that is no reason that its heart should not be just as great as that of the greatest nation in the world. There is no reason why the tiniest country in this whole world can't give to each of us larger nations new ideas, new inspiration; because often indeed the example of sacrifice made by the weak is something that can shame us into doing more ourselves.

I say to you that all of these things that we seek must have, of course, at their foundation a better economic strength in each of the peoples in which we are interested—the free nations. This means that for both of these chambers of commerce there is a great mission, a great opportunity: not just to make Manila more beautiful, more attractive—and indeed, that is rather impossible—not just to make this nation bigger, stronger, although you do that as part of your problem. You are making your nation capable economically to develop its spiritual and intellectual strength so that in all circumstances and in all areas you are a true leader for peace—for peace with justice in freedom.

Now, my friends, I have been highly complimented here from this platform. Indeed, Mr. Balatbat, with his nomination of me for the Presidency of the world, forgot one thing: the frailty of the human; although I am proud to say that I use my entire strength, my entire life, to try to promote the ideals and the concepts of which I have so haltingly spoken. Yet we cannot look to one man, no matter how great he could have been—a man with the wisdom of Solomon, the patience of a Lincoln, the military genius of a Napoleon, the philosophical insight of a Socrates. Even such a man could not carry on this crusade and this necessary work by himself.

Every one of us that knows in his heart that he can help, if he so chooses, can help. In so doing he becomes a leader, a leader for the noblest cause that man has ever held—and has indeed held for centuries, even millennia: peace with justice in freedom.

If we keep this thought before us, then every gain we make is no longer a selfish one, no longer is it merely the result of selfish ambition. It is something to do to strengthen you, to make better and stronger your efforts for the attainment of this great goal.

I realize I am talking of something that is a bit idealistic. But I believe this with my whole heart. Only as each of us makes himself a little better in this regard, does the world become better.

I refer again to human frailty. I and every man I have ever known have some evidence of this frailty. We are not omnipotent. We pray to God for guidance, but it is on our own shoulders that the responsibility rests to reach the objective I have tried to outline. None of us will do it perfectly, but each can do it a little better.

And if we can do this, in this one audience alone, the aggregate of improvement will be revolutionary.

Ladies and gentlemen, I congratulate you all for what I have seen in this city and this country, which shows the capabilities of the people and the organizations that you here represent. I simply say this: my confidence in the Philippines, and my confidence in the United States, and my confidence in the solidarity of their partnership will do still better in the future. And you have the great opportunity to be one of the agents of that betterment.

Thank you very much indeed.

NOTE: The President spoke at 1:15 p.m. in the Fiesta Pavilion of the Manila Hotel. In his opening words he referred to José Orosa, the master of ceremonies, Marcelo Balatbat, President of the Chamber of Commerce of the Philippines, and Merle S. Robie, Acting President of the American Chamber of Commerce of the Philippines. Later in his remarks he referred to the Secretary of Foreign Affairs, Felixberto Serrano.

188 ¶ Remarks at a Civic Reception at the Luneta in Manila. *June* 16, 1960

MR. PRESIDENT, you, on behalf of the Filipino people, have just bestowed a great honor upon me.

Proudly, I accept, in the name of the American people, the award of Rajah in the Ancient Order of Sikatuna.

My friends, this Luneta was for more than 4 years the scene of my habitual evening walks. To this day it lives in memory as one of the most pleasant, indeed even one of the most romantic spots, I have known in this entire world. Leaving the front entrance of the Manila Hotel of an evening, I could walk to the right to view the busy docks where Philippine commerce with the world was loaded and unloaded. From here, looking across the peaceful waters of Manila Bay, I could see the gorgeous sunsets over Miravales. Walking toward the Club of the Army and the Navy, and looking down toward the city itself, I nearly always paused for a moment before the statue of the great José Rizal before returning to my quarters. One thing that made those evening promenades so pleasant, so meaningful, was the deep sense of feeling I had of Philippine-American friendship.

To you, assembled before this platform—to Filipinos and Americans everywhere, and to those who are gone from among us—is due the credit of having our close friendship in war and in peace.

Now, upon both our peoples still rests the grave responsibility of working together tirelessly in the promotion of liberty and world peace.

The voluntary association of free peoples produces, from the sharing of common ideals of justice, equality and liberty, a strength and a moral fiber which tyrannies never attain by coercion, control, and oppression. Such tyrannies can, of course, concentrate upon a single objective—the toil of millions upon millions of men and women, working endless hours, denied even the smallest happiness of human living, sometimes whipped, sometimes cajoled, always treated as robots bereft of human dignity. For a space of years, particularly if the peoples they regiment have known little of freedom or of a decent prosperity, such dictatorships may seem to achieve marvels. But in their denial of human dignity—their destruction of individual self-esteem—they write the eventual doom of their system.

Long before many of us here today were born, a great Filipino, José Rizal, in vivid and eloquent language, foretold the eruption of these tyrannies and predicted their ultimate fate. He said:

"Deprive a man of his dignity, and you not only deprive him of his moral strength but you also make him useless even for those that wish to make use of him. Every creature has its stimulus, its mainspring.

Man's is his self-esteem.   Take it away from him and he is a corpse. . . ."

Now tyrannies of many sorts still exist in the world.   All are rejected by free men.   Some authoritarian governments, being narrow in ambition, content themselves with local and confined dominance.   Others are blatant in their boasts of eventual supremacy over continents and even the world; constant in their boast that eventually they will bury all systems of freedom.

That boast will never come true.   Even in the lands that Communists now master with an iron rule, the eternal aspirations of humanity cannot be forever suppressed.   The truth enunciated by José Rizal is universal in its application.   But tyrannies, before their fated deterioration and disappearance, can, sometimes for many years, engulf and enslave free peoples unable to resist them.

In that knowledge, the free world—two-thirds of the earth's population—step by step moves forward toward a more effective partnership that freedom, human dignity, the noble heritages of many centuries may withstand successfully all aggression.

Some nations are still reluctant to commit themselves fully; others are divided on commitments already made.   Minorities in some—possibly the victims of subversion or of bribe, possibly confused by propaganda and threat—oppose even the most obviously profitable associations.   But most stand firmly together.

The free world must increase its strength—in military defenses, in economic growth, in spiritual dedication.   Thus the free world will withstand aggressive pressures, and move ever forward in its search for enduring peace.

Your government has recently reaffirmed your determination to stand steadfast by joining only 2 weeks ago in the communique issued in Washington by the Council of Ministers of the eight nations of SEATO. They stated clearly that:

"The Council availed itself of this timely opportunity to reemphasize the firm unity of purpose of the member countries of SEATO and their determination to maintain and develop, both individually and collectively, their capacity to meet all forms of Communist threat to the peace and security of the Treaty Area."

May I say here that the United States is proud and indeed is thankful to be so closely associated and so staunchly allied with the Philippines both in SEATO and in the Mutual Defense Treaty between our two countries.

But in this world of continuing tension and yearnings for social change, it is insufficient that the free world stand static in its defense of freedom.

We must, all of us, move ahead with imagination and positive programs to improve conditions in which human freedom can flourish.

We must, collectively and individually, strive for a world in which the rule of law replaces the rule of force.

Your country and mine have reaffirmed our faith in the principles of the United Nations Charter. We share a common desire to settle international disputes by peaceful means. The task is not an easy one. Communist intransigence at the conference table, whenever they do agree to sit at one, makes the attainment of an equitable agreement most difficult. Moreover, the record of Communist violations of agreements is a long one—indeed, a sad one. The continuation of Communist provocations, subversion, and terrorism while negotiations are underway serves only to compound the difficulty of arriving at peaceful settlements.

But we shall never close the door to peaceful negotiations. All of us, all free nations, always hold out the hand of friendship as long as it is grasped in honesty and in integrity. We shall continue to make it clear that reason and common sense must prevail over senseless antagonism and distorted misunderstandings and propaganda. The arms race must be brought under control and the nuclear menace that is poised in delicate suspension over the heads of all mankind must be eliminated. This, I am convinced, can be done, without appeasement or surrender, by continuing a course of patient, resourceful and businesslike dealings with the Soviet leaders.

The goal of a world at peace in friendship with freedom is so worth the attaining that every feasible and honorable avenue must be explored. The support, understanding, and participation of all who cherish freedom is essential to this noblest endeavor in history. The Philippine contribution will be mighty in its impact on the future.

And now, my friends, I cannot close without attempting once more to express my very deep appreciation of all the cordial hospitality and friendliness that has been exhibited to me and to all the members of my party during our all too brief stay in this lovely country.

We know that in greeting us along the highway or in magnificent crowds such as this, you are really expressing your basic affection for the American people.

And I assure you—all of you—as the spokesman of the American people, that their concern for you, your faith, your future, your well-being, their affection for you is equally deep with yours.

Thank you and goodbye.

NOTE: The President spoke at 5:03 p.m. from the band shell in Luneta Park, where he and President Garcia reviewed a military parade. The Order of Sikatuna, Rajah, is the highest decoration awarded by the Philippine Government.

During the parade the President learned that the Japanese Government had requested a postponement of his visit to Japan. A White House release of the same date stated that although the President would have liked to fulfill his long-held ambition to pay his respects to the Emperor and to the people of this great sister-democracy and ally of the United States, he, of course, fully accepted the decision of the Japanese authorities and therefore would not visit Japan at the scheduled time.

"In so doing," the release continued, "the President wishes to express his full and sympathetic understanding of the decision taken by the Japanese Government. He would like also to express his regrets that a small organized minority, led by professional Communist agitators acting under external direction and control, have been able by resort to force and violence to prevent his good will visit and to mar the celebration of this centennial in Japanese-American relations.

"At the same time the President remains confident that the deliberate challenges to law and order which have caused the Japanese Government to reach its decision will not and cannot disrupt the abiding friendship and understanding which unite our two nations and our two peoples."

189 ❡ Joint Statement Following Discussions With President Garcia. *June* 16, 1960

PRESIDENT EISENHOWER, at the invitation of President Garcia, paid a state visit to the Philippines on June 14 to 16, 1960, returning the visit of President Garcia to the United States two years ago.

President Eisenhower recalled his personal association with the Philippines extending over a period of many years. As the first President of the United States to visit the Philippines while in office, he expressed his deep sense of satisfaction that he had been afforded this opportunity to attest to the admiration and affection which the government and people of the United States feel toward their Philippine allies.

President Garcia, on his part, viewed the affection shown to President Eisenhower by the Filipino people as a grateful remembrance of the latter's tour of duty in the Philippines some twenty-five years ago and their admiration for his military leadership in the second world war and his dedicated labors for a just and lasting world peace.

The visit afforded President Garcia and President Eisenhower, together with other officials of both governments, an opportunity for a frank and cordial exchange of views on matters of mutual interest. In a review of the international situation and of the bilateral relations of the two countries, the two Presidents:

1. Reaffirmed the bonds of friendship and mutual understanding which have historically joined the Filipino and American governments and peoples.

2. Noted the problems facing the free world at the beginning of the new decade and discussed the possibility of increased tensions in view of recent statements by Communist leaders in Moscow and Peiping. They renewed their determination to support the work of the United Nations and the objectives of the United Nations' Charter in the interest of true international peace and progress based on justice and the dignity of the individual.

3. Assessed the continuing threat to peace in the Far East posed by Communist China. They reaffirmed the importance of regional cooperation in insuring the independence of the nations of Southeast Asia. They emphasized the important role of the Southeast Asia Treaty Organization in furthering such cooperation and in developing a sense of regional solidarity; and they noted with satisfaction the contribution being made by the Philippines toward strengthening its ties with its Asian neighbors.

4. Noted that President Eisenhower's visit and the warm response thereto by the Filipino people provided renewed evidence of the strength and vitality of the alliance between the Philippines and the United States and of its essential contribution to the security of Southeast Asia. To promote the continuing strength of the alliance and to enable the Philippines to discharge its obligation thereunder, they emphasized the importance of close military collaboration and planning between the appropriate authorities of their countries. They further expressed the view that this close military collaboration and planning should be aimed at the maximum effectiveness in formulating and executing United States military assistance programs and in furthering Philippine defensive capability in the light of modern requirements.

5. Noted the recent meeting of the Council of Foreign Ministers of the SEATO held in Washington and expressed satisfaction with the continuing effectiveness of the SEATO as a deterrent to Communist aggression in Southeast Asia. They were also gratified that the Washington conference had given attention to the economic objectives of the

SEATO, recognizing the importance of economic cooperation between and among the members.

6. Recalled the provisions of the Mutual Defense Treaty. President Eisenhower, on his part, renewed the assurance he had made to President Garcia in Washington that under the provisions of this treaty and other defensive agreements between the Philippines and the United States and in accordance with the deployments and dispositions thereunder, any armed attack against the Philippines would involve an attack against the United States Forces stationed there and against the United States and would instantly be repelled. It was noted that this understanding was included in the agreement reached between the Secretary of Foreign Affairs of the Philippines and the Ambassador of the United States on October 12, 1959.

7. Noted with satisfaction the considerable progress that had been made in talks between the Secretary of Foreign Affairs of the Philippines and the Ambassador of the United States towards settlement of problems arising from the presence of United States bases in the Philippines. They expressed confidence that the few remaining problems will be similarly resolved to the mutual satisfaction of the two governments.

8. Reemphasized the importance of strong, stable economies in furthering the objectives of peaceful development in the free world. President Eisenhower expressed his gratification at the evident progress which has been made in the Philippine economy, including notable advances in industrializaton. The contribution which the United States aid programs have made and will continue to make to Philippine economic development was emphasized. In recognition of the economic interdependence of all nations in the modern world, they discussed opportunities for increased private investment and expanded trade between the two countries in a climate favorable to free enterprise and to the free movement of capital.

President Garcia and President Eisenhower concluded that the exchange of views and the renewal of personal associations made possible by President Eisenhower's visit will further strengthen the traditional ties between the two countries and will contribute significantly to the advancement of their cooperative efforts on behalf of peace and progress in this vital part of the world.

NOTE: The joint statement was released in Manila.

190 ¶ Remarks in Manila Before Leaving for Taipei. *June* 16, 1960

Mr. President, Your Excellencies, members of the Armed Services of the Philippines, and friends:

After this very brief visit to this beautiful country, the time has come for me to say goodbye. To you, Mr. President, and to your associates I must express the very deep appreciation of all my party and myself for your many kindnesses and many courtesies. Truly we feel that we have found in you, here in your own country, what we always knew you were when you came to see us: a true friend, a true friend personally, as friends live in affection with each other, but friends as the head of a friendly government and a friendly people—a government and people that stands with other free nations in defense of all the values that all of us hold dear.

So as we go, we don't truly go. Our memories, our hopes, and our hearts will be with you—always.

And frankly, when the burdens of my present office have been passed on to someone else, and I can become a freer man than I am now, I still nurture the hope that again I can come back here and with even less restrictions than now, wander around this land and learn it once again as I thought I knew it a quarter century ago.

Thank you, and through you I want to thank every single individual who along the street or in crowds exposed to me a friendly face and shouted a friendly *mabuhay*.

It has been heartwarming. And goodbye.

NOTE: The President spoke at 11:10 p.m. at the Presidential Landing near the Manila Hotel, following a dinner given in honor of President and Mrs. Garcia at the Chancery. The President then took a launch to the U.S.S. St. Paul, which was anchored in the South Harbor waiting to take him to Taipei.

191 ¶ Remarks to the Officers and Men of the 7th Fleet. *June* 18, 1960

[Broadcast from the President's Quarters aboard the U.S.S. St. Paul]

GOOD MORNING. I take this opportunity to tell all of you how grateful my party and I are for all your effort to make this wonderful cruise possible.

Because of your hard work, thoughtfulness, and courtesy, we have enjoyed ourselves thoroughly and are indeed appreciative.

More important, however, than the gratitude of my party and myself, is the gratitude the American people feel for you and our servicemen all over the world for protecting our country.

Until the nations of the world find a way to insure their security without armaments, the Seventh Fleet must be strong enough to support our allies, maintain our interests, and help keep the peace in the Far East.

That strength is measured largely by the devotion to duty and professional skill of you, the men of the Seventh Fleet.

The American people know you are doing your job well. They and the people of the free world are not deceived by the false propaganda of the Communists.

And now may I say goodbye, good luck, and smooth sailing. Thank you and God bless you.

192 ¶ Remarks Upon Arrival at the Sungshan Airport, Taipei. *June* 18, 1960

President Chiang, ladies and gentlemen:

First, Mr. President, I must thank you for your cordial words of welcome. I am indeed gratified that you saw fit to acknowledge the significance of this visit as one that attempts to bring even closer together our two countries.

For a long time I have hoped that I might be able to visit Taiwan. Therefore, I was delighted when I found I could accept your President's gracious invitation to come here.

I look forward to fruitful conversations with him as well as to the opportunity to salute the Chinese people on the rapid progress made on this island.

Our friendship, tested in war and in peace, is a real source of strength in our development of Free World security.

The ideals that we share: our common commitment to self-government in our respective countries; our aspiration for a world of freedom, justice and peace and friendship under the rule of law; all these demand of us—as they do of all the Free World—increased vigilance and closer cooperation in the face of the threats posed by Communist imperialism.

Mr. President, to your people I bring the personal assurance of America's steadfast solidarity with you and your Government in the defense of these ideals and in the pursuit of our common aspirations.

Thank you very much.

NOTE: The President spoke at 10:01 a.m. He was greeted by President Chiang Kai-shek, Vice President Chen Cheng, and other Chinese Government officials, U.S. Ambassador Everett F. Drumright, and Vice Adm. Roland N. Smoot, Commander of the Taiwan Defense Command.

193 ¶ Address at a Mass Rally in Taipei. *June* 18, 1960

Mr. President, distinguished guests, and friends:

I address this gathering today fully aware of the honor you have bestowed on my Country and myself in inviting me to speak here. I bring to your Nation greetings from the American people.

We Americans are in a very real sense your close neighbors: we look out with you upon the same ocean—the Pacific. This largest of oceans has been narrowed by the marvels of modern communication and transportation. No longer is it a formidable barrier separating America from the Nations of the Far East.

We in America have accepted this tremendously important fact of international life, and recognize its implications for the future of our country. Therefore, I come to you, as to the other countries of the Pacific which I am privileged to visit, as a friend and neighbor deeply concerned with your—and our common interests.

This concern has shaped my country's policies toward the nations of the Pacific. The realization that America's security and welfare are intimately bound up with their security and welfare has led us to foster the concept of collective defense; and to contribute money, materials and technical assistance to promote their economic stability and development.

But though the United States provides assistance to the nations of the Pacific Region, many of them recently emerged from Colonial status, we have not sought to impose upon them our own way of life or system of government. We respect their sovereignty as we do our own.

To do otherwise would be a betrayal of America's own traditions. Our purpose is to help protect the right of our neighbors of the Pacific to develop in accordance with their own National aspirations and their own traditions.

In this era of mass destruction weapons, the increasing intimacy in which the peoples of the world live makes resort to global war, even by the smallest of them, dangerous to the whole community of nations.

I come to you representing a country determined, despite all setbacks, to press on in search of effective means to outlaw war and to promote the rule of law among nations.

History has repeatedly shown that this high purpose is not served by yielding to threats or by weakening defenses against potential aggressors. Indeed such weakness would increase the danger of war.

You may be assured that our continuing search for peaceful solutions to outstanding international problems does not reflect the slightest lessening of our determination to stand with you, and with all our free neighbors of the Pacific, against aggression.

The United States does not of course recognize the claim of the warlike and tyrannical Communist regime in Peiping. In the United Nations we support the Republic of China, a founding member, as the only rightful representative of China in that organization.

The American people deeply admire your courage in striving so well to keep the cause of liberty alive here in Taiwan in the face of the menacing power of Communist Imperialism. Your accomplishments provide inspiration to us all.

The search for lasting peace comprehends much more than the erection of sure military defenses. Perhaps nothing offers greater hope to a war weary world than the new opportunities for a better life which have been opened up in the past few decades by the magnificent achievements of science and technology. If the peoples of the world can not only master the forces of nature but can find also the way to use them for peaceful ends, we are on the threshold of a new era.

One of the great peaceful battles for a better life—which the Republic of China is now in the midst of fighting here on Taiwan—is on the front of economic progress. For you, the past has been full of hardships. But for the people of this island each difficulty was a challenge to be mastered.

During the years of this progress, freedom has not been a free ingredient, like air or water. Indeed, freedom has been the costliest component of your daily lives. Even in sheer economic terms you have devoted a larger share of your incomes to keeping your independence than have most other peoples on the globe. To do this you have had to adopt progressive measures.

A great economic accomplishment of the past ten years was your program in land reform. Due to its fair and democratic conception and execution it has become a model for similar reforms in other lands. It dealt successfully with one of the fundamental problems the Chinese people have faced throughout history. Moreover, in it you achieved much more than a fair and equitable adjustment—you produced both social dynamism and economic growth.

That reform, founded on Sun Yat-Sen's three peoples principles and executed with due regard for law and for private property, stands in sharp contrast to the brutal regimentation of your countrymen on the mainland. There they are often herded into the soul-destroying labor brigades of the Commune System. But Free China knows that a system in which the farmer owns the land he tills gives him the incentive to adopt advanced fertilization, irrigation and other farming techniques.

We are proud that we have been of some help technically, in carrying through your agricultural reform program. We too have learned much from our association in the Chinese-American joint commission on rural reconstruction. We have been able to use this experience to good advantage in helping other countries. In the industrial field your friends in the United States and all over the world have watched with satisfaction your growing productivity and diversification. You have demonstrated, under adverse conditions, the moral and physical strength, the imagination and the perseverance to achieve this near miracle. Now I learn that, not satisfied with the impressive rate of progress already attained, you are entering upon a new program for further speeding up your economic growth.

In today's world, where many new nations of Asia and Africa are seeking a path of economic development to satisfy the growing expectations of their people, Free China provides a shining example. Thanks in large measure to the vigor and talents of its population and its leaders, it has advanced to the threshold of the kind of self-sustaining economic growth that has brought other free nations to wealth and power.

Free China thus has an opportunity, which is at the same time a responsibility, to demonstrate to less developed nations the way to economic growth in freedom. Confronted with the harsh example of the Communist way on the mainland, you here are in a position to show how a nation can achieve material strength and advance the well-being of its people without sacrificing its most valued traditions.

Your success in this field can sustain and guarantee your secure standing in the community of nations. And it will become, for your own fellow countrymen on the mainland, an ever more insistent refutation of the false Communist thesis that modern economic development can be purchased only at the price of freedom.

We in the United States have studied your plans for social and economic changes and do not underestimate the difficulties you will have to endure during a period of transition. Economic growth, especially accelerated growth, constantly calls for recurring revolutions in thinking, in the way we do things, indeed in every phase of our lives.

As you know, we intend to join hands with you in this great enterprise. By doing so we shall not lighten your load because you have already pledged yourselves to maximum effort, but our partnership should demonstrate how rapid progress can be achieved by the methods of free peoples freely joined in friendship for mutual benefit.

As representatives of the great and numerous Chinese Nation, heirs to one of the world's most ancient and honored cultures, you—the people of Free China—can play a unique role in the future of mankind. By grasping the opportunities for the improvement of human welfare now made possible by the advancement of science and technology, you can blaze a trail of progress here on Taiwan that may ultimately shape the destiny of all your fellow countrymen, of nearly one-quarter of the human race. This is indeed a challenge of gigantic proportions.

In meeting that challenge, the United States—and all the free world— wishes you every success.

My friends, this morning I encountered an unforgettable experience. I met thousands of you people along the road from the airport and everywhere I encountered only friendliness, courteous greetings and a face lighted up with smiles. To each of you who lined that route, to each of you who today came out to do me the courtesy of listening to what I had to say, I give you my grateful thanks on behalf of my party, myself— indeed for the American people, whose concern for every one of you is deep and lasting. So from your President to the humblest citizen of the land, I say thank you very much, and God be with you.

NOTE: The President spoke at 5 p.m. from a balcony on the Presidential Office Building overlooking the Plaza. His opening words "Mr. President" referred to President Chiang Kai-shek.

194   ¶ Toast by the President at a Dinner Given in His Honor by President Chiang Kai-shek. *June* 18, 1960

President Chiang, Madame Chiang, and distinguished guests:

Mr. President, I am deeply grateful for your recounting the record—the long record—of Sino-American cooperation through the years. I think we must never forget that effective, successful cooperation demands mutual understanding. Where cooperation has been successful in the past it is unquestionably because there was at that moment real understanding.

And where it has been less successful, it is because one or the other has not understood the problem as did the other. I think if we have one problem always before us, it is to make certain that this understanding, of ourselves and of the other and of our mutual problems, is so clear, so sharp, that there can be no mistake in judgment made that can have its effect—a—anything less than true cooperation in pursuit of the ideals we both believe in.

And now with your permission, sir, I should like to respond specifically to your gracious remarks. Additionally, of course, I am grateful for the wonderful reception I received from the Chinese people today.

And I am particularly happy to renew my personal acquaintance and friendship with President Chiang, whom I first met in Cairo in 1943. Lasting associations between nations are founded not in personal relationships, but in community of interest, mutual respect, shared ideals and aspirations, and common purpose. But international relations, like historical events, cannot be divorced from the persons who play a part in them.

For a third of a century, President Chiang has played a decisive role in the shaping of relations between our two countries. He first won America's admiration and respect as a brilliant young revolutionary leader who unified China in a series of masterly campaigns. He set it on the road to becoming a modern democratic nation. He further deepened our respect and earned our gratitude by his indomitable leadership of our great Far Eastern ally in the second World War.

As the President has noted, this is my second visit to the government of the Republic of China. In 1946, when I visited China, as Chief of Staff of the Army, President Chiang had just led his embattled people to victory in the face of tremendous odds. He was then acutely conscious that China faced a new threat, one as yet scarcely recognized in the rest of the world.

President Chiang, with undiminished courage and vigor, still leads China in resistance to the menace he saw so clearly 14 years ago. He stands now as our partner in a great alliance of free peoples, who have come to share his own appreciation of the need for unity against the global threat of Communist imperialism.

Our solidarity with the Republic of China has been proclaimed in many forms—in our close political, economic, and cultural relations, in our mutual defense treaty, in our common opposition to Communist aggression, in the joint communique during the last visit of the late Secretary Dulles to this island.

My presence here this evening will be taken, I hope, as another token of that solidarity. It is also an occasion for reaffirming our steadfast confidence, as Secretary Dulles said in 1957, "that international communism's rule of strict conformity is, in China as elsewhere, a passing and not a perpetual phase."

With these thoughts in mind I would like to propose a toast to President Chiang and his charming wife to our lasting friendship, to his success in his third term as President, and to the prosperity in freedom and peace of the Chinese people.

Ladies and gentlemen, the President!

NOTE: The President proposed the toast at 8:30 p.m. at a state banquet in the Presidential Office Building.

195 ¶ Joint Statement Following Discussions With President Chiang Kai-shek. *June 19, 1960*

AT THE INVITATION of President Chiang Kai-shek, President Dwight D. Eisenhower visited the Republic of China from June 18 to June 19, 1960. This historic journey of the President of the United States of America and the warmth and enthusiasm with which he was received by the Chinese people demonstrated anew the strong bonds of friendship between the two countries.

Both President Chiang and President Eisenhower welcomed the opportunity afforded them by this visit for an intimate exchange of views on various matters of common interest and concern, calling to mind that the two countries have always stood closely together as staunch allies in war as well as in peace.   The talks between the two Chiefs of State were held in an atmosphere of utmost cordiality.

In the course of their discussions, the two Presidents reaffirmed the dedication of the two Governments to an untiring quest for peace with freedom and justice.   They recognize that peace and security are indivisible and that justice among nations demands the freedom and dignity of all men in all lands.

Taking note of the continuing threat of Communist aggression against the free world in general and the Far Eastern free countries in particular, the two Presidents expressed full agreement on the vital necessity of achieving closer unity and strength among all free nations.

They pledged once again that both their Governments would continue to stand solidly behind the Sino-U.S. Mutual Defense Treaty in meeting the challenge posed by the Chinese Communists in this area.   They deplored the outrageous and barbaric practice of the Chinese Communists in shelling and ruthlessly killing Chinese people on alternate days and noted that this practice emphasized the necessity for continued vigilance and firmness in the face of violence.

Discussions were also held on the importance of accelerating the economic expansion of the Republic of China in order to enhance the prosperity and well-being of its people.   President Chiang explained the steps which his Government is taking to assure the early accomplishment of his goal.   He expressed the appreciation of his Government and people for the valuable assistance which the United States of America has rendered to the Republic of China.   President Eisenhower expressed the admiration of the American people for the progress achieved by the Republic of China in various fields in recent years and gave assurance of continuing United States assistance.

Finally, the two Presidents voiced their common determination that the two Governments should continue to dedicate themselves to the principles of the United Nations and devote their unremitting efforts to the intensifying of their cooperation and to the further strengthening of the traditional friendship between the Chinese and American peoples.

NOTE: The joint statement was released in Taipei.

196 ¶ Remarks at the Sungshan Airport, Taipei, Upon Leaving for Okinawa. *June* 19, 1960

Mr. President, and ladies and gentlemen:

I leave the Republic of China with only one regret, that my visit has been so short. But I leave with a lasting impression of the warmth of your welcome, and renewed appreciation of the depth and permanence of the friendly ties that unite the Chinese and American peoples. I leave with an unforgettable impression of the dedication of the Chinese people to the cause of freedom.

My visit has been most instructive, as well as pleasant. My discussions with your distinguished Chief of State and members of the government have confirmed my belief that we have no more staunch friends anywhere than right here in Taiwan.

I have learned at first hand of the strides you have made in developing the military and economic strength of your country. I believe the plans that your leaders have developed will make of this land a living demonstration of the better life, political, economic, and social, and that this can be done by free men. Such a beacon of hope for your enslaved countrymen on the mainland will, I believe, hasten the dawn of freedom.

Finally—and I would speak also to the Americans here today, for they too are engaged in this endeavor—let me assure you again of the full and unwavering support of the American Government and people for the important part you are playing in our joint efforts toward a world of peace with justice, in freedom. I know the American people would join me in saying God be with you, and may He bring you the measure of success which your deep dedication deserves.

NOTE: The President spoke at 9:45 a.m.

197 ¶ Remarks Upon Arrival at Kadena Air Force Base, Okinawa. *June* 19, 1960

Chief Executive Ota, General Booth, members of the military services here, citizens of this Island, ladies and gentlemen:

The Ryukyuan people have a vital role for the free world in the circumstances of this era. Consequently, when the opportunity presented itself, I decided to make a stop on Okinawa.

I have come here, as to other areas of free Asia, on a mission of peace, friendship, good will, to learn at first hand more about the region. A fine relationship exists, I am informed, between the Ryukyuans and the Americans stationed in these Islands. I assure you that this feeling of friendship is shared by the American people as a whole. They and their government, conscious of the heavy responsibility they bear to the Ryukyuans, have a deep and an abiding interest in the welfare of all who live on these Islands, and in the steady improvement of their livelihood and economy.

Together we of the Ryukyus and America present to the world a splendid example of the mutual benefits that result when people of good will work toward the common goal of peace and friendship in freedom.

On behalf of the American people, for what you have done, for what you are doing, I thank you with all my heart, and I assure you personally that I am delighted to have these few hours here to visit with you of the Services and with the citizens of this Island.

NOTE: The President spoke at 11:22 a.m. In his opening remarks he referred to Seisaku Ota, Chief Executive of the Ryukyu Administration, and Lt. Gen. Donald P. Booth, High Commissioner of the Ryukyu Islands and Commanding General of the U.S. Army on the Islands.

198 ¶ Remarks Upon Arrival at Kimpo International Airport in Seoul. *June* 19, 1960

Mr. Prime Minister, Your Excellencies, officers and men of the armed services of Korea and of the United States, ladies and gentlemen:

First of all, Mr. Prime Minister, permit me to thank you most sincerely for your kind address of welcome to me and to my party.

For me and my party, as for all who love freedom, a visit here vividly recalls the memory of many months when Korea was a rallying place for the fighting men of the free world.

Here they came from every continent and hemisphere. Here, in their blood and valor, they proved that their devotion to freedom knew no boundary of land or of ocean. Here they demonstrated that a people determined to preserve their freedom against brutal aggression can depend on help, men and for arms and food—from all over the world.

I first came here only months after the Korean Republic was established. Six years later, in 1952, I saw the winter fighting in the mountains and felt the spirit and the will for sacrifice, and the courage out of which greatness in freedom is built.

This third time I come here to learn better and at first hand the progress you have made since war devastated your land; to discuss with the leaders of the Republic our common concerns and purposes; to help fortify and strengthen our mutual efforts in support of collective security, and to assure you that the United States, with all its heart, works for the noblest goal of mankind—peace and friendship in freedom.

I am proud to salute the men and women of Korea who have so amply proven their love of liberty, and I bring from the people of the United States their heartfelt wish for Korean growth and progress in the years ahead.

Thank you very much.

NOTE: The President spoke at 4:05 p.m. He was greeted by Prime Minister and Mme. Huh Chung, other Korean Government officials, members of the diplomatic corps, Mayor Kee Young Chang, and U.S. Ambassador and Mrs. Walter P. McConaughy.

199 ❡ Remarks to the American Community in Seoul. *June* 20, 1960

WELL, FOLKS, to say that I am complimented by your conducting this mobilization so I could meet you, is an understatement. I am delighted to see you, not only those that are connected directly with government, but those who are in business, who are in missionary work, or are otherwise engaged in work in Korea. I have the feeling that everybody who goes abroad absorbs and takes over an additional responsibility than that of merely becoming a good citizen of the United States. He owes something to the country that he visits, because anyone who comes here merely for profit or into a foreign country—any foreign country—merely for a profit, finds soon that he has not made friends and therefore is not making the profit he should like to make.

We have an obligation of service, in other words, to the country in which we are guests, as well as we have to our own. This of course applies with special force to anyone that is in the service of the United States Government. If we are discharging our responsibilities properly, we are trying to serve society. True, this may be the work of our own choice, and we have a right to develop in it. And naturally we expect to be happy in it. But we can be happy only if we are successful in rendering service to the society of which we are a part. And therefore we, knowing that it is to America's interest to make friends in the world everywhere, have a similar obligation.

In a very real sense, every American in this crowd is an ambassador, an ambassador of goodwill. You have exactly the same function, I think—let us say a side function—that I have as a direct function, that I am trying to perform by making this trip.

I would like to assure Korea that the United States recognizes an identity of interest between this country and our own, and that this identity of interest comes about because of shared ideals, shared convictions in the dignity of man, shared beliefs in the equality of every citizen before the law regardless of inconsequential things like color or race or religion.

This is the kind of thing, I believe, that makes foreign service challenging and interesting. For my own part, a great deal of my governmental service was performed in foreign countries, and I found it one always challenging, always interesting, and of course frequently I felt that I had not lived up to my own responsibilities. And I think that since humans are frail, we all have that feeling at times.

But I am merely trying to say that you have here a great opportunity as well as just the mere routine duties in which you are engaged, be it in business, in government, in educational work, or anything else.

Now, on the personal side, I was delighted to see the Little Leaguers here. I have got a grandson who is a very good second baseman and in hitting. Now he doesn't field very well, and so the reason I delayed down there was to ask these fellows how they were doing in fielding and in hitting. I didn't get a chance to talk to them in detail. I am disappointed that I did not, but I should like, really, to talk to every one of you about what you are doing, what is the interest that keeps you here, the one that really keeps you working—working to fulfill your own obligation to America, and to yourself, and to your family. I certainly don't mean to preach any doctrine that is so idealistic that none of us can live up to.

We start out by taking the advantaging of ourselves as an incentive that keeps us working, and the advantaging of our families and everything else—our communities. But I would like to find, by conversation with each individual here, what we really are believing and trying to do. Because I am convinced that only as we understand each other better in this world, and particularly those parts that we are pleased to call the free world, are we going to achieve the success we want for America, for ourselves, and for humankind.

We must think of their—and our—spiritual aspirations, our moral standards, our intellectual attainments, our economic strength, so that we may have decent and rising living standards throughout the world. Only as we understand these things and put our shoulders to the common wheel is humankind going to achieve that future that we know it must achieve if it is not going to risk the very grave dangers of global war—or even less than that, just complete chaos and unease and fear.

We want to live as confident people. And if we are going to live as confident people, we must live as a cooperative people.

So I think that we have identical missions, you and I. You will probably have them longer because I am going to lose my job pretty soon. But as long as I am in it, I am going to continue to work for that understanding between peoples that spells success for freedom and for liberty and for dignity of men in this world.

Now coming out of the house a minute ago, I had no idea what I was going to say—and you may have no idea of what I was saying, because I have been wandering around, playing with an idea that intrigues me and consumes my attention all the time. Because I am so confident that in cooperation is safety and progress, and in lack of cooperation is defeat if not disaster, that I think it is a subject all of us should think of every day.

And I am certain that those of you who are living here have found unusual opportunities to ponder these matters because of the very great dangers that the Republic of Korea has been exposed to—her trials and tribulations as she is developing into true democracy. And you have this lesson in front of you all the time. And I think as you show sympathetic understanding and readiness to help, you are really doing a very great service to your country and to yourselves.

To the youngsters around here, I can promise only one thing: insofar as I can go around the perimeter of this crowd and they have cameras, I will wait until at least they can get one picture, if they want it. And some of them, I see, seem to be well-armed with cameras—I saw one with two.

Thank you again for coming out. It has been a great privilege to meet you, the kind of meeting that thrills me every time I encounter this same opportunity in countries clear around the globe. So, thank you again. Good luck to all of you. God bless you.

NOTE: The President spoke at 10:15 a.m. on the lawn at the American Embassy Residence.

200 ¶ Toast by the President at a Luncheon Given in His Honor by Prime Minister Huh Chung of Korea. *June* 20, 1960

Mr. Prime Minister, Your Excellencies, friends:

In the short span of its independence the Republic of Korea has provided inspiration to those engaged in the common struggle against Communist aggression.

This inspiration springs from the courageous and selfless attitude which the Korean people have displayed both in times of conflict and in times of uneasy peace. They have proved their readiness to die for those principles under which they desire to live. May their example give heart to those of every land who dedicate their lives to the defense and independence of country, and to the strengthening of representative government.

Ladies and gentlemen, I ask you to join with me in a toast to His Excellency, the Prime Minister of the Republic of Korea.

NOTE: The President proposed the toast at 1 p.m. at a luncheon at Kyung Mu Dai, the official residence of the Prime Minister.

201 ¶ Address Before the National Assembly of
Korea. *June* 20, 1960

*Mr. Speaker, Members of the National Assembly, distinguished guests,
ladies and gentlemen:*

First, I offer my apologies to the Members of this Chamber because of
my tardiness in arriving here. I assure you that the delay was un-
intentional.

You have signally honored me by your invitation to address this National Assembly. To you is entrusted the realization of the Korean
people's hopes and aspirations. This is no local, narrow or limited
mission. What you do and what you say in the discharge of your trust
is of deep significance and powerful impact far beyond the boundaries
of this Republic. You are watched by the entire world.

Korea, once a battlefield for survival over aggression, is now a proving
ground for responsible, representative self-government. This is a testing
time of Korean integrity, perseverance in the democratic process, loyalty
to the ideals on which the Republic was founded.

In all your efforts you have the sympathetic understanding and the
best wishes of the American people.

Impressive changes of many kinds have occurred here since I visited
your country in 1952. Then your land bore the deep scars of war. But
you of free Korea have struggled to rehabilitate your war-torn nation.
You have achieved better standards of living against odds that for a less
sturdy people would have been overwhelming.

Equally inspiring to us all in recent days has been the purposeful re-
vitalization of the free institutions and practices on which democracy
rests.

You have reason today to be confident that your military forces,
together with those of your friends and allies, will permit no intrusion
across the borders of Free Korea. On behalf of the Government and
people of the United States I solemnly reaffirm the pledge of full American support to the Republic of Korea in accordance with our commitments under the Mutual Defense Treaty.

The primary responsibility, of course, rests squarely on the Korean
people and their Government. External aid to any nation can be used
effectively and indeed is deserved only as the recipient shows by stability,

energy, unity and steadfastness of purpose its determination to sacrifice for the ideals it deems paramount in its way of life.

Certainly, in its agonizing tests during three years of war, Korea showed itself so determined.   We shall forever pay tribute to the heroic soldiers, sailors and airmen of Korea who, together with their fellow fighting men from sixteen member nations of the United Nations, gave their lives in the cause of freedom.

So long as a like spirit, a like will to sacrifice, animates the people of Korea other nations will be inspired and, I think, anxious to help you in every way they can.   They have already proved such a readiness.

The United Nations response to the attack in 1950 was one of the significant events of history.   This united determination of free countries will not be forgotten by those who would wage aggression or by those who seek to maintain their full independence and security.

The cause for which free nations fought here in Korea transcended physical stemming of Communist aggression.   Their greater and more far-reaching purpose was to strengthen and safeguard, on the mainland of Asia, a nation founded on the principles of government by and for the people.

This kind of government cannot endure without such basic institutions and practices as:

1.—a free press;

2.—responsible expression of popular will;

3.—a system of public education;

4.—an assembly truly representative of the Korean people.

Events over the past few months in the Republic of Korea have demonstrated how aware its citizens are of the rights and obligations of a free people.

Members of the National Assembly, I repeat that yours is a great trust.   You, and those new members who will soon be gathering here in the next Assembly, have the opportunity and the heavy responsibility to show that human freedom and advancement of the people's welfare thrive even in the very shadow of Communist aggression.

The prompt and judicious fulfillment of the recently expressed wishes of the Korean people is a momentous challenge.   Your friends throughout the world hope and believe you will meet this challenge with courage and with moderation.   And success in this undertaking will provide inspiration to your countrymen to the north who, I earnestly pray will one day join you in a free, united Korea.

Over the past years, I have had an unusual opportunity to visit many people throughout the world. In race, in color, in language, in creed they were a cross-section of all mankind. But they were united in their recognition that responsible and representative self-government best serves the needs and welfare of free men. This National Assembly, for example, has its counterpart in all free countries, which like you, are striving for liberty, progress and peace with justice.

All free nations cherish these goals. All aspire to achieve them. But not a single one—even the most rich and powerful—can hope, of itself, for fullness of attainment in the circumstances of this time. All of us— Asian and European, American and African—must work together in cooperative purpose or we shall lose the right to work at all in freedom.

That we may effectively work together we must come to understand more clearly and fully how much we have in common—the great goals of free men, their eternal aspirations; a common destiny.

As we grow in such understanding, I am firmly convinced that all artificial, man-made differences will shrink and disappear. In their stead will develop full recognition of the tremendous opportunities for mutual advancement that lie in cooperative endeavor. And we will use these opportunities for our own good and the good of all mankind.

Free people, of course, must stand together resolutely against aggression. But they must also stand together in combat against the enemies of humanity: hunger, privation and disease. The American people have devoted much of their resources to this cause. Here in Korea are some of our largest programs for contributing to the economic progress of a close ally and for strengthening its military capabilities.

Cooperation between our two countries has, as you know, extended into many spheres—education, industry, defense, agriculture, social welfare. Through Korean-American cooperation in all these diverse fields, we have come better to understand each other. This common understanding, which reflects our common stake, will, I am convinced, grow deeper and firmer as we continue jointly to face the problems and demands of the future.

Now, on the eve of the tenth anniversary of the Communist invasion of your nation, let us rededicate ourselves to the cause of peace and friendship in freedom among nations and men.

My friends, I come before you this afternoon as a representative of one sovereign nation speaking to the legislative representatives of another sovereign nation. My message from America to you is this: we will be watching your progress with ever growing concern. You can always count on our friendship so long as we endure.

NOTE: The President spoke at 3:51 p.m. His opening words "Mr. Speaker" referred to the Vice Speaker of the Assembly, Do Yun Kim.

202 ¶ Remarks at the Headquarters of the Korean Army's Sixth Corps.   *June 20, 1960*

Mr. Prime Minister, General Yu, General Magruder, distinguished guests, members of the United Nations Command, ladies and gentlemen:

Fighting men from the Republic of Korea, the Republic of Turkey, the Kingdom of Thailand, the United Kingdom, Ethiopia, and the United States are formed here on this field. In the reviewing stand are officers and men representing Australia, Canada, France, Greece, New Zealand. The parade field is flanked, I note, by the flags of the 16 nations which served the United Nations cause here during the Korean conflict. Through those of the "16" who are represented here today, as well as those who are not, I pay tribute to the contribution and sacrifice of their people and fighting men in the Korean war.

And taking the privilege of a fellow citizen, in my case, I cannot fail to observe with pride the men in American uniforms in the ranks before me. Our countrymen in the United States join me in a prideful salute to you who represent us in this land that lies along the frontier of freedom.

But in particular, I pay a special tribute to the Armed Forces of the Republic of Korea. No one can forget the fortitude and bravery of the Korean Army when, almost 10 years ago this very day, it went into action against Communist aggression from the north. The utmost of self-sacrifice was manifested by the Korean soldiers, and the sailors, and their airmen defending these rugged hills that surround us, sparkling today in their summer beauty, bleak and forbidding in the cold winter months.

This heroism is fittingly commemorated by the Unknown Soldier's monument where a few minutes ago I was privileged to place a wreath. All of us—soldiers and civilians alike—from all these 16 nations, salute the soldier who lies there. He, like countless thousands of others, gave his life not only in the defense of Free Korea but in the defense of freedom for all people everywhere.

NOTE: The President spoke at 6:50 p.m. In his opening words he referred to Prime Minister Huh Chung, Lt. Gen. Yu Jai Heung, Commanding General, First Army of the Republic of Korea, and Gen. Carter B. Magruder, Commander in Chief, United Nations Command.

203 ¶ Joint Statement Following Discussions With Prime Minister Huh Chung. *June* 20, 1960

ACCEPTING an invitation of long standing from the Government of the Republic of Korea, President Eisenhower today visited Korea where he met with Prime Minister Huh Chung and other Korean leaders, including members of the Korean National Assembly, which he addressed. President Eisenhower also visited the United Nations Command and reviewed contingents representing United Nations Forces which are helping to defend this key Free World position.

President Eisenhower's visit highlighted the vital purposes served by collective Free World action to preserve peace initiated almost exactly ten years ago in response to international communism's attack on the Republic of Korea.   The manner in which the United Nations responded in June, 1950 to aggression and the retention over the past decade of a strong Free World position in the Republic of Korea have been major factors in preserving the peace in Asia and creating a climate in which Free Asia nations can enjoy independence, promote human rights and improve the spiritual and material welfare of these people.

The visit impressively reaffirmed the strong bonds of friendship and close cooperation between the Republic of Korea and the United States. The visit also provided an opportunity for discussions between Prime Minister Huh Chung and President Eisenhower on questions of common concern to their two countries.   President Eisenhower reaffirmed the assurance of the Government and people of the United States of their continued support for the Republic of Korea and their solemn pledge to preserve the independence of Korea.

The two leaders gave unqualified endorsement to the principles of the United Nations Charter as standards for international behavior.   They pledged that their countries would continue to uphold United Nations principles and work unreservedly and unceasingly toward maintaining

peace. To this end, both leaders recognized the vital importance of preserving the alliance between the Republic of Korea and the United States
of America and of maintaining vigilance and strength, patience and fore-
sightedness, in carrying out the purposes for which this alliance stands.

In the course of the discussions, Prime Minister Huh Chung and President Eisenhower took cognizance of the deep longing of the Korean
people for reunification of their homeland. They agreed that every
effort must be continued to bring a peaceful end to this tragic division in
accordance with the principles set forth in United Nations resolutions,
envisaging the achievement by peaceful means of a unified, independent
and democratic Korea under a representative form of government and
full restoration of peace and security in the area.

Prime Minister Huh Chung outlined measures being taken by his country to broaden its international ties and he affirmed his nation's strong
desire to be a full member of the United Nations. Prime Minister Huh
Chung and President Eisenhower agreed that the Republic of Korea is
entitled to United Nations membership and that its membership would
strengthen the United Nations.

Prime Minister Huh Chung and President Eisenhower agreed that
efforts should be made to encourage private investment and increase the
flow of trade between countries of the Free World.

Prime Minister Huh Chung and President Eisenhower examined
Korean and American economic and social programs and agreed that
they should be designed and executed so as to foster economic independence, assist social progress, and provide a strong foundation for democratic institutions. Both leaders agreed that continued United States
economic assistance is required to help the Republic of Korea maintain
economic growth and achieve economic viability as soon as possible.

Prime Minister Huh Chung and President Eisenhower expressed their
resolve to continue to serve the cause of peace and strengthen the bonds of
friendship between their two peoples.

NOTE: The joint statement was released in Seoul.

204 ¶ Remarks in Seoul Upon Leaving for Honolulu. *June* 20, 1960

Mr. Prime Minister and citizens of Korea:

My all too brief stay here in Korea has for me been full of interest and inspiration. I have seen the strength and vigilance of the forces guarding an unnatural boundary which keeps Koreans in the north from their fellow countrymen in the Republic of Korea.

I have seen how free world forces from many nations are joined here together in preserving a vital frontier of freedom and in furthering the purposes of the United Nations Charter. I have had interesting and profitable discussions with Prime Minister Huh Chung and other Korean leaders. I have had the privilege of addressing your National Assembly and meeting some of its members who bear such important responsibilities in fulfilling the wishes of the Korean people.

I have had the memorable experience of seeing so many Korean people along the routes of travel I have followed. To them, and to countless numbers whom I could not see, I extend my warmest thanks for Korea's hospitality.

I regret very much that some parts of my planned route for yesterday became so greatly congested by friendly spectators that I could not ride through all of the streets where people were waiting to welcome me and my party. To them, who waited so long, I express a particular word of thanks.

I must now say goodbye to you and to your fellow countrymen. On behalf of all the members of my party, I wish to express our deep appreciation for the wonderful day we have spent here as your guests. We are profoundly grateful.

Every best wish to you and to all the people of Korea wherever they may be. And God go with you.

NOTE: The President spoke at 7:50 p.m. at the Kimpo International Airport.

205 ¶ Remarks Upon Arrival at the Honolulu International Airport. *June 20, 1960*

Governor Quinn, Admiral Felt, and all members of the armed services here in Hawaii, and my friends:

It is a signal privilege that is mine to land here on this beautiful island for the first time since it has been a State.

As your Governor has said, this is something that had been on my heart for a long time, and more particularly since 1942. To my theater was sent the first Japanese-American unit, the 100th Battalion, which covered itself with glory in a number of hard fought fields. Then came the 442d, and apparently the desire to enlist was so great that it was an over-strength regiment. Every man seemed to be anxious to prove not only his loyalty to his adopted country, to America, but his readiness to die for the principles that that country stands for.

To both those units and particularly to every man here who was ever a part of those two units, I send my warmest and affectionate greetings, and render them the salute due to brave men.

Hawaii, I think, should long have been a State for another reason. Here we have a true example of men living together in human dignity, men of every race and creed that can possibly exist on this earth. And they have lived so together to their mutual benefit, mutual profit, and their mutual satisfaction—and possibly even deeper than that, to their mutual self-respect.

I cannot tell you what good I believe can come out of the effort or the activities that will go on here in Hawaii, where it will act as really the meeting place between the Western and Eastern Hemispheres in the Pacific.

I understand the East-West Center is really getting off the ground and going. I can't imagine anything better than for us to use this place, and by this I mean Hawaiians using this opportunity in this area to bring about a better feeling between the peoples bordering the Pacific all the way around, so that among us we may live in greater strength, in greater cooperation, and in mutual harmony.

So it is truly an eventful day for me. I thank the members of the Honor Guard for coming out, and each citizen for doing me the courtesy to come out here today in order that I might greet them.

Thank you very much.

NOTE: The President spoke at 12:15 p.m. In his opening words he referred to Governor William F. Quinn of Hawaii and Adm. Harry Donald Felt, Commander in Chief, Pacific Fleet.

206 ¶ Remarks at Hickam Air Force Base, Honolulu, Upon Leaving for Washington. *June 25, 1960*

Governor Quinn, Admiral Felt, officers and men of the armed services, and my friends of Hawaii:

All of you have made my few days here in Hawaii a memorable experience, a most pleasant and enjoyable one—and indeed an instructive one. I have learned more about your history, your industrial development, your agriculture, your educational and cultural pursuits.

And incidentally, I want to say from all I have heard about this East-West Cultural Center, that I assure you that you have my prayers for its great success. I hope it will be supported properly, because I am quite sure it will be one mechanism through which the friendly States bordering the Pacific ocean will be brought closer together.

Now I cannot, of course, thank each of you individually for all you have done to make the stay here of my party and myself so enjoyable.

There is only one thing actually you could have done for me, and that was to show me how to beat number nine at Kaneohe. It looks easy, but it fooled me.

To all of you, my thanks, my heartiest *alohas* and my prayers that this State is going to develop to fulfill the highest aspirations and hopes and dreams of all of your people—particularly those who have done so much to bring about the present state of development in this lovely region—and those who saw that it should be indeed a sister State of the Union.

I am indeed proud that Governor Quinn has handed to me this medal, because it was for me a very great honor to urge Statehood for Hawaii and to sign the bill that made it a State.

So again as I go, thanks to all of you—particularly to everybody I saw that was grinning and shouting along the road the other day, when I left this city.

Thank you very much. Goodbye.

NOTE: The President spoke at 4:30 p.m.
In his remarks he referred to Kaneohe,
the Marine Corps Air Station where he
stayed during his stopover in Honolulu.

The medal presented to the President
was inscribed as followed: "The Aloha
State, August 21, 1959—Hawaii, 50th
State."

207 ¶ Message to President Tsiranana on the Occasion of the Independence of the Malagasy Republic. *June 26, 1960*

[Released June 26, 1960. Dated June 25, 1960]

Dear Mr. President:

On the occasion of the independence of the Malagasy Republic, I extend in my own name and on behalf of the people of the United States most cordial greetings and felicitations to you and your countrymen.

The independence of the Malagasy Republic achieved in friendly co-operation with France is a source of deep satisfaction to the United States. The Government and people of Madagascar and of France in their efforts to achieve social and economic advancement in Madagascar through democratic means have earned the admiration of all free nations.

On this historic occasion the Government and the people of the United States look forward to close and friendly relations with the Government and people of the Malagasy Republic.

Sincerely,

DWIGHT D. EISENHOWER

208 ¶ Remarks Recorded for the Governors' Conference at Glacier National Park, Montana. *June 27, 1960*

Governor Boggs, Governor Aronson, members of the Governors' Conference, friends and guests:

I am recording this message on the eve of my departure for the Far East.

Ever since I addressed you in Seattle 7 years ago, I have been concerned with the problems that engage the interest of the Nation's Governors and the Federal Government.

Our common philosophy through the years, I think, can be thus expressed:

The first responsibility of the Federal Government is to maintain the Republic strong and safe and free; to create a favorable climate for the expansion of the national economy; to carry out the Constitutional guarantees of full equality under law for all persons; to promote the general welfare wherever and whenever national action is necessary to insure common objectives.

The first responsibility of State governments is to provide all those services, necessary to the welfare of our people, which can best be provided by legislatures and executives close to the people; sharply aware of local needs; free from the need to compromise conflicting claims by section and region.

Through a preceding period, the traditional role of State governments within our Federal Government was, or at least seemed to be, in the process of reduction to secondary status.

At Seattle, I expressed to you my conviction that this role had to be restored and maintained.

Moreover, I pledged frequent consultation with you concerning our mutual problems.

Only so, I felt, might be developed a true partnership between the National and State administrations.

The first step was an examination of the situation.

That was accomplished by the Kestnbaum Commission on Intergovernmental Relations—the first official study of Federal-State relations since our Constitution was written.

Thereafter, 3 years ago in Williamsburg, I proposed that the National government and the States cooperate in establishing an action committee to consider the many facets of Federal-State relations.

Congress last year, with my approval, enlarged this joint enterprise into a continuing, permanent, advisory commission with membership representing all levels of American government.

Accomplishments are measurable.

In areas of responsibility where the States have major concern—education, highways and public works, health, welfare and conservation—they are spending twice as much today as they were 10 years ago.

This increase in money is an accurate index, I think, to the increase in the States' acceptance of responsibility—an index to the restoration of the traditional role of the State governments.

Take one example.

At your conference in New York in 1954, the Vice President presented on my behalf a proposal that the States and the national government work together on a gigantic project to modernize our nationwide highway system.

You approved and appointed a committee to work jointly with the Committee appointed by me.

Together, we developed the greatest highway program in our history.

Nine thousand miles of the interstate system are now completed.

Another two thousand are scheduled for completion this year.

Of course, the program needs more money. But with your help, this money will be found.

On many fronts, we have been engaged in an exciting and historic effort to make our unique Federal system work, and to work better.

Our cooperative effort, I am certain, will be carried forward and improved upon by our successors.

Certainly, in the talks I shall have overseas during the next 2 weeks, I can speak with greater assurance than ever of our success and strength in representative government, with greater confidence that we shall continue our advance toward a more effective democracy at home, a more vigorous leadership in the world.

In that sense, the trip ahead of me is a sequel to the philosophy and the programs that have joined us in mutual effort.

Before closing, I should like to pay my respects to your distinguished guest, the Prime Minister of Canada—the outstanding leader of our neighbors and partners and friends to the north. And on behalf of all our people, I salute him and the nation he represents.

To all of you and to the representatives of our neighbors to the south, my best wishes for a productive and successful conference.

NOTE: The President recorded the message on June 11. In his opening words he referred to Governor J. Caleb Boggs of Delaware and Governor J. Hugo Aronson of Montana. In his closing remarks he referred to Prime Minister John Diefenbaker of Canada.

209 ¶ Radio and Television Report to the American People on the Trip to the Far East. *June 27, 1960*

[Delivered from the President's office at 7:30 p.m.]

My friends:

I have just returned to Washington from a trip to the Far East. It has been a trip so marked by events of significance that I shall try this evening to give you a simple background of fact, against which these recent events can be viewed in perspective.

To begin, a few personal observations on the trip I have just concluded:

First, American relations with the Philippines, Taiwan, Korea and Okinawa have been strengthened.

Second, the people of these Far Eastern lands took advantage of the opportunity given by this visit to demonstrate anew their long and ardent friendship with and for the people of America. The American people are gratified, I am sure, as am I, by these heartwarming demonstrations.

Third, the ratification of the Mutual Security Treaty between the United States and Japan represents an important victory for the Free World—a defeat for international communism.

And now, let's look at the background of this trip—and the others I have taken in the interest of world peace.

This trip was planned as one of a series which have, in toto, taken me nearly around the world, to twenty-seven nations of Europe, the Middle East, South Asia, North Africa, the Americas, and the Far East. Those nations I have visited during the last ten months have populations reaching an aggregate of over a billion people.

To understand where these visits fit into the over-all foreign relations of this government we must go back to 1953, to the time when I was assessing the world situation with the late Secretary of State Dulles, preparatory to my assumption of the office of the Presidency.

At that time we recognized that the Communists had, for some years following the conclusion of World War II, taken advantage of the chaotic aftermath of conflict—and of our own self-imposed military disarmament—to indulge in a continuous campaign of aggression and subversion in Asia and Eastern Europe. They had disrupted the lives of millions of free people, causing lowered living standards and exhausted economies. China and its half billion people had been lost to the Free World. The war in Korea, then in condition of stalemate, still dragged on.

We began our studies with one essential fact before us. It had become clear, by 1953, that the accumulation of atomic weapon stockpiles, whose use could destroy civilization, made resort to force an intolerable means for settling international disputes. Only in the rule of law—which meant the attainment of an enduring peace with justice could mankind hope for guarantee against extinction.

With these facts in mind we concluded, and have since been guided by the conviction, that there were several things which we should do simultaneously, all of them in conformity with the ideals expressed in the Charter of the United Nations.

It was, and is, mandatory to present before the world, constantly and vigorously, America's great desire for peace and her readiness to sit at the conference table to discuss specific problems with anyone who would show an equal readiness to negotiate honestly and in good faith. This we continue to do in spite of difficulties such as the regrettable action of the Soviet delegation in walking out of the 10-nation Disarmament Conference at Geneva this morning. But, from the very beginning we have made it clear that until real progress toward mutual disarmament could be achieved, our first concern would be to keep our own defenses strong, modern, and alert.

We tried to identify all those areas in the world where serious trouble could erupt suddenly, and developed suggestions for correcting the causes of unrest and of enhancing stability in such localities. Through cooperation with our friends we have succeeded in removing causes of friction in many of these areas.

In support of these purposes, we have sought, from the beginning, frequent personal contact with responsible governmental officials of friendly nations. Indeed, we have felt it wise, also, to seek to improve communications between ourselves and the Soviet government. Akin to this effort was one which has come to be called the people-to-people program—a completely new type of venture in international relations which has been amazingly successful.

Along with these objectives, we have constantly striven to devise better methods of cooperation with our friends, working out with them programs by which together we could improve our common security and raise living standards. Our Mutual Security Program has been and is a vital means of making such cooperation effective.

To carry out the purpose of proclaiming and demonstrating to the world America's peaceful intentions, we first made a number of policy statements and a series of concrete proposals that might lead to fruitful discussions with the Soviets.

As early as April of 1953, I suggested disarmament talks with the Soviets and pledged that I would urge the United States to apply a substantial portion of any savings realized through mutually acceptable disarmament to the improvement of living standards in the less developed nations.

Later that year I proposed, before the United Nations General Assembly, that we devote all discoveries in atomic science to peaceful uses. Nineteen months later at Geneva I suggested the Open Skies method of mutual inspection.

In the meantime, the Secretary of State set out tirelessly to make calls on friendly governments and to strengthen collective security. In return we issued invitations to Heads of State to visit America and her people. Other good will visits were concurrently made by the Vice President and other personal representatives.

Many Heads of Government or State responded promptly to our invitations to visit this country. In the past seven and a half years, more than seventy Heads of State and Prime Ministers have come to the United States (some of them several times) in visits extending from a few days to some weeks. In this respect the period has been without precedent. Other visitors are to come in the near future. Indeed, tomorrow we shall be honored by the arrival in Washington on such a visit of the King and Queen of Thailand, and later in the year the Crown Prince and Princess of Japan, and the King and Queen of Denmark.

I early began to receive urgent invitations to make return visits to the countries whose Heads had paid us the courtesy of coming to see America and our way of life

Many months ago we concluded that I should personally accept some of these invitations, as opportunity should present itself. Secretary Herter, first as Under Secretary of State and later as Secretary of State, enthusiastically concurred. Overseas visits by me, all of us felt, would be a strong support of other successful programs.

The great value resulting from these journeys to twenty-seven nations has been obvious here and abroad. Throughout the world there has been opportunity to emphasize and re-emphasize America's devotion to peace with justice; her determination to sustain freedom and to strengthen Free World security through our cooperative programs; her readiness to sacrifice in helping to build the kind of world we want.

These visits involved, of course, valuable conversations between Heads of State and Government, as well as the promotion of understanding among peoples.

However, except for so-called Summit and the NATO Heads of Government meeting, none of my visits has been planned or carried out solely as a diplomatic mission seeking specific agreements, even though discussions have invariably involved important issues.

Incidentally, I believe that Heads of State and Government can, occasionally, and preferably on an informal basis, profitably meet for conversations on broad problems and principles. They can, of course, also convene to give solemn approval to agreements previously prepared by normal diplomatic methods.

But Heads of Government meetings are not effective mechanisms for developing detailed provisions of international compacts, and have never been so considered by this government.

On the other hand, the good will aspects of a visit by a Head of Government can frequently bring about favorable results far transcending those of normal diplomatic conferences. They have resulted in the creation of a more friendly atmosphere and mutual confidence between peoples. They have proved effective in bringing closer together nations that respect human dignity and are dedicated to freedom.

Indeed it seems apparent that the Communists, some time ago, reached the conclusion that these visits were of such positive value to the Free World as to obstruct Communist imperialism. Thus they have sought every possible method to stop them. Through their propaganda they bitterly opposed my entry into the Philippines, in Taiwan, in Okinawa, in Korea, and, of course, Japan.

In Paris last month they advanced false and elaborate excuses for cancelling my invitation to visit the Soviet Union, when all that was necessary to say was that they found it inconvenient to receive me.

With their associates in Peiping, they went to great lengths and expense to create disorders in Tokyo that compelled the Japanese government to decide, under conditions then existing, that it should revoke its long-standing invitation for me to visit that sister democracy.

These disorders were not occasioned by America. We in the United States must not fall into the error of blaming ourselves for what the Communists do; after all, Communists will act like Communists.

One clear proof of the value, to us, of these visits is the intensity of the opposition the Communists have developed against them.

Respecting Japan, in spite of the outrageous conduct of a violent and disorderly minority, I have been assured that the people there were, in overwhelming majority, anxious to welcome me as a representative of a nation with which they wished to cooperate and to have friendly relations.

Of course, the basic objective of the Communist-inspired disorders in Tokyo was to bring about the rejection by the Japanese government of the Treaty. That the Communists were defeated in their frantic efforts to prevent ratification of that Treaty speaks well for the future of Japanese-American relations. Obviously that signal defeat for International Communism far outweighs, in importance, the blocking of my scheduled visit.

Another purpose of the Communist-inspired riots in Tokyo was to weaken confidence between our peoples and to persuade the United States to change its basic policies toward Japan. It would be a tremendous victory for International Communism if we were to permit the unhappy events of the past several weeks in Japan to disrupt our economic relationships with that nation; or to weaken the feeling of friendship and understanding which unites the vast majority of the Japanese and American people.

Japan has once again become a great nation. Over the postwar years she has painstakingly created a new image of herself, the image of a responsible, peaceful and cooperative Free World nation, mindful of her obligations and of the rights of others. Japan has made a fine record in the United Nations as well as elsewhere on the international stage.

Since the loss of mainland China to the Communists in 1949, the need to link the other nations of the Far East with the United States more strongly, in their mutual interest, should be apparent to all. We seek, and continue to build and strengthen these links, with Japan as well as with the other countries, by actions of many kinds—of which my recent trip was but a single example. In the present circumstances, a Far

Eastern policy of "waiting for the dust to settle" will not meet the Free World's need.

The other free countries of the Far East, small in relation to the massive area and immense population of Red China, can survive in freedom and flourish only in cooperative association with the United States and a free Japan. Through our aid programs, through our bilateral and collective defensive arrangements such as SEATO, through our very presence in the area, we help them greatly. And a free and friendly Japan can reinforce this American effort, as indeed she is already doing through aid programs of her own.

Because of the Prime Minister's necessary withdrawal of his urgent invitation of last winter for me to visit Japan on June 19th, I was of course unable to meet with the Japanese Government and people, or to bring to them assurances of American good will. This was disappointing, but we should not forget the favorable effects of visits elsewhere in the Far East, as well as the final approval of the Japanese-American treaty by both Governments. Moreover, the general improvement that has come about through exchanges of visits by friendly Heads of Government is recognized and appreciated throughout the Free World.

I wish that every one of you could have accompanied me to Manila, Taipei, and Korea and thus witnessed for yourselves the outpouring of friendship, gratitude and respect for America. The throngs of people there, like the many millions who, during earlier journeys, lined the streets of great cities in the Mid-East, Europe, North Africa, South America—as well as in Canada and Mexico—had one overwhelming message for our nation.

That message, expressed in glowing faces, friendly shouts, songs, gaily painted placards, and home made signs, was that they wanted to be partners with the United States. They share our ideals of dignity of man and the equality of all before the law—they believe in their God; they believe that the American people are their friends. They believe that Americans are sincerely devoted to their progress which means so much to them, and which is so evident on every side.

These demonstrations have been inspiring to all who have not closed their eyes and minds to their meaning. Moreover, the leaders of the free peoples I have met here or abroad have assured me, privately and publicly, that they approve of America's purposes and policies, even though details of implementation are frequently subjects for discussion or negotiation. They have expressed the hope that visits to their countries by the senior officials of our Government might be of greater frequency. They have shown to me evidence of their marked material progress through American cooperation. They have testified to the reborn hope and restored confidence of their peoples.

Let me stress, however, that all the profit gained by past and any possible future trips will be quickly dissipated should we Americans abandon our present course in foreign relations or slacken our efforts in cooperative programs with our friends.

This is what the Communists want. It is imperative that we act with mature judgment.

We must recognize their tactics as a deliberate attempt to split the Free World, causing friction between allies and friends. We must not fall into this trap; all of us must remain firm and steadfast in our united dedication to freedom, and, to peace with justice.

Above all, we must bear in mind that successful implementation of any policy against Communist imperialism requires that we never be bluffed, cajoled, blinded or frightened. We cannot win out against the Communist purpose to dominate the world by being timid, passive, or apologetic when we are acting in our own and the Free World's interests. We must accept the risks of bold action with coolness and courage. We must always be strong but we must never forget that peace can never be won by arms alone; we will be firm but never truculent; we will be fair but never fearful; we will always extend friendship wherever friendship is offered honestly to us.

Now a final, personal word—

So far as any future visits of my own are involved, I have no plans, no other particular trip in mind. Considering the shortness of the time before next January, and the unavoidable preoccupations of the few months remaining, it would be difficult to accept any invitation for me, again, to go abroad.

But so long as the threat of Communist domination may hang over the Free World, I believe that any future President will conclude that reciprocal visits by Heads of friendly Governments have great value in promoting Free World solidarity.

And this I assure you. If any unforeseen situation or circumstances arising in the near future should convince me that another journey of mine would still further strengthen the bonds of friendship between us and others, I would not hesitate a second in deciding to make still an additional effort of this kind.

No consideration of personal fatigue or inconvenience, no threat or argument would deter me from once again setting out on a course that has meant much for our country, for her friends, and for the cause of freedom—and peace with justice in the world.

Thank you and—good night.

2 1 0　¶ Memorandum to Federal Agencies on the United Fund and Community Chest Campaigns. *June 28, 1960*

To the Heads of Executive Departments and Agencies:

Last year, Government personnel demonstrated their individual concern for the health and welfare of their fellow men by voluntarily helping to raise part of the record $455,000,000 collected throughout the Nation during the United Fund and Community Chest campaigns.

Again this coming fall the United Community Campaigns will seek our support for 27,000 national—and local—health, welfare and recreational organizations. The American National Red Cross will be included in a number of these, along with other national organizations, such as the Salvation Army, the USO, the Scouts and the Y's. By united charity, we are able to support the work of hospitals, clinics, visiting nurses' associations and homes for the sick and aged in our local communities. We are also able to strengthen various recreational and character-building groups working among our youth.

The Honorable Thomas S. Gates, Jr., Secretary of Defense, has agreed to serve as Vice Chairman of the United Community Campaigns for the Federal Government. He merits our heartiest cooperation.

We, in Government, must bear our full citizens' share in the great humanitarian efforts which advance the welfare of our fellow citizens and communities. The support given by you and your personnel in the past has been heart-warming. I know that Government employees will continue their fine record of voluntary giving.

DWIGHT D. EISENHOWER

211 ¶ Remarks of Welcome to the King and Queen of Thailand at the Washington National Airport. *June* 28, 1960

Your Majesties and members of our visiting party from Thailand, and friends:

Your Majesty, it is indeed a great privilege to welcome you to this country. The record of the friendly relationships between our two countries is a bright one, and it is therefore with unusual pleasure that we welcome here in this country the head of that nation.

You will find, sir, in all parts of this Nation a similar readiness to bid you welcome and to express their friendship for your fine country in southeast Asia. We sincerely trust that the journey that you make through our country will be for you and for Her Majesty, the Queen, very interesting and enjoyable, and indeed we hope to some extent instructive, as you will learn more of our country and of our people and of their way of life, just as visitors to your country learn about yours.

So, sir, again welcome to you and to Her Majesty, and our very best wishes for an enjoyable stay in our Nation.

Thank you.

NOTE: The President spoke at 12 noon. King Bhumibol Adulyadej responded as follows:

Thank you so much, Mr. President, and thank you for the kind words you have just spoken now, and for the rousing welcome you have given us. In fact, we have arrived in this country when we set foot on the island of Hawaii, just on the 14th, and then to California and to Pittsburgh. Everywhere we received a very friendly welcome. So we are all very grateful to you, Mr. President, for making this visit possible.

And before coming on this tour, I had told my people the object of such a state visit; that is, when we are friends, between friends and relatives we like to go and visit each other, for the ties of friendship; but now, with nations, it is quite impossible for the people of each nation— 24 million of them—for my people to come and visit your 190 million people in this country. So I have to come as the head of state and as their representative.

That is why I am here, and the people understood very well. The day we left Bangkok they gave us a very big send-off and they showed by that they were quite ready to give me support and to give their good will. So now, as the representative of my people, I bring to you as the representative of the American nation the greetings and the good will of the Thai people.

Both countries have had long and very happy relations for a long time. That is because we have the same convictions. We say that we cannot have happiness without freedom and independence. Since we have been here we have seen many similarities. Among the similarities, in dress—ordinarily, privately, the Thai people don't like to dress too formally, they like to be easily comfortable, as you people do. And between

537

meals we take snacks, as you do. But the difference is in the food—you have popcorn, you have hot dogs and ice cream. Oh, that is very good. We have noodle soup. And we have pickled fruit. So among the differences we have many similarities. And especially in the train of thought; that is, we like to live simply. And above all, we like freedom.

Now this visit is something more for me personally. In Thailand we say—we call the motherland the land of our birth, the land where we live (*the King spoke in Thai*). I was born here in this country, so I can say that the United States is half my motherland. This visit is somewhat of a sentimental journey, and this I feel with quite genuine emotion in coming back here. I say, "coming back here." I never say "come" or "go" to the United States. I say return to the United States. All that emotion gives me the conviction that our visit here will be of great use for the strengthening and reinforcement of the bonds of friendship which have existed for a long time already between the United States and my country.

So I thank you once again, Mr. President.

212 ¶ Citation Accompanying Legion of Merit, Degree of Chief Commander, Presented to the King of Thailand. *June* 28, 1960

THE PRESIDENT of the United States of America, authorized by Act of Congress, July 20, 1942, has awarded the Legion of Merit, Degree of Chief Commander, to

HIS MAJESTY, KING BHUMIBOL ADULYADEJ

COMMANDER-IN-CHIEF, ROYAL THAI ARMED FORCES

for exceptionally meritorious conduct in the performance of outstanding services:

His Majesty, King Bhumibol Adulyadej, defender of the faith and Commander-in-Chief of the Royal Thai Armed Forces, has since his coronation on 5 May 1950, served as a symbol of unity and steadfastness in the Free World. His Majesty's manifold tasks have demanded sagacity and breadth of vision in perceiving that in a turbulent world swept by war and ideological conflict, causes of freedom required collective efforts and mutual aid devoted to the interests of his country and preservation of its freedom and ways of life. His Majesty has been a staunch supporter of the South East Asia Treaty Organization since its inception in 1955 and has significantly contributed to its growth and development. His Majesty's personal efforts through extensive travel to other nations have been singularly fruitful in developing a closer understanding among these countries. Indicative of the marked progress of

His Majesty's Armed Forces under his guidance and leadership is the high esteem accorded to them by the United Nations Command, Korea, and all nations of the Free World.

NOTE: The President made the presentation at the White House at 7:40 p.m.

213 ¶ Toasts of the President and the King of Thailand. *June* 28, 1960

Your Majesty the King, Your Majesty the Queen, ladies and gentlemen:

It is a very particular privilege that we have this evening in welcoming to this city and to this house the King and Queen of Thailand. Fortunately, between these two countries there are no great problems. Our history is that of friendship. And the experience that I have had over the last few hours with the King and Queen convinced me that we are just personal friends as well as official. We welcome them not only as the head of a friendly and great state of Southeast Asia, but as a true friend.

Now I have seen some speculation in papers, and heard it, as to what heads of state can possibly talk about when they meet. People worry about this. Now so far as we are concerned, we can talk of course about the differing cultures. I can't tell him much about ours, because he was born here. But I can learn something about his, which is helpful. But by and large those are subjects that are just, I say, auxiliary to our main purpose, and that is to find out what each is like.

Well, he likes noodle soup. He said so publicly today, and so I think we have the right to ask him for the recipe. After all, I have four grandchildren who demand that the old gentleman occasionally get out and take charge of a cookout; and when I can surprise them with a new dish, it's a great triumph, and if I can do it with noodle soup, sir, I am going to be very grateful to you.

So this is the kind of thing we talk about. And he showed me reproductions of his paintings, which he tells me he has been practicing only a few months. I promptly retired my brushes, because he is talented and mine is what you would call a daub.

I find that they have four children, one boy and three girls. That's just how many grandchildren I was able to get, so everything seems to be going along splendidly on the basis of friendship.

What I am trying to say in this rather round-about fashion is that it is indeed a pleasure and a great privilege and honor to meet someone who bears the responsibilities that fall upon the King in his country, in his great country of 24 million people, and still who comes with the same family concerns, the same human feelings toward his children, toward what he and his wife are doing, as each of us does. This kind of thought brings us closer.

So when I ask you to stand and drink a Toast this evening to the King and to the Queen, and to the happiness and prosperity of the people of Thailand, I do so not as just my duty to ask you to drink a Toast to the head of a friendly state, but to true and real friends of America. Ladies and gentlemen, the King!

NOTE: The President proposed the toast at 10:12 p.m. at a state dinner at the White House. King Bhumibol responded as follows:

Mr. President and ladies and gentlemen:

In a formal dinner like this, I usually have this prepared speech to read to you, but this speech has been prepared for many days, so perhaps it would not reflect the true sentiment that is in our heart, only what we thought that would be. I had put in about the appreciation of the kind words. Well, I appreciate very much the very kind words and touching words that Mr. Eisenhower just spoke now. I wanted to tell you that since our arrival in this country we have received many marks of friendship and good will.

Now, tonight, I have experienced something more, to know, really know, Mr. Eisenhower, Mrs. Eisenhower, personally—and to know like I thought they were: very human. So this is the confirmation of my—what you call thoughts that I had thought beforehand.

And so I don't have anything to say very much because Mr. President has stolen my words—something about the noodle soup. It's the same thing as I asked Mr. President to make ice cream for me. Well, I asked the recipe for ice cream, and perhaps I will find out the recipe for noodle soup so I can give to Mr. President for his grandchildren.

And ice cream is the delight of my children. They have, since their arrival in the United States, always asked for ice cream, and yesterday, as a parting or as a farewell ice cream party, we brought them to an ice cream shop near Los Angeles and they enjoyed it very much.

So for all this, I must say that it is because Mr. President has invited us to come that it has been possible to show my children what a great country America is. And all the people here are so friendly. That is a great lesson to show our children, that the world is big and everybody is friendly if you are friendly.

Now I want you to rise and drink to the health of Mr. Eisenhower, Mrs. Eisenhower, and to the great American nation.

214 ¶ Letter to the President of the American Red Cross on the Nation's Voluntary Disaster Relief in Chile. *June* 29, 1960

Dear General Gruenther:

Your heartwarming preliminary report of our Nation's voluntary relief efforts in Chile was on my desk when I arrived home.

The total value of cash and supplies donated by our people was most gratifying to me. It symbolizes an even greater asset: namely, the united response of Americans—of all creeds and races—to their neighbors in need.

This great outpouring of charity has served as a most human supplement to the official relief actions taken by our Government on behalf of our stricken friends in Chile. I am sure it will help them to recover from the shattering effects of disaster. This whole experience serves to strengthen the bonds of affection and respect which unite our two countries.

I would like to make an additional comment about one section of your report which carried particular promise. That was the part dealing with the needs of the 80,000 stricken school children of Chile and the major effort by our young people on their behalf. I am proud that the youth of America are demonstrating their concern for these children. This is further proof that our best traditions are in good hands!

With warm regard,

Sincerely,

DWIGHT D. EISENHOWER

NOTE: General Gruenther's preliminary report was enclosed in a letter to the President dated June 24, 1960. The report outlined the activities of each of the voluntary agencies participating with the American Red Cross in the relief effort.

In his letter General Gruenther stated that the response of the American people to the President's appeal for aid to the victims of the Chilean earthquake had been very gratifying, and that, as of July 24, the total value of cash and supplies contributed was nearly $4,500,000.

The letter and the report (9 pp., mimeographed) were released with the President's reply.

215   ¶ Remarks at the AFL–CIO Testimonial Dinner in Honor of Secretary of Labor James P. Mitchell.   *June 29, 1960*

Mr. Chairman and distinguished guests:

I feel that there is something possibly symbolic about my appearance here this evening.   I stand in front of you in plain view and for some years I have been the target for some of the sharpest barbs that some of you had to launch in my direction.   And I don't know of any time when I have been more exposed than I am this moment.

But there are two specific areas outside of our common patriotism and love of country in which I find myself always in agreement with the AFL–CIO and indeed the other unions here represented.   Those two are:

In our recognition that we are but one nation in the world and that our own prosperity, our own progress, and our own peace depend upon our friendship with other nations and our leadership with them in the paths of peace.

And second, our common admiration for your guest of honor, Jim Mitchell.

Now I would like to talk for just a moment about these two subjects. Time and again I have been encouraged in heartwarming fashion by the members of all our unions in efforts to increase the spirit of friendship and the depth of understanding between this nation and other nations who, like us, believe in the dignity of man and his possession of the inalienable rights given to him by his Creator.

There is in the Cabinet a committee that has as its job trying to better markets through the world so that our economy may prosper as we help others to prosper.   As their purchasing power rises, our prosperity rises with it.   This is the kind of thing that we understand together, and this is the kind of thing in which the AFL–CIO has always been in the forefront in supporting.

I cannot tell you how much this has meant to me, because there are those short-sighted people who believe that by building around ourselves walls—walls of guns and walls of tariff—that we can live in a secure and prosperous isolation.

My friends, you at least—the people of your organizations—have shown that they recognize the falsity of any such belief and, indeed, have been on the positive side, working to destroy such illusions and delusions in this country. Fortunately, the number of the people that so believe are diminishing. I am completely sure that part of that result has been because of your enlightened efforts. And for this, on behalf of the entire nation, I must thank you.

Now I get to my second subject, Jim Mitchell. I was once told by a very distinguished soldier that practically every general's reputation as it was recorded in history was the result of his skill in picking a chief of staff.

I rather think that if I am going to live in history, one of the reasons is the wisdom I had in selecting Jim Mitchell as Secretary of Labor.

He and I both have learned this about the leaders of labor. They may not see eye to eye with us always, but they respect a man of courage, of honesty, of integrity and who tries to dig under the facade of slogan, of wisecrack, and to get at the facts—get them out so that peoples looking together at the same problem are not talking about something that is false or disorted but things as they are, the realities of situations.

I have had the great good fortune of having Secretary Mitchell at my side now these 7 years. For that good fortune I thank the Almighty. Secretary Mitchell has constantly championed the cause of labor, as such, and its right to get its proper due. The people who with their hands and their heads and their thinking produce the wealth of this country are entitled to their proper dues and at the same time saying that in a free enterprise country if we are to be preserved as such, we must recognize the needs for profit, because if there are no profits, there will be no investments, and free labor as we know it will not continue to exist.

This is the kind of thing he has taught, the kind of thing he has preached, outside and within the confines of the Cabinet Room.

Each of us—you of labor—we of Government—have got a very deep responsibility to the United States, the Nation that we believe under God is destined to lead the entire earth to better paths—finer paths—toward peace and justice in this world.

And so I think, regardless of the points of difference you have found and discovered and criticized within this administration—which is your right—but I say this: no man has ever been more dedicated to the idea of whatever is good for the United States is good for labor than has Jim Mitchell.

And therefore, as I salute you—all of you—of the labor movement,

I salute him and his family who are so fortunate to be here as part of the group that you are honoring along with him this evening.

Thank you and good night.

NOTE: The President spoke at the Statler Hilton Hotel in Washington. His opening words "Mr. Chairman" referred to George Meany, President of the AFL–CIO.

216 ¶ Message to President Kasavubu on the Occasion of the Independence of the Republic of the Congo. *June* 30, 1960

Dear Mr. President:

On the occasion of the independence of the Republic of the Congo I extend in my own name and on behalf of the people of the United States most cordial greetings and felicitations to you and the Congolese people.

The independence of the Republic of the Congo is a source of deep satisfaction to the United States, especially since this freedom was achieved in friendly cooperation with Belgium. The attainment of independence by 13.5 million Congolese is one of the most significant events in Africa during this unprecedented year of 1960.

On this historic occasion the Government and people of the United States look forward to close and friendly relations with the Government and people of the Republic of the Congo.

Sincerely,

DWIGHT D. EISENHOWER

217 ¶ Veto of a Bill To Increase the Salaries of Federal Employees. *June* 30, 1960

To the House of Representatives:

I return herewith, without my approval, H.R. 9883, a bill to increase the salaries of Federal employees.

Whenever I have been presented with legislation providing for increases in Federal salaries that were justified and warranted, I have unhesitatingly given my approval to such legislation—and I would gladly do so again.

H.R. 9883, however, is indefensible by any light. This hastily drawn bill violates every concept of fairness, every rule of reason and logic. Were this measure to become law, the already conspicuous unfairness and discrimination in our antiquated Federal pay system would be greatly intensified. Instead of making progress—by improving the Federal pay structure—we would actually be taking a long step backward.

The money cost of all this retrogression—not to mention its intangible costs—would impose an annual burden on the American taxpayer of three quarters of a billion dollars, and the money would not be wisely spent. Such fiscal and legislative irresponsibility, and particularly the bill's basic unfairness and the discrimination it would perpetuate, offend all thinking citizens, Federal employees among them, and make this legislation entirely unacceptable.

More specifically, H.R. 9883 is defective in the following respects:

1. The bill totally ignores the recognized precept that the only sound basis for setting Federal salaries is reasonable comparability to rates paid for similar work in private industry. Judged by this standard there is reason to believe, from such information as is now available, that a number of Federal salaries already exceed private rates of pay for similar work and, conversely, that other Federal salaries are below corresponding private compensation. H.R. 9883 in no respect addresses itself to these disparities and, in fact, actually perpetuates and intensifies them.

Furthermore, in the haste to pass some kind of pay legislation in this particular year, the national salary survey currently being made by the Department of Labor to ascertain the comparability of Federal salaries, grade-by-grade, with those paid in private business was completely ignored—notwithstanding that the Congress itself appropriated $500,000 to finance it. This survey, which will be completed in September,[1] was intended to provide a sound and defensible basis for adjustments in the Federal pay structure—and it still will. To that end, such recommendations as are indicated by the survey and other relevant evidence will be made to the Congress in January.

2. The inequities already present in our Federal pay structure would be sharply accentuated by H.R. 9883. It increases by the largest

---

[1] The "National Survey of Professional, Administrative, Technical, and Clerical Pay, Winter 1959–60" (49 pp., Government Printing Office, 1960) was released by the Bureau of Labor Statistics, Department of Labor, December 4, 1960.

A related report of the President's Committee on Government Employment Policy on "Trends in the Employment of Negro-Americans in Upper-Level White-Collar Positions in the Federal Government" (4 pp., mimeographed) was released by the White House on October 5.

percentages those salaries which are already apparently in excess of compensation rates for similar work in private industry. On the other hand, the lowest percentage increases are accorded those who appear to be underpaid in relation to their counterparts in private business. To thus heighten the present distortion would be grossly unfair and highly discriminatory.

3. Even within itself H.R. 9883 is manifestly unjust. For a large number of employees it would increase salaries by nearly 9%, but for others performing exactly the same work the increase would be only slightly over 7½%. Further, employees in the postal field service would, in general, be given larger percentage increases than those provided for nearly twice as many persons who are compensated under the Classification Act and other statutory pay schedules.

4. The claim by proponents of the bill that the pay increases it would provide are justified by a rise in the cost of living is utterly without foundation in fact. Since June of 1958, when a 10% pay increase for Federal employees was approved, the cost of living as measured by the Consumers' Price Index has advanced 2.1%. More importantly, since the beginning of this Administration in January of 1953, Federal civilian employees have received two general pay adjustments, increasing average salaries 17½ to 20 percent in the aggregate, while during the same period the Consumers' Price Index has advanced less than 11 percent.

5. By not providing offsetting revenues for the $248 million a year it would add to Post Office Department costs, the bill stands in complete disregard of the policy which the Congress itself established in 1958 that postal revenues should approximately equal postal costs less those costs deemed attributable to the performance of public services. The consequences of this disregard, were H.R. 9883 to become law, would be to increase the postal deficit, which must be met by the American taxpayer, to $851 million a year.

6. The bill would unwarrantedly extend Federal retirement and life and health insurance benefits to employees of locally-elected county stabilization and conservation committees who are not Federal employees because not appointed or supervised by Government officers. The Federal system should apply only to Federal employees. The legitimate needs of these people for such retirement and insurance opportunities should be met and the Department of Agriculture, accordingly, has for some months now been exploring means by which the Government

might appropriately act. I have asked the Secretary of Agriculture to expedite these efforts.

Looking to the future, I urge the Congress, in accordance with my recommendation of last January, promptly to enact legislation which will make permanent the 2½ percent temporary salary increase accorded postal field service employees two years ago in 1958. That increase is now scheduled to expire in January of next year, so action prior to adjournment of the current session is advisable.

With regard to general pay legislation, I am convinced, as I have indicated, that it is not presently required and should not be enacted until we can at the same time intelligently modernize our pay system. Evidently, however, this view is not shared by the Congress. In an effort to resolve the difference, therefore, I would be willing at this time to approve a modest increase reasonably commensurate with the percentage rise in the Consumers' Price Index since the last general pay increase became effective. This is the only increase that could possibly be justified under present circumstances. In fairness to the American taxpayer, however, new postal revenues should be provided sufficient not only to offset the cost of any such increase to the Post Office Department, but also to eliminate the current postal deficit.

I must preface my following remarks on another aspect of this legislation by emphasizing that I have an abiding admiration and respect for the great mass of those who work in the Government service. It has been my privilege to have lived and worked with them, in Washington and throughout the world, for half a century. They deserve and rightfully expect fair and enlightened treatment, in personnel matters, on the part of the Government. At the same time, with regard to their remuneration, they desire only that the accepted principles of reward for merit, length of service and especial competence be followed. I bear all of this in mind in what I am about to say and I wish to make it clear that the remarks which follow are directed only to a small minority, and in particular their leadership, of what are in the main a fine and outstanding group of public servants.

The other aspect of this legislation to which I refer is unrelated to its merits and is to me deeply disturbing. I am informed that the enactment of H.R. 9883 was attended by intensive and unconcealed political pressure exerted flagrantly and in concert on Members of Congress by a number of postal field service employees, particularly their leadership.

I fully respect the legal right of every Federal employee—indeed of all our citizens—to petition the Government. But the activity of which I have been advised so far exceeds a proper exercise of that right, and so grossly abuses it, as to make of it a mockery.

I am further informed that, in anticipation of my disapproval of this bill, it is planned to resume these deplorable tactics, to an even greater degree.

That public servants might be so unmindful of the national good as to even entertain thoughts of forcing the Congress to bow to their will would be cause for serious alarm. To have evidence that a number of them in the postal field service, led by a few, have actually sought to do so is to say the least shocking. Were the pressure tactics surrounding the passage of this bill, and apparently further intended in the event of its veto, widely known to the American people, their indignation and outrage in all its power would be quickly felt—and rightly so.

Dwight D. Eisenhower

NOTE: On July 1, 1960, the Congress passed the bill over the President's veto. Thereupon the Press Secretary issued a release stating that for the second time pressure and pork barrel tactics had overridden a Presidential veto. "Nevertheless," the release added, "the President will not abandon—but will continue unabated—his efforts to further responsibility in government."

As enacted, H.R. 9883 is Public Law 86–568 (74 Stat. 296).

218   ¶ Joint Statement Following Discussions With the King of Thailand.   *July 1, 1960*

THE PRESIDENT of the United States and His Majesty the King of Thailand have held a friendly and useful exchange of views on matters of mutual interest.

Their Majesties the King and Queen of Thailand are visiting the United States upon the invitation of the President. At the conclusion of their stay in Washington on July 2, during which His Majesty the King addressed a joint session of the United States Congress, Their Majesties will begin a twelve-day coast-to-coast tour of the United States, during which they will meet with various civic, cultural and business leaders.

The President recalled the fact that the King was born in the United States and expressed the hope that this personal link would enhance the pleasure of His Majesty's visit to the land of his birth.

The President expressed great admiration for the steps taken under the King's leadership to foster the economic and social development of Thailand in harmony with the aspirations and ideals of the Thai people. He voiced profound respect for the moral inspiration which the King's devotion to the welfare of his people continues to provide.

In their review of the world situation, the President and the King expressed their mutual concern with the vital problem of preserving freedom and independence as well as achieving lasting peace and establishing a world order based on international justice. They reasserted their determination to work towards these goals, the achievement of which will contribute immensely to the general progress, prosperity, and welfare of mankind. They noted that the staunch adherence of Thailand and the United States to the Southeast Asia Treaty Organization demonstrates a mutual belief in the indispensability of collective security as a means of preserving the frontiers of the free world from aggression and of promoting the peaceful objectives shared by both countries. The President took this occasion to pay tribute to the steadfast partnership of Thailand and the United States in all fields and reaffirmed to His Majesty the unwavering determination of the United States fully to honor its treaty commitments undertaken in the cause of collective security.

The President and the King expressed a common belief in the ideal of enhancing human dignity as the well-spring by which a free society prospers and is nourished. They agreed that the American and Thai peoples are dedicated to abiding respect for the principles of the sovereignty and independence of nations and of genuine noninterference in the affairs of others. They voiced their profound conviction that any attempt by any nation to impose its own economic system or political beliefs on any other country should be condemned.

In recalling the long and fruitful tradition of friendship which binds the United States and Thailand the President assured the King of the continuing determination of the United States to assist the Royal Government of Thailand in its noble objective of promoting the economic and social development of the country for the lasting benefit of the Thai people. The President and the King expressed their mutual desire to maintain and further to strengthen the bonds of close and cordial collaboration between Thailand and the United States, both directly and through the United Nations and other appropriate international organizations in which the two countries share membership, confident that in so doing they are responsive to the highest aspirations of their peoples for a world in which peace, freedom and the sanctity of human dignity are honored and cherished.

219   ¶ Message to President Osman on the Occasion of the Independence of the Somali Republic. *July* 1, 1960

Dear Mr. President:

It is with the greatest of pleasure that I extend in my own name and on behalf of the people of the United States most cordial greetings and heartfelt congratulations upon the independence of the Somali Republic.

We share deeply in your joy in this occasion for not only does a new state join the family of nations but your country's accession to independence marks the successful conclusion of another United Nations trusteeship. This, understandably, is a source of great pride and satisfaction to all who have dedicated themselves to making the United Nations an effective instrument of world peace and progress and I am confident that in the years to come your country will strengthen the ranks of those devoted to this noble purpose.

The Government and people of the United States welcome the independence of your country and look forward to a lasting friendship with your Government and people.

Sincerely,

DWIGHT D. EISENHOWER

220 ¶ Message to President Nkrumah on the Occasion of the Accession of Ghana to the Status of Republic. *July* 1, 1960

Dear Mr. President:

Upon the accession of your country to the status of Republic and upon your inauguration as its first President I extend in my own name and on behalf of the people of the United States most cordial greetings and felicitations to you and your countrymen.

In the more than three years of close relations between an independent Ghana and this country strong bonds of friendship and mutual interests have developed. It is the sincere hope of the Government and people of the United States that these bonds will continue to grow stronger in the years to come.

Sincerely,

DWIGHT D. EISENHOWER

221 ¶ Statement by the President on the United Nations Freedom-From-Hunger Campaign. *July* 1, 1960

ON THIS DAY, the Food and Agriculture Organization of the United Nations has begun an international Freedom-from-Hunger Campaign. The basic objectives of this campaign are to raise levels of food production and nutrition for the people of the world. These objectives have the earnest support of us all.

The world is confronted by two great problems in hunger: The needs of the present and the future. And the last is greater than the first. We must try to raise the level of nutrition for many millions who now subsist on an inadequate diet and we must find new sources of food for the rapidly expanding family of man.

To achieve this end, all countries will have to exert supreme efforts and inventiveness.

The United States took an active part in the formation and development of the Food and Agriculture Organization. We continue to support it as an instrument for intergovernmental consultation, for the exchange of information, and to sponsor separate and collective actions by its member countries in raising levels of nutrition. We wish the Director General of FAO and his staff all success as they carry forward their Program of Work of which this Campaign is a special part. Through our Food-for-Peace efforts we are advancing the objectives of the Campaign, and we are working with other countries in the common task of improving humanity's standard of living which gives substance to our hopes for the peace and freedom of all peoples.

222   ¶ The President's News Conference of July 6, 1960

THE PRESIDENT. Good morning. Please sit down.

Do you have any questions?

Q. Merriman Smith, United Press International: Mr. President, I wonder if you could give us your general reaction to the situation in Cuba. Is there any limit, Mr. President, to this country's policy of nonintervention, and is there anything that can or will be done about the expropriation of American-owned property?

THE PRESIDENT. Well, first of all, the Sugar Act just passed by the Congress—it came to my desk just a few minutes ago with the reports from the several departments, and along with that there are our plans for staff study and conferences with me during the course of the day. And I am sure that there will be something said on the whole situation—if not today, then early tomorrow.

And I think the part of wisdom, therefore, would be not to make any casual statements until that has been done.

Q. David Kraslow, Knight Newspapers: Mr. President, Senator Johnson said yesterday that we can look forward to the establishment of a Russian submarine base in Cuba. First, sir, do you agree with his estimate and, secondly, assuming that this occurs, what would you suggest that the United States and the other nations of the hemisphere do, if anything?

THE PRESIDENT. Well, I think there is not only the Caracas Resolution, but there is the OAS that is constantly—has a permanent body in which these things are assessed and what might be done about them.

Now I am not going to make any guesses about the possibilities of which the Senator spoke. Always there are such possibilities in the world, but I don't think it is a likelihood. I do say that through the OAS, but if necessary to protect our own interests and to make sure that we are not threatened, why we would have to act as we saw fit.

Q. Ray L. Scherer, National Broadcasting Company: Sir, can you conceive of a situation where a Russian military base and a United States base would coexist on Cuban soil?

THE PRESIDENT. Well, I don't believe I will comment or try to predict on that one.

Q. Mr. Scherer: Mr. President, you have traveled almost 100,000 miles in the cause of peace this past year and yet, for a number of reasons, your hopes have not been fulfilled. It has not been possible to reach a detente with the Soviet Union. There was no summit, and the Japan visit was canceled. Could you tell us how you feel about all this, in personal terms—whether, for instance, you think it might affect your place in history, and what part these recent developments in foreign policy might play in the election campaign?

THE PRESIDENT. Well, you certainly asked a big question. [*Laughter*]

Well, let's dismiss the simple part at once. My place in history will be decided by historians, and they will probably give consideration to these years and to the war years that they think they deserve, and then they will make a conclusion. And I don't think I will be around to differ with them.

Now, as to the effort to produce better understanding among the free nations, and in the hope that this will lead to a better road for seeking out agreements—negotiations—with the Iron Curtain countries—the Soviets—of course, I have worked on this for a long, long time, and I tried in my talk of a couple weeks ago to try to put this thing in perspective. I see no reason, either, for despairing because such successes as were achieved were not all that you would like to have been. On the other hand, I see no reason for getting pessimistic and not continuing to work.

And I said then, I believe that any future President will find some value in the occasional visit to other countries, and certainly I know that if he is going to respond to the American wishes—the wishes of the American people—he is going to be doing his very best to promote peace. Now, that is all I can say.

Q. Lloyd M. Schwartz, Fairchild Publications: Mr. President, an increasing number of economists appear to be expressing the view that a recession may be edging up on us or may actually be under way. I wonder what your own assessment is of the economic prospects.

THE PRESIDENT. Will you name the economists?

Q. Mr. Schwartz: Well, one in particular is the research director for the Investment Bankers Association, who says that we actually may already be in such a recession.

THE PRESIDENT. I have seen two letters from interested parties, but in the second quarter our GNP was $503 billion, which is an alltime high. In May, the last month for which we have figures, the employment went up a million. The personal income is over 400 billion.

Now, the one thing on which they must be predicting this recession is the fact that steel is operating on the order of 50 percent.

Now, there are two things to remember. One, that such a tremendous capacity—productive capacity of steel—was built in the few years in the past that now the 50 percent activity is something on the order of 75 some very few years back. And possibly there is a reserve capacity that is a very good thing. And you would not expect it to operate at 100 percent all the time, because then you would have to build some more and then you would still have a low percentage or a lower percentage.

And the other thing is right after the conclusion of the steel strike, everybody was astonished by the rate of steel production. And inventories were built up, and there is not now the same demand that there was at that moment.

That is the only thing that I know on the horizon that gives legitimate cause for the concern these people have expressed.

Q. Rowland Evans, Jr., New York Herald Tribune: Governor Rockefeller of New York, sir, made a series of statements recently questioning the relative position of the United States versus the Soviet Union. Specifically, he says that we have declined in terms of military, psychological, and economic strength in relation to the Soviet Union.

I wonder, sir, whether you agree with the Governor's assessment, and, too, what effect do you think his campaign along these lines will have on the Republican Party politics?

THE PRESIDENT. Well, now, let's talk about this thing, about defense and how we have declined militarily. I have put in, I think it is now, a total of eight budgets. In five of those budgets the Congress has reduced the amounts for which I asked. Three of those budgets—and only incidentally I remark that they were election years—they have raised those budgets. Now, what I am at least getting at is this: that the judgment of the Executive Department, which is reached after—well, tortuously, you might say, through the long channels that have to follow before you get to the making up of the budget, has been, by and large, approved by the Democratic-controlled Congress during these years. There is not, in other words, a very great deal of difference between us.

Now, there are individuals, of course, who get very deeply concerned, and possibly even worried, about some of these things and believe that just more money would do a better job.

I will say the Governor is not only entitled to his own opinions but is entitled to express them. And I don't believe that that mere expression will itself tend to wreck any party. That is—it happens to be his conviction; it is not mine.

Q. John M. Hightower, Associated Press: Mr. President, Mr. Khrushchev has set up his plans so that shortly after a new administration takes office, he may be in position to make very radical or dramatic proposals with respect to Berlin, and so on. Have you given any thought yet, sir, to the idea of a transitional arrangement with a new administration respecting foreign affairs?

THE PRESIDENT. Well, I'd say only this: When the election is carried out and the results known, my successor, no matter who he may be, will be given every facility to familiarize himself with every going policy, every activity, every connection we have, and he and his associates that he will appoint to take the place of my associates will be given like opportunity, so that this Government can go forward according to the convictions of the administration that comes in and can be informed in so doing.

Now, so far as Mr. Khrushchev's opinions on this and his statements are concerned, I don't believe that either party is—should be—concerned about them, and I don't believe they are concerned about them. They are very crude attempts to involve himself and his influence, if any, in this country into our affairs, and I don't believe that either side is going to try to find any advantage in whatever his advice to both of us may be.

Q. Charles W. Bailey, Minneapolis Star and Tribune: Sir, in the light of your two terms in the White House, I wonder if you could give us your judgment, all other things being equal, on the importance of age as a factor in choosing a President.

THE PRESIDENT. Well, I don't suppose there is any ideal age, because we've had people of all ages. As a matter of fact in my own case, if the good Lord allows me to fill out my term, I'll be the oldest man that ever served in this office.

Now, I have not, in spite of three illnesses, felt that physical defects or a weakness has been any decisive factor with me and in the way I have conducted my office. At times I may doubt a little bit my mind and intellectual capacity and my good judgment, but I'll tell you one thing: I never doubt my own heart and where it stands with America. And I don't think that the physical has had a great deal to do with whatever good I've been able to accomplish or the mistakes I have made.

Q. Raymond P. Brandt, St. Louis Post-Dispatch: Mr. President, have you received a report on the amount of the Treasury surplus for 1960, and have you made an estimate of how much, or guess as to what, the 1961 surplus will be?

THE PRESIDENT. Well, we've got an estimate, but it has not yet been finalized, and therefore I don't want to put the figure out prematurely. I do think it is fair to say that, respecting the '61, after all, we asked for the money that would make up the Post Office deficit and to raise the taxes for aviation gasoline and the tax we—the additional half cent we asked for in highways, of course, went into the trust fund and not into the budget. On top of that, there has been a great deal of money, including just an $800 million slug just the other day for each year; so it would be a miracle if the surplus for '61 should be what I then estimated.

But let's remember that that budgetary estimate lays down the conditions on which it is made; that is, the additional revenues and the estimate as to the prosperity of the country at the time.

Q. John V. Horner, Washington Star: Mr. President, on the subject of Cuba, is the United States making any serious efforts to get across its story to the Cuban people so they will fully understand, some time in the future, that our quarrel is not with them but with the present policies of their present government?

THE PRESIDENT. Yes, we are. Now, I haven't had a recent report as to how effective that is. But that is exactly what we are trying to do.

And I have stated before this group time and again we not only have no quarrel with the Cuban people, we want to be their friends and, indeed, I think we both need each other. They are great producers of sugar, and we consume—or we import—something like over 3 million tons a year from them. It seems to me we have a very fine mutually beneficial arrangement. And it is only the inexplicable actions of the government that caused the trouble, as we see it.

Q. L. Edgar Prina, Washington Star: Mr. President, you and Mr. Nixon have just had a long political talk, we understand. Can you tell us anything about how active a role you plan to play in the coming campaign?

THE PRESIDENT. Well, the only thing I know at this moment, I am to be at—I'm to make a talk on the night of the 26th at the Republican Convention and to be there the following morning for breakfast. And then my wife apparently gets a free lunch, and then we are going on from there.

Q. Mr. Prina: But beyond that——

THE PRESIDENT. Now, beyond that there are no plans made that I know of.

Now, I do have, for some reason, an unusual number of prior engagements for nonpolitical meetings and all over the place, but I haven't got any political engagements made for the time being, except that one.

Q. Spencer Davis, Associated Press: Communist China has been contending that war is inevitable with the capitalist countries, and the Soviet Union has been saying otherwise. What is your opinion of this and to what extent should it guide our future policies?

THE PRESIDENT. Well, you mean in the effort to split these two peoples apart, or what do you mean—in our policy in avoiding war? What are you talking about?

Q. Mr. Davis: Our policy in meeting the threat of a nation that believes war is inevitable.

THE PRESIDENT. Well, I will say this: if you will go back into the writings of Lenin and even, I think, you will find it in Stalin's book on the problems of Leninism, these same statements were made. Now, as these people have gotten more productive, they have a much bigger collection of productive mechanisms. In other words, they have accumulated wealth, and they've also got a great arsenal of powerful weapons; I think that there is—there comes a time when their views as to the methods they will use to dominate the world should be—might be changed. And I think that there is a change going on there that probably the Red Chinese have not yet decided upon. As of this moment, they seem to be much more belligerent and much more, you might say, quarrelsome than are their associates.

But I would think this: just as always in this world, vigilance, alertness, and strength are the base from which you must work, as you try to bring about conditions in which these things will not come about.

Q. David P. Sentner, Hearst Newspapers: Mr. President, as a followup to that subject, would you care to comment on the statement of Khrushchev in Austria that he would like to have the Communist flag fly over the whole world during his lifetime?

THE PRESIDENT. Well, I think he once said in that same statement that he wasn't talking about doing it by violence and by war; he said this was a hope of his, but he said not an expectation.

Now, I may be quoting from a reporter from your newspapers; I'm not sure. But he said it was a hope and not an expectation.

In other words, they, the Communists, have never retreated one step from their conviction, their belief, that the Communist flag ought to fly over the whole world from pole to pole. And so their intention is still the same.

Q. Robert C. Pierpoint, CBS News: Mr. President, in view of Premier Khrushchev's derailment of East-West negotiations in the last few months, do you see any way that we could get these talks and negotiations back on the track during the remainder of your administration?

THE PRESIDENT. I have directed and I've made sure that there is a clear understanding on the part of the Soviets that we are ready to talk any time, honestly and without any equivocation or evasiveness, on the problems that have been attracting our attention—I mean our common attention. These are disarmament, nuclear testing, liberalizing movements, and exchange of ideas, and all that sort of thing between our two sides.

Q. Lillian Levy, Science Service: Mr. President, on the subject of disarmament, what were the plans we would have presented on nuclear disarmament at Geneva had not the Russians walked out, and has their walkout affected our decision concerning the resumption of nuclear testing?

THE PRESIDENT. Well, to take the second part, the nuclear testing, there is not yet any indication that they intend to walk out on these particular negotiations.

The five nations on our side—Canada, Italy, Britain, ourselves, and France—that are the part of the 10-nation conference, are staying there for a while, because this gives them such a fine opportunity to refine and agree upon the details of the plan that we should—would have submitted to the Russians on the day they walked out.

Now, this plan has been exposed in its general terms and, as I say, is now undergoing some refinement, and that's all there is to be done on this thing.

Q. Laurence H. Burd, Chicago Tribune: Mr. President, this is the first press conference we've had in 8 weeks, and part of that time you've been away, but part of that time you've been in the city. My question is: do you base your decision on whether or not to hold a press conference on some policy consideration, apart from the time element that you have, or how do you decide whether or not to hold a press conference?

THE PRESIDENT. Well, as a matter of fact, I suppose that there is some little bit of whim that comes in there once in a while. But, in fact, I don't try to be talking all the time. I don't try to take charge of the microphone and carry that as my baton.

But the fact is now, one week I made a speech on Monday. I said about all on the subject then that seemed to be engaging the headlines that I could think of, and there seemed to be very little reason for a press conference. And then, as you say, I'm away at times, and other things come up. Whenever the day seems to be free and I can do it, well, frankly, I enjoy many of them, you know. And so it is not any running out on the thing; it's just, as I say, how it happens to strike me, I guess.

Q. Felix Belair, New York Times: In the matter of nuclear testing, Mr. President, I think it is now approaching 2 years since we volunteered the ban on further testing, and there have not been, of course, any controls or assurance that Russia is not continuing its tests. Is it the intention to continue the ban on our testing as long as the negotiations continue, in view of—what I am getting at, Mr. President, the charge frequently heard that this is gambling with the national security, of which we'll hear more in the weeks ahead, I am sure.

THE PRESIDENT. As of this moment, of course, we are actually proposing certain tests in which the three countries will participate and on, you might say, an equal basis so far as that can be established. There are very many legal and technical problems or obstacles to overcome, and our hope would be that in this matter we would have this much—we would have a sufficient, you might say, assurance—sufficient assurance of progress and of honest intent on the part of the other fellow that we could afford to stand for a few more months without testing.

Now, I've made quite clear about—I think it was about last January, or something of that kind—that our promise no longer held. We had said we will not test in the atmosphere, we will not do anything to pollute it. We reserved the right, however, if we cannot get any kind of agreement, to make such underground tests as we would choose.

Well, that decision has not been changed. On the other hand, when we will make a decision that we now have to go in our own—in the interests of our own security and defense—that is one that has to be made when we see what happens. I can't—I must say it hasn't been too hopeful in its outlook, but I think it is still worthwhile pressing for some kind of an agreement.

Q. Charles H. Mohr, Time Magazine: During the period right after the summit, Mr. President, when Mr. Khrushchev was releasing a whole waterfall of words and abuse about you, he made a statement that at Camp David you had said that you weren't in favor of German reunification, and that's been dealt with by a White House statement. But it seems Mr. Khrushchev is embarrassed somewhat now because of his own friendly attitude during this period, in view of the Chinese attacks on him. Can you tell us some of the concessions he might have suggested at Camp David and some of the other things that had passed between you on this Berlin question over the months in communications?

THE PRESIDENT. Well, frankly, this talk, like between most heads of state, heads of government, was of informal character, taking from one end of the spectrum and going to the other. And the only concession that was made that I know of was the one that I announced the following morning, I think—let's say Tuesday or Wednesday after that—I guess even before this body, that so far as his attitude on Berlin and his policy on Berlin was concerned he had removed the time limit.

You remember, he had had a time limit that at first he put 6 months, and then he hinted at another one, and he said there would be no time limit, although he said he wanted to negotiate honestly, and we said we wanted to negotiate honestly always, having in mind the basic problem of the reunification of Germany.

Now, that was all that was—that I remember of a substantive concession made by him and certainly we didn't make any, because we didn't have any to make.

Q. Charles W. Roberts, Newsweek: Sir, in the past, you have praised Governor Rockefeller as a good Republican. Has your view of him changed, or do you still consider him qualified for a place on the Republican ticket?

THE PRESIDENT. Well, I don't know what I've said—I've said this: I've had a good number of years of experience with Nelson Rockefeller, and I have found him a dedicated, honest, hard-working man, and that's what I still think about him. Now this doesn't mean that I necessarily agree with all the conclusions that he has made in a number of fields.

Q. Roscoe Drummond, New York Herald Tribune: Mr. President, I would like to return to an earlier question and ask whether you feel, in view of the great uncertainty of foreign developments, after the election there should be close and recurring personal consultation between you and the incoming President regardless of who is elected?

THE PRESIDENT. Well, I don't feel—after all, just like it takes two to make a fight, it takes two to make an agreement. And assuming that any individual wants this kind of consultation, he will certainly find me quite ready and willing.

Now, I would say this: in my own case, I found that to get into the documents, the budgets that were being proposed at that time—you see, I have to make up a '62 budget and propose it; I have to make up a State of the Union Message, and a whole—recommendations, including those about my convictions about the necessary reorganization of Government and all that. Now, we do have those documents which I think would do him more good than too many—just talks. But he will always be welcome to come in, I assure you.

Q. Kenneth M. Scheibel, Gannett Newspapers: Mr. President, in view of the recent election in North Dakota, do you think the Republican Party ought to adopt a new farm program, or some new policies?

THE PRESIDENT. I don't think any general policies. I will say this: right now I think it would be very good for the farmers, to take this one— this troublesome wheat thing—and pass the bill that the Senate did pass and sent over to the House.   It has not been passed yet, and I think it would be a very great thing for them.

Actually, we talk about the farm problem like there is just one.   There are as many farm problems as there are commodities, as there are different localities in this country, and it is a real mishmash of problems.   And there is nobody that I know of that is ever going to cure it completely by governmental action.   And anyone that believes that either the economic or the general economic or, more specifically, the farm problems are going to be cured completely by legislation is fooling himself.   That's all there is to it.

Marvin L. Arrowsmith, Associated Press: Thank you, Mr. President.

NOTE: President Eisenhower's one hundred and eighty-sixth news conference was held in the Executive Office Building from 10:31 to 11:02 o'clock on Wednesday morning, July 6, 1960.   In attendance: 215.

223   ¶ Statement by the President Upon Signing Bill and Proclamation Relating to the Cuban Sugar Quota.   *July* 6, 1960

I HAVE today approved legislation enacted by the Congress which authorizes the President to determine Cuba's sugar quota for the balance of calendar year 1960 and for the three-month period ending March 31, 1961.   In conformity with this legislation I have signed a proclamation which, in the national interest, establishes the Cuban sugar quota for the balance of 1960 at 39,752 short tons, plus the sugar certified for entry prior to July 3, 1960.   This represents a reduction of 700,000 short tons from the original 1960 Cuban quota of 3,119,655 short tons.

This deficit will be filled by purchases from other free world suppliers.

The importance of the United States Government's action relating to sugar quota legislation makes it desirable, I believe, to set forth the reasons which led the Congress to authorize and the Executive to take this action in the national interest.

Normally about one-third of our total sugar supply comes from Cuba. Despite every effort on our part to maintain traditionally friendly relations, the Government of Cuba is now following a course which raises serious question as to whether the United States can, in the long-run, continue to rely upon that country for such large quantities of sugar.   I believe that we would fail in our obligation to our people if we did not take steps to reduce our reliance for a major food product upon a nation which has embarked upon a deliberate policy of hostility toward the United States.

The Government of Cuba has committed itself to purchase substantial quantities of goods from the Soviet Union under barter arrangements. It has chosen to undertake to pay for these goods with sugar—traded at prices well below those which it has obtained in the United States. The inescapable conclusion is that Cuba has embarked on a course of action to commit steadily increasing amounts of its sugar crop to trade with the Communist bloc, thus making its future ability to fill the sugar needs of the United States ever more uncertain.

It has been with the most genuine regret that this Government has been compelled to alter the heretofore mutually beneficial sugar trade between the United States and Cuba. Under the system which has existed up to this time, the people of Cuba, particularly those who labor in the cane fields and in the mills, have benefited from the maintenance of an assured market in the United States, where Cuban sugar commands a price well above that which could be obtained in the world market. These benefits also reached many others whose livelihood was related to the sugar industry on the island.

The American people will always maintain their friendly feelings for the people of Cuba. We look forward to the day when the Cuban Government will once again allow this friendship to be fully expressed in the relations between our two countries.

NOTE: The act (Sugar Act Amendments) is Public Law 86–592 (74 Stat. 330). Proclamation 3355 "Determination of Cuban Sugar Quota" is published in the Federal Register (25 F.R. 6414). See also Item 373.

224 ¶ Memorandum of Disapproval of Bill for Relief of Juan D. Quintos and Others. *July 7, 1960*

[Released July 7, 1960. Dated July 6, 1960]

I AM withholding my approval from H.R. 1516, "For the relief of Juan D. Quintos, Jaime Hernandez, Delfin Buencamino, Soledad Gomez,

60295—61——39

Nieves G. Argonza, Felididad G. Sarayba, Carmen Vda de Gomez, Perfecta B. Quintos, and Bienvenida San Agustin."

The bill would waive the applicable statute of limitations and confer jurisdiction upon the Court of Claims to hear the claims of these individuals for losses of jewelry, coins, relics, and currency which were somehow included in one of four large wooden boxes delivered to the United States High Commissioner to the Philippines by the Philippine National Bank in response to the Commissioner's direction, in December 1941, that the bank deliver to him "all cash reserves, bullion, negotiable securities, and other negotiable papers held by your bank, or held by you in trust for others." The purpose of the directive was to prevent such items from falling into the hands of the enemy who, at that moment, was invading the islands. When the property of these claimants was discovered, it was turned over to a representative of the Philippine government, who rejected suggestions of United States Army officers that it be sent out on an American submarine. Instead, he voluntarily placed the property in a safe at Corregidor where it was confiscated by the Japanese. From these facts it is apparent that the possibility of a valid claim against the United States is very remote.

More importantly, these claimants had ample opportunity to present their claims in a timely manner. Under the applicable statute of limitations, they had until December 1947—two years after the end of the war—to file suit in the Court of Claims. They had five months after the Treasury Department, on July 25, 1947, advised that there was no statute or appropriation permitting the administrative settlement of such claims. They waited, however, for four years, until 1951, before petitioning the Court of Claims.

Nothing in the record justifies special treatment for these claimants, particularly when it is remembered that many others filed suit against the United States in the Court of Claims for damages arising out of incidents in the Philippines during the war years and had their cases dismissed because of the expiration of the statute of limitations.

DWIGHT D. EISENHOWER

225 ¶ Memorandum of Disapproval of Bill To Provide for the Economic Regulation of the Alaska Railroad Under the Interstate Commerce Act.
July 7, 1960

[Released July 7, 1960. Dated July 6, 1960]

I AM withholding my approval from S. 1508, a bill "To provide for economic regulation of the Alaska Railroad under the Interstate Commerce Act, and for other purposes."

I cannot approve the bill because it would (1) subordinate certain of the President's statutory powers to those of a regulatory commission, (2) allow a State to regulate a Federal agency, and (3) apply to the Alaska Railroad laws, rules, and procedures which are intended solely for application to privately owned and operated railroads and which are completely inappropriate for a Government agency established to carry out a public purpose.

The power to construct and operate the Alaska Railroad and to set the rates charged by it are vested in the President. To subject the President's exercise of these powers to the review and perhaps disapproval of the Interstate Commerce Commission would be repugnant to our constitutional system.

By allowing the State of Alaska to regulate the Railroad, which is a Federal agency, the bill violates the principle that the Federal Government's authority shall be supreme. Under S. 1508, the State could thwart public purposes declared by the President and the Congress, but it would have no responsibility for the success or for the financing of the Railroad.

The laws, rules, standards, and procedures concerning tariffs, rates, accounts, services, and employees of private railroads are not suited to a Government agency. Accounting standards established by the Interstate Commerce Commission for private railroads cannot, for example, assure the President and the Congress of adequate control over the use of Federal funds by a Federal agency. In requiring the Commission to consider the needs of Government financial agencies, and in other exceptions it makes, the bill itself recognizes that standards applied to private industry cannot be applied to the Alaska Railroad.

By extending the Employers' Liability Act to cover the Alaska Railroad's liability to its employees, who are already covered by the Federal Employees' Compensation Act, the bill may give this group of federal employees either dual compensation from the Federal Government for a single injury or the right to choose between two methods of obtaining compensation. Either result would be inconsistent with the federal workmen's compensation policy that all employees be treated equally.

The President and the Congress have ample authority to insure that the Railroad operates in the public interest. In due course, it will be determined that the Railroad's federal purposes have been achieved. At that time the Congress should authorize disposition of the Railroad to a non-Federal agency, and it would then automatically become subject to Interstate Commerce Commission regulation.

Dwight D. Eisenhower

226   ¶ Memorandum of Disapproval of Bill for Relief of Sam J. Buzzanca. *July* 7, 1960

I AM withholding my approval from H.R. 6712, a bill "For the relief of Sam J. Buzzanca."

Mr. Buzzanca, at a Federal tax sale in 1954, purchased certain real estate which had an estimated market value of $21,000, but which was subject to a mortgage prior in time to the Federal tax lien. It was announced at the tax sale that principal and interest in the amount of $8,320 was due under this prior mortgage. The real estate was sold to Mr. Buzzanca for $8,100—far less than the amount of the Federal tax lien which exceeded the market value of the property.

Two months later the holder of the first mortgage, who also had acquired whatever rights the heirs of the delinquent taxpayer and former owner had in the property, successfully sued Mr. Buzzanca to obtain possession of the property. Although the United States was not a party to this action, the District Director for the area did render informal assistance to Mr. Buzzanca. On appeal, the Supreme Court of Alabama affirmed.

Mr. Buzzanca's claim for relief appears to rest on the contention that the first mortgagee obtained a judgment for possession of the property because the tax sale to Mr. Buzzanca was defective and did not convey to Mr. Buzzanca the former owner's interest.

Internal Revenue Service records reveal no defect in the seizure and sale. This being so, Mr. Buzzanca has no ground for complaint against the United States. Because the existence of the first mortgage was made known at the time, the tax sale did not purport to convey rights superior to a valid first mortgage.

The United States cannot and does not attempt to warrant or defend title to property seized and sold under the internal revenue laws. No warranty is available to a purchaser at a tax sale and a deed is not a warranty of the title conveyed. The right, title, and interest conveyed is derivative, and the purchaser acquires only the interest of the delinquent taxpayer. To compel the United States to warrant and defend the title to all property sold by it for taxes would be costly and inadvisable.

For these reasons I cannot, on the facts at hand, approve this bill for it would create a precedent that would encourage dissatisfied purchasers at Federal tax sales to ask Congress to underwrite their losses and guarantee their titles.

Were Mr. Buzzanca, however, to adduce direct evidence establishing incontrovertibly that the tax deed in question was defective, I would of course be willing to sign a similar bill subsequently enacted.

DWIGHT D. EISENHOWER

227   ¶ Statement by the President Concerning Premier Khrushchev's Announcement of Support for the Castro Regime in Cuba.   *July* 9, 1960

THE STATEMENT which has just been made by Mr. Khrushchev in which he promises full support to the Castro regime in Cuba is revealing in two respects. It underscores the close ties that have developed between the Soviet and Cuban governments. It also shows the clear intention to establish Cuba in a role serving Soviet purposes in this hemisphere.

The statement of the Soviet Premier reflects the effort of an outside nation and of international Communism to intervene in the affairs of the Western Hemisphere. There is irony in Mr. Khrushchev's portrayal of the Soviet Union as the protector of the independence of an American nation when viewed against the history of the enslavement of countless other peoples by Soviet imperialism.

The Inter-American system has declared itself, on more than one occasion, beginning with the Rio Treaty, as opposed to any such interference. We are committed to uphold those agreements. I affirm in the most emphatic terms that the United States will not be deterred from its responsibilities by the threats Mr. Khrushchev is making. Nor will the United States, in conformity with its treaty obligations, permit the establishment of a regime dominated by international Communism in the Western Hemisphere.

NOTE: Mr. Khrushchev's statement was made in Moscow on July 9 in an address to a group of teachers from the Russian Soviet Federal Socialist Republic. The President's statement was released at the U.S. Naval Base, Newport, R.I.

228 ¶ The President's News Conference at Newport, Rhode Island. *July* 11, 1960

THE PRESIDENT [*reading*]. During my trip to South America in February and in numerous talks in Washington, I have obtained the views of leading Latin American statesmen on the problems which their countries and the area in general now face. They have told me of the aspirations and needs of their peoples for homes and land and a better life, and of their efforts to meet those needs.

I know that other leaders in the Americas are thinking and working along similar lines. I have given a good deal of thought to how the United States might do more in helping these efforts.

The National Advisory Committee on Inter-American Affairs, which I appointed last year to advise the Secretary of State and myself on matters of hemispheric concern, has given us the benefit of its knowledge and experience.

II.

Within the Organization of American States, joint action is underway. The Council of that Organization, on the initiative of Venezuela, voted three days ago to call a meeting of their Foreign Ministers to consider matters of extreme gravity in the Caribbean area—matters that involve a challenge to the ideals and purposes of the American community. The United States supported this move.

In September, the economic representatives of the twenty-one American Republics will convene in Bogotá, Colombia, to consider an equally important component of our hemispheric future—the problem of social reform and economic growth. This problem is embraced within a joint hemispheric concept known as Operation Pan-America—a concept initially suggested by President Kubitschek of Brazil. This will be further developed at Bogotá.[1]

These two meetings will give the United States opportunities for frank consultations with our sister republics on measures to advance the political, economic, and social welfare of the peoples of the Americas.

III.

I believe it would be well for me to state the basic ideas which will guide the United States' participation in these forthcoming meetings.

First, widespread social progress and economic growth benefiting all the people and achieved within a framework of free institutions are the imperatives of our time.

Second, our nation's history and traditions place us in accord with those who seek to fulfill the promise of the future through methods consistent with the dignity of free men. Our interests and sympathies are with them.

Third, a new affirmation of purpose is called for in our cooperation with friendly developing countries in their efforts to progress.

In the Americas as elsewhere change is the law of life, and the interests of the people will be better served if that change is effected constructively and peacefully, not violently. Clearly, the aspirations and needs of the peoples of the Americas for free institutions and a better way of life must be met. Our desire is to help the American nations to meet their own responsibilities—to help them develop their institutional and human resources, to strengthen the framework of freedom, to protect individual dignity, and to gain a better life for those who are underprivileged, underemployed and undereducated.

Latin America is passing through a social and political transformation. Dictatorships are falling by the wayside.

---

[1] A statement released July 8 by the Press Secretary to the President noted that the President had been working with the Department of State for some time on a comprehensive plan to be submitted to the meeting at Bogotá "in the hope of making more effective our mutual cooperative work in raising the living and social standards of our respective populations." "The plan," the statement further noted, "will deal particularly with methods for making United States participation more effective."

Moderate groups, seeking orderly reform, are contesting with dictators of both right and left who favor violence and authoritarianism. Many of the extremists frequently endeavor to introduce dogmas which are inimical to the traditions of the Western Hemisphere. Indeed, the Foreign Ministers of the American Republics met last August in Santiago, Chile, to consider the problems caused by the blatant intervention of certain extremists in their neighbors' affairs.

The interests of the United States no less than those of all the Americas are directly involved in this struggle, a threat to the security of the hemisphere. It is imperative that institutions be developed and strengthened sufficiently to permit the peoples' needs to be met through orderly processes of change.

A renewed hemispheric determination to preserve principles of liberty and the dignity of man is needed. There is also an urgent need for a broader and more vigorous cooperative attack by all American governments and peoples if adequate economic progress with freedom, is to be achieved.

IV.

Among the specific needs which it seems to me must be met through cooperative action are:

First, we need to consider with the other American Republics practicable ways in which developing countries can make faster progress in meeting their own needs and ways in which their friends can most effectively cooperate with them. A better knowledge and mobilization of resources, their more effective use, and the improvement of legal and institutional means for promoting economic growth are among the subjects which require special consideration.

I have in mind the opening of new areas of arable land for settlement and productive use. I have in mind better land utilization, within a system which provides opportunities for free, self-reliant men to own land, without violating the rights of others. I have in mind housing with emphasis, where appropriate, on individual ownership of small homes. And I have in mind other essential minimums for decent living in both urban and rural environments.

Second, in our common efforts towards these goals more attention needs to be given, in a manner which respects the dignity and rights of all, to improving the opportunities of the bulk of the population to share in and contribute to an expanding national product. Soundly based economic and social progress in any of our countries is of benefit to all. Each nation must of course resolve its own social problems in its own way and without the imposition of alien dogmas.

Third, within this framework we need to consider whether there are better ways to accelerate the trend which is already evident toward greater respect for human rights and democratic government based on the will of the people as expressed in free and periodic elections. The United States with its tradition of democracy is opposed to tyranny in any form— whether of the left or of the right.

v.

Each period in history brings its call for supreme human effort. At times in the past it took the form of war. Today it takes the form of social evolution or revolution. The United States will not, cannot stand aloof. We must help find constructive means for the under-privileged masses of mankind to work their way toward a better life. Indeed, so far as this Hemisphere is concerned, every American nation must cooperate in this mighty endeavor. Even the poorest nation can contribute its spiritual and intellectual strength. The important consideration is that every member of the American family of nations should feel responsible for promoting the welfare of all.

I have requested the Secretary of State to take the lead in conferring with our Latin American friends on these principles and purposes. Assuming their agreement, he will prepare for my approval as promptly as possible specific recommendations along these lines.

I intend to submit a message on this subject to the Congress promptly. I shall seek authority for such additional public funds as we may deem appropriate to assist free men and neighbors in Latin America in cooperative efforts to develop their nations and achieve better lives. [*Ends reading*]

Now, as far as the message itself is concerned, I am ready to entertain two or three questions.

Q. Robert C. Pierpoint, CBS News: Mr. President, you mentioned here, I believe, that every American nation must cooperate in this new plan or program. Would that include Cuba, the present Cuban Government?

THE PRESIDENT. It would be only those nations who have shown a willingness and a readiness to cooperate with the others in this great effort—specifically with ourselves, because we are the ones that are making the statement.

Q. Felix Belair, New York Times: Mr. President, is it possible at this time to give any kind of estimate as to the order of magnitude of assistance contemplated, and would the proposed program operate as did the European recovery program with the so-called shopping lists?

THE PRESIDENT. No. You are talking about the so-called Marshall plan?

Q. Mr. Belair: Yes, sir.

THE PRESIDENT. Well, the Marshall plan was to repair and rehabilitate a destroyed industrial plant already existing. This is an entirely different problem, and I think it would be unfair to compare the effort we are now talking about—raising the social and economic standards of the people—with the effort of the Marshall plan.

Now, when it comes to terms of magnitude of the sums that would be affected, let us remember this, that I am talking about two meetings still in the future which we are calling with our own friends and which we are examining our own efforts, and it would be impossible to make any kind of even rough guess.

But I do want to say this, which I have said so often: the only real investment that is going to flow into countries that will be useful to them in the long term, is private investment. It is many times the amount that can be put in from the public coffers. And normally, the public loans are made so as to encourage and make better opportunities for the private investments that follow.

Q. Mr. Belair: Does it follow from what you just said, Mr. President, that no larger expenditure would be made than is now being made?

THE PRESIDENT. No. I would think this—I just say this: that in my own opinion, some additional sums would be probably necessary. But there are many ways in which this could be done. For example, all nations could agree to increase the capital and the lending capacity of the American Bank. In other words, I would not think of it just as a great—anything as remotely resembling the Marshall plan.

Q. Marvin L. Arrowsmith, Associated Press: Mr. President, I wonder if you would be willing to tell us in what context the current Cuban crisis was considered in your and the Secretary's discussion of this program? We have been told that you were analyzing that situation, too. Is there anything further you can say this morning?

THE PRESIDENT. Well, Marvin, this has been on our minds and think-ing and even almost written preparation for some months—ever since I came back from South America—and with my associates and the Presi-dents of those countries that I met or visited, this Cuban problem was discussed. Very naturally, every day that this thing has been under preparation, there has been discussion of the Cuban problem. But I don't for the moment see any benefit in going further in giving our atti-tude than was expressed in my statement, I think it was the day before yesterday, in answer to the Khrushchev rather crude threat. And I think that statement speaks for itself.

Q. Mr. Arrowsmith: I wonder, you probably have seen that the Presi-dent of Cuba last night strongly implied that Cuba might demand that we give up the Guantanamo Naval Base. Did you have any discussion of that? Do you have any reaction to that?

THE PRESIDENT. Well, I will wait till I hear the demand on that one.

Q. Charles W. Roberts, Newsweek: Mr. President, do you have the feeling, or do you have assurances from the other American Republics that they favor going ahead on this regional hemispheric basis rather than appealing to the aid—or accepting aid from powers outside of this hemisphere?

THE PRESIDENT. Well, so far as all the countries I have spoken to personally, this particular question has not been placed in specific terms. But the whole attitude and atmosphere of our conversation was, to make a more effective and stronger organization among all the States to work in a cooperative—I mean all the American States—to work in a co-operative basis rather than to go each individually seeking outside help somewhere. Now, if there's any specific difference outside of what we have seen in Cuba, why I think you should ask the question of the State Department, because I am not aware of it.

Q. Mr. Roberts: If I might rephrase that——

THE PRESIDENT. Yes.

Q. Mr. Roberts:——do you feel the other powers are opposed to any aid coming from outside this hemisphere to any country in the Western Hemisphere—such as the aid that Russia has offered to Cuba?

THE PRESIDENT. Well, I would—I don't want to speculate on what their general attitude is. I know the very cooperative attitude they have shown to me in conversations with me, and I think it's a question I would rather have you put to the State Department, and put it in more specific fashion, and let them give a specific answer.

Q. M. Stewart Hensley, United Press International: Mr. President, you of course talked at some length with Mr. Kubitschek, Mr. Alessandri, Mr. Frondizi, about this plan. From what you know of their aspirations, and what you have in mind in the nature of the size of the American contribution, do you believe that your plan is going to satisfy all their hopes in that respect?

THE PRESIDENT. Well, what I would say is this: if we can ever get a true coordination and meeting of minds on the problem itself, and its scope, and how it should be arranged in priorities, then I think the United States would feel it should do its own proper share.

Now I do not believe that any nation can be saved merely by outside help. The first need is the heart and the brains and the wills and the determination and the morale in a nation itself, and to do those things which it can itself do.

When it comes, though, to the need of foreign exchange, and so on, and assistance in technical and scientific fields which can be given from a country such as ours, I think that our nation will never quail from doing what it needs to do. But I do not believe that just great sums of money is the answer.

Q. Daniel Karasik, NBC News: Mr. President, would a question on your Saturday statement be in order?

THE PRESIDENT. Well, I put it on this—I wanted to put the questions directly on this, and therefore I don't believe this is the place for that, because I think you'll start a precedent for me.

Q. Frederic W. Collins, Providence Journal: In your soundings, do you have a feeling that the other Latin American Republics would go ahead with a general cooperative plan of this nature if it excluded Cuba?

THE PRESIDENT. Well, I think that no nation of course can come in unless it wants to cooperate, and I would see no reason why the others— so that the remaining 20 of us could not go ahead—and as a matter of fact, even if there were 2 or 3 excluded for any reasons of their own choosing, I think this would still be a practicable thing.

Q. Laurence H. Burd, Chicago Tribune: Does this require any action by Congress, apart from the funds, for this plan?

THE PRESIDENT. I can't tell for sure yet, Larry, for a very simple reason, that there may be something in the authorization. For example, suppose they want to authorize a little bit different kind of loan in the American Bank, then each country's Congress would have to approve.

Q. Mr. Burd: Are you hoping to get it through in the next session of Congress——

THE PRESIDENT. I don't know. And the timing is just something that I cannot predict.

Q. Mr. Burd: Otherwise it might be done after you are gone—after you have left office?

THE PRESIDENT. Well, I would think that this plan would appeal to any thinking American and so I would—if I have—now I would like to get it done better, of course—quicker, but always as I think it's a soldier's attitude, if you know what you want to do, get it done in a hurry. But in this, you take some time to get exactly the agreements that you want.

Q. Mr. Burd: Have you had any discussions with the Democrats on this?

THE PRESIDENT. Not on this one.

Well, I think, gentlemen, that will cover the subject.

[Speaker unidentified]: Thank you very much, Mr. President.

THE PRESIDENT. Didn't know there were so many of you up here!

NOTE: President Eisenhower's one hundred and eighty-seventh news conference was held in the Upstairs Press Room, Naval Headquarters Station Building, U.S. Naval Base, Newport, R.I., at 10 a.m., on Monday, July 11, 1960. The attendance was not recorded.

Secretary Herter was also present at the conference.

229 ¶ Statement by the President Upon Signing the Independent Offices Appropriation Act. *July* 12, 1960

I HAVE today approved H.R. 11776, the Independent Offices Appropriation Act, 1961.

In enacting this law the Congress refused to provide recommended funds which would have enabled the General Services Administration, at small cost, to include fallout shelters in certain appropriate new and existing Federal buildings. In fact, by a general provision, the law actually precludes the construction of fallout shelters in Government-owned or leased buildings unless specifically authorized.

It is an aspect of the Federal Government's policy in this area to provide leadership by example.   The incorporation of fallout shelters in appropriate new and existing Federal buildings is intended to stimulate State and local governments and the public to undertake shelter projects on their own initiative.

State Governors attending a recent White House meeting on civil defense unanimously agreed that providing protection from fallout was an essential requirement of national policy.   Last year, in Puerto Rico, and again this year in Montana, the Governors' Conference reached the same conclusion.

The Congress accordingly should appropriate the omitted funds when it convenes again in August.   Such positive action would be in the best interest of our national security.

NOTE: As enacted, H.R. 11776 is Public   The statement was released at the U.S.
Law 86–626 (74 Stat. 425).   Naval Base, Newport, R.I.

230   ¶ Memorandum of Disapproval of Bill Concerning Wage Rates at the Portsmouth Naval Shipyard.   *July* 12, 1960

I AM withholding my approval from S. 19, "To provide a method for regulating and fixing wage rates for employees of Portsmouth, New Hampshire, Naval Shipyard."

My reasons for disapproving an identical enactment of the 85th Congress still apply.   This bill, like its predecessor, strikes at the heart of the statutory principle that rates of pay for 673,000 Federal wage board employees shall conform, as nearly as is consistent with the public interest, with private rates of pay in the immediate vicinity of the particular Federal activity.

This principle is sound.   It insures Federal employees a fair wage.   It insures against the payment of unwarranted hourly rates by the Government.   And it insures that Federal rates of pay will not upset the economy of the community in which the Federal establishment is located.

S. 19 would disregard this principle by providing that hourly rates for Portsmouth Naval Shipyard employees should be based on those which obtain, not in Portsmouth, but rather in the Boston industrial complex,

60 miles distant. Private industrial rates are substantially higher in Boston than in Portsmouth—and therein lies the explanation of the bill.

But why should the Government pay a much higher hourly wage rate than do fair-minded private employers in the Portsmouth area? If the Portsmouth Naval Shipyard were a private establishment, there would be no question of a differential. The going rate for the area would be paid. But because the Government is the employer, and just because it is, there is apparently an expectation that the Government should pay more than these hourly employees in fairness and equity have a right to expect. Further, it is seemingly of little or no concern that in so doing the Government would be departing from sound principle and business practice and would be unsettling the economy of the Portsmouth community.

This kind of legislation—this expectation of something-for-nothing from the Government just because it is the Government—weakens our national fabric and with each occurrence leaves it more seriously impaired. The spread of this expectation, and its reflection in an increase of such legislation, are profoundly disturbing for the future of America.

In this one instance, for example, S. 19 as a law would provide a ready precedent for the eventual dissolution of the wage board principle and system. The Portsmouth Naval Shipyard in no way presents an unusual situation. Several Federal establishments, less distant from Boston than Portsmouth, have *lower* pay scales than those of the Portsmouth Naval Shipyard.

By no rationale can this bill be justified. Wage disparities exist throughout the United States but under the wage board principle the Government pays the fair and equitable hourly rates of the particular area in which it finds itself—and so it should.

For these reasons I am unable to approve the bill.

Dwight D. Eisenhower

NOTE: The memorandum was released at the U.S. Naval Base, Newport, R.I.

231 ¶ Statement by the President on the Downing of an RB–47 Plane by the U.S.S.R. *July* 13, 1960

THE UNITED STATES Government is ready and willing to go to the Security Council for a full discussion of the Soviet's wanton shooting down of the United States Air Force RB–47 airplane in international waters July 1.

This Government itself had contemplated recourse to the Security Council but only after trying the bi-lateral remedies specified in the United Nations Charter. The United States has in fact proposed in its note of July 12 to the Soviet Government that a joint investigation be made. The Soviet Government has ignored the provisions of the Charter which call upon the parties to an international dispute to attempt to settle their differences by negotiation or similar means prior to any action within the United Nations itself.

The United States will focus attention in the Security Council on the lawless actions and reckless threats of the Soviet Government.

NOTE: The Press Secretary to the President, in a release dated July 12, stated that the American RB–47 plane was over international waters and at no time flew over Soviet territory, Soviet territorial waters, or Soviet air space. "The shooting down of this plane, as the Soviet Government alleges," the release continued, "can only have been a deliberate and reckless attempt to create an international incident." The release further stated that the plane had been missing 11 days and that it had been reported that at least one Soviet ship was assisting, in good faith, in the search for the missing aircraft. "Any attempt to connect the flight of this aircraft with the U–2 flight of May is completely without foundation and the Soviet authorities, including Mr. Khrushchev, know this," the release added.

The note of July 12 to the Soviet Government is published in the Department of State Bulletin (vol. 43, p. 163).

The President's statement was released at the U.S. Naval Base, Newport, R.I.

232 ¶ Telegram to Senator Mansfield Welcoming a Security Council Discussion of the RB–47 Plane Incident. *July* 13, 1960

Dear Senator Mansfield:

Thank you for your telegram in which you suggest that the matter of the shooting down of the U.S. Air Force RB–47 airplane be brought before the Security Council of the United Nations.

As you will have noted from this government's reply of July 12th to the Soviet note of July 11th, the United States has proposed to the Soviet government that a joint investigation be made. This action was taken pursuant to the provisions of the United Nations Charter, which calls upon the parties to an international dispute to attempt to settle their differences by negotiation or similar means prior to any action within the United Nations itself.

Press reports just received indicate that instead of responding to our proposal, the Soviet government is requesting a meeting of the Security Council on this subject. While we had contemplated recourse to the Security Council only after trying bilateral remedies specified in the Charter, we welcome the Security Council consideration of this question. We propose to make full use of this opportunity to focus world attention on the lawless actions and reckless threats of the Soviet government.

Sincerely,

DWIGHT D. EISENHOWER

NOTE: The letter was released at the U.S. Naval Base, Newport, R.I.

233 ¶ Statement by the President Upon Signing Bill Providing for the Admission of Refugees. *July* 14, 1960

I HAVE today approved H.J. Res. 397, "To enable the United States to participate in the resettlement of certain refugees, and for other purposes," because of its general merit and the urgent need to accomplish the purposes of the measure. Under this provision, the special authority of the Attorney General to parole into the United States certain refugees could be terminated upon the adoption of a simple resolution to that effect by either House of Congress. The Attorney General has advised me that there is a serious question as to whether this provision is constitutional. Nevertheless, in view of the short period for which this power is given and the improbability that the issue will arise, it is believed that it would be better to defer a determination of the effect of such possible action until it is taken.

NOTE: As enacted, H.J. Res. 397 is Public Law 86–648 (74 Stat. 504).

The statement was released at the U.S. Naval Base, Newport, R.I.

234 ¶ Memorandum of Disapproval of Bill for the Relief of Margaret P. Copin. *July* 14, 1960

I AM withholding my approval from H.R. 4546 "For the relief of Margaret P. Copin."

This bill would direct that its beneficiary be credited with a 20-year service period for purposes of civil service retirement annuity, payable commencing October 1, 1958.

This claimant, during three periods beginning in August 1920 and ending in June 1949, was on the employment rolls of the Treasury Department for a total time of 20 years and 29 days. This included, however, 7 months and 21 days of leave without pay in calendar year 1922. Her actual service therefore, totals only 19 years, 5 months and 8 days. Nevertheless, in computing Mrs. Copin's length of service for retirement annuity purposes, the normal rules of the law were applied, namely, free credit of 6 months of leave without pay taken in 1922 and exclusion of the excess amount.

Despite the credit of 6 months, the claimant still lacks 22 days of the 20 years of creditable service which would have given her the right to an immediate reduced annuity beginning October 1, 1958, when disability annuity payments theretofore received were terminated pursuant to a finding that she was reemployable. Instead, her status is that of a deferred annuitant, and retirement annuity will not be payable until March 1, 1964 after she has attained 62 years of age. The difference in the total value of the two annuities, based on life expectancy, is $4,200, which would be, in effect, a gratuity from the Federal Government.

The record on H.R. 4546 discloses no valid justification for the favored position the bill would accord this claimant. To confer such a preferential advantage on one individual participant in the retirement program would be highly discriminatory and contrary to the principles of fair play and equality of treatment which are basic to sound personnel administration.

DWIGHT D. EISENHOWER

NOTE: The memorandum was released at the U.S. Naval Base, Newport, R.I.

235   ¶ Memorandum of Disapproval of Bill Relating to Payments to Bernalillo County, New Mexico, for Care of Indians.   *July* 14, 1960

I AM withholding my approval from H.R. 11545, "To amend the Act of October 31, 1949, with respect to payments to Bernalillo County, New Mexico, for furnishing hospital care for certain Indians."

A 1949 law authorized the Government to contribute $1,500,000 toward construction of a hospital in Bernalillo County upon Government donated land. In return, the county must make available, when required, at least 100 beds for the care of eligible Indians. Further, the cost of caring for Indians admitted to the hospital was to be paid by the United States and, as an experiment, the Government undertook to guarantee the county a payment at least equal to the cost of operating 80 per cent of the beds reserved for Indians irrespective of the number actually hospitalized.

The minimum guaranty provision, previously twice extended and now expired as of June 30, 1960, would be extended for still another year under H.R. 11545.

Ordinarily in such cases the United States pays for Indian care on the basis of actual hospitalization. Accordingly, the Department of Health, Education, and Welfare, in reporting to the Congress in 1957 pursuant to the original law, recommended that the experimental 80 per cent minimum guaranty be permitted to expire. The Congress nevertheless extended the guaranty provision for another three years.

Funds for contract hospital care should be available for expenditure wherever the health needs of Indian patients so require, and no portion of them should be mandatorily tied to a single contract facility without regard to actual need or use. Moreover, because other Government service contracts for Indian care do not include a minimum payment guaranty, it would be highly inequitable to continue this provision solely for the Bernalillo County Hospital.

Finally, the completion of other facilities now under construction will in all likelihood reduce the number of Indian patients at Bernalillo Hospital and the bill would thus mean unnecessary expense to the

Government and without any corresponding advantage, either to the Government or to this program.

For these reasons, I am unable to approve this bill.

Dwight D. Eisenhower

NOTE: The memorandum was released at the U.S. Naval Base, Newport, R.I.

236 ¶ Telegrams to Senators Kennedy and Johnson Offering Them Briefings by the Central Intelligence Agency.   *July 18, 1960*

The Honorable John F. Kennedy
Hyannisport, Mass.

I believe it to be in the national interest, and I hope it conforms to your desire, for you, as the duly designated candidate of one of the major parties for the Presidency of the United States, to have periodic briefings on the international scene from a responsible official in the Central Intelligence Agency. Acting on the assumption that you likewise believe such briefings to be in the national interest, I have already requested the Director of the Central Intelligence Agency, Allen Dulles, to arrange procedural details with you or with some designated member of your staff.

Because of the secret character of the information that would be furnished you, it would be exclusively for your personal knowledge. Otherwise, however, the receipt of such information would impose no restriction on full and free discussion.

On the assumption that you desire me to authorize similar briefings for the Honorable Lyndon Johnson, your Vice Presidential candidate, I am offering them to him by telegram today, and these briefings will go forward unless you advise of any view to the contrary that you might have.

Dwight D. Eisenhower

NOTE: The telegram to Senator Johnson, similar to the foregoing but without the last paragraph, was released with the telegram to Senator Kennedy and the latter's reply of acceptance at the U.S. Naval Base, Newport, R.I.

237 ¶ Statement by the President on the Budget Surplus for Fiscal Year 1960. *July* 20, 1960

THE FEDERAL GOVERNMENT finished fiscal year 1960, which ended last June 30, with not only a balanced budget but a surplus of $1.1 billion. This represents a very encouraging turnaround from the prior fiscal year when the Government incurred a recession-induced deficit of almost $12½ billions.

The Budget surplus results from revenues of $78.4 billion and expenditures of $77.3 billion. Full details of receipts and expenditures are available in a joint announcement being made at this time in Washington by the Secretary of the Treasury and the Director of the Bureau of the Budget.

This demonstration of fiscal responsibility not only reinforces economic strength here at home, but reaffirms to the world that the United States intends to run its financial affairs on a sound basis.

NOTE: Details of receipts and expenditures, as announced by the Secretary of the Treasury and the Director of the Bureau of the Budget on July 20, are published in the "Monthly Statement of Receipts and Expenditures of the United States Government—For the Period July 1, 1959, through June 30, 1960" (Government Printing Office, 1960).

The President's statement was released at the U.S. Naval Base, Newport, R.I.

238 ¶ Statement by the President on the Need for an Early Meeting of the Disarmament Commission of the United Nations. *July* 21, 1960

I HAVE been greatly concerned that everything possible be done to make progress on the question of disarmament.

The abrupt breakup of the ten nation talks in Geneva by the Soviet Union last month makes it desirable to take further steps so that the vital issue of disarmament can be considered promptly once again. Our efforts to get the Soviet Union to return to the conference table through normal diplomatic channels have not met with success. The need for disarmament in the present world situation is too important to set aside at the present time when deliberate efforts are being made to increase tensions.

The United Nations under the charter has primary responsibility in this field. I have therefore today instructed Ambassador Henry Cabot Lodge to request an early meeting of the Disarmament Commission of the United Nations so that we and other members of the international community can continue to search for ways and means to achieve the universal desire to reduce the risk of war by controlled steps of disarmament.

NOTE: The statement was released at the U.S. Naval Base, Newport, R.I.

239 ¶ Remarks at the Dedication of Eisenhower Park, Newport, Rhode Island.   *July* 22, 1960

Mr. Mayor, Mr. Wilkinson, and fellow Americans and citizens of this beautiful city:

It is an understatement for my wife and me to say that we are deeply honored by the graciousness of the City Fathers in naming this spot for us. I am deeply touched by this kind of gracious incident and thought, for the simple reason that a name given to a place like this endures.

There will be future classes and groups of these Coggeshall Continentals on down the decades and possibly even centuries that will learn of this rather long and unusual name, and will possibly wonder how it happens that it was so named within this city.

But so long as they are people in those future times that live true to the traditions that have inspired the people of Rhode Island and of Newport in the past centuries, then it will make little difference as to what they think of the name of this spot at that time. But if they think of it only that this is a place where freedom has flourished, where the dignity of man has been respected, and they themselves can have the privileges we have today, even to change the name of this park, but do whatever may seem to them to be fitting, then indeed we will be fortunate people— and so will they.

I was particularly honored that at this occasion they would bring here this little group of the Continentals of the Coggeshall School. I have been told it steals every parade and it is the great feature of every ceremony that is held in Newport.

I can well understand it because they, I can see, are exactly the age of at least two of my own grandchildren, and I wish that my grandchildren had that kind of uniform and could play fifes and drums as they do. I congratulate the city and the school that has perpetuated this organization, and the leaders that have trained it so well.

As Mr. Wilkinson has said, this is our third visit here. We look forward to an opportunity for staying even a little longer, but the interruptions in the summer's vacation are not of our making but have to do with some of the regular political activities of our country that break things up into conventions and into recessed sessions of the Congress. So I am afraid we cannot stay here as long as we had hoped and prayed we could, because I assure you our gratitude to the people of Newport, for the courtesies and thoughtfulness they have displayed towards us all the time, makes it one of the places we truly like to come back to. And possibly maybe next summer—in the summer—we can come here and be sitting with the crowd to view somebody else who will then be in the center of attention because of his particular position. Because I suspect that future Presidents will learn something about this place and the fun we have had here, and possibly they will even come to try it themselves. And if they do they will repeat.

So again I say thank you most sincerely for the honor you have done us. Again thank you for your courtesies, for the simplicity and yet the niceness and beauty of this little ceremony. And I do hope that you will never find any reason for changing your mind that the name of this park is a good name.

Thank you very much.

NOTE: The President spoke at 2:35 p.m. in Washington Square. His opening words "Mr. Mayor, Mr. Wilkinson" referred to James Maher, Mayor of Newport, and former Mayor Henry C. Wilkinson.

240   ¶ Letter to Dr. Henry M. Wriston on the Progress Made by the Commission on National Goals.   *July* 22, 1960

[Released July 22, 1960. Dated July 11, 1960]

Dear Henry:

I was very happy to receive your letter of June twenty-seventh outlining the progress and work of the Commission on National Goals. I am amazed at the speed with which you have put this project together, and I am, of course, pleased that you now think it will be possible to have a report by December.

Your recommendations, I am sure, will be most timely. I feel more strongly than ever that your committee has the opportunity to make an historic addition to our knowledge and understanding of the democratic processes and our national ideals and purposes.

Again, my sincerest thanks for undertaking this most vital assignment.

With warm regard,

Sincerely,

DWIGHT D. EISENHOWER

NOTE: Dr. Wriston's letter stated that since the appointment of the Commission in February (see Items 29, 30) the members had held both full scale and informal meetings, appointed a small but highly competent staff, and adopted a set of procedures and a time schedule. Dr. Wriston further stated that the final report would be a unified and self-contained statement of the basic elements that, in their judgment, should be included in the national agenda over a workable time span, in most cases 5 to 10 years. "We intend to re-state what we conceive to be the ultimate goals of the nation," his letter continued, "but we shall give equal weight to practical measures and priorities of effort needed to make progress toward those goals to the limit of our powers."

The release containing the text of the letters announced that they would form the basis of conversations on July 22 between the President, Dr. Wriston, and Frank Pace, Jr., Vice Chairman of the Commission.

The letters were released at the U.S. Naval Base, Newport, R.I.

241 ¶ Letter to Frederick M. Eaton Following the Closing of the Ten-Nation Committee on Disarmament. *July* 22, 1960

[Released July 22, 1960. Dated July 20, 1960]

Dear Mr. Eaton:

Upon the closing of the Ten-Nation Committee on Disarmament, I want you to know how deeply grateful I am to you for undertaking the Chairmanship and for your efforts to find an agreement which would halt the building up of armaments.

Your strong, courageous and imaginative leadership has been a source of pride to all of us who have been working with you. It was not due to any fault on the part of yourself and your associates that no agreement was reached. In any event you have made the United States position of dedication to peace clear to the world.

You have my congratulations and best wishes.

With warm regard,

Sincerely,

DWIGHT D. EISENHOWER

NOTE: Mr. Eaton served as Chairman of the U.S. delegation to the Conference of the Ten-Nation Committee on Disarmament in Geneva. His letter, dated July 5, was released with the President's reply at the U.S. Naval Base, Newport, R.I.

242 ¶ Statement by the President Making Public an Interim Report on the Food-for-Peace Program. *July* 24, 1960

I HAVE received an interim report on the Food-For-Peace program. This commendable effort provides a constructive use of our agricultural capabilities and is our chief weapon in the world-wide war against want and hunger.

There is no form of overseas assistance which this country is better able to provide than the supplying of American farm products and agricultural science.

The overwhelming share of our Food-For-Peace effort is going to the nations of Asia, Latin America, the Mediterranean area, and Africa which need it most.

I note with gratification the achievements of the program thus far. I am heartened by the prospect that our accomplishment can be further improved, with emphasis on a continuing effort to make sure that the hazards of the program will be minimized.

I am making this report public since it deals with matters of current and prospective importance at home and abroad.

NOTE: The report "Food-for-Peace" (8 pp., mimeographed) was prepared by Don Paarlberg, Food for Peace Coordinator. It was released with the President's statement at the U.S. Naval Base, Newport, R.I.

In his report Mr. Paarlberg stated that altogether, from 1954 through 1959, approximately the following quantities (in shiploads) of surplus agricultural products had been moved: sales for foreign currency—under Public Law 480, 3000, through the Mutual Security Act, 1250; relief of disaster (government-to-government), 275; donations through charitable agencies (people-to-people), 400; bartered for strategic and other material, 1500; for a total of 6,425 shiploads.

243   ¶ Letter to the Administrator of General Services Concerning the Design of Proposed Buildings on Lafayette Square.   *July 25, 1960*

Dear Mr. Floete:

The Congress has recently enacted, and I have approved, an appropriation act which provides for the design and construction of several Federal buildings throughout the United States. I have a particular interest in the design of two of these buildings which are to be located on Lafayette Square near the White House. One of these buildings is to house certain court facilities on the east side of the Square, and the other is to provide additional space for the Executive Office of the President on the west side of the Square.

It is extremely important that the architectural plans for these buildings be carried out with the greatest of thought and with attention to the present and future dignity and beauty of Lafayette Square and its historic past. Because this is a splendid opportunity to revive the historical and architectural significance of this Square, I earnestly request that all preliminary plans and thinking in connection with these buildings be developed in close consultation with the National Capital Planning Commission and the Commission of Fine Arts.

It would be also advisable that whoever the architect may be, he will approach the planning not only with his attention and inspiration fixed upon the dignity and simplicity of some of the older buildings—the White House, St. John's Church, the Treasury and Decatur House—but also taking into account the planning for the west side of the Square as it develops.

We should use this opportunity to leave Lafayette Square for posterity as an architectural symbol of the simplicity, beauty and clean lines traditional to the American style.

Funds for the construction of a building for the courts on the east side of the Square are appropriated for the fiscal year 1961, and I understand that it will be possible to develop plans for Federal Office No. 7 in sufficient time to permit construction funds to be included in the 1962 budget.

I am sending a copy of this letter to the Chairman of the National Capital Planning Commission and to the Chairman of the Commission of Fine Arts.

Sincerely,

DWIGHT D. EISENHOWER

NOTE: The letter was released at the U.S. Naval Base, Newport, R.I.

244 ¶ Statement by the President Following the Firing of the Polaris Missile by the Submarine Patrick Henry. *July* 25, 1960

THIS DEMONSTRATION exceeds in significance for the nation's security even the most optimistic predictions that I had heard about the expected efficiency of this new weapons system. I am proud of the patriotic and competent personnel who have brought about this great achievement. Moreover, in the crew, officers and men, I find another example of traditional morale and training of our armed services personnel.

NOTE: The President made a noon tour of the submarine U.S.S. Patrick Henry, then boarded the Barbara Anne, from which he watched the firing of two Polaris missiles from the submarine.

245 ¶ Address at the Republican National Convention in Chicago. *July* 26, 1960

Mr. Chairman, members of this convention, your guests, and my fellow citizens across this broad land:

From our hearts, Mamie and I thank you for the warmth of your greeting.

My friends, there is no individual who has been in political life for five minutes that has not felt at times discouragement and disappointment. But such a demonstration as you have given to my wife and me tonight, after we have for seven and a half years been occupying the positions we now hold, is indeed a tribute that warms our hearts. We shall never forget you.

The enthusiasm I find throughout this Convention evidences your support of the domestic and international leadership that has been provided by Republicans during the past seven and a half years.

This means to me that, under sound Republican direction, you want, first of all, to stimulate—never weaken—the sturdy self-reliance and self-confidence of the American citizen, and sustain his equality before the law.

Next, that you believe moral law to be the sure foundation of every constructive human action.

Third, that you want to continue to foster a strong, expanding economy.

Next, that you are determined to continue the maintenance of a national security position second to none.

Next, that your deepest hope is that each of us may do his or her part in furthering the age-old dream of mankind—a universal peace with justice.

And finally, that each of you is ready to roll up your sleeves and to work tirelessly and in every conceivable, honorable way to help achieve these great purposes.

———

My friends, I have come before you to testify to my great pride in the America of today; and my confidence in the brightness of her future. I glory in the moral, economic and military strength of this nation, in the ideals that she upholds before the world, and in her readiness to assist the less fortunate of the earth to obtain and enjoy the blessings of freedom.

So to this convention I bring no words of despair or doubt about my country—no doleful prediction of impending disaster.

In this election campaign of 1960, I pray that Republicans will always remember the greatness of our nation and will talk only the truth about her—because, my friends, in spreading the truth we are not only being true to our national ideals but we are planting the fertile seeds of political victory.

We need not and we shall not distort or ignore the facts. The truth—the whole truth—will lead the American people to wise decisions in selecting the men and women to occupy positions of responsibility in government, including the man who will ride with me up Pennsylvania Avenue next January to be inaugurated as our next President.

And if we present the facts fervently, persistently, and widely, the next President of the United States will be a Republican—and that will indeed be a blessing for America.

So this campaign is nothing less than a vast educational endeavor—presenting to the citizens the evidence they need in order to arrive at their individual judgments on the issues and the candidates.

Whoever misleads by calculated use of some but not all the facts, whoever distorts the truth to serve selfish ambition, whoever asserts weakness where strength exists—makes a mockery of the democratic process and misrepresents our beloved country in the eyes of a watching world.

The irrefutable truths are that the United States is enjoying an unprecedented prosperity; that it has, in cooperation with its friends and allies, the strongest security system in the world, and that it is working ceaselessly and effectively for a peace with justice, in freedom.

Our own mounting living standards and the history of these Republican years, provide the proof that these are facts.

It's not my purpose tonight to review the detailed story of these past seven and a half years. But our people are so deeply and naturally interested in the status and progress of American economic, military and foreign activities that to those fields I direct my particular attention.

Our foremost objective is the pursuit of peace with justice. To make any progress toward this goal we must have both a strong economy and adequate military strength. I will talk first of these two essential conditions.

The economic story can be quickly, succinctly, and accurately told. There are more Americans today employed, at higher wages and with more take-home pay than ever before in our history. And with this they have more confidence in the stability of their money than they have enjoyed in three decades.

Included in this record there is one economic comparison that has particular interest in this election year. It involves what the economists call the Gross National Product. Concerning it we are fed a great deal of information—and much more of mis-information. Now the interesting fact to which I refer is that in these past seven and a half years the annual Gross National Product has increased by one hundred billion dollars—or 25 per cent.

This figure, though stupendous, is asserted by some to be unnecessarily low. But what would they say if they knew that during the almost eight-year duration of the prior, Democratic, Administration, the Gross National Product actually declined in every single peacetime year, save one.

Are we not justified in drawing some appropriate conclusions from this fact? And by the way, the facts that I am giving you are in terms of constant dollars.

It is clear that whatever economic growth was realized during the previous Administration occurred mainly under wartime circumstances. Surely it is not suggested that this is the way for the United States to seek prosperity!

During all the years of this Administration, I've heard much from the opposition—especially from its free-spending clique—about increasing the rate of economic growth, by depending principally on governmental activity, with vastly increased Federal expenditures.

Here we encounter a major difference between the two parties: we, as Republicans, reject the argument that healthy growth can thus be bought from the funds of the Federal Treasury.

We believe profoundly that constant and unnecessary governmental meddling in our economy leads to a standardized, weakened, and taste-less society that encourages dull mediocrity; whereas private enterprise, dependent upon the vigor of healthful competition, leads to individual responsibility, pride of accomplishment, and, above all, national strength. This has always been, is now—and I pray will always be—basic Republican doctrine.

Our total picture of economic well-being contains another fact vitally important to every citizen: the amazing growth in national prosperity since 1953 has been accompanied by a radical reduction in the rate of inflation.

Inflation—the most insidious and cruel form of taxation ever devised— drove prices up 48 per cent in the previous Administration, thus robbing millions of our people of savings and of purchasing power.

In the last seven and a half years, we have succeeded in keeping the total price rise below eleven per cent. And, at least this is my fixed opinion, this record could have been even better if I might have had the privilege of working all these years with a Republican Congress.

Now over and above strictly material accomplishments, the American people have every reason to be proud of their many domestic achievements during these Republican years.

Our educational structure has been expanded and assisted to perform better its traditional functions.

A higher percentage of Americans than ever before own their own homes.

In science and technology, advances have been unprecedented.

My Science Adviser informs me that funds going into research and development are two and a half times greater than they were seven years ago.

Fifty million more Americans have been covered by private medical and hospital insurance.

Medical research has expanded five times.

Seven and a half million more of our people have been covered by Social Security.

And, in the face of all the efforts of the reckless spenders to thwart the Administration, a budgetary surplus has been achieved, fiscal responsibility has been maintained, and confidence restored.

Such results are the fruit of sound, deliberate policies—including Executive veto of irresponsible, narrowly-conceived, pork-barrel legislation. These surpluses create new confidence in the principle of fiscal responsibility in the Federal government, they lessen inflationary pressures and offer new hope for some debt reduction.

We have, of course, serious domestic problems still requiring attention. Mere recitation of a few of these emphasizes the moral obligation of the nation as a whole and each of its individual citizens in these matters.

Education must be improved.

Juvenile delinquency and crime cry out for renewed attack at every level.

Constructive solutions must be found for difficult agricultural problems.

Racial and religious discrimination must be combatted.

City slums must be erased, and depressed regions in our prosperous nation, where they exist, must be restored to economic health.

There can be no dispute about the necessity of getting on with the job in these and other pressing matters. But the major question is how shall it be done.

I repeat, it is Republican policy in such matters to rely first on the ingenuity and initiative of citizens themselves. Because it is the people in whom we place our faith. When government must undertake a program, we look wherever possible, to the State and local governments to assume the responsibility. The Federal government undertakes only those necessary tasks which cannot otherwise be accomplished. But even so, the central government finds itself deeply involved, and the proper performance of these duties requires time, resources, experience and judgment.

It is an irresponsible misrepresentation for any party to allege that all the human and economic problems of this nation can be overcome in a short time, or accomplished by reckless spending of our grandchildren's resources—and all this, they claim, without increasing taxes or incurring new deficits.

We demand that the Federal government give needed assistance cheerfully, but in ways that will protect the traditional relationship between Federal and local government, and promote the dynamism of our total economy. Republicans support the concepts that animated the Founding Fathers, who feared nothing else so much as they did the concentration of power and responsibility in the central government.

Our record proves that we have lived and worked in these convictions.

Now I come to the military field.

In the sum of our capabilities we have become the strongest military power on earth.

But just as the Biblical Job had his boils, so we have a cult of professional pessimists who, taking counsel of their fears, continually mouth the allegation that America has become a second rate military power.

This extraordinary assertion amazes our friends in the world who know better; it even bewilders many of our own people who have examined our seven and a half year record of military expansion and who are not used to hearing their gigantic defense efforts so belittled.

But let me give you a few glimpses of the comparative record.

Let us go back to the last peacetime year of the previous Administration. Defense expenditures during the twelve months preceding the outbreak of the Korean War were less than $12 billion. Today, we are spending, after seven years without hostilities, over three times that much—more than $41 billion annually on a powerful, flexible and adequate defense establishment, which commands world-wide respect.

In 1953 our mainstay in the Strategic Air Command was the B-36. We still had many old World War II B-29s in operating squadrons.

Since then our fleet of heavy bombers has nearly doubled. And the bombers with which the Strategic Air Command is now equipped are B-52s, giant intercontinental jets which dwarf the power of the obsolete B-36.

New supersonic B-58s are entering our operational forces to replace some of the older, medium range B-47 jets.

A third of this great force, deployed strategically around the world, is maintained on continuous ground alert, able to take off within minutes, carrying an unimaginable destructive power.

When this Administration took office, continental U.S. defense was almost non-existent. Today, under single command, our continental defense against manned aircraft has virtually been completed. Against the threat of long range ballistic missiles, we are pressing forward with vast programs featuring 3,000-mile range radar stations and satellite warning systems.

In 1953, our Navy had yet to launch its first nuclear-powered ship. Aside from a handful of destroyer types, not a single modern first-line ship had joined the Fleet since the end of the construction program of World War II.

Now the Navy has been progressively reshaped. Fifty new guided missile ships have been authorized since 1953. We have provided for approximately the same number of nuclear-powered vessels. And two of the revolutionary Polaris submarines will be operational this year—and this has been done in two-thirds of the time predicted by the most optimistic of the scientists and sailors.

Incidentally, the Polaris submarine has just passed its final tests with flying colors. And here is another interesting fact: this revolutionary and practically invulnerable ballistic missile system was brought from initial concept to operational status entirely within the years of the present Administration.

How boastfully the Kremlin dictatorship would have gloated, had it been capable of this great achievement!

Now this nation did not have a single long-range ballistic missile in 1953, and no real effort to produce such ballistic missiles was under way. The total expenditure in this field by the previous Administration during its entire tenure was less than 7 million dollars.

Now promptly after the close of World War II, the Soviet Union began concentrating on missile development. But the present Administration, entering office in 1953, had to start practically from scratch. And what have we accomplished?

We have developed a whole family of intermediate and intercontinental ballistic missiles. And missile squadrons are operational in Western Europe. Our first operational intercontinental ballistic missiles have gone into place. The whole effort becomes more and more efficient and is being accelerated.

The American space satellites, now providing answers to great scientific problems, were ignored during the previous Administration. In this kind of scientific exploration we now lead the world.

The Army of the United States, which was sent into the Korean War, was but a slightly updated version of the Army with which we fought World War II. Since then, the Army and the Marines have been reorganized and re-equipped to fight under every conceivable condition. New man-carried guided missiles and nuclear-capable rockets are giving the foot soldier a vastly greater power than even that of a big bomber of World War II.

Fellow Americans: the United States today possesses a military establishment of incalculable power. Combined with the strength of our NATO, SEATO, and other allies, the Free World is prepared to meet any threat, and, by its retaliatory strength, to face any potential aggressor with a mighty deterrent.

Over all these years we have given priority to the nation's security above other purposes and programs.

But, in addition to all this, competent military, scientific, intelligence and State Department staffs keep daily touch with changing international conditions as well as new possibilities for the technical improvement of our forces.

I have time and again announced my purpose of recommending to the Congress new methods and, where necessary, new appropriations to meet new situations and take advantage of new opportunities for increasing our security. Such vigilance will never be relaxed.

All this—all this has been brought about by vigorous and imaginative leadership, the genius of our scientists, the skill of our armed forces, and by the sacrifices of the American people. To belittle this might, prestige, pride and capabilities of these groups does such violence to my sense of what is right that I have difficulty in restraining my feelings of indignation.

And mark this well: the world knows that this awesome strength is maintained for one principal purpose: to make war so completely unthinkable that any would-be aggressor will not dare to attack us. And with such a deterrent and defensive power, we have the opportunity to work patiently toward the time when we can gradually transfer production from arms to the true needs of mankind. And this is America's goal.

And now I turn to our dealings with other nations.

In this Administration we have employed the whole might of our military, economic, political and moral strength to prevent war and to build a solid structure of peace. If we can be blessed with experienced and steady leadership in Washington, the possibility of the outbreak of future war will be minimized and we can eventually win the peace.

By conducting foreign relations with patience and on firm principle, we have made in these past years measurable progress in solidifying dependable cooperation among our allies; the uncommitted nations have come to have a clearer understanding of our purposes; the world is better aware of the fundamental nature of the mighty struggle in which we are engaged—a struggle to preserve the basic concepts which undergird our free way of life.

In this vast effort we have experienced a great sweep of progress. Now in such a gigantic program, working toward such great goals as these, we of course encounter some disappointments—witness the difficulties in Cuba, the unrest in the Congo, and Communist-inspired mob violence in Japan. But such as these we have to expect, and each is a spur to harder work—never shall we cease or tire in this task.

In the pursuit of world peace, I have personally journeyed more than 90,000 miles during the past year, and I have visited the peoples of more than a score of nations on four continents. I have heard the insistent demands of multitudes for the right to live their lives in peace, and I have seen and taken part in many impressive American initiatives directed toward this crucial goal.

In Europe, our friends are more prosperous and stronger than at any time in history, and NATO stands more solidly united with greater resources of strength than ever before.

The independence of South Korea endures, as does that of South Vietnam and Taiwan. The Southeast Asia Treaty Organization, organized in 1954, manifests our deep interest in the freedom and welfare of 175 million people in that quarter of the world, as does the new Security Treaty between Japan and ourselves.

The American family of nations is more closely knit than ever before, with new instruments for effective cooperation. We have created the Inter-American Development Bank with our Latin American friends. We have established the Development Loan Fund in order to avoid placing unreasonable burdens upon developing nations—we have increased the lending capacity of the Export-Import Bank by approximately $2 billion. Despite the lawlessness and violence in one area of this Hemisphere, there has been an increased recognition of the mutuality of interest of the countries of the Americas in cultural, economic and military ways; our importance one to another has been reaffirmed.

We have given of our strength, our skills, and our material abundance in the task of building a strong, stable, secure and powerful community of free nations. And from this work we shall not be deterred, despite the blustering threats of Communists leaders.

Another matter engaging our constant concern is to make steady progress toward controlled disarmament. The United States has made proposal after proposal, each in good faith, in an effort to reduce tension in the world and to lessen the economic burden of armaments. Moreover, we are prepared always to consider any reasonable proposal made by others.

But on one point we must never waver—and that is our insistence that agreements toward disarmament be accompanied by sound methods of inspection and control. The absolute necessity of this caution is readily understood when one recalls that the government with which we must deal in these matters has, since 1945, broken an uncounted number of solemn agreements made with us and other nations of the free world.

The ideas, policies and cooperative programs among democratic countries must accommodate themselves to the frequent and erratic change in the Soviet attitudes.

Only a few months ago, the men in the Kremlin were calling for complete and total disarmament. But suddenly thereafter they began devising one crisis after another.

They brutally wrecked the Summit Conference.

They have threatened us with missiles.

And today they cold-bloodedly boast of shooting down one of our planes legitimately travelling over intercontinental waters.

All such events, emphasizing the tactical unpredictability and shiftiness of Soviet leaders, call for constant analysis and reappraisal.

At this moment I am planning on an early conference with Congressional leaders of both parties on these significant events. And depending upon developments in the meantime, I shall make such recommendations for any changes in our own national programs as may then seem appropriate.

High in our thinking about the future of the world must be the fact that millions of people are crushed under the heavy heel of Communist imperialism. The conscience of America can never be completely clear until the precious right of freedom of choice is extended to all people, everywhere.

Now when the men of the Kremlin flagrantly misrepresent the facts by saying that we seek to subjugate one of our near neighbors, when they threaten us with missiles, they are apparently hoping to divert world attention from the domination they maintain over once free and proud peoples—these are people who have been guilty of nothing under the sun save a craving for the right to live as they themselves choose to live.

The Soviet dictator has said that he has, in his recent journeys and speeches, succeeded in damaging the prestige of America. Now this is indeed an empty boast.

Concerning this matter of comparative national prestige, I challenge him to this test: will he agree to the holding of free elections under the sponsorship of the United Nations—to permit people everywhere—in every nation and on every continent, to vote on one single simple issue:

That issue is: do you want to live under a Communist regime or under a free system such as found in the United States?

My friends, are the Soviets willing to measure their world prestige by the results of such elections? Well, you know the answer to that one.

But the United States would gladly do so.

To replace misunderstanding with genuine human comprehension—to develop and maintain sound relations among the nations—to find ways to share the bounty of our harvests with others, without disrupting normal world markets—to have sympathetic identification with all peaceful revolutions which seek greater freedom and better living—and to do all these things without violating our basic policies of nonintervention and freedom of choice for all—these are among the complex world problems with which the United States must deal.

And I profoundly believe that Republican policies and Republican leaders provide us with our best opportunity to carry these, as well as our domestic, tasks to completion.

And now, permit me a word about our personal approach to the business of this Convention, and to our duty to ourselves, to our Party, to our Nation.

You delegates assembled here are a significant part of American life. You are the leaders, the representatives and the workers of the Republican Party.

You have come here on business of the utmost seriousness to the Nation. Your purpose is not merely partisan victory, for political victory except as it is for the achievement of noble aims is devoid of meaning and value. But you are here to convince America that you, our Party, by its record of integrity and accomplishment—and by reason of the character and stature of the candidates it will put forward—is worthy of the great national responsibilities and leadership which victory in November will bring to them.

Your continuing objective is to serve every citizen—not a favored few. You recognize each as a creature of God's creation; you make no distinction in according him equality before the law and respecting his rightful dignity.

Now in the course of a year the members of this Convention come in contact with uncounted numbers of our citizens. I think you would agree that there has been a great change in their attitude about politics in the years since World War II.

They are no longer willing to condone or to brush aside trickery and insincerity with the phrase, "That's just politics."

They expect and demand honesty, integrity and moral courage from the men and women who bear public responsibilities. They know that political office should be—and demand it be—a position of trust and honor; qualification for it must comprehend more than mere personal ambition. They realize, as never before, that the stakes in today's world are too high to risk their futures to the hands of frivolous, irresponsible or inexperienced government.

Now within this Convention I hear that there is some dispute among the delegates concerning the Platform. Now there is nothing wrong in this. It is good! Only through open, sincere discussion can we as a Party present our united conclusions on the great issues that confront Americans both at home and abroad. Your Party expects that you, the delegates of the Republican Party, will work out these differences in a spirit of patriotic dedication, and will adopt out of your collective wisdom, a Platform that our nation can proudly support.

Though there is room for healthy argument within our Party, you have come to this Convention with a unity of basic conviction and philosophy unprecedented in the nation's political history. This is because the purposes and ideals for which your Party has striven, have commanded your loyal cooperation and the respect of the public. And under them our people have realized great gains.

In the successes of the past seven and a half years you have a solid foundation on which to build toward new levels of attainment. But thank God there is no smugness or complacency about your accomplishments.

Indeed, today's world demands that we be alert and responsive to every national requirement, attacking it at every appropriate level of government—as well as in every private sector—with vigor, judgment and imagination.

My friends, finally, I express my confidence that we shall do nothing here to insult the intelligence—to injure the pride or destroy the confidence of the American people in the great nation they have built. We shall do nothing here to serve the cult of pessimism, to spread false gospel among our allies or create misunderstanding among ourselves. You will make your decisions of your own free will—uninfluenced by any outside designs and pressures.

You will return to your homes—as you came—serious, patriotic American citizens, with a fuller confidence that you can lead our country onward, always to greater heights.

You will go back with your spirits and your hopes held high. You will be armed with far-sighted and progressive plans for the years ahead, and an unquenchable determination to bring the truth to every citizen everywhere. So doing you will assure victory once more for sound, courageous and enlightened government in the United States.

Now—my friends, one more word. May I say that my wife and I look forward, next January twentieth to meeting all of you, knowing that you will come with the happy, glowing faces of victors.

Thank you very much.

NOTE: The President spoke at 9:42 p.m. at the Union Stockyards Amphitheater in Chicago. His opening words "Mr. Chairman" referred to Thruston B. Morton, Chairman of the Republican National Committee and U.S. Senator from Kentucky.

246   ¶ Remarks at the Republican National Committee Breakfast, Chicago, Illinois. *July 27, 1960*

My friends of the Republican Party:

Any man who is compelled, and who, as a matter of duty and because of circumstances of his office, to face constantly these microphones gets a little bit weary of his own voice.

This morning I had a little incident that made me even a little more discouraged with my efforts to limit my appearances before these devilish mechanisms. I was getting up and, as you know, it was rather late when we all got to bed last night; but my faithful helper, sure that I would want to hear something on television surprised me when, by turning around, I found myself talking to myself about things in the speech last night.

It did seem a little bit too much.

Now, the first thing I should like to do is to mention the great compliment paid to me by Governor Stratton and the people of Illinois in presenting me with this bust of Lincoln. I might tell you that for eight— for seven and a half long years—there have always been in my office four prints. All of us certainly know who they are; four men I admire extravagantly. They are Benjamin Franklin, George Washington, Abraham Lincoln and General Lee. I cannot think of any four men whose histories and whose records could do more to inspire anyone to try to do his best.

You people have got a very tough job—I do not know whether it is finished yet or not—and that is: getting up the platform. Now, this is not merely a matter of composing differing views among able and dedicated people; in addition they have got this in the background: I am still President of the United States for six months.

You cannot obviously put out a platform that tells exactly what Republicans are going to do in the future until there is some effort to make sure that that is exactly what I am going to do.

I just give this as one of their complicating factors. I have no advice for them. As a matter of fact, from all the things I have heard, they have certainly got into a state of composition that does no violence to my beliefs. But it does make a three-cornered, rather than merely a bilateral, sort of argument.

You know, as an aside, I want to make one remark to you people who, if you stop to think, would have known this anyway. It is this: foreign affairs is today the greatest preoccupation of all people in positions of political responsibility, for a very simple reason. Foreign affairs and our relations with others affect every other problem we have. It involves our taxes, our inner feelings of confidence or apprehension. It affects our trade.

We have, right now, in the Cabinet a committee that, among other things, has the job of trying to promote more foreign trade. Very naturally the State Department has to be in this, because the relations of our countries, one to the other, is always involved.

But now here is a point: there is practically no such thing as a bilateral arrangement between two nations—just as your platform makers have to take me into account in a small way, so does every diplomatic interchange—let us say between Arabia and the United States or Britain and the United States or Japan and the United States—such negotiations always affect other nations.

And this is the thing that makes it so difficult to get these nice, clean-cut decisions that so many of our experts—who are not carrying responsibilities as some of us do—can develop.

Just as all international trade is almost invariably a multi-lateral affair, when we develop our food-for-peace plan we have to think how it affects Canada, Australia, the Argentine, and any other wheat or surplus-wheat producing country, or any country that produces the same surplus as we do.

This is a serious matter.

So it is not merely a matter of saying we have 10 bushel of wheat we would like to get rid of—of course that has to have an exponent on that 10. If we do it in unwise ways, we damage very fine friends who want to stay in the very same corner we are, fighting and working for the freedom of men and the independence of their own countries—and the safety of their own countries.

So I think the tenor of my little simple message this morning is this: in human affairs there is no such thing—in vast organisms, at least—as nice clean-cut "two and two is four" and set it aside and forget it. These are matters of judgment, of long study, of—let us say—experienced conclusions and, finally, readiness to make the particular decision, no

matter even if it might be only the least harmful of three or four that
are possible.

And that is the one reason that I was delighted that your Chairman
introduced to you this morning some of the men who have been my close
associates over these years. They, with Republican leaders of the Congress, have met with me during different weekly meetings, and their conclusions, their analyses of problems, and their recommendations are made
not lightly, but through the study in midnight hours and with a lot of oil
burned in the lamps, in order that they may bring out something that they
believe is the best for the United States.

And then, of course, something that I shall approve.

And I want to say this about them: after all, they are all men of my
selection. I am not going to admit that I made too many mistakes in
naming them. And I cannot remember more than two or three occasions
when, with the overwhelming majority of my advisers saying, "Do this,"
that I have felt it necessary to "do that." And when I so did decide, I
have never had a single one of that Cabinet show any inclination to go
counter to that decision.

What I am saying here is we have had a group of the ablest and most
loyal men I know in America, and people who realize this one great
truth: in the operation of any great human organism, constructive plans
and programs must be developed in what we call the great middle road.

I always liken, in my own mind, the people marching forward into
tomorrow as occupying a great road. Most of them instinctively grow
to like the broad highway stretching before them and they understand
here is where human progress is achieved. Those that insist on marching
in the gutters in the extremes of the right and the left are, in the long
run, always defeated. People instinctively think of themselves—and now
I am excluding from this the moral field—you cannot, of course, use a
lie, then a smaller lie and believe that such a process brings you to the
truth. That doesn't work. I am talking about the practical affairs of
getting humans in great numbers to work together. You must find the
broad highway and you must ignore the gutters.

Fortunately, in our party, I find few if any people are in the gutters.
We Republicans have a broad spectrum of thinking. Unfortunately,
politics is too often described as a conservative against a liberal, or the
right against the left. But just as all America comprehends people,
good sound citizens who want to go ahead and do not feel they should

insist upon getting into the extremes of action—so does the Republican Party.

Now, I think that all of us should hold this one truth in mind: every Republican, everybody he reaches, every independent, every discerning Democrat should be appealed to on the basis that we are truly a middle-of-the-road party and by that I don't mean just walking a wishy-washy path between right and wrong, not at all. The middle road is a kind of path that is always difficult to defend, or at least requires intelligent explanation to defend, because you get your attacks from both flanks. And no commander going into battle of any kind likes to be compelled to fight on both flanks as he is trying to go forward, but that is exactly what a middle-of-the-roader has to do. But because so many people want to go exactly in that direction we have a tremendous strength in our party, and we must make it our business to explain what we mean by middle-of-the-road government.

This is the courageous, the constructive path that all of us must take. We are deeply unified in our support of basic principles: our belief in stability in our financial structure, in our determination we must have fiscal responsibility, in our determination not to establish and operate a paternalistic sort of government where a man's initiative is almost taken away from him by force.

Only in the last few weeks, I have been reading quite an article on the experiment of almost complete paternalism in a friendly European country. This country has a tremendous record for socialistic operation, following a socialistic philosophy, and the record shows that their rate of suicide has gone up almost unbelievably and I think they were almost the lowest nation in the world for that. Now, they have more than twice our rate. Drunkenness has gone up. Lack of ambition is discernible on all sides. Therefore, with that kind of example, let's always remember Lincoln's admonition. Let's do in the Federal Government only those things that people themselves cannot do at all, or cannot so well do in their individual capacities.

Now, my friends, I know that these words have been repeated to you time and time again until you're tired of them. But I ask you only this, to contemplate them and remember this—Lincoln added another sentence to that statement. He said that in all those things where the individual can solve his own problems the Government ought not to interfere, for all are domestic affairs and this comprehends the things

that the individual is normally concerned with, because foreign affairs
does belong to the President by the Constitution—and they are things
that really require constant governmental action.   But for the citizen
himself, this is still to my mind the true, fine way of defining the "middle
of the road."   I would like us to make it not just a casual explanation
of what we want to do.   We ought to have it as a flaming battle flag at
the highest mast that the Republican Party can put up, and fight for it
always, because this is the way to make this great truth of Lincoln's
popular, understood, and followed.

Thank you very much.

——————

May I add: in the home state of Governor Stratton, and because both
a Governor and a Senator are up for election this year, I want to give
my moral support and every kind of influence that I can honorably give
in favor of Governor Stratton and Mr. Witwer, who are to be elected
along with their congressional colleagues.

I wanted to get that plug in.

Thank you again.

NOTE: The President spoke at the Morrison Hotel in Chicago.

247   ¶ Statement by the President Concerning a Program for the Development of Peru.
July 28, 1960

THE PURPOSES of this program are closely in accord with those which
I had in mind on July 11 when I stated that a new affirmation of purpose was called for in our cooperation with friendly developing Latin
American countries in their efforts to progress.   I stated that the aspirations and needs of the peoples of the Americas for free institutions and a
better way of life must be met, and that among the things I had in mind
were the opening of new areas for settlement and opportunities for free
self-reliant men to own their own land and their own homes.

The Government of Peru has succeeded in establishing internal financial
stability and strengthening its economy, essential foundations for accelerated economic and social progress.   It has established a concrete
program to achieve such progress and it will dedicate substantial resources to this end.   Its program is to open for settlement virgin lands

in the rich Upper Selva, to make better use of land now under cultivation, and to give urban working families the opportunity to own their own homes.

Representatives of the Export-Import Bank, the Development Loan Fund, the International Cooperation Administration, and the Department of State recently visited Peru and discussed the details of this program with President Prado, Prime Minister Beltran, Cabinet Ministers and other officials responsible for the program. They personally inspected, from the air and on the ground, typical areas already settled and to be settled, and urban areas where new homes are being built for workers and their families.

NOTE: The statement was released at Denver, Colo., following the announcement of a loan of $53.2 million to Peru for land development and low-cost housing.

For the President's statement of July 11, see Item 228.

248 ¶ Exchange of Messages Between the President and President Nkrumah on the Airlift of Ghanaian Forces to the Congo. *July 31, 1960*

Dear Mr. President:

Thank you very much for your letter of July twenty-seventh expressing your thanks for the assistance which my Government has been able to provide in airlifting from Accra to Leopoldville Ghanaian forces contributed to the United Nations. The prompt and generous manner in which your Government made its forces available in response to the appeal of the United Nations is deserving of the highest praise.

I agree with you that the United Nations action in the Congo is a most heartening demonstration of the effectiveness with which the world community can cooperate.

The American Government is particularly gratified that it has been able to play a part in this operation, and I want to thank you for the indispensable assistance Ghana has given United States aircraft operating through Accra, not only those transporting Ghanaian troops but also those making transit stops with Moroccan and Tunisian forces. This splendid support has been a vital element in the success of our common effort.

I have learned of the military proficiency and the high morale with which the forces of Ghana have carried out their duties under the United Nations Command in the Congo. I extend to you and the people of Ghana my admiration and that of the American people for the conspicuously successful contribution of Ghana in support of the United Nations mission of peace in the Congo.

Sincerely,

DWIGHT D. EISENHOWER

NOTE: President Nkrumah's message follows:

Dear Mr. Eisenhower:

Now that the airlift of Ghana forces to Congo is complete and all Ghana troops have been carried safely to Leopoldville, I should like to send you my personal thanks for the assistance which America has rendered in this regard.

I am particularly happy that United States of America, United Kingdom, Union of Soviet Socialist Republics and United Arab Republic aircraft were able to use Accra Airfield to cooperate with Ghanaian civil aviation in support of the United Nations. It gives me great pleasure that we have had in Accra so practical a demonstration of international cooperation in carrying out the Security Council Resolution.

I hope that you will be able to convey to the pilots and the crews who took part in the operation, my thanks and the thanks of the people of Ghana for the service which they have rendered so ably and efficiently in the cause of upholding the principles of the United Nations.

Yours sincerely,

KWAME NKRUMAH

The messages were released at the U.S. Naval Base, Newport, R.I.

249 ¶ Message to Prime Minister Maga on the Occasion of the Independence of the Republic of Dahomey. *August 1, 1960*

Dear Mr. Prime Minister:

On the occasion of the independence of the Republic of Dahomey, I extend in my own name and on behalf of the United States most cordial greetings and felicitations to you and the people of Dahomey.

The United States has followed with great interest the progress of Dahomey towards independence and it is with deep satisfaction that we welcome this historic event, achieved in friendly cooperation with France.

On this memorable occasion the Government and people of the United States look forward to close and friendly relations with the Government and people of Dahomey.

Sincerely,

DWIGHT D. EISENHOWER

NOTE: The message was released at the U.S. Naval Base, Newport, R.I.

250   ¶ Message to the Students of Korea.
August 2, 1960

To the students of the Republic of Korea:

Throughout my life I will cherish the memory of the warm and gracious welcome recently accorded me by the people of Korea.   For this I wish to express my heartfelt gratitude.   Your welcome afforded convincing proof, if it were necessary, of the friendly and strong bonds between our two peoples.

The world well knows the dedication of the youth and students of Korea to the cause of freedom.   You have proven your courage and your willingness to defend man's most precious possession.   You and your country are now embarked upon the intricate, more difficult task of ensuring that the liberties you have won will find lasting expression in the Republic of Korea.

Youth has the priceless assets of vigor and enthusiasm.   Yet you must also bring to your tasks a sense of infinite patience, broad vision, and deep humility if you are to meet the challenge which faces Korea and the world.   Courage alone will not suffice.   You must demonstrate that sense of individual responsibility and self-restraint which will serve to guarantee both freedom and its inseparable twin, justice.   Free men face a difficult choice; whether they will dissipate their liberty through license; or whether they will take up the burdens which liberty imposes and go forward in the service of mankind.   For freedom must be served as well as sought.   It imposes duties and obligations, as well as bestowing rights and liberties.   Your success in fulfilling these obligations will determine whether your generation will succeed in maintaining a balance between the extremes of license on the one hand and repression on the other.

There are those who would deny you your freedom to achieve their aims—indeed they want to dominate the world.   They exploit both anarchy and servitude.   They seek to convince you that the free world poses a threat to peace and progress.   In this they persist despite clear evidence that they, not we, have brought a third of the world's people into brutal subjugation; that they, not we, foment anarchy in troubled lands; that they, not we, refuse to disarm and, instead, threaten to rain down instruments of destruction upon the weak and the powerful alike. There is, indeed, existing a threat to peace and progress, to your right of self-determination and your liberties; it is posed by the ruthless colonial aggressions which characterize international communism.

Your generation, in Korea and elsewhere, faces as none before it the issue as to whether mankind is to progress united in freedom and justice or whether nations will fall victim one by one to a new and deadly colonialism. Upon your response depend the future of your nation and, in considerable measure, the future of the free world. I have deep confidence that you are equal to the task before you, and I wish you full and complete success in this great responsibility.

Sincerely,

Dwight D. Eisenhower

NOTE: The White House release of the text stated that this message had been requested by Daeyung Kim, a member of the editorial staff of the Chungang Herald, a student newspaper published at Chungang University in Seoul.

The message was released at the U.S. Naval Base, Newport, R.I.

251 ¶ Message to Prime Minister Diori on the Occasion of the Independence of the Republic of Niger. *August 3, 1960*

Dear Mr. Prime Minister:

Upon the accession to independence of the Republic of Niger, I extend in my own name and on behalf of the United States most cordial greetings and felicitations to you and the people of Niger.

The United States has followed with great interest the progress of Niger towards independence and welcomes with deep satisfaction this historic event which was achieved in friendly cooperation with France.

On this memorable day the Government and the people of the United States look forward to close and friendly relations with the Government and people of Niger.

Sincerely,

Dwight D. Eisenhower

NOTE: The message was released at the U.S. Naval Base, Newport, R.I.

252 ¶ Exchange of Messages Between the President and Prime Minister Ikeda of Japan. *August 4, 1960*

Dear Mr. Prime Minister:

I extend my congratulations and best wishes on your election as Prime Minister. I look forward to working closely with your government on all matters of mutual interest and to strengthening the bonds that link our two countries in their dedication to the preservation of peace and human freedom.

Sincerely,

DWIGHT D. EISENHOWER

NOTE: Prime Minister Ikeda's reply follows:

Dear Mr. President:

I am most grateful for your cordial message of congratulations on my election as Prime Minister. I shall continue to work for the strengthening of the ties of friendship and cooperation between our two countries for the cause of world peace and prosperity.

HAYATO IKEDA

The messages were released at the U.S. Naval Base, Newport, R.I.

253 ¶ Message to Prime Minister Yameogo on the Occasion of the Independence of the Republic of Upper Volta. *August 5, 1960*

Dear Mr. Prime Minister:

On the occasion of the independence of the Republic of Upper Volta, I extend in my own name and on behalf of the United States most cordial greetings and felicitations to you and the people of the Upper Volta.

The accession to independence of the Upper Volta is a source of great satisfaction to the United States, especially since this freedom was achieved in friendly cooperation with France.

On this historic day the Government and people of the United States look forward to close and friendly relations with the Government and people of the Upper Volta.

Sincerely,

DWIGHT D. EISENHOWER

NOTE: The message was released at the U.S. Naval Base, Newport, R.I.

254 ¶ Message to Prime Minister Houphouet-Boigny on the Occasion of the Independence of the Republic of the Ivory Coast. *August 7, 1960*

Dear Mr. Prime Minister:

On the occasion of the independence of the Republic of the Ivory Coast, I extend in my own name and on behalf of the United States most cordial greetings and felicitations to you and the people of the Ivory Coast.

The independence of the Ivory Coast is a source of deep satisfaction to the United States, particularly since this freedom was achieved in friendly cooperation with France. We shall follow with keen interest as the newly independent Ivory Coast takes its important place in the community of nations.

I recall with great pleasure our frank and thorough conversation during your visit to Washington last November. Your clear exposition of problems in Africa was of the highest interest to me.

On this historic occasion the Government and people of the United States look forward to close and friendly relations with the Government and people of the Ivory Coast.

Sincerely,

DWIGHT D. EISENHOWER

NOTE: The message was released at the U.S. Naval Base, Newport, R.I.

255 ¶ Special Message to the Congress Upon Its Reconvening. *August 8, 1960*

To the Congress of the United States:

I welcome the return of the Congress. There is much important legislative work still pending that cannot await the selection and assembly of a new Congress and a new Administration. The Executive and Legislative branches must act together on these pressing needs these next few weeks. I shall do my part. I am sure that the Congress will be similarly disposed.

First, the world situation, with its great significance to us.

Fundamentally, it is as it was. The free world still faces a Communist imperialism fixed upon conquest of all the world.

Vigilance, therefore, must still be our watchword. Continuing strength, military, economic, spiritual, must remain our reliance. Our basic objective—to secure a permanent peace—is yet to be won. Our programs have long been keyed to this situation. They must continue.

During the Congressional recess events have dramatized tensions that still plague the world.

We have seen an intensification of Communist truculence.

Indeed, the Soviet dictator has talked loosely and irresponsibly about a possible missile attack on the United States.

An American aircraft has been attacked over international waters. Our resolution requesting an investigation of this matter has been vetoed by the Soviets in the United Nations Security Council. Surviving crew members are still being held prisoner.

The Soviet Delegation has walked out of the Geneva disarmament negotiations.

The Communists continue to exploit situations of unrest, flagrantly striving to turn to their ends the struggles and hopes of peoples for a better world. These Communist efforts have recently reached new extremes in Central Africa.

All of us know about Cuba.

As a result of continuous appraisal of changing Communist tactics and attitudes, I have ordered the military services to take certain practical measures affecting the readiness and posture of our military commands. These include the deployment of additional aircraft carriers to the Sixth and Seventh Fleets. A number of B–47 medium bombers and their accompanying tankers, which had been scheduled to be phased out of our forces, will be retained in service for the time being; and the tempo of operation of the Strategic Air Command will be increased and its deployment further dispersed. The readiness of our ground forces will be further improved by expanding the number and scope of strategic field and airborne exercises.

I have also directed expansion of certain long-range programs. The Strategic Air Command capability to conduct a continuous airborne alert will be further strengthened. More funds will be applied to the modernization of the Army combat equipment and to military airlift. Additional effort will be devoted to the development of the B–70 and the reconnaissance satellite SAMOS.

During the Congressional recess we have made extraordinary progress in testing one of America's most important weapons systems—the Polaris Ballistic Missile Submarine. It is with great satisfaction that I report to the Congress that the first test firings of the Polaris missile from the submerged nuclear submarine GEORGE WASHINGTON had rifle shot accuracy at great ranges. Never in my long military career has a weapon system of such complexity been brought from its original conception to the operational stage with such sureness and speed—an achievement that in its entirety has taken less than five years.

The time is now right to increase the scope of the Polaris program and five instead of three more submarines have been started this fiscal year. Furthermore, I have directed the development of a much longer range version of the Polaris missile, which will give America a weapon of even greater versatility, power and invulnerability.

The Defense Department will carry out these defense measures with its available resources insofar as possible. Measures pertaining to weapons systems programs will be carried out by utilizing appropriations already made in this session. Total resources are adequate, although a modest increase in military personnel and in operation and maintenance funds may prove to be necessary to carry out the readiness measures. If such an increase should be required, I shall promptly request the necessary funds.

Incidentally, provision will have to be made after the first of the year to fund the civilian pay increases imposed by Congress a few weeks ago. These will add permanently to our defense costs some $200 million a year.

Once again I assure the Congress that this Nation's military power is second to none and will be kept that way. Our long range strategic bombers and air to ground missiles, our intermediate and long range ballistic missiles, our Polaris submarines, our attack carriers, the tactical air units overseas, the air defense forces, and the atomic and conventional firepower of our ground forces world-wide are indeed a retaliatory and defensive force unmatched anywhere.

So much for administrative actions which I have recently taken. Congressional actions, too, are required.

Our national security needs encompass more than excellence and strength in our own military establishment. They include measures to build free world strength everywhere. These require, and I therefore request, appropriations of the full amount authorized by the Congress for the Mutual Security Program. At this point in the legislative process, these appropriations have been cut by well over a half billion dollars. The Nation's security and our inescapable interest in a stable world require that these amounts be restored.

In addition, I request a $100 million increase in the authorization and appropriation for the Mutual Security Contingency Fund. This increase is needed to keep America poised for sudden developments such as those in the Congo where a United States airlift and other efforts were needed suddenly and critically. Happily, in this instance, we were able to respond in a matter of hours. We must maintain ourselves in a position to give rapid backing to the efforts of the United Nations in this troubled region.

At my direction, two other matters will be presented to Congress, their purpose being to promote free world stability by stimulating the hopes, morale and efforts of our friends everywhere. These programs are:

First, an authorization in the magnitude of $600 million to help our Latin American neighbors accelerate their efforts to strengthen the social and economic structure of their nations and improve the status of their individual citizens. This program, which should include further assistance for the rehabilitation of devastated Chile, will promote the dynamism and effectiveness of all our efforts in this Hemisphere. I urgently request enactment of this authorization prior to the Economic Conference of the American Republics, which convenes at Bogota on September 5, so that discussions leading to the development of detailed plans may be initiated there.

Second, a proposal to be presented in September before the General Assembly of the United Nations, whereby we and other fortunate nations can, together, make greater use of our combined agricultural abundance to help feed the hungry of the world. The United Nations provides a multilateral forum admirably suited to initiate consideration of this effort.

I consider it important that Congress approve a Resolution endorsing such a program before the United Nations Assembly convenes.

_____

Turning to domestic problems, clearly we face a legislative log jam, the possibility of which I suggested, by special message, on the third of May.

Only one major measure—civil rights—had then been passed, and this had two major deletions which I hope will now be restored in keeping with the bipartisan support evidenced for these items last month.

Legislating time is now short, and so far in this session only six of the twenty-seven measures I cited last May as required by the Nation's interests have been enacted into law.   Because those that fail of enactment before adjournment will go begging for months to come, I urge the Congress to attend to them now.   In addition to those already mentioned, I cite these:

—Federal assistance in the construction of facilities for colleges, universities and elementary and secondary schools;

—assistance to older people to meet serious illnesses;

—expansion of coverage of the Fair Labor Standards Act;

—a moderate upward adjustment of the minimum wage;

—constructive measures to meet existing farm problems;

—a sound area assistance program directed specifically to the areas in need;

—the authorizing of 40 new judgeships to expedite the rendering of justice;

—proper financing to avoid delays in our Interstate Highway Program;

—an increase in the aviation fuel tax to facilitate proper financing of our Airways Modernization Program;

—removal of the interest rate limitation on long-term Treasury bonds;

—a postal rate increase to avoid saddling the next administration and taxpayers generally, wholly unjustifiably, with a postal deficit nearing a billion dollars a year;

—liberalization of our immigration laws;

—continuation of the long-established authority for the President to reorganize the Executive branch;

—and a grouping of measures generally in the conservation field.

Also still needed and long ago recommended are Senate ratification of the important Antarctica Treaty, amendments to speed our space exploration efforts, and a restoration of the traditional relationship between the active duty and the retired pay of our military personnel.

All of these items are at least as urgently needed for America as when first recommended. So I urge that we stay on the job until it is done.

Certainly we cannot adjourn the public interest.

I have a special comment on two of these matters.

First, agriculture. I reiterate the theme of my February ninth and May third messages on this subject. The well-being of our farm people still demands that we act with good sense on their pressing problems, notably wheat. The public will have every right to register its serious protest should the Congress adjourn without responsible action in this area.

The recent history of this problem has been deadlock. The Congress has refused to accept my recommendations and insisted upon unrealistic programs which, of course, I have rejected.

Last January I made one further attempt to resolve this issue. I urged Congress simply to work its will, provided only that the end result fitted within broad guidelines assuring a truly beneficial result for the farmer and the Nation. My own preferred program, leading to greater freedom for the farmer, is widely known. I repeat, however, what I have said many times—if a different approach is desired, and kept within the guidelines, I will unhesitatingly approve it.

Our farmers need constructive action and for years have been entitled to it. They know, as does all America, that this Administration has been unable substantially to alter the existing type of wheat program because of lack of Congressional cooperation. It has been a program attuned to calamity—war, depression or drought—but which in these years of peace and great productivity has resulted in staggering surpluses which overhang the market, depress prices, and threaten the farmer's future.

The Congress should promptly provide the constructive remedies for agriculture so long and so urgently needed.

For five years in a row I have recommended area assistance legislation. Regrettably I had no choice but to veto the legislation the Congress did pass this session. It would have frittered the taxpayers' money away in areas where it was not needed and on programs that would not have benefited those truly in need of help.

A new area assistance bill, with Administration backing, was introduced immediately after my veto. It would channel more help directly into stricken areas than any previous measure proposed. Failure to act will deny this help for months to come. Human distress demands action now. If later we find there should be changes either in the dollar amounts or the methods used, experience will dictate the kind of adjustments to be made.

Last January I estimated that, if the Congress would adhere to my appropriation and revenue recommendations, we could look forward to a budgetary surplus of $4 billion. Since then, however, the spending programs enacted and pending—coupled with the failure of Congress to enact proposed new revenue measures—threaten to consume the entire expected surplus.

This situation relates very importantly to your forthcoming deliberations because of the need of avoiding further deficit spending and of making, in years of prosperity, savings to be applied either to debt reduction or to tax reform.

In meeting this need I shall not abdicate my responsibility to use the Executive power to help keep the Nation's economy strong and sound while we carry forward our urgent work at home and in the world.

This means that I shall not be a party to reckless spending schemes which would increase the burden of debt of our grandchildren, by resuming, in prosperous times, the practice of deficit financing. I shall not fail to resist inflationary pressures by whatever means are available to me.

This truth we must take to heart: in good times, we must at the very least pay our way. This is the fundamental condition for a dependable future for our working men and women, for management, for consumers, and for the Government. If we will but handle responsibly the taxpayers' money, as I am firmly determined that we shall, private and public action can continue to move confidently ahead.

This simply means that we must adhere to necessary programs and sensible priorities. I have herein suggested those in which I believe.

If the Congress prefers other priorities at greater national cost, responsibility dictates that it accompany them with the additional taxes to pay the bill.

I recognize the magnitude of the task still before the Congress, and, of course, I am not unaware of the other matters attracting public attention in this year 1960.

But I repeat—if during the critical months ahead we hold to the standard of national interest, the future will be bright for America—indeed, for all the free world.

DWIGHT D. EISENHOWER

NOTE: The President recorded the message in his office at 12 noon the same day for news broadcasts over radio and television networks.

On August 5 the Director of the Bureau of the Budget submitted, in response to the President's request, a summary of the effect of congressional actions on the President's budget recommendations for fiscal year 1961. This summary (7 pages) was released by the White House on August 9.

In brief, the summary stated that as of that date the net fiscal impact of all congressional actions in the second session was as follows:

1. Net expenditures (i.e. spending and losses of revenue required by congressional action over budget requests, plus revenues requested by the President but not granted) were increased by $1.6 billion for the fiscal year 1961 and by $11.8 billion over a period of years.

2. Pending legislation passed by one or both Houses, and awaiting further congressional action in August, would further increase expenditures and reduce revenues for 1961 by $2.4 billion and over a period of years by $7.8 billion.

The summary noted that if the pending legislation were enacted, in addition to actions already taken, the result would be total revenue decreases and expenditure increases amounting to over $4 billion for fiscal 1961. "This would practically wipe out the $4.2 billion surplus estimated in the 1961 budget," the summary further noted, "and if revenues were to turn out less than estimated, a deficit would result."

256 ¶ The President's News Conference of *August* 10, 1960

THE PRESIDENT. Good morning. Please sit down.

I have a very short statement about this Congolese situation.

[*Reading*] I believe that the Security Council resolution, adopted early yesterday, represents another step forward in the United Nations determination, under the Secretary General's tireless efforts, to find a peaceful solution to the difficult situation in the Congo. The United States welcomes the steps Belgium has already taken and has said it will take in conformity with the Security Council resolutions.

Belgium has contributed much in past years to the development of the Congo. The United States hopes that loyal cooperation with the United Nations on the part of all concerned will restore confidence between the

Belgian and Congolese peoples and enable Belgian civilians to continue their contributions in the development of the new Congolese State. [*Ends reading*]

Any questions?

Q. Jack Bell, Associated Press: Mr. President, both party platforms promised, pledged, an acceleration in defense, and despite the steps you have taken in the last few days and those that you outlined, Senator Lyndon Johnson says that you still do not intend to spend $621 million of the money Congress has made available. Could you tell us why you decided against spending that money?

THE PRESIDENT. Well, can you tell me how you decided that his statement was correct?

Q. Mr. Bell: Sir, I didn't say that his statement was correct. I just said that Senator Johnson——

THE PRESIDENT. You asked me why I decided it. Well, let's don't go that far.

Q. Mr. Bell: All right. If you——

THE PRESIDENT. I know of no reason for anyone to say that I have decided not to spend this money. But I'll tell you this—when you make changes in programs that remove from the budget some one and three-quarters billions of money and put back into it about $1.1 billion for other purposes, now there's a lot of study and tedious allocation and priorities to be settled and it's not done in a few weeks. It's a very difficult thing. And to say that this money has been frozen is—the proposition hasn't even been put before me in those terms at all, whatsoever.

Q. Robert C. Pierpoint, CBS News: Mr. President, I wonder if you could give us your reaction to the possibility that Premier Khrushchev may lead the Soviet delegation to the discussion of disarmament in the United Nations, and could you tell us if you might possibly do the same for the American delegation?

THE PRESIDENT. Well, by no means would I disbar myself from going up if I thought it were necessary. Now, Mr. Khrushchev proposed that all heads of state apparently, or of government, head their delegations when it comes to the General Assembly of September 20th, and that was obviously a propaganda thing.

Now someone told me that he has suggested he might bring his disarmament delegation. I haven't even given any thought to that, I just heard of it this morning sometime. [*Confers with Mr. Hagerty*]

Excuse me, I used the wrong date—September the 15th instead of September 20th.

Q. William McGaffin, Chicago Daily News: Mr. President, do you regret having kept Ezra Benson on as Secretary of Agriculture in view of the unresolved farm problem that is giving Mr. Nixon such a hard time in his campaign?

THE PRESIDENT. Ezra Benson has, to my mind, been very honest and forthright and courageous in trying to get enacted into legislation plans and programs that I think are correct. And, therefore, for me to regret that he has been working would be almost a betrayal of my own views in this matter. I think we must find ways to give greater freedom to the farmer and make his whole business more responsive to market, rather than just to political considerations.

Now, this is what we have been trying to do and, as you know, in January I said—well, I've done everything I could to try to get the Congress to accept sensible measures, and told them—I gave some very broad outlines, largely economic in nature—that if they would bring up a program that they thought was better, or that anywhere fell within these guidelines, I would approve it. Well, they've never done anything about it and the only bill that was passed that I know of was the Senate wheat bill which was killed by the House.

Q. Frank van der Linden, Nashville Banner: Sir, Republicans are saying that it's very likely that you will do a good deal of campaigning in the South in behalf of the Nixon-Lodge ticket because you received so many votes down there yourself in the last two elections. I'd like to ask, sir, are you planning to come south on several speaking trips and do you feel confident that the Nixon-Lodge ticket will do very well down there?

THE PRESIDENT. I think the Nixon-Lodge ticket is going to do well. And whatever I can do to promote it, and its success, because of my conviction that it would be good for the country, I shall do. Now this doesn't mean that I possibly should be out on hustings and making partisan speeches. I'm not so sure that it is—that it would be a good thing. I've got a lot of other responsibilities and I've got a lot of other commitments around the country. But I think these two fellows can take care of themselves pretty well and I think they are tops.

Q. Rowland Evans, Jr., New York Herald Tribune: Mr. President, in this special session will you spend more time discussing strategy with the presidential nominee of your party and will you give him a greater voice in your final determination on vetoes for signing various legislation than you have in the past, in view of his responsibility as the candidate or nominee of the Republican Party?

THE PRESIDENT. In the final analysis my decisions have to be made on what is best, what I believe to be best for our country—whether it is a veto or approval of a bill or anything else. Now, I don't see how the Vice President could be more closely drawn into the consultative process than he has been in the past. He's always been there, in every important meeting of which I can remember. But, I repeat, this is my responsibility and will be until noon on January 20th and until—as long as any question is put up before me involving what I believe is the good of the country, I'm going to decide it according to my judgment.

Q. David Kraslow, Knight Newspapers: Mr. President, the Democrats have charged that the administration proposed civil rights legislation at this time simply to seek political advantage. Would you care to comment on that, sir?

THE PRESIDENT. I made a proposal in January. I called special attention May the 3d, I believe it was, in this year, and I think it would be completely inconsistent if I failed to point out that in the legislation passed this spring, the one major bill that had been passed before May 3d, two of the provisions that I asked for were omitted and that's what I did. I repeated those and I should like to point out that all this talk about me starting a bunch of new programs is just a little bit silly. Go back and look at what I have been recommending, not only during the months past, but for years in some instances. For example, I know for 5 years I have been recommending an area assistance bill, and have had to veto one that was so completely beside the point that it was no good. But I still want one. Now, I'm just asking for what I have always believed.

Q. Mrs. May Craig, Portland (Maine) Press Herald: Sir, I believe you said that we could not permit a Communist-dominated regime to come into our hemisphere. Do we not now have such a regime in Cuba, and what can we do about it in a domination form?

THE PRESIDENT. Well, Mrs. Craig, I am not going to propose specific plans of what we might do. But what I have said is: any organization, I mean any government, that was dominated and controlled by international communism—that is, if it were in the same status, let us say, as a satellite—any other satellite—state, this to my mind would call for very definite action.

Now, the mere fact that someone that might believe in a different form of government than I do and established it themselves freely, then I don't see how the United States could properly object or intervene. Now, I don't believe this is going to happen. I don't believe there is any case in the whole world when any group of people have freely voted to make themselves—to regiment themselves. Therefore I think that you have got to take the situation itself, analyze it—what does it mean? What is its significance in the international world? And then finally devise those means that will defeat it.

Q. Felix Belair, New York Times: Despite assurances from leaders of both parties in the Senate, sir, and as some of the questions here this morning would indicate, the first 3 days of the session have gotten off to a rather partisan political framework. I wonder if you intend to address yourself to this point when you meet with the leaders of both parties next week, or whenever it is, and when would that be?

THE PRESIDENT. I am not going to address myself to the business of lecturing them how they should carry out their own duties and to perform in conformity with their own consciences.

Now, what I shall do is lay out a situation in the international field, which I think is important, and I'll put it this way: I'll invite them to come if they should like, to explain further the details of the international situation as I see it and which have been responsible for some changes in my own programs.

Q. Mr. Belair: Has any date been set?

THE PRESIDENT. No.

Q. Laurence H. Burd, Chicago Tribune: This is a question about the agreement that the Vice President and Governor Rockefeller reached just before the Republican Convention. What do you think of the principles that they set forth, and do you think, as some members of the party seem to, that the Vice President went too far perhaps in appeasing the Governor?

THE PRESIDENT. Well, I don't think he feels that he was appeasing. I think he thought here was a proper activity for two major figures in the political future of our party, and he decided that he should meet with the Governor, and they did, and they came out with certain things. I don't think any one of us would possibly agree with every single comma and period and word, but I think this: I think that certain of the people have already stated—here is a platform that the Republican Party can follow with honor and with the certainty that it would be good for the United States.

Q. Chalmers M. Roberts, Washington Post: On that same point, sir, the Nixon-Rockefeller agreement, it was reported in Chicago at the time of the Convention that you were personally upset at what that agreement had to say about defense on the grounds that it was implicitly critical of your administration. Were you upset and did you try to get the platform language changed at Chicago?

THE PRESIDENT. No. I don't remember that I was upset. As a matter of fact, I didn't see the details of the platform until after I reached—I think it was the following morning, I think it was Wednesday morning, they gave me a pamphlet that had the platform and I read it, frankly, on the way out to Denver.

Now, there were many calls as to what I thought would be a good thing to put in, in the planks of the platform that had to do with defense, and I conferred by telephone with a good many people and for a good many hours. I don't recall anything that I found that I thought of as particularly critical. I have always insisted that you are dealing in a platform with the years as you see them coming up. I've been having to deal with the years that are now in the past, and therefore it would be miraculous if you just said, "This is adequate for the future." And what they say in one decade is not necessarily the same as another. I say one era or one period or one atmosphere might justify one type of action; another era, another atmosphere, might justify something else. In other words, I thought of it as something as building; I hadn't looked at it in the terms that you asked your question.

Q. John M. Hightower, Associated Press: Mr. President, if Mr. Khrushchev should come either to the Disarmament Commission meeting or to the General Assembly meeting, would you see any advantage in having him down here for a talk, or a meeting in New York?

THE PRESIDENT. Well, frankly, Mr. Hightower, I have considered the possibility so remote that I haven't given it a thought. Now, if I were to come to the conclusion that it was useful for me to see him, why, I would of course invite him to come down if he so chose. But, I haven't even given it the kind of thought that would allow me to make a decision at this time.

Q. Peter Lisagor, Chicago Daily News: The Vice President is said to be inhibited by the fact that he cannot speak on the Senate floor. Would you have any objections to his holding press conferences about the legislative program?

THE PRESIDENT. I would have none, no. As a matter of fact I am quite sure that while, with the exception of minute detail, he would be saying exactly the same thing I would be, I have no objection to his going and making any kind of public talk any time, anywhere at a place that is applicable or appropriate and say just exactly what he pleases. Certainly the others do. [*Laughter*]

Q. John R. Gibson, Wall Street Journal: Mr. President, there is a lot of discussion and certain amount of uncertainty as to what the economy can be doing between now and the end of the year. What do your advisers tell you about it?

THE PRESIDENT. Well, of course, the one spot in the economy that everybody watches is steel, which finally got down to 50 percent and is now going back a little bit. Now, we've got to remember about steel, that because of the rather hysterical production before and after the strike that we were operating almost at 100 percent, and this country cannot now consume and absorb a steel production that we are capable of turning out. After all, I think we can do almost 150 million tons a year. So, it would—we couldn't possibly expect to be operating at 100 percent, but that is nevertheless showing one of these ups and downs in the steel production that is always bothersome.

As of now this is the latest report I have from the economic advisers. Gross national product is—for the second quarter—is even higher than we had estimated. Personal income is over $400 billion. Both of these are records. Employment is almost 69 million, another record; and retail sales continue to go up at a record.

Now, these are very hopeful signs and certainly there is no reason to read what you might call a receding or any kind of depressionlike situation in our economy. People have talked a little about housing, how right now they are building houses at a rate of 1,300,000, which is, I think with one exception, as high as we have ever been. And automobiles—in July were not very good, but one reason is that they are making their—still we are going on a 6 million basis this year and it looks like we will make something over 6 million, which is really a very fine year.

And on top of that the models are probably coming up earlier this year, I have heard, and therefore there may be some hesitancy in buying the new automobiles.

All in all, while you do not see a picture of a burgeoning economy at this particular period you certainly don't see any signs that anyone can call a recession or depression.

Q. Spencer Davis, Associated Press: Do you see any need, sir, for the United States to reexamine or reappraise its economic and military aid program to Laos in view of the rebel regime that has ousted the government there and invited our forces to leave?

THE PRESIDENT. Well, actually, for I guess about 30 hours now, I have been trying to get some real details on the Laos situation, and we really don't know anything about it. It does appear that all of the country except the capital, taken over by a battalion of parachuters, remains loyal to the royal government. So, until there is some clarification, I don't think we can make any answer whatsoever.

Q. Sarah McClendon, El Paso Times: Sir, there is some puzzlement about your message that you sent to Congress Monday on the military program. Is this an about-face on your program to expand the ground forces and give them more modern equipment and increase the capability of SAC and B-70 bombers, is this an about-face or is it a change that you took in light of the world situation or were you influenced to do this by Mr. Nixon or Mr. Rockefeller? [*Laughter*]

THE PRESIDENT. Well, I wasn't influenced by anybody except my own military and State Department advisers and my own judgment. Now, anyone who does not see evidence that the Soviets have been trying to create a very different atmosphere than what it had been trying to create over the past couple of years is not reading very closely. This being so, it seems to me that it's all a matter of keeping the confidence of your allies and your own people that you are taking anything that within reason shows your awareness of this kind of change and take such effective and reasonable steps as you believe will do something to counteract them.

Q. Charles L. Bartlett, Chattanooga Times: Mr. President, what is your present thinking on the question of underground nuclear testing, and is there any difference on this point between you and the Vice President?

THE PRESIDENT. Well I can't recall what he has ever said specifically about nuclear underground testing. As you will recall, I think it was in December of last year, I said we would be no longer bound by any gentleman's agreement on this matter, but that we were going to hold our hand until we could exhaust every possibility of reaching some worthwhile agreement.

Now, this has been a very disappointing and discouraging thing and we've apparently made no progress. But, I will just simply say this: when we come to the place that progress is not possible, then we have to take care of ourselves. But I will adhere, as long as I am here, to the one promise I made: I will not allow anything to be exploded in the atmosphere that would add anything to the apprehensions of people about their health.

Q. Carleton Kent, Chicago Sun-Times: Can you tell us if there is any substance to reports that there is a possible Soviet overt move in the offing in Europe or in Asia this late summer or fall, perhaps against Berlin or——

THE PRESIDENT. I haven't—where?

Q. Mr. Kent: Against West Berlin or somewhere else in Europe.

THE PRESIDENT. Well, the only thing I could think of that is related to your question, is that Mr. Khrushchev continually says something to the effect that he will be ready to sign a peace treaty with East Germany at such and such a time. I believe that he made that statement most recently in connection with his objection to the meeting of the Bundestag in West Berlin. Well, this is something that has been going on for a long time, and I don't know any reason why he should make this statement at this moment. But otherwise, I don't know of anything that would indicate any intention on their part to do anything major.

Q. Ralph de Toledano, King Features: The Democrats have indicated that they will block all attempts to enact the programs that you sent up to the Hill. Do you have any plans for going over the head of Congress to the people?

THE PRESIDENT. Well, I don't know; possibly I'm doing it right now. [*Laughter*]

I am just simply trying to say that I have been standing for a number of things for quite a while, and I think to—now to desert them and say we'll do nothing about them merely because Congress saw fit to recess and then have what they say is a short session, we cannot just simply say that politicking is more important than the Nation's business, and I don't think it is. I think that the Nation's interest comes first, and we should do what we can about it. And I personally think this: I think all this talk about Congress having to take weeks and months and months to get simple actions carried out and accomplished is a little bit silly. If there is a determination on the great majority that there is now in the Congress, to enact a constructive program, it could be done very quickly, because they've got a 2 to 1 majority in both houses.

Q. S. Douglass Cater, Jr., Reporter Magazine: Mr. President, are you, in your discussions with the Vice President, do you feel that there is any serious difference between you on the size of the defense acceleration that is needed at this time?

THE PRESIDENT. No, I don't think so. Certainly if there is, he hasn't come to me with it, and we've talked about it.

Q. James B. Reston, New York Times: Mr. President, would you spell out for us the ideas you have in mind for your new Latin American program?

THE PRESIDENT. Well, by and large it's this: to find better ways of getting a cooperative effort in these nations to bring about the thing they are always talking about—a rise of living standards throughout their nations. Many of our lending institutions are not geared to this kind of thing. You build roads and docks with what you call soft loans because they are not immediately productive, and you help mines and industry, initiating new industries and all the rest of it with different types like the Ex-Im Bank, but what we need is something, and programs which we can work out ourselves and have enough authorization or intent behind them that we can begin to give more hope directly to people throughout this hemisphere.

Q. Mr. Reston: Could I ask another question about that?
THE PRESIDENT. Yes.

Q. Mr. Reston: Well if you do not get in this month, these 3 weeks, the program you want, will you then summon the Congress back at a later date?

THE PRESIDENT. I wouldn't think it—well, it's not a matter I have thought of yet. Congress has been here quite a bit this year, but I am not asking for a specific program, Mr. Reston. I'm saying I would like to have an expression of the sentiment in the Congress and its intent that we would, together, find ways to bring about this raising of living standards and bringing better life to these people generally, rather than just confining ourselves to these particular different types of loans of which I speak.

Now, if we have that then we can go to the Bogota conference and talk definitely—what are the kinds of plans and what are the programs

I don't want to make the programs from here for South America, as you can well see. They are the ones that have to make the programs or cooperate with them. Then, if we can find that we can support them with a good heart and knowing that we are serving our own interests as well as theirs, then I think we'd have something really worthwhile.

Jack Bell, Associated Press: Thank you, Mr. President.

NOTE: President Eisenhower's one hundred and eighty-eighth news conference was held in the Executive Office Building from 10:29 to 10:59 o'clock on Wednesday morning, August 10, 1960. In attendance: 206.

257 ¶ Message to Prime Minister Tombalbaye on the Occasion of the Independence of the Republic of Chad. *August 11, 1960*

Dear Mr. Prime Minister:

On the occasion of the independence of the Republic of Chad, I extend in my own name and on behalf of the United States most cordial greetings and felicitations to you and the people of Chad.

The accession to independence of the Republic of Chad is a source of great satisfaction to the United States especially since it was achieved in friendly cooperation with France.

The development of democratic traditions under your leadership at the Crossroads of Africa is encouraging for the future of Chad.

On this historic day, the Government and people of the United States look forward to close and friendly relations with the Government and people of Chad.

Sincerely,

DWIGHT D. EISENHOWER

258 ¶ Message Recorded for Transmission Via Communication Satellite Echo I. *August* 12, 1960

THIS IS President Eisenhower speaking.

It is a great personal satisfaction to participate in this first experiment in communications involving the use of a satellite balloon known as Echo. This is one more significant step in the United States program of space research and exploration. The program is being carried forward vigorously by the United States for peaceful purposes for the benefit of all mankind.

The satellite balloon which has reflected these words may be used freely by any nation for similar experiments in its own interests. Information necessary to prepare for such participation was widely distributed some weeks ago.

The United States will continue to make freely available to the world the scientific information acquired from this and other experiments in its program of space exploration.

NOTE: The message was transmitted from the Jet Propulsion Laboratory station at Goldstone, Calif., as Echo I was completing its first orbit, and was relayed by the satellite to the Bell Telephone Laboratories station in Holmdel, N.J.

259 ¶ Message to Prime Minister Dacko on the Occasion of the Independence of the Central African Republic. *August* 13, 1960

Dear Mr. Prime Minister:

On the occasion of the independence of the Central African Republic, I extend in my own name and on behalf of the United States most cordial greetings and felicitations to you and the people of the Central African Republic.

The United States has followed with great interest the progress of the Central African Republic towards independence while carrying out the traditions of the late Barthelemy Boganda. That this independence is being reached in harmony and friendship with France is a source of great satisfaction.

On this memorable day, the Government and people of the United

States look forward to close and friendly relations with the Government and people of the Central African Republic.

Sincerely,

DWIGHT D. EISENHOWER

260 ¶ Message to President Youlou on the Occasion of the Independence of the Republic of Congo. *August* 15, 1960

Dear Mr. President:

On the occasion of the independence of the Republic of Congo, I extend in my own name and on behalf of the United States most cordial greetings and felicitations to you and the people of Congo.

The United States has followed with great interest the progress of the Congo towards independence in harmony and friendship with France. It is with deep satisfaction that we welcome this historic event.

I recall with great pleasure and appreciation the thoughtful gift which you made to me last year in the name of the Community. This tangible token of affection of the Community and of yourself for the United States will long be remembered.

On this historic day, the Government and people of the United States look forward to close and friendly relations with the Government and people of Congo.

Sincerely,

DWIGHT D. EISENHOWER

NOTE: The President referred to the gift of a baby elephant presented at the time of his visit to Paris in 1959 (see 1959 volume, this series, p. 652).

261 ¶ Remarks Upon Inspection of the Capsule Retrieved From the Satellite Discoverer XIII. *August* 15, 1960

I SHOULD LIKE to think of some way that I could properly commend the people who are responsible for this remarkable achievement. I know that mere medals and ribbons don't do this. But I do think that I can in a feeble way attempt to assure all of you that the American people are indeed proud of what you have done.

This is another incident in a remarkable series of accomplishments that show how rapidly America has forged far ahead into worthwhile exploration of space. This one has so much promise for future development of the same kind of achievement and possibly even, finally, having men to come back to tell us about it.

The great achievement of the sun satellite that for 22 million miles and 3 months continued to telemeter back to the United States and to the world—to the earth—information that never before had been achieved.

And finally another recent one, this one about the balloon—this big balloon. I just had a report this morning from scientific circles outside of Government which said that this was the greatest advance in the science of communications that had been achieved in many years.

So to have this remarkable achievement we have here today climax this long series must indeed give every American a great deal of pride and particularly those of you and all your associates that had a part in it.

Quite naturally, I am proud that someone thought of the thoughtful gesture, so far as I was personally concerned, of giving me this little flag that has certainly now for itself a unique history. I will try to see that it is put into a place where all Americans can see it and be reminded of this great accomplishment.

Thank you very much.

NOTE: The President spoke in the Conference Room at the White House where the capsule was on exhibit.

Gen. Thomas D. White, Chief of Staff of the U.S. Air Force, presented the President with a flag taken from the capsule, which was recovered from the Pacific Ocean on August 12. In presenting the flag General White noted that the capsule had been released from orbit in outer space in the vicinity of our 49th State, Alaska, and recovered in the vicinity of the 50th State, Hawaii. Secretary of Defense Thomas S. Gates, Jr., also spoke at the ceremonies.

The remarks of General White and Secretary Gates were released with those of the President.

262 ¶ Message to President Makarios on the Occasion of the Independence of the Republic of Cyprus. *August 16, 1960*

Dear Mr. President:

Upon the achievement of independence by the Republic of Cyprus, I am happy to extend in my own name and on behalf of the people of the United States most cordial greetings and felicitations to you, the members of your Government, and the Cypriot people in the Greek, Turkish, and other communities of the Republic.

The emergence of an independent and democratic Cyprus is a tribute to your statesmanship as well as that of Vice President Kutchuck and all those whose dedicated efforts have brought to a successful conclusion the negotiations of the past year and a half. The United States is a close friend of all parties to these negotiations, and is therefore especially gratified at their happy outcome.

The Government and people of the United States welcome the independent and democratic Republic of Cyprus to the family of nations, and look forward to maintaining close and cordial relations with the Government and people of Cyprus.

Sincerely,

DWIGHT D. EISENHOWER

263 ¶ The President's News Conference of *August 17, 1960*

THE PRESIDENT. Good morning. Please sit down.

I had a few questions about the accomplishments of the Space Agency over the past week, and so I had a short memorandum prepared this morning that will be available at Mr. Hagerty's office if any of you want them. It lists the unusual accomplishments of the week.[1]

Any questions?

Q. Frank Eleazer, United Press International: Mr. President, Francis Powers, the U–2 pilot, pleaded guilty today to spying. Does this indicate

---

[1] See item 264.

to you in any way that he may have been brainwashed or do you have any other comments, sir, on the conduct of the trial so far?

THE PRESIDENT. Well, no, it doesn't show evidence that he has been brainwashed. The only thing I would like to comment on would be the past history of the case.

Under international usage—custom—any foreigner who is accused of a crime in any country has been accorded the right to see counsel of his own choosing and to see interested consuls or people of that kind of the other government. In this case, of course, Mr. Powers has been given no such privilege and we have asked that he should have it.

Now, in the actual conduct of the trial, as it goes on, I would have no comment because it certainly wouldn't be helpful to Mr. Powers' case for anyone in my position to be commenting on the conduct of a trial in that other country.

Q. Ray L. Scherer, National Broadcasting Company: Mr. President, a number of us talked to Mr. Dirksen and Mr. Halleck after they conferred with you yesterday, and they said that generally they don't look for much from this post-Convention session of Congress. Some of us got the impression that Republican strategy will be to label this a "do-little" Congress. Is that the way you see it, Mr. President?

THE PRESIDENT. Well, that is the first time that I have heard that word "do-little" Congress and I didn't—I suppose they were speaking as legislators, and possibly from past experience. You know, strangely enough, someone called my attention to the fact that the Congress passed in 2 weeks last year 436 bills. And now we have a program that was not only presented last January for consideration during these past some 7 or 8 months, but it has been repeated to the Congress in messages of various kinds during the time. This is not a new program. It is one that was presented some months back. And I don't see any reason why there shouldn't be some action.

Q. Lloyd M. Schwartz, Fairchild Publications: Mr. President, in the closing months of any administration, the President usually has the problem of persuading people not to leave their posts and go back to their private businesses. I wonder if you are having that problem already, or anticipate having it soon?

THE PRESIDENT. No, I haven't in any—there certainly has been no volume of it. I remember one of my staff was offered a different position, and he accepted, with my blessing. But I have always done that, and I have seen no great influx of letters of resignation at the moment.

Q. Chalmers M. Roberts, Washington Post: Mr. President, since the Democrats do not seem disposed to enact any, or much, of your 21-point program, are you considering at all the possibility that you might call Congress back into session before the elections, or do you prefer to leave the issue to the voters in November?

THE PRESIDENT. Well, Mr. Roberts, I think it would be a very unwise thing to call a special session of Congress under the atmosphere in which we are now living, unless actual emergency demands it. If Congress doesn't want to act now, what would be the point in bringing them back?

If we are thinking of the public interest and not just of political maneuvering, why, there can be done what needs to be done. Then if the voters are dissatisfied with either side, why, they can make their views known.

Q. Edward P. Morgan, American Broadcasting Company: Mr. President, this is a question about your project for an emergency fund for the Congo and Africa, which the Senate Foreign Relations Committee approved yesterday. Do you think that a case can be made, particularly at this juncture, for use of some of those funds through the United Nations, or does the administration think it would be wiser and easier to spend the money independently?

THE PRESIDENT. Well, I wouldn't want to comment in such detailed fashion about this question that I would appear to set up a new policy on the spur of the moment. Actually, I believe that we must depend on the United Nations to take the leadership in meeting these situations as they arise. Actually, there haven't been too many of them, you know, when you stop to think that, I believe, with the six nations now soon to come into existence we have got something like 34 or 35 coming into existence since World War II. And in many—most cases—these transitions have been accomplished not only peacefully but in such ways that a certain degree of stability has been achieved almost at once. Here we have had the unfortunate spectacle of disorder and disruption of governmental processes occurring. The United Nations ought to take the lead, and we support it. Therefore, if some of the funds that we have to give to this place go through them, it will be, I think, a proper way to do it.

Q. Mr. Morgan: How do you envision, sir, the use of those funds in other ways? The funds that would not go through the United Nations—how do you expect them to be applied?

THE PRESIDENT. You will recall, I think it says not merely the Congo, but in the other areas of Africa. So you couldn't always do it through the United Nations, because the United Nations probably wouldn't have taken any cognizance of the need expressed to us by that nation.

I would think each one would have to be decided on its merits as it came up. But I think if you will read Mr. Dillon's statement in detail, the one he made before the Committee the other day, it was very explanatory.

Q. Felix Belair, New York Times: Mr. President, you spoke a moment ago of the U.N. taking the lead in Africa with our support. What will you do, if you can say, sir—what do we do when U.N. troops are arrested over there and also do you have any correspondence on this?

THE PRESIDENT. Well, this last incident—you mean when Lumumba arrested some of them and then released them? Well, you have got conditions that are deplorable, and there seem to be many actions taken impulsively. I still say this: the United Nations must shoulder its responsibilities in such matters, and we must support them. And I think that the vast bulk of the free nations will feel exactly as we do about this. Now, this doesn't mean that things are always going to be easy, and we are not going to have such incidents as occurred the other day—or yesterday, I guess it was. But I think that on the whole, the record of the United Nations gives a great deal of promise that it can continue to handle matters like this expeditiously.

Q. Mrs. May Craig, Portland (Maine) Press Herald: Mr. President, regardless of whether Congress did or didn't do what it should since January, do you think it is possible for them now to deal with all of your more than a score of points when the time is so short, or do you think that they should go out and explain their future policies and platforms to the voters between now and November?

THE PRESIDENT. Well, we have a Congress of the United States, set up in the Constitution, to pass the laws that are seemingly needed for the United States. And under that system we have developed the two-party system. We have now in each House of Congress a two-thirds majority. And as a matter of fact, from my viewpoint at least, such of this legislation as is constructive, and I believe those that I have recommended are supported by the Republican group, I see no reason why you couldn't get a lot of action, particularly when, as I pointed out, there were 436 bills passed in 2 weeks last year.

Q. Robert C. Pierpoint, CBS News: Mr. President, I wonder if you

have some kind of a priority among these 21 proposals that you could list
for us.

THE PRESIDENT. No, no. Actually, after having put these things
before the Congress, the Congress will have to decide what it is going to
do and what it is not going to do.

Q. Peter Lisagor, Chicago Daily News: Suggestions were made in the
Senate this week that perhaps it would be wise to devise a program, a
multibillion-dollar program, for Latin American aid, something on the
concept of the Marshall plan. Can you tell us how you would feel about
such a program?

THE PRESIDENT. The Marshall plan was developed for a specific purpose. This specific purpose was the restoration of a damaged and, in
some cases, destroyed industrial fabric in Western Europe—mostly in
Western Europe. Now, this was—this had, in other words, a foreseeable
terminating date because it had a specific objective.

When you go into the problem of helping people raising living standards, this has no foreseeable end at the moment; it is a thing that has to
be studied year by year, adapted, changed to meet changing conditions,
and this is an entirely different thing. I don't believe any man is wise
enough today to foresee what will be the ultimate need and set up the
program and the money to meet it. I think that this is the kind of thing
where a family of nations, like a family of individuals, have to understand
they live together; and in living together, new needs come up. And if
they are met cooperatively by everybody putting his brains and his
resources into it, we will get somewhere. But I don't believe that any
nation could at this moment, for all the other 20, say, "We will put x
billion dollars, and here is a program, and if you do this you will be all
right." I don't believe that for a minute.

Q. Lambert Brose, Lutheran Layman: Mr. President, there has been
some criticism in the press of the hopeful signs you gave of our economy
at last week's news conference. And Newsweek magazine has taken some
of the Government statistics you quoted and shows that, according to
Newsweek, that they are not so favorable. May I quote several of them
to you?

THE PRESIDENT. It's all right with me. [*Laughter*]

Q. Mr. Brose: You said last week: "Retail sales continue to go up at
a record," and Newsweek says, "Total retail sales dropped during July
to 18.3 billion, lowest level in 3 months. It is no higher than it was a

year ago, despite rising population and rising prices."

And then you said last week: "Right now, they are building houses at a rate of 1.3 million, which is, I think with one exception, as high as we have ever been." Newsweek says: "Home builders are in fact having their worst year, with one exception, since 1954."

And one more—[*laughter*]—I just want to mention. You stated: "Employment is almost 69 million, another record." Newsweek says: "Unemployment, which the President didn't mention, is over 4 million, a high 5.4 percent of the labor force."

My question is: do you think—[*laughter*]—the public may have received a slightly more favorable outlook of the economy at last week's press conference than really is justified?

THE PRESIDENT. Allowing for the possibility that any man can always misspeak himself a little bit, I don't admit that I made any error. But I will tell you: you are talking now about a quarrel between Newsweek and the Council of Economic Advisers, and I ask you to go and meet them, and see what they have to say about it. [*Laughter*]

Q. Edward T. Folliard, Washington Post: Mr. President, last week you were asked about your role in the campaign. As I remember it, you said that you would do whatever you could to help the Nixon-Lodge ticket, but you didn't think it would be wise to go out on the hustings. And since then, it has been announced that you are going to make a couple of nonpolitical speeches. What is your reasoning there, Mr. President, that nonpolitical speeches, so called, would be more helpful to the Nixon-Lodge ticket? I was a little puzzled.

THE PRESIDENT. Well, certainly I wouldn't want to hurt that ticket, because I think it is fine. But let's get this thing straight.

There becomes a division of responsibility with respect to the future— you might say the political future of this country—that must be obvious to everybody. I necessarily remain as President of the United States, and I am responsible for every decision taken up, as I say, until January 20, on the actions of this Government.

Now, there is a political campaign up, when by Constitution I am no longer included. I am just a spectator in a way. Therefore, the direction of the political campaign as such—not the Government, but the political campaign—falls into other hands.

Now, they come to me, because after all we have been working together a long time, and they do realize that what I do will have some definite influence on that election. Then they will tell me what they want done.

What I am saying is that I have already accepted, oh, months back, some engagements—like I am going up to speak for my old friend, Cardinal Spellman, in the Catholic Church. I guess we have announced this, haven't we?

Mr. Hagerty: Yes, sir.

THE PRESIDENT. And in Philadelphia, and places like that. Now, what I would do otherwise, I know that there is one—there is one performance coming in where I am going to be part of the political picture, and make a political speech. I don't know how many. But they will give me their ideas, and if I agree, why, that is exactly what I will do, because I am going to do whatever I can to elect Mr. Nixon and Mr. Lodge; you can bet on that.

Q. David Kraslow, Knight Newspapers: Mr. President, this administration has prided itself on being budget conscious, yet it is sponsoring a medical care program for the aged that will make a sizable dent in the general Treasury, while the Democratic leadership, which has been criticized in the past on spending issues, is sponsoring a so-called self-funding plan, pay as you go, as they put it. Will you comment on that, sir?

THE PRESIDENT. Well, I say this. I am for a plan that will be truly helpful to the aged, particularly against illnesses which become so expensive, but one that is freely accepted by the individual. I am against compulsory medicine, and that is exactly what I am against, and I don't care if that does cost the Treasury a little bit more money there. But after all, the price of freedom is not always measured just in dollars.

Q. Sarah McClendon, Manchester (N.H.) Union Leader: Mr. President, I presume from the reappointments in the State Department that you have taken some look recently at the background and actions of—both actions and policy in the State Department on the things that brought about the Communist encroachment in Cuba. Now, I wonder if from your look at that, if you have found mistakes that were made, and if you would tell us who were making the mistakes?

THE PRESIDENT. Well, you must be asking for some kind of white paper—[*laughter*]—that will tell everything that we have ever done in Cuba. I have not heard of any circumstances that would justify the question you have just asked. And I know of no blunder which I can attach blame to anyone for. Therefore—and I have had these reports on

Cuba every day, I think, for the last month, either by telephone or personally—I don't know of any reason for apologizing for what we have done in the past.

Q. Mrs. McClendon: Well, sir, may I——

THE PRESIDENT. No, thank you.

Q. E. W. Kenworthy, New York Times: A further question, sir, on aid to Latin America. While the situations confronting the Marshall plan countries and Latin America are quite different, would it be helpful if the Latin American countries would set up an equivalent organization to the——

THE PRESIDENT. Would set up a what?

Q. Mr. Kenworthy:——an equivalent organization to the OEEC, which the Marshall plan countries have, to help plan the aid they want?

THE PRESIDENT. Well, I wouldn't be too quick to give a specific answer on this. I think it would be good. And I am speaking personally, and not having discussed this particular point with others—very competent people in this field. I am sure of this: that the OAS must provide a mechanism where this whole development is going to be on a cooperative basis, and where there is the actual decision made on a group basis, because if it is made unilaterally, and we pretend to be the great experts on Latin America, and everything that we say is to be done and nothing else, then it will not work. It has got to be a very cooperative effort, and if it is an organization something as we developed in the OEEC, why, fine.

Q. Paul Martin, Gannett Newspapers: Mr. President, Marion Folsom said the other day that, on this health bill, Congress should not act this year in a political atmosphere. He suggested that we appoint a study commission, composed of representatives of the insurance industry, medical profession, employers, labor, and so on, with instructions to report next year, and let the next administration and the next Congress, with the basis of facts, determine what they should do. What do you think about that idea?

THE PRESIDENT. Well, first of all, I have great admiration for Marion Folsom. Secondly, I very thoroughly believe in a thorough analysis of all the facts that we can find in such thing—in such affairs, in such vast programs, before we take action.

Now, the fact is that there has been an awful lot of study. We have conferred with the American Medical Association, with the insurance companies, and everybody that seemed to have an authoritative voice in this matter.

And I am not adverse to the studies. I doubt that you ever get a really favorable year to do anything as difficult. People say it is either election year or it is not an election year. Either one seems to be a good excuse for not doing anything. But the fact is that if such studies would give us a better and clearer idea, why, of course, I would have no objections. But I do believe that something ought to be done now, because these people are truly in need for this kind of support and help.

Q. Spencer Davis, Associated Press: Would you say, sir, how the situation in Laos looks to you now, and if you contemplate any need to pull out American aid and military missions in that country?

THE PRESIDENT. Well, Laos is a very confused situation. Of course, the new prime minister is getting ready to present his newly established government to the Assembly, and that is about the only development since last week. And I can say only this: that both in Laos and here in Washington we are following the situation just as earnestly as we can, and certainly to take any kind of action that seems to be indicated.

Q. John V. Horner, Washington Star: Mr. President, now that the American foreign ministers are in session, what do you think that they should do, or what would you like to see them do, about Cuba?

THE PRESIDENT. Well, I think that they are brought together there to study everything that is of interest, and particularly that seems to disturb the public opinion in all the Americas, from here on southward. Both by the report made to the foreign—to the Council—yesterday, both Trujillo, the Dominican problem, and the Cuban problem are cited as two of the items which they must study, and decide among themselves what to do. And further than that, I would not want to comment, because I am quite clear in my mind that these matters are for all the states of the OAS. It is not merely because we have had some specific problems and difficulties in these areas. This does not make it our problem alone. If we can't solve it on a cooperative and general basis, then indeed it would look quite bad.

Q. Lillian Levy, Science Service: Mr. President, there have been reports, sir, that there is some feeling among our allies that an agreement on the cessation of nuclear tests cannot be achieved between East and West before the end of your administration. What is your appraisal of the possibility of an agreement between now and January?

THE PRESIDENT. Well, of course the history of the whole thing doesn't seem too good, for the simple reason that we have been working so hard on this thing up to now. And I would say this: nothing could gratify me more than to achieve, between the East and West, some agreement that would bring a bit more of peace of mind to all our people, and would do so by making certain that that agreement could be policed on both sides— that is, inspected and kept everybody up to snuff.

Q. Frank van der Linden, Nashville Banner: Mr. President, the polls are now beginning to show that Vice President Nixon is pulling ahead of Mr. Kennedy in the presidential race, and his press secretary says he now has closed the gap, and they are running neck to neck. I wonder, sir, if you have any advice to Mr. Nixon's friends and the Republicans not to get a little overconfident as was done in 1948, and maybe keep working.

THE PRESIDENT. Well, I wasn't here in '48. But I would say this: in any competitive enterprise, whether it is war or politics or anything else, no one should be pessimistic or discouraged by some straw in the wind, and certainly he should not be complacent with another straw that seems to point favorably in his direction. I am quite sure that Mr. Nixon is correct when he says he is starting a fight as rapidly as he can, and he is going to wage it right down to the last minute of the campaign, because I think he is too old a campaigner to take anything for granted.

Q. John M. Hightower, Associated Press: I would like to raise the question of the Powers case again, sir. The major Soviet propaganda line in connection with this case is that the United States itself is on trial. I wondered whether you had occasion to give this matter some thought, and what your reaction is to this line.

THE PRESIDENT. Well, I don't think it is, whatsoever. When we admitted publicly that the U-2 belonged to us and that it was on a reconnaissance mission, we were doing something that in a modern world was the only way we could find out, to get any information, about a closed society, and a society that is constantly threatening us by their strength, boasting about what they could do to the world, and all the rest of it.

Now, this does not put the United States on trial whatsoever. If they want to say that they are putting me on trial, that is their privilege. But to put the United States on trial in this way is just another piece of their propaganda that distorts fact into their own line of charge and allegation.

Q. Benjamin R. Cole, Indianapolis Star: Mr. President, in connection with that, if the Soviets put the President of the United States on trial, how, then, can they put an American citizen on trial for carrying out a mission under the command of his Commander in Chief?

THE PRESIDENT. Well, they can't put him on trial, because they can't take jurisdiction in the sense that you are speaking. What they are trying—they are trying to say that they are condemning the United States before world opinion. Well, I think they have no case whatsoever. The number of spies that we have caught, and cases of bribery and subversion, which have been proved all over the world, gives their—just denies any validity whatsoever to this kind of a charge on their part.

Jack Bell, Associated Press: Thank you, Mr. President.

NOTE: President Eisenhower's one hundred and eighty-ninth news conference was held in the Executive Office Building from 10:30 to 10:59 o'clock on Wednesday morning, August 17, 1960. In attendance: 215.

264 ¶ Statement by the President on U.S. Achievements in Space. *August* 17, 1960

THE EVENTS of the past weeks have demonstrated beyond all doubt the vigor, capabilities and leadership of the United States in the conquest of the frontiers of science and technology and, in particular, in the exploration and utilization of space. The entire nation is proud of the impressive array of successful experiments carried out by the United States this year:

—Pioneer V, the sun satellite, which continued to receive and transmit radio messages over a period of three months and to a distance of 22,500,-000 miles from earth;

—Tiros I, the meteorological satellite which took 23,000 cloud cover pictures during its operating life of three months and provided increased assurance that revolutionary improvements in the science of weather forecasting will be achieved;

—the success that has attended the efforts in the satellite-based navigation program called Transit I;

—the orbiting of Echo I, the 100-foot balloon which circles the earth at a distance of approximately 1000 miles and a speed in excess of 15,000 miles per hour serving as a reflector of radio signals from one point to another and distant point on the surface of the earth;

—the record-breaking flights of the X–15 research airplane;

—and finally, the spectacular recovery of the data capsule of the Discoverer XIII satellite.

All these are the results of a well planned and determined attack on this new field—an attack that promises very real and useful results for all mankind. Each of these satellites is destined to play an important part in broadening man's understanding of the cosmos in which he lives. While no one of them has been undertaken solely in an effort to achieve a "spectacular first" in the eyes of the world, each has resulted in just such a "spectacular first" in support of the desires of mankind for greater knowledge and understanding.

The United States leads the world in the activities in the space field that promise real benefits to mankind.

265   ¶ Message to President M'ba on the Occasion of the Independence of the Republic of Gabon.   *August 17, 1960*

Dear Mr. President:

On the occasion of the independence of the Republic of Gabon, I extend in my own name and on behalf of the United States most cordial greetings and felicitations to you and the people of the Republic of Gabon.

The United States has followed with great interest the progress of Gabon toward independence in harmony and friendship with France. It welcomes this historic event with deep satisfaction.

The close ties between our countries and the excellent climate Gabon has provided for United States and other Western investments constitute a favorable omen for the future of your country.

On this memorable occasion, the Government and people of the United States look forward to continued close and friendly relations with the Government and people of Gabon.

Sincerely,

DWIGHT D. EISENHOWER

266 ¶ Letter Accepting Resignation of Henry Cabot Lodge as U.S. Representative to the United Nations. *August 19, 1960*

Dear Cabot:

In the past seven and a half years the United Nations has indeed, as you say, grown greatly in influence and as an agency for the preservation of peace. This has not been so because of any one nation or any one man. But the United States has sought to nurture that growth. As her Representative you have applied extraordinary talents of firmness, perseverance, and imagination to pressing in that forum our aims of peace with freedom and justice.

For your services in this cause and to the United States you have, I am sure, the gratitude of all the American people—especially, perhaps, groups of our citizens most recently of foreign origin. In behalf of all Americans and for my own part, I thank you.

I accept your resignation as the Representative of the United States to the United Nations and to the Security Council, effective, as you wish, September third. The deep regret I feel at contemplating your leaving your United Nations post is mitigated by the knowledge that you do so only to offer yourself to the nation in an elective post of high responsibility and opportunity for service. In this effort you have, as you know, my heartiest endorsement. The country could ill afford in these times to lose the service of a man of your abilities.

With warm regard,

As ever,

DWIGHT D. EISENHOWER

NOTE: Mr. Lodge became Representative of the United States to the United Nations on January 23, 1953. His letter of resignation, dated August 17, was released with the President's reply.

267   ¶ Special Message to the Congress on the
Sugar Quota of the Dominican Republic.
August 23, 1960

To the Congress of the United States:

The meeting of Foreign Ministers of the American Republics at San
Jose, Costa Rica, has just completed its deliberations on the charges made
against the Dominican Republic by the Government of Venezuela, as well
as on the flagrant violation of human rights by the Trujillo regime. The
Foreign Ministers voted unanimously to condemn the Dominican acts of
aggression and intervention against Venezuela, culminating in the attempt on the life of the President of that country, and resolved to (1)
break diplomatic relations with the Dominican Republic, and (2) inter-
rupt partially economic relations with that country beginning with a
suspension of trade in arms and implements of war, with the provision
that the Council of the Organization of American States shall study the
feasibility and desirability of extending this trade suspension to other
articles. The United States joined with the other American Republics in
approving these measures.

Some 322,000 short tons of the sugar not being purchased from Cuba
pursuant to the reduction in the Cuban quota is, under the July amendment to the Sugar Act, to be allocated to the Dominican Republic. This
allocation is in addition to the Dominican Republic's 1960 quota amounting to approximately 130,000 tons. Since total imports of sugar from the
Dominican Republic in 1959 amounted only to about 84,000 tons, the
statutory allocation would give that country a large sugar bonus seriously
embarrassing to the United States in the conduct of our foreign relations
throughout the hemisphere.

In view of the foregoing considerations, the Government should have
discretion to purchase elsewhere the quantity apportioned to the Dominican Republic pursuant to the July Amendment to the Sugar Act. I
therefore request legislation providing that amounts which would be purchased in the Dominican Republic pursuant to the July Amendment need
not be purchased there, but may be purchased from any foreign countries
without regard to allocation.

I would also remind the Congress that the Sugar Act's present termination date of March 31, 1961—only three months after the reconvening of

Congress next January—could cause a serious gap in supplies, because it often takes as much as one or two months after purchase for sugar from distant areas to reach our refineries.   Thus an extension of the Sugar Act beyond its present termination date is necessary at this session in order to protect consumers in the United States against the possibility of unreasonable prices for sugar next February and March.

I request that the Congress give urgent consideration to and take favorable action on the proposed legislation.

DWIGHT D. EISENHOWER

NOTE: On September 1 a White House release was issued as follows:

"Replying to inquiries from Congressional leaders, the President has indicated that he has no new measures to place before the Congress.

"He still supports the measures which he has already recommended.

"As for sugar legislation, he regards the situation resulting from failure to act as extremely serious.   He is disappointed that a measure similar to the one passed last evening by the Senate failed of enactment."

268   ¶ The President's News Conference of *August 24, 1960*

THE PRESIDENT. Good morning, please sit down.

For the benefit of the radio and television industry, I'll tell them that I signed this bill on equal time this morning.[1]

Any questions?

Q. Jack Bell, Associated Press: Mr. President, after his version of the medical aid bill was rejected by the Senate yesterday, Senator Kennedy said, and I quote, "If we are going to have effective legislation, we are going to have to have an administration that will provide leadership and a Congress that will act." Would you care to comment on that?

THE PRESIDENT. Well, I don't know whether I have got equal time in this debate. [*Laughter*] I have to watch these things, because I am not a candidate.

The Democrats have a 2 to 1 majority in the Congress, in both Houses. And I don't see how they could want more, or if they do, how. They are having enough difficulty controlling this, because they apparently are not getting anywhere with it.   Now, I just say this, for the leadership end of it, they are saying that a brand new program was put before them just

---

[1] The President referred to Public Law 86–677 (74 Stat. 554) suspending for the 1960 campaign the equal opportunity requirements of section 315 of the Communications Act of 1934 for nominees for the offices of President and Vice President.

to enact within the last few weeks, or couple of weeks. And I have called your attention time and time again, the very same things I sent down in August, I sent in January and in May, and in numerous special sessions. So I don't know why the complaints. They have got the majority—such great majorities they can do anything they want to, if they get together.

Q. Ray L. Scherer, National Broadcasting Company: Mr. President, now that you have signed the bill which you mentioned a moment ago, could you tell us how you look upon the prospect of debates between Mr. Nixon and Mr. Kennedy, as a factor in the campaign and in the election?

THE PRESIDENT. Well, I am not certain that it all has to be on debates. I think equal time doesn't necessarily have to be in a debating atmosphere. I do think that it is a very fine thing in the public service that the networks will be performing by allowing these people to do this on an equal time basis and without cost. Actually, it seems to me over these years the costs of presenting the issues and cases and personalities to the public has gone way up, and if these networks can help out on this equal time basis, it will be a fine thing.

Q. David P. Sentner, Hearst Newspapers: Mr. President, would you please give us your latest opinion as to the major issues in the campaign?

THE PRESIDENT. Well, I think that we have always agreed that politics ends at the water's edge. But the conduct apparently of foreign affairs is going to be a very important issue, whether or not I would believe it should be. It apparently is going to be, because it has been talked so much.

At home I would say that the basic material question would be the farm, and of course I think we will make, most certainly, sound money or—not sound money but preventing the debasement of our currency, and with fiscal responsibility.

So I think things of that kind are going to be probably debated more than anything else in the campaign.

Q. Robert C. Pierpoint, CBS News: Mr. President, I wonder if you could tell us why you feel, as Mr. Hagerty mentioned the other day you do, that Captain Powers' sentence was too severe,[1] in view of the fact

---

[1] On August 19 the Press Secretary to the President issued the following statement:

"The President has been informed of the sentence imposed on Mr. Powers by the Soviet court, and he deplores the Soviet propaganda activity in connection with the entire episode, beginning last May, and regrets the severity of the sentence. He extends his sincere sympathy to the members of Mr. Powers' family."

that, for instance, the United States sentenced Colonel Abel to, I believe, 30 years, and we have given less severe sentences to other Russian spies.

THE PRESIDENT. Well, I think I regretted that it was so long; I hoped for less, when you come down to it. I have no measure of just what has been done in like cases over the years, for the simple reason that this particular kind of case has never before come up.

Q. John M. Hightower, Associated Press: Mr. President, I wondered if you could tell us under what circumstances and for what purpose you might address the United Nations. Ambassador Lodge said it was a matter under serious consideration.

THE PRESIDENT. Well, it's a matter that is discussed every year when there comes up the opening of the General Assembly. I did this in 1953, and one other time. I am not sure whether it was on the opening day, but another time.

Now, this time there are so many things that are not completed. We have had this long session of the nuclear tests which now is recessed, and there are a lot of things that probably need to be repeated. But this doesn't mean that I personally would do this unless I think it was something that I wanted sufficiently to emphasize as to ask for time before them. Normally, the Secretary of State would do this.

Q. William H. Y. Knighton, Jr., Baltimore Sun: Mr. President, a few weeks ago Mr. Hagerty, in discussing your political campaign plans for this year, suggested that a great amount of your activities would not be of a traditional nature. He has declined to explain that so far. I wonder if you would care to enlighten us on that now, sir.

THE PRESIDENT. Well, I will have to say, quoting Mr. Hagerty, he hasn't explained that to me, either. [*Laughter*]

What I think: we have got a thing coming up now where a President wants to help perpetuate his party in the White House, and to increase their strength in the Legislature, of course.

Now, as I pointed out the other day, there are two types of authority, so far as party affairs, that are now to be observed. One of them is the man still responsible for the running of this Government, and will continue to be so until January 20. The other is the mapping out of these campaigns.

Now, I would expect there will be two or three occasions when—and probably no more—where the party as such wants me to do something, and I will probably respond, so far as I can.

Now, on the other hand, I have already a number of engagements that take me through a great deal of this United States, and under various bodies—economic, educational, accountants, charitable institutions. And those I shall fulfill. But they will not be political. So I guess he meant that my activities were going to be nonpolitical as well as political during this time.

Q. Edward T. Folliard, Washington Post: Mr. President, you just said that the farm problem might be an issue—was likely to be an issue. Over the weekend a statement was made that the administration, including Mr. Nixon and Mr. Benson, had brought disaster to the farmers. There are usually two sides to these questions. Would you care to comment on that, sir?

THE PRESIDENT. We are operating under laws—some of them go back, way back into the late thirties. The laws have never been reformed. We have struggled for 8 years to get real reform in the farm laws with a basic purpose of making the farm production more nearly responsive to the demand. And we have tried to increase world demand, or at least world consumption, through PL 480, by expanding markets—commercial markets. That is one of the reasons that Secretary Benson has traveled so much and is still traveling—to produce better markets. But to say that Mr. Benson and the administration have brought this problem—this farm problem into its acute stage, whether you call it disastrous or not, is just to my mind a distortion that is used for political purposes, and nothing else.

Q. Andrew F. Tully, Jr., Scripps-Howard Newspapers: Sir, there has been considerable comment that Pilot Powers didn't have a chance because the United States had already pleaded guilty for him. Do you think now, in retrospect, that there might have been an alternative to our acknowledging that flight?

THE PRESIDENT. To my mind, the young man, Powers, that found himself in that position, could not possibly be repudiated by the Government. And therefore, to have tried to have done so would have made him some kind of adventurous fellow that suddenly had designed, manufactured a plane, flew it for himself, for no reason whatsoever. Now, this doesn't make sense to me. And as far as I am concerned, for my part of this, taking responsibility for this kind of action, I have no reason for thinking I would change my mind.

Q. Felix Belair, New York Times: Mr. President, in view of the indictment of the Castro regime by the American Republics foreign ministers, and particularly the United States white paper along this same line, do you consider that the Cuban problem is now beyond the realm of personal diplomacy, involving yourself; and as a second part, has the Monroe Doctrine been effectively supplanted by the Rio and other non-intervention treaties?

THE PRESIDENT. Well, let's take the second part. From my viewpoint, Mr. Belair, I think that the Monroe Doctrine has by no means been supplanted. It has been merely extended. When the Monroe Doctrine was written and enunciated, it had in mind such things as happened when the Austrians and the French—or an Austrian Emperor with some French troops—came into Mexico. Times have changed, and there are different kinds of penetration and subversion that can be very dangerous to the welfare of the OAS.

Now, the OAS is an organization that, for a long, long time we have been supporting, just as strongly as we can. We do want it to use its collective influence, its moral and political influence, in straightening out these things. But that does not, as I see it, inhibit any government, when it comes down to—when the chips are finally down, to looking after its own interests. They must be represented, of course—I mean they must be protected, of course.

Q. Edward V. Koterba, United Features: Mr. President, in a followup to Eddie Folliard's question, a Midwestern poll shows an apparent resurgence of strong support for the Republicans across the Farm Belt. Sir, would you say this indicated a renewed confidence for Ezra Benson, who one Republican referred to last week as a scapegoat for all the farmers' troubles? And could you at this time, sir, give us your judgment on this man who has served as your Secretary of Agriculture for 7½ years?

THE PRESIDENT. Well, I think I did that a couple of weeks ago, when I said that I have never known a man who was more honest, more dedicated, and more informed in his particular work. He is, moreover, a courageous man in presenting the views of the administration, and with his work I have not only had the greatest sympathy, but wherever I could possibly find a way to do it, I have supported exactly what he has been trying to do.

Now, I don't know about—anything about the effects in the Farm Belt at this moment, for the simple reason I haven't had any recent reports of opinion there. I do know this: in the long run, people respect honesty and courage and selflessness in the governmental service. And I don't believe that any of us should be so free as to crucify Secretary Benson. I think he has done a wonderful service.

Q. Raymond P. Brandt, St. Louis Post-Dispatch: Mr. President, have you specific plans for active participation in the congressional campaigns comparable to '56 and '58?

THE PRESIDENT. No. I have—as I recall, there are three tentative dates that could be called political on my calendar. Now, I don't think they have yet been announced, so I won't try to get things balled up by being too quick about it. [*Confers with Mr. Hagerty*] Oh, September 29th. That is the fundraising—and I am going to speak in one of the things. That will be a 10-minute speech, something like that, during the half hour.

Q. James B. Reston, New York Times: In the last 7½ years, sir, you have appointed a great many Presidential commissions that have done a great deal of very good work in studying various national problems. My question is whether you have thought of getting those commissions to bring their work up to date, so that their conclusions could be modernized and presented to your successor, to guide him at the end of the election.

THE PRESIDENT. Yes. Mr. Reston, I didn't think of it in those same terms. But you have put a thought in my head, and I am going to look and see whether something of this kind could be done. I did appoint a commission to look into all the administrative activities of the Government, and it reported some years back. And we have had the question up right now, whether we should not either reappoint that one or appoint a new one, and to bring this up, because it will take some months. And so in the—since the commission would be questioning and investigating people of real experience, that this would be something to turn over to a successor and would be very valuable. I do not for a moment question the value of this if we can find a practical way of doing these things.

Q. Sarah McClendon, El Paso Times: Mr. President, will you tell us some of the big decisions that Mr. Nixon has participated in since you have been in the White House and he, as Vice President, has been helping you?

THE PRESIDENT. Well, Mrs. McClendon, no one participates in the decisions. Now let's see, we just—I don't see why people can't understand this: no one can make a decision except me if it is in the national executive area. I have all sorts of advisers, and one of the principal ones is Mr. Nixon. But any Vice President that I should have, even if I did not admire and respect Mr. Nixon as I do, I would still keep him close in all these things, because I think any President owes it to the country to have the next individual in line of succession completely aware of what is going on. Otherwise, you have a break that is unconscionable and unnecessary.

Now, if just when you talk about other people sharing a decision, how can they? No one can, because then who is going to be responsible? And because I have been raised as an Army individual and have used staffs, I think you will find no staff has ever thought that they made a decision as to what should be done or should not be done when I was a commander. And I don't think anyone in the Government will find or you can find anyone that would say differently.

Q. Lillian Levy, Science Service: Mr. President, on May 13 you signed an Executive order which allows each interested Federal agency to fix its own radiation safety standards and to exceed, if it deems necessary, the standards recommended by the Federal Radiation Council. Is there any reason why the Executive order did not provide that any standards set by the individual agency which would exceed the radiation safety levels recommended by your Council be subject to review and approval by the Federal Radiation Council which originally was established, I believe, for the purpose of recommending radiation safety standards for all agencies, so that the confusion and conflict—*[laughter]*—within an agency between keeping to standards of safety on the one hand, and performing its functions in developing nuclear energy on the other, might be eliminated? *[Laughter]*

THE PRESIDENT. Well, as a matter of fact, the question is sensible, because I assume, from the way you have read it, that there could be some confusion here if any excess radiation were allowed to escape and were not reported to the proper people. If the order is defective, I will try to find out about it.[1]

Q. Frank van der Linden, Nashville Banner: Mr. President, the Democrats apparently are going to let Congress go home without passing your oft requested bill for additional Federal judgeships. They are apparently turning down your offer to share these between the two parties, in a gamble that maybe they can get all of them next year. I wonder, sir, do you think maybe they are playing politics with this, or are you going to make another appeal to them before they leave?

THE PRESIDENT. They will have to make their own decision. Whether they are just ignoring the welfare of the United States and the administering of justice, or for any other reason, I don't know what it is. But I think in every year that I have been here, I have recommended these judges. And I don't know why it was not done.

Q. E. W. Kenworthy, New York Times: Reports from San Jose, sir, this morning indicate that a number of the Latin American foreign ministers have been appealing to Mr. Roa, the Cuban Foreign Minister, to speak moderately when his turn comes. Evidently, this has made some impression, because it has been reported that Mr. Roa has asked Premier Castro if he may moderate his remarks.

My question is whether you think the situation is really irretrievable. You spoke just now of cooperation in these matters. Do you think it would be useful if a number of heads of government of the American Republics met with Mr. Castro to try to prevent this situation from deteriorating any further?

THE PRESIDENT. Well, of course, every time you bring up this question of heads of government meeting, why then there is so much speculation, and then next you have almost an intention, and sometimes you

---

[1] On May 13 the President approved seven recommendations contained in a memorandum entitled "Radiation Protection Guidance for Federal Agencies" addressed to him by Secretary Arthur S. Flemming, who served as chairman of the Federal Radiation Council. The memorandum, prepared as a report by the Council following a study of the hazards and use of radiation, was made public by the White House on May 17 and was published together with the President's statement of approval in the Federal Register of May 18, 1960 (25 F.R. 4402).

A further memorandum from Chairman Flemming, made public on October 13 by the White House, stated that 14 Federal agencies had indicated in replies to the Council's letter of July 15 that they were conducting radiation protection activities in accordance with the approved guides, and that no deviations from the guides were in effect or planned at the time of reporting. Mr. Flemming noted that a mechanism for regular reporting on these matters had been established.

practically have your ticket bought—at least in the papers.

Now, I repeat what I have said many times. Whenever we can see—a number of us, I mean, not only in our own Government but in others—that something of this kind will be useful, I will always be ready to participate. By no means do I want to admit or charge that this situation is irretrievable. Cuba has been one of our finest friends. We were the ones that conducted the war that set them free. And when they got in trouble, we had an occupation, back about 1908, and again we set them on their feet, and set them free. And we have had a long history of friendly relationships, and we have tried to keep our hands out of their internal political affairs. We have not tried to throw out someone we didn't like, or anything like that.

So I would think that the very welfare of the Cuban people finally demands some kind of composition of the difficulties between the American states, including our own on the one hand and Cuba on the other.

Q. Carleton Kent, Chicago Sun-Times: Mr. President, a news story based on another look at the Potsdam papers quotes Marshal Stalin as having called you an honest man who turned over 135,000 German soldiers to the Russians. Would you care to comment on this historical footnote?

THE PRESIDENT. Well, I don't know about this. And now I have to call on memory. Under the treaty, or the arrangements made by the several allies—and remember then Russia was an ally—I was ordered to go into the German—the prison camps in our areas and get these people and send them back to Russia. How many there were, I don't remember. But I do remember this: there was trouble because some of them didn't want to go back. And even after the—I think the mass movement was accomplished, then we had to allow on both sides of the line missions to go in to search and to find out whether there was anyone else who should go back to the country of origin.

Now, it is a feeble memory that I have, but that was the story, and I don't remember that there was any 135,000. It strikes me there were more but maybe I'm wrong.

Q. Rutherford M. Poats, United Press International: Mr. President, a moment ago you expressed regret at the possibility that the conduct as well as the issues in foreign affairs would become a major issue in the campaign. There has also been published speculation that both candidates might try to outdo each other in demonstrating how they would stand up to Khrushchev. I wonder, sir, if you could elaborate on your expression of regret and tell us whether you regard this issue of standing up to Khrushchev as one of the dangers you see in bringing foreign policy into the campaign.

THE PRESIDENT. It never even occurred to me to make that as one of the basic issues—what to do with Mr. Khrushchev. I assumed that anyone who has got strong convictions as to the line he should take in negotiation to protect and advance the interests of his own country would push them forthrightly and courageously, and the point of mannerisms would not be particularly important.

Now, this other part of your question—my regret. You must remember I was in the Army a long time, and I had no politics. I served my most important military positions under two Democratic Presidents, and it never occurred to me to—and certainly never occurred to any of them— to ask me what my politics were, if any.

Now, it is in this kind—with this kind of a background, that I would have hoped that our foreign affairs could be truly—and as a matter of tradition almost—conducted in a bipartisan spirit, and true bipartisan action.

If we are going to make these things such an important part of political or partisan debate, I think it is a little bit too bad.

Q. Edward P. Morgan, American Broadcasting Company: Mr. President, according to published reports, anti-Catholic propaganda has markedly increased in the campaign. You have already told us that as far as you are concerned, a candidate's religion should not make any difference and should not be an issue. But a man whom you have publicly esteemed, Evangelist Billy Graham, now says that it is a legitimate issue and could be a decisive one in this election. Do you have any comments on that, and do you have any further thoughts on the problem in general?

THE PRESIDENT. Well, as I say, my usual answer to this, I go back to the Constitution. We do have freedom of worship, and I think the Constitution means exactly what it says. And I think it is incumbent on all of us to respect the rights of others.

Now, I haven't seen Billy Graham's statement, and therefore I don't know whether it is in context or not.

I would say this: it should not be an issue. But I, on the other hand— I am not so naive that I think that in some areas it will not be. It is just almost certain, because as long as you have got strong emotional convictions and reactions in these areas, there is going to be some of it; you can't help it. But I certainly never encouraged it. And I don't think I would ever admit that it is really a legitimate question.

Q. Charles H. Mohr, Time Magazine: Mr. President, one of your answers to a previous question raises this question: one of the issues in this campaign is seeming to turn on the question of Mr. Nixon's experience, and the Republicans to some extent almost want to claim that he has had a great deal of practice at being President. Now, in answer to the other question, I wonder if it would be fair to assume that what you mean is that he has been primarily an observer and not a participant in the executive branch of the Government. In other words, many people have been trying to get at the degree that he has—I don't want to use that word "participated"—but acted in important decisions, and it is hard to pin down.

THE PRESIDENT. Well, it seems to me that there is some confusion here—haziness—that possibly needs a lot of clarification.

I said he was not a part of decision-making. That has to be in the mind and heart of one man. All right. Every commander that I have ever known, or every leader, or every head of a big organization, has needed and sought consultative conferences with his principal subordinates. In this case, they are normally Cabinet officers. They include also such people as the head of GSA, the Budget Bureau, and the Vice President as one of the very top. So the Vice President has participated for 8 years, or 7½ years, in all of the consultative meetings that have been held. And he has never hesitated—and if he had I would have been quite disappointed—he has never hesitated to express his opinion, and when he has been asked for it, expressed his opinion in terms of recommendation as to decision. But no one, and no matter how many differences or whether they are all unanimous—no one has the decisive power. There is no voting.

It is just—you could take this body here, and say, "Look, we are going to do something about the streets down here, about parking around here for you people." All right. Now, everybody has got his say. But I have to handle, let's say, around the White House, and so who is going to decide—I am; not this body. So Mr. Nixon has taken a full part in every principal discussion.

Q. Mr. Mohr: We understand that the power of decision is entirely yours, Mr. President. I just wondered if you could give us an example of a major idea of his that you had adopted in that role, as the decider and final——

THE PRESIDENT. If you give me a week, I might think of one. I don't remember.

Jack Bell, Associated Press: Thank you, Mr. President.

NOTE: President Eisenhower's one hundred and ninetieth news conference was held in the Executive Office Building from 10:30 to 11:01 o'clock on Wednesday morning, August 24, 1960. In attendance: 203.

269 ¶ Statement by the President on the 40th Anniversary of the Women's Suffrage Amendment. *August 26, 1960*

FORTY YEARS AGO today, the 19th Amendment to the Constitution of the United States became effective. This Amendment gave the women of America the right to become full voting partners with the men of America.

In observing this anniversary, it is fitting to honor such women as Susan B. Anthony and Carrie Chapman Catt whose courageous work paved the way for the passage of the 19th Amendment. I would also like to pay tribute to the women of today who exercise their inherited voting rights with pride and judgment. Their lively political concern— at election time and whenever an issue of public moment arises in their communities—contributes greatly to the strength of our local, State and Federal Governments. As they study the issues, work for their Party's candidates, and cast their responsible ballots at the polls, they illustrate to people the world over the privileges and rights of a free society, selecting by free choice the leaders who will represent them in the nation and the world.

270 ¶ Statement by the President Concerning
Mutual Security Appropriations.
August 26, 1960

I AM gravely concerned by the Conference action on Mutual Security appropriations.

I have repeatedly stated that the appropriation of the full $4,086 million authorized is vitally needed. Moreover, needs which have developed since my original request, particularly the emergency in the Congo, have made necessary an additional $100 million for the Contingency Fund.

Only day before yesterday, by a 67–26 vote, the Senate approved the additional $100 million and at the same time increased last month's House appropriation of $3,584 million by $297 million. The Conference, while approving the $100 million increase in Contingency funds, virtually disregarded the Senate restoration in the basic Mutual Security budget. It accepted only $31 million—one-tenth of the $297 million restoration that the Senate had just overwhelmingly approved.

In short, the Conference recognized the need for $100 million of new funds but at the same time slashed by $265 million the budget to which these new funds are to be added.

This cut would sharply curtail support indispensable to the defense of allies now under intensified Soviet pressure and deny aid urgently needed by other friendly nations struggling under the gravest difficulties to make progress in freedom.

Not only are the funds now provided by the Conference inadequate, but also a number of administrative restrictions were retained which would impair the management of the Mutual Security Program.

Surely, in the world situation now confronting our country, the Congress will not accept these recommendations which fall so short of the need.

I urge that this appropriation be returned to Conference. We must, for America, correct its deficiencies.

A Congressional rejection of this request will hamper greatly the Nation's Chief Executive who succeeds me next January. Upon him will fall the heavy responsibility of continuing to guide our country in a troubled world. He, no less than I, must have adequate funds to do the job.

NOTE: The President's statement was released with the letters comprising Items
271 and 272, below.
    The Mutual Security and Related

Agencies Appropriation Act, 1961 (Pub.
Law 86–704, 74 Stat. 776), was approved
September 2, 1960.

271   ¶ Letter to the Majority and Minority Leaders of the Senate on Mutual Security Appropriations.   *August 26, 1960*

Dear Senator —————:

I am deeply disturbed by the action yesterday of the conference on the mutual security appropriation. I cannot state too strongly my belief that a cut of this size will jeopardize the security of the country.

I hope the Senate will reject the Conference Report should the House approve it. Both political parties and all of the major national candidates are publicly committed to the support of an adequate mutual security program. No one can responsibly contend that this Conference Report and the amounts approved constitute adequacy in today's world.

In view of the world-wide scope of this program and the necessity for planning so far ahead in such an effort, time is of the essence. These critical matters simply will not wait until the Congress returns in January, then to assess the results of its actions taken now. There is at the moment such an acceleration of events in the world that we must be forearmed at all times and ready to deal with critical situations as they develop. It must be evident to the Congress from the speed with which the situation in Africa recently developed that we must stay ready and that our free world security programs, economic and military, must be kept continuously adequate. Postponement of these funds needed now may irretrievably cripple us later.

I enclose a public statement that I have just released.

I am sending an identical letter to Senator (Johnson) (Dirksen) and similar communications to the House Leaders.

Sincerely,

DWIGHT D. EISENHOWER

NOTE: This is the text of identical letters
addressed to the Honorable Lyndon B.
Johnson and to the Honorable Everett

McKinley Dirksen, Majority and Minority
Leaders of the Senate, respectively.
    For the public statement, see Item 270.

272 ¶ Letter to the Speaker and to the Minority Leader of the House of Representatives on Mutual Security Appropriations. *August* 26, 1960

Dear Mr. ————:

I am deeply disturbed by the action yesterday of the conference on the mutual security appropriation. I cannot state too strongly my belief that a cut of this size will jeopardize the security of the country.

I am writing Senator Johnson and Senator Dirksen urging that the Senate reject this Conference Report should, despite all our efforts, the House approve it. I hope I can count on your cooperation in leading the House to recommit the bill so that the final action can conform fully to the national interest.

Both political parties and all of the major national candidates are publicly committed to the support of an adequate mutual security program. No one can responsibly contend that this Conference Report and the amounts approved constitute adequacy in today's world.

In view of the world-wide scope of this program and the necessity for planning so far ahead in such an effort, time is of the essence. These critical matters simply will not wait until the Congress returns in January, then to assess the results of its actions taken now. There is at the moment such an acceleration of events in the world that we must be forearmed at all times and ready to deal with critical situations as they develop. It must be evident to the Congress from the speed with which the situation in Africa recently developed that we must stay ready and that our free world security programs, economic and military, must be kept continuously adequate. Postponement of these funds needed now may irretrievably cripple us later.

I enclose a public statement that I have just released.

I am sending an identical letter to (Speaker Rayburn) (Mr. Halleck).
> Sincerely,

> Dwight D. Eisenhower

NOTE: This is the text of identical letters addressed to the Honorable Sam Rayburn and to the Honorable Charles A. Halleck, Speaker and Minority Leader of the House of Representatives, respectively. For the public statement, see Item 270.

273 ¶ Message to President Po Sun Yun of Korea. *August* 29, 1960

Dear Mr. President:

It is with great pleasure that I extend my congratulations and best wishes to you upon your assumption of the office of President of the Republic of Korea.

I wish you all success in discharging the responsibilities of this high office, your accession to which bears eloquent testimony to the trust and confidence reposed in you as a distinguished leader of a great people.

Sincerely,

DWIGHT D. EISENHOWER

274 ¶ Message to Prime Minister Chang Myon of Korea. *August* 29, 1960

Dear Mr. Prime Minister:

Please accept my congratulations and warm good wishes upon your accession to the post of Prime Minister of the Republic of Korea. This honor is fitting recognition of your record of distinguished service to your country.

I remember with pleasure our enjoyable and useful conversation at breakfast during my visit to Seoul, and I wish you every success in carrying out the heavy burden of your office and in fulfilling the trust which has been placed in your hands.

Sincerely,

DWIGHT D. EISENHOWER

275 ¶ Letter to Judge E. Barrett Prettyman Requesting Him To Serve as Chairman of the President's Conference on Administrative Procedure. *August 29, 1960*

Dear Judge Prettyman:

The Chairmen of six of the independent regulatory agencies of the Federal government, in a letter to me dated August 25, 1960, a copy of which is enclosed, have proposed that there be a new President's Conference looking to a continuation of the study of administrative problems such as was achieved under the President's Conference on Administrative Procedure in 1953–54 under your leadership. I have concurred in their proposal.

I have also received from the Chief Justice a strong recommendation for such a Conference and the endorsement of the Judicial Conference of the District of Columbia, the American Bar Association and the Federal Bar Association. It would appear that the Conference would be advisory, provide for the exchange of information and experience, and make such suggestions as might reasonably improve agency procedure.

The suggestion, which I heartily approve, has been made that you act as Temporary Chairman of the Conference and arrange for its initial organization. I earnestly hope that you will be willing to do so.

Sincerely,

DWIGHT D. EISENHOWER

NOTE: Judge Prettyman was serving as Chief Judge of the U.S. Court of Appeals for the District of Columbia.

The letter from the Chairmen of the six regulatory agencies was released with the President's letter to Judge Prettyman.

276 ¶ Remarks at the Assembly Session of the American Bar Association. *August 29, 1960*

President Randall, Mr. Chief Justice, distinguished guests from many nations, members of the American Bar, and friends:

It is a great privilege and a personal honor to be permitted to welcome this body to the Nation's Capital and to address to you a few thoughts that I should like to bring to your attention.

We are, of course, flattered and complimented that such a group would come from abroad to meet with our own Bar Association in studying and contemplating common problems and seeking some kind of common solution. We are particularly complimented by the arrival of 700 British members to this conference. Our own lawyers have told me about the hearty welcome they received when they went to British shores a couple of years ago, but there is more significance in the British-American lawyer relationship than mere exchange of visits in such groups as this.

There were 55 drafters of our Constitution. Of those, 34 were students of law and most of them had studied law in Britain. The writers of our Constitution were heirs to centuries of development and practice of law in Britain, and when it came to the time for publication of that document—which Gladstone said was the most wonderful work that ever came out of the mind and purpose of men at a single time—they were well aware of all of this legal history. They were aware of what was then modern thinking in the development of law, and there is no question whatsoever that our Constitution, as we know it, could not have been written in 1787 except for this great heritage obtained from the mother country.

It was probably no mere coincidence that one authority says that in the decade of the 1780's there was a higher proportion of able and distinguished Americans dedicated and committed to public service than at any other time in our entire history. And from that decade we received this great and lasting document.

Now, of course, as much as we value our friendship with Britain and our close relationship with her as inheritors of all these values, we seek, hope for, and value friends everywhere in the world—and more especially in what we call the free world.

It is my conviction that such friends and such relationships can be obtained and held only under a rule of law—a law that can develop and maintain the relationships between nations that domestic law maintains and develops among individuals.

Of course, all of us understand that the rule of law among nations cannot, in any near future, have behind it the force of national power that obtains in every free nation. But there is a mighty force behind it, and that is world opinion. World opinion is not lightly to be disregarded. Both in the constitution of such a court and in the observance of its decisions and opinions, anyone who does so flagrantly disregard its authority and prestige will be guilty of a very grievous error.

It strikes me that of all of the people who should work for the rule of law, lawyers should be among the forefront. I cannot conceive that a good lawyer can think primarily—and above anything else—of the size of his fee or the success he may have in achieving a good verdict for his client. He is, I think above all, a public servant. He serves our courts, as in all free countries, in order that the Nation, as we know it, may prosper and be strong. In that atmosphere his client likewise can prosper, and be confident of receiving justice in any quarrel with his fellows, whether it is civil or any other kind.

So within the domestic scene lawyers uphold this main purpose of service. I think we must extend our minds to the breadth of the earth when we speak of law that is comparable to the kind of law we so respect within our own nations.

Now, American lawyers are not always right. I know they can't always be right, because they have differences. By the way, here I might tell one little story. I had a friend who was just out of law school, and not having many other things occupying his attention, it was his habit to go into the local courts, possibly hoping for a piece of business to come his way, but to learn about the practices and procedures of the courts.

Well, one day there was a man held under a charge of petty larceny, and the judge turned to him and said, "I'm sure you know you are entitled to a lawyer. Do you have one?"

"No," he said.

"Do you want the court to appoint one?" Yes, he thought he should. And the judge said, "Well, we have three available. Here is Mr. Allen, and here is Mr. Blair, and Mr. Kirk is another, but not here just now. These three are available. Have you got any choice?"

He looked at the two present, and said, "The other one!"

Now, I am not saying that the American lawyers are either of the two in the room or the other one who was selected. The fact is that American lawyers do have differing characteristics and convictions. They differ very strongly about America's relationship to the World Court.[1]

I am not a lawyer, and so they don't have to pay much attention to my opinions. But, far be it from me to fail to express it.

---

[1] Resolutions relating to the Connally Reservation concerning U.S. participation in the World Court were under consideration by the Bar Association at this time.

In so expressing it, the first thing I want to say is this: are we seeking peace with justice? Which means, are we seeking a world of law, or are we seeking to find ways in which we can cater to our own views and ideas in the legal field rather than to put our minds to finding some way of achieving peace?

So, while I have been criticized—and praised also in other instances—for asking for the deletion of the self-judging clause in our laws, I believe that this is one of those times where we must put our minds on the major issue. We must adopt a rule of reason. Let's not ask for defeat by pleading every kind of petty or important obstacle that can be imagined, not every kind of difficulty that might be in the way of a perfect administration of international justice.

What we ought to put our eyes on is what is now attainable, including methods and schemes and plans. Under the world as we know it, and with our eyes on the rule of reason, we must take a stand that will make this accomplishment realizable.

So I merely say—and unfortunately, I have a lawyer in my own family whom I haven't yet converted—I merely say to all of them: "Look at the great objective, look what peace means."

How are we ever going to travel that road unless we are ready to make some concessions—concessions that, as I see it, cannot possibly hurt us?

So, with that little contribution to your own family quarrel, I have just one other statement to make. There was apparently some kind of agreement that involved a degree of selection in the guests who are to come to the White House this evening for the garden party. And I believe the confusion came about through the anxiety of your officers to make sure that everybody could get into an area that is, after all, limited in size.

I want to tell you that I still believe in keeping the brighter, larger goal in front of my eyes, not its difficulties. I say to you, all are welcome, and I shall expect you this evening at 6 o'clock—or 7, whatever it is. You will have to get detailed instructions from your own president, but I expect to see you.

Goodbye.

NOTE: The President spoke at 2:40 p.m. at the Sheraton-Park Hotel in Washington. In his opening words he referred to John D. Randall, President of the Association, and to Chief Justice Earl Warren. Near the close of his remarks he referred to his older brother, Edgar Eisenhower, who attended the meeting.

277　❡ Message to the King of Jordan on the Death of Prime Minister Hazza al-Majali.
August 30, 1960

Your Majesty:

It is with profound regret and sorrow that I have learned of the tragic death of His Excellency Hazza al-Majali, Prime Minister of Jordan. I know that you personally as well as the people of Jordan have suffered a grievous loss through the wanton criminal act which resulted in his and other deaths.

Please accept the sincerest condolences of the people of the United States.

DWIGHT D. EISENHOWER

278　❡ Remarks to a Group of Republican Candidates for Congress.　*August 31, 1960*

WELL, it's quite a ceremony we went through in there. I hope that the pictures with each of you won't hurt any of you in your districts.

It is, of course, a very great honor for any man to receive the nomination of a major party for the Congress. So I congratulate you—each of you—for the many steps you have taken to reach this point in your political progress, and I wish you good luck in the election and in the years to come.

There is a coincidence about 1960 that may have escaped the notice of some of you. The last time that all four of the principal candidates on the national ticket came from or had had experience in the Congress was in 1860—and that, I remind you, was a Republican year.

When I was a boy, 99 percent of the electorate voted for their Congressmen when they voted for the President. Now we have gotten to the point that just under 90 percent of the population votes at the same time for their Congressional nominee and for their national nominee.

I think this indicates that each of you has a job not merely of being a member of a team that is promoting a common cause and promoting a common philosophy. You have got to do a lot of walking and wearing out of shoe leather and ringing of door bells and things on your own, not just leaving it to other people. You have got to meet everybody in your district if you can.

Someone pointed out that among the qualifications that a candidate must have is a personality that is outgiving. You cannot, I think, sit inside an office and direct strategy and be remote. People have got to know you, and they have got to like what they know. So I would say four-fifths of our work is knowing what we want to do, promoting the kind of country in which we want to live, and then working.

The other fifth is devoted to a number of other causes and activities. But working and knowing what you are working for would be my prescription.

I can't tell you how much I hope for each of you real success—resounding success. I am convinced that it is through such people as you that we are going to keep this country secure, fiscally sound, and on the straight, tough middle way to future progress.

And after all, no man has a right to be in politics unless he is thinking, first of all, of the United States. I am sure that every single one of you does.

Goodbye and good luck.

NOTE: The President spoke in the Rose Garden at the White House. He was photographed with each of the candi- dates, who were attending a conference sponsored by the National Republican Congressional Committee.

279 ¶ Remarks at the Fifth International Congress on Nutrition. *September 1, 1960*

Dr. King, and ladies and gentlemen:

I am delighted to open this Fifth International Congress on Nutrition, a Congress attended by representatives from 59 countries, including every continent on the globe. Since you have previously met in London, Basel, Amsterdam, and Paris, but this is your first visit to Washington, I bid you a hearty welcome to this side of the Atlantic and to this city.

May I remark, President King, that I envy you in your association with this Congress. You will not need to veto any of its actions. Now this, of course, is because each of you is selflessly and wholeheartedly dedicated to the advancement of a science that underlies human health. You have come with a vision to build a better world, now and for years to come.

The twentieth century is unique in many ways—not the least of which is the fact that ours is the first generation which has dared to think in terms of food enough for all. And our age is the first to be deeply concerned about the quality as well as the quantity of the food supply. For the first time in history, man's ancient enemies—hunger and malnutrition—are on the defensive. They are not whipped. But ours is the first generation to catch the scent of victory.

Let me turn for a moment to one phase of the free world's campaign against hunger, a program to send crop surpluses to needy areas. I take as an example the case with which I am most familiar, that of my own country. But first a word of caution. Any transaction involving the transfer of commodities from one nation to another is of more than bilateral interest. Thus, in moving our abundant surplus of food products overseas, we must be diligent to avoid disrupting the markets of others. Irresponsible handling of our huge stocks of wheat, for example, could unjustifiably harm a nation which is heavily dependent on foreign exchange earnings from wheat and other cereal exports. My concern regarding this problem is one of the reasons for recommending increased use of the United Nations so as to distribute surplus crops under methods that will benefit all.

During the past 6 years, the United States Government has sent more than four thousand shiploads of food abroad in exchange for foreign currencies.

In similar transactions, we have done or engaged to do things like the following—to one country 16 million tons of wheat and 1 million of rice; for disaster relief, in earthquakes and hurricanes, 300 shiploads of food have gone abroad—through voluntary charitable agencies 400 shiploads of food to help 60 million stricken peoples.

Twelve hundred United States agricultural technicians are now working overseas, translating agricultural science into better living for the world's millions. Last year we received more than three thousand agricultural visitors from other countries, who came here to study food production, agricultural research, and education, and to meet our farmers and to see how they work.

We have loaned over $265 million abroad to build irrigation projects, fertilizer plants, and to improve transportation facilities.

Now these activities of my own country are only a part of the total free world program to lift the scourge of hunger. Great efforts are being made by the developing countries themselves. Much help has come from other industrialized nations. The special agencies of the United Nations—the World Health Organization, the United Children's Fund, and the Food and Agriculture Organization—have all made outstanding contributions in our common effort to eliminate hunger from this planet.

And the combined effort has been effective. There have been no major famines in the free world during the past decade, and to my knowledge this cannot be said of any previous decade. Nutritional levels in most of the developing countries, while still distressingly low, have nevertheless crept up slightly. World agriculture has generally kept abreast or ahead of the population increase.

While we have thus helped lift production capabilities abroad, the stream of agricultural and industrial exports from the more industrialized nations has increased, not diminished. The reason is a simple one: a better-fed neighbor is a better customer.

This is as it should be, and reflects the wisdom of programs which meet current needs while building long-term self-reliance. To make the recipient countries indefinitely dependent upon our assistance would be disadvantageous to them and to us. Compassion and prudence are equally important in this undertaking; our food-for-peace program partakes of both.

There is a Danish proverb which says: "You may light another's candle at your own without loss." Indeed there is gain in the lighting of many candles; in the brighter light we can all see better.

There are risks, indeed, in our undertaking. But the risks of failing to face up to our opportunities are greater than those involved in considered action. Political explosions can result, in a shrinking world, from a widening gap between the wealthy and the underdeveloped nations.

And science has given us a set of tools designed for human betterment. Farm people, in the United States and elsewhere, have translated these tools into a capability for constructive action. Though the task is gigantic, we seek opportunity to move ahead rather than becoming preoccupied with despair.

The world cups its ear to hear the rattling of rockets. It listens less closely to the sounds of peace and well-being which emanate from the slow but steady improvement in world health and nutrition.

For centuries orators and writers have developed the habit of warning about the crossroads that the world was facing at the very moment of the particular speaking or writing. Many of these crossroads have existed only in a lively imagination. Yet if history, which will one day view the events of this period in perspective, could only say that it was at this moment the world began truly to take the high road of health, and plenty, leading toward peace, leaving forever the path of strife and anxiety, then indeed would our great-grandchildren call this the brightest era of all time.

To each of you, my best wishes for a successful Congress. To the degree that you succeed, the human family in the nations here represented will step from under the shadow of want. This is the purpose that has brought you half-way around the world. The earth's nearly three billion people join me, I am sure, in my good wishes for your success. And may God ever be your helper.

Thank you very much.

NOTE: The President spoke at 11:05 a.m. at the Sheraton-Park Hotel in Washington. His opening words "Dr. King" referred to Dr. Charles Glen King, Scientific Director of the Nutrition Foundation, Inc., of New York City, and President of the Fifth International Congress on Nutrition.

280　¶ Memorandum of Disapproval of Bill Authorizing the Payment of Subsidies to Producers of Lead and Zinc. *September* 2, 1960

I HAVE WITHHELD approval of H.R. 8860, "To stabilize the mining of lead and zinc by small domestic producers on public, Indian, and other lands, and for other purposes."

H.R. 8860 authorizes lead and zinc subsidies based on the difference between market prices and a price of 17 cents per pound for lead and 14½ cents per pound for zinc. The subsidies would be paid on the output of mines producing not more than 2,000 tons annually of each commodity.

The problems of our lead and zinc miners have caused me concern for some time. To help solve these problems, the Administration has taken administrative actions and has twice proposed legislation which the Congress did not enact. Thereafter, in October of 1958, I reduced imports by imposing quantitative controls.

Now the Congress has enacted H.R. 8860, but unfortunately it would harm rather than help the lead-zinc industry. It would negate the progress of recent years, increase the problems of lead-zinc producers, subject the market to instability, and burden our taxpayers with unsound subsidies. Apart from the fact that the appropriations authorized by the bill would be completely inadequate to pay the proposed subsidies—with the result that the bill's intended beneficiaries could be misled into production for which they would not receive the promised subsidies—the bill has these fatal defects:

First, H.R. 8860 would intensify the industry's problems by generating substantial additional production at the expense of other miners' jobs. Its subsidies would induce the opening for full-time production of many mines which are not now operating, some of which have operated only intermittently in the past. The substantial additions to supply would depress lead and zinc prices and thus cause cut-backs and lay-offs of mine workers in the unsubsidized mines.

Second, the subsidized production induced by this bill would complicate, even frustrate, programs now in effect that are gradually bringing the production and demand of these commodities into balance. As a result of existing import controls and continuing international cooperation, the volume of imports is at the lowest levels, and constitutes the smallest percentage of total lead-zinc in supply, in nearly a decade. This has made it possible during 1959 for domestic lead and zinc producers to reduce excess stocks and to increase mine output. While consumption of these two metals has been at disappointing levels, the domestic industry should, with increased demand, again move rapidly forward to normal and stable operation at reasonable prices. The depressed prices that would result from the subsidy program would represent a backward step. A lasting solution can best be achieved through a world-wide balance of production and consumption, and that is the object of past and current international consultations.

Third, approval of H.R. 8860 would generate demands for equal treatment and similar subsidies from other producers of lead and zinc as well as producers of many other minerals. Such a system of subsidies would make a substantial portion of domestic mining totally dependent on Federal appropriations and would thereby lessen incentives for the technological improvement vital to the continued health of American mining.

For these reasons, I am compelled to withhold my approval of H.R. 8860.

DWIGHT D. EISENHOWER

281 ⁋ Letter to the Chairman, Civil Aeronautics Board, Concerning International Local Service to Regina, Saskatchewan. *September* 2, 1960

Dear Mr. Chairman:

I have reviewed the Board's recommendations in the Service to Regina Case on the basis of the broad national welfare, foreign policy and defense considerations, and other matters within my special responsibilities. I am compelled to return the Board's proposed order without my approval.

International local service should not, in general, be instituted in the absence of a reasonable probability that such service can survive. Can it be expected, for example, that traffic on this route would expand sufficiently to satisfy the Board's present "use-it-or-lose-it" policy within the three-year duration proposed for this certificate? If so, does the Board find that the carrier's operations on this route could become self-supporting? And if these questions can be answered in a manner favorable to certification, there remains the necessity of judging whether the subsidies involved are or would become excessive.

These questions are not intended to be exhaustive but only to suggest the difficulties of judging the public interest in this international case in the absence of policy and findings more closely defined than I find in the record before me.

On several occasions, as you know, I have expressed concern about the great and increasing cost of government subsidies to local service airlines. I hope that the Board will intensify its efforts to review and restate its policies governing the certification and subsidization of local service.

Sincerely,

DWIGHT D. EISENHOWER

The Honorable Whitney Gillilland
Chairman, Civil Aeronautics Board
Washington, D.C.

282 ¶ Statement by the President: Labor Day. *September 5, 1960*

IN THIS, my final Labor Day message as President, I reaffirm my faith in the traditions of America's working men and women.

Over 184 years ago, the people of the thirteen colonies declared themselves free, proclaiming their purpose of upholding the principles of justice, dignity, and equal opportunity for each citizen in the land. Upon the foundation of these principles Americans have built a dynamic society which has earned the respect and raised the hopes of working people throughout the world.

As a Nation of free men and women, we have worked—with abundant success—to convert our principles into reality. By freely asserting our rights as citizens, we have improved our standard of living, bettered our working conditions, and achieved greater security for ourselves and our families than any other society in the history of mankind.

Today we are challenged to show that our society can make progress in freedom—challenged by an aggressive rival, communism, which seeks adherents to its brand of progress. This rival system is based upon an attitude of life diametrically opposed to ours. Under its flag, the individual worker is harnessed to an enterprise directed by the State. Their system is a powerful machine, capable and ruthless, but it lacks one essential element: the spark of freedom which Americans hold most dear, and without which no sustained or satisfying achievement is possible.

On Labor Day 1960, I am proud to salute the working men and women of America.

DWIGHT D. EISENHOWER

283 ¶ Remarks at the Dedication of a New Building at the Industrial College of the Armed Forces, Fort McNair. *September 6, 1960*

General Mundy, General Lemnitzer, the Chiefs of Staff of the Services, and friends of the Industrial College:

It is a distinct pleasure to come here and take part in the ceremony dedicating this new building to the service of the United States. This structure is a far cry from the humble habitation of the old Army Industrial College with which I was identified in the early thirties, just as the atomic-age curriculum of this year's class is far removed from the course of study in the college almost three decades ago.

Before I give to you the few thoughts I have—before formally dedicating this building—I think it might be fitting for me to indulge in a few of the reminiscences to which Mr. Ward has alluded, as he told you about the beginnings of this Industrial College.

I came into the Office of the Assistant Secretary of War about 1930, when the Industrial College was limping along in its course for about 7 years. Limping, I assure you, is an exaggeration of the progress it was making.

But a few civilians had a great vision. The one with whom I came in closest contact was Mr. Baruch. When I was assigned to the Assistant Secretary's Office and told that one of my principal functions would be to be a liaison with the Industrial College, because the Assistant Secretary of War was then its boss, I thought that my career in the Army had come to an end. Service people at that time looked down a very long and disdainful nose when they thought about the Industrial College and its mission—indeed, they rather thought that it had no mission.

I was impressed here today by two of the speakers talking about the quality of the officers selected now for these classes. At the time I am talking about, selection was completely in the hands of the Chief of the Supply Services of the Army, and that officer had trouble in filling the quotas. Because they did, the Industrial College became known among the knowledgeable as rather a year of rest for the poor officer who no longer was desired by his chief but who nevertheless had a long record on which he could not be classed B.

In fact, so wide was the difference of outlook on the part of those who really had the vision about the Industrial College, that the Chief of Staff, in my time, issued instructions to his general staff that they would not enter the Office of the Assistant Secretary of War, because he felt that they would, apparently, thereby be contaminated.

If I have any claim to the allegation that I have helped toward the development of this College at all, it came about by one thing: I had just come recently from the Army War College—the building right across the way—and I had found out, working under the Assistant Secretary of War and the Chief of Staff, that officers could come there only if they qualified in the very highest ranks so far as their particular and respective fitness reports and efficiency reports were concerned. Well, I thought this was a good idea, if we were going to raise the quality of the Industrial College. So I induced our bosses to say no one could come to the Industrial College as a student, unless his efficiency report in quality fell within a certain high category of priority and excellence.

Well, there was a great outcry. There were many people that were going to be taken out of some comfortable billets and we did have to make a compromise to say that those who were then currently in the school would not be fired. But from that time on, people began to realize there was a distinction to be assigned to this school. Why? Because they knew among their fellows that their efficiency reports were high and this was an advertisement that never ceased to have a great deal of effect on the character of this school.

I lived in that atmosphere, I think, until 1935, and I can tell you that even within those very few years, the change, in spite of the meager accommodations that we then had, was indeed remarkable.

Times indeed have changed. In 1930 few among us gave serious and comprehensive thought to national security. The defense budget totaled a bit over 1 percent of our gross national product. The United States Army, which included the Air Corps and the Philippine Scouts, totaled some 140,000 people. In the Armed Forces even a sketchy knowledge of tactics was deemed far more important than the deepest understanding of the productive capacity of the United States. Indeed one of the purposes of the Industrial College was to bring about a firm and permanent relationship between the fighting forces and the economy on which they necessarily had to exist.

Today, national security is one of the central facts of our existence. Ten percent of our gross national product is devoted to it; over one-third of our scientists and engineers are engaged in it; half our research moneys are committed to it. No fewer than five million of our citizens are directly and wholly involved in its programs.

Thus there has been an intrusion of defense matters into our national life on a scale never before approached except in time of war. And this condition will continue until powerful aggressors renounce their aims of world conquest. Until that time arrives, our first priority task is to develop and sustain a deterrent commanding the respect of any potential aggressor and to prepare to face resolutely the dangers of any possible war.

At the same time, we of course cannot neglect the vital problems of a nation at peace. This places a heavy responsibility upon Government and especially upon those charged with the management of the human and material resources which we devote to our national security. The wise and prudent administration of the vast resources required by defense calls for extraordinary skill in meshing the military, political, economic, and social machinery of our modern life. It requires the finest understanding of how a complex industrial economy may best be put at the service of the Nation's defense so that the greatest effective use is made of resources with a minimum of waste and misapplication.

Our liberties rest with our people, upon the scope and depth of their understanding of the spiritual, political, and economic realities which underlie our national purpose and sustain our Nation's security. It is the high mission of the Industrial College of the Armed Forces to develop such understanding among our people and their military and civilian leaders. So doing, we will make the wisest use of our own resources in promoting our common defense. The Industrial College has been a guidepost pointing to the greatly increased quality of our defensive capacity; it must continue to point to an ever-ascending progress for the years ahead.

This splendid structure, which now we dedicate, will enable the College to do its work more efficiently, and it is a tribute to the continuing high public esteem in which it is held. To all who had a part in making this possible, I offer my warm congratulations, and officially dedicate this College to the service of the United States of America.

NOTE: The President's opening words "General Mundy, General Lemnitzer" referred to Lt. Gen. George W. Mundy, USAF, Commandant of the Industrial College of the Armed Forces, and Gen. Lyman L. Lemnitzer, Chief of Staff of the U.S. Army. Later he referred to J. Carlton Ward, Jr., Chairman of the Board of Advisers of the College, and Bernard Baruch who lectured at the College during the period of the President's association with it.

284 ¶ The President's News Conference of September 7, 1960

THE PRESIDENT. Good morning. Please sit down.

In a very depressing world picture that we see so often, there is one bright spot that seems to me worthy of mention, and that is the settling of the Indus River water problem between Pakistan and India. I think the world—at least, certainly, the free world—should offer a vote of thanks to the people that have been so instrumental: not only President Ayub and Prime Minister Nehru, but Eugene Black of the World Bank and his deputy, Mr. Iliff. This has been brought about by long, patient negotiations with concessions on both sides, and among the governments that of course necessarily had to assist in financing over and beyond what the World Bank could do, and the countries themselves. In both cases I know that this—particularly between the two governmental heads—this negotiation has gone on for a long time. When I was in these two countries we talked about the matter, and their expressed intention there to settle it has finally come to a fruition for which all of us should be very grateful and gratified.

Q. Rutherford M. Poats, United Press International: Sir, in that connection can you suggest to us the breadth of the political possibilities in this step toward a rapprochement between India and Pakistan? Do you see this as a step toward, say, tackling the problem of Kashmir?

THE PRESIDENT. In this sense, yes: that with both these countries water is a tremendous matter—problem, and the agreement here cannot fail to lead, in my opinion, to the settlement of other problems about their refugees and displaced persons, and even it might have some effect on this very touchy question of Kashmir. Certainly that is the hope.

Q. Kenneth M. Scheibel, Gannett Newspapers: Mr. President, Vice President Nixon has said that he will not make religion an issue in this campaign. Now, the other day a prominent American said that the Republican Party is bringing religion into the campaign as an issue through the back door. Do you have any comment?

THE PRESIDENT. Mr. Nixon and I agreed long ago that one thing that we would never raise, and never mention, is the religious issue in this coming campaign. I have made my position clear before this group, and I suppose I do not need to repeat it.

I not only don't believe in voicing prejudice, I want to assure you I feel none. And I am sure that Mr. Nixon feels exactly the same.

Now, the very need for—apparently for—protesting innocence in this regard now, in itself, seems to exacerbate the situation rather than to quiet it. I know of no one, certainly no Republican has come to me and said, "I believe we should use religion as an issue," or intimate that he intends to use it either locally or nationally. I do not believe that any group of leaders has been more emphatic upon this point than have the Republican leaders. And, I would hope that it could be one of those subjects that could be laid on the shelf and forgotten until after the election is over.

Q. Ray L. Scherer, National Broadcasting Company: Mr. President, how do you evaluate reports from the Congo that Russian planes are being used to transport troops outside U.N. jurisdiction?

THE PRESIDENT. Mr. Scherer, that's one question I knew I was going to get—*[laughter]*—and so, I have written an answer because I want to make perfectly clear what we feel about it.

[*Reading*] The United States deplores the unilateral action of the Soviet Union in supplying aircraft and other equipment for military purposes to the Congo, thereby aggravating an already serious situation which finds Africans killing other Africans. If these planes are flown by Soviet military personnel this would be contrary to the principles so far applied regarding use in the Congo of military contingents from the larger powers.

As far as I know, these rules have previously been upheld by the Soviet Union itself. Therefore, it would be doubly serious if such participation by military units were part of an operation in the civil war which has recently taken on very ugly overtones.

The main responsibility in the case of the Congo has been thrown on the United Nations as the only organization able to act without adding to the risks of spreading the conflict. The United Nations maintains very strict principles regarding foreign military intervention in the Congo or in any country. I am sure that within the limits set by the Charter itself, the United Nations is doing what it can to uphold these principles and will do so in the future.

The constitutional structure of the Congo Republic is a question which should be worked out peacefully by the Congolese themselves.

This objective is threatened by the Soviet action which seems to be motivated entirely by the Soviet Union's political designs in Africa. I must repeat that the United States takes a most serious view of this action by the Soviet Union. In the interest of a peaceful solution in Africa, acceptable to all parties concerned, I urge the Soviet Union to desist from its unilateral activities and to demand its support—to lend its support instead to the practice of collective effort through the United Nations. [*Ends reading*]

And I might add that the United States intends to give its support to the United Nations to whatever they find it necessary within the limits of the Charter to keep peace in this region.

Q. William McGaffin, Chicago Daily News: Sir, continuing this discussion upon a very grave question, do you—could you give us the benefit of your thinking as far as you can within security reasons, on our chances of keeping the lid on the Congo, of keeping it from succumbing to communism, and of avoiding another war, Korean-type war there?

THE PRESIDENT. Well, I don't know that you could describe the type of war. I think this: this job can be done if others see the problem in the same serious way that the United States, and I think the United Nations, does see it. But if they, someone, or if the Soviets insist on acting unilaterally, I can say this would create a situation that would indeed be serious.

Q. Thomas N. Schroth, Congressional Quarterly: Sir, it's often been said that you preferred to stand above politics. I wonder if you would give us your views on the role of the Presidency in political campaigns, and would you tell us whether you personally enjoy political activities?

THE PRESIDENT. Well, first of all, I of course am not responsible for the opinions of others saying I like to stay above politics. I've never said so. I recognize that I have, or have had, the responsibility to be the head of a party, a party that upholds the basic philosophy that I believe to be correct for application in this Nation to keep our economy strong and expanding.

Now, believing that, and having been responsible for directing the operations of the executive department for the past 7½ years, it would be odd if I simply became a sphinx and refused to show why I believe these things and what were my hopes for it in the future. Now, I do think this: I think that the President, as long as he is President, still has an obligation to every single individual in this Nation. Therefore, the rule of reason and of logic and of good sense has got to apply in these things if a man in such position, concerned with the dignity of the office, concerned with its standing, he cannot just go out and be in the hustings and shouting some of the things that we see stated often irresponsibly. I believe he does have a right to make his views known to Americans wherever they are.

Q. Mrs. May Craig, Portland (Maine) Press Herald: Sir, Senator Kennedy said yesterday that you cannot get Mr. Khrushchev to bargain seriously about peace either by arguing with him or smiling with him.

Now, you've tried "summitry" and you tried inviting him here. Do you think it would have been better if you had taken a tougher road, and would you so advise Vice President Nixon?

THE PRESIDENT. What do you mean by "tougher road"?

Q. Mrs. Craig: Not stop nuclear testing, perhaps not had him here.

THE PRESIDENT. I don't see anything that would be tough about refusing to see a man as long as there was any possible chance of his agreeing to one of the main efforts we are making toward disarmament. I do not see that it is merely in, as part of the contest between, in perfecting weapons that we want to stop testing. We are talking about everything we can do to bring some peace to the world; that's what we are trying to do. Now, toughness comes in standing in front of the man and telling him what you will do and you won't do. Our country is peaceable; we want peace. Is it tough just to say we won't even talk peace? That makes—that seems to me to be silly. Now, I don't care who says it, you have got to explore every avenue there is, and you've got to work on it day and night and think about it day and night. And I am not concerned about any criticism about my past actions. I have worked for what I thought was the good of the United States and the peace of the world, and I will continue to do so.

Q. William H. Y. Knighton, Jr., Baltimore Sun: Mr. President, on a less serious subject, it appears as though now the world series will be played possibly only 40 miles from here. [*Laughter*] Would you consider attending one of the games, sir?

THE PRESIDENT. Yes, sir.

Q. Mr. Knighton: Thank you.

Q. Robert C. Pierpoint, CBS News: Mr. President, on a more serious subject again—[*laughter*]—you have indicated that you are considering going to the United Nations General Assembly and I am wondering if you have made your decision to go, if you could tell us about that decision; and, secondly, will you possibly see Mr. Khrushchev when he's here?

THE PRESIDENT. Well, I would think the chances of the latter were very, very slim indeed. And there would have to, again, to be some conditions fulfilled because—before that could happen.

I think we must start off with this premise: we must respect the United Nations; we must believe in the United Nations or the case for relieving some of the burdens that mankind is now carrying, for removing some of the worries and the fears that plague men's minds and hearts, will never be achieved. Therefore, I do not intend to debase the United Nations by being a party to a, well, a battle of invective and propaganda.

Now, I have been thinking even more this year than formerly of the possibility of making a pilgrimage to the United Nations. I have done it twice. But every year it comes up. This year there would appear to be very definite reasons for going there, but at the same time I must insist I am not going there in any attempt to, you might say, to debase that organization in the minds of people everywhere.[1]

Q. David P. Sentner, Hearst Newspapers: Mr. President, would you please give us your reaction to the recognition of Communist China by the Castro regime in Cuba?

THE PRESIDENT. Well, it seems that it's what you might have expected. I think it is a very grave error.

Q. David Kraslow, Knight Newspapers: Mr. President, there has been quite a bit of soul searching of late about our national purpose. How would you define our national purpose, and do you think the American people are losing sight of it?

THE PRESIDENT. You know, I think there's a lot of talk about this. The United States purpose was stated in its Declaration of Independence and very definitely in the first ten amendments to the Constitution, and as well as the preamble to that document.

I am not concerned about America losing its sense of purpose. We may not be articulate about it, and we may not give daily the kind of thought to it that we should; but I believe America wants to live first in freedom and the kind of liberty that is guaranteed to us through our founding documents; and, secondly, they want to live at peace with all their neighbors, so that we may jointly find a better life for humanity as we go forward.

This, to me, is the simple purpose of the United States.

We have to take many avenues and routes to achieve it. We have to keep tremendous defensive arrangements. We must help others in different fashions, but that is always the purpose, and I see no reason for blinking it or dimming it or being afraid to speak it.

---

[1] On September 14 the Press Secretary announced that the President would go to New York on the morning of September 22 for the purpose of addressing the General Assembly of the United Nations. It was further stated that the President would make specific proposals to the United Nations delegates at that time.

Q. Marvin L. Arrowsmith, Associated Press: Mr. President, how do you feel about these NSA defectors, and do you think there is anything that should be done to try to prevent the hiring of this type by our top security agencies?

THE PRESIDENT. Mr. Arrowsmith, I don't know of anything that has—any internal or procedural problem—that has more engaged my attention for these past years. And this is only natural, I think.

I was a commander of an enormous force, an allied force, in which the dangers of leaks and defectors and spies in our midst were always very great and I have possibly been more sensitive to the dangers to our country as created by this kind of weakness, human weakness, than have most people.

Now, I believe that an incident such as this shows that we must be always on the alert, very alert. I would think we must go through our entire procedures to see if there is any one way we could better it. We have every kind of organization—every kind of group—that is possible to be party to these investigations into the backgrounds and character of the people in sensitive positions. I believe we must continue to do so. And, for my part, whenever it's a choice of the Nation's safety in keeping an individual, I will do something to get him out of a place—where he cannot hurt us.

I recognize that even in Government—although Government employment is a privilege and not a right—that the rights of the individual must be respected, but this incident, I believe, should be a lesson to all of us that we must never cease our vigilance in the large and small places at any time.

Q. M. Stewart Hensley, United Press International: Mr. President, you have spoken of the Russian, use of Russian planes to transport Lumumba's troops within the Congo. Do you have any evidence that the Russians, in addition to this, are supplying any arms to Lumumba's forces?

THE PRESIDENT. I have no—and, as a matter of fact, two things: we do not know as of now that there are any Russian [military] crews operating these planes, and we do not know that there are any weapons in the cargoes.

Now, there were 10 planes that, on the request of the Russians, landed in Athens on the condition that they were inspected for the character of their cargo and it was all of a legitimate type for peaceful uses. But I believe, understand that there have been no more requests made to land at Athens. [*Confers with Mr. Hagerty*]

Well, Russian military crews, I'll correct that.

Q. John Scali, Associated Press: Mr. President, in answer to an earlier question you said you thought the chances were very, very slim of your meeting with Premier Khrushchev until some conditions were fulfilled beforehand. Could you spell that out a bit; by "conditions" would you have in mind something like freeing the RB–47 fliers which they are now holding in jail?

THE PRESIDENT. That would be one thing that I would expect, yes. But I don't believe I will go into the entire gamut of the possibilities. I think I will let your imagination answer that one.

Q. Edward V. Koterba, United Features: Mr. President, again in a lighter vein, on next October 4th, just 10 days before your 70th birthday, you will have passed the age record of Andrew Jackson who became the oldest Chief Executive in history, as he left office at the age of 69 years, 11 months, and 19 days. As this milestone in presidential history approaches, sir, could you give us a few hints on how you've succeeded in maintaining such apparent good health despite the tremendous burdens of your office?

THE PRESIDENT. Well, now, first of all, I believe it's a tradition in baseball that when a pitcher has a no-hitter going, no one reminds him of it. [*Laughter*] So, I don't take it very kindly that you are taking for granted that I am going to reach October 4th.

As a matter of fact, I see no particular virtue or not that a man should be the eldest President ever to serve. I do think about age in the terms of two men that were going down the road, and one of them was very woeful about the fact that he was getting into so many advanced years. And he complained about this and all of the joys of youth and middle age that he was now missing, and finally the other one could stand it no longer and he says, "Well, I'm certainly glad I'm old." And the fellow said, "Well, what's the matter; are you crazy?" "Well," he says, "considering when I was born, if I weren't old, I'd be dead." [*Laughter*]

Now, I, the way I feel of it, concerning, considering the day I was born, why, I'm glad I'm old!

Q. Frank van der Linden, Nashville Banner: Sir, the Congress has gone home without acting on nearly all of the requests you made for legislation. And Senator Kennedy and the other Democratic leaders are saying it's mostly your fault, or the Republicans' fault. And I wondered if you have other reasons than that.

THE PRESIDENT. Well, apparently this other—this other party then is making me responsible for splitting theirs. I think that should be something for self-examination and not for calling for comment from me.

Next, they had a 2-to-1 majority. They were in session for a long time, and they did very little indeed.

I think the record was disappointing and certainly it was disappointing to me, but that isn't important. I think that it should be disappointing to the United States.

Within any little bit of give-and-take which, after all, is necessary in the legislative process, we could certainly have had a reasonable raise in the minimum wage. The administration had asked for it. We could have had some schoolrooms constructed, and which would have been the kind of thing that I think the Federal Government could well help out. And we could have had other things like that done with a little bit of give-and-take.

Now, I am not going to start castigating people for motives or anything else. I am merely relating the facts which I think are such as to cause some disappointment, if not dismay, throughout the American Nation.

Q. Mikhail R. Sagatelyan, Tass Telegraph Agency: Sir, at several recent news conferences you repeated, repeatedly stated, that the United States and you personally are ready to do everything which may appear necessary for strengthening peace with justice, and mainly for progress in the field of world disarmament. Would you, sir, tell us what new steps for obtaining the above-mentioned aims the United States and you personally are going to make during the coming session of the General Assembly in which a certain number of heads of governments will participate?

THE PRESIDENT. Well, I don't know whether you can say that there is anything new. There will be renewed effort made, there will be renewed effort to place the whole record of America in this field before the world again, to show where are the areas where we want to negotiate, concessions we are ready to make, the kind of agreements we are ready to make, provided only that every agreement has with it the kind of control and inspection that can make each side confident that both are acting in good faith. That is the sole reservation we make in these negotiations, and I think it will be, of course, reemphasized.

Now, as far as any new proposal, I believe there have been one or two made in the United Nations again about a good many tons of U–235, and so on, ready to—[*confers with Mr. Hagerty*]—I think made by— Mr. Lodge made this before the United Nations just in a matter of a month.   We will continue to stand by such offers as that.   But in every place we will review the whole situation and say, "Here is what we stand ready to do."

Q. Robert G. Spivack, New York Post: Mr. President, in appraising the short session of Congress, how much responsibility do you think the Southern Democrats and conservative Republicans, the coalition, must bear for not getting through the domestic, social welfare legislation you spoke of?

THE PRESIDENT. Well, it turns out, Mr. Spivack, that this contest now in which everybody is so interested, and in the context of which all of this record of the Congress is viewed, is between Democrats and Republicans.   So, there is where I would leave the Congress.

Q. Charles W. Roberts, Newsweek: Sir, in the statements made by the two NSA defectors in Moscow, they indicated that they had made known their unhappiness here, made to a Member of Congress, and there was an indication that the State Department was informed that they were unhappy and contemplating defection.   I wonder if any reports coming to you show that there was evidence anywhere in the Government that these men were under surveillance or were suspected of defecting prior to the time they left?

THE PRESIDENT. No.   I haven't—this is a new statement in the thing, so far as I am concerned.   And, I would say this: the Defense Department has already made quite a statement in—and one of these men, I believe, is—he was investigated by the, originally, by the Navy, the other by the Army, and I think those two services could give you more detailed information on this matter than I can.   I know nothing about this, as a specific charge.

Marvin L. Arrowsmith, Associated Press: Thank you, Mr. President.

NOTE: President Eisenhower's one hundred and ninety-first news conference was held in the Executive Office Building from 10:30 to 11:01 o'clock on Wednesday morning, September 7, 1960.   In attendance: 243.

285   ¶ Memorandum of Disapproval of Bill Concerning the Marking of Imported Articles and Containers.   *September 7, 1960*

[Released September 7, 1960. Dated September 6, 1960]

I AM withholding my approval from H.R. 5054, "To amend the Tariff Act of 1930 with respect to the marking of imported articles and containers."

The bill would provide that new packaging for articles imported in containers required by present law to be marked with the name of the country of origin must be similarly marked by the repackager, whether the importer, distributor, retailer, or other handler of the merchandise. Goods in packages not so marked would be subject to seizure and forfeiture. The requirement could be waived only where found to necessitate such substantial changes in customary trade practices as to cause "undue" hardship.

H.R. 5054 runs counter to one of our major foreign policy objectives— the reduction of unnecessary barriers and hindrances to trade. The burdens the bill would impose are unnecessary because the Federal Trade Commission requires the disclosure of the foreign origin of repackaged imported articles when it is in the public interest to do so.

The United States and other principal trading nations of the world have recognized that burdensome marking requirements can be a hindrance to trade and have agreed to the principle that such hindrances should be reduced to a minimum. H.R. 5054 might well result in successive domestic handlers requiring written assurances of proper marking in order to avoid the severe penalty of seizure and forfeiture. The cost and the complications involved in such cumbersome paper work would tend to discourage such imports. Moreover, this measure could prove ultimately damaging to our export-expansion efforts, for needlessly restrictive action on our part could readily lead to similarly restrictive action by other countries against American goods.

In addition, the bill would unnecessarily extend the Bureau of Customs into new areas by requiring the Bureau to follow goods after they have entered the stream of domestic commerce and to act against handlers of merchandise who are not importers. The Bureau would be required to determine the nature of customary trade practices and the possibility of "undue" hardship in a field outside its normal competence. Aside from the unnecessary additional expense, these new responsibilities would be most awkward for the Bureau to administer.

For these reasons I am withholding my approval of H.R. 5054.

DWIGHT D. EISENHOWER

286 ¶ Message for the SEATO Day Ceremonies at Bangkok.   *September 8, 1960*

TODAY, the eighth of September, 1960, marks the Sixth Anniversary of the signing, at Manila, of the Southeast Asia Collective Defense Treaty which brought into being the Southeast Asia Treaty Organization, more commonly known as SEATO.   Joining together in accordance with the purposes set forth in the charter of the United Nations, the member nations of SEATO—Australia, France, New Zealand, Pakistan, the Philippines, Thailand, the United Kingdom and the United States—have demonstrated a firm adherence to the principle of equal rights and self-determination of peoples, have subscribed to the attainment of self-government through peaceful means and are supporting the development of economic and social well-being of all peoples in the Treaty Area.

SEATO has, in its six years of existence, performed admirably the task of coordinating the efforts of its members in collective defense for the preservation of peace and security against the threat of Communist imperialism.   At the same time, SEATO's accomplishments in fostering social and economic progress have been noteworthy.   It is working towards the eradication of the scourge of cholera in Southeast Asia and is conducting other medical research in the area.   It is training and developing a needed reservoir of skilled Asian technicians.   It is advancing education through grants of scholarships and fellowships, cultural exchanges and lecture tours by persons eminent in their fields of achievement.   It has established a Graduate School of Engineering, now in its second successful year in Bangkok, for the advanced training of Asian engineers and scientists.   It is currently planning for an area-wide radio meteorological network and for an institute of tropical agriculture.   All these constitute examples of the way SEATO is carrying out its objectives.

The United States is proud to share in these accomplishments and it was honored by having the opportunity last May to act as host for the Sixth Annual Meeting of the SEATO Council of Ministers in Washington. On that occasion I had the great honor and pleasure of greeting personally the Council members, their senior civil and military advisers, the Secretary-General and the Chief of the Military Planning Office of SEATO. At the Sixth Annual Meeting, the member nations renewed their pledges to insure mutual security, reaffirmed their determination to resist Communist aggression and subversion and further developed their plans to foster and support the economic and social advancement of the Treaty Area. On this occasion, I am happy to reaffirm United States support for these solemn pledges.

DWIGHT D. EISENHOWER

287 ¶ Remarks at the Dedication of the George C. Marshall Space Flight Center, Huntsville, Alabama. *September 8, 1960*

Governor Patterson, Mrs. Marshall, Mayor Searcy, Dr. Glennan, Dr. Von Braun, Members of the Congress here present, other distinguished guests, and my fellow Americans—all of you:

It is always good to come back to our Southland, this region of traditional hospitality and friendliness. I thank you, Governor, for making me feel so much at home, and so welcome in your State.

I have long looked forward to visiting this spot. I know that, for an old foot soldier, it will be a revelation to see at firsthand the efforts here under way to probe into the mysteries of the universe millions of miles from our earth.

Already, in brief visits with your distinguished men of rocketry, I have made a significant discovery of my own.

I find that the leaders of the new space science feel as if Venus and Mars are more accessible to them than a regimental headquarters was to me more than 40 years ago, when I was a platoon commander.

To move conceptually, in one generation, from the hundreds of yards that once bounded my tactical world to the unending millions of miles that beckon these men forward, is a startling transformation.

Now I freely admit to sentimentality in my contemplation of these advances, because so much of this dramatic accomplishment was pioneered in the United States Army, which until recently was my home and my life.

Here, under Army guidance, Redstone and Jupiter and a whole family of missiles have taken form. Here, too, was created Explorer I, America's first earth satellite. I share with the Army its gratification in these trail-blazing achievements, which have their counterparts in other services. These achievements have thrilled the American people and won plaudits throughout the world.

The momentum thus gained accelerates today under the civilian management of the new National Aeronautics and Space Administration, guided by Dr. Glennan, and his Deputy, Dr. Dryden. The gifted scientists, engineers, and technicians who splendidly served the Army are now eagerly developing, for this new organization, the gigantic launch vehicle Saturn.

No doubt this mighty rocket system makes its presence known loudly— possibly too loudly—in Huntsville. But it is a significant forward step in our conquest of space and for growth in human comprehension.

Already we have improved our understanding of matter, energy, motion, and life processes through our early efforts in space.

The characteristics of the radiation belts girdling the earth—the true nature of our space environment, including solar storms—the appearance of the earth's total cloud cover—the feasibility of a worldwide communications system utilizing satellites—these and other space ventures have opened new vistas of thought, of understanding, and of opportunity.

These, of course, are only beginnings. This past month new milestones in space exploration have been headlined throughout the world. As the months go by we shall see many more.

But marvel as we will at these technical achievements, we must not overlook this truth:

All that we have already accomplished, and all in the future that we shall achieve, is the outgrowth not of a soulless, barren technology, nor of a grasping state imperialism. Rather, it is the product of unrestrained human talent and energy restlessly probing for the betterment of humanity. We are propelled in these efforts by ingenuity and industry, by courage to overcome disappointment and failure, by free-ranging imagination, by insistence upon excellence—with none of this imposed by fiat, none of it ordered by a domineering bureaucracy. In this fact is proof once again that hard work, toughness of spirit, and self-reliant enterprise are not mere catchwords of an era dead and gone. They remain the imperatives for the fulfillment of America's dream.

Not pushbuttons nor electronic devices, therefore, but superlative human qualities have brought success and fame to this place. These qualities I mention because they typify a distinguished American, George Catlett Marshall, in whose name we carry forward this activity.

General Marshall was supremely endowed. He was a man of war, yet a builder of peace—forceful and dynamic as a leader, calculating and prudent in judgment, yet warmly regarded by his associates. He was selfless, indeed self-effacing, yet known and admired throughout the world. Though dominating in personal force, in action and thought he was humble and considerate.

Northern born and Southern schooled, all-American through military service, he ultimately became a citizen of the world. I, of course, knew him best during the prosecution of World War II. I found him immune to discouragement, relentless in carrying the war to the enemy, and unsparing of himself in his leadership of the great forces he directed. But so profound was his devotion to the constructive works of peace, so outspokenly was he their advocate as Secretary of State, that he later became the symbol of renewed hope for scores of millions of suffering people through his great plan for Europe that will forever bear his name. He became, in consequence, the only professional soldier ever to be honored with the Nobel Peace Prize.

During his final 20 years he lived with, he counselled and influenced, the greatest men and movements of his time. Through it all he remained unaffected, reserved, completely disinterested in self, and dedicated to our Nation's highest ideals.

We, participating in this brief ceremony, agree with Sir Winston Churchill, who said that succeeding generations must not be allowed to forget General Marshall's achievements and his example.

There are ways to do this that General Marshall would have prized far more than what we do here today. It is not enough that we rest with praise of his name.

But we can newly resolve to work ceaselessly, with all our hearts and with such talents as we may possess, as he did throughout his life, for the good of this land and its freedoms.

Thus we shall carry forward the noble mission of our Republic, ever striving to strengthen peace, ever advancing the cause of human liberty, ever doing our best to build a better life for all.

That is what George Marshall would wish from us today.

In this spirit, and with deep satisfaction in having shared in this tribute to a revered friend, I dedicate this, the George C. Marshall Space Flight Center.

May this great Center be ever worthy of its honored name.

Now, Governor Patterson and friends, I have an additional comment that is especially meaningful to me. With us is Katherine Marshall, General Marshall's constant helpmeet during the world events of which I have spoken. Without her inspiration, loyal support, and companionship, the great American whom we honor here today could not have hoped to achieve the heights I have briefly outlined.

I salute this distinguished lady. I am, with all of you, delighted that she could be with us today, as we permanently enshrine a bust of her husband which will serve as an inspiration to all who work and visit here.

Mrs. Marshall, I would be deeply grateful if you would step forward with me and unveil this sculpture of General George C. Marshall.

NOTE: The President spoke at 10:35 a.m. in the Administration Building. His opening words referred to John Patterson, Governor of Alabama, Mrs. George C. Marshall, R. B. Searcy, Mayor of Hunts-ville, T. Keith Glennan, Administrator, National Aeronautics and Space Administration, and Wernher von Braun, Director of the George C. Marshall Space Flight Center.

288 ¶ Memorandum of Disapproval of Bill for the Relief of Raymond Baurkot. *September 9, 1960*

[Released September 9, 1960. Dated September 8, 1960]

I HAVE WITHHELD my approval from H.R. 6767, "For the relief of Raymond Baurkot."

This bill would permit the filing of a tax refund claim that was in fact filed after the deadline date set by law.

Public Law 85–859 provided for the refund of internal revenue taxes paid on certain liquors lost as the result of a major disaster occurring prior to the date of enactment, September 2, 1958. It required that claims be filed on or before March 2, 1959. The claimant filed on March 16, 1959 for a refund of $382.10 paid in taxes on beer destroyed in a 1955 flood. He asserted that he had telephoned the branch office of the District Director's office in Easton, Pennsylvania, on February 26, 1959, and was informed by an unidentified person that he had a "couple of months" in which to file.

The Easton branch office has no record of any such request for information from Mr. Baurkot. That office, moreover, does not itself handle alcohol tax problems. Its standard procedure is to refer such inquiries to the Assistant Regional Commissioner's office in Philadelphia which has general supervision over such matters.

Information concerning Public Law 85–859 and its filing requirements were widely disseminated to the liquor industry by the Internal Revenue Service. It appears that the claimant received the Industry Circular published by the Service but thereafter misplaced it. This Circular set forth the March second deadline and specifically provided that inquiries regarding claims should be addressed to the Assistant Regional Commissioner's office.

Under these circumstances I am unable to approve this bill. The statutory period of limitations, which the Congress has included in the revenue system as a matter of sound policy, is essential to the achievement of finality in tax administration. Efficient administration of the tax laws is dependent upon taxpayers meeting statutory deadlines. To grant special relief in this case would be to discriminate against other similarly situated taxpayers and to create an undesirable precedent.

DWIGHT D. EISENHOWER

289 ¶ Memorandum of Disapproval of Bill Amending the Bankruptcy Act.
September 9, 1960

[Released September 9, 1960. Dated September 8, 1960]

I HAVE WITHHELD my approval of H.R. 7242, "To amend sections 1, 57j, 64a(5), 67b, 67c, and 70c of the Bankruptcy Act, and for other purposes."

I recognize the need for legislation to solve certain problems regarding the priority of liens in bankruptcy, but this bill is not a satisfactory solution.

It would unduly and unnecessarily prejudice the sound administration of Federal tax laws. In some cases, for example, mortgages would be given an unwarranted priority over Federal tax liens even though the mortgage is recorded after the filing of the tax lien.

This and other defects of the bill can, I believe, be corrected without compromising its primary and commendable purpose. The Treasury Department and the proponents of H.R. 7242 have been working toward solution of recognized problems in present law. Further cooperative effort should produce satisfactory legislation that would avoid the undesirable effects of this bill.

Dwight D. Eisenhower

290 ¶ Remarks at the Opening of the Republican Campaign, Friendship International Airport Near Baltimore.   *September* 12, 1960

Mr. Vice President, Senator Lodge, my associates in Government of whom I see so many here on the platform, and my friends:

When I was first invited to come over here this morning, I really demurred on the grounds that it was a mistake to have me here. This is the starting of a campaign, and we have new faces, new energies, new candidates. It seemed a time to just look forward, never backward.

Well, I was wrong, I think, because as an old war horse—sort of smelling a bit of the dust of battle—I have not only changed my mind, I am glad I am here. I am not even using the notes that I so laboriously scrawled down. I just want to chat with you as I have so often in the past.

First of all, I have heard this rain and this hurricane mentioned. To my mind, it is a good omen. I recall that back in 1952 in June, I was finally persuaded to come back from Europe and announce that if nominated, I would be glad to run for the Presidency of the United States. My first meeting was in Abilene, Kansas. And such a rainstorm you have never seen. Then we had no nice big room where we could have a ceremony. It was out in the ball park, and we had to take it. So I see nothing at all to be downhearted about because there is a rainstorm that impeded some of your movements.

Next, this seems to be a really good place to start a campaign such as we are now beginning. You have a record of sending champions out for the last couple of years—at least the Colts, as I understand, have been champions. I expect you can sort of adopt Dick and Cabot as another team and send them out also to win the championship. And I might mention that right behind me here is a little boy carrying a unique sign. It says: "I am for Nixon, I am for Lodge, I am for Blum." I am not exactly sure who Mr. Blum is, but down at the bottom the sign says: "I am for the Orioles." So I think this particular crowd at least could, by adoption of Dick and Cabot into their teams, possibly bring some luck.

As Republicans, we have selected our leaders for a campaign and for a Government that we hope and trust will be established in Washington for the next 4 years. They are going out as messengers—messengers to carry to every nook and corner of this country the story of the record that has been established by Republican leadership in the House, the Senate, and in the executive department over the past years. They are going out with a promise to build upon that record, respectful of its past accomplishments, but never satisfied that the answers have yet been reached to America's problems. They are going out, therefore, to stand on the platform of the Republican Party as written in Chicago. They are going to make pledges on their own part, as to the responsibilities they see before them, and how they will carry them out and perform them when elected.

They will do this honestly, as men of proved integrity. By no means will they be placing before the American people something that they think certain sections or certain groups may like, and do this presentation only in the hope of attracting votes. Whatever they say to the American people about programs, about pledges, will be a promise and a prelude for action.

They are men of demonstrated capacity in every kind of activity in carrying heavy responsibilities in the vicissitudes of foreign visits and in carrying the American flag in the United Nations debate. We have, by all odds, the finest team America could choose—for showing to America what we as a Nation are standing for in the world, what we shall fight for. We shall never be content with less.

They will fight, then, for peace. They will fight for those things that should help us toward the road to peace. They will fight for disarmament, continuing the struggle that has been going on along these years, to find whether the two opposing camps cannot, by honest negotiation, lift from the backs of men some of this burden that mankind is now condemned to carry.

There are many facets to this problem of disarmament. In the past we have proposed every conceivable kind of approach to that problem. They will possibly find new ones. But I know this: they will stand firm on this one principle—we shall have methods by which the good faith of each side may be proved, or we shall never lay down one single necessary weapon of our own.

As long as the other side is willing to adopt methods which will show the good faith of both sides—in other words, inspection—to see that both sides are doing what they say they are doing, Dick and Cabot will never cease, will never tire in this effort that means so much to people everywhere.

They will be concerned always also with the welfare, the progress of our citizens. They will look for everything to inspire, to lead our people to better heights, using Government where necessary, but depending first of all upon the initiative, the pride, and the self-respect of every single American individual wherever he is.

And of one thing they will always talk about—our liberties. They will remind every American that we will never put personal convenience, material gain, above our personal, priceless liberties. Because if ever we put any other value above liberty and above principle, we shall lose both.

Now, my friends, I am not here to make a campaign speech. I was supposed to be down by the airplane to say goodbye to two of my very best friends in Government as they start on this pilgrimage—this campaign—for the benefit of the United States and the free world.

I believe they are—I repeat—the finest team that all America could have chosen for this effort. All of us wish for them Godspeed and good luck. And all of us—if I may speak now for you—each of you—pledge them our support, even the little girl who was wearing a badge which said: "If I were 21, I would vote for Nixon," right up to the oldest patriarch—this whole audience—because across the board we need good government, we need Nixon and Lodge.

Thank you very much and goodbye.

NOTE: The President spoke at 10:27 a.m. In the fourth paragraph he referred to David Blum, Republican candidate from the 7th Congressional District of Maryland.

291 ⁋ Memorandum of Disapproval of Bill for the Relief of Eric and Ida Mae Hjerpe.
September 14, 1960

I AM withholding my approval from H.R. 2074, for the relief of Eric and Ida Mae Hjerpe.

In their income tax return for 1952 these taxpayers reported as income certain disability payments received by Mr. Hjerpe from his employer. During 1952, however, the Court of Appeals for the Seventh Circuit had held such disability payments excludable from gross income, even though the Internal Revenue Service had ruled to the contrary, and in 1957 the United States Supreme Court affirmed.

The taxpayers' claim for refund, based upon the excludability of the disability pay received by Mr. Hjerpe, was filed almost four years after the 1952 return had been filed and approximately 10½ months after the expiration of the applicable three-year statutory period of limitations. The claim was accordingly disallowed.

The last Congress enacted legislation to grant general relief, on a non-discriminatory basis, to taxpayers who had paid income tax on disability pay excludable from gross income under the Supreme Court decision. Relief was not provided, however, for taxpayers who, as in the case at hand, had not attempted to protect their rights by filing timely claims for refund.

H.R. 2074 would direct the payment to Mr. and Mrs. Hjerpe of $1,096.48 as a refund notwithstanding their late filing and failure to qualify under the general relief legislation. The bill is similar to several others from which I have withheld my approval in the past.

The statutory period of limitations, which the Congress has included in the revenue system as a matter of sound policy, is essential in order to achieve finality in tax administration. A substantial number of taxpayers paid income tax on disability payments received by them and failed to file timely claims for refund. To grant special relief in this case, where a refund was not claimed within the time prescribed by law, would constitute a discrimination against other similarly situated taxpayers and would create an undesirable precedent.

Under the circumstances, therefore, I am compelled to withhold my approval of the bill.

DWIGHT D. EISENHOWER

292 ¶ Memorandum of Disapproval of Bill for the Relief of H. P. Lambert Company, Incorporated, and Southeastern Drilling Corporation. *September* 14, 1960

I AM withholding my approval from H.R. 7618, a bill "For the relief of H. P. Lambert Company, Incorporated, and Southeastern Drilling Corporation."

The bill would waive the applicable statute of limitations and permit a claim for refund of duty paid on certain non-dutiable equipment imported into the United States.

The claimants requested that certain oil field equipment be entered under provisions of the Tariff Act affording duty-free status to property originally manufactured in the United States. The equipment was admitted duty-free after the Lambert Company, the brokerage firm in the case, had posted a bond to assure production of the documentation required to establish United States origin. At the request of the brokerage firm, the time covered by the bond was extended on several occasions. At the end of two years and when no further request for extension had been received, customs officials personally contacted the firm and advised that the duty would be payable if the requisite documentation were not furnished promptly. Despite this notice and despite a subsequent assessment of the duty, of which the brokerage firm was apprised and which it could have protested within 60 days, the Lambert Company failed to produce proof of United States origin until after its consideration was barred by applicable law and regulations.

Statutes of limitations should be set aside only when justified by compelling equitable considerations. No such considerations appear here. The only extenuating circumstance advanced in this case is that the notice of the assessment of duty was sent to the wrong party. I am advised, however, that the notice was properly sent to the brokerage firm as the party liable for the payment of duty. Furthermore, the firm, presumably well-versed in the customs laws, had not only been given repeated extensions on the bond it posted but had also been specifically advised of the imminence of an assessment of duty.

For these reasons, I am unable to approve this bill.

DWIGHT D. EISENHOWER

293 ¶ Statement Recorded for the Opening of the United Community Campaigns.
September 15, 1960

IT IS a privilege to serve as an "advance herald" for the united community campaigns. From now until Thanksgiving, these charitable campaigns will be conducted in cities and towns across the country.

In your home town the campaign may be known either as the United Fund or Community Chest. In both, many health and welfare agencies join together to ask our help once a year, in one campaign.

Much depends on the results of these nationwide efforts. They supply the funds for many of our local welfare groups and for some great national organizations like the American Red Cross and the USO. Money given in these campaigns also goes to the support of health agencies and medical research.

America has a proud reputation in the field of charity. It is true that we have more of the world's goods than many other nations. But it is also true that we share them generously, with the world and with each other. We do this primarily, I believe, because our spiritual heritage includes a deep sense of responsibility for our fellow men. The united community campaigns testify to the vitality of this heritage.

294 ¶ Exchange of Letters Between the President and Prime Minister Ikeda of Japan.
September 16, 1960

Dear Mr. Prime Minister:

I deeply appreciate the warm sentiment for the United States expressed in your personal letter to me which Foreign Minister Kosaka handed to Secretary Herter.

The American people share with the vast majority of Japanese the earnest wish for lasting American-Japanese friendship. Let me assure you that the American people fully understand the circumstances which led to the request by your government to postpone my visit to Japan. I share the regret, which you were kind enough to express, that the planned visit could not be carried out at that moment. But I assure you that the ties that link Japan and the United States are much too strong to be impaired by such momentary developments.

Rather than dwelling unnecessarily on events of the past, I would prefer to stress my great confidence in the future of relations between our two countries. The partnership existing between Japan and the United States today is built on a solid foundation of common interest, mutual confidence, and mutual trust. I am certain that we can look forward with assurance to even closer ties between our two countries in the coming years. I trust, too, that at some future time I may have an opportunity to accept your cordial invitation.

Sincerely,

Dwight D. Eisenhower

NOTE: Prime Minister Ikeda's letter follows:

My dear Mr. President:

It affords me the greatest of pleasure to send this personal letter to you by our Minister for Foreign Affairs, Mr. Kosaka, who is visiting Washington to have a frank exchange of views on matters of mutual interest with your Secretary of State, Mr. Herter, and other leaders of your country, prior to attending the 15th General Assembly of the United Nations.

I wish to express my profound regrets that the Japanese Government was compelled to ask you to postpone your visit to our shores in June and, at the same time, my deep gratitude for the sympathetic understanding shown by you, Mr. President, and by the American people, of the most unfortunate circumstances. I also wish to convey to you the deep feeling of friendship which the overwhelming majority of the Japanese people entertain toward you and the American people and our hopes that we shall be able to welcome you to our country in the near future.

It is our affirmed policy to maintain and to develop the broad basis of cooperation and partnership between our two countries which have the common aim of a peace based on freedom and justice and the betterment of human welfare. I am firmly resolved to adhere to this basic policy and sincerely hope that the mutual understanding between our two peoples will be further strengthened and that our relations of goodwill and friendship will be further promoted.

Finally, I wish to take this opportunity to express our sincere appreciation to you for extending a cordial invitation to Their Highnesses the Crown Prince and Crown Princess to visit your country. I am confident that their forthcoming visit to your country in this auspicious year which marks the centennial of Japan-United States relations will serve immeasurably toward further cementing the ties of friendship between our two peoples.

With kindest personal regards and best wishes for your continued good health,

Sincerely yours,

Hayato Ikeda

295 ¶ Statement by the President Upon Signing Bill Raising Support Prices for Butterfat and Manufacturing Milk. *September 16, 1960*

I HAVE TODAY signed S. 2917, setting minimum price supports until March 31, 1961 for butterfat and milk for manufacturing purposes. The price of fluid milk, not subject to price support legislation, is not dealt with in the bill.

In 1954, the Congress turned away from rigid price supports and authorized the administrative determination of price support levels, within a stated range, so that agricultural production could be brought into line with demand. S. 2917 elevates minimum support prices for butterfat and manufacturing milk above present support levels and, if continued in effect beyond its termination date, could pose the threat of a return to the disastrous dairy surplus situation of only a few years ago.

The bill would have little practical effect, however, for present prices in the market place for butterfat and manufacturing milk are, depending on the item, above, at or only slightly below the minimum prices that S. 2917 would establish. Moreover, the bill by its own terms will expire on March 31st of the new year.

The bill, therefore, can do little, if anything, to benefit the dairy farmer and, even more important, will do him little harm. Nor should it add materially to the cost of the Federal Government's dairy product price support programs or have a significant effect, if any at all, on the prices of dairy products to consumers.

For these reasons, and because I am mindful that the Congress—which passed the bill overwhelmingly—has by its adjournment no opportunity to attempt to override a veto, I concluded that the bill could and should be signed. These reasons seem to me the more compelling because this is an election year. Had the bill been presented to me under different circumstances, however, I doubtless would have withheld my approval because the bill on its face violates long established and well-known policies of this Administration. But because its practical effects are negligible—and hence the violations more theoretical than real—I believe it my duty this year to avoid so far as possible any action on my part that would only serve to engender intensely partisan political charges and counter-charges in the dairy regions.

Early next year the new administration will be confronted with this problem, but it will then be very real, for any extension of S. 2917 would pose the serious threat I have described. At that time, however, the matter can be discussed and resolved in an atmosphere free of election year politics. In that regard, I wish it to be perfectly clear that for my part I shall continue to support the policy that agricultural production must eventually be controlled by economic law rather than by political maneuvering. Until this has happened, there can be no settlement of the so-called "farm problem" and no sound prosperity for the family-size farm.

NOTE: As enacted, S. 2917 is Public Law 86–799 (74 Stat. 1054).

296　¶　Statement by the President Concerning the Attendance of Chiefs of State and Heads of Government at the U.N. General Assembly. *September* 17, 1960

THE UNITED STATES Government and State and local authorities are faced with an extremely difficult security problem in view of the forthcoming attendance at the United Nations General Assembly of nearly a score of Chiefs of State or Heads of Government, several of whom have been bitterly antagonistic to the United States.

In this situation, I am confident that I can count on the traditional dignity and cooperation of our people. Although the Chiefs of State or Heads of Government are coming to New York to attend the United Nations and not to visit the United States, it is essential that their activities in connection with the United Nations be in no way impaired. The United States Government, by its Agreement with the United Nations, has guaranteed free and unimpeded access to the United Nations so that the representatives of foreign governments may properly discharge their functions in connection with that organization.

The calm and reasonable conduct of our citizens will give a renewed demonstration of our nation's sense of responsibility.

NOTE: The statement was released at Camp David, Md.

297 ¶ Statement by the President on the Signing of the Treaty Between Pakistan and India Relating to the Waters of the Indus River.
September 19, 1960

I WARMLY WELCOME the signing today at Karachi of the Treaty between Pakistan and India by President Ayub and Prime Minister Nehru on the use of the waters of the Indus River and its tributaries. This brings to a salutary close a dispute of major proportions which had existed between these two free world countries since their independence 13 years ago. The livelihood of some 50 million people will be enhanced by the solution of this problem.

The peaceful settlement of this issue marks the inauguration of a new chapter in the conduct of international relations wherein the expert "good offices" of an international organization have served to assist two equally determined nations to reconcile their opposing viewpoints and to reach an amicable agreement over a highly contentious dispute.

President Ayub and Prime Minister Nehru together with their representatives have demonstrated to the world a quality of the highest statesmanship in reaching the compromises necessary to an agreement on this question. President Eugene R. Black and Vice President W. A. B. Iliff of the International Bank for Reconstruction and Development deserve the highest praise for their years of patient effort in assisting India and Pakistan to negotiate their differences in this matter.

The World Bank must also be commended for subscribing its own financial support and in enlisting the support of six friendly governments to participate in the financing of this enormous project of development of the Indus Basin, without which agreement would not have been possible despite the large investments being made by Pakistan and India themselves.

The United States is proud to be able to participate in this cooperative endeavor in the interest of the economic growth and security of these newly developing nations. It was with great interest that I was able to discuss this matter with President Ayub and Prime Minister Nehru when I was in their capitals last autumn.

The amicable and friendly resolution of this difficult issue with multilateral assistance is a striking example of the value of international cooperation and good will in the pursuit of a lasting peace with justice for all the world.

298 ¶ Remarks to Members of the American Nationalities for Nixon-Lodge. *September* 19, 1960

SOMEONE told me there are 20 million Americans that are classed as belonging to the Nationality Groups. I asked a few minutes ago why aren't there 180 million that belong to the same groups. We all came from somewhere, that's sure.

I asked, "Why don't I belong to the Germanic, with my name?" Well, I was told I would have to get the permission of, I think it was, my great-great-grandfather.

In any event, what I am saying in this awkward fashion is that I have difficulty in addressing a group when I feel that they are different from other Americans. All of us are Americans. I don't know how to speak to a Jewish group or a Catholic group or a Presbyterian group, or any other. I like to talk to Americans.

So as I welcome you here to our Capital City for your conferences, I would very much like to urge that all of us, in these days which seem now to be unusually troublous—with at least what seems to be trouble-makers trying to come to our country—that we all stand behind a strong, firm, national policy that really spells out our determination to be free, and to help others enjoy the same freedom that we in this Nation won so many years ago.

World problems color our domestic problems. Sometimes though our domestic problems seem very severe and urgent—the farm problem or arguments about easy money or inflation or anything else—they are dwarfed when you come to compare them with the age-old struggle of mankind to achieve international order and peace.

You people with your identity to these national groups are more closely related, possibly, than some other citizens. With individuals and with populations from which you or your forebears have more recently come, these national groups enlist your interest, your support, so that we all may achieve this international order. I am convinced that if enough people in the world—whether it's in Africa or Asia or all the Americas, or in Europe—if each of us puts his mind to this one great problem, eventually we shall solve it.

Possibly first we have to solve it by making certain that we cannot be attacked successfully, penetrated successfully, and certainly not subverted successfully. If we can in our hearts and in our minds and by the strength of our economies—and where necessary by our military strength—make ourselves absolutely sure and secure, then in the long run we win.

I must say this does not include any aggressive intent toward any person. The time has come when anyone talking about an aggressive war on a global scale is also talking about suicide. I think at least all of us have got that much sense.

So as you talk about your common problems in these groups—I care not what they are in detail—I do say let's all of us dedicate ourselves anew to unionizing the thinking and the spiritual, economic and material strength of our whole free world in order to make ourselves secure. By being secure and living these principles in which we all are talking about now—the principles of freedom and of human liberty and of dignity—finally we win.

And that's the thing I would like to see the whole world do.

Goodbye. Good luck.

NOTE: The President spoke in the Rose Garden at the White House.

299 ¶ Statement by the President: National Science Youth Month. *September* 20, 1960

THIS present age requires a constant renewal of the Nation's supply of trained scientific personnel to meet the demands of industry, government, and research. Young Americans with aptitudes in science and technology must be given every opportunity to develop their abilities. At the same time, we can encourage all citizens to work toward a deeper understanding of these subjects.

America's future is dependent to a large degree upon the strengthening of every area of education. I hope the annual observance of National Science Youth Month will further stimulate our people's desire to learn and will help increase their respect for the quality of intellectual excellence.

DWIGHT D. EISENHOWER

300   ¶ Statement by the President: The Jewish High Holy Days.   *September* 21, 1960

DURING the season of the Jewish High Holy Days it is always a pleasure to extend greetings to my fellow citizens of the Jewish faith.

I know this is a time of deep meaning for them. In the honored tradition of their ancient faith they are led to special acts of contrition, thanksgiving and praise. Sustained by the creative and moral power of their fathers' God they enter their new year with confidence.

This is my last opportunity to extend greetings on this occasion but as a private citizen I shall continue to remember these Holy Days each year with warmth and respect.

DWIGHT D. EISENHOWER

301   ¶ Message to the Fourth General Conference of the International Atomic Energy Agency. *September* 21, 1960

[Read by John A. McCone, Chairman of the United States delegation]

Mr. President and delegates:

Nearly seven years ago, at the United Nations General Assembly, it was my privilege to give voice to a hope that was rising in many minds and many places.

The hope was to harness the new force of the atom for the benefit of all peoples of all Nations. The challenge was to do it.

The almost universal approval of the Atoms for Peace proposal demonstrated the hope of people everywhere that the great new force of atomic energy would be devoted to the peaceful advancement of mankind.

This International Atomic Energy Agency is one expression of that hope. The historic mission of the Agency was to make a new approach in international cooperation to translate the concept of the peaceful atom into a practical, positive program on a world basis.

In three short years, the Agency has become the prime international organization in the nuclear field. Its activities are stimulating much of the global effort to bring to more people more benefits of this still new atomic age. It is providing sound advice and guidance for the management of the many new atomic projects underway in its member states.

The Agency is making substantial contributions on an international basis in such fields as education and training and technical assistance. It is making great strides in spreading the knowledge of the many uses of the radioisotopes in the fields of medicine, agriculture and industry. In addition, the Agency has a paramount role in the development of the necessary health and safety standards.

This Agency is an organization that has no secrets; an organization devoted to the sharing of effort, research and information; one in which the major powers can lay aside political differences to work for the common good.

In broad outline, I can see the Agency fulfilling the basic purposes of its historic charter and thereby contributing to world peace. I can see it as a unique forum where technical skills and resources are pooled for the benefit of mankind.

The United States is gratified and encouraged at what has been done in three short years. My country will continue to support this organization and I wish for it continued progress and success.

Sincerely,

Dwight D. Eisenhower

NOTE: The opening words "Mr. President" referred to Gueorgui Nadjakov, chairman of the Bulgarian delegation. The conference was held in Vienna, September 20–October 1, 1960.

302 ❡ Address Before the 15th General Assembly of the United Nations, New York City. *September 22, 1960*

Mr. President, Mr. Secretary General, members of the General Assembly, and guests:

The people of the United States join me in saluting those countries which, at this session of the General Assembly, are represented here for the first time. With the admission of new members, mainly from the giant continent of Africa, almost 100 nations will be joined in a common effort to construct permanent peace, with justice, in a sorely troubled world.

The drive of self-determination and of rising human aspirations is creating a new world of independent nations in Africa, even as it is producing a new world of both ferment and of promise in all developing areas. An awakening humanity in these regions demands as never before that we make a renewed attack on poverty, illiteracy, and disease.

Side by side with these startling changes, technology is also in revolution. It has brought forth terrifying weapons of destruction, which for the future of civilization, must be brought under control through a workable system of disarmament. And it has also opened up a new world of outer space—a celestial world filled with both bewildering problems and dazzling promise.

This is, indeed, a moment for honest appraisal and historic decision.

We can strive to master these problems for narrow national advantage or we can begin at once to undertake a period of constructive action which will subordinate selfish interest to the general well-being of the international community.

The choice is truly a momentous one.

Today, I come before you because our human commonwealth is once again in a state of anxiety and turmoil. Urgent issues confront us.

II.

The first proposition I place before you is that only through the United Nations Organization and its truly democratic processes can humanity make real and universal progress toward the goal of peace with justice. Therefore, I believe that to support the United Nations Organization and its properly constituted mechanisms and its selected officers is the road of greatest promise in peaceful progress. To attempt to hinder or stultify the United Nations or to deprecate its importance is to contribute to world unrest and, indeed, to incite the crises that from time to time so disturb all men. The United States stands squarely and unequivocally in support of the United Nations and those acting under its mandate in the interest of peace.

Nowhere is the challenge to the international community and to peace and orderly progress more evident than in Africa, rich in human and natural resources and bright with promise. Recent events there have brought into being what is, in effect, a vast continent of newly independent nations.

Outside interference with these newly emerging nations, all eager to undertake the tasks of modernization, has created a serious challenge to the authority of the United Nations.

That authority has grown steadily during the 15 years since the United Nations pledged, in the words of its own Charter, "to bring about by peaceful means, and in conformity with the principles of justice and international law, adjustments or settlement of international disputes or situations which might lead to a breach of the peace."

And during those years, the United Nations successfully supported Iran's efforts to obtain the withdrawal of foreign military forces; played a significant role in preserving the independence of Greece, rallied world resistance to aggression against the Republic of Korea; helped to settle the Suez crisis; countered the threat to Lebanon's integrity; and most recently, has taken on an even more important task.

In response to the call of the Republic of the Congo, the United Nations under its outstanding Secretary General, has recently mounted a large-scale effort to provide that new Republic with help. That effort has been flagrantly attacked by a few nations which wish to prolong strife in the Congo for their own purposes. The criticism directed by these nations against the Secretary General, who has honorably and effectively fulfilled the mandate which he received from the United Nations, is nothing less than a direct attack upon the United Nations itself. In my opinion, he, the Secretary General, has earned the support and gratitude of every peace loving nation.

The people of the Congo are entitled to build up their country in peace and freedom. Intervention by other nations in their internal affairs would deny them that right and create a focus of conflict in the heart of Africa.

The issue thus posed in the Congo could well arise elsewhere in Africa.

The resolution of this issue will determine whether the United Nations is able to protect not only the new nations of Africa, but also other countries against outside pressures.

It is the smaller nations that have the greatest stake in the effective functioning of the United Nations.

If the United Nations system is successfully subverted in Africa, the world will be on its way back to the traditional exercise of power politics, in which small countries will be used as pawns by aggressive major powers. Any nation, seduced by glittering promises into becoming a catspaw for an imperialistic power, thereby undermines the United Nations and places in jeopardy the independence of itself and all others.

It is imperative that the international community protect the newly emerging nations of Africa from outside pressures that threaten their independence and their sovereign rights.

To this end, I propose a program which contains five major elements:

First: A pledge by all countries represented at this Assembly to respect the African peoples' right to choose their own way of life and to determine for themselves the course they choose to follow. And this pledge would involve three specific commitments:

To refrain from intervening in these new nations' internal affairs—by subversion, force, propaganda, or any other means.

To refrain from generating disputes between the states of this area or from encouraging them to wasteful and dangerous competition in armaments.

And to refrain from any action to intensify or exploit present unsettled conditions in the Congo—by sending arms or forces into that troubled area, or by inciting its leaders and peoples to violence against each other.

These actions my country—and many others—are now avoiding. I hope this Assembly will call upon all its members to do likewise, and that each speaker who follows me to this platform will solemnly pledge his country to honor this call.

Second: The United Nations should be prepared to help the African countries maintain their security without wasteful and dangerous competition in armaments.

United Nations experts are being asked to train the Congo's security forces. If the Secretary General should find it useful to undertake increased activity in order to meet requests of this nature elsewhere, my country would be glad to join other Member States in making essential contributions to such United Nations activity.

More importantly I hope that the African states will use existing or establish new regional machinery in order to avert an arms race in this area. In so doing, they would help to spare their continent the ravages which the excesses of chauvinism have elsewhere inflicted in the past. If, through concerted effort, these nations can choke off competition in armaments, they can give the whole world a welcome lesson in international relations.

The speed and success of the United Nations in dispatching substantial forces to the Congo should give these states assurance that they can rely on the United Nations to organize an effective response if their security is threatened. This should reduce any pressures on them to raise larger forces than are required to maintain internal security. Thus they would help to free their resources for more constructive purposes.

Third: We should all support the United Nations response to emergency needs in the Republic of the Congo which the Secretary General has shown such skill in organizing. I hope that states represented here will pledge substantial resources to this international program, and agree that it should be the preferred means of meeting the Congo's emergency needs. The United States supports the establishment of a United Nations fund for the Congo. We are prepared to join other countries by contributing substantially for immediate emergency needs to the $100 million program that the Secretary General is proposing.

Fourth: The United Nations should help newly developing African countries to shape their long-term modernization programs. To this end:

The United Nations Special Fund and Expanded Technical Assistance Program should be increased so that in combination they can reach their annual $100 million goal in 1961. The Special Fund's functions should be expanded so that it can assist countries in planning economic development.

The United Nations Operational and Executive Personnel program for making available trained administrators to newly developing countries should be expanded and placed on a permanent basis. The United States is prepared to join other countries in contributing increased funds for this program, and for the Special Fund, and for the United Nations Technical Assistance Program.

The World Bank and International Monetary Fund should be encouraged increasingly to provide counsel to the developing countries of Africa through missions and resident advisers. We should also look forward to appropriate and timely financial assistance from these two multilateral financial sources as the emerging countries qualify for their aid.

Of course, many forms of aid will be needed: both public and private, and on a bilateral and multilateral basis. For this assistance to be most effective it must be related to the basic problems and changing needs of the African countries themselves.

Fifth: As the final element of this program, I propose an all-out United Nations effort to help African countries launch such educational activities as they may wish to undertake.

711

It is not enough that loud speakers in the public square exhort people to freedom. It is also essential that the people should be furnished with the mental tools to preserve and develop their freedom.

The United States is ready to contribute to an expanded program of educational assistance to Africa by the family of United Nations organizations, carried out as the Secretary General may deem appropriate, and according to the ideas of the African nations themselves.

One of the first purposes of this assistance, after consultation and approval by the governments involved, might be to establish, staff and maintain—until these governments or private agencies could take over—Institutes for Health Education, for Vocational Training, for Public Administration and Statistics, and perhaps other purposes.

Each institute could be appropriately located and specifically dedicated to training the young men and women of that vast region, who are now called upon to assume the incredibly complex and important responsibilities inherent in an explosive emergence into nationhood.

If the African States should wish to send large numbers of their citizens for training abroad under this program, my country would be glad to set up a special commission to cooperate with the United Nations in arranging to accommodate many more of these students in our institutions of learning.

These then are the five ingredients of the Program I propose for Africa:

Non-interference in the African countries' internal affairs;

Help in assuring their security without wasteful and dangerous competition in armaments;

Emergency aid to the Congo;

International assistance in shaping long-term African development programs;

United Nations aid for education.

III.

Such a program could go far to assure the African countries the clear chance at the freedom, domestic tranquility and progress they deserve.

The changes which are occurring in Africa are also evident elsewhere. Indeed, Africa is but one part of the new world of change and progress which is emerging in all the developing areas.

We must carry forward and intensify our programs of assistance for the economic and social development in freedom of other areas, particularly in Latin America, Asia, and the Middle East.

Beyond this, we must never forget that there are hundreds of millions of people, particularly in the less developed parts of the world, suffering from hunger and malnutrition, even though a number of countries, my own included, are producing food in surplus. This paradox should not be allowed to continue.

The United States is already carrying out substantial programs to make its surpluses available to countries of greatest need. My country is also ready to join with other members of the United Nations in devising a workable scheme to provide food to member states through the United Nations system, relying on the advice and assistance of the Food and Agriculture Organization.

I hope this Assembly will seriously consider a specific program for carrying forward the promising Food for Peace Program.

IV.

In the developing areas, we must seek to promote peaceful change, as well as to assist economic and social progress. To do this—to assist peaceful change—the international community must be able to manifest its presence in emergencies through United Nations observers or forces.

I should like to see member countries take positive action on the suggestions in the Secretary General's report looking to the creation of a qualified staff within the Secretariat to assist him in meeting future needs for United Nations forces.

To regularize the United Nations emergency force potential, I proposed in 1958 creation of stand-by arrangements for United Nations forces. Some progress has been made since that time. Much remains to be done.

The Secretary General has now suggested that members should maintain a readiness to meet possible future requests from the United Nations for contributions to such forces. All countries represented here should respond to this need, by earmarking national contingents which could take part in United Nations forces in case of need.

The time to do it is now—at this Assembly.

I assure countries which now receive assistance from the United States that we favor use of that assistance to help them maintain such contingents in the state of readiness suggested by the Secretary General. To assist the Secretary General's efforts, the United States is prepared to earmark also substantial air and sea transport facilities on a stand-by basis, to help move contingents requested by the United Nations in any future emergency.

Over the long run, further progress toward increasing the United Nations' ability to respond to future needs is surely possible. The prospects for such progress, however, will remain just that—prospects—unless we move now to exploit the immediate possibilities for practical action suggested by the Secretary General.

v.

Another problem confronting us involves outer space.

The emergence of this new world poses a vital issue: will outer space be preserved for peaceful use and developed for the benefit of all mankind? Or will it become another focus for the arms race—and thus an area of dangerous and sterile competition?

The choice is urgent. And it is ours to make.

The nations of the world have recently united in declaring the continent of Antarctica "off limits" to military preparations. We could extend this principle to an even more important sphere. National vested interests have not yet been developed in space or in celestial bodies. Barriers to agreement are now lower than they will ever be again.

The opportunity may be fleeting. Before many years have passed, the point of no return may have passed.

Let us remind ourselves that we had a chance in 1946 to ensure that atomic energy be devoted exclusively to peaceful purposes. That chance was missed when the Soviet Union turned down the comprehensive plan submitted by the United States for placing atomic energy under international control.

We must not lose the chance we still have to control the future of outer space.

I propose that:

1. We agree that celestial bodies are not subject to national appropriation by any claims of sovereignty.

2. We agree that the nations of the world shall not engage in warlike activities on these bodies.

3. We agree, subject to appropriate verification, that no nation will put into orbit or station in outer space weapons of mass destruction. All launchings of space craft should be verified in advance by the United Nations.

4. We press forward with a program of international cooperation for constructive peaceful uses of outer space under the United Nations. Better weather forecasting, improved world-wide communications, and more effective exploration not only of outer space but of our own earth— these are but a few of the benefits of such cooperation.

Agreement on these proposals would enable future generations to find peaceful and scientific progress, not another fearful dimension to the arms race, as they explore the universe.

VI.

But armaments must also be controlled here on earth, if civilization is to be assured of survival. These efforts must extend both to conventional and non-conventional armaments.

My country has made specific proposals to this end during the past year. New United States proposals were put forward on June 27, with the hope that they could serve as the basis for negotiations to achieve general disarmament. The United States still supports these proposals.

The communist nations' walk-out at Geneva, when they learned that we were about to submit these proposals, brought negotiations to an abrupt halt. Their unexplained action does not, however, reduce the urgent need for arms control.

My country believes that negotiations can—and should—soon be resumed.

Our aim is to reach agreement on all the various measures that will bring general and complete disarmament. Any honest appraisal, however, must recognize that this is an immense task. It will take time.

We should not have to wait until we have agreed on all the detailed measures to reach this goal before we begin to move toward disarmament. Specific and promising steps to this end were suggested in our June 27 proposals.

If negotiations can be resumed, it may be possible to deal particularly with two pressing dangers—that of war by miscalculation and that of mounting nuclear weapons stockpiles.

The advent of missiles, with ever shorter reaction times, makes measures to curtail the danger of war by miscalculation increasingly necessary. States must be able quickly to assure each other that they are not preparing aggressive moves—particularly in international crises, when each side takes steps to improve its own defenses, which actions might be misinterpreted by the other. Such misinterpretation in the absence of machinery to verify that neither was preparing to attack the other, could lead to a war which no one had intended or wanted.

Today the danger of war by miscalculation could be reduced, in times of crisis, by the intervention, when requested by any nation seeking to prove its own peaceful intention, of an appropriate United Nations surveillance body. The question of methods can be left to the experts.

Thus the vital issue is not a matter of technical feasibility but the political willingness of individual countries to submit to inspection. The United States has taken the lead in this field.

Today, I solemnly declare, on behalf of the United States, that we are prepared to submit to any international inspection, provided only that it is effective and truly reciprocal. This step we will take willingly as an earnest of our determination to uphold the preamble of the United Nations Charter which says its purpose is "to save succeeding generations from the scourge of war, which twice in our lifetime has brought untold sorrow to mankind . . ."

The United States wants the Soviet Union and all the nations of the world to know enough about United States defense preparations to be assured that United States forces exist only for deterrence and defense— not for surprise attack. I hope the Soviet Union will similarly wish to assure the United States and other nations of the nonaggressive character of its security preparations.

There is a more basic point: in an age of rapidly developing technology, secrecy is not only an anachronism—it is downright dangerous. To seek to maintain a society in which a military move can be taken in complete secrecy, while professing a desire to reduce the risk of war through arms control, is a contradiction.

A second danger which ought to be dealt with in early negotiations is posed by the growth and prospective spread of nuclear weapons stockpiles.

To reverse this trend, I propose that the nations producing nuclear weapons immediately convene experts to design a system for terminating, under verification procedures, all production of fissionable materials for weapons purposes.

That termination would take effect as soon as the agreed inspection system has been installed and is operating effectively, while progress in other disarmament fields is also being sought.

The United States is prepared, in the event of a termination of production, to join the USSR in transferring substantial quantities of fissionable materials to international stockpiles. The United Nations Disarmament Commission has already heard the proposal of Ambassador Lodge, to set aside not pounds, as was proposed by the United States in 1954, but tons of fissionable materials for peaceful purposes. Additional transfers would be made as progress in other aspects of disarmament is accomplished.

If the USSR will agree to a cessation of production of fissionable materials for weapons purposes, some production facilities could be closed without delay. The United States would be willing to match the USSR in shutting down major plants producing fissionable materials, one by one, under international inspection and verification.

The proposed working group of experts could also consider how to verify the complete elimination of nuclear weapons, which is part of the third stage of our proposed disarmament program of June 27. There is as yet no known means of demonstrably accomplishing this; we would hope that the experts could develop such a system.

United States officials are willing to meet immediately with representatives of other countries for a preliminary exchange of views on these proposals.

Some who have followed closely the many fruitless disarmament talks since the war tend to become cynical—to assume that the task is hopeless. This is not the position of the United States.

Men everywhere want to disarm. They want their wealth and labor to be spent not for war, but for food, for clothing, for shelter, for medicines, for schools.

Time and again, the American people have voiced this yearning—to join with men of good will everywhere in building a better world. We always stand ready to consider any feasible proposal to this end. And as I have said so many times, the United States is always ready to negotiate with any country which in integrity and sincerity shows itself ready to talk about any of these problems. We ask only this—that such a program not give military advantage to any nation and that it permit men to inspect the disarmament of other nations.

A disarmament program which was not inspected and guaranteed would increase, not reduce, the risk of war.

The international control of atomic energy and general and complete disarmament can no more be accomplished by rhetoric than can the economic development of newly independent countries. Both of these immense tasks facing mankind call for serious, painstaking, costly, laborious and non-propaganda approaches.

VII.

I have specifically avoided in this address mention of several immediate problems that are troubling the United States and other nations. My failure to do so does not mean in any sense that they are not of great concern both to the United States and to the entire international community.

For example, accumulating evidence of threatening encroachments to the freedom of the people of West Berlin continues to disturb us deeply.

Another instance, though, of special concern to the United States, the shooting down of an American aircraft last July first over international waters, the apparent killing of four of its crew members and the imprisonment of two others on trumped-up spy charges, is a shocking affront to the right of all nations to peaceful passage on and over the high seas. By its veto in the Security Council the Soviet Union prevented a full investigation of the facts of the case. But these facts still demand to be heard as a proper matter for the consideration of an impartial tribunal.

The particular problems I have just mentioned are not merely isolated instances of disagreements among a few nations. They are central to the issue of peace itself, and illustrative of the continuous and interdependent nature of our respective national concerns. They must be confronted with the earnestness and seriousness which their settlement demands.

VIII.

The basic fact today of all change in the domain of international affairs is the need to forge the bonds and build the structure of a true world community.

The United Nations is available to mankind to help it create just such a community. It has accomplished what no nation singly, or any limited group of nations, could have accomplished. It has become the forum of all peoples, and the structure about which they can center their joint endeavors to create a better future for our world.

We must guard jealously against those who in alternating moods look upon the United Nations as an instrument for use or abuse. The United

Nations was not conceived as an Olympian organ to amplify the propaganda tunes of individual nations.

The generating force behind a successful United Nations must be the noble idea that a true international community can build a peace with justice if only people will work together patiently in an atmosphere of open trust.

In urging progress toward a world community, I cite the American concept of the destiny of a progressive society. Here in this land, in what was once a wilderness we have generated a society and a civilization drawn from many sources. Yet out of the mixture of many peoples and faiths we have developed unity in freedom—a unity designed to protect the rights of each individual while enhancing the freedom and well-being of all.

This concept of unity in freedom, drawn from the diversity of many racial strains and cultures, we would like to see made a reality for all mankind. This concept should apply within every nation as it does among nations. We believe that the right of every man to participate through his or her vote in self-government is as precious as the right of each nation here represented to vote its own convictions in this Assembly. I should like to see a universal plebiscite in which every individual in the world would be given the opportunity freely and secretly to answer this question: Do you want this right? Opposed to the idea of two hostile, embittered worlds in perpetual conflict, we envisage a single world community, as yet unrealized but advancing steadily toward fulfillment through our plans, our efforts, and our collective ideas.

Thus we see as our goal, not a super-state above nations, but a world community embracing them all, rooted in law and justice and enhancing the potentialities and common purposes of all peoples.

As we enter the decade of the 1960's, let us launch a renewed effort to strengthen this international community; to forge new bonds between its members in undertaking new ventures on behalf of all mankind.

As we take up this task, let us not delude ourselves that the absence of war alone is a sufficient basis for a peaceful world. I repeat, we must also build a world of justice under law, and we must overcome poverty, illiteracy, and disease.

We of the United States will join with you in making a mounting effort to build the structure of true peace—a peace in which all peoples may progress constantly to higher levels of human achievement. The means are at hand.　We have but to use them with a wisdom and energy worthy of our cause.

I commend this great task to your hearts, to your minds, and to your willing hands.　Let us go forward together, leaving none behind.

Thank you, and God bless you.

NOTE: The President spoke at 11:12 a.m. His opening words "Mr. President, Mr. Secretary General" referred to Frederick H. Boland, Permanent Representative to the United Nations for Ireland, and Secretary General Dag Hammarskjöld.

303　¶ Remarks at a Luncheon for Latin American Delegates to the U.N. General Assembly, New York City.　*September 22, 1960*

THIS IS the time, I think, to re-affirm some of our convictions and our beliefs that are important to all of us.　I have, someone told me today, 2 days less than 4 months still to serve in my present office, and possibly this is the last time I shall have an opportunity to tell you, as representatives of your several governments, something of my affection for the people of Latin America with whom I have worked, and the affection of my government for these governments, all of which have served and worked so closely with us.

I tried to tell you this morning something of the importance that we of America attach to the functioning and indeed the existence of the United Nations, and the possibility it has for furthering the aspirations of men.　But I want to tell you in somewhat more intimate fashion how deeply I believe in the Organization of American States, organized within the limits prescribed by the charter of the United Nations.

Gentlemen, our nations are bound together not merely by inescapable ties of geography.　We are strong, and we are worthwhile only because we are bound together by things of the spirit.　The dedication we have to imperishable values, of human dignity and liberty, and the sovereignty of our respective nations—these are the things that are worthwhile.

But because we do believe in these values and have these same dedications, we must devote ourselves as a unit to the production of that kind of atmosphere, that kind of situation in the world that will let us progress, with the help of the God in which we all believe, toward a better life, not merely for such people as sit around this table, but for the lowliest peon, the lowliest farmer, the lowliest dweller in Harlem and the East Side toward a better life.

My friends, our neighboring Republic to the South and ourselves decided to build a dam, and it began by being called, according to the name of where it was situated, El Diablo.   The President of Mexico and I decided to change that name, and it is now the Amistad Dam.   This is the word that, it seems to me, all of us can well adopt as our motto, because we do have, as I said, the same dedications, the same devotions, and the same beliefs.

Now although I had already promised there would be no speech, I found I have already violated my promise, but I will ask you all to stand with me to drink a toast to *Amistad.*

NOTE: The President spoke at a luncheon which he gave in honor of the chiefs of the 18 Latin-American delegations to the United Nations at the headquarters of the United States delegation in the Wal-dorf-Astoria Hotel, New York City.

304   ¶ Address in Philadelphia Before the American Institute of Certified Public Accountants. *September* 26, 1960

President Seidman, members of the American Institute of Certified Public Accountants, and friends:

I am particularly delighted to be with you this morning.   I have never had the privilege before of talking to a big group of accountants all in one spot.   I run into them in my daily life, but not in such numbers.

One of the more statistically-minded people in the Government told me not long ago that I had appointed more certified public accountants to Government positions than any prior President.   I certainly did not do this just because they are accountants.   I have been for all these 8 years searching for talent—people of dedication, of training, of education, of capability—people who have a sense of civic responsibility.   So, since I have appointed so many of this type of person who have been public accountants, I suppose it's a fair conclusion that your profession averages very high up among those that are so dedicated and so capable.

The Director of the Budget—Mr. Stans—is a public accountant.   I have heard that he rather divides Government officials into two classes— those who are certified public accountants, and those who are not quite so able. I make allowances, of course, for his somewhat prejudiced viewpoint. Nevertheless, I do agree that the excellent performance of the some two thousand of accountants who are now in the Federal Government is one of satisfaction to me, and I am sure to yourselves.

I shall not try to talk about your profession. Certainly you know more about it than I do. I assume that one of your great functions in American industry and in American business life is to make certain that corporations, companies, and others that are conducting businesses do not go bankrupt because of reckless financial and business practices. If they show tendencies this way, you are there to point out where the error is and what they must do if they are going to keep in the black.

My friends, the biggest business in the world is the United States Government. It employs directly 5 million people, and it spends each year, $80 billion of your money. I cannot conceive of a greater need anywhere for certified accountants than in the Federal Government.

I want to talk to you a little while this morning about Government rather than about your profession, and indeed, even your functions within the Government. Since this big Government business of ours is owned by all our people, affects all our people, and depends upon all our people, then indeed this is something that must be the concern of every serious thinking person.

I want to make an observation—a sort of truism from my old military life. There was an old adage that went something like this: in war you can do nothing positive except as you do it from a firm base. This means that unless a commander has an area in the rear from which he can draw his replacements for casualties, his new ammunition supplies and food—all the things that an army needs in a campaign—then in the long run he cannot win. Most of you know that Hannibal, a great general of early times, campaigned successfully up and down Italy for some dozen years trying to win a war, but finally lost it because he had no firm base.

Ladies and gentlemen, the firm base for the problem of leading the world toward the achievement of human aspirations—toward peace with justice in freedom—must be the United States. America's moral, spiritual, and intellectual strength is vitally important, but I do not intend to discuss these strengths this morning. What I want to discuss today is the need, within the United States, for a strong, expanding, and growing economy.

Going back to a comparison with business, I said that if a business is reckless in its spending, if it doesn't know what its accounts are, it is going to find itself at the end of the year in a very bad spot—if not bankrupt, at least in need of reform. I pointed out that the Government—the Government of the United States, the biggest business of all—is not exempt from the practice of these basic principles of financial integrity, of knowledge of what we are doing and where we are going, of efficiency and effectiveness in its operations.

The biggest thing, then, about budgeting is to try to pay as you go. If a business or the Government does not pay for its current costs out of current revenues when the business and the Government seem to be in prosperous times, then when is it ever going to pay its bills? If it doesn't pay its bills—if it depends upon deficit spending, upon piling up the debt which our grandchildren, if anybody, will have to pay—then I submit that the Federal Government is in a very tough position. Deficit spending is not only robbing our children of their rightful heritage, but it brings with it the evils of recklessness in Government, of rising costs; indeed, it is one of the great factors in bringing about the evil of inflation.

So if I should be able to give you one conviction this morning, it would be this: the Government of the United States, in view of the long-term nature of the program facing it, must look carefully to its financial processes and its fiscal operations, so that rather than ruining its economy by inflationary practices, it will make up its mind that every new program must have the revenues in sight that are going to support it.

All this means efficient government because no government can afford to ignore the priority needs of its people. Each need of the people, whether it be in health or in education, or in insurance or anything else, must be carefully weighed in order that we do not go overboard in expenditures without knowing where we are going. On the other hand, we must not ignore any need. This extends, of course, to the needs of our security. By security I mean not only our own military defenses and mechanisms, but the help we give those people who with us want to live in freedom, who are dedicating themselves to the ideals in which we believe, and whose combined strength will make our position in the world better, stronger, and higher.

So, knowing that all of these functions are not only necessary but essential to our existence, it is more and more a duty of those who believe in efficient government to lay out before the American people—all 180 million of them—the day-by-day record of the Government's operations, so that everyone may know whether or not these things are being done as the mass of our people want them done.

This brings me to the last point I should like to make. We must remind ourselves all the time that in our open society only the force of a public opinion provides the motivation for all that Government does. Senators and Congressmen and Presidents are sensitive to the force of public opinion. If that public opinion is well informed of the facts of our present existence, of the aspirations and hopes we hold out for ourselves and for those things that make for effectiveness and efficiency, then indeed we will have representative government—self-government at its best.

With such principles as these in our minds, we look forward not backward. It is not that we merely look at "pie in the sky." As someone said, "we keep our heads in the clouds but our feet on the earth," and that probably is still a good adage.

What I mean is this: in looking at any bright prospect—any glittering promise held up before our eyes—we must see those things through basic principles of responsibility, of effectiveness, and of efficiency, if we are going to put them in their right focus. Before we adopt them, we must measure them against those principles. This we must never forget.

I believe that people who have been trained and educated like yourselves, people who have spent their time in thinking as you people have done, have a great responsibility for informing and organizing this public opinion of which I speak, which is the force that will always keep us going.

You must talk to all people in terms of principles, of soundness, of progress, of responsibility. If we all do this, we will have a great country. There is no reason why it cannot be done. In such a problem and in such a function—such a duty—I can think of no greater body than this one because I am told that there are seventy thousand of you in the United States.

I want to point out this one feature of this job. If you will do your part, you have undertaken a lifetime enlistment. There is no short term. No election—no single administration—can mark the end of the efforts of such a body. Rather, this must be a dedication of yourselves and your successors and those you train and those that may come after you, right on down to the end of time. You and your successors must teach and believe these principles so that the United States will be ever a stronger influence in the world—commanding the respect of others, winning their adherence to her lofty ideals and principles—and finally, leading all the world to that great day when we can believe that we have achieved peace with justice in freedom.

Thank you very much.

NOTE: The President spoke at 10 a.m. at the Academy of Music in Philadelphia. His opening words "President Seidman" referred to J. S. Seidman, President of the American Institute of Certified Public Accountants.

305 ❡ Remarks in Philadelphia to a Group of Eisenhower Exchange Fellows.
September 26, 1960

Mr. McCabe, Fellows of the Eisenhower Exchange Program, Trustees and friends:

I have been more or less in a public position—a publicized position—for the past 18 or 19 years. By this time, I should think, it would be impossible to surprise me. When Mr. McCabe asked me to come over here this morning, I had a vision of going into his office to chat a little bit about this program. I had no idea that the Fellows themselves were going to be here or that I would have such an audience as this.

Nevertheless, far be it from me, with 8 years of political experience behind me, to hesitate to take advantage of such an opportunity and express some views which I hope will have some value.

I have had many presents given to me in my life. None has touched me more deeply—none has seemed to me more significant—than the one which in 1953 was given me and presented to me by some of my devoted friends.

The Eisenhower Fellowships are a living, vital present—one that promises and is already producing greater understanding in the world. This present is helping to bring about those conditions which all mankind realizes must be brought about before we can achieve the deepest of our aspirations.

There are many fine research organizations in the United States that support basic research in science, applied research in all kinds of industries, and everything we can think of—pure knowledge and applied knowledge. But it is very difficult to conceive of a research program that is going to produce that quality of leadership—much more elusive than the factor of pure knowledge.

I don't know exactly how you could define the characteristics and qualities that are most promising in the production of these things. Those of us looking at our own grandchildren and children have some probably prejudiced viewpoints. But we think we know what they will do. There's a story, you know, of a grandfather looking at his children and someone asked their ages. He replies, "Well, the doctor is 7 and the lawyer is 5."

Possibly someday we will have some mechanized brain that at the very earliest stages of human life will determine what the characteristics of these children will be and what functions they will perform best as they grow up, and particularly whether or not they will be natural leaders. I don't believe that we can yet visualize such a machine, and if it is on the horizon, I would suspect it is probably about the smallest item that we can detect.

So therefore, this group, under the leadership of Tom McCabe, had the theory that some leadership could be developed by this Exchange Program. They wanted, naturally, young men. There is not much use, for example, educating me much further. By the time you got done with it, I wouldn't be much use to many of you. But they did want people that had experience and had proved their qualities of leadership. And these people—the men that make up the members of these Fellowship groups, whether you are going abroad or whether you are coming here—have produced or multiplied their own capacity for learning and for understanding by hundreds of times, because they have already proved their qualities of leadership. This, I submit, is a quality that is the most needed of any I can think of in the world.

Leadership is not merely trying to satisfy personal ambition. Leadership must have some quality in it, of desiring to give service to others—your country—your community—your business—humankind. Indeed, I believe it would be a generality that could be sustained, that those men who have been most successful in business are those who thought far more of making that business successful than themselves successful. This particular characteristic must be in everybody who is going to be a leader, because only in that way can he influence others along the right path.

We know the world is changing, and I believe these Fellowship exchanges bring about an understanding of everyone who comes to the United States, or who goes out and brings back an understanding of how much this world is changing. Whether you come from New Delhi to Washington, or from here to the Philippines or anywhere else—South America, Asia, Europe—we do find that changes are taking place, and we don't resist these changes. We merely want to direct these changes into those things that will bring about this basic objective: peace with justice.

This means, as I see it, each one doing his self soul-searching, making certain that he knows what he wants to do, preparing himself for doing it, and then using the greatest possible influence that he can exert on getting everybody else to do the same thing—or at least to follow the same basic principles.

For our part—for our own country—our country is going to be strong as long as leaders—and I mean leaders in business, in education, in philosophy, in the professions, and in Government—recognize the need for obeying and respecting the great principles that have brought us to our high position of today. They must adapt the changes that must take place in such a way that those principles will not be violated. We do not want to fall prey to the belief that merely spending will bring about progress. We want to set up our needs in order of priority, starting with the security of our Nation, the soundness of our economy, and all the methods that will keep us strong.

Our strength will be useful not merely to us, but our strength will be useful to the world if we are the kind of leader I have been so feebly trying to describe. If we have the kind of leader who informs himself, by studies of his own, by mingling with peoples of his own nation and others, developing his understanding of humankind and of its problems, and above all, wants to see the society of which he is a part advance to ever higher standards—spiritually, intellectually, materially—and can keep producing them in the United States, our country, then, on a national basis will always be in a better position to lead the world toward the great objective of all.

It is for reasons such as these that I express my congratulations to every person here who has had a part in this Exchange Program, particularly to the groups that belong to the Exchange Program—to those leaders and its director—because in spite of the machine—the imaginary machine of which I spoke—I think the methods that Mr. McCabe and his associates have developed to get these proven young leaders, are still the methods on which we must depend.

So, to all of you, my felicitations, my congratulations, and my deep thanks for your attention.

Goodbye.

NOTE: The President spoke at 10:30 a.m. at the Bellevue-Stratford Hotel in Philadelphia. His opening words "Mr. McCabe" referred to Thomas B. McCabe, Chairman of the Board of Trustees and of the Executive Committee of the Eisenhower Exchange Fellowships.

306   ¶ Address at the Golden Jubilee Dinner of the National Conference of Catholic Charities, New York City.   *September 26, 1960*

Cardinal Spellman, Your Eminences, Your Excellencies, Governor Rockefeller, Mayor Wagner, the Republican Senatorial delegation from Washington, members of the National Conference of Catholic Charities, and my friends:

The approach in early November of an all-important event upon which the eyes of the nation are centered, suggests that I begin my remarks tonight with a special footnote. The problem prompts me to cite the case of a tormented man in a troublesome time in Ireland's history who, feeling the need to relieve his conscience, sought out his local pastor. Having been admitted to the priest's study, the man said, "Father, I have just killed a man." To which the priest replied, "This is neither the time nor the place for discussing politics."

So it is that I am sure we can all agree that we are gathered here tonight in a wholly unpartisan spirit. We have come to honor one of the noblest of all human qualities—charity—the benevolence of men of good will toward their brothers.

I have heard too often the word "charity" disparaged in public discussions, people saying there should be no need for charity and we should have none of it. I personally hold that when our country has lost the spirit of charity, then our government and our form of life will be changed for the worse.

Charity helps the recipient but if given in the right spirit it ennobles the giver, whether the gift be only a kind word or a fortune. So I make no apology for speaking of charity as one of the noblest of man's virtues.

Now quite possibly it would seem natural this evening to spend my time before such an audience in recounting the extraordinary accomplishments of the Catholic Charities. The list is indeed long and impressive. Moreover, Cardinal Spellman's record of alleviating human suffering would, in itself, provide material to interest, and excite the admiration, of every American.

But I have chosen as my subject not gifts themselves. For, as Lowell the American poet so movingly said, "The gift without the giver is bare." It is through the spirit of the giver and in the preservation of this spirit that we sustain one of the indispensable bulwarks of American life.

Over a century ago a keen French observer visiting our land wrote that the greatness of America springs out of the goodness of its people. More cynically minded persons, too deeply impressed by our unquestioned wealth and material progress, have tried to refute the truth of this conclusion. Such people not only ignore the transcendence of spiritual values—they are blind to our nation's history. Concern for a neighbor's welfare and a warm generosity have been more typical of the American way than any alleged worship of money or preoccupation with material success.

Our literature abounds with tales of how early settlers helped one another build homes, clear land, establish schools, tend the sick, and rally when disaster struck. I remember very well that in my days of youth in Central Kansas, charity was primarily an individual matter. Helping one another was as common for parents as raising their own children.

But today, charity has taken on a corporate character and national breadth. Yet the spirit of true charity is the same.

The American people accept as a clear responsibility the combatting of privation and suffering. The growth in private philanthropic contributions in the past ten years has exceeded both the rate of growth of our population and our personal income. Another amazing fact is that in this year 1960, 45 million Americans will lend their time and talents in raising over 9 billion dollars for philanthropic causes.

Now this responsibility is not laid upon us by any constitutional or legal mandate. Our belief, that men are brothers in divine origin and destiny, is a part of our religious heritage that reaches back to the hills of Galilee and imposes upon each of us a spiritually-rooted obligation. Moreover, the methods by which we discharge this obligation must conform to the true spirit of the giver. And, today, they involve a lasting and fruitful partnership between citizens and their government.

While the government must be concerned about the welfare of all the people, we must exercise great care lest we encroach upon the domain of private philanthropy. We must be especially careful not to dilute local responsibility, self-reliance and the spirit of "taking care of one's own."

Of course in those humanitarian undertakings that are so complex in character and so wide in scope as to make futile the efforts of the individual, whether acting singly or in voluntary cooperation, the responsibility for major action falls upon government—either local or central. But money raised by taxes, although willingly paid, can never wholly replace voluntary giving by individuals and groups.

Even as government cannot guarantee us happiness or satisfy the deepest aspirations of mankind, the State cannot more than partially and in special circumstances satisfy the obligation—the compulsion within us—to help our neighbor. Were it to assume entirely this or any other fundamentally personal obligation, the government—the instrument— would eventually become the master. Political considerations might easily become paramount over human values. A concern of heart and spirit would degenerate into a machine-like operation of bureaucratic processes. The will to sacrifice for others would be replaced by reliance on governmental administrative procedures.

The American people, instinctively sensitive to this, have developed a way, a method, an approach to charitable giving unmatched in its scale in human history. Thereby, men and women join voluntarily in discharge of self-imposed obligations, confident that proper goals can be achieved by individuals and organizations of citizens, either by supplementing or making unnecessary governmental activity in the same field.

Now we are met this evening to commemorate fifty years of service by one of these organizations—the National Conference of Catholic Charities. I suggest that, for a moment, we look at the spirit, purposes, and values exemplified by the Conference against a world-wide background of governments and men absorbed in the frantic pursuit of transistory temporal power, unworthy ambitions, and false greatness.

In our season of history, beyond any previous era, the world spectacle seems most violent in its surface turmoil; most intense in its inner passion; most titanic in its destructive potential. Our waking and working hours seem too often filled with the alarms of new threats, the clamor of the aggressive, and the cries of the fearful.

Against the dangers inherent in the attitude and announced purposes of a powerful, secretive dictatorship, we steadfastly maintain the military, moral, economic and political strength to assure the nation's safety. Further, knowing that peace and freedom are weakened if not shared, we help other nations which, like ourselves, uphold the dignity of men and maintain their liberty. But in spite of these inescapable burdens, America, if true to herself, will never be tempted to abandon her noble goals.

For close to two centuries our nation has thrived under the bracing influence of belief in God and the dignity of the individual. Should this spiritual base of our society ever become dimmed, our faith in the destiny of America would disappear before a vain reliance on materialism, and crass political maneuver.

Then, even should we seem, for a while, victorious over world circumstances and all visible foes, we would be tragic losers—robbed of our heritage in ideals and our destiny as a leader for world peace with justice. An apparent triumph would become a soon-exposed illusion. A materialistic America—bereft of spiritual purpose—could be nothing more than a rudderless ship of state, and eventually a victim of the fury of international storms and internal decay.

That tragedy will never be visited upon us so long as our churches and our synagogues and chapels—and people who believe in God and in themselves—continue to give of their spirit, of their time, and of their substance, that they may be secure and their fellow men may have faith and hope and courage.

Clear it is that a great charitable and intensely dedicated organization like the Conference of Catholic Charities is far more than an agency for alleviating suffering; it is the collective expression of the spirit of the giver; it is a great bulwark against collapse into materialism and utter dependence on the omnipotent State.

The physical evidence of your work is, of course, immense; without such effort our American communities would lack priceless institutions to help the needy, to relieve suffering, to heal the sick.

Nevertheless, I say again that your greatest contribution is not your gifts; rather it is the example of selfless service you and others set for all Americans; the inspiration you give to your fellow citizens, and to the world; and the direct call you make to their hearts, whatever their creed.

For I am sure—and in this, I think Cardinal Spellman will be quick to support me—your works could hardly in these days be accomplished had you not the help and the prayers of many, many Americans who are not of your Church.

By the same token the men and women who support this Conference participate also in the good works of others. For the spirit of the giver is not narrow—it is as broad as his understanding of human need.

So, at this Golden Jubilee Dinner, I salute the devoted men and women—clergy and lay—joined in the National Conference of Catholic Charities. I applaud their record of achievement in helping the less fortunate, for the proof they provide that we live not by bread alone—or by dollars, or by machines.

So long as our America is served by such people and such organizations we shall go forward in self-reliance and confidence; we shall be recognized as good neighbors by all the world's people and we will remember that, despite our fears and ignorance of each other, we are of one brotherhood under God.

Thank you.

NOTE: The President spoke at 9:52 p.m. at the Statler Hilton Hotel in New York City.

307 ¶ Joint Statement Following Meeting With Prime Minister Macmillan To Discuss the Situation Before the United Nations. *September 27, 1960*

THE PRESIDENT of the United States and the Prime Minister of Great Britain had a breakfast meeting this morning starting at 8:00 o'clock in the President's suite in the Waldorf Astoria Hotel. They were joined at 9:00 A.M. by the Secretary of State and British Foreign Secretary Lord Home.

The President and the Prime Minister reviewed the situation in the General Assembly of the United Nations and considered the policies best pursued by their two countries towards their common goal. They were in complete agreement as to the vital role of the United Nations, particularly in the Congo crisis and the need to give full support to the Secretary General in his task. They greatly hope that after a stormy start the General Assembly will now be able to concentrate on serious, sober and constructive work, notably in the matter of disarmament.

NOTE: The joint statement was released in New York City.

308 ❡ Toasts of the President and the Crown Prince of Japan. *September 27, 1960*

Your Imperial Highnesses, ladies and gentlemen:

In the past 8 years that it has been the good fortune of my wife and myself to entertain representatives of nations great and small at this table, one thing is certain, we have never entertained a couple who showed such youth, vitality, and charm as the couple that we are so fortunate as to have this evening.

Possibly they won the hearts of America as they have come across our continent partially because of their youth, because our country is a young country. But we must remember also that Japan, although a very old nation, is also young. Starting just a century ago, there began in that country a great renaissance. We are proud that we had a small part in bringing about its beginning.

Today it is flowering into a great production and prosperity that will certainly continue on into the future, and Japan stands again as one of the proud countries that values its independence and with us believes in the democratic ideal of life.

So I think all of us will deem it a great privilege, as we honor the Crown Prince and the Crown Princess at this table, to drink a Toast also to this country and its Emperor, His Imperial Majesty, the Emperor of Japan.

NOTE: The President proposed the toast at 10:04 p.m. at a state dinner at the White House. Prince Akihito responded as follows:

Mr. President, Mrs. Eisenhower, and distinguished guests:

I am deeply moved, Mr. President, by the cordial words addressed directly to me and to the Princess, and through us, I believe, to the people of my country.

May I say, Mr. President, that you are held by all free peoples the world over in the highest respect and affection because of your candor and sincerity, your warmness of heart, and above all your love of peace.

Ladies and gentlemen, I have the honor to propose a Toast to the great friend and pre-eminent leader of the free world, the President of the United States and his gracious Lady.

309 ¶ Address in Chicago at the 1960 Victory Fund Dinner Rally. *September 29, 1960*

Mr. Chairman, fellow Republicans, and all dedicated citizens everywhere:

For 8 years I have been introduced at party gatherings and many public affairs functions by a good friend of mine, the Vice President of the United States. Tonight, with your permission, I would like to have the privilege of reversing that order. But first, some brief remarks:

In this gathering, all of us are joined to make certain, through our own dedication and our sacrifice of time, effort, and pocketbooks, that we will assure victory on November 8th for Richard Nixon and Cabot Lodge, and with them the continuation of sound government.

The reason we work for their election is our confidence in their capacity to provide the Nation with the best possible leadership in the years immediately ahead. For my part, this confidence is based upon an intimate acquaintance with their talents, their experience, and their character.

I have known Cabot Lodge for many years.

During World War II, I knew him as a soldier.

He was the only man in the United States Senate since the Civil War to resign from his seat to fight in the Armed Forces.

He served in the North African campaign, and continued to serve with distinction until the close of the war, after which the voters of Massachusetts gratefully returned him to the Senate.

His career in the Senate was in keeping with the brilliant record of his family. Five of his ancestors served in that body. He began his own active political career in the Massachusetts Legislature.

There, Cabot Lodge quickly came to understand that good representative government requires a system under which certain responsibilities and powers are allocated to each level—local, State, and national government.

In his most recent role, as our representative to the United Nations the past 7 years, Ambassador Lodge has demonstrated, day by day, his superb qualities of leadership. He has stood firmly on a platform of truth to confound the delegates of the Soviet Union and its satellites who have falsely misrepresented the peaceful intentions of the United States. We salute him for his enviable record as a public servant, because he has been a stout and skillful representative of the United States, and because his performance in the United Nations has brought growing respect and admiration for that great international institution among our countrymen.

It is upon such a record that we acclaim Cabot Lodge as our vice presidential candidate.

Heading our ticket is Richard Nixon, the possessor of a vast richness of experience in domestic affairs, foreign relations, and person-to-person diplomacy. In important functions in executive work, he has served the Nation well. In some half-hundred countries around the world the Vice President has carried out assignments at my request—assignments requiring tact, sound judgment, and courage—in all of these he has been extraordinarily successful.

In the 171 years of this Republic, 34 men have occupied the high position of trust and responsibility of the American presidency. Today, possibly more than ever before, the office is the principal channel for the expression of our national purpose—of our hopes, beliefs, and aspirations for a world living in peace with justice.

In the years ahead your President must be a man capable of calm decision in the midst of frenzy—a man who is neither intimidated by selfish pressure groups at home nor tyrants abroad.

Richard Nixon is such a man.

Of late I have noted allegations that the Vice President has contributed little to the affairs of government. On this matter, let me set the record straight—and certainly no one is in a better position to do so.

For 8 years I have worked closely with him. During these years Dick Nixon has participated with me and high officials of your Government in hundreds of important deliberative proceedings of the Cabinet, the National Security Council, and other agencies. In these meetings he has proved himself time and again to be a man with a comprehensive understanding of both the problems of our age and the demands upon government.

His counsel has been invaluable. He is dedicated, decisive, persistent in pursuing new ways for improving government, and a man possessed of the character, patience, and sound judgment so essential for effective leadership in the troubled world of tomorrow.

Leadership is not proved by a mere whirling across the public stage in a burst of glib oratory. It is forged of experience in the many workshops of public affairs—at the council table, at the diplomatic conference; it is ripened in unlimited contacts with those who work at the summit and those who labor in the vineyard. It gains deeper insight as it explores into the ideas and problems that disturb world leaders and bewilder humankind the world over.

It is on this basis I make this unequivocable statement. As a man qualified to enter on the duties of the presidential office, Dick Nixon has the broadest and deepest preparation and experience of any man I know.

Alexander Hamilton once prophesied of a time to come when "every vital question of state will be merged in the question," he said, " 'Who will be the next President?' "

In this election such a time is at hand.

We want presidential leadership that rejects both irresponsible promises and deceptively simple solutions to national problems. We are against leadership that seeks to center all government in Washington. We want leadership that sees government as the willing partner, not the controller of human progress and achievement.

We do not want leadership that recklessly exhausts the rightful heritage of our grandchildren. We do want leadership that will fight against the debasement of the dollar at the grocery counter, and the erosion of our pensions and personal savings.

We do not want leadership that sees only dark continents of despair in American life—leadership that has a stultifying preoccupation with our faults. We do want leadership that gauges our problems with definitive care, and then produces a solution patterned carefully to the problem, regardless of the carping of the irresponsible.

I ask you: do we want leadership from a trained team, unmatched in experience in the affairs of modern diplomacy, to continue and enlarge upon what we have done to build peace with justice?

Of course we do—we want Nixon and Lodge.

The Nation needs this team. So, under the bracing influence of our philosophy of freedom and dignity of the individual, let us pledge ourselves to an all-out drive to assure victory for our national ticket. And let's back them up by giving them a big crew of Republican Congressmen in Washington and Governors in the Nation's statehouses.

So doing, we shall begin our second century of Republican leadership with a sound assurance that America's bright hopes for a better world will be steadily advanced.

And now, ladies and gentlemen, it is my privilege and honor to introduce Richard Nixon, the next President of the United States!

NOTE: The President spoke at 9:26 p.m. at the Conrad Hilton Hotel in Chicago. His opening words "Mr. Chairman" referred to U.S. Senator Thruston Morton of Kentucky, Chairman of the Republican National Committee.

The address was broadcast to similar dinner rallies in 35 cities joined by closed-circuit television. The Vice President spoke in Boston; Senator Morton, who served as toastmaster, spoke in Philadelphia.

310   ¶ Remarks at the Polish-American Congress in Chicago.   *September 30, 1960*

Mr. Rozmarek, distinguished guests, and my fellow Americans:

First of all, I must thank you personally, Mr. Rozmarek, for the very generous terms in which you have introduced me.

I want to say, first, that I am especially delighted to have a chance to meet briefly with the Polish-American Congress. This is not a mere formality, because from time immemorial, the people of Poland have shown such a fierce dedication to the conception of liberty and personal freedom, that they have been an example for all the world.

We must remember that spirit is, after all, the major force that animates all human action. Material strength we have, and we are fortunate in having it; we have economic strength and intellectual strength— but what is in the heart of the human is, after all, the thing we must seek when we say he is our friend or our ally, or our brother in the convictions and beliefs that we hold.

So, from the days of Kosciuszko (and here I must pause for a moment, because once in Poland they used that name quite often, and it was a whole day before I knew what they were saying, but my pronunciation is Kosciuszko) from the day he came to help in our struggle for independence in this country, there has never been a time when the Polish people and Polish fortunes have been absent from the hearts and minds of the American people.

Only in the time of Woodrow Wilson, one of his Fourteen Points that he laid out as his formula for peace with Germany after World War I, was the permanent independence and the territorial integrity of Poland.

That the people of our country and the people of Poland have been akin in spirit, I think was again demonstrated very definitely when Vice

737

President Nixon went to that country only a year or so ago, and had a quarter of a million people cheering him, voluntarily bringing in arms of flowers to throw in his path, trying to let him know that through him they hoped to send a message to America, "We still, with you, believe in freedom."

In 1952, I promised the American people that whatever I could do by peaceful means would be done, in order that those people who are held in bondage by a tyrannical dictatorship might finally have the right to determine their own fates by their own free votes.

This is still a tenet in the faith of every right-thinking American. It is as yet unachieved, but this does not mean that anyone must give up hope. We must continue, by our unity and freedom throughout the world, to oppose the bloc that by making the State a deity and the individual just a plodding animal do the bidding of that State.

So, just as we keep faithful to our religious teachings, and the religious background on which this Nation was formed, we keep faithful to that ideal of freedom, well realizing that freedom and peace are in the long run indivisible.

There must be peace for the world, or no nation can truly enjoy it.

People of your blood have come to this country. You are citizens of the United States. Your loyalty to the United States is exactly as that of your forefathers, of yourselves, to your mother country. But citizenship is not a mere matter of expressing our pride in our traditions, in our historical figures. Citizenship is the carrying forward of the ideals on which nations based on freedom are maintained and sustained. It is a matter of discharging our responsibilities.

The individual's way of discharging his responsibilities is found in many channels. It is in obedience to the law; it is performing with others the cooperative works of communities and sects and organizations that have to do with the alleviation of suffering. But there is one thing that right now is uppermost in our minds: it is discharging your responsibility of expressing your view about the political future or the immediate political future of our country.

This you do by registering and by placing your vote in the ballot box. It makes no difference, so far as I am concerned—but I don't mean to say I am disinterested—but it makes no difference for what individual or party you vote, as long as you are voting your own honest convictions. And if you do not do that, you are not discharging your responsibilities either to this great country, or to the traditions that you have brought with you from the culture from which you came.

I cannot tell you what great importance I attach to this business of making certain that our government is surely a representative one. It is not representative of us at all if anyone fails to perform this duty. You know, after I go, but before you people leave this room, I would like each person here to turn to his two neighbors or her two neighbors and say, "Have you registered? Are you going to vote?" If you can get a hundred percent "yes," this will be one of the most magnificent meetings that I have ever attended—and it will be an example for all the United States. And then, as you go out, and you meet two other people—in your home, at your work, wherever you are living—and say "Have you registered and are you going to vote?" This is truly what we must do, if self-government, representative government, is going to exist permanently and healthily.

Because, if you are doing this, you are also thinking of what are the issues, who are the leaders you want to follow. You are going to do it thoughtfully, you are not going to let a brand name, or anything else, influence you. And I cannot tell you how earnestly I pray that every person here will do just that.

Now there's one other phase of this relationship among free countries that I should like to mention, before I close these brief and very informal remarks.

I was told the other day that there are 213 nationalities recognized by our Immigration Service—213 nationalities that have in some way or other contributed to the development of our civilization in this country. There is one point I want to make. Our country has found it necessary to establish quotas, quotas on immigration. Whether or not you and I happen to think that quotas are correct at this time, and used properly, or we may think they are not generous enough, the fact is we have had quotas.

Has any Communist country had to establish quotas to keep people from immigrating to their nation?

So when we talk about this prestige between free countries and Communist countries, I would like to make that simple test: how many of you here want to apply for passports and visas to go to Russia?

In other words, we are not only proud of our citizenship, we are proud of every nation that, with us, gives the opportunity to the individual to realize the most out of his talents and his opportunities. In other words, it is the human spirit that must be free. And this is the thing that brings 213 nationalities finally into one single nation.

I think that each of these nations should be proud of its heritage. It should be proud of the traditions and the faiths that it brings, because with that kind of pride in traditions it helps to build our country. Our country is a great amalgamation, and we each live with the other in friendship, with mutual self-respect, and because we find that in this great mixture of cultures and thinking, and traditions and history, each of us is enriched.

Now among the free nations of the world, we have got to have something of that kind of spirit. We must not, as I see it, appear superior to any other country that is, like ourselves, working for the same kind of civilization which respects the dignity of men. We must not be either patronizing, resentful, or either because of race or religion or color or background or some other inconsequential factor treat them as a stranger or enemy.

Just as we seek peace and order and progress and greater unification among our own people, we must seek it through all those people who like ourselves believe in God and base their whole ideals concerning humanity on that faith.

Now, my friends, I was told I was to come over here and just greet you, and wish you well, but I guess possibly I have been so long in political life that I can't help, when I've got an opportunity, to just start talking.

But I might tell you one little story about that. We had one State that had in its laws a provision that anyone convicted for murder and was to be executed, was to be given 5 minutes to say anything he wanted to, before the final act.

And there was in this State a man who was so convicted and was just about on the brink. And the sheriff, in front of the assembled crowd— and they had come from everywhere to see this thing—offered this man very solemnly and officially his 5 minutes.

Well, the man promptly refused it. But another man in the gathering jumped up quickly and says he's running for Congress, "Can I have the 5 minutes?"

I didn't mean to take the time that somebody else should have had— although not in those circumstances, of course. But I cannot tell you how much I wish you well, how proud I am of the record of your country, its convictions, of the great contributions the people of Polish extraction have brought to this New World.

And again to say, don't forget to make sure that you have registered and your two neighbors have. And vote for somebody!

Thank you very much indeed.

NOTE: The President spoke at the Sherman Hotel in Chicago. His opening words "Mr. Rozmarek" referred to Charles Rozmarek, President of the Polish-American Congress.

311 ¶ Message to the People of the Federation of Nigeria on the Occasion of Their Independence. *October 1, 1960*

ON BEHALF OF the people of the United States of America, I wish to extend to the Government and people of Nigeria heartiest congratulations on the occasion of their independence.

We in the United States have watched with sympathy and admiration the progress of the people of Nigeria toward this historic and welcome event which is the result of fruitful cooperation between the people of Nigeria and the Government and people of the United Kingdom. We are confident that this spirit of cooperation will inspire Nigeria's future relationships with all who hold freedom dear.

In expressing the best wishes of my country, I speak for a people who cherish individual liberty and independence, and who have made great sacrifices so that these vital principles might endure. It is with special pleasure, therefore, that we witness the assumption by this new nation of its sovereign place in the world community.

I am keenly conscious of the friendship which has marked the relations of our two countries. We take great pride in bonds established by Nigerian government leaders whom we were privileged to receive as guests, and by the many Nigerians who have studied in our land.

For the future, we in the United States stand ready to work with the people of Nigeria to reach the goals we all share of health, enlightenment and material well being. I am confident that in years to come our two countries will stand as one in safeguarding the greatest of all bonds between us, our common belief in a free and democratic way of life.

DWIGHT D. EISENHOWER

312   ¶ Joint Statement Following Meeting With Prime Minister Macmillan and Prime Minister Menzies.   *October* 2, 1960

THE PRIME MINISTER of Australia met for an hour and a half at the White House this morning with the President of the United States and the Prime Minister of the United Kingdom. They continued the discussion of current problems at the United Nations which the President and Mr. Macmillan had started in New York on Tuesday last. They adjourned their meeting at 10:50 A.M.

All three were agreed in the hope that the General Assembly will now be able to achieve real progress on the problems confronting it, notably that of disarmament.

The United States and British Secretaries of State plan to meet again this afternoon at the British Embassy at 2:30 to carry forward the review of certain of the points under discussion this morning.

313   ¶ Letter in Reply to a Proposal for a Meeting of the President and Chairman Khrushchev.   *October* 2, 1960

Dear ————:

I have received your letter of September 29, informing me of your intention to submit to the current session of the General Assembly a resolution calling for a meeting between the Chairman of the Council of Ministers of the USSR and myself. I assure you again that I share the concern expressed in this communication over the present state of international relations, and I understand and sympathize with the motives which led you to propose this step.

As President of the United States I have sought on every occasion to explore to the full any possibility for the resolution of outstanding international questions by negotiation.

Following the refusal last May of the Soviet government to participate in the long awaited Summit Conference which was to deal with certain of these questions, especially disarmament and problems arising out of the war, the President of France, the Prime Minister of the United Kingdom and I issued a declaration which stated: "They remain unshaken in their conviction that all outstanding international questions should not be settled by threat or the use of force but by peaceful means through negotiation. They themselves remain ready to take part in such negotiations at any suitable time in the future."

Speaking for the United States this statement still holds good.

I have at no time utilized any threats whatsoever with reference to any international question. This is, I am sure you will agree, a matter of historical record.

On the other hand, the Soviet Union far from following a comparable policy of restraint appears to have undertaken with deliberate intent a policy of increasing tension throughout the world and in particular of damaging relations with the United States.

Instead of avoiding threats of the use of force, the Soviet Government has threatened rocket retaliation against many members of the United Nations including the United States on the pretext of contrived and imaginary intentions on the part of these countries. While these threats have necessarily only strengthened our resolve to maintain our readiness to deter and, if necessary, to resist any aggression, they have nevertheless caused uneasiness throughout the world.

The Soviet Government has refused any thought of an impartial international body to investigate the shooting down on July 1 of an aircraft of the United States Air Force, and is still holding incommunicado two members of its crew.

The Soviets have unilaterally disrupted the ten-nation disarmament talks in Geneva with full knowledge that the Western Powers there represented were about to submit new proposals which took into account those made earlier by the Soviet Union.

I believe that a comparison of the international behavior of the participants of the Paris Meeting since its collapse demonstrates where the responsibility lies for the increase of international tension and the failure to make any progress in the solution of outstanding problems.

I reiterate what I said in my speech before the General Assembly on September 22: The United States is always ready to undertake serious negotiations with the Soviet Union and other interested countries on any unresolved international question, and especially in the field of disarmament. I also pointed out that there are needs for great constructive action, for which I have made proposals to the General Assembly, that are primary in their importance to the peace and progress of major areas of the world. However, the chief problems in the world today are not due to differences between the Soviet Union and the United States alone, and therefore are not possible of solution on a bilateral basis.

The questions which are disrupting the world at the present time are of immediate and vital concern to other nations as well. The importance of these matters is such as to go beyond personal or official relations between any two individuals to impede their solution, and I have many times personally pledged myself, regardless of every kind of personal consideration, to meet with anyone at anytime if there is any serious promise of productive results. There is nothing in the words or actions of the government of the Soviet Union which gives me any reason to believe that the meeting you suggest would hold any such promise. I would not wish to participate in a mere gesture which, in present circumstances, might convey a thoroughly misleading and unfortunate impression to the peoples of the world.

If the Soviet Union seriously desires a reduction in tensions it can readily pave the way for useful negotiations by actions in the United Nations and elsewhere. If Soviet representatives should wish to discuss concrete measures to reduce tensions my representatives, including the Secretary of State, are always available for this purpose. Should such exploratory discussions reveal that the Soviet Union is prepared to return to the path of peaceful negotiation with some prospect of fruitful results then I personally would be prepared to meet and negotiate with the representative of the Soviet Government and with the heads of other governments as their interests were involved.

Sincerely,

Dwight D. Eisenhower

NOTE: This is the text of identical letters addressed to President Nkrumah of Ghana, President Sukarno of Indonesia, President Nasser of the United Arab Republic, President Tito of Yugoslavia, and Prime Minister Nehru of India.

314 ¶ Remarks to the 67th Annual Conference of the International Association of Chiefs of Police. *October 4, 1960*

President Woodson, Chief Murray, and members of the International Association of Chiefs of Police:

Very shortly I am going to be out of government, and I won't have some of the arrangements that are normally conducted around me—to make sure I don't misbehave. I don't know of any crowd that I want to make stronger friends of mine in the years to come than the police chiefs—so if I get out of line they will be very lenient with me.

It is truly a privilege to come here to welcome such a body as this, a body that stands for law and order in the world. I understand there are gathered here not only the chiefs of police throughout my own country, but representatives of 39 countries.

If this world needs anything more than law and order, I would defy anyone here to tell me what it is. I am quite sure that if we could only get your dedication to this concept of law and order and decent behavior adopted on the part of all humans—if we could get that concept understood and practiced in the nations—indeed your work would be much easier. It is the tensions and the problems and the worries of the world that I think often lead individuals themselves to conduct themselves improperly.

My thanks are due not only to the police of my own country for the many courtesies and favors they have given to me and my party as I have gone around this country during the past years, but to those of other nations which I have visited. In all these visits, I have never seen a single case of discourtesy or of lack of attention to his duty by police officers in any single one of these countries. My admiration for the discipline that is maintained in their organizations, for the obvious dedication of each man to his duty, is indeed high.

So as you go about your work, I would like you to know that it is not only someone like myself who is the recipient of so much attention because of the office, but America and the world—the people in the nations represented here—who also recognize the value of your work. They know the difficulties you have, particularly when, after having apprehended some guilty persons and by some kind of technicality they are

745

freed and you think your work has all to be done over, you may get discouraged. You should understand that people who read your newspapers also appreciate this problem, and as a matter of fact pray with the rest of us that these things can be corrected.

I say I will not again have the opportunity to greet such a body as this. But I would not want to go away without explaining to you that my appreciation is sincere.

I want also to call your attention to one police body that I have recently seen operating effectively and at full force and overtime. This is the New York City Police, which is operating under a man, a friend of mine who cannot be here today, Commissioner Kennedy. Because of the extraordinary burdens placed upon that force, they are working according to the records shown me recently, from 12 to 18 hours, 7 days a week. Commissioner Kennedy has his entire force denied any leave or any furlough, all equipment is mobilized, and even those that were on furlough or leave were in many instances recalled. So I would personally like to think that all of the people here understand what the responsibilities of such a job are—and I myself know something about it because I have been on these motorcades and I know the police haven't got very easy jobs. I would like to see you give him and his force at least a silent salute for the way he and they are working, not only for all of New York City, but for the Nation and indeed for all freedom-loving people everywhere.

I merely cite his case, which may be duplicated in many other instances in different ways in all your cities, for all I know. I happen to know that that one is now, you might say, at the dramatic height of its activities, and is doing a very splendid job, as I can well testify.

So again, to all of you, thank you for inviting me here. Good luck to you, and may everyone that you have caught and is found guilty get his proper punishment. Similarly I hope that in every case where you apprehend a man and you are doubtful about the case, if you can find real evidence to show that he is innocent, that again will be something that will bring up in the minds of people everywhere the value of a true police force.

Thank you, and goodbye.

NOTE: The President spoke at the Statler Hilton Hotel in Washington. His opening words "President Woodson, Chief Murray" referred to Col. Charles W. Woodson, Jr., President of the International Association of Chiefs of Police, and Robert V. Murray, Chief of Police of the District of Columbia.

315   ¶ Remarks to a Group of Engineers From India Upon Completion of a Training Program in the United States.   *October 5, 1960*

Mr. Minister, Mr. Riddleberger, and alumni of this training and educational program:

I shall not attempt to make a commencement address in the traditional sense that we do in this country at least, whenever a class graduates from an institution of learning.   But first I should like to welcome you here to this Capital where I understand you have gathered from the various institutions and industries in which you have been training, and now you are going to talk among yourselves and with others about the training you have had and how you can help each other with the special instruction you have received.

The United States has been committed for a long time to what we call a people-to-people program.   We think this is one of the most brilliant features of this kind of getting together of nations, of different philosophies—at times, of different races—and certainly of different backgrounds and histories.

So we are indeed happy that you are here in this country and have gone through these institutions which we believe you will find helpful. More than that we hope that aside from the individual advantage you get, there will be real improvements brought about between the understanding—mutual understanding—of our two countries.

Now I would like to talk a little bit about my own country and its purposes, particularly in this kind of operation.

We believe by helping other peoples to bring up their economic standards—individual standards of living—that this is good for the United States.   We want to live in a peaceful world.   We are an industrious people.   We are not combative—but we are determined to take care of ourselves.

You have been in institutions that are operated under the free enterprise system.   Of this we are very proud.   We have grown up in that tradition, and we believe in it, and we want to maintain it.

You have seen something of the way it operates here.   In your own country industries are operated sometimes differently, sometimes in the same pattern. To us that makes no difference. You do it your way. What we believe is this: it is important to us that the mind and spirit of man is free so he can himself decide what it is that he as one of the representatives of his own country—what that country wants to do. As long as the man has a free mind and a free spirit, we believe he is no danger to peace.

On the contrary, we believe that the great populations of the world, every one of them, wants peace. Governments—and possibly I as one member of my Government—can sometimes be stupid or ignorant or lack in understanding. But there is one thing sure: we do know that peoples want peace. They want to act according to their own ideas and convictions and deeper feelings—and their religions. That is what they want to do, instinctively, because we are humans.

Our country would like to see that done, and indeed our Government would like to see that done. It has been the main policy of our Government for many, many years, long before I came here. We will attempt to proceed along that line. We hope that more of you people will come here and carry back with you, as you will, a clear understanding of how we do things. We will say this should help you to make up your mind on the matter of how you want to do it. We don't say that you should have our system. Maybe our system isn't necessarily good for others. After all, we came here as a very small population into a vast region of rich resources.

Countries today that are trying to industrialize are not in that situation. So therefore they have got different problems. We merely ask you to remain free in mind and spirit, and on that basis you will certainly have a friend in the United States of America.

We want nothing—no territory. We want no influence, or domination that comes about either by military or economic power, or political power. We want to be friends with people on a basis of mutual understanding and respect, and a common dedication to the concept of the dignity of man.

I hope as you learn something more about engineering and industrial production and about steel—I can't talk about them, I wouldn't know anything about them, and you would laugh at me—but I do know this: you have learned something more because you have come out from your own environment and lived with people who are doing things somewhat differently than you do. Living under those conditions and all the rest of it, this is good.

Any one of us that goes to another nation, even for brief hours, learns something. You have gotten a real comprehension of United States thinking because you have talked not just to Presidents and politicians and Senators, you have talked to people that work, and in the production of the things that the world needs.

So I say, as you go, good luck, Godspeed. We are looking forward to having more of you here. I believe during 1961 your six hundred-man program is going to be completed. I think all of us should thank the Iron and Steel Institute for the help it has given, but I am quite sure that private enterprise and private industries and the Government will want to see this continued in some way. One of these days you people, in turn, are going to have to bring others in to show them your plants—whether it be in Africa or Asia or anywhere else, showing them how you do it there, and how you do it better than the United States.

Thank you very much.

NOTE: The President spoke in the Rose Garden at the White House. His opening words "Mr. Minister, Mr. Riddleberger" referred to D. N. Chatterjee, Minister of the Indian Embassy, and James W. Riddleberger, Director of the International Cooperation Administration.

The group of 90 Indian engineers had just completed 7 months training under the Indian Steel Training and Education Program. This program, sponsored by the Ford Foundation and the International Cooperation Administration, is designed to provide India with 600 trained engineers by the end of 1961.

316 ❡ Letter to Secretary Mitchell on Receiving Report on the Effectiveness of the Labor-Management Act. *October 7*, 1960

[Released October 7, 1960. Dated October 6, 1960]

Dear Mr. Secretary:

I have read with interest your October first report to me on the Labor Department's first year of operations under the Labor-Management Reporting and Disclosure Act of 1959.

It is indeed heartening to see how the provisions of this law are being utilized by America's working men and women to safeguard against the corruption and abuses of power it was designed to correct. While such corruption and abuses have occurred only among a small minority of those in the labor-management field, all of us are agreed that in a free society these practices cannot be tolerated no matter how few may engage in them.

Clearly, the experience of the past year under this statute attests to the wisdom of those who worked so diligently for passage of an adequate labor reform law, and it particularly supports the judgment of those in the House of Representatives who voted for the Landrum-Griffin bill to replace the weak and ineffective measure approved earlier by the Senate.

It is my hope that our working men and women will continue to use the provisions of this law where they are appropriate, and that our Nation will continue its advance toward truly responsible labor-management relations.

Sincerely,

DWIGHT D. EISENHOWER

NOTE: Secretary Mitchell's report stated that the law had brought about a renewed awareness and participation on the part of union members in the affairs of their unions; a restoration, where it had been denied, of the democratic rights of union members to manage their own affairs; the protection of the dues moneys paid by union members from their wages; and the curbing of improper practices and collusion between union officials and management, or by management and their representatives against the interest of working people.

The report, in the form of a letter dated October 1, 1960, was released with the President's reply.

317 ¶ Toasts of the President and Prince Albert of Belgium.   *October 7, 1960*

Your Royal Highnesses, ladies and gentlemen:

We are privileged today to have as our honored guests Their Royal Highnesses the Prince and Princess of Liege. It is a peculiar privilege also to tell you people about one thing that I have learned here today. The Princess is a citizen of the United States by reason of the fact that she is a descendant of Lafayette.

I have been trying to persuade her to stay here until November 8th, and I am doing a little bit of electioneering to see her vote is on the right side.

However, it is a great honor to tell you about this particular relationship of hers, because as far as I am concerned, it is the first time I have met one of the relatives of any of the descendants of our great French hero in America.

The country of Belgium is one of America's closest friends. We served with Belgium in two wars, and we saw her bring about her renaissance after the tremendous destruction of World War II. Today she is a happy, prosperous country, a champion of liberty. And because she is a champion of liberty, she is a close relative of ours, because any two peoples that have this kind of similar dedication cannot fail to be brothers.

So I today deem it a great privilege that I can ask you—this company—to rise with me to drink a Toast to His Majesty the King of the Belgians.

NOTE: The President proposed this toast at a luncheon at the White House in honor of Prince Albert and Princess Paola. Prince Albert responded as follows:

Mr. President, Madame, ladies and gentlemen:

First of all, I want to apologize for doing very, very short and uninteresting speech, because of my knowledge in English is incomplete. I hope you will excuse me.

Mr. President, I want to thank you for your very kind words to us, my wife and I, and to our country—and also to my brother.

Madame, let me thank you in the name of my wife and me for that delicious meal. We enjoyed it.

As you know, I have the honor of heading an Economic Mission which main purpose is to foster economic cooperation, especially from the industrial point of view. In name of the Belgian Economic Mission, I want to thank you especially, Mr. President, and all the American people, for the warm welcome they have given to us everywhere where we have been until now. We have received the nicest welcome we have ever received. When we were talking together, my wife and I, over our mutual impressions of America and the American people—we were completely *de le coeur* to use a French word—that really the American people are terribly kind and terribly nice. I am sure that this visit will have as a result to bind us more—if I can use this expression—the relationships between Belgium and America.

May I ask you, ladies and gentlemen, to join me in drinking a Toast to the health and the happiness of Mr. President of the United States, and Madame Eisenhower.

318 ¶ Remarks to Regional Office and Hospital Managers of the Veterans Administration. *October 8, 1960*

GOOD MORNING. Maybe it's a little bit early for some of you, but I am an old soldier. Actually, I am a veteran—some of you people some day are going to have to take care of me.

I wanted to chat with you a little bit because of the great importance your organization achieves in the United States Government, and your part in that organization. After all, the third item in our budget is for the Veterans Administration, and it gets something over five and a half billion and with 170,000 of you people—office managers and hospital managers—dealing with this matter of some 22 million veterans all over the United States, it is not only important that you meet in such places as Washington to talk among yourselves about your problems and how you can improve the service, but it is also important that all of the United States knows that you are doing your job well.

Since the United States does provide generously for, as Lincoln said, "the widow and the orphan and those who have been disabled in the service of their country," then, in order that that generosity may be properly expressed, you people have to do it. Mr. Whittier or any other individual here in this office can set a tone. You people do the work.

Consequently, from all these angles of the great amounts the Nation provides, the need and the numbers of veterans who have in some form or other been receiving help through your hands, this is a very important and really a vital function that you perform.

Now in the last few years I have been more than gratified by the reports I have from Mr. Whittier's office of the increasing efficiency. He tells me that there is something on the order of 3 percent of all our appropriations that can be allocated to overhead. This, to my mind, is really great efficiency. I am sure in view of the reports that have come to me from leaders of the Veterans Administration, about the way that our veterans are treated, you are also doing your part in making this a human organization. I realize that it is through your recommendations that many of the administrative improvements are achieved. But when you come down to it, it is the 170,000 people, starting with the Philippines and Hawaii and Alaska and down into the heart of our country here, our Continental United States, it is through you that the human touch that is so important to these people is brought about.

So not only do I congratulate you for the work you have been doing, I urge that every one of you continues to make his ideas and beliefs and convictions known to the headquarters concerning efficiency, effectiveness, and even reporting how to take care of these people—not that they are given a dole, but that they are treated as human beings who have deserved well of their country. All of this, it seems to me, from every report that has come to me, outside of Government and inside, you people have been doing.

So I have, then, besides the duty of thanking you, one of expressing very great personal satisfaction in this matter. I had, in Europe, the greatest number of people ever sent into the field under one command, and of that command over three million were Americans. They are the ones that are our responsibility. I saw them—many of you saw them—there and in the Pacific, dirty, muddy, sometimes cold and freezing, nearly always tired—and looking for a coca cola.

But today, as I go back in my memory to the days when I was living among those people all the time, I feel again that tremendous hope that some way they would get to know America's real appreciation of the sacrifices they make, and I think it is through you people more than anyone else that they do.

So, my personal thanks on behalf of all those people who served and for the widows and orphans or dependents of those who did not come back.

I apologize again for bringing you out here at this early hour of the morning, but it was the only way I could see to meet you, and I did want to do that. I thank you for coming out, because it has been a great pleasure to talk with and see such a great group of dedicated Americans.

Thank you very much. Goodbye.

NOTE: The President spoke in the Rose Garden at the White House. In the course of his remarks he referred to Sumner G. Whittier, Administrator of Veterans Affairs.

319 ❡ Remarks to Participants in the International Field Hockey Festival.
October 11, 1960

Colonel Eagan and gentlemen:

I have never seen a field hockey game. The nearest I ever came to it was as a boy we played a game called "shinny," and you got whatever club you could and then you took a tin can and you "batted" it into the shape of a ball and then you really went at it. You could sometimes have very unfortunate results.

But I am very much interested in this group for two reasons. First, because of your interest and participation in sports, and secondly, because of your love of sports, you are involved also in the people-to-people program which Colonel Eagan had a part in establishing some years back.

I think most of you know about my deep conviction that through formation of friendships between groups of people from different nations we can progress toward the road of mutual understanding. That means in the long run a common peace for all of us with justice. If we can do this, or we can further it just one tiny bit, then I think we have all done something worthwhile. If there is anything this poor old world needs more than anything else, it is a better understanding in one nation of the people of another.

Through this kind of sport participation, you meet your opponents and your associates and you form friendships that in some cases will exist throughout your lives. And through that, and through the communications, there will radiate out from your own knowledge and consciousness, something of this friendship for others that you yourselves feel. So the sport itself is important because it produces healthy bodies and strong attitudes of sportsmanship and decency and fair play. But even more do I applaud this practice because of its bringing together of the peoples of different nations. Colonel Eagan tells me you are planning soon, or in the next couple of years, a very large tournament in which there is going to be a lot of nations participating—a world's championship. That will be something.

I don't know whether any of you are particularly interested—outside of the citizens of our own country—in football or baseball, but right now it happens we are in the midst of both. We are just trying to end up a world series in baseball, and our collegiate football is right at its height. I hope some of you will get to see one of these games, as I hope to see one of your field hockey games. They tell me the only real relationship between it and the games I played was that they had 11 men. When I played football at the Academy, we did have 11 men.

Now I don't know how long all of you from the other countries are going to be here. I know that you speak several languages, but I suppose most of you speak enough English to get along and to get things to eat and places to sleep. So I do hope you will take advantage of the opportunity to see different parts of the United States. There are different modes of life here and there, and you will find many differences in accent and all the rest of it. But I will tell you one thing: everywhere you go you will find first, hospitality; second, you will find a complete dedication to the idea of peace with justice, and of minding our own business. In countries that we help in this world, we do it with no thought of domination. We want no one else's territory. We don't want to have any influence over others, whether it be economic, military, political, or even social. We want partners. We want partners, and that's all we do want.

So I just ask you to check, as you see these people of America, and find out whether you do not agree with me that that is their basic feeling about other nations in the world.

So as I congratulate you on your opportunities to participate in this kind of sports—and all sports are fun, so I know you have had a lot of fun—I do want also to say you are a valuable instrument in bringing about this understanding we so greatly need.

Thank you very much—I'll be seeing you.

NOTE: The President spoke in the Rose Garden at the White House. His opening words "Colonel Eagan" referred to Col. Edward P. F. Eagan, Chairman of the People-to-People Sports Committee, with headquarters in New York City.

The group consisted of members of field hockey teams from Venezuela, Bermuda, Holland, West Germany, and the United States.

320 ❡ Remarks of Welcome to the King and Queen of Denmark at the Washington National Airport. *October* 11, 1960

Your Majesties and friends:

It is indeed a pleasure to welcome to Washington the King and Queen of Denmark. Their country, like our own, is a member of the NATO alliance, standing to defend the security of their countries and the freedom of their people and of all those others of the alliance, and as a great bulwark against the loss of freedom in any other section of the world.

This is a country I have visited during my different tours of duty in Europe and found it hospitable and its people always courteous and ready to help.

I learned something of the country there, but I learned far more about it from one of my oldest friends who was born a Dane and came to this country—I think he was 14, Your Majesty. But he has been a great citizen of our country and one of my warmest and oldest friends. From him I have learned more about your people, and I have found that he is typical of their worth to this Nation—their industriousness, their readiness to cooperate with others, their ability to adapt themselves to our customs and to our practices.

I feel that while all of our own people and your people feel a great kinship among themselves, for me I have achieved through this companionship and this friendship of this individual and his family and his friends an especially warm feeling of sentiment toward your nation and its people. So I feel almost as if I can speak for my friend, Aksel Nielsen, in saying we are especially glad that you two have come here to honor us with your visit. We express the great hope, Your Majesties, that even, as you say, you have found on part of your trip that you have already accomplished something interesting and instructive, we hope that it will continue to be interesting and enjoyable until the day you leave our shores—a day, I assure you, we shall regret.

So again, sir, welcome to Washington and to this country.

NOTE: King Frederik responded as follows:

I thank you, Mr. President, very much for this heartwarming reception at the outset of our visit in Washington.

First of all, I should like to thank you, Mr. President, for your and Mrs. Eisenhower's invitation to the Queen and me to visit your country. We have now been here 7 days and have visited Los Angeles and San Francisco and Chicago. Everywhere we have been received with unsurpassable hospitality and friendliness, and our experiences have been many and unforgettable.

We have been looking forward to this moment when we would meet again with you and Mrs. Eisenhower, whom we feel are close and true friends of Denmark. Our past experiences in a common cause and the present wholehearted cooperation between our countries within many fields, form a solid foundation for a verity and a real friendship—a friendship that is shared by the Danish Government and by the Danish people, from whom I bring you warm and sincere greetings and best wishes for the future of your country.

I thank you.

321 ¶ Toasts of the President and King Frederik of Denmark. *October 11, 1960*

Your Majesties, and ladies and gentlemen:

It is indeed a signal honor to welcome to this Capital and to this house Their Majesties the King and Queen of Denmark. It is a country with which we are bound by ties of common ideals and principles, and ties of blood. Many of their people have come to this country—and indeed, in their country, they celebrate one of our holidays. It has a long and interesting history. And of course, standing as it does as a buttress between the Baltic and the North Seas, it is not strange that they have had a long maritime history.

But in these later days it is one of the key countries in the NATO alliance. It is a forward country. Geographically it looks across a very narrow gap to the threatening dictatorship that creates so much tension and indeed so much ill will in this world.

So we are proud to call them friend and ally. We need them. We hope that they feel, on their part, a sense of partnership and need for us. I am sure they do.

It is a romantic country. Many of you no doubt visited the Castle of Hamlet, and for my part at least, I was astonished to find out that Hamlet never lived in Denmark.

It is a country of people calm and serene; they seem never to be startled, never to be hysterical. One great man said of his people: they were always hysterical in victory and panicky in defeat. I think the people of Denmark would be the last people that you could say that about, if you went there and wanted to make a generalization.

In any event, it is a great country—a prosperous country—and above all, one with us, believing in the dignity of man and ready to put everything on the line; to risk even their existence in the defense of these values that free men feel are above all else in life.

So you can realize that it is with a great sense of distinction that I ask you all to rise with me to drink to Their Majesties, the King and Queen of Denmark.

NOTE: The President proposed the toast at a state dinner in honor of King Frederik and Queen Ingrid at the White House. King Frederik responded as follows:

Mr. President:

The Queen and I are deeply moved by the kind words you have addressed to us and by the hearty welcome which you and Mrs. Eisenhower as well as the inhabitants of this beautiful city of Washington have given us.

The kind hospitality with which we have been met by everybody during this first part of our stay in the United States has made a great impression on us and will always be kept in grateful memory by the Queen and myself.

We have been looking forward with great expectations to this visit which I am sure will contribute to further strengthening of the ties of friendship which so happily unite our two countries. Twenty-one years have elapsed since in 1939 we had the opportunity of paying our first visit to the United States—a tour of which we retain the most happy memories—21 years full of dramatic historic events.

A world war with its terror and suffering for millions of people lies between then and now. During the dark years of war our two countries—each with the means at her disposal—aimed at promoting a common cause. We Danes realize how much we owe to the United States, to the courage and sacrifice of the American people, to the indomitable leadership of outstanding individuals as your memorable predecessors and you yourself, Mr. President, and to the dedicated efforts of the United States to achieve a peace based on freedom and justice for all nations. I wish to take this opportunity to express on behalf of all my countrymen our gratitude towards the United States for their share in the liberation of our country.

When peace had been achieved, we were faced with a series of new problems. As a result of the war the economy of my country—like that of most other European countries—had suffered severe setbacks. The rebuilding and expansion of our means of production and our merchant fleet and the revival of our commerce would not have been completed today had not the United States Government carried out their large-scale aid programs. Through this assistance the United States significantly helped the cause of economic integration in Western Europe. Your country thereby made an inestimable contribution to the unity of the states in our region. It is in my view a major interest, not only of Western Europe, but also of its friends in this hemisphere, that the cause of ever closer cooperation between European nations should enjoy the sympathy and active support of the United States of America.

At the same time dark and menacing clouds were again gathering on the international horizon and prevented the peoples of the world from enjoying the peace for which they had fought so bitterly. Certainly those clouds still darken the sun, but thanks to inspiration and support from the United States the free nations of the Western World have joined their efforts to avert the threats to their national existence and their free way of life.

Our country and yours are united in NATO. During the past 11 years we have had ample proof of the solidarity of the United States with NATO. We have benefited from the magnanimous aid which has enabled Denmark to build up a defense system without endangering the economic and social stability which are also important links in total defense. The contribution of Denmark to the defense of the whole NATO area is, of course, bound to be on a moderate scale. However, we are fully aware that solidarity with our allies is a necessity if the alliance is to fulfill its mission. The establishment of common defense areas in Greenland, upon which Denmark and the United States agreed in 1951, is one of the Danish contributions to that end. During our recent visit to Greenland the Queen and I had the pleasure to visit one of these areas and to inspect the forces stationed there. The high efficiency of these forces gained and deserved our sincere admiration.

While both of us see in the alliance which unites us a purely defensive instrument and a successful means to avert the horrors of a new war, we are not closing our eyes to, but indeed seeking, all possible means to diminish the present tension in the world. We are grateful to you, Mr. President, for your untiring, personal efforts in the cause of peace and good will. They are the ultimate proof of the peaceful aims to which the policy of the United States as well as Denmark are dedicated.

The close cooperation between our two countries—in the United Nations and other international organizations—is based on an identity of views with respect to the fundamental elements of life and stamped by mutual respect and sympathy. To this contribute in no slight degree the ties which unite many Americans of Danish origin with the land of their ancestors. For centuries Danes have gone to the United States to work and study. Many of them stayed on and founded their new homes in their country of adoption; we are happy to meet them here as esteemed and mostly prosperous citizens of this great country. New bonds of friendship have been created by the ever increasing numbers of American visitors coming to Denmark and Danes going to the United States. A most useful and ever increasing exchange of scientists, students, teachers, etc., has developed since the war—thanks to American generosity and planning. This constitutes an essential factor in the cultural relations between our two countries. Tourist travel also is becoming possible for wider and wider groups of our citizens, thanks to the rising standards of living and the progress in the means of transportation. We Danes have always been proud of our merchant marine. In the field of air transportation we have—by pooling our resources with our sister nations, Norway and Sweden—significantly assisted in making connections between your country and Scandinavia easier and closer. These personal links across oceans and borders bear evidence of the freedom reigning in our countries. Let us unite in the hope that the torch of freedom which we received from our fathers may also illuminate the path of our descendants for generations to come.

I raise my glass in honor of the President of the United States and Mrs. Eisenhower, for the prosperity and happiness of the people of the United States.

322   ¶ Statement by the President Upon Receiving Fifth Annual Report on the Rural Development Program.   *October* 13, 1960

I HAVE today received the Fifth Annual Report on the Rural Development Program, which was presented to me by the Under Secretary of Agriculture, True D. Morse, on behalf of the six Departments of the Federal Government which carry major responsibility.

Prior to inauguration of the Rural Development Program in 1955, there had not been a concerted attack on the complex problems of families living on small and inadequate farms.

Half of the farm families, those on small farms, together produce only about nine percent of the farm products marketed. The result is low income, inadequate social service, wasted manpower and a loss of America's potential strength. This is not solely an agricultural problem, nor does the solution lie wholly within agriculture. There must be supplemental employment and additional sources of income, which the Rural Development Program helps provide.

Thirty-one States and Puerto Rico have work underway in 262 counties. By June 30, 1961, the program will be operating in more than 350 counties in at least 36 States and Puerto Rico.

The program demonstrates the effectiveness of the American concept that the role of government is to help people to help themselves.

The initial pilot and demonstration phase of the Rural Development Program has been successful. The program can now be expanded and intensified.   It deserves greatly increased governmental effort and the support of all Americans.

NOTE: The Fifth Annual Report on the   by the Government Printing Office (24
Rural Development Program is published   pp., 1960).

323   ¶ Statement by the President: National Newspaper Week.   *October* 14, 1960

To the Newspapers of the Nation:

It is a privilege to join in the annual observance of National Newspaper Week.

"Your Newspaper—Freedom's Guardian" is a timely theme for 1960. This is the year of our national elections, and it is a year of great decisions in lands around the world.

In our newspapers, we expect to find an accurate, responsible and lively source of public information.   We live in an "open society" and by reporting the news accurately and promptly to us, our reporters help to keep it open.   At the same time, we live in a threatening world where news can be distorted and exploited by the enemies of freedom.   So for freedom's sake our newspapers, too, must be zealously guarded by the sentinels of truth and vigilance.

DWIGHT D. EISENHOWER

324   ¶ Remarks to the Heads of U.N. Delegations From New African Nations and Cyprus. *October* 14, 1960

I UNFORTUNATELY can't speak in French, so I will have the interpreter to interpret just a few words I have to say to you here in a group.

First of all, it is a great privilege for me to have the opportunity of seeing you, and I thank all of you for taking the trouble to come down to Washington so that I could have a word with you.

As you can well know, we in this country have followed with very great interest your various steps in reaching the state of independence, and each of you being accorded a seat in the United Nations organization.

Some of you may have heard the speech I made before the United Nations, expressing not only the friendship of this country for the peoples of Africa, but our hope that we may be of some help to you, and our refusal to attempt interference in the affairs of any other nation, and to refuse to achieve or try to achieve, any kind of domination—military, political, or economic. We want only willing partners—that's all we want.

I have only a few months left in the office I now occupy, but no matter who shall succeed me in this office, I know that his interest will be no less than mine in the efforts you will be making to advance the standards of living of your people and to lead them toward a free and democratic, self-governing type of organization which will give the greatest possible satisfaction to each of you and to the individuals of your nation.

The proposals I have made before the United Nations may not be exactly those that you believe to be correct. All I was trying to point out was the kind of thing that the United States would be prepared to join with others in attempting to do, through the United Nations. But this does not mean that your own views, your own ideas of the details of such schemes should not have a very great influence on exactly how these cooperative programs will be launched.

Now, gentlemen, with just a word of apology for our Washington weather that delayed your landing here, I suggest that we adjourn to the gallery for some orange juice and coffee, and this would give me an opportunity—which I am seeking—to talk to little groups more intimately than I can here, making a speech.

[*Following these remarks in his office, the President accompanied the representatives of the new states to an adjoining gallery. There he responded as follows to remarks addressed to him by Issofou Djermakoye, Minister of Justice of the Republic of Niger:*]

In a rather long life I have received few commendations on my efforts for peace in this world that have touched me more deeply.

While I have never visited the middle of Africa, I am quite sure in my heart that I understand clearly your desires and the desires of your people in this world of tensions and fears. I understand when you say that "we in Africa are without great material strength" and that you stand between two great hostile blocs.

But, sir, we are not a bloc. We are not hostile. But we are determined that those forces which want to destroy liberty, the dignity of man, and human freedom shall not prevail in this world. When there is a militant dictatorship that has proclaimed openly and time again its intention to communize the world and control it from Moscow, then it is time for all of us—all free nations—so to order our affairs as to prevent selfish, dictatorial forces from having their way in the world.

We do not urge—indeed we do not desire—that you should belong to one camp or to the other. You cannot afford to waste your money which is needed to build the hospitals, the schools, the roads that your people need—you cannot afford to put that money into costly armaments.

So, we are not talking about membership in any association—even though it may be a voluntary association to defend militarily against the threat that does exist in the world.

It is because of this that I said earlier to you that the United States does not want either militarily, politically, or economically, to dominate, control or subvert the peoples of your nations. The only thing we ask is that through your own love of freedom and the determination of your people to live their own lives as they choose, you will resist others who have military, economic, or political intent to dominate you. These people should not—cannot—penetrate your people and use them for their own evil purposes.

Gentlemen, I assure you, as I told some of you at the tables, my leaving this office will not terminate my devotion to world peace with justice. Whenever and wherever I see liberty threatened throughout this world, so long as I can write, so long as I can speak, I shall always be on the side of freedom.

One thing I can assure you, the Government of this Nation will always continue to express for its people the same sentiments I have outlined here today.

Thank you for coming to visit with me.

NOTE: The delegates arrived in Washington aboard the Presidential plane "Columbine." The new nations were represented as follows: Republic of Cameroun by Charles Okala, Minister of Foreign Affairs; Central African Republic by Michel Gallin-Douathe, chairman, U.N. delegation; Republic of Chad by Jules Toura Gaba, Minister of Foreign Affairs; Republic of Congo (Brazzaville) by Stephane Tchichelle, Vice Premier and Minister of Foreign Affairs; Republic of Cyprus by Zenon Rossides, chairman of the U.N. delegation; Republic of Dahomey by Ignacio Pinto, chairman of the U.N. delegation; Gabonese Republic by Joseph N'Goua, chairman of the U.N. delegation; Republic of Ivory Coast by Mathieu Ekra, chairman of the U.N. delegation; Malagasy Republic by Louis Rakotomalala, Minister of Foreign Affairs; Republic of Mali by Ousmane Ba, Minister of Labor; Republic of Niger by Issofou Djermakoye, Minister of Justice; Federation of Nigeria by Jaja Wachuku, Minister of Economic Development; Republic of Senegal by Ibrahima Sarr, Minister of Labor and Civil Service; Republic of Togo by Paulin Freitas, Minister of Foreign Affairs; Somali Republic by Abdullahi Issa, Minister of Foreign Affairs; and Republic of Upper Volta by Frederic Guirma, chairman of the U.N. delegation.

The delegates were invited by the President to remain for a tour of the United States as guests of the Government.

325 ¶ Remarks at the Tree-Planting Ceremony at the White House on the President's 70th Birthday. *October* 14, 1960

Mr. Commissioner and citizens of the District:

I take great pride from the fact that after almost 8 years in the White House and having been compelled at times to make decisions that could not possibly have pleased all of you—and I can understand that from your viewpoint so close at hand that you can point out what you at least believe to be errors of mine—yet you have found the time to come in on a 70th birthday of mine and by your presence give me encouragement and strength for the tasks that still lie ahead.

I owe you an apology for being late to my own birthday party. But, when I tell you its reason, I am sure you will applaud my decision to stay a few extra minutes in my office.

I have just been visited by the heads of United Nations delegations from 15 new African states, and from the state of Cyprus, all of these newly independent and coming for the first time as official delegates to the United Nations.

Now the message I want to give to you I bring from them. It is this: these new nations are anxious to follow the leadership of the United States in the great work of promoting justice in the world, promoting the opportunities of men everywhere to raise their standards of living so that they may truly lead lives of dignity and prize the liberty and the independence that they have so recently achieved.

They expressed for the people of the United States the warmest sentiments of friendship and hope that our relations will be so strong and so understanding between ourselves that the world will thereby profit in the pursuit of this age-old goal of peace in justice and in freedom.

So as I thank the people of this city for their great kindness in coming this morning—and the Commissioners for so thoughtfully presenting to me this tree which will one day be a towering giant long after I have gone—I want to say that I believe that we can have a little stronger conviction from the words and the sentiments expressed by these 15 delegations, we can have greater confidence that the world is moving in the direction we want it to go.

We must never—in spite of all the provocations of personal deportment or open or veiled threat as to our existence—we must never be discouraged from achieving those friendships and that kind of cooperation in the world that will eventually lead to the result for which man has so long longed.

I find it difficult here in this period just before I turn over the responsibilities of my office next January, to tell you how much I owe to the people of this city. Never in a single instance, whether from one individual, or people gathered in groups, or two or three or more, have I had anything but the utmost of courtesy, greatest encouragement from their smiles and their words of cheer. I owe the same kind of gratitude to the Commissioners and to all the officials of the District—the policemen of every type, the Park, and the White House, and the City Police—the firemen—all of them who have helped to make so many occasions memorable for visiting dignitaries, and for keeping order where necessary.

So to everybody that had the slightest part, in spirit or just in friendly word, in making this occasion one to be indelibly impressed upon my memory, I say thank you with my whole heart. I hope and wish for you in the years to come a constantly growing confidence in the leadership of your country and the progress of the world, partly because of its leadership toward the goal of peace.

Thank you very much.

NOTE: The President spoke from a platform on the South Grounds following the planting of a red oak tree presented to him by Commissioner Robert E. McLaughlin on behalf of the District of Columbia.

326 ¶ Remarks at the City-County Building in Detroit. *October* 17, 1960

Mr. Mayor, members of the Common Council, and fellow Americans:

I am indeed proud to be here, to know that you have come out on a busy day to greet me and to have your Mayor and the Council present to me these mementoes which I shall cherish always.

I am delighted to come back to this city, which is of course known throughout the world as the motor capital of all the earth. I am delighted to come back because I have so many friends here and throughout the State, and I know that gathering at this convention this evening I shall have the great privilege of meeting many more of them.

Detroiters have a great right to be proud of their city, not merely because of its material accomplishments but because it is a city where people with good jobs have lived in self-respect, in decency, and in perfect awareness of the fact that all America wants to live in exactly the same way.

We are engaged in a great political struggle to determine which candidates and which parties will control Washington in the coming 4 years. I am not here as a proponent of either party or of anything else except for this one thing: I urge all our people to vote their own convictions, their own consciences, and not to be swayed by any kind of false or extreme propaganda—no matter what its source.

Along this time of a campaign, always there are extremists, people who think they can find an advantage in distorting America before the world, making it appear a people and a Nation that is evil, who do not know the truth, who do not have regard for the normal commitments of honor and decency.

I believe that anyone who is guilty in America of putting out any kind of document that tries to tear down our self-respect, which tries to make us believe that we are not trying to do the good and best things for ourselves and for the world, this is a disservice to the United States.

And I repeat, I care not from what source any such calumnies can come, but I say to the people of Detroit, as I should like to say it to all America: just be true to yourselves, and don't be misled by anyone who for any reason would seek advantage in distortions, falsehoods, and wrongdoing.

I realize that these things are only a drop in the bucket as compared to the entire program of speaking and talking and writing that is done and is accomplished in these campaigns. But anything that attempts to degrade America calls for something from me, as long as I live and no matter what my position may be. Because this country, above all in the world that I know of, has reason to respect itself, and by respecting itself it also respects others—and it respects those great virtues in which we all hope to live.

I came in here this morning just to thank you most sincerely for your kindness and for these presents. It is only because I am so jealous of the character of America, because America is her people and what they do, and I am so proud of that vast majority of great, hardworking Americans, that whenever there is any attempt to besmirch their record, I want to be on the side opposing it.

So I hope you will forgive me for turning a little serious in my talk when I intended, as I said, to thank you very much for your welcome, to express my pride in the invitation to come back to this spot where I was 8 years ago—and in any event, to all of you good luck and my best wishes for success and happiness ahead.

Thank you again.

NOTE: The President spoke at 12:35 p.m. from a platform on the square in front of the City-County Building. Mayor Louis C. Miriani presented him with the key to the city; Marshall M. Fredericks gave the President a small replica of his statue "Spirit of Detroit."

327 ¶ Remarks in Detroit to a Group of Business and Professional Women. *October* 17, 1960

Madam Chairman and my fellow Americans:

I am always frightened when I have the temerity to face an audience of women, and yet never have I experienced more enjoyable meetings than I have on those occasions when I have been able to greet a convocation exactly like this one.

I recognize that you are the representatives of women of all Michigan. You represent the homes of Michigan. I often think that the function of government is to make it possible for the home to remain always what it was intended to be: the place where there is nurtured in us a love of freedom, a respect for constituted authority—and more than this, the concern of each individual in the world for every other individual. I point out that if we are not, indeed, brothers under the sonship of God, then all of this civilization of which we are so proud begins to lose meaning.

Our own Founding Fathers, in attempting to explain this new form of government which was brought so brilliantly forward in the early days, had to say, "We hold that all men are endowed by their Creator with certain unalienable rights." The point is, you were "endowed by your Creator," and this means to me that underlying all of our political institutions, indeed our entire system of government, is a deeply felt religious faith somewhere.

It matters not exactly the form that faith takes, exactly what its doctrinal tenets are, but if we don't have that belief that we have these "unalienable rights," given to us by someone more powerful than ourselves, then why should we be so respectful of each other? Why do *I* insist that my rights are as equal to those of any other citizen, and *his* are as equal to mine?

This is what I believe we mean by freedom, and because we believe in this freedom we are impelled to form and establish democratic governments—self-government.

Now all of this, as I see it, derives from the home, and one of the names that has always been applied to the women of our Nation or any other nation is that they are the homemakers.

I cannot imagine a greater responsibility, a greater opportunity than falls to the lot of the woman who is the central figure in the home. They, far more than the men, remind us of the values of decency, of fair play, of rightness, of our own self-respect—and respecting ourselves always ready to respect others.

The debt that all men owe to women is not merely that through women we are brought forth on this world, it is because they have done far more than we have to sustain and teach those ideals that make our kind of life worth while.

So, my friends, I am going to have just one word to say about the election that is coming up. About this time in every campaign, there comes forward some evil kind of propaganda, it matters not what its source may be, but this evil propaganda is trying to make someone forget that we are a Nation that loves decency, that believes in fair play, and that we are ready to vote our convictions according to the conscience of each of us.

I say that no propaganda of any kind allows you to desert your own determination to have the kind of government that you choose, and to elect the candidates that you want. This is your bounden duty, and we should never let those of evil intent besmirch the fair name of the United States by lies, distortions, and indeed every kind of crooked statement that it is possible to conceive.

As I say, always this happens, and I think that it has had very little effect in any of the elections of which I have known. I remember as far back as 1896, I carried a torch in a parade—I was 6 years old. And in that election I heard some people around in my little town carrying terrible stories about prominent figures in that election. I don't think it has ever ceased but I just pray that none of you lets himself be unbalanced by it, but sticks right behind his own ideals, his own convictions about the United States, and certainly his own opinions as to how—I have been saying "he" I should have been saying "she"—sorry—her own opinions as to how this election should come out. That is between you and your conscience, and inside the secret booth.

Now I brought up this subject down in the square, and I hope that all of you can understand how sincerely I mean it, and how honestly I mean it, because my great faith is: America is a political expression of a religious faith. We believe in integrity, in honesty, and decency, and if we ever are swayed by a loss of those, then indeed we will be in a sorry fix.

Now I express to each of you my regrets that my wife could not be with me. I will take your present to her with great glee, and of course I shall not be allowed to know what it is, because I know she is going to be the one to open it.

And I thank you for the courtesy you have paid me in meeting here, where I might greet you, express my pleasure again in being in Detroit in meeting with such a body, and wishing you—every single one of you—all the happiness, all of the satisfaction in life that you deserve as a straightforward American.

So, with that, goodbye and good luck.

NOTE: The President spoke at approximately 1 p.m. in the Ball Room of the Sheraton Cadillac Hotel in Detroit. His opening words "Madam Chairman" referred to Mrs. Dorothy S. Reynolds, chairman of the Women of Michigan Committee which sponsored the luncheon.

328 ¶ Address in Detroit at the National
Automobile Show Industry Dinner.
October 17, 1960

*President Colbert, Governor Williams, Mayor Miriani, Directors of
the Automobile Manufacturers Association, distinguished guests, and
my friends:*

Tonight, though we are in the midst of a political campaign in which
most of us are not completely disinterested, I want to speak to you in a
non-partisan spirit.

I am happy to meet with you, who are among our business and labor
leaders in America's productive enterprises. The nation admires the
material accomplishments for which you, here, have been so greatly
responsible, particularly in your own chosen field. Administrators, scientists, artists, labor, and representatives from a dozen professions have had
a part in the marvelous growth of our motor industry. I salute them all.

Yet this evening, I do not address myself solely to this particular part
or even all of the American economy. Instead I shall present to you
some reflections about our nation, our people, and the world—touching
upon truths and trends which, it seems to me, have insistent meaning
for us now and for the future.

Around the world, one of the most widely known features of the United
States today is its unprecedented wealth. But much less understood
abroad is the great spread, throughout the peoples of our nation, of the
benefits of the American system. Other peoples find it hard to believe
that an American working man can own his own comfortable home and
a car and send his children to well-equipped elementary and high schools
and to colleges as well. They fail to realize that he is not the downtrodden,
impoverished vassal of whom Karl Marx wrote. He is a self-sustaining,
thriving individual, living in dignity and in freedom. Annual family
income now averages $6,500. The Gross National Product has passed
$500 billion, and national income has soared to over $400 billion a year.

In spite of certain localities in which there is economic weakness this
level of material well-being stands in startling contrast to that of most
of the world's peoples. Yet we confidently expect that our standard of
living will continue to rise at a rate of 3 or 4 percent per year, while for

millions of others elsewhere productivity will scarcely keep pace with population growth.

In many other areas of the earth, once isolated peoples are acquiring a knowledge of the world in which we live. The poverty-stricken masses of a score of nations cannot fail, with some bitterness, to compare their lot with ours, and to that of the other industrialized and currently prosperous nations. Hundreds of millions of human beings, denied any real opportunity, out of their own resources, to bring their living standards up to respectable levels will certainly, if abandoned by others, tend to develop a feeling of helplessness, hopelessness and despair. Out of these would emerge increasing world tensions and unrest. Vast areas of resentment and turmoil, especially if combined under a despotic and aggressive dictatorship, could destroy the material prosperity we now so freely enjoy and so confidently expect to increase. Freedom would be endangered.

Clearly the economic status of others affects both our own prosperity and world peace. The more intense and widely spread becomes the resentment against poverty abroad, the more serious will become the consequent problems on our own doorstep.

I believe that the vast majority of Americans is aware of these facts and, consciously or subconsciously, is determined to make the world a better place for all.

For us, a free world leader by reasons of size, productivity and strength, the question really becomes "How are we to use our wealth and the strength and influence deriving from it?" Should we merely strive jealously to guard, in a materialistic philosophy and static isolation, the possessions we already have? Or, recognizing the dangers of inaction, are we boldly to strike out for the preservation of our cherished values of freedom, by striving to see that others may, with us, possess and enjoy them?

Since freedom is strengthened by its sharing and can be destroyed by withholding from others the opportunities also to possess it, for us there can be only one response.

How then may we best help in building the kind of world we seek?

In our search for the means by which we can best render help, we must learn more about the economies of others. I suggest, for example, that preliminary surveys should, in each case, try to pinpoint the areas in which a particular nation may be lacking. We know that indiscriminate transfers of materials and money will not suffice. But if each underdeveloped nation can, with competent technical help, discover its own special weaknesses and plan their correction, then outside help can be both effective and economically used. One of the functions of the Special Fund of the United Nations is to help develop such facts.

But complicating the problem of steady reduction of poverty in the free world is the greatest obstacle that our way of life has ever known. The principal and immediate challenger to these values is a government which hates all that we hold most dear. The challenge we face is many sided, and in each of its aspects it is intensified by the never ending threat of the use of force.

The problem is, partly, philosophic—that is, spiritual and moral. We begin all our reasoning about man's destiny and the purpose of social organization with the conviction that man, in his sonship to God, is precious as an individual and has absolutely inviolable rights. The Communists scornfully deny this belief. Marx, Engels, Lenin, Stalin, and Khrushchev have all, in turn, proclaimed that the religious view of man with dignity is false. They have taught that material factors alone are responsible for man's life and aspirations; that any means, no matter how repugnant, to achieve Communist ends, is acceptable.

The Communist philosophy denies to man the right of self-government, and herein lies another phase of the critical world contest in which we are engaged. Because of our convictions about the nature of man and his natural rights, we adhere to democratic methods. The basic political power resides with our people, and the decisions of government are their decisions. Since, in the Communist view, man possesses no natural rights, in theory all power is vested in the state—in practice, in the hands of a few elite members of the ruling party. The people are regimented. They know only what their rulers want them to know; they do only what their rulers tell them to do. Whether they live at peace or are forced into war is decided by an omnipotent few.

But these two aspects of the struggle, obvious to us, are deliberately obscured by vicious Communist propaganda. Communists know that men and women whose minds have been conditioned by hunger, are tempted to follow any system that promises—no matter how falsely—a better life. Starving people can be brought to look with envious eyes at the Communist system which, hiding the price its people must pay in loss of individual freedom, has made in a few short years violent but effective strides in the production of foods, goods and armaments.

Where individual income may be as little as 50 or 100 dollar a year, where population increases more rapidly than production, where the major rewards of enterprise are reaped by a relatively few, the doctrine of communized production is seductive.

Viewed uncritically by those who allow the great fundamental philosophical and political differences to be obscured, the comparison between the free and the communistic systems assumes a false simplicity.

When impoverished peoples and nations look, with envy, at the economic achievements of the Soviet Union, they make one serious mistake: in their impatience with the slowness of their own progress, they tend to confuse their particular system of private enterprise with that of the United States. They are not fully aware of the basic factors of America's growth. Many things and forces have molded our national experience, and each has often been cited as the touchstone of our success. Yet none of them belongs exclusively to us. America has no monopoly on the prime movers of progress.

An abundance of natural resources, a system of private, competitive enterprise, a physical size and political system that insure a great free trade area, a way of life based on the bedrock of deep religious commitment, a massive dynamic educational system, and the great thrust of a hybrid energy derived from many cultures—all these we have.

Beyond these, one is of special importance. It is our national social conscience. Lack of knowledge, abroad, concerning it, is largely responsible for the erroneous concept that many have of the American system of production and distribution.

Relatively few nations have the socially conscious type of private enterprise that we enjoy. Here private enterprise, with minimal intervention by government, strives to benefit all the people. Now this was not always so but the whole philosophy and spirit of our historic enterprise have led us through evolutionary changes which have given us our present socially responsive, and responsible economic system.

So while we depend primarily upon the initiative of the individual, for economic and social progress, yet what the people cannot do for themselves, they expect their government to undertake in the degree demonstrated as necessary. The share of public enterprise has necessarily increased with the growing complexity of our lives. The costs of national defense, promotion of the general welfare, and other aspects of public effort by Federal, State and local governments mount with the years; government expenditures at all levels now approximate $130 billion a year. This means that nearly one-third of our total national income is taken in taxes and spent for public purposes.

Parenthetically, I should here remark that one of our greatest internal problems is to see to it that we maintain the health and strength of our private competitive system, including always the stability of its currency.

All the public services, with defense in the first line priority, must be financed by our free economy. If government costs become greater than we can meet now, in the most prosperous period of our history, then either we must disastrously go deeper in debt—or take so much in taxes that the economy will lose the ability to maintain the dynamism that it must have for continued growth. Only a steadily growing economy, and one devoid of harmful inflation and mushrooming debt, can support our ever-increasing number of public services.

Now to return to my theme: in many countries of the free world private enterprise is greatly different from what we know here. In some, a few families are fabulously wealthy, contribute far less than they should in taxes, and are indifferent to the poverty of the great masses of the people. Broad purchasing power does not, therefore, exist, even for the domestic products of the nation. A country in this situation is fraught with continual instability. It is ripe for revolution. The mass of the people want and demand a change for the better, and hence two questions arise: First, will reform come in a peaceful, orderly way, or violently with ensuing chaos? Second, will essential reform be within a system of private enterprise, or will production be socialized?

The Communist propagandists, playing their Pied Piper's tune, tempt the disadvantaged to believe that Communism is the only way. Thus, they boast that the Soviet Union will soon outstrip even the United States in production.

We must continue to try to get the underprivileged to look behind this claim.

It is not surprising that productivity is now increasing at a faster rate in Russia than it is in the United States. Indeed, it would be surprising if this were not so, for the Bolsheviks started, some forty years ago, at a very low level, and since then have channeled all production according to political need. By imitation and seizure, the Kremlin has been able to use many advanced practices developed over the years by free world scientists and technologists. But even so, with three times as many people engaged in agriculture, for example, Russia is producing less food and fiber than is the United States. Russian industrial production is less than half as great as ours. Only in defense production does Russia approach us—and let me emphasize: even in this, she does not exceed us.

Yet even if we accepted the claim that a communized system will eventually equal our productivity—which, of course, we do not—we would still reject it. For a complete communization of the means of production will succeed only under a dictatorship. We would prefer poverty in freedom to riches in slavery.

But, my friends, how fortunate it is that this is not the choice.

If the free nations will recognize the need for, and practice effective cooperation among themselves, they can make certain of their common security in freedom and advance their common prosperity.

Not so many years ago we felt we could keep safely to ourselves. But now our economy has become interdependent with that of many other nations. Modern transportation and communication have narrowed continents and oceans, and modern capabilities for destruction have wiped out the last shreds of safety in isolation.

Understanding these truths, the United States since World War II has devoted much of its time and energy, and has given with unprecedented generosity of its resources, in helping to protect freedom and to promote rising levels of well-being in all nations wishing to be independent and free.

There can be no retreat from this course.

But changing situations call for new thinking and action, more study of priorities.

First, it becomes urgent that every nation of the free world do all it can to advance itself and bear its own appropriate responsibility to all the other nations of that family. This means that there must be a new, true spirit of common dedication to freedom pervading the relationships of all free nations.

It has no doubt been necessary in the postwar years that the United States be the leader in providing assistance to the free world. But all these nations must realize that our resources are not unlimited; yet more must be done.

If the Free World Community is to persevere and prosper, every one of the nations must contribute to the total cooperative enterprise to the utmost of its ability. No nation is so rich or strong that it dares to stand aloof. No nation is so poor that it cannot make a vital contribution. All must share in forming the principles and carrying out the total program for the search of peace with justice and ever-rising levels of human well-being. While all will properly work in their own self-interest, they must also act on a commitment for the common good.

Another new action is called for: as each of the nations of the free economy examines its own actions and unflinchingly takes the greatest possible responsibility for its own economic advance, it must make certain that the blessings of production benefit all its people, not only a favored few. The internal revisions found necessary must be undertaken by each nation promptly and peacefully. Delay incites violence, and not only retards the achievement of domestic goals, but also causes damage to all free nations, as we have lately witnessed.

I do not say these things complacently. I know, as you do, that we in the United States have many improvements to make, and we know the dangers inherent in being self-righteous and content. We do not preach— we cooperate to produce the moral, intellectual and material strength needed in the free world.

Since time began, opulence has too often paved for a nation the way to depravity and ultimate destruction. Rich, sluggish societies have put comfort, ease and luxury ahead of spiritual vigor, intellectual development and the energetic pursuit of noble goals. The ancient civilizations of Egypt, Greece, Rome and more recently the splendid court of Louis XV fell thus, each having developed a false sense of values and its people having lost their sense of national destiny.

This could be a threat to the United States but for the fact that we are not motivated by materialism. We hold dear the things of the spirit and the intellect. Our ideals of freedom, democracy, human dignity and social justice shine through all our institutions. These are the supreme purposes of our people and the motivating force of our government.

Our own weaknesses must be understood and corrected. We have problems of crime, juvenile delinquency, physical and mental health, deficiencies in education, slum housing, and racial and religious discrimination—all of which call for massive attacks. This we shall always try to do, but not by government alone, rather by localities and by an informed and aroused citizenry. These matters are peoples' problems and must be met by a broad peoples' effort.

The stop-watch of history is running. The race is on to see whether the material and spiritual needs of the world will be better met through dictatorial control, communized enterprise, immorality and inhumanity, or through freedom, private enterprise, and cooperative action, inspired by the concepts of morality and respect for human dignity. This emphasizes the necessity in every free nation to have leaders of integrity, understanding, strength, compassion, and patience.

In our nation we want men who keep us alert to the priorities toward which all efforts should be directed. They must sustain policies needed to keep our economy strong, while at the same time fulfilling the nation's domestic and foreign responsibilities—especially that of defense. Such leaders are needed in governmental, industrial, labor, political, educational, cultural and moral areas.

Of special concern to this audience is leadership in industry, including particularly, labor-management relationships and responsibility.

We properly cherish the American system of labor-management relations and collective bargaining. It has many unique characteristics, not the least of which is its virtual independence of governmental interference. This is a great strength, for it constantly encourages labor and management to grow in self-reliance and responsibility. These are important factors in our national greatness.

But just as some other elements of our national life are today being sorely tested, so is our labor-management system on trial. Questions have arisen as to whether it can continue effectively to meet the complex problems of modern industrial society; whether it can provide the necessary acceleration in vital production areas; whether it can control the wage-price relation in ways that will permit world competition and are fair to labor, management, consumers, and the nation; whether it can use with maximum efficiency the increasingly complex technology our scientists and engineers are designing; or whether because of self-interest labor and management, unmindful of the general good, and the essentiality of constantly growing strength, will fail to do what must be done.

My friends, only yesterday I read in the newspaper a statement made by a professor—an economist, I believe—at least he is said to be one—

and he made this statement: "Capitalism as we know it is merely a step in the inexorable march from feudalism to socialism." I do not pretend to quote him exactly, but that was the tenor of his words.

We have gone through several phases in the development of labor-management relations.

The phase we are in now calls for a supreme effort on the part of both to conduct their affairs with ever-increasing responsibility for the national welfare.

We can, we must banish poverty.

But we cannot, if labor and management behave as adolescents instead of adults—not if they ignore the national welfare by deadlocking for protracted periods with painful effects upon the economy before composing their differences.

No longer can this nation permit either group to drag its feet in adopting preventive measures for the prompt settlement of industrial disputes.

Two Irishmen were riding up a hill on a tandem bicycle. When they barely made the top, the front rider jumped off, mopped his brow, and gasped about the ordeal of the climb: "Begorrah," he said, "it was so steep I thought we'd never make it." Whereupon the rear rider added: "And faith if I hadn't kept my foot on the brake, I think we'd have rolled backwards."

The obvious point is that the task of climbing above the lower slopes of human achievement in our highly industrialized society calls for a communion of purpose and effort, not mutual antagonism.

For the American people, I say to you of management and to the leaders of labor that there must be an ever-increasing understanding of the total national interest, of its vital needs at each moment in history, and of the historic mission in which it is engaged. Differences of opinion are natural and good, but there is no room for mutual distrust, or bitterness. Labor and business leaders must sit down in a calm atmosphere and regularly discuss—far removed from the bargaining table—their philosophy, their needs, and, above all, their common responsibility to this free nation.

Your future and the future of our country are dependent on the success you of business and of labor have in this matter. Labor-management statesmanship is today as imperative as labor-management bargaining.

In speaking this way, I assure you I don't mean to scold. Frankly, I have been amazed and highly delighted at the progress that I have seen made in the last few years in the fields I have been discussing. I say to you that no single one of us can escape the responsibility, though, for bettering this relationship.

Finally, in a larger sense, our nation's leaders in all fields must deeply believe in the brotherhood of man—the nobility of a democratic people exercising the political power. They must have the vision and stature neither to give up our national commitment to the rightness of freedom nor—even under great duress—to forget that the freedom of the individual is an essential source of our vitality.

I am grateful that in these past eight years our nation has been spared war, has been steadily growing in its total strength, and, under the most trying circumstances, has been working for world order. Moreover, as I peer down the lane of years ahead, I express my unshakable faith that new leaders will, through their character, experience, judgment and ability, lead our nation steadily to greater heights and closer to a cooperative and just peace in freedom.

Good night—and thank you.

NOTE: The President spoke at 9:30 p.m. in Cobo Hall in Detroit. His opening words referred to L. L. Colbert, President of the Automobile Manufacturers Association, Governor G. Mennen Williams of Michigan, and Mayor Louis C. Miriani of Detroit.

329 ¶ Remarks at a Republican Rally at the Minneapolis-St. Paul International Airport. *October* 18, 1960

Mr. Chairman, Your Excellencies, and my fellow Americans:

I am delighted to come back to the Twin City area, and I am happy that I have the opportunity to go over to Red Wing this morning to dedicate a very fine new bridge that will span a river between Wisconsin and this State.

It is absolutely correct that the people of Minnesota had a very great part in deciding for me that I should lay aside the military career in which I had so long lived, and offer myself for the Presidency—or for the candidacy for the Presidency in 1952. The write-in vote of that year was more effective than anything else—certainly far more effective than all the arguments that the politicians and political leaders brought to me over in Paris—and your Congressman Judd was one of them that came. Now in his own right he is very persuasive, but not quite so persuasive as the fact of so many Americans—finding my name nowhere else, many of them putting it in just as "Ike," which again pleased me.

So as I look back over these 8 years, I would be very much too modest to say that I have been responsible for the great advances of these 8 years, but I do want to say to you I am grateful that they have taken place. With national income, national product, employment—everything that you can think of—up dramatically over these 8 years, it is idle to say that this country is not proud of itself and doesn't hold its head up with self-respect in any place in the world.

We are looking forward to leaders who will carry forward, enlarge upon, and improve the programs that have been followed for the past 8 years. Those programs which have been developed have not always been completely successful. They have been modified by others, but as long as we are on the right track, with determination to secure ourselves in the world, to lead other people into an opportunity for enjoying freedom—as long as we pay our bills, and be solvent as a nation, then we are doing those things that must be done, and at the same time bringing to the people of the United States greater opportunities in the whole fields of health and education and welfare than they have ever had before

So I say, these programs have not yet been completely successful; indeed they never will be—we are human—but they are going to be improved under the leadership that you people now have the right and the opportunity to choose.

And I am myself grateful for all the help that you people have given me, and you have given me help unconsciously at times, when you have simply gone about your business, refusing to panic under fear-mongering people who like to peddle gloom—you have gone and done your business like sturdy, human Americans, and not like fearful vassals of some other kind of government.

I think that every single one of us has reason to be prouder today of his country than he was 8 years ago—and I certainly am. And the fact that all of you people would come out on what I am told is the first bad day of the Minneapolis-St. Paul fall weather, to come out today to give me a chance to greet you and to say thanks to you, means to me that you believe that this country has not been so badly off as some would like to believe.

So thank you very much, and I hope most of you will come to the inauguration to see the next man inaugurated as President—the man of our choice.

Goodbye.

NOTE: The President's opening words "Mr. Chairman" referred to Leonard L. Lindquist, chairman of the civic committee for the President's visit.

330 ¶ Remarks at the Dedication of the Hiawatha Bridge, Red Wing, Minnesota. *October* 18, 1960

Mr. Chairman, Congressman Quie, Governor Freeman, Mayor Rardin, Senator Humphrey, Congressman Judd, Lieutenant Governor Nash, Congressman Johnson, and my fellow Americans:

I welcome the opportunity to revisit Minnesota and to attend these ceremonies here in Red Wing. It is a real experience to stand here near the head of Lake Pepin and contemplate the contours and rugged beauty of this part of the upper Mississippi Valley. This area through which Father Hennepin passed almost three centuries ago, and known for such romantic figures of the past as Red Wing, Wabasha, and Winona, fills a large page in the history of America.

The dedication of this great new bridge across the Mississippi is another effective example of Federal-State partnership in meeting both local and national needs. Hiawatha Bridge, now spanning the Father of Waters, is a part of the Federal-State highway program. While this particular partnership dates back over 40 years, to 1916, it assumed a tremendous new work load in 1956 with the enactment of the Federal Aid Highway Act—a program which Vice President Nixon first publicly presented on my behalf at the 1954 Governors' Conference.

I am proud of this program for a number of reasons:

First, it is financed on a sound pay-as-you-go basis.

—It gives the States primary responsibility and initiative within their own borders.

—The program will eventually build 41,000 miles of interstate highways. Already, in the few years since its inception, 12,000 miles of high-ways have been built or are presently under construction.

And more important than all of these things, when the Interstate System is completed, it is estimated that it will save 4,000 lives every year.

And so I salute all those in Minnesota, Wisconsin, and across the Nation, who have made this partnership the efficient and effective union it is today.

And now may I dwell a moment on the name of this useful but equally handsome structure. I am not thinking of the Hiawatha in that charming legend of Longfellow's poem in which I found such enchantment when I read it as a boy. Today, it is the real Indian, Hiawatha, not the poetic legend, that I find so meaningful and whose work seems to me so relevant to the season of history that is now upon us.

The American Indian Chief Hiawatha is said to have lived about 400 years ago. But his deeds in the 16th century in what was then Stone Age America, are strikingly reminiscent of the work we are undertaking today. Except that his work was carried on four centuries back, it would today, in a different and wider scope, be noted by our daily newspapers and excite discussion throughout the world.

Hiawatha was a founder of a United Nations organization in America.

His United Nations or League of Nations had five members. They were the Iroquois tribes. He undertook the organization of a permanent league for the purpose of stopping for all time the shedding of human blood by violence. The constitution Hiawatha championed had as its founding principles, justice, righteousness, and power, or authority, and was intended to "safeguard human life, health, and welfare." Wisely, it did not limit membership in their United Nations to the five Iroquois tribes. The founding nations proposed for themselves and their successors the great task of gradually bringing into their organization to preserve peace, in the words of the constitution quoted: "all the known tribes of men, not as subject peoples, but as confederates." The end of that quotation.

Hiawatha's league failed, though for several generations it was remarkably successful in the achievement of its objectives. But failure does not dim the validity of his idea. Indeed it demonstrates the timelessness of mankind's desire for peace.

Hiawatha's experiment had an historical repetition in the sad fate of the League of Nations, founded in this century at the close of World War I. In retrospect we realize that there had been for the League of Nations insufficient intellectual preparation for such a world system. Its purposes were admirable but no firm ideology existed to sustain it.

We must not through lack of faith or understanding so endanger the United Nations of our own time.

Humankind has painfully discovered that peace with justice cannot be had merely by proclaiming a charter of confederation, no matter how skillfully devised, any more than freedom can be sustained by mere ritualistic worship of the concept of liberty. It must be undergirded by understanding, dedication, sacrifice, and effective machinery.

The problem has always been—in Hiawatha's time as in ours—to channel governments into peaceful ways, to build institutions that make peace easier and war more difficult and eventually impossible.

Such institutions we are now patiently building under the United Nations. One such example is an international police force.

All of us must struggle ceaselessly for the success of the United Nations; we must support its ideals and its operations. From this commonwealth of nations there must be eliminated the causes of war. A concomitant task is to banish poverty and disease, which have so much to do in disturbing the peace.

Day by day it becomes more clear that our faith in the United Nations is justified—that the system under which it operates is valuable in seeking solutions, for turning heat into light, and for keeping the true desires of nations and of peoples exposed to world opinion.

On Monday of next week—United Nations Day—we celebrate the 15th birthday of this organization. This is a time for reaffirming in unmistakable terms our determination that this time our effort to find peace through cooperation shall not fail.

In the 8 years I have occupied my present office, several truly remarkable achievements have been gained through this organization.

For example:

—America's atoms-for-peace proposal, under United Nations auspices, has become a reality and is gradually making its influence felt throughout the world.

—The Suez crisis in 1956 was resolved through the United Nations.

—The 1958 crisis in Lebanon was dealt with successfully when, through the United Nations, we sent our troops to the Middle East and then promptly withdrew them when the situation so warranted.

—Since early 1957 the United Nations' Emergency Force has effectively stopped the dangerous raids and reprisals in the Gaza Strip which continually threatened the peace of the Middle East.

These are merely a few sporadic instances. The great and sustained contribution of the United Nations is the opportunity it affords for composing, through discussion, mutually antagonistic viewpoints.

Today, my friends, truth and freedom and peace are forced to fight for survival. We must strengthen the United Nations as the great forum for ventilating differences, for the opportunity to present the truth, and for seeking workable compromises among our respective societies.

I say again, we can write a recipe for international cooperation and justice, but it cannot become a reality until we live it.

We dare not stumble. We must prepare our citizenry and our children intellectually for the task of sustaining the United Nations. Noble ideas must be supported by education and hard work. Unless we surrender to the possibility of being thrown back to the age of flint and steel, we will use wisely every instrument and means at hand to find peace with justice.

Only through the collective force of a strong and informed public opinion, united in its belief in the free spirit, shall we succeed. With such intellectual strength and spiritual faith, we shall not fail. To your hands and to the hands of your children, I commend this task. Indeed, that task can never be called completely finished, for peace, like freedom, will always demand the price of vigilance. I pray that this structure bridging a river between two commonwealths of our nation, and its name may ever symbolize the purpose of forging and sustaining indestructible bonds between free peoples.

Thank you very much.

NOTE: The President spoke at 10:45 a.m. from a platform erected at the intersection of Main and Broad Streets in Red Wing. His opening words referred to Henry A. Swanson, Jr., program chairman for the Hiawatha Bridge Opening Committee, U.S. Representative Albert H. Quie and Governor Orville L. Freeman of Minnesota, Mayor Harry Rardin of Red Wing, U.S. Senator Hubert H. Humphrey and U.S. Representative Walter H. Judd of Minnesota, Lieutenant Governor Philleo Nash and U.S. Representative Lester R. Johnson of Wisconsin.

331   ¶ Statement by the President Concerning the Agreement With Canada on the Water Resources of the Columbia River Basin.   *October* 19, 1960

IT IS with pleasure that I announce basic agreement in the negotiations, initiated in January of this year, between the United States and Canada looking toward the formulation of a treaty for the cooperative development of the water resources of the Columbia River Basin.

The negotiators have transmitted to the two governments a joint report, dated September 28, recommending the basis upon which the drafting of a treaty should proceed. For the Government of the United States I have today approved that report and am making it public herewith. Prime Minister Diefenbaker is today making a similar announcement on behalf of the Government of Canada.

The agreement is heartening proof that two neighboring nations sharing a common resource can sit down together and plan a mutually advantageous development. In these days of international tensions, not the least important aspect of these negotiations is the example they provide for the resolution of international problems through a process of mutual examination and mutual accommodation of views which has traditionally characterized relationships between Canada and the United States.

The translation of this basic agreement into a draft treaty will now be undertaken by the negotiators of the two Governments.

NOTE: The statement was released at Palm Springs, Calif., together with the joint report of the two Governments (6 pp. and annexes, mimeographed) and a White House statement summarizing the report and the benefits to be derived from the proposed development of the Columbia River Basin.

332   ¶ Address in San Francisco to the Commonwealth Club of California. *October* 20, 1960

President Graybiel, Mayor Christopher, and my fellow Americans:

To say that I am grateful for the cordiality of the welcome given to me today by this lovely City and its people, is a sheer understatement. My heart is full with thanks to all.

I am glad to be here this evening to sustain your perfect score of having as a speaker, every President of the United States since this Club was founded at the beginning of the Century. I sincerely hope that my appearance gives you no reason to abandon the practice.

Moved by a wisdom, developed out of experience, the organizers of this Club devised for their new creation a noble and necessary purpose—better government in their State. Its energizing spark was the belief that—and I take these words from the document of the time: "California suffers greatly because the best elements of the population fail to cooperate for the common good as effectively as the bad elements cooperate for evil purposes." The dedication of that group, and the unremitting efforts of its membership to pursue the course of sound government have remained undimmed for the almost six decades of the Club's existence.

The word commonwealth signifies a group united by common interests. But equally significant is the fact that in the political realm, a commonwealth as Mr. Webster defines it, has come to mean generally, if not always, an association based upon free choice.

Tonight I shall try to apply to some aspects of the world of international affairs the founding principles of this organization—that this State suffered because of the failure of some elements to cooperate as effectively for good as others did for evil.

No groups, no matter how well-intentioned, can cooperate fruitfully unless there is first established a firm basis of common understanding. This the founders of your Club recognized, by noting that one of the great difficulties was that different groups in California did not know each other—they were separated at that time by wide areas—and they also distrusted each other.

Just as the California of 1903, the year your Club was founded, was a far cry from the Commonwealth of California today, so the world as we turned into the Twentieth Century is scarcely recognizable as the one we know in 1960.

The multiplication of differences and problems before the international community recalls an old alumnus who returned to visit his college after a half-century's absence. Delighted to find one of his old physical science professors still teaching, he was amazed to find him still using the same old questions on examinations that he employed 50 years before. "Why is this?" the alumnus wanted to know. "Very simple," answered his former teacher, "The questions are the same, but the answers always become different!"

So today, instead of 53 members in the family of nations, we have 106. Instead of 1½ billion people in the world, we have 2½ billion; instead of weaponry whose maximum range was a few thousand yards, we have nuclear tipped missiles that can hurtle 9,000 miles to bring wholesale death and destruction. Parenthetically, in this particular field, our marvelous progress is not measured in decades. Our scientists and government have brought us in a few years from a position of former neglect and indifference to a level of extraordinary efficiency and strength. Here is an example of the absurdity of the allegation that America and its economy and its progress are static. I point out that now we spend on long range ballistic missiles 10 million dollars a day— every day—more than all the entire aggregate of all the expenditures for this purpose in all the years from 1945 to 1952. This example could be repeated in a dozen fields.

In 1903 man was still earthbound except for the exploits of a few adventurous balloonists and the Wright brothers, who made their historic flight in December of that year. Today, man-made objects whirl around the sun independent of the earth's movements—and the same ones will continue to do so for a future measured in millennia. 1903 was the year of the first automobile crossing from San Francisco to New York. It took 64 days—just seven less than it took Columbus to sail from Spain to America. Now it is not uncommon for air travelers to cross the country twice in a single day.

In the early years of this century, the only impression most voters ever received of a Presidential candidate came to them from a printed page; now an electronic miracle brings his voice and his face into forty million living rooms across the land.

On all fronts, there have been wrought on the earth great changes that are in themselves important, some almost miraculous—similar changes are now extending into the celestial regions as well.

Now in contemplating these great changes and the problems that have followed in their wake, it is essential that we recognize two important truths:

First, almost no problem arising between nations today is strictly bilateral.   Whether we consider the difficulties arising out of the relation-ships between Israel and the Arab States or the necessity for our recent embargo on most exports to Cuba, inevitably other nations are affected. We cannot conceive today of an international community operating as a system of bilateral partnerships travelling in unordered and reckless orbit. Every arrangement we effect with another nation, whether political, com-mercial, or even cultural, seems inevitably to have an impact on other societies.   Some degree of world coordination and cooperation obviously becomes necessary.

The recognized need for a cooperative international community was responsible for the founding here in this City of the United Nations in 1945.   It has been, in some areas, remarkably successful—yet, as in the early days of California, we have found that the mere existence of an appropriate organizational mechanism cannot maintain the law, order and progress so much desired.   In the United Nations we have a Charter and agreements supposed to insure order and avoidance of conflict, but these can be successful only as the understanding and dedication of the members become equal to the task.

A second important truth is that the dimensions of the task that lies before us, in helping to straighten out this poor old world, are so vast and complex as to make its accomplishment beyond the capacity of leaders, governments and peoples except those of experience, inexhaustible strength, patience, understanding and faith.

The supreme need of this Century is to find a way to produce an effec-tive international order, and the most obvious way to do this is through improvement of the United Nations.   Certainly the way is not through domineering empires, the rise and fall of which the world has witnessed for the past five thousand years, but through a free and mutually bene-ficial association of nations.   To realize such an international order, of course, great leadership is required.

It must be a leadership that conceives of nations as partners and equals. It must be leadership that accepts the responsibility of power, but one that exercises it in a spirit of trusteeship, through just and patient proc-esses of mutual adjustment.   It must always base policies upon a clear identification of long-range common interests.

Now upon America has fallen the heavy responsibility of providing this kind of leadership.

Unmistakably we are called upon at this precise moment in the course of human events to renew and revitalize our efforts to insure the health and strength of a mighty, international, commonwealth.

Our own conception of an ordered international community conforms roughly to our own political system.

The American system presupposes full information and active participation by every citizen in the processes of both local and Federal government. The more nearly universal this informed participation, the healthier and stronger is our government, our nation's policies, and our entire social structure.

In our complex industrial society, no thoughtful person would contend that every citizen can become truly informed on so many and such perplexing problems of domestic policy as those involving defense, social services, taxation, employment, public debt, budget, and inflation. Yet on each of these subjects, there is first hand information and personal experience available in almost every sector of our nation and, as a consequence, the average of general understanding is reasonably high.

But achievement of a satisfactory level of understanding is far more difficult in the field of foreign affairs.

Consider, for example, Korea, Indochina, the Suez Canal, Quemoy and Matsu, the Middle East, the turmoil in the Caribbean, the Berlin difficulty, the economic development of India, or the fifteen newly developing nations in Africa.

To extend the range and fullness of understanding on foreign affairs heroic efforts are made here at home by news-gathering and news-distributing agencies, and by great numbers of private foundations, as well as by study, research and educational institutions. But because no substantial segment of our population has had first hand experience in international affairs, these particular problems are far more likely to excite our emotions and prejudices rather than to inspire a painstaking search for all the facts pertaining to a problem and their relation to each other.

Yet every citizen is becoming more and more vitally affected by the issues of foreign policy, and his need for knowledge grows correspondingly greater.

We cannot anticipate any hasty or simple solution to such a large and complicated problem. But no matter is more urgent than the establishment of an effective working relationship between the American people and their government for the conduct of foreign affairs and assuring the nation's security. This problem completely overshadows, at this period of our history, any other we face.

As we push ahead to strengthen the partnership of the citizen with his government, there are, as I see it, some pitfalls to be avoided.

First, we must not be afraid to look at ourselves honestly. We must steadily maintain critical self-examination. Our nation must always concern itself with any failure to realize our national and legitimate aspirations.

But while maintaining a healthy critical insight, let us not be misled by those who, inexplicably, seem so fond of deprecating the standing, condition, and performance of the entire nation.

Surely we must avoid smugness and complacency. But when in the face of a bright record of progress and development, we hear some misguided people wail that the United States is stumbling into the status of a second-class power and that our prestige has slumped to an all-time low, we are simply listening to debasement of the truth.[1]

Now related to this irresponsible practice of defacing the true American portrait, is the development of an almost compulsive desire to make counterfeit comparisons, especially between our nation and others.

Because of differing backgrounds and cultures such comparisons rarely contain any validity whatever. The economic and social statistics of a nation cannot be conveniently compared like Olympic track records.

Consider a country—the Soviets, for example—through a violent upheaval, rich in natural resources and abundantly stocked with manpower that suddenly emerges from a strictly feudal agrarian society into a nation with an expanding and centrally controlled industrialism. What about

---

[1] On the same day the White House made public the following statement by Mansfield D. Sprague, chairman of the President's Committee on Information Activities Abroad:

"A newspaper story today with respect to the activities of the President's Committee on U.S. Information Activities Abroad is grossly in error.

"In the first place this Committee has made no report. In the second place it has made no findings. In the third place, while it is true that this Committee is concerning itself with ways and means of improving Government activities in the international information field, the Committee has made no conclusions as to the status of U.S. prestige abroad, and statements that it has done so are completely erroneous. That is not the business of this Committee. So much for that.

"Speaking personally, in my considered judgment, based on all the facts of which I am aware, the United States is today the most respected nation on the face of the earth and its prestige is preeminent."

its rate, its rate of economic growth? Obviously the tempo of its economic growth can, for a time, leap ahead at a rate faster than a nation which had long since become highly industrialized.

If a village has a single telephone—which in many cases in the world it does—or even less, the acquisition of another in a single year is a 100% increase in growth. In a mature society such increases are necessarily measured in fractions of the whole.

Now in a broader sense any attempt at comparison between national patterns of economic organization leads to unfortunate and widespread misunderstandings. The issue today in the supreme effort to build a thriving international community that can live in peace with justice, is not merely capitalism versus socialism.

We believe that our free and socially responsible enterprise has demonstrated definite advantages over an economy based upon a socialistic pattern of organization. But we do recognize that those nations whose particular problems lead them to adopt a socialist economy should not be condemned for doing so.

What we do contend is that the issue today is not capitalism versus socialism, but rather democracy versus dictatorship—the open society against the closed and secret society.

Recognition of this fact compels us to warn newly developing nations of the perils of authoritarianism lest they gravitate toward communist control because of the seductive promises of immediate benefits.

So we see the vital importance of having the free world understand the true basis of the world struggle.

To return to our own country the problems before us in the conduct of foreign affairs involve an endless flow of concrete decisions upon specific issues.

The difficulties involved are infinite—they arise hour by hour in some instances; day by day or week to week in others. Each problem, of course, will have to be met by those charged with the particular sphere of responsibility. But though this work is one of the duties of government, the citizenry cannot abandon its inherent function of critical, self-examination of performance.

All of us must see that the policy decisions of our government officials are responsive to the needs, objectives, values, and historic tendencies of the American people. One vital purpose is to see that while meeting the requirements of foreign affairs, we simultaneously sustain our domestic institutions and traditional liberties. For example, to further progress in our country, and indeed throughout the free world, we must be certain that there is no cheapening and no debasement of our currency. Tasks like this impose a heavy, but necessary, strain upon our citizenry.

It calls for experienced and mature leadership.

This is not a task for a leadership that insists upon agitating small points to the neglect of the nation's true good.

This is not a task for a leadership that sees the nation as a giant supermarket for the distribution of special favor.

This is not a task for any leadership that scorns fiscal integrity and sees no national disadvantage in deficit spending.

Nor is it a task for leadership that, falsely trumpeting an incompetence within the body politic, assigns to a centralized government the responsibility for all progress.

It is a task for leadership which understands that our job today is to intensify the beliefs that made America great; leadership which recognizes that sound policy arises out of the inner wisdom and experience of countless communities and people throughout America fully capable, as always before, of responding to a summons to greatness.

To return now to the theme of your organization which I have borrowed tonight—the importance of cooperating effectively for good— I repeat that the central need in all international affairs today is to forge a commonwealth of nations—a United Nations that will steadily strengthen the bonds and build the structure of a true world community that can live in peace with justice.

Before us still is the opportunity to take by firm, steady steps, practicable action toward disarmament.

The position of the United States remains as I have often stated, that our appropriate representatives are willing to meet immediately with those of other countries to consider any feasible and enforceable proposal that will lead mankind to outlaw for all time, the terrifying tools of war. We have repeatedly made fair and specific proposals to this end—as yet the Soviets have refused to negotiate seriously on them.

In declaring ourselves ever ready to negotiate the problems of disarmament we ask only that any program advanced shall not give military advantage to a particular country and that it assures the right to inspect the armaments of other nations.

A disarmament program failing to offer such assurance is a devious device that could only result in raising, rather than decreasing, the probability of war.

Many other serious international disagreements await resolution.

We must never retreat from these purposes even in face of discouragement by the wrecking crew antics of those who want to demolish the United Nations.

We know that peace with justice is not just a matter of bringing about the absence of war. Peace is, rather, a world living its human ideals and aspirations. Moreover, there is one kind of righteous war—one we must all wage. It is against poverty, illiteracy, and disease.

This we shall do—this we propose to do—as we take up our individual tasks without subordinating the national character of our individual societies.

Because progress will not be found in a super state run by super powers.

We believe that cooperation in freedom is the way to build the necessary structure for permanent peace.

As I reflect upon the course of American history, I have full confidence that the political genius and wisdom of the American people are equal to their vital responsibility that the world has now conferred upon them.

The search for solutions will be a long one. But fortified by a conviction born of the spirit, and with a national strength unmatched by any other, I know the American people will lead the way on the greatest mission upon which we have ever embarked—the establishment of a durable peace with justice.

Thank you very much.

NOTE: The President spoke at 9:10 p.m. at the Sheraton Palace Hotel in San Francisco. His opening words "President Graybiel, Mayor Christopher" referred to Lloyd E. Graybiel, President of the Commonwealth Club of California, and Mayor George Christopher of San Francisco.

333 ¶ Remarks in San Diego Before the Inter-American Congress of Municipalities.
October 21, 1960

Mayor Dail, Mayor McAllister, Senator Kuchel, and Congressmen Wilson and Utt, President Brewer Casey and Rotarians, and members of the Inter-American Municipal Congress, guests and my friends:

I am honored by this opportunity to address a few words to the Eighth Inter-American Congress of Municipalities, and to add my own welcome to that of Mayor Dail and the other United States delegates who have been your hosts these past 5 days. I have been told that you have been hard at work since the sessions began. I hope, however, that your duties have permitted you at least some time to relax and enjoy yourselves, to use this golf course, and to have a good look at the City of San Diego, its people, and the surrounding countryside.

Now this Congress is an immediate people-to-people approach to the furthering of good hemispheric relations. Our respective national governments are not involved in your special effort. It has been planned and carried out entirely by private citizens and municipal governmental officials. I give my enthusiastic support to the unique form of person-to-person understanding which these important meetings make possible. Indeed, I look forward a few days hence to the pleasure of another person-to-person contact when I meet my good friend, President Lopez Mateos of Mexico in Ciudad Acuña next Monday. And through him, I shall have the opportunity to send once more my friendly greetings to all Mexico and the Mexican people.

———

For over 20 years the Inter-American municipal organization has helped strengthen the ties of international cooperation and promoted better municipal government throughout the Western Hemisphere.

Perhaps no area attracts our common concern more than that of municipal administration. Sweeping changes are remaking and enlarging our old cities and building new ones—and so rapidly that we are hard put to keep pace with their demands. New industries spring up overnight in the most unlikely places; villages become cities whose bulging borders merge with other cities; there is an insatiable demand for more roads, surface transportation facilities, more airports, more water resources, better methods of cleaning the air, more schools, hospitals, churches, homes—the list is endless.

These conditions in turn create an endless series of problems for the cities and towns in which they occur. Providing the basic administrative services to a stabilized community is a real challenge itself. But meeting the needs of one literally exploding in all directions demands the finest qualities of imagination, dedication, and leadership, not to mention a healthy sense of humor. Yet the challenge must be met and the problems surmounted, and it must largely be done by the municipal administration working in its own field—often, it alone can effectively handle these basic relationships between the citizen and his government.

No other body has the intimate knowledge of the needs and desires of the community. None but the local official can develop the machinery and civic support needed to solve effectively the manifold problems of a busy, complex metropolis. The central and provincial governments have their own vital responsibilities to meet. They cannot and should not be burdened with tasks which can better be performed by the municipalities themselves. To require them to do so results not only in cumbersome and inefficient administration, but it immeasurably lessens the control of the municipalities over their own affairs.

Nevertheless, situations arising out of national disasters or even merely out of the dimensions of rapid municipal growth can call for cooperation among the several levels of government. In my own country, for example, a hurricane may call for the immediate and effective intervention into a city's affairs by both State and national Governments. The spreading out of a metropolitan center over the boundaries of two or more of our States produces a necessity for cooperation among the States affected. Indeed to meet such a situation we have devised operative organizations called "authorities," never contemplated by our Constitution.

Solutions to other urban problems beyond the capacity of localities to meet themselves call for credits and grants provided by State and Federal Governments which, if denied, would bring hardship to thousands of human beings. And the very nature of these problems creates another, that of determining when State or Federal help should be asked and accepted or should be rejected. I feel that in any case of doubt the help should be refused, but when the necessity becomes clear the higher governments should act promptly and effectively. Help that is accepted for a need that is not real, can damage self-reliance and self-confidence. And I assure you of my conviction that the two greatest qualities that have made this country great are self-reliance and self-confidence.

So all of you know that by and large, free, effective local government is in the common tradition of all our American Republics. It is the cornerstone of our whole structure of representative government which ranges from the town council to the national assembly. It must be strengthened by intelligent understanding of a field which grows yearly in size and complexity.

This is why meetings such as this are of such great value. By sharing our knowledge and experience on these problems which are common to us all, we strengthen the important cause of local self-government in every city in the hemisphere. There is not one of our countries which cannot profit from this example of mutual cooperation; none which cannot help the others; none which cannot be helped by the others.

By providing for this exchange of needed information and encouraging the spirit of cooperation, this Congress and its parent organization are making a real contribution to good government and good will in the Western Hemisphere. And I can think of nothing in this whole vast region that is of more importance to all our nations, large and small, than is the increasing of good will among us.

I congratulate you all on what you are doing, not only on your work in improving city government in our respective nations, but on the increasing growth of mutual understanding among our peoples thereby brought about.

I salute you and your nations, and extend to you every good wish for a pleasant and profitable session. It has been a real personal pleasure to be with you. So I thank you and say *vaya con Dios*—goodbye.

NOTE: The President spoke at 1:23 p.m. at the San Diego Country Club. His opening words referred to Charles C. Dail, Mayor of San Diego, Robert R. McAllister, Mayor of Chula Vista, U.S. Senator Thomas H. Kuchel and U.S. Representatives Bob Wilson and James B. Utt of California, and Dr. C. Brewer Casey, President of the Chula Vista Rotary Club. The Chula Vista Rotary Club was host to the Inter-American Congress of Municipalities.

334   ¶ Remarks Broadcast to the Mexican People, Ciudad Acuña, Mexico.   *October 24, 1960*

Mr. President and my Mexican friends of this lovely city:

In my journey from southern California to Houston, Texas, I could not possibly have come this close to the territory of our great country and friend here to our southward without attempting to make a call upon your President and your people.

Your President and I first met in Acapulco. We then made one resolve, to make certain that our two peoples would be greater friends than ever before, and that between us—us two—there would be a friendship that would be indestructible.

For this particular visit there are certain particular reasons. This is the 150th anniversary this year—the 150th anniversary of Mexican independence, an event I assure you that means just as much to the people of my country as it does to the people of yours.

This is also probably the last time I shall be able to visit your country and your President as long as I hold my particular office, and it was only fitting, I thought, that I should attempt to make upon your President an official call, as well as a personal one, to assure him of the high value I have placed upon the friendship that he has shown to my people and to me. And this visit gives to your great and distinguished President, and to me, an opportunity jointly to promise to your people and to our people to the northward that the Amistad Dam will be built.

We know what this will mean to people on both sides of this river, in flood protection, in production of power, and in production of more irrigated lands. But it is more than this; this is a symbol of what two countries working together in peace can accomplish. And I point out that this thing here that marks the 150th anniversary of your independence also marks the 15th anniversary of the United Nations.

We two nations have given to the United Nations a real example of how to solve their problems through peaceful negotiation, through refusing to be balked by technical difficulties, but with the spirit on both sides aimed at high and noble purposes that can bring about the kind of thing that the United Nations should do every day, every month, every year, until peace has finally been achieved in the world.

Mr. President, I thank you from my heart for your invitation that enabled me to come here and personally and officially express to you and to your people the esteemed admiration and affection of our people, and again to reaffirm to you personally my great and affectionate regard for a man whom I deem to be one of the leaders of this world, and a man who will be so useful in the United Nations to make certain that the world does progress toward peace.

[*At this point the Mayor of Ciudad Acuña, Lucina Sanchez Martinez, presented the President with the key to the city. The President's response follows:*]

Mr. Mayor:

I am honored by this gift, but I must warn you, sir, that this is not something that I intend to give up along with my office. It will be my hope, one day, to come across the bridge and unlock the gates of this city, so that I may come again to see you.

Thank you very much.

NOTE: The President's remarks, which were delivered from the balcony of the Municipal Building in Ciudad Acuña at 12:50 p.m., were also broadcast locally over the radio. His opening words "Mr. President" referred to President Adolfo Lopez Mateos of Mexico.

335   ¶ Joint Declaration by the President and President Lopez Mateos Concerning the Construction of Amistad Dam.   *October 24, 1960*

DWIGHT D. EISENHOWER, President of the United States of America, and Adolfo Lopez Mateos, President of the United Mexican States, inspired by the true friendship that binds the Governments and peoples of the United States of America and Mexico and by the fruitful cooperation that has characterized their relations;

Considering that international hydraulic works constitute one of the most valued examples of this cooperation, the bases of which were established in the Water Treaty between the United States of America and Mexico signed on February 3, 1944;

Considering that Amistad Dam will complement Falcon Dam and will form part of the system of international dams provided for in the above-mentioned treaty;

Considering that Amistad Dam will serve to control floods of the Rio

Grande, which repeatedly have caused very serious damage to border communities and agricultural areas of both countries; to provide additional waters for irrigation needs of both countries; and to permit production of hydroelectric energy as required;

Have agreed that:

The Government of the United States of America and the Government of Mexico will proceed with the construction of Amistad Dam as soon as possible after the two Governments have approved the technical recommendations that are to be made for that purpose by the International Boundary and Water Commission, United States and Mexico.

NOTE: The joint declaration was released in Ciudad Acuña.

336   ¶ Address in Houston Before the Faculty and Students of Rice University.   *October* 24, 1960

Mr. Mayor, Mr. Croneis, Mr. Brown, Mrs. Hobby, members of the faculty, student body, and friends of Rice University:

As we are all aware, there is a political campaign in progress. This meeting with you ladies and gentlemen is not intended by me to be any part of that contest. What I have to say to you this evening is representative of my own convictions and is not intended to be a disparagement to anyone. After all, there are, possibly, a few Democrats in this audience.

This evening I find myself once again in Texas, a State that has had a special and lifelong place in my memories and affections. This is the State where I was born seventy years ago; it is where I met the girl who became my wife; where I began a long career in military and civil service and where I was stationed on the day that Pearl Harbor hurled our nation once again into war.

When, in 1915, I came to join the Army at San Antonio, the alert Texas newspapers found nothing newsworthy in the arrival here of another 2nd Lieutenant of Infantry, but they properly gave much space to the completion and to the dedication of Rice Institute at Houston.

During the forty-five intervening years, the Institute, since become Rice University, has steadily added lustre to the name of her founder. It is a great personal privilege to come to this spacious campus, to see its structures of classic beauty and to pay tribute to Rice as one of America's great institutions of learning.

It is customary on occasions such as this for Age to speak to Youth, to hold up before the young, lessons from the past, to offer counsel for the future. Each generation, reflecting on its successes and mistakes, earnestly wants to bequeath to its successor a formula for a much better world than it, itself, has ever been able to produce. We have learned the futility of this, but we continue to attempt it. And so each generation is obliged to make its own way as best it can because, for one reason, it always inherits new and unforeseen problems along with whatever advantages it may have gained from its predecessors.

Now of course, a new generation is not compelled to accept its eventual responsibilities all at once. There is no clear dividing line, in point of time, between the duties and influence of any one generation and its successor. Invariably there is a gradual transition—a full changing of the guard takes years to complete. Now this is well, for the factor of experience inevitably plays an essential part in any important undertaking, but the transfer is, nevertheless, relentless and it is final. Sooner or later the day will come when the decisions which control the affairs of your community, your nation, your world, must be made by another generation—yours. The nation's future is what you make it.

Now what can you expect to find in these years of challenge and decision which lie ahead?

None of us needs to be reminded that, internationally, they will be years of unremitting struggle—for peace, for security, for freedom and for justice. With the best will in the world on the part of all sides, the peaceful resolution of basic world differences would be a most complex process.

Complicating the problem, it is inevitable that whenever one nation tries to dominate or enslave others, freedom-loving nations will always resist—and the result will be increased tension and strain. We know that the Soviet Union is using its vast power not for world betterment, but as weapons of political and economic warfare and for human enslavement.

For this basic problem of living on the same planet with the Communist bloc there is no ready-made solution.

Through our own strength we can assure that the Communists clearly appreciate the utter folly of any attempt to gain their ends by military aggression. Even they would not willingly choose suicide. In science, both of the earth and of space, we can continue our great aggregate advantages over them. Through patience we may relieve by negotiation some dangerous pressures, both local and national. Free nations, when they unite effectively, can defeat specific efforts at economic penetration and political subversion in newly developing areas.

But our experience of the past warns us not to expect miracles of the future; the road to genuine peace will be long and hard and costly.

An enormous stake lies in the less developed areas of the world. Many of these nations are old, by present standards. Others are very new. Seventeen new nations were admitted last month to the United Nations.

Yet whether they are new or old, whether from Asia, Africa or Latin America, these nations have a common problem and a common objective. All are fiercely determined to preserve their national independence and most need to break the age-old bonds of grinding poverty. These people must have hope; they must be enabled to realize their legitimate aspirations, or internal pressures may burst all bounds. Alone the progress of these people is far too slow. But with help from us and other free nations they can reach their goals, and contribute thereby to a stable and peaceful world.

We have done much in the past to help other nations, and I count our Mutual Security Program as being one of the most important, necessary and successful ventures for sustaining world peace and stability that our nation has ever undertaken. But what we and others have so far done is only a fair beginning in helping the under-developed peoples toward progress in freedom. If we abandon them, desperation could drive them to Moscow. Consequently the free world dare not fail. It must succeed—and it can do so only in true cooperation. This is an international imperative.

And this road, too, will be long and hard and costly.

Now at home there will be urgent problems that must be faced. By 1970 there will be some 35 million more Americans. They will be needing millions of new homes, 300,000 more school classrooms and as many additional hospital beds, and a veritable catalog of other essential services. Indeed, the future of America is as great as our vision.

The many necessary new jobs thus created will produce new national wealth, new security, new business. The cost will be vast.

Just to produce the plants, tools and equipment for the anticipated 13 million new jobs in 1970 will require a minimum of $140 billions of investment. Yet the gigantic yield to labor, capital and our nation will be far beyond anything that can be comprehended by those who are fearful of the future.

These commitments to the future—both at home and abroad—represent a tremendous challenge to our vision, ingenuity and our productive capacity. We can employ our resources—both material and spiritual—in ways which can bring forth a better world for all people—including ourselves. Or we can waste and dissipate them, and so lose the last clear chance in our time for freedom for all those who want it and are ready to work for it.

Our clear mission is to produce a better life in freedom for ourselves and help to do so for the world and, so doing, make the attainment of a just peace more probable. This will demand a massive, sustained, coordinated effort by all our people and by all peoples devoted to freedom.

The genius of a free people lies in the fact that they can produce such an effort by their own volition, without the coercive power of a dictatorial government. But they can do so only to the extent of their capacity for self-discipline and the subordination of selfish interests to national good. Within even the freest nation there must exist certain imperatives in policy, without which no great purpose can go forward.

Now there is little I can give you in the way of specific advice. But I suggest to you the value of three domestic imperatives which, among others, might be stated as axioms:

First—public programs—local or national—must be guided by long-term and easily recognizable goals. Short-term expediency, resulting in rapid change in effort, is a most wasteful process. It makes practically impossible the sustaining of responsible government.

Second—national solvency is mandatory to the continuance of national security, steadily rising productivity, and individual well-being.

Third—only by the maintenance of a carefully balanced system of local-Federal authority that discourages the dumping on the Federal Government of problems that can be solved close to home, can we assure continuance of the widespread liberties our citizenry has enjoyed for a century and three quarters.

Consider, then, the first of these axioms—steadiness, both of purpose and of method. Nothing is more destructive of orderly progress than wild fluctuation between the extremes of panic and complacency. It is our aim to build steadily and soundly the economic and military strength we shall need—possibly over decades—to meet, every minute, every day, our responsibilities in the momentous decade ahead. And this is not done by hasty or ill-considered actions, crash programs, efforts that stop and go like traffic at a busy intersection. This is not only costly; it is flagrantly inefficient. It betrays a myopic vision, a weakness of will and a lack of inner conviction that our long-term goals are worthy and our methods correct.

If we, today, look at ourselves in true perspective, we see a great nation—the most powerful the world has seen, with a confident, virile people, a vigorous, expanding economy. We are pursuing defense policies and programs which provide us with real security now and, if our nation remains alert and flexible in meeting changes in the world situation, will do so on into the future. Our economic health and outlook are good, and our rate of private investment is equal to the demands for needed expansion of production and facilities. Just as we need no giant new arms programs, we need no governmentally administered massive economic shots in the arm to stimulate the growth of business.

What, indeed, our economy needs for growth is less government interference in its affairs, not more. Private saving and investment—not public spending—is the real basis of economic growth.

If we resolutely and steadfastly go about our business, refusing to respond to false fears and empty promises, we will have built a firm material foundation that will sustain security, prosperity, self-respect and confidence.

One of my strongest allies in opposing centralization of power in Washington is Secretary of the Treasury Anderson, from your State.

The second imperative is solvency, measured in terms of a sound currency. The cause of freedom in the world depends critically upon the material and moral strength of the United States of America. Our continued ability to defend against Communist aggression, to help build a stable, peaceable world community, to provide abundantly for the millions of new Americans who will presently join us, all these depend upon our economy.

Now with this, all of us agree. Yet on an issue as basic as national solvency many people are misled by false arguments which would be readily transparent if applied to their own personal circumstances.

No one argues that the average person can spend what he has not earned, or that he can long continue to write checks against a bank account not covered by deposits. Yet some who readily see how these principles apply to individuals can be persuaded that they may somehow be ignored by a nation.

The Republic of Texas had its own bitter experience with deficit financing a hundred and twenty years ago. General Sam Houston is justly honored as the Hero of the Revolution, but few realize that he fought as hard for the solvency of Texas as for the independence of Texas. In his second administration he inherited a vast public debt, a currency ruined by a flood of worthless "Redbacks" and a completely demoralized economy—all caused by just one thing: unjustified deficit spending. One of the great achievements of his second administration was to redeem the nation's credit and restore order to its economy.

But today we are often told that our nation is so large and so rich that it really doesn't have to balance accounts, that a little inflation doesn't hurt; that we can spend lavishly to "stimulate growth" and make up the deficits out of some increases in the future. There is the carefree assumption that we have gone along happily during most of these recent decades without paying the full fare, and that this fine arrangement can be continued indefinitely. But the truth is that we have paid, and will continue to pay, to the tune of hundreds of billions in lost purchasing power of dollars that have shrunk to less than half the value they represented in 1939. This is inflation.

And who, in particular, has paid? I have, you have, and so have your mothers and fathers, your professors, people who own bonds and insurance policies, people drawing pensions and Social Security payments, people who have savings accounts, people who work on salaries, and this University. We have all paid. More than this, our grandchildren will pay.

Wealth, whether it be that of a nation or an individual, is the product of useful work. It can be created in no other way. It cannot be legislated, conjured or commanded into existence. And everything that is consumed must eventually be paid for by someone, in some way. Every governmental expenditure is a charge against the productive effort of the American people, and it must and will be paid, as surely as the sun rises. And to the extent that we cannot pay it out of current income, it must and will be paid out of the future. Moreover, if we fail to balance our budget and to hold our dollar at a stable value, the confidence of other nations in the United States will falter. Fiscal and monetary policies that are essentially inflationary have very grave international consequences, with serious impact on ourselves. This is a fact of life over which all the present-day advocates of heavy Federal spending, regardless of deficits, could properly reflect very seriously.

I cite a quotation from my friend, Dr. Gabriel Hauge. He says: "Living in an economy with an unstable currency is like living in a society in which no one tells the truth. The ability of modern governments to keep their money straight is an essential condition of their ability to govern."

And with that quotation I completely agree.

————

Now the third imperative of which I speak is the maintenance of State and local authority against the unhealthy growth of power in the Federal Government. Our booming population, the growth of huge metropolitan areas, the shrinkage of our countryside by rapid transport and communications—are reducing our nation to a neighborhood and creating complex new problems in cooperative living.

Some of these problems can indeed be solved only through participation by the Federal Government. This I readily concede, and I have supported many measures in which Federal cooperation was necessary to the success of State and local problems.

But I do believe deeply that every problem should be solved as close to home as it is possible to do so. Federal assistance should be requested only when the case for it is clear—and continued only for the minimum time necessary. The tendency to look needlessly to the Federal Government for help in purely local problems has been far too prevalent over recent decades, and the price has invariably been paid in terms of a steady and unwarranted Federal encroachment upon the authority of the States. For rights are inseparable from responsibility, and the State which abdicates its responsibilities in any field will surely find that it has bargained away its rights there as well.

The South has long been a staunch defender of the rights of the sovereign States—to its great and everlasting credit. And this matter has special meaning to the residents of this State which was for ten years a Republic. I counsel you to continue to guard jealously the rights reserved to your State under our Constitution—to keep your Government close to home, your local affairs out of the hands of a meddlesome, bumbling bureaucracy thousands of miles away. Weigh carefully the words of those who carelessly say "let the Federal Government do it or pay for it." For in the end it is the people—not the Government—who pay, and they not only pay in money, but in a currency far more precious—in their hard-won right to run their own affairs in their own way. This is fundamental.

––––––––––

So now I have discussed briefly:

Steadiness, solvency, balance. These may seem prosaic and uninteresting to talk about in times when people are being promised, without cost, the good life for all. Yet these unglamorous realities are the bedrock upon which all our strength is based, and the necessary precondition for the great labors we must perform both at home and abroad in the interest of world peace and progress.

Today is United Nations Day—set aside for Americans to honor the organization which has become an indispensable force for peace in a troubled world. We of the United States bear a heavy responsibility for assuring the continued success of this great experiment in international cooperation. I recently had the privilege of addressing the United Nations General Assembly, and of making certain proposals to that body on the peaceful uses of outer space, arms control, and assistance to the less developed nations, particularly the emerging States of Africa. These proposals are evidence of America's deep and continuing interest in the United Nations and its work. They are also evidence of the depth and scope of the vast unresolved problems with which the human community must deal, and to whose solution we must make our contribution.

This contribution will be measured by our capacity and our will, and its success will be assured not by a few great and valorous deeds, but rather by all of us doing a great many small tasks sensibly and well.

To you now learning and maturing in this great institution, and to your comrades of college age everywhere in the land, I can make no prophecies for which I would claim the slightest shred of validity, dealing with the future's great imponderables. But I can express to you an unshakable faith, derived and developed through years of living, in the character and capacity of young Americans, to meet life's problems as they exist or arise. On battlefields, in peaceful countrysides and in great cities, on busy campuses, I have seen America's youth developing and producing leaders that, in every quality and in every walk of life, measure up to the world's finest.

These we need in ever-growing numbers, so that through them and throughout our nation, and finally throughout the world, all people everywhere will come to understand that the oldest aspiration of mankind—peace with justice—must be provided by their governments, or their governments will be repudiated. People must meet and understand other people, and so doing make it ever more difficult for governments, responding to false prides or even worse, personal ambitions, to sustain dictatorships, foreign domination, or unjust and unworthy practices.

These things can be done—your part in bringing them to pass will be measured by the intensity of your dedication—your readiness to sacrifice.

These are the abilities and capacities I have in mind as I say—I have faith in America's young men and women, and in the future they will build.

I thank you very much indeed.

NOTE: The President spoke at 8:30 p.m. in the University gymnasium. His opening words referred to Lewis Cutrer, Mayor of Houston, Dr. Carey Croneis, Provost of the University, George R. Brown, Chairman of the Board of Trustees, and Mrs. Oveta Culp Hobby, editor and president of the Houston Post and former Secretary of Health, Education, and Welfare.

337   ¶ Telegram Accepting Invitation To Address a Rally of the Nixon for President Committee of Pennsylvania.   *October* 25, 1960

I AM HAPPY to confirm my acceptance of your invitation to join you for a dinner meeting in Philadelphia on Friday, October 28th. Looking ahead to the future of our country and to the freedom we want for our children and grandchildren the decision to be made by the American people on November eighth is, I think, one of the most important in our history.

I propose on Friday evening to give my own convictions and try to clear the air on why this is so and on the choice our fellow citizens must make. I am particularly happy that your group will include Democrats and Independents as well as Republicans.

DWIGHT D. EISENHOWER

NOTE: Winfield C. Cook and Mrs. Hilda H. Robbins, chairman and vice chairman respectively, of the Montgomery County Nixon for President Club, Norristown, Pa., had requested the President to speak on "important issues of the campaign and Vice President Nixon's qualifications to handle these issues." Their telegram was released with the President's reply. For the address in Philadelphia, see Item 341.

338 ❡ Message to President Diem on the Fifth Anniversary of the Independence of Viet-Nam. *October 26, 1960*

Dear Mr. President:

My countrymen and I are proud to convey our good wishes to you and to the citizens of Viet-Nam on the fifth anniversary of the birth of the Republic of Viet-Nam.

We have watched the courage and daring with which you and the Vietnamese people attained independence in a situation so perilous that many thought it hopeless. We have admired the rapidity with which chaos yielded to order and progress replaced despair.

During the years of your independence it has been refreshing for us to observe how clearly the Government and the citizens of Viet-Nam have faced the fact that the greatest danger to their independence was Communism. You and your countrymen have used your strength well in accepting the double challenge of building your country and resisting Communist imperialism. In five short years since the founding of the Republic, the Vietnamese people have developed their country in almost every sector. I was particularly impressed by one example. I am informed that last year over 1,200,000 Vietnamese children were able to go to elementary school; three times as many as were enrolled five years earlier. This is certainly a heartening development for Viet-Nam's future. At the same time Viet-Nam's ability to defend itself from the Communists has grown immeasurably since its successful struggle to become an independent Republic.

Viet-Nam's very success as well as its potential wealth and its strategic location have led the Communists of Hanoi, goaded by the bitterness of their failure to enslave all Viet-Nam, to use increasing violence in their attempts to destroy your country's freedom.

This grave threat, added to the strains and fatigues of the long struggle to achieve and strengthen independence, must be a burden that would cause moments of tension and concern in almost any human heart. Yet from long observation I sense how deeply the Vietnamese value their country's independence and strength and I know how well you used your boldness when you led your countrymen in winning it. I also know that your determination has been a vital factor in guarding that independence while steadily advancing the economic development of your country. I am confident that these same qualities of determination and boldness will meet the renewed threat as well as the needs and desires of your countrymen for further progress on all fronts.

Although the main responsibility for guarding that independence will always, as it has in the past, belong to the Vietnamese people and their government, I want to assure you that for so long as our strength can be useful, the United States will continue to assist Viet-Nam in the difficult yet hopeful struggle ahead.

Sincerely,

Dwight D. Eisenhower

339   ¶ Toasts of the President and the Prime Minister of Malaya.   *October* 26, 1960

Mr. Prime Minister and gentlemen:

We are gathered here today to honor the Prime Minister of the Federation of Malaya. Malaya is an independent nation of 3 years of age. In spite of its youth, it is one of our staunchest friends, and one of the partners that we value highly. It is a staunch defender of freedom in the world and individual liberty for its people. This is why I call it our partner because we are dedicated to the same principles.

To give you something of the Prime Minister's spirit and heart as he interprets it for his own people, I would hope that each of you could obtain from the State Department a copy of the speech he made when he sent the Malayan contingent to the Congo to take its part in the United

Nations' efforts in that country, and to prevent communism from taking it over. In his speech, you will read his exposition of the evils of colonialism in the past, and which he pointed out, were of the past. Now, he continued, we all face a Communist colonialism far greater in its threat to freedom and to civilization than any we have known in the past. His country, he said, is dedicated to the defeat of that kind of colonialism and to the support of freedom and peace and justice in the world.

He is the Prime Minister of the Federation. I have been receiving an explanation from the Prime Minister and from the Ambassador of just how their Federation is formed. They have a parliamentary form of government—and what we would call a President they call a King. But, their King does not have any hereditary rights; he is elected for 5 years and then his term is over. It's a little bit unique, but the principle is there: a self-governing people, people that are developing themselves economically. By the same token they are developing their self-respect, their self-confidence and their determination to be what they are now— a free people.

So, it is a great pleasure to ask you gentlemen to join me in a Toast to the King, the Supreme Ruler of the Federation of Malaya.

NOTE: The President proposed the toast at a luncheon at the White House. The Prime Minister responded as follows:

Mr. President and gentlemen:

I thank you most warmly for your very kind words and your account of my little country and our contribution towards the peace of the world. I do appreciate it most heartily.

I have come here, sir, at your very, very kind invitation. I and my friends are overwhelmed with the kindness and the warmth of your welcome. When we arrived yesterday, we were received most royally. Today, sir, you have given a banquet in my honor, with a fine gathering of gentlemen whom it is a pleasure to know. Last night, Mr. Secretary of State also gave me a most enjoyable banquet, and we had a most enjoyable evening. All these kindnesses which you have shown me, I feel have been done not only for me but for my little country.

I have said, and I repeat it here, that when I return to my country, there is a lot that I could tell my people about your American people and the kindness which you have shown us and also their appreciation of the situation at home. As I said, and as you have rightly said, we are always happy to make a little contribution towards what you are trying to do—that is to maintain peace in this world. Therefore, in spite of our smallness and in spite of the very small army we have, and having just emerged from the 12-years' war which we had, we still find time to send a little force to the Congo. I hope the action on our part is accepted in the form in which it is given, and with the intention of the aid or the idea behind it, that is, to show how much we value peace.

I realize that you have, under your constitution, to leave your office. I would like to tell you that your name is, of course, a household word even in the small and primitive houses we have in our country. The example which you have set to the world, the guidance and the leadership which you have shown and proclaimed to the world, is very, very much admired by every person, not only persons of intellect but even persons in their primitive state. And let me tell you, sir, that we feel that the example which you have set has come to stay. I feel whoever comes in your place can't help but carry on the good work which you have done.

I can only say that I wish you all the happiness in your retirement, and I wish you all the good health and all the best in the days to come.

Gentlemen, may I ask you to rise and join me in a Toast to the President.

340 ¶ Address at Ceremonies Honoring the Memory of Woodrow Wilson, Staunton, Virginia. *October 27, 1960*

Mr. Mayor, Senator Byrd, Senator Robertson, members of the Woodrow Wilson Birthplace Foundation, the President, Faculty and student body, and friends of Mary Baldwin College, and my friends:

I am indeed happy to share this platform with, and to be introduced by my old and esteemed friend, Harry Byrd. He and I share, I might add, a number of similarities in background and in viewpoint.

Both of our mothers were born in Virginia. We both entered the public service the same year—45 years ago—Mr. Byrd as a freshman State Senator, while I joined the Army as a Second Lieutenant. And though our starting points were different, our careers eventually converged across the lines of party policies to wage a campaign as allies against a common enemy, excessive costs in government. I am proud to have been able to fight for fiscal responsibility shoulder to shoulder with your distinguished Senior Senator. And I am sure that I speak for him also when I say we are both proud that your Junior Senator, Willis Robertson, could be here, because he belongs in that same fighting army.

Harry Byrd's integrity, statesmanship, and character have earned for him the respect of those dedicated to sound government. And I salute this legislative warrior, and devoutly hope that he may long continue annually to trot up the Old Rag Mountain—which he apparently does to condition himself for his service in the United States Senate.

My friends, I have come here today as Senator Byrd has said, to pay honor to the memory of a very great man, a man of ideals and high purpose, and a fighter for what he believed to be right. And I had the opportunity to visit the birthplace of my mother, born two years after Mr.

Wilson, so you can understand that this journey today is, for me, full of sentiment and deep feeling for this area in which two people who were so important in my life were born.

So we are joined here today to honor the memory of Woodrow Wilson, the seventh of the Presidents of the United States to be produced by the Commonwealth of Virginia.

Incidentally, throughout my remarks, I shall quote often from President Wilson, without attempting to identify the quotations as such.

It is now just two years short of a half-century since Wilson returned to Staunton for a triumphal homecoming after his election as President in 1912.

Today again, another connection I had with Mr. Wilson, in 1913 I was a Cadet corporal at West Point, and I marched in his first Inaugural parade.

Neither of the two warmly anecdotal talks he gave on that occasion— one at Mary Baldwin College and the other at Staunton Military Academy—could in any sense be construed as major addresses. Yet in both we catch glimpses of the progression of ideas that formed the touchstone of Wilson's faith—the ideas which had slowly taken shape and firm root during a career that gave him such rich preparation for the presidency. In that career he enjoyed a varied and valuable experience—he was a scholar—a man of thought; a college president; a Governor of one of our largest eastern States where he necessarily exercised both executive and political functions.

Wilson paid special tribute to his native State on his homecoming to Staunton and to the important influence Virginia's dedication to freedom played in his own development. On an earlier occasion he had already made a masterly presentation of the vital role of state government in our republic.

"We are certified by all political history," he said, "that centralization is not vitalization."

Today we know the wisdom of this principle is still applicable despite the great changes in our society that massive industrialization and population growth have brought about. Yet we are beseeched on all fronts to deposit more and more functions and authority in the hands of central government.

Sometimes we abdicate local responsibility, consciously, in the false hope of permanently ridding ourselves of some nagging problem; in other instances it is done unknowingly as we become too preoccupied with other matters to observe the extending reach of centralized authority. In either case the net result is to diminish further the freedom that flourishes best where responsibility is held and authority is exercised, close to home. I trust that as each of us reflects upon the working partnership of the Federal-State system, he will become increasingly mindful of Wilson's perceptive warning that "Centralization is not vitalization." The need for eternal vigilance of the people against the insidious maneuverings of centralized bureaucracy is constant.

Virginia's valiant struggle against oppressive centralism antedates the American Revolution by at least a hundred years. The citizens of this State have never faltered in their support of this cause. I salute them for their stalwart defense of one of the most vital features of America's free government—the reserved rights of the sovereign states.

When Woodrow Wilson stood here in December of 1912, at the age of 56, he sensed a new responsibility descending upon America. Abundantly furnished with wealth and extraordinarily furnished with opportunity though we were, he remarked, we tended to forget that our mission was not to pile up this wealth, but to serve mankind in humanity and justice. Indeed, he said, all the world was coming to this view.

Wilson was profoundly conscious of this turning point. He knew that the human commonwealth could not remain a trackless society, unsupported by rules of conduct that could sustain peace with justice. And he gave a wealth of thought to this problem.

Finally, six years later, he presented the arguments for adoption of his famous 14 points. What we seek, he declared, is "The reign of law, based upon consent of the governed, and sustained by the organized opinion of mankind."

This indeed was the goal that Wilson sought without success. But today we have a second chance to win through to that goal. And we dare not fail.

This week we commemorated an event that President Wilson would have applauded—the fifteenth anniversary of the United Nations Organization. He would have seen it as a lineal descendant of the League of Nations. It would please him to know that above the multilingual communication that goes on daily in the United Nations, a mighty effort is being waged by men and women of good will to learn a new language—a new universal language of mutual trust and faith. It can be learned but only through the mutual understanding that must be established in the human commonwealth. Its purpose is to lighten, not darken, the mind; it is a common tongue whose dialect knows neither suspicion nor hatred.

Over the years the stir of ideas was what Wilson loved most. Once in his teaching days he noted that "the use of a university is to make young gentlemen as unlike their fathers as possible." Most of us might be momentarily startled by such an assertion, but on reflection we would see that he was merely decrying an excessive worship of habit, ritual, dogma, and even labels.

To him, the fact that an idea was not presently attainable in no way dimmed its validity. "Sometimes people call me an idealist," he said. "Well that's the only way I know I am an American. America is the only idealistic nation in the world."

While Wilson was very definitely a man engrossed in the world of intellectual thought, he had a profound distrust of cloistered study. "Would I not be a better professor of public law for having been Assistant Secretary of State?" he asked, testifying to the value he placed on experience.

And his ideal of leadership was the concept of the thinking man in action. And the strength of the true leader, as he sensed it with great conviction, was not force, but persuasion; not matter, but the spirit.

The great problems of humankind, President Wilson held, could only be successfully overcome through the union of thought and action in enlightened leadership. He recognized that leaders must generate momentum. But this does not require a cunning and facile tongue, he told the students at Staunton. Momentum does not require eloquence. "It just needs the kind of serenity which enables you to steer by the stars, not by the ground."

He was not a man who believed in bruising the ears of his fellow men with shrill cries of alarm. Only clear expression of ideas "wins entrance into minds," he argued—and their sincerity into their hearts.

Wilson displayed an almost prophetic vision in the times that were even then swiftly descending upon us, and which could require from all peoples an effort to organize the world for a peace with justice. As we push forward with the hard, serious tasks ahead we can take satisfaction that an American idealist tried to chart the way for us.

His sweeping grasp of history made him acutely conscious that men and societies have often been inclined to follow false leaders to their destruction. Thus the great task of a society, as he saw it, was to be able to recognize who are the safe leaders. The citizen, in short, must distinguish between two alternatives, he said—"one trimming to the inclinations of the moment, the other obedient to the permanent purposes of the public mind. The one adjusts his sail to the breeze of the day; the other makes his plans to ripen with the slow progress of the years. While one solicitously watches the capricious changes of the weather, the other diligently sows grains in their seasons."

With this in mind, societies must choose between the conflicting teachings of political expediency on the one hand and the pursuit of noble, long term goals on the other. This is the kind of decision that free peoples are often called upon to make—and we can only pray that Wilson's counsel will always be their guide.

Certainly, if we heed Wilson we shall never hesitate to pay for freedom whatever price may be required. And in such a determination on the part of all of us, there is the constant assurance of victory. Let us remember another passage from President Wilson: "The highest and best form of efficiency," he said, "is the spontaneous cooperation of a free people."

The greatest tribute we can pay him is to reflect seriously on his life, his thoughts, his work, realizing that in the self-discipline he preached lies the one true way by which free peoples may sustain freedom and live fruitful and meaningful lives in peace.

Thank you very much indeed.

NOTE: The President spoke at 1:35 p.m. on the porch of the Administration Building at Mary Baldwin College, upon invitation of the Woodrow Wilson Birthplace Foundation. His opening words referred to Thomas E. Hassett, Mayor of Staunton, U.S. Senators Harry F. Byrd and A. Willis Robertson of Virginia, and Dr. Samuel R. Spencer, Jr., President of Mary Baldwin College.

On his trip to Virginia the President visited the birthplace of his mother, Mrs. Ida Stover Eisenhower, near Mt. Sydney in Augusta County.

341 ¶ Address in Philadelphia at a Rally of the Nixon for President Committee of Pennsylvania. *October 28, 1960*

General Baker and my fellow citizens:

We have 10 critical days left in which to evaluate the issues and personalities of this campaign. We are thankful that we vote secretly in America—that regardless of party affiliation or party registration we can freely and conscientiously choose the best leader for our country.

Almost 8 years have gone by since millions of us—Republicans, Democrats, and Independents—enthusiastically joined together to build a better America. We have had, I feel, a happy and fruitful partnership.

Measured in the dollars that have remained relatively stable these past 8 years, you—the American people—have come a long way since 1952—

You have increased personal income by $132 billion—by 48 percent.

You have increased average weekly earnings from $68 a week to $91 a week—by over a third.

You have increased your individual annual savings by $7 billion—up 37 percent.

You are building 70 thousand elementary classrooms this year alone. That is 22 thousand more than were built in 1952—or 46 percent.

You have increased college enrollments from 2 million to almost 3½ million—up 75 percent.

You have built 9 million new homes—more than ever were built before in the same length of time.

You have added $280 billion in capital expenditures on plants and equipment—more in this job-making field than in the preceding 30 years.

You have increased the gross national product by $158 billion—almost 45 percent.

Our Interstate Highway System was talked about for many years, but not started. Now we are building 41 thousand miles of these great new avenues of commerce—and paying for them as we go. When completed, they will save four thousand American lives a year.

The St. Lawrence Seaway was for decades a dream; finally it came true. At last we have brought the oceans of the world to the very heart of America.

In the meantime, you expanded social security, improved our national parks, forced passage of a good labor reform bill, and took the only significant steps in civil rights in 80 years. You, the American people, kept inflation down, balanced the budget four times, with another one on the way. You did these and a multitude of other things—and all this with a reduction of a quarter of a million in governmental positions.

Now, in all these years, a primary contribution of Government and national leadership was to create a climate fostering confidence, enterprise, and a willingness to venture and risk. At the same time, we stopped a wasteful war and prevented others, always with honor. By removing stifling economic controls, we allowed the men and women of America once again to concentrate on getting ahead. Under enlightened governmental policies you, the American people, have been responsible for all this surging progress.

And what about our military strength?

It is the most powerful on earth.

Into our Armed Forces we integrated weapons of tremendous deterrence, many of them unknown 8 years ago, through a program more than three times larger, in dollar amount, than only 10 years ago. And we have proof of the respect the Soviets have for our power and our resolution: the Communists have been turned from a strategy of military penetration to a strategy of infiltration by political and economic means.

So, I am proud of you—proud of what you have done, and proud of what has been done by America. Let no one diminish your pride and confidence in yourselves or belittle these accomplishments. My friends, never have Americans achieved so much in so short a time.

Now in glib political oratory we have heard this progress called "standing still."

Now in glib political oratory we have heard this progress called "stand-America needs more of it.

Now, shortly you must select a new leader for our country. Because I know what he must face—because I feel so earnestly that your choice will have far-reaching effects—possibly for decades—I trust you will think it fitting that I share with you my deep personal convictions on this matter.

There are four key qualities by which I believe America would like to measure the candidates in this election. They are:

Character; ability; responsibility; experience.

From 8 years of intimate association, I know Richard Nixon has these qualities and will use them wisely and decisively. And so will Cabot Lodge. This is why I trust and I believe that the American people will elect this splendid team on November 8.

My friends, this is a subject on which I will have more to say next Wednesday from New York.

Your President, of course, will have to be many things. As Chief of State and of Government, he will be your spokesman, presenting to the world your ideals; your firmness in the right; your strength—in fact, the true image of your country.

To perform this task he must thoroughly think through the problems of our time. In this he cannot succeed unless he is free of rashness; of arrogance; of headlong action; of the inclination to easy compromise. I hear that one candidate says he will act first and act fast. My friends, America needs a man who will think first, and then act wisely.

We need a leader who will not, one day, say that the United States Government should intervene in Cuba and then retract it the next day.

We need a leader who will not, one day, say he would give up territory to the Communists, then change his mind on it a day or so later.

Because, my friends, upon such decisions can hinge peace or war. Upon your President will fall problems like disarmament—like nuclear testing—like Berlin and Quemoy—like Cuba—and, beyond these, the task of continuing to win the hearts and minds of millions of struggling peoples. By the morality, justice, and steadiness of his decisions, he must be able to rally world support.

Your President will also be the Commander in Chief of your Armed Forces. National security will be one of his basic responsibilities and will depend greatly upon his understanding, born of experience. Just wanting to keep out of war will not be enough—as our three major wars in this century have proved. Your President must see to it that your Armed Forces are kept alert and modern, always ready to meet whatever threat may exist in this world. They are that now.

Now a strong defense necessarily rests upon a strong economy. Defense is vastly expensive. Even now you, the people, are spending $10 million a day on long-range ballistic missiles alone—more each day, every day, than the total spent for this purpose in all the years before I took office.

Now as long as high level spending is necessary for your security, the Commander in Chief will need to be mindful that unless he holds firmly to policies that promote the growth of free, competitive economic enterprise in the United States, the entire defense effort will be weakened.

Now I have given these few examples of Presidential duties to make clear the momentous significance to you and your children of your vote on November 8.

I have lived a fairly long and full life, so I tend to think of this Nation in terms of my children's and grandchildren's problems. In thinking of their future I am profoundly concerned by some statements in this campaign that have had world-wide circulation and have cruelly distorted the image of America. These statements demonstrate an amazing irresponsibility. They demand, from me, emphatic correction.

This week Pravda, one of Moscow's propaganda newspapers, reproduced speeches by some American politicians—you know who they are— bewailing alleged weaknesses in our country. The Soviet leaders are gleefully quoting from these same speeches in their effort to prove that our influence with other governments of the world is shrinking.

My friends, too many people are talking carelessly and ignorantly about America's standing, as if our Republic were in a popularity contest.

The word prestige has become so badly used and misused as to have lost any real meaning. But of this we can be sure: the Nation's prestige is not measured by the stridency of a politician's voice; it is measured by proved accomplishment. Aside from the great economic development for which you have been responsible, we have, among other things, stopped a futile and costly war, moved to halt Communist advances in Viet-Nam, prevented attacks on Formosa, helped our Philippine friends eliminate Communist guerrilla warfare, achieved, through the United Nations, a decent solution for the Suez affair, saved Iran, removed the sore spot of Trieste, by our sacrifices and cooperative effort strengthened free nations all along the periphery of the Communist bloc, and forged new and strong ties with our neighbors to the South. Now these successes were not won by any lack of strength or decisiveness. It is on such a record that Americans measure prestige rather than upon self-serving political assertions.

The important thing in our foreign affairs is that our Nation's purposes and programs be right. I should like to ask you all to give your closest study to this thing of foreign relations and foreign activities. Foreign problems color every other problem we have in the world—indeed, they cause almost every other problem we have. This is the basic problem that all of us must think about, and select leaders that will know how to handle them. That these programs are right is proved in one area by the eagerness with which the heads of other governments seek our counsel and support, and by our record in the United Nations.

More than 120 heads of state and government have visited our Nation's Capital in the past 8 years, an unprecedented occurrence. The heads of government who went to the United Nations in its last session, excepting those from behind the Iron Curtain, requested to see me, as your chief spokesman, to assure me of their purpose of keeping their relations with us sound and firm. And all the new nations formed—gaining their independence since World War II, have chosen a democratic form of government—not Communist. They, at least, have no doubts about America's prestige.

And too many of our people talk loosely about relative military strength. Such talk is an exercise in calculated confusion. I remind these self-appointed experts that the past 8 years comprise the only period in the entire history of the United States in which peacetime military preparation has been adequate and tailored to meet any possible emergency. I remind you that I have served in these Forces for more than 40 years. I think I know whereof I speak. Moreover, our defense has been tuned to the continuity of the threat and to long-range goals, avoiding the wild fluctuations that too often follow upon the incidence of either panic or complacency. This is one of the important reasons why the United States is today militarily the strongest nation in the world.

In any case: whatever was America's image abroad at the beginning of this political campaign, it tends to become blurred today. This is because of unwarranted disparagement of our own moral, military, and economic power. And what American is entitled to criticize the accomplishments of 180 million other Americans?

My friends, anyone who seeks to grasp the reins of world leadership should not spend all his time wringing his hands.

As another example of unwise politicking, I call attention to the recent speculations in gold on the London market.

Today your dollar is still the strongest currency in the world. We can keep it that way if we continue to hold firmly to the right policies on our budget, our money, and our national debt.

This we have worked tirelessly to achieve for 8 years. We have successfully fought against the big-spending schemes and irresponsible monetary policies that lead to currency debasement and a weak dollar.

But recently, the price of gold in the free market has risen above our official price of $35 per ounce. The foreign press—the European press—reports that this development is based in part on a growing fear of the cheap money policies and radical spending promised in the Los Angeles platform.

If these promises should be carried out, the impact on our economic position—and on the free world—could be catastrophic. Very quickly, confidence in our dollar could be impaired.

This places an immediate obligation upon the political leaders who support that platform.

That obligation is to spell out, specifically, in dollars and cents, how they would pay for the many billions of additional Federal spending pledged by that platform. We know that they could not pay for them with high hopes alone.

If they would pay for these lavish programs by raising taxes, let them say so.

And if they would cut going programs of the Government, let them specify what they are.

But if they would pay for these programs by deficit spending, raising the debt of our children and grandchildren, and thereby debase our currency, let them so confess.

In such a case let them understand that they and their party assume not only full responsibility for the present dangerous speculation in gold, but also for the developing fear about the future worth of the American dollar.

In all these things, my friends, we will need judgment and experience as our surest guide.

Of course "America must move." But forward—not backward. Not back to inflation—not back to bureaucratic controls—not back to deficit spending—not back to higher taxes, and bigger government. We found all these in 1952.

America must continue to go forward—with maturity, with judgment, with balance. I see no sense in America galloping in reverse to what has been called a New Frontier.

This is why, my fellow Americans, we must not settle for leadership other than the very best. We cannot afford anything less.

And clearly the best is the team of Nixon and Lodge.

Dick Nixon is superbly experienced, maturely conditioned in the critical affairs of the world. For 8 years he has been a full participant in the deliberations that have produced the great decisions affecting our Nation's security and have kept us at peace. He has shared more intimately in the great affairs of government than any Vice President in all our history.

He has traveled the world, studying at first hand the hopes and needs of more than 50 nations. He knows in person the leaders of those nations—knowledge of immeasurable value to a future President. He has represented us with distinction in situations demanding diplomacy, wisdom, tact, and courage.

By all odds, Richard Nixon is the best qualified man to be the next President of the United States.

Likewise unique in experience is Ambassador Henry Cabot Lodge. Where could we find a man, better qualified by stature and service in the world arena, to assume the responsibility whose burden must always be the knowledge that at any instant he may have to assume the Presidency of the United States? Cabot Lodge will be prepared.

Here is a superlative team, prepared in every respect to lead our country responsibly and well.

Fellow Americans—in the days ahead, I ask you to reflect soberly on these thoughts. However you are registered, consider it only a passkey to a secret ballot governed solely by your own convictions and your own conscience. Cast your ballot not for party, nor for any other lesser consideration. Vote for the team that can more fully lead us toward peace with justice. Vote what is best for America.

In that spirit, and joined, I hope, by a vast majority of Americans regardless of party, I shall vote for Vice President Nixon and Ambassador Lodge on November eighth.

NOTE: The President spoke at 8:30 p.m. at the Bellevue Stratford Hotel in Philadelphia. His opening words "General Baker" referred to Lt. Gen. Milton G. Baker, superintendent of the Valley Forge Military Academy, who served as chairman of the Nixon for President Committee for Pennsylvania.

342 ¶ Statement by the President Regarding the U.S. Naval Base at Guantanamo, Cuba.
November 1, 1960

WHILE THE POSITION of the Government of the United States with respect to the Naval Base at Guantanamo has, I believe, been made very clear, I would like to reiterate it briefly.

Our rights in Guantanamo are based on international agreements with Cuba, and include the exercise by the United States of complete jurisdiction and control over the area. These agreements with Cuba can be modified or abrogated only by agreement between the two parties, that is, the United States and Cuba. Our Government has no intention of agreeing to the modification or abrogation of these agreements and will take whatever steps may be appropriate to defend the Base.

The people of the United States, and all of the peoples of the world, can be assured that the United States' presence in Guantanamo and use of the Base pose no threat whatever to the sovereignty of Cuba, to the peace and security of its people or to the independence of any of the American countries. Because of its importance to the defense of the entire hemisphere, particularly in the light of the intimate relations which now exist between the present Government of Cuba and the Sino-Soviet bloc, it is essential that our position in Guantanamo be clearly understood.

343 ¶ Statement by the President Concerning the Agreement Reached in the Railway Industry.
November 1, 1960

A LANDMARK in the history of labor-management relations in the United States—

Both sides for many years have been concerned about the problems deeply affecting the livelihood of the men who run the trains and the future of the industry itself. I am sure the American people applaud as I do the high principle which has brought railway labor and management together in this agreement which adds greatly to the substance of the fabric of our free enterprise system.

Certainly this agreement is living proof that free collective bargaining is successful if left in the hands of dedicated, capable men who desire to see it work. It is also another indication of the maturity that has been achieved in industrial relations in this country in recent years.

NOTE: The President's statement was made on the occasion of the signing of Executive Order 10891 "Establishing a Commission to Inquire Into a Controversy Between Certain Carriers and Certain of Their Employees" (25 F.R. 10525). Representatives of the railroads and of the five railway operating brotherhoods had agreed to submit their dispute over work rules and practices to a Presidential commission on which the unions, the carriers, and the public would be represented.

For statement by the President announcing the appointment of members of the commission see Item 378.

344 ¶ Remarks Recorded for a Telecast Sponsored by the Independent Television Committee for Nixon and Lodge.
November 1, 1960

My fellow Americans:

We are going to talk tonight about a subject of fundamental importance to all Americans and the free world. We are going to hear about the vital importance of maintaining the buying power of the dollar and the confidence of people not only here at home, but abroad, in the future value of that dollar.

Soundness of our money is important to all people who earn wages for what they need; for people who are putting aside money for any number of purposes; for people already on some form of retirement income. The soundness of the U.S. dollar is also important because the dollar has become the reserve back of most of the currencies of the free world.

Let us make no mistake about it—the preservation of the soundness of the dollar, as well as preservation of the confidence that the dollar will remain sound is absolutely essential both for the welfare of our citizens at home and the rest of the free world.

We have been working mightily in the 8 years of this Administration to do the things in our Government that will help maintain a sound, honest dollar. In budget policy, this means the avoidance of deficit spending which can lead only to inflationary pressures. It means managing our debt so as to be as non-inflationary as possible. It means Federal Reserve operation of monetary policy to provide soundly for credit and money needs of a growing economy while avoiding creating excessive money and credit.

We shall hear tonight the Secretary of the Treasury, Robert B. Anderson, discuss in more detail these vital matters which should impress on American citizens the urgent need for voting to continue the proven and prudent financial and economic policies which have been followed in the past 8 years. I now present to you the Secretary of the Treasury, Mr. Anderson, and some distinguished citizens from American private life who will interview Secretary Anderson.

NOTE: The President's remarks were part of a half-hour program which was telecast over the Columbia Broadcasting System at 8 p.m. Following his remarks Secretary Anderson was interviewed by Dr. Deane W. Mallott, president of Cornell University, Thomas Lazzio, president of Local 300, AFL–CIO, United Auto Workers, Paterson, N.J., and Alfred H. Williams, chairman of the Board of Trustees of the University of Pennsylvania and former president of the Federal Reserve Bank of Philadelphia.

345 ¶ Remarks at a Rally in Garden City, New York. *November 2, 1960*

My fellow Americans:

I know that some of you are blanketed by the television cameras, but I would hope this is some little inconvenience with which you can put up, for the simple reason that these men also have a job, and they are trying to record these proceedings for the public. So while I recognize that you would like to throw a bulb at them, or something of that kind, I do plead that they are performing a service for the public and for this meeting and its proceedings.

I think there is a word of explanation due you people. I am a man who has lived fairly long, served a long time in the public service, and within some 2 months and 20 days I am to lay down the burdens of my office and put them in the hands of someone else.

So I have two reasons that I want to give you, as to why I am here. My concern for the United States, my readiness to work for the peace of the world, will be and are now just as great as they were from the days I was a second lieutenant and from the first day that I took my oath as President in 1953. I am concerned about the kind of leadership that America is going to have in these next critical years, in order that these things in which we all believe—peace with justice in freedom and in the opportunity of America to fulfill itself both in its national character and in its individual person—we are concerned about these things; and we all live in the hope that we will have a leadership that can create the atmosphere, point the way, so that we may more effectively do our parts, each of us, as we follow this road.

My second reason is this: for 8 years I have worked intimately with the two men who are today your national candidates. I know them intimately. I have seen them undertake the tasks which I have requested of them, with the utmost enthusiasm, never with a complaint or with any excuses for avoiding a duty. Instead, no matter how difficult the task, no matter what it meant in personal inconvenience, no matter what it meant in sleepless nights and long roads of travel, they have always been ready to do it. And the point is, they have done it effectively.

They know. They know about the problems that are brought before the President and his Cabinet, problems on which depend the opportunities of the United States to expand its growth, to be stronger, to keep its own self-respect and the respect of other nations. They know the problems that come up when the crises are developed by the Communists with threats about military activity, economic penetration, and just plain lying propaganda. They know these things. They have lived with them.

I think this: we should go into our voting booths on November 8th and think of several things. One is this—I would like to compare the two candidates, or the two teams of candidates, the way I would like to express it, on the basis of character. What have they shown to you people over these 8 years in their moral courage, their capacity, their readiness to undertake any task no matter how disagreeable, their experience—of which you have been a witness.

You have seen what they do, and you know how they do it, and their ability on their feet, or in producing studies, making decisions—and above all, their devotion and dedication to the United States; not attempting to emphasize too much their own virtues, not being controlled too much by a personal ambition. They want to serve the United States. They want to serve it, as it has been served through so many years by people from Washington on down to this day, who have taken as their watchword: what is good for the United States is good for me and for the party of which I am a part.

So I come here then again to tell you of my convictions that Richard

Nixon and Henry Cabot Lodge offer to America the finest type of leadership that is today available in this Nation.

And I want to express my utter faith that as I peer down the lane of the years ahead, that these are the two men that can do better than any others I know in keeping the peace, in bringing us and leading us more surely and firmly to a better peace, to one in which we can have faith and confidence, and which will one day lift from the backs of mankind the burdens of armaments and allow us to use our toil, our talents and all the resources we have to the betterment of mankind.

No glittering promises, no glib oratory will give you this kind of leadership. This leadership, I repeat, is born of character, ability, and experience—and a dedication to the United States.

So these are the reasons I have for coming here today, and I pray that all of those who joined together with me 8 years ago in the crusade to bring about what we believed was a better situation in government, in our Nation, in the freedom of our economy, and the opportunity for growth, that you today will be even more emphatic in your efforts and your readiness to make certain that these two men, Mr. Nixon and Mr. Lodge, take the work over of leadership for the next 4 years—and that you will see to it on November 8th that they do so.

These are the things that I ask you to do.

Goodbye.

NOTE: The President spoke at 10 a.m. at the Roosevelt Field Shopping Center in Garden City.

346 ¶ Remarks in New York at a Rally at the Westchester County Airport. *November 2, 1960*

My fellow Americans:

You know, I am enjoying this morning. If I weren't so old, I think I would like campaigning again.

I think there is nothing so inspirational for any man who seeks to serve the public than to meet with the public and have it borne into his conscience just how wonderful these people are that we call Americans.

There are many compliments that come to men during the course of a distinguished career such as have been accomplished by so many men and women here today, but there is no greater compliment that Americans can pay to any individual than to come out from their busy lives, from their homes, and buck traffic jams, just to come to give him a friendly hello and say, "We're for you, boy."

I had a number of things I was going to talk about this morning. I have mentally thrown them away because Dick Nixon has just made one of the best political speeches that I have ever heard. So I am going to content myself with something very brief and very short.

I have been very proud of the fact that 8 years ago thousands of you, millions of you, joined with me and with others to bring about a reformation in the United States, bring about a new growth. You will recall we were then living under economic controls, prices were controlled and wages were controlled, and goodness knows what all. We decided we wanted to be free. We decided there was a war that should be stopped because it was futile and had no real objective except a defense, and that had already been accomplished. We decided that we must band together to make sure that no more wars were allowed to occur—certainly they were not to be allowed to occur because of weakness—military weakness, or indecision, or vagueness in America's purposes in the war.

These things we have done.

And then we decided that we should have the kind of atmosphere in this world in which the United States could go ahead—as it has. The last 8 years have been the most remarkable in the growth of the United States than in any other peacetime period in its history.

Bob Barry told me a minute ago—and I hope his figure is correct—that in the town of Tarrytown there were 164 thousand automobiles made in these 10 months of this year. And in all of Russia in the same period there were 132 thousand made. It looks to me that if Tarrytown can outproduce them, that at least we have got one statistical figure that will show something about the relative strength, prestige, and standing of these two countries.

Now my friends, the only real purpose that I have today is to tell you this, that these men on this platform, and particularly Vice President Nixon and Ambassador Lodge, have been my close associates and great helpers over these past 7½ years. They have been among my most trusted counselors and advisers, associates, and have always been ready to perform any task that I requested from them.

Now in other words, we have been members of a team. I think of them as a team. And these two men as presented to you today are themselves a team, a team of leadership that it is my prayer will build upon the record that you the people of the United States have accomplished during these last 8 years—build upon it in the same direction, with the same regard for your pocketbooks, your economy, your health, your education, that has characterized the administration of the past 8 years.

Now I have heard complaints about the country not moving. My contention is that isn't good enough. Of course you can move easily—you can move back to inflation, you can move back to deficit spending, you can move back to the military weakness that allowed the Korean war to occur, you can move back to a lot of things—no trouble at all.

But Americans, if they are going to work, to study, to band together to make better lives for themselves and for this Nation, they are going to do it by going forward, and that is exactly what the program that the Republican document that was established and written at Chicago promises to you.

And you have the record of two people who have not written a platform to catch votes. They have written a platform of intent—honest intent; and they intend to see it go ahead.

So I come to you because of my experience with these men, to endorse them as men of character, vision, human concern—and above all experience in the tough jobs that will be before the leadership of this country during the next 4 years.

I believe and I commend them to you as men in whom you can have confidence that they will never do anything that is rashly risking the cataclysm of war; and on the other hand, they will always be proudly standing for every principle that has made the United States great.

This team, then, offers you an opportunity to vote for experience and character. It gives you an opportunity to vote enthusiastically your own conscience, your own interests, and above all the interests of the United States of America.

I am going to vote that way on November 8th, and I hope the rest of you do—and get 10 people for each one here to do the same thing.

Goodbye.

NOTE: The President spoke at 10:40 a.m.   sentative Robert R. Barry, of New York.
In his remarks he referred to U.S. Repre-

347   ¶ Remarks at a Rally in Herald Square, New York City.   *November 2, 1960*

My fellow Americans:

I would like to talk to you just a minute or two, and I want to talk to you as citizens who are facing a very heavy responsibility: deciding upon your leadership for the next 4 years in the Government of the United States.

I come here not to talk about Republicanism. I am not talking about any kind of partisan politics when I appeal to you—each of you—to use your own good judgment and your own conscience in deciding which of the two teams you have heard described and have heard speak, which of those you trust most to lead America.

From my viewpoint this will take very little deciding. The issues have been brought out into the open. The characters and types of the personalities who will be your leaders have been exposed to the public, and certainly, as Lincoln said, "You can't fool all the people all the time."

I am perfectly certain that the speech that I have prepared in my own mind to make is now unnecessary, because the people of New York have given it for me. I came here to tell you why I knew that Nixon and Lodge were so much better for the world and for the United States than anybody we could meet, that I feel now it would be futile for me to attempt anything else in the way of words.

As we came up this broad highway, with the ticker tape floating down by the ton, I had the assurance in my own heart and in my own mind that New York knows much better than I do, even, the answer. Possibly I know a few more intimate answers—more intimate reasons about these two people. I don't need to name them, I don't need to describe them any more. What I am going to say is just this: as I walked to this platform, I saw old comrades of mine in war, men of the Herzian Forest, men of D-Day and of North Africa and of Bastogne.

And then I was told as I came up that there are representatives in this crowd of every single nation behind the iron curtain, and indeed of every single nation in the world. This is more than just a meeting of the League of Nations. There you have instructed delegates fighting to get everything for its own government, for its nation, what it believes to be justice and for right for itself and for its people.

Here you have people who are representing other people, who are feeling as other people. The kind of leadership we are talking about is: the people that can understand this crowd, that can walk their way through it, who know the triumphs over poverty, who have experienced the joy of work and have grown in stature, in intelligence, and in spirit because they have worked and because each has the right to feel that he has helped, along with others, to make this country great.

So to all the people here representing every possible ethnic group, to my old comrades, I bring the warmest greetings and my deepest gratitude for your readiness to come out and by your presence show your support of policies and programs that will take this country on to new heights, on for your children and your grandchildren, and not merely succumb to the glib arguments of the "pie in the sky" promises that so many of us have read.

I have one more word only: we saw thousands and thousands of signs which said "the first team." It has always been my feeling that the Government of America is truly a team when it properly represents the people of the United States. You—each of you—is a member of the team, as I am and as these people are.

It happens that the two men we are talking about today happen to be the captains of the team. They have to create the atmosphere in which you can exercise your rights, in which you can live in liberty, prosperity, and with the certainty that you are respected as a nation abroad and as an individual here at home.

They are the first team, in the sense that they can and will do this. They will make you prouder of America, because they will represent properly the ideals and aspirations of our great country. They will see that its strengths, its spiritual and its economic and its military strength, will never be weakened. They will guide, during their tenure of office, this great country to such heights that your pride may be greater and your chest pushed out a little further and your chin a little higher.

Now this is what we are talking about when we are talking about leaders. You know people that promise you a life of ease with no work. The day that we don't have to work, that's the day you will have to call the United States second rate.

So these two men are not going to make you promises that couldn't be kept, and that even if they were kept they wouldn't be good for us.

This evening at least will probably be the last political gathering that I will attend in New York City, certainly during my term of office. I just want to make this one pledge: when I leave my office, no matter what I may then be doing, my struggle to help bring the world a little closer to the goal of peace, my hope of helping the United States to be stronger in every possible way, will never flag; and wherever I can, by word or a piece of writing, or by merely a handclasp with someone, help nurture and strengthen that feeling in any other person in the world, that I shall do. Because this is not something that I have indulged in merely because I was for these 8 years your President. I believe these things with my heart and soul.

We must have peace.

We must not succumb to the threats of communism.

We must hold freedom high.

And as I become within a few score days a private citizen like you, I will have exactly your same responsibilities, to do that—to do my part toward holding freedom high. And under these two people I believe we can all march together to a new confidence, a new position of leadership in the whole world.

Thank you very much.

NOTE: The President spoke at 1:15 p.m.

348   ¶ Address at a Republican Rally in the New York Coliseum.   *November 2, 1960*

My fellow Americans:

I have spent my adult life in public service. This I have been proud to do because of my unshakable belief in America's great destiny as the world leader for freedom, and because America represents the mightiest temporal power that has ever been developed here on this earth.

For almost 8 years I have served as the elected head of this Nation and its spokesman in the world scene.

Mindful of the many perplexing problems that have inescapably demanded from me a multitude of decisions of world-wide import, I present to you this evening reasons why I think this election to be a momentous event for us and for the free world. Beyond this I give you additional reasons for my support of Richard Nixon and Cabot Lodge.

Every one of us knows that the subject that most engages our national attention and causes the greatest concern to every individual, is the aggressive intentions of powerful Communist imperialism. Another is the family budget—its market basket. This I shall talk about in a day or so, possibly Friday evening.

But this struggle with the Kremlin has been with us for a long time and it will be with us for a long time to come.

Yet the world of today is not what it was when I took office 8 years ago. At home our economy has become immeasurably stronger. In every index by which we measure strength and development, the past 8 years have been the brightest of our history. Such strength and development form the sturdy foundation on which are built all our necessary programs for national prosperity and security at home and waging peace abroad.

The first difference the years have brought about internationally is that we were then fighting in Korea.

America was at war—a war into which the Nation had been allowed to drift by its leadership through weakness, through indecision, and through vagueness of purpose.

We were weak because the Government had cut back our Armed Forces to their lowest ebb since the beginning of World War II, leaving Korea undefended—

—indecision, because the Government had no intelligible plan for dealing with the Communist power in the Far East—

—vagueness, because neither our friends nor our enemies knew in advance of the attack where we stood on the issue of South Korea's independence and territorial integrity.

Six months after this administration took office, a cease fire order had been achieved that assured the safety of South Korea and ended the fighting.

Since that time we have had no single battle casualty in our Nation.

There have been no further gains of territory or population by Communist imperialism in any area where American influence and arms were involved.

We have successfully withstood an intensive campaign by the Soviet Union to absorb all of Berlin.

Moreover, the number of people who defect from Communist-controlled states is measured annually in the hundreds of thousands. And I point out that when people by the countless thousands will risk everything, including their lives, for the chance to join us on freedom's side of the Iron Curtain—there is no question in their minds about America's leadership.

My friends, there is no question in your minds. In fact, there seems to be only one individual who is bewailing America's strength and weakness, and he happens to be a political—the only one who is doing this thing is a political candidate, and he isn't here tonight.

My friends, this Government has spelled out our intentions to the world in unmistakable terms, for all to see and understand, as, for example, in NATO, Korea, the Formosan Straits, in SEATO, and in the Middle East.

We have built up the strength of our Armed Forces steadily, for the long pull. Our retaliatory forces are at a peak of power and readiness never before attained.

And, we have closely associated ourselves with other free nations in a common effort to preserve and expand freedom, to promote economic growth and political stability, and to help make life more meaningful for people the world over.

My friends, I do not cite these achievements, domestic and foreign, as a cause for smugness, either by our Nation or by me.

But neither can I understand how, in face of the record, anyone can seriously argue that the world leadership of the United States has been impaired. Perhaps only a wealth of personal experience can truly develop a reservoir of personal faith.

This is why I am so concerned about the leadership that our Nation will have next January.

The Nation needs leaders who have been immersed in the hard facts of public affairs in a great variety of situations—men of character who are able to take the long-range view and hold long-range goals—leaders who do not mistake minor setbacks for major disasters—and leaders who by their own records have demonstrated a capacity to get on with the job. We want men of inexhaustible strength and inexhaustible faith.

This is why I am so wholeheartedly in back of Richard Nixon and Cabot Lodge.

My friends, in their preparation for high office, the experience of Cabot Lodge and Dick Nixon has never been equaled.

These men didn't learn their lessons merely out of books—not even by writing books. They learned these lessons by meeting the day-in, day-out problems of our changing world.

As my personal representative, I have sent Richard Nixon on major missions to most of the countries of the world. I have carefully weighed his advice and have made changes as a result of his insight and experience.

The work of Cabot Lodge as our permanent representative to the United Nations is universally known. The televised debates at the UN have brought into our very homes the proof of his two-fisted courage and skill.

Richard Nixon and Cabot Lodge have advised and helped me well for 8 years. They have my respect, my admiration, my friendship. They have character, ability, experience, and courage.

The problems they will have to face in the years ahead will not always be the same problems I have faced. But with Vice President Nixon and Ambassador Lodge at the helm, I can have full confidence that the fate of my country and your country is in strong and trustworthy hands. My friends, I promised Dick I would make this talk in 10 minutes, and I have got 30 seconds to go. Yet for myself, I shall always be on the side of those who work for the betterment of America and the goal of a just peace in the world.

This is what these two men will do. In this sense, my friends, I shall always be part of their team. In these critical years before us, we need leadership with clarity of vision and steadiness of purpose.

We need leadership of maturity, proven experience and decision.

We need the leadership of Richard Nixon and Cabot Lodge.

NOTE: The President spoke at 8:40 p.m.

349 ¶ Letter to Dr. Milton S. Eisenhower on the Occasion of His Resignation From Two Advisory Committees. *November 3, 1960*

Dear Milton:

With great reluctance, I am accepting your resignation as a member of the President's Advisory Committee on Government Organization, and am informing the Secretary of State that you wish to be relieved as a member of the National Advisory Committee on Inter-American Affairs.

I am delighted that, at the suggestion of the Department of the Navy and in accordance with our recent conversation, you will continue to serve on the Board of Visitors of the United States Naval Academy.

I know how difficult it has been for you, as President of the Johns Hopkins University, to give time to these important advisory committees, and additionally to serve as my personal representative on many major missions to Latin America. Your wisdom, experience, and common sense have time and again led to constructive recommendations for difficult problems. Your judgments and advice have been sound—practically, as well as morally.

Your work and concrete suggestions on government organization have been of substantial help in keeping the government abreast of changing requirements and in promoting economy and efficiency in government operations. You should take particular satisfaction from the fact that since 1953, fourteen reorganization plans have become effective, and seven other important reorganization measures have been put into operation by executive action. As a member of the Advisory Committee on Government Organization, you can take justifiable pride in having played an important role in the establishment of the Department of Health, Education and Welfare, the United States Information Agency, the International Cooperation Administration, the Federal Aviation Agency, the National Aeronautics and Space Agency, and the Federal Council on Science and Technology.

Many ideas useful both to me and the Secretary of State have already come from the National Advisory Committee on Inter-American Affairs, which you first proposed in December, 1958, and your work in the area of Inter-American relations has been an inspiration to all people who believe that common problems can be resolved through mutual efforts.

In accepting your resignations from these two significant Advisory Committees, I want you to know that your counsel during the years I have occupied the Presidency has been a source of steady satisfaction to me personally. Your contribution to the cause of good government will be self-evident.

Sincerely,

DWIGHT D. EISENHOWER

NOTE: Dr. Eisenhower's letter to the President, and a letter to Dr. Eisenhower from Secretary Herter relieving him of duty on the National Advisory Committee on Inter-American Affairs, were also released.

350   ¶ Address in Cleveland at a Rally in the Public Square.   *November 4, 1960*

Mr. Chairman, and fellow Americans:

Cleveland has been a source of strength to the United States for generations and, certainly, to the administration I have headed for the last 8 years.

George Humphrey, for example, came to Washington and helped to restore to the American economy a dependable American dollar. Keith Glennan came to Washington and helped develop a space program that, in this field, has far outstripped the Soviet's performance. Chappy Rose came to Washington and animated everyone who met him with the enthusiasm of his responsible citizenship. And Frances Bolton and Bill Minshall have been towers of strength in supporting programs designed to speed the sound, forward progress of America.

Many others from this city and State, of like dedication and genius, have helped make the country more secure, more prosperous, more worthy of its own aspirations.

Of course, also, I always feel some personal satisfaction in coming to Cleveland—now an ocean port because of the St. Lawrence Seaway. That great project stood still, stock-still, through many years—even decades. Then during this administration—which some politicians, I understand, call a period of standing still—we did something about it; and it was carried to completion.

Now there is something almost amazing about the way some politicians can twist things up. Here is an example: within the last few days I have heard of a plan for forming a great corps of "workers for peace" abroad. The time given to this project by its members—for which the Federal Government would of course pay—would be a substitute for a tour of duty in the uniformed service. Now this plan is apparently intended as one of the new ideas that will help produce the New Frontier. But strangely enough, this brand new plan is amazingly similar to a proposal made in 1954 in a book by Heinz Rollman, who is not a member of the party whose spokesman made the recent announcement on November 2d. Mr. Rollman, the original author, is the Republican candidate for Congress from the 12th District of North Carolina. It makes us wonder how many other proposals are equally not original and not new, but are merely immature.

My principal purpose in this visit is to assure everyone in this State, which has given so many Presidents to the United States, that I am completely committed to the election to the Presidency of another Ohioan, once removed—Dick Nixon. Now for 8 years he has been immersed in the problems and the responsibilities of leadership. He is prepared now to take over national leadership next January. And I must remark that the White House is one place where we should not depend upon, and cannot afford, on-the-job training of the occupant.

I support Dick Nixon and Cabot Lodge because of deep-seated convictions about the source of American strength and the dangers that threaten it. These two men, I know, will amplify the sources of our strength. They will guard tirelessly against all threats to us, of whatever character.

THE SOURCE OF AMERICAN STRENGTH

America is the product of faith, deeply felt, religiously held. The builders of America, our forebears, were fired by faith in God; faith in themselves; faith in the American principles that proclaimed man's right to freedom and justice.

And that faith still endures. And its product is the world's mightiest temporal power, America. Now our Nation is dedicated—not to aggression or conquest or material aggrandizement—but to the fostering of human freedom; the promotion of human welfare; the achievement of a just peace; and the maintenance of a peace for all mankind.

Yet, the might and grandeur of the United States could be torn down by our own citizens. We can destroy ourselves, for example, by:

Trading faith in ourselves for faith in big government.

By division into voting blocs.

By abandonment of citizenship responsibility.

Now let me speak first on our faith in big government.

In this campaign, once again, we hear political candidates preach the false gospel of big government. They take it for granted, and imply, that we have lost faith in ourselves.

My friends, some of you are old enough to remember a man by the name of Coué, and Coué said, "Every day, day by day, we grow better and better." But we have got politicians today who are saying and repeating Mr. Coué in reverse, and say "Every day, each day, we are growing worse and worse." And on that premise they attempt to persuade us that only the Federal Government can solve our problems and they present vast programs for Federal action. They are going, they say, to solve every imaginable human problem; blithely they proclaim that their federalized wisdom will give to each of us a life of ease, security, and plenty.

But they don't tell us how the bills—running into additional billions—will be paid.

But they say they will save money by reducing the cost of the farm program. From what farmers, let us ask, will these savings come? Let them tell us specifically.

More money, they say, will be saved by military reorganization. I have heard the figure of $1 and $1½ billion. Now where did this young genius acquire the knowledge, experience, and the wisdom through which he will make such vast improvements over the work of the Joint Chiefs of Staff, and the dedicated civilian and service men who have given their lives to this work?

And one of these men who so worked for you was your fellow Ohioan, Neil McElroy.

They will reduce, they say, the cost of servicing the national debt by reducing interest rates.

Now what individual among you wants his currency debased? Certainly not the man who is living on a pension or looking forward to receiving one. Certainly not the man who is buying an insurance policy, or putting his savings into a bank.

And then they tell us all of these things are going to be paid by growth. And how are we going to get the growth? Why, easy!—more Federal spending, out of your pockets.

The growth of the United States is the product of the hearts and hands and minds of the workers of the United States, working in the fields and the factories and the offices. Wherever we need productive work, there is where our growth is coming from, and not from some magic Federal program of spending.

These people can't pay these enormous bills with any or all of such phony schemes as this, and so we can only presume that they intend a return to deficit spending and resultant inflation, the kind which we slowed down 8 years ago and brought to a virtual stop.

In no more sure way than by deficit spending and currency debasement can we destroy the individual initiative and enterprise which have been responsible for America's growth.

In no more sure way can the economic strength of the Republic be destroyed, because inflation removes the individual's assurance against financial catastrophe. Let me give you an example.

Some of you are retired people living on monthly checks that constitute your principal or only income. And all of us expect to be retired some day.

In many cases—probably for most of you—these payments will not increase regardless of whether inflation occurs or not. But if inflation occurs, this simply means that the value of each dollar goes down, or stated another way, that the price of everything you pay for goes up— your rent, your groceries, your heating bill, your utilities, every other kind of service—goes up.

If you are barely making ends meet now at the end of each month, this means that with inflation you will be unable to pay your living costs out of your retirement income. But as we fight against the debasement of our currency, as we have been doing since 1953, then your retired income and purchasing power will be preserved. You will have nothing to fear. My conscience would give me no rest without making it clear that this is the choice you will be making next Tuesday: an inflation fired by deficit spending, or sticking with the sound fiscal policies of this administration.

And, my friends, for those who are working actively, steady inflation would be almost equally hopeless. In runaway inflation, wage increases rarely keep up with the soaring cost of living. The dollars added to a paycheck will be devoured by the increase in prices of every item in the family market basket. There is no profit whatsoever in a pay increase of $5.00 a week when living costs go up to $6.00 a week.

Just that was happening to us when you—you people—stepped in and stopped it by electing the present administration in 1952. It will stay stopped if you vote for Dick Nixon and Cabot Lodge on Tuesday, because these men will sustain fiscal sanity in the operation of the Federal Government. By this I mean they will not pile upon our huge national debt still more debt. They will eliminate excessive spending and will make sure that income exceeds expenditures. And this is one great contribution the Federal Government can make to preserving the value of your money.

Then again, in this campaign, we witness a deliberate appeal to Americans, not as Americans but as members of specific groups. This can only promote an intolerable antagonism between economic and social elements of our country. In that, there is no profit for anyone. No group in our sort of society can for long prosper unless all groups prosper.

When we cease to recognize ourselves as full and equal citizens of the United States and act as selfish members of a selfish group concerned only with our own interests, we fragmentize America.

When we are more concerned with the profit or the honor or the strength of one faction or group or party than we are with the profit and honor and strength of America, the lessons of history tell us that we are engaged in self-destruction.

When you go in a voting booth you are responsible only to your own conscience and convictions. No matter what label you may wear, in what party you are now registered, what voting habits you have observed, you are in that booth to do your part in making America's future be what you think it should be.

You should, at that moment, think only of America, not a part of it. Your decision should be your own—no one else's. Because in that booth you are alone, alone with your own conscience and facing yourself, what you think of the policies and the projects and the programs of the two parties—and the character and the standing and the experience of the people for whom you vote.

Now just a word about this matter of *abandonment of citizen responsibility:*

America is strong today because men and women—the families of America—strive in their homes, on their jobs, in their communities, in the world beyond our shores, to live by their faith as Americans. They are self-starters in making this country a better place for human living. When they cannot do a job by themselves alone, they go into partnership with government. But they don't need and they don't want government as a boss. The miracle of American progress during the past 8 years is the product of individuals working on their own and in an atmosphere fostered by government.

We are told, however, that the world of today is far too big and complex for the individual to accomplish anything. Only mass effort, organized and controlled by government, can have any effective impact, they say. They want us, it seems to me, to abandon citizen responsibility.

But only responsible citizenship makes America great and increases her prestige. It encourages ever-greater achievement by individuals following leaders they respect because of their character, ability, and experience.

My friends, a sound, progressive government, a Nation with a constantly expanding economy, and a people dedicated to the pursuit of a just world peace in freedom—these are the basic aspirations that should guide the voting of all of us on November 8th. They are the basis of the platform on which Richard M. Nixon and Henry Cabot Lodge stand. And it is for this reason that I shall cast my vote for these two men.

Thank you very much.

NOTE: The President spoke at 12:15 p.m. His opening words "Mr. Chairman" referred to A. L. DeMaioribus, Chairman of the Republican Central and Executive Committee of Cuyahoga County. In the second paragraph he referred to George M. Humphrey, former Secretary of the Treasury, Dr. T. Keith Glennan, Administrator of the National Aeronautics and Space Administration, H. Chapman Rose, former Under Secretary of the Treasury following a term of service as Assistant Secretary, and U.S. Representatives Frances P. Bolton and William E. Minshall of Ohio. Later he referred to Neil H. McElroy, former Secretary of Defense.

351 ¶ Remarks at a Republican Men's Luncheon in Cleveland. *November 4, 1960*

My friends:

Of course we don't have to be reminded we are in the midst of a political campaign, and I have been a little amused by some of the descriptions of my part in this campaign. This morning my headlines in the Washington papers said that I was a member of a rescue squad.

I said this is right, in 1952 I joined with a good many million Americans to rescue us from a lot. We were able to rescue the Nation from a war that no longer had any real meaning except calling for casualties every day, where we had already the objective we said we wanted, which was to gain the safety of South Korea. So that was solved—and with honor. Then we rescued it from inflation, and George Humphrey and I were called a good many names in trying to rescue it from a lot of controls that were then over our economy, prices on both labor and the costs of things and services. And we were rescued from military weakness which was the principal cause of ever getting into the Korean struggle in the first place.

And finally we were rescued from the philosophy that could see China go down the drain with five hundred million people, by far the vast majority of whom wanted to stay on this side of freedom and indeed looked to America as their great friend and champion.

So I am very proud to be in this rescue squad, because I think that the millions with whom I joined at that time have done a very splendid job.

And then of course we hear about the country standing still. I would just like to see this one test: when we say America and the American economy, in a way sort of an amorphous idea, the entity that we are thinking about is just so vast we don't grasp it very well. But I would like to see on billboards around this town—I would like to see Cleveland put up somewhere, what they have done, how many more homes you have built, how many hospitals, how many more roads, how many businesses have come in, what is the increase in population, the increase in its real wages, and the very great flattened-out curve of the cost of living since 1952. I would like to see those things just on a billboard to remind ourselves that we haven't exactly stood still. Either that, or I don't understand the word—the term.

Now I am on my way today to go to Pittsburgh for a little politicking, but I just want to make one observation: too many candidates—and here I am talking about the one on the opposing side, seems to me to think of this election as a little bit like we do a hundred-yard sprint. You put everything you have got into it, you call on every resource of mind and heart and muscles just to get over that line. That's the election day. Now the proper way to look at election day, in my opinion, is: what are you going to do after you get over that line? It is not in the race. In the race, all you have to do is break that tape and that's that. You are number one. In this race it is not good enough to be just number one. What are you going to do now?

I think of going back to the sports field again, and let's take a baseball game. Well, you have cracked out a grounder and you put in your last ounce of energy and you just happen to make first base. But you don't stop there. First base is the beginning. Now you call on all your alertness, your skill, your energy—and you count on your teammates, you count on the people that are working with you. And the purpose of that getting on first base was to get you around to count a run.

Now we want to think of the things that are coming behind this election. It is necessary to be number one over the line, but after you get there, we are going to do something about it, not merely to stand up and "huzza" after the results and say, "Well, we were number one," and go on about our business.

The Nation is too important to think of this race in those terms, and I think it is too often thought of in exactly that way.

And then finally I have this one observation: we talk so much or we hear so much about a second-rate country, second-rate in this and that and the other thing, whether it's space or whether it's schoolrooms or whatever. By the way, all these things are so ridiculous that they don't have to be refuted, but it leads me to this observation: suppose you had one of the players on Ohio State and he was forever saying, "You are a second-rate bunch of 'muckers.'" "You don't look good to me." "Now if you just make me your coach, this will be a much better team and we would go places, we would be world champions without even walking on the field."

Now I submit that any of the players that is running down his own squad all through the season, all through the year, is not himself going to make a very good coach.

Thank you very much and goodbye.

NOTE: The President spoke at 2:28 p.m. in the Wedgwood Room at the Sheraton-Cleveland Hotel.

352 ❡ Remarks in Cleveland at a Reception of Republican Women. *November 4, 1960*

My friends:

Having had now 8 years experience in political life, I have made it a point never to miss a gathering of women. I have found out through my statistical department that there are some millions more of you than there are of men, and this alone makes a meeting with a women's crowd something endearing to the politician's heart.

Now we know that we are in a political struggle today, and I just want to say as my first word this: I do hope that each of you will remember that when you are in the voting booth that for once you are not part of a crowd, you are not part of a group, you are not a part of a sect or anything else—you are there alone with your conscience and your convictions. No matter what your convictions, you pull down the lever or you make your mark in that place; because the opportunity we have in voting is to do our part in this particular point in our history in trying to make the United States what our highest ideals and what our deepest aspirations want it to be.

So I say this with all the seriousness and the solemnity that I can bring to bear. This is something that you must not do carelessly. This must be something that comes from both your head and your heart.

Now in this political campaign I find my part of it is criticised for this and that, or I am told what I should do or should not do. This morning in my Washington paper, big headlines said that it was very bad that I had become a part of a rescue squad.

Well, I told my friends, and I have told the crowd of men a few minutes ago, that I was very proud to be in a rescue squad. I joined one in 1952, and it was made up of millions and millions of Americans who believed that our country should be rescued from certain things:

A war that no longer meant anything, where we had gained the basic objective of protecting South Korea and it was ended with honor.

We wanted to be rescued from inflation. We wanted to be rescued from controls that were then existing all over the costs of wages and things and services and everything that we used and bought. We wanted to be rescued from military weakness which itself was one of the reasons for drifting into that Korean mess—and we certainly wanted to be rescued from the mess in Washington.

Now the millions of you that joined that rescue squad and joined in that rescue work have something that I think you will be proud of all your lives.

In the last 8 years you not only stopped some of the things that we thought were bad for the United States, but you helped this Nation get on a path that led toward the realization of our ideals and our aspirations.

You have, in your material accomplishments, written an 8-year history that is the brightest of our entire American history.

If you of Cleveland—each of you—would compare Cleveland today, or your own home for that matter, with 1952—in this city, though: how many homes have you built, how many hospitals, how many new roads, new schoolrooms? What have we done in increasing the real wages of our workers? What have we done to make this a better city?

I believe if you could really carry your memory back to 1952, you would find that you have been part of an operation that was not only one of rescue, it was one of constructive work, to bring this Nation to the place which you think it ought to go.

Now of course this is work that is never done, and there I just want to compare an election, any election, with a sort of a sprint race.

Of course the big task in a sprint is to get across the line first, because in the hundred yards that you are running, you put your entire heart, your head, every muscle, all your training, all your knowledge, just to break that tape, and then when you have broken that tape, you are done.

But an election is not quite that. After you break the tape you have won this sprint in the election—now what are you going to do?

A fire department does not run through the streets just to make a record in timing. What it does is to get there to put out the fire and do something constructive to save the things that need to be saved, and possibly even to establish the conditions under which the householders can begin to rebuild.

There is something to be done after this election is won. That is again something that I think we ought to give our heads and our hearts a chance to ponder, because we are sometimes—and certainly I think that one of our young hopefuls thinks of our election too much this way, just to get across that line first.

We need to do that in order to get the chance to do something constructive, but that is where the real work begins.

This Nation is the first in power, first in free world leadership. It is first in its intellectual capacity throughout the Nation. You people— every one of you—have a right to be proud of your Nation and what you have done in these past 8 years—indeed, in what you have done with your lives.

But you still have the distance to go, and in the last day let us all pray that each of us is worthy of this Nation and each of us can say, "I have done my best to help it be the country that we believe it should be."

So—goodbye.

NOTE: The President spoke at 2:40 p.m. in the Whitehall Room at the Sheraton-Cleveland Hotel.

353 ❡ Remarks Upon Arrival in Pittsburgh. *November* 4, 1960

My friends:

Thank you very much for this welcome, but I must get this record straight. My name is not Dick Groat, it is not Mazeroski—I am not Vern Law.

But I am most sincerely grateful to you for the warmth of this welcome.

I have just come from Cleveland where I saw another great crowd, and I saw the same signs "Vote for Nixon and Lodge."

And that is what I am going to do.

Thank you very much.

NOTE: The President spoke just before entering the Pittsburgh-Hilton Hotel. In the opening paragraph he referred to members of the Pittsburgh Pirates baseball team.

354   ¶ Address in Pittsburgh at a Dinner Sponsored by the Allegheny County Republican Executive Committee.   *November 4, 1960*

Congressman Judd, Mr. Graham, Mr. Flaherty, Senator Scott, the congressional delegation, and my fellow Americans:

After a half century in the service of the Republic, I address you tonight.

I am not here merely because of friendship for any person or out of any sense of obligation to any individual or organization of individuals. Such influences carry a great appeal but they cannot be controlling in this time of decision.

I am here solely because of my concern for the future of the United States and your hopes of peace with justice and in freedom.

That future and your deepest hopes are at stake. And they can be compressed right now to a choice between two men and their running mates.

For me, drawing on a lifetime of experience with men who want to lead and men who can lead, there is no question about the choice.

I support Richard Nixon and Henry Cabot Lodge.

In speaking to you tonight, I am sharply conscious:

Of the debt I owe this country.

Of the pride I feel as I review the long march of America, generation after generation, to leadership among the nations.

Of the hope that our grandchildren and their grandchildren will recall our days and our decisions with a like pride.

All these reasons, deep-seated in my heart, demand that I speak out on our right and duty as American citizens next Tuesday to vote—to vote our sober, serious convictions.

So doing, we shall once again justify the American faith that free men and women, voting in secret ballot, answerable only to conscience, will judge wisely as honest stewards of a grand heritage; as farsighted designers of a grand destiny.

We will not justify this faith if we are moved by selfish interest or specious promise or emotional appeal; or if we vote as members of a bloc.

The major, the over-riding, problem of today is the global struggle between those who seek to impose dictatorial domination over all men and those who seek to help all men achieve a good life in freedom.

On the outcome of this struggle depends the preservation of everything that we hold dear; the liberty that we enjoy; the opportunities we possess; the just peace we purpose.

Should we lose this struggle, Communism would darken the light of the world.

This international struggle defines the character, scope and importance of every domestic question argued and publicized in this political campaign. The primary importance of these debated issues is their effect upon our ability to win the ideological war.

To make America's world leadership felt and effective in this vast conflict, we must be strong—strong morally, economically and, indeed, militarily—as we are tonight.

Strength cannot be conjured out of glittering generalities and promises; out of fanciful pictures of a life of ease—devoid of labor, sacrifice and self-dedication; out of a grab-bag of easy answers for hard questions.

If we are to be respected and our leadership willingly accepted, the substance of our strength must be realized and felt. Every individual among us must find his greatest happiness in constructive work—work for himself, his family, his community, our Nation.

Our moral strength must never waver; never weaken before the blackmail of threat; never degenerate into surrender-infected compromise with a gun-enforced tyranny.

Our military strength must be, at whatever cost, so maintained that never again will the United States through military weakness be plunged into war—as it was three times within this century.

To fortify our economic strength, we must pay our way, not thoughtlessly piling an ever-mounting debt upon the shoulders of our children and our grandchildren and forfeiting the confidence of other nations.

We must be proud of our heritage, diligent in its maintenance and determined in its continued development; neither deserting our traditions, nor downgrading ourselves.

We must have leadership—leadership of the very finest kind that we can produce. In this campaign, only in Richard Nixon and Ambassador Lodge is the best of such leadership to be found.

I say this because they possess a rich experience in waging the kind of war in which we are now engaged; in meeting the needs of our Nation to support our world purposes; and in leading us to victory.

What I am talking about is not a matter of predicting the number of motels to be built in a given time; of forecasting to the dollar the amount of money that will be spent on gadgets and luxuries in the next four years; or of guaranteeing precisely the number of jobs that will be filled at a distant date.

The matter of which I speak—of indescribable and lasting importance to every individual among us—is the application of integrity and intellect and experience to countless problems, always directly affecting our domestic strength and our progress toward peace; they are always changing in their context and in their priorities; but always changeless in their demand for sober, resolute, steady minds.

In the campaign of our opponents, the juggling of promises by the inexperienced, the appeal to immediate gain and selfishness, the distortion of fact, the quick changes from fantastic charge to covert retreat—all these are intended to confuse the voter; not to enlighten him.

And this is nothing new. The tactics of confusion have always been a device to cover weakness in principle or in purpose or in proposal. They are still the arsenal of those who lack a constructive program founded on tested principle.

Out of the complexities of modern living, our political opponents construct a jungle of problems which, they say, are impossible of solution except by the formulas they have dreamed up and would like to test— on us and on the world. If allowed to do so—if elected—they will call the tune, but we—and those who come after us—will pay the piper, and we will have to pay, because their announced plans call for swollen costs and mushrooming expenditures.

Now our opponents of course are experts at assuring us that neither higher taxes nor deficit spending will be used to meet these additional costs. But all history shows the absurdity of this claim.

Now this is a time for woodshed honesty—even if the American people have to apply a little woodshed discipline to get it. Unless they do, the American family will pay the costs out of its family budget because either Federal taxes will skyrocket once again or the cheap dollar and higher prices will return.

Now, of course, political opponents promise us more dollars in our pockets so that we can meet the cost of their schemes. But purchasing power at the corner grocery comes from creative and productive work, not from Federal printing presses grinding out dollars that constantly buy less—less food—less clothing—less shelter.

My friends, all gains made by labor rest on one foundation—a stable dollar. Possibly, for a time, a wage earner receiving a constantly increasing number of dollars in his pay envelope may imagine he is keeping even with the speed that his dollars cheapen. But accelerated inflation soon destroys even this poor hope and reduces it to futility.

But think of the man living on a fixed pension, or the man whose savings are in bonds and insurance policies, or the one who has nothing but his social security.

The effect on him is catastrophic.

Does this show concern for our senior citizens? A concern so prated about in some of the other platforms we read—platform planks in Los Angeles.

These wizards in fiscal shell games try to prove that all problems can be solved by bigger government, bigger spending, bigger promises. They are idolatrous worshippers of bigness—especially of big government.

But we must recognize that:

All our problems are still human problems.

All our goals are still human goals.

Therefore, for the proper conduct of human affairs, we must have:

Character that endures; not campaign promises that evaporate.

Ability that elevates; not ambition that corrupts.

Responsibility that deliberates; not rashness that stampedes.

Experience in duty that sobers; not eagerness for power that intoxicates.

Richard Nixon and Cabot Lodge, in this light, are worthy of your choice as well as mine. They have been tried and trained, tested and proved worthy.

One thought more.

Almost sixteen and a half years ago, almost on the very eve of D-Day, I became absorbed in a soul-wracking problem. A senior staff officer of mine, a tested and gallant battle leader, came to me to express his conviction that part of the plan that I had devised and approved would require the destruction of two fine American divisions—two airborne divisions of gallant soldiers. He prophesied that if I went on with this movement, these two divisions would suffer at least 90 percent casualties, even before they could land. Manifestly, if this were true, their sacrifice would be futile, because there would be no remaining strength.

If he were right, it appeared that the attack on Utah Beach was probably hopeless, and this meant that the whole operation suddenly acquired a degree of risk, even foolhardiness, that could generate a gigantic failure, possibly Allied defeat in Europe.

And the decision was squarely up to me. There was no one to help me. Professional and technical advice and counsel had been exhausted.

There was nothing for me to do but to go to my tent and think out this problem alone. I realized, of course, that if I disregarded the advice of my technical expert and trusted associate, and if his predictions should be true, then I would carry to my grave the unbearable burden of a conscience justly accusing me of indifference to the lives of thousands of Americans, and of a stupid, blind sacrifice of thousands of the flower of America's sons. Outweighing any personal burden, however, was the fact that if he were right the effect of the disaster would be far more than local; it would likely affect the entire force and probably cause a gigantic repulse on the beaches.

Now seriously I reviewed every single step in my battle plan. Having completed that study—I phoned to him and said the attack would go as stated.

Now events proved, happily, his prediction to be wrong. And I am glad to say that the first notice that came to me of the successful landing was from this same man, whose joy knew no limits.

But for years thereafter, I felt that only once in a lifetime could a problem of that sort weigh so heavily upon a man's mind and heart.

Now my fellow Americans, now that I know that in this age the President encounters soul-wracking problems many times in a single term of office, I really realize what we are asking the next President to do. This kind of problem comes to him in every conceivable form, almost every day that he is in office.

Not the fate of two divisions or even of an entire landing force but the fate of millions of Americans—young and old, military and civilian, city dwellers and farm families—the fate of the Republic itself might depend on his decision.

When the push of a button may mean obliteration of countless humans, the President of the United States must be forever on guard against any inclination on his part to impetuosity; to arrogance; to headlong action; to expediency; to facile maneuvers; even to the popularity of an action as opposed to the rightness of an action.

He cannot worry about headlines; how the next opinion poll will rate him; how his political future will be affected.

He must worry only about the good—the long-term, abiding, permanent good—of all America.

The nakedness of the battlefield when the soldier is all alone in the smoke and the clamor and the terror of war is comparable to the loneliness—at times—of the Presidency. These are the times when one man must conscientiously, deliberately, prayerfully, scrutinize every argument, every proposal, every prediction, every alternative, every probable outcome of his action and then—all alone—make his decision.

In that moment he can draw on no brain trust; no pressure group; no warehouse of trick phrases, no facile answers. Even his most trusted associates and friends cannot help him in that moment. He can draw only upon the truths and principles responsible for America's birth and development, applying them to the problem immediately before him in the light of a broad experience with men and nations.

He will be face to face with himself, his conscience, his measure of wisdom. And he will have to pray for Divine guidance from Almighty God.

And that is exactly where every thoughtful American will be, and what he should do, when he marks his secret ballot next Tuesday.

Out of that knowledge of the duties and the burdens of the Presidency, and of the responsibility of the good citizen, I must vote for Richard Nixon and Cabot Lodge November 8th.

Thank you and good night.

NOTE: The President spoke at 9:06 p.m. at the Pittsburgh-Hilton Hotel. His opening words referred to U.S. Representative Walter H. Judd of Minnesota, the Reverend William F. Graham, Edward L. Flaherty, chairman of the Allegheny County Republican Executive Committee and coordinator of the dinner meeting, and U.S. Senator Hugh Scott of Pennsylvania.

355   ¶ Radio and Television Remarks on Election Eve.   *November 7, 1960*

My fellow citizens:

Eight years ago on the eve of the 1952 election, I came into your homes through the magic of radio and television to thank the many millions of you—of all parties—of all faiths—from all sections of our land—I thanked you that evening because you supported Richard Nixon and me in our campaign to restore the unimpeded opportunity to America to develop her economic, military, and spiritual strength to the full.

Your response on election day in 1952—renewed in even greater measure in 1956—was overwhelming proof of the identity of beliefs and convictions that you and your families have shared with us over these past 8 years.

It has been a good partnership—and much good for our nation has resulted from it.

For myself, I shall always be humble and grateful because of the confidence you have placed in me and my associates in the Government.

Tonight—on the eve of another election—I again come into your homes.

Tomorrow, we choose the next President of the United States and the Commander in Chief of our Armed Forces—as each of us going into the polling booth finds himself alone with his God and his conscience.   In that booth, each of us makes his own imprint on the future prosperity, security, and peace of the Republic—and of mankind.

Much more than your and my immediate good is at stake.

After church yesterday, I paid a visit to the home, on the outskirts of Gettysburg, where my son and his wife and their four children live. These grandchildren of mine, ranging in years from 12 to 4, are naturally very dear to me.

Though young, they have definite opinions of their own about this election—opinions in which, I must say, I heartily concur.   Of course, like all other children, they are lighthearted and very personal in their approach to an election.   They cannot appreciate what its impact will be upon their lives in the future.

But as I drove away, I could not help pondering on the far-reaching effects that tomorrow's election will inevitably have on them and on all the other Americans—your children and grandchildren—now too young to vote.

Will they, years from now, live in a country still strong and free; still prosperous, its economy undamaged by the cancer of inflation; still dynamic in its philosophy of free enterprise—with Government the partner of the people, not the boss? Will our nation still be the respected leader of free peoples in a world at peace?

This is what all of us want, but none of us tonight can answer these questions. I do pray that we, here and now, in this election do our part to give to these young Americans the best possible chance of inheriting from us a sound Republic.

I do pray that the man we choose to be your—and my—President for the next 4 years is endowed with wisdom, common sense, experience, and character. Then the heritage of our children and grandchildren will be well served.

———

Since the beginning of the Republic, great decisions influencing our destiny have been wrought by the President in deliberation with his Cabinet. In such deliberations, the measure of every participant is soon taken by those around him.

Since January of 1953, in the Cabinet Room of the White House, in the weekly sessions of the Cabinet and the National Security Council, Richard Nixon sat directly across the table from me—a mere few feet away.

I came to know him as a man cannot be known from headlines or interviews or speeches. I lived with him in hours of intense discussion and thought and soul-searching.

Around the Cabinet table were gathered at every meeting men and women who constituted in their dedication to the public good, a gathering worthy of America's highest purposes.

The matters before us were always important to the well-being of Americans; often of grave moment; sometimes fraught with the peril of war, sometimes critical in their impact on the nation's prosperity and security.

They included such matters as:

Korea and Formosa and Lebanon;

Suez and Indo-China;

a halt to Communist engulfment that began in 1946;

a buildup, for the first time in our peacetime history, of an adequate military posture including the initiation and development of missile systems never before attempted;

orderly expansion at Cabinet level of programs in health, education and welfare;

an end to Federal controls on your economy and a halt to rapid rises in the cost of living.

The constant effort was to create conditions in which America might live in bright hope; might have the opportunity to better themselves and the living of their families; might be confident that their Government cared about people.

In every discussion during these 8 years of Cabinet and National Security Council sessions, all of us were always unified in fundamental principle. Our single guide was the welfare of the United States. But in the application of principle, there were often expressed honest and wide differences of opinion. This was democracy at work—and quite naturally these differences inspired full, even heated, debate.

Through all these meetings, I could watch Richard Nixon; absorbed in the thoughtful, sober, silent weighing of every word and idea.

Then, after others had spoken, I frequently asked him to present a consensus of the judgments expressed. This he did, avoiding the trivial, the irrelevant, the imprudent; adding, from his own insight and knowledge and conviction, counsel that took into account every factor important to my final decision.

Eight years ago, I pledged to you that I and my Administration would serve all the people of America in every human way. Four years ago, I repeated that pledge—to lead and serve in devotion to the national interest; in a program of hard work; and in the purpose of seeking always a universal peace with justice. I hope you believe we have kept that pledge.

Acting for you, we fostered a climate of enterprise and hope.

And you—the people of America—took effective advantage of the opportunities so created. In all the works of heart and mind and hand you have set new records of achievement.

You made the United States the most powerful nation on earth— militarily, economically, spiritually.

In partnership with local and State and Federal Government, you built schools in your communities; expanded colleges and universities; erased slums; linked cities with expressways; advanced the horizons of knowledge in the science of health, of security, of space; pushed to new standards of living—as no people ever before has been able to do in a comparable period.

Far from standing still, you have advanced dramatically. My pride in you is beyond anything I can express—but I do suggest to you: just look around. See for yourselves what you have accomplished. And you will continue so to advance—given assurance that the climate of confidence will be sustained and that the system of free, competitive enterprise will never be weakened by political meddling.

That assurance you will have with the right kind of leadership, steeped in the philosophy of enterprise and of hope; experienced in working for an America, confident of her destiny, secure against the devastation of war, in a world moving toward peace with justice in freedom.

In those countless hours in the Cabinet Room, in many more hours of consultation with him at my own desk, I took the measure of the man that is Richard Nixon. He will provide that sort of leadership.

Side by side with him, the other member of a remarkable team, is Henry Cabot Lodge, esteemed by the entire free world and grudgingly respected by Communist bosses. He will give Richard Nixon the sturdy help, advice, and support that only a man who has proved himself a statesman, a diplomat, a great American, can give his President.

Cabot Lodge, for 8 years, has dealt with international problems at the highest level. And he has performed superbly, as the many million Americans who have watched him at the United Nations well understand. Incidentally, Ambassador Lodge will be the next to follow me on this program.

———————

My friends, I have one all-consuming desire: I want our country to continue along the paths of peace and progress that she has trod so confidently for 8 years. I want America to have the most experienced, the most responsible leadership that we can produce.

You want the same, I know. But I am told that millions of you still are called "undecided voters." I deeply hope that this means only that you are still undecided as to your choice. I trust that you are decided in a determination to vote your choice tomorrow after you make it.

Let us remember that the right to vote was won for you in the toil and sacrifice and blood of all the fighting men of all America's wars. You must not ignore or reject that right.

My friends—exactly 18 years ago tomorrow, on November 8, 1942, it was my responsibility to lead an invading force of young Americans and their allies, landing in Africa in the first great land operation of World War II to eliminate the Hitler-Mussolini axis. Those two men had decided to destroy the right of freedom and of the free vote in the world. Our men were there to prevent this.

In all that command everybody was far from home; none had decent shelter, rarely any hot food; they were lonesome, tired, hungry; they were constantly exposed to the dangers of bullets and bombs. Thousands of them were wounded or disabled. Many others died. But their comrades pushed on until at least in Africa they forced the surrender of the Fascists and the Nazis.

They then went on to over-run Pantelleria, capture Sicily, invade Italy—finally, they and their comrades and their brothers who came after them invaded northern Europe. Finally we reached the culmination with the surrender of the Nazis at Berlin. Now they fought their way through danger and terror, under the constant threat of extinction, until they penetrated the Nazi heartland and destroyed that menace to freedom.

The primary purpose of their courage and sacrifice was to assure that there could not be taken from us the right of free government, the freedom of responsible citizenship—a citizenship that demands of us all the exercise of our right to vote.

I shall exercise my right tomorrow, as I hope you will, also. For myself, because of my firsthand knowledge of their capacity, dedication and character, I shall vote for Richard M. Nixon and Henry Cabot Lodge, as again I hope you will.

And now, after the last campaign speech that as your President I shall ever make to you, I say good night—may God bless you all and our beloved country.

NOTE: The President spoke at 10:30 p.m. at a studio of the Columbia Broadcasting System in Washington.

356 ¶ Telegrams of Congratulations to the President- and Vice President-Elect. *November 9, 1960*

Senator John F. Kennedy
Hyannis Port, Massachusetts

My congratulations to you for the victory you have just won at the polls. I will be sending you promptly a more comprehensive telegram suggesting certain measures that may commend themselves to you as you prepare to take over next January the responsibilities of the Presidency.

DWIGHT D. EISENHOWER

Senator Lyndon B. Johnson
Driskill Hotel
Austin, Texas

The American people have spoken. Congratulations and best wishes on your victory as Vice President-elect.

DWIGHT D. EISENHOWER

357 ¶ Telegrams to Vice President Nixon and Henry Cabot Lodge. *November 9, 1960*

The Vice President of the United States
Ambassador Hotel
Los Angeles, California

Your hard-fought courageous campaign to carry forward the principle of sound government will have my lasting respect. It has been a matter of deep personal satisfaction to have served closely with you these past eight years and I shall always cherish your friendship. Best wishes to Pat and a salute to you both for your spirited and sustained work in the cause of good government.

DWIGHT D. EISENHOWER

Ambassador Henry Cabot Lodge
Sheraton Park Hotel
Washington, D.C.

I salute you for a magnificent campaign in the finest tradition of a great American family. I shall be forever grateful for your effective service to my Administration and the country during these past eight years. Please extend my regards to Emily, and my best wishes in whatever your future may hold.

DWIGHT D. EISENHOWER

358 ¶ Letter to Secretary Mueller Concerning Participation in the New York World's Fair of 1964-65. *November* 12, 1960

My dear Mr. Secretary:

It will be desirable to give early consideration to the advisability of participation by the United States in the New York World's Fair to be held in New York City in 1964 and 1965. It is also desirable that preliminary consideration be given to the character and scope of any such participation.

It is accordingly requested that the Secretary of Commerce take the lead in considering the question of Federal participation in the New York World's Fair and present to me his recommendations thereon not later than January 1, 1961.

In connection with the carrying out of the foregoing assignment, it is requested that the appropriate Federal agencies be consulted. I suggest that you consult the Departments of State, Treasury, Agriculture, the Interior, Labor, and Health, Education and Welfare, the Atomic Energy Commission, the National Aeronautics and Space Administration, the National Science Foundation, the United States Information Agency, and the Housing and Home Finance Agency.

Expenditures arising in connection with the above shall be paid from the appropriation appearing under the heading "Special Projects" in Title I of the General Government Matters Appropriation Act, 1961 (Public Law 86–642; 74 Stat. 473–474).

I am sending a copy of this letter to the head of each of the foregoing agencies.

Sincerely,

DWIGHT D. EISENHOWER

NOTE: The letter was released at Augusta, Ga.

359 ¶ Exchange of Messages Between the President and President Garcia on the Occasion of Philippine-American Day. *November* 14, 1960

Dear President Garcia:

It gives me great pleasure to reaffirm the close ties between our two countries on this day designated by the late President Magsaysay as Philippine-American Day.

Our two nations share a common heritage. For over six decades we have worked together to create and maintain strong democratic institutions. Our task has not been easy. During the fourth decade we fought side by side to defend our way of life. Now we are challenged by the imperialistic ambitions of a ruthless ideology. It is especially fitting, therefore, that we pause on this day which marks the twenty-fifth anniversary of the inauguration of the Commonwealth of the Philippines to rededicate ourselves to the principles of free government and to reaffirm our conviction that we shall eventually have a world in which all men are brothers, and in which the outstretched hand is not that of a tyrant, but the hand of friendship.

Sincerely,

DWIGHT D. EISENHOWER

NOTE: President Garcia's message follows:

The President
The White House

The Philippine Government has designated November fifteen as Philippine-American Day, primarily as a fitting reminder to the peoples on both sides of the Pacific of the special ties of friendship that have characterized several decades of intimate and close relationship between the Philippines and the United States of America.

To twenty-seven million Filipinos, this date bears additional significance as it also commemorates the Twenty-Fifth Anniversary of the Philippine Commonwealth, the transition period which preceded the final attainment of Philippine independence and which in the minds of Filipinos was the climax and fruit of many years of special Philippine-American relations.

Let this day, therefore, be the occasion for Filipinos and Americans to jointly reiterate their high goals and noble objec-

60295—61——58

tives for continued and lasting friendship based on mutual respect. Let this also be the time for a rededication of our common determination to meet and deter further encroachment by Communist imperialism on our accepted free and democratic way of life.

CARLOS P. GARCIA

The messages were released at Augusta, Ga.

360   ¶ Statement by the President on the Entrance Into Sea Duty of the Polaris Submarine George Washington.   *November* 15, 1960

TODAY the Polaris submarine U.S.S. *George Washington* leaves the United States for the high seas. It will be the first of its kind to become operational and inaugurates a new technique of deterrence. Roving and hidden under the seas with 16 thermonuclear missiles apiece, the *George Washington* and her following sisterships possess a power and relative invulnerability which will make suicidal any attempt by an aggressor to attack the free world by surprise. The *George Washington,* the *Patrick Henry,* the *Abraham Lincoln* and other Polaris submarines will perform a service to world peace worthy of the great American names they bear.

NOTE: On November 1, following Prime Minister Macmillan's announcement that Great Britain had agreed to provide a base for U.S. nuclear submarines armed with Polaris missiles, the Press Secretary to the President issued a release concerning the arrangements made with Great Britain for support facilities for the submarines. The release stated that the President welcomed the arrangements as further evidence of United States-British cooperation for the mutual benefit of both countries and the NATO Alliance.

The President's statement of November 15 was released at Augusta, Ga.

361   ¶ Letter to Dr. Nnamdi Azikiwe on the Occasion of His Investiture as Governor General of the Federation of Nigeria.   *November* 16, 1960

Dear Dr. Azikiwe:

On the occasion of your investiture as Governor General of the Federation of Nigeria, it gives me great pleasure to extend to you, both personally and officially, cordial greetings and heartiest congratulations.

This great honor, which happily comes to you on your birthday anniversary, is a fitting tribute to your long years of devoted service to your country and to Africa. I know that your many friends in the United States join with me in expressing the hope that your years in this high office will be marked by peace and prosperity for your people and by ever-closer relations between Nigeria and the United States.

Sincerely,

DWIGHT D. EISENHOWER

NOTE: The letter was released at Augusta, Ga.

362   ¶ The President's News Conference at Augusta, Georgia.   *November* 16, 1960

THE PRESIDENT. Ladies and gentlemen, this is not a press conference as such, but we are distributing today a paper—which you will get after we have finished here—that is of such importance that I thought it was worthwhile to come down and tell you something of my own feelings about it.

It has to do with the balance of payments problem. This is a problem that has been engaging the concern of government officials for a number of years. Financial circles and financial pages have been watching it, and, moreover, foreign financial institutions also have been very much concerned about it.

Of course, as the balance of payments gets too unfavorable with respect to any country—in this case ours—you have either to settle your debts with gold or you have to increase your dollar obligations. Therefore the risks or the threat of a sudden movement of gold that could have very bad inflationary effects in our own country are such as to demand great care on the part of governmental officials.

We have been doing what we could over some years. For example, one of the things that you can do to avoid this unfavorable balance of payments is to continue sound fiscal policies here at home and avoid inflation. By avoiding inflation you keep down the costs of your products and as a result you can compete, you can get your share of the income, and you sell enough to pay for all of the outflow of dollars and credits to other nations.

Except for the year 1959, our exports have been very fine. They always have shown a surplus, but I think in 1959 there was only about a

$1 billion balance. This year it may reach $4 billion. But that is still not enough to support the outflow that we have.

One of the things that happens is this: if people—other nations which use dollars as well as gold in their financial reserves—get fearful of the American dollar, then there can be what you call a run on it. They want to convert into gold right away, and the outflow of gold would be so rapid that we could, of course, be greatly embarrassed.

Now there are many things we can do. The paper that you will receive today not only describes for you in considerable detail what the problem is, but it will describe what are the actions that we can take now administratively—or at least some of them.

Without going into detail, they are measures to check the unnecessary flow of dollars and credit abroad, and to increase our own sales abroad.

For a long time we have had a committee in the Cabinet that has been coordinating all of our efforts toward increasing exports. Indeed we have worked with our industrial and agricultural activities and institutions, in order to increase these exports—and we have done so. But more needs to be done, both in increasing our exports and decreasing the outflow of credits and dollars.

Now they are outlined, as I said, in the paper you will receive. One of them, for example, is a reduction in the number of dependents of the armed services abroad, and a similar reduction by all of the departments that have personnel stationed overseas—to cut them down to the minimum. But as I say, you will read it in more detail in the paper.[1]

Now I think that's about the story as I see it. I repeat that this problem of balance of payments is not separated from sound fiscal practices in our own country, because as long as other people know that we can, and will, pay our bills as we go, they will not get frightened of our dollar; they will not demand that dollars be exchanged into gold. That is the kind of thing that is always important.

I think that's the story as I wanted to give it to you, and with respect to this one problem, if there are any additional comments of your own, any additional questions, why I would be glad to talk about them.

Q. John Scali, Associated Press: Mr. President, will you discuss this problem tomorrow at the National Security Council meeting?

---

[1] The President referred to his directive of November 16 concerning the U.S. balance of payments problem. The directive is published in the Federal Register (25 F.R. 12221) and in the 1960 Supplement to title 3 of the Code of Federal Regulations.

THE PRESIDENT. Well, it may be brought up. I should have pointed out that, of course, our national security as well as our own soundness of our economy are affected by a healthy situation in this balance of payments, but as such, I doubt whether it would be on the agenda. No.

Q. Felix Belair, New York Times: Mr. President, are there any estimates at all of the amount potentially that might be saved as a result of the directives being issued today?

THE PRESIDENT. Well, I didn't ask for that estimate, Felix, but— (*confers with Mr. Hagerty*)—I just hear from Jim that the Treasury Department is actually trying to make such an estimate today and later in the day may be able to give you such an estimate. I do know that as of now we have about a half million dependents in the Military Establishment abroad. This is a rather expensive business. No one likes to break up families, but when you are sending out gold dollars all the time—that's what they are now under the present situation—why we have to set a limit, and that is what we are trying to do.

Q. William J. Eaton, United Press International: Mr. President, can you tell us roughly how many dependents will be pulled back?

THE PRESIDENT. Well, it's in the paper. I think they want to come down at the rate of 3 percent and down to a maximum of about two hundred thousand. Three percent per month, I should have said, and down to a maximum of two hundred thousand.

Q. Robert C. Young, Chicago Tribune: Mr. President, do you anticipate that this cut in the military dependents would—well, in view of the effect it would have on this balance of payments deficit—would be working any kind of hardship on military personnel?

THE PRESIDENT. Well, of course, it is a most unhappy occasion when you have to set up regulations that do separate families for a period of their service. For example, we have never allowed dependents to go to Korea, but we have shortened the tour of our military personnel. And while there may be some unfavorable budgetary effects here—in other words, we may have to spend more of our own dollars here, but we will spend them at home. So I would say that one of the compensations would be, possibly, by shorter tours of service. That is normally done.

Q. Daniel Karasik, National Broadcasting Company: Mr. President, in the proposed ways of saving dollars, is there any suggestion of having the NATO countries help support dependents abroad?

THE PRESIDENT. Well, yes. As a matter of fact, this whole problem is the principal purpose of Mr. Anderson and Mr. Dillon going abroad this Saturday.[2] We have been discussing the problem, of course, with numbers of people. We are going to insist that NATO, and particularly the more fortunate countries industrially, which are now accumulating great reserves, should be asked to do their part in carrying the economic aid program to other nations that we want to help have better conditions in the interests of world peace. The industrially strong countries must help to meet the payments that are so burdensome to us, when we are spread all over the world with troops and with aid and all that sort of thing. Of course, we shall insist that they help. That's in the paper, by the way.

Q. John Scali, Associated Press: Mr. President, in the past, there have been persistent reports that crop up to the effect that in order to help close this gap we might consider reducing the actual number of troops that we maintain in Western Europe as a shield for NATO. Could you say anything about this?

THE PRESIDENT. Well, of course this comes up all the time, because it's a very expensive business keeping troops abroad. As you know, the American soldier is the highest paid soldier in the world, and there's all sorts of discussions come up when we have them stationed abroad in large numbers. But I would say this: the last thing we would want to do would be to diminish the combat strength of our forces until the NATO countries have found it possible so to solve their problems that they can fill the gaps.

Now, I could go back to January 1951 when I was sent to NATO. It was always thought of as an emergency operation, just as the Marshall plan was thought of as an emergency program. In the Marshall plan you were rebuilding an economy. With NATO you were trying to rebuild a

---

[2] On November 15 the White House released a statement by Secretary Anderson after his meeting with the President to discuss the forthcoming visit to Bonn with Under Secretary of State Dillon. The statement announced that the President had instructed Secretary Anderson to pursue with Chancellor Adenauer and other representatives of the German Republic matters of mutual interest in the international financial field, including the cost of U.S. troops in West Germany, and assistance to developing countries.

The statement added that the President had asked Secretary Anderson to convey his warmest personal greetings to Chancellor Adenauer, as well as his personal hopes that the talks would result in even greater understanding and mutually beneficial results in the interest of the strength of the free world.

The full text of Secretary Anderson's statement is printed in the Department of State Bulletin (vol. 43, p. 864).

defense until they—Europe—picked up the burden. Well, I think we should never want to reduce our forces so far that people would think we had abandoned the area, or we had lowered our flag in that area. Not at all. But I do think that the time is coming when all of us will have to study very carefully what should be our proper portion of the load.

Q. Harold Davis, Atlanta Journal: Mr. President, is there some thought of reducing diplomatic and ICA personnel also?

THE PRESIDENT. Well, that's in the directive all right. I propose that the State Department, through its ambassadors, go over this whole business with a fine-tooth comb and see whether there are some people we can take out. I think personally that most of us that have traveled throughout the world have had the impression, at least, that we could do with fewer people. I think there must be a real study job done on it. That would be one way to help, all right.

Q. William J. Eaton, United Press International: Mr. President, is there any consideration being given to reducing or curtailing traveling by Americans abroad?

THE PRESIDENT. I think that would be one of the things we should not do. Remember our great purpose of promoting progress toward peace. One thing we don't want to do is to develop an isolationist practice of staying at home. I would add this: I would like to see our people go abroad, but I would like also to see more Europeans and other people that have money come to our country. Let's have a little reciprocity around here. That would be very helpful. At the same time we want them, not merely because of the dollars, but for the general effect it has on the progress toward peace.

Well, now, ladies and gentlemen, that's the problem, and the subject for the day. And I would again add this: I do think that the paper deserves your very closest study, because it has been tightly reasoned. It has been prepared carefully over a good many days and weeks. I think you will find paragraphs right in the middle of it that are just as important as those that you find at the opening of the paper.

Thank you very much.

NOTE: President Eisenhower's one hundred and ninety-second news conference was held in the press room of the Hotel Richmond in August, Ga., at 3:35 o'clock on Wednesday afternoon, November 16, 1960. The attendance was not recorded.

363   ¶ Statement by the President on Making
Public a Report by the Science Advisory Committee.
November 20, 1960

[Released November 20, 1960. Dated November 17, 1960]

THIS REPORT is part of a continuing study by my Science Advisory
Committee of ways in which the Federal Government can best assure the
strength and progress of American science, one of our essential resources
for national security and welfare. I hope it will be favorably received
and widely studied by everyone in our national community concerned
with the advancement of scientific knowledge through basic research
and with the education of young scientists.

I call particular attention to the conclusion of the Science Advisory
Committee that the process of basic scientific research and the process of
graduate education in universities must be viewed as an integrated task
if the nation is to produce the research results and the new scientists that
will maintain the leadership of American science. In this great endeavor,
the partnership between the Federal Government and the nation's universities will assume growing importance in the future.

NOTE: The report "Scientific Progress, the
Universities, and the Federal Government," dated November 15 (33 pp., Government Printing Office, 1960), was
prepared by a special Panel on Basic Research and Graduate Education of the
President's Science Advisory Committee.

The President's statement was issued as
part of a White House release which also
included a summary of the panel's conclusions and of its recommendations by Dr.
George B. Kistiakowsky, Chairman of the
President's Science Advisory Committee,
together with his letter to the President
submitting the report.

This statement was released at Augusta,
Ga.

364   ¶ Exchange of Messages Between the President and President Touré of Guinea Regarding U.S. Policy Toward the Congo.
November 26, 1960

[Released November 26, 1960. Dated November 25, 1960]

Dear Mr. President:

Your cable on November 20, 1960, I regret to say, reflects a serious misunderstanding of the policy of the United States Government in support of African freedom. I am prompted, therefore, to recall to you that the United States has been in the forefront of those nations who have favored emancipation of all peoples, including Africans, in accordance with the purposes and principles of the Charter of the United Nations. The record of our actions over many years in support of African emancipation is open for all to see.

With specific reference to the Republic of the Congo, the United States warmly welcomed its independence. We have recognized and upheld its unity and territorial integrity through United Nations actions. We have refrained from unilateral intervention in its internal affairs. Although considerable partisanship has been demonstrated by some states, our support for the recognition by the United Nations of M. Kasavubu as Chief of State, a constitutional position which is universally accepted and recognized in the recent report of the U.N., is not a question of partisanship but an attempt to strengthen one of the essential foundations of stable and effective government in that unhappy country. This, I believe, is in strict conformity with the interests of the Congolese Government and people. As you are aware, a large number of African states have taken a similar stand. In view of the support by most countries for the United Nations role in the Congo and the fact that United Nations success is vital for the welfare of the Congolese, I sincerely hope that you will give full support to the United Nations effort there.

Sincerely,

DWIGHT D. EISENHOWER

NOTE: President Touré's message follows:
    I have the honor to inform you of our concern at the development of a partisan position by the United States in the situation in the Congo. We earnestly request that you cease supporting the position of

the enemies of African emancipation, who are employing every possible means against the legitimate government of the Congo to attack the unity and territorial integrity of the Congolese Nation. If the United States maintains its present posi-

tion the Government of Guinea will refuse to take any part in the Conciliation Commission and will take any position in African affairs consistent with Congolese interests. High consideration.

SEKOU TOURÉ

365 ¶ Statement by the President Upon Completion of the Mission of Secretary Anderson and Under Secretary Dillon to West Germany. *November 28, 1960*

THE SECRETARY of the Treasury and the Under Secretary of State this morning reported to me, personally, on conversations they conducted last week with officials of the Federal Republic of Germany which were conducted in a cooperative and friendly spirit by the delegations on both sides, with a complete mutual willingness to explore proposals.

I believe that the discussions were most useful. They developed agreement between the two countries on the necessity of maintaining a sound international financial system, not only for the economic well-being of the countries involved but so that each country may continue to provide the resources basic to the common security of the nations of the Free World.

As a result of these talks there is a greater acceptance of the United States view that there must be basic improvement in the United States balance of payments position as an essential part of maintaining the Free World's financial system, depending as it does upon the dollar as a cornerstone.

Secretary Anderson and Secretary Dillon, both in substance and in presentation, carried out my instructions. These had been fully coordinated with the Secretary of State and the Secretary of Defense and had been made known in advance to the Government of the Federal Republic of Germany.

Although the matter of sharing in some way a portion of the total cost of United States Troops in West Germany was discussed, in accordance with the announcement made in Augusta on November 15,[1] it did not

---

[1] The President referred to a statement by Secretary Anderson. See Item 362, footnote 2.

result in agreement. However, the discussion contributed greatly to a growing understanding of the problem.

It was agreed with the Federal Republic of Germany that there should be a continuation of discussions on a number of other points which could not be fully explored in a short meeting but which are designed to lead to the betterment of the United States balance of payments position. These various proposals, some suggested by the Germans and some by the American representatives as possible partial aids to our common problem, will continue to be negotiated in Bonn and in Washington.

The American delegation expressed appreciation of the decided speedup and greater flexibility of a proposed German program for development aid to developing countries, recognizing fully the major importance of this new program recently introduced by the Federal Republic of Germany.

Among other problems upon which there will be continuing discussions are the removal of remaining restrictions on imports of agricultural products from the United States, an enlargement of procurement of military items by the Federal Republic of Germany for its own forces, and consideration of procuring military items which might be supplied to other countries of the NATO alliance.

On the way home from Bonn, Secretaries Anderson and Dillon informally exchanged views with French and British officials as well as United States officials in Paris and London on matters of mutual interest, particularly the world financial system.

I am confident that greater world understanding will result from the conversations, and will serve both our national and international interests by helping to reinforce the soundness of the Free World's financial system.

The United States is determined to take whatever decisions are necessary and appropriate consistent with its devotion to a free economy and as are necessary to protect the integrity of the dollar.

366 ¶ Exchange of Messages Between the President and Prime Minister Ikeda on the Election in Japan. *November 28, 1960*

Dear Mr. Prime Minister:

I extend my congratulations to you and to the Liberal-Democratic Party on your election victory on November twentieth. I end my term of office as President of the United States with deep satisfaction over the close cooperation between our two countries, and with the knowledge that this cooperation will continue to grow and increase in the years ahead.

Sincerely,

DWIGHT D. EISENHOWER

NOTE: Prime Minister Ikeda's reply follows:

Dear Mr. President:

I wish to thank you most sincerely for your kind message of congratulations on our election victory on November twentieth.

It is indeed most reassuring to know that the majority of the Japanese people endorsed our consistent policy to cooperate closely with the United States for the furtherance of world peace and prosperity. The Government and the people of Japan deeply appreciate the kind cooperation of the United States under your great leadership during eight long years of your tenure of office as President of the United States, and I wish to avail myself of this opportunity to express, on behalf of the Government and the people of Japan, our heartfelt gratitude to you.

Sincerely,

HAYATO IKEDA

367 ¶ Exchange of Messages Between the President and Prime Minister Nash of New Zealand. *November 30, 1960*

Dear Prime Minister:

Thank you for your two letters of October tenth, and particularly for your renewed invitation to visit New Zealand as the guest of your Government. Such a visit would, I can assure you, be a source of happiness to Mrs. Eisenhower and me, for we have often wished to see your beautiful country and to get better acquainted with the people of New Zealand. Since we have made no plans for the period after I leave office, I can unfortunately make no commitment in this regard, but I most sincerely appreciate your kindness in renewing this gracious invitation.

    With warm personal regard,

Sincerely,

DWIGHT D. EISENHOWER

NOTE: Only one of the two letters from Prime Minister Nash, dated October 10, was released with the President's reply. Its text follows:

My dear Mr. President:

    May I again reiterate the personal invitation that I extended to you during my last visit to Washington to come to New Zealand as the guest of the Government of New Zealand. Any time that you and Mrs. Eisenhower feel that you have the time available and would like to come down to the South Pacific we will take particular care to ensure that your visit is of interest and it would we hope bring you and Mrs. Eisenhower much joy and happiness in visiting a smaller country which, for many years, has had very happy relations with the great United States of which you have been in charge for the last eight years.

    With kind personal regards and all good wishes to Mrs. Eisenhower and yourself,

    I am,

Yours sincerely,

WALTER NASH

368 ¶ Exchange of Messages Between the President and President Ydigoras Fuentes on U.S. Naval Aid to Guatemala. *December 2, 1960*

[Released December 2, 1960. Dated November 28, 1960]

Dear Mr. President:

I should like to thank you for your very kind message of November nineteenth. The steps taken by the United States Government have enabled us to be in a position to respond to the request received from Your Excellency's Government on November sixteenth for assistance in preventing Communist-directed efforts to intervene in the internal affairs of your country through the landing of armed forces or supplies from abroad. I am gratified to learn that constitutional order is being maintained in Guatemala.

The American people join me in expressing warm good wishes to the Guatemalan people and to Your Excellency personally.

    Sincerely,

DWIGHT D. EISENHOWER

NOTE: The message from President Ydigoras Fuentes follows:

His Excellency
Dwight D. Eisenhower

I take pleasure in sending you the cordial greetings and the great gratitude of the people and government of Guatemala for the effective aid you were good enough to grant by ordering a watch on the seas adjacent to Central America by units of the glorious United States Navy, which prevented outside forces from giving support to the Communist-inspired revolutionary movement which, in connection with Fidel Castro, broke out in Guatemala on the thirteenth of the current month in order to overthrow the constitutional and anti-Communist Government over which I have the honor to preside.

This watch you ordered was decisive in stopping the development of the movement and greater bloodshed in my country and preventing eventual establishment of a new Communist government in the Americas.

The people of Guatemala, my Government, and I personally reiterate our friendship and gratitude to the great people of the United States, to its democratic government, and its illustrious President.

MIGUEL YDIGORAS FUENTES

In a White House release dated December 7 it was noted that in response to requests by the governments of Guatemala and Nicaragua the United States had announced on November 17 that "surface and air units are in a position in which they could assist the governments, should it become necessary, to seek out and prevent intervention on the part of Communist-directed elements in the internal affairs of Guatemala and Nicaragua through the landing of armed forces or supplies from abroad." The December 7 release further noted that the emergency which led to their request had passed and that all participating naval surface and air units had been ordered to return to normal operations.

369 ¶ Joint Statement by the President and President-Elect Kennedy. *December 6, 1960*

THE PRESIDENT of the United States of America and the President-elect conferred today at the White House.

They first met alone in the President's office and then were joined in the Cabinet Room by the Secretaries of State, Defense and Treasury. Also attending this latter meeting were The Assistant to the President and Mr. Clark Clifford, who have been acting as representatives of their two principals during the post-election period.

At the conclusion of the discussions the President and the President-elect agreed to the following statement:

We have had an informal personal meeting on continuing problems, particularly in the international arena, that confront and will continue to confront the Chief Executive of our nation.

The discussions, later joined in by the three Secretaries, covered such foreign affairs matters as major problems of peace, security, and freedom throughout the world, particularly including the American balance of payments and the position of the American dollar; and such domestic matters as the operation of certain aspects of the Executive Branch of the Government, including those related to our national security, as well as the manner in which the White House staff machinery has assisted the President in his Executive responsibilities.

There was of course full understanding that under the Constitution the President of the United States maintains sole jurisdiction for the conduct of the Government until his successor is inaugurated. The meetings, however, were extremely informative in nature. Thus, we feel that we were able in our discussions to provide a better foundation for our representatives who are working on the necessary orderly transfer of Executive responsibility from one Administration to another. The progress to date of this work has been most satisfactory.

We believe that through such orderly processes the continuity of Government affairs will be assured and our people will continue to demonstrate that they are united in the nation's leadership toward peace.

We reaffirm the historic American position that this nation does not covet the territory of any people nor does it seek to dominate or control any other nation.

The American people and their government have consistently sought to protect freedom and have tried to help people throughout the world better their standards of living. These national objectives will be vigorously pursued by the incoming Administration.

The Government of the United States has and will continue to seek peace with justice in freedom for all peoples.

370 ¶ Proclamation 3382: Civil War Centennial. December 7, 1960

By the President of the United States of America a Proclamation:

The years 1961 to 1965 will mark the one-hundredth anniversary of the American Civil War.

That war was America's most tragic experience. But like most truly great tragedies, it carries with it an enduring lesson and a profound inspiration. It was a demonstration of heroism and sacrifice by men and women of both sides who valued principle above life itself and whose devotion to duty is a part of our Nation's noblest tradition.

Both sections of our now magnificently reunited country sent into their armies men who became soldiers as good as any who ever fought under any flag.   Military history records nothing finer than the courage and spirit displayed at such battles as Chickamauga, Antietam, Kenesaw Mountain, and Gettysburg.   That America could produce men so valiant and so enduring is a matter for deep and abiding pride.

The same spirit on the part of the people at home supported and strengthened those soldiers through four years of great trial.   That a Nation which contained hardly more than thirty million people, North and South together, could sustain six hundred thousand deaths without faltering is a lasting testimonial to something unconquerable in the American spirit.   And that a transcending sense of unity and larger common purpose could, in the end, cause the men and women who had suffered so greatly to close ranks once the contest ended and to go on together to build a greater, freer, and happier America must be a source of inspiration as long as our country may last.

By a joint resolution approved on September 7, 1957 (71 Stat. 626), the Congress established the Civil War Centennial Commission to prepare plans and programs for the nationwide observances of the one-hundredth anniversary of the Civil War, and requested the President to issue proclamations inviting the people of the United States to participate in those observances.

NOW, THEREFORE, I, DWIGHT D. EISENHOWER, President of the United States of America, do hereby invite all of the people of our country to take a direct and active part in the Centennial of the Civil War.

I request all units and agencies of government—Federal, State, and local—and their officials to encourage, foster, and participate in Centennial observances.   And I especially urge our Nation's schools and colleges, its libraries and museums, its churches and religious bodies, its civic, service, and patriotic organizations, its learned and professional societies, its arts, sciences, and industries, and its informational media, to plan and carry out their own appropriate Centennial observances during the years 1961 to 1965; all to the end of enriching our knowledge and appreciation of this momentous chapter in our Nation's history and of making this memorable period truly a Centennial for all Americans.

IN WITNESS WHEREOF, I have hereunto set my hand and caused the Seal of the United States of America to be affixed.

DONE at the City of Washington this sixth day of December in the year of our Lord nineteen hundred and sixty, and of the Independence of the United States of America the one hundred and eighty-fifth.

[SEAL]

DWIGHT D. EISENHOWER

By the President:
CHRISTIAN A. HERTER
Secretary of State

371 ¶ Letter to Cardinal Spellman Concerning Aid to Cuban Refugees. *December 9, 1960*

Dear Cardinal Spellman:

I am deeply appreciative of your telegram concerning the Cuban refugees and of your very generous contribution toward the efforts which America is making to deal adequately with the plight of these thousands of Cubans who have fled to our shores to escape oppression.

Mr. Tracy Voorhees, who is acting in this matter for me, has already told me of the inspiring work of the Diocese of Miami under Bishop Carroll and of the instant response of the National Catholic Welfare Conference under Bishop Swanstrom to his requests for action. May I ask that you express to them my gratitude for their important part in the traditional response of the United States and its citizens to such tragic situations.

With warm personal regard, in which Mrs. Eisenhower joins,

Sincerely,

DWIGHT D. EISENHOWER

NOTE: Cardinal Spellman's telegram, also released, stated that he was gratified to learn of the President's appropriation of $1,000,000 to aid Cuban refugees, and that he was forwarding a check for $10,000.

372 ¶ Statement by the President on the Death of Meyer Kestnbaum. *December 14, 1960*

I HAVE JUST HEARD the news of the sudden and tragic passing of Meyer Kestnbaum. As Special Assistant, Mr. Kestnbaum's wisdom and advice were of great value to me in his special fields of Federal-State relationships and in the implementation of the recommendations of the Hoover Commission. An outstanding businessman, he unhesitatingly entered government service and contributed his talents to the public good. Mrs. Eisenhower and I join with his many friends in extending our deep sympathy to his family.

373   ¶ Exchange of Messages Between the President and Prime Minister Holyoake of New Zealand. *December 16, 1960*

Dear Prime Minister:

Please accept my hearty congratulations and best wishes for you and your colleagues in the new Cabinet. I am confident that the close cooperation and friendship between the Governments and peoples of New Zealand and the United States of America will continue to grow during your administration.

With warm regard,

Sincerely,

DWIGHT D. EISENHOWER

NOTE: Prime Minister Holyoake's reply follows:

I was delighted to receive your message of congratulations to my colleagues and me on our assumption of office in New Zealand on 12 December. You may be assured that under my Administration everything possible will be done to ensure the maintenance of the close cooperation and warm friendship that exists between the governments and peoples of New Zea-land and the United States of America.

May I take this opportunity of expressing to you, Mr. President, sincere appreciation of your own great services to the progress and peace of the world and the warmest good wishes of the government and people of New Zealand in my years that lie ahead.

Yours sincerely,

KEITH HOLYOAKE

374 ¶ Statement by the President Upon Issuing Proclamation Fixing the Cuban Sugar Quota at Zero. *December* 16, 1960

I HAVE TODAY by proclamation fixed at zero the quota for imports of Cuban sugar during the first quarter of 1961. The proclamation expresses my finding that such action is in the national interest of the United States. It is applicable to imports of Cuban sugar through March 31, 1961, the expiration date of the present Sugar Act.

Since my proclamation of July 6 of this year the Government of Cuba has continued to follow a policy of deliberate hostility toward the United States and to commit steadily increasing amounts of its sugar crop to Communist countries. This further confirms the view I expressed at that time that the United States cannot now rely upon Cuba to supply a large part of the sugar needs of American consumers.

To replace supplies normally obtained from Cuba, the Department of Agriculture will shortly authorize the importation of non-quota sugar from other countries. These authorizations will be made in accordance with the formula laid down in the present Sugar Act as amended.

Despite my urgent recommendations to the contrary, Congress has provided that one of the countries from which replacement sugar must be purchased under this Act is the Dominican Republic. In view of the unanimous condemnation of the present Government of the Dominican Republic by the Organization of American States, replacement sugar purchases from that country will continue to be subject to special import fees. When the new Congress convenes next month I shall again recommend that it relieve the Executive from the obligation to purchase such sugar from the Dominican Republic.

NOTE: Proclamation 3383 "Determination of Cuban Sugar Quota to Supplement Proclamation No. 3355" is published in the Federal Register (25 F.R. 13131) and in the 1960 Supplement to title 3 of the Code of Federal Regulations. See also Item 223.

375   ¶ Citation Accompanying the National Security Medal Presented to Robert Murphy. *December* 19, 1960

CITATION TO ACCOMPANY THE AWARD OF

THE NATIONAL SECURITY MEDAL

TO

ROBERT MURPHY

ROBERT MURPHY is hereby awarded the National Security Medal.

As Foreign Service Officer, Ambassador, Deputy Under Secretary of State, and Under Secretary of State for Political Affairs he has made an outstanding contribution to the security of the United States. A man of legendary achievement in the cause of freedom during World War II, he has brought to the subsequent councils of the nation rare qualities of idealism and statesmanship in the analysis and resolution of international problems of the greatest complexity. A shrewd observer, a wise counselor, a strong leader, and a diplomat of skill and decision, he has provided steady guidance and made an invaluable contribution to the conduct of foreign affairs and to the development of national intelligence in support of our national security.

NOTE: The President read the citation and presented the award at a ceremony in the Cabinet Room at the White House.

Mr. Murphy served as Assistant Secretary of State from July 28, 1953, to December 18, 1953; as Deputy Under Secretary of State to August 14, 1959; and as Under Secretary of State for Political Affairs to December 3, 1959. He was recalled as career ambassador for special assignment and served until December 31, 1959.

376   ¶ Letter to Secretary Mueller Concerning U.S. Participation in the New York World's Fair of 1964-65. *December* 20, 1960

Dear Mr. Secretary:

I have received your report of December 15, 1960, regarding United States participation in the New York World's Fair, and I approve your recommendations.

There is no doubt in my mind that the Federal Government should participate in the Fair. While I realize that the Congress must authorize formal participation and make the necessary appropriations, I believe that because of the urgency as to time and the strong probability of participation, the theme development and other planning required should be initiated immediately.

I, therefore, authorize and direct the Secretary of Commerce to be in charge of theme development and planning for the United States exhibit and further request that for policy guidance he should organize an appropriate interdepartmental committee and an advisory group of select leaders of American thought and action. The Director of the Bureau of the Budget will assist you in making the necessary arrangements for financing this activity.

Sincerely,

DWIGHT D. EISENHOWER

NOTE: Secretary Mueller's report, in the form of a letter dated December 15 and released with the President's reply, recommended United States participation in the fair. It further recommended that the theme of the U.S. exhibit should be broadly based, "reflecting what America is and will be—its abiding concern for individual freedom and responsibility—its developing opportunities for the individual, rather than, for example, just what America makes or can do."

377 ¶ Presidential Citation Honoring James Forbis Brownlee. *December* 21, 1960

CITATION

JAMES FORBIS BROWNLEE

FOR HIS LIFETIME of public service, the people of the United States owe to James F. Brownlee their profound thanks.

In World War II and the Korean War, Mr. Brownlee occupied governmental positions of great responsibility and contributed markedly to the success of the Nation's efforts. During the past two decades, at critical periods in our national life, in war and peace, he has repeatedly contributed to the Federal Government counsel and strength of outstanding value.

For exceptionally meritorious conduct and outstanding performance on behalf of his countrymen, I cite this record of a patriot.

DWIGHT D. EISENHOWER

NOTE: The President presented the citation to Mrs. Brownlee at a ceremony in his office at the White House. Mr. Brownlee died October 12, 1960.

378   ¶ Statement by the President on Appointing the Presidential Railroad Commission.
December 22, 1960

THE MEMBERS of this Commission, representing management, labor and the public, are embarking upon an effort that will have far-reaching and lasting consequences for the railroad industry. The appointment of this Commission represents a major and constructive innovation that will prove to be a significant achievement in the progress of labor-management relations toward greater maturity and stability. In resolving this problem in a manner fair to the men, helpful to the industry, and in the best interests of our country, the members of this Commission will provide service of incalculable value.

Representatives of the railroads and railway labor organizations concerned have, in a letter to me, jointly recommended that Secretary of Labor James P. Mitchell serve as chairman of the Commission. I am particularly pleased that Secretary Mitchell has agreed to provide this additional and significant service to our Nation in the cause of industrial peace.

NOTE: A list of the 15 members of the Commission was attached to the statement.

379   ¶ Message to President Kubitschek on the Occasion of the Ceremonies in Brazil Honoring the Dead of World War II.   *December 22, 1960*

Dear Mr. President:

The memorial ceremonies which are being held today in honor of the Brazilians who gave their lives in the Second World War have a special significance for me personally and for the people of my country. As wartime Commander of the Allied Forces, I had personal knowledge of Brazilian courage on the field of battle, where members of the armed forces of the United States of Brazil and of the United States of America, allied in the struggle against totalitarianism, fought and died together. I am convinced that the spirit of common endeavor, which characterized our relations then, still permeates them today.

Now we are partners in a common struggle to develop and strengthen our free institutions, to make the benefits of our growing economies available to all our citizens, and to find ways to further understanding among all nations.   On behalf of myself and the people of the United States, I salute the memory of your countrymen who, in time of war, made the ultimate sacrifice.   Remembering their courage, we can continue to work together in time of peace for the high purposes they so gallantly defended.

    With warm regard,

                                        Sincerely,

                                DWIGHT D. EISENHOWER

380   ¶ The President's Certification as to His Forbidding Disclosure to Congress of Certain Documents Relating to Aid to South American Countries.   *December* 23, 1960

[Released December 23, 1960. Dated December 2, 1960]

I AM ADVISED that on October 31, 1960, there were delivered to the Secretary of State, the Director of the International Cooperation, and the Managing Director of the Development Loan Fund written requests from the Chairman of the Subcommittee on Foreign Operations and Monetary Affairs of the Committee on Government Operations of the House of Representatives for certain documents relating to the United States aid program in seven South American countries.

    As I have stated on other occasions, it is the established policy of the Executive Branch to provide the Congress and the public with the fullest possible information consistent with the national interest.   However, the Executive also has a recognized Constitutional duty and power with respect to the disclosure of information, documents and other materials relating to its operations.

    It is vital to the national interest that the officials and employees of the Executive Branch be able to conduct its operations in an effective manner. It is essential to effective operations that such officials and employees be in a position to be fully candid in advising with each other on policy, personnel or other official matters, that they be able to engage in frank and informal exchanges of views with foreign officials and other foreign persons, and that they be in a position to conduct effective investigations into the conduct and suitability of personnel and other matters. The disclosure of certain conversations, communications or documents relating to the foregoing matters can tend to impair or inhibit essential investigative, reporting or decision-making processes or the proper conduct of our foreign relations, and such disclosure must therefore be forbidden, as contrary to the national interest, where that is deemed necessary for the protection of the orderly and effective operation of the Executive Branch.

I have accordingly found it necessary to forbid the disclosure of certain of the documents which are included or understood to be included in the written requests referred to above. These documents are identified in the lists attached to this certificate.

1. Of these documents, those which contain references to statements or policy of the National Security Council or the Operations Coordinating Board recommend changes in such statements or policy or reflect the advice to the President of members of his cabinet and others of his principal advisers. Another document requested contains advice to the Secretary of State by one of his principal assistants concerning policy matters as to which recommendations were to be made to the President. The President must be free to receive the confidential advice of his officers in the Executive Branch. Such documents as these have traditionally not been disclosed outside of the Executive Branch and in my opinion such disclosure would be contrary to the national interest.

2. A number of the documents requested relate to informal conversations or communications between United States officials and foreign officials of the highest rank or other foreign persons of importance. The disclosure of documents of this character outside of the Executive Branch would have an adverse effect upon the willingness of such foreign officials and other persons to engage in the frank and informal exchanges of views which are essential to the proper conduct of our foreign relations.

3. Several of the documents requested relate to personnel matters and contain statements as to the performance, efficiency, loyalty, character or other qualities of particular personnel of the United States Government. It has been the traditional policy of the Government that the disclosure of documents of this character outside of the Executive Branch would be contrary to the proper protection of individuals and could tend to inhibit the candid evaluation of personnel.

4. A number of the documents requested contain investigative matter such as unsubstantiated allegations, confidential sources of information, techniques of investigation and the like. The disclosure of documents of this character would be unfair to the individuals concerned and would tend to impair the ability of the Executive to conduct effective investigations.

5. The requests are also understood to include evaluation reports and exchanges of several airgrams describing recommendations or otherwise referring to such reports as to the Mutual Security Program, prepared by the Department of State or the International Cooperation Administration. For the reasons which I have stated in connection with prior requests for similar reports, such documents may not be released, but the facts shown by such reports are to be furnished.

6. One document requested contains a statement given in confidence to a United States Ambassador by a person who specifically requested that his confidence be respected. The protection of such confidences is necessary to preserve the ability of United States officials abroad to obtain information in the course of their duties as representatives of the President.

In the case of a number of documents requested, more than one of the above reasons for not furnishing the document is applicable.

I accordingly certify, pursuant to Section 101(d) of the Mutual Security and Related Agencies Appropriation Act, 1961, that for the reasons set forth above I have forbidden the furnishing, pursuant to the requests referred to above, of the documents identified on the attached list.

DWIGHT D. EISENHOWER

NOTE: The list of documents comprising the attachment to the President's certification was not released.

The certification was made public together with a letter from the Deputy Assistant to the President to the Attorney General, dated December 9, stating that the Comptroller General had advised the Secretary of State that unless the documents were furnished the use of certain funds would be disallowed pursuant to section 533 A(d) of the Mutual Security Act, and further stating that the President requested an opinion in the matter.

The Attorney General, in a letter dated December 22 and also released, advised the President that the Comptroller General's view concerning section 533 A(d) was erroneous, and that the funds continued to be available.

381   ¶ Remarks at the Pageant of Peace Ceremonies.   *December 23, 1960*

[Delivered over radio and television at 5:15 p.m.]

THROUGH THE AGES men have felt the uplift of the spirit of Christmas. We commemorate the birth of the Christ Child by the giving of gifts, by joining in carols of celebration, by giving expression to our gratitude for the great things that His coming has brought about in the world. Such words as faith and hope and charity and compassion come naturally and gladly to our lips at this wondrous time of the year.

And Christmas inspires in us feelings even deeper than those of rejoicing. It impels us to test the sincerity of our own dedication to the ideals so beautifully expressed in the Christian ethic. We are led to self-examination.

We are grateful for all the material comforts with which we have been blessed. We take great pride in our country's pre-eminent position in the family of nations.

Yet, as we look into the mirror of conscience, we see blots and blemishes that mar the picture of a nation of people who devoutly believe that they were created in the image of their Maker.

Too often we discern an apathy toward violations of law and standards of public and private integrity. When, through bitter prejudice and because of differences in skin pigmentation, individuals cannot enjoy equality of political and economic opportunity, we see another of these imperfections, one that is equally plain to those living beyond our borders. Whenever there is denied the right of anyone, because he dares to live by the moral code, to earn for himself and his family a living, this failure, too, is a blot on the brightness of America's image.

But one of America's imperishable virtues is her pride in the national ideals proclaimed at her birth. When danger to them threatens, America will fight for her spiritual heritage to the expenditure of the last atom of her material wealth; she will put justice above life itself. America will never cease in her striving to remove the blemishes on her own reflection.

Though we boast that ours is a government of laws, completeness in this work cannot be achieved by laws alone, necessary though these be. Law, to be truly effective, must command the respect and earnest support of public opinion, both generally and locally. And each of us helps form public opinion.

Before us, then, is a task that each must himself define and himself perform. Good it is that Christmas helps to make us aware of our imperfections. Better it is that we rededicate ourselves to the work of their eradication.

A year ago last night I returned from a trip that took me to the other side of the world, to eleven nations of wide variations in race, color, religion, and outlook. That homecoming had added meaning for me because I came back at this time of year, when we are unfailingly reminded that, under God, we are all brothers in one world.

In this season next year a new President will address you as I address you now. Each succeeding Christmas will, we pray, see ever greater striving by each of us to rekindle in our hearts and minds zeal for America's progress in fulfilling her own high purposes. In doing so, our veneration of Christmas and its meaning will be better understood throughout the world and we shall be true to ourselves, to our Nation, and to the Man whose birth, 2,000 years ago, we now celebrate.

And now, I ask Mrs. Eisenhower to join me. It is our privilege to turn on the lights of our National Christmas Tree.

NOTE: The President spoke just before lighting the National Community Christ- mas Tree at the Pageant of Peace cere- monies on the Ellipse.

382 ¶ Memorandum to the Secretary of the Army on the Operation of Steamships by the Panama Canal Company. *December* 24, 1960

[Released December 24, 1960. Dated December 21, 1960]

Memorandum for the Secretary of the Army:

I have studied the analyses of the Panama Line that have been made by the Board of Directors of the Panama Canal Company and by the Director of the Bureau of the Budget. I have concluded that its transportation of nongovernmental passengers and cargo for commercial shippers is wholly inconsistent with the intended role of Government in a free enterprise economy.

Accordingly, the Board of Directors of the Panama Canal Company should immediately give the necessary notice, and discontinue the commercial operations of the Panama Line by February 10, 1961. Thereafter the activities of the Line should be confined solely to the transportation of passengers and freight for the account of the Panama Canal Company and the Canal Zone Government.

This action will, of course, necessitate a reappraisal of the Line's operation. The Board of Directors should, therefore, immediately restudy its position that the operation of the steamships is essential to the mission of the Panama Canal Company and promptly report its findings to the Director of the Bureau of the Budget.

DWIGHT D. EISENHOWER

383 ¶ Statement by the President Upon Issuing Proclamation Relating to Petroleum Imports. *December 24, 1960*

I AM TODAY making a technical amendment to Proclamation 3279 which established a mandatory control program for adjusting and regulating imports of crude oil and its principal products into the United States.

The amendment provides for adjustments in oil import levels for over-estimates and under-estimates of total oil demand in Districts I–IV by the Department of the Interior's Bureau of Mines. It is on the basis of such estimates that import levels into these Districts are presently established. The amendment will require the Secretary of the Interior to make corrective adjustments in the mandatory oil import program, in order to prevent over-estimates and under-estimates of total demand from having an unintended impact on levels of importation of oil into the United States.

Districts I–IV include all of the United States with the exception of Alaska, Arizona, California, Hawaii, Nevada, Oregon, Washington, and the Commonwealth of Puerto Rico.

NOTE: Proclamation 3386, amending Proclamation 3279, is published in the Federal Register (25 F.R. 13945) and in title 3 of the 1960 Supplement to the Code of Federal Regulations.

384 ¶ Letter Accepting Resignation of Leo A. Hoegh as Director, Office of Civil and Defense Mobilization. *December 30, 1960*

[Released December 30, 1960. Dated December 29, 1960]

Dear Leo:

Through your efforts as Director of the Office of Civil and Defense Mobilization, our Nation has taken great strides in building a strong non-military deterrent to war. As I accept your resignation, effective January 20, 1961, I assure you of the Nation's debt to you for your personal contribution.

I was particularly pleased to note in your report that the National Shelter Policy, issued in May 1958, has already resulted in the construction of over one million family fallout shelters, that, under the National Plan for Civil Defense and Defense Mobilization, all states and 2500 county and city governments have completed Survival Plans, and that 38 states now have adopted continuity of government measures. Today, OCDM officers could, in the event of dire emergency, warn all states and hundreds of local areas within 15 seconds after an attack is detected. More than half the Nation's high schools have received radiological instruments for instruction; more than 25,000 leaders have received training at the OCDM Staff College; 20 million Americans have received written instruction on fallout shelters. These are some of the outstanding achievements for which you deserve the grateful thanks of the Nation.

I deeply appreciate the work you have done to alert every American to the importance of this vital part of our total security. You have my very best wishes as you return to private life. May the future hold much health and happiness.

With warm regard,

Sincerely,

DWIGHT D. EISENHOWER

NOTE: Mr. Hoegh served as Administrator of the Federal Civil Defense Administration from July 19, 1957, to July 1, 1958, at which time he was appointed Director of the Office of Defense and Civilian Mobilization (redesignated Office of Civil and Defense Mobilization on August 26, 1958). His letter of resignation and report were released with the President's reply.

385 ¶ Letter Accepting Resignation of Arthur E. Summerfield as Postmaster General.
January 1, 1961

[Released January 1, 1961. Dated December 30, 1960]

Dear Arthur:

The operation of the United States postal system during the past eight years under your direction has been better and more efficient than ever before in our history. I am accepting your resignation, effective January 20, 1961, and in so doing I wish to pay tribute to your dedication and management skill, and to the valuable services of your fine staff.

Particularly do I wish to thank you for your fine report of achievements of your Department. You have introduced outstanding improvements in the postal service: the Department's archaic accounting system has been corrected; a new Bureau of Personnel now makes the Department a model of modern personnel practices; an aggressive building and leasing program again enables the Post Office to keep up with increasing volumes of mail; a long-range program explores avenues for greater mechanization in the future.

Americans in all parts of the country are receiving faster postal service. As your report points out, the reorganized handling of local mail now brings next-day delivery to 168 million people in our dense population centers, expanded carrier service now accommodates the 9.3 million families in the growing suburbs, and 1.4 million farm families have been added to the rural delivery service.

I thank you for these services to the Nation and for your friendship over these past eight years. You have my very best wishes for the future as you return to private life. May good health and happiness be yours in the years ahead.

    With warm regard,

As ever,

Dwight D. Eisenhower

NOTE: Mr. Summerfield served during the entire 8 years of President Eisenhower's administration. His letter of resignation, dated December 27, and his report, in the form of a letter, were released with the President's reply.

386 ¶ Statement by the President Concerning Commercial Use of Communication Satellites. *January 1, 1961*

THE COMMERCIAL APPLICATION of communication satellites, hopefully within the next several years, will bring all the nations of the world closer together in peaceful relationships as a product of this nation's program of space exploration.

The world's requirements for communication facilities will increase several fold during the next decade and communication satellites promise the most economical and effective means of satisfying these requirements.

Increased facilities for overseas telephone, international telegraph, and other forms of long-distance person-to-person communications, as well as new facilities for transoceanic television broadcasts, through the use of man-made satellites, will constitute a very real benefit to all the peoples of the world.

This nation has traditionally followed a policy of conducting international telephone, telegraph and other communications services through private enterprise subject to Governmental licensing and regulation. We have achieved communications facilities second to none among the nations of the world. Accordingly, the government should aggressively encourage private enterprise in the establishment and operation of satellite relays for revenue-producing purposes.

To achieve the early establishment of a communication satellite system which can be used on a commercial basis is a national objective which will require the concerted capabilities and funds of both Government and private enterprise and the cooperative participation of communications organizations in foreign countries.

Various agencies of Government, including the Department of State, the Department of Defense and the Office of Civil and Defense Mobilization, have important interests and responsibilities in the field of communications.

With regard to communication satellites, I have directed the National Aeronautics and Space Administration to take the lead within the Executive Branch both to advance the needed research and development and to encourage private industry to apply its resources toward the earliest practicable utilization of space technology for commercial civil communications requirements. In carrying out this task NASA will cooperate closely with the Federal Communications Commission to make certain that the high standards of this nation for communications services will be maintained in the utilization of communication satellites.

387 ¶ Letter Accepting Resignation of Frederick H. Mueller as Secretary of Commerce. *January 2, 1961*

[Released January 2, 1961. Dated December 31, 1960]

Dear Fritz:

Under your leadership, the Department of Commerce has continued to be an articulate and effective voice for the American free enterprise system. You have always encouraged private initiative and you have been a major contributor to the constant fight against inflationary pressures. In accepting your resignation as Secretary of Commerce, effective January 20, 1961, I take the opportunity to pay tribute to you and your excellent staff.

Among the many significant accomplishments of your Department these past eight years, two deserve special mention—the Interstate and Defense Highway Program and the Export Expansion Program. As you point out in your report, the new 41,000 mile highway system has already opened vast new territory for recreation, homes and industry. Not only is it progressing at a most satisfactory rate, but the system is being constructed on a sound "pay-as-you-go" basis. The new National Export Expansion Program, started this year, has done much to improve and expand services and information to help American business sell more abroad. The rise in non-military exports this year must, in large part, be credited to the interest you have helped create in overseas business.

For these activities, as well as the broad range of other functions you have supervised, you have my appreciation and thanks. As you leave government service, I wish you health and happiness in the years to come.

With warm regard,

As ever,

DWIGHT D. EISENHOWER

NOTE: Mr. Mueller served as Secretary of Commerce from August 10, 1959, to January 20, 1961. His letter of resigna- tion, dated December 30, and his report were released with the President's reply.

388 ¶ Statement by the President on Terminating Diplomatic Relations With Cuba. *January 3, 1961*

BETWEEN ONE and two o'clock this morning, the Government of Cuba delivered to the United States Charge d'Affaires ad interim of the United States Embassy in Habana a note stating that the Government of Cuba had decided to limit the personnel of our Embassy and Consulate in Habana to eleven persons. Forty-eight hours was granted for the departure of our entire staff with the exception of eleven. This unusual action on the part of the Castro Government can have no other purpose than to render impossible the conduct of normal diplomatic relations with that Government.

Accordingly, I have instructed the Secretary of State to deliver a note to the Charge d'Affaires ad interim of Cuba in Washington which refers to the demand of his Government and states that the Government of the United States is hereby formally terminating diplomatic and consular relations with the Government of Cuba. Copies of both notes are being made available to the press.

This calculated action on the part of the Castro Government is only the latest of a long series of harassments, baseless accusations, and vilification. There is a limit to what the United States in self-respect can endure. That limit has now been reached. Our friendship for the Cuban people is not affected. It is my hope and my conviction that in the not too distant future it will be possible for the historic friendship between us once again to find its reflection in normal relations of every sort. Meanwhile, our sympathy goes out to the people of Cuba now suffering under the yoke of a dictator.

NOTE: The text of the notes exchanged by the United States and Cuban Governments and released with the President's statement is published in the Department of State Bulletin (vol. 44, p. 103).

On January 4 the Press Secretary to the President stated in a release that the termination of diplomatic and consular relations with Cuba had no effect on the status of the naval station at Guantánamo. He added that the treaty rights under which the naval station is maintained may not be abrogated without the consent of the United States.

389 ¶ Statement by the President Following Announcement of Recipients of the President's Award for Distinguished Federal Civilian Service. *January 3, 1961*

THE EXEMPLARY achievements of these individuals in the fields of communications, science, administration, conservation, and employee relations have contributed significantly to the furtherance of our national goals. Their distinguished careers are in the finest tradition of service to the American people.

Through these awards a grateful nation honors these men who have dedicated their highest abilities to serving the best interests of this great country.

Our progress toward fulfillment of the high purposes of government depends on the ability of the people who devote their careers to the public service. This progress has been enhanced by the outstanding achievements of many of our civil servants. I take this opportunity to express my faith in the skill and devotion to duty that characterize the Federal work force. These characteristics provide a firm basis for the nation's continued progress in the future.

NOTE: The President made this statement in announcing his selection of the following persons to receive the awards: Bert B. Barnes, Assistant Postmaster General, Bureau of Operations, Post Office Department, for "a vital role in providing a vastly improved postal service for the American people despite unprecedented increases in mail volume"; Wilbur S. Hinman, Jr., Technical Director, Diamond Ordnance Fuze Laboratories, Department of the Army, for "brilliant leadership of scientists and engineers in the creation of new electronic techniques and devices having both military and civilian uses, and his own technical contributions"; Frederick J. Lawton, Commissioner, U.S. Civil Service Commission, for "signal success in improving Government management, in perfecting the Federal budget system, and in furthering advancements in personnel management"; Richard E. McArdle, Chief, Forest Service, Department of Agriculture, for "imagination, vision, and inspiring leadership [which] have brought exceptional progress in the development and protection of vital forest resources for the American people now and for generations to follow"; William R. McCauley, Director, Bureau of Employees' Compensation, Department of Labor, for "unusual foresight, judgment and executive competence [through which] he has exercised a profound influence in developing the Federal employees' compensation system to serve the human needs of the times."

Gold medals were presented by the President to the award winners in a White House ceremony on January 11.

390 ¶ Message to Tuanku Syed Putra, Paramount Ruler of the Federation of Malaya.
January 4, 1961

Your Majesty:

On behalf of the American people, I extend congratulations and sincere best wishes on the occasion of Your Majesty's installation as Yang di-Pertuan Agong of the Federation of Malaya. I also take this opportunity to express the hope that the close and friendly relations which have developed between our two countries and our peoples will continue to grow and prosper.

Sincerely,

DWIGHT D. EISENHOWER

391 ¶ Letter Accepting Resignation of Ezra Taft Benson as Secretary of Agriculture.
January 5, 1961

[Released January 5, 1961. Dated January 4, 1961]

Dear Ezra:

As Secretary of Agriculture for the past eight years, you have been of immeasurable aid to me, and in accepting your resignation, effective January 20, 1961, I wish to thank you for the many contributions you have made to the Nation, and especially to its rural population.

Among the vital programs that you have worked for so effectively, these immediately come to mind: The Rural Development Program, which has been the first concerted effort to provide low-income farming areas with technical assistance; the Food for Peace Program, which has helped raise the value of farm exports over the past seven years to $26.5 billion, a record for any seven year period; many of the sound flexible price support programs now working toward better balanced production and consumption; and the greatly intensified research programs that are responsible for expanding markets and finding new uses for our farm products.

Although Agriculture still faces many problems, through your determined and dedicated work, and the efforts of your fine staff, the way has been pointed toward solution of our farm problems.

I again thank you and wish you a future life of good health and happiness as you leave government service.

With warm regard,

As ever,

Dwight D. Eisenhower

NOTE: Secretary Benson served the entire 8 years of President Eisenhower's administration. His letter of resignation, dated January 3, and his report were released with the President's reply.

392 ¶ Statement by the President: The Centennial of the American Civil War.
January 5, 1961

THIS COMING SUNDAY, we citizens of the United States begin observance of the 100th anniversary of the American Civil War. This observance affords us a special opportunity to pay tribute to those Americans whose heroism and sacrifice, a century ago, comprise a part of our national heritage.

America then was a nation divided; today she possesses a national and spiritual unity which has been nurtured and developed over the years, and sometimes defended at great price. This unity provides a base for all that we do as a people.

At the center of American greatness lies something far more than the breadth of our physical expanse with its rich endowment of natural resources. What makes America a leader among nations is a devotion to principle which endures any imaginable strain—a devotion which brings men and women to value something more than they value life itself. Out of that devotion comes an understanding of our national purpose and a deep determination to make that purpose endure.

No event in our history ever tested that devotion, that understanding and that determination more profoundly than did the American Civil War. The memory of that event is shadowed with its story of sacrifice, of loss, of dark tragedy long endured; yet somehow, today, it is the magnificent unity of spirit that came out of it—and the realization that every man is made for freedom and accountable for the freedom of his neighbor—that should be most clearly remembered.

Let us join in the forthcoming Centennial observances with pride. The tragedy is passed, but the way in which Americans of North and South met and eventually overcame that tragedy is a living memory forever.

393 ¶ Letter to Alan T. Waterman on Receiving Report of the National Science Foundation. *January 6, 1961*

Dear Dr. Waterman:

In acknowledging receipt of your report on "Major Activities of the National Science Foundation," I wish to pay tribute to the effective job you and your dedicated staff have done to promote the progress of science.

As you indicate, the work of the National Science Foundation is an excellent barometer of the extent to which the Nation is responding to the urgent need for increasing the scientific effort. It is therefore gratifying that NSF appropriations have risen from $4.7 million in 1953 to $154.7 million in 1960.

Your organization has given outstanding support to works of basic research, the hard core of our national effort in science. In this field NSF grants have gone from $1.8 million to $57.2 million in eight years.

Equally important has been the international research program. Your work during the International Geophysical Year has established beyond question the universality of science.

The NSF has also provided important assistance in providing research facilities and research tools, which, in many cases, have become too expensive to be financed by local institutions.

Through fellowships, training institutes, and other programs, NSF has made dramatic contributions to the training of scientific manpower in the United States.

In making this report public, I should particularly like to call attention to your final sentence: "The realization that today leadership among nations is synonymous with leadership in science presents the United States with the grave responsibility for assuring the continued acceleration and advancement not only of American science but of science throughout the free world."

I thank you for your valuable contributions to the Nation during this Administration.

With warm regard,

Sincerely,

DWIGHT D. EISENHOWER

NOTE: The report (13 pp., mimeographed) was released with the President's letter.

394 ¶ Letter to Archibald J. Carey, Jr., Regarding Report of the President's Committee on Government Employment Policy. *January 6, 1961*

Dear Dr. Carey:

Thank you for your report on the record of the President's Committee on Government Employment Policy. Because I consider this such an important statement, I am making it available to the public.

Yours has been a difficult task. Your high degree of success reflects great credit on your ability and wisdom and the devotion of your excellent staff.

I wish to pay special tribute to the Committee's commendable record in acting on complaints of discrimination. Of the 1,053 cases in which you were called upon to render opinion, corrective actions have been taken in 96 percent of these cases.

The Nation can ill afford discrimination. The Committee of which you are Chairman has made great strides in correcting grievous wrongs.

With warm regard,

Sincerely,

DWIGHT D. EISENHOWER

NOTE: The report, in the form of a letter dated December 30, was released with the President's reply.

395 ¶ Remarks at a Luncheon Honoring the President Given by the Republican National Committee. *January* 6, 1961

THANK YOU. Thank you. It is certainly nice to know that your friends haven't forgotten you.

Mr. Chairman and Mrs. Williams, and my friends:

In my young years—high school and college—I was a member of some athletic teams, and in all of those years there were coaches who were men of character who were always telling us boys that when you had to take a defeat you had to be a good sport about it.

I believed that, and I still believe it. But I never had a coach that told me I had to get used to it. Now the contest ahead of us is for the Congress. That is the next one. When we look into the Congressional results, we find that in 1954, 1956, 1958, and 1960 we failed to get a majority in either House. Now, four times is aplenty and that gets to be a habit, and we will have no more of it.

I will go back to my coaches. I find that every time there was a loss, they just took you out and instead of scrimmaging once a week or twice, you were doing it four times. You practiced not an hour and a half but two hours and a half. Then you got down to the fundamentals, whether it was in football or baseball or any other game you were playing.

Now we are playing something that is far more important than games. The principle of winning contests as honorable individuals—but winning them honorably—means just exactly what you have to do when you are an athletic team: you have to work.

Here and there, there are some people who are supremely endowed. My memory goes back to Jim Thorpe. He never practiced in his life and he could do anything better than any other football player I ever saw.

If we have any of those geniuses around here, they don't have to work—but all the rest of us do.

And if I could leave just one little message, as I try to thank you for the great support that you have given me and the people you represent have given me over these 8 years—and the support you have given to this party and the leadership to this party—if I could leave one little message with you, it would be: no matter how hard we have worked, we can still do better.

I still go back to athletics. There was a team, down in your State, Thruston, called Centre College. One year—antediluvian for most of you—they cleaned up on every great team in the United States. They were called the Praying Colonels. But here is a strange thing, they did pray before every game. But they did not pray for success; they did not pray to win. Their coach had them down on their knees praying that every man there would do his best. That's all they prayed for.

If we would pray that every day for these next 2 years that every one of us, and everybody we can contact, will do his best, we will have a Republican Congress.

Thank you very much.

NOTE: The President spoke in the Cotillion Room at the Sheraton-Park Hotel in Washington. His opening words "Mr. Chairman and Mrs. Williams" referred to Senator Thruston B. Morton and Mrs. Clare B. Williams, Chairman and Assistant Chairman of the Republican National Committee, respectively.

396 ¶ Remarks at Troop Review Ceremonies, Fort Gordon, Georgia. *January 7, 1961*

General Adams, General Hobson, Mr. Mayor, officers and men of Camp Gordon, and members of the garrison:

For me this is a distinct privilege and honor. I have long been wanting to visit Fort Gordon in order that I might thank the personnel which has been so helpful to my friends and my family and me during the intermittent trips that I make to Augusta. I assure you that our obligation to you is deep and lasting.

But I have a very special reason this morning to thank you for the opportunity you have given me to see again soldiers in ranks as I have just witnessed. Fifty years ago I entered the military service and even in the last 8 years, although I call myself a civilian—even sometimes a politician—I am still by law Commander in Chief and therefore I feel a part of you.

This is the last review that I shall ever receive in my life. I have been part of such ceremonies during this half-century. None has been more meaningful than this one. It gives me a chance, through you, to say goodbye to the Army—an Army that has had all these years not only my admiration and affection but my deep feeling of confidence that in such bodies as this, and in your sister services, the United States has a shield that no enemy dare attack or attempt to break down.

So this morning, as I have this chance to say goodbye to you, I hope that you will understand that my heart will always be filled with admiration for you, and there will be in my soul a certain nostalgia as I see a uniform, whether it be a single soldier on the streets or when I see a unit marching in a parade.

God bless you—and keep going.   I have seen a command this morning that would thrill the heart of any soldier, and so I send with you my very best wishes for your future.

NOTE: The President spoke from the reviewing stand on the parade ground. His opening words referred to Lt. Gen. Paul D. Adams, commanding general of the Third United States Army, Fort McPher- son, Ga., Brig. Gen. Howard M. Hobson, commanding general of Fort Gordon and commandant of the Provost Marshal General School, and Mayor Millard Beckum of Augusta, Ga.

397   ¶ Letter Accepting Resignation of Thomas S. Gates as Secretary of Defense.   *January* 8, 1961

Dear Tom:

On the successful discharge of the duties that you have borne, the safety of our nation has vitally depended.   In accepting your resignation as Secretary of Defense, effective January 20, 1961, I assure you of my deep appreciation and admiration of the distinguished contribution you have made in carrying out this task.

Today the United States has a military strength second to none, with the greatest striking power in our history.   At the same time, provision has been made to see that this pre-eminence can be sustained in future years.   In the building and maintaining of this deterrent power, the work of you and your splendid team of associates has been outstanding. But you have not only seen that our armed forces are well designed, fit and ready for their tasks; you have shown a keen understanding that we maintain these forces for purposes that are entirely peaceful—to preserve security, justice and freedom.

In each of the offices you have held in this Administration, your service has been marked by fairness and open-mindedness in approaching your problems, as well as hard work and willingness to consider all points of view, coupled with decisiveness and good judgment.   You have stood like a rock for honest judgments and responsible military programs against the unsound and spurious, from whatever quarter advanced.

I add one personal note. For a President, there is a special cause for gratitude when he can feel certain, always, of the unfailing loyal and able support of his chief lieutenants, as I do of yours.

I hope you will take with you, as your term of service ends, the satisfaction of a difficult, vital job always superbly done.

My very best wishes to you and your family now and in the future, and my warm regard.

As ever,

DWIGHT D. EISENHOWER

NOTE: During President Eisenhower's administration Mr. Gates served as Under Secretary of the Navy from October 7, 1953, to March 31, 1957; as Secretary of the Navy to June 7, 1959; as Deputy Secretary of Defense to December 1, 1959; and as Secretary of Defense to January 20, 1961. His letter of resignation and his report were released with the President's reply.

398 ¶ Remarks at Opening Session of the White House Conference on Aging.   *January* 9, 1961

Mr. Secretary and delegates to this White House Conference:

This is the last time I shall have the privilege of bidding welcome to a group of Americans assembled here in the Capital City to confer among themselves about problems interesting to a particular group or indeed to the whole Nation.

This one, of course, is about the problems of the aged—or the aging, because I don't want to get too definite about this aged business!

It is one, of course, in which many views are held. Some of these, I notice in the press, have been so earnestly stated that they think there shouldn't even be any conference, because their views don't agree with those of some of the others attending.

Now I thought that was the purpose of conferences, to get opposing or opposite views, to see whether there's ground or a program or a platform that can satisfy the sound sense of logic of people of goodwill.

So I applaud the conference, and I think the Congress did a good thing in passing a Joint Resolution asking the President to call this conference. Indeed, I think the Governors in responding so promptly to the request for nominations did also a real service. So I welcome you here, not merely as the head of our Nation hoping that you will have an enjoyable time, but that out of your labors will develop something interesting and profitable for the United States.

Now, as to substantive subjects, there is no reason for me to express my views. I think they are well known, and besides I am not a delegate. But all of us certainly do recognize that in a world changing as rapidly as is ours, when we have gone from a pioneer civilization to a highly industrialized and complicated civilization in a matter of less than a century, there are new problems emerging all the time and that affect often with peculiar force people in special groups, and in this case what we call our senior citizens.

So I feel very privileged to express to you my hope that this will be a profitable conference where every conceivable opinion, no matter how bitterly opposed it may be to some other opinion, will be fully aired, and out of your deliberations will come some kind of guidance that the Congress can use as it proceeds in its own deliberations later.

So, to each of you—welcome. My very best wishes for a good conference, prosperity in the coming year, and indeed in America's labors for maintaining peace and justice, and for raising the standards of our own people in all forms—spiritual, intellectual, and economic.

Thank you. Goodbye.

NOTE: The President spoke in Constitution Hall. His opening words "Mr. Secretary" referred to Arthur S. Flemming, Secretary of Health, Education, and Welfare.

399 ¶ Message to General Cemal Gursel on the Occasion of the Opening of the Turkish Constituent Assembly. *January* 9, 1961

Dear General Gursel:

It is a great pleasure for me to send greetings to you and to the Turkish people on the occasion of the opening of the Turkish Constituent Assembly.

This historic event is a further tangible demonstration of Turkish dedication to democratic ideals and of its determination to build a solid foundation for the future.

Please extend my best wishes to the members of this Assembly for the success of the important work on which they are embarking.

Sincerely,

Dwight D. Eisenhower

400 ¶ Letter Accepting Resignation of George B. Kistiakowsky as Special Assistant to the President for Science and Technology. *January* 9, 1961

[Released January 9, 1961. Dated January 6, 1961]

Dear George:

I accept, as I must, your resignation as my Special Assistant for Science and Technology, effective January 20, 1961. I do so with real regret, for the association we have enjoyed has meant a great deal to me. You have served not only with the utmost professional distinction but with a spirit of constructive helpfulness and outstanding dedication.

For your public-spirited service to your country and your unfailing assistance to me, I am everlastingly grateful. I especially appreciate your offer to continue to be available to me for future assistance.

As you return to the life of teaching and research—to which I know you are so deeply dedicated—you take with you my very best wishes for a future as rewarding and productive, both for yourself and for our country, as has been the period just ending. For my part, I shall continue to prize the opportunity we have shared, in company with your colleagues of the Science Advisory Committee and its panels, to work together for the good of the nation.

With warm regard,

As ever,

Dwight D. Eisenhower

NOTE: Mr. Kistiakowsky served as Special Assistant to the President for Science and Technology and as Chairman of the President's Science Advisory Committee from July 15, 1959, to January 20, 1961. His letter of resignation, dated December 22, was released with the President's reply.

401 ¶ Letter Accepting Resignation of James P. Mitchell as Secretary of Labor. *January* 9, 1961

[Released January 9, 1961. Dated January 6, 1961]

Dear Jim:

With great understanding, skill, and respect for all viewpoints, you have established in the Department of Labor new standards of usefulness to the Nation. In accepting your resignation as Secretary of Labor, as of January 20, 1961, I express my high regard for you and your capable staff.

There are many ways to measure the effectiveness of your work. One important indicator is that time lost because of strikes has been half that lost in the previous eight years.

Important new programs and administrative and structural changes have been initiated in the Department, as your report indicates. States have been encouraged and assisted in improving the welfare of their wage earners. Significant legislation has been passed, including the Landrum-Griffin Act in 1959, which guards against corruption and abuse of trust and power in labor-management affairs.

As you return to private life, you carry with you my deep appreciation for a job admirably done. May your future years bring good health and much happiness.

With warm regard,

As ever,

Dwight D. Eisenhower

NOTE: Mr. Mitchell served as Secretary of Labor from October 9, 1953, to January 20, 1961. His letter of resignation, dated January 4, and his report were released with the President's reply.

402 ¶ Letter Accepting Resignation of Fred A. Seaton as Secretary of the Interior. *January* 9, 1961

Dear Fred:

I accept your resignation as of January 20, 1961. You can take great pride in having discharged your duties as Secretary of the Interior with vigor, wisdom, and imagination.

Your report of the accomplishments of your Department during these last eight years is an account of what wise and responsible government can do to advance the well-being of our people.

I am particularly impressed that our production of hydroelectric power far surpasses that of any other nation in the world; that presently underway is the largest water resources construction program in our history; that the Mission 66 program has taken great strides in preserving, protecting, and improving our National Parks System; that there has been a remarkable increase in our Wildlife Refuge System; that considerable progress has been made on saline water conversion; that education and health programs for our Indian population have been expanded and improved; that an Office of Coal Research has been established; and, of course, that statehood has been achieved for Alaska and Hawaii.

As you return to Nebraska, I want to officially express my thanks and appreciation. In the years ahead, may you always have good health and happiness.

With warm regard,

As ever,

DWIGHT D. EISENHOWER

NOTE: Mr. Seaton served as Secretary of the Interior from June 8, 1956, to January 20, 1961. His letter of resignation, dated January 5, 1961, and his report were released with the President's reply.

403 ¶ Remarks at the Vice President's Birthday Party. *January 9, 1961*

Mr. Chairman, Mr. Vice President, Mrs. Nixon, ladies and gentlemen:

This evening I was looking at my daily schedule and knowing that I was going to come to Dick's birthday party, I thought I would look and see what the staff had down on this particular spot, and the first thing I saw was that I was to go to a party and immediately after the first course I was to go home.

Well, I said, this is rather short shrift, isn't it, just to throw you out after the soup? And I said it wouldn't be polite for me to go, and secondly I would be hungry, and thirdly I wanted to be here for the party, and fourthly I wouldn't get to make a speech if I went that soon— and that is one thing I like to do, is talk to Republicans.

I wanted to pay my little tribute to one who has served his country well, and certainly in these long 8 years has been one of the main-stays of the Republican administration and to me personally has been not only an invaluable associate in Government but a warm friend.

So it is my privilege to present to him, on your behalf, a memento of his birthday. And of course another reason I wanted to come is because it's always fun to see one just having his 48th birthday. Isn't that something?

I am going to read to you the inscription that is on this beautiful little silver bowl—"Richard Milhous Nixon, Vice President of the United States of America, in grateful recognition of his devoted service to our country. January 9, 1961."

I should like to endorse the sentiment expressed on that bowl from the very depths of my heart. I shall never cease to be grateful to him for his loyalty, his absolute readiness to undertake any chore, no matter what the inconvenience to himself and to his family—and whenever he has undertaken such a chore, to perform it brilliantly and to the credit of the United States of America.

So it is an honor for me to present to you this bowl—after all, I am only an honorary member of this club, you know—so it is particularly a distinction for me, Dick. But I hope that this will always remind you that this room is filled with your friends, your admirers, and people that want for you and Pat the very best that this life has to offer.

NOTE: The President spoke at the Mayflower Hotel in Washington. His opening words "Mr. Chairman" referred to U.S. Representative B. Carroll Reece of Tennessee, President of the Capitol Hill Club which sponsored the dinner honoring the Vice President.

404 ¶ Remarks Upon Receiving the Big Brother of the Year Award. *January 10, 1961*

I HAVE BEEN witness to many of these occasions, but it did not occur to me at those times that I was going to be one of the recipients, and I am very grateful.

This kind of movement is a thing that is so worthwhile in this world. We live so much by prejudice, a readiness to view every stranger with suspicion at least—if not worse—and we forget the great value of meeting others and trying to understand them, trying to put ourselves in their place or in their circumstances. And I don't care whether we are talking about difficulties in our own country or abroad.

All these movements that tend toward promotion of understanding are, I think, worthy of the best efforts of every individual. By this I mean that no matter how he is earning his living or whatever his vocation, all of us have the time and the opportunity to do something decent in the world with respect to the individual, and to which he is bound to respond. There is no question about it, if an individual thinks you like him, he just can't help it, he reacts in that same fashion towards you.

I am very proud of being put in this company with you, although my efforts may not have been those that deserve such language—but I am still happy to be in your company. I assure you I will do my best in the years left to me to promote this same kind of understanding, this same kind of feeling in the world. And maybe in doing so—all of us doing so—we will make progress that is noticeable even to us.

Thank you a lot.

NOTE: The President spoke at the White House upon receiving the 1960 award from the Big Brothers of the U.S. and Canada for his "outstanding accomplishments and personal contributions toward a better understanding and brotherhood among peoples of the world." In making the presentation, Charles G. Berwind, President of Big Brothers of America, read a citation to which the President referred in his concluding remarks.

405   ¶ Remarks Upon Receiving the Hoover Medal Award.   *January* 10, 1961

Mr. President and distinguished guests of this distinguished audience:

I am indeed proud to join that company of men which has been awarded this medal during these years since Mr. Hoover first accepted it. And that reminds me that 30 years is just too long a time to elapse between Republican Presidents. And that is a sentiment which I think Mr. Hoover would share.

Ladies and gentlemen, as I listened to the statistics with which I was overwhelmed by General—and we called him "Slam" Marshall—I had the feeling it was a rather good thing he didn't know all those figures, and give them to me somewhere along about December of 1944. I would have been so impressed that I think my mind would have been taken off the war. And certainly it is enlightening, even at this late date, to find out exactly what such devoted and professionally competent people achieved.

And indeed it was the confidence of military men that our technical and professional people could do this. That was at the bottom of the plan that came later to be known as Operation Overlord. This plan came finally to a preliminary state of completion in about April of 1942. It was placed before General Marshall and all of the possibilities were explained to him, and he approved and later got the approval, of course, of the President and the British counterparts. But the point is that the planners knew there would be no ports to use, that the beaches would be mined and defended. But they also had the great faith that the American engineering profession could provide us the equipment and the materiel that would be needed, finally, for victory.

There are one or two incidents that General Marshall did not mention. I am not going to go too deeply into statistics, but there is a story—a true one—that I thought always was interesting. The American engineers equipped with the kind of mechanisms such as he mentioned, went over to Malta; and there was a British air officer, General Park, a very competent and gallant man, who knew that the Americans needed a new fighter field right close by. The only spot that was possible to use was an island and I think it was named Gozo, but if I am wrong General Gruenther will tell me after we leave this meeting. But anyway it was nothing but a mountain. And the British having long ago given up with their hand tools on building this field, said to the engineer colonel visiting for the evening, "How long would it take you to get this field ready?" And the British thought, at least, that anything under a year, if you could do it at all, would be all right. And this man took a look and said, "Oh, 12 to 14 days." And the British officer was so astonished, and really so insulted in a sense, he said, "When can you start?" "Well," he said, "let's see what headquarters will give me." And he cabled back to Africa—he was over in Sicily—and it happened that all this equipment was in a harbor in Philippeville and ready to go, so it went right over.

From the time the equipment reached there, 13 days later, our first fighter flew on and off the field. And General Park made a special flight to me and said, "I take back everything about American bragging; it's all true."

And then, many months later, we were about to go across the Rhine, and we made finally, down near Wesel, what we called a power crossing.

It was way down toward the mouth—it was flooded rivers and it looked pretty bad—all the bridges of course were blown, as the general said.

But we wanted a railroad bridge just to the north of the river, and so the supply people, showing their confidence in themselves, invited me— and I think it was 12 days later—to ride on the first train that was to go across the Rhine on their bridge. They had not yet gotten all the piles and equipment on the side. Well, the amazing thing is that 11 days I went up and they were ready to go, and I didn't have time to stay, but they cut off a piece of rail and gave it to me as a trinket to show that they had done it. That was another of those great accomplishments that people called impossible and therefore took a little time to do.

But finally there was one little incident that impressed me almost more than any other. We had in Normandy what is called the "bocage" country, and it's a country that is very closely bounded and broken up with hedges, fields the size of this room are not uncommon, and these hedges are so old that they have banks of earth formed up around them. And so you have these big hedges—enormous—sometimes 20 feet high— 15 feet and that kind, growing out of these big banks of earth. Every time our tanks would try to go across, of course, they would "belly up," and even a machine gun would go through them, and we were losing tanks and pretty helpless.

There was a little sergeant. His name was Culin, and he had an idea. And his idea was that we could fasten knives, great big steel knives in front of these tanks, and as they came along they would cut off these banks right at the ground level—they would go through on the level keel—would carry with themselves a little bit of camouflage for awhile. And this idea was brought to the captain, to the major and to the colonel, and it got high enough that somebody did something about it— and that was General Bradley—and he did it very quickly.

Because this seemed like a crazy idea, they did not even go to the engineers very fast, because they were afraid of the technical advice, but then someone did have a big question, "Where are you going to get the steel for all this thing?" Well now, happily, the Germans tried to keep us from going on the beaches with great steel "chevaux de frise"—big crosses, they were all big bars of steel down on the beach where the Germans left it. And he got it—got these things sharpened up—and it worked fine. The biggest and happiest group I suppose in all the Allied Armies that night were those that knew that this thing worked. And it worked beautifully.

Now Sergeant Culin later had a leg shot off, but he is still strong and healthy—in New York the last time I saw him—a salesman. And he is one of those humble Americans who had an idea, who had the courage to bring it up to someone who could do something about it. And unquestionably he saved—the idea, properly implemented, of course, by technical and professional men—saved thousands of lives.

So that I submit that sometimes your engineering profession can profit by a little bit of "lay" imagination and wit.

By no means, my friends, did I mean to supplement General Marshall's history with these little accounts, but I couldn't help having my mind jumping around to the theatre of those years, and exciting years.

I cannot tell you how proud I am for the award I have been given, how complimented I am by General Marshall's brilliant remarks this evening, and how happy indeed that I have met so many of you this evening. It is a great privilege. I shall hope to see you again one day, when I am not quite so busy as today.

Goodbye.

NOTE: The President spoke at the Statler Hilton Hotel in Washington on the occasion of the annual Hoover Medal award dinner. The award is sponsored by four leading engineering societies.

The President's opening words "Mr. President" referred to Walker L. Cisler, president of the American Society of Mechanical Engineers, who presented the medal and accompanying citation. Later in his remarks, the President referred to Brig. Gen. Samuel L. A. Marshall, Gen. George C. Marshall, Gen. Alfred M. Gruenther, Air Vice Marshal Sir Keith Rodney Park, and Sergeant Curtis J. Culin.

406   ⟨ Letter Accepting Resignation of Maurice H. Stans as Director, Bureau of the Budget. *January* 11, 1961

[Released January 11, 1961. Dated January 10, 1961]

Dear Maury:

Your efforts on behalf of sound budgetary policies and the promotion of efficiency throughout the Executive Branch of government have been of invaluable assistance to me. In accepting your resignation as Director of the Bureau of the Budget, effective January 20, 1961, I wish to tell you what a superb job you have done.

You have worked tirelessly to insure that the Federal government provides adequately for national needs, while maintaining responsible fiscal policy. Your labors have helped to show that government can be run humanely within the framework of a balanced budget.

Your intensive attention to improving financial management practices in the Federal government has resulted in great savings in time and money and increased efficiency and service to the taxpayer. Your report outlines these improvements—the work of the Office of Financial Management in the Bureau of the Budget, improved accounting systems, training institutes, important changes in the annual budget process, adoption of Hoover Commission recommendations, new automatic data processing.

As you reenter private life, please accept my deep appreciation and gratitude. Good luck on your safari and best wishes for a future of good health and happiness.

With warm regard,

As ever,

Dwight D. Eisenhower

NOTE: Mr. Stans served as Director of the Bureau of the Budget from March 18, 1958, to January 20, 1961. His letter of resignation, dated January 9, and his report were released with the President's reply.

407   ¶ Statement by the President on Receiving Report of the President's Committee on Government Contracts.   *January 11, 1961*

I URGENTLY call the attention of every American to the recommendations made to me today in the final report of the President's Committee on Government Contracts under the able chairmanship of Vice President Nixon. These recommendations, if acted upon, will bring our people closer to the great goal of full equality of opportunity.

This Committee has served the Nation well. It has had a most successful experience in promoting employment equality. The response to its efforts by Government contractors, employing hundreds of thousands of workers, has been gratifying.

Our national policy calls for equal job opportunity irrespective of race, color, religion, or national origin. Our world image as a nation and as a people depends to a great extent on how well we implement that policy. I am confident that every American will strive to make equal job opportunity in the United States a reality. The work of this Committee and its recommendations will go far in helping to achieve that worthy objective.

I want personally to thank all members of the Committee for their dedicated service.

NOTE: The final report of the President's Committee on Government Contracts entitled "Pattern for Progress" was published by the Government Printing Office (24 pp., 1960).

408 ¶ Memorandum Concerning the International Phase of the Large Irregular Air Carrier Investigation. *January* 12, 1961

[Released January 12, 1961. Dated January 9, 1961]

Memorandum for the Chairman, Civil Aeronautics Board:

I have carefully considered the recommendation of the Civil Aeronautics Board in the international phase of the *Large Irregular Air Carrier Investigation,* Docket No. 5132 et al. I have reviewed the case on the basis of foreign policy and defense considerations together with other elements of the national interest that are within my particular responsibilities and have decided (a) to approve the Board's denial of applications and (b) to withhold my approval in other respects.

I appreciate the Board's objectives in proposing temporary certificates authorizing each of the twenty-two "supplemental" carriers to conduct foreign and overseas cargo operations and overseas passenger transportation on an unlimited number of charter flights and on ten individually way-billed or ticketed flights per month in each direction between each of any pair of points. I also recognize that the present limitation on such operations—irregularity in the number and pattern of flights—creates many difficulties.

In view of present levels of competition, however, the number and breadth of the proposed certificates imply a potentially serious economic impact upon the existing overseas and foreign route operations of United States carriers.   This concern is not met by the record now before me. Even that record, moreover, has become out-dated over the period during which I have withheld action on the recommended certificates because of the still-unresolved question—which arose in the separate domestic phase of the case—concerning the Board's legal authority to issue certificates of the proposed type.

DWIGHT D. EISENHOWER

409   ¶ Letter Accepting Resignation of Christian A. Herter as Secretary of State.   *January* 12, 1961

Dear Chris:

As Secretary of State for nearly two years, and for the two years just preceding as Under Secretary, you have made a distinguished contribution, for which the people of our country have cause for deep gratitude. As I accept your resignation, concluding your official service in this vital and important field as of January twentieth, I pay tribute to both your ability and devotion.

Never have you lost sight of our main goals.   First, of course, we have sought to stay at peace, and this we have done.   I know you find deep satisfaction in this, just as I do.

Notwithstanding the periods of crisis and peril the years have brought— and will continue to bring—we have demonstrated our will for peace, while safeguarding security and furthering justice and freedom.   Collective security arrangements have been maintained and strengthened, preserving free peoples against Communist encroachment and oppression. We have worked hard and long to bring under control the threat of nuclear war, through proposals for safeguarded international control measures, and patient and persistent negotiation to this end.   We have sought to advance the use of the atom for peace.   We have ranged our influence on the side of human dignity, and national and individual freedom and sought to achieve greater mutual understanding between the United States and other nations.   We have helped other countries in the course of self-development through our mutual security programs and efforts.   Despite all provocation and hostility, we have avoided being drawn away from our constructive efforts into a mere sterile struggle with the Communist bloc.

For the years that lie ahead, bound to be marked by grave and complex problems but bearing bright promise of progress, I know we both believe that the nation's best hope lies in continued pursuit of these objectives, and we both pray that our country may continue to march successfully toward them.

For your steady hand and wise counsel throughout our service together, and for the privilege I have had of working with you in close association, I am deeply grateful.

You have my best wishes for happy years ahead for yourself and your family.

With warm regard,

Sincerely,

DWIGHT D. EISENHOWER

NOTE: Mr. Herter served as Under Secretary from February 21, 1957, to April 22, 1959, and as Secretary to January 20, 1961. His letter of resignation and his report were released with the President's reply.

410 ¶ Annual Message to the Congress on the State of the Union. *January* 12, 1961

To the Congress of the United States:

Once again it is my Constitutional duty to assess the state of the Union.

On each such previous occasion during these past eight years I have outlined a forward course designed to achieve our mutual objective—a better America in a world of peace. This time my function is different.

The American people, in free election, have selected new leadership which soon will be entrusted with the management of our government. A new President shortly will lay before you his proposals to shape the future of our great land. To him, every citizen, whatever his political beliefs, prayerfully extends best wishes for good health and for wisdom and success in coping with the problems that confront our Nation.

For my part, I should like, first, to express to you of the Congress, my appreciation of your devotion to the common good and your friendship over these difficult years. I will carry with me pleasant memories of this association in endeavors profoundly significant to all our people.

We have been through a lengthy period in which the control over the executive and legislative branches of government has been divided between our two great political parties. Differences, of course, we have had, particularly in domestic affairs. But in a united determination to keep this Nation strong and free and to utilize our vast resources for the advancement of all mankind, we have carried America to unprecedented heights.

For this cooperative achievement I thank the American people and those in the Congress of both parties who have supported programs in the interest of our country.

I should also like to give special thanks for the devoted service of my associates in the Executive Branch and the hundreds of thousands of career employees who have implemented our diverse government programs.

My second purpose is to review briefly the record of these past eight years in the hope that, out of the sum of these experiences, lessons will emerge that are useful to our Nation. Supporting this review are detailed reports from the several agencies and departments, all of which are now or will shortly be available to the Congress.

Throughout the world the years since 1953 have been a period of profound change. The human problems in the world grow more acute hour by hour; yet new gains in science and technology continually extend the promise of a better life. People yearn to be free, to govern themselves; yet a third of the people of the world have no freedom, do not govern themselves. The world recognizes the catastrophic nature of nuclear war; yet it sees the wondrous potential of nuclear peace.

During the period, the United States has forged ahead under a constructive foreign policy. The continuing goal is peace, liberty, and well-being—for others as well as ourselves. The aspirations of all peoples are one—peace with justice in freedom. Peace can only be attained collectively as peoples everywhere unite in their determination that liberty and well-being come to all mankind.

Yet while we have worked to advance national aspirations for freedom, a divisive force has been at work to divert that aspiration into dangerous channels. The Communist movement throughout the world exploits the natural striving of all to be free and attempts to subjugate men rather than free them. These activities have caused and are continuing to cause grave troubles in the world.

Here at home these have been times for careful adjustment of our economy from the artificial impetus of a hot war to constructive growth in a precarious peace. While building a new economic vitality without inflation, we have also increased public expenditures to keep abreast of the needs of a growing population and its attendant new problems, as well as our added international responsibilities. We have worked toward these ends in a context of shared responsibility—conscious of the need for maximum scope to private effort and for State and local, as well as Federal, governmental action.

Success in designing and executing national purposes, domestically and abroad, can only come from a steadfast resolution that integrity in the operation of government and in our relations with each other be fully maintained. Only in this way could our spiritual goals be fully advanced.

FOREIGN POLICY

On January 20, 1953, when I took office, the United States was at war. Since the signing of the Korean Armistice in 1953, Americans have lived in peace in highly troubled times.

During the 1956 Suez crisis, the United States government strongly supported United Nations' action—resulting in the ending of the hostilities in Egypt.

Again in 1958, peace was preserved in the Middle East despite new discord. Our government responded to the request of the friendly Lebanese Government for military help, and promptly withdrew American forces as soon as the situation was stabilized.

In 1958 our support of the Republic of China during the all-out bombardment of Quemoy restrained the Communist Chinese from attempting to invade the off-shore islands.

Although, unhappily, Communist penetration of Cuba is real and poses a serious threat, Communist dominated regimes have been deposed in Guatemala and Iran. The occupation of Austria has ended and the Trieste question has been settled.

Despite constant threats to its integrity, West Berlin has remained free.

Important advances have been made in building mutual security arrangements—which lie at the heart of our hopes for future peace and security in the world. The Southeast Asia Treaty Organization has been established; the NATO alliance has been militarily strengthened; the Organization of American States has been further developed as an instrument of inter-American cooperation; the Anzus treaty has strengthened ties with Australia and New Zealand, and a mutual security treaty with Japan has been signed. In addition, the CENTO pact has been concluded, and while we are not officially a member of this alliance we have participated closely in its deliberations.

The "Atoms for Peace" proposal to the United Nations led to the creation of the International Atomic Energy Agency. Our policy has been to push for enforceable programs of inspection against surprise attack, suspension of nuclear testing, arms reduction, and peaceful use of outer space.

The United Nations has been vigorously supported in all of its actions, including the condemnations of the wholesale murder of the people of Tibet by the Chinese Communists and the brutal Soviet repression of the people of Hungary, as well as the more recent UN actions in the Congo.

The United States took the initiative in negotiating the significant treaty to guarantee the peaceful use of vast Antarctica.

The United States Information Agency has been transformed into a greatly improved medium for explaining our policies and actions to audiences overseas, answering the lies of communist propaganda, and projecting a clearer image of American life and culture.

Cultural, technological and educational exchanges with the Soviet Union have been encouraged, and a comprehensive agreement was made which authorized, among other things, the distribution of our Russian language magazine Amerika and the highly successful American Exhibition in Moscow.

This country has continued to withhold recognition of Communist China and to oppose vigorously the admission of this belligerent and unrepentant nation into the United Nations. Red China has yet to demonstrate that it deserves to be considered a "peace-loving" nation.

With communist imperialism held in check, constructive actions were undertaken to strengthen the economies of free world nations. The United States government has given sturdy support to the economic and technical assistance activities of the UN. This country stimulated a doubling of the capital of the World Bank and a 50 percent capital increase in the International Monetary Fund. The Development Loan

Fund and the International Development Association were established. The United States also took the lead in creating the Inter-American Development Bank.

Vice President Nixon, Secretaries of State Dulles and Herter and I travelled extensively through the world for the purpose of strengthening the cause of peace, freedom, and international understanding. So rewarding were these visits that their very success became a significant factor in causing the Soviet Union to wreck the planned Summit Conference of 1960.

These vital programs must go on. New tactics will have to be developed, of course, to meet new situations, but the underlying principles should be constant. Our great moral and material commitments to collective security, deterrence of force, international law, negotiations that lead to self-enforcing agreements, and the economic interdependence of free nations should remain the cornerstone of a foreign policy that will ultimately bring permanent peace with justice in freedom to all mankind. The continuing need of all free nations today is for each to recognize clearly the essentiality of an unbreakable bond among themselves based upon a complete dedication to the principles of collective security, effective cooperation and peace with justice.

NATIONAL DEFENSE

For the first time in our nation's history we have consistently maintained in peacetime, military forces of a magnitude sufficient to deter and if need be to destroy predatory forces in the world.

Tremendous advances in strategic weapons systems have been made in the past eight years. Not until 1953 were expenditures on long-range ballistic missile programs even as much as a million dollars a year; today we spend ten times as much each day on these programs as was spent in all of 1952.

No guided ballistic missiles were operational at the beginning of 1953. Today many types give our armed forces unprecedented effectiveness. The explosive power of our weapons systems for all purposes is almost inconceivable.

Today the United States has operational ATLAS missiles which can strike a target 5000 miles away in a half-hour. The POLARIS weapons system became operational last fall and the TITAN is scheduled to become so this year. Next year, more than a year ahead of schedule, a vastly improved ICBM, the solid propellant MINUTEMAN, is expected to be ready.

Squadrons of accurate Intermediate Range Ballistic Missiles are now operational. The THOR and JUPITER IRBMs based in forward areas can hit targets 1500 miles away in 18 minutes.

Aircraft which fly at speeds faster than sound were still in a developmental stage eight years ago. Today American fighting planes go twice the speed of sound. And either our B–58 Medium Range Jet Bomber or our B–52 Long Range Jet Bomber can carry more explosive power than was used by all combatants in World War II—Allies and Axis combined.

Eight years ago we had no nuclear-powered ships. Today 49 nuclear warships have been authorized. Of these, 14 have been commissioned, including three of the revolutionary POLARIS submarines. Our nuclear submarines have cruised under the North Pole and circumnavigated the earth while submerged. Sea warfare has been revolutionized, and the United States is far and away the leader.

Our tactical air units overseas and our aircraft carriers are alert; Army units, guarding the frontiers of freedom in Europe and the Far East, are in the highest state of readiness in peacetime history; our Marines, a third of whom are deployed in the Far East, are constantly prepared for action; our Reserve establishment has maintained high standards of proficiency, and the Ready Reserve now numbers over 2½ million citizen-soldiers.

The Department of Defense, a young and still evolving organization, has twice been improved and the line of command has been shortened in order to meet the demands of modern warfare. These major reorganizations have provided a more effective structure for unified planning and direction of the vast defense establishment. Gradual improvements in its structure and procedures are to be expected.

United States civil defense and nonmilitary defense capacity has been greatly strengthened and these activities have been consolidated in one Federal agency.

The defense forces of our Allies now number five million men, several thousand combatant ships, and over 25,000 aircraft. Programs to strengthen these allies have been consistently supported by the Administration. U.S. military assistance goes almost exclusively to friendly nations on the rim of the communist world. This American contribution to nations who have the will to defend their freedom, but insufficient means, should be vigorously continued. Combined with our Allies, the free world now has a far stronger shield than we could provide alone.

Since 1953, our defense policy has been based on the assumption that the international situation would require heavy defense expenditures for an indefinite period to come, probably for years. In this protracted struggle, good management dictates that we resist overspending as resolutely as we oppose underspending. Every dollar uselessly spent on military mechanisms decreases our total strength and, therefore, our security. We must not return to the "crash-program" psychology of the past when each new feint by the Communists was responded to in panic. The "bomber gap" of several years ago was always a fiction, and the "missile gap" shows every sign of being the same.

The nation can ill afford to abandon a national policy which provides for a fully adequate and steady level of effort, designed for the long pull; a fast adjustment to new scientific and technological advances; a balanced force of such strength as to deter general war, to effectively meet local situations and to retaliate to attack and destroy the attacker; and a strengthened system of free world collective security.

THE ECONOMY

The expanding American economy passed the half-trillion dollar mark in gross national product early in 1960. The Nation's output of goods and services is now nearly 25 percent higher than in 1952.

In 1959, the average American family had an income of $6,520, 15 percent higher in dollars of constant buying power than in 1952, and the real wages of American factory workers have risen 20 percent during the past eight years. These facts reflect the rising standard of individual and family well-being enjoyed by Americans.

Our Nation benefits also from a remarkable improvement in general industrial peace through strengthened processes of free collective bargaining. Time lost since 1952 because of strikes has been half that lost in the eight years prior to that date. Legislation now requires that union members have the opportunity for full participation in the affairs of their unions. The Administration supported the Landrum-Griffin Act, which I believe is greatly helpful to the vast bulk of American Labor and its leaders, and also is a major step in getting racketeers and gangsters out of labor-management affairs.

The economic security of working men and women has been strengthened by an extension of unemployment insurance coverage to 2.5 million ex-servicemen, 2.4 million Federal employees, and 1.2 million employees of small businesses, and by a strengthening of the Railroad Unemployment Insurance Act. States have been encouraged to improve their unemployment compensation benefits, so that today average weekly benefits are 40 percent higher than in 1953.

Determined efforts have improved workers' safety standards. Enforceable safety standards have been established for longshoremen and ship repair workers; Federal Safety Councils have been increased from 14 to over 100; safety awards have been initiated, and a national construction safety program has been developed.

A major factor in strengthening our competitive enterprise system, and promoting economic growth, has been the vigorous enforcement of antitrust laws over the last eight years and a continuing effort to reduce artificial restraints on competition and trade and enhance our economic liberties. This purpose was also significantly advanced in 1953 when, as one of the first acts of this Administration, restrictive wage and price controls were ended.

An additional measure to strengthen the American system of competitive enterprise was the creation of the Small Business Administration in 1953 to assist existing small businesses and encourage new ones. This agency has approved over $1 billion in loans, initiated a new program to provide long-term capital for small businesses, aided in setting aside $3½ billion in government contracts for award to small business concerns, and brought to the attention of individual businessmen, through programs of information and education, new developments in management and production techniques. Since 1952, important tax revisions have been made to encourage small businesses.

Many major improvements in the Nation's transportation system have been made:

—After long years of debate, the dream of a great St. Lawrence Seaway, opening the heartland of America to ocean commerce, has been fulfilled.

—The new Federal Aviation Agency is fostering greater safety in air travel.

—The largest public construction program in history—the 41,000 mile national system of Interstate and Defense highways—has been pushed rapidly forward. Twenty-five percent of this system is now open to traffic.

Efforts to help every American build a better life have included also a vigorous program for expanding our trade with other nations. A 4-year renewal of the Reciprocal Trade Agreements Act was passed in 1958, and a continuing and rewarding effort has been made to persuade other countries to remove restrictions against our exports. A new export expansion program was launched in 1960, inaugurating improvement of export credit insurance and broadening research and information programs to awaken Americans to business opportunities overseas. These actions and generally prosperous conditions abroad have helped push America's export trade to a level of $20 billion in 1960.

Although intermittent declines in economic activity persist as a problem in our enterprise system, recent downturns have been moderate and of short duration. There is, however, little room for complacency. Currently our economy is operating at high levels, but unemployment rates are higher than any of us would like, and chronic pockets of high unemployment persist. Clearly, continued sound and broadly shared economic growth remains a major national objective toward which we must strive through joint private and public efforts.

If government continues to work to assure every American the fullest opportunity to develop and utilize his ability and talent, it will be performing one of its most vital functions, that of advancing the welfare and protecting the dignity, rights, and freedom of all Americans.

GOVERNMENT FINANCE AND ADMINISTRATION

In January 1953, the consumer's dollar was worth only 52 cents in terms of the food, clothing, shelter and other items it would buy compared to 1939. Today, the inflationary spiral which had raised the cost of living by 36 percent between 1946 and 1952 has all but ceased and the value of the dollar virtually stabilized.

In 1954 we had the largest tax cut in history, amounting to $7.4 billion annually, of which over 62 percent went to individuals mostly in the small income brackets.

This Administration has directed constant efforts toward fiscal responsibility. Balanced budgets have been sought when the economy was advancing, and a rigorous evaluation of spending programs has been maintained at all times. Resort to deficit financing in prosperous times could easily erode international confidence in the dollar and contribute to inflation at home.   In this belief, I shall submit a balanced budget for fiscal 1962 to the Congress next week.

There has been a firm policy of reducing government competition with private enterprise.   This has resulted in the discontinuance of some 2,000 commercial industrial installations and in addition the curtailment of approximately 550 industrial installations operated directly by government agencies.

Also an aggressive surplus disposal program has been carried on to identify and dispose of unneeded government-owned real property.   This has resulted in the addition of a substantial number of valuable properties to local tax rolls, and a significant monetary return to the government.

Earnest and persistent attempts have been made to strengthen the position of State and local governments and thereby to stop the dangerous drift toward centralization of governmental power in Washington.

Significant strides have been made in increasing the effectiveness of government.   Important new agencies have been established, such as the Department of Health, Education, and Welfare, the Federal Aviation Agency, and the National Aeronautics and Space Administration.   The Council of Economic Advisers was reconstituted.

The operation of our postal system has been modernized to get better and more efficient service.   Modernized handling of local mail now brings next-day delivery to 168 million people in our population centers, expanded carrier service now accommodates 9.3 million families in the growing suburbs, and 1.4 million families have been added to the rural delivery service.   Common sense dictates that the Postal Service should be on a self-financing basis.

The concept of a trained and dedicated government career service has been strengthened by the provision of life and health insurance benefits, a vastly improved retirement system, a new merit promotion program, and the first effective incentive awards program.   With no sacrifice in efficiency, Federal civilian employment since 1953 has been reduced by over a quarter of a million persons.

I am deeply gratified that it was under the urging of this Administration that Alaska and Hawaii became our 49th and 50th States.

AGRICULTURE

Despite the difficulties of administering Congressional programs which apply outmoded prescriptions and which aggravate rather than solve problems, the past eight years brought notable advances in agriculture.

Total agricultural assets are approximately $200 billion—up $36 billion in eight years.

Farm owner equities are at the near record high of $174 billion.

Farm ownership is at a record high with fewer farmers in a tenant and sharecropper status than at any time in our nation's history.

The "Food-for-Peace" program has demonstrated how surplus of American food and fiber can be effectively used to feed and clothe the needy abroad. Aided by this humanitarian program, total agricultural exports have grown from $2.8 billion in 1953 to an average of about $4 billion annually for the past three years. For 1960, exports are estimated at $4.5 billion, the highest volume on record. Under the Food-for-Peace program, the largest wheat transaction in history was consummated with India in 1960.

The problems of low-income farm families received systematic attention for the first time in the Rural Development Program. This program has gone forward in 39 States, yielding higher incomes and a better living for rural people most in need.

The Rural Electrification Administration has helped meet the growing demand for power and telephones in agricultural areas. Ninety-seven percent of all farms now have central station electric power. Dependence upon Federal financing should no longer be necessary.

The Farm Credit Administration has been made an independent agency more responsive to the farmer's needs.

The search for new uses for our farm abundance and to develop new crops for current needs has made major progress. Agricultural research appropriations have increased by 171 percent since 1953.

Farmers are being saved approximately $80 million a year by the repeal in 1956 of Federal taxes on gasoline used in tractors and other machinery.

Since 1953, appropriations have been doubled for county agents, home agents and the Extension Service.

Eligibility for Social Security benefits has been extended to farmers and their families.

Yet in certain aspects our agricultural surplus situation is increasingly grave. For example, our wheat stocks now total 1.3 billion bushels. If we did not harvest one bushel of wheat in this coming year, we would still have all we could eat, all we could sell abroad, all we could give away, and still have a substantial carryover. Extraordinary costs are involved just in management and disposal of this burdensome surplus. Obviously important adjustments must still come. Congress must enact additional legislation to permit wheat and other farm commodities to move into regular marketing channels in an orderly manner and at the same time afford the needed price protection to the farmer. Only then will agriculture again be free, sound, and profitable.

NATURAL RESOURCES

New emphasis has been placed on the care of our national parks. A ten year development program of our National Park System—Mission 66—was initiated and 633,000 acres of park land have been added since 1953.

Appropriations for fish and wildlife operations have more than doubled. Thirty-five new refuges, containing 11,342,000 acres, have been added to the national wildlife management system.

Our Nation's forests have been improved at the most rapid rate in history.

The largest sustained effort in water resources development in our history has taken place. In the field of reclamation alone, over 50 new projects, or project units, have been authorized since 1953—including the billion dollar Colorado River Storage Project. When all these projects have been completed they will have a storage capacity of nearly 43 million acre-feet—an increase of 50 percent over the Bureau of Reclamation's storage capacity in mid-1953. In addition, since 1953 over 450 new navigation flood control and multiple purpose projects of the Corps of Engineers have been started, costing nearly 6 billion dollars.

Soil and water conservation has been advanced as never before. One hundred forty-one projects are now being constructed under the Watershed Protection Program.

Hydroelectric power has been impressively developed through a policy which recognizes that the job to be done requires comprehensive development by Federal, State, and local governments and private enterprise. Teamwork is essential to achieve this objective.

The Federal Columbia River power system has grown from two multipurpose dams with a 2.6 million kilowatt capacity to 17 multipurpose projects completed or under construction with an ultimate installed capacity of 8.1 million kilowatts. After years of negotiation, a Columbia River Storage Development agreement with Canada now opens the way for early realization of unparalleled power, flood control and resource conservation benefits for the Pacific Northwest. A treaty implementing this agreement will shortly be submitted to the Senate.

A farsighted and highly successful program for meeting urgent water needs is being carried out by converting salt water to fresh water. A 75 percent reduction in the cost of this process has already been realized.

Continuous resource development is essential for our expanding economy. We must continue vigorous, combined Federal, State and private programs, at the same time preserving to the maximum extent possible our natural and scenic heritage for future generations.

EDUCATION, SCIENCE, AND TECHNOLOGY

The National Defense Education Act of 1958 is already a milestone in the history of American education. It provides broad opportunities for the intellectual development of all children by strengthening courses of study in science, mathematics, and foreign languages, by developing new graduate programs to train additional teachers, and by providing loans for young people who need financial help to go to college.

The Administration proposed on numerous occasions a broad new five-year program of Federal aid to help overcome the classroom shortage in public elementary and secondary schools. Recommendations were also made to give assistance to colleges and universities for the construction of academic and residential buildings to meet future enrollment increases.

This Administration greatly expanded Federal loans for building dormitories for students, teachers, and nurses training, a program assisting in the construction of approximately 200,000 living accommodations during the past 8 years.

There has been a vigorous acceleration of health, resource and education programs designed to advance the role of the American Indian in our society. Last fall, for example, 91 percent of the Indian children between the ages of 6 and 18 on reservations were enrolled in school. This is a rise of 12 percent since 1953.

In the field of science and technology, startling strides have been made by the new National Aeronautics and Space Administration. In little more than two years, NASA has successfully launched meteorological satellites, such as Tiros I and Tiros II, that promise to revolutionize methods of weather forecasting; demonstrated the feasibility of satellites for global communications by the successful launching of Echo I; produced an enormous amount of valuable scientific data, such as the discovery of the Van Allen Radiation Belt; successfully launched deep-space probes that maintained communication over the greatest range man has ever tracked; and made real progress toward the goal of manned space flights.

These achievements unquestionably make us preeminent today in space exploration for the betterment of mankind. I believe the present organizational arrangements in this area, with the revisions proposed last year, are completely adequate for the tasks ahead.

Americans can look forward to new achievements in space exploration. The near future will hold such wonders as the orbital flight of an astronaut, the landing of instruments on the moon, the launching of the powerful giant Saturn rocket vehicles, and the reconnaissance of Mars and Venus by unmanned vehicles.

The application of atomic energy to industry, agriculture, and medicine has progressed from hope and experiment to reality. American industry and agriculture are making increasing use of radioisotopes to improve manufacturing, testing, and crop-raising. Atomic energy has improved the ability of the healing professions to combat disease, and holds promise for an eventual increase in man's life span.

Education, science, technology and balanced programs of every kind—these are the roadways to progress. With appropriate Federal support, the States and localities can assure opportunities for achieving excellence at all levels of the educational system; and with the Federal government continuing to give wholehearted support to basic scientific research and technology, we can expect to maintain our position of leadership in the world.

CIVIL RIGHTS

The first consequential Federal Civil Rights legislation in 85 years was enacted by Congress on recommendation of the Administration in 1957 and 1960.

A new Civil Rights Division in the Department of Justice has already moved to enforce constitutional rights in such areas as voting and the elimination of Jim Crow laws.

Greater equality of job opportunity in Federal employment and employment with Federal contractors has been effectively provided through the President's Committees on Government Contracts and Government Employment Practices.

The Civil Rights Commission has undertaken important surveys in the fields of housing, voting, and education.

Segregation has been abolished in the Armed Forces, in Veterans' Hospitals, in all Federal employment, and throughout the District of Columbia—administratively accomplished progress in this field that is unmatched in America's recent history.

This pioneering work in civil rights must go on. Not only because discrimination is morally wrong, but also because its impact is more than national—it is world-wide.

HEALTH AND WELFARE

Federal medical research expenditures have increased more than four-fold since 1954.

A vast variety of the approaches known to medical science has been explored to find better methods of treatment and prevention of major diseases, particularly heart diseases, cancer, and mental illness.

The control of air and water pollution has been greatly strengthened.

Americans now have greater protection against harmful, unclean, or misrepresented foods, drugs, or cosmetics through a strengthened Food and Drug Administration and by new legislation which requires that food additives be proved safe for human consumption before use.

A newly established Federal Radiation Council, along with the Department of Health, Education, and Welfare, analyzes and coordinates information regarding radiological activities which affect the public health.

Medical manpower has been increased by Federal grants for teaching and research.

Construction of new medical facilities has been stepped up and extended to include nursing homes, diagnostic and treatment centers, and rehabilitation facilities.

The vocational rehabilitation program has been significantly expanded. About 90,000 handicapped people are now being rehabilitated annually so they are again able to earn their own living with self-respect and dignity.

New legislation provides for better medical care for the needy aged, including those older persons, who, while otherwise self-sufficient, need help in meeting their health care costs. The Administration recommended a major expansion of this effort.

The coverage of the Social Security Act has been broadened since 1953 to make 11 million additional people eligible for retirement, disability or survivor benefits for themselves or their dependents, and the Social Security benefits have been substantially improved.

Grants to the States for maternal and child welfare services have been increased.

The States, aided by Federal grants, now assist some 6 million needy people through the programs of Old Age Assistance, Aid to Dependent Children, Aid to the Blind, and Aid to the Totally and Permanently Disabled.

HOUSING AND URBAN DEVELOPMENT

More houses have been built during the past eight years—over nine million—than during any previous eight years in history.

An historic new approach—Urban Renewal—now replaces piecemeal thrusts at slum pockets and urban blight. Communities engaged in urban renewal have doubled and renewal projects have more than tripled since 1953. An estimated 68 projects in 50 cities will be completed by the end of the current fiscal year; another 577 projects will be underway, and planning for 310 more will be in process. A total of $2 billion in Federal grants will ultimately be required to finance these 955 projects.

New programs have been initiated to provide more and better housing for elderly people. Approximately 25,000 units especially designed for the elderly have been built, started, or approved in the past three years.

For the first time, because of Federal help and encouragement, 90 metropolitan areas and urban regions and 1140 smaller towns throughout the country are making comprehensive development plans for their future growth and development.

American communities have been helped to plan water and sanitation systems and schools through planning advances for 1600 public works projects with a construction cost of nearly $2 billion.

Mortgage insurance on individual homes has been greatly expanded. During the past eight years, the Federal Housing Administration alone insured over 2½ million home mortgages valued at $27 billion, and in addition, insured more than ten million property improvement loans.

The Federal government must continue to provide leadership in order to make our cities and communities better places in which to live, work, and raise families, but without usurping rightful local authority, replacing individual responsibility, or stifling private initiative.

IMMIGRATION

Over 32,000 victims of Communist tyranny in Hungary were brought to our shores, and at this time our country is working to assist refugees from tyranny in Cuba.

Since 1953, the waiting period for naturalization applicants has been reduced from 18 months to 45 days.

The Administration also has made legislative recommendations to liberalize existing restrictions upon immigration while still safeguarding the national interest. It is imperative that our immigration policy be in the finest American tradition of providing a haven for oppressed peoples and fully in accord with our obligation as a leader of the free world.

VETERANS

In discharging the nation's obligation to our veterans, during the past eight years there have been:

The readjustment of World War II veterans was completed, and the five million Korean conflict veterans were assisted in achieving successful readjustment to civilian life;

Increases in compensation benefits for all eligible veterans with service connected disabilities;

Higher non-service connected pension benefits for needy veterans;

Greatly improved benefits to survivors of veterans dying in or as a result of service;

Authorization, by Presidential directive, of an increase in the number of beds available for sick and disabled veterans;

Development of a 12-year, $900 million construction program to modernize and improve our veterans hospitals;

New modern techniques brought into the administration of Veterans Affairs to provide the highest quality service possible to those who have defended us.

CONCLUSION

In concluding my final message to the Congress, it is fitting to look back to my first—to the aims and ideals I set forth on February 2, 1953: To use America's influence in world affairs to advance the cause of peace and justice, to conduct the affairs of the Executive Branch with integrity and efficiency, to encourage creative initiative in our economy, and to work toward the attainment of the well-being and equality of opportunity of all citizens.

Equally, we have honored our commitment to pursue and attain specific objectives.   Among them, as stated eight years ago: strengthening of the mutual security program; development of world trade and commerce; ending of hostilities in Korea; creation of a powerful deterrent force; practicing fiscal responsibility; checking the menace of inflation; reducing the tax burden; providing an effective internal security program; developing and conserving our natural resources; reducing governmental interference in the affairs of the farmer; strengthening and improving services by the Department of Labor, and the vigilant guarding of civil and social rights.

I do not close this message implying that all is well—that all problems are solved.   For progress implies both new and continuing problems and, unlike Presidential administrations, problems rarely have terminal dates.

Abroad, there is the continuing Communist threat to the freedom of Berlin, an explosive situation in Laos, the problems caused by Communist penetration of Cuba, as well as the many problems connected with the development of the new nations in Africa.   These areas, in particular, call for delicate handling and constant review.

At home, several conspicuous problems remain: promoting higher levels of employment, with special emphasis on areas in which heavy unemployment has persisted; continuing to provide for steady economic growth and preserving a sound currency; bringing our balance of payments into more reasonable equilibrium and continuing a high level of confidence in our national and international systems; eliminating heavily excessive surpluses of a few farm commodities; and overcoming deficiencies in our health and educational programs.

Our goal always has been to add to the spiritual, moral, and material strength of our nation.   I believe we have done this.   But it is a process that must never end.   Let us pray that leaders of both the near and distant future will be able to keep the nation strong and at peace, that they will advance the well-being of all our people, that they will lead us on to still higher moral standards, and that, in achieving these goals, they will maintain a reasonable balance between private and governmental responsibility.

Dwight D. Eisenhower

NOTE: The message was transmitted to the House of Representatives on January 12 and to the Senate (not being in session that day) on January 13.

411 ¶ Letter Accepting Resignation of William P. Rogers as Attorney General.   *January* 13, 1961

[Released January 13, 1961. Dated January 11, 1961]

Dear Bill:

Under your direction, the Department of Justice has been noted for its impartial and effective administration of Federal law. In accepting your resignation as Attorney General, effective January 20, 1961, I take the opportunity to emphasize the outstanding record you have achieved with the assistance of your competent staff.

I am particularly gratified by the establishment and functioning of the new Civil Rights Division. Then too, the outstanding record of the Department in bringing anti-trust actions—a 25 per cent increase over the previous eight-year period—is most impressive. Indeed, as your report so well relates, every section of your Department has made commendable advances.

For guiding these achievements, as well as many more that come to mind, you have my thanks and deep appreciation. May the future hold good health and happiness. You leave government service with my respect and sincere friendship.

With warm regard,

As ever,

DWIGHT D. EISENHOWER

NOTE: Mr. Rogers served as Attorney General from November 8, 1957, to January 20, 1961. His letter of resignation, dated January 10, and his report were released with the President's reply.

412 ¶ Letter Accepting Resignation of Gordon Gray as Special Assistant to the President for National Security Affairs. *January* 13, 1961

Dear Gordon:

In accepting your resignation as my Special Assistant for National Security Affairs, effective January 20, 1961, as you request, I thank you not only for your outstanding service in this and earlier assignments, but also for your clear and thoughtful observations concerning the National Security Council.

You have been almost uniquely in position to know its value to me and to the vital work of assuring our country's security now and in the future. The Council itself has admirably fulfilled its function of advice and counsel at the top echelon of government, with thorough, searching and far-ranging debate and deliberation upon the great issues of U.S. national security. In addition, the Council has, as you say, served as the "capstone of mechanisms for assisting you in the formulation of policy and in assuring the timely and effective implementation of policy decisions taken by you." I am especially grateful for your report because somehow, despite our previous efforts, our people have not received an accurate and valid appreciation of the National Security Council's effectiveness—in which you and your predecessors, as well as your staff, have had such an important part.

But my appreciation to you does not stop with your current contribution to the work of the National Security Council, nor even with your previous distinguished service in prior positions. Over the whole wide range of security affairs, it has been a great help to me to have had, as one of my closest associates, a man of your wise understanding, integrity and dedication to our nation's interests. I deem myself, and our country, indeed fortunate.

To you and your fine family I extend my best wishes for happy and rewarding future years.

With warm regard,

         Sincerely,

            DWIGHT D. EISENHOWER

NOTE: Mr. Gray served as Special Assistant to the President for National Security Affairs from July 22, 1958, and as Chairman of the Operations Coordinating Board from January 13, 1960. Earlier he served as Assistant Secretary of Defense, as Defense member of the National Security Council Planning Board, and as Director of the Office of Defense Mobilization.

His letter of resignation, dated January 13, 1961, which includes his observations and report on the National Security Council and related organizations, was released with the President's reply.

413 ¶ Letter Accepting Resignation of Arthur S. Flemming as Secretary of Health, Education, and Welfare. *January* 15, 1961

Dear Arthur:

The dramatic progress in raising the level of health, education, and economic security, through the broad programs administered by the Department of Health, Education and Welfare under your leadership, is a monumental tribute to your organizational skill, understanding of human problems, and ability to see a job through. In accepting your resignation, effective January 20, 1961, I wish to express my deep appreciation to you and your able staff.

On all fronts great gains have been made since my recommendation to establish the Department was approved in 1953. As your report indicates, medical research and health facilities have been significantly expanded; a new Division of Radiological Health has been created; major improvements have been made in fighting air and water pollution; the National Defense Education Act of 1958 has already become a landmark in the history of American education, and Social Security coverage has been broadened and benefits increased.

As you return to private life, I wish you a future of good health and happiness. You take with you my deep thanks and lasting friendship.

With warm regard,

As ever,

DWIGHT D. EISENHOWER

NOTE: Secretary Flemming served from August 1, 1958, to January 20, 1961. His letter of resignation and his report were released with the President's reply.

414   ¶ Annual Budget Message to the Congress: Fiscal Year 1962.   *January* 16, 1961

To the Congress of the United States:

For the fiscal year 1962 I send you budget and legislative proposals which will meet the essential domestic needs of the Nation, provide for the national defense, and at the same time preserve the integrity and strength of our Federal Government's finances.

With this budget, I leave to the new administration and the Congress a progressive and workable financial plan which recognizes national priorities and which reflects my confidence in the strength of our economy now and in the years to come.

A budget surplus was achieved in the fiscal year which ended on June 30, 1960. A narrowly balanced budget is anticipated for fiscal year 1961. The recommendations in this budget provide for still another balanced budget, with a surplus, in fiscal year 1962. The achievement of balanced budgets this year and in the coming fiscal year will help foster noninflationary prosperity at home and strengthen confidence in the dollar abroad.

Despite the persistence of hardship in some local areas, economic activity continues at a high level. It is imperative for the extension of economic growth at a high and sustainable rate that the budget be kept balanced and that we act responsibly in financial matters.

For 1962 the budget estimates reflect expected gains in the national economy and provide for carrying programs forward in an efficient and orderly manner. The estimates also reflect, as in previous years, the budgetary effects of proposed changes in legislation, including the cost of certain new programs. Most of the legislative proposals have been previously recommended. I again urge their enactment.

In total and in its parts, this budget embodies a sensible and forward-looking plan of action for the Government. In brief, it provides for:

1. Increasing our own military capabilities and promoting increased strength in other free world forces;

2. Advancing activities important to economic growth and domestic welfare;

3. Continuing assistance to the less-developed nations of the world whose peoples are striving to improve their standards of living;

4. Increasing support for scientific activities in outer space;

5. Achieving savings by making desirable modifications in existing programs and by charging users the costs of special benefits received by them; and

6. Continuing present tax rates to maintain the revenues needed for a sound fiscal plan.

The policies and proposals in this budget will enable us to meet fully our national and international responsibilities and to promote real and sustainable national progress.

GENERAL BUDGET POLICY

This budget, like each of the seven which I have previously sent to the Congress, reflects the conviction that military strength and domestic advancement must be based on a sound economy, and that fiscal integrity is essential to the responsible conduct of governmental affairs.　A surplus in good times, as provided in this budget, helps make up the deficits which inevitably occur during periods of recession.　To ignore these principles is to undermine our strength as a Nation through deficits, unmanageable debt, and the resulting inflation and cheapening of our currency.

An 8-year effort has been made by this administration to stabilize the purchasing power of the dollar.　This effort, which was a necessary undertaking in view of the heavy depreciation of the dollar's purchasing power following World War II, has had a large measure of success, but the problem of maintaining reasonable price stability will require close and continuing attention in the future.

Our national economy is strong and our national welfare continues to advance.　Despite a leveling out in economic activity during the latter part of the calendar year just ended, the total market value of all goods and services produced in our country in the calendar year 1960 increased by approximately $20 billion over the preceding year and crossed the half-trillion-dollar mark for the first time in our history.　Personal incomes increased more than 5% over 1959, the previous record high.　The Economic Report will describe the trends which indicate that further substantial increases can be expected during the calendar year 1961, carrying the gross national product and personal incomes to new highs.

The budgetary outlook for the future reinforces the need for self-discipline in meeting current national demands.　Over the next 10 years and beyond, we will be faced with the consequences of many commitments under present laws for nondefense expenditures, in addition to the heavy military burden we must continue to bear.

We can confidently expect that a growing economy will help pay for these commitments. As the labor force grows and employment expands, as business discovers new techniques of production and invests in a larger and more efficient productive base, the national output and income will grow, and with them our ability to finance needed public services. But our resources will not be unlimited. New and expanded Federal programs being urged by special groups are frequently appealing, but, added to existing commitments, they threaten to swell expenditures beyond the available resources.

The Federal Government cannot reasonably satisfy all demands at the same time. We must proceed first to meet those which are most pressing, and find economies to help pay their costs by reappraising old programs in the light of emerging priorities. We must encourage States and localities to increase further their participation in programs for meeting the needs of their citizens. And we must preserve and strengthen the environment in which individual initiative and responsibility can make their maximum contribution.

Our unsatisfactory balance of international payments provides another compelling reason for pursuing sound financial policies. The relationship between our budgetary actions and the balance of payments needs to be carefully examined to assure a minimum adverse effect. Whether the dollar will continue to enjoy high prestige and confidence in the international financial community will depend on the containment of inflation at home and on the exercise of wise restraint and selectivity in our expenditures abroad.

The need for concern about our spending abroad is not strange or surprising. It results from the recovery, profoundly desired and deliberately encouraged by our country, of the major centers of production in Western Europe and Japan following the devastation and disruption caused by war. To reflect this developing state of affairs, changes are now required in some policies established in earlier years. Therefore, I have prescribed certain actions in international transactions under direct governmental control and others are under study. Such measures, combined with proper financial prudence in the handling of domestic affairs and strong export promotion, should significantly improve our balance of payments.

In summary, if we plan wisely and allocate our resources carefully, we can have both public and private advancement. Sound fiscal policies and balanced budgets will sustain sound economic growth and, eventually, will make possible a reduced tax burden. At the same time, we can have necessary improvements in Federal programs to meet the demands of an ever-changing world. If, however, we deliberately run the Government by credit cards, improvidently spending today at the expense of tomorrow, we will break faith with the American people and their children, and with those joined with us in freedom throughout the world.

Budget Totals—1961

Current estimates indicate a close balance in the 1961 budget. On the newly adopted basis of excluding interfund transactions, expenditures are estimated at $78.9 billion and receipts at $79.0 billion, resulting in a budget surplus of $0.1 billion. The revenue estimate reflects a justifiably optimistic view as to the course of our economy, based on circumstances described in my Economic Report.

Last January, I proposed a budget for 1961 that showed a surplus of $4.2 billion. The enactment by the Congress of unrecommended expenditures and the unwillingness of the Congress to increase postal rates reduced this prospect by approximately $2 billion. In the meantime, lower corporate profits have materially reduced our expectation of tax collections from this source.

The small surplus of $79 million currently estimated for 1961 takes into account an assumption that postal rates will be increased not later than April 1, 1961.

Despite the congressional increases in the budget last year, the present estimate of $78.9 billion for 1961 expenditures is about $900 million less than the figure of $79.8 billion which appeared in the budget a year ago. The apparent reduction results from (1) the elimination, as announced in last year's budget, of certain interfund transactions totaling $0.7 billion from the current estimate of expenditures and (2) the shift of employment security grants of $0.3 billion to trust fund financing as provided by law. As explained elsewhere in this budget, these changes affect receipts as well as expenditures and do not affect the surplus.

Apart from these accounting adjustments, the increases and decreases from last year's estimate of 1961 expenditures are approximately offsetting.

Major increases from the original budget include $766 million for Federal employee pay raises; $554 million in losses of the postal service because rates were not increased as proposed; $269 million for defense programs; $188 million for health, education, and welfare activities; and $164 million for civil space activities.

Major decreases from the original estimates include $600 million for interest on the public debt; $496 million for the activities of the Commodity Credit Corporation; $311 million for veterans compensation, pensions, and readjustment benefits; $93 million for the Export-Import Bank; and $50 million for military assistance. In addition, a reduction of $160 million is estimated under the proposal to reduce the postal deficit in 1961 by increasing postal rates effective April 1. Other reductions, including a normal downward revision in the allowance for contingencies, total $210 million.

BUDGET TOTALS—1962

For the fiscal year 1962, my recommendations provide for $82.3 billion in budget receipts and $80.9 billion in budget expenditures. The resulting budgetary surplus of $1.5 billion will permit another modest payment on the public debt.

The estimate of receipts in 1962 is $3.3 billion higher than the current estimate for 1961, and $4.6 billion more than the receipts actually collected in 1960. Expenditures are also increasing, from a total of $76.5 billion in 1960 to $78.9 billion currently estimated for 1961 and $80.9 billion proposed for 1962.

BUDGET EXPENDITURES.—The increase of $1.9 billion in estimated expenditures between 1961 and 1962 reflects several factors which are worthy of special note.

First, outlays for our Nation's defenses are estimated to rise by $1.4 billion in 1962 to a total of $42.9 billion. Much of this increase reflects continued emphasis on certain expanding defense programs, such as Polaris submarines, the Minuteman missile, the B–70 long-range bomber, a strengthened airborne alert capability, airlift modernization, and modernization of Army equipment. These improvements are for the purpose of keeping our military might the strongest in the world.

Second, the budget provides for substantial continuing efforts to support the cause of freedom through the mutual security program. Expenditures for this program in 1962 are estimated at $3.6 billion, an increase of $250 million over 1961.

Third, civil space vehicles and space exploration will require $965 million in 1962, up $195 million from 1961, and $564 million more than in 1960.   In total, the recommendations in this budget provide for $9.4 billion in expenditures in 1962 for carrying forward research and development efforts, of which $7.4 billion is for major national security purposes. The total represents an increase of $770 million over 1961.   As part of the overall research and development effort, increasing Federal support for basic research is being provided.   This budget includes $1 billion for the conduct and support of basic research in universities, industrial establishments, Government laboratories, and other centers of research.

Fourth, increases in expenditures are proposed for certain activities important to domestic well-being and to the future development of our Nation.   These include, among others, broadening medical care for the aged; making major improvements in transportation programs; continuing development of our natural resources at a new record level of expenditures; improving our health and welfare programs; providing assistance for construction of elementary and secondary schools and college facilities; assisting areas of substantial and persistent unemployment; and fostering rural development.   Expenditures in 1962 for labor, education, health, welfare, community development, transportation aids and services, and conservation of natural resources are estimated to total $8.6 billion, an increase of $627 million over 1961.

To some extent these recommended budget increases are offset by proposed reductions which can be effected in existing programs through improved operations and through changes in present laws.   These reductions result from a continuous search for ways to restrain unnecessary expenditures in going activities, to recognize real priorities of need, and to assure that Federal programs are carried out in an efficient manner.

Savings are proposed and can be achieved through modification of activities which, in their existing form, require a disproportionate or wasteful expenditure of Federal funds.   For example, States, localities, and other non-Federal interests should assume a greater share of the costs of urban renewal, local flood protection, and the building and operating of schools in federally affected areas.   The Congress should act on proposals to encourage nongovernmental financing, and reduce reliance on direct Federal financing, in such activities as home loans for veterans and for military personnel, and the expansion of rural electrification and telephone systems.   Certain grants and benefits should also be reviewed and revised, including those for agricultural conservation, civil airport construction, airline subsidies, housing aids no longer needed for readjustment of World War II veterans, and agricultural price supports, particularly for wheat.

Benefits to the general taxpayer are also proposed in the coming fiscal year and later years through the enactment of measures to charge users for special services which they derive from particular Government activities. Among these are proposals to eliminate the postal deficit and to provide more adequate taxes on aviation and highway fuels.

BUDGET RECEIPTS.—Estimated budget receipts of $82.3 billion in 1962 are based on an outlook for higher production, employment, and income as the calendar year 1961 progresses.   The accompanying table shows the sources of budget receipts for the fiscal years 1960, 1961, and 1962.

BUDGET RECEIPTS

[Fiscal years. In billions]

Source	1960 actual	1961 estimate	1962 estimate
Individual income taxes	$40. 7	$43. 3	$45. 5
Corporation income taxes	21. 5	20. 4	20. 9
Excise taxes	9. 1	9. 3	9. 7
All other receipts	7. 1	6. 7	6. 9
Total	78. 5	79. 7	83. 0
Deduct interfund transactions (included in both receipts and expenditures)	. 7	. 7	. 7
Budget receipts	77. 8	79. 0	82. 3

Extension of present tax rates.—It is necessary to extend for another year the present tax rates on corporation income and the excise taxes which are scheduled for reduction or termination on July 1, 1961.   The excise tax rates scheduled for reduction include those on distilled spirits, beer, wines, cigarettes, passenger automobiles, automobile parts and accessories, and transportation of persons; the 10% tax on general telephone service is scheduled to expire.   Unless these tax rates are extended, the Federal Government will lose an estimated $2.6 billion in revenues in 1962, and $3.7 billion on a full annual basis.

Changes in fees and charges.—In the conduct of certain of its activities, the Government provides special services, sells products, and leases federally owned resources, which convey to the recipients benefits above and beyond those which accrue to the public at large. In fairness to the general taxpayer, the cost of these services or the fair market value of the products and resources which are transferred to private use should be recovered, wherever feasible, through adequate fees and charges. To this end, the Congress was requested last year to provide increased fees and charges for a number of special benefits. With the one exception of fees for non-competitive oil and gas leases no final action was taken. The Congress is again requested to raise postal rates to eliminate the postal deficit and to act favorably on the proposals for increased highway and aviation fuel taxes and for a number of other fees or charges.

The present highway fuel tax rate should be increased by one-half cent per gallon and the resulting rate of 4½ cents should be continued through 1972. This step is necessary to permit timely completion of the Interstate System. It will also make possible the repeal of the unwise diversion from the general fund to the trust fund of excise tax receipts amounting to 5% of the manufacturers' price of passenger automobiles and automobile parts and accessories; this diversion is presently scheduled by law to begin July 1, 1961, and to continue for the fiscal years 1962 through 1964. The Congress should also raise the excise tax rate on aviation gasoline from 2 to 4½ cents per gallon; impose the same excise tax rate on jet fuels, now untaxed; and retain the receipts from these taxes in the general fund to help pay the cost of the Federal airways system. Other aspects of these recommendations are set forth in the discussion of transportation programs in this message.

ESTIMATED SAVINGS TO THE GENERAL TAXPAYERS FROM MORE ADEQUATE FEES AND CHARGES

[In millions]

Proposal	Fiscal year 1962
Increase postal rates	$843
Support highway expenditures by highway use taxes:	
Repeal pending diversion of general fund excise taxes to trust fund (and increase motor fuel tax)	810
Transfer financing of forest and public lands highways to trust fund	38
Charge users for share of cost of Federal airways:	
Increase taxes on aviation gasoline and retain in general fund	38
Tax jet fuels	62
Increase patent fees	7
Increase miscellaneous fees now below costs	9
Total savings	1,807

PUBLIC DEBT.—Achievement of the proposed budget surplus for 1962 will enable the Federal Government to make another modest reduction in the public debt. It is estimated that the public debt, which stood at $286.3 billion on June 30, 1960, will decline to $284.9 billion by the end of fiscal year 1961 and to $283.4 billion on June 30, 1962.

If the Congress accepts the proposals in this budget, and the proposed budget surplus for fiscal year 1962 is achieved, at the end of that year the Government will have some operating leeway within the permanent debt limit of $285 billion. Due to the seasonal pattern of tax collections, however, it will again be necessary for the Congress to provide a temporary increase in the debt limit during 1962. The present temporary debt limit of $293 billion expires June 30, 1961.

The Congress is again urged to remove the 4¼% statutory limitation on new issues of Treasury bonds, which remains a serious obstacle to efficient long-run management of the public debt. The marketable debt is still too heavily concentrated in securities of relatively short maturity, with almost 80% of the total coming due within 5 years. Although interest rates have declined in recent months, the continued existence of the interest rate ceiling limits the flexibility of debt operations by the Treasury. It effectively prevents the Treasury under certain circumstances from lengthening the debt by offering longer term securities or exchanges at maturity and, more importantly, it reduces considerably the possible use of the advance refunding technique, which offers the greatest promise for lengthening the average maturity of the debt.

RECEIPTS FROM AND PAYMENTS TO THE PUBLIC

The budget totals exclude the transactions of funds held in trust by the Federal Government as well as certain other transactions affecting the flow of money between the public and the Federal Government as a whole. Trust fund operations are an important factor in this flow and are consolidated with budget transactions to measure the Federal Government's cash receipts from and payments to the public. In this consolidation, certain transactions involving no flow of cash between the Government and the public are eliminated.

Expenditures from trust funds are financed through taxes and other receipts which are specifically designated to serve the special purposes for which the funds were established. About one-half of total trust fund transactions are accounted for by the old-age and survivors insurance system.   Other important programs carried on through trust funds include the railroad retirement system, the Federal employees' retirement systems, disability insurance, unemployment compensation, grants for highway construction, purchase of insured and guaranteed mortgages, and veterans life insurance.   In certain areas of Government activity, notably labor and welfare, trust fund expenditures far exceed the amounts spent through budget funds and, with the taxes levied to finance them, exert a considerable influence on the economy of the Nation.

Total receipts and expenditures of trust funds more than tripled during the decade of the fifties, and passed the $20 billion mark in 1960.   In 1962, they are both estimated to total $25.2 billion.   Total receipts from the public in 1962 are estimated at $103.1 billion and payments to the public at $101.8 billion, with a resulting excess of receipts of $1.3 billion.

FEDERAL GOVERNMENT RECEIPTS FROM AND PAYMENTS TO THE PUBLIC

[Fiscal years.   In billions]

	1960 actual	1961 estimate	1962 estimate
Receipts from the public	$95.1	$99.0	$103.1
Payments to the public	94.3	97.9	101.8
Excess of receipts over payments	+.8	+1.1	+1.3

IMPROVEMENTS IN THE TAX SYSTEM

There is a continuing need for a reappraisal of the tax system to assure that it operates equitably and with a minimum of repressive effects on incentives to work, save, and invest.   Continued close cooperation between the Treasury and the committees of the Congress is necessary to formulate sound and attainable proposals for the long-range improvement of the tax laws.

However, as the development of a comprehensive tax revision program will take time, the Congress should consider promptly this year certain changes in the tax laws to correct inequities.   For example, it is again recommended that the Congress promptly consider amending the laws on taxation of cooperatives to provide for more equitable taxation by insuring that taxes are paid on the income of these businesses either by the cooperative or by its members.

It has been many years since certain of the tax laws which now apply to the Nation's various private lending institutions and to fire and casualty insurance companies became effective.   The Congress should re-

943

view these statutes and the tax burdens now carried by lending institutions and insurance companies to determine whether or not inequities exist and to remedy any inequitable situations which may be found. The Treasury Department has under way studies relating to the operation of the existing statutes in this area. These studies should be of assistance to the Congress in any such review.

There is a need for review of present depreciation allowances and procedures. More liberal and flexible depreciation can make a major contribution toward neutralizing the deterrent effects of high tax rates on investment. A better system of capital recovery allowances would provide benefits to those who invest in productive plant and equipment and would encourage business expenditures for modernization and greater efficiency, thus helping to foster long-range economic growth. By bringing the allowances for American business more nearly into line with those available to many foreign producers, improved depreciation procedures would not only strengthen the competitive position of American producers, but their benefits would also accrue to American workers through increased productivity and greater job opportunity.

The depreciation rules should not be substantially liberalized, however, without accompanying remedial legislation with respect to the taxation of gains from sale of depreciable property. The legislation recommended last year to treat income on disposition of depreciable property as ordinary income to the extent of the depreciation deductions previously taken on the property is an essential first step.

IMPROVEMENTS IN GOVERNMENT ORGANIZATION

During the past 8 years major improvements have been made in the organization of the executive branch of the Government. An executive Department of Health, Education, and Welfare was established to give Cabinet status to its important programs. The organization of the Department of Defense was strengthened to bring it more closely into line with the requirements of modern warfare. A National Aeronautics and Space Administration was created to provide effective civilian leadership over appropriate parts of our national space program. The Council of Economic Advisers was reconstituted and reorganized to strengthen its internal administration and clarify its relationships with the President. Functions of coordinating governmental planning for defense mobilization and civil defense were consolidated. The establishment of the Federal

Aviation Agency brought about substantial improvements in aviation programs.

Many of the numerous organizational improvements were effected by Presidential reorganization plans authorized by the Reorganization Act of 1949, which has now expired. The Congress should renew that authority and make it permanently available for all future Presidents in the effective form as originally enacted. The task of conforming Government organization to current needs is a continuing one in our ever-changing times.

Executive Office of the President.—The duties placed on the President by the Constitution and the statutes demand the most careful attention to the staffing and organization of the President's Office. While the present organization of the Executive Office of the President reflects many constructive steps taken over a period of years, much remains to be done to improve the facilities available to the President. The first requirement for improvement is for the Congress to give the President greater flexibility in organizing his own Office to meet his great responsibilities.

Specifically, the Congress should enact legislation authorizing the President to reorganize the Executive Office of the President, including the authority to redistribute statutory functions among the units of the Office; to change the names of units and titles of officers within the Office; to make changes in the membership of statutory bodies in the Office; and, within the limits of existing laws and available appropriations, to establish new units in the Executive Office and fix the compensation of officers. Such action would insure that future Presidents will possess the latitude to design the working structure of the Presidential office as they deem necessary for the effective conduct of their duties under the Constitution and the laws. Enactment of such legislation would be a major step forward in strengthening the Office of the President for the critical tests that will surely continue to face our Nation in the years to come. These matters are obviously devoid of partisan considerations.

My experience leads me to suggest the establishment of an Office of Executive Management in the Executive Office of the President in which would be grouped the staff functions necessary to assist the President in the discharge of his managerial responsibilities. In an enterprise as large and diversified as the executive branch of the Government, there is an imperative need for effective and imaginative central management to strengthen program planning and evaluation, promote efficiency, identify and eliminate waste and duplication, and coordinate numerous inter-agency operations within approved policy and statutory objectives. The establishment of an Office of Executive Management is highly desirable to help the President achieve the high standards of effective management that the Congress and the people rightfully expect.

I have given much personal study to the assistance the President needs in meeting the multitude of demands placed upon him in conducting and correlating all aspects of foreign political, economic, social, and military affairs. I have reached the conclusion that serious attention should be given to providing in the President's Office an official ranking higher than Cabinet members, possibly with the title of First Secretary of the Government, to assist the President in consulting with the departments on the formulation of national security objectives, in coordinating international programs, and in representing the President at meetings with foreign officials above the rank of Foreign Minister and below the rank of Head of State.

Recognizing the personal nature of the relationship of each President to his Cabinet and staff, I am not submitting formal legislative proposals to implement these latter two suggestions, but I do commend them for earnest study.

Other improvements.—Several other organizational reforms should be considered by the Congress:

First, a Department of Transportation should be established so as to bring together at Cabinet level the presently fragmented Federal functions regarding transportation activities.

Second, legislation should be enacted to strengthen the position of the chairmen of the Interstate Commerce Commission, the Federal Communications Commission, and the National Labor Relations Board by vesting in them the executive and administrative duties of their agencies. The legislation should provide that the Chairman of the Interstate Commerce Commission be designated by the President. These steps would place these chairmen generally on a comparable basis with the chairmen of other regulatory bodies. In the case of the National Labor Relations Board, the legislation should vest all regulatory responsibilities under the National Labor Relations Act in the Board. Additionally, the responsibility of the President to control and supervise the exercise of executive functions by all Federal regulatory bodies should be clarified.

Third, action should be taken to consolidate the civil water resources functions of the Corps of Engineers of the Department of the Army, the Department of the Interior, and the responsibilities of the Federal Power Commission for river basin surveys, in order to bring about long needed improvements in the coordination of the increasingly important Federal civil water resources activities.

REVIEW OF AUTHORIZATIONS AND EXPENDITURES BY MAJOR FUNCTIONS

The remaining sections of this message discuss the budget and legislative proposals for 1962 in terms of the functions they serve. In the following table, estimated expenditures for 1962 are compared with the actual figures for 1960 and the current estimates for 1961 for each of 9 major functional categories.

The expenditure total for 1962 includes an allowance for contingencies, which is intended to provide for unforeseen developments in existing programs and for programs proposed in this budget but not itemized separately.

BUDGET EXPENDITURES

[Fiscal years. In billions]

Function	1960 actual	1961 estimate	1962 estimate
Major national security	$45. 6	$45. 9	$47. 4
International affairs and finance	1. 8	2. 3	2. 7
Commerce, housing, and space technology	2. 8	3. 8	3. 4
Agriculture and agricultural resources	4. 8	4. 9	5. 1
Natural resources	1. 7	2. 0	2. 1
Labor and welfare	4. 4	4. 5	4. 8
Veterans services and benefits	5. 1	5. 2	5. 3
Interest	9. 3	9. 0	8. 6
General government	1. 7	2. 0	2. 1
Allowance for contingencies	....	([1])	. 1
Total	77. 2	79. 6	81. 5
Deduct interfund transactions (included in both receipts and expenditures)	. 7	. 7	. 7
Budget expenditures	76. 5	78. 9	80. 9

[1] Less than $50 million.

MAJOR NATIONAL SECURITY

The deterrent power of our Armed Forces and the forces of our allies is based on a carefully planned combination of nuclear retaliatory weapons systems together with worldwide deployment of ground, naval, and air forces in essential forward areas, backed up by strong ready reserves.

These forces make up a collective security system for the Free World more versatile and powerful than any military alliance in world history.

Our Nation's objective in pursuing a policy of collective security is peace with justice for all peoples. However, while we strive to eliminate the fear of war among nations, we must maintain our military strength. The recommendations made in this budget provide for an increasingly strong defense posture along with a strong national economy.

Expenditures for major national security programs in fiscal year 1962 are estimated to be $47,392 million, or $1,462 million more than for 1961. The bulk of the increase is for the military functions of the Department of Defense, reflecting mainly evolutionary growth in our country's defense programs. Military assistance in conjunction with the efforts of our allies will continue to provide the Free World with modern weapons and equipment, thus strengthening the collective defense. Programs of the Atomic Energy Commission continue to emphasize weapons development and production while also providing increases for research and development on peaceful applications of atomic energy. Expenditures for stockpiling and for expansion of defense production will again decline as nearly all stockpile objectives have been met.

MAJOR NATIONAL SECURITY

[Fiscal years. In millions]

Program or agency	Budget expenditures			Recommended new obligational authority for 1962
	1960 actual	1961 estimate	1962 estimate	
Department of Defense—Military:				
Military functions:				
Present programs	$41,215	$41,500	$42,879	$41,809
Proposed retirement pay legislation	....	....	31	31
Military assistance	1,609	1,700	1,750	1,800
Atomic energy	2,623	2,660	2,680	2,598
Stockpiling and expansion of defense production	180	70	52	40
Total	45,627	45,930	47,392	[1] 46,278

[1] Compares with new obligational authority of $44,761 million enacted for 1960 and $45,912 million (including $289 million in anticipated supplemental appropriations) estimated for 1961.

DEPARTMENT OF DEFENSE—MILITARY.—Recommended new obligational authority of $41,840 million for the military functions of the

Department of Defense for fiscal year 1962 reflects the continued policy of adapting the Defense Establishment to expected long-run requirements. Expenditures in 1962 are estimated at $42,910 million, which is $1,410 million more than the estimate for the current fiscal year.

This increase reflects, in part, certain steps recently taken to increase the readiness of our military commands. These steps can be financed in 1961 mainly within available appropriations. However, some supplemental appropriations will be required for this year and are included in this budget.

The recommendations for 1962 continue a strong posture of readiness and add to the capability of our military forces.

To take full advantage of the results of scientific and technological developments, rapid and sometimes drastic changes must continually be made in military forces and programs. Just a few years ago the United States was programing twice as much money for manned bomber systems as for strategic missile systems. The budget for the coming fiscal year, by contrast, programs more than four times as much for strategic missile systems as for manned bomber systems. Similarly, defense against ballistic missile attack took only a small part of the total capital investment in continental air defense as recently as the fiscal year 1957, whereas in the coming fiscal year it will be a substantial percentage of the total. There has been a gradual shift from guns to missiles on surface ships, and from conventional to nuclear power for submarines. For surface ships, the relative utility of nuclear or conventional power is a question that requires case by case consideration in each year's shipbuilding program. In total, there has been an increased emphasis on versatile and modern multipurpose military units equipped and prepared for all forms of military action—from limited emergencies to a general war.

Forces and military personnel.—To carry out basic military missions, this budget provides for a total strength in our Active Forces of 2,492,900 men and women on June 30, 1962, the same as now estimated for the end of fiscal year 1961 and 4,000 over the year-end strength originally planned for this year. A supplemental appropriation is being requested to provide for this 1961 increase, which is primarily to bring our naval forces to a greater degree of preparedness.

The Active Forces to be supported include an Army of 14 divisions and 870,000 men; a Navy of 817 active ships and 625,000 men; a Marine Corps of 3 divisions and 3 aircraft wings with 175,000 men;

and an Air Force of 84 combat wings and 822,900 men.

Worldwide deployment of these forces, and of civilian employees of the Department of Defense as well, requires a considerable amount of travel to and from duty stations. The dollar limitation on travel established by the Congress in the 1961 appropriation for the Department is not sufficient to cover all essential travel costs of military and civilian personnel. Accordingly, it is recommended that this limitation be increased by $54 million for the fiscal year 1961 and that no limitation be imposed for 1962.

If the reserve components of our Armed Forces are to serve effectively in time of war, their basic organization and objectives must conform to the changing character and missions of the Active Forces. Under modern conditions the quality and combat readiness of the reserve forces are more important than numbers. The nature of warfare has changed so drastically during the last decade that the whole concept of the roles and missions of the reserve forces must be reevaluated.

Accordingly, the Secretary of Defense and the Joint Chiefs of Staff have been directed to make a new study of the reserve missions and requirements. This should be aimed at the objectives of efficiency, economy, and promoting administrative effectiveness. As a first step toward a more fundamental revision, this budget provides for a reduction in the number in the Army National Guard and Army Reserve paid for participation in reserve training from the present 400,000 and 300,000, respectively, to 360,000 and 270,000 by the end of fiscal year 1962. These recommended reserve personnel strengths are fully adequate to meet the needs of our national defense. The statutory minimum placed on the personnel strength of the Army National Guard in the 1961 Department of Defense Appropriation Act should not be continued. The excess strengths which have been provided by the Congress above my recommendations in the last several years are unnecessarily costing the American people over $80 million annually and have been too long based on other than strictly military needs. Even with the proposed lower reserve personnel strengths, the cost of pay, allowances, travel, and operation and maintenance for the military reserves will amount to well over $1 billion in 1962.

Strategic forces.—The strategic forces provided for in this budget consist of a combination of nuclear weapons systems of land-based and carrier-based aircraft, fixed and mobile missiles of intercontinental and intermediate range, and overseas missile systems under the military command of mutual defense treaty organizations. The composite capability of these forces represents an enormous destructive potential and should deter any potential aggressor.

Up to the present time our strategic striking forces have relied in large measure on manned bombers. Manned bombers—both land-based and carrier-based—will continue to be required. However, with the advent of operational missile systems, more and more of the strategic force in the years ahead will be composed of fixed-base and mobile ballistic missiles—both land- and sea-based. The recommendations in this budget reflect this change.

By the end of fiscal year 1962, the largest part of the planned squadrons of the Atlas ballistic missile system will be operational, and a significant number of the planned Titan missiles will be in place and ready. The solid propellant Minuteman missile system is now well along in development, and the first missiles are scheduled to become operational during the calendar year 1962. Funds are requested for 5 additional Polaris submarines, making a total of 19 submarines which will have been fully funded, and for the procurement of long leadtime components of 5 more; procurement of the appropriate number of Polaris missiles to arm these submarines is also planned, as is the continued development of a much longer range version of the Polaris missile.

Thor and Jupiter intermediate range ballistic missiles, provided to our allies overseas under the military assistance portion of the mutual security program, add still another important element of strength to the strategic forces.

All production of B–52 and B–58 manned bomber aircraft is scheduled to end in the calendar year 1962. However, as indicated in my special message to the Congress last August, additional effort is being devoted to the development of the B–70 long-range bomber. Funds are included in this budget to continue work in 1962 on the airframe and engine, and on the essential subsystems.

In addition to the forces equipped uniquely for nuclear attack, the tactical fighters and missiles of the Air Force also contribute importantly to our strategic capability. Deployed overseas, with an increasing all-weather strike capability, these tactical forces can deliver megaton-class nuclear weapons to potential enemy targets.

As a further step in strengthening the strategic forces, the Navy has been authorized to increase significantly the proportion of attack aircraft aboard carriers of the 6th and 7th Fleets. This action will substantially increase the capability of those fleets to strike enemy targets.

The very diversity of our weapons systems has created an increasing need for fully integrated operational planning. To meet this need, the Secretary of Defense has established a special staff group composed of members of the services and representatives of unified commands contributing forces to our nuclear strike capability. I have recently approved the integrated strategic operational plan prepared by that group and recommended by the Secretary of Defense and the Joint Chiefs of Staff.

The advent of nuclear-armed intercontinental ballistic missiles in the hands of a potential adversary has confronted this Nation with a problem entirely new to its experience. The speed with which these weapons could be delivered against us and their tremendous destructive power make them suited to use by an enemy for surprise attack. Accordingly, this budget will continue the major effort under way during the last few years to increase the protection of our forces from surprise attack. Except for the first few squadrons of Atlas, all Atlas and Titan missiles are being deployed in hardened underground sites. All fixed-base Minuteman missiles will be so deployed. There will also be mobile squadrons of the Minuteman. The submarine Polaris system, of course, lends itself ideally to mobility and concealment and should be able to survive under all conditions.

There has also been an intensive effort to make the manned bomber force increasingly less vulnerable. Some 4 years ago the Air Force began the dispersal of these aircraft and commenced construction of special alert facilities to assure that one-third of the force could be airborne within 15 minutes of warning of an attack. Both of these programs are substantially completed. Under emergency conditions, the long-range bomber force could also use a large number of additional bases throughout the country.

As a further measure, steps have been taken to provide the heavy bomber force with an airborne alert capability. Funds are provided in this budget to continue to train crews and to acquire spare parts and other materiel so that a substantial portion of the heavy bomber force could immediately mount a 24-hours-a-day, 365-days-a-year airborne alert, should that step ever become necessary in an emergency.

Air defense forces.—The emergence of the ballistic missile threat has, of course, required a revamping of our air defense forces. The speed and destructiveness of the nuclear armed ballistic missile have placed an extremely high premium on timely warning of an attack. Therefore, systems designed to provide such warning have been receiving urgent attention.

The ground-based Ballistic Missile Early Warning System (BMEWS), involving a cost of nearly a billion dollars, has already been largely financed. Work on this system has been greatly accelerated and is proceeding as fast as practicable. The first of the three sites is now in operation. The second site will be in operation this year, substantially increasing the coverage. The third site is planned to become operational somewhat later. When the entire system is in full operation, our air defense forces and civilian population, as well as the strategic retaliatory forces, should have 15 minutes of warning of intercontinental ballistic missile attack.

The matter of reliable warning of ballistic missile attack is of such crucial importance to the safety of the Nation, however, that a number of other approaches are also being explored. The most advanced of these is the satellite-borne missile early warning system, Midas, which is now under accelerated development. Midas is designed to detect an enemy missile attack at the time of launching; this could about double the amount of warning time available to our military forces and civilian population. Substantial funds are included in this budget to continue development of this system at a high rate.

With the increasing reliability, accuracy, payload, and sophistication of the ballistic missile, our problem of safeguarding against surprise attack will become ever more onerous. Development of an active defense against ballistic missiles is progressing. The Nike-Zeus antimissile system is proceeding under the highest national priority, and funds for its Pacific range test facilities are included in this budget. Funds should not be committed to production until development tests are satisfactorily completed.

The entire problem of detection, tracking, and destruction of the attacking missile must be dealt with as a whole. Every avenue of research which offers any reasonable chance of success must be explored beyond the present frontiers of knowledge. That is the purpose of the group of studies now under way, which has been designated by the Department of Defense as Project Defender. Additional funds to continue this project through the coming fiscal year are also included in this budget.

As long as a manned bomber threat to this Nation exists, we shall have to maintain a reasonable degree of defense against it. The Air Force now has under way a large-scale program for improving the capability of its existing fighter interceptor force, particularly against the low level manned bomber. The Bomarc B ground-to-air-missile program has already been funded. Production is going forward, and missiles will be delivered to the air defense units over the next few years. Additional funds are recommended to complete and modernize the Nike-Hercules ground-to-air-missile system.

The Bomarc B and Nike-Hercules, together with the early models of these missiles and the very substantial force of supersonic manned interceptors armed with air-to-air guided missiles, provide a formidable defense against manned bomber attack. To provide the detection, warning, and control for these forces, an extensive network of radars and communications lines is being maintained and modernized. Funds for additional construction and for the procurement of equipment are included in this budget.

Sea control forces.—Control of the seas is vital to the maintenance of our national security. The naval forces, which are being provided during this fiscal year with new combat ships and increased personnel, carry the primary responsibility for this important mission.

The 1962 budget provides for active naval forces consisting of 817 combatant and support ships, including 14 attack carriers, 16 attack carrier air groups, 11 carrier antisubmarine air groups, and 37 patrol and warning air squadrons.

New and modernized ships to be delivered in 1962 from prior year authorizations will enhance the combat capability of the naval forces and permit the replacement of older ships. Among the new and modernized ships to join the fleet in 1962 will be the first nuclear-powered attack aircraft, the *Enterprise;* the first nuclear-powered cruiser, the *Long Beach,* armed with Talos and Terrier surface-to-air missiles; three nuclear-powered attack submarines; four Polaris submarines; and several guided missile destroyers.

The 1962 shipbuilding program provided in this budget will further improve the fleet and help offset the increasing number of over-age ships. The program consists of construction of 30 new ships and conversion of 22 others. In addition to the 5 Polaris fleet ballistic missile submarines, new ships will include 7 guided missile frigates, 3 nuclear-powered attack submarines, 6 escort vessels, and 9 amphibious, supply, and research ships. The conversion program includes 14 destroyers, 1 communications relay ship, 1 missile range instrumentation ship, and 6 conventionally powered attack submarines.

A great deal of emphasis in the 1962 shipbuilding program is on anti-submarine warfare. Progress has been made in antisubmarine warfare organization and tactics. Improvements have been made in weapons and equipment, particularly antisubmarine rockets, torpedoes, and sound detection gear. However, the fast, deep running, nuclear-powered sub-marine of today is exceedingly difficult to detect and attack. An increase in the capability to detect and destroy enemy submarines is needed. Additional funds are requested in this budget for research and develop-ment in this area.

Tactical forces.—The tactical forces include ground, naval, and air elements which are organized and trained to deal with cold war emergen-cies and limited war situations, as well as to be prepared for combat roles in the event of a general war. Recommendations in this budget will continue the modernization and improve the effectiveness of the tactical forces.

This budget provides for a further increase in procurement for the ground forces. Procurement of additional quantities of rifles and machineguns employing standard ammunition of the North Atlantic Treaty Organization will fill the high priority needs of the Army and Marine Corps forces; the M–113 armored personnel carrier will be made available for high priority active Army forces; the M–60 tank will be provided for the Army's highest priority deployed forces; and increasing quantities of new field communications equipment, vehicles, and self-propelled weapons will be produced.

The Army and Marine Corps will continue to buy a wide variety of tactical guided missiles and rockets, including initial quantities of the Pershing, a solid-propellant missile; a new lightweight shoulder-fired assault weapon; the Davy Crockett, which provides infantry units with a close range atomic support weapon; and missiles such as Hawk and Redeye for defense of field forces against air attack.

Army aircraft procurement proposed for 1962 provides for 261 new aircraft compared to 229 in the 1961 program, and includes funds for surveillance and utility planes, as well as for medium cargo helicopters.

The tactical forces of the Army are supported by the tactical air wings of the Air Force, which will also be provided with an increased capability under these budget recommendations. Funds are provided for continued procurement of F–105 supersonic all-weather fighter-bombers. These aircraft, with their low-altitude performance characteristics and large carrying capacities for both nuclear and non-nuclear weapons, will strengthen significantly the air support available to tactical ground units.

Continued modernization of our existing fleet of military airlift aircraft is needed. Although the cargo and troop transport airlift now available is generally adequate, much of the fleet is approaching obsolescence. Last year a program was started to acquire the best existing transports for the most immediate needs and also to develop a new aircraft specifically designed for cargo and transport needs. The budget includes funds to continue the orderly development of this program.

Proposed legislation.—Legislation is again recommended to make the necessary adjustments in military retirement pay so as to reestablish for all retired personnel the traditional relationship of their pay with active duty pay. This relationship was broken for those retired prior to June 1, 1958, when the 1958 Military Pay Act increased active duty pay without a comparable increase for those on the retirement rolls. The people affected are in most cases those who have fought through two or three of our major wars. Legislation to correct this situation should no longer be delayed.

Basic long lines communications systems in Alaska which are now operated by the Army, Air Force, and the Federal Aviation Agency should be sold to private enterprise for operation and development under appropriate regulatory supervision. Legislation is recommended which will permit the sale of these Government-owned communications facilities under adequate safeguards.

The need for maintaining the relatively small naval petroleum reserves for strictly military purposes no longer exists. Legislation is therefore recommended to transfer responsibility for the administration of these petroleum reserves from the Department of the Navy to the Department of the Interior.

The need for manned aircraft, and for the pilots and other persons necessary to fly them, is declining gradually as more and more missiles enter the inventory of our operating forces. During the transitional period it will be necessary to remove from flying status a number of officers whose professional and managerial skills are still required by the services. The complete loss of flight pay which such removal now entails would represent a serious hardship to many officers who have served their country well and who believed they would qualify for flight pay as long as they maintained their flying proficiency. To help ease the transition which this group faces as a result of conversion to new weapons systems, the Congress should make provision for appropriate financial relief by reducing flight pay gradually for officers removed from flying status because of changing technology.

The provision of section 412(b) of the Military Construction Act of 1959 requiring prior congressional authorization of appropriations for the procurement of aircraft, missiles, and naval vessels is inappropriate and should be repealed. Pending its repeal, the required authorizations for 1962 should be enacted promptly so that national security planning and preparation can go forward with the least possible delay. Further, in enacting the authorizations, the Congress should allow flexibility in the administration of the Department of Defense procurement programs to meet changing threats and take advantage of technological breakthroughs.

The Capehart military family housing program has admirably served its purpose. Over the last 6 years, more than 100,000 such family units were provided at a time when they were badly needed. It is now apparent that the most urgent family housing needs of the Department of Defense have been met. However, in order to place under contract presently authorized projects and to provide for a final increment of 2,025 units in 1962, it is recommended that a 1-year extension of the existing authority be enacted.

In 1958, I recommended to the Congress a comprehensive program for reorganizing the Department of Defense. While many of these recommendations were enacted, and substantial progress has been made in implementing them, one area still needing attention is the method of providing funds for the Department. As a first step, appropriations have now been enacted on a broad category basis but with specific limitations by Service. I now recommend that the Congress, in acting upon the appropriation structure for the fiscal year 1962 for the Department of Defense, give earnest consideration to a plan which would make the necessary authorizations and appropriations to that Department to be administered by the Secretary, but with a substructure of sufficient

identification which will retain for the Congress its constitutional preroga-
tives of raising and supporting the military forces of the United States.

North Atlantic Treaty Organization.—The evolutionary changes in
warfare that have taken place over the last decade have had a profound
effect on the military plans and programs of the North Atlantic Treaty
Organization. These plans are again being reviewed and studied to take
account of new weapons, better organization of the NATO military forces,
and more direct channels of command to carry out NATO objectives
effectively.

It is expected that the revised military plans for NATO will recognize
the changes that have taken place. However, the menace of Communist
military strength is growing. The NATO alliance remains vital to the
security of the United States, no less than to the security of the other
NATO allies. The United States will continue to contribute to the
constructive and defensive tasks it has assumed.

Some changes in U.S. force deployments may become advisable in
light of continuing studies of overall U.S. programs. Nevertheless, the
United States will continue to provide a fully effective strategic deterrent
force and will contribute to the forward deployed forces of NATO.

MILITARY ASSISTANCE.—U.S. military planning has long recognized
the importance of allied forces in maintaining the security of the free
world. Military assistance under the mutual security program helps to
strengthen the forces of more than 40 nations. New obligational authority of $1.8 billion is recommended for military assistance for 1962
to provide training and materiel for essential maintenance and modernization of forces in the countries receiving aid.

In light of the expanding scope and cost of vital military programs
being borne by the United States, we cannot continue indefinitely to
provide military equipment on a grant basis to nations which now have
the economic and financial capability to shoulder more of the burden of
the common defense. The recent improvement in the financial position
of many of our allies has highlighted the need for greater sharing of this
burden.

Some of the Western European countries have now assumed full financial responsibility for equipping their own military forces, in which the
United States had assisted earlier. We are confident that as full partners
in the common defense all nations of the North Atlantic Treaty Organization who are able to assume this responsibility will do so. In 1962,

military assistance to our Western European allies will be concentrated on selected types of new weapons and on the training required for their effective use.

This budget also reflects the continuing need to develop and maintain effective forces in other nations which are faced with serious threats of internal subversion or external aggression. Individually, and within mutual defense organizations, such as the South East Asia Treaty Organization (SEATO) and the Central Treaty Organization (CENTO), these forces play vital roles in the defense of vast areas, predominantly in Asia and the Near East. Assistance to these nations will be concentrated largely on the strengthening of conventional forces. In addition to its military value, this assistance in the common defense effort contributes to the sharing of technical knowledge and strengthens the bonds of friendship and mutual respect among the nations of the Free World.

ATOMIC ENERGY ACTIVITIES.—In 1962, expenditures by the Atomic Energy Commission are estimated to be $2,680 million, compared with an estimated $2,660 million in 1961. There will be increases in several program areas, but these will be largely offset by reductions elsewhere, notably in the procurement of uranium concentrates.

Expenditures for the production of nuclear weapons in 1962 will increase over 1961, while those for the development of weapons will continue at the same rate. Work will be carried forward in 1962 to improve methods for seismic detection of underground nuclear weapons tests. The Atomic Energy Commission is also cooperating with the Department of Defense in the improvement of methods for detecting high altitude tests.

In the naval reactor program, continued efforts will be made to develop longer lived nuclear fuel. The development of a nuclear ramjet engine for missiles and of nuclear powerplants for use at remote military installations will be pursued. The efforts to develop a nuclear engine for military aircraft will be continued in 1962 on one technical approach.

Peaceful uses of atomic energy.—Fundamental to progress in the peaceful uses of atomic energy is a sound and balanced program of basic research in the physical and life sciences. An important segment of this work is high energy physics. Last July, the United States began operating the alternating gradient synchrotron at the Atomic Energy Commission's Brookhaven National Laboratory on Long Island at the highest energy level ever attained anywhere in the world. During fiscal year

1962 two more high energy accelerators, at Cambridge, Mass., and Princeton, N.J., will begin operation. A high intensity accelerator is under construction at the Commission's Argonne National Laboratory near Chicago, Ill. Legislation is again proposed to authorize construction at Stanford University of a high energy linear electron accelerator which will be 2 miles long.

The development of civilian atomic power is being carried forward intensively. Expenditures of $250 million estimated for 1962 will support major development efforts on seven reactor types, and preliminary studies and experimental work on a number of other reactor concepts. The breadth and scope of our technology in this field are unmatched in the world.

The next 18 months will see further advances toward our long-term objective of making atomic energy an alternative and economic source of power at home and abroad. The total number of major Government-owned experimental power reactors in operation will increase by 5 to a total of 10, and the number of power reactors operating in public and private utility systems will increase from 3 to 10. The 1962 budget proposes additional funds for cooperative arrangements with private and public power groups in undertaking atomic power projects which would further the objectives of the program.

Jointly with the National Aeronautics and Space Administration, the Atomic Energy Commission is pursuing Project Rover to develop a nuclear powered rocket for possible future space missions. Expenditures for this project will increase in 1962. Continued emphasis will be given to development of small, long-lived nuclear power sources for space vehicles and other special applications. With the completion of a major experimental device in 1961, expenditures for long-term development of thermonuclear power will decrease somewhat, but the research work will continue at about current levels.

STOCKPILING AND EXPANSION OF DEFENSE PRODUCTION.—Expenditures for stockpiling and expansion of defense production are estimated to decrease from $70 million in 1961 to $52 million in 1962, as outstanding contracts for delivery of strategic materials are progressively completed or terminated. Most of the objectives for the strategic stockpile are completed, and no new expansion programs are in prospect.

Of major concern now are the storage and maintenance of large quantities of strategic materials and the orderly disposal over a period of years of surplus materials. Efficient management is hampered because these materials are in several inventories, each subject to different statutory requirements. Therefore, legislation is being developed to enable consolidation of the inventories of strategic materials and provide uniform procedures for disposing of surplus materials whenever disposal will not seriously disrupt markets or adversely affect our international relations.

NONMILITARY DEFENSE.—Closely related to the major national security programs are the civil defense activities of the Government. These activities are discussed with other community facilities programs in the commerce, housing, and space technology section of this message, under which the expenditures for civil and defense mobilization are classified.

INTERNATIONAL AFFAIRS AND FINANCE

The national security and prosperity of the United States under conditions of peace and freedom require us to maintain our position of world leadership. Thus we must continue to assist in developing the resources and skills needed in many parts of the non-Communist world for the common defense and for economic growth.

Since the end of World War II, military and economic programs launched by the United States have helped to make possible the reconstruction of Europe and have thwarted the advance of Communist domination in most other areas. In recent years, the focus of these efforts has been shifting increasingly to the broader and more difficult problems of helping less-developed countries maintain their independence, build the foundations of growth, and advance the welfare of their people. Accordingly, increasing emphasis is being placed on such aspects of our international programs as development loans, technical assistance, and educational exchange. Greater use of multilateral channels is being fostered.

Expenditures for international affairs and finance programs in fiscal year 1962 are estimated at $2,712 million. The increase of $401 million over 1961 expenditures is due mainly to a greater volume of loan disbursements by the Development Loan Fund, to the second payment of our subscription to the Inter-American Development Bank, and to the expansion of activities in Latin America and Africa.

New obligational authority of $3,102 million is recommended for fiscal year 1962. This is a decrease of $105 million from the amount estimated for 1961. Increases for special assistance, commodity grant programs, and the second subscription to the Inter-American Development Bank are more than offset by the nonrecurrence of the 1961 supplemental appropriation requested for the new Inter-American Social and Economic Cooperation Program.

MUTUAL SECURITY PROGRAM.—The military portion of the mutual security program was discussed as an integral part of our national security effort in the preceding section of this message. For the total mutual security program, this budget recommends new obligational authority of $4,000 million for 1962, of which $1,800 million is for military assistance, $1,950 million for economic and technical programs, and $250 million for contingencies.

The 1962 recommendation has been determined with consideration for our present balance of payments situation and the steps being taken to improve it. I have recently directed that the use of the funds provided for assistance abroad should emphasize the purchase of the necessary goods and services in the United States. Such foreign procurement as may continue will be largely confined to less-developed countries, most of which do not increase their dollar reserves to any significant extent but tend rather to use their earnings to increase their imports.

Organization and financing of international programs.—Attention has been given constantly to the problem of improving the organization and administration of our international programs. For example, most of the recommendations of the President's Committee To Study the Military Assistance Program have already been fully or partially adopted. As required by section 604 of the Mutual Security Act of 1960, further analysis is being made of ways to improve the overall management and coordination of our various assistance programs. These studies will provide the basis for specific recommendations on organization later in the year when the detailed mutual security program for 1962 is presented to the Congress. Other studies concerning possible changes in the appropriation structure are currently under way.

In addition to possible improvements in the organization of foreign economic activities, the Congress is urged to consider means by which funds can be provided through the normal budgetary process to meet the needs of more than one specific fiscal year. This applies particularly to programs of long-term economic development and technical assistance in the training of manpower and the creation of basic economic, social, and governmental institutions. The provision of longer term financing should not only enable a more effective use of aid but, in the long run, should be more economical.

INTERNATIONAL AFFAIRS AND FINANCE

[Fiscal years. In millions]

Program or agency	Budget expenditures			Recommended new obligational authority for 1962
	1960 actual	1961 estimate	1962 estimate	
Economic and financial assistance:				
Mutual security—economic:				
Development Loan Fund	$202	$275	$425	$700
Defense support	741	705	665	650
Special assistance	255	250	256	298
Technical cooperation	172	183	190	203
Other	114	112	119	99
Mutual security—contingencies	129	150	220	250
Subtotal, mutual security—economic and contingencies	1,613	1,675	1,875	2,200
Inter-American Social and Economic Cooperation Program	......	......	50	......
Inter-American Development Bank	80	......	110	110
International Development Association	......	74	62	62
Export-Import Bank	−323	−100	−4	......
Commodity grants for emergency relief and development abroad (title II, Public Law 480) and other	107	285	151	257
Subtotal, economic and financial assistance	1,477	1,934	2,243	2,628
Conduct of foreign affairs:				
Department of State, administration of foreign affairs	215	210	228	233
Proposed legislation for Philippine claims	......	......	49	49
Tariff Commission and other	4	4	3	3
Foreign information and exchange activities:				
United States Information Agency	113	125	138	140
Department of State, exchange of persons	24	37	50	48
Total	1,833	2,310	2,712	[1] 3,102

[1] Compares with new obligational authority of $2,672 million enacted for 1960 and $3,207 million (including $666 million of anticipated supplemental appropriations) estimated for 1961.

MUTUAL SECURITY PROGRAM

[Fiscal years. In millions]

Program	Budget expenditures			Recommended new obligational authority for 1962
	1960 actual	1961 estimate	1962 estimate	
Military assistance..................	$1,609	$1,700	$1,750	$1,800
Economic (including technical) assistance	1,484	1,525	1,655	1,950
Contingencies....................	129	150	220	250
Total, mutual security..........	3,223	3,375	3,625	[1] 4,000

[1] Compares with new obligational authority of $3,226 million enacted for 1960 ($1,331 million military, $1,895 million economic and contingencies) and $3,931 million estimated for 1961 ($1,800 million military, $2,131 million economic and contingencies).

Eligibility for assistance.—Legislation is again requested to allow greater flexibility in providing assistance to certain countries which are not in a position to meet the requirements of the Mutual Defense Assistance Control Act (Battle Act). Complex, time-consuming waiver procedures are now required for cases in which our own interests would be clearly fostered by the prompt extension of aid to countries endeavoring to reduce their dependence on the Soviet bloc.

ECONOMIC AND FINANCIAL ASSISTANCE.—The efforts of less-developed countries in mobilizing their domestic resources for economic growth will have to be supplemented during the next decade by continued investment from the economically more advanced countries. This investment will have to come from four major sources.

First, an increasing share should be private capital, which could increase directly the productive capacities within these countries. Among the steps taken by the U.S. Government to foster this goal are the negotiation of investment treaties and the provision of information on investment opportunities. Efforts are also being made to use, where appropriate, existing guarantee authority. Private sources, such as foundations and other specialized groups, should also continue their substantial contributions to the overseas schools, hospitals, and churches, so important in promoting democratic society.

Second, increased investment may be expected through international organizations. In addition to the International Bank for Reconstruction and Development there are now the International Development Association and the Inter-American Development Bank. These institutions are supported by contributions from many countries. Also, the United Nations Special Fund is receiving increasing subscriptions from member countries. Further, the Congress should authorize the United States to join the countries of Europe and Canada in the new Organization for Economic Cooperation and Development which will replace the Organization for European Economic Cooperation. The new organization will extend and invigorate the practice of consultation among its members and will help find ways to facilitate the flow of investment funds to less-developed countries.

Third, a greatly increased share of the needed investment must come from the bilateral programs of other industrialized nations. In the post-World War II era many of the other developed countries have succeeded in rebuilding their economies and have established a high rate of economic growth. In recent years they have substantially increased their gold and foreign exchange reserves. The time has come for such countries to augment materially their financing of the growth of the less-developed areas, and there is evidence of growing willingness on their part to do so. Strenuous efforts are being made to persuade our partner nations to accelerate significantly the pace at which they are taking on responsibilities for economic assistance as well as for the common defense.

Finally, common sense, goodwill, and national interest require that the U.S. Government continue substantial assistance. The needs of the less-developed countries cannot be met wholly by the efforts of private investors, international organizations, or other industrial countries.

Loans for economic development.—In 1962, the United States will pay the second installments of its subscriptions to both the International Development Association and the Inter-American Development Bank. However, successful development in many countries is dependent upon additional loans from outside sources. The Export-Import Bank expects to commit $602 million for development loans, and this budget proposes that $700 million be made available in 1962 to the Development Loan Fund. Both agencies now have requests for a variety of productive projects in such fields as electric power, transportation, and industrial facilities. In some countries, such as India and Pakistan, loans will be needed on a basis broader than individual projects to insure the success of development plans.

There is a pressing need to approve financing for development projects in several countries over and above the level of funds presently available to the Development Loan Fund. Accordingly, a supplemental appropriation of $150 million for 1961 is required. This supplemental request, if approved, together with funds already appropriated for 1961, would make available the full amount requested in the 1961 budget.

Mainly because of earlier commitments, expenditures by the Development Loan Fund are estimated at $425 million in 1962, an increase of $150 million over 1961. The Export-Import Bank plans to finance its operations without incurring net budget expenditures in 1962 by encouraging private lenders to participate in its loan programs, by using funds obtained from repayments and interest on prior loans, and by selling notes from its large portfolio.

Loans of the Development Loan Fund will continue to be made repayable largely in local currencies in order not to draw on the limited foreign exchange resources of the recipient countries.

Latin America.—A supplemental appropriation of $500 million is recommended for 1961 for the Inter-American Social and Economic Cooperation Program which was authorized by the last Congress. This amount represents the total authorization and therefore no further appropriation will be required for 1962. These funds will be used for a broad range of projects of direct benefit to the people of Latin America in such fields as housing, education, agricultural improvements, and land utilization.

When plans become firmer, a supplemental appropriation for 1961 should be requested for earthquake reconstruction in Chile under the $100 million authorization enacted by the last Congress. To cover interim needs a $20 million grant from mutual security contingency funds has been made available to Chile, and surplus agricultural commodities valued at $29 million are being shipped under the Agricultural Trade Development and Assistance Act of 1954 (Public Law 480).

Defense support and special assistance.—New obligational authority of $650 million for 1962 is proposed for defense support, a reduction of $25 million from 1961, and $298 million is recommended for special assistance, an increase of $66 million over 1961. These programs not only help maintain substantial military strength by free world countries rimming the Soviet bloc, but also include special economic programs in certain vital countries, and provide for the continuance of other special programs such as malaria eradication. The increase in special assistance funds recommended for 1962 is due principally to the growing need for aid to Africa. Other countries which have had a traditional interest in that continent may be expected to continue the constructive work started there, and their assistance, like ours, should increasingly be channeled through an expanded United Nations effort which we have proposed.

In estimating the requirements for defense support and special assistance, full account has again been taken of the substantial amount of economic assistance in the form of surplus agricultural commodities which may be programed under Public Law 480. For 1962, the budget estimates provide for placing almost complete reliance on Public Law 480 for financing the Government programs for export of surplus farm products, but the mutual security program will continue to finance exports which cannot readily be programed under Public Law 480. The requirement that a specified portion of mutual security funds be used to finance exports of these commodities should be eliminated.

Technical cooperation.—The scope and effectiveness of our technical assistance activities have been expanding, and this trend may be expected to continue. Experience has shown that improved human resources within a country are just as vital to development as capital assistance from without. New obligational authority of $203 million is requested for 1962 for technical cooperation programs, compared with $184 million enacted for 1961. Part of the increase is for a larger contribution to the United Nations Special Fund and United Nations technical assistance programs to support the continuing expansion of their work which has been made possible by larger contributions from other countries.

Contingency fund and other assistance.—Events of the past year have reemphasized the need for a fund to provide the President with the flexibility to meet international contingencies which cannot be foreseen in the budget. The situation in Africa continues fluid, and major emergency requirements are possible in other areas as well. To provide for such contingencies new obligational authority of $250 million is recommended under the mutual security program for 1962, about the same as provided for 1961. This is the minimum amount required for the coming year consonant with the responsibilities of the President.

Funds are also authorized under the Mutual Security Act for administration and for contributions to specialized programs such as those for refugees, Atoms for Peace, and children's welfare. For these purposes, new obligational authority of $99 million for 1962 is recommended. This amount is $6 million higher than available for 1961, due mainly to expanding administrative needs in Africa and Latin America.

CONDUCT OF FOREIGN AFFAIRS.—In 1962, the Department of State plans to expand further its activities in three important areas of its work. The number of diplomatic and consular posts in Africa is expected to increase from 36 in 1960 to 49 by the end of 1962. A Disarmament Administration has been established within the Department of State, and expansion of this activity is proposed. The Department will also intensify its efforts to increase U.S. exports, complementing efforts of the Department of Commerce.

During the calendar year 1960, there were 17 countries in Africa which gained their independence. Official representation with these new governments must be established as early as possible and preparation must be made for representation in other countries soon to become independent. Because of the large number of new nations, a supplemental appropriation for 1961 is requested to cover costs of establishing new diplomatic and consular posts in Africa and raising certain existing consulates to embassy status.

Legislation previously recommended to authorize payment of certain war damage claims of the Philippine Government should be enacted at an early date. The Congress should also act promptly to remove the existing reservation on acceptance by the United States of jurisdiction of the International Court of Justice (the World Court).

FOREIGN INFORMATION AND EXCHANGE ACTIVITIES.—Substantial increases have been recommended in the 1962 budget for exchange programs and the programs of the United States Information Agency in Latin America and Africa, made possible, in part, by reductions in activities in Western Europe. It is essential that these activities be stepped up in these areas to the extent of our ability to do so effectively. The 1962 budget recognizes this need. However, if the developing situation indicates both a further need for additional resources and an ability effectively to utilize them, we should stand ready to expand further these efforts. In Africa, 20 new information centers requiring sizable initial costs will be put into operation in 1961 and 1962, mostly in the newly independent countries. In Latin America, special efforts will continue toward expanding and strengthening activities of the binational cultural centers. Construction of new, more powerful radio facilities for world-wide broadcasting is under way in North Carolina, with completion expected in December 1962. Initial activities are under way toward the construction of a radio facility in Liberia. In 1962, further improvement of facilities of the Voice of America abroad is proposed by quintupling the transmitter power in the United Kingdom and by procurement of a transportable radio relay station to meet special needs on short notice.

The budget also provides for an expansion of cultural presentation activities and exhibits at international fairs abroad. Funds for this purpose are included in the estimates for the United States Information Agency instead of being appropriated to the President as in previous years. The trade mission segment of the program is included in the estimates for the Department of Commerce.

Activities under our cultural exchange agreement with the Soviet Union continue to progress mainly under private auspices. There are plans to exchange three Government-sponsored exhibits beginning this spring, each of which will be shown in several cities. A supplemental appropriation is proposed for 1961 to take advantage of this opportunity to demonstrate American achievements to a wide segment of the Russian people.

Further expansion in the programs of the Department of State for the exchange of persons is proposed in 1962, particularly in Africa. Continuing support of workshops and foreign university chairs in American studies, as well as assistance to American-sponsored schools abroad, is planned. An increase in the Department's new program of cultural and educational development abroad will permit many new contacts between foreign and American universities. The 1962 estimates include funds for the continued development of the Hawaii Center for Cultural and Technical Interchange between East and West.

COMMERCE, HOUSING, AND SPACE TECHNOLOGY

The Federal Government provides a wide variety of aids to transportation, operates the postal service, fosters local and private initiative in housing and urban renewal, provides financial and other aids to small businesses and to areas suffering from substantial and persistent unemployment, and helps finance civil defense preparations. Expenditures for many of these and other commerce and housing programs will continue to increase as workloads rise and past commitments for construction and expansion fall due. Moreover, the Government's outer space activities are requiring substantially increased expenditures. Nevertheless, the total expenditures of $3.4 billion estimated for the fiscal year 1962 for commerce, housing, and space technology are $413 million less than the expenditures now estimated for 1961, primarily because legislation is proposed to increase postal rates and thus eliminate the postal deficit financed from the general fund.

SPACE EXPLORATION AND FLIGHT TECHNOLOGY.—Civil space activities being carried forward under the National Aeronautics and Space Administration include: (1) the development of larger and improved space vehicles, new types of propulsion and equipment, and a wide range of necessary supporting research and development; (2) the development of systems of meteorological and communications satellites; and (3) the search for new knowledge about the universe through unmanned, and eventually manned, space exploration. The NASA also carries on research related to new and improved types of aircraft and missiles, chiefly to support programs of the military services.

Expenditures for civil space programs are estimated at $965 million during fiscal year 1962, which is $195 million more than in 1961 and $564 million more than in 1960. Appropriations of $1,110 million for 1962, and supplemental appropriations of $50 million for 1961, are recommended in this budget. Legislation is being proposed to authorize the appropriations required for 1962 and to provide permanent authorization for later years. In addition, amendments to the National Aeronautics and Space Act of 1958 are again being proposed to improve the organization and management of the space programs.

We have just cause to be proud of the accomplishments of our space programs to date and can look forward with confidence to future achievements which will succeed in extending ever further the horizons of our knowledge.

The first attempts to develop communications systems have met with outstanding success with both the Echo I passive communications satellite, which has reflected signals between widely distant stations on the ground, and the Courier active communications satellite of the Department of Defense, which has stored and relayed messages transmitted to it from the ground. We are now ready, therefore, to take the first steps leading to a practical satellite communications system for commercial use. While

COMMERCE, HOUSING, AND SPACE TECHNOLOGY

[Fiscal years. In millions]

Program or agency	Budget expenditures			Recommended new obligational authority for 1962
	1960 actual	1961 estimate	1962 estimate	
Space exploration and flight technology......	$401	$770	$965	$1,110
Promotion of aviation:				
Federal Aviation Agency.................	508	640	730	686
Civil Aeronautics Board.................	60	87	82	84
Promotion of water transportation:				
Department of Commerce................	269	279	338	293
Coast Guard..........................	238	262	272	296
Panama Canal Company.................	(¹)	16	10	......
Provision of highways.....................	38	39	(¹)(²)	(²)
Postal service:				
Public service costs.....................	37	49	63	63
Postal deficit under present law...........	488	897	843	843
Proposed rate revisions..................	......	−160	−843	−843
Community development and facilities:				
Urban Renewal Administration...........	108	159	208	310
Other	22	25	31	4
Public housing programs..................	134	153	170	183
Other aids to housing:				
Federal Savings and Loan Insurance Corporation:				
Present program.....................	−20	−35	−64	......
Proposed premium increase.............	......	......	−164	......
Federal Housing Administration...........	−53	3	21	53
Veterans housing loans:				
Present program.....................	206	100	115	150
Proposed limitation on eligibility.........	......	......	−30	......
Federal National Mortgage Association.....	−30	113	75	285
College housing loans...................	201	172	200	100
Farm housing loans and other.............	−25	−39	26	12
Other aids to business:				
Small Business Administration............	63	68	94	24
Proposed area assistance legislation........	......	......	10	83
Other	33	56	58	71
Regulation of commerce and finance.........	58	67	74	73
Civil and defense mobilization..............	46	50	81	104
Disaster loans and relief...................	−1	14	7	9
Total..............................	2,782	3,784	3,371	³ 3,993

¹ Less than one-half million dollars.

² Reflects proposed financing of Federal-aid highways in national forests and public lands from highway trust fund.

³ Compares with new obligational authority of $3,784 million enacted for 1960 and $4,612 million (including $203 million of anticipated supplemental appropriations) estimated for 1961.

the special nature of space operations makes it necessary and proper for the Government to take the lead in advancing the needed research and development of satellites for commercial communications use and to conduct the launchings, private industry should participate in the development phase and should be aggressively encouraged to assume the costs of the establishment and operation of the commercial system. The recommendations in the 1962 budget, including a supplemental estimate for 1961, provide for moving ahead rapidly with the development of an active communications satellite system for commercial use, and anticipate that private concerns will provide $10 million in 1962 in support of the program.

In the field of meteorology we have also achieved success with the Tiros I and Tiros II satellites. The 1962 recommendations provide for further experiments with more advanced Tiros and Nimbus satellites, which may provide the basis for an operational system for weather forecasting and research.

In the program for manned space flight, the reliability of complex booster, capsule, escape, and life-support components of the Mercury system is now being tested to assure a safe manned ballistic flight into space, and hopefully a manned orbital flight, in calendar year 1961. Further testing and experimentation will be necessary to establish whether there are any valid scientific reasons for extending manned space flight beyond the Mercury program.

In unmanned space exploration, the scientific information received from our earth satellites and space probes has taught us a great deal about the earth and surrounding space. In the near future, the first launching under the Ranger unmanned lunar exploration program will take place. This program will eventually include the increasingly complex Surveyor and Prospector series. Investigations in the vicinity of the planets Mars and Venus are planned under Project Mariner with initial launchings scheduled for 1962. Large earth-orbiting astronomical and geophysical observatories are also planned as successors to our present scientific satellites.

The success of many of the advanced projects planned for 1962 and future years will depend on the success of the new and powerful Centaur and Saturn launch vehicles. Steady progress has been made on these boosters, which use proven liquid propellant in the lower stages and advanced liquid hydrogen propellant in the upper stages. The weightlifting capability of the Saturn launch vehicle will surpass any currently known to exist.

TRANSPORTATION AND COMMUNICATION.—Few segments of our economic system are more essential to economic growth and national defense than an adequate and efficient transportation and communication network. This budget reflects important actions under way to modernize Federal transportation and communication programs. As a basis for future legislation, the Congress also has before it a comprehensive study of our Nation's transportation system completed last year by the Secretary of Commerce.

Aviation.—The expanded program to improve air traffic control and navigation services, begun in 1957, is advancing rapidly under the direction of the Federal Aviation Agency. Over this period budget expenditures for the promotion of civil aviation have risen from $219 million to an estimated $811 million for 1962. Large numbers of radars and instrument landing aids, as well as many new navigation aids and other airway facilities, have been placed in operation. Substantial progress has been made in achieving joint use of facilities for air defense and air traffic management purposes. The improvements being provided and those now under active development by the Federal Aviation Agency will help assure accommodation of a growing volume of air traffic with maximum safety and efficiency.

The continuing expansion of the modernization effort will cause expenditures of the Federal Aviation Agency to rise by $90 million to an estimated $730 million in 1962. New obligational authority of $686 million is being requested, primarily for procurement of additional equipment, for operating the airways system, and for conducting research and development of new equipment and techniques.

New legislation is recommended to authorize appropriations for continuing Federal grants-in-aid for airport construction beyond 1961. In this legislation, the present method of providing new obligational authority by contract authorization in substantive legislation should be changed to appropriations which are subject to the normal executive and congressional review process, but still provide for adequate advance planning by localities. For 1962, this budget includes recommended appropriations of $40 million, which is $23 million less than the presently authorized level. The reduction reflects the sound policy that the level should progressively be reduced and that, after a reasonable transition period, users and benefiting communities should assume full responsibility for the construction of airports, which should be largely self-financed.

Legislation is again recommended to establish a Federal corporation to operate the Washington National and Dulles International Airports in the Washington, D.C., metropolitan area. This arrangement will provide greater management flexibility to meet changing requirements and permit more business-like operations.

Subsidies to local-service airlines, including intra-Alaska operations and helicopter services in Chicago, Los Angeles, and New York, continue to be excessive. These Federal payments currently average about $12 per passenger-trip for all trips of local-service carriers. The reduction in subsidy expenditures of the Civil Aeronautics Board from $87 million in 1961 to $82 million in 1962 reflects the large non-recurring payments in 1961 to reduce the backlog of unpaid subsidies from prior years rather than any reduction in accruing subsidies. According to current Board estimates, subsidies will rise to a peak in fiscal year 1963 and will remain above $80 million through 1966. Strong demands for additional services and for new routes to smaller communities could cause further increases in subsidies because the potential traffic is inadequate to pay the full costs of the services.

The dependence of these local-service carriers on the Federal Government should be reduced. Toward this end positive action is needed from both the Civil Aeronautics Board and the Congress. The Board should discontinue the least essential routes and stops in accordance with its use-it-or-lose-it policy, and should also develop other means of limiting Federal support. The Congress should review the basic promotional policy of the Federal Aviation Act, giving special attention to the question of whether the national interest justifies continuing substantial Federal payments to sustain deficit operations for service to points with very limited traffic.

Domestic trunk airlines, now self-supporting, provide more passenger miles of transportation than any other common carriers. In view of this evidence of the industry's growing maturity, the Congress should enact legislation to make trunk lines ineligible for subsidies after a period of subsidy-free operations. This will remove a potential burden on Federal resources.

Airway user charges.—The civilian users of the Federal airways system enjoy substantial benefits from the large and growing Government outlays for improved traffic control and navigation services. Federal costs for operating and improving the airways system, excluding airport grants and weather and other indirect services, now approach $600 million a year. It is wholly appropriate that civilian users begin to assume a more reasonable share of these costs, most of which are now borne by the general taxpayer.

To achieve this purpose, it is again recommended that the present tax on aviation gasoline be increased from 2 to $4\frac{1}{2}$ cents per gallon and that the $4\frac{1}{2}$-cent tax rate be extended to jet fuels, which are now tax free. In addition, receipts from the existing and proposed aviation gasoline taxes should be placed in the general fund rather than transferred to the highway trust fund as at present. There is no sound reason for using these taxes to finance highway construction. The airlines should be assured that these tax increases may be reflected promptly in fare adjustments.

Promotion of water transportation.—The steadily rising cost of operating U.S. merchant ships is seriously hampering our efforts to achieve a healthy, competitive merchant marine industry. Net expenditures by the Department of Commerce, chiefly the Maritime Administration, in 1962 are estimated at $338 million, up from $279 million in 1961. Expenditures for replacement of war-built cargo ships are estimated to rise by $23 million, and outlays for operating subsidies are expected to be $32 million more than in 1961.

In order to assist the shipping industry to achieve lower costs and a stronger competitive position, the Government has recently initiated a new research and development program. A primary objective of this program is to make available the new equipment necessary to mechanize shipboard operations along the lines already well established in shoreside industries. The full cooperation of Government, industry, and labor will be required to assure the success of this program. Established practices and legislative policies must be reassessed, and attention must be focused on measures most likely to enhance the competitive position of U.S. merchantmen in international trade. If the United States is to maintain its position as a maritime nation, if the industry is to be reasonably profitable and less dependent upon Government aid, and if maritime employment is to be stable and wages high, continuous bold innovations are necessary.

It is again requested that the inflexible 3½% interest rate on ship mortgage loans made by the Maritime Administration be replaced by authority to charge the Government's full cost for such loans.

Expenditures by the Coast Guard are estimated at $272 million in 1962, which is $10 million more than in 1961. This increase reflects the operation of new loran stations, higher repair and maintenance costs, modernization of facilities, and replacement of equipment, such as patrol vessels, rescue helicopters, and aids to navigation.

Construction will continue on the Balboa Bridge across the Panama Canal. Widening of the canal from 300 to 500 feet in the area of the Continental Divide will also continue, in order to accommodate increased ship traffic. As a result of some increase in toll revenues and some decrease in capital outlays, budget expenditures of the Panama Canal Company in 1962 will be $6 million less than in 1961. The Company should be authorized to reimburse the U.S. Treasury for various costs associated with its operations which are not now recovered, including the increased annuity payable to the Republic of Panama in accordance with the treaty of 1955, and legislation to this end is proposed.

Following extensive study, I have concluded that the commercial activities of the Panama Steamship Line should be discontinued and the Board of Directors of the Panama Canal Company has been requested to take appropriate steps to do so. Commercial shippers now using the Panama Line have been notified of this action, and complete cessation of commercial activities of the Line is to be accomplished by February 10, 1961. Thereafter, the activities of the Line should be confined solely to the transportation of passengers and freight for the account of the Panama Canal Company and the Canal Zone Government. This action will undoubtedly require a reappraisal of the Line's operations, including a review of the need for supplying Company-owned shipping services to the Panama Canal Company from the continental United States, in the light of national maritime considerations and established Government policy to avoid undue competition with private enterprise.

Highways.—The Interstate Highway System has progressed considerably since the enactment of the Highway Act of 1956, with almost 10,000 miles now open to traffic. Active work is under way on another 14,600 miles, of which approximately 1,600 miles are expected to be open to traffic by the end of calendar year 1961. To continue this progress and assure timely completion of the Interstate System, two important legislative actions are required. The highway fuel tax should be increased to 4½ cents per gallon, as previously recommended, and the rate should be continued at this level through 1972, instead of reverting to 3 cents on July 1, 1961, as provided by present law. The unwise diversion of automotive excise taxes from the general fund to the highway trust fund, also scheduled for July 1, 1961, should be rescinded.

Adoption of these recommendations will make it possible to complete the Interstate System in 1973 to meet the traffic needs for which it is designed. The enactment of my previous recommendations to (1) transfer financing of forest and public lands highways, which for the most part are components of the Federal-aid systems, from the general fund to the highway trust fund and (2) retain the receipts from aviation gas taxes in the general fund, will not extend this planned completion date. Under the proposed program, Federal payments from the trust fund for highways in fiscal year 1962 are estimated at $3,029 million, up from $2,868 million in 1961.

The Secretary of Commerce, in a report submitted to the Congress this month, is presenting a current estimate of $37 billion as the total Federal cost of the Interstate System. The estimated construction costs of this 41,000-mile system are about $1 billion less than in the 1958 estimate, but the new total includes the cost of highway planning and administration not previously included.

Postal service.—During recent years, the Post Office Department has been conducting a large-scale modernization program to improve the delivery of mail and to reduce handling costs per unit. For example, a new system of mail transportation and distribution is now providing overnight delivery of letter mail within all principal metropolitan areas. Modern mail processing systems with electronic and mechanical equipment developed under the direction of the Department are already in operation in 17 major postal facilities, and similar installations will soon be in use in 48 others.

While the modernization program has increased the efficiency of postal operations and will contribute to savings in future costs, it cannot materially reduce the enormous postal deficit. In fiscal year 1962 this deficit is estimated at $843 million, after deduction of the $63 million estimated cost of services benefiting the public at large computed in accordance with the principles used by the Congress in previous years. The deficit is largely the result of the enactment by the Congress in the postwar years of postal pay increases without corresponding rate increases.

In the Postal Policy Act of 1958, the Congress established the policy that postal rates should be kept high enough to recover postal expenses except for the cost of certain public services as fixed by appropriation acts. In accordance with this policy, rate increases adequate to cover such expenses were proposed to the Congress in 1959 and again in 1960. No rate legislation was enacted in either year. With record postal deficits in prospect for the current fiscal year and for 1962, rate increases must be provided promptly to achieve a self-supporting postal service. Accordingly, I strongly urge that additional revenue of $843 million be provided for the fiscal year 1962 and that the higher rates be made effective by April 1, 1961, in order to reduce the postal deficit for the fiscal year 1961. Such action is necessary to eliminate the drain upon the Treasury of this mounting deficit for which there is no justification in law or in equity.

HOUSING AND COMMUNITY DEVELOPMENT.—During the past decade, housing construction and improvement have gone forward at the highest level in history. The housing shortages of the postwar period have been largely met, and the housing conditions of the great bulk of the population improved. At the same time, major new governmental and private programs have begun to reverse the blight and deterioration afflicting our urban areas. Thus, a solid base has been laid for greater progress in the decade of the sixties.

In the future, as in the past, the best results will be obtained by emphasizing leadership and financial participation by private industry and by local and State public agencies. Federal assistance can be most effective, most consistent with our free institutions, and least costly to the taxpayers if it emphasizes the supplementary action needed to help overcome obstacles to private and local accomplishment.

The major needs for the immediate future can best be met by assuring private groups and local governments of the continuing availability of existing Federal programs. Unfortunately, at the present time most housing programs require legislative action at frequent intervals merely to continue present operations. These programs are no longer experimental. Their continued availability should not depend upon the enactment of legislation which also often includes controversial changes. Rather, the major existing housing programs, like most other Federal programs, should be authorized permanently, subject only to normal annual budgetary review by the executive branch and the Congress.

Urban renewal.—The nationwide program to rebuild and rehabilitate our cities continues to grow. By the close of the current fiscal year, an estimated 68 projects in 50 cities will be completed, another 577 projects will be under way, and planning for 310 more will be in process. These 955 projects will ultimately have required a total of almost $2 billion in Federal grants to pay two-thirds of the net cost. If present trends continue, approximately the same amount may also be needed for Federal purchases of mortgages to finance construction of housing connected with the same projects. This Federal aid will generate much greater private and local investment and will result in substantial increases in property values and in tax revenues to local public agencies.

This vital program should move forward on a basis which gives adequate assurance to local communities of continuing Federal assistance and also places proper emphasis on local participation. Accordingly, permanent authority should replace the present annual statutory limitations on Federal grants, with annual amounts provided through the normal appropriation process. Further, the local share in project costs should be increased from one-third to one-half to reflect more adequately the increases in local tax revenues and other direct benefits to the communities participating in the program. For the fiscal year 1962 new obligational authority of $300 million is recommended.

Urban planning.—The various housing and urban renewal programs and the Federal-aid highway program have important impacts on the character and development of our rapidly growing metropolitan areas. To help assure that these aids make the maximum contribution to sound community development, the Secretary of Commerce and the Housing and Home Finance Administrator have established a new procedure for the joint use of urban planning grants and Federal-aid highway research and planning funds for comprehensive metropolitan planning. This procedure is intended not only to produce better planning for the use of Federal, State, and local funds, but also to encourage effective coordination and cooperation among the many local governments and the State and Federal agencies engaged in metropolitan development activities. To help carry out the new approach, as well as to aid mass-transit planning and to meet other expanding requirements, it is recommended that the present statutory limitations on appropriations for urban planning grants be removed and that the appropriation for such grants be increased to $10 million for 1962 from the $4 million appropriated for 1961.

Public housing programs.—By the close of the fiscal year 1962 an estimated 522,000 federally aided public housing units will be occupied, and construction will be underway on 49,000 more units. Another 49,000 units will be under contract for Federal contributions but construction will not yet have been started on these units. In view of the large number of authorized units not yet under construction, no additional authorization is recommended in this budget. Expenditures for contributions to local authorities will increase in 1962 largely because of subsidies required on newly occupied units.

Federal Savings and Loan Insurance Corporation.—A year ago legislation was recommended to provide needed increases in the insurance reserve of the Federal Savings and Loan Insurance Corporation, which insures the share accounts of institutions representing the largest source of home mortgage financing. Because of the continuing rapid growth of these institutions, the Corporation's reserves are still only 0.66% of the insured liability, and legislation is even more necessary now. Therefore, it is recommended that the present unnecessarily high requirement for investment in stock of the Federal Home Loan banks be reduced, and that insured savings and loan associations be required to make additional prepayments of insurance premiums of approximately the amounts of that reduction. The objective should be to build up the secondary reserves of the Corporation until total reserves reach 2% of the insurance liabilities. This proposal would cause a much more rapid increase in the insurance reserves of the Corporation, by adding an extra $164 million in 1962. It would not significantly increase the costs to member associations, but would allocate more realistically the combined resources of the Home Loan banks and the Corporation.

Insurance of private mortgages.—The Federal Housing Administration expects to increase its commitments to insure mortgages from about 800,000 housing units in the fiscal year 1961 to over 900,000 units in 1962; about 40% of the 1962 commitments will be mortgages on newly built houses. However, since the present amount of insurance authority will be used up within the next few months, prompt action is needed to prevent interruption of this important program. The Congress should remove the present ceiling on this authority so that home buyers, builders, and lenders can count upon the continued availability of Federal mortgage insurance.

Legislation should also be enacted to make permanent the authority to insure loans on home improvements, which expires October 1, 1961. This program, initiated in 1934, has proved to be an important aid to modernization of existing homes, and its continuance should no longer depend on periodic congressional action.

Statutory ceilings on interest rates for certain types of mortgages insured by the Federal Housing Administration, as well as for direct and guaranteed loans of the Veterans Administration, have from time to time limited the effectiveness of these programs. In the past, the Congress has recognized the need for some increased flexibility in such interest rates in order to attract adequate private capital. In the present situation, the interest rate ceiling of 5¼% on housing loans guaranteed by the Veterans Administration is a serious obstacle to adequate private financing. The similar ceiling on insured mortgages for rental housing, especially for the new housing program for the elderly, and the ceiling of 4½% on family housing for members of the armed services also discourage private financing. As previously recommended, these ceilings should be increased or removed by the Congress. The success of the new mortgage insurance program for nursing homes in obtaining private funds through slightly higher interest rates illustrates the importance of adequate flexibility in such rates.

Veterans housing loans.—The last Congress extended the veterans direct housing loan program of the Veterans Administration for another 2 years, provided new obligational authority of $150 million for such loans for each of the fiscal years 1961 and 1962, and provided for a 2-year extension of the loan guarantee program for World War II veterans. The need for continuing the readjustment benefit programs of direct loans and loan guarantees for World War II veterans has long since passed.

Changes are recommended in the direct loan program to (1) confine this program, beginning July 26, 1961, to veterans of the Korean conflict, (2) extend the program for Korean conflict veterans from the present termination date of July 25, 1962, until February 1, 1965 (the same termination date as for loan guarantees for these veterans), and (3) finance the extended program from funds already authorized, augmented by funds from repayment of loans previously made. These changes will permit a satisfactory program of aid for veterans of the Korean conflict with expenditures of $85 million in 1962, a reduction of $15 million from 1961.

Voluntary Home Mortgage Credit Program.—Authority for the Voluntary Home Mortgage Credit Committee expires October 1, 1961. Under present unrealistic interest rate limitations, this program cannot contribute substantially to the financing of guaranteed home loans to veterans in remote areas. Other federally insured loans are, however, being placed for borrowers in such areas and for members of minority groups. The Committee is also now trying to find private financing for mortgages eligible for special assistance by the Federal National Mortgage Association. This program should, therefore, be extended for another 2 years.

Mortgage purchases.—Mortgage financing requirements for housing for displaced families, for elderly families, and in urban renewal areas, will continue to increase in 1962. Despite the progress made by the Voluntary Home Mortgage Credit Committee in finding some private financing, the bulk of the financing needs for these types of housing will continue to be met through mortgage purchases by the Federal National Mortgage Association under its special assistance functions. The Association will require, for this purpose, additional new obligational authority of $250 million in 1962; the legislation should authorize provision of this amount through the appropriation process.

Through its secondary market operations trust fund, the Federal National Mortgage Association will purchase an estimated $1 billion of insured and guaranteed mortgages of all types at market prices. Unlike the special assistance program, which is wholly financed by the Federal Government, almost all of the necessary funds for secondary market operations will be provided by sale of debentures to private investors and by purchase of common stock by mortgage sellers. New obligational authority of $35 million, however, is estimated to be required for additional Treasury subscriptions to the Association's preferred stock.

College housing.—Legislation enacted by the last Congress provided sufficient authority to continue the present college housing program into the fiscal year 1962. I have previously recommended a new program to be administered by the Department of Health, Education, and Welfare to provide Federal assistance for university facilities of all types through loan guarantees and grants. As a transition to that new and broader program, new obligational authority of $100 million for college housing loans is recommended for 1962. Together with funds from existing authorizations, this will permit new loan commitments of $200 million in 1962.

PROMOTION AND REGULATION OF BUSINESS.—The Federal Government provides a variety of direct and indirect aids to business enterprises. At the same time, Federal regulatory agencies and programs enforce competition and regulate monopoly in many specific areas.

Small business.—Federal assistance to small business will continue to grow in 1962. Financial aid under the Small Business Investment Act to both small business investment companies and to State and local development companies is increasing at a rapid rate. The number of such investment companies is expected to exceed 400 by the end of June 1962, compared to 109 in June 1960, thus expanding the supply of private capital available to small businesses. Other loans by the Small Business Administration will continue at a high level, as will the efforts to assist small businesses in obtaining a larger share of Federal procurement and research contracts and in improving management methods. Special efforts are being made to provide assistance to firms displaced by urban renewal projects and firms in labor surplus areas.

Legislation should be enacted to extend the important program of loans to local development companies, which otherwise expires at the end of the current fiscal year. In addition, legislation is again requested to extend the privilege of simplified filings under the Securities Act of 1933 to a wider range of securities issues, and thus to facilitate small business financing.

Area assistance.—The Department of Commerce, with the assistance of 16 other departments and major agencies, has further extended in the past year the wide range of Federal aids to local communities suffering from severe and chronic unemployment. However, private groups and local public officials must provide the primary initiative in finding successful permanent solutions for the difficult problems of their specific areas.

For the past 5 years I have repeatedly recommended legislation which would provide the authority necessary for more effective Federal assistance without merely substituting temporary Federal aid for indispensable local leadership. Alternative proposals enacted by the Congress, which would have been less effective and more expensive, have been vetoed. The Congress is again urged to enact sound legislation to permit reasonable increases in Federal aid through a program of loans and grants. This program should continue to be administered by the Secretary of Commerce to avoid establishment of an unnecessary new agency. Appropriations of $83 million for 1962 are requested to initiate the expanded Federal program.

Export expansion.—The national export expansion program launched early last year by the Department of Commerce has already had considerable success. This budget includes recommendations for additional appropriations to help achieve further increases in exports and to place greater emphasis on encouraging travel to the United States.

New York World's Fair.—The Secretary of Commerce, at my request, is developing plans, in anticipation of authorizing legislation, for Federal participation in the New York World's Fair scheduled to open in the spring of 1964.

Regulation of commerce and finance.—Under this budget, the Federal Communications Commission, the Federal Trade Commission, the Interstate Commerce Commission, the Securities and Exchange Commission, and the Civil Aeronautics Board will be further strengthened. The appropriations recommended for these five independent regulatory agencies will finance a staff 40% greater than at the end of 1956, an expansion clearly required by the growth of regulated industries, by new legislative responsibilities, and by the increased complexity of the problems involved. Numerous improvements in agency operations to simplify procedures and reduce backlogs are anticipated from a series of management studies made in recent months. The increasing workload of these agencies increases the need to adjust or impose charges on the regulated industries or activities sufficient to cover the costs of administration.

The antitrust laws should be strengthened by legislation (1) requiring large businesses to notify the antitrust agencies of proposed mergers, (2) empowering the Attorney General to issue civil investigative demands in antitrust cases when civil procedures are planned, and (3) authorizing the Federal Trade Commission to seek preliminary injunctions when it is likely that a proposed merger would violate the law.

CIVIL AND DEFENSE MOBILIZATION.—Prudent concern for the protection of the civilian population from hazards in a nuclear world makes it necessary to recommend increases for 1962 in appropriations for civil defense. The largest increases for nonmilitary defense will provide funds for increasing medical stockpiles and for the first full-year cost of a program begun in 1961 to match State and local costs for civil defense personnel and administration.   Additional funds are also requested for procurement of radiological equipment and for strengthening Federal activities in emergency health and manpower programs.

The Congress and the executive branch have recognized that civil defense is the joint responsibility of Federal, State, and local governments. As exercise of its partnership, the Federal Government has, by leadership and example, implemented a national shelter policy, which recognizes the fallout shelter as the best single nonmilitary defense measure for the protection of the greatest number of people.   Under this policy the Federal Government has instructed people in protective measures, conducted a sample survey of existing shelter capabilities, accelerated shelter research, and constructed prototype shelters for example and guidance. Moreover, the Congress has been urged to provide funds for inclusion of fallout shelters in appropriate new and existing Federal buildings.   Funds and appropriate legislation are being requested to accelerate these activities in 1962.

In order to strengthen the program, legislation is being proposed to require appropriate fallout shelters in certain new private construction where the Federal Government provides some form of financial assistance. This legislation will also provide for a 1-year program of grants to States to assist in the construction of fallout protection shelters in selected State buildings.   Upon the enactment of this legislation, supplemental appropriations will be required.

AGRICULTURE AND AGRICULTURAL RESOURCES

In the fiscal year 1962, Federal programs for agriculture will continue to require heavy expenditures for much the same reason as in the immediately preceding years: the lack of adequate modifications in the price-support laws to make them conform to the increased efficiency and growing productive capacity of the agricultural industry.

Estimated expenditures for agriculture and agricultural resources in 1962 are $5.1 billion, which is $165 million more than the estimate for the current year and $263 million more than was spent in 1960.   Total new authority to incur obligations requested for 1962 is $4.6 billion, which includes $936 million to restore, to the extent necessary, the capital impairment of the Commodity Credit Corporation resulting from previous price-support losses, and $1.7 billion to reimburse the Corporation for estimated costs and losses through fiscal year 1961 of other programs financed through that agency.

AGRICULTURE AND AGRICULTURAL RESOURCES

[Fiscal years. In millions]

Program or agency	Budget expenditures			Recommended new obligational authority for 1962
	1960 actual	1961 estimate	1962 estimate	
Stabilization of farm prices and farm income:				
Commodity Credit Corporation—price support, supply, and purchase programs.....	$1,480	$1,423	$1,537	$936
Commodity Credit Corporation—special activities:				
Public Law 480 (titles I and IV)........	1,232	1,285	1,303	1,353
International Wheat Agreement.........	66	72	71	89
National Wool Act....................	93	62	66	59
Transfer of bartered materials to supplemental stockpile....................	192	208	175	163
Other...........................	6	—2	—2	......
Removal of surplus agricultural commodities.	90	100	110	284
Sugar Act............................	74	74	85	81
Other	44	42	51	51
Subtotal........................	3,278	3,264	3,396	3,017
Financing rural electrification and rural telephones	330	328	340	255
Financing farm ownership and operation:				
Farmers Home Administration............	249	264	231	225
Farm Credit Administration..............	—3	4	4	3
Conservation of agricultural land and water resources:				
Conservation reserve:				
Present program.....................	324	354	357	330
Proposed legislation for extension and expansion............................	......	......	19	19
Agricultural conservation program:				
Program total.......................	237	236	234	238
Under CCC special activities..........	(1)	(—4)	(—8)	......
Soil Conservation Service (including watershed protection and Great Plains program)................................	131	151	163	166
Research and other agricultural services......	293	336	357	352
Total............................	4,838	4,936	5,101	[2] 4,605

[1] Less than one-half million dollars.

[2] Compares with new obligational authority of $5,151 million enacted for 1960 and $4,696 million (including $23 million in anticipated supplemental appropriations) estimated for 1961.

Each year that the current unrealistic price-support program is continued complicates further the production adjustments that will have to be made before present Government controls over farm operations can be relaxed. Carryover stocks of wheat continue to rise. Current indications are that by July 1, 1961, wheat stocks will amount to about 1.5 billion bushels, which is more than an average year's production and 2½ times an average year's domestic consumption. Carryover stocks of corn and other feed grains have risen each year since 1952, and by the fall of 1961 are expected to reach 82 million tons, or about one-half an average year's production. While cotton carryover stocks are expected to be down slightly by the beginning of the fiscal year 1962 as compared with a year earlier, the cotton program continues to be a substantial drain on the budget, principally as a result of the sale of cotton abroad at prices substantially lower than support levels.

Among the many aspects of the price-support program in need of major changes, the most urgent is the enactment of realistic price-support legislation for wheat. It is imperative that the Congress take early action so that farmers can make the necessary adjustments in their plans. Because of the time lag between enactment of new price-support legislation and its budgetary impact, legislation enacted in this session of the Congress can have little effect before the 1963 budget. My previous recommendations for wheat legislation allow for considerable latitude in method of approach as long as the legislation deals realistically with the problem.

The last session of the Congress did not extend the authority of the Secretary of Agriculture to bring additional land into the conservation reserve. Since the rental rates needed to induce farmers to place large quantities of surplus-producing land in the conservation reserve depend in large part on levels of price supports, it would be unsound to attempt to set such rates high enough to compete with the present unrealistic level of price supports, particularly for wheat. Therefore, legislation proposed by this administration to extend the conservation reserve through the calendar year 1964 and to expand the program from the present level of 28.6 million acres to a maximum of 60 million acres should be enacted only if satisfactory legislation for wheat is also enacted. An expanded conservation reserve would not be effective unless largely concentrated in areas producing wheat and other surplus commodities. For this reason, the Secretary of Agriculture should be provided with specific authority to give special consideration, in allocating conservation reserve funds, to those States and regions where curtailment of the production of wheat or other surplus commodities is consistent with long-range goals for adjusting production.

Stabilization of farm prices and income.—In fiscal year 1962, expenditures for price supports and other programs to stabilize farm prices and income are estimated at $3.4 billion, which is $132 million more than the amount currently estimated for 1961, and $118 million more than expenditures in 1960. Expenditures for these programs are not subject to regular annual budgetary control, since they are determined mainly by the loan, commodity purchase, and other price-supporting activities that the Commodity Credit Corporation is required to carry out under existing laws. In 1962 farm price support and related activities account for about two-thirds of the estimated expenditures for agricultural programs. The budget estimate assumes that yields per acre of price-supported crops for the 1961 crop year will be in line with recent years. It also assumes a continued favorable level of exports of farm commodities.

This high level of expenditures reflects, directly or indirectly, the continuation of present price supports in the face of a volume of agricultural production that cannot be absorbed by the domestic and world markets at currently supported prices. Total farm production for the calendar year 1960 established an all-time record both on an absolute and a per capita basis. It was 29% above the 1947–49 average, and was achieved with 30% fewer farmworkers and 6% fewer crop acres.

Surplus wheat, cotton, corn, rice, and other commodities are being utilized in our Food for Peace program to promote economic development and common defense and to provide emergency relief for needy people abroad. The largest part of the program is the sale of farm commodities for foreign currencies under title I of the Agricultural Trade Development and Assistance Act of 1954 (Public Law 480). Because of the size of past sales, particularly a 4-year agreement with India, additional authority of $1.1 billion is recommended for the remainder of the calendar year 1961. Titles II and III of this act provide for donating surplus commodities to foreign governments primarily for emergency relief needs and to private relief organizations in support of their activities abroad; over 55 million people benefited this past year from these donations. Continuation of the programs currently carried on under titles I and II will require legislation this year to extend them beyond December 31, 1961.

Surplus agricultural commodities are also made available to the needy at home through the direct distribution program of the Department of Agriculture, which is carried on under the permanent appropriation for the removal of surplus agricultural commodities and through the Commodity Credit Corporation's surplus disposal operations. In the fiscal year 1960, there were donations of 526 million pounds of surplus food, valued at $59 million, directly to needy families in the United States. In October 1960, there were 3.3 million people in the United States receiving surplus foods through these programs; additional persons benefited from food donations to the school lunch program and to institutions providing aid to the needy.

Since the Sugar Act expires on March 31, 1961, prompt legislative action extending this program is required. In line with my previous recommendation, the Congress should amend the Act to provide the President with urgently needed flexibility in the allocation of quotas.

The National Wool Act, which expires on March 31, 1962, should be extended, and its financing should be shifted to a direct appropriation basis.

To conserve fiscal resources and to implement the principle that identifiable recipients of certain special services should pay for them, legislation is again proposed to permit the Federal Crop Insurance Corporation to include its administrative expenses in determining appropriate premium rates for crop insurance.

Rural electrification and telephones.—Expenditures of the Rural Electrification Administration are estimated at $340 million for 1962, and new obligational authority of $255 million is recommended, including $100 million for telephone loans and $145 million for electrification loans.

The Rural Electrification Administration has made a major contribution to the development of rural America. About 97% of our farms now have central station electric service as compared with 11% in 1935. The telephone program also is making a real contribution to a better rural America by improving rural telephone service.

The expanding use of power in the areas served by electric cooperatives, however, requires substantial amounts of new capital each year to provide additional generating capacity and heavier transmission and distribution facilities. More than half of the total power sales by the REA system are made to rural industrial, recreational, and other nonfarm users. These nonfarm users comprise about 80% of the new customers being added.

The capital needs of the Rural Electrification Administration are being financed currently by loans from the Treasury at 2% interest. Loans are made to borrowers at this same rate. While special treatment of these programs through favorable Federal financing was justified in earlier years, the progress that has been made by the local systems in achieving the objectives of the Rural Electrification Act and in developing financial stability indicates that the time has come to plan for methods of financing other than through the Federal Government. To that end, legislation should be developed for a federally chartered institution to finance the future requirements of the rural electrification and rural telephone programs. Such an institution should be owned and managed by the REA borrowers subject to the examination and supervision of the Secretary of Agriculture. To launch the new institution on a sound basis, it should be assisted initially by a Federal loan, with provision for orderly retirement of the loan. Future capital needs of the REA borrowers should be met by the sale of the institution's obligations to the public. Provision should also be made for loans by the institution on behalf of the Secretary of Agriculture to borrowers who are unable to qualify for regular loans.

Farm ownership and operation.—Expenditures for the loan programs of the Farmers Home Administration are estimated at $231 million for 1962, compared with $264 million estimated for 1961. Loans are made by the Farmers Home Administration to borrowers who are unable to obtain credit from other sources at interest rates currently prevailing in their communities, in order to finance farm ownership and enlargement, farm operations, and soil and water conservation. Direct loans for farm ownership and soil and water conservation are supplemented with private loans insured by the Federal Government.

Legislation previously recommended to simplify, consolidate, and improve the authority of the Secretary of Agriculture to make these types of loans should be enacted. Included in this legislation is a proposal to place the operations of the Farmers Home Administration on a revolving fund basis.

Authority to make loans under the farm housing loan program expires June 30, 1961. Extension of this separate farm housing loan authority is not recommended, since loans similar to the farm housing loans would be authorized under the general legislation being recommended relating to the loan authority of the Secretary of Agriculture.

Legislation should be enacted, as recommended previously, to require the States to share a greater part of the costs of farm disaster relief assistance.

Conservation of agricultural resources.—Expenditures in 1962 under the conservation reserve program are expected to be $357 million under existing legislation. If legislation extending and expanding this program is enacted as proposed in this budget, additional expenditures of $19 million in 1962 would result. Under the proposal, there would be a net increase of 10.5 million acres during the 1962 program year, bringing the total at the end of that year to 39 million acres. However, most of the increase in expenditures required for the 1962 program would not occur until 1963 and later fiscal years. To the extent that additions of land to the conservation reserve result in curtailment of the production of price-supported agricultural commodities, the added expenditures resulting from extension and expansion of this program will be accompanied by lower outlays for price supports.

An advance authorization of $100 million is recommended for the 1962 agricultural conservation program. This will affect primarily the expenditures for the fiscal year 1963. In recent appropriation acts the Congress maintained this program at a level which far exceeded my recommendations. As a result, expenditures for the agricultural conservation program are estimated to be $236 million in 1961 and $234 million in 1962. The $100 million advance authorization, together with other aids for soil and water conservation, will provide substantial incentives for the Nation's farmers to meet our high-priority conservation needs.

Federal cost-sharing assistance in the future under this program should be concentrated on conservation measures which will foster needed shifts to less intensive uses of cropland, and assistance should be eliminated for practices which increase capacity to produce agricultural commodities already in surplus supply. Continuation of cost sharing for output-increasing practices directly conflicts with the recommended expansion of the conservation reserve program under which cropland is removed from production.

New obligational authority of $66 million is recommended for the upstream watershed programs, including $46 million under the Water-

shed Protection and Flood Prevention Act. Of this amount, $10 million
is for initiating construction of projects involving an estimated total
Federal cost of $70 million. Expenditures under these programs are
expected to be $65 million in 1962, which is an increase of $12 million
over 1961 and $21 million over 1960. New obligational authority re-
quested for the Great Plains program totals $10 million, the same as for
1961.

Research and other agricultural services.—Expenditures for research,
education, and other agricultural services in 1962, including $17 million
for purchases of foreign currencies to finance research and market development programs abroad, are estimated at $357 million, which is an increase
of $22 million over 1961. This increase reflects primarily additional sup-
port for the research programs of the Agricultural Research Service and
continuing progress on laboratory construction.

Rural development.—The rural development program inaugurated
by this administration is successfully stimulating economic progress and
growth in low-income farming areas of the Nation. It is becoming
widely accepted as a major national approach to helping families in these
areas. By June 30, 1961, it is expected that some 350 counties in 39
States will be participating in the program. Among the impressive gains
reported in participating areas are the following: (1) new farm crops
have been introduced and production on small farms improved; (2) the
number of jobs has increased through the establishment of new industries
and enlargement of others; (3) income has increased from nonfarm
sources such as recreation, tourist services, and expanded business activities; and (4) educational and training programs have been inaugurated
for those who have little opportunity to enter commercial farming.

The Federal Government supports this program principally through
a redirection and strengthening of existing services and activities. Emphasis is placed on cooperation among Federal and State agencies and
local groups. In the Department of Agriculture, the program is conducted as a part of the continuing responsibilities of 10 of its agencies,
with general leadership furnished by the Extension Service, for which
an increase of $2 million is estimated in this budget. Other Federal
departments and agencies have accelerated their activities that contribute
to the aims of the rural development program. These agencies include
the Small Business Administration, and the Departments of the Interior,
Commerce, Labor, and Health, Education, and Welfare. All of these

activities are carried out under the general guidance of the Committee for Rural Development Program which was established by Executive order.

NATURAL RESOURCES

Sound development of our natural resources is necessary to meet the needs of our growing population and expanding economy. The budget recommendations for the fiscal year 1962 provide for appropriate Federal participation in the development, conservation, and use of these resources, in cooperation with State and local agencies and private interests.

Federal expenditures for natural resources are estimated to be $2.1 billion in 1962 compared with $2 billion in 1961. These expenditures are higher than in any previous year.

Water resources.—Approximately two-thirds of the Federal expenditures for natural resources in 1962 will be for water resources activities. The programs of the Corps of Engineers and the Bureau of Reclamation will require expenditures estimated at $1.2 billion—a record level. Of this amount, $1 billion will be spent on construction. This includes $976 million for continuation of work on projects started in 1961 or prior years, $11 million for first-year expenditures on 37 proposed new project starts, and $13 million for advance planning of projects needed in later years. A large share of the construction expenditures of these agencies will be for multiple-purpose river basin projects, including flood control, navigation, irrigation, water supply, hydroelectric power, and in some cases related recreational and fish and wildlife benefits.

For the Corps of Engineers, the budget includes appropriations of $15 million for starting 31 new projects and an additional number of smaller projects costing less than $400 thousand each. The estimated total cost of building these new projects is $302 million. Appropriations of $6 million are also recommended to enable the Bureau of Reclamation to begin construction on five new projects, with an estimated total cost of $141 million, and to make a loan for one small reclamation project for which the total Federal commitment will be $5 million.

The 1962 program of the Bureau of Reclamation includes protective works for the Rainbow Bridge National Monument, as required by law in connection with construction of Glen Canyon Dam.

It is again recommended that the Congress authorize construction by the Bureau of Reclamation of the Fryingpan-Arkansas project in Colorado.

A few months ago agreement was reached between the United States and Canada on the basic terms of a treaty for the cooperative development of the water resources of the Columbia River Basin. The proposal envisages the construction in Canada, within a 10-year period, of three major reservoirs and the construction by the United States of the authorized Libby project in northern Montana. The substantial flood control and power benefits which will result from this agreement will be realized at a much earlier date with materially less cost than would be the case if they were provided by unilateral rather than by cooperative endeavor. The location of the proposed storage reservoirs will not interfere with the cycle for salmon and other anadromous fish, which constitute an important economic and recreational asset of the Pacific Northwest. The Senate should give prompt attention to the ratification of the treaty when it is presented. Following this ratification, preconstruction planning of Libby Dam should be started by the Corps of Engineers.

NATURAL RESOURCES

[Fiscal years. In millions]

Program or agency	Budget expenditures			Recommended new obligational authority for 1962
	1960 actual	1961 estimate	1962 estimate	
Land and water resources:				
Corps of Engineers	$867	$930	$930	$932
Department of the Interior:				
Bureau of Reclamation	209	240	305	290
Power marketing agencies	34	41	36	36
Indian lands resources	59	68	63	64
Public domain lands and other	35	45	50	50
Tennessee Valley Authority	12	55	103	30
Federal Power Commission	7	8	9	9
International Boundary and Water Commission and other	12	15	19	20
Forest resources	220	263	311	248
Mineral resources	65	66	67	82
Recreational resources	74	87	101	105
Fish and wildlife resources	68	75	84	85
General resource surveys and administration	51	58	60	61
Total	1,713	1,951	2,138	[1] 2,012

[1] Compares with new obligational authority of $2,533 million enacted for 1960 and $2,049 million (including $139 million of anticipated supplemental appropriations) estimated for 1961.

The previous Congress enacted legislation to authorize negotiation of an agreement between the United States and Mexico for the joint construction of Amistad (Friendship) Dam on the Rio Grande, and appropriated $5 million for this project. The 1962 budget includes $12 million to finance further work on the dam as soon as the technical details relating to its construction are approved by the two Governments.

Legislation should be enacted to place the financing of the Bureau of Reclamation and the power marketing agencies of the Department of the Interior on a revolving fund basis, retaining annual review and control by the Congress.

Net budget expenditures of the Tennessee Valley Authority are estimated at $103 million in the fiscal year 1962. The increase of $48 million over the current year will be largely for construction of power and navigation facilities. Under the authority to sell revenue bonds, enacted in August 1959, the TVA issued $50 million of such bonds in November 1960. The Authority plans to issue an additional $140 million in the fiscal year 1962 which, together with power revenues, will provide funds for continuing construction of power facilities and for starting construction of a new steam powerplant in the eastern part of the TVA power area. Construction will continue on Wheeler and Wilson locks and on the navigation features of the Melton Hill project, financed by appropriated funds. The Authority plans to make a payment of $50 million from power proceeds to the Treasury in fiscal year 1962, of which $40 million is a dividend and $10 million is a return of Government capital. A similar payment, estimated at $51 million, is being made in 1961.

The 1961 and 1962 programs of the TVA contemplate the acquisition of certain coal land or mining rights, on which options have been taken, in the eastern portion of its coal supply area. Since it has not been clearly established that such acquisitions are necessary to assure an adequate reserve of coal for TVA's operations, I have directed that these actions not be taken without specific Presidential approval.

Research conducted by the Department of the Interior over the past several years has reduced substantially the cost of obtaining fresh water from saline water. Two demonstration plants for conversion of sea and brackish water into fresh water will be completed in the fiscal year 1962. Appropriations of $3.5 million are recommended for starting two additional plants in 1962, one at Roswell, N. Mex., and the other at a location to be selected on the east coast.

River basin planning commissions.—In addition to the Corps of Engineers, Bureau of Reclamation, Tennessee Valley Authority, and International Boundary and Water Commission, several other Federal agencies participate in phases of water resources programs. The Department of Agriculture assists local groups in watershed protection and flood prevention; the Department of Health, Education, and Welfare has responsibility relating to control of water pollution; and the Federal Power Commission has broad river basin planning authority in connection with licensing construction of private power projects. The Fish and Wildlife Service, National Park Service, and other agencies also participate in certain aspects of water resources projects. Furthermore, activities of State and local agencies and private interests in the field of water resources are of increasing importance. Only with coordinated planning on the part of all groups concerned can there be assurance that all possible uses of water are adequately considered.

To provide for comprehensive, coordinated planning, legislation is being submitted to authorize the President to establish water resources planning commissions as needed in the various river basins or regions. These commissions would be composed of Presidentially appointed members from the various Federal agencies and the States. They would prepare and keep current comprehensive, integrated river basin plans. This proposed general authority would be an improvement over separate laws such as those which established the two *ad hoc* river basin study commissions for the Southeastern and Texas areas.

Cost sharing for local flood protection.—The varied requirements for financial participation by State and local interests in local flood protection projects have resulted in inequities among the various beneficiaries of such projects. In the case of projects of the Corps of Engineers, the Bureau of Reclamation, and the Department of Agriculture, non-Federal contributions range from zero to over 60% of flood protection costs. In previous budget messages, legislation has been recommended to provide an equitable, uniform minimum of 30% non-Federal cost sharing for all flood protection projects. Although the Congress did not act on that proposal, a forward step was taken in the Flood Control Act of 1960, which provides for a uniform minimum of 20% non-Federal cost sharing on local flood protection projects of the Corps of Engineers authorized by that act. The Congress is urged to broaden this action by requiring a minimum of 30% cost sharing on all local projects providing flood protection benefits which are authorized in the future for the Corps of Engineers, the Bureau of Reclamation, and the Department of Agriculture.

Public domain and Indian lands.—In the fiscal year 1962, expenditures for the conservation and development of the public domain lands, administered by the Bureau of Land Management, will be $43 million, somewhat higher than in 1961. Receipts from grazing fees, timber sales, and mineral leases on the public domain lands, including the Outer Continental Shelf, are estimated at $221 million in the fiscal year 1962, an increase of $55 million over the revenues estimated for the current year. A portion of the estimated increase will result from the increases authorized last year in the fees for noncompetitive oil and gas leases. Some of these revenues are shared with States and counties. Shared-revenue payments to these governmental units in 1962 from the public domain lands amount to $58 million.

Estimated expenditures of $63 million for the management of Indian lands in the fiscal year 1962 include $33 million for construction of roads; for irrigation facilities; and for buildings and utilities, mainly additional school facilities for Indian children who reside on lands held in trust by the United States.

Forest resources.—Some increases in expenditures of the Forest Service in 1962 are needed to carry forward its long-range development program for the national forests. These increases will be for forest roads and trails and for forest protection and utilization, including forestry research, fire prevention, and recreational facilities. A supplemental appropriation of $69 million is being requested for the fiscal year 1961 to enable the Forest Service to pay for those portions of the forest lands of the Klamath Indians which are not sold to competitive bidders by April 1, 1961 (as required by Public Law 85–731), with expenditures estimated in the fiscal year 1962. These increases will be offset in part by an expected decrease from the expenditures of $33 million in 1961 for fire fighting in the national forests—the highest annual expenditures on record.

Management of the national forest lands yields substantial revenues, mostly from timber sales and grazing permits. These receipts—which are in addition to the amounts cited earlier under public domain lands—are estimated at $156 million in the fiscal year 1962. Shared revenue payments to the States in 1962 are estimated at $29 million.

Legislation is recommended to provide authority for the Secretary of Agriculture to complete acquisition of the remaining lands in the Boundary Waters Canoe Area of the Superior National Forest in order to preserve this unique wilderness area for public use.

Mineral resources.—Amendments to the Helium Act during the last session of the Congress authorize a long-range program for conserving vital helium resources. Under these amendments, effective March 1, 1961, private industry will be encouraged to finance, build, and operate plants to recover helium for sale to the Department of the Interior. Where necessary, the Secretary of the Interior may take direct steps to conserve this important resource. The program is to be financed from borrowing authority, subject to the appropriation process. Supplemental borrowing authority of $12 million for the fiscal year 1961 is recommended so that the Bureau of Mines can start the program promptly, and provision is made in the 1962 budget to augment this initial amount by $15 million.

The Bureau of Mines will continue its research on improved methods of production and utilization of coal and other minerals. Under recent legislation, the Department of the Interior will contract with educational, trade, and other organizations for research aimed at early solutions to some of the problems confronting the coal industry.

Recreational resources.—The rapidly expanding use of public recreational facilities is placing great demands on the resources of our national park system. The estimated increase of $14 million in expenditures of the National Park Service from 1961 to 1962 will provide for needed maintenance and rehabilitation of the park areas and for operation of new facilities and areas added to the system in recent years. Prompt action should be taken on legislation, as recommended last year, to permit the Secretary of the Interior to acquire three of the remaining undeveloped seashore areas for the national park system. Such action will enable these areas to be preserved for public benefit.

The forthcoming report of the Outdoor Recreation Resources Review Commission will provide a comprehensive survey of outdoor recreational resources and needs. The report should be useful as a guide for Federal, State, local, and private interests in their plans for meeting increasing needs for recreation.

Fish and wildlife resources.—Expenditures for fish and wildlife resources in the fiscal year 1962 are estimated at $84 million, an increase of

$9 million over the current year. Part of the increase will be for management and operation of fish hatcheries and wildlife refuges by the Bureau of Sport Fisheries and Wildlife. Outstanding refuges recently established by the Secretary of the Interior are the Arctic, Kuskokwim, and Izembek wildlife ranges in Alaska, comprising 11.2 million acres, with unique values as waterfowl breeding grounds and with wilderness areas of scenic beauty. Increases for the Bureau of Commercial Fisheries are for construction of oceanographic research facilities, and for biological and technological research to be initiated in 1962 under a special foreign currency program to aid the fishing industry.

General resource surveys.—Expenditures of the Geological Survey will increase primarily as a result of increased interest and participation by the States in the cooperative programs for topographic and geological mapping and water resources investigations.

LABOR AND WELFARE

The labor and welfare programs of the Federal Government have assumed in the last decade a growing role in meeting human needs in our increasingly complex, urbanized society. These programs provide manpower, health, education, science, economic security, and welfare services of great importance to the entire population and also assist many special groups such as the aged, the children, the disabled, the unemployed, and the needy.

Budget expenditures for labor and welfare programs in the fiscal year 1962 are estimated at $4.8 billion, an increase of $276 million over 1961. In the last decade these budget expenditures have more than doubled. Labor and welfare benefit payments from the social security and other trust funds, supported largely by payroll taxes on employers and employees, have increased fivefold in the same period to an estimated $19.6 billion in 1962.

Of estimated expenditures of $24.4 billion from budget and trust accounts for labor and welfare programs for 1962, an estimated $13 billion will be for benefits and services for elderly persons. When benefits for veterans and others are added, total estimated expenditures in 1962 for benefits and services for persons who are 65 and over exceed $16 billion.

New obligational authority recommended for 1962 for labor and welfare programs in the budget totals $5 billion, and is $88 million more than estimated for the current fiscal year. The largest program increase

LABOR AND WELFARE

[Fiscal years. In millions]

Program or agency	Budget expenditures			Recommended new obligational authority for 1962
	1960 actual	1961 estimate	1962 estimate	
Promotion of education:				
National Science Foundation, science education	$57	$65	$69	$74
Department of Health, Education, and Welfare:				
Assistance to schools in federally affected areas:				
Present programs	258	264	173	102
Proposed legislation			60	93
Defense education program	129	161	190	194
Vocational education and other	65	73	79	80
Other, primarily Bureau of Indian Affairs	60	64	69	73
Promotion of science, research, libraries, and museums:				
National Science Foundation, basic research	63	90	119	138
Department of Commerce:				
Bureau of the Census	100	38	19	17
National Bureau of Standards and other	17	28	54	77
Other	31	47	58	40
Labor and manpower:				
Department of Labor:				
Grants for administration of employment services and unemployment compensation[1]	325			
Repayable advances to unemployment trust fund		36	−42	
Other	29	47	48	47
Other, primarily Selective Service System and National Labor Relations Board	57	64	66	67
Promotion of public health:				
National Institutes of Health	348	439	516	540
Hospital construction and research grants and activities	146	157	170	153
Grants for construction of health research facilities	26	26	25	30
Community and environmental health	58	75	101	104
Grants for construction of waste treatment facilities	40	41	43	50
Other	199	234	240	251
Public assistance:				
Present programs	2,061	2,162	2,290	2,291
Proposed legislation for medical care for the aged			25	25
Correctional and penal institutions	46	49	52	52

LABOR AND WELFARE—Continued

[Fiscal years. In millions]

Program or agency	Budget expenditures			Recommended new obligational authority for 1962
	1960 actual	1961 estimate	1962 estimate	
Other welfare services:				
School lunch and special milk programs:				
Present programs	234	245	155	326
Proposed legislation to extend special milk program	......	......	94	95
Other, primarily vocational rehabilitation	68	78	84	105
Total	4,419	4,483	4,759	[2] 5,025

[1] By law the receipts and expenditures for employment security grants are shown as trust fund transactions for 1961 and 1962, and as budget transactions for 1960.

[2] Compares with new obligational authority of $4,574 million enacted for 1960 and $4,937 million (including $34 million in anticipated supplemental appropriations) estimated for 1961.

is for public assistance, including medical care for the aged. The proposed appropriations for hospital construction grants are lower than the amounts enacted for 1961, but expenditures will increase by $13 million as a result of commitments under obligational authority provided in prior years. Recommended appropriations, as well as estimated expenditures, for programs to assist federally affected school districts are reduced for 1962 in view of the modifications proposed in those programs.

EDUCATION.—The vitality of our democracy and the productivity of our economy depend in large measure on the development of our human resources through an effective educational system. Primary responsibility for education rests with the local communities and States and with private institutions and groups. The strength of our American educational system flows from its freedom and this broad basis of support. Thus, the Federal role in education is properly a supplementary one, limited primarily to providing assistance where there is a special national concern. For such assistance, the Federal Government will spend in all budget categories about $1 billion in 1962 for educational activities, including college housing loans and readjustment aid to veterans, but excluding indirect assistance through research contracts and grants.

In the last few years, it has become increasingly clear that the national interest requires an expansion of Federal activities in the field of education. Accordingly, I recommended in 1958, and the Congress enacted, the

National Defense Education Act to assist students, particularly those interested in science, mathematics, and languages, and to help States improve school facilities and services. I have also recommended repeatedly and again recommend the enactment of temporary legislation to provide Federal assistance for construction of primary and secondary school classrooms and for construction of college classrooms and supporting facilities.

As outlined in last year's budget message, the proposed program would stimulate and assist in the construction of $3 billion of public elementary and secondary schools in the next 5 years by a Federal commitment to pay half the debt service (principal and interest) on school bonds. The cost to the Federal Government over a 30-year period would be about $2 billion. To help institutions of higher education finance construction of required facilities, the legislation would authorize a 5-year program which would provide (1) Federal guarantees of principal and interest on $1 billion of non-tax-exempt bonds to be sold by colleges to private investors and (2) Federal grants, payable over 20 to 35 years, of 30% of the principal of $2 billion of bonds to be issued by colleges. The aggregate Federal cost of the aid to institutions of higher education would be about $600 million.

The precise requirements for Federal aid to local school districts are difficult to determine because of the inadequacy of available information on the classroom needs of districts in various parts of the country and on their financial capacity to meet these needs. Accordingly, funds are included in the budget for improvement of education statistics, including data on local school construction requirements and the actions local communities and States are taking to meet them.

National Science Foundation educational activities.—Expenditures of $69 million in 1962 are estimated for graduate fellowships in science and mathematics and for other programs to train new scientists, to improve the teaching of science and mathematics, and to stimulate interest in scientific careers. This represents more than a fourfold expansion in the training programs of the National Science Foundation in 5 years.

Schools in federally affected areas.—The Federal Government has recognized an obligation to assist school districts in which enrollments are significantly increased by its activities. Legislation for this purpose was enacted as a temporary measure during the Korean emergency. However, legislation providing aid to districts with children whose parents both reside and work on Federal property was made permanent in 1958. The budget provides funds required to meet Federal obligations under this program.

The programs of assistance to school districts on behalf of pupils whose parents work on Federal property but live on private taxable property expire on June 30, 1961. This budget includes $93 million to cover the cost of extending the program for operating grants, but on a modified basis which would discharge more equitably than the expiring legislation the Federal responsibility to these districts. In the case of construction grants, where general aid for needy districts is again proposed, no separate provision is included for continuing the special program for federally affected districts. It is recommended, furthermore, that the Congress defer consideration of any extension legislation until after it has considered and enacted the broad program of Federal aid for school construction which is being recommended. The Congress would then be in a better position to determine the kind of support which should be provided to discharge the Government's obligations to these areas.

Defense education program.—The National Defense Education Act, which will be in its fourth year in 1962, the last under the current authorization, has provided outstanding assistance to American education. Expenditures under this act in 1962 are estimated to be $190 million, an increase of $29 million from 1961. The proposed 1962 appropriation of $194 million will provide modest increases for fellowships, language and cultural training centers, counseling institutes, and area vocational programs. The amount requested for student loans for 1962 is estimated at the 1961 level pending further information as to the rate of applications.

I am again recommending repeal of the provision of the National Defense Education Act that requires a student seeking aid to supply an affidavit stating that he does not believe in or belong to any organization that teaches the illegal overthrow of the Government. This requirement is unwarranted and discriminatory.

SCIENCE AND RESEARCH (INCLUDING LIBRARIES AND MUSEUMS).—The advancement of our national security and welfare depends in great measure upon the strength and progress of American science. The Federal Government plays a major role in the development of the Nation's scientific capacity through the research programs of many agencies.

Expenditures for promotion of science, research, libraries, and museums in 1962 are estimated to be $251 million, which is $48 million more than in 1961 and over three times the amount 5 years earlier. In addition to these figures, there are large amounts of expenditures for research and development included in other functional categories.

New scientific knowledge which stems from basic research is indispensable to the technological progress of modern industrialized society. Expenditures of $119 million are estimated for general purpose basic research grants by the National Science Foundation, chiefly for research projects and facilities, including the support of national research centers and the improvement of graduate school laboratories. This represents an increase of $29 million over 1961 and a sevenfold expansion in these activities in 5 years. Many other agencies are engaged in the support and conduct of basic research where it is recognized that such fundamental research is important and desirable in the attainment of their objectives.

Increased funds are included in the budget for the National Bureau of Standards, particularly for the completion of the major laboratories and service buildings at its new Gaithersburg, Md. site. Expansion is also provided in the regular scientific program of the Bureau, including initiation of a program for research projects abroad financed with foreign currencies which the Government holds in excess of its normal needs.

Certain scientific areas of broad national interest have been given special attention in recent years by the Federal Council for Science and Technology. These include long-range programs for oceanography, high-energy physics, and the atmospheric sciences, which will be further expanded under this budget. Part of the financing of these activities is included in other functional categories.

The scientific program for the Antarctic is developed, financed, and managed by the National Science Foundation with logistic support from the Department of Defense. Under this program the United States is cooperating with many other nations in the peaceful development of the Antarctic.

Government statistical services.—An estimated $56 million in obligations is provided throughout the budget for gathering, processing, and disseminating the statistical information which is used by Government, private institutions, and individuals in policy formulation and decision making. Increases in 1962 for collecting the regular recurring statistics are more than offset by the decrease from the funds required in 1961 for the Eighteenth Decennial Census.

Further improvement is planned in the scope and reliability of statistical data on current economic and social conditions. These include information on retail and service trade, foreign trade, manufacturing, construction, crop and livestock production, prices, manpower utilization, characteristics of the unemployed labor force, health and medical care, vital statistics, and education. Provision is also made for completion of the processing and publication of the results of the 1960 decennial census, for taking the 1962 Census of Governments, for planning the 1963 economic censuses, and for continuing a substantial portion of the work, begun over a year ago, looking toward a major revision of the Consumer Price Index.

LABOR AND MANPOWER.—The manpower programs of the Department of Labor and other labor agencies help maintain an efficient labor market and a healthy national climate in labor-management relations.

Employment security.—Of particular importance are the job placement services and unemployment compensation payments made through the State employment security offices. In addition to general job placement services, farm people are assisted in finding industrial work and workers in depressed areas are helped in finding jobs in other areas.

Last year the administration proposed, and the Congress enacted, amendments to the Social Security Act that placed Federal receipts and expenditures for the employment security program on a trust fund basis starting July 1, 1960. This is the same arrangement that is used for other social insurance programs. Expenditures for this program are now expected to exceed the 1961 tax receipts, and the Treasury, as authorized by present law, will advance to the trust fund the additional $36 million needed in 1961. This advance will be repaid with interest in 1962 from the excess of receipts which will come from the increased Federal unemployment tax rate taking effect on January 1, 1961, from 0.3% to 0.4% of covered payrolls.

Based on the level of claims for unemployment compensation, this budget estimates $41 million more than enacted to date for the limitation on 1961 grants to States for administering unemployment insurance and employment services. Together with the $326 million already enacted, this brings the estimated 1961 requirement to $366 million, which is in excess of the $350 million annual ceiling established by the Social Security Act Amendments of 1960. In view of the number of workers now filing claims for unemployment compensation, it is necessary to ask the Congress to remove this ceiling so that adequate funds can be provided to pay claims promptly.

Last year, coverage of unemployment compensation was extended to about 60,000 additional workers, but further legislation is still needed to extend unemployment compensation to some 3 million workers, most of whom are employed in small businesses employing fewer than 4 workers each. Such action, together with action by States to increase the amount and duration of unemployment compensation benefits, would provide more adequately against economic hardship for the Nation's work force. This program has proved to be one of the most successful means for combining the interest of the economy as a whole with the interest of the individual worker.

Other labor programs.—In the last several years the operating programs of the Department of Labor have been strengthened by additional funds and new legislation. The 1962 budget provides an increase of $4 million in appropriations to strengthen further such activities of the Department as the enforcement of the Labor-Management Reports Act and the statistical and research programs of the Bureau of Labor Statistics.

Last year the Secretary of Labor endorsed expanded coverage and a moderate adjustment in the level of the minimum wage under the Fair Labor Standards Act. This recommendation is repeated. Legislation should also be enacted to make the Welfare and Pension Plan Disclosure Act more effective. Legislation is again proposed to assure equal pay for equal work and to improve the laws relating to hours of work and overtime pay on Federal construction projects.

HEALTH.—Americans enjoy a high standard of health service. About three-quarters of the more than $25 billion devoted annually to health services and facilities in this country is being spent through private channels. However, State and local as well as Federal agencies also play an important role.

Promotion of public health.—The Federal Government's contribution toward improved health care for the American people has been increasing rapidly in recent years. Expenditures for the promotion of public health in 1962 are estimated at $1.1 billion, more than twice the amount spent only 5 years earlier. Total Federal expenditures for all health programs in the various categories of this budget (including military and veterans hospitals) are about $4 billion.

In 1962, expenditures by the National Institutes of Health for medical research and training will represent about half the total spent for promotion of public health. The programs of the National Institutes will have multiplied more than threefold from 1957 to 1962.

The budget for 1962 recommends appropriations of $540 million for the National Institutes, compared to the $560 million enacted by the Congress for 1961. While this is $20 million less than the 1961 appropriation, it actually represents a substantial program increase for medical research and training. The reduction results from the elimination in 1962 of nonrecurring projects and from the transfer of programs to other parts of the Public Health Service which were included in the total for the National Institutes of Health for 1961. These decreases more than offset increases for new research activities. Expenditures by the Institutes will rise by an estimated $76 million in 1962.

Appropriations of $153 million for hospitals, mainly construction grants, are recommended for 1962. Although this is less than the level of appropriations for 1961, it will not result in a decrease in federally assisted hospital construction. On the contrary, it is anticipated that expenditures in 1962 for this program will be at an alltime high because of the prior authorizations and the volume of construction which has been initiated but not yet completed. The appropriation recommended for 1962 will permit initiation of new projects for general hospital beds, which, together with construction not federally assisted, will be sufficient to provide for growth in population, cover current obsolescence, and reduce the backlog by over 5,000 beds. The 1962 appropriation will also permit starting the same volume of new projects for specialized facilities for long-term care as is provided for in the appropriation for the current year. In recognition of the need for medical care facilities and the continuing rise in the cost of hospital services, new legislation is proposed to encourage coordinated community and regional planning of hospital facilities, to augment research on design and operation of hospitals, and to permit use of grants for high priority modernization projects.

Federal grants for construction of health research facilities in the last 5 years have materially helped expand our Nation's medical research capacity. This budget continues appropriations for this purpose at the full authorization of $30 million.

One of our greatest national health needs is the expansion of existing schools and establishment of new schools to train doctors and dentists. The shortage of physicians, already a critical factor in the rising cost of medical care, will become increasingly acute as the population and the demand for medical services increase. The Congress should at an early date enact legislation to authorize $100 million of matching grants over a 5-year period to stimulate construction of additional medical and dental school facilities.

Legislation should also be enacted to authorize a loan guarantee program to facilitate the construction of clinics for the group practice of medicine and dentistry. The sharing of such clinics by groups of physicians and dentists is economical in terms of reducing capital expenditures for such purposes and leads to more complete care for the patient by enabling the practitioners to combine their diverse skills.

In our urbanized and industrial society, environmental and community health is assuming increasing importance. Appropriations of $104 million for 1962 are proposed for Public Health Service activities in these fields. Increased funds are provided to augment the research and operating arms of the Public Health Service in the fields of air pollution, water pollution, community sanitation, and radiological health control activities. Larger amounts are also proposed for community health service activities to make the benefits of improved medical knowledge more widely and quickly available. Legislation is again recommended to authorize greater Federal leadership in combating air pollution.

The budget also includes an appropriation of $50 million for construction of waste treatment works, the full amount authorized for this program. These funds will help stimulate local action to correct immediate pollution problems. The control of water pollution is principally a local responsibility and requires greater financial and enforcement efforts by local interests. The Federal Government can most appropriately assist State and local governments through legislation (1) to strengthen its enforcement powers under the Federal Water Pollution Control Act and (2) to provide flexibility assuring that highest priority is given to waste treatment construction grants for projects which contribute to the reduction of pollution of interstate and coastal streams. Legislation to accomplish these and related objectives should be enacted by the Congress.

Of daily importance to each of us is the work of the Food and Drug Administration in establishing and enforcing standards of safety for food and drugs. The 1962 budget continues a long-standing policy of strengthening this agency, which in 1962 will spend three times as much as it did 5 years earlier.

Legislation should be enacted to transfer Freedmen's Hospital to Howard University and to provide for construction of a new teaching hospital. Such legislation would give essential support to Howard University's program of medical education and end the divided responsibility and control now existing.

SOCIAL INSURANCE AND OTHER WELFARE.—Since the Social Security Act first became law in 1935, the United States has made great strides in its public income maintenance programs, both under the social security system and other public retirement systems. Today 93% of our workers are protected under the basic old-age, survivors, and disability insurance program or under other Federal or State-local retirement systems. To assist the unemployed we also have the Federal-State unemployment insurance system, and the Federal Government further provides or helps finance assistance to needy groups through other programs.

In 10 years the benefit payments made because of loss of income due to old age, death, disability, or unemployment under Federal, State, and local programs have trebled, rising in the calendar year 1960 to approximately $26 billion, of which about $24 billion was paid from federally administered or federally aided programs. Benefits were paid during the calendar year 1960 to an average of more than 20 million families or single persons. The cost of these benefits, 6% of our national income, is funded from employee and employer contributions and taxes. Benefit payments and taxes under laws already in effect will increase greatly over the years.

Social insurance.—The Federal old-age, survivors, and disability insurance system now covers 9 out of 10 American workers and their families. In fiscal year 1962 it will pay $12.9 billion in benefits to an average of 16.5 million people of all ages, including 12 million persons aged 65 and over. Coverage should be extended to Federal civilian employees and self-employed physicians, the largest groups of regularly employed persons in our economy not now covered by this system.

Benefit payments and administrative costs are paid from trust funds supported by payroll taxes shared equally by workers and employers and from contributions of the self-employed. The combined employer-employee rate is now 6% of covered payrolls. Under present law it will rise by steps to 9% in calendar year 1969. Expenditures for the administration of this vast insurance system will be increased in fiscal year 1962 to cope with the increased workloads resulting from extension of disability protection to workers below age 50 and from other amendments enacted by the last Congress.

Public assistance.—Total Federal expenditures for public assistance and medical aid in 1962 under existing law are estimated to increase by $128 million over 1961, largely reflecting the cost of the newly enacted medical assistance program for the aged. In 1962, the Federal share of payments for an average of 6.3 million recipients is estimated to be $2.3 billion, which is 58% of the total. Caseloads for old-age assistance and aid to the blind are declining moderately, while caseloads for aid to dependent children and aid to the permanently and totally disabled are increasing.

Medical care for the aged.—In recent years, the American people have greatly improved their ability to obtain and pay for medical care through private and nonprofit health organizations. This approach has produced excellent results and should be preserved.

However, some aged persons are finding it increasingly difficult to pay for the medical services which they require. Medical and institutional care for the aged financed by public funds (Federal, State, and local) is currently estimated to cost over $1 billion annually. The last Congress authorized substantial expansion in Federal assistance for medical care of the aged through (1) increased Federal participation under the regular old-age assistance program and (2) a new program of medical assistance for the aged who are not recipients of public assistance but who nevertheless require aid to pay their medical and hospital bills.

In the 1962 budget, $400 million is included in the amount shown for public assistance for the old and the new programs of medical care for the aged. There will be a substantial increase in these expenditures in future years under existing law as additional States participate in these programs.

Extension of medical care assistance to the aged through a voluntary program under Federal-State-local auspices—as authorized by the Congress—is sound national policy both from a fiscal standpoint and from the standpoint of encouraging the widest participation of private as well as public agencies in the improvement of medical care for this group. However, under the program approved by the Congress many of the aged will still not be able to obtain needed protection against catastrophic hospital and medical expenses even though under ordinary circumstances they are able to pay their normal medical bills. The Congress is therefore urged to broaden the existing program in keeping with the recommendations which were made by this administration last spring. This would further increase the number who receive assistance.

Public action in providing assistance for medical care and the sharply rising costs of hospital and medical care underline the need for more adequate information regarding medical costs and the best methods of organizing to meet them. This budget provides for augmented research in medical economics under the Department of Health, Education, and Welfare. Likewise, it expands the related program of research and demonstration projects on causes of dependency for which appropriations were first authorized last year.

Military service credits.—Both the Railroad Retirement Act and the Social Security Act provide that military service during certain periods of military conflict should be counted toward the rights of employees in determining benefits even though the employee made no contribution during this period. As has been previously indicated, it is appropriate for the Federal Government to reimburse the trust funds for the cost of benefits paid on the basis of such military service credits. But it is not sound policy for the Government to pay more than the true cost of such benefits or to pay both the railroad retirement and old-age and survivors and disability insurance trust funds for the same military service credits, as the present law requires.

Under statutes now in effect the Federal Government has paid the railroad retirement account an estimated $400 million more than the estimated cost of military service benefits. At the same time the Federal Government is obliged to reimburse the old-age and survivors and disability insurance trust funds for an estimated $450 million for military service benefits. The Congress is again urged to enact legislation to recover the overpayments to the railroad retirement account and to transfer them to the social security trust funds to cover the Government liability. Pending action on such legislation, no appropriations are included in this budget for military service payments to these trust funds.

Other welfare services.—Between 1950 and 1960, the number of disabled people rehabilitated annually through the Federal-State rehabilitation program increased by 48%, to 88,000. The budget for 1962 includes enlarged appropriations of $97 million for this program, mostly for grants to State agencies for the rehabilitation of an estimated 103,000 persons.

The authorization for the special milk program, financed by the Commodity Credit Corporation, expires June 30, 1961. Appropriations are recommended in this budget to reimburse the Corporation for costs of the 1960 and 1961 operations. This program was originally established as a temporary measure to aid the dairy industry. An evaluation presently under way in the Department of Agriculture will provide a basis for determining the proper level of the program. Pending the results of this evaluation, an appropriation of $95 million is included under proposed legislation to provide for a continuation of the special milk program in 1962 through a regular annual appropriation. Including this amount, grants to the States through the school lunch and special milk programs of the Department of Agriculture would be $250 million in 1962.

Our society must continue to encourage all our citizens to achieve the maximum degree of self-realization and economic independence. There are two large groups which as a nation we have recognized must be given special attention—the 16 million aged persons and the 65 million children and young people under 18. A White House Conference on Children and Youth was held last spring. Widespread local and State preparations have been made also for this month's White House Conference on Aging. Such conferences can help State, local, and Federal agencies, as well as private organizations and individuals, to increase opportunities for the aged and for the youth of our land.

VETERANS SERVICES AND BENEFITS

Budget expenditures for veterans programs are estimated to total $5.3 billion in 1962, which is $69 million more than in 1961. Continued increases in pensions for non-service-connected disabilities and deaths and in costs of medical care are expected to be largely offset by a decrease in readjustment benefits for veterans of the Korean conflict.

Expenditures for pensions are estimated to increase in 1962 principally because World War I veterans and survivors of World War II veterans will continue to be added to the pension rolls. These additions reflect both the number of World War I veterans reaching age 65 by 1962 who will be able to meet the eligibility standards, and the effect of the liberalizations provided in the Veterans' Pension Act of 1959.

The decline in the education and training assistance provided to veterans of the Korean conflict foreshadows the approaching end of this second historic venture in providing readjustment assistance for wartime service. Henceforth, the bulk of the veterans expenditures will be for pensions, compensation, and medical care benefits. Because of the growth in non-service-connected disability and survivor pension costs, veterans expenditures will continue to increase for many years under laws now in effect.

In the 6-year period 1957–62, annual pension, compensation, and medical care expenditures will have risen by over $1 billion. This increase is in part the result of liberalizations in pension laws and improved standards of medical care. It also results from the advancing age of our veterans, which makes more of them or their survivors eligible for benefits. The trends are illustrated by the fact that from 1957 to 1962 there will be a net increase of 750,000, or about 20%, in disability and survivor cases on the rolls. Of the 22½ million living veterans, 1 out of every 7 will be receiving compensation or pension benefits at the end of 1962.

An increasing proportion of the total expenditures of the Veterans Administration is attributable to disabilities, diseases, or deaths not related to military service. Between 1957 and 1962, non-service-connected costs will increase by 70%, rising from less than one-third to nearly one-half of all budget expenditures for veterans services and benefits.

This trend raises serious questions about the further expansion of veterans programs, particularly since veterans, their dependents, and survivors of veterans total about 80 million people or over two-fifths of our total population. The improvement in recent years of general welfare programs, for which veterans as well as others are eligible, coupled with the improvements in veterans programs, has reduced the justification for providing additional special benefits to veterans on the basis of non-service-connected factors. Any further expansion of non-service-connected benefits would create serious inequities of treatment between veterans and others in our population. I particularly oppose measures which would increase or make available non-service-connected pensions for veterans of World War I contrary to the principle of need incorporated in the Veterans' Pension Act of 1959.

VETERANS SERVICES AND BENEFITS

[Fiscal years. In millions]

Program or agency	Budget expenditures			Recommended new obligational authority for 1962
	1960 actual	1961 estimate	1962 estimate	
Readjustment benefits:				
Education and training	$383	$233	$128	$72
Loan guarantee and other benefits	132	131	77	9
Unemployment compensation	5	......	......	......
Compensation and pensions:				
Service-connected compensation	2,049	2,038	2,026	2,026
Non-service-connected pensions	1,263	1,512	1,717	1,487
Burial and other allowances	56	55	55	55
Hospitals and medical care	904	982	1,025	1,025
Hospital construction	57	63	66	75
Insurance and servicemen's indemnities	33	31	27	40
Other services and administration	179	182	174	174
Total	5,060	5,227	5,296	[1]4,963

[1] Compares with new obligational authority of $5,169 million enacted for 1960 and $5,438 million (including $58 million in anticipated supplemental appropriations) estimated for 1961.

Readjustment benefits.—Expenditures for readjustment assistance, estimated in 1962 at $205 million, continue their decline from a post-Korean high mark of about $900 million in 1957. The principal reduction is in the education and training program, in which the average number of Korean conflict veterans participating will be reduced to 85,000 in 1962, compared to 288,000 in 1960 and 170,000 in 1961.

The previous Congress extended until July 25, 1962, the home loan guarantee program as it applies to veterans of World War II. The direct loan program was similarly extended for both Korean conflict veterans and World War II veterans. It is clear that continuation of direct loan assistance and of loan guarantee assistance is no longer required to help World War II veterans in their readjustment to civilian life 15 years after the end of that war.

Veterans, like other citizens, can and should participate in the regular housing programs when their special readjustment needs resulting from military service have passed. The loan guarantee program for World War II veterans should therefore be terminated as of July 25, 1961. Changes proposed in the veterans direct loan program have been described with other housing programs elsewhere in this message.

Legislation is again recommended to provide vocational rehabilitation for peacetime ex-servicemen having substantial service-connected disabilities. This would add to other benefits which the Federal Government provides peacetime ex-servicemen, such as unemployment compensation, employment service, and reemployment rights. On the other hand, there is no justification for the extension of special educational or housing benefits to peacetime ex-servicemen. Such benefits cannot be justified by conditions of military service and are inconsistent with the incentives which have been provided to make military service an attractive career for capable individuals.

Compensation and pensions.—Expenditures for service-connected death and disability compensation benefits continue a slow decline from their 1959 peak as compensation rolls are reduced by the deaths of veterans or their widows and by the transfer of many aging veterans to pension rolls. These decreases are offset in small part by the addition of veterans of the Korean conflict and of peacetime ex-servicemen or their survivors. Compensation will be paid to an average of 2,397,000 veterans and survivors of veterans in 1962 compared to 2,410,000 in 1961 and 2,428,000 in 1960.

The continued rise in expenditures for non-service-connected pensions, however, will more than offset the decline in compensation payments. Approximately half of all World War I veterans over 65 will be receiving pensions by the end of 1962, and the pension rolls will carry an average of nearly 2 million veterans and survivors in 1962. The Veterans' Pension Act of 1959 is expected to increase expenditures by adding over 100,000 new beneficiaries to the rolls at an estimated additional cost of $77 million in 1961. These additional expenditures also reflect higher rates for many veterans on the rolls before July 1, 1960.

Hospitals and medical care.—The budget includes expenditures of approximately $1 billion for hospital and medical care for eligible veterans in 1962, an increase of $43 million over 1961. The increase will permit continued improvement in the quality of medical care in the hospitals and clinics. The new 1,000-bed hospital at Brecksville, Ohio, is scheduled to be opened in 1962 and the new Palo Alto, Calif., hospital addition will be fully activated. Hospital and domiciliary care will be provided for an average of 141,500 beneficiaries per day in Veterans Administration, contract, and State facilities, and a total of 3,622,000 visits for medical services are expected to be made by veterans to out-patient clinics and to private physicians on a fee basis.

Hospital construction.—An appropriation of $75 million is proposed for 1962, the same as for 1961, as the second step in carrying out a 12-year hospital modernization program of $900 million initiated in 1961. Of the 1962 appropriation, $26 million will be for construction of a 1,250-bed replacement hospital at Wood (Milwaukee), Wis., $11 million will be for replacement of 500 beds at Charleston, S.C.; the remainder will be for planning a new 580-bed general hospital at Atlanta, Ga., planning the replacement of approximately 1,000 beds in the Los Angeles, Calif., area, and for a large number of modernization projects.

Administration.—The general operating expenses of the Veterans Administration (other than the direct costs of administration of medical, dental, and hospital services) in 1962 are expected to be $162 million, slightly less than in 1961. Reductions in administrative costs are expected to accrue in future years from the program now under way to convert the recording and payment of veterans benefits to automatic data processing equipment.

INTEREST

Interest payments are estimated to decrease by $400 million to $8.6 billion in the fiscal year 1962. These payments are almost entirely for interest on the public debt and represent 11% of budget expenditures.

INTEREST

[Fiscal years. In millions]

	New obligational authority and budget expenditures		
Item	1960 actual	1961 estimate	1962 estimate
Interest on public debt	$9,180	$8,900	$8,500
Interest on refunds of receipts	76	83	83
Interest on uninvested funds	10	10	10
Total	9,266	8,993	8,593

Market rates of interest have been decreasing from the levels prevailing last year. This makes it possible for the Treasury to pay, on the average, lower interest on securities issued to refinance maturing obligations. The reduction in the public debt during the year, facilitated by the surplus in the budget in 1960 as well as currently, is also helping to a lesser extent to reduce interest payments.

GENERAL GOVERNMENT

Expenditures for general government activities are estimated to rise by $89 million to $2.1 billion in the fiscal year 1962. The increase is primarily for more construction of Government buildings and for strengthening the tax collection system.

Central fiscal operations.—The 1962 budget includes an increase of $36 million in new obligational authority to $450 million for the Internal Revenue Service. This will finance the second year's cost of a program to provide more effective enforcement of our tax laws and will thus reduce the revenue losses which arise from the failure of some individuals and businesses to report their incomes fully or accurately. Ultimately, all aspects of tax administration capable of being mechanized will be handled electronically. With the growth of the economy, tax returns are increasing in volume and necessarily become more complex. Installation of the new and modernized system for the processing of these returns will make possible the collection of taxes with lower expenditures than would otherwise be the case. Legislation should be enacted to authorize the adoption of tax account numbers which are needed for mechanical and electronic processing.

Legislation to authorize the consolidated reporting by employers of wages for income tax and social security purposes should also be enacted. Such legislation would produce considerable savings for both employers and the Government by reducing paperwork and would also help in enforcing the tax laws. Nearly 4 million employers could be relieved of the need to file for social security purposes 14 million separate quarterly wage reports each year covering over 230 million wage items. The Treasury Department and the Department of Health, Education, and Welfare have already agreed on the cooperative steps to be taken for improved administration of the tax laws and the social security system once such legislation is enacted.

Presidential office space.—There is pressing need for providing future Presidents with modern and efficient office facilities. My experience during the last 8 years strongly confirms the conclusion of the Advisory Commission on Presidential Office Space that present facilities "are outmoded, overcrowded, inefficient, and not consistent with effective and well coordinated management of the highest office of the executive branch of the Government." The Commission recommended: (1) a new build-

GENERAL GOVERNMENT

[Fiscal years. In millions]

| Program or agency | Budget expenditures | | | Recommended new obligational authority for 1962 |
	1960 actual	1961 estimate	1962 estimate	
Legislative functions	$109	$137	$130	$100
Judicial functions	49	53	56	56
Executive direction and management	12	14	15	15
Central fiscal operations:				
Internal Revenue Service	360	412	446	450
Other	198	207	218	218
General property and records management	367	417	467	516
Central personnel management and employment costs:				
Department of Labor	190	212	216	216
Civil Service Commission:				
Present programs	21	74	95	95
Proposed legislation	.....	.....	−45	−45
Civilian weather services	54	57	66	70
Protective services and alien control	217	241	247	250
Territories and possessions, and the District of Columbia:				
District of Columbia	28	48	66	63
Other	63	75	81	75
Other general government	28	34	12	17
Total	1,695	1,982	2,071	[1] 2,096

[1] Compares with new obligational authority of $1,664 million enacted for 1960 and $2,073 million (including $131 million in anticipated supplemental appropriations) estimated for 1961.

ing to house only the White House office on the site of the existing Executive Office Building; (2) a new building for other units of the Executive Office; and (3) remodeling of the west wing of the White House for use as quarters for visiting dignitaries.

As a first step in carrying out these recommendations, the Congress should provide funds for constructing a new Executive Office Building on the west side of Lafayette Square, and this budget includes $26 million of new obligational authority for this purpose. More than two decades ago, the Congress wisely provided new quarters for the Supreme Court of the United States. In recent years, major improvements and expansions have been made in the facilities necessary to carry on the increasingly complex and important duties of the legislative branch. The next logical step is to remedy the serious deficiencies in the office space of the Chief Executive of the United States. I strongly urge the Congress to give early attention to the needed building as well as to the other recommendations of the Commission.

General property and records management.—New obligational authority of $516 million is requested for the general property and records management activities of the General Services Administration, predominantly for management of existing buildings, construction of new buildings, purchase and distribution of supplies, and custody of Government records. Of this total, $212 million is for the construction of Federal office buildings, $26 million more than enacted for 1961. Budget expenditures for new buildings will be $169 million in 1962, nearly 50% above the 1961 level. This large increase results from an acceleration in construction initiated in 1959 to remedy some serious deficiencies of space which interfere with effective operations in many Federal agencies.

The expanded program of the General Services Administration for improving the utilization of excess Federal personal property is accomplishing significant results. Transfers of property in 1962 from agencies having an excess to those which can use it are expected to be $350 million valued at acquisition cost, compared to $218 million in 1960.

As a part of an overall program for improving supply management, the responsibility for the procurement and distribution of subsistence items for the civilian agencies has been centralized in the Veterans Administration. Substantial progress has also been made toward centralizing in the Veterans Administration the procurement and distribution of medicines, drugs, and pharmaceuticals for the civilian agencies. Progress is also being made in transferring from the Department of Defense to the General Services Administration responsibility for managing the supplies of certain items which are used by civilian agencies as well as by the military services.

Central personnel management and employment costs.—Appropriations of $147 million are recommended in 1962 for the Department of Labor to provide unemployment compensation for former Federal civilian employees and ex-servicemen. Another $69 million will be required for workmen's compensation for present and past Federal employees. The new obligational authority recommended for the Civil Service Commission includes $26 million to finance the Government's share of the new health benefits programs for retired Federal personnel. The remaining appropriations in this category are predominantly for administration of the civil service system.

A long-range policy should be established for financing the civil service retirement system, which covers over 90% of Federal civilian employment. Previous recommendations to accomplish this objective should be enacted. This legislation would assure continued availability in the fund of the full amount of the net accumulations from employee contributions and would establish a definite basis for meeting the Government's share of the costs consistent with the principle that its full faith and credit support the authorized benefits.

Under present law, an appropriation of $45 million would be required for 1962 to finance the cost of civil service retirement benefits enacted in 1958 for certain retired employees and certain widows or widowers of former employees. Without this appropriation these benefits could not be continued. Legislation is again recommended to assure that in 1962 and later years such benefits are paid from the civil service retirement and disability fund on the same basis as other benefits, without specific annual appropriation.

A number of outmoded and inconsistent statutes now regulate the employment and compensation of retired military personnel in civilian positions with the Government. We should replace this legal maze with a single, rational statute which would eliminate unnecessary dual payments, adequately safeguard the civilian career service, and permit the Government to hire members of this group possessing needed skills under conditions that are fair to the individual.

Efforts must be continued to improve Federal job evaluation and other pay practices so as to make Federal pay, including that at the executive level, more comparable with private enterprise. This is essential to recruit and retain superior personnel for Federal programs, particularly in the middle and upper professional and managerial positions, and to overcome the severe competitive disadvantages with which the Federal Government must now contend in recruiting personnel.

To help attain this objective, the accuracy of comparisons of Federal salary rates with private business rates should be improved. Funds are recommended in this budget for the Department of Labor to continue its recently expanded surveys which provide annual reports on salaries currently paid in private business. In time the Federal Government should make full use of this information as a guide in fixing salaries for its own officers and employees.

Legislation should be enacted to provide a system of survivorship annuities for the widows and dependent children of judges of the Tax Court of the United States comparable to the system already in effect with respect to the other Federal courts.

Civilian weather services.—The successful launching of meteorological satellites has created vast possibilities for increasing our knowledge about the atmosphere and for improving daily weather services and forecasts. To realize some of this potential, an appropriation increase of $9 million over 1961, to a total of $70 million, is recommended for the Weather Bureau for 1962. This increase will provide for the establishment of processing facilities to permit the immediate use of worldwide cloud data received from satellites, as well as for increased research in applying this new source of information to improve understanding of atmospheric motion. The budget also continues the efforts of the past several years to transfer to Weather Bureau appropriations the financing of certain meteorological activities of other Federal agencies which are national in scope and serve both civilian and military needs.

Territories, possessions, and District of Columbia.—The expenditures required to meet the Federal share of the financing of governmental operations in the District of Columbia will increase substantially in 1962, primarily because of loans authorized in prior years to meet capital requirements of the area, including a metropolitan sewage system to connect with the Dulles International Airport.

A constitutional amendment to permit residents of the District to vote for President and Vice President is now before the States for ratification. The States should act promptly on this amendment.

Another basic step, recommended on many past occasions, would be the restoration of home rule for the 764,000 District of Columbia residents. I repeat my recommendation in this respect. Such local self-government is essential not only to carry out our democratic principles but also to remove excessive and unnecessary responsibilities from the Federal Government.

To promote the further development of democratic institutions, and in keeping with the growth of local self-government, the Congress should authorize representation of the Virgin Islands and Guam in the Congress through nonvoting territorial deputies.

Intergovernmental relations.—Federal financial assistance to State and local governments plays a large role in financing their operations. In 1962 such aid, including budget and trust funds, will amount to $7.9

billion and account for a substantial portion of total annual State and local revenues. Continuous attention must be given to Federal-State-local fiscal interrelationships so that they reflect the proper distribution of responsibilities. The Advisory Commission on Intergovernmental Relations established in 1959 can make an important contribution through its work in reexamining intergovernmental relations and fiscal problems.

In this field, a uniform Federal policy is needed (1) defining immunity from local taxation on the use or possession of Federal property in the custody of contractors and lessees, and (2) governing payments in lieu of taxes made by the Government to localities on certain real properties. Legislation on these matters should be enacted in accordance with the recommendations made by the administration in the last session of the Congress, which call for partial restoration of immunity from taxation of Federal property in the hands of contractors or lessees and authorization of a system of payments in lieu of taxation on certain real properties in cases of local hardship.

Other recommendations.—It is again recommended that the Employment Act of 1946 be amended to make reasonable price stability an explicit goal of Federal economic policy, coordinate with the goals of maximum production, employment, and purchasing power now specified in that Act.

In support of our position of world leadership, legislation is again recommended to liberalize and modernize our immigration laws. The quota system should be brought up to date by revising the methods of determining, distributing, and transferring quotas, and the total number of immigrants admitted under quotas should be doubled. A permanent program for admission of refugees should also replace the inadequate and piecemeal legislation now in effect.

The enactment of the Civil Rights Acts of 1957 and 1960, the activities of the Department of Justice in enforcing these statutes, and the contribution of the Civil Rights Commission in identifying basic problems and legislative action required, represent significant progress in the field of civil rights. To permit the Commission to explore more thoroughly the necessity for further legislation in this field, its life should be extended for another 2 years. As part of an effort to extend civil rights in education to all our citizens, the Congress should enact legislation to assist State and local agencies to meet costs of special professional services needed in carrying out public school desegregation programs. Also, legislation should be enacted to establish a Commission on Equal Job Opportunity to make permanent and expand, with legislative backing, the important work of the President's Committee on Government Contracts.

The seriously congested conditions in the courts require that the Congress give early consideration to the creation of additional Federal judgeships as proposed by the Judicial Conference.

It is important that the Congress enact legislation, such as that passed by the House of Representatives last year, to reimburse Americans for certain World War II property damage.

A system of awards to recognize outstanding civilian achievements should also be established, as previously recommended.

Legislation should be enacted to incorporate the Alaska Railroad to place its operations on the same basis as other Federal activities of this type.

Last spring, legislation was introduced in the Congress to enlarge and change the boundaries of the site for the National Cultural Center in accordance with the design for the structure contemplated as a national center for the performing arts on the banks of the Potomac. It is important that such legislation be enacted as early as possible so that the fund-raising activities of the Center's Board of Trustees may be energetically continued.

I have repeatedly urged construction of a freedom monument symbolizing the ideals of our democracy as embodied in the freedoms of speech, religion, press, assembly, and petition. I still believe such a living, ever-building monument would be fitting.

IMPROVEMENTS IN BUDGETING

The budget process is a means of establishing Government policies, improving the management of Government operations, and planning and conducting the Government's fiscal role in the life of the Nation. Whether that role is increasing, decreasing, or remaining unchanged, the budget process is perhaps our most significant device for planning, controlling, and coordinating our programs and policies as well as our finances. Thus, the President and the Congress will always need to give attention to the improvement and full utilization of the budget system.

Improvements in presentation.—The budget totals in this document reflect a technical accounting adjustment which affects budget expenditures and budget receipts equally, and does not affect the budget surplus for any year. This is the exclusion from the totals of expenditures and receipts, for all years shown in this document, of certain interfund transactions, mainly interest payments to the general fund of the Treasury by wholly owned Government enterprises which have borrowed from the Treasury. The amounts involved continue to be included in the figures for each function and for each agency, but are deducted in one sum to reach expenditure totals. Similarly, they continue to be included as miscellaneous budget receipts of the Treasury, but are deducted to arrive at the total of budget receipts. Since the beginning of the present fiscal year, various statements and reports on Government financial operations have been eliminating these interfund payments from budget totals.

Steady progress is being made in applying the principles of performance budgeting. In this budget, the appropriation pattern or activity classifications of several agencies and bureaus have been improved and greater use is being made of program and workload measurement data. Cost-type budgets, which present the most adequate measure of financial performance, are used for more than 80 appropriation accounts for the first time. With these additions, about two-thirds of the appropriation accounts are now presented on a cost-type basis.

Funding arrangements.—Recommendations placed before the Congress in this budget are again based upon the principle that authority to incur budget obligations and make expenditures should be granted in appropriation acts, rather than in substantive legislation handled outside the regular appropriation process. Of course, the budget totals include—as they have for many years—all of the new obligational authority actually granted each year and the subsequent spending, no matter what the method by which provided. The Congress ought to pass upon all new obligational authority in a regular systematic way as part of the appropriation process. We must never be led into thinking that special funding arrangements, which are a claim against budget receipts or borrowing, are somehow not a part of the budget or not a cost to the taxpayers.

From time to time, the Congress has enacted legislation and appropriations under which additional sums become available for obligation and expenditure annually without further congressional action. These are so-called permanent appropriations. In a few cases, such as interest on the public debt, permanent obligational authority may be desirable. In many other cases, however, permanent appropriations give unnecessary preferential treatment. A complete congressional review is needed of all such provisions of permanent authority, including those to use borrowed money, to enter into contracts ahead of appropriations, and to use collections to supplement appropriations. Those provisions which cannot be fully justified at this time should be repealed.

It is again recommended that major business-type activities of the Government be placed on a revolving fund basis, through which receipts can be used to meet obligations and expenditures, subject to annual review and control by the Congress. Such a system, which is presently applied successfully to all of the Government-owned corporations and many unincorporated Government enterprises, provides a clear display of the business-type nature of these activities, their income or loss from current operations, and the extent to which they are adding to or using up the Government's capital assets. In accordance with legislation enacted in response to a previous recommendation, the loan guarantee program of the Veterans Administration is thus presented in this budget. Legislation should be enacted to provide revolving funds for the Farmers Home Administration, the Bureau of Reclamation, and the power marketing agencies of the Department of the Interior.

A few mixed-ownership Government corporations having authority to draw money from the Treasury or to commit the Treasury for future expenditures are presently outside the Government's budget system. This is largely because of the unrealistic and inconsistent distinction the law now makes between wholly owned and mixed-ownership Government corporations, even though both may affect the Government's finances. All Government corporations with such authority, namely, the Federal Deposit Insurance Corporation, the banks for cooperatives, and the Federal intermediate credit banks, should be brought within the flexible budget provisions of the Government Corporation Control Act, and thus within the normal budgetary and reporting structure of the Government.

The extensive recommendations made a year ago for the control of foreign currencies generally were adopted by the Congress, and this action has proved helpful in obtaining more adequate budget control of these resources. However, there still remain various special provisions of law, requiring reservations of currencies for certain programs, that hinder the Government in making the wisest use of the foreign currencies coming into its hands. They should be repealed. Expenditures of all foreign currencies owned by the Government and used for its activities should be controlled through the annual budget process and should be accounted for in the same way as dollar expenditures.

The budget process in the Congress.—Although the President presents one budget for the entire Government to the Congress each year, the Congress considers the budget in a multitude of pieces rather than as a whole. The financing methods outside the regular appropriation process, already mentioned, are but one phase of this problem. Another is the tendency to require a double budget process each year for certain agencies—requiring them, first, to seek legislation to authorize appropriations annually and, second, to seek their appropriations. The subcommittee arrangement and time schedule for processing appropriation requests further fragments the budget process. The complete separation of the handling of tax legislation from the consideration of appropriations and expenditures adds to the total problem.

The Congress should therefore provide a mechanism by which total receipts and total appropriations (and expenditures) can regularly be considered in relation to each other. Further, substantive legislation with respect to all continuing programs should be written so that new legislation is not required each year, thus permitting the budget and appropriation process to proceed in an orderly manner.

In accordance with recommendations of the second Hoover Commission, legislation was enacted in 1958 authorizing the Congress to establish limitations on accrued expenditures as a means of enabling more direct control over spending. Limitations were proposed for selected accounts in the last two budgets, but were rejected by the Congress without exception. Therefore, and since the law providing for accrued expenditure limitations expires in April 1962, no such limitations are proposed in this budget.

Provision of item veto.—Future Presidents should have the authority to veto items of appropriation measures without the necessity of disapproving an entire appropriation bill. Many Presidents have recommended that this authority be given to our Chief Executive, and more than 80% of the States have given it to their Governors. It is a necessary procedure for strengthening fiscal responsibility. As in the case of other vetoes, the Congress should have the authority to override an item veto.

In my first budget message to the Congress, I described the philosophy of this administration in the following words:

"By using necessity—rather than mere desirability—as the test for our expenditures, we will reduce the share of the national income which is spent by the Government. We are convinced that more progress and sounder progress will be made over the years as the largest possible share of our national income is left with individual citizens to make their own countless decisions as to what they will spend, what they will buy, and what they will save and invest. Government must play a vital role in maintaining economic growth and stability. But I believe that our development, since the early days of the Republic, has been based on the fact that we left a great share of our national income to be used by a provident people with a will to venture. Their actions have stimulated the American genius for creative initiative and thus multiplied our productivity."

This philosophy is as appropriate today as it was in 1954. And it should continue to guide us in the future.

Over the past 8 years, we have sought to keep the role of the Federal Government within its proper sphere, resisting the ever-present pressures to initiate or expand activities which could be more appropriately carried out by others. At the same time, the record of this administration has been one of action to help meet the urgent and real needs of a growing population and a changing economy. For example, Federal expenditures between 1953 and 1961 for aids to education have more than doubled; outlays for public health have more than tripled; civil aviation expenditures have more than quadrupled; highway expenditures are five times the 1953 level; and urban renewal expenditures are more than seven times as great.

The major increases in spending which have taken place have not been devoted to the tools of war and destruction. A military posture of great effectiveness and strong retaliatory capability has been maintained without increasing defense expenditures above 1953, despite rising costs. We have, fortunately, been able to direct more of our public resources toward the improvement of living conditions and the enlargement of opportunities for the future growth and development of the Nation.

By applying the test of necessity rather than desirability to the expenditures of government, we have made significant progress in both public and private affairs during the past 8 years. And it is significant that requirements have been met while holding budget expenditures to a lesser proportion of the national income than in 1953.

The 1962 budget has been designed to promote further advancement for all of our people on a sound and secure basis. In that spirit, I commend it to the consideration of the next administration and the Congress.

DWIGHT D. EISENHOWER

NOTE: As printed above, the following have been deleted: (1) illustrative diagrams and highlight summaries; (2) references to special analyses appearing in the budget document.

415 ¶ Letter Accepting Resignation of Robert B. Anderson as Secretary of the Treasury. *January 16, 1961*

[Released January 16, 1961. Dated January 13, 1961]

Dear Bob:

I shall never be able to tell you of the depth of my gratitude for your readiness to return three and a half years ago to governmental service as Secretary of the Treasury. Your sound grasp of fiscal, financial and general governmental problems have made you a real stalwart in this Administration and invaluable to me. In accepting your resignation, effective January 20, 1961, as Secretary of the Treasury and from the other offices referred to in your letter of January ninth, it would be difficult indeed to over-emphasize the sense of obligation I feel to you and your staff.

Under your leadership the Treasury has provided constructive guidance in this Administration's efforts to stabilize the dollar, balance the Federal budget, correct the balance of payments deficit, plan for tax revision and simplification, and manage the Federal debt. The story of the actions of the Department of the Treasury in these areas is clearly presented in your report and I shall release it to the press in order that these major accomplishments can be made a part of the public record.

I earnestly hope that opportunities will develop from time to time for you and me to meet; no matter what my future activities may be, I shall always deem it a privilege to renew with you the conversations and exchange of views that have meant so much to me over these many months.

As for you and your future, I am completely confident that your demonstrated capacity, ability and strength of character will make you a brilliant success in whatever calling you may see fit to follow.

To you and your family, I send my warm regard and, of course, my very best wishes for your continued health and vigor.

Sincerely,

DWIGHT D. EISENHOWER

NOTE: Secretary Anderson served from July 29, 1957, to January 20, 1961. His letter of resignation, dated January 6, and his report were released with the President's reply. In his letter of January 9, also released, Mr. Anderson resigned as U.S. Governor of the International Monetary Fund, as U.S. Governor of the International Bank for Reconstruction and Development, as U.S. Governor of the Inter-American Development Bank, and as a member of the Advisory Commission on Intergovernmental Relations.

416 ¶ Remarks at the Signing of the Columbia River Basin Treaty With Canada. *January* 17, 1961

Gentlemen:

The signing of this treaty marks the culmination of a long effort—indeed 16 years long—between Canada and the United States to reach a common ground of agreement on the development of the Upper Columbia.

I personally believe that the work which will now go ahead, when these treaties are properly approved, will be one of the great developments for the benefit of both our countries.

Moreover, in more intangible benefits, there is a tremendously important advance. That comes about because these two nations living so close together have to watch each other, probably, at times. Nevertheless, we are such great friends, as Mr. Diefenbaker has also said, that we serve as a model for other countries.

This is another step in cementing that friendship and making it more lasting and useful to the whole world.

So, for me to be able to sign this treaty, in the last 2 or 3 days of this administration, is indeed a great personal gratification and satisfaction.

I thank you, Mr. Prime Minister, and your associates for the work you have done to facilitate this treaty and to be a part of this great step in the future cooperation of our countries.

NOTE: Prime Minister Diefenbaker's remarks follow:

Mr. President:

This, I believe, is an historic milestone in Canadian-American relations. As you have said, this project is one of the greatest projects that has ever been undertaken. Indeed, it is the first occasion in history when two nations, side by side, have agreed to the distribution of power as between their two countries, and the sharing of the development of an international river to the same extent as will be the result in the years ahead.

And as you have said, this relationship between our countries is something that is a model for all mankind. Indeed, it would be difficult to understand the relationship between our two countries when placed alongside the relationships that prevail between other countries in the world today. My hope is that, in the years ahead, this day will be looked back on as one that represents the greatest advance that has ever been made in intranational relations between countries.

While we are joined in sentiment and in a common dedication to freedom, we are, under this project, joined as well in an economic development for the benefit of both our countries.

And I want to say this, Mr. President, as you approach the end of your term of office, and in deep sincerity, how much your friendship has meant to me. And I speak for all Canadians when I wish you good health, long years of service on behalf of peace. Indeed we think of you as the great leader of the legions of freedom in the darkest days of war. We think of you as well as the architect of international relationships. Your dedication to the achievement and the attainment of peace is something that has been an inspiration to all of us in the free world.

I think that this day is the culmination of your dedication to the assurance that each nation is indeed its brother's keeper and that only in the raising of the opportunities economically can there be a true foundation for peace.

We, in our cooperation, are building for the future. And if only the other nations could catch something of this relationship so that each of us would through economic endeavor and cooperation help others less enjoyably placed economically, a long step forward can be made.

This is a great day. I wish you well, and I know that in the days ahead your contribution everywhere in the world, with the prestige that is yours, will do much to bring about the attainment of peace in this generation.

417   ¶ Citation Presented to General Melvin J. Maas.   *January* 17, 1961

[Text read by Gerald D. Morgan, The Deputy Assistant to the President]

CITATION:

Major General Melvin Joseph Maas (U.S. Marine Corps, Retired), has served the people of the United States in peace and war with vigor, ability and devotion.

As a Congressman, as a Marine in both World Wars, as Chairman of the President's Committee on Employment of the Physically Handicapped, Melvin Maas has become an example of inspired citizenship to all Americans.

Total blindness and diverse physical afflictions have not been able to stop him in his prosecution of good works. He is a symbol of the proud motto of the handicapped: "It's ability, not disability, that counts." In him the physically handicapped have a brave and effective champion.

For his life-long dedication to the service of the American people; for his outstanding leadership of the President's Committee on Employment of the Physically Handicapped; and for his courage in action over and beyond the call of duty, it is most fitting that Melvin Maas receive the grateful recognition of his countrymen.

DWIGHT D. EISENHOWER

NOTE: The citation was presented at the Bethesda Naval Medical Center, where General Maas was recuperating from an illness. General Maas was appointed Chairman of the President's Committee on Employment of the Physically Handicapped on April 13, 1954.

418 ¶ Statement by the President on the Sugar Act. *January* 17, 1961

I HAVE instructed the Secretary of Agriculture to transmit to the Congress of the United States a recommendation for extension and amendment of the Sugar Act of 1948, as amended, from its present expiration date of March 31, 1961, through December 31, 1961. I have also indicated my belief that a nine-months extension is imperative to maintain a stable sugar market in the interest of domestic producers and consumers, if the Congress is to have time enough to develop longer range legislation.

In accordance with my statement of December 16, 1960, I have again asked the Congress to relieve the Executive of the obligation to purchase from the Dominican Republic a portion of the sugar needed to replace that formerly obtained from Cuba.

NOTE: For the President's statement of December 16, 1960, see Item 374.

419   ¶ Special Message to the Senate
Transmitting the Columbia River Basin Treaty
With Canada.   *January* 17, 1961

To the Senate of the United States:

With a view to receiving the advice and consent of the Senate to ratification, I transmit herewith a treaty between the United States of America and Canada concerning the cooperative development of the water resources of the Columbia River Basin, signed at Washington January 17, 1961, together with a report of the Secretary of State.

The treaty is an important step toward achieving optimum development of the water resources of the Columbia River basin as a whole from which the United States and Canada will each receive benefits materially larger than either could obtain independently.

The United States will secure a large block of power at low cost, substantial flood control benefits, and additional incidental benefits for irrigation, navigation, pollution abatement, and other uses resulting from controlled storage. Canada will also receive a large block of power at a low cost, as well as flood control and other benefits resulting from the control of water flow.

The treaty envisages the construction, in the Columbia River basin in Canada within a nine-year period, of reservoirs providing 15.5 million acre-feet of storage. The treaty also clears the way for construction by the United States, at its option, of the Libby project on the Kootenai River in northern Montana, which was authorized by the Congress in the Flood Control Act of 1950. The reservoir area for this project extends forty-two miles into the Canadian province of British Columbia.

The flood control and power benefits resulting from the treaty will be realized at a much earlier date and at a cost materially less than would be the case were they to be provided exclusively through projects in the United States.

The developments brought about under the treaty will be of great significance for their human values as well as for the material gains they will provide.

The flood control objectives of the United States for the lower Columbia River in Oregon and Washington which have been a pressing need for many years will be brought to substantial realization within a span of less than a decade. The Libby project will resolve the critical flood control problem in the Bonners Ferry area in Idaho. Removal of the hazard of periodic floods will pay incalculable dividends in the saving of human life and the avoidance of suffering, as well as through economic improvement in areas heretofore subject to recurring flood damage.

The initial power benefits realizable in the United States from Canadian storage under the treaty are comparable to another Grand Coulee dam, the largest hydroelectric project now in operation in the United States. The Libby clearance presents the opportunity to gain an additional block of power substantially greater than the output of Bonneville dam. The total initial result is a gain to the United States of over 1,686,000 kilowatts of low-cost prime power.

Over the longer term, this large block of storage will make more valuable the existing projects in the Columbia River basin, representing an investment of some $3.5 billion, by accelerating the time at which their full potential can be realized. The large blocks of power that will result will be a tremendous asset in fostering the nation's economic growth and in augmenting our national resources.

Due to the location of the storage, there will be no interference with the cycle for salmon and other anadromous fish which constitute such an important economic and recreational asset for the people of the Pacific Northwest.

To provide flood control and power benefits equivalent to those provided by the Canadian storage as of 1970 entirely from projects in the United States would require an investment in the United States of about $710,000,000 (including the cost of necessary additional transmission facilities) over this decade. To realize the treaty benefits, on the other hand, the costs in the United States over the next 10 years are estimated at not over $150,000,000. Between 1970 and 1985 an additional estimated $268,000,000 of United States expenditures will be required. Most of this added expenditure will go to install additional generating facilities in the United States to take full advantage of the Canadian storage. In all, the total capital outlay in the United States by reason of the treaty (exclusive of the cost of the Libby project) is estimated at about $418,000,000.

I recommend that the Senate give early and favorable consideration to the treaty which should not be considered from the aspect of economic

benefit alone but also as a further demonstration of the spirit of cooperation and mutual accommodation which has traditionally characterized
relationships between Canada and the United States of America.

DWIGHT D. EISENHOWER

NOTE: The report of the Secretary of   lished in the Department of State Bulletin
State and the text of the treaty are pub-   (vol. 24, p. 229).

420   ¶ Special Message to the Congress Transmitting Agreement With Italy for Cooperation on Uses of Atomic Energy for Mutual Defense.   *January 17, 1961*

To the Congress of the United States:

In December 1957 the Heads of Government of the nations members
of the North Atlantic Treaty Organization reached agreement in principle on the desirability of achieving the most effective pattern of NATO
military defensive strength, taking into account the most recent developments in weapons and techniques.   In enunciating this agreement in
principle the Heads of Government made it clear that this decision was
the result of the fact that the Soviet leaders, while preventing a general
disarmament agreement, had left no doubt that the most modern and
destructive weapons of all kinds were being introduced into the Soviet
armed forces.   The introduction of modern weapons into NATO forces
should be no cause for concern on the part of other countries, since NATO
is purely a defensive alliance.

It is our conviction and the conviction of our NATO allies that the
introduction into NATO defenses of the most modern weapons available
is essential in maintaining the strength necessary to the Alliance.   Any
alliance depends in the last analysis upon the sense of shared mutual
interests among its members, and by sharing with our Allies certain training information we are demonstrating concretely our sense of partnership
in NATO's defensive planning.   Failure on our part to contribute to the
improvement of the state of operational readiness of the forces of other
members of NATO will only encourage the Soviet Union to believe that
it can eventually succeed in its goal of destroying NATO's effectiveness.

To facilitate the necessary cooperation on our part legislation amending
the Atomic Energy Act of 1954 was enacted by the Congress in 1958.

Pursuant to that legislation agreements for cooperation were concluded with four of our NATO partners in May and June 1959. A similar agreement was also recently concluded with our NATO ally, the Republic of Italy. All of these agreements are designed to implement in important respects the agreed NATO program.

This agreement with the Government of Italy will enable the United States to cooperate effectively in mutual defense planning with Italy and in the training of Italian NATO forces in order that, if an attack on NATO should occur, Italian forces could, under the direction of the Supreme Allied Commander for Europe, effectively use nuclear weapons in their defense.

These agreements previously concluded and this Italian Agreement represent only a portion of the work necessary for complete implementation of the decision taken by the North Atlantic Treaty Organization in December 1957. I anticipate the conclusion of similar agreements for cooperation with certain other NATO nations as the Alliance's defensive planning continues.

Pursuant to the Atomic Energy Act of 1954, as amended, I am submitting to each House of the Congress an authoritative copy of the agreement with the Government of Italy. I am also transmitting a copy of the Secretary of State's letter accompanying an authoritative copy of the signed agreement, a copy of a joint letter from the Secretary of Defense and the Chairman of the Atomic Energy Commission recommending my approval of this document and a copy of my memorandum in reply thereto setting forth my approval.

DWIGHT D. EISENHOWER

NOTE: The text of the agreement and related documents is published in the Congressional Record of March 7, 1961 (vol. 107, p. 3095).

421 ¶ Farewell Radio and Television Address to the American People. *January* 17, 1961

[Delivered from the President's Office at 8:30 p.m.]

My fellow Americans:

Three days from now, after half a century in the service of our country, I shall lay down the responsibilities of office as, in traditional and solemn ceremony, the authority of the Presidency is vested in my successor.

This evening I come to you with a message of leave-taking and farewell, and to share a few final thoughts with you, my countrymen.

Like every other citizen, I wish the new President, and all who will labor with him, Godspeed. I pray that the coming years will be blessed with peace and prosperity for all.

———

Our people expect their President and the Congress to find essential agreement on issues of great moment, the wise resolution of which will better shape the future of the Nation.

My own relations with the Congress, which began on a remote and tenuous basis when, long ago, a member of the Senate appointed me to West Point, have since ranged to the intimate during the war and immediate post-war period, and, finally, to the mutually interdependent during these past eight years.

In this final relationship, the Congress and the Administration have, on most vital issues, cooperated well, to serve the national good rather than mere partisanship, and so have assured that the business of the Nation should go forward. So, my official relationship with the Congress ends in a feeling, on my part, of gratitude that we have been able to do so much together.

II.

We now stand ten years past the midpoint of a century that has witnessed four major wars among great nations. Three of these involved our own country. Despite these holocausts America is today the strongest, the most influential and most productive nation in the world. Understandably proud of this pre-eminence, we yet realize that America's leadership and prestige depend, not merely upon our unmatched material progress, riches and military strength, but on how we use our power in the interests of world peace and human betterment.

III.

Throughout America's adventure in free government, our basic purposes have been to keep the peace; to foster progress in human achievement, and to enhance liberty, dignity and integrity among people and among nations. To strive for less would be unworthy of a free and religious people. Any failure traceable to arrogance, or our lack of comprehension or readiness to sacrifice would inflict upon us grievous hurt both at home and abroad.

Progress toward these noble goals is persistently threatened by the conflict now engulfing the world. It commands our whole attention, absorbs our very beings. We face a hostile ideology—global in scope, atheistic in character, ruthless in purpose, and insidious in method. Unhappily the danger it poses promises to be of indefinite duration. To meet it successfully, there is called for, not so much the emotional and transitory sacrifices of crisis, but rather those which enable us to carry forward steadily, surely, and without complaint the burdens of a prolonged and complex struggle—with liberty the stake. Only thus shall we remain, despite every provocation, on our charted course toward permanent peace and human betterment.

Crises there will continue to be. In meeting them, whether foreign or domestic, great or small, there is a recurring temptation to feel that some spectacular and costly action could become the miraculous solution to all current difficulties. A huge increase in newer elements of our defense; development of unrealistic programs to cure every ill in agriculture; a dramatic expansion in basic and applied research—these and many other possibilities, each possibly promising in itself, may be suggested as the only way to the road we wish to travel.

But each proposal must be weighed in the light of a broader consideration: the need to maintain balance in and among national programs—balance between the private and the public economy, balance between cost and hoped for advantage—balance between the clearly necessary and the comfortably desirable; balance between our essential requirements as a nation and the duties imposed by the nation upon the individual; balance between actions of the moment and the national welfare of the future. Good judgment seeks balance and progress; lack of it eventually finds imbalance and frustration.

The record of many decades stands as proof that our people and their government have, in the main, understood these truths and have responded to them well, in the face of stress and threat. But threats, new in kind or degree, constantly arise. I mention two only.

IV.

A vital element in keeping the peace is our military establishment. Our arms must be mighty, ready for instant action, so that no potential aggressor may be tempted to risk his own destruction.

Our military organization today bears little relation to that known by any of my predecessors in peacetime, or indeed by the fighting men of World War II or Korea.

Until the latest of our world conflicts, the United States had no armaments industry. American makers of plowshares could, with time and as required, make swords as well. But now we can no longer risk emergency improvisation of national defense; we have been compelled to create a permanent armaments industry of vast proportions. Added to this, three and a half million men and women are directly engaged in the defense establishment. We annually spend on military security more than the net income of all United States corporations.

This conjunction of an immense military establishment and a large arms industry is new in the American experience. The total influence—economic, political, even spiritual—is felt in every city, every State house, every office of the Federal government. We recognize the imperative need for this development. Yet we must not fail to comprehend its grave implications. Our toil, resources and livelihood are all involved; so is the very structure of our society.

In the councils of government, we must guard against the acquisition of unwarranted influence, whether sought or unsought, by the military-industrial complex. The potential for the disastrous rise of misplaced power exists and will persist.

We must never let the weight of this combination endanger our liberties or democratic processes. We should take nothing for granted. Only an alert and knowledgeable citizenry can compel the proper meshing of the huge industrial and military machinery of defense with our peaceful methods and goals, so that security and liberty may prosper together.

Akin to, and largely responsible for the sweeping changes in our industrial-military posture, has been the technological revolution during recent decades.

In this revolution, research has become central; it also becomes more formalized, complex, and costly. A steadily increasing share is conducted for, by, or at the direction of, the Federal government.

Today, the solitary inventor, tinkering in his shop, has been overshadowed by task forces of scientists in laboratories and testing fields. In the same fashion, the free university, historically the fountainhead of free ideas and scientific discovery, has experienced a revolution in the conduct of research. Partly because of the huge costs involved, a government contract becomes virtually a substitute for intellectual curiosity. For every old blackboard there are now hundreds of new electronic computers.

The prospect of domination of the nation's scholars by Federal employment, project allocations, and the power of money is ever present—and is gravely to be regarded.

Yet, in holding scientific research and discovery in respect, as we should, we must also be alert to the equal and opposite danger that public policy could itself become the captive of a scientific-technological elite.

It is the task of statesmanship to mold, to balance, and to integrate these and other forces, new and old, within the principles of our democratic system—ever aiming toward the supreme goals of our free society.

v.

Another factor in maintaining balance involves the element of time. As we peer into society's future, we—you and I, and our government—must avoid the impulse to live only for today, plundering, for our own ease and convenience, the precious resources of tomorrow. We cannot mortgage the material assets of our grandchildren without risking the loss also of their political and spiritual heritage. We want democracy to survive for all generations to come, not to become the insolvent phantom of tomorrow.

vi.

Down the long lane of the history yet to be written America knows that this world of ours, ever growing smaller, must avoid becoming a community of dreadful fear and hate, and be, instead, a proud confederation of mutual trust and respect.

Such a confederation must be one of equals. The weakest must come to the conference table with the same confidence as do we, protected as we are by our moral, economic, and military strength. That table, though scarred by many past frustrations, cannot be abandoned for the certain agony of the battlefield.

Disarmament, with mutual honor and confidence, is a continuing imperative. Together we must learn how to compose differences, not with arms, but with intellect and decent purpose. Because this need is so sharp and apparent I confess that I lay down my official responsibilities in this field with a definite sense of disappointment. As one who has witnessed the horror and the lingering sadness of war—as one who knows that another war could utterly destroy this civilization which has been so slowly and painfully built over thousands of years—I wish I could say tonight that a lasting peace is in sight.

Happily, I can say that war has been avoided.   Steady progress toward our ultimate goal has been made.   But, so much remains to be done. As a private citizen, I shall never cease to do what little I can to help the world advance along that road.

VII.

So—in this my last good night to you as your President—I thank you for the many opportunities you have given me for public service in war and peace.   I trust that in that service you find some things worthy; as for the rest of it, I know you will find ways to improve performance in the future.

You and I—my fellow citizens—need to be strong in our faith that all nations, under God, will reach the goal of peace with justice.   May we be ever unswerving in devotion to principle, confident but humble with power, diligent in pursuit of the Nation's great goals.

To all the peoples of the world, I once more give expression to America's prayerful and continuing aspiration:

We pray that peoples of all faiths, all races, all nations, may have their great human needs satisfied; that those now denied opportunity shall come to enjoy it to the full; that all who yearn for freedom may experience its spiritual blessings; that those who have freedom will understand, also, its heavy responsibilities; that all who are insensitive to the needs of others will learn charity; that the scourges of poverty, disease and ignorance will be made to disappear from the earth, and that, in the goodness of time, all peoples will come to live together in a peace guaranteed by the binding force of mutual respect and love.

422   ¶ The President's News Conference of *January* 18, 1961

THE PRESIDENT. Good morning. Please sit down.

I came this morning not with any particularly brilliant ideas about the future, but I did want the opportunity to say goodbye to people that I have been associated with now for 8 years, mostly I think on a friendly basis—[*laughter*]—and at least it certainly has always been interesting.

There is one man here who has attended every press conference that I have had, at home and abroad, and who has been of inestimable service to the Government and to all of you, and I think most of you have never seen him. It's Jack Romagna, and I am going to ask him to stand up. [*Shouting and applause*]

Now, if we have any questions, past, present, or future, why——

Q. William J. Eaton, United Press International: Mr. President, more than 2 months have elapsed since Senator Kennedy's election and the problem of transition began. Do you feel this transition period should be shortened or changed in any way?

THE PRESIDENT. Well, my ideas are more radical than that. I think that we ought to get a constitutional amendment to change the time of the inauguration and to give dates for election and assumption of office in such fashion that a new President ought to have at least 80 days or something of that kind before he meets his first Congress.

Q. Thomas N. Schroth, Congressional Quarterly: Mr. President, in the 8 years of your Presidency you have had a Congress of the other party for 6 years. How do you, would you describe that experience? Has the loyal opposition been pretty loyal or have you been frustrated by Congress?

THE PRESIDENT. I think I said, I made a little talk last evening you may have heard—[*laughter*]—and I said on vital issues I thought that the record of the Congress was really cooperative and no one could fault upon that.

Q. Ray L. Scherer, National Broadcasting Company: Mr. President, you had one talk with Mr. Kennedy; you are about to have another. I wonder if you could give us your personal impression of the man.

THE PRESIDENT. Well, now you know that's the last thing I would do. After all, this is a new President coming in and I don't think it's up to me to talk about personalities. As I said last evening, I wish him God-speed in his work because I'll tell you——

Q. Mr. Scherer: I mean, what I mean more specifically, how do you think the transition is going?

THE PRESIDENT. Oh! The transition.

Q. Mr. Scherer: Yes, sir.

THE PRESIDENT. I think it's going splendidly, splendidly. As a matter of fact there are no complaints on our part.

Q. William McGaffin, Chicago Daily News: Mr. President, you sounded a warning last night of the dangers to our democratic processes implicit in unparalleled peacetime military establishment. But some of your critics contend that one liberty, the people's right to know, has suffered under your administration because you have tolerated the abuse of Executive privilege in the Defense Department and other departments and agencies and because you did not hold frequent enough press conferences.

THE PRESIDENT. Well, they are critics and they have the right to criticize.

Q. Robert G. Spivack, New York Post: Mr. President, at your first press conference you came into the room here and you said there had been some speculation in the press that there would be a great deal of antagonism develop between you and the reporters over the years. You said that "through the war years and ever since, I have found nothing but a desire to dig at the truth, so far as I was concerned, and be openhanded and forthright about it. That is the kind of relationship I hope we can continue."

Do you think during these 8 years we have continued it?

THE PRESIDENT. Well, I will say this: so far as I have known the facts I have given them responsively to every question, and where I thought the national security was involved, I was honest enough to say so.

Q. Mr. Spivack: I meant, did you feel that reporters had been fair to you, too, in their questions?

THE PRESIDENT. Well, when you come down to it, I don't see what a reporter could do much to a President, do you? [*Laughter*]

Q. Robert J. Donovan, New York Herald Tribune: Could you expand a little more on your ideas about a constitutional amendment on the re-election of the President? Do you have any particular dates in mind when the election should be held or——

THE PRESIDENT. Well, I am going to be talking, as I warned someone the other day, much more in the future than I thought I would; so, I am going to put these ideas out. I don't mind giving the general idea that I just did, but I wouldn't want to put the details and dates right down until I had studied them completely through in this way. But I do think that a President ought to have the task of completing and finishing his Budget Message, his Economic Reports, and recommendations, and his State of the Union Message during a period while he is still responsible.

Q. Mr. Donovan: The new President?

THE PRESIDENT. The new President. That's right. So we can give him a period in which he is responsible for that, before you go before the Congress. Because now the old President has got to put these things in and the new President has different ideas, he just has to start changing them right away. It seems a little bit silly to me.

Q. Mr. Donovan: I wonder if you could tell us for the historical record, this has come up a number of times, could you say whether at any time you advised or counseled Vice President Nixon against engaging in televised debates, and whether you felt that you, your participating in the campaign began as early as it should have?

THE PRESIDENT. Well, you have a lot of questions this morning. [*Laughter*]

First, I was not asked for any advice on debates. Secondly, I carried out exactly the schedule that the headquarters of the Campaign Committee asked me to do.

Q. Mrs. May Craig, Portland (Maine) Press Herald: Mr. President, can you tell us yet what you think has been your most satisfying achievement and the most heartbreaking failure in your 8 years? You came into the office, I know, with many desires of what you could do.

THE PRESIDENT. Well, I think possibly, Mrs. Craig, that there will have to be more reflection on my part to give you truly a definitive answer.

The big disappointment I felt is one not of a mere incident, it was the fact that we could not in these 8 years get to the place where we could say it now looks as if permanent peace with justice is really in sight. But, on the other hand, if you take achievement over the long run, let us remember what has happened in these 8 years. Our opponents achieved the nitrogen—hydrogen bomb. They began to build up an arsenal which, of course, we know is many thousands of megatons in expressed power, in its power; and at the same time during those days we were already fighting one war, there was danger that there was going to be a spread of those hostilities. During the entire first 4 years, I think, the Red Chinese were constantly threatening war, saying they were and they were not only threatening, but often making moves in that direction and at the same time the Russians were saying, "We are going to support our Red China allies."

Now, there was I believe in this—in the governmental actions of the 8 years, the kind of understanding and firmness and readiness to take the risk that prevented those things from happening because I am perfectly sure that weakness would have allowed them to, and a display of weakness, and I mean either moral or physical would have allowed them to spread this war to the great and disastrous consequences of all the earth.   So, the achievement I think, one of the achievements has been that we actually have stopped many of these risks from becoming realities, and on the other hand the disappointment is that we haven't done better in getting a more constructive and positive indication that real disarmament is around the corner.

Now if you want, if you want a very particular incident, I'd say November 8th was one of another bad disappointments.   [*Laughter*]

Q. Robert C. Pierpoint, CBS News: Mr. President, I wonder if you could tell us in some detail your work and travel plans for the near future, and also whether you want to do this, or prefer to do this work and travel as a civilian, an ex-President, or would you like to have Congress restore your five-star military rank?

THE PRESIDENT. Well, let's start, so I may not remember all your questions, I will start with the end of it.

By Democratic friends of mine in the Congress it has been proposed to give me back my rank that I resigned in July of 1952 and that, of course, would be a satisfying thing to me simply because it was the 40 years that I put in the military service that would give me a title of my own rather than—how do you say "Mr. ex-President"?   I don't know.   [*Laughter*]

But anyway, I understand that that is to be merely a title and no additional pay so that there is no conflict there.

Now, as to what I want to do, I do want to explore my own mind and have a bit of perspective in looking at these 8 years rather than being in the midst of them and seeing whether I have anything that I think is worthwhile to providing for the public; and in doing that, I will possibly do some traveling.

I have, as I think some of you know, I have tentatively agreed to go to Japan in—some time later, I don't know just when, but later and as a matter of fact it has been very gratifying to know of the extraordinary numbers of groups and the really, literally the millions of people that have expressed a desire for me to come back.   But that is not as gratifying as the fact that every single election held in that country since last June has been very, very favorable to the United States and to the treaty that was really at the heart of the whole affair.

Q. William H. Y. Knighton, Jr., Baltimore Sun: Mr. President, have you come to a firm decision on the value of the third-term amendment— no third-term amendment?

THE PRESIDENT. A funny thing, ever since this election the Republicans have been asking me this. [*Laughter*]

No, I think I told you that I had come or, I think at first way back even when I had no intention of ever going more than once that I was sort of against the third-term amendment because I thought the American people had the right to choose who they wanted. But we do know there are possibilities of building up great machines in a democracy and so on, and finally I came, on balance, and I think I so said to this body, on balance to decide that I believe the two-term amendment was probably a pretty good thing.

Q. Edward P. Morgan, American Broadcasting Company: Mr. President, this is a question about the past and the future.

Could you tell us what you personally think were the major points which lost the Republicans the election; and do you have any counsel for the Republicans in '62 and '64 to avoid a repetition of November 8th?

THE PRESIDENT. Well, I would think this: yes, of course I have ideas but here is one case that I think it would be better for me to keep still for the moment. I have to meet with these Republican leaders of the future and talk to them and give them the lessons I think I have learned, and where together we can point out what we believe are mistakes, and where together we can say what we believe is the best method to make sure that this country will have balanced government.

Q. Lillian Levy, Science Service: Mr. President, last night you called attention to the danger that public policy could become the captive of a scientific technological elite. What specific steps would you recommend to prevent this?

THE PRESIDENT. I know nothing here that is possible, or useful, except the performance of the duties of responsible citizenship. It is only a citizenry, an alert and informed citizenry which can keep these abuses from coming about. And I did point out last evening that some of this misuse of influence and power could come about unwittingly but just by the very nature of the thing. When you see almost every one of your magazines, no matter what they are advertising, has a picture of the Titan missile or the Atlas or solid fuel or other things, there is becoming a great influence, almost an insidious penetration of our own minds that the only thing this country is engaged in is weaponry and missiles. And, I'll tell you we just can't afford to do that. The reason we have them is to protect the great values in which we believe, and they are far deeper even than our own lives and our own property, as I see it.

Q. Edward V. Koterba, United Features Syndicate: Mr. President, in line with your opening statement and a question earlier, it is agreed that at times over the last 8 years we at the press conferences may not have been too charitable in our questioning of you. Now could you elaborate, sir, and relate to us your feeling about your relations with the press and these press conferences in particular?

THE PRESIDENT. Well, I don't know that I can elaborate very much. I'll say this, the other evening I asked the people that they call the regulars around the White House, and you people know them as well as I do, and I guess there was, what, seventy? Seventy people. Now I didn't ask them whether they were critics or particular friends of mine, some of them are, they've been warm personal friends, whether they were Democrats or Republicans or Socialists—but we had a good time I think, everybody seemed to, and I think on a personal basis it was a friendly thing. So I have never objected to penetrating and searching questions. The only thing I object to is something that tries to—it's like the beating of your wife question, I don't like that, and—[*laughter*]—but I have no one that I could single out and say that they have been annoying nor have I anyone to argue with.

Q. Sarah McClendon, El Paso Times: Mr. President, this question concerns your budget, this proposal on the Office of Executive Management. Would you discuss that for us some and tell us, does this not mean that there will be more centralized control over our public works projects, as to whether or not they would be started or they would be stopped?

THE PRESIDENT. Oh, no, not at all. There, you can have supervision not only subjectively, like the Secretary of the Interior over the Interior subjects, but you can have it functionally because you have two great areas that cause a President work and study every single day of his life. One is everything that touches foreign relations. This is his constitutional duty, and here where we used to think of it, those things falling only within the Department of State, we have now—we have representatives of the Labor Department, of the Commerce Department, of the Agriculture Department, we have ICA, we have USIA, and then the Defense Department which now obviously with the stationing of troops abroad everywhere, has a great effect on foreign policy.

Now, it is therefore a very tough problem to keep all of these things always on the same road going the same way. This would be the job of the First Secretary, as I see it, not that he takes the place of the President at all, in the foreign field, but to day by day watch what is going on in the world—keep everybody in all the several departments aware of what they must do so as to have a completely coordinated policy.

Now, in the management field you have everything from rates of pay that are different in all sorts of different departments, you have all different kinds of accounting methods in different departments, you have got different methods of procurement and all of this sort of thing in my opinion ought to be coordinated. Now, you don't get into their business of running the Defense Department or the State Department or the USIA. You make sure that the business arrangements that they carry out are good, and this has nothing to do with the starting of a new dam or not. That is a political decision.

Q. Raymond P. Brandt, St. Louis Post-Dispatch: Can you tell us, sir, what you think is the greatest problem confronting your successor?

THE PRESIDENT. Well, I think that is answered almost by the fact that the thing that causes all our problems is the intransigent, unreasonable attitude of the Communist bloc and therefore his basic problem and as a matter of fact not just the President's, everybody else's, is what do to keep ourselves strong and firm and yet conciliatory in trying to meet this—this terrible problem that is none of our making.

Q. Richard L. Wilson, Cowles Publications: One indication of what the succeeding administration may have in mind is apparently contained in the report by Professor Samuelson in which he recommends an increase of $3 billion to $5 billion immediately in certain domestic programs. Do you take the view that the economy is moving into a dangerous period that would require this additional governmental action, or do you feel that the proposals made may be extreme and not necessary?

THE PRESIDENT. Well, put it this way: of course I'm no—while I'm one of seven sons, I'm not the seventh son of a seventh son, so I'm not a prophet.

Now, we believe, and I'm now talking not out of my guesswork, I'm talking about the economic analyses, that the economy is swinging and it will be swinging up gradually but steadily so as to provide more revenue than it currently is doing, I mean Federal revenue.

Now, this business of going into public works all of a sudden to cure what someone believes is a recession, or to stop a recession—I have had a very, very searching study made of this thing and it's not quite complete, but I am going to use it someday in trying to point out that that kind of a problem, or that kind of dependence upon stopping a recession usually gets into effect about 18 months after the recession is all over and you are in your boom period. If people exaggerate the number of men that are going to be put back to work because you appropriate 3 billion or 5 billion, in fact I believe as we go back to this last one of— '58—the biggest thing that the Federal Government did, was most helpful, was this: it picked up the tab for all of the unemployment insurance benefits that had been exhausted by people in the several States and where there was no help. So the Federal Government I think probably put, I don't remember the figures, let's say 600 or 700 million and that 600 or 700 million was far better because it alleviated suffering at the moment and restored some confidence and people naturally began to build and buy again.

I really don't go in very much for the theory that by suddenly expanding $3 or $4 or $5 billion worth of Federal programs that you get a tremendous boost. We are talking of $503 or $504 billion GNP, and this is 3 or 4 or 5 billions now that we are going to put somewhere, and it takes a long, long time to get it used. But it does mean that it stays permanently as a debt that we have to pay sometime.

Q. L. Edgar Prina, Washington Star: How active a role do you plan to play in the effort to strengthen the Republican Party; and can you tell us whether this role will be nearly as active, for example, as Mr. Truman's in his own party? You mentioned making a lot of speeches.

THE PRESIDENT. Well, I won't make any comparisons—*[laughter]*— I'll just say this: I'm now, I think this is the fourth time that I am supposedly going to retire, and I feel this, the Republican Party is necessary to this country, I believe in its general policies and if the leaders of that party want me for any service in which I can be helpful and by that I would assume we were talking about consultation from time to time and not any truly active thing, I will be available. I won't be around trying to lecture them, but I should like to converse with them if they want me.

Q. Mr. Prina: You mentioned you were going to make a great many more speeches than you had planned. Would that be——

THE PRESIDENT. Not speeches; no, not speeches, I'll probably stop that.

Q. Spencer Davis, Associated Press: Mr. President, you mentioned a short time back the need for the United States to remain firm and strong and at the same time conciliatory. Would you relate that to our policy toward Laos, sir, particularly the reports that the United States had turned down the invitation of Cambodia to attend a 14-nation conference?

THE PRESIDENT. Well, at the moment there is no point, of course, of going into a conference unless everybody thinks this would be a good idea. You can't haul anybody into a conference.

Now, the thing that has been proposed most has been a reconvening of the ICC and if that could be done in proper auspices and where it was recognized that the government of Phoumi, which has been now approved by the Parliament, if that was recognized as the proper government I think there might be a useful purpose of reconvening this ICC to be served.

Actually what again causes the trouble is the determination of the Communist bloc, as expressed again yesterday in Mr. Khrushchev's speech to exacerbate and support what he calls wars of liberation and which are revolts of Communist elements to overturn constituted governments in authority.

Now, the United States has tried to do this within the limits of the United Nations Charter. We believe that unless there can become a greater adherence to these principles, and unless that charter can be supported by more of our nations, then the outlook for peace becomes dimmer.

On the other hand, as all of us take the United Nations Charter as our guide and as we have tried to do so earnestly, and I think most of the Western nations have tried to do also, then I think the chances of settling this as well as other problems will be greater.

Q. Frank van der Linden, Nashville Banner: Sir, the House of Representatives will vote soon on a proposal by Speaker Rayburn to add two Democrats and one Republican to the Rules Committee for the announced purpose of clearing the way for some of these welfare and spending bills that you vetoed in the past. Would you advise the Republicans in the House to vote solidly against this proposal which has been called the packing plan?

THE PRESIDENT. Well, I think one thing that is scarcely proper for me to comment on is how the two bodies of Congress rule themselves. This, for the reason that I believe the Constitution says that they have established their own methods of operation and I don't think the President has any real right to interfere.

Q. David P. Sentner, Hearst Newspapers: Mr. President, you referred earlier to the great values to be considered in our way of living.   Would you sum up for us your idea of what kind of a United States you would like your grandchildren to live in?

THE PRESIDENT. I'd say in a peaceful world and enjoying all of the privileges and carrying forward all the responsibilities envisioned for the good citizen of the United States, and this means among other things the effort always to raise the standards of our people in their spiritual, their intellectual, their economic strength and generally and specifically and that's what I would like to see them have.

Sterling F. Green, Associated Press: Thank you, Mr. President.

[*The Press Conference was concluded with a standing ovation and applause by the members present as the President left the conference room.*]

NOTE: President Eisenhower's one hundred and ninety-third news conference was held in the Executive Office Building from 10 to 10:29 o'clock on Wednesday morning, January 18, 1961.   In attendance: 309.

423   ¶ Annual Message Presenting the Economic Report to the Congress.   *January* 18, 1961

To the Congress of the United States:

I present herewith my Economic Report, as required by Section 3(a) of the Employment Act of 1946.

The Report was prepared with the advice and assistance of the Council of Economic Advisers, who, in turn, have had the assistance of the heads of the executive departments and independent agencies directly concerned with the matters discussed.   Pursuant to the requirements of the Employment Act, the Report summarizes the economic developments of the year and the policy actions taken to promote balanced growth of the economy, appraises the economic outlook, and puts forward a number of legislative proposals designed to help achieve the purposes of the Act.   The Report also reviews the performance of the economy under the Employment Act, and particularly during the period of this Administration, and discusses policies for the future in the light of this experience.

The major conclusions and recommendations of the Report are set forth below, in part in the words of the Report itself.

As the year 1960 came to a close, the Nation was producing goods and services at an annual rate of $503.5 billion, the same as in the third quarter of the year, though slightly less than in the second quarter. For the year as a whole, the total output of our economy, in dollars of constant buying power, was 2.6 percent greater than in 1959.

Production and employment declined in the latter part of 1960, and unemployment rose, owing in large measure to an inventory adjustment. In the first quarter, inventories were being built up at an annual rate of $11.4 billion, but in the fourth quarter they were being reduced at an annual rate of $4.0 billion. It is encouraging, however, that the declines in production and income were moderate. And it is especially important that final demands for goods and services—that is, the sum of the Nation's expenditures except those resulting in inventory change—rose without interruption during the year and in the final quarter reached the level of $507.5 billion.

The achievement of a reasonable equilibrium in the Nation's international transactions continued to be a goal of our policies in 1960. The over-all deficit in the United States balance of payments last year remained close to that in each of the two preceding years, but the structure of the deficit changed markedly. Short-term capital outflows accelerated, mainly in response to a widening of the margin by which interest rates abroad exceeded those in this country. But the deficit on all other transactions diminished greatly, as a result of a rapid rise in exports.

The underlying strength of our economy, manifested in final demand for goods and services, is a distinctly favorable element in appraising the economic outlook. So, also, is the fact that economic conditions today are free of maladjustments and imbalances which, to be corrected, would require prolonged contraction. Businessmen and consumers have kept their use of credit within reasonable limits, and speculative excesses have been generally avoided. Inflationary pressure has been restrained. While this may have affected inventory policies and, perhaps, other demands for goods and services, it has helped to prepare a solid foundation for a resumption of sustainable growth. Because action to maintain balance and to consolidate gains was taken in good time, we can look forward, provided public and private policies are favorable, to a period of sound economic growth from a firm base.

The Federal policies needed to promote balanced growth can, to a considerable extent, be applied under existing administrative authority. But there are certain areas in which legislative action is needed.

First, funds appropriated by the Congress for the fiscal year 1962 should be held within the limits of expected revenues. A budget conforming to this standard has been presented to the Congress. It makes certain suggestions for revenues to cover projected expenditures, including necessary extensions of taxes that would otherwise terminate or be reduced on July 1, 1961; an increase in the highway fuel tax to $4\frac{1}{2}$ cents per gallon, to supply needed funds in the Highway Trust Fund; the rescinding by the Congress of action taken in 1959 which would divert funds from the general fund of the Treasury for road construction; and a rate increase to place the postal system on a self-supporting basis.

Second, Congress should give the Secretary of the Treasury authority to raise funds in the long-term capital market when, in his judgment, this is in the public interest, even if the cost of the funds is above $4\frac{1}{4}$ percent. The existing ceiling remains an important impediment to the Treasury's flexibility in achieving significant debt lengthening.

Third, as I have pointed out to the Congress each year since 1955, legislation is needed to enable the Federal Government to give constructive assistance to areas where there is high and persistent unemployment. The character of the legislation needed is described in the Economic Report, and an Administration proposal drafted to meet the standards indicated has been placed before the Congress.

Fourth, legislative needs in the areas of health, education and welfare, antitrust enforcement, long-term agricultural adjustment, unemployment compensation, and housing and community development are outlined in the Report. These are also described in the Budget Message.

Finally, I recommend again that Congress amend the Employment Act of 1946 to make reasonable price stability an explicit goal of national economic policy, coordinate with the goals of maximum employment, production, and purchasing power now stated in the Act. The amendment proposed is limited to a change in the language of the Act's declaration of policy and would accomplish its aim without placing restrictions on the effective operation of economic markets. It would strengthen the Employment Act which, as the Economic Report shows, has been a useful statute under which our citizens have made notable further advances in their welfare.

DWIGHT D. EISENHOWER

NOTE: The message and the complete report (214 pp.) are published in "Economic Report of the President, 1961" (Government Printing Office, 1961).

424 ¶ Message to the Congress Transmitting the Third Annual Report on U.S. Aeronautics and Space Activities. *January* 18, 1961

To the Congress of the United States:

In accordance with Section 206(b) of the National Aeronautics and Space Act of 1958, I am transmitting herewith the third annual report on the Nation's activities in the fields of aeronautics and space.

As this report testifies, 1960 witnessed a vast expansion of man's knowledge of the earth's atmosphere and of the limitless regions of space beyond. The Vanguard, Explorer, and Pioneer spacecraft have added substantially to our knowledge of the earth's environment and of the sun-earth relationship. Experiments with Projects Echo and COURIER, TIROS I and II, and TRANSIT I and II have shown the promise of spacecraft application in the fields of communications, meteorology, and navigation. Among the outstanding accomplishments in technology were a series of successful recoveries from orbit of capsules from the DISCOVERER satellites and the increasing degree of reliability in stabilizing these satellites in the required orbit.

Significant advances were made in the manned space flight program and in the preparation of a small fleet of powerful launch vehicles to carry out a wide variety of space missions.

Underlying the Nation's aeronautics and space programs was a strong basic and applied research effort which resulted in constantly broadening scientific and technological horizons. Finally, the entire effort has been drawn together in a long-range program of space exploration which offers every promise that in the years to come benefits for all mankind will be extensive.

Summarized within this report are contributions of Federal agencies participating in the space effort.

DWIGHT D. EISENHOWER

NOTE: The report is printed in House Document 56 (87th Cong., 1st sess.).

425   ¶ Citation Accompanying the Medal of
Freedom Presented to James H. Douglas.
January 18, 1961

[Text read by Brig. Gen. A. J. Goodpaster, Staff Secretary to the President]

CITATION TO ACCOMPANY THE AWARD OF
THE MEDAL OF FREEDOM
TO
JAMES H. DOUGLAS
FOR EXCEPTIONALLY MERITORIOUS SERVICE
AND DISTINGUISHED CONTRIBUTION
TO THE SECURITY OF THE UNITED STATES

For nearly eight years—as Under Secretary of the Air Force, Secretary of the Air Force and currently as Deputy Secretary of Defense, James Douglas has borne major responsibilities in the shaping of military policy and programs, and in key decisions guiding the use of military resources.

Through sound judgment, wise leadership and great devotion to his country he has made an outstanding contribution to the effective direction of the Defense establishment, to our international security operations, and to the strengthening of cooperation and confidence between the United States and nations joined with us in collective security. For his firm and unyielding dedication to principles of good government, and for his many contributions to the nation's security, I award to him the Medal of Freedom.

DWIGHT D. EISENHOWER

NOTE: The presentation was made by the President at a ceremony held in the Cabinet Room at the White House.

426 ¶ Citation Accompanying the Medal of Freedom Presented to Thomas S. Gates. *January* 18, 1961

[Text read by Brig. Gen. A. J. Goodpaster, Staff Secretary to the President]

CITATION TO ACCOMPANY THE AWARD OF

THE MEDAL OF FREEDOM

TO

THOMAS S. GATES

FOR EXCEPTIONALLY MERITORIOUS SERVICE

AND DISTINGUISHED CONTRIBUTION

TO THE SECURITY OF THE UNITED STATES

Through nearly seven years of service in the Department of Defense—as Under Secretary of the Navy, Secretary of the Navy, Deputy Secretary of Defense, and currently Secretary of Defense—Thomas Gates has worked with selfless dedication for the security of the United States and the Free World. He has brought experienced leadership, sound judgment, and unswerving loyalty and courage to the heavy responsibilities assigned to him.

Through his effective leadership in the direction of the United States military forces, and his statesmanship and diplomatic skill in numerous international conferences on security affairs, he has made outstanding contributions to the constant effort of our Nation to attain the goal of world peace with freedom and honor. It is with great pleasure that I award to him the Medal of Freedom.

DWIGHT D. EISENHOWER

NOTE: The presentation was made by the President at a ceremony held in the Cabinet Room at the White House.

427 ¶ Citation Accompanying the Medal of Freedom Presented to Gordon Gray. *January 18, 1961*

[Text read by Brig. Gen. A. J. Goodpaster, Staff Secretary to the President]

CITATION TO ACCOMPANY THE AWARD OF

THE MEDAL OF FREEDOM

TO

GORDON GRAY

FOR EXCEPTIONALLY MERITORIOUS SERVICE

AND DISTINGUISHED CONTRIBUTION

TO THE SECURITY OF THE UNITED STATES

Over a period of many years, Gordon Gray has given dedicated service to the cause of peace and security. An outstanding public servant, he has borne with distinction and devotion responsibilities as Assistant Secretary, Under Secretary and Secretary of the Army, Director of the Psychological Strategy Board, Assistant Secretary of Defense for International Security Affairs, Director of the Office of Defense Mobilization, and Special Assistant to the President for National Security Affairs. In all of these duties, he has shown wisdom, integrity and responsibility of the highest order. He has made a major contribution to the effective development and execution of policies for our national security and has served with statesmanship and understanding in international conferences on security affairs. With deep appreciation, I award him the Medal of Freedom.

DWIGHT D. EISENHOWER

NOTE: The presentation was made by the President at a ceremony held in the Cabinet Room at the White House.

428 ¶ Citation Accompanying the Medal of Freedom Presented to Christian A. Herter. *January* 18, 1961

[Text read by Brig. Gen. A. J. Goodpaster, Staff Secretary to the President]

CITATION TO ACCOMPANY THE AWARD OF

THE MEDAL OF FREEDOM

TO

CHRISTIAN A. HERTER

FOR EXCEPTIONALLY MERITORIOUS SERVICE

AND DISTINGUISHED CONTRIBUTION

TO THE SECURITY OF THE UNITED STATES

During a lifetime of dedicated service, Christian Herter has made a distinguished contribution to world peace and to the safety of his nation. Selfless patriot and distinguished gentleman, he has brought a clear and lucid mind, a sense of history, intense devotion and steadfast courage to the cause of justice and well-being for his fellow man. He has borne heavy responsibilities with sagacity, imagination and patience coupled with perseverance.

As Secretary of State during one of the most trying times of our history, Christian Herter has stood as a symbol of strength and inspiration to those who love freedom.

It is with great appreciation and gratitude for his services to his country that I award him the Medal of Freedom.

DWIGHT D. EISENHOWER

NOTE: The presentation was made by the President at a ceremony held in the Cabinet Room at the White House.

429 ¶ Citation Accompanying the Medal of Freedom Presented to George B. Kistiakowsky. *January 18, 1961*

[Text read by Brig. Gen. A. J. Goodpaster, Staff Secretary to the President]

CITATION TO ACCOMPANY THE AWARD OF

THE MEDAL OF FREEDOM

TO

GEORGE BOGDAN KISTIAKOWSKY

FOR EXCEPTIONALLY MERITORIOUS SERVICE

AND DISTINGUISHED CONTRIBUTION

TO THE SECURITY OF THE UNITED STATES

For more than two decades George Kistiakowsky has worked tirelessly for the advancement of science and for the development of military technology.

During World War II and in the years since, he has been a major contributor to the success of vital defense projects—a courageous spirit and guiding force in the forefront of development activities, giving generously of his time while continuing his important work as a distinguished scientist and teacher.   He has labored to promote the progress and understanding of science in the interests of mankind everywhere. Seeking safeguarded arms control in the interest of security and peace, he served at the international conference table on measures to prevent surprise attack.

As my Special Assistant for Science and Technology, he has combined scientific judgment and statesmanship, lending wise counsel, knowledge and experience to the framing of national policies that have served to keep our country strong and secure.   In recognition of his outstanding service and his abiding dedication to the national interest, I award him the Medal of Freedom.

DWIGHT D. EISENHOWER

NOTE: The presentation was made by the President at a ceremony held in the Cabinet Room at the White House.

430 ¶ Citation Accompanying the Medal of Freedom Presented to General Andrew J. Goodpaster. *January* 18, 1961

[Text read by Lt. Col. John D. S. Eisenhower, Assistant Staff Secretary]

CITATION TO ACCOMPANY THE AWARD OF
THE MEDAL OF FREEDOM
TO
BRIGADIER GENERAL ANDREW J. GOODPASTER, USA
FOR DISTINGUISHED SERVICE IN A POSITION OF
GRAVE RESPONSIBILITY

During the period 1954 to 1961, General Goodpaster has served in the position of Staff Secretary to the President of the United States, and as Liaison Officer of the Department of Defense to the White House. In these capacities he has been the President's operational assistant and has distinguished himself by his unparalleled devotion to duty, his courage and wisdom, and his remarkable ability as administrator and coordinator.

General Goodpaster's unique service throughout this period was in the finest military tradition and reflects the highest credit upon himself and upon the United States Army.

DWIGHT D. EISENHOWER

NOTE: The presentation was made by the President at a ceremony held in the Cabinet Room at the White House.

431 ¶ Statement by the President on Releasing a Report on Cuban Refugee Problems. *January* 18, 1961

I AM RELEASING herewith the final report on Cuban refugee problems by Tracy Voorhees who has been acting as my personal representative in this matter.

In appointing Mr. Voorhees for this task last November, and in giving him funds and added powers on December 2, I sought to express by effective action the interest which, as President of the United States, I felt in these troubled people, as well as my deep sympathy for them and desire to be of help to them.

This latest exodus of persons fleeing from Communist oppression is the first time in many years in which our nation has become the country of first asylum for any such number of refugees.   To grant such asylum is in accordance with the long standing traditions of the United States. Our people opened their homes and hearts to the Hungarian refugees four years ago.   I am sure we will do no less for these distressed Cubans.

I would like to pay public tribute to Mr. Voorhees for his willingness once again to give of his time and energy in the public interest.   Steps have been initiated to implement his additional recommendations including the assignment of State Department personnel evacuated from Cuba to the Refugee Center in Miami.

NOTE: The report (15 pp.) includes 10 recommendations concerning the Cuban refugee problem and a partial list of reports and surveys made at Mr. Voorhees' request.   It supplements an interim report of December 19 (10 pp.).   Both reports were printed by the Government Printing Office.

432   ¶ Statement by the President Upon Signing Proclamation Modifying Petroleum Import Control Program.   *January* 18, 1961

I AM TODAY further modifying Proclamation 3279, March 10, 1959, which established a mandatory oil import control program within the Department of the Interior.

The purpose of this amendment is to permit, effective April 1, 1961, the orderly entrance of new importers, who do not currently qualify as importers, into the residual fuel oil markets of the East Coast.   These new importers must be sellers in that area of residual fuel oil and will be granted residual fuel oil allocations on the basis of their deep-water terminal inputs of that fuel.   Furthermore, the amendment will also result in more equitable residual fuel oil import allocations to several established importers.

This change in the method of allocating residual fuel oil imports will be effective in District I, which includes the states of Maine, New Hampshire, Vermont, Massachusetts, Connecticut, Rhode Island, New York, New Jersey, Pennsylvania, Maryland, Delaware, West Virginia, Virginia, North Carolina, South Carolina, Georgia, Florida, and the

District of Columbia. Imports of residual fuel oil into other parts of the Nation are negligible, and current importing practices in those areas are not changed.

The Proclamation issued today also contains other technical amendatory language made necessary by adoption of the new method of issuing residual fuel oil allocations. These changes do not affect current procedures under which other portions of the mandatory oil import program are operated.

The Department of the Interior will shortly issue regulations implementing this proclamation, along the lines of the proposal published by that Department in the Federal Register on October 7, 1960.

NOTE: Proclamation 3389 modifying Proclamation 3279 is published in the Federal Register (26 F.R. 507, 811).

433 ¶ Letter to Arthur S. Flemming Concerning the President's Advisory Committee on Government Organization. *January* 18, 1961

[Released January 18, 1961. Dated January 17, 1961]

Dear Arthur:

Thank you for the summary of the work of the Advisory Committee on Government Organization.

The constructive advice of this Committee has played a large part in promoting economy and efficiency in the Executive Branch of the Government. I am especially pleased with the Committee's contribution to the reorganization of the Department of Defense and the creation of three major agencies of government—the Department of Health, Education, and Welfare, the Federal Aviation Agency, and the National Aeronautics and Space Administration.

I again wish to express my appreciation to you, as Chairman, and to your colleagues on the Committee.

With warm regard,

As ever,

DWIGHT D. EISENHOWER

NOTE: Mr. Flemming's letter of January 14 and his report summarizing the principal activities of the committee for the past 8 years were released with the President's reply.

434 ¶ Letter to Secretary Gates Concerning the Effect of the President's Directive on Balance of Payments. *January* 18, 1961

Dear Mr. Secretary:

I fully agree that the understandings and views outlined in your letter of January 18, 1961 with respect to the Directive of November 16, 1960 on the United States balance of payments should be placed on record.

Fundamentally, as you say, these measures were taken to improve our difficult balance of payments situation and to show our seriousness and our determination to meet this problem. It has been my constant hope that it would be possible eventually to relieve hardships occasioned by these actions, giving priority to those which involve family separation. I know that you have, for this purpose, been studying reductions in the length of overseas tours. Also, I have been in full agreement that, over any extended period of time, the treatment applied to Defense personnel must be as far as possible comparable to that applied throughout the rest of government. To this end all departments of the government are under instructions to continue to examine the size of their staffs abroad and the number of their dependents accompanying these staffs with the objective of making further reductions wherever possible.

As you know, my Directive has been viewed as one that should appropriately be under close and continued review, and at my direction specific follow-up procedures are in effect. Among the matters requiring continued attention are the further development of our balance of payments situation in light of actions taken, any possibility of making some reduction of our forces deployed overseas (thus reducing separations from dependents) and any evidence of undue adverse effect on our military forces.

In light of the above, I approve your recommendation to acquaint your successor with your letter of January 18, 1961 and this reply.

Sincerely,

DWIGHT D. EISENHOWER

NOTE: Secretary Gates, in his letter released with the President's reply, noted that the Defense Department had initiated action on all of the points specified in the President's Directive of November 16, 1960 (25 F.R. 12221). With respect to dependents, he stated that the Department had recognized from the outset that it would be desirable to alleviate the problem of separation of families as soon as practicable. He further stated that the adverse impact of the separation of families was substantial and, in his opinion, relief should be sought as soon as feasible. He noted that this impact had been heightened by the fact that other agencies were not planning to reduce the number of their dependents significantly.

435   ¶ Letter to the Director, Bureau of the Budget, Upon Receiving Reports on Government Operations.   *January* 19, 1961

Dear Maury:

I have the seven reports which you transmitted to me recently:

Federal Fiscal Behavior During the Recession of 1957–58
User Charges
Ten-Year Projection of Federal Budget Expenditures
Program for Disposal of Surplus Federal Real Property
Government Competition with Business
Management Improvement in the Executive Branch
Progress in Improving Budget Practice 1953 to 1961

These are excellent reports, individually and collectively. They not only reflect significant progress in improving Government operations, but in addition they suggest further courses of action for the consideration of our successors, who will have the responsibility for seeking efficiency, economy, and sound measures of budgetary and fiscal management.

I am glad to leave these valuable reports as part of my legacy to the next administration and to the Nation.

Sincerely,

DWIGHT D. EISENHOWER

NOTE: The reports were made available by the Bureau of the Budget.

436 ¶ Memorandum Concerning the Trans-Pacific Route Case.   *January* 19, 1961

[Released January 19, 1961. Dated January 18, 1961]

Memorandum for the Chairman, Civil Aeronautics Board:

After considerable deliberation I have concluded that the recommendations of the Civil Aeronautics Board in the *Trans-Pacific Route Case, Docket 7723 et al.,* should, with minor exceptions set forth at the end of this memorandum, be disapproved.

When I requested in February 1959 that this proceeding be undertaken by the Board, I sincerely hoped that it would be possible at the conclusion of the case to provide greater competition among United States flag carriers in the Pacific.

The study made by the Board is excellent. Much evidence is set forth in support of the Board's recommendations for additional United States flag service on major routes to the Orient. My decision not to approve the Board's principal recommendations is predicated solely on considerations of foreign policy, a responsibility that is mine and which the Board, of course, does not share.

My review of the record in this case persuades me that our foreign relations would be adversely affected were we at this time to add second carriers on our major routes to the Orient. Duplication of service on major routes presently served by a single carrier means inevitably—as history shows—that greater United States flag capacity would be offered. This result is made all the more certain by the advent in recent months of jet service which in and of itself means greater capacity because much larger and much faster aircraft are involved.

Greatly increased capacity—always of considerable concern to other nations engaged in international commercial aviation—should not in my judgment be approved unless traffic forecasts for the routes in question plainly show that the additional capacity can be absorbed without engendering a legitimate fear abroad that United States flag carriers will collect so much of the traffic as to make service on the route by a foreign carrier economically untenable or marginal at best. The evidence in the case at hand, including particularly the traffic forecasts does not establish the circumstances I have described. It is reasonable, therefore, to predict that approval of the Board's major recommendations in this case would unsettle our international relations—particularly with Japan which would be faced with an additional United States carrier on all but one of the now existing four routes from the United States to Tokyo.

For these reasons I have concluded that the Board's major recommendations should be disapproved, but I recommend to the Board that within the next several years it update the evidence in this case and again consider the addition of second United States flag carriers on major routes to the Orient.

The Board in the Mainland-Hawaii part of this case has concluded that another airline—until now a carrier engaged solely in service on the North American continent—should be authorized to provide service between San Francisco and Los Angeles and Honolulu. Due to the advent of Hawaii as a State, the President, under the law, no longer has jurisdiction over service between the Mainland and Hawaii. It would be my hope, however, that the Board would reconsider its decision to authorize additional service between the Mainland and Hawaii by a carrier which heretofore has not been engaged in service over the Pacific. At some future time it may be deemed advisable from every standpoint to add a second United States carrier on the California-Hawaii-Tokyo route. The carrier selected—which would presumably be a carrier customarily engaged in international commercial aviation in the Pacific—should also be authorized to carry local traffic between the Mainland and Hawaii. To do otherwise would be to handicap such a second carrier in terms of its ability to compete with the carrier now serving this route to the Orient, a carrier which already has full traffic rights between the Mainland and Hawaii and which is thus able materially to support its overall route to the Orient.

Those of the Board's recommendations that I do approve are (a) the renewal for an indefinite period of Northwest Airlines' authority to serve Okinawa, Korea, Taiwan, Hong Kong, and the Philippines; (b) the renewal for an indefinite period of Pan American World Airways' authority to serve Japan, Viet Nam, Singapore, Sumatra, Java, Federation of Malaya, Thailand, Burma, and points within India and Pakistan lying north of the twentieth parallel; (c) the amendment of Pan American's certificate to redesignate Australia as an intermediate point and adding Java as a new intermediate point on its South Pacific route; (d) the renewal and amendment of South Pacific Airlines' certificate as recommended by the Board; (e) the amendment of Trans World Airlines' certificate as recommended by the Board; (f) the Board's denial of applications.

DWIGHT D. EISENHOWER

Appendix A—White House Press Releases, 1960-61

NOTE: Includes releases covering matters with which the President was closely concerned, except announcements of Presidential personnel appointments and approvals of legislation with which there was no accompanying statement.

Releases relating to Proclamations and Executive Orders have not been included. These documents are separately listed in Appendix B.

For list of Press and Radio Conferences, see subject index under "News Conferences."

January	Subject
1	Letter to the Attorney General on receiving his report on deceptive practices in broadcasting media
2	White House announcement of the President's forthcoming meeting with the Special Committee on Civil Defense of the Governors' Conference
4	Exchange of New Year greetings between the United States and the Soviet Union
6	White House announcement of the President's forthcoming trip to South America
6	White House announcement of the forthcoming visit of President de Gaulle of France
7	Statement by the President on the death of Representative Simpson of Pennsylvania
7	Annual message to the Congress on the State of the Union
8	Letter to Senator Cooper on Federal programs and activities in aid of chronic labor surplus areas
12	Special message to the Congress on removal of the interest rate ceiling on Government bonds
13	Letter to Gordon Gray designating him chairman of the Operations Coordinating Board
13	Letter to Karl G. Harr, Jr., concerning his duties with the Operations Coordinating Board
14	Special message to the Congress on transfers from the Department of Defense to the National Aeronautics and Space Administration
14	Special message to the Congress recommending amendments to the National Aeronautics and Space Act

January	Subject
14	Letter to T. Keith Glennan, Administrator, National Aeronautics and Space Administration, on high thrust space vehicles
17	White House announcement of the date of the President's forthcoming visit to the Soviet Union
18	Annual Budget Message to the Congress: Fiscal Year 1961
19	Toasts of the President and Prime Minister Kishi of Japan
19	Remarks at the signing of the Treaty of Mutual Cooperation and Security between Japan and the United States
19	White House announcement of the presentation to Prime Minister Kishi of a medal commemorating the arrival of the first Japanese Diplomatic Mission in April 1860
19	Joint statement following discussions with Prime Minister Kishi of Japan
20	White House announcement concerning the President's forthcoming visit to Japan
20	Annual message presenting the economic report to the Congress
20	Remarks to participants in the Young Republican National Leadership Training School
21	White House statement following receipt of report by the President's Committee for Traffic Safety
21	White House release of summary report of the President's Committee for Traffic Safety
25	Remarks at the annual midwinter meeting of the National Association of Real Estate Boards
25	White House statement following meeting with Governor Rockefeller to discuss transferring the tax on local telephone service to the States

Appendix A

Appendix A

Appendix A

Appendix A

April   *Subject*

28 Joint statement following discussions with King Mahendra

May

2 Remarks at the annual meeting of the U.S. Chamber of Commerce

2 Address at a dinner sponsored by the Committee for International Economic Growth and the Committee to Strengthen the Frontiers of Freedom

3 Special message to the Congress on the legislative program

3 Statement by the President on the occasion of the centennial of the first Japanese diplomatic mission to the United States

3 Remarks at Fort Benning, Ga., after watching a demonstration of new army equipment

4 Statement by the President upon signing "Food for Peace" agreement between the United States and India

4 White House statement concerning the agricultural commodities agreement between the United States and India

4 White House announcement concerning sewage disposal at Dulles International Airport

6 Statement by the President upon signing the Civil Rights Act of 1960

6 Exchange of messages between the President and Queen Juliana upon completion of the monument presented by the people of the Netherlands

6 Remarks at the opening of the 1960 AFL–CIO union-industries show

7 Statement by the President announcing the forthcoming visit of the Crown Prince and Princess of Japan

7 Statement concerning the President's approval of an expanded seismic research and development program

9 White House announcement of the forthcoming visit of Prime Minister Diefenbaker of Canada

9 Letter to Syngman Rhee upon his withdrawal from political life in Korea

10 Citation accompanying award of Legion of Merit to Captain Edward L. Beach, USN

May   *Subject*

11 Statement by the President concerning the U–2 incident

12 Statement by the President on the the death of John D. Rockefeller, Jr.

12 Remarks to the members of the American Helicopter Society

13 Veto of the area redevelopment bill

14 White House statement making public the report of the panel on food additives

15 Remarks upon arrival at Orly Airport in Paris

16 White House statement on report of Board of Visitors to the U.S. Air Force Academy

16 Statement by the President upon signing the Mutual Security Act

16 Message to the Congress transmitting the Civil Service Commission's first report under the Government Employees Training Act

16 Veto of a bill relating to the income tax treatment of non-refundable capital contributions to Federal National Mortgage Association

16 Veto of bill for relief of Universal Trades, Inc.

16 Special message to the Congress concerning the proposed Freedom Monument

16 Memorandum to Federal agencies on the United Givers Fund campaign in the National Capital Area

16 Letter accepting resignation of John H. Williams, member, Atomic Energy Commission

16 Letter accepting resignation of John F. Floberg, member, Atomic Energy Commission

16 Statement by the President concerning the position taken by Chairman Khrushchev at the opening of the summit conference

17 White House announcement of members of U.S. delegation to attend ceremonies in connection with the 150th anniversary of the independence of Argentina

17 Statement approving recommendations contained in memorandum "Radiation protection guidance for Federal agencies"

| *May* | *Subject* | *June* | *Subject* |

June	*Subject*
15	Remarks to the staff of the U.S. Embassy and the American Community in Manila
15	Toast by the President at a dinner given in his honor by President Garcia
16	Remarks at the University of the Philippines upon receiving an honorary degree
16	Remarks at a luncheon given by the Chamber of Commerce in Manila
16	White House announcement of delegations to ceremonies marking the independence of the Congo Republic and of Somalia, and the inauguration of the Republic of Ghana
16	Remarks at a civic reception at the Luneta in Manila
16	Joint statement following discussions with President Garcia
16	Statement by the Press Secretary on the postponement of the President's visit to Japan
16	Remarks in Manila before leaving for Taipei
18	Remarks to the officers and men of the 7th Fleet
18	Remarks upon arrival at the Sungshan Airport, Taipei
18	Address at a mass rally in Taipei
18	Toast by the President at a dinner given in his honor by President Chiang Kai-shek
19	Joint statement following discussions with President Chiang Kai-shek
19	Remarks at the Sungshan Airport, Taipei, upon leaving for Okinawa
19	Remarks upon arrival at Kadena Air Force Base, Okinawa
19	Remarks upon arrival at Kimpo International Airport in Seoul
20	Remarks to the American Community in Seoul
20	Toast by the President at a luncheon given in his honor by Prime Minister Huh Chung of Korea
20	Address before the National Assembly of Korea
20	Remarks at the headquarters of the Korean Army's Sixth Corps
20	Joint statement following discussions with Prime Minister Huh Chung
20	Remarks in Seoul upon leaving for Honolulu

June	*Subject*
20	Remarks upon arrival at the Honolulu International Airport
25	Remarks at Hickam Air Force Base, Honolulu, upon leaving for Washington
26	Message to President Tsiranana on the occasion of the independence of the Malagasy Republic
27	Remarks recorded for the Governors conference at Glacier National Park, Mont.
27	Radio and television report to the American people on the trip to the Far East
28	Letter accepting resignation of Maj. Gen. J. Stewart Bragdon, Special Assistant to the President for Public Works Planning
28	Memorandum to Federal agencies on the United Fund and Community Chest campaigns
28	Remarks of welcome to the King and Queen of Thailand at the Washington National Airport
28	Citation accompanying Legion of Merit, Degree of Chief Commander, presented to the King of Thailand
28	Toasts of the President and the King of Thailand
29	Letter to the President of the American Red Cross on the Nation's voluntary disaster relief in Chile
29	Remarks at the AFL–CIO testimonial dinner in honor of Secretary of Labor Mitchell
30	Message to President Kasavubu on the occasion of the independence of the Republic of the Congo
30	Veto of a bill to increase the salaries of Federal employees

July	
1	Joint statement following discussions with the King of Thailand
1	Letter accepting resignation of Julian F. Harrington, Ambassador to Panama
1	Letter accepting resignation of Gerald A. Drew, Ambassador to Haiti
1	Statement by the Press Secretary on congressional action overriding the veto of the Federal employees pay raise bill

July	Subject
1	Message to President Osman on the occasion of the independence of the Somali Republic
1	Message to President Nkrumah on the occasion of the accession of Ghana to the status of Republic
1	Statement by the President on the United Nations Freedom-from-Hunger campaign
6	White House statement concerning tariff on clinical thermometers
6	Statement by the President upon signing bill and proclamation relating to the Cuban sugar quota
7	Memorandum of disapproval of bill for relief of Juan D. Quintos and others
7	Memorandum of disapproval of bill for relief of Sam J. Buzzanca
7	Memorandum of disapproval of bill to provide for the economic regulation of the Alaska Railroad under the Interstate Commerce Act
8	Statement by the Press Secretary concerning a plan for more effective U.S. participation in raising standards in the Americas
9	Letter accepting resignation of Andrew D. Orrick, member, Securities and Exchange Commission
9	Statement by the President concerning Premier Khrushchev's announcement of support for the Castro regime in Cuba
11	Statement by the President pledging U.S. cooperation to strengthen the framework of freedom through social and economic progress in the Americas
12	Statement by the Press Secretary on the downing of an RB–47 plane by the U.S.S.R.
12	Statement by the President upon signing the Independent Offices Appropriation Act
12	Memorandum of disapproval of bill concerning wage rates at the Portsmouth Naval Shipyard
13	Statement by the President on the downing of an RB–47 plane by the U.S.S.R.
13	Telegram to Senator Mansfield welcoming a Security Council discussion of the RB–47 plane incident

July	Subject
14	Statement by the Press Secretary on the U.S. response to the U.N. appeal for emergency food supplies for Leopoldville
14	Statement by the President upon signing bill providing for the admission of refugees
14	Memorandum of disapproval of bill for the relief of Margaret P. Copin
14	Memorandum of disapproval of bill relating to payments to Bernalillo County, N. Mex., for care of Indians
16	Message to the Congress transmitting the fourth annual report on the operation of the Trade Agreements Program
18	Telegrams to Senators Kennedy and Johnson offering them briefings by the Central Intelligence Agency
18	Letter to the President from Senator Kennedy accepting his offer of briefings on foreign affairs
20	White House announcement of forthcoming visit of Prime Minister Rahman of Malaya
20	Statement by the President on the budget surplus for fiscal year 1960
21	Letter accepting resignation of Dallas S. Townsend, Assistant Attorney General
21	Letter accepting resignation of Mason Sears, U.S. Representative on U.N. Trusteeship Council
21	Statement by the President on the need for an early meeting of the Disarmament Commission of the United Nations
22	Remarks at the dedication of Eisenhower Park, Newport, R.I.
22	Letter to Henry M. Wriston on the progress made by the Commission on National Goals
22	Letter to Lynn U. Stambaugh at the close of his term of service as first vice president of the Export-Import Bank of Washington
22	Letter to Frederick M. Eaton following the closing of the Ten-Nation Committee on Disarmament
24	Statement by the President making public an interim report on the Food-for-Peace program

July	Subject
25	Letter to the Administrator of General Services concerning the design of proposed buildings on Lafayette Square
25	Statement by the President following the firing of the Polaris missile by the submarine Patrick Henry
26	Address at the Republican National Convention in Chicago
27	Remarks at the Republican National Committee Breakfast, Chicago, Ill.
28	Statement by the President concerning a program for the development of Peru
29	White House statement concerning the appointment of Roy R. Rubottom as Ambassador to Argentina and Thomas C. Mann as Assistant Secretary of State for Inter-American Affairs
31	Exchange of messages between the President and President Nkrumah on the airlift of Ghanaian forces to the Congo

August	
1	Message to Prime Minister Maga on the occasion of the independence of the Republic of Dahomey
2	Message to the students of Korea
3	Message to Prime Minister Diori on the occasion of the independence of the Republic of Niger
4	Exchange of messages between the President and Prime Minister Ikeda of Japan
5	Message to Prime Minister Yameogo on the occasion of the independence of the Republic of Upper Volta
7	Message to Prime Minister Houphouet-Boigny on the occasion of the independence of the Republic of the Ivory Coast
8	Special message to the Congress upon its reconvening
9	White House statement on report of Board of Visitors to the U.S. Military Academy
9	Memorandum from the Director, Bureau of the Budget, submitting report on congressional actions affecting the budget recommendations for fiscal year 1961

August	Subject
10	Statement by the President on the Security Council resolution on the Congo
10	Message to the Congress transmitting the 12th semiannual report under Public Law 480 (83d Cong.)
11	Message to Prime Minister Tombalbaye on the occasion of the independence of the Republic of Chad
12	Message recorded for transmission via communication satellite Echo I
13	Message to Prime Minister Dacko on the occasion of the independence of the Central African Republic
15	Message to President Youlou on the occasion of the independence of the Republic of Congo
15	Remarks upon inspection of the capsule retrieved from the satellite Discoverer XIII
16	Message to President Makarios on the occasion of independence of the Republic of Cyprus
17	Message to President M'ba on the occasion of the independence of the Republic of Gabon
17	Statement by the President on U.S. achievements in space
19	Letter accepting resignation of Henry Cabot Lodge as U.S. Representative to the United Nations
19	Statement by the Press Secretary concerning the sentence imposed on U-2 pilot Powers by the Soviet court
20	Letter accepting resignation of William J. Hallahan, member, Federal Home Loan Bank Board
20	Letter accepting resignation of Clyde A. Wheeler, Jr., Staff Assistant to the President
23	Special message to the Congress on the sugar quota of the Dominican Republic
23	White House statement on the Tariff Commission report on cotton imports
23	White House statement on the tariff on linen toweling and watch movements imports
23	Letter accepting resignation of Ervin L. Petersen, Assistant Secretary of Agriculture

Appendix A

Appendix A

Appendix A

Appendix A

Appendix A

Appendix A

January   Subject

19 Letter accepting resignation of Franklin B. Lincoln, Jr., Assistant Secretary of Defense (Comptroller)

19 Letter accepting resignation of Robert A. Forsythe, Assistant Secretary, Department of Health, Education, and Welfare

19 Letter accepting resignation of Elmer F. Bennett, Under Secretary of the Interior

19 Letter accepting resignation of David A. Lindsay, General Counsel of the Treasury

20 Letter to the Chairman, Tariff Commission, regarding cotton imports

20 Letter accepting resignation of Dudley C. Sharp, Secretary of the Air Force

20 Letter accepting resignation of Wilber M. Brucker, Secretary of the Army

January   Subject

20 Letter accepting resignation of John A. Roosevelt, member, President's Committee on Government Contracts

20 Letter accepting resignation of John J. Gilhooley, Assistant Secretary of Labor for Labor-Management Relations

20 Letter to Dr. Leroy E. Burney regarding his retirement as Surgeon General

20 Letter accepting resignation of Rowland Jones, Jr., member, Advisory Board, Post Office Department

20 Letter accepting resignation of Herbert B. Warburton, General Counsel, Post Office Department

20 Letter accepting resignation of Ivy Baker Priest, Treasurer of the United States

Appendix B—Presidential Documents Published in the Federal Register, 1960-61

PROCLAMATIONS

EXECUTIVE ORDERS

Appendix B

Appendix B

Appendix B

Appendix C—Presidential Reports to the Congress, 1960–61

Subject	Published	Sent to the Congress, 1960	Date of White House release
Mutual Security Program	H. Doc. 299	Jan. 14	. . . .
	H. Doc. 373	May 2	. . . .
Housing and Home Finance Agency:			
Twelfth Annual	. . . . .	Jan. 14	. . . .
Thirteenth Annual	. . . . .	Aug. 23	. . . .
Corregidor Bataan Memorial Commission . .	H. Doc. 298	Jan. 14	. . . .
National Science Foundation	H. Doc. 300	Jan. 18	. . . .
Economic Report of the President	H. Doc. 268	Jan. 20	Jan. 20
Public Law 480 (83rd Congress):			
Eleventh Semiannual	H. Doc. 335	Feb. 11	Feb. 11
Twelfth Semiannual	H. Doc. 449	Aug. 10 (S)	Aug. 10
		Aug. 16 (H)	. . . .
Commodity Credit Corporation	. . . . .	Feb. 15	. . . .
Middle East:			
Fourth Annual	H. Doc. 342	Feb. 15	. . . .
Fifth Annual	H. Doc. 448	Aug. 16	. . . .
Health Research Facilities Program	H. Doc. 344	Feb. 17	. . . .
National Aeronautics and Space Administration:			
Second Annual	H. Doc. 349	Feb. 24 (S)	. . . .
		Feb. 25 (H)	. . . .
Second Semiannual	H. Doc. 361	Mar. 18	. . . .
Third Semiannual	H. Doc. 454	Aug. 30	. . . .
Civil Service Commission	H. Doc. 253	Mar. 10	. . . .
Civil Service Commission Report on Government Employees Training	. . . . .	May 16	. . . .
Railroad Retirement Board	H. Doc. 267	Mar. 10	. . . .
Semiannual Report of the Secretary of the Interior on Mineral Reserves	. . . . .	Mar. 21	. . . .
Saint Lawrence Seaway Development Corporation	H. Doc. 376	Apr. 11	. . . .
Commission on International Rules of Judicial Procedure	. . . . .	May 9	. . . .
National Monument Commission	. . . . .	May 16	. . . .
National Capital Housing Authority	. . . . .	May 16	. . . .
International Cultural Exchange and Trade Fair Participation Act	. . . . .	June 2	. . . .
Weather Modification	H. Doc. 438	June 28	. . . .

Appendix C

Subject	Published	Sent to the Congress, 1960	Date of White House release
Lend-Lease Operations	H. Doc. 429	Aug. 1 (Secy. of Senate)	. . . .
		Aug. 1 (Clerk of House)	. . . .
Office of Alien Property	. . . . . .	Aug. 16	. . . .
U.S. Participation in the United Nations for the year 1959	H. Doc. 378	Aug. 16	. . . .
Trade Argeements Program	H. Doc. 447	Aug. 16	. . . .

1961

Subject	Published	Sent to the Congress	Date of White House release
International Cultural Exchange and Trade Fair Participation Act	. . . . . .	Jan. 10 (S)	. . . .
		Jan. 12 (H)	. . . .
Corregidor Bataan Memorial Commission . .	H. Doc. 48	Jan. 10 (S)	. . . .
		Jan. 12 (H)	. . . .
Semiannual Report of the Secretary of the Interior on Mineral Reserves	. . . . . .	Jan. 10 (S)	. . . .
		Jan. 12 (H)	. . . .
Eighteenth Decennial Census of the Population	H. Doc. 46	Jan. 10 (S)	. . . .
		Jan. 12 (H)	. . . .
United States Participation in the International Atomic Energy Agency	H. Doc. 45	Jan. 10 (S)	. . . .
		Jan. 12 (H)	. . . .
Civil Service Commission	H. Doc. 13	Jan. 10 (S)	. . . .
		Jan. 12 (H)	. . . .
Expenditures and allocations to States for Disaster Relief	H. Doc. 47	Jan. 10 (S)	. . . .
		Jan. 12 (H)	. . . .
Mutual Security Program	H. Doc. 50	Jan. 17 (S)	. . . .
		Jan. 18 (H)	. . . .
National Science Foundation	H. Doc. 57	Jan. 17 (S)	. . . .
		Jan. 18 (H)	. . . .
Economic Report of the President	. . . . . .	Jan. 18 (H)	. . . .
		Jan. 20 (S)	. . . .
National Aeronautics and Space Administration: Third Annual	H. Doc. 56	Jan. 18 (H)	. . . .
		Jan. 20 (S)	. . . .
Fourth Semiannual	H. Doc. 58	Jan. 18 (H)	. . . .
		Jan. 20 (S)	. . . .

Appendix D—Rules Governing This Publication

[Reprinted from the Federal Register, vol. 24, p. 2354, dated March 26, 1959]

TITLE 1—GENERAL PROVISIONS

Chapter I—Administrative Committee of the Federal Register

PART 32—PUBLIC PAPERS OF THE PRESIDENTS OF THE UNITED STATES

PUBLICATIONS AND FORMAT

Sec.
32.1 Publication required.
32.2 Coverage of prior years.
32.3 Format, indexes, ancillaries.

SCOPE

32.10 Basic criteria.
32.11 Sources.

FREE DISTRIBUTION

32.15 Members of Congress.
32.16 The Supreme Court.
32.17 Executive agencies.

PAID DISTRIBUTION

32.20 Agency requisitions.
32.21 Extra copies.
32.22 Sale to public.

AUTHORITY: §§ 32.1 to 32.22 issued under sec. 6, 49 Stat. 501, as amended; 44 U.S.C. 306.

PUBLICATION AND FORMAT

§ 32.1 *Publication required.* There shall be published forthwith at the end of each calendar year, beginning with the year 1957, a special edition of the FEDERAL REGISTER designated "Public Papers of the Presidents of the United States." Each volume shall cover one calendar year and shall be identified further by the name of the President and the year covered.

§ 32.2 *Coverage of prior years.* After conferring with the National Historical Publications Commission with respect to the need therefor, the Administrative Committee may from time to time authorize the publication of similar volumes covering specified calendar years prior to 1957.

§ 32.3 *Format, indexes, ancillaries.* Each annual volume, divided into books whenever appropriate, shall be separately published in the binding and style deemed by the Administrative Committee to be suitable to the dignity of the office of President of the United States. Each volume shall be appropriately indexed and shall contain appropriate ancillary information respecting significant Presidential documents not published in full text.

SCOPE

§ 32.10 *Basic criteria.* The basic text of the volumes shall consist of oral utterances by the President or of writings subscribed by him. All materials selected for inclusion under these criteria must also be in the public domain by virtue of White House press release or otherwise.

§ 32.11 *Sources.* (a) The basic text of the volumes shall be selected from the official text of: (1) Communications to the Congress, (2) public addresses, (3) transcripts of press conferences, (4) public letters, (5) messages to heads of state, (6) statements released on miscellaneous subjects, and (7) formal executive documents promulgated in accordance with law.

(b) Ancillary text, notes, and tables shall be derived from official sources only.

FREE DISTRIBUTION

§ 32.15 *Members of Congress.* Each Member of Congress, during his term of office, shall be entitled to one copy of each annual volume published during such term: *Provided,* That authorization for furnishing such copies shall be submitted in writing to the Director and signed by the authorizing Member. [As amended effective Dec. 30, 1960, 25 F.R. 14009]

§ 32.16 *The Supreme Court.* The Supreme Court of the United States shall be entitled to twelve copies of the annual volumes.

§ 32.17 *Executive agencies.* The head of each department and the head of each independent agency in the executive branch of the Government shall be entitled to one copy of each annual volume upon application therefor in writing to the Director.

PAID DISTRIBUTION

§ 32.20 *Agency requisitions.* Each Federal agency shall be entitled to obtain at cost copies of the annual volumes for official use upon the timely submission to the Government Printing Office of a printing and binding requisition (Standard Form No. 1).

§ 32.21 *Extra copies.* All requests for extra copies of the annual volumes shall be addressed to the Superintendent of Documents, Government Printing Office, Washington 25, D.C. Extra copies shall be paid for by the agency or official requesting them.

§ 32.22 *Sale to public.* The annual volumes shall be placed on sale to the public by the Superintendent of Documents at prices determined by him under the general direction of the Administrative Committee.

*   *   *   *   *

ADMINISTRATIVE COMMITTEE OF
THE FEDERAL REGISTER,
WAYNE C. GROVER,
*Archivist of the United States,
Chairman.*

RAYMOND BLATTENBERGER,
*The Public Printer,
Member.*

WILLIAM O. BURTNER,
*Representative of the Attorney
General, Member.*

Approved March 20, 1959.

WILLIAM P. ROGERS,
Attorney General.
FRANKLIN FLOETE,
Administrator of General Services.

[F.R. Doc. 59–2517; Filed, Mar. 25, 1959; 8:45 a.m.]

INDEX

[References are to items except as otherwise indicated]

Index

Index

[References are to items except as otherwise indicated]

Index

[References are to items except as otherwise indicated]

Index

Index

Index

[References are to items except as otherwise indicated]

Index

[References are to items except as otherwise indicated]

Index

Index

Index

[References are to items except as otherwise indicated]

Index

Index

Index

Index

Index

Index

[References are to items except as otherwise indicated]

Index

Index

Hospitals and medical care facilities—
Continued
Veterans, 13 (pp. 97, 100), 414 (pp. 1015, 1016)
See also Medical care
Hound Dog missile. *See* Missiles
Houphouet-Boigny, Felix, message, 254
Housing, 341, 410
Budget messages, 13 (pp. 65, 71–75), 414 (pp. 957, 978–983, 1014)
Tables, 13 (p. 67), 414 (p. 971)
College, 13 (p. 75), 414 (pp. 982, 983)
Military personnel, 414 (p. 957)
News conference remarks, 143, 256, 263
Older persons, 410
Public, 13 (pp. 72, 73), 414 (p. 980)
Veterans, 13 (p. 74), 414 (pp. 981, 982, 1014)
Housing bill, 143
Housing and Home Finance Agency, 5, 358
Budget messages, 13 (p. 72), 414 (p. 979)
Public facility loans, 13 (p. 72), 146
Houston, Samuel, 336
Houston, Tex.
Address at Rice University, 336
Mayor Lewis Cutrer, 336 n.
Howard University
Budget message, 414 (p. 1009)
Choir, 23
Howe, Walter, 69 n., 72 n., 75 n.
Huh Chung, 198, 202, 204
Joint statement with, 203
Toast to, 200
Huh Chung, Madame, 198 n.
Humphrey, George M., 350, 351
Humphrey, Sen. Hubert H., 93, 330
Hungary
Refugees from, 410, 431
Soviet repression, 410
Huntsville, Ala.
George C. Marshall Space Flight Center, dedication, remarks, 287
Mayor R. B. Searcy, 287
Hussein I, message, 277

Hydroelectric power projects, 402, 410
Hydrogen bomb
Soviet possession of, 422
See also Nuclear weapons; Nuclear weapons tests

ICA. *See* International Cooperation Administration
ICBM (intercontinental ballistic missile). *See* Missiles
Idaho, Gov. Robert Smylie, letter, 115
Ikeda, Hayato
Election as Prime Minister, message, 252
Letter, 294
Messages, 252, 366
Iliff, W. A. B., 284, 297
Illinois
Candidates for public office, 246
Chicago, 23 n., 245, 246, 310, 320 n.
Dirksen, Sen. Everett McK., 132, 143, 263, 271, 272
Stratton, Gov. William G., 246
Immigration, 410
Admission of refugees, 96, 133
Approval of bill, 233
Budget messages, 13 (p. 105), 414 (p. 1022)
Immigration laws, revision proposed, 96, 133, 255
Message to Congress, 96
Quotas, 310
Immigration and Naturalization Service, 310
Imports, 132
Coffee, 54
Country of origin of repackaged articles and containers, marking of, disapproval, 285
Lead and zinc, 280
Petroleum, 383, 432
Sugar quotas
Cuba, 21, 38, 93, 167 n., 222, 223, 267, 374
Dominican Republic, 267, 374, 418
Letter to Senator Bennett, 167
Philippines, 106

1124

Index

Index

Index

Index

Justice, Department of—Continued
Civil Rights Division, 410, 411
Eligibility of President for office of Vice President, report, 21
Record of accomplishment, report, 411
Juvenile delinquency, 100

Kaiser, William J., relief of, veto, 113
Kansas
Abilene, 45, 290
Eisenhower Library, 21, 118
Docking, Gov. George, 118 n.
Eisenhower Presidential Library Commission, 118
Governor's National Committee for the Eisenhower Presidential Library, 118 n.
Karachi, Pakistan, 297
Karasik, Daniel, 228, 362
Kasavubu, Joseph, 364
Message, 216
Kashmir dispute between India and Pakistan, 284
Kastenmeier, Repr. Robert W., 7
Kearsarge, U.S.S., 97
Keating, Sen. Kenneth B., 173
Kee Young Chang, 198 n.
Kelly, John B., 103
Kenesaw Mountain, battle, 370
Kennedy, Sen. John F.
Candidacy for President, 93, 263
Briefings by CIA, telegram, 236
Election victory, telegram, 356
Television debates, 268
News conference remarks on, 93, 263, 268, 284, 422
President-elect, 356, 422
Joint statement with, 369
Kennedy, Stephen P., 314
Kent, Carleton, 24, 103, 127, 256, 268
Kentucky
Cooper, Sen. John Sherman, 5, 176
Depressed areas, 176 n.
Morton, Sen. Thruston B., 23, 245 n., 309 n., 395
Kenworthy, E. W., 103, 127, 263, 268
Kerr, Clark, 30 n.

Kestnbaum, Meyer, 208
Death of, statement, 372
Khrushchev, Nikita S., 21 ftn. (p. 131), 36, 147, 173, 231 n., 328
Announcement of support for Castro regime in Cuba, statement, 227
Disarmament proposal, 93
Meeting with President, proposed, letter on, 313
Messages, 2, 97
News conference remarks on, 7, 24, 34, 38, 93, 127, 143, 222, 228, 256, 268, 284, 422
Position taken at summit conference, 154, 155, 163, 313
U.N. General Assembly meeting, 256, 284
Visit to U.S. (1959), 38
Killian, James, 30 n.
Kim, Daeyung, 250 n.
King, Dr. Charles Glen, 279
Kishi, Nobusuke, 15, 140, 209
Exchange of toasts, 14
Joint statement with, 16
Kistiakowsky, George B., 143, 363 n.
Medal of Freedom, citation, 429
Resignation, letter, 400
Knighton, William H., Jr., 7, 21, 24, 93, 268, 284, 422
Kootenai River, Libby Dam, 419
Budget message, 414 (p. 994)
Korea, 23, 133, 245, 302
Armed forces, 202
Assistance, 36, 203
Campaign remarks, 348, 351, 352
Chang Myon, message, 274
Economy, 203
Election, 93, 127
Huh Chung, 198, 200, 202, 204
Joint statement with, 203
Membership in United Nations, question of, 203
Mutual Defense Treaty, 201
News conference remarks, 93, 127, 143
Po Sun Yun, message, 273
Political changes, 127
Relations with U.S., 201, 203

Index

[References are to items except as otherwise indicated]

Index

Index

Index

Index

[References are to items except as otherwise indicated]

Index

Index

[References are to items except as otherwise indicated]

Index

Index

Index

[References are to items except as otherwise indicated]

Presidential documents published in Federal Register (1960), Appendix B, p. 1086

Presidential nomination, Democratic, 93

Presidential nomination, Republican, comments on, 7, 24, 93, 103

Presidential Railroad Commission, 343 n.
Appointment of members, statement, 378

Presidential reports to Congress
List, Appendix C, p. 1091
See also Congress, reports to, messages transmitting

President's Advisory Commission on Presidential Office Space, 414 (p. 1017)

President's Advisory Committee on Government Organization, 349
Report, letter, 433

President's Award for Distinguished Federal Civilian Service, 68, 389

President's Committee on Employment of the Physically Handicapped, 417

President's Committee on Government Contracts, 410
Budget message, 414 (p. 1023)
Report, statement, 407

President's Committee on Government Employment Policy, 410
Report, 217 ftn. (p. 545), 394

President's Committee on Information Activities Abroad, 332 ftn. (p. 789)

President's Committee to Study the U.S. Military Assistance Program, 36
Budget messages, 13 (p. 57), 414 (p. 962)

President's Conference on Administrative Procedure, letter to Chairman, 275

President's papers, 21
Offer as gift to U.S., 118

President's Science Advisory Committee, 143, 400
Report, statement, 363

Press conferences. *See* News conferences

Prestige abroad, U.S., 245, 332, 341

Prettyman, Judge E. Barrett, letter, 275

Price controls, 346, 410

Price stability, 117

Price Stability for Economic Growth, Cabinet Committee on, report, statement, 117

Price supports, 32, 391
Budget messages, 13 (pp. 77, 79), 414 (pp. 985–988)
News conference remarks, 38, 127
See also specific commodities

Prices, 4, 17, 23, 143, 423
Campaign remarks, 350, 354
Coffee, 111 n.
Rise in, 245
See also specific commodities

Prina, L. Edgar, 7, 93, 222, 422

Princeton University, 21

Printing press, invention of, 58

Prisoners of World War II, returned to Soviet Union, 268

Privileged information, 422
Certification forbidding disclosure to Congress of documents re aid to South America, 380

Proclamations, 374, 383, 432
Civil War Centennial, 370
List, Appendix B, p. 1086

Procurement, military. *See* Defense procurement

Production, decline in, 423

Production controls (farm products), 32

Project Defender, 414 (pp. 953, 954)

Project Mariner, 414 (p. 972)

Project Mercury (man-in-space), 13 (p. 66), 414 (p. 972)

Project Rover, 414 (p. 960)

Project VELA, 143 ftn. (p. 410)

Property, Federal, 410
Budget messages, 13 (pp. 101, 102, 105), 414 (pp. 1017, 1019)

Public assistance, 127 and ftn. (p. 362)
Budget messages, 13 (pp. 87, 95), 414 (pp. 1001, 1010, 1011)

Public debt. *See* Debt, national

Public facility loans, 13 (p. 72)

Public health, 13 (pp. 87, 93, 94), 414 (pp. 1006–1009)

Public Health Service, 13 (p. 94), 414 (pp. 1007, 1008)

Index

Index

Index

Index

Index

[References are to items except as otherwise indicated]

Index

Index

Index

Index

Index

Index

[References are to items except as otherwise indicated]

Index

Index

Index

[References are to items except as otherwise indicated]

Index

[References are to items except as otherwise indicated]